Mary Louise Parks
315 Grace Street
Council Bluffs,
Iowa

August, 1935

THE MODERN LIBRARY

of the World's Best Books

RENAISSANCE IN ITALY

>>

>>>

RENAISSANCE IN ITALY

BY

JOHN ADDINGTON SYMONDS

VOLUME II

BENNETT A. CERF · DONALD S. KLOPFER
THE MODERN LIBRARY
NEW YORK

FIRST MODERN LIBRARY EDITION, 1935

By arrangement with
CHARLES SCRIBNER'S SONS

Manufactured in the United States of America
Bound for THE MODERN LIBRARY *by H. Wolff*

CONTENTS

ITALIAN LITERATURE (*Continued*)

CHAPTER IV

POPULAR SECULAR POETRY

CHAPTER V

POPULAR RELIGIOUS POETRY

CHAPTER VI

LORENZO DE' MEDICI AND POLIZIANO

CHAPTER VII

PULCI AND BOIARDO

CHAPTER VIII

ARIOSTO

CHAPTER IX

THE 'ORLANDO FURIOSO'

CHAPTER X

THE NOVELLIERI

CHAPTER XI

THE DRAMA

CHAPTER XII

PASTORAL AND DIDACTIC POETRY

CHAPTER XIII

THE PURISTS

CHAPTER XVII

CONCLUSION

APPENDICES

PAGE

No. IV.—Jacopone's 'Presepio,' 'Corrotto,' and 'Cantico dell' Amore Superardente' translated into English Verse 475
No. V.—Passages translated from the 'Morgante Maggiore' of Pulci . . . 483
No. VI.—Translations of Elegiac Verses by Girolamo Benivieni and Michelangelo Buonarroti 495
No. VII—Italian Comic Prologues 496
No. VIII.—Passages translated from Folengo and Berni, which illustrate the Lutheran opinions of the Burlesque Poets 498
No. IX.—On Palmieri's 'Città di Vita' 506

THE CATHOLIC REACTION

CHAPTER I

THE SPANISH HEGEMONY

PAGE

Italy in the Renaissance—The Five Great Powers—The Kingdom of Naples—The Papacy—The Duchy of Milan—Venice—The Florentine Republic—Wars of Invasion closed by the Sack of Rome in 1527—Concordat between Clement VII. and Charles V.—Treaty of Barcelona and Paix des Dames—Charles lands at Genoa—His Journey to Bologna—Entrance into Bologna and Reception by Clement—Mustering of Italian Princes—Francesco Sforza replaced in the Duchy of Milan—Venetian Embassy—Italian League signed on Christmas Eve 1529—Florence alone excluded—The Siege of Florence pressed by the Prince of Orange—Charles's Coronation as King of Italy and Holy Roman Emperor—The Significance of this Ceremony at Bologna—Ceremony in S. Petronio—Settlement of the Duchy of Ferrara—Men of Letters and Arts at Bologna—The Emperor's Use of the Spanish Habit—Charles and Clement leave Bologna in March 1530—Review of the Settlement of Italy effected by Emperor and Pope—Extinction of Republics—Subsequent Absorption of Ferrara and Urbino into the Papal States—Savoy becomes an Italian Power—Period between Charles's Coronation and the Peace of Cateau Cambrésis in 1559—Economical and Social Condition of the Italians under Spanish Hegemony—The Nation still exists in Separate Communities—Intellectual Conditions—Predominance of Spain and Rome—Both Cosmopolitan Powers—Levelling down of the Component Portions of the Nation in a Common Servitude—The Evils of Spanish Rule . . . 517

CHAPTER II

THE PAPACY AND THE TRIDENTINE COUNCIL

The Counter-Reformation—Its Intellectual and Moral Character—Causes of the Gradual Extinction of Renaissance Energy—Transition from the Renaissance to the Catholic Revival—New Religious Spirit in Italy—Attitude of Italians toward German Reformation—Oratory of Divine Love—Gasparo Contarini and the Moderate Reformers—New Religious Orders—Paul III.—His early History and Education—Political Attitude between France and Spain—Creation of the Duchy of Parma—Imminence of a General Council—Review of previous Councils—Paul's Uneasiness—Opens a Council at

CHAPTER III

THE INQUISITION AND THE INDEX

CHAPTER IV

THE COMPANY OF JESUS

CHAPTER V

SOCIAL AND DOMESTIC MORALS: PART I

CHAPTER VI

SOCIAL AND DOMESTIC MORALS: PART II

CHAPTER VII

TORQUATO TASSO

CHAPTER VIII

THE 'GERUSALEMME LIBERATA'

CHAPTER IX

GIORDANO BRUNO

CHAPTER X

FRA PAOLO SARPI

CHAPTER XI

GUARINI, MARINO, CHIABRERA, TASSONI

CHAPTER XII

PALESTRINA AND THE ORIGINS OF MODERN MUSIC

CHAPTER XIII

THE BOLOGNESE SCHOOL OF PAINTERS

CHAPTER XIV

CONCLUSION

CHAPTER IV

POPULAR SECULAR POETRY

Separation between Cultivated Persons and the People—Italian despised by the Learned—Contempt for Vernacular Literature—The 'Certamen Coronarium'—Literature of Instruction for the Proletariat—Growth of Italian Prose—Abundance of Popular Poetry—The People in the Quattrocento take the Lead—Qualities of Italian Genius—Arthurian and Carolingian Romances—'I Reali di Francia'—Andrea of Barberino and his Works—Numerous Romances in Prose and Verse—Positive Spirit—Versified Tales from Boccaccio—Popular Legends—Ginevra degli Almieri—Novel of 'Il Grasso'—Histories in Verse—'Lamenti'—The Poets of the People—'Cantatori in Banca'—Antonio Pucci—His 'Sermintesi'—Political Songs—Satires—Burchiello—His Life and Writings—Dance-Songs—Derived from Cultivated Literature, or produced by the People—Poliziano—Love-Songs—'Rispetti' and 'Stornelli'—The Special Meaning of 'Strambotti'—Diffusion of this Poetry over Italy—Its Permanence—Question of its Original Home—Intercommunication and Exchange of Dialects—'Incatenature' and 'Rappresaglie'—Travelling in Mediæval Italy—The Subject-Matter of this Poetry—Deficiency in Ballad Elements—Canti Monferrini—The Ballad of 'L'Avvelenato' and Lord Ronald.

During the fifteenth century there was an almost complete separation between the cultivated classes and the people. Humanists, intent upon the exploration of the classics, deemed it below their dignity to use the vulgar tongue. They thought and wrote in Latin, and had no time to bestow upon the education of the common folk. A polite public was formed, who in the Courts of princes and the palaces of noblemen amused themselves with the ephemeral literature of pamphlets, essays, and epistles in the Latin tongue. For these well-educated readers Poggio and Pontano wrote their Latin novels. The same learned audience applauded the gladiators of the moment, Valla and Filelfo, when they descended into the arena and plied each other with pseudo-Ciceronian invectives. To quit this refined circle, and address the vulgar crowd, was thought unworthy of a man of erudition. Even Alberti, as we have seen, felt bound to apologise for sending his 'Teogenio' in Italian to Lionello d' Este. Only here and there a humanist of the first rank is found who, like Bruni, devoted a portion of his industry to the Italian lives of Dante and Petrarch, or, like Filelfo, lectured on the 'Divine Comedy,' or again, like Landino, composed a Dantesque commentary in the mother tongue. Moreover, Dante and Petrarch passed for almost classical; and in nearly all such instances of condescension, pecuniary interest swayed the scholar from his wonted orbit. It was want of skill in Latin rather than love for his own idiom which induced Vespasiano to pen his lives of great men in Italian. Not spontaneous inspiration, but the whim of a ducal patron forced Filelfo to use *terza rima* for his worthless poem on S. John, and to write a commentary upon Petrarch in the vernacular.[1] One of this man's letters reveals the humanist's contempt for the people's language, and his rooted belief in the immortality of Latin. It is worth translating.[2] 'I will answer you,' he says, 'not in the vulgar language, as you ask, but in Latin and our own true speech; for I have ever had an abhorrence for the talk of grooms and servants, equal to my detestation of their life and manners. You, however, call that dialect vernacular which, when I use the Tuscan tongue, I sometimes write. All Italians agree in praise of Tuscan. Yet I only employ it for such matters as I do not choose to transmit to posterity. Moreover, even that Tuscan idiom is hardly current throughout Italy, while Latin is far and wide diffused throughout the habitable world.' From this interesting epistle we gather that even professional scholars in the middle of the fifteenth century recognised Tuscan as a quasi-literary language, superior in polish to the other Italian dialects, but not to be compared for dignity and durability with Latin. It also proves that the language of Boccaccio was for them almost a foreign speech.

This attitude of learned writers produced a curious obtuseness of critical insight. Niccolò Niccoli, though he was a Florentine, called Dante 'a poet for bakers and cobblers.' Pico della Mirandola preferred Lorenzo de' Medici's verses to Petrarch. Landino complained, not, indeed, without good reason in that century, that the vulgar language could boast of no great authors. Filippo Villani, in the proem to his biographies, apologised for his father Matteo, who exerted humble faculties and scanty culture to his best ability. Lorenzo de' Medici defended himself for paying attention to an idiom which men of good judgment blamed for 'lowness, incapacity and unworthiness to deal with high themes or grave material.' Benedetto Varchi, who lived to be an excellent though somewhat cumbrous writer of Italian prose, gives this account of his early training:[3] 'I remember that when I was a lad, the first and strictest rule of a father to his sons, and of a master to his pupils, was that they should on no account and for no object read anything in the vulgar speech (*non legesseno cose volgari, per dirlo barbaramente come loro*); and Master Guasparre Mariscotti da Marradi, who was my teacher in grammar, a man of hard and rough but pure and

[1] See Rosmini, *Vita di Filelfo*, vol. ii. p. 13, for Filelfo's dislike of Italian. In the dedication of his Commentary to Filippo Maria Visconti he says: 'Tanto più volentieri ho intrapreso questo comento, quanto dalla tua eccellente Signoria non solo invitato sono stato, ma pregato, lusingato et provocato.' The first Canto opens thus:

> O Philippo Maria Anglo possente,
> Perchè mi strengi a quel che non poss' io?
> Vuoi tu ch' io sia ludibrio d' ogni gente?

[2] Dated Milan, Feb. 1477. Rosmini, *op. cit.* p. 282.

[3] *Ercolano* (in Vinetia, Giunti, 1570), p. 185.

excellent manners, having once heard, I know not how, that Schiatta di Bernardo Bagnesi and I were wont to read Petrarch on the sly, gave us a sound rating for it, and nearly expelled us from his school.' Some of Varchi's own stylistic pedantries may be attributed to this Latinising education.

Even when they wrote their mother tongue, it followed that the men of humanistic culture had a false conception of style. Alberti could not abstain from Latinistic rhetoric. Cristoforo Landino went the length of asserting that 'he who would fain be a good Tuscan writer, must first be a Latin scholar.' The Italian of familiar correspondence was mingled in almost equal quantities with Latin phrases. Thus Poliziano, writing from Venice to Lorenzo de' Medici, employs the following strange maccaronic jargon[4]:

> Visitai stamattina Messer Zaccheria Barbero; e mostrandoli io l' affezione vostra ec., mi rispose sempre lagrimando, et ut visum est, de cuore; risolvendosi in questo, in te uno spem esse. Ostendit se nosse quantum tibi debeat; sicchè fate quello ragionaste, ut favens ad majora. Quello Legato che torna da Roma, et qui tecum locutus est Florentiæ, non è punto a loro proposito, ut ajunt.

Poliziano, however, showed by his letters to the ladies of the Medicean family, and by some sermons composed for a religious brotherhood of which he was a member, that he had no difficulty in writing Tuscan prose of the best quality.[5] It seems to have been a contemptuous fashion among men of learning, when they used the mother tongue for correspondence, to load it with Latin—just as a German of the age of Frederick proved his superiority by French phrases. The acme of this affectation was reached in the 'Hypnerotomachia,' where the vice of Latinism sought perpetuation through the printing press. Meanwhile, the genius of the Florentine people was saving Italian literature from the extreme consequences to which caricatures of this kind, inspired by humanistic pedantry and sciolism, exposed it.

A characteristic incident of the year 1441 brings before us a set of men who, though obscure and devoted to the service of the common folk, exercised no slight influence over the destinies of the Italian language. After the reinstatement of the Medici, and while Alberti was resident in Florence, it occurred to him to propose the prize of a silver crown for the best poem upon Friendship, in the vulgar tongue. Piero de' Medici approving of this scheme, it was arranged that the contest for the prize should take place in S. Maria del Fiore, the competitors reciting their own compositions. The secretaries of Pope Eugenius IV. consented to be umpires. Eight poets entered the lists—Michele di Noferi del Gigante, Francesco d' Altobianco degli Alberti, and six others not less unknown to fame. We still possess their compositions in octave

[4] *Prose Volgari*, &c., edite da I. del Lungo (Firenze, Barbèra, 1867), p. 80.
[5] *Prose*, &c., *op. cit.* pp. 45 *et seq.*, pp. 3 *et seq.*

stanzas, *terza rima*, sapphics, hexameters and lyric strophes.[6] The poems were so bad that even the judges of that period refused to award the crown; nor could the most indulgent student of forgotten literature arraign this verdict for severity. Yet the men who engaged in Alberti's 'Certamen Coronarium,' as it was called, fairly represented a class of literary workers, who occupied a middle place between the learned and the laity, and on whom devolved the task of writing for the people.

Since that unique moment in the history of Tuscan civilisation when the lyrics of Dante and Guido Cavalcanti were heard upon the lips of blacksmiths, the artisans of Florence had not wholly lost their thirst for culture. Style and erudition retired into the schools of the humanists and the studies of the nobles. But this curiosity of the *volgo*, as Boccaccio contemptuously called them, was satisfied by the production of a vernacular literature, which brought the ruder elements of knowledge within their reach. Mention has already been made of Latini's 'Tesoro' and 'Tesoretto,' Uberti's 'Dittamondo' and similar encyclopædic works of mediæval learning. To these may now be added Leonardo Dati's cosmographical history in octave stanzas, the Schiavo da Bari's aphorisms on morality, and Pucci's *terza rima* version of Villani's Chronicle. Genealogical poems on popes, emperors and kings; episodes from national Italian history; novels, romances and tales of chivalry; pious biographies; the rudiments of education, from the 'Dottrinale' of Jacopo Alighieri down to Feo Belcari's 'A B C,' helped to complete the handicraftsman's library. Further to describe this plebeian literature is hardly necessary. The authors advanced no pretensions to artistic elegance or stateliness of style. They sought to render knowledge accessible to unlettered readers, or to please an open-air audience with stirring and romantic narratives. Their language broke only at rare intervals into poetry and rhetoric, when the subject-matter forced a note of unaffected feeling from the improvisatore. Yet it has always the merit of purity, and, in point of idiom, is superior to the Latinistic periods of Alberti. By means of the neglected labours of these nameless writers, the style of the fourteenth century, so winning in its infantine grace, was gradually transformed and rendered capable of stronger literary utterance. Those who have studied a single prose work of this period—'I Reali di Francia,' for instance, or Belcari's 'Vita del Beato Colombino,' or the 'Governo della Famiglia' ascribed to

[6] Alberti, *Op. Volg.* vol. i. pp. clxvii-ccxxxiii. The quality of these Latin metres may be judged from the following hexameters:

> Ma non prima sarà che 'l Dato la musa corona
> Invochi, allora subito cantando l' avete,
> Tal qual si gode presso il celeste Tonante.

Of the sapphics the following is a specimen:

> Eccomi, i' son qui Dea degli amici,
> Quella qual tutti li omini solete
> Mordere, e falso fugitiva dirli,
> Or la volete.

Pandolfini—will be convinced that a real progress toward grammatical cohesion and massiveness of structure was made during those years of the fifteenth century which are usually counted barren of achievement by literary historians. Italian prose had entered on the period of adolescence, leading to the manhood of Machiavelli.

The popular poetry of the *quattrocento* is still more interesting than its prose. No period of Italian history was probably more fruitful of songs poured forth from the very heart of the people, on the fields and in the city. The music of these lyrics still lingers about the Tuscan highlands and the shores of Sicily, where much that now passes for original composition is but the echo of most ancient melody stored in the retentive memory of peasants. To investigate the several species of this poetry, together with kindred works of prose fiction, under the several classes of (i) epics and romances, (ii) histories in verse and satires, (iii) love-poems, (iv) religious lyrics, and (v) dramas, will be my object in the present and the following chapters. This survey of popular literature forms a necessary introduction to the renascence which was simultaneously effected for Italian at Florence, Ferrara and Naples during the last years of the century. The material prepared by the people was then resumed and artistically elaborated by learned authors.

It has been well said that Italian poetry exhibits a continual reciprocity of exchange between the cultivated classes and the proletariat. In this respect the literature of the Italians corresponds to their fine art. Taken together with painting, sculpture, and music, it offers a more complete embodiment of the national spirit than can be shown by any other modern race. Dante's Francesca and Count Ugolino, Ariosto's golden cantos, and the romantic episodes of the 'Gerusalemme' are known by heart throughout the length and breadth of the Peninsula. The people have appropriated these masterpieces of finished art. On the other hand, the literary poets have been ever careful to borrow subjects, forms, and motives from the populace. The close *rapport* which thus connects the tastes and instincts of the proletariat with the culture of the aristocracy, is rooted in peculiar conditions of Italian society. Traditions of a very ancient civilisation, derived without apparent rupture from the Roman age, have penetrated and refined the whole nation. From the highest to the lowest, the Italians are born with sensibility to beauty. This people and its poets live in sympathy so vital that, though their mutual good understanding may have been suspended for short intervals, it has never been broken. The vibrations of intercourse between the peasant and the learned writer are incessant; and if we notice some intermittency of influence on one side or the other, it is only because at one epoch the destinies of the national genius were committed to the people, at another to the cultivated classes. In the fifteenth century, one of these temporary ruptures occurred. The Revival of Learning had to be effected by an isolation of the scholars. Meanwhile, the people carried on the work of literary transmutation, which was to connect Boccaccio with Pulci and Poliziano. Their instinct rejected all elements alien to the national temperament. Out of the many models bequeathed by the fourteenth century, only those which suited the sensuous realism of the Florentines survived. The traditions of Ciullo d' Alcamo and Jacopone da Todi, of Rustico di Filippo and Lapo Gianni, of Folgore da S. Gemignano and Cene dalla Chitarra, of Cecco Angiolieri and Guido Cavalcanti, of Boccaccio and Sacchetti, of Ser Giovanni and Alesso Donati, triumphed over the scholasticism of those learned poets—'half Provençal and half Latin, half chivalrous and half *bourgeois*, half monastic and half sensual, half aristocratic and half plebeian'[7]—who had unsuccessfully experimentalised in the dawn of Tuscan culture. The artificial chivalry, lifeless mysticism, barren metaphysics, and hypocritical piety of the rhyming doctors were eliminated. Common sense expressed itself in a reaction against their conventional philosophy. Giotto's blunt critique of Franciscan poverty, Orcagna's burlesque definition of Love, not as a blind boy with wings and arrows, but thus:

> L' amore è un trastullo;
> Non è composto di legno nè d' osso;
> E a molta gente fa rompere il dosso:

struck the keynote of the new literature.[8] It is true that much was sacrificed. Both Dante and Petrarch seemed to be forgotten. Yet this was inevitable. Dante represented a bygone age of faith and reason. Petrarch's humanity was too exquisitely veiled. The Florentine people required expression more simple and direct, movement more brusque, emotion of a coarser fibre. Meanwhile the 'Divine Comedy' and the 'Canzoniere' were the inalienable possessions of the nation. They had already taken rank as classics.

The Italians had no national Epic, if we except the 'Æneid.' We have seen how the romances of Charlemagne and Arthur were imported with the languages of France and Provence into Northern Italy, and how they passed into the national literature of Lombardy and Tuscany.[9] Both cycles were eminently popular. The 'Tavola Ritonda' ranks among the earliest monuments of Tuscan prose.[10] The 'Cento Novelle' contain frequent references to Merlin, Lancelot and Tristram. Folgore da S. Gemignano compares the members of his Joyous Company to King Ban's children. In the 'Laberinto d' Amore' Boccaccio speaks of Arthurian tales as the favourite studies of idle women, and Sacchetti bids his blacksmith turn from Dante to legends of the Round Table. Yet there is no doubt that from a very early period the Carolingian

[7] Carducci, 'Delle Rime di Dante Alighieri,' *Studi*, p. 154.

[8] For Giotto's and Orcagna's poems, see Trucchi, vol. ii. pp. 8 and 25.

[9] See Vol. I, pp. 850 *et seq.*

[10] The *Tavola Ritonda* has been reprinted, 2 vols., Bologna, Romagnoli, 1864. It corresponds very closely in material to our *Mort d'Arthur*, beginning with the history of Uther Pendragon and ending with Arthur's wound and departure to the island of Morgan le Fay.

cycle gained the preference of the Italian people.[11] It is also noticeable that, not the main legend of Roland, but the episode of Rinaldo, and other offshoots from the history of the Frankish peers, furnished plebeian poets with their favourite material.[12] MSS. written in Venetian and Franco-Italian dialects before the middle of the fourteenth century attest to the popularity of these subordinate romances, and reveal an independent handling of the borrowed subject. In form they do not diverge widely from French originals. Yet there is one prominent characteristic which distinguishes the Italian *rifacimenti*. A Christian hero falls in love with a pagan heroine on pagan soil. His pursuit of her, their difficulties and adventures, and the evangelisation of her people by the knightly lover, furnish a series of incidents which recur with singular persistence.[13] When the romances in question had been translated into Tuscan, a destiny of special splendour was reserved for two of them, in no way distinguished by any apparent merit above the rest. These were the tales of Buovo d' Antona, of which we possess an early version in octave stanzas, and of Fioravante, which exists in still older prose. About the beginning of the fifteenth century, the 'Buovo' and the 'Fioravante,' together with other material drawn from the Carolingian epic, were combined into the great prose work called 'I Reali di Francia.'[14] Since its first appearance to the present day, this romance has never ceased to be the most widely popular of all books written in Italian. 'There is nothing,' says Signor Rajna, 'so assiduously read from the Alps to the furthest headlands of Sicily. Wherever a reader exists, there is it certain to be found in honour.'[15] Not the earliest but the latest product of a long elaboration of romantic matter by the people, it seems to have assimilated the very essence of the popular imagination. When we inquire into its authorship, we find good reason to ascribe it to Andrea dei Mangalotti of Barberino in the Val d' Elsa, one of the best and most indefatigable workmen for the literary market of the proletariat.[16] It was he who compiled the 'Aspromonte,' the 'Aiolfo,' the seven books of 'Storie Nerbonesi,' the 'Ugone d' Avernia,' and the 'Guerino il Meschino,' reducing these tales from elder poems and prose sources into Tuscan of sterling lucidity and vigour, and attempting, it would seem, to embrace the whole Carolingian cycle in a series of episodical romances.[17] 'Guerino il Meschino' rivalled for a while the 'Reali' in popularity; but for some unknown reason, which

[11] See Vol. I, p. 851. The subject of these romances has been ably treated by Pio Rajna in his works, *I Reali di Francia* (Bologna, Romagnoli, 1872), and *Le Fonti dell' Orlando Furioso* (Firenze, Sansoni, 1876).

[12] The *Rinaldino*, a prose romance recently published (Bologna, Romagnoli, 1865), might be selected as a thoroughly Italian *fioritura* on the ancient Carolingian theme.

[13] We have here the germ of the *Orlando* and of the first part of the *Morgante*.

[14] Rajna, *I Reali*, p. 320, fixes the date of its composition at a little before 1420.

[15] *Ibid.* p. 3.

[16] *Ibid.* pp. 311-319.

[17] The *Storie Nerbonesi* were published in 2 vols. (Bologna, Romagnoli, 1877), under the editorship of I. G. Isola. The third volume forms a copious philological and critical appendix.

would have to be sought in the instinctive partialities of the people, it was gradually superseded by the latter. The 'Reali' alone has descended in its original form through the press to this century.[18]

Andrea da Barberino, if we are right in ascribing the 'Reali' to his pen, conferred a benefit on the Italians parallel to that which the English owed to Sir Thomas Mallory in his 'Mort d'Arthur.' He not only collected and condensed the scattered tales of numerous unknown predecessors, but he also bequeathed to the nation a monument of unaffected prose at a moment when the language was still ingenuous and plastic. It would be not uninteresting to compare the fate of the 'Reali' with that of our own 'Mort d'Arthur.' The latter was the more artistic performance of the two. It achieved a truer epical unity, and was composed in a richer, more romantic style. The former remained episodical and incomplete; and its language, though solid and efficient, lacked the charm of Mallory's all golden prose. Yet the 'Reali' is still a household classic. It is found in every *contadino's* cottage, and supplies the peasantry with subjects for their 'Maggi.' The 'Mort d'Arthur,' on the contrary, has become the plaything of mediævalising folk in modern England. Read for its unique beauty by students, it is still unknown to the people, and, in the opinion of the dull majority, it is reckoned inferior to Tennyson's smooth imitations.

When we come to consider the romantic poems of Pulci, Boiardo, and Ariosto, we shall be able to estimate the service rendered by men like Andrea da Barberino to polite Italian literature. The popularity of the cycle to which the 'Reali' belonged, decided the choice of the Carolingian epic by the poets of Florence and Ferrara. Nor were the above-mentioned romances by any means the only works of their kind produced for a plebeian audience in the *quattrocento*. It is enough to mention 'La Regina Ancroja,' 'La Spagna,' 'Trebisonda con la Vita e Morte di Rinaldo.' Both in prose and verse an abundant literature of the kind was manufactured. Without being positively burlesqued, the heroes of chivalrous story were travestied to suit the taste of artisans and burghers. The element of the marvellous was surcharged; comic and pathetic episodes were multiplied; beneath the armour of the Paladins Italian characters were substituted with spontaneous malice for the obsolete ideals of feudalism. It only needed a touch of conscious irony to convert the material thus elaborated by the people into the airy fabric of Ariosto's art. At the same time the form which the epic of romance was destined to assume, had been determined. The streets and squares of town and village rang with the chants of improvisatori, turning the prose periods of Andrea da Barberino and his predecessors into wordy octave stanzas, rehandling ancient 'Chansons de Geste,' and adapting the mannerism of chivalrous minstrelsy to the requirements of a subtle-witted Tuscan crowd. The old-fashioned invocations of God, Madonna, or some saint were preserved at the be-

[18] *Guerino* was versified in octave stanzas, by a poet of the people called L'Altissimo, in the sixteenth century.

ginning of each canto, while the audience received their *congé* from the author at its close. When the poems thus produced were committed to writing, the plebeian author feigned at least the inspiration of a bard.

While the traditions of mediæval song were thus preserved, the prose romances followed, as closely as possible, the style of a chronicle, and aimed at the verisimilitude of authentic history. The 'Reali,' for example, opens with this sentence: 'Fuvvi in Roma un santo pastore della Chiesa, che aveva nome papa Silvestro.' The 'Fioravante,' recently edited by Signor Rajna, begins: 'Nel tempo che Gostantino imperadore regiea & Mantenea corte in Roma grandissima.' This parade of historic seriousness, observed by the subsequent romantic poets, contributed in no small measure to the irony at which they aimed. But with the story-tellers of the *quattrocento* it was no mere affectation. Like their predecessors of the fourteenth century, they treated legend from the standpoint of experience. It was due in no small measure to this circumstance that the Italian prose romances are devoid of charm. Nowhere do we find in them that magic touch of poetry which makes the forests, seas and castles of the 'Mort d'Arthur' enchanted ground. Notwithstanding all their extravagances, they remain positive in spirit, presenting the material of fancy in the sober garb of fact. The Italian genius lacked a something of imaginative potency possessed in overflowing measure by the Northern nations. It required the stimulus of satire, the infusion of idyllic sentiment, the consciousness of art, to raise the romantic epic to the height it reached in Ariosto. Then, and not till then, when the matter of the legend had become the sport of the æsthetic sense, were the inexhaustible riches of Italian fancy, dealing delicately and humorously with a subject which could no longer be apprehended seriously, revealed to the world in a masterpiece of beauty. But that work of consummate art was what it was, by reason of the master's wise employment of a style transmitted to him through generations of plebeian predecessors.

The same positive and workmanly method is discernible in the versified *Novelle* of this period.[19] The popular poets were wont to recast tales from the 'Decameron' and other sources in octave stanzas. Of such compositions we have excellent specimens in Girolamo Benivieni's version of the novel of Tancredi, and in an anonymous rhymed paraphrase of Patient Grizzel.[20] The latter is especially interesting when we compare it with the series of panels attributed to Pinturicchio in

[19] See *I Novellieri Italiani in Verso* by Giamb. Passano (Romagnoli, 1868). The whole *Decameron* was turned into octave stanzas by V. Brugiantino, and published by Marcolini at Venice in 1554. Among *Novelle* versified for popular reading may be cited, *Masetto the Gardener* (*Decam.* Giorn. iii. 1), *Romeo and Juliet* (Verona, 1553), *Il Grasso, Legnaiuolo* (by B. Davanzati, Florence, 1480), *Prasildo and Lisbina* (from the *Orlando Innamorato*), *Oliva, Fiorio e Biancifiore* (the tale of the *Filocopo*). Of classical tales we find *Sesto Tarquinio et Lucretia, Orpheo, Perseo, Piramo, Giasone e Medea.*

[20] *Tancredi Principe di Salerno*, Bologna, Romagnoli, 1863. *Il Marchese di Saluzzo e la Griselda*, Bologna, Romagnoli, 1862.

the National Gallery, where a painter of the same period has exercised his fancy in illustrating the legend which the poet versified. Detached episodes of semi-mythical Florentine history were similarly treated. Allusion has already been made to the love-tale of Ippolito and Leonora, attributed on doubtful grounds to Alberti.[21] But by far the most beautiful is the story of Ginevra degli Almieri, told in octave stanzas by Agostino Velletti.[22] This poem has rare value as a genuine product of the plebeian muse. The heroine Ginevra's father was a pork-butcher, says the minstrel, and lived in the Marcato Vecchio, where he carried on the best business of the sort in Florence. It is also important for students of comparative literature because it clearly illustrates the difference between Italian and Northern treatment of an all but contemporary incident. The events narrated are supposed to have really happened in the year 1396. On the Scotch Border they would have furnished materials for a ballad similar to Gil Morrice or Clerk Saunders. In Florence they take the form of a *Novella*, and the *Novella* is expanded in octave stanzas.[23] Ginevra had two lovers, Antonio de' Rondinelli and Francesco degli Agolanti. Antonio loved her the more tenderly; but her parents gave her in marriage to Francesco. Soon after the ceremony, she sickened and fell into a trance; and since Florence was then threatened with the plague, the girl was buried over-hastily in this deep slumber. Her weeping parents laid her in a cippus or *avello* between the two doors of S. Reparata, where the workmen, unable to finish their job before sunset, left the lid of her sepulchre unsoldered. In the middle of the night Ginevra woke, and discovered to her horror that she had been sent to the grave alive. Happily the moon was shining, and a ray of light fell through a chink upon her bier. She arose, wrapped her shroud around her, and struggled from her marble chest into the silent cathedral square. Giotto's bell-tower rose above her, silvery and beautiful, and slender in the moonlight. Like a ghost, sheeted in her grave-clothes, Ginevra ran through the streets, and knocked first at Francesco's door. He was seated awake by the fireside, sorrowing for his young bride's loss:

> Andonne alla finestra e aprilla un poco:
> Chi è là? Chi batte? Io son la tua Ginevra;
> Non m' odi tu? Col suo parlar persevera.

[21] See Vol. I, p. 959. The literary hesitations of an age as yet uncertain of its aim might be illustrated from these romances. Of *Ippolito e Leonora* we have a prose, an *ottava rima*, and a Latin version. Of *Griselda* we have Boccaccio's Italian, and Petrarch's Latin prose, in addition to the anonymous *ottava rima* version. Of the *Principe di Salerno* we have Boccaccio's Italian, and Lionardo Bruni's Latin versions in prose, together with Filippo Beroaldo's Latin elegiacs, Francesco di Michele Accolti's *terza rima* and Benivieni's octave stanzas. Lami in his *Novelle letterarie* (Bologna, Romagnoli, 1859) prints an Italian *Novella* on the same story, which he judges anterior to the *Decameron*. Later on, Annibal Guasco produced another *ottava rima* version; and the tale was used by several playwrights in the composition of tragedies.

[22] *La Storia di Ginevra Almieri che fu sepolta viva in Firenze* (Pisa, Nistri, 1863).

[23] The same point is illustrated by the tales of the Marchese di Saluzzo and the Principe di Salerno, which produced the novels of *Griselda* and *Tancredi*. See notes above.

Her husband doubts not that it is a spirit calling to him, bids her rest till masses shall be said for her repose, and shuts the window. Then she turns to her mother's house. The mother, too, is sitting sorrowful by the hearth, when she is startled by Ginevra's cry:

> E spaventata e piena di paura
> Disse: va in pace, anima benedetta,
> Bella figliuola mia, onesta e pura;
> E riserrò la finestra con fretta.

Rejected by husband and mother, Ginevra next tries her uncle, and calls on him for succour in God's name:

> Fugli risposto; anima benedetta,
> Va che Dio ti conservi in santa pace.

The poor wretch now feels that there is nothing left for her but to lie down on the pavement and die of cold. But while she is preparing herself for this fate, she bethinks her of Antonio. To his house she hurries, cries for aid, and falls exhausted on the doorstep. Then comes the finest touch in the poem. Antonio knows Ginevra's voice; and loving her so tenderly, he hurries with delight to greet her risen from the grave. He alone has no fear and no misgiving; for love in him is stronger than death. At the street door, when he reaches it, he finds no ghost, but his own dear lady yet alive. She is half frozen and unconscious; yet her heart still beats. How he calls the women of his household to attend her, prepares a bed, and feeds her with warm soups and wine, and how she revives, and how Antonio claims her for his wife, and wins his cause against her former bridegroom in the Bishop's court, may be read at length in the concluding portion of the tale. The intrinsic pathos of this story makes it a real poem; for though the wizard's wand of Northern imagination lay beyond the grasp of the Italian genius, the *Novelle* are rarely deficient in poetry evoked by sympathy with injured innocence and loyal love.

Of truly popular *Novelle* belonging to the fifteenth century, none is racier or more characteristic than the anonymous tale of 'Il Grasso, Legnaiuolo.'[24] It is written in pure Florentine dialect, and might be selected as the finest extant specimen of homespun Tuscan humour. We have already seen that the point of Sacchetti's stories is nearly always a practical joke, where comedy combines with heartless cruelty in almost equal parts. The theme of 'Il Grasso' is a superlatively comic *beffa* of this sort, played by Filippo Brunelleschi on a friend of his. The incident is dated 1409, and is supposed to have really occurred. Manetto Ammannatini, a *tarsiatore* or worker in carved and inlaid wood, was called 'Il Grasso,' because he was a fine stout fellow of twenty-eight years. He had his *bottega* on the Piazza S. Giovanni and lived with his brother in a house hard by. Among his most intimate associates were Filippo di Ser Brunellesco, Donatello, *intagliatore di marmi*,

[24] *Raccolta dei Novellieri Italiani*, vol. xiii.

Giovanni di Messer Francesco Rucellai, and others, partly gentlemen and partly handicraftsmen; for there was no abrupt division of classes at Florence, and this story shows how artisans and men of high condition dwelt together in good fellowship. The practical joke devised by Brunelleschi consisted in persuading Manetto that he had been changed into a certain Matteo. The whole society of friends were in the secret, and the affair was so cunningly conducted that at last they attained the desired object. They caused Manetto to be arrested for a debt of Matteo, sent Matteo's brothers and then the clergyman of the parish to reason with him on his spendthrift habits, and fooled him so that he fairly lost his sense of identity. The whole series of incidents, beginning with Manetto's indignant assertion of his proper personality, passing through his doubts, and closing with his mystification, is conducted by fine gradations of irresistibly comic humour. At last the poor man resolves to quit Florence and to seek refuge with King Mathias Corvinus in Hungary; which it seems he subsequently did, in company with a certain Lo Spano. There is no reason to suppose that this practical joke did not actually take place.

I have enlarged upon the *novella* of 'Il Grasso,' because it is typical of the genuinely popular literature, written to delight the folk of Florence, appealing to their subtlest as well as broadest sense of fun, and bringing on the scene two famous artists, Brunelleschi, whose cupola is 'raised above the heavens,' and Donatello, whose S. George seems stepping from his pedestal to challenge all the evil of the world and conquer it. Unfortunately, our published collections are not rich in novels of this date; and next to the anonymous tale of 'Il Grasso, Legnaiuolo' it is difficult to cite one of at all equal value, till we come to Luigi Pulci's story of Messer Goro and Pius II. This is really a satire on the Sienese, whom Pulci represents with Florentine malice as almost inconceivably silly. The Tuscan style is piquant in the extreme, and the picture of manners very brilliant.[25]

From epical and narrative literature to poems written for the people upon contemporary events and public history, is not an unnatural transition. These compositions divide themselves into 'Storie' and 'Lamenti.' We have abundant examples of both kinds in lyric measures and also in octave stanzas and *terza rima*.[26] A few of their titles will suffice to indicate their scope. 'Il Lamento di Giuliano de' Medici' relates the tragic ending of the Pazzi conspiracy; 'Il Lamento del Duca Galeazzo Maria' tells how that Duke was murdered in the church of S. Stefano at Milan; 'El Lamento di Otranto' is an echo of the disaster which shook all Italy to her foundations in the year 1480; 'El Lamento e la Discordia de Italia universale' sounds the death-note of Italian

[25] *Op. cit.* vol. xiii. An allusion to Masuccio in this novel is interesting, since it proves the influence he had acquired even in Florence: 'Masuccio, grande onore della città di Salerno, molto imitatore del nostro messer Giovanni Boccaccio,' *ibid.* p. 34. Pulci goes on to say that the reading of the *Novellino* had encouraged him to write his tale.

[26] See D' Ancona, *La Poesia Popolare Italiana*, pp. 64-79.

freedom in the last years of the century. After that period the 'Pianti' and 'Lamenti,' attesting to the sorrows of a nation, increase in frequency until all voices from the people are hushed in the leaden sleep of Spanish despotism.[27] The 'Storie' in like manner are more abundant between the years 1494 and 1530, when the wars of foreign invaders supplied the bards of the market-place with continual matter for improvisation. Among the earliest may be mentioned two poems on the Battle of Anghiari and the taking of Serezana.[28] Then the list proceeds with the tale of the Borgias, 'Guerre Orrende,' 'Rotta di Ravenna,' 'Mali deportamenti de Franciosi fato in Italia,' and so forth, till it ends with 'La Presa di Roma' and 'Rotta di Ferruccio.' A last echo of these 'Storie' and 'Lamenti'—for alas! in Italy of the sixteenth century history and lamentation were all one—still sounds about the hillsides of Siena[29]:

O Piero Strozzi, 'ndù sono i tuoi bravoni?
Al Poggio delle Donne in que' burroni.
O Piero Strozzi, 'ndù sono i tuoi soldati?
Al Poggio delle Donne in quei fossati.
O Piero Strozzi, 'ndù son le tue genti?
Al Poggio delle Donne a côr le lenti.

It may be well to say how these poems reached the people, before they were committed to writing or the press. There existed a professional class of rhymesters, usually blind men, if we may judge by the frequent affix of *Cieco* to their names, who tuned their guitar in the streets, and when a crowd had gathered round them, broke into some legend of romance, or told a tale of national misfortune. The Italian designation of these minstrels is *Cantatore in Banca* or *Cantore di piazza*. In the high tide of Florentine freedom the *Cantore di piazza* exercised a noble calling; for through his verse the choice of the common folk made itself heard beneath the very windows of the Signoria. In 1342, when the war with Pisa turned against the Florentines owing to the incompetence of their generals, Antonio Pucci, who was the most celebrated *Cantatore* of the day, took his lute and placed himself upon the steps beneath the Palazzo, and having invoked the Virgin Mary, struck up a *Sermintese* on the duty of making peace[30]:

Signor, pognàm ch' i' sia di vil nascenza,
I' pur nacqui nel corpo di Firenza,
Come qual c' è di più sofficienza:
Onde 'l mi duole

[27] A fine example of these later *Lamenti* has been republished at Bologna by Romagnoli, 1864. It is the *Lamento di Fiorenza* upon the siege and slavery of 1529-30.

[28] A mediæval specimen of this species of composition is the *Ballata* for the *Reali di Napoli* in the defeat of Montecatini. See Carducci's *Cino e Altri*, p. 603.

[29] D' Ancona, *op. cit.* p. 78.

[30] *Sermintese Storico di A. Pucci*, Livorno, Vigo, 1876. It will be remembered that Dante in the *Vita Nuova* (section vi.) says he composed a *Serventese* on sixty ladies of Florence. The name was derived from Provence, and altered into *Sermintese* by the Florentines. We possess a poem of this sort by A. Pucci on the Florentine ladies, printed by D' Ancona in his edition of the *Vita Nuova* (Pisa, Nistri, p. 71), together with a valuable discourse upon this form of poetry. Carducci in his *Cino e Altri* prints two *Sermintesi* by Pucci on the beauties of women.

Di lei, considerando che esser suole
Tenuta più che madre da figliuole;
Oggi ogni bestia soggiogar la vuole
E occupare.

Other poems of the same kind by Antonio Pucci belong to the year 1346, or celebrate the purchase of Lucca from Mastino della Scala, or the victory of Messer Piero Rosso at Padua, or the expulsion of the Duke of Athens from Florence in 1348. It must not be supposed that the *Cantatori in Banca* of the next century enjoyed so much liberty of censure or had so high a sense of their vocation as Antonio Pucci. Yet the people made their opinions freely heard in rhymes sung even by the children through the streets, as when they angered Martin V. in 1420 by crying beneath his very windows:[31]

Papa Martino, Signor di Piombino,
Conte de Urbino, non vale un quattrino.

During the ascendency of Savonarola and the party struggles of the Medici the rival cries of *Palle* and *Viva Cristo Rè* were turned into street songs;[32] but at last, after the siege and the victory of Clement, the voice of the people was finally stifled by authority.[33]

The element of satire in these ditties of the people leads me to speak of one very prominent poet of the fifteenth century—Domenico di Giovanni, called Il Burchiello, the rhyming barber.[34] He was born probably in 1403 at Florence, where his father, who was a Pisan, had acquired the rights of citizenship and followed the trade of a barber. Their shop was situated in Calimala, and formed a meeting-place for the wits, who carried Burchiello's verses over the town. The boy seems to have studied at Pisa, and acquired some slight knowledge of medicine.[35] At the age of four-and-twenty we find him married, with three

[31] D' Ancona, *Poesia Popolare Italiana*, pp. 47-50, has collected from Leonardo Bruno and other sources many interesting facts about Pope Martin's anger at this ditty. He seems to have gone to the length of putting Florence under an interdict.

[32] D' Ancona, *op. cit.* pp. 51-56.

[33] One of the last plebeian rhymes on politics comes from Siena, where, in the year 1552, the people used to sing this couplet in derision of the Cardinal of the Mignanelli family sent to rule them:

Mignanello, Mignanello,
Non ci piace il tuo modello.

See Benci's *Storia di Montepulciano* (Fiorenza, Massi e Landi, 1641), p. 104. An anecdote from Busini (*Lettere al Varchi*, Firenze, Le Monnier, p. 220) is so characteristic of the popular temper under the oppression of Spanish tyranny that its indecency may be excused. He says that a law had been passed awarding 'quattro tratti di corda ad uno che, tirando una c . . . . . . disse: Poi che non si può parlare con la bocca, io parlerò col c . . . .'

[34] See the work entitled *Sulle Poesie Toscane di Domenico il Burchiello nel secolo xv*, G. Gargani, Firenze, Tip. Cenn. 1877.

[35] Intendi a me, che già studiai a Pisa,
E ogni mal conosco senza signo.

Sonetti del Burchiello, del Bellincioni, e d' altri, 1757, Londra, p. 125. See, too, the whole sonnet *Son medico in volgar.*

children and no property.[36] Soon after this date, he separated from his wife; or else she left him on account of his irregular and dissolute habits. Peering through the obscurity of his somewhat sordid history, we see him getting into trouble with the Inquisition on account of profane speech, and then espousing the cause of the Albizzi against the Medicean faction. On the return of Cosimo de' Medici in 1434, Burchiello was obliged to leave Florence. He settled at Siena, and opened a shop in the Corso di Camollia, hoping to attract the Florentines whose business brought them to that quarter. Here he nearly ruined his health by debauchery, and narrowly escaped assassination at the hands of a certain Ser Rosello.[37] Leaving Siena about 1440, Burchiello spent the last years of his life in wandering through the cities of Italy. We hear of him at Venice entertained by one of the Alberti family, then at Naples, finally in Rome, where he died in 1448, poisoned probably by Robert, a bastard of Pandolfo Sigismondo Malatesta, at the instigation of his ancient enemy, Cosimo de' Medici.[38] Such long arms and such retentive memory had the merchant despot.

Burchiello's sonnets were collected some thirty years after his death and published simultaneously at various places.[39] They owed their popularity partly to their political subject-matter, but more to their strange humour. A foreigner can scarcely understand their language, far less appreciate their fun; for not only are they composed in Florentine slang of the fifteenth century, but this slang itself consists of detached phrases and burlesque allusions, chipped as it were from current speech, broken into splinters, and then wrought into a grotesque mosaic. That Burchiello had the merit of originality, and that he caught the very note of plebeian utterance, is manifest from the numerous editions and imitations of his sonnets.[40] His Muse was a *volgivaga Venus* bred among the taverns and low haunts of vulgar company, whose biting wit introduced her to the society of the learned. Yet her utterances, at this distance of time, are so obscure and their point has been so blunted that to profess an admiration for Burchiello savours of literary affectation.[41] He was a poet of the transition; and the burlesque style which he made popular was destined to be superseded by the more refined and subtle Bernesque manner. Il Lasca, writing in the sixteenth

[36] Gargani, *op. cit.* p. 23, extract from the *Catasto*, 1427: 'Domenicho di Giovanni barbiere non ha nulla.'

[37] The parallel between these passages of Burchiello's life and Filelfo's at the same period is singular. See *Revival of Learning*, p. 455.

[38] Gargani, *op. cit.* p. 90.

[39] The best edition bears the date Londra, 1757.

[40] The edition cited above includes *Sonetti alla Burchiellesca* by a variety of writers. The strange book called *Pataffio*, which used to be ascribed to Brunetto Latini, seems born of similar conditions.

[41] Florentines themselves take this view, as is proved by the following sentence from Capponi: 'È pure qui obbligo di registrare anche il Burchiello, barbiere di nome rimasto famoso, perchè fece d' un certo suo gergo poesia forse arguta ma triviale; oscura oggi, ma popolare nei tempi suoi e che ebbe inclusive imitatori' (*Storia della Rep. di Firenze*, ii. 176).

century, expressed himself strongly against those who still ventured to compare Burchiello with the author of 'Le Pesche.' 'Let no one talk to me of Burchiello; to rank him with Berni is no better than to couple the fiend Charon with the Angel Gabriel.'[42]

Not the least important branch of popular poetry in its bearing on the future of Italian literature was the strictly lyrical. In treating of these *Volkslieder*, it will be necessary to consider them under the two aspects of secular and religious—the former destined to supply Poliziano and Lorenzo de' Medici with models for their purest works of literary art, the latter containing the germs of the Florentine Sacred Play within the strophes of a hymn.

If we return to the golden days of the fourteenth century, we find that Dante's, Boccaccio's and Sacchetti's *Ballate* descended to the people and were easily adapted to their needs.[43] Minute comparison of Dante's dance-song of the *Ghirlandetta* with the version in use among the common folk will show what slight alterations were needed in order to render it the property of 'prentice lads and spinning maidens, and at the same time how subtle those changes were.[44] Dante's song might be likened to a florin fresh from the mint; the popular ditty to the same coin after it has circulated for a year or two, exchanging something of its sharp lines for the smoothness of currency and usage. The same is true of Boccaccio's *Ballata*, 'Il fior che 'l valor perde;' except that here the transformation has gone deeper, and, if such a criticism may be hazarded, has bettered the original by rendering the sentiment more universal.[45] Sacchetti's charming song 'O vaghe montanine pasturelle' underwent the same process of metamorphosis before it assumed the form in which it passed for a composition of Poliziano.[46] Starting with poems of this quality, the rhymesters of the market-place had noble models, and the use they made of them was adequate. We cannot from the wreck of time recover very many that were absolutely written for the people by the people; but we can judge of their quality by Angelo Poliziano's imitations.[47] He borrowed so largely from all sources, and his debts can be so accurately traced in his *Rispetti*, that it is fair to credit the popular Muse with even such delicate work as 'La Brunettina,' while the disputed authorship of the May-song 'Ben venga Maggio' and of the *Ballata* 'Vaghe le montanine e pastorelle' is sufficient

[42] See the Sonnet quoted in Note 59 to Mazzuchelli's Life of Berni, *Scrittori d' Italia*, vol. iv.

[43] The *Ballata* or *Canzone a Ballo*, as its name implies, was a poem intended to be sung during the dance. A musician played the lute while young women executed the movements of the Carola (so beautifully depicted by Benozzo Gozzoli in his Pisan frescoes), alone or in the company of young men, singing the words of the song. The *Ballata* consisted of lyric stanzas with a recurrent couplet. It is difficult to distinguish the *Ballate* from the *Canzonette d' Amore*.

[44] See Carducci, *Cantilene e Ballate* (Pisa, 1871), pp. 82, 83.

[45] *Ibid.* pp. 171-173.

[46] *Ibid.* pp. 214-217.

[47] A volume of ancient *Canzoni a Ballo* was published at Florence in 1562, by Sermatelli, and again in 1568.

to prove at least their widespread fame.[48] Whoever wrote them, they became the heirlooms of the people. If proof were needed of the vast number of such compositions in the fifteenth century—erotic, humorous, and not unfrequently obscene—it might be derived from the rubrics of the *Laude* or hymns, which were almost invariably parodies of popular dance-songs and intended to be sung to the same tunes.[49] Every festivity—May-morning tournaments, summer evening dances on the squares of Florence, weddings, carnival processions, and vintage-banquets at the villa—had their own lyrics accompanied with music and the Carola.

The dance-songs and canzonets, of which we have been speaking, were chiefly of town growth and Tuscan. Another kind of popular love-poem, common to all the dialects of Italy, may be regarded as a special production of the country. Much has lately been written concerning these *Rispetti*, *Strambotti* and *Stornelli*.[50] Ample collections have been made to illustrate their local peculiarities. Their points of resemblance and dissimilarity have been subjected to critical analysis, and great ingenuity has been expended on the problem of their origin. It will be well to preface what has to be said about them with some explanation of terms. There are, to begin with, two distinct species. The *Stornello*, *Ritornello* or *Fiore*, called also *Ciure* in Sicily, properly consists of two or three verses starting with the name of a flower. Thus:[51]

> Fior di Granato!
> Bella, lo nome tuo sta scritto in cielo,
> Lo mio sta scritto sull' onda del mare.

Rispetto and *Strambotto* are two names for the same kind of song, which in the north-eastern provinces is also called *Villotta* and in Sicily *Can-*

[48] *Le Rime di Messer A. Poliziano*, pp. 295, 346.

[49] See *Laude Spirituali di Feo Belcari e di Altri*, Firenze, 1863. The hymn *Crocifisso a capo chino*, for example, has this heading: 'Cantasi come—Una donna d' amor fino,' which was by no means a moral song (*ibid.* p. 16). D' Ancona, in his *Poesia Pop. It.* pp. 431-436, has extracted the titles of these profane songs, some of which are to be found in the *Canzoni a Ballo* (Firenze, 1568), and *Canti Carnascialeschi* (Cosmopoli, 1750), while the majority are lost.

[50] The books which I have consulted on this branch of vernacular poetry are (1) Tommaseo, *Canti popolari toscani, corsi, illirici e greci* Venezia, 1841. (2) Tigri, *Canti popolari toscani*, Firenze, 1869. (3) Pitrè, *Canti popolari siciliani*, and *Studi di poesia popolare*, Palermo, 1870-1872. (4) D' Ancona, *La Poesia popolare italiana*, Livorno, 1878. (5) Rubieri, *Storia della poesia popolare italiana*, Firenze, 1877. Also numerous collections of local songs, of which a good list is furnished in D 'Ancona's work just cited. Bolza's edition of Comasque poetry, Dal Medico's of Venetian, Ferraro's of *Canti Monferrini* (district of Montferrat), Vigo's of Sicilian, together with Imbriani's of Southern and Marcoaldo's of Central dialects, deserve to be specially cited. The literature in question is already voluminous, and bids fair to receive considerable additions.

[51] I take this example at random from Blessig's *Romische Ritornelle* (Leipzig, 1860), p. 48:

> Flower of Pomegranate tree!
> Your name, O my fair one, is written in heaven;
> My name it is writ on the waves of the sea.

zune.[52] Strictly speaking, the term *Strambotto* should be confined to literary imitations of the popular *Rispetto*. In Tuscany the lyric in question consists, in its normal form, of four alternately rhyming hendecasyllabic lines, followed by what is technically called the *ripresa*, or repetition, which may be composed of two, four, or even more verses. Though not strictly an octave stanza, it sometimes falls into this shape, and has then two pairs of three alternate rhymes, finished up with a couplet. In the following instance the quatrain and the *ripresa* are well marked:[53]

Quando sarà quel benedetto giorno,
Che le tue scale salirò pian piano?
I tuoi fratelli mi verranno intorno,
Ad un ad un gli toccherò la mano.
Quando sarà quel dì, cara colonna,
Che la tua mamma chiamerò madonna?
Quando sarà quel dì, caro amor mio?
Io sarò vostra, e voi sarete mio!

In Sicily the *Canzune* exhibits a stanza of eight lines rhyming alternately throughout upon two sounds. Certain peculiarities, however, in the structure of the strophe render it probable that it was originally a quatrain followed by a *ripresa* of the same length. Thus:[54]

Quannu nascisti tu, stidda lucenti,
'N terra calaru tri ancili santi;
Vinniru li Tri Re d' Orienti,
Purtannu cosi d' oru e di brillanti;
Tri aculi vularu prestamenti,
Dannu la nova a penenti e a livanti;
Bella, li to' billizzi su' putenti!
Avi nov' anni chi ti sugnu amanti.

52 The term *Villotta* or *Vilota* is special, I believe, to Venice and the Friuli. D' Ancona identifies it with *Rispetto*, Rubieri with *Stornello*. But it has the character of a quatrain, and seems therefore more properly to belong to the former.

53 Tigri, p. 123. Translated by me thus:

Ah, when will dawn that blissful day
When I shall softly mount your stair,
Your brothers meet me on the way,
And one by one I greet them there!
When comes the day, my staff, my strength,
To call your mother mine at length?
When will the day come, love of mine,
I shall be yours and you be mine?

54 Pitrè, vol. i. p. 185. Translated by me thus, with an alteration in the last couplet:

When thou wert born, O beaming star!
Three holy angels flew to earth;
The three kings from the East afar
Brought gold and jewels of great worth;
Three eagles on wings light as air
Bore the news East and West and North.
O jewel fair, O jewel rare,
So glad was heaven to greet thy birth.

In the north-east the *Villotta* consists of a simple quatrain. Of this form the following is an example:[55]

> Quanti ghe n' è, che me sente a cantare,
> E i dise;—Custia canta dal bon tempo.—
> Che prego 'l ciel che me possa agiutare;
> Quando che canto, alora me lamento.

Though these are the leading types of the *Rispetto*, *Canzune* and *Villotta*, each district exhibits a variety of subordinate and complex forms. The same may be said about the *Stornello*, *Ritornello* and *Ciure*. The names, too, are very variously applied; nor without pedantry would it be possible to maintain perfect precision in their usage.[56] It is enough to have indicated the two broad classes into which popular poetry of this kind is divided. For the future I shall refer to the one sort as *Rispetti*, to the other as *Stornelli*.

Comparative analysis makes it clear that the *Rispetti* and *Stornelli* scattered over all the provinces of Italy, constitute a common fund. That is to say, we do not meet with the *Rispetti* of each dialect confined to their own region; but the same original *Rispetto*, perhaps now lost to sight, has been adapted and transformed to suit the taste and idiom of the several provinces. To reconstitute the primitive type, to decide with certainty in each case the true source of these lyrics, is probably impossible. All we know for certain is that beneath apparent dialectical divergences the vulgar poetry of the Italians presents unmistakable signs of identity.[57] Which province was the primitive home of the *Rispetti*; whether Sicily, where the faculty for reproducing them is still most vivid;[58] or Tuscany, where they certainly attain their purest form and highest beauty; or whether all Italian country districts have contributed their quota to the general stock; are difficult questions, as yet by no means satisfactorily decided. Professor d' Ancona advances a theory, which is too plausible to be ignored in silence. *Rispetti*, he suggests, were first produced in Sicily, whence they travelled through Central Italy, receiving dialectical transmutation in Tuscany, and there also

[55] Dalmedico, *Canti Ven.* p. 69:

> Many there are who when they hear me sing,
> Cry: There goes one whose joy runs o'er in song!
> But I pray God to give me succouring;
> For when I sing, 'tis then I grieve full strong.

[56] For instance, *Rispetti* in the valley of the Po are called *Romanelle*. In some parts of Central Italy the *Stornello* becomes *Mottetto* or *Raccommandare*. The little Southern lyrics known as *Arii* and *Ariette* at Naples and in Sicily, are elsewhere called *Villanelle* or *Napolitane* and *Siciliane*. It is clear that in this matter of nomenclature great exactitude cannot be sought.

[57] The proofs adduced by D' Ancona in his *Poesia popolare*, pp. 177-284, seem to me conclusive on this point.

[58] See Pitrè, *Studi di Poesia popolare* (Palermo, Lauriel, 1872), two essays on 'I Poeti del Popolo Siciliano,' and 'Pietro Fullone e le sfide popolari,' pp. 81-184. He gives particulars relating to contemporary improvisations. See, too, the Essays by L. Vigo, *Opere* (Catania, 1870-74), vol. ii.

attaining to the perfection of their structure.[59] Numerous slight indications lead to the conclusion that their original linguistic type was Southern. The imagery also which is common in verses sung to this day by the peasants of the Pistoja highlands, including frequent references to the sea with metaphors borrowed from orange-trees and palms, seems to indicate a Sicilian birthplace.[60] We have, moreover, the early evidence of six *Napolitane* copied from a Magliabecchian MS. of the fourteenth century, which exhibit the transition from Southern to Tuscan idiom and structure.[61] One of these still exists in several dialects, under the title of 'La Rondinella importuna.'[62] It is therefore certain that many *Rispetti* are very ancient, dating from the Suabian period, when Sicilian poetry, as we have seen, underwent the process of *toscaneggiamento*. However, D' Ancona's theory is too hypothetical, and it may also be said, too neat, to be accepted without reservation.

One point, at any rate, may be considered certain. Though the *Rispetti* are still alive upon the lips of *contadini*; though we may hear them echoing from farm and field through all the length and breadth of Italy; though the voluminous collections we possess have recently been gathered from *viva voce* recitation; yet they are perhaps as ancient as the dialects. The proof of this antiquity lies in the fact that whether we take the literary *Strambotti* of Poliziano for our standard, or the *pasticci*, *incatenature* and *intrecciature* of the sixteenth century for guides, we find the phrases and the style that are familiar to us in the rural lyrics of to-day.[63] Bronzino's *Serenata* and the *Incatenatura* of Bianchino contain, embedded in their structure, ditties which were universally known in the sixteenth century, and which are being sung still with unimportant alterations by the people. The attention of learned men was directed in the renascence of Tuscan literature to the beauty of these lyrics. Poliziano, writing to Lorenzo de' Medici in 1488, and describing his journey with Pietro through Montepulciano and Acquapendente in the month of May, says that he and his companions amused themselves with *rappresaglie* or adaptations of the songs they heard upon the way.[64] His road took him through what is still one of the

[59] *Op. cit.* pp. 285, 288-294.

[60] I may refer at large to Tigri's collection, and to my translations of these *Rispetti* in *Sketches in Italy and Greece.*

[61] Carducci, *Cantilene*, p. 57.

[62] See Rubieri, *Storia della poesia popolare,* pp 352-356, for a selection of variants.

[63] The terms employed above require some illustration. Poliziano's Canzonet, *La pastorella si leva per tempo*, is a *pasticcio* composed of fragments from popular songs in vogue at his day. We possess three valuable poems—one by Bronzino, published in 1567; one by Il Cieco Bianchino of Florence, published at Verona in 1629; the third by Il Cieco Britti of Venice, published in the same year—which consist of extracts from popular lyrics united together by the rhymester. Hence their name *incatenatura*. See Rubieri, *op. cit.* pp. 212, 121, 130. See, too, D' Ancona, *op. cit.* pp. 100-105, 146-172, for the text and copious illustrations from contemporary sources of Bronzino's and Il Cieco Bianchino's poems.

[64] *Prose Volgari, ecc., di A. A. Poliziano* (Firenze, Barbèra, 1867), p. 74. 'Siamo tutti allegri, e facciamo buona cera, e becchiamo per tutta la via di qualche rappresaglia e Canzone di Calen di Maggio, che mi sono parute più fantastiche qui in Acquapendente alla Romanesca, vel nota ipsa vel argumento.'

best sources of local verse and music; and we may believe that at the close of the fifteenth century, the *contadini* of that district were singing nearly the same words as now. Nor, when we examine the points of similarity and difference in the Italian *Rispetti* and *Stornelli*, as they now exist, is there anything improbable in this antiquity. Nothing but great age can account for their adaptation to the tone, feeling, fancy, habits, and language of so many regions. It must have taken more than a century or two to rub down their original angles, to efface the specific stamp of their birthplace, and to make them pass for home productions in Venice no less than Palermo, in Tuscan Montalcino and Ligurian Chiavari.

The retentiveness of the popular memory, before it has been spoiled by education, is quite sufficient to account for the preservation of these lyrics through several hundred years. Nor need their wide diffusion suggest difficulties. Italy in the middle ages offered readier means of intercommunication between the inhabitants of her provinces than she has done since the settlement of the country in 1530. When the liberation of the Communes gave a new impulse to intellectual and commercial activity, there began a steady and continually increasing movement from one city to another. Commercial enterprise led the burghers of Pisa, Lucca, Florence, Venice, Genoa, to establish themselves as bankers and middlemen, brokers and manufacturers, in Rome and Naples. Soldiers of adventure flocked from the south, and made the northern towns their temporary home. The sanctuaries of Gargano, Loretto and Assisi drew pilgrims from all quarters. Noblemen of Romagna acted as *podestà* beyond the Apennines, while Lombards opened shops in Palermo. Churchmen bred upon the Riviera wore the mitre in the March; natives of the Spoletano taught in the schools of Bologna and Pavia. Men of letters, humanists and artists had no fixed dwelling-place, but wandered, like mercenary soldiers, from town to town in search of better pay. Students roamed from school to school according as the fame of great professors drew them. Party quarrels in the commonwealths drove whole families, such as the Florentine Uberti, Alberti, Albizzi, Strozzi, into exile. Conquered cities, like Pisa, sent forth their burghers by hundreds as emigrants, too proud to bear the yoke of foes they had resisted. Nor were the Courts of princes without their influence in mingling the natives of different districts. Whether, then, we study the *Novelle*, or the histories of great houses, or the biographies of eminent Italians, or the records of the universities, we shall be led to the conclusion that from the year 1200 to the year 1550 there was a perpetual and lively intercourse by land and sea between the departments of Italy. This reciprocity of influence did not cease until the two despotic races, Austrian and Spaniard, threw each separate province into solitary chains. Such being the conditions of social exchange at the epoch when the language was in process of formation, there is nothing strange in finding the rural poetry of the South acclimatised in central and northern Italy. But the very facility of communication and the probable antiquity of these lyrics should make us cautious in adopting any rigid hypothesis about their origin. It is reasonable to suppose that such transferable property as love-poems might have been everywhere produced and rapidly diffused, the best from each centre surviving by a natural process of selection. Lastly, whatever view may be taken of their formation and their age, we have every reason to believe that the fifteenth century was a fruitful period of production and accumulation. Toward the close of the *quattrocento* they attracted the curiosity of lettered poets, who began to imitate them, and in the next hundred years they were committed in large numbers to the press.[65]

In addition to the influence exercised by these popular lyrics over polite literature in the golden age of the Renaissance, extraordinary interest attaches to them as an indigenous species of verse, dating from remote antiquity and still surviving in all corners of the country. In them we analyse the Italian poetic genius at its source and under its most genuine conditions. Both from their qualities and their defects inferences may be drawn, which find application and illustration in the solemn works of laurelled singers. The one theme of *Rispetti* and *Stornelli* is love; but love in all its phases and with all its retinue of associated emotions—expectation, fruition, disappointment, jealousy, despair, rejection, treachery, desertion, pleading, scorn—the joys of presence, the pangs of absence, the ecstasy of union, the agony of parting—love, natural and unaffected, turbulent or placid, chaste or troubled with desire, imperious or humble, tempestuously passionate or toned to tranquil acquiescence—love varying through all moods and tempers, yet never losing its note of spontaneity, sincerity and truth. The instincts of the people are pure, and their utterances of affection are singularly free from grossness. This at least is almost universally the case with lyrics gathered from the country. Approaching town-life, they lose their delicacy; and the products of the city are not unfrequently distinguished by the crudest obscenity.[66] The literary form of many of these masterpieces exhibits the beauty of rhythm, the refinement of outline, which we associate with melodies of the best Italian period—with chants of Pergolese, songs of Salvator Rosa. When we compare their subject-matter with that of our Northern Ballads, we notice a marked deficiency of legend, superstition or grotesque fancy.

[65] See D' Ancona, *op. cit.* pp. 354-420, for copious and interesting notices of the popular press in several Italian towns. The *Avallone* of Naples, *Cordella* of Venice, *Marescandoli* of Florence, *Bertini* and *Baroni* of Lucca, *Colomba* of Bologna, all served the special requirements of the proletariat in town and country. G. B. Verini of Florence made anthologies called *L' Ardor d' Amore* and *Crudeltà d' Amore* in the sixteenth century, both of which are still reprinted. The same is true of the *Olimpia* and *Gloria* of Olimpo degli Alessandri of Sassoferrato. The subordinate titles commonly used in these popular Golden Treasuries are, 'Canzoni di amore,' 'di gelosia,' 'di sdegno,' 'di pace e di partenza.' Their classification and description appear from the following rubrics: 'Mattinate,' 'Serenate,' 'Partenze,' 'Strambotti,' 'Sdegni,' 'Sonetti,' 'Villanelle,' 'Lettere,' 'Affetti d' Amore,' &c.

[66] Upon this point consult Rubieri, *op. cit.* chap. xiv. In Sicily the *Ciure,* says Pitrè, is reckoned unfit for an honest woman's mouth.

There are no witches, dragons, demon-lovers, no enchanted forests, no mythical heroes, no noble personages, few ghosts, few dreams and visions, in these songs poured forth among the olive-trees and myrtle-groves of Italy. Human nature, conscious of pleasure and of pain, finding its primitive emotion an adequate motive for verse subtly modulated through a thousand keys, is here sufficient to itself. The echoes imported from an outer world of passion and romance and action into this charmed region of the lover's heart are rare and feeble. Through all their national vicissitudes, the Italian peasants followed one sole aim in verse. The *Rispetti* of all times, localities and dialects form one protracted, ever varying Duo between Thou and I, the *dama* and the *damo*, the eternal protagonists in the play of youth and love.

This absence of legendary and historical material marks a main difference between Italian and Teutonic inspiration. Among the Italic communities the practical historic sense was early developed, and sustained by the tradition of a classic past. It demanded a positive rather than imaginative treatment of contemporary fact and mythus. Among the people this requirement was satisfied by *Storie*, *Lamenti*, and prose Chronicles. Very few, indeed, are the relics of either romantic or actual history surviving in the lyrics of the rural population. Only here and there, in dim allusions to the Sicilian Vespers and the Norman Conquest, in the tale of the Baronessa di Carini, or in the Northern legend of Rosmunda, under its popular form of 'La Donna Lombarda,' do we find a faint analogy between the Italian and Teutonic ballads.[67] Dramatic, mythical and epical elements are almost wholly wanting in the genuine lyrics of the people.

This statement requires some qualification. The four volumes of 'Fiabe, Novelle e Racconti' recently published by Signor Pitrè, prove that the Sicilians in prose at least have a copious literature corresponding to German *Märchen* and Norse tales.[68] This literature, however, has not received poetic treatment in any existing Southern songs that have been published, excepting in the few already noticed. At the same time, it must be mentioned that the collections of lyrics in north-western dialects—especially the 'Canti Monferrini,' 'Canzoni Comasche,' and 'Canti Leccesi'—exhibit specimens of genuine ballads. It would seem that contact with French and German borderers along the Alpine rampart had introduced into Piedmont and Lombardy a form of lyric which is not essentially Italian. Had I space sufficient at disposal, I should like to quote the 'Donna Lombarda,' 'Moglie Infedele,' 'Giuseppina Parricida,' 'Principessa Giovanna,' 'Giuliano della Croce Bianca,' 'Cecilia,' 'Rè Carlino,' 'Morando,' and several others from Ferraro's collection.[69] They illustrate, what is exceedingly rare in popular Italian

[67] The South seems richer in this material than the Centre. See Pitrè's *Canti Pop. Sic.* vol. ii., among the *Leggende e Storie*, especially *La Comare*, *Minni-spartuti*, *Principessa di Carini*, *L'Innamorata del Diavolo*, and some of the bandit songs.

[68] Palermo, Lauriel, 1875.

[69] *Canti Monferrini* (Torino-Firenze, Loescher, 1870), pp. 1, 6, 14, 26, 28, 34, 42. One of the ballads cited above, *La Sisilia*, is found in Sicily.

poetry, both the subject-matter and the manner peculiar to the Northern Ballad. Let the following verses from 'La Sposa per Forza' suffice:[70]

Ra soi madona a r' ha brassaja
    Suvra u so coffu a r' ha minèe;
    Uardèe qui, ra me noiretta,
    Le bele gioje che vi vôi dunèe.
Mi n' ho csa fè dle vostre gioje;
    E manc ancur dla vostra cà;
    Cma ca voja dir bel gioje
    Ra me mama m' na mandirà.

To comparative mythologists in general, and to English students in particular, the most interesting of these rare Italian Ballads is undoubtedly one known as 'L' Avvelenato.'[71] So far as I am aware, it is unique in the Italian language; nor had its correspondences with Northern Ballad literature been noticed until I pointed them out in 1879.[72] In his work on popular Italian poetry, Professor D' Ancona included the following song, which he had heard upon the lips of a young peasant of the Pisan district:[73]

Dov' eri 'ersera a cena
Caro mio figlio, savio e gentil?
    Mi fai morire
        Ohimè!

Dov' eri 'ersera a cena
Gentile mio cavalier?—
Ero dalla mia dama;
    Mio core stà male,
    Che male mi stà!
Ero dalla mia dama;
'L mio core che se ne và.—
Che ti diènno da cena,
Caro mio figlio, savio e gentil?
    Mi fai morire,
        Ohimè!

Che ti diènno da cena,
Gentile mio cavalier?—
Un anguilletta arrosto,
    Cara mia madre;
    Mio core stà male,
    Che male mi stà!
Un anguilletta arrosto,
'L mio core che se ne và.

Other versions of the same poem occur in the dialects of Venice, Como and Lecco with such variations as prove them all to be the offshoots

[70] *Ibid.* p. 48.
[71] It does not occur in the *Canti Monferrini*.
[72] See my letter to the *Rassegna Settimanale*, March 9, 1879, on the subject of this ballad. Though I begged Italian students for information respecting similar compositions my letter only elicited a Tuscan version of the *Donna Lombarda*.
[73] *Op. cit.* p. 106.

from some original now lost in great antiquity. That it existed and was famous so far back as the middle of the seventeenth century, is proved by an allusion in the 'Cicalata in lode della Padella e della Frittura,' recited before the Accademia della Crusca by Lorenzo Panciatichi in 1656.[74] A few lines are also quoted in the *incatenatura* of the Cieco Fiorentino, published at Verona in 1629.[75] Anyone who is familiar with our Border Minstrelsy will perceive at once that this is only an Italian version of the Ballad of Lord Donald or Lord Randal.[76] The identity between the two is rendered still more striking by an analysis of the several Lombard versions. In that of Como, for example, the young man makes his will; and this is the last verse:[77]

> Cossa lassè alla vostra dama,
> Figliuol mio caro, fiorito e gentil,
> Cossa lassè alla vostra dama?
> La fôrca da impiccarla,
> Signora mama, mio cor sta mal!
> La fôrca da impiccarla:
> Ohimè, ch' io moro, ohimè!

The same version furnishes the episode of the poisoned hounds:[78]

> Coss' avì fâ dell' altra mezza,
> Figliuol mio caro, fiorito e gentil?
> Cossa avì fâ dell' altra mezza?
> L' hô dada alla cagnòla:
> Signôra mama, mio core sta mal!
> L' hô dada alla cagnòla:
> Ohimè, ch' io moro, ohimè!
> Cossa avì fâ della cagnòla,
> Figliuol mio caro, fiorito e gentil?
> Cossa avì râ della cagnòla?
> L' è morta drè la strada;
> Signora mama, mio core sta mal!
> L' è morta drè la strada:
> Ohimè, ch' io moro, ohimè!

It is worth mentioning that the same Ballad belongs under slightly different forms to the Germans, Swedes, and other nations of the Teu-

[74] D' Ancona *op. cit.* p. 106.

[75] *Ibid.* pp. 99, 105.

[76] See Child's *English and Scottish Ballads*, vol. ii. pp. 244 *et seqq.*

[77] Bolza, *Canz. Pop. Comasche,* No. 49. Here is the Scotch version from Lord Donald:

> What will ye leave to your true-love, Lord Donald, my son?
> What will ye leave to your true-love, my jollie young man?
> The tow and the halter, for to hang on yon tree,
> And lat her hang there for the poisoning o' me.

[78] This is the Scotch version, with the variant of Lord Randal:

> What gat ye to your dinner, Lord Randal, my son?
> What gat ye to your dinner, my handsome young man?
> I gat eels boiled in broo; mother, make my bed soon,
> For I'm weary wi' hunting, and fain wald lie down.
> What became of your bloodhounds, Lord Randal, my son?

tonic stock; but so far as I have yet been able to discover, it remains the sole instance of that species of popular literature in Italy.[79] The phenomenon is singular, and though conjectures may be hazarded in explanation, it is impossible, until further researches for parallel examples have been made, to advance a theory of how this Ballad penetrated so far south as Tuscany.

> What became of your bloodhounds, my handsome young man?
> O, they swelled and they died; mother, make my bed soon,
> For I'm weary wi' hunting, and fain wald lie down.

[79] In Passano's *I Novellieri Italiani in Verso* I find, at p. 20, the notice of a poem, in octave stanzas, which corresponds exactly to the *Heir of Lynn*. Published at Venice, 1530, 1531, 1542, it bears this title: 'Essempio dun giovane ricchissimo; qual consumata la ricchezza: disperato a un trave si sospese. Nel qual il padre previsto il suo fatal corso gia molti anni avanti infinito tesoro posto havea, et quello per il carico fracassato, la occulta moneta scoperse.' The young man's name is Fenitio. I have not seen this poem, and since it is composed in *ottava rima* it cannot be classed exactly with the *Avvelenato*. Passano also catalogues the *Historia di tre Giovani disperati e di tre fate*, and the *Historia di Leon Bruno*, which seem to contain ballad elements.

CHAPTER V

POPULAR RELIGIOUS POETRY

The Thirteenth Century—Outburst of Flagellant Fanaticism—The 'Battuti,' 'Bianchi,' 'Disciplinati'—Acquire the name of Laudesi—Jacopone da Todi—His Life—His Hymns—The 'Corrotto'—Franciscan Poetry—Tresatti's Collection—Grades of Spiritual Ecstasy—Lauds of the Confraternities—Benivieni—Feo Belcari and the Florentine Hymn-writers—Relation to Secular Dance-songs—Origins of the Theatre—Italy had hardly any true Miracle Plays—Umbrian Divozioni—The Laud becomes Dramatic—Passion Plays—Mediæval Properties—The Stage in Church or in the Oratory—The 'Sacra Rappresentazione'—A Florentine Species—Fraternities for Boys—Names of the 'Festa'—Theory of its Origin—Shows in Mediæval Italy—Pageants of S. John's Day at Florence—Their Machinery—Florentine Ingegnieri—Forty-three Plays in D' Ancona's Collection—Their Authors—The Prodigal Son—Elements of Farce—Interludes and Music—Three Classes of 'Sacre Rappresentazioni' —Biblical Subjects—Legends of Saints—Popular 'Novelle'—Conversion of the Magdalen—Analysis of Plays.

THE history of popular religious poetry takes us back to the first age of Italian literature and to the discords of the thirteenth century. All Italy had been torn asunder by the internecine struggle of Frederick II. with Innocent III. and Gregory IX. The people saw the two chiefs of Christendom at open warfare, exchanging anathemas, and doing each what in him lay to render peace and amity impossible. Milan resounded to the shrieks of *paterini*, burned upon the public square by order of an intolerant pontiff. Padua echoed with the groans of Ezzelino's victims, doomed to death by hundreds and by thousands in his dungeons, or cast forth maimed and mutilated to perish in the fields. The southern provinces swarmed with Saracens, whom an infidel Emperor had summoned to his aid against a fanatical Pope. It seemed as though the age, which had witnessed the assertion of Italian independence and the growth of the free cities, was about to end in a chaos of bloodshed, fire and frantic cruelty. The climax of misery and fury was reached in the Crusade launched by Alexander IV. against the tyrants of the Trevisan Marches. When Ezzelino died like a dog in 1259, the maddened populace believed that his demon had now been loosed from chains of flesh, and sent forth to the elements to work its will in freedom. The prince of darkness was abroad and menacing. Though the monster had perished, the myth of evil that survived him had power to fascinate, and was intolerable.

The conscience of the people, crazed by the sight of such iniquity and suffering, bereft of spiritual guidance, abandoned to bad government, made itself suddenly felt in an indescribable movement of religious terror. 'In the year 1260,' wrote the Chronicler of Padua,[1] 'when Italy was defiled by many horrible crimes, a sudden and new perturbation seized at first upon the folk of Perugia, next upon the Romans, and lastly on the population of all Italy, who, stung by the fear of God, went forth processionally, gentle and base-born, old and young, together, through the city streets and squares, naked save for a waistband round their loins, holding a whip of leather in their hands, with tears and groans, scourging their shoulders till the blood flowed down. Not by day alone, but through the night in the intense cold of winter, with lighted torches they roamed by hundreds, by thousands, by tens of thousands through the churches, and flung themselves down before the altars, led by priests with crosses and banners. The same happened in all villages and hamlets, so that the fields and mountains resounded with the cries of sinners calling upon God. All instruments of music and songs of love were hushed; only the dismal wail of penitents was heard in town and country.'

It will be noticed that this fanaticism of the Flagellants began among the Umbrian highlands, the home of S. Francis and the centre of pietistic art, where the passions of the people have ever been more quickly stirred by pathos than elsewhere in Italy. The *Battuti*, as they were called, formed no mere sect. Populations of whole cities, goaded by an irresistible impulse, which had something of the Dionysiac madness in it, went forth as though a migration of the race had been initiated. Blind instinct, the intoxication of religious frenzy, urged them restlessly and aimlessly from place to place. They had no Holy Land, no martyr's shrine, in view. Only the ineffable horror of a coming judgment, only the stings of spiritual apprehension, the fierce craving after sympathy in common acts of delirium, the allurements of an exaltation shared by thousands, drove them on, lugubrious herds, like Mænads of the wrath of God. This insurgence of all classes, swelling upward from the lowest, gaining the middle regions, and confounding the highest in the flood of one promiscuous multitude, threatened the very fabric of society.[2] Repentance and compunction, exhibited upon a scale of such colossal magnitude, attended by incidents of such impassioned frenzy, assumed the aspect of vice and of insanity. Florence shut her gates to the half-naked *Battuti*. At Milan the tyrants of the Della Torre blood raised 600 gibbets as a warning. Manfred drew a military cordon round his southern States to save them from contagion. The revival was diagnosed by cold observers as an epidemic, or as a craving akin to that which sets in motion droves of bisons on a trackless plain. It needed drastic measures of Draconian justice to curb a disease which threatened the whole nation. Gradually, the first fury of this fanatical enthusiasm subsided. It was but the symptom of moral and intellectual bewilder-

[1] Muratori, *Rer. Ital. Script.* viii. 712.

[2] A curious letter describing the entrance of the *Battuti* into Rome in 1399 may be read in Romagnoli's publication *Le Compagnie de' Battuti in Roma*, Bologna, 1862. It refers to a period later by a century than the first outbreak of the enthusiasm.

ment, of what the French would call *ahurissement*, in a race of naturally firm and patient fibre. Yet, when it passed, durable traces of the agitation remained. Lay fraternities were formed, not only in Umbria and Tuscany, but in almost all provinces of the peninsula, who called themselves *Disciplinati di Gesù Cristo*. These societies aimed at continuing the ascetic practices of the Flagellants, and at prolonging their passion of penitence in a more sober spirit. Scourging formed an essential part of their observances, but it was used with decency and moderation. Their constitution was strictly democratic, within limits sanctioned by the clergy. They existed for the people, supplementing and not superseding the offices of the Church. From the date of their foundation they seem to have paid much attention to the recitation of hymns in the vernacular. These hymns were called *Laude*. Written for and by the people, they were distinguished from the Latin hymns of the Church by greater spontaneity and rudeness. No limit of taste or literary art was set to the expression of a fervent piety. The Lauds dwelt chiefly on the Passion of our Lord, and were used as a stimulus to compunction. In course of time this part of their system became so prominent that the *Battuti* or *Disciplinati* acquired the milder title of *Laudesi*.[3]

From the *Laudesi* of the fourteenth century rose one great lyric poet, Jacopone da Todi, whose hymns embrace the whole gamut of religious passion, from tender emotions of love to sombre anticipations of death and thrilling visions of judgment. Reading him, we listen to the true lyrical cry of the people's heart in its intolerance of self-restraint, blending the language of erotic ecstasy with sobs and sighs of soul-consuming devotion, aspiring to heaven on wings sped by the energy of human desire. The flight of his inebriated piety transcends and out-soars the strongest pinion of ecclesiastical hymnology. Such lines as—

> Fac me plagis vulnerari,
> Cruce hac inebriari
> Ob amorem filii—

[3] Some banners—*Gonfaloni* or *Stendardi*—of the Perugian fraternities, preserved in the Pinacoteca of that town, are interesting for their illustration of these religious companies at a later date. The Gonfalone of S. Bernardino by Bonfigli represents the saint between heaven and earth pleading for his votaries. Their Oratory (Cappella di Giustizia) is seen behind, and in front are the men and women of the order. That of the *Societas Annuntiatæ*, with date 1466, shows a like band of lay brethren and sisters. That of the Giustizia by Perugino has a similar group, kneeling and looking up to Madonna, who is adored by S. Francis and S. Bernardino in the heavens. Behind is a landscape with a portion of Perugia near the Church of S. Francis. The Stendardo of the Confraternità di S. Agostino by Pinturicchio exhibits three white-clothed members of the body, kneeling and gazing up to their patron. There is also a fine picture in the Perugian Pinacoteca by Giov. Boccati of Camerino (signed and dated 1447) representing Madonna enthroned in a kind of garden, surrounded by child-like angels with beautiful blonde hair, singing and reading from choir books in a double row of semi-circular choir-stalls. Below, S. Francis and S. Dominic are leading each two white *Disciplinati* to the throne. These penitents carry their scourges, and holes cut in the backs of their monastic cloaks show the skin red with stripes. One on either side has his face uncovered: the other wears the hood down, with eye-holes pierced in it. This picture belonged to the Confraternity of S. Domenico.

do but supply the theme for Jacopone's descant. Violently discordant notes clash and mingle in his chords, and are resolved in bursts of ardour bordering on delirium. He leaps from the grotesque of plebeian imagery to pictures of sublime pathos, from incoherent gaspings to sentences pregnant with shrewd knowledge of the heart, by sudden and spontaneous transitions, which reveal the religious sentiment in its simplest form, unspoiled by dogma, unstiffened by scholasticism. None, for example, but a true child of the people could have found the following expression of a desire to suffer with Christ:[4]

O Signor per cortesia
  Mandame la malsania
A me la freve quartana
  la contina e la terzana,
  la doppia cottidiana
  Colla grande ydropesia.
A me venga mal de dente
  Mal de capo e mal de ventre,
  a lo stomaco dolor pungente
  en canna l' asquinantia.
Mal de occhi e doglia de fianco
  e la postema al lato manco
  tyseco me ionga enalco
  e omne tempo la frenesia.
Agia el fegato rescaldato
  la milza grossa el ventre enfiato,
  lo polmone sia piagato
  Con gran tossa e parlasia.

In order to understand Jacopone da Todi and to form any true conception of the medium from which his poems sprang, it is necessary to study the legend of his life, which, though a legend, bears upon its face the stamp of truth. It is an offshoot from the Saga of S. Francis, a vivid utterance of the times which gave it birth.[5] Jacopone was born at Todi, one of those isolated ancient cities which rear themselves upon their hill-tops between the valleys of the Nera and the Tiber, on the old post-road from Narni to Perugia. He belonged to the family of the Benedetti, who were reckoned among the noblest of the district. In his youth he followed secular studies, took the degree of Doctor of Laws, and practised with a keen eye for gain and with not less, his biographer hints, than the customary legal indifference for justice. He married a beautiful young wife, whom he dressed splendidly and sent among his equals to all places of mediæval amusement. She was, however, inwardly religious. The spirit of S. Francis had passed over her; and unknown to all the crowd around her, unknown to her husband, she practised the extremities of ascetic piety. One day she went, at

[4] *Cantici di Jacopone da Todi* (Roma, Salviano, 1558), p. 64. I quote from this edition as the most authentic, and reproduce its orthography.
[5] This Life is prefixed to Salviano's Roman edition of Jacopone's hymns, 1558.

her husband's bidding, to a merry-making of the nobles of Todi; and it so happened that 'while she was dancing and taking pleasure with the rest, an accident occurred, fit to move the greatest pity. For the platform whereupon the party were assembled, fell in and was broken to pieces, causing grievous injury to those who stood upon it. She was so hurt in the fall that she lost the power of speech, and in a few hours after died. Jacopo, who by God's mercy was not there, no sooner heard the sad news of his wife than he ran to the place. He found her on the point of death, and sought, as is usual in those cases, to unlace her; but she, though she could not speak, offered resistance to her husband's unlacing her. However, he used force and overcame her, and unlaced and carried her to his house. There, when she had died, he unclothed her with his own hands, and found that underneath those costly robes and next to her naked flesh she wore a hair-shirt of the roughest texture. Jacopone, who up to now had believed his wife, since she was young and beautiful, to be like other women, worldly and luxurious, stood as it were astonied and struck dumb when he beheld a thing so contrary to his opinion. Wherefore from that time forward he went among men like to one who is stunned, and appeared no longer to be a reasonable man as theretofore. The cause of this his change to outward view was not a sudden infirmity of health, or extraordinary sorrow for the cruel death of his wife, or any such-like occurrence, but an overwhelming compunction of the heart begotten in him by this ensample, and a new recognition of what he was and of his own wretchedness. Wherefore turning back to his own heart, and reckoning with bitterness the many years that had been spent so badly, and seeing the peril in which he had continued up to that time, he set himself to change the manner of his life, and even as he had lived heretofore wholly for the world, so now he resolved to live wholly for Christ.'

Jacopone's biographer goes on to tell us how, after this shock, he became an altered man. He sold all his goods and gave away his substance to the poor, retaining nothing for himself, but seeking by every device within his power to render himself vile and ridiculous in the eyes of men. At one time he stripped himself naked, and put upon his back the trappings of an ass, and so appeared among the gentles of his earlier acquaintance. On another occasion he entered a company of merry-making folk in his brother's house, without clothes, smeared with turpentine and rolled in feathers like a bird.[6] By these mad pranks he acquired the reputation of one half-witted, and the people called him Jacopone instead of Messer Jacopo de' Benedetti. Yet there was a keen spirit living in the man, who had determined literally to become a fool for Christ's sake. A citizen once bought a fowl and bade Jacopone carry it to his house. Jacopone took the bird and placed it in the man's family vault, where it was found. To all remonstrances he answered with a solemnity which inspired terror, that *there* was the citizen's real

[6] The biographer adds, 'Ma fu si horribile e spiacevole a vedere che conturbò tutta quella festa, lasciando ogniuno pieno di amaritudine.'

home. At the end of ten years spent in self-abasement of this sort, Jacopone entered the lowest rank of the Franciscan brotherhood. The composition of a Laud so full of spiritual fire that its inspiration seemed indubitable, won for the apparent madman this grace. There was something noble in his bearing, even though his actions and his utterance proved his brain distempered. No fear of hell nor hope of heaven, says his biographer, but God's infinite goodness and beauty impelled him to embrace the monastic life and to subject himself to the severest discipline. Meditating on the Divine perfection, he came to regard himself as 'entirely hideous, vile and stinking, beyond the most abominable carrion.' It was part of his religious exaltation to prove this to himself by ghastly penances, instead of seeking to render his body a fit temple for God's Spirit by healthy and clean living. He had a carnal partiality for liver; and in order to mortify this vile affection, he procured the liver of a beast and hung it in his cell. It became putrid, swarmed with vermin, and infected the convent with its stench. The friars discovered Jacopone rejoicing in the sight and odour of this corruption. With sound good sense they then condemned him to imprisonment in the common privies; but he rejoiced in this punishment, and composed one of his most impassioned odes in that foul place. Still, though he was clearly mad, he had the soul of a Christian and a poet. His ecstasies were not always repugnant to our sense of delicacy. Contemplating the wounds of Christ, it entered into his heart to desire all suffering which it could be possible for man to undergo—the pangs of all the souls condemned to purgatory, the torments of all the damned in hell, the infinite anguish of all the devils—if only by this bearing of the pains of others he might be made like Christ, and go at length, the last of all the world, to Paradise. Not only the passion but the love of Jesus inflamed him with indescribable raptures. He spent whole days in singing, weeping, groaning, and ejaculation. 'He ran,' says the biographer, 'in a fury of love, and under the impression that he was embracing and clasping Jesus Christ, would fling his arms about a tree.' It is not possible to imagine more potent workings of religious insanity in a distempered and at the same time nobly-gifted character. That obscene antipathy to nature which characterised mediæval asceticism, becomes poetic in a lunatic of genius like Jacopone. Nor was his natural acumen blunted. He discerned how far the Papacy diverged from Christianity in practice, and assailed Boniface VIII. with bitterest invectives. Among other prophetic sayings ascribed to him, we find this, which corresponds most nearly to the truth of history: 'Pope Boniface, like a fox thou didst enter on the Papacy, like a wolf thou reignest, and like a dog shalt thou depart from it.' For his free speech Boniface had him sent to prison; and in his dungeon, rejoicing, Jacopone composed the finest of his Canticles.

Such was the man who struck the key-note of religious popular poetry in Italy, and whose Lauds may be regarded as the germ of a voluminous literature. Passing from his life to his writings, it will suffice to give a few specimens of those hymns which are most characteristic of his temper. We have already seen how he brought together the most repulsive details of disease, in order to express his desire to suffer with Christ.[7] Here is the beginning of a canticle in praise of the madness he embraced with a similar object:[8]

Senno me pare e cortesia
 empazir per lo bel messia.
Ello me fa sì gran sapere
 a chi per dio vol empazire
 en parige non se vidde
 ancor si gran phylosofia.

These words found an echo after many years in Benivieni's even more hysterical hymn upon divine madness, which was substituted in Savonarola's Carnivals for the *Trionfi* of Lorenzo de' Medici.

A trace of the Franciscan worship of poverty gives some interest to a hymn on the advantages of pauperism. The theme, however, is supported with solid arguments after the fashion of Juvenal's *vacuus viator*:[9]

Povertate muore en pace,
 nullo testamento face,
 lassa el mondo como jace
 e la gente concordate.
Non a judice ne notaro
 a corte non porta salaro,
 ridese del omo avaro
 che sta en tanta anxietate.

Truer to the inebriation of Jacopone's piety are the following stanzas, incoherent from excess of passion, which seem to be the ebullition of one of his most frenzied moments:[10]

Amore amore che si mai ferito
 altro che amore non posso gridare,
 amore amore teco so unito
 altro non posso che te abbracciare,
 amore amore forte mai rapito
 lo cor sempre si spande per amore
 per te voglio pasmare: Amor ch' io teco sia
 amor per cortesia: Fammi morir d' amore.

Amor amor Jesu so gionto aporto
 amor amor Jesu tu m' ai menato,
 amor amor Jesu damme conforto,
 amor amor Jesu si m' ai enflammato,
 amor amor Jesu pensa lo porto
 fammete star amor sempre abracciato,
 con teco trasformato: En vera caritate
 en somma veritate: De trasformato amore.

[7] See above, p. 32. The seventeenth-century editor of Jacopone and his followers, Tresatti, has justly styled this repulsive but characteristic utterance, 'invettiva terribile contro di se.'

[8] *Cantici di Jacopone da Todi* (Roma, Salviano, 1558), p. 109.

[9] *Ibid.* p. 77.

[10] *Ibid.* p. 122. See Appendix.

Amor amore grida tuttol mondo
amor amore omne cosa clama,
amore amore tanto se profondo
chi piu t' abraccia sempre piu t' abrama,
amor amor tu se' cherchio rotondo
con tuttol cor chi c' entra sempre t' ama,
che tu se' stame e trama: chi t' ama per vestire
cusi dolce sentire: Che sempre grida amore.

Amor amor Jesus desideroso
amor voglio morire a te abracciando,
amor amor Jesu dolce mio sposo
amor amor la morte l' ademando,
amor amor Jesu si delectoso
tu me t' arendi en te transformando,
pensa ch' io vo pasmando: Amor non so o me sia
Jesu speranza mia; Abyssame en amore.

A still more mysterious depth is sounded in another hymn in praise of self-annihilation—the Nirvana of asceticism:[11]

Non posso esser renato
s' io en me non so morto,
anichilato en tucto
el esser conservare,
del nihil glorioso
nelom ne gusta fructo,
se Dio non fal conducto
che om non cia que fare,
o glorioso stare
en nihil quietato,
lontellecto posato
e laffecto dormire.

Ciocho veduto e pensato
tutto e feccia e bruttura
pensando de laltura
del virtuoso stato,
nel pelago chio veggio
non ce so notatura
faro somergitura
del om che anegato
sommece inarenato
nonor de smesuranza
vincto de labundanza
del dolce mio sire.

One of Jacopone's authentic poems so far detaches itself in character and composition from the rest, and is so important, as will shortly be seen, for the history of Italian dramatic art, that it demands separate consideration.[12] It assumes the form of a dialogue between Mary and

[11] *Ibid.* p. 45.

[12] It is printed in Salviano's, and reproduced in Tresatti's edition. I have followed the reading offered by D' Ancona, *Origini del Teatro*, vol. i. p. 142. See Translation in Appendix.

Christ upon the Cross, followed by the lamentation of the Virgin over her dead Son. A messenger informs the Mother that Christ has been taken prisoner:

> Donna del Paradiso,
> Lo tuo figliole è priso,
> Jesu Cristo beato.
> Accurre, donna, e vide
> Che la gente l' allide;
> Credo che llo s' occide,
> Tanto l' on flagellato.

Attended by the Magdalen, whom she summons to her aid, Mary hurries to the judgment-seat of Pilate, and begs for mercy:

> O Pilato, non fare
> 'L figlio mio tormentare,
> Ch' io te posso mostrare
> Como a torto è accusato.

But here the voices of the Chorus, representing the Jewish multitude, are heard:

> Crucifige, crucifige!
> Omo che se fa rege,
> Secondo nostra lege,
> Contradice al Senato.

Christ is removed to the place of suffering, and Mary cries:

> O figlio, figlio, figlio,
> Figlio, amoroso figlio,
> Figlio, chi dà consiglio
> Al cor mio angustiato!
> Figlio, occhi giocondi,
> Figlio, co' non rispondi?
> Figlio, perchè t' ascondi
> Dal petto o' se' lattato?

They show her the cross:

> Madonna, ecco la cruce
> Che la gente l' adduce,
> Ove la vera luce
> De' essere levato.

They tell her how Jesus is being nailed to it, sparing none of the agonising details. Then she exclaims:

> E io comencio el corrotto;
> Figliolo, mio deporto,
> Figlio, chi mi t' à morto,
> Figlio mio delicato!
> Meglio averien fatto
> Che 'l cor m' avesser tratto,
> Che nella croce tratto
> Starci desciliato.

Jesus now breaks silence, and comforts her, pointing out that she must live for His disciples, and naming John. He dies, and she continues the 'Corrotto'[13]:

Figlio, l' alma t' è uscita,
Figlio de la smarrita,
Figlio de la sparita,
Figlio [mio] attossicato!
Figlio bianco e vermiglio,
Figlio senza simiglio,
Figlio, a chi m' apiglio,
Figlio, pur m' hai lassato!
Figlio bianco e biondo,
Figlio, volto jocondo,
Figlio, perchè t' à el mondo,
Figlio, cusì sprezato!
Figlio dolce e piacente,
Figlio de la dolente,
Figlio, à te la gente
Malamente trattato!
Joanne, figlio novello,
Morto è lo tuo fratello;
Sentito aggio 'l coltello
Che fo profetizzato,
Che morto à figlio e mate,
De dura morte afferrate;
Trovârsi abbracciate
Mate e figlio a un cruciato.

Upon this note of anguish the poem closes. It is conducted throughout in dialogue, and is penetrated with dramatic energy. For Passion Music of a noble and yet flowing type, such as Pergolese might have composed, it is still admirably adapted.

Each strophe of Fra Jacopone's Canticles might be likened to a seed cast into the then fertile soil of the Franciscan Order, which bore fruit a thousand-fold in its own kind of spiritual poetry. The vast collection of hymns, published by Tresatti in the seventeenth century, bears the name of Jacopone, and incorporates his genuine compositions.[14] But we must regard the main body of the work as rather belonging to Jacopone's school than to the master. Taken collectively, these poems

[13] The word *Corrotto*, used by Mary, means lamentation for the dead. It corresponds to the Greek *Threnos*, Corsican *Vocero*, Gaelic *Coronach*.

[14] *Le Poesie spirituali del Beato Jacopone da Todi*. In Venetia, appresso Niccolò Miserrimi, MDCXVII. The book is a thick 4to, consisting of 1,055 pages, closely printed. It contains a voluminous running commentary. The editor, Tresatti, a Minorite Friar, says he had extracted 211 *Cantici* of Jacopone from MSS. belonging to his Order, whereas the Roman and Florentine editions, taken together, contained 102 in all. He divides them into seven sections: (1) Satires, (2) Moral Songs, (3) Odes, (4) Penitential Hymns, (5) The Theory of Divine Love, (6) Spiritual Love Poems, (7) Spiritual Secrets. This division corresponds to seven stages in the soul's progress toward perfection. The arrangement is excellent, though the sections in some places interpenetrate. For variety of subjects, the collection is a kind of lyrical encyclopædia, touching all needs and states of the devout soul. It might supply material for meditation through a lifetime to a heart in harmony with its ascetic and erotically enthusiastic tone.

bear upon their face the stamp of considerable age, and there is no reason to suppose that their editor doubted of their authenticity. A critical reader of the present time, however, discerns innumerable evidences of collaboration, and detects expansion and dilution of more pregnant themes in the copious outpourings of this cloistral inspiration. What the Giotteschi are to Giotto, Tresatti's collection is to Salviano's imprint of Jacopone. It forms a complete manual of devotion, framed according to the spirit of S. Francis. In its pages we read the progress of the soul from a state of worldliness and vice, through moral virtue, into the outer court of religious conviction. Thence we pass to penitence and the profound terror of sin. Having traversed the region of purgatory upon earth, we are introduced to the theory of Divine Love, which is reasoned out and developed upon themes borrowed from each previous step gained by the spirit in its heavenward journey. Here ends the soul's novitiate; and we enter on a realm of ecstasy. The poet bathes in an illimitable ocean of intoxicating love, summons the images of sense and makes them adumbrate his rapture of devotion, reproducing in a myriad modes the Oriental metaphors of the soul's marriage to Christ suggested by the Canticle of Canticles. A final grade in this ascent to spiritual perfection is attained in the closing odes, which celebrate annihilation—the fusion of the mortal in immortal personality, the bliss of beatific vision, Nirvana realised on earth in ecstasy by man. At this final point sense swoons, the tongue stammers, language refuses to perform her office, the reason finds no place, the universe is whirled in spires of flame, we float in waves of metaphor, we drown in floods of contemplation, the whole is closed with an 'O Altiduto!'

It is not possible to render scantiest justice to this extraordinary monument of the Franciscan fervour by any extracts or descriptions. Its full force can only be felt by prolonged and, if possible, continuous perusal. S. Catherine and S. Teresa attend us while we read; and when the book is finished, we feel, perhaps for the first time, the might, the majesty, the overmastering attraction of that sea of faith which swept all Europe in the thirteenth century. We understand how *naufragar in questo mar fù dolce.*

Though the task is ungrateful, it behoves the historian of popular Italian poetry to extract some specimens from this immense repertory of anonymous lyrics. Omitting the satires, which are composed upon the familiar monastic rubrics of vanity, human misery, the loathsomeness of the flesh, and contempt of the world, I will select one stanza upon Chastity from among the moral songs:[15]

O Castità bel fiore,
Che ti sostiene amore.
 O fior di Castitate,
Odorifero giglio,
Con gran soavitate,
Sei di color vermiglio,
Et a la Trinitate
Tu ripresenti odore.

[15] *Op. cit.* p. 149.

Chastity in another place is thus described:[16]

La Castitate pura,
Più bella che viola,
Cotanto ha chiaro viso
Che par un paradiso.

Poverty, the Cardinal Virtues, and the Theological Virtues receive their full meed of praise in a succession of hymns. Then comes a long string of proverbs, which contain much sober wisdom, with passages of poetic feeling like the following:[17]

Li pesciarelli piccoli
Scampan la rete in mare;
Grand' ucel prende l' aquila,
Non può 'l moscon pigliare;
Enchinasi la vergola,
L' acqua lassa passare;
Ma fa giù cader l' arbore,
Che non si può inchinare.

Among the odes we may first choose this portion of a carol written to be sung before the manger, or *presepe*, which it was usual to set up in churches at Christmas:[18]

Veggiamo il suo Bambino
Gammettare nel fieno,
E le braccia scoperte
Porgere ad ella in seno,
Ed essa lo ricopre
El meglio che può almeno,
Mettendoli la poppa
Entro la sua bocchina.
Cioppava lo Bambino
Con le sue labbruccia;
Sol la dolciata cioppa
Volea, non minestruccia;
Stringeala con la bocca
Che non avea dentuccia,
Il figliuolino bello,
Ne la dolce bocchina.
A la sua man manca,
Cullava lo Bambino,
E con sante carole
Nenciava il suo amor fino
Gli Angioletti d' intorno
Se ne gian danzando,
Facendo dolci versi
E d' amor favellando.

There is a fresco by Giotto behind the altar in the Arena Chapel at Padua, which illustrates part of this hymn. A picture attributed to Botticelli in our National Gallery illustrates the rest. The spirit of the

[16] *Ibid.* p. 244.
[17] *Op. cit.* p. 253.
[18] *Ibid.* p. 266. See Translation in Appendix.

carol has been reproduced with less sincerity in a Jesuit's Latin hymn, 'Dormi, fili, dormi, mater.'

Close upon the joys of Mary follow her sorrows. The following is a popular echo of the 'Stabat Mater:'[19]

Or si incomincia lo duro pianto
Che fa la Madre di Christo tanto;
Or intendete l' amaro canto,
Fu crocifisso quel capo santo.

Ma quando che s' inchiodava,
Presso al figliuolo la Madre stava;
Quando a la croce gli occhi levava,
Per troppa doglia ci trangosciava.

La Madre viddelo incoronato,
Et ne la croce tutto piagato,
Per le pene e pel sangue versato
Sitibondo gridar Consummato.

Many of the odes are devoted to S. Francis. One passage recording the miracle of the Stigmata deserves to be extracted:[20]

La settima a Laverna,
Stando in orazione,
Ne la parte superna,
Con gran divozione,
Mirabil visione
Seraphin apparuto
Crucifisso è veduto,
Con sei ale mostrato:
Incorporotti stimmate
A lato piedi e mano;
Duro già fora a credere
Se nol contiam di piano,
Staendo vivo et sano
Molti l' han mirate,
L' ha morte dichiarate,
Da molti fu palpato.
La sua carne bianchissima
Pareva puerile;
Avanti era brunissima
Per gli freddi nevili;
La fe amor si gentile,
Parea glorificata,
Da ogni gente ammirata
Del mirabil ornato.

The Penitential Hymns resound with trumpets of Judgment and groans of lost souls. There is one terrible lament of a man who repented *after death*; another of one arising from the grave, *damned*.[21]

[19] *Op. cit.* p. 306.
[20] *Ibid.* p. 343.
[21] *Op. cit.* pp. 416, 420.

The Day of Judgment inspires stanzas heavy with lugubrious chords and a leaden fall:[22]

> Tutta la terra tornerà a niente,
> Le pietre piangeranno duramente,
> Conturbaronsi tutti i monumente,
> Per la sententia di Dio onnipotente
> Che tutti sentiranno.
> . . . .
> Allora udrai dal ciel trombe sonare,
> Et tutti morti vedrai suscitare,
> Avanti al tribunal di Christo andare,
> E 'l fuoco ardente per l' aria volare
> Con gran velocitate.
> . . . .
> Porgine aiuto, alto Signor verace,
> E campane da quel foco penace,
> E danne penitentia si verace
> Che 'n ciel possiam venir a quella pace
> Dove in eterno regni.

This is the 'Dies Iræ' adapted for the people, and expanded in its motives.

The exposition and the expression of Divine Love occupy a larger space than any other section of the series. Mystical psychology, elaborated with scholastic subtlety of argument and fine analysis of all the grades of feeling, culminates in lyric raptures, only less chaotic than the stanzas already quoted from Jacopone. The poet breaks out into short ejaculations:[23]

> O alta Nichilitate,
> Dhe mi di dove tu stai!

He faints and swoons before the altar in the languors of emotion:[24]

> Languisco per amore
> Di Gesù mio Amatore.

We see before our eyes the trances of S. Catherine, so well portrayed with sensuous force by Sodoma. Then he resumes the Song of Solomon in stanzas to be counted by the hundred, celebrates the marriage of Christ and the soul, or seeks crude carnal metaphors to convey his meaning:[25]

> Del tuo bacio, amore,
> Degnami di baciare.
>   Dhe baciami, dolcezza
> Di contrizione,
> Et dolce soavezza
> Di compunzione,
> O santa allegrezza
> Di devozione,
> Per nulla stagione
> Non m' abandonare.

[22] *Ibid.* p. 433.
[23] *Op. cit.* p. 703.
[24] *Ibid.* p. 741.
[25] *Ibid.* p. 715.

Poì che 'l bacio sento
Bevo a le mammelle
C' hanno odore d' unguento;
Pur le tue scintille
A bever non so lento
Con le mie maxille,
Più che volte mille
Vò me inebriare.

Let this suffice. With the language of sweetness and monastic love we are soon surfeited. Were it not that the *crescendo* of erotic exaltation ends at last in a jubilee of incomprehensible passion, blending the incoherence of delirium with fragments of theosophy which might have been imported from old Alexandrian sources or from dim regions of the East, a student of our century would shrink aghast from some of these hermaphroditic hymns, as though he had been witness of wild acts of nympholepsy in a girl he reckoned sane.

Through the two centuries which followed Jacopone's death (1306?) the Lauds of the Confraternities continued to form a special branch of popular poetry; and in the fifteenth century they were written in considerable quantities by men of polite education. Like all hymns, these spiritual songs are less remarkable for literary quality than devoutness. It is difficult to find one rising to the height of Jacopone's inspiration. Many of the later compositions even lack religious feeling, and seem to have been written as taskwork. Those, for example, by Lorenzo de' Medici bear the same relation to his 'Canti Carnascialeschi' as Pontano's odes to the Saints bear to his elegies and Baian lyrics. This was inevitable in an age saturated with the adverse ideals of the classical Revival, when Platonic theism threatened to supplant Christianity, and society was clogged with frigid cynicism. Yet even in the sixteenth century, those hymns which came directly from the people's heart, thrilling with the strong vibrations of Savonarola's preaching, are still remarkable for almost frantic piety. Among the many Florentine hymn-writers who felt that influence, Girolamo Benivieni holds the most distinguished place, both for the purity of his style and for the sincerity of his religious feeling. I will set side by side two versions from his book of Lauds, illustrating the extreme limits of devout emotion—the calmness of a meditative piety and the spasms of passionate enthusiasm. The first is a little hymn to Jesus, profoundly felt and expressed with exquisite simplicity:[26]

Jesus, whoso with Thee
Hangs not in pain and loss
Pierced on the cruel cross,
At peace shall never be.

Lord, unto me be kind:
Give me that peace of mind,
Which in this world so blind
And false dwells but with Thee.

[26] *Opere di Girolamo Benivieni* (Venegia, G. de Gregori, 1524), p. 151.

Give me that strife and pain,
Apart from which 'twere vain
Thy love on earth to gain
Or seek a share in Thee.

If, Lord, with Thee alone
Heart's peace and love be known,
My heart shall be Thine own,
Ever to rest with Thee.

Here in my heart be lit
Thy fire, to feed on it,
Till burning bit by bit
It dies to live with Thee.

Jesus, whoso with Thee
Hangs not in pain or loss,
Pierced on the cruel cross,
At peace shall never be.

The second is an echo of Jacopone's eulogy of madness, prolonged and developed with amorous extravagance:[27]

Never was there so sweet a gladness,
Joy of so pure and strong a fashion
As with zeal and love and passion
Thus to embrace Christ's holy madness.
They who are mad in Jesus, slight
All that the wise man seeks and prizes;
Wealth and place, pomp, pride, delight,
Pleasure and fame, their soul despises;
Sorrow and tears and sacrifices,
Poverty, pain, and low estate,
All that the wise men loathe and hate,
Are sought by the Christian in his madness.

They who are fools for Christ in heaven,
Should they be praised peradventure, mourn,
Seeing the praise that to them is given
Was taken from God; but hate and scorn
With joy and gladness of soul are borne;
The Christian listens and smiles for glee
When he hears the taunt of his foe, for he
Glories and triumphs in holy madness.

Many collections of Lauds were early committed to the press; and of these we have an excellent modern reprint in the 'Laude Spirituali di Feo Belcari e di altri,' which includes hymns by Castellano Castellani, Bernardo Giambullari, Francesco Albizzi, Lorenzo de' Medici, Lucrezia Tornabuoni, and the Pulci brothers.[28] Studying this miscellany, we perceive that between the *Laude* and *Ballate* of the people there is often little but a formal difference. Large numbers are parodies of amatory

[27] *Op. cit.* p. 143. I have only translated the opening stanzas of this hymn.
[28] Published at Florence by Molini and Cecchi, 1863. Compare the two collections printed by Prof. G. Ferraro from Ferrarese MSS. *Poesie popolari religiose del secolo xiv.* Bologna, Romagnoli, 1877.

or obscene songs, beginning with nearly the same words and intended to be sung to the same tunes, Thus the famous ballad, 'O vaghe montanine e pastorelle' becomes 'O vaghe di Gesù, o verginelle.'[29] The direction for singing 'Crucifisso a capo chino' is 'Cantasi come—Una donna di fino amore,' which was a coarse street-song in vogue among the common folk.[30] 'Vergine, alta regina,' is modelled upon 'Galantina, morosina; I' son quella pecorella' upon 'I' son quella vilanella;' 'Giù per la mala via l'anima mia ne va' on 'Giù per la villa lunga la bella se ne va.'[31] Others are imitations of carnival choruses noted for their grossness and lewd innuendoes.[32] It is clear that the *Laudesi*, long before the days of Rowland Hill, discerned the advantage of not letting the devil have all the good tunes. Other parallels between the Florentine Lauds and the revival hymns of the present century might be pointed out. Yet in proportion as the Italian religious sentiment is more sensuous and erotic than that of the Teutonic nations, so are the Lauds more unreservedly emotional than the most audacious utterances of American or English Evangelicalism. As an excellent Italian critic has recently observed, the amorous and religious poems of the people were only distinguished by the difference of their object. Expression, versification, melody, pitch of sentiment, remained unaltered. Men sang the same *strambotti* to the Virgin and the lady of their love, to the rose of Jericho and the red rose of the balcony.'[33] No notion of impropriety seems to have been suggested by this confusion of divergent feelings. Otherwise, Savonarola would hardly have suffered his proselytes to roam the streets chanting stanzas which are little better than echoes from the brothel or travesties of Poliziano's chorus of the Mænads. The Italians have never been pious in the same sense as the Northern nations. Their popular religious poetry is the lyric of emotion, the lyric of the senses losing self-restraint in an outpouring of voluptuous ecstasy. With them 'music is a love-lament or a prayer addressed to God;' and both constituents of music blend and mingle indistinguishably in their hymns. As they lack the sublime Chorales of the Reformation period in Germany, so they lack the grave and meditative psalms for which Bach made his melodies.

The origins of the Italian theatre were closely connected with the services of the *Laudesi*. And here it has to be distinctly pointed out that the evolution of the Sacred Drama in Italy followed a different course from that with which we are familiar in France and England. Miracle-plays and Mysteries, properly so called, do not appear to have been common among the Italians in the early middle ages. There is, indeed, one exception to this general statement, which warns us to be cautious, and which proves that the cyclical sacred play had been ex-

[29] *Laude*, &c., p. 105.
[30] *Op. cit.* p. 16. See *Canzone a Pallo*, &c. (Firenze, 1568), p. 30, for this song.
[31] *Op. cit.* pp. 96, 227, 50.
[32] See *op. cit.* pp. 227, 234, and *passim.*
[33] Carducci, *Dello Svolgimento della Letteratura Nazionale*, p. 90.

hibited at least in one place at a very early date. At Cividale, in the district of Friuli, a 'Ludus Christi,' embracing the principal events of Christian history from the Passion to the Second Advent, was twice acted, in 1298 and 1303. From the scanty notices concerning it, we are able to form an opinion that it lasted over three days, that it was recited by the clergy, almost certainly in Latin, and that the representation did not take place in church.[34] The Friulian 'Ludi Christi' were, in fact, a Mystery of the more primitive type, corresponding to Greban's 'Mystère de la Passion' and to our Coventry or Widkirk Miracles. But, so far as present knowledge goes, this sacred play was an isolated phenomenon, and proved unfruitful of results. We are only able to infer from it, what the close intercourse of the Italians with the French would otherwise make evident, that Mysteries were not entirely unknown in the peninsula. Yet it seems clear, upon the other hand, that the two forms of the sacred drama specific to Italy, the Umbrian 'Divozione' and the Florentine 'Sacra Rappresentazione,' were not a direct outgrowth from the Mystery. We have to trace their origin in the religious practices of the *Laudesi*, from which a species of dramatic performance was developed, and which placed the sacred drama in the hands of these lay confraternities.

At first the 'Disciplinati di Gesù' intoned their Lauds in the hall of the Company, standing before the crucifix or tabernacle of a saint, as they are represented in old woodcuts.[35] From simple singing they passed to antiphonal chaunting, and thence made a natural transition to dialogue, and lastly to dramatic action. To trace the steps of this progress is by no means easy; nor must we imagine that it was effected wholly within the meeting-places of the confraternities without external influence. Though the Italians may not have brought the Miracle-play to the perfection it attained among the Northern nations, they were, as we have seen, undoubtedly aware of its existence. Furthermore, they were familiar with ecclesiastical shows but little removed in character from that form of mediæval art. Representations of the manger at Bethlehem made part of Christmas ceremonies in Umbria, as we learn from a passage in the works of S. Bonaventura referring to the year 1223.[36] Nor were occasions wanting when pageants enlivened the ritual of the Church. Among liturgical dramas, enacted by priests and choristers at service time, may be mentioned the descent of the Angel Gabriel at the feast of the Annunciation, the procession of the Magi at Epiphany, the descent of the dove at Pentecost, and the Eastern representation of a sepulchre from which the body of Christ had been removed. Thus the *Laudesi* found precedents in the Liturgy itself for introducing a dramatic element into their offices.

Having assumed a more or less dramatic form, the Laud acquired the name of 'Divozione' as early as the middle of the fourteenth century.

[34] See Muratori, *Rer. Ital. Script.* xxiv. 1205, and *ibid.* 1209, Friulian Chronicle.
[35] See the frontispiece to *Laude di Feo Belcari e di altri.*
[36] D' Ancona, *Or. del T. op. cit.* vol. i. p. 109.

It was written in various lyric metres, beginning with six-lined stanzas in *ottonari*, passing through hendecasyllabic *sesta rima*, and finally settling down into *ottava rima*, which became the common stanza for all forms of popular poetry in the fifteenth century.[37] The Passion of our Lord formed the principal theme of the 'Divozioni;' for the *Laudesi* were bound by their original constitution to a special contemplation of His suffering upon the cross for sinners. The Perugian Chronicles refer to compositions of this type under the name of 'Corrotto,' or song of mourning. In its highest form it was the passionate outpouring of Mary's anguish over her crucified Son—the counterpart in poetry to the 'Pietà' of painting, for which the Giottesque masters, the Umbrian school, Crivelli, and afterwards Mantegna, reserved the strongest exhibition of their powers as dramatists. We have already seen with what a noble and dramatic dialogue Jacopone da Todi initiated this species of composition.[38] At the same time, the 'Divozioni' and the Lauds from which they sprang, embraced a wide variety of subjects, following the passages of Scripture appointed to be read in church on festivals and Sundays. Thus the Laud for Advent dramatised the Apocalypse and introduced the episode of Antichrist. The story of the Prodigal furnished a theme for the vigil when that parable was used. It was customary to sing these compositions in the oratories after the discipline of the confraternity had been duly performed; and that they were sung, is a fact of importance which must never be forgotten. Every Company had its own collection of dramatic Lauds, forming a cycle of sacred melodramas, composed with no literary end and no theatrical effect in view, but with the simple purpose of expressing by dialogue the substance of a Scripture narrative.

An inventory of the Perugian Confraternity of S. Domenico, dated in the year 1339, includes wings and crowns for sixty-eight angels, masks for devils, a star for the Magi, a crimson robe for Christ, black veils for the Maries, two lay figures of thieves, a dove to symbolise the Holy Ghost, a coat of mail for Longinus, and other properties which prove that not Passion-plays alone but dramas suited to Epiphany, Pentecost and the Annunciation must have been enacted at that period. Yet we have no exact means of ascertaining when the *Laudesi* left their oratories and began to recite 'Divozioni' with action in church or on the open square. The Compagnia del Gonfalone are said to have presented a play to the Roman people in the Coliseum in 1260; but though the brotherhood was founded in that year, it is more than doubtful

[37] The phases of this progress from *ottonari* to *ottava rima* have been carefully traced by D' Ancona (*op. cit.* vol. i. pp. 151-165). *Ottonari* are lines of eight syllables with a loose trochaic rhythm, in which great licenses of extra syllables are allowed. The stanza rhymes *a b a b c c*. The *sesta rima* of the transition has the same rhyming structure. The *Corrotto* by Jacopone da Todi, analysed above, shows a similar system of rhymes to that of some Latin hymns: *a a a b c c c b*, the *b* rhyme in *ato* being carried through the whole poem.

[38] See above, pp. 31-38, and Appendix.

whether their famous Passion dates from so early an epoch.[39] By the year 1375 it had become customary for *Laudesi* to give representations in church, accompanied by a sermon from the pulpit. The audience assembled in the nave, and a scaffold was erected along the screen which divided the nave and transepts from the choir. Here the brethren played their pieces, while the preacher at appropriate intervals addressed the people, explaining what they were about to see upon the stage or commenting on what had been performed.[40] The actors were the Chorus, the preacher the Choregus. The stage was technically called *talamo*.[41] It had a large central compartment, corresponding to the 'Logeion' of the Attic theatre, with several smaller rooms termed *luoghi deputati*, and galleries above reserved for the celestial personages. The actors entered from a central and two side doors called *reggi*.

These Umbrian 'Divozioni' form a link between the Laud of the thirteenth and the 'Sacra Rappresentazione' of the fifteenth century. They still—in form at least, if not in sacred character—survive in the 'Maggi' of the Tuscan peasantry, which are yearly acted among the villages of the Lucchese and Pistojese highlands.[42] It is difficult to say how far we are justified in regarding them as wholly different in type from the Northern Miracle-plays. That they originated in the oratories of lay brotherhoods, and that they retained the character of Lauds to be sung after they had assumed dramatic shape, may be reckoned as established points. Moreover, they lack the cyclical extension and the copious admixture of grotesquely comic elements which mark the French and English Mysteries. Yet we have already seen that such Mysteries were not entirely unknown in Italy, and that the liturgical drama, performed by ecclesiastics, had been from early times a part of Church ceremonial on holy days. We are, therefore, justified in accepting the 'Divozioni' as the Italian species of a genus which was common to the mediæval nations. The development of Gothic architecture in Central Italy might furnish an illustration. Its differentiation from the grander and more perfect type of French and English Gothic does not constitute a separate style.

To bridge the interval between the 'Divozione,' used in Umbria, and the 'Sacra Rappresentazione,' as it appeared at Florence, is rendered impossible by the present lack of documents. Still there seems sufficient reason to believe that the latter was evolved from the former within the precincts of the confraternities. In the 'Sacra Rappresentazione'

[39] D' Ancona, *op. cit.* p. 108. At p. 282 he gives some curious details relating to the Coliseum Passion in the fifteenth and sixteenth centuries. In 1539 it was suppressed by Paul III., because the Romans, infuriated by the drama of the Crucifixion, were wont to adjourn from the Flavian amphitheatre to the Ghetto, and begin a murderous crusade against the Jews!

[40] In the directions for a 'Devotione de Veneredì sancto,' analysed by D' Ancona (*op. cit.* pp. 176-182), we read: '*predica, e como fa signo* che Cristo sia posto in croce, li Judei li chiavano una mano e poi l' altra' . . . . 'a quello loco quando Pilato comanda che Cristo sia posto a la colona, *lo Predicatore tase*.'

[41] Ducange explains *thalamum* by *tabulatum*.

[42] See Appendix to vol. ii. of D' Ancona's *Origini del Teatro*.

the religious drama of Italy reached its highest point of development, and produced a form of art peculiar to Florence and the Tuscan cities. Though it betrays certain affinities to the Northern Miracle-play, which prove familiarity with the French 'Mystères' on the part at least of some among the playwrights, it is clearly a distinct kind. As in the case of the Umbrian 'Divozioni,' so here the absence of grotesque episodes is striking; nor do we find connected series of 'Sacre Rappresentazioni,' embracing the Christian history in a cyclical dramatic work. This species flourished for about fifty years, from 1470 to 1520. These dates are given approximately; for though we know that the Sacred Drama of Florence did not long survive the second decade of the sixteenth century, we cannot ascertain the period of its origin. The 'Sacre Rappresentazioni' we possess in print, almost all written within the last thirty years of the fifteenth century, present so marked a similarity of style and structure that they must have been preceded by a series of experiments which fixed and conventionalised their form. Like the 'Divozioni,' they were in the hands of confraternities, who caused them to be acted at their own expense. Since these Companies were wealthy, and included members of the best Florentine families, their plays were put upon the stage with pomp. The actors were boys belonging to the brotherhoods, directed by a Chorodidascalus called *Festajuolo*. S. Antonino, the good archbishop, promoted the custom of enrolling youths of all classes in religious Companies, seeking by such influences to encourage sound morality and sober living. The most fashionable brotherhoods were those of San Bastiano or Del Freccione, Del Vangelista or Dell' Aquila, Dell' Arcangelo Raffaello or Della Scala—the name of the saint or his ensign being indifferently used. Representations took place either in the oratory of the Company or in the refectory of a convent. Meadows at Fiesole and public squares were also chosen for open-air performances.[43] The *libretti* were composed in octave stanzas, with

[43] In the prologues of the later comedies of learning (*commedia erudita*) allusions to the rude style of Fiesolan shows are pretty frequent. The playwrights speak of them as our Elizabethan dramatists spoke of Bartholomew Fair. The whole method of a Fiesolan *Sacra Rappresentazione* is well explained in the induction to the play of *Abraam e Sara* (Siena, 1581). A father and his son set out from Florence, at the boy's request:

> Et vo che noi andiamo
> a Fiesolani poggi,
> Ch' io mi ricordo c' hoggi
> una festa non più vista
> Mai piu el Vangelista
> vi fa e rappresenta.

On the road they wonder, will the booth be too full for them to find places, will they get hot by walking fast up hill, will their clothes be decent? They meet the Festajuolo at the booth-door, distracted because:

> manca una voce
> Et è ito un veloce
> a Firenze per lui.

Voce was the technical name for the actor.

passages of *terza rima*, and were sung to a recitative air. Interludes of part-songs, with accompaniment of lute and viol, enlivened the simple *cantilena*; and there is no doubt, from contemporary notices, that this music was of the best. The time selected was usually after vespers. The audience were admitted free of cost, but probably by invitation only to the friends and relatives of the young actors. 'Sacra Rappresentazione' was the generic name of the show; but we meet with these subordinate titles, 'Festa,' 'Mistero,' 'Storia,' 'Vangelo,' 'Figura,' 'Esemplo,' 'Passione,' 'Martirio,' 'Miracolo,' according to the special subject-matter of the play in question.

D' Ancona, in his book on the 'Origins of the Italian Drama,' suggests that the 'Sacre Rappresentazioni' were developed by a blending of the Umbrian 'Divozioni' with the civic pageants of S. John's Day at Florence. This theory is plausible enough to deserve investigation; especially as many points relating to the nature of the performances will be elucidated in the course of the inquiry. We must, however, be cautious not to take for granted that D' Ancona's conclusions have been proved. The researches of that eminent literary antiquarian, in combination with those made by Professor Monaci, are but just beginning to throw light on this hitherto neglected topic.

From the Chroniclers of the fifteenth century we have abundant testimony that in all parts of Italy sacred and profane shows formed a prominent feature of municipal festivals, and were exhibited by the burghers of the cities when they wished to welcome a distinguished foreigner, or to celebrate the election of their chief magistrates.[44] Thus Sigismund, King of the Romans, was greeted at Lucca in 1432 by a solemn triumph. Perugia gratified Eugenius IV. in 1444 with the story of the Minotaur, the tragedy of Iphigenia, the Nativity and the Ascension.[45] The popular respect for S. Bernardino found expression at Siena in a pageant, when the Papal Curia, in 1450, issued letters for his canonisation.[46] Frederick III. was received in 1452 at Naples with the spectacle of the Passion. Leonora of Aragon, on her way through Rome in 1473 to Ferrara, witnessed a series of pantomimes, profane and sacred, splendidly provided by Pietro Riario, the Cardinal of San Sisto.[47] The triumphs of the Popes on entering office filled the streets of Rome with dramatic exhibitions, indifferently borrowed from Biblical and classic history. At Parma in 1414 the students celebrated the election of Andrea di Sicilia to a chair in their university by a procession of the Magi.[48] When the head of S. Andrew entered Rome in 1462, the citizens and prelates testified their joy with figurative pomps.[49] Viterbo

[44] See D' Ancona, *op. cit.* pp. 245-267. Compare the section on 'Geselligkeit und die Feste' in Burckhardt's *Cultur der Renaissance in Italien.*

[45] Graziani, *Arch. Stor.* xvi. 344.

[46] Allegretti, Muratori, xxxiii. 767.

[47] Corio, quoted by me, Vol. I., *Age of the Despots*, p. 196.

[48] See D' Ancona, *op. cit.* p. 245, and compare the account of a similar show in Galvano Flamma's *Chronicle of Milan.*

[49] *Pii Secundi Commentarii* (Romæ, 1584), viii. 365.

in the same year enjoyed a variety of splendid exhibitions, Cardinal vying with Cardinal in magnificence, upon the festival of Corpus Domini.[50]

The pageants above mentioned formed but prolusions to the yearly feast of S. John at Florence.[51] Florence had, as it were, the monopoly of such shows; and we know from many sources that Florentine artists were employed in distant cities for the preparation of spectacles which they had brought to perfection in their own town. An extract from Matteo Palmieri's Chronicle, referring to the year 1454, brings this Midsummer rejoicing vividly before the reader's mind.[52] It is an accurate description of the order followed at that period in the exhibition of pantomimic pageants by the guilds and merchants of the town. 'On the 22nd day of June the Cross of S. Maria del Fiore moved first, with all the clergy and children, and behind them seven singing men. Then the Companies of James the wool-shearer and Nofri the shoemaker, with some thirty boys in white and angels. Thirdly, the Tower (*edifizio*) of S. Michael, whereupon stood God the Father in a cloud (*nuvola*); and on the Piazza, before the Signoria, they gave the show (*rappresentazione*) of the Battle of the Angels, when Lucifer was cast out of heaven. Fourthly, the Company of Ser Antonio and Piero di Mariano, with some thirty boys clothed in white, and angels. Fifthly, the Tower of Adam, the which on the Piazza gave the show of how God created Adam and Eve, with the Temptation by the serpent and all thereto pertaining. Sixthly, a Moses upon horseback, attended by many mounted men of the chiefs in Israel and others. Seventhly, the Tower of Moses, which upon the Piazza gave the show of the Delivery of the Law. Eighthly, many Prophets and Sibyls, including Hermes Trismegistus and others who foretold the Incarnation of our Lord.' With this list Palmieri proceeds at great length, reckoning in all twenty-two Towers. The procession, it seems, stopped upon its passage to exhibit tableaux; and these were so arranged that the whole Scripture history was set forth in dumb show, down to the Last Day. The representation of each tableau and the moving of the pageant through the streets and squares of Florence lasted sixteen hours. It will be observed that, here at least, a cyclical exposition of Christian doctrine, corresponding to the comprehensive Mysteries of the North, was attempted in pantomime. The Towers, we may remark in passing, were wooden cars, surmounted with appropriate machinery, on which the actors sat and grouped themselves according to their subject. They differed in no essentials from the Triumphal Chariots of carnival time, as described by Vasari in his Lives of Piero di Cosimo and Pontormo. From an anonymous Greek writer who visited Florence in the train of

[50] Niccolò della Tuccia, *Cron. di Viterbo* (Firenze, Vieusseux, 1872), p. 84.

[51] See Vol. I, pp. 870-872, for passages from Goro Dati's Chronicle and other sources, touching on the summer festivals of Florence.

[52] This passage from Palmieri's MS. will be found, together with full information on the subject of S. John's Day, in Cambiagi, *Memorie istoriche riguardanti le feste, ecc.* (Firenze, Stamp. Gran-ducale, 1766), p. 65.

John Palæologus, we gather some notion of the effect produced upon a stranger by these pageants.[53] He describes the concourse of the Florentines, and gives the measure of his own astonishment by saying: 'They work prodigies in this feast, and miracles, or at least the representation of miracles.'

Vasari in his Life of Il Cecca contributes much valuable information concerning the machinery used in the shows of S. John's Day.[54] The piazza of the Duomo was covered in with a broad blue awning—similar, we may suppose, to that veil of deeper and lighter azure bands which forms the background to Fra Lippi's 'Crowning of the Virgin.' This was sown with golden lilies, and was called a Heaven. Beneath it were the clouds, or *Nuvole*, exhibited by various civic guilds. They were constructed of substantial wooden frames, supporting an almond-shaped aureole, which was thickly covered with wool, and surrounded with lights and cherub faces. Inside it sat the person who represented the saint, just as Christ and Madonna are represented in the pictures of the Umbrian school. Lower down, projected branches made of iron, bearing children dressed like angels, and secured by waistbands in the same way as the fairies of our transformation scenes. The wood-work and the wires were hidden from sight by wool and cloth, plentifully sprinkled with tinsel stars. The whole moved slowly on the backs of bearers concealed beneath the frame. Vasari attributes the first invention of these and similar *ingegni* to Filippo Brunelleschi. Their similarity to what we know about the *pegmata* of Roman triumphs, renders this assertion probable. Brunelleschi's study of ancient art may have induced him to adapt a classical device to the requirements of Christian pageantry. When designed on a colossal scale and stationary, these *Nuvole* were known by the name of *Paradiso*. Another prominent feature in the Midsummer Show was the procession of giants and giantesses mounted upon stilts, and hooded with fantastic masks. Men marched in front, holding a pike to balance these unwieldy creatures; but Vasari states that some specialists in this craft were able to walk the streets on stilts six cubits high, without assistance. Then there were *spiritelli*—lighter and winged beings, raised aloft to the same height, and shining down like genii from their giddy altitude in sunlight on the crowd.

Whether we are right or not in assuming with D' Ancona that the 'Sacra Rappresentazione' was a hybrid between the Umbrian 'Divozione' and these pageants, there is no doubt that the Florentine artists, and *ingegnieri*, were equal to furnishing the stage with richness. The fraternities spared no expense, but secured the services of the best designers. They also employed versifiers of repute to compose their libretti. It must be remembered that these texts were written for boys, and were meant to be acted by boys. Thus there came into existence a peculiar type of sacred drama, displaying something childish in its style,

[53] D' Ancona, *op. cit.* p. 205. This use of the term Miracle seems to indicate that the Florentines applied to them the generic term for Northern Sacred Plays.

[54] Lemonnier's edition, vol. v.

but taxing the ingenuity of scene-painters, mechanicians, architects, musicians, and poets, to produce a certain calculated theatrical effect. When we remember how these kindred arts flourished in the last decades of the fifteenth century, we are justified in believing that the 'Sacre Rappresentazioni' offered a spectacle no less beautiful than curious and rare.

An examination of a few of these plays in detail will help us to understand one of the most original products of the popular Italian literature. With this object, I propose to consider the three volumes of reprints, edited with copious illustrations by Professor Alessandro d' Ancona.[55] But before proceeding to render an account of the forty-three plays included in this collection, it will be well to give some notice of the men who wrote them, to describe their general character, and to explain the manner of their presentation on the stage.

The authors of 'Sacre Rappresentazioni' are frequently anonymous; but Lorenzo de' Medici, Antonio Alamanni, Bernardo Pulci and his wife Monna Antonia contribute each a sacred drama. The best were written by Feo Belcari and Castellano Castellani. Of the latter very little is known, except that in the year 1517 he exercised the priestly functions at Florence and was a prolific writer of Lauds. Feo Belcari, a Florentine citizen, born in 1410, held civic offices of distinction during the ascendency of Casa Medici. He was a man of birth and some learning, who devoted himself to the production of literature in prose and verse intended for popular edification. His Lauds are among the best which have descended from the fifteenth century, and his translation of the Lives of the Fathers into Tuscan is praised for purity of style. When he died, in 1484, 'poor, weak, and white-haired,' Girolamo Benivieni, the disciple of Savonarola and the greatest sacred singer of that age, composed his elegy in verses of mingled sweetness and fervour:[56]

Tace il celeste suon, già spenta e morta
  È l' armonia di quella dolce lira,
  Che 'l mondo afflitto or lascia, e 'l ciel conforta.
È come parimenti si sospira
  Qui la sua morte, così in ciel s' allegra
  Chi alla nuova armonia si volge e gira.
Felice lui che dalla infetta e negra
  Valle di pianti al ciel n' è gito, e 'n terra
  Lasciata ha sol la veste inferma ed egra,
Ed or dal mondo e dall' orribil guerra
  De' vizi sciolto, il suo splendor vagheggia
  Nel volto di Colui che mai non erra.

[55] *Sacre Rappresentazioni*, Florence, Lemonnier, 3 vols. 1872.

[56] It may be not uninteresting to compare this *terza rima* with a passage written fifty years later by Michelangelo Buonarroti on his father's death, grander in style but less simply Christian:

Tu se' del morir morto e fatto divo,
  Nè tem' or più cangiar vita nè voglia;
  Che quasì senza invidia non lo scrivo.
Fortuna e 'l tempo dentro a vostra soglia
  Non tenta trapassar, per cui s' adduce

As regards their form, the 'Sacre Rappresentazioni' are never divided into acts; but the copious stage-directions prove that the scenes were shifted, and in one or two instances secular interludes are introduced in the pauses of the action.[57] The drama follows the tale or legend without artistic structure of plot; nor do the authors appear to have aimed, except in subordinate episodes, at much development of character. What they found ready to their hand in prose, they versified. The same fixed personages, and the same traditional phrases recur with singular monotony, proving that a conventional framework and style had become stereotyped. The end in view was religious edification. Therefore mere types of virtue in saints and martyrs, types of wickedness in tyrants and persecutors, sufficed alike for authors, actors, and audience. True dramatic genius emerges only in the minor parts, where a certain freedom of handling and effort after character-drawing are discernible. The success of the play depended on the movement of the story, and the attractions of the scenery, costumes, and music. It was customary for an angel to prologise and to dismiss the audience;[58] but his place is once at least taken by a young man with a lute.[59] A more dramatic opening was occasionally attempted in a conversation between two boys of Florence, the one good and the other bad; and instead of the *licenza* the scene sometimes closed with a 'Te Deum,' or a Laud, sung by the actors and probably taken up by the spectators. Castellani in his 'Figliuol Prodigo' made good use of the dramatic opening, gradually working the matter of his play out of a dialogue which begins with a smart interchange of Florentine chaff.[60] It would be useless even to attempt a translation of this scene. The raciness of its obsolete street-slang would evaporate, and the fibre of the piece is not strong enough to bear rude handling. It must suffice to indicate its rare dramatic quality. Students of our own Elizabethan literature may profitably compare this picture of manners with similar passages in 'Hycke Scorner' or 'Lusty Juventus.' But the Florentine interlude is more fairly representative of actual life than any part of our Mor-

Fra no' dubbia letizia e cierta doglia.
Nube non è che scuri vostra luce,
L' ore distinte a voi non fanno forza,
Caso o necessità non vi conduce.
Vostro splendor per notte non s' ammorza,
Nè crescie ma' per giorno benchè chiaro,
Sie quand' el sol fra no' il caldo rinforza.

In the Appendix will be found translations.

[57] Cecchi's *Elevation of the Cross* aims at the dignity of a five-act tragedy; but it was not represented until 1589. *Santa Uliva* illustrates the interludes; and a very interesting example is supplied by the *Miracolo di S. Maria Maddalena* where two boys prologise in dialogue, comment at intervals upon the action, and conclude the exhibition with a Laud.

[58] 'L' Angelo annunzia la festa,' is the common stage-direction at the beginning; and at the end 'L' Angelo dà licenza.'

[59] 'Constant no Imperatore,' *Sacre Rappr.* ii. 187. 'Un Giovine con la citara annunzia.'

[60] *Op. cit.* vol. i. pp. 357-359.

alities. Castellani's Prodigal Son, however, rises altogether to a higher artistic level than the ordinary; and the same may be said about the Miracolo di S. Maria Maddalena,' where a simple dramatic motive is interwoven with the action of the whole piece and made to supply a proper ending.[61]

As a rule, the 'Sacre Rappresentazioni' partook of the character of a religious service. Their tone is uniformly pious. Yet the spirit of the age and the nature of the Italians were alike unfavourable to piety of a true temper. Here it is unctuous, caressing, sentimental—anything but vigorous or virile. The monastic virtues are highly extolled; and an unwholesome view of life seen from the cloister by some would-be saint, who 'winks and shuts his apprehension up' to common facts of experience, is too often presented. Vice is sincerely condemned; yet the morality of these exhibitions cannot be applauded. Instead of the stern lessons of humanity conveyed in a drama like that of Athens or of England, the precepts of the pulpit and confessional are enforced with a childish simplicity that savours more of cloistral pietism than of true knowledge of the world. Mere belief in the intercession of saints and the efficacy of reliques is made to cover all crimes; while the anti-social enthusiasms of dreamy boys and girls are held up for imitation. We feel that we are reading what a set of feeble spiritual directors wrote with a touch of conscious but well-meaning insincerity for children. The glaring contrast between the professed asceticism of the fraternities and the future conduct of their youthful members in the world of the Renaissance leaves a suspicion of hypocrisy.[62] This impression is powerfully excited by Lorenzo de' Medici's 'Rappresentazione di S. Giovanni e Paolo,' which was acted by his children. The tone is not, indeed, so unctuous as that of Castellani. Yet when we remember what manner of man was Lorenzo; when we reflect what parts were played by his sons, Piero and Leo X., upon the stage of Italy; the sanctimonious tone of its frigid octave stanzas fails to impose on our credulity.

An adequate notion of the scenic apparatus of the 'Rappresentazioni' may be gathered from the stage-directions to 'S. Uliva' and from the interludes described in Giovanmaria Cecchi's 'Esaltazione della Croce.'[63] The latter piece was acted in Florence on the occasion of Ferrando de' Medici's marriage to Cristina of Lorraine, in 1589. It belongs, therefore, to the very last of these productions. Yet, judging by Vasari's account of the *ingegni*, we may assume that the style of presentation was traditional, and that a Florentine Company of the fifteenth century might have put a play upon the stage with at least equal pomp. The prose description of the apparatus and the interludes reads exactly like the narrative portion of Ben Jonson's Masques at Court, in which the

[61] *Sacre Rappr.* i. 391. Cp. the *Abraam* quoted in a note above p. 49.

[62] Compare, for example, Vespasiano's *naïve* astonishment at the virginity of the Cardinal di Portogallo with the protestations of chastity in the *Tre Pellegrini* (*Sacre Rappr.* iii. 467).

[63] *Sacre Rappr.* iii. p. 235 and p. 1.

poet awards due praise to the 'design and invention' of Master Inigo Jones and to the millinery of Signor Forobosco.[64] It was, indeed, a custom derived by England from Italy for the poet to set forth a minute record of his own designs together with their execution by the co-operating architects, scene-painters, musicians, dress-makers, and morris-dancers. The architect, says Cecchi, was one Taddeo di Leonardo Landini, a member of the Compagnia, skilled in sculpture as well as an excellent machinist. He arranged the field, or *prato*, of the Compagnia di S. Giovanni in the form of a theatre, covered with a red tent, and painted with pictures of the Cross considered as an instrument of shameful death, as a precious relique, and as the reward of virtue in this life. Emblems, scrolls and heraldic achievements completed the adornment of the theatre. When the curtain rose for the first time, Jacob was seen in a meadow, 'asleep with his head on certain stones, dressed in costly furs slung across his shoulder, with a thin shirt of fine linen beneath, cloth-of-silver stockings and fair buskins on his feet, and in his hand a gilt wand.' While he slept, heaven opened, and seven angels appeared, seated upon clouds, and making 'a most pleasant noise with horns, greater and less viols, lutes and organ . . . . the music of this and all the other interludes was the composition of Luca Bati, a man in this art most excellent.' When they had played and sung, the cloud disclosed, and showed a second heaven, where sat God the Father.[65] All the angels worshipped Him, and heaven increased in splendour. Then a ladder was let down, and God, leaning upon it, turned to Jacob and 'sang majestically to the sound of many instruments, in a sonorous bass voice.' Thereupon angels descended and ascended by the ladder, singing a hymn in honour of the Cross; and at last the clouds closed round, heaven disappeared, and Jacob woke from sleep. Such was the introduction to the drama. Between the first and second acts was shown, with no less exuberance of scenical resources, the exodus of Israel from Egypt; between the second and third, the miracle of Aaron's rod that blossomed; between the third and fourth, the elevation of the Brazen Serpent; between the fourth and fifth, the ecstasy of David dancing before the ark 'to the sound of a large lute, a violin, a trombone, but more especially to his own harp.' After the fifth act the play was concluded with a pageant of religious chivalry—the Knights of Malta, S. James, S. Maurice, and the Teutonic Order—who had fought for the Cross, and to whom, amid thunderings and lightnings, as they stood upon the stage, was granted the vision of 'Religion, habited in purest white, full of majesty, with the triple tiara and the crossed keys of S. Peter, holding in her hand a large and most resplendent cross, adorned with diamonds, rubies and emeralds.' The resources of a theatre which could place so many actors on the stage at once, and attempt the illusion of clouds and angels, bringing into play the machinery of transformation scenes, and enriching the whole with

[64] *Sacre Rappr.* p. 121. Shakespeare Soc. Publ. vol. xvii.

[65] For the technical terms *Nuvola* and *Paradiso* see above, p. 52.

a varied accompaniment of music, must have been considerable. Those who have spent an hour in the Teatro Farnese at Parma, erected of wood for a similar occasion, may be able to summon by the aid of the imagination a shadow of this spectacle before their eyes. That the effect was not wholly grotesque, though the motives were so hazardous, can be understood from Milton's description of the descent of Mercy in his Christmas Ode.[66]

For the play of 'S. Uliva,' though first known to us in a Florentine reprint of 1568, we may assume a more popular origin than that of Cecchi's Mystery of the Cross. It abounds in rare Renaissance combinations of pagan with Christian mythology. The action extended over two days and was interrupted at intervals by dumb shows and lyrical interludes connected only by a slight thread with the story. At one time a chase was brought upon the stage. On other occasions pictures, described with minute attention to details, were presented to the audience in Tableaux Vivants. These pictures vividly recall the style of Florentine masters, Piero di Cosimo or Sandro Botticelli. 'In the interval,' say the stage-directions to the players, 'you will cause three women, well-beseen, to issue, one of them attired in white, one in red, the other in green, with golden balls in their hands, and with them a young man robed in white; and let him, after looking many times first on one and then on another of these damsels, at last stay still and say the following verses, gazing at her who is clad in green.' This is the Masque of Hope. In another part the fable of Narcissus has to be presented, and directions are given for the disappearance of Echo, who is to repeat the final syllables of the boy's lament. 'After he has uttered all these complaints, let him thrice with a loud voice cry slowly Ahimè, Ahimè, Ahimè! and let the nymph reply, and having thus spoken let him stretch himself upon the ground and lie like one dead; and within a little space let there issue forth four or more nymphs clad in white, without bows and with dishevelled hair, who, when they have come where the youth lies dead, shall surround him in a circle, and at last having wrapped him in a white cloth, carry him within, singing this song:[67]

> Fly forth in bliss to heaven,
> Thou happy soul and fair,
> To find thy planet there, and haunt the skies;
> Leaving the tears and sighs
> Of this low-lying earth,
> Where man hath sorry mirth, as thou dost know!
> Bask in the fervent glow
> Of that pure light divine,

[66] It is probable that the painting of the period yields a fair notion of the scenic effects attempted in these shows. Or, what is perhaps a better analogue, we can illustrate the pages of the libretti by remembering the terra-cotta groups of the Sacro Monte at Varallo. Designed by excellent artists and painted in accordance with the traditions of the Milanese school, it is not impossible that these life-size representations of Christ's Birth and Passion reproduce the Sacred Drama with fidelity.

[67] *Sacre Rappr.* iii. 270.

Which on thy path shall shine, and be thy guide.
Nay, soul, thou hast not died,
But still more life hast thou,
Albeit unbodied now thou art at rest.
O soul, divinely blest,
Enjoy the eternal mind,
There dwelling unconfined through nights and days!
Heaven's angels stand and gaze
Upon thy glorious eyes,
Up there in Paradise! In crowds they come!
Now hast thou found thy home:
Now art thou blithe and blest:
Dwell now for aye at rest, pure placid soul!

For another interlude a May-day band of girls attired in flower-embroidered dresses and youths with crowns of ivy on their heads are marshalled by Dan Cupid. They sing a song of which the following is a free translation:

Let earth herself adorn
With grasses and fresh flowers,
And let cold hearts, these hours, in love's fire burn.
Let field, let forest turn
To bloom this morn of May,
That the whole world to-day may leap and sing.
Let love within us spring,
Banishing winter's smart,
Waking within our heart sweet thoughts and fair.
Let little birds in air
Sing yonder boughs above;
Each young man tell his love to his own maid;
And girls through mead and glade,
With honest eyes and meek
Fixed on their lovers, seek true troth to plight.
From field and mountain height
To-day cold snows are fled;
No clouds sail overhead; up springs clear morn.
Let violets be born,
Let leaves and grasses sprout,
And children wander out, garlands to twine.
In every dingle shine
Flowers white and blue and red,
Roses and lilies shed perfume around.
Maidens with May-blooms crowned
Through copse and meadow stray,
Singing their thoughts to-day, their sweet thoughts pure.
Let none be too demure;
Innocence marries mirth,
And from the jocund earth green laurels spring.
Come, Love, and blessings bring;
Chase sorrow, scatter care;
Make all men happy there, soul-full of ease.
Soothe pain, soothe jealousies,
That with their restless flame
Feed on man's heart: no shame no grief be near.

Night and the God of Sleep again amuse the audience with an allegorical masque; and the seven deadly sins, figured as men, women, and beasts, march across the stage. At no great distance from a vision of Judgment, the Sirens are introduced after this fashion: 'Now goes the King to Rome; and you, meanwhile, make four women, naked, or else clothed in flesh-coloured cloth, rise waist-high from the sea, with tresses to the wind, and let them sing as sweetly as may be the ensuing stanzas twice; in the which while shall two or three of you come forth, and seem to fall asleep on earth at the hearing of the song, except one only, who shall be armed, and with closed ears shall pass the sea unstayed, and let the said women take those who sleep and cast them in the waves.' When we reach Uliva's wedding, we meet with the following quaint rubric: 'If you wish to beguile the weariness caused by the length of the show, and to make the spectators take more delight in this than in any other interlude, then you must give them some taste of these bridals by providing a general banquet; but if you mislike the expense, then entertain the players only.' It would seem that 'S. Uliva' was acted on the *prato* of the confraternity, where a booth had been erected.

The forty-three plays comprised in D' Ancona's volumes may be arranged in three classes—those which deal with Bible stories or Church doctrine based on Scripture; dramatised Legends of the Saints; and *Novelle* transformed into religious fables. Among the first sort may be mentioned plays of Abraham and Isaac, Joseph, Tobias and Raphael, and Esther; the Annunciation, the Nativity, S. John in the Desert, Christ preaching in the Temple, the Conversion of the Magdalen, the Prodigal Son, the Passion and Resurrection of our Lord, and the Last Judgment. The 'Natività di Cristo' opens with a pastoral reminding us of French Mystères and English Miracle-plays.[68] The shepherds are bivouacking on the hills of Bethlehem when the angel appears to them. For Tudde, Harvye, Houcken, and Trowle of our Chester play, we find these Southern names, Bobi di Farucchio, Nencio di Pucchio, Randello, Nencietto, and so forth. But the conduct of the piece is the same. The Italian hinds discuss their cheese and wine and bread just as the clowns of Cheshire talk about 'ale of Hatton,' 'sheep's head sowsed in ale,' and 'sour milk.' Such points of similarity are rare, however; for the 'Rappresentazioni' were the growth of more refined conditions, and showed their origin in sentiment and pathos. The anonymous play of 'Mary Magdalen' rises to a higher level of dramatic art than any sacred play in English.[69] Her story, as told in these scenes, is the versified *novella* of a Vittoria Accoramboni or a Bella Imperia converted by the preaching of S. Bernardino or Savonarola. It might have happened in Rome or Florence or Perugia. Magdalen, the lady of noble blood but famous with ill-fame, fair of person and of heaven-bright countenance, who dresses splendidly and lives with many lovers, spending her days in the pleasure of rich banquets and perfumed baths, delighting her heart with the music of lyres and flutes

[68] *Sacre Rappr.* i. 193. See Shakespeare Society's Publications i. 119.
[69] *Sacre Rappr.* i. 255.

and the voices of young men, appears before us with a reality that proves how deep a hold upon the poet's fancy her picturesque tale had taken. Martha, her good but commonplace sister, forms a foil to the more impassioned and radiant figure of Magdalen. She has been cured by Christ, and has heard Him preach. Now she entreats her sister but to go and listen, for never man spake words like His. Magdalen scoffs: 'Why should I be damned because I do not follow your strange life? There is time for me to enjoy my youth, and then to make my peace with God, and Paradise will open wide for me at last.' Her friend Marcella enters with another argument: 'O Magdalen, if you did but know how fair and gracious are His eyes! Surely He has come forth straight from heaven; could you but see Him once, your heart would never be divided from Him.' This touches the right spring in Magdalen's mind. She will not go to hear the words of Christ, but the face and form that came from Paradise allure her. Besides, in the church where Christ will preach, there will be found new lovers and men in multitudes to gaze at her. Her maidens array her in gold and crimson, and bind up her yellow hair; and forth she rides in all her bravery surrounded by her suitors. What follows may best be told by a translation of the stage-directions and a passage of the play itself.

And at these last verses Jesus enters the temple; and having gone up into the pulpit, He begins to preach and to say with a loud voice, 'Homo quidam peregre proficiscens vocavit servos suos et tradidit illis bona sua.' Now comes Magdalen with her company, and her young men prepare for her a seat before the pulpit, and she in all her pomp takes her place upon it, regarding her own pleasure, nor paying heed as yet to Jesus. Afterward, Jesus looks at her and goes on preaching, always keeping His most holy gaze bent upon her; and she, after the first stanza of the sermon, looks at Him, and her eyes meet those of Jesus. Then He goes on preaching, and says as follows:—

A certain lord who on a journey went,
Called unto him each of his serving men,
And of his goods gave them arbitrament:
To one he dealt five talents, to one ten,
To another two, to try their heart's intent,
And see how far they should be careless; then
Unto the last he left but one alone:
According to their powers, he charged each one.

And when he had departed, instantly
That servant unto whom he gave the five,
Went forth, and labouring with much industry,
Increased them, and therewith so well did thrive
That other five he gained immediately,
To render when his master should arrive;
He who received but twain, did even so,
And added to his sum another two.

But he on whom one talent was bestowed,
Went forthwith and concealed it in the soil:
Careless, unthankful for the debt he owed,
While he hath peace, he seeks but strife and toil:

Called like his fellows in that lord's abode,
He answers not, but doth himself despoil;
And, as a worthless steward, hides away
The money of his master day by day.

Woe to thee, slothful servant and remiss,
That hast thy talent buried in the ground!
When reckoning comes, thou'lt yield account for this!
Nay, think how stern and rigorous he'll be found!
Weep, then, in time for what thou'st done amiss,
Before the trumpets of the judgment sound:
O soul, I tell thee thou hast gone astray,
Hiding thy talent in the earth away!

He who on earth sets his affections still,
Forgetful of the promised heavenly treasure;
He who loves self more than his Maker's will,
And in ill-doing finds continual pleasure;
He who remembers not that sin must kill,
Nor thinks how Hell will plague him above measure;
He who against himself makes fast heaven's gate;
Hideth in earth his talent till too late.

He who loves father, mother, more than God,
Not reckoning His great gifts bestowed on man;
He who the path of worldly gain hath trod,
Publishes for himself damnation's ban:
Woe, woe to that bad servant sunk in fraud,
Who leaves the good and doth what ill he can!
He who on this world seeks his joy to find,
His talent hides in earth, perversely blind.

He who is grasping, proud, discourteous, base,
Who dreameth not that he may come to want,
Who seeks for flattery, praise, and pride of place,
Lording it with high airs and arrogant;
Who to the world gives all, and still doth chase
Delight in songs and pomps exorbitant;
Who in this life is fain to rest and sleep—
His talent in the earth lies hidden deep.

Woe for that servant who through negligence
Hath hearkened not to the command divine!
Yea, he shall hear the dreadful doom: Go hence!
Go forth, accursed, in endless fire to pine!
There shall be then no time for penitence:
Bound hand and foot with punishment condign,
He shall abide among lost souls beneath,
Where is great weeping and great gnashing of teeth.

O soul, so full of sins, what shalt thou do?
Of all thy countless crimes abominable,
Look to the end! Look to it! Hell for you
Lies open, with damned folk innumerable!
Whence thou shalt never issue, ever rue
In vain remorse and pangs intolerable!
Weep, soul, ah weep for thy most vile estate,
Now that repentance need not come too late!

Seek in this life to feel sincere contrition,
Before the judge so just and so severe
Summons thee to His throne, for inquisition
Into each sin, each thought that wandered here:
There shalt thou find no merciful remission,
But justice shall be dealt with truth austere;
And he who fails shall go to burn with shame
For ever, ever, in eternal flame.

Quis ex vobis centum oves habens,
Si forte unam ex illis perdiderit,
Nonne nonagintas novem dimittens
Et illam querit, donec ipsam ivenerit?
Et cum invenerit, in humeros ponens,
Gaudens, in domum suam cito venerit,
And calls his kinsfolk and his friends to make
Festival for the new-found wanderer's sake?

The soul, she is that lost and wandering sheep;
Eternal God is the true shepherd: He
Seeks her, lest on His lamb the wolf should leap,
The fiend, who slays with guile and treachery.
He spends his life, her safe to seek and keep,
And leaves those ninety-nine in bliss to be;
And when He finds her, makes great joy in heaven,
With all the angelic host, o'er one forgiven.

There was a father who had children twain;
The younger son began to speak and pray
That he might take his share, for he was fain,
Furnished therewith, from home to wend his way:
The father gently urged him to remain,
But at the last was bounden to obey:
Far, far away he roamed, and spent his all,
Sad wretch, on carnal joys and prodigal.

But when he came to want, repenting sore,
Unto his father, all ashamed, he knelt;
His father clothed him with new robes, and bore
Even more tender love than first he felt:
So doth high God, who lives for evermore,
Unto the souls that with repentance melt;
Let them but seek His love with contrite will,
He is most merciful, and pardons still.

Soul, thou hast wounded many hearts, I wis,
Dwelling in delicate and vain delight;
With many a lover thou wouldst toy and kiss,
And art o'erfull of evil appetite;
Thy heart is big with strifes and jealousies:
Turn unto me; I wait to wash thee white;
That with the rest thy talent thou may'st double,
And dwell with them in heaven secure from trouble.

After the blessing of Jesus, Magdalen, weeping, and with her head covered, can have no rest for the great confusion that she felt; and all the people wept, and in great astonishment were waiting agaze to see what should ensue.

O alma peccatrice, che farai?—Christ's voice with its recurrences of gravely sweet persuasion melts Magdalen's heart. She may not speak one word, until her sister has led her home and comforted her a space. Then she answers:

Deh, priega Iddio che m' allumini il core!

After this, left alone with her own soul, awakened to the purer consciousness that Christ has stirred, she takes the box of ointment, and, despoiled of all her goodly raiment, with her hair dishevelled, goes to the house of the Pharisee. There at last, with the breaking of the alabaster, she dissolves in tears, and her heart finds peace. In these scenes, if anywhere, we have the stuff from which the drama might have been evolved. Magdalen is a living woman, such as Palma might have painted; and Christ is a real man gifted with power to penetrate the soul.

The 'Figliuol Prodigo' illustrates the same effort on the poet's part to steep an old-world story in the vivid colours of to-day.[70] In the Prodigal himself we find a coarse-hearted villain, like Hogarth's Idle Apprentice—vain, silly, lustful, gluttonous, careless of the honour and love that belong to him in his father's home. The scenes with the innkeeper, the gamblers, and the ruffians, among whom he runs to ruin, portray the vulgar dissipations of Florence, and justify the common identification of taverns with places of ill-fame.[71] There is a touch of true pathos at the end of the play in the grief of the father who has lost his son. The conflict of feelings in the heart of the elder brother, vexed at first with the prodigals' reception, but melting into love and pity at the fervour of his penitence, is also not without dramatic spirit. At the very end 'a boy with the lyre' enters and 'speaks the moral of the parable.'[72]

The movement of these two plays is not impeded by the sanctity of the subject. When, however, the legend belongs more immediately to the narrative of Christ's life, the form of the Representation is more severe. This is especially true of Castellani's 'Cena e Passione,' where the incidents of the Last Supper, the Agony in the Garden, the trials before Pilate and Caiaphas, the Flagellation, and the Crucifixion are narrated with reverential brevity.[73] In reading these scenes, we must summon to our memory Lucca della Robbia's bas-reliefs or the realistic groups of the Lombard Sacri Monti. The coloured terra-cotta figures

[70] *Sacre Rappr.* i. 357.

[71] All the novelists might be cited to illustrate this point.

[72] At the end of the *Rappresentazione di un Pellegrino* (*Sacre Rappr.* iii. 430) a little farce is printed, bearing no relation to the play It is a dialogue between a good and a bad apprentice, who discuss the question of gambling. Here and in the *Figliuol Prodigo* and the induction to the *Miracolo di S. Maddalena* we have the elements of comedy, which, however, unfortunately came to nothing. These scenes remind us of Heywood's tavern pictures, Marston's 'Eastward Ho!' and other precious pieces of English Elizabethan farce.

[73] *Sacre Rappr.* i. 304.

in those chapels among the chestnut trees above the Sesia are but Castellani's poetry conveyed in tableaux, while the Florentine actors undoubtedly aimed at presenting by their grouping, dresses and attitudes a living image of such plastic work. But the peculiar pathos of the Italians found finer expression in picture or fresco—in Luini's 'Flagellation' at S. Maurizio or the pallid anguish of Tintoretto's women sunk beneath the Cross in the Scuola di San Rocco—than in the fluent stanzas of the sacred playwrights. On the walls of church or oratory the sweetness and languor of emotion became as dignified in beauty as the melodies of Pergolese, and its fervour touched at times the sublimity of tragic passion. Not words but plastic forms were ever the noblest vehicle of Italian feeling. Yet each kind of art may be profitably used to illustrate the other, and the simple phrases of the 'Rappresentazioni' are often the best comments on finished works of painting. Here, for example, is Raphael's 'Lo Spasimo' in words:[74]

> Oimè, figliuol, è questo il viso
> Ch' era tanto formoso e tanto bello?
> Omè, dove si specchia el paradiso
> Oggi è percosso in tanto gran flagello!
> Io vengo a morte, figliuol mio diletto,
> Se non ti tengo nelle braccia stretto.

Mary faints, and the Magdalen supports her, weeping:[75]

> Omè, che per dolor Maria vien meno:
> Noi perderem la madre col figliuolo.
> Pallido è il volta già tanto sereno,
> Quale è tutto mutato pel gran duolo.
> El polso manca, e nel sacrato seno
> El cuor suo resta respirante solo.
> Soccorso, aiuto; ognun gli dia conforto,
> Sendo aghiacciato il corpo e quasi morto.

The hearts of these rude poets were very tender for Mary, Mother of our Lord. There is a touching passage in the 'Disputa al Tempio,' when Joseph and the Virgin are walking toward the Temple with the boy who is to them a sacred charge:[76]

> *Iosef.* I' guido e son guidato, e reggo quello
> Che regge me, e muovo chi mi muove:

[74] *Ibid.* p. 319.
[75] *Ibid.* p. 229.
[76] This play ends with a pretty moralisation of the episode that forms its motive, addressed by Mary to the people (*Sacre Rappr.* i. 240).

> Figliuo' diletti, che cercate in terra
> Trovar il figliuol mio, pietoso Iddio,
> Non vi fermate in questa rozza terra,
> Chè Jesù non istà nel mondo rio.
> Chi vel crede trovar, fortement' erra,
> E come stolto morrà nel disio.
> Al tempio, chi lo vuol, venghi oggi drento,
> Chè 'l viver vostro è come foglia al vento.

Pastor mi fo di quel ch' io son agnello;
O quanta grazia in questo servo piove!
Maria. S' i' alzo gli occhi alquanto per vederlo,
Contemplo nel mirar cose alte e nuove.
Per la virtù di sua divina forma
L' amante ne l' amato si trasforma.

Something artless and caressing in these words brings before us Luini's Joseph with his golden-brown robes and white hair, Mary in her blue and crimson with the beautiful braided curls of gold. The Magdalen, again, moves through all these solemn scenes with a grace peculiar to her story. The poet, like the painter, never forgets that her sins were forgiven *quia multum amavit.* She who in Luini's fresco at Lugano kneels with outstretched arms and long fair rippling loosened hair, beneath the Cross, is shown in the 'Resurrezione di Gesù Cristo' upon her knees before the gardener whose one word tells her that she sees her risen Lord.[77] It is a scene from Fra Angelico, a touch of tenderness falling like a faint soft light athwart the mass of orthodox tradition.

The sympathy between these shows and the plastic arts may be still further traced in Belcari's 'Dì del Giudizio.'[78] After the usual prologue an angel thrice blows the trumpet-blast that wakes the dead, crying aloud *Surgite!* Minos assembles his fiends, and Christ bids the archangel separate the good from the bad.[79] Michael, obedient to this order, seeks a hypocrite hidden among the just and sets him on the left hand, while Trajan is taken from the damned and placed among the saved. Solomon rises alone,[80] and remains undecided in the middle space, till Michael, charging him with carnal sin, forces him to take his station with the goats. S. Peter now disputes with wicked friars who think to save themselves by pointing to their cowls and girdles. The poor appeal to S. Francis, but he answers that poverty is no atonement for a sinful life. Magdalen refuses help to women who have lived impenitent. Christ and Mary reply that the hour of grace is past. Then the representatives of the seven deadly sins step forth and reason with the virtuous—the proud man with the humble, the glutton with the temperate. Sons upbraid their fathers for neglect or evil education. Others thank God for the discipline that saved them in their youth. At the last Christ awards judgment, crying to the just: 'Ye saw Me hungry and ye fed Me, naked and ye clothed Me!' and to the unjust, 'I was hungry and ye fed Me not, naked and ye clothed Me not.' Just and unjust answer, as in Scripture, with those words whereof the double irony is so dramatic. The damned are driven off to Hell, and angels open for the blessed the doors of Paradise.

[77] *Sacre Rappr.* i. 342.

[78] *Ibid.* iii. 439.

[79] For these incidents we may think of Signorelli's huge angels and swarming devils at Orvieto. What follows suggests the Lorenzetti fresco at Pisa, and the Orcagna of the Strozzi Chapel. Fra Angelico and Fra Bartolommeo also supply pictorial parallels.

[80] Poetry forced Castellani to decide where Solomon should go; Lorenzetti left it vague.

The 'Rappresentazioni' of the second class offer fewer points of interest; almost the sole lesson they inculcate being the superiority of the monastic over the secular life. S. Anthony leaves the world in which he has lived prosperous and wealthy, incarcerates his sister in a convent, and becomes a hermit.[81] Satan assembles the hosts of hell and makes fierce war upon his resolution; but the temptation is a poor affair, and Anthony gets through it by the help of an angel. The play ends with an assault of the foiled fiend of Avarice upon three rogues—Tagliagambe, Scaramuccia, and Carabello—who cut each other's throats over their ill-gotten booty. 'S. Guglielmo Gualtero,' like S. Francis, sells all that he possesses, embraces poverty, and becomes a saint [82] 'S. Margaret' subdues the dragon, and is beheaded by a Roman prefect for refusing homage to the pagan deities.[83] 'S. Giovanni e Paolo' are Latin confessors of the conventional type.[84] The legends of the 'Seven Sleepers,' 'S. Ursula,' and 'S. Onofrio' are treated after a like fashion. 'S. Eufrasia' still further illustrates the mediæval ideal of monastic chastity.[85] She leaves her betrothed husband and her mother to enter a convent. Nothing befalls her, and her life is good for nothing, except that she exhales the odour of conventual sanctity and dies 'S. Teodora' is a variation on the same theme.[86] She refuses Quintiliano, the governor of Asia, in marriage; and is sent to a bad house, whence Eurialo, a Christian, delivers her. Both are immediately despatched to execution. It is probable that the two last-mentioned plays were intended for representation within the walls of a nunnery. 'S. Barbara' presents the same motive, with a more marked theological bias.[87] Dioscoro, the father of the saint, hears from his astrologers that she is fated to set herself against the old gods of his worship. To avert this calamity, he builds a tower with two windows, where he shuts her up in the company of orthodox pagan teachers. Barbara becomes learned in her retirement, and refuses, upon the authority of Plato, to pay homage to idols. Faith, instead of Love, finds this new Danaë, in the person, not of Zeus, but of a priest despatched by Origen from Alexandria to convert her to Christianity. The princess learns her catechism, is baptized, and adds a third window to her tower, in recognition of the Trinity. It only remains for her father to torture her cruelly to death.

The outline of these stories is often singularly beautiful, and capable of poetic treatment. Remembering what Massinger and Decker made of the 'Virgin Martyr,' we turn with curiosity to 'S. Teodora' or 'S. Ursula.' Yet we are doomed to disappointment. The ingenuous charm, again, which painters threw over the puerilities of the monastic fancy, is absent from these plays. Sodoma's legend of S. Benedict in fresco

[81] *Sacre Rappr.* ii. 33.
[82] *Ibid.* iii. 140.
[83] *Ibid.* ii. 124.
[84] *Ibid.* ii. 235.
[85] *Ibid.* ii. 269.
[86] *Ibid.* ii. 323.
[87] *Sacre Rappr.* ii. 71.

on the walls of Monte Oliveto, Carpaccio's romance of S. Ursula painted for her Scuola at Venice, are touched with the grace of a child's fairy-story. The 'Rappresentazioni' eliminate all elements of mystery and magic from the fables, and reduce them to bare prose. The core of the myth or tale is rarely reached; the depths of character are never penetrated; and still the wizardry of wonderland is gone. In the hands of these Italian playwrights the most pregnant story of the Orient or North assumed the thin slight character of ordinary life. Its richness disappeared. Its beauty evanesced. Nothing remained but the dry bones of a *novella*. Indeed, the prose legends of the fourteenth century are far more fascinating than these dramatised tales of the Renaissance, which might be used to prove, if further proof were needed, that the Italian imagination is not in the highest sense romantic or fantastic, not far-reaching by symbol or by vision into the depths of nature human and impersonal. The sense of infinity which gives value to Northern works of fancy, is unknown in Italy. Sir Thomas Mallory wrote of Arthur's passage into dreamland:[88] 'And when they were at the water's side, even fast by the banke hoved a little barge with many faire ladies in it, and among them all was a queene, and all they had blacke hoods, and they wept and shriked when they saw King Arthur.' The author of the 'Tavola Ritonda' makes the event quite otherwise precise:[89]

> E stando per un poco, ed ecco per lo mare venire una navicella, tutta coperta di bianco . . . e la nave s' accostò allo re, e alquante braccia uscirono della nave, che presono lo re Artù, e visibilemente il misono nella nave, e portàrollo via per mare . . . si crede che la fata Morgana venisse per arte in quella navicella, e portòllo via in una isoletta di mare; e quivi morì di sue ferite, e la fata il sopellì in quella isoletta.

This anxiety after verification and distinctness is almost invariable in Italian literature. The very devil becomes a definite and oftentimes prosaic personage. External Nature is credited with no inner spirit, reaching forth from wood or wave or cloud to touch the soul of man in reverie or trance, or breaking on his charmed senses in the form of gnome or water-sprite or fairy. Men and women move in clear sunlight, disenchanted of the gloom or glory, as of star-irradiate vapour, which a Northern mytho-poet wraps around them, making their humanity thereby more poignant.

Those who care to connect the genius of a people with the country of their birth, may find the source of these mental qualities in the nobly beautiful, serene and gracious, but never mystical Italian land. The Latin Camœnæ have neither in ancient nor in modern years evoked the forms of mythic fable from that landscape. Far less is there the touch of Celtic or Teutonic inspiration—the light that never was on sea

[88] *La Mort d' Arthur* (Wright's edition), vol. iii. p. 331.
[89] Polidori's edition, vol. i. p. 542.

or land. The nightingales of Sorrento or Nettuno in no poet's vision have

> Charmed magic casements, opening on the foam
> Of perilous seas, in faery lands forlorn.

Down the hillsides between Lucca and Pistoja, where the cypresses stand in rows and olives cast their shadows on the grey tilled soil, no lover has dreamed he met Queen Guinevere in spring riding through flowers with Lancelot. Instead of Morgan le Fay, turning men to lichened and mist-moistened stones upon the heath, the Italian witch was ever Locusta, the poison-brewer, or Alcina, the temptress.

This peculiarity of the Italian genius made their architects incapable of understanding Gothic. This deprived Italian art of that sublimity which needs a grain of the grotesque for its perfection, a touch of the uncouth for its accomplishment. The instinct of poets and artists alike induced them to bring mystery within the sphere of definition, to limit the marvellous by reducing it to actual conditions, and to impoverish the terrible by measuring its boundaries. But since every defect has its corresponding quality, this same instinct secured for the modern age a world of immaculate loveliness in art and undimmed joyousness in poetry. If the wonderland of fancy is eliminated, the monstrous and unshaped have disappeared. With the grotesque vanishes disproportion. Humanity, conscious of its own emotion, displaces the shadowy people of the legends. We move in a well-ordered world of cheerfulness and beauty, made for man, where symmetry of parts is music. Ariosto's jocund irony is no slight compensation for the imagery of a Northern mythus.

Returning to the 'Rappresentazioni' we are forced to admit that the defect of the Italian fancy is more apparent than its quality, in a species of dramatic art which, being childish, needed some magic spell to reconcile an adult taste to its puerility.[90] They were written at the most prosaic moment of the national development, by men who could not afford to substitute the true Italian poetry of irony and idyllic sensuousness for the ancient religious spirit. The bondage of the middle ages was upon them. They were forced to take the extravagance of the monastic imagination for fact. But they did not really believe; and so the fact was apprehended frigidly, prosaically. Instead of poetry we get rhetoric; instead of marvels, gross incredibilities are forced upon

[90] The greater maturity of the plastic than of the poetic arts in the fifteenth century is apparent when we contrast the *Rappresentazioni* with Masaccio's, Ghirlandajo's, Mantegna's, or Carpaccio's paintings. Art, as I have frequently had to observe, emancipated the human faculties, and humanised the figments of the middle age by investing them with corporeal shape and forms of æsthetic beauty. The deliverance of the Italian genius was thus effected in painting earlier than in poetry, and in those very spheres of religious art where the poets were helpless to attain true freedom. Italian poetry first became free when it turned round and regarded the myths with an amused smile. I do not say that this was absolutely necessary, that an heroic Christian poetry might not have been produced in the fifteenth century by another race. But for the Italians it was necessary.

us in the lives of men and women fashioned like the folk who crowd the streets we know. Another step in the realistic direction would have transformed all these religious myths into *Novelle*; and then a new beauty, the beauty of the 'Decameron' and *Novellino*, would have been shed upon them. But it was precisely this step that Castellani and Belcari dared not take, since their purpose remained religious edification. Nay, their instinct led them in the opposite direction. Unable to escape the influence of the *Novella*, which was the truest literary form peculiar to Italy in that age, they converted it into a sacred legend and treated it with the same rhetorical and insincere pietism as the stories of the Saints. From S. Barbara to the third-class 'Rappresentazioni' the transition is easy.

The interest of this group of stories, as illustrating the psychological conditions of the Italian imagination, is great. Stripped of mediæval mystery, reduced to the proportions of a *Novella*, but not yet invested with its worldly charms, denuded of the pregnant symbolism or tragic intensity of their originals, these plays reveal the poverty of the fifteenth century, the incapacity of the Florentine genius at that moment to create poetry outside the sphere of figurative art, and in a region where irony and sensuality and natural passion were alike excluded. They might be compared to dead bones awaiting the spirit-breath of mirth and sarcasm to rouse them into life. 'Teofilo' is the Italian Faustus.[91] A devil accuses him to the bishop he is serving. Outcast and dishonoured, he seeks Manovello, a Jewish sorcerer, who takes him to a crossway and raises the fiend, Beelzebub. Teofilo abjures Christ, adores the devil, and signs a promise to be Satan's bondsman. In return, Beelzebub despatches a goblin, Farfalletto, to the bishop, who believes that an angel has come to bid him restore Teofilo to honour. Consequently Teofilo regains his post. But in the midst of his prosperity the renegade is wretched. Stung by conscience, he throws himself upon the mercy of our Lady. She pleads for him with Christ, summons the devil, and wrests from his grasp the parchment given by Teofilo. Poetic justice is satisfied by Manovello's descent to hell. Such is the prosaic form which the Faust legend assumed in Italy. Instead of the lust for power and knowledge which consumed the doctor of Wittenberg, making him exclaim:

> Had I as many souls as there be stars,
> I'd give them all for Mephistophilis!

we have this commonplace story of a bishop's almoner, driven by a vulgar trial of his patience to abjure the faith. The intercession of Mary introduces a farcical element into the piece; the audience is amused by seeing the devil's contract snatched from him after a jocular altercation with the Queen of Heaven. Our Mephistophilis is either fantastically grotesque as in the old prose-legend, or tragically saturnine as in Marlowe's tragedy. The fiend of this Florentine play is a sort

[91] *Sacre Rappr.* ii. 447.

of supernatural usurer, who lends at a short date upon exorbitant interest, and is nonsuited for fraud in the supreme court of appeal. To charge the Italian imagination in general with this dwarfing and defining of a legend that had in it such elements of grandeur, might be scarcely fair. The fault lies more perhaps with Florence of the fifteenth century; yet Florence was the brain of Italy, and if the people there could find no more of salt or savour in a myth like that of Theophilus, this fact gives food for deep reflection to the student of their culture.

In the 'Rè Superbo' we have one of those stories which travelled from the far East in the middle ages over the whole of Europe, acquiring a somewhat different form in every country.[92] The proud king in the midst of his prosperity falls sick. He takes a short day's journey to a watering-place, and bathes. By night an angel assumes his shape, dons his royal robes, summons his folk, and fares homeward to his palace. The king, meanwhile, is treated by the innkeeper as an impudent rascal. He begs some rags to cover his nakedness, and arrives in due time at the city he had left the day before. There his servants think him mad; but he obtains an audience with the angel, who reads him a sermon on humility, and then restores him to his throne. In this tale there lay nothing beyond the scope of the Italian imagination. Consequently the treatment is adequate, and the situations copied from real life are really amusing. The play of 'Barlaam e Josafat' by Bernardo Pulci is more ambitious.[93] Josafat's father hears from his astrologers that the child will turn Christian. Accordingly he builds a tower, and places his son there, surrounded with all things pleasant to the senses and cheering to the heart of man. His servants receive strict orders that the boy should never leave his prison, lest haply, meeting with old age or poverty or sickness, he should think of Christ. On one occasion they neglect this rule. Josafat rides forth and sees a leper and a blind man, and learns that age and death and pain are in store for all. This stirs reflection, and prepares him to receive the message of one Barlaam, who comes disguised as a merchant to the tower. Barlaam offers him a jewel which restores sight to the blind, hearing to the deaf, speech to the dumb, and which turns a fool to wisdom. The jewel is the faith of Christ. Josafat is instantly converted and baptized; nor can the persuasions of wise men or the allurements of women overcome his fixed resolve. So firmly rooted is his new faith, so wonderful his eloquence, that he converts his father and the Court, and receives for his great wisdom the crown of his ancestors. Yet an earthly throne savours too much in his eyes of worldly pride. Therefore he renounces it, and lives thenceforth a holy hermit. This legend, it will be perceived, is a dim echo of the wonderful history of Siddârtha, the founder of Buddhism. Beautiful as are the outlines, too beautiful to be spoiled by any telling, Pulci has done his best to draw it from the dream-world of romance into the sphere of prose. At the same time, while depriving

[92] *Sacre Rappr.* iii. 177.
[93] *Sacre Rappr.* ii. 163.

it of romance, he has not succeeded in dramatising it. We do not feel the psychological necessity for the changes in any of the characters; the charm of each strange revolution is destroyed by the clumsy preparation of the motives. We are forced to feel that the playwright was working on the lines of a legend he did not understand and could not vitalise. The wonder is that he thought of choosing it and found it ready to his hand.

Few of the 'Rappresentazioni' are so interesting as 'S. Uliva.'[94] Uliva is no saint of the Catholic calendar, but a daughter of world-old romance. Her legend may be read in the 'Gesta Romanorum,' in Philip de Beaumanoir's 'Roman de la Mannelline,' in Ser Giovanni's 'Pecorone,' in Chaucer's 'Man of Law's Tale,' in Grimm's 'Handless Maiden,' and in Russian and Servian variations on the same theme. It is in truth the relic of some very ancient myth, used by the poets of all ages for the sake of its lesson of patience in affliction, its pathos of persecuted innocence. The form the tale assumed in Italy is this: Uliva, daughter of the Roman Emperor, Giuliano, is begged in marriage by her own father, who says she has more beautiful hands than any other princess. She cuts her hands off, and Giuliano sends her to Britain to be killed. But her intending murderers take pity on her, and leave her in a wood alone. There the King of Britain finds her and places her under the protection of his queen. After many misfortunes the Virgin Mary restores her hands, and she is married to the King of Castille. She bears him a son; but by this time she has roused the jealousy and hatred of the queen-mother, who takes the opportunity of the king's absence to poison his mind against her by letters, and shortly after drives her forth with her child. Uliva reaches Rome, and lives there twelve years unknown, till her husband, who has discovered and punished his mother's treason, and has sought his wronged wife sorrowing, at last rejoins her and recognises in her son his heir. The play ends with a reconciliation scene between the Emperor, the King, and Uliva, the Pope pronouncing benedictions on the whole party. It will be seen from this brief abstract of the legend that the 'Rappresentazione' is a chivalrous *Novella* dramatised. Several old pathetic stories have been woven into one, and the heroine has been dignified with the title of saint because of the pity she inspires. Uliva belongs to the sisterhood of Boccaccio's Griselda, Ariosto's Ginevra, and the Queen in our old ballad of Sir Aldingar. The mediæval imagination, after creating types of stateliness like Guinevere, of malice like Morgana, of love like Iseult, turned aside and dwelt upon the tender delicacy of a woman, whose whole strength is her beauty, gentleness, and patience; who suffers all things in the spirit of charity; whom the angels love and whom our Lady cherishes; who wins all hearts of men by her goodliness; and who, like Una, passes unscathed through peril and persecution until at last her joy is perfected by the fruition of her lawful love. It was precisely this element of romance that touched the Italian fancy; and the playwright of 'S. Uliva' has

[94] *Sacre Rappr.* iii. 235. Also edited separately with an introduction by D' Ancona.

shown considerable skill in his treatment of it. Piteous details are accumulated with remorseless pertinacity upon the head of the unfortunate Uliva, in order to increase the pathos of her situation. There is no mitigation of her hardships except in her own innocence, and in the loving compassion wrung by her beauty from her rude tormentors. This want of relief, together with the brusque passage from one incident to another, betrays a lack of dramatic art. But the poet, whoever he was, succeeded in sustaining the ideal of purity and beauty he conceived. He shows how all Uliva's sufferings as well as her good fortune were due to the passions her beauty inspired, and how it was her purity that held her harmless to the end.

'Stella' is the same story slightly altered, with a somewhat different cast of characters and an evil-hearted stepmother in the place of the malignant queen.[95] If we compare both fables with Grimm's version of the 'Handless Maiden,' the superiority of the Northern conception cannot fail to strike us. The Italian *Novella*, though written for the people, exhibits the external pomp and grandeur of royalty. All its motives are drawn from the clash of human passions. Yet these are hidden beneath a superincumbent mass of trivialities. The German tale has a background of spiritual mystery—good and evil powers striving for the possession of a blameless soul. When the husband, who has been deceived by feminine malice, takes his long journey without food as a penitent to find his injured wife, how far deeper is the pathos and the poetry of the situation than the Italian apparatus of couriers with letter-bags, chancellors, tournaments, and royal progresses undertaken with a vast parade, can compass! The Northern fancy, stimulated by the simple beauty of the situation, confines itself to the passionate experience of the heart and soul. The Florentine playwright adheres to the material facts of life, and takes a childish pleasure in passing the splendours of kings and princes in review. By this method he vulgarises the legend he handles. Beneath his touch it ceases to be holy ground. The enchantment of the myth has evanesced.

'Rosana' is simply the story of 'Floire et Blanchefleur,' which Boccaccio had already worked into his 'Filocopo.'[96] Austero, King of Rome, goes with his wife on pilgrimage to Holy Land. He falls into the hands of the King of Cesaria, and is slain with all his folk, except the queen. She is taken captive to Cesaria, where she gives birth to Rosana on the same day that Ulimeno is born to her master. When Ulimeno grows up, he loves the daughter of his father's slave. His parents seek to cure this passion by sending him to France, and at the same time sell Rosana to some merchants, who convey her to the Sultan's harem. Ulimeno returns to Cesaria in deep distress, and vows that he will never rest till he has regained his love. After a proper number of adventures, he finds Rosana in the seraglio, where, notwithstanding the Sultan's admiration of her beauty, she has preserved her virginity.

[95] *Sacre Rappr.* iii. 319.
[96] *Sacre Rappr.* iii. 362.

They are married, and Ulimeno is converted, with his realm, to Christianity. The prettiest parts of this play are the scenes in the seraglio, where Rosana refuses comfort from the Sultan's women, and the contrivances devised by Ulimeno to get speech with her. Except that Rosana and her parents are Christian and that the saints protect her, there is nothing to justify the title of 'Sacra Rappresentazione.' It is a love-romance, like Shakspere's 'Pericles.'

Another *Novella* of less poetic interest is dramatised in 'Agnolo Ebreo.'[97] Agnolo, the Jew, has a Christian wife, who persuades him instead of putting out his money at usury to lend it to Christ by giving it away in alms. Having thus cast his bread upon the waters, he recovers it again after not many days by picking up money in the streets and finding a jewel in a fish's belly. He is baptized, because he sees clearly that the God of the Christians can make him rich. Only its tedious solemnity prevents this play from being a farce.

Three 'Rappresentazioni' are written upon incidents of pilgrimage to the shrine of S. James of Compostella—Il Santo Barone, as he is always called. The first of these is entitled 'Rappresentazione di un Pellegrino.'[98] It tells the tale of a certain Guglielmo who vowed the journey to Compostella on his sick bed. Upon the road he meets with a fiend in the disguise of S. James, who persuades him to commit suicide. No sooner is he dead, than the devil grasps his soul, as may be seen in Lorenzetti's fresco of the Campo Santo, and makes away with it toward hell. S. James stops him, and a voluble altercation takes place between them, at the end of which the soul, who keeps crying *misericordia* at intervals, is rescued and restored to its body. Then Guglielmo completes his vow, and returns joyfully to his wife. 'I due Pellegrini' is more complex.[99] Arrigo Coletta leaves his wife and son at Rome; Constantino Constante leaves his wife and three sons at Genoa; and both set forth to Compostella. On the way they meet and make friends; but the Genoese dies before they have got far upon their journey. His Roman friend carries the dead body to Compostella, where S. James restores it to life, and both return in safety to their homes. After sojourning some time in Rome, Arrigo falls sick of leprosy, and has to go forth and wander up and down the earth. Chance brings him to the house of the Genoese who had received such benefits from him upon their pilgrimage. They consult doctors and wise men together, who assure them that no cure can be wrought unless the leper bathe from head to foot in the blood of virgins. This determines Constantino to sacrifice all that he holds dearest in the world. He kills his three sons, and prepares a bath of their blood, which restores his old benefactor to health. But the Saint of Compostella has still his eye upon his servants. A miracle brings the three boys back to life. They are found with golden apples in their hands, and the play ends with a general thanks-

[97] *Sacre Rappr.* iii. 485.
[98] *Ibid.* iii. 416.
[99] *Sacre Rappr.* iii. 439.

giving. The prosy bluntness with which the incidents of this strange story are treated as matter of fact, is scarcely less remarkable than the immorality which substitutes mere thaumaturgy for the finer instincts of humanity. The exaggerated generosity of Constantino might be paralleled from hundreds of *Novelle*. This one virtue seems to have had extraordinary fascination for the Italians. 'I tre Pellegrini' is based upon a legend of mediæval celebrity, versified by Southey in his 'Pilgrimage to Compostella.'[100] A father, a mother, and a son of great personal beauty set forth together for the shrine of S. Iago. On the road they put up at an inn, where Falconetta, the host's daughter, falls in love with the boy and tempts him. Thwarted in her will, she vows to ruin him; and for this purpose, puts a silver cup into his travelling bag. In the morning the pilgrims are overtaken by the police, who find the cup and hang the beautiful young man. The parents complete their vow, and on the way back discover their son upon the gallows alive and well. Falconetta is burned, and her parents are hanged—the old host remarking, not without humour, that, though he was innocent of this crime, he had murdered enough people in his day to have deserved his fate. The style of this play merits more praise than can be bestowed on the 'Rappresentazioni' in general. Falconetta is a real theatrical character, and the bustle of the inn on the arrival of the guests is executed with dramatic vigour.

In their 'Sacre Rappresentazioni' the Florentines advanced to the very verge of the true drama. After adapting the Miracle-plays of mediæval orthodoxy to their stage, they versified the Legends of the Saints, and went so far as to dramatise novels of a purely secular character. The 'Figliuol Prodigo' and the farce appended to the 'Pellegrino' contain the germs of vernacular comedy. S. Maddalena is a complete character. S. Uliva is delicately sketched and well sustained. The situation at the opening of the 'Tre Pellegrini' is worked out with real artistic skill. Lastly, in the 'Esaltazione della Croce' a regular five-act tragedy was attempted.

From the oratories of the Compagnie and the parlours of the convents this peculiar form of art was extended to the Courts and public theatres. Poliziano composed a 'Rappresentazione' on the classical fable of Orpheus, and Niccolò da Correggio another on the myth of Cephalus and Procris.[101] Other attempts to secularise the religious drama followed, until, in 1521, Francesco Mantovano put the contemporary history of the French General Lautrec upon the boards.

Still the fact remains that the 'Sacre Rappresentazioni' did not lead to the production of a national Italian theatre. If we turn to the history of our Elizabethan stage, we shall find that, after the age of the Miracles and Moralities had passed, a new and independent work of art, emanating from the creative genius of Marlowe and Shakspere, put England in the possession of that great rarity, a Drama commensurate

[100] *Ibid.* iii. 466.
[101] The date of the former is probably 1472, of the latter 1486.

with the whole life of the nation at one of its most brilliant epochs. To this accomplishment of the dramatic art the Italians never attained. The causes of their failure will form the subject of a separate inquiry when we come to consider the new direction taken by the playwrights at the Courts of Ferrara and Rome.

As an apology for the space here devoted to the analysis of plays childish in their subject-matter, prosaic in their treatment, and fruitless of results, it may be urged that in the 'Sacre Rappresentazioni' better than elsewhere we can study the limitations of the popular Italian genius at the moment when the junction was effected between humanism and the spirit of the people.

CHAPTER VI

LORENZO DE' MEDICI AND POLIZIANO

Period from 1470 to 1530—Methods of treating it—By Chronology—By Places—By Subjects—Renascence of Italian—At Florence, Ferrara, Naples—The New Italy—Forty Years of Peace—Lorenzo de' Medici—His Admiration for and Judgment of Italian Poetry—His Privileges as a Patron—His Rime—The Death of Simonetta—Lucrezia Donati—Lorenzo's Descriptive Power—The 'Selve'—The 'Ambra'—'La Nencia'—'I Beoni'—His Sacred Poems—Carnival and Dance Songs—Carri and Trionfi—Savonarola—The Masque of Penitence—Leo X. in Florence, 1513—Pageant of the Golden Age—Angelo Poliziano—His Place in Italian Literature—'Le Stanze'—Treatment of the Octave Stanza—Court Poetry—Mechanism and Adornment—The 'Orfeo'—Orpheus, the Ideal of the Cinque Cento—Its Dramatic Qualities —Chorus of Mænads—Poliziano's Love Poems—Rispetti—Florentine Love—La Bella Simonetta—Study and Country Life.

In dealing with the mass of Italian literature between the dates 1470 and 1530, several methods suggest themselves, each of which offers certain advantages, while none is wholly satisfactory. In the *first* place we might adopt a chronological division, and arrange the chief authors of whom we have to treat, by periods. Lorenzo de' Medici, Poliziano, Luigi Pulci, Boiardo, and Sannazzaro would be the leading names in the first group. In the second we should place Ariosto, Machiavelli, Guicciardini and the minor historians of Florence. Bembo would lead a third class, including Castiglione, La Casa, and the Petrarchistic poets of the Academies. A fourth would be headed by Pietro Aretino, and would embrace the burlesque writers and minor critical prosaists of the decadence. The advantage of this method is that it corresponds to a certain regular progression in the evolution of Italian genius during that brief space of brilliant activity. Yet the chronological stages are not sufficiently well marked to justify its exclusive adoption. The first group is separated from the rest by a real interval, since the men who compose it died, with one exception, before the close of the fifteenth century, about the year of Charles VIII.'s entrance into Italy.[1] But the authors of the second, third, and fourth groups lived almost contemporaneously, covering the whole period of Italy's greatest literary glory and deepest national discomfiture, and witnessing the final extinction of her liberty in the settlement effected by the policy of Charles V.[2]

[1] Lorenzo de' Medici, b. 1448, d. 1492. Poliziano, b. 1454, d. 1494. Luigi Pulci, b. 1432, d. about 1487. Boiardo, b. about 1434, d. 1494. Sannazzaro, b. 1458, d. 1530.

[2] Machiavelli, b. 1469, d. 1527. Ariosto, b. 1474, d. 1533. Guicciardini, b. 1482, d. 1540. Bembo, b. 1470, d. 1547. Castiglione, b. 1478, d. 1529. La Casa b. 1503, d. 1556. Pietro Aretino, b. 1492, d. 1557.

Nor, again, can we trace in the several phases of literature they represent, so clear a process of expansion as may be detected in the successive stages of artistic or humanistic development. When the work effected by the first group was accomplished, both the language and the literature of Italy became in a true sense national, and the cultivated classes of all districts, trained in the common discipline of humanistic studies, set themselves with one accord and simultaneously to the task of polishing the mother-tongue. This fact in the history of Italian literature suggests a *second* method of classification. We might take the three chief centres of renascence at the close of the fifteenth century—Florence, Ferrara, Naples—and show how the local characteristics of these cities affected their great writers. Rome during the pontificate of Leo X.; Urbino under the rule of Guidobaldo Montefeltre; Milan in the days of the last Sforzas; Venice at the epoch of Aldo's settlement; might next be chosen to illustrate the subsequent growth of Italian culture, when it ceased to be Tuscan, Neapolitan, and Ferrarese. Yet though this local method of arrangement offers many advantages, and has the grand merit of fixing the attention upon one important feature of intellectual life in Italy—its many-sidedness and diversity, due to the specific qualities of cities vying with each other in a common exercise of energy—still it would not do for the historian of Italian culture at one of its most brilliant moments to accentuate minor differences, when it ought to be his object to portray the genius of the people as a whole. In a word, this classification has the same defect as the treatment of the arts by Schools.[3] Moreover, it cannot fail to lead to repetition and confusion; for though the work we have to analyse was carried on in several provinces, yet each Court and each city produced material of the same general character. Novels, for example, were written at Florence as well as Milan. Rome saw the first representation of comedies no less than Ferrara. The romantic epic was not confined to the Court of the Estensi, nor dissertations on the gentle life to that of Urbino. We are led by the foregoing considerations to yet a *third* method of arrangement. Would it not be scientific to divide the literature of the Renaissance into its chief branches, and to treat of the romantic epic, the *novella*, the stage, the idyll, lyric verse, essays in prose, histories, and so forth, under separate chapters? Undoubtedly there is much to say for such a treatment of the subject. Yet when we consider that it necessitates our bringing the same authors under review in several successive sections, confuses chronology, and effaces local distinctions, it will be seen that to follow this system exclusively would be unwise. It is too strictly analytical for our purpose. That purpose is to draw a portrait of the Italian spirit as expressed in the vernacular literature of about seventy years of exceptional splendour; and perhaps it will be conceded by the student that instinct, conscious of the end in view, conscious also of these several methods, but unwilling to be hampered

[3] See Vol. I., *The Fine Arts*, p. 671.

by any one of them too rigorously followed out, will be a safer guide than formal accuracy.

I therefore propose in the remaining chapters of this book to adopt a mixed method, partaking of the chronological in so far as I shall attempt to show a certain process of evolution from the renascence led by Lorenzo de' Medici to the decadence typified in Pietro Aretino, insisting upon local peculiarities where it can be clearly proved that these contributed an important element to the total result, and relying on the classification by subjects for bringing scattered details under general consideration. Five men of the highest eminence mark stages in the history we have to review. These are Poliziano, Ariosto and Machiavelli, Bembo, and Pietro Aretino. Chronologically, they represent four moments of development—the initial, the consummate, the academical, and the decadent. But if we discard chronology and regard their intellectual qualities alone, we might reduce them to three. Merging Poliziano and Bembo in Ariosto, retaining Machiavelli and Pietro Aretino, we obtain the three prominent phases of Renaissance culture in Italy—firstly, serene, self-satisfied, triumphant art, glorying in the beauty of form for form's sake, and aiming at perfection in style of sunny and delightful loveliness; secondly, profound scientific analysis, taking society for its object, dissecting human history and institutions without prejudice or prepossession, unqualified by religious or ethical principles, pushing its logical method to the utmost verge of audacity, and startling the world with terror by the results of its materialistic philosophy; thirdly, moral corruption unabashed and unrestrained, destitute of shame because devoid of conscience, boldly asserting itself and claiming the right to rule society with cynical effrontery. Round Ariosto are grouped the romantic and idyllic poets, the novelists and comic playwrights, all the tribe of joyous merry-makers, who translated into prose and verse the beauty found in painting of the golden age. With Machiavelli march the historians and political philosophers, the school of Pomponazzi and the materialistic analysts, who led the way for a new birth of science in the Baconian speculations of the Cosentine academy. Aretino is the coryphæus of a multitude of scribes and courtiers, literary gladiators, burlesque authors of obscene *Capitoli*, men of evil character, who used the pen for poniard, and were the fit successors of invective-writers.

If we turn from men to cities, and seek to define the parts played by the several communities in this work of creating an Italian literature, we shall find that Florence fixes the standard of language, and dominates the nation by the fame of her three poets of the fourteenth century. Florence, moreover, gives birth to Machiavelli, Guicciardini, and the political theorists who form a group around them. Florentine wit and humour lend a certain pungency to all the products of the golden age. Naples adds the luxury of southern colour, felt in Sannazzaro's waxen paragraphs and Pontano's voluptuous hendecasyllables. Ferrara develops the chivalrous elements of the romantic epic, shelters Ariosto, and produces the pastoral drama, that eminently characteristic product of the late Renaissance. Milan is the home of Bandello, who takes the first rank among the novelists and leads a school of Lombard writers in that style. Rome does little for the general culture of the nation, except that in the age of Leo the Papal Court formed a centre for studious men of all classes and qualities. Her place in literature is therefore analogous to that she occupies in art and scholarship.[4] Aretino chooses the city of the lagoons for his retreat, not without a certain propriety; for Venice had become the Paris of the sixteenth century, and here the press was more active than elsewhere in Italy. His instinct led the master of lampoon, the prince of pamphleteers, to the city which combined the utmost license of printing with the most highly developed immorality of manners. Thus, seen from many points of view and approached with different objects of study, men, places, and matter alike furnish their own pivots for treatment. Italy, unlike England and France, has no political and intellectual metropolis, no London and no Paris, where the historian may take his stand securely to survey the manifold activities of the race as from a natural centre. He must be content to shift his ground and vary his analytic method, keeping steadily in mind those factors which by their interaction and combination determine the phenomena he has in view.

We are now at length upon the threshold of the true Renaissance. The division between popular literature and humanistic culture is about to end. Classic form, appropriated by the scholars, will be given to the prose and poetry of the Italian language. The fusion, divined and attempted, rather than accomplished by Alberti, will be achieved. Men as great as Machiavelli and Ariosto henceforth need not preface their *cose volgari* with apologies. The new literature is no longer Tuscan, but Italian—national in the widest and deepest sense of the word, when Venetian Bembo, Neapolitan Sannazzaro, Ariosto from Reggio, Boiardo Count of Scandiano, Castiglione the Mantuan and Tasso the Bergamasque vie with Tuscan Pulci and Poliziano, Machiavelli and Guicciardini, in the creation of the golden age.

The renascence of Italian took place almost simultaneously in three centres: at Florence under the protection of the Medici, at Ferrara in the castle of the Estensi, and at Naples in the Aragonese Court. Rome from the pontificate of Innocent VIII. to that of Leo X. was almost dumb and deaf to literature. Venice waited till the period of the press. Milan produced nothing. It was but gradually that the wave of national culture reached the minor States. The three cities to which Italy owed the resurrection of her genius were ruled by princes, and the new literature felt the influence of Courts from the commencement. Indeed, the whole conditions of Italy had been altered since the death of Boccaccio in 1375. The middle ages had been swept away. Of their modes of thought, religious beliefs, political ideals, scholastic theories, scarcely a vestige remained. Among the cities which had won or kept their

[4] See Vol. I., *Revival of Learning*, pp. 427 *et seq.*; *The Fine Arts*, pp. 671 *et seq.*

independence during the fourteenth century, only one remained free from a master's yoke; and even Venice, though she showed no outward signs of decadence, had reached the utmost verge of her development. The citizens who had fought the battles of the Communes round their banners and their sacred cars, were now quiet burghers, paying captains of adventure to wage mimic warfare with political or commercial rivals in neighbouring States. A class of professional diplomatists corresponding to these mercenary war-contractors had arisen, selected from the ranks of the scholars for their rhetorical gifts and command of Latin style. The humanists themselves constituted a new and powerful body, a nation within the nation, separated from its higher social and political interests, selfish, restless, greedy for celebrity, nomadic, disengaged from local ties, conscious of their strength, and swaying with the vast prestige of learning in that age the intellectual destinies of the race. Insolent and ambitious in all that concerned their literary pretensions, these men were servile in their private life. They gained their daily bread by flatteries and menaces, hanging about the Courts of petty despots, whose liberality they paid with adulation or quickened with the threat of infamy in libels. At the same time the humanists, steeped in the best and worst that could be extracted from the classics, confounding the dross of Greek and Roman literature with its precious metal in their indiscriminate worship of antiquity, and debarred through want of criticism from assimilating the noblest spirit of the pagan culture, had created a new mental atmosphere. The work they accomplished for Italy, though mixed in quality, had two undeniable merits. Not only had they restored the heritage of the past and broken down the barrier between the ancient and the modern world, bringing back the human consciousness from the torpor of the middle ages to a keen and vivid sense of its own unity; but they so penetrated and imbued each portion of the Italian nation with their enthusiasm, that, intellectually at least, the nation was now one, and ready for a simultaneous progress on the path of culture.[5]

It so happened that at this very moment, when the unity of Italy in art and scholarship had been achieved, external quiet succeeded to the discords of three centuries. The ancient party-cries of Emperor and Church, of Guelf and Ghibelline, of noble and burgher, of German and Latin ingredients within the body politic had gradually ceased and been forgotten. The Italic element, deriving its instincts from Roman civilisation, triumphed over the alien and the feudal; and though this victory was attended with the decay of the Communes that had striven to achieve it, yet the final outcome was a certain homogeneity of conditions in all the great centres of national life. Italy became a network of cultivated democracies, ruled by tyrants of different degrees. The middle of the fifteenth century witnessed the commencement of that

[5] It is right to say here that considerable portions of Southern Italy, the Marches of Ancona and Romagna, Piedmont and Liguria, remained outside the Renaissance movement at this period.

halcyon period of forty years' tranquillity, destined to be broken by the descent of Charles VIII., in 1494, upon which Machiavelli and Guicciardini from amid the tempests of the next half-century looked back with eyes of wonder and of envy. Constantinople fell, and the undoubted primacy of the civilised races came to the Italians. Lorenzo de' Medici was regarded as the man who, by his political ability and firm grasp of the requisite conditions for maintaining peace in the peninsula, had established and secured the equilibrium between mutually jealous and antagonistic States. Whether the merit of that repose, so fruitful of results in art and literature for the Italians, was really due to Lorenzo's sagacity, or whether the shifting forces of the nation had become stationary for a season by the operation of circumstances, may fairly be questioned. Yet there is no doubt that the unprecedented prosperity of the people coincided with his administration of Florence, and ended when he ceased to guide the commonwealth. It was at any rate a singular good fortune that connected the name of this extraordinary man with the high-tide of material prosperity in Italy and with the resurrection of her national literature.

The figure of Lorenzo de' Medici has more than once already crossed the stage of this history.[6] Whether dealing with the political conditions, or the scholarship, or the fine arts of the Renaissance, it is impossible to omit his name. There is therefore now no need to sketch his character or to inquire into the incidents of his Florentine administration. It will suffice to remind the readers of this book that he finally succeeded in so clinching the power of the Casa Medici that no subsequent revolutions were able to destroy it. The part he played as a patron of artists and scholars, and as a writer of Italian, was subordinate to his political activity in circumstances of peculiar difficulty. While controlling the turbulent democracy of Florence and gaining recognition for his tyranny from jealous princes, he still contrived to lead his age in every branch of culture, deserving the magnificent eulogium of Poliziano, who sang of him in the 'Nutricia:'[7]

> Tu vero æternam, per avi vestigia Cosmi
> Perque patris (quis enim pietate insignior illo?),
> Ad famam eluctans, cujus securus ad umbram
> Fulmina bellorum ridens procul aspicit Arnus,
> Mæoniæ caput, o Laurens, quem plena senatu
> Curia quemque gravi populus stupet ore loquentem,
> Si fas est, tua nunc humili patere otia cantu
> Secessusque sacros avidas me ferre sub auras.
> Namque, importunas mulcentem pectine curas,
> Umbrosæ recolo te quondam vallis in antrum
> Monticolam traxisse deam: vidi ipse corollas
> Nexantem, numerosque tuos prona aure bibentem. . . .
> Quodque alii studiumque vocant durumque laborem,

[6] See Vol. I., *Age of the Despots*, pp. 116, 253, 261; *Revival of Learning*, pp. 473-477; *Fine Arts*, pp. 707, 764. See also *Sketches and Studies in Italy*, Article on Florence and the Medici.

[7] *Op. Lat.* p. 423.

Hìc tibi ludus erit: fessus civilibus actis,
Huc is emeritas acuens ad carmina vires.
Felix ingenio! felix cui pectore tantas
Instaurare vices, cui fas tam magna capaci
Alternare animo, et varias ita nectere curas!

Lorenzo de' Medici was the last apologist for the mother speech, as he was the first and chief inaugurator of the age when such apologies were no longer to be needed. He took a line somewhat different from Alberti's in his defence of Italian, proving not merely its utility, but boldly declaring its equality with the classic languages. We possess a short essay of his, written with this purpose, where he bestows due praise on Dante, Boccaccio, and Guido Cavalcanti, and affirms in the teeth of the humanists that Petrarch wrote better love-poems than Ovid, Tibullus, Catullus, or Propertius.[8] Again, in his epistle to Federigo of Aragon, sent with a MS. volume containing a collection of early Tuscan poetry, he passes acute and sympathetic judgments on the lyrists from Guittone of Arezzo to Cino da Pistoja, proving that he had studied their works to good purpose, and had formed a correct opinion of the origins of Italian literature.[9] Lorenzo does not write like a man ashamed of the vernacular or forced to use it because he can command no better. He is sure of the justice of his cause, and determined by precept and example and by the prestige of his princely rank to bring the literature he loves into repute again.

No one could have been better fitted for the task. Unlike Alberti, Lorenzo was a Florentine of the Florentines, Tuscan to the backbone, imbued with the spirit of his city, a passionate lover of her customs and pastimes, a complete master of her vernacular. His education, though it fitted him for Platonic discussions with Ficino and rendered him an amateur of humanistic culture, had failed to make a pedant of him. Much as he appreciated the classics, he preferred his Tuscan poets; and what he learned at school, he brought to bear upon the study of the native literature. Consequently his style is always idiomatic; whether he seeks the elevation of grave diction or reproduces the talk of the streets, he uses language like a man who has habitually spoken the words which he commits to paper. His brain was vigorous, and his critical faculty acute. He lived, moreover, in close sympathy with his age, never rising above it, but accurately representing its main tendencies. At the same time he was sufficiently a poet to delight a generation that had seen no great writer of verse since Boccaccio. Though his work is in no sense absolutely first rate, he wrote nothing that a man of ability might not have been pleased to own.

Lorenzo's first essays in poetry were sonnets and *canzoni* in the style of the *Trecento*. It is a mistake to classify him, as some historians of literature have done, with the deliberate imitators of Petrarch, or to

[8] *Poesie di Lorenzo de' Medici* (Firenze, Barbèra, 1859), pp. 10-19.

[9] *Poesie di Lorenzo de' Medici*, pp. 24-34. Notice especially the verdict on Cino and Dante, p. 33.

judge his work by its deflection from the Petrarchistic standard of pure style. His youthful lyrics show the appreciative study of Dante and Guido Cavalcanti no less than of the poet of Vaucluse; and though they affect the conventional melancholy of the Petrarchistic mannerism, they owe their force to the strong objective spirit of the fifteenth century. Lorenzo's originality consists in the fusion he effected between the form of the love-lyric handed down from Petrarch and the realistic genius of the age of Ghirlandajo. This is especially noticeable in the sonnets that describe the beauties of the country. They are not penetrated with emotion permeating and blurring the impressions made by natural objects on the poet's mind. His landscapes are not hazy with the atmosphere, now luminous, now sombre, of a lover's varying mood. On the contrary, every object is defined and classified; and the lady sits like a beautiful figure in a garden, painted with no less loving care in all its details than herself.[10] These pictures, very delicate in their minute and truthful touches, affect our fancy like a panel of Benozzo Gozzoli, who omits no circumstance of the scene he undertakes to reproduce, crowds it with incidents and bestows the same attention upon the principal subjects and the accessories. The central emotion of Lorenzo's verse is scarcely love, but delight in the country—the Florentine's enjoyment of the villa, with its woods and rivulets, the pines upon the hillsides, the song-birds, and the pleasures of the chase.

The following sonnet might be chosen as a fair specimen of the new manner introduced into literature by Lorenzo. Its classical colouring, deeply felt and yet somewhat frigid, has the true stamp of the *quattrocento*:[11]

> Leave thy belovèd isle, thou Cyprian queen;
> Leave thy enchanted realm so delicate,
> Goddess of love! Come where the rivulet
> Bathes the short turf and blades of tenderest green!
> Come to these shades, these airs that stir the screen
> Of whispering branches and their murmurs set
> To Philomel's enamoured canzonet:
> Choose this for thine own land, thy loved demesne!
> And if thou com'st by these clear rills to reign,
> Bring thy dear son, thy darling son, with thee;
> For there be none that own his empire here.
> From Dian steal the vestals of her train,
> Who roam the woods at will, from danger free,
> And know not Love, nor his dread anger fear.

That Lorenzo was incapable of loving as Dante or Petrarch or even Boccaccio loved, is obvious in every verse he wrote. The spirit in him neither triumphs over the flesh nor struggles with it, nor yet submits a willing and intoxicated victim. It remains apart and cold, playing with fancies, curiously surveying the carnival of lusts that hold their revel

[10] Read for instance No. xii. in the edition above cited, 'Vidi madonna sopra un fresco rio;' No. xviii., 'Con passi sparti,' &c.; No. xlvii., 'Bello fresche e purpuree viole.'
[11] *Ibid.* p. 97.

in the breast whereof it is the lord. Under these conditions he could take the wife his mother found for him at Rome, and record the fact in his diary;[12] he could while away his leisure with venal beauties or country girls at his villas; but of love in the poet's sense he had no knowledge. It is true that, nurtured as he was in the traditions of fourteenth-century verse, he thought it necessary to establish a titular mistress of his heart. The account he gives of this proceeding in a commentary on his own sonnets, composed after the model of the 'Vita Nuova,' is one of his best pieces of writing. He describes the day when the beautiful Simonetta Cattaneo, his brother Giuliano's lady, was carried to her grave with face uncovered, lying beneath the sunlight on her open bier. All Florence was touched to tears by the sight, and the poets poured forth elegies. The month was April, and the young earth seemed to have put on her robe of flowers only to make the pathos of that death more poignant. Then, says Lorenzo: 'Night came; and I with a friend most dear to me went communing about the loss we all had suffered. While we spoke, the air being exceedingly serene, we turned our eyes to a star of surpassing brightness, which toward the west shone forth with such lustre as not only to conquer all the other stars, but even to cast a shadow from the objects that intercepted its light. We marvelled at it awhile; and then, turning to my friend, I said: "There is no need for wonder, since the soul of that most gentle lady has either been transformed into yon new star or has joined herself to it. And if this be so, that splendour of the star is nowise to be wondered at; and even as her beauty in life was of great solace to our eyes, so now let us comfort ourselves at the present moment with the sight of so much brilliance. And if our eyes be weak and frail to bear such brightness, pray we to the god, that is to her deity, to give them virtue, in order that without injury unto our sight we may awhile contemplate it." . . . Then, forasmuch as it appeared to me that this colloquy furnished good material for a sonnet, I left my friend and composed the following verses, in which I speak about the star aforesaid:

O lucid star, that with transcendent light
Quenchest of all those neighbouring stars the gleam,
Why thus beyond thine usage dost thou stream,
Why art thou fain with Phoebus still to fight?
Haply those beauteous eyes, which from our sight
Death stole, who now doth vaunt himself supreme,
Thou hast assumed: clad with their glorious beam,
Well may'st thou claim the sun-god's chariot bright.
Listen, new star, new regent of the day,
Who with unwonted radiance gilds our heaven,
O listen, goddess, to the prayers we pray!
Let so much splendour from thy sphere be riven
That to these eyes, which fain would weep alway,
Unblinded, thy glad sight may yet be given!'

[12] 'Tolsi donna . . . ovvero mi fu data,' from the *Ricordi* printed in the Appendix to Roscoe's *Life*.

From that moment Lorenzo began to write poems. He wandered alone and meditated on the sunflower, playing delightfully unto himself with thoughts of Love and Death. Yet his heart was empty; and, like Augustine or Alastor, he could say: 'nondum amabam, sed amare amabam, quærebam quod amarem amans amare.' When a young man is in this mood it is not long before he finds an object for his adoration. Lorenzo went one day in the same spring with friends to a house of feasting, where he met with a lady lovelier in his eyes even than La Simonetta. After the fashion of his age, he describes her physical and mental perfections with a minuteness which need not be enforced upon a modern reader.[13] Suffice it to say that Lucrezia Donati—such was the lady's name—supplied Lorenzo with exactly what he had been seeking, an object for his literary exercises. The 'Sonetti,' 'Canzoni,' and 'Selve d' Amore' were the fruits of this first passion.

Though Lorenzo was neither a poet nor a lover after the stamp of Dante, these juvenile verses and the prose with which he prefaced them, show him in a light that cannot fail to interest those who only know the statesman and the literary cynic of his later years. There is sincere fervour of romantic feeling in the picture of the evening after Simonetta's funeral, even though the analytical temper of the poet's mind is revealed in his exact description of the shadow cast by the planet he was watching. The first meeting with Lucrezia, again, is prettily described in these stanzas of the 'Selve:'

What time the chain was forged which then I bore,
Air, earth, and heavens were linked in one delight;
The air was never so serene before,
The sun ne'er shed such pure and tranquil light;
Young leaves and flowers upon the grassy floor
Gladdened the earth where ran a streamlet bright,
While Venus in her father's bosom lay
And smiled from heaven upon the spot that day.

She from her brows divine and amorous breast
Took with both hands roses of many a hue,
And showered them through the heavens that slept in rest,
Covering my lady with their gracious dew;
Jove, full of gladness, on that day released
The ears of men, that they might hear the true
Echoes of melody and dance divine,
Which fell from heaven in songs and sounds benign.

Fair women to that music moved their feet,
Inflamed with gentle fire by Love's breath fanned:
Behold yon lover with his lady sweet—
Her hand long yearned for clasped in his loved hand;
Their sighs, their looks, which pangs of longing cheat;
Brief words that none but they can understand;
The flowers that she lets fall, resumed and pressed,
With kisses covered, to his head or breast.

[13] 'Innamoramento,' *Poesie*, pp. 58-62. Compare 'Selve d'Amore,' *ibid.* pp. 172-174.

Amid so many pleasant things and fair,
My loveliest lady with surpassing grace
Eclipsed and crowned all beauties that were there;
Her robe was white and delicate as lace;
And still her eyes, with silent speech and rare,
Talked to the heart, leaving the lips at peace:
Come to me, come, dear heart of mine, she said,
Here shall thy long desires at rest be laid.

The impression of these verses is hardly marred by the prosy catalogue of Lucrezia's beauties furnished in the 'Innamoramento.' Lorenzo was an analyst. He could not escape from that quality so useful to the observer, so fatal to artists, if they cannot recompose the data furnished by observation in a new subjective synthesis. When we compare his description of the Age of Gold in the 'Selve,'[14] justly celebrated for its brilliancy and wealth of detail, with the shorter passage from Poliziano's 'Stanze,' we measure the distance between intelligent study of nature and the imagination which unifies and gives new forms of life to every detail. The same end may be more briefly attained by a comparison of this passage about roses from Lorenzo's 'Corinto' with a musical *Ballata* of Poliziano:[15]

Into a little close of mine I went
  One morning, when the sun with his fresh light
  Was rising all refulgent and unshent.
Rose-trees are planted there in order bright,
  Whereto I turned charmed eyes, and long did stay
  Taking my fill of that new-found delight.
Red and white roses bloomed upon the spray;
  One opened, leaf by leaf, to greet the morn,
  Shyly at first, then in sweet disarray;
Another, yet a youngling, newly born,
  Scarce struggled from the bud, and there were some
  Whose petals closed them from the air forlorn;
Another fell, and showered the grass with bloom;
  Thus I beheld the roses dawn and die,
  And one short hour their loveliness consume.
But while I watched those languid petals lie
  Colourless on cold earth, I could but think
  How vain a thing is youthful bravery.
Trees have their time to bloom on winter's brink;
  Then the rathe blossoms wither in an hour,
  When the brief days of spring toward summer sink;
The fruit, as yet unformed, is tart and sour;
  Little by little it grows large, and weighs
  The strong boughs down with slow persistent power;
Nor without peril can the branches raise
  Their burden; now they stagger 'neath the weight
  Still growing, and are bent above the ways;
Soon autumn comes, and the ripe ruddy freight
  Is gathered: the glad season will not stay;
  Flowers, fruits, and leaves are now all desolate.
Pluck the rose, therefore, maiden, while 'tis May!

[14] *Poesie*, pp. 206-213. [15] *Poesie*, p. 236.

That is good. It is the best kind of poetry within Lorenzo's grasp. But here is Poliziano's dance-song:

I went a-roaming, maidens, one bright day,
In a green garden in mid month of May.

Violets and lilies grew on every side
  Mid the green grass, and young flowers wonderful,
Golden and white and red and azure-eyed;
  Toward which I stretched my hands, eager to pull
  Plenty to make my fair curls beautiful,
To crown my rippling curls with garlands gay.

I went a-roaming, maidens, one bright day
In a green garden in mid month of May.

But when my lap was full of flowers I spied
  Roses at last, roses of every hue;
Therefore I ran to pluck their ruddy pride,
  Because their perfume was so sweet and true
  That all my soul went forth whith pleasure new,
With yearning and desire too soft to say.

I went a-roaming, maidens, one bright day,
In a green garden in mid month of May,

I gazed and gazed. Hard task it were to tell
  How lovely were the roses in that hour:
One was but peeping from her verdant shell,
  And some were faded, some were scarce in flower.
  Then Love said: Go, pluck from the blooming bower
Those that thou seest ripe upon the spray.

I went a-roaming, maidens, one bright day,
In a green garden in mid month of May.

For when the full rose quits her tender sheath,
  When she is sweetest and most fair to see,
Then is the time to place her in thy wreath,
  Before her beauty and her freshness flee.
  Gather ye therefore roses with great glee,
Sweet girls, or ere their perfume pass away.

I went a-roaming, maidens, one bright day,
In a green garden in mid month of May.

Both in this *Ballata* and also in the stanzas on the Age of Gold, it might almost seem as though Poliziano had rewritten Lorenzo's exercise with a view to showing the world the difference between true poetry and what is only very like it.

The 'Selve d' Amore' and the 'Corinto' belong to Lorenzo's early manner, when his heart was yet fresh and statecraft had not made him cynical. The latter is a musical eclogue in *terza rima*; the former a discursive love-poem, with allegorical episodes, in octave stanzas. Up to the date of the 'Selve' the *ottava rima* had, so far as I know, been only used for semi-epical poems and short love-songs. Lorenzo proved his originality by suiting it to a style of composition which aimed at brilliant descriptions in the manner of Ovid. He also handled it with an ease and brightness hitherto unknown. The pageant of Love and Jealousy and the allegory of Hope in the second part are both such poetry as only needed something magical from the touch of Ariosto to make them perfect.[16] As it is, Lorenzo's studies in verse produce the same impression as Bronzino's in painting. They are brilliant, but hard, cold, calculated, never fused by the final charm of poetry or music into a delightful vision. What is lacking is less technical skill or invention than feeling in the artist, the glow of passion, or the charm of spiritual harmony. Here is a picture of Hope's attendant train:

> Following this luckless dame, where'er she goes,
> Flit dreams in crowds, with auguries and lies,
> Chiromants, arts that cozen and impose,
> Chances, diviners, and false prophecies,
> Spoken or writ in foolish scroll and glose,
> Whose forecast brings time flown before our eyes,
> Alchemy, all who heaven from our earth measure,
> And free conjectures made at will and pleasure.
>
> Neath the dark shadow of her mighty wings
> The whole deluded world at last must cower:—
> O blindness that involves all mortal things,
> Frail ignorance that treads on human power!—
> He who can count the woes her empire brings,
> Could number every star, each fish, each flower,
> Tell all the birds that cross the autumnal seas,
> Or leaves that flutter from the naked trees.

His 'Ambra' is another poem in the same style as the 'Selve.' It records Lorenzo's love for that Tuscan farm which Poliziano afterwards made famous in the sonorous hexameters he dedicated to the memory of Homer.[17] Following the steps of Ovid, Lorenzo feigns that a shepherd Lauro loved the nymph Ambra, whom Umbrone, the river-god, pursued through vale and meadow to the shores of Arno. There he would have done her violence, but that Diana changed her to a rock in her sore need:

> Ma pur, che fussi già donna ancor credi;
> Le membra mostran, come suol figura
> Bozzata e non finita in pietra dura.

This simile is characteristic both of Lorenzo's love for familiar illustration, and also of the age that dawned on Michelangelo's genius. In the same metre, but in a less ambitious style, is 'La Caccia col Falcone.' This poem is the simple record of a Tuscan hawking-party, written to amuse Lorenzo's guests, but never meant assuredly to be discussed by critics after the lapse of four centuries. These pastorals, whether trifling like 'La Caccia,' romantic like 'Corinto,' or pictorial like 'Ambra,' sink

[16] *Poesie*, pp. 190-194, 200-204.
[17] See the peroration to Ambra, in the *Sylvæ*; Poliziano, *Prose Volgari e Poesie Latine*, &c. (Firenze, 1867), p. 365; Et nos ergo illi, &c.

into insignificance beside 'La Nencia da Barberino'—a masterpiece of true genius and humour, displaying intimate knowledge of rustic manners, and using the dialect of the Tuscan *contadini*.[18] Like the 'Polyphemus' of Theocritus, but with even more of racy detail and homely fun, 'La Nencia' versifies the love-lament of a hind, Vallera, who describes the charms of his sweetheart with quaint fancy, wooing her in a thousand ways, all natural, all equally in keeping with rural simplicity. It can scarcely be called a parody of village life and feeling, although we cannot fail to see that the town is laughing at the country all through the exuberant stanzas, so rich in fancy, so incomparably vivid in description. What lifts it above parody is the truth of the picture and the close imitation of rustic popular poetry:[19]

> Le labbre rosse paion di corallo:
> Ed havvi drento due filar di denti
> Che son più bianchi che quei di cavallo:
> E d' ogni lato ella n' ha più di venti.
> Le gote bianche paion di cristallo
> Senz' altri lisci ovver scorticamenti:
> Ed in quel mezzo ell' è come una rosa.
> Nel mondo non fu mai sì bella cosa.
>
> Ben si potrà tenere avventurato
> Che sia marito di sì bella moglie;
> Ben si potrà tener in buon dì nato
> Chi arà quel fioraliso senza foglie;
> Ben si potrà tener santo e beato,
> Che sì contenti tutte le sue voglie
> D' aver la Nencia e tenersela in braccio
> Morbida e bianca che pare un sugnaccio.

These lines, chosen at random from the poem, might be paralleled from *Rispetti* that are sung to-day in Tuscany. The vividness and vigour of 'La Nencia' secured for it immediate popularity. It was speedily imitated by Luigi Pulci in the 'Beca da Dicomano,' a village poem that, aiming at cruder realism than Lorenzo's, broke the style and lapsed into vulgarity. 'La Nencia' long continued to have imitators; for one of the principal objects of educated poets in the Renaissance was to echo the manner of popular verse. None, however, succeeded so well as Lorenzo in touching the facts of country life and the truth of country feeling with a fine irony that had in it at least as much of sympathy as of sarcasm.

'I Beoni' is a plebeian poem of a different and more displeasing type. Written in *terza rima*, it distinctly parodies the style of the 'Divine Comedy,' using the same phrases to indicate action and to mark the turns of dialogue, introducing similes in the manner of Dante, burlesquing Virgil and Beatrice in the disgusting Bartolino and Nastagio.[20] The poem might be called The Paradise of Drunkards, or their Hell; for it consists of a succession of scenes in which intoxication in all stages and

[18] *Poesie*, p. 238.
[19] *Poesie*, p. 239.
[20] *Poesie*, p. 294.

topers of every calibre are introduced. The tone is coldly satirical, sardonically comic. The old man of Tennyson's 'Vision of Sin' might have written 'I Beoni' after a merry bout with the wrinkled ostler. When Lorenzo composed it, he was already corrupt and weary, sated with the world, worn with disease, disillusioned by a life of compromise, hypocrisy, diplomacy, and treason to the State he ruled. Yet the humour of this poem has nothing truly sinister or tragic. Its brutality is redeemed by no fierce Swiftian rage. If some of the descriptions in Lorenzo's earlier work remind us of Dutch flower and landscape painters, Breughel or Van Huysum, the scenes of 'I Beoni' recall the realism of Dutch tavern-pictures and Kermessen. It has the same humour, gross and yet keen, the same intellectual enjoyment of sensuality, the same animalism studied by an acute æsthetic spirit.[21]

To turn from 'I Beoni' to Lorenzo's Lauds, written at his mother's request, and to the sacred play of 'S. Giovanni e Paolo,' acted by his children, is to make one of those bewildering transitions which are so common in Renaissance Italy. Without rating Lorenzo's sacred poetry very high, either for religious fervour or æsthetic quality, it is yet surprising that the author of the 'Beoni' and the Platonic sage of Careggi should have caught so much of the pietistic tone. We know that 'S. Giovanni e Paolo' was written when he was advanced in years;[22] and the latent allusions to his illness and the cares of state which weighed upon him, give it an interest it would not otherwise excite. This couplet,

> Spesso chi chiama Costantin felice
> Sta meglio assai di me e 'l ver non dice,

seems to be a sigh from his own weariness. Lorenzo may not improbably have envied Constantine, the puppet of his fancy, at the moment of abdication. And yet when Savonarola called upon him ere his death to deal justly with Florence, the true nature of the man was seen. Had he liked it or not, he could not then have laid down the load of care and crime which it had been the business of his whole life to accumulate by crooked ways in the enslavement of Florence and the perdition of his soul's peace. The Lauds, which may be referred to an earlier period of Lorenzo's life, when his mother ruled his education, and the pious Bishop of Arezzo watched his exemplary behaviour in church with admiration, have here and there in them a touch of profound feeling;[23] nor are they in all respects inferior to the average of those included in the Florentine collection of 1863. The men of the Renaissance were so constituted that to turn from vice, and cruelty, and crime, from the deliberate corruption and enslavement of a people by licentious pleasures and the persecution of an enemy in secret, with a fervid and impassioned

[21] If anything had to be quoted from *I Beoni*, I should select the episode of Adovardo and his humorous discourse on thirst, cap. ii. *ibid.* p. 229. For a loathsome parody of Dante see cap. v. *ibid.* p. 315.

[22] The date is 1489.

[23] Especially 'O Dio, o sommo bene,' and 'Poi ch' io gustai, Gesù,' *ibid.* pp. 444, 447. Likewise 'Veni a me,' *ibid.* p. 449.

movement of the soul to God, was nowise impossible. Their temper admitted of this anomaly, as we may plainly see in Cellini's Autobiography. Therefore, though it is probable that Lorenzo cultivated the Laud chiefly as a form of art, we are not justified in assuming that the passages in which we seem to detect a note of ardent piety are sincere.

The versatility of Lorenzo s talent showed itself to greater advantage when he quitted the uncongenial ground of sacred literature, and gave a free rein to his fancy in the composition of *Ballate* and Carnival songs. This species of poetry offered full scope to a temperament excessive in all pleasures of the senses.[24] It also enabled him to indulge a deeply rooted sympathy with the common folk. Nor must it be supposed that Lorenzo was following a merely artistic impulse. This strange man, in whose complex nature opponent qualities were harmonised and intertwined, made his very sensuality subserve his statecraft. The Medici had based their power upon the favour of the proletariat. Since the days of the Cionpi riot they had pursued one line of self-aggrandisement by siding with the plebeians in their quarrels with the oligarchs. The serious purpose which underlay Lorenzo's cultivation of popular poetry, was to amuse the crowd with pageantry and music, to distract their attention from State concerns and to blunt their political interest, to flatter them by descending to their level and mixing freely with them in their sports, and to acquire a popularity which should secure him from the aristocratic jealousies of the Acciaiuoli, the Frescobaldi, the Salviati, Soderini, and other ancestral foemen of his house. The frontispiece to an old edition of Florentine carnival songs shows him surrounded with masquers in quaint dresses, leading the revel beneath the walls of the Palazzo, while women gaze upon them from the windows.[25] That we are justified in attributing a policy of calculated enervation to Lorenzo is proved by the verdict of Machiavelli and Guicciardini, both of whom connect his successful despotism with the pageants he provided for the populace,[26] and also by this passage in Savonarola's treatise on the Government of Florence: 'The tyrant, especially in times of peace and plenty, is wont to occupy the people with shows and festivals, in order that they may think of their own pastimes and not of his designs, and, growing unused to the conduct of the commonwealth,

[24] Guicciardini, in his *Storia Fiorentina* (*Op. Ined.* vol. iii. 88), writes of Lorenzo: 'Fu libidinoso, e tutto venereo e constante negli amori suoi, che duravano parecchi anni; la quale cosa, a giudicio di molti, gli indebolì tanto il corpo, che lo fece morire, si può dire, giovane.' Then, after describing his night-adventures outside Florence, he proceeds: 'Cosa pazza a considerare che uno di tanta grandezza, riputazione e prudenza, di età di anni quaranta, fussi sì preso di una dama non bella e già piena di anni, che si conducessi a fare cose, che sarebbono state disoneste a ogni fanciullo.'

[25] *Canzone per andare in maschera, facte da più persone.* No place or date or printer's name; but probably issued in the lifetime of Lorenzo from Mongiani's press. There is a similar woodcut on the title-page of the *Canzone a Ballo*, Firenze, 1568. It represents the angle of the Medicean Palace in the Via Larga, girls dancing in a ring upon the street, one with a wreath and thyrsus kneeling, another presenting Lorenzo with a book.

[26] *Ist. Fior.* viii.; *Stor. Fior.* ix.

may leave the reins of government in his hands.'[27] At the same time he would err who should suppose that Lorenzo's enjoyment of these pleasures, which he found in vogue among the people, was not genuine. He represented the worst as well as the best spirit of his age; and if he knew how to enslave Florence, it was because his own temperament shared the instincts of the crowd, while his genius enabled him to clothe obscenity with beauty.

We know that it was an ancient Florentine custom for young men and girls to meet upon the squares and dance, while a boy sang with treble voice to lute or viol, or a company of minstrels chaunted part-songs. The dancers joined in the refrain, vaunting the pleasures of the May and the delights of love in rhythms suited to the *Carola*. Taking this form of poetry from the people, Lorenzo gave it the dignity of art. Sometimes he told the tale of an unhappy lover, or pretended to be pleading with a coy mistress, or broke forth into the exultation of a passion crowned with success. Again, he urged both boys and girls to stay the flight of time nor suffer the rose-buds of their youth to fade unplucked. In more wanton moods, he satirised the very love he praised, or, casting off the mask of decency, ran riot in base bestiality. These *Canzoni a Ballo*, though they lack the supreme beauty of Poliziano's style, are stylistically graceful. Their tone never rises above sensuality. Not only has the gravity of Dante's passion passed away from Florence, but Boccaccio's sensuous ideality is gone, and the *naïveté* of popular erotic poetry is clouded with gross innuendoes. We find in them the æsthetic immorality, the brilliant materialism of the Renaissance, conveyed with careless self-abandonment to carnal impulse.

The name of Lorenzo de' Medici is still more closely connected with the *Canti Carnascialeschi* or Carnival Songs, of which he is said to have been the first author, than with the *Ballate*, which he only used as they were handed to him. In Carnival time it was the custom of the Florentines to walk the streets, masked and singing satiric ballads. Lorenzo saw that here was an opportunity for delighting the people with the magnificence of pageantry. He caused the Triumphs in which he took a part to be carefully prepared by the best artists, the dresses of the masquers to be accurately studied, and their chariots to be adorned with illustrative paintings. Then he wrote songs appropriate to the characters represented on the cars. Singing and dancing and displaying their costumes, the band paraded Florence. Il Lasca in his introduction to the Triumphs and Carnival Songs dedicated to Don Francesco de' Medici gives the history of their invention:[28] 'This festival was invented by the Magnificent Lorenzo de' Medici. Before his time, when the cars bore mythological or allegorical masques, they were called *Trionfi*; but when they carried representatives of arts and trades, they kept the simpler name of *Carri*.' The lyrics written for the Triumphs

[27] *Trattato circa il Reggimento e Governo della Citta di Firenze* (Florence, 1847), ii. 2.
[28] *Tutti i Trionfi, Carri*, &c., Firenze, 1559. See also the edition dated Cosmopoli, 1750.

were stately, in the style of antique odes; those intended to be sung upon the *Carri*, employed plebeian turns of phrase and dealt in almost undisguised obscenity. It was their wont, says Il Lasca, 'to go forth after dinner, and often they lasted till three or four hours into the night, with a multitude of masked men on horseback following, richly dressed, exceeding sometimes three hundred in number, and as many men on foot with lighted torches. Thus they traversed the city, singing to the accompaniment of music arranged for four, eight, twelve, or even fifteen voices, supported by various instruments.'

Lorenzo's fancy took the Florentine mind. From his days onward these shows were repeated every year, the best artists and poets contributing their genius to make them splendid. In the collection of songs written for the Carnival, we find Masques of Scholars, Artisans, Frog-catchers, Furies, Tinkers, Women selling grapes, Old men and Young wives, Jewellers, German Lansknechts, Gypsies, Wool-carders Penitents, Devils, Jews, Hypocrites, Young men who have lost their fathers, Wiseacres, Damned Souls, Tortoiseshell Cats, Perfumers, Masons, Mountebanks, Mirror-makers, Confectioners, Prudent persons, Lawyers, Nymphs in love, Nuns escaped from convent—not to mention the Four Ages of Man, the Winds, the Elements, Peace, Calumny, Death, Madness, and a hundred abstractions of that kind. The tone of these songs is uniformly and deliberately immoral. One might fancy them composed for some old phallic festival. Their wit is keen and lively, presenting to the fancy of the student all the humours of a brilliant bygone age. A strange and splendid spectacle it must have been, when Florence, the city of art and philosophy, ran wild in Dionysiac revels proclaiming the luxury and license of the senses! Beautiful maidens, young men in rich clothes on prancing steeds, showers of lilies and violets, triumphal arches of spring flowers and ribbons, hailstorms of comfits, torches flaring to the sallow evening sky—we can see the whole procession as it winds across the Ponte Vecchio, emerges into the great square, and slowly gains the open space beneath the dome of Brunelleschi and the tower of Giotto. The air rings with music as they come, bass and tenor and shrill treble mingling with the sound of lute and cymbal. The people hush their cheers to listen. It is Lorenzo's Triumph of Bacchus, and here are the words they sing:

Fair is youth and void of sorrow;
  But it hourly flies away.—
  Youths and maids enjoy to-day;
Nought ye know about to-morrow.

This is Bacchus and the bright
  Ariadne, lovers true!
They, in flying time's despite
  Each with each find pleasure new;
These their Nymphs, and all their crew
  Keep perpetual holiday.—
  Youths and maids, enjoy to-day;
Nought ye know about to-morrow.

These blithe Satyrs, wanton-eyed,
Of the Nymphs are paramours:
Through the caves and forests wide
They have snared them mid the flowers.
Warmed with Bacchus, in his bowers,
Now they dance and leap alway.—
Youths and maids, enjoy to-day;
Nought ye know about to-morrow.

These fair Nymphs, they are not loth
To entice their lovers' wiles.
None but thankless folk and rough
Can resist when Love beguiles.
Now enlaced with wreathèd smiles,
All together dance and play.—
Youths and maids, enjoy to-day;
Nought ye know about to-morrow.

See this load behind them plodding
On the ass, Silenus he,
Old and drunken, merry, nodding,
Full of years and jollity;
Though he goes so swayingly,
Yet he laughs and quaffs alway.—
Youths and maids, enjoy to-day;
Nought ye know about to-morrow.

Midas treads a wearier measure:
All he touches turns to gold:
If there be no taste of pleasure,
What's the use of wealth untold?
What's the joy his fingers hold,
When he's forced to thirst for aye?—
Youths and maids, enjoy to-day;
Nought ye know about to-morrow.

Listen well to what we're saying;
Of to-morrow have no care!
Young and old together playing,
Boys and girls, be blithe as air!
Every sorry thought forswear!
Keep perpetual holiday.—
Youths and maids, enjoy to-day;
Nought ye know about to-morrow.

Ladies and gay lovers young!
Long live Bacchus, live Desire!
Dance and play, let songs be sung;
Let sweet Love your bosoms fire;
In the future come what may!—
Youths and maids, enjoy to-day;
Nought ye know about to-morrow.

On rolls the car, and the crowd closes round it, rending the old walls with shattering hurrahs. Then a corner of the street is turned; while soaring still above the hubbub of the town we hear at intervals that musical refrain. Gradually it dies away in the distance, and fainter and more faintly still the treble floats to us in broken waifs of sound—the echo of a lyric heard in dreams.

Such were the songs that reached Savonarola's ears, writing or meditating in his cloister at S. Marco. Such were the sights that moved his indignation as he trod the streets of Florence. Then he bethought him of his famous parody of the Carnival, the bonfire of Vanities, and the hymn in praise of divine madness sung by children dressed in white like angels.[29] Yet Florence, warned in vain by the friar, took no thought for the morrow; and the morrow came to all Italy with war, invasion, pestilence, innumerable woes. In the last year of Pier Soderini's Gonfalonierato (1512) it seemed as though the Italians had been quickened to a consciousness of their impending ruin. The siege of Brescia, the battle of Ravenna, the League of Cambray, the massacres of Prato, the sack of Rome, the fall of Florence, were all imminent. A fascination of intolerable fear thrilled the people in the midst of their heedlessness, and this fear found voice and form in a strange Carnival pageant described by Vasari:[30] 'The triumphal car was covered with black cloth,

[29] In this place should be noticed a sinister Carnival Song, by an unknown author, which belongs, I think, to the period of Savonarola's democracy. It is called *Trionfo del Vaglio*, or 'Triumph of the Sieve' (*Cant. Carn.* p. 33):

To the Sieve, to the Sieve, to the Sieve,
Ho, all ye folk, descend!
With groans your bosoms rend!
And find in this our Sieve
Wrath, anguish, travail, doom for all who live!
To winnow, sift and purge, full well we know,
And grind your souls like corn:
Ye who our puissance scorn,
Come ye to trial, ho!
For we will prove and show
How fares the man who enters in our Sieve.
Send us no groats nor scrannel seed nor rye
But good fat ears of grain,
Which shall endure our strain,
And be of sturdy stuff.
Torment full stern and rough
Abides for him who resteth in our Sieve.
Who comes into this Sieve, who issues thence,
Hath tears and sighs, and mourns:
But the Sieve ever turns,
And gathers vehemence.
Ye who feel sin's offence,
Shun ye the rage, the peril of our Sieve.
A thousand times the day, our Sieve is crowned;
A thousand times 'tis drained:
Let the Sieve once be strained,
And, grain by grain, around
Ye shall behold the ground
Covered with folk, cast from the boltering Sieve.
Ye who are not well-grained and strong to bear,
Abide ye not this fate!
Penitence comes too late!
Seek ye some milder doom!
Nay, better were the tomb
Than to endure the torment of our Sieve!

[30] Life of Piero di Cosimo.

and was of vast size; it had skeletons and white crosses painted upon its surface, and was drawn by buffaloes, all of which were totally black: within the car stood the colossal figure of Death, bearing the scythe in his hand; while around him were covered tombs, which opened at all the places where the procession halted, while those who formed it, chanted lugubrious songs, when certain figures stole forth, clothed in black cloth, on whose vestments the bones of a skeleton were depicted in white; the arms, breast, ribs, and legs, namely, all which gleamed horribly forth on the black beneath. At a certain distance appeared figures bearing torches, and wearing masks presenting the face of a death's head both before and behind; these heads of death as well as the skeleton necks beneath them, also exhibited to view, were not only painted with the utmost fidelity to nature, but had besides a frightful expression which was horrible to behold. At the sound of a wailing summons, sent forth with a hollow moan from trumpets of muffled yet inexorable clangour, the figures of the dead raised themselves half out of their tombs, and seating their skeleton forms thereon, they sang the following words, now so much extolled and admired, to music of the most plaintive and melancholy character. Before and after the car rode a train of the dead on horses, carefully selected from the most wretched and meagre animals that could be found: the caparisons of those worn, half-dying beasts were black, covered with white crosses; each was conducted by four attendants, clothed in the vestments of the grave; these last-mentioned figures, bearing black torches and a large black standard, covered with crosses, bones, and death's heads. While this train proceeded on its way, each sang, with a trembling voice, and all in dismal unison, that psalm of David called the Miserere. The novelty and the terrible character of this singular spectacle, filled the whole city, as I have before said, with a mingled sensation of terror and admiration; and although at the first sight it did not seem well calculated for a Carnival show, yet being new, and within the reach of every man's comprehension, it obtained the highest encomium for Piero as the author and contriver of the whole, and was the cause as well as commencement of numerous representations, so ingenious and effective that by these things Florence acquired a reputation for the conduct of such subjects and the arrangement of similar spectacles such as was never equalled by any other city.'

Of this Carnival song, composed by Antonio Alamanni, I here give an English version.

Sorrow, tears, and penitence
Are our doom of pain for aye;
This dead concourse riding by
Hath no cry but Penitence.

Even as you are, once were we:
You shall be as now we are:
We are dead men, as you see:
We shall see you dead men, where

Nought avails to take great care
After sins of penitence.

We too in the Carnival
Sang our love-song through the town;
Thus from sin to sin we all
Headlong, heedless, tumbled down;
Now we cry, the world around,
Penitence, oh penitence!

Senseless, blind, and stubborn fools!
Time steals all things as he rides:
Honours, glories, states, and schools,
Pass away, and nought abides;
Till the tomb our carcase hides,
And compels grim penitence.

This sharp scythe you see us bear,
Brings the world at length to woe;
But from life to life we fare;
And that life is joy or woe;
All heaven's bliss on him doth flow,
Who on earth does penitence.

Living here, we all must die;
Dying, every soul shall live,
For the King of kings on high
This fixed ordinance doth give:
Lo! you all are fugitive:
Penitence, cry penitence!

Torment great and grievous dole
Hath the thankless heart mid you:
But the man of piteous soul
Finds much honour in our crew:
Love for loving is the due
That prevents this penitence.

These words sounded in the ears of the people, already terrified by the unforgotten voice of Savonarola, like a trump of doom. The pageant was, indeed, an acted allegory of the death of Italy, the repentance after judgment of a nation fallen in its sins. Yet a few months passed, and the same streets echoed with the music of yet another show, which has also been described by Vasari.[31] If the Car of Death expressed the uneasy dread that fell on the Italians at the opening of the century, the shows of 1513 allegorised their mad confidence in the fortune of the age, which was still more deeply felt and widely shared. Giovanni de' Medici had just been elevated to the Papal Chair, and was paying a holiday visit to his native city. Giuliano de' Medici, his brother, the Duke of Nemours, was also resident in Florence, where he had formed a club of noble youths called the Diamond. Lorenzo, Duke of Urbino, the titular chief of the house, presided over a rival Company named Il Broncone—with a withered laurel-branch, whence leaves were sprouting, for its emblem. The Diamond signified the constancy of Casa

[31] Life of Pontormo.

Medici; the withered branch their power of self-recovery. These two men, Giuliano and Lorenzo, are the same who now confront each other upon their pedestals in Michelangelo's Sacristy of S. Lorenzo. Both were doomed to an untimely death; but in the year 1513, when Leo's election shed new lustre on their house, they were still in the heyday of prosperity and hope. Giuliano resolved that the Diamond should make a goodly show. Therefore he entrusted the invention and the poems to Andrea Dazzi, who then held Poliziano's chair of Greek and Latin literature. Dazzi devised three Cars after the fashion of a Roman triumph. For the construction of each chariot an excellent architect was chosen; for their decoration the painter Pontormo was appointed. In the first rode beautiful boys; in the second, powerful men; in the third, reverend grandsires. Lorenzo, in competition with his uncle, determined that the Laurel branch should outrival the Diamond. He applied to Jacopo Nardi, the historian of Florence and translator of Livy. Nardi composed a procession of seven chariots to symbolise the Golden Age, and wrote appropriate poems for each, which are still extant. In the first car rode Saturn and Janus, attended by six shepherds of goodly form, naked, on horses without harness. In the second sat Numa Pompilius, surrounded by priests in antique raiment. The third carried Titus Manlius, whose consulship beheld the close of the first Punic war. In the fifth Augustus sat enthroned, accompanied by twelve laurelled poets. The horses that drew him, were winged. The sixth carried Trajan, the just emperor, with doctors of the law on either side. All these chariots were adorned with emblems painted by Pontormo. The seventh car held a globe to represent the world. Upon it lay a dead man in a suit of rusty iron armour, from the cloven plates of which emerged a living child, naked and gilt with glistening leaf of gold. This signified the passing of the Iron, and the opening of the Golden Age—the succession of the Renaissance to feudalism—the fortunes of Italy reviving after her disasters in the sunlight of the smiles of Leo. 'Magnus sæclorum nascitur ordo!' 'The world's great age begins anew; the golden years return!' Thus the artists, scholars, and poets of Florence symbolised in a Carnival show the advent of the Renaissance. The boy who represented the Golden Age, died of the sufferings he endured beneath his gilding; and his father, who was a baker, received ten scudi of indemnity. A fanciful historian might read in this little incident the irony of fate, warning the Italians that the age they welcomed would perish for them in its bloom. In the year 1513 Luther was already thirty years of age, and Charles V. in the Low Countries was a boy of thirteen, accumulating knowledge under the direction of the future Adrian VI. Whatever destiny of gold the Renaissance might through Italy be offering to Europe, it was on the point of pouring blood and fastening heavier chains on every city of the sacred land.

In my desire to bring together these three representative festivals—Lorenzo's Triumph of Bacchus, Alamanni's Car of Death, and Pontormo's Pageant of the Golden Age—marking three moments in the Florentine Renaissance, and three diverse moods of feeling in the people —I have transgressed the chronological limits of this chapter. I must now return to the year 1464, when a boy of ten years old, destined to revive the glories of Italian literature with far greater lustre than Lorenzo, came from Montepulciano to Florence, and soon won the notice of the Medicean princes. Angelo Ambrogini, surnamed Poliziano from his home above the Chiana, has already occupied a prominent place in this work.[32] It is not, therefore, needful to retrace the history of his uneventful life, or again to fix his proper rank among the scholars of the fifteenth century. He was the greatest student, and the greatest poet in Greek and Latin, that Italy has produced. In the history of European scholarship, he stands midway between Petrarch and Erasmus, taking the post of honour at the moment when erudition had acquired ease and elegance, but had not yet passed on into the final stage of scientific criticism. What concerns us here, is Poliziano's achievement as an Italian poet. In the history of the vulgar literature he fills a place midway between Petrarch and Ariosto, corresponding to the station of distinction I have assigned to him in humanistic culture. Of few men can it be said that they have held the same high rank in poetry and learning; and had the moral fibre of Poliziano, his intellectual tension and his spiritual aim, been at all commensurate with his twofold ability, the Italians might have shown in him a fourth singer equal in magnitude to their greatest. As it was, the excellence of his work was marred by the defect of his temperament, and has far less value for the general reader than for the student of versification.

Lorenzo de' Medici could boast of having restored the mother tongue to a place of honour among the learned. But he was far from being the complete artist that the age required. 'That exquisite flower of sentiment we call good taste, that harmony of intellect we call judgment, lies not within the grasp of power or riches.'[33] A man was needed who should combine creative genius with refined tact in the use of language; who should be competent to carry the tradition of Italian poetry beyond the point where Boccaccio dropped it, while giving to his work the polish and the splendour of a classic masterpiece. It was further necessary that this new dictator of the literary commonwealth should have left the Middle Age so far behind as not to be aware of its stern spirit. He must have acquired the erudition of his eminently learned century—a century in which knowledge was the pearl of great price; not the knowledge of righteousness; not the knowledge of nature and her laws; but the knowledge of the life that throbbed in ancient peoples, the life that might, it seemed, yet make the old world young again. Moreover, he must be strong enough to carry this erudition without bending beneath its weight; dexterous enough to use it without

[32] Vol. I., *Revival of Learning*, pp. 487-492, 536-543.

[33] Carducci, Preface to his edition of *Le Stanze, L'Orfeo e Le Rime di Messer Angelo Ambrogini Poliziano* (Firenze, 1863), p. xxiii.

pedantry; exuberant enough in natural resources to reduce his stores of learning, his wealth of fancy, his thronging emotions, to one ruling harmony—fusing all reminiscences in one style of pure and copious Italian. He must be gifted with that reverent sense of beauty, which was the sole surviving greatness of his century, animating the imagination of its artists, and justifying the proud boast of its students. This man was found in Angelo Poliziano. He, and only he, was destined, by combining the finish of the classics with the freshness of a language still in use, to inaugurate the golden age of form. Faustus, the genius of the middle ages, had wedded Helen, the vision of the ancient world. Their son, Euphorion, the inheritor of all their gifts, we hail in Poliziano.

When Poliziano composed 'Le Stanze' he was nearly twenty-four years of age.[34] He had steeped himself in the classic literatures. Endowed with a marvellous memory, he possessed their spirit and their substance. Not less familiar with Tuscan poetry of the fourteenth century, he commanded the stores of Dante's, Petrarch's and Boccaccio's diction. Long practice in Greek and Latin composition had given him mastery over the metrical systems of the ancient languages.[35] The daily habit of inditing songs for music to please the ladies of the Medicean household, had accustomed him to the use of fluent Italian. The translation of the 'Iliad,' performed in part before he was eighteen, had made him a faithful imitator, while it added dignity and fulness to his style.[36] Besides these qualifications for his future task of raising Italian to an equality with Latin poetry, he brought with him to this achievement a genius apt to comprehend the spirit of the Renaissance in its pomp and liberty and tranquil loveliness. The noble and yet sensuous manner of the great Venetian painters, their dignity of form, their luxury of colour, their boldness and decision, their imperturbable serenity of mundane joy—the choicer delicacy of the Florentine masters, their refinement of outline, selection of type, suggestion of restrained emotion—the pure design of the Tuscan sculptors, the suavity and flexibility of the Lombard *plasticatori*—all these qualities of Italian figurative art appear, as it were in bud, in the 'Stanze.' Poliziano's crowning merit as a stylist was that he knew how to blend the antique and the romantic, correct drawing with fleshly fulness. Breadth of design and harmony of colour have rarely been produced in more magnificent admixture. The octave stanza, which in the hands of Boccaccio

[34] This poem must have been written between 1476, the date of Simonetta's death, and 1478, the date of Giuliano's murder, when Poliziano was about twenty-four. Chronology prevents us from regarding it as the work of a boy of fourteen, as Roscoe thought, or of sixteen, as Hallam concluded.

[35] His Latin elegies on Simonetta and on Albiera degli Albizzi, and those Greek epigrams which Scaliger preferred to the Latin verses of his maturity, had been already written.

[36] From *Le Stanze*, i. 7, we learn that he interrupted the translation of the *Iliad* in order to begin this poem in Italian. He never took it up again. It remains a noble torso, the most splendid extant version of a Greek poem in Latin by a modern hand.

was languid and diffuse, in the hands of Lorenzo harsh, in the hands of Pulci rugged, became under Poliziano's treatment an inexhaustible instrument of varying melodies. At one time, beneath his touch, the metre takes an epic dignity; again it sinks to idyllic sweetness, or mourns with the elegy, or exults with the ode. Its movement is rapid or relaxed, smooth or vibrating, undulatory or impetuous, as he has chosen. When we reflect how many generations of poets it required to bring the Sonnet to completeness, we may marvel at this youth, in an age when scholarship absorbed inventive genius, who was able at one stroke to do for the octave stanza what Marlowe did for our Blank Verse. Poliziano gave to Ariosto the Italian epical metre perfected, and established a standard of style amid the anarchy which threatened the literature of Italy with ruin.

Yet it must be confessed that, after all, it is chiefly the style of Poliziano that deserves praise. Like so much else of Renaissance work—ike the Farnesina frescoes in Rome, or Giulio Romano's luxuriant arabesques at Mantua, or the efflorescence of foliage and cupids in the bas-reliefs of palace portals at Venice—there is but little solid thought or serious feeling underneath this decorative richness. Those who cannot find a pleasure in form for its own sake, independent of matter, will never be able to do Poliziano justice. This brings us to the subject of the 'Stanze.' They were written to celebrate the prowess of Giuliano de' Medici, Lorenzo's brother, in a tournament held at Florence in the beginning of the year 1478. This fact is worth consideration. The poem which opened a new age for Italian literature, had no nobler theme than a Court pageant. Dante had been inspired to sing the epic of the human soul. Petrarch finished a portrait of the life through love of an impassioned man. Boccaccio bound up in one volume a hundred tales, delineating society in all its aspects. Then the Muse of Italy fell asleep. Poliziano aroused her with the full deep intonations of a golden instrument. But what was the burden of his song? Giuliano de' Medici loved the fair Simonetta, and bore away the prize in a toy-tournament.

This marks the change effected by a century of prince-craft. Henceforth great poets were to care less for what they sang than for the style in which they sang. Henceforth poetry in Italy was written to please—to please patrons who were flattered with false pedigrees and absurd mythologies, with the imputation of virtues they never possessed, and with the impudent palliation of shame apparent to the world. Henceforth the bards of Ausonia deigned to tickle the ears of lustful boys and debauched cardinals, buying the bread of courtly sloth—how salt it tasted let Tasso and Guarini tell—with jests or panegyrics. Liberty could scarcely be named in verse when natives and strangers vied together in enslaving Italy. To praise the great deeds of bygone heroes within hearing of pusillanimous princes, would have been an insult. Even satires upon a degraded present, aspirations after a noble future, prophecies of resurrection from the tomb—those last resorts of a national literature that retains its strength through evil days—were unknown upon the lips of the Renaissance poets. Art had become a thing of pleasure, sometimes infamous, too often nugatory. The fault of this can scarcely be said to have rested with one man more than with another; nor can we lay the blame on Poliziano, though he undoubtedly represented the class who were destined to continue literature upon these lines. It was the combined result of scholarship, which for a whole century had diverted the minds of men to the form and words of literature; of court-life, which had enfeebled the recipients of princely patronage; of tyranny, which encouraged flattery, dissimulation, and fraud; of foreign oppression, which already was beginning to enervate a race of slaves; of revived paganism, which set the earlier beliefs and aspirations of the soul at unequal warfare with emancipated lusts and sensualities; of indolence, which loved to toy with trifles, instead of thinking and creating thought; of social inequalities, which forced the poet to eat a master's bread, and turned the scholars of Italy into a crowd of servile and yet arrogant beggars. All these circumstances, and many more of the same kind, were slowly and surely undermining the vigour of the Italian intellect. Over the meridian splendour of 'Le Stanze' we already see their influences floating like a vaporous miasma.

Italy, though never so chivalrous as the rest of Europe, yet preserved the pompous festivities of feudalism. Jousts were held in all great cities, and it was reckoned part of a courtier's business to be a skilful cavalier. At Florence the custom survived of celebrating the first of May with tournaments, and on great occasions the wealthy families spent large sums of money in providing pastimes of this sort. February 7, 1468, witnessed a splendid spectacle, when Lorenzo de' Medici mounted successively on chargers presented to him by the Duke of Ferrara and the King of Naples, attired in armour given by the Duke of Milan, bearing the *fleurs de lys* of France conferred upon the Medici by Louis XI., and displaying on his pennon for a motto *Le Tems revient*, won the prize of valour before the populace assembled in the square of S. Croce. Luca Pulci, the descendant of an ancient house of Tuscan nobles, composed an adulatory poem in octave stanzas on this event. So changed were the times that this scion of Florentine aristocracy felt no shame in fawning on a despot risen from the people to enslave his city. Yet the spectacle was worthy celebration. Lorenzo, the banker's son, the Platonist, the diplomatist and tyrant, charging in the lists of feudalism beneath Arnolfo's tower, with the lilies of France upon his shield and the device of the Renaissance on his banner—this figured symbol of the meeting of two ages in a single man was no mean subject for a poem!

From Poliziano's 'Stanze' we learn no such characteristic details concerning Giuliano's later tournament. Though the poem is called 'La Giostra,' the insignificant subject disappears beneath a wealth of illustration. The episodes, including the pictures of the Golden Age and of the garden and palace of Venus, form the real strength of a masterpiece which blent the ancient and the modern world in a work of art glowing with Italian fancy. That 'La Giostra' has no subject-matter, no theme of weight to wear the poet thin through years of anxious toil, no progress from point to point, no chain of incidents and no romantic evolution, is a matter of little moment. When Giuliano de' Medici died before the altar by the hand of an assassin on April 26, 1478, Poliziano laid down his pen and left the 'Stanze' unfinished.[37] It cannot bc said that the poem suffered, or that posterity lost by this abrupt termination of a work conceived without a central thought. Enough had been already done to present Italy with a model of the style she needed; and if we ask why 'La Giostra' should have become immediately popular in spite of its peculiar texture and its abrupt conclusion, the answer is not far to seek. Poliziano incarnated the spirit of his age, and gave the public what satisfied their sense of fitness. The three chief enthusiasms of the fifteenth century—for classical literature, for artistic beauty, and for nature tranquilly enjoyed—were so fused and harmonised within the poet's soul as to produce a style of unmistakable originality and charming ease. Poliziano felt the delights of the country with serene idyllic rapture, not at second hand through the ancients, but with the voluptuous enjoyment of the Florentine who loved his villa. He had, besides, a sense of form analogous to that possessed by the artists of his age, which guided him in the selection and description of the scenes he painted. Again, his profound and refined erudition enabled him 'to shower,' as Giovio phrased it, 'the finest flowers of antique poetry upon the people.' Therefore, while he felt nature like one who worshipped her for her own sake and for the joy she gave him, he saw in her the subjects of a thousand graceful pictures, and these pictures he studied through a radiant haze of antique reminiscences. Each stanza of 'La Giostra' is a mimic world of beauty, art, and scholarship: a painting where the object stands before us modelled with relief of light and shade in finely modulated hues; a brief anthology of daintily culled phrases, wafting to our memories the perfume of Greece, Rome, and Florence in her prime. These delicate little masterpieces are, turn by turn, a picture of Botticelli, a fresco by Giulio Romano, an engraving of Mantegna, a bas-relief of young Buonarroti, or a garden-scene of Gozzoli, expressed in the purest diction of all literatures by a poet who, while imitating, never ceased to be original.[38] Nothing more was needed by a nation of idyllic dreamers, artists and scholars.

[37] By a strange coincidence this was the anniversary of his love, Simonetta's, death in 1476. The close connexion between her untimely end—celebrated by Lorenzo de' Medici in his earlier *Rime*, by Poliziano in his Latin Elegy and again in the *Giostra*—and the renascence of Italian poetry, making her portrait by Botticelli in the Pitti interesting.

[38] I must refer my readers to the original, and to the translations published by me in *Sketches and Studies in Italy*, pp. 217-224. The description of Simonetta in the meadow (*Giostra*, i. 43 and following) might be compared to a Florentine Idyll by Benozzo Gozzoli; the birth of Venus from the waves (i. 99-107) is a blending of

What Poliziano might have achieved, if he had found a worthy theme for the employment of his powers, it would be idle to ask. It is perhaps the condemnation of the man and of his age that the former did not seek heroic subjects for song, and the latter did not demand them—in a word, that neither poet nor public had in them anything heroic whatsoever. The fact is undeniably true; but this does not deprive Poliziano of the merit of such verses as the following:

> After such happy wise, in ancient years,
> Dwelt the old nations in the age of gold;
> Nor had the fount been stirr'd of mothers' tears
> For sons in war's fell labour stark and cold;
> Nor trusted they to ships the wild wind steers,
> Nor yet had oxen groaning ploughed the wold;
> Their houses were huge oaks, whose trunks had store
> Of honey, and whose boughs thick acorns bore.
>
> Nor yet, in that glad time, the accursèd thirst
> Of cruel gold had fallen on this fair earth:
> Joyous in liberty they lived at first;
> Unploughed the fields sent forth their teeming birth:
> Till fortune, envious of such concord, burst
> The bond of law, and pity banned and worth;
> Within their breasts sprang luxury and that rage
> Which men call love in our degenerate age.

A somewhat earlier composition than 'La Giostra' was 'La Favola di Orfeo,' a dramatic poem similar in form to the 'Sacra Rappresentazione' with a classical instead of a religious subject.[39] To call it a tragedy would be to dignify it with too grand a title. To class it with pastorals is equally impossible, though the songs of the shepherds and wood-nymphs may be said to have anticipated the style of Tasso's 'Aminta' and Guarini's 'Pastor Fido.' Nor, again, is it properly speaking an opera, though it was undoubtedly meant for music. The 'Orfeo' combined tragedy, the pastoral, and the opera in a mixed work of melodramatic art, which by its great popularity inspired the poets of Italy to produce specimens of each kind, and prepared the public to

Botticelli's *Venus* in the Uffizzi with his *Primavera* in the Belle Arti; the picture of Venus in the lap of Mars (i. 122-124) might be compared to work by Piero di Cosimo, or, since poetry embraces many suggestions, to paintings from the schools of Venice. The metamorphoses of Jupiter (i. 104-107) remind us of Giulio Romano. The episode of Ariadne and the Bacchic revel (i. 110-112) is in the style of Mantegna's engravings. All these passages will be found translated by me in the book above quoted.

[39] I believe the *Favola di Orfeo*, first published in 1494, and republished from time to time up to the year 1776, was the original play acted at Mantua before the Cardinal Gonzaga. It is not divided into acts, and has the usual 'Annunziatore della Festa' of the *Sacre Rappresentazioni*. The *Orphei Tragœdia*, published by the Padre Ireneo Affò at Venice in 1776, from two MSS. collated by him, may be regarded as a subsequent recension of his own work made by Poliziano. It is divided into five acts, and is far richer in lyrical passages. Carducci prints both in his excellent edition of Poliziano's Italian poems. I may refer English readers to my own translation of the *Orfeo* and the note upon its text, *Studies and Sketches in Italy*, pp. 226-242, 429, 430.

receive them.[40] Still, in form and movement, it adhered to the traditions of the 'Sacra Rappresentazione' and its originality consisted in the substitution of a Pagan for a Christian fable.

Unerring instinct guided Poliziano in the choice of his subject. Orpheus was the proper hero of Renaissance Italy—the civiliser of a barbarous world by art and poetry, the lover of beauty, who dared to invade Hell and moved the iron heart of Pluto with a song. Long before the composition of 'Orfeo,' Boccaccio had presented the same conception of society humanised by culture in his 'Ninfale Fiesolano.' This was the ideal of the Renaissance; and, what is more, it accurately symbolised the part played by Italy after the dissolution of the middle ages. In the myth of Orpheus the humanism of the Revival became conscious of itself. This fable was the Mystery of the new age, the allegory of the work appointed for the nation. Did we dare to press a metaphor to the verge of the fantastic, we might even read in the martyrdom of Orpheus by the Mænads a prophecy of the Italian doom. Italy, who had aroused Europe from lethargy with the voice of poetry and learning, who had inaugurated a new age of civil and social refinement, who thought she could resist the will of God by arts and elegant accomplishments, after triumphing over the rude forces of nature, was now about to violate the laws of nature in her vices, and to fall a victim to the Mænads of incurrent barbarism, inebriate with wine and blood, indifferent to the magic of the lyre, avengers blindly following the dictates of a power that rules the destinies of nations. Of this Italy, Poliziano, the author of 'Orfeo,' was himself the representative hero, the protagonist, the intellectual dictator.[41]

The 'Orfeo' was sent with a letter of dedication to Messer Carlo Canale, the obsequious husband of that Vannozza who bore Cesare and Lucrezia Borgia to the Pope Alexander VI. Poliziano says that he 'wrote this play at the request of the Most Reverend the Cardinal of Mantua, in the space of two days, among continual disturbances, and in the vulgar tongue, that it might be the better comprehended by the spectators.' He adds: 'This child of mine is of a sort to bring more shame than honour on its father.'

There is good reason to believe that the year 1472, when the Cardinal Francesco Gonzaga returned from Bologna to Mantua, and was received with 'triumphs and pomps, great feasts and banquets,' was the

[40] The popularity of Poliziano's poems is proved by the frequency of their editions. The *Orfeo* and the *Stanze* were printed together or separately twenty-two times between 1494 and 1541, thirteen times between 1541 and 1653. A redaction of the *Orfeo* in octave stanzas was published at Florence in 1558 for the use of the common people. It was entitled *La Historia e Favola d' Orfeo alla dolce lira.* This narrative version of Poliziano's play is still reprinted from time to time for the Tuscan *contadini.* Carducci cites an edition of Prato, 1860.

[41] No one who has read Poliziano's Greek epigrams on Chrysocomus, or who knows the scandal falsely circulated regarding his death, will have failed to connect the sentiments put into the mouth of Orpheus (Carducci, pp. 109-110) with the personality of the poet-scholar. That the passage in question could have been recited with applause before a Cardinal is a fact of much significance.

date of its composition. If so, the 'Orfeo' was written at the age of eighteen. It could not have been played later than 1483, for in that year the Cardinal died. At eighteen Poliziano was already famous for his translation of the 'Iliad.' He had gained the title of *Homericus Juvenis*, and was celebrated for his powers of improvisation.[42] That he should have put the 'Orfeo' together in forty-eight hours is hardly so remarkable as that he should have translated Herodian in the space of a few days, while walking and dictating. For the 'Orfeo' is but a slight piece, though beautiful and pregnant with the germs of many styles to be developed from its scenes. The plot is simple, and the whole play numbers no more than 434 lines.

To do the 'Orfeo' justice, we ought to have heard it with its own accompaniment of music. Viewed as a tragedy, judged by the standard of our Northern drama, it will always prove a disappointment. That mastery over the complex springs of human nature which distinguished the first efforts of Marlowe, is almost wholly absent. A certain adaptation of the language to the characters, in the rudeness of Thyrsis when contrasted with the rustic elegance of Aristæus; a touch of feeling in Eurydice's outcry of farewell; a discrimination between the tender sympathy of Proserpine and Pluto's stern relenting; a spirited representation of Bacchanalian enthusiasm in the Mænads; an attempt to model the Satyr Mnesillus as apart from human nature and yet conscious of its anguish—these points constitute the chief dramatic features of the melodrama. But where there was the opportunity of a really tragic movement, Poliziano failed. We have only to read the lament uttered by Orpheus for the loss of Eurydice, in order to perceive how fine a situation has been spoiled. The pathos which might have made us sympathise with the lover in his misery, the passion approaching frenzy which might have justified his misogyny, are absent. Poliziano seems to have already felt the inspiration of the Bacchic chorus which concludes the play, and to have forgotten his duty to his hero, whose sorrow for Eurydice is stultified and made unmeaning by the prosaic expression of a base resolve. Yet, when we return from these criticisms to the real merit of the piece, we find in it a charm of musical language, a subtlety of musical movement, which are irresistibly fascinating. Thought and feeling seem alike refined to a limpidity that suits the flow of melody in song. The very words evaporate and lose themselves in floods of sound. Orpheus himself is a purely lyrical personage. Of character, he can scarcely be said to have anything marked; and his part rises to its height precisely in the passage where the singer has to be displayed. Thus the 'Orfeo' is a good poem only where the situation is less dramatic than lyrical, and its finest scene was, fortunately for

[42] Perhaps Ficino was the first to give him this title. In a letter of his to Lorenzo de' Medici we read: 'Nutris domi Homericum illum adolescentem Angelum Politianum qui Græcam Homeri personam Latinis coloribus exprimat. Exprimit jam; atque, id quod mirum est ita tenerâ ætate, ita exprimit ut nisi quivis Græcum fuisse Homerum noverit dubitaturus sit e duobus uter naturalis sit et uter pictus Homerus' (*Ep.* ed. Flor. 1494 lib. i. p. 6). Ficino always addressed Poliziano as 'Poeta Homericus.'

the author, one in which the dramatic motive could be lyrically expressed. Before the gates of Hades and the throne of Proserpine, Orpheus sings, and his singing is the right outpouring of a musician-poet's soul. Each octave resumes the theme of the last stanza with a swell of utterance, a *crescendo* of intonation, that recalls the passionate and unpremeditated descant of a bird upon the boughs alone. To this true quality of music is added the persuasiveness of pleading. Even while we read, the air seems to vibrate with pure sound, and the rich recurrence of the tune is felt upon the opening of each successive stanza. That the melody of this incomparable song is lost, must be reckoned a misfortune. We have reason to believe that the part of Orpheus was taken by Messer Baccio Ugolini, singing to the viol.[43]

Space does not permit me to detach the whole scene in Hades from the play and print it here; to quote a portion of it would be nothing less than mutilation.[44] I must content myself with this Chorus of the Mænads, which contains, as in a kernel, the whole dithyrambic poetry of the Italians:

Bacchus! we all must follow thee!
Bacchus! Bacchus! Ohé! Ohé!

With ivy coronals, bunch and berry,
Crown we our heads to worship thee!
Thou hast bidden us to make merry
Day and night with jollity!
Drink then! Bacchus is here! Drink free,
And hand ye the drinking-cup to me!
Bacchus! we all must follow thee!
Bacchus! Bacchus! Ohé! Ohé!

See, I have emptied my horn already;
Stretch hither your beaker to me, I pray;
Are the hills and the lawns where we roam unsteady?
Or is it my brain that reels away?
Let everyone run to and fro through the hay,
As ye see me run! Ho! after me!
Bacchus! we all must follow thee!
Bacchus! Bacchus! Ohé! Ohé!

Methinks I am dropping in swoon or slumber;
Am I drunken or sober, yes or no?
What are these weights my feet encumber?
You too are tipsy, well I know!
Let everyone do as ye see me do,

[43] Among the frescoes by Signorelli at Orvieto there is a *tondo* in monochrome, representing Orpheus before the throne of Pluto. He is dressed like a poet, with a laurel crown, and he is playing on a violin of antique form. Mediæval demons are guarding the prostrate Eurydice. It would be curious to know whether a rumour of the Mantuan pageant had reached the ears of the Cortonese painter, or whether he had read the edition of 1494.

[44] The original should be read in the version first published by the Padre Affò (Carducci, pp. 148-154). My translation will be found in *Studies and Sketches in Italy*, pp. 235-237.

Let everyone drink and quaff like me!
  Bacchus! we all must follow thee!
  Bacchus! Bacchus! Ohé! Ohé!

Cry Bacchus! Cry Bacchus! Be blithe and merry,
  Tossing wine down your throats away!
Let sleep then come and our gladness bury:
  Drink you, and you, and you, while ye may!
Dancing is over for me to-day.
Let everyone cry aloud Evohé!
  Bacchus! we all must follow thee!
  Bacchus! Bacchus! Ohé! Ohé!

It remains to speak of the third class of poems which the great scholar and supple courtier flung like wild flowers with a careless hand from the chariot of his triumph to the Capitolian heights of erudition. Small store, indeed, he set by them—these Italian love-songs, hastily composed to please Donna Ippolita Leoncina, the titular mistress of his heart; thrown off to serve the turn of Giuliano and his younger friends; or improvised, half jestingly, to meet the humour of his princely patron, when Lorenzo, quitting the laurel-crowned bust of Plato, or the groves of Careggi, or the audience-chamber where he parleyed with the envoys of the Sforza, went abroad like King Manfred of old with lute and mandoline and viol to serenade the windows of some facile beauty in the twilight of a night of June.[45] Little did Poliziano dream that his learning would pass away almost unreckoned, but that men of after time would gather the honey of the golden days of the Renaissance from these wilding garlands.[46] Yet, however slightly Poliziano may have prized these productions of his early manhood, he proved that the *Canzone*, the *Rispetto* and the *Ballata* were as much his own in all their multiformity of lyric loveliness, as were the rich sonorous measures of the octave stanza. Expressing severally the depths of tender emotion, the caprices of adoring passion, and the rhythmic sentiment that winds in myriad movements of the dance, these three kinds of poem already belonged to the people and to love. Poliziano displayed his inborn taste and mastery of art in nothing more than in the ease with which he preserved the passionate simplicity of the Tuscan *Volkslied*, while giving it a place among the lyrics of the learned. We have already seen how that had been achieved by Boccaccio and Sacchetti, and afterwards in a measure by Lorenzo de' Medici. But the problem of

[45] 'La notte esceva per Barletta (rè Manfredi) cantando strambotti e canzoni, che iva pigliando lo frisco, e con isso ivano due musici Siciliani ch' erano gran romanzatori.' M. Spinello, in *Scr. Rer. Ital.* vii. Spinello's Chronicles are, however, probably a sixteenth-century forgery.

[46] A letter addressed by Poliziano to Lorenzo in 1488 from Acquapendente justifies the belief that the cultivation of popular poetry had become a kind of pastime in the Medicean circle. He says: 'Yesterday we set off for Viterbo. We are all gay, and make good cheer, and all along the road we whet our wits at furbishing up some song or May-day ditty, which here in Acquapendente with their Roman costume seem to me more fanciful than those at home.' See Del Lungo's edition of the *Prose Volgari*, &c., p. 75.

writing love-poetry for the people in their own forms, without irony and innuendo, was not now so easy as it had been in the fourteenth century, when no barrier had yet arisen between educated poets and the folk. Nor had even Boccaccio, far less Lorenzo, solved it with the exquisite tact and purity of style we find in all Poliziano's verses. In order to comprehend their charm, we must transfer ourselves to Florence on a summer night, when the prince is abroad upon the streets attended by singing-boys as beautiful as Sandro's angels. The professor's chair is forgotten, and Plato's spheres are left to turn unheeded. Pulci and Poliziano join hands with girls from the workshop and the attic. Lorenzo and Pico figure in the dance with prentice-lads and carvers of wood-work or marble. All through the night beneath the stars the music of their lutes is ringing; and when the dancing stops, they gather round some balcony, or hold their own upon the square in matches of improvised melody with the unknown rhymesters of the people. What can be prettier than the ballad of roses made for 'such a night' by Angelo Poliziano?[47]

Poliziano's *Rispetti* are written for the most part in *ottava rima*. This form alone suffices to mark them out as literary reproductions of the poetry upon which they are modelled. In the *Rispetti* more than the *Ballate* we notice a certain want of *naïveté*, which distinguishes them from the racier inspirations of the popular Muse. That passionate insight into the soul and essence of emotion which rarely fails the peasant in his verse, however rude, is here replaced by *concetti* rounded into pearls of fancy with the daintiest art. Those brusque and vehement images that flash the light of imagination on the movements of the heart, throbbing with intensest natural feeling, yield to carefully selected metaphors, developed with a strict sense of economy. Instead of the young *contadino* willing to mortgage paradise for his *dama*, worshipping her with body, will and soul, compelling the morning and the evening star and the lilies of the field and the bells that swing their notes of warning over Rome, to serve the bidding of his passion, we have the scholar-courtier, who touches love with the finger-tips for pastime, and who imitates the gold of the heart with baser metal of fine rhetoric. Still we find in these *Rispetti* a quality which their rustic models lack. This is the roseate fluency and honeyed rapture of their author—an exquisite limpidity and ease of diction that reveal the inborn gift of art. Language in Poliziano's hand is plastic, taking form like softest wax, so that no effort of composition, no labour of the file can be discerned.

Nec pluteum cædit nec demorsos sapit ungues.

This line of Persius denotes the excellences no less than the faults of his erotic poetry, so charming in its flow, so fit to please a facile ear, so powerless to stir the depths of the soul or wring relenting from re-

[47] See above, p. 87. For translations of several *Ballate* by Poliziano I may refer to my *Sketches and Studies in Italy*, pp. 190-225.

luctant hearts. Compared with the love-poetry of elder poets, these *Rispetti* are what the artificial epigrams of Callimachus or the Anacreontics of the Alexandrian versifiers were to the ardent stanzas of Sappho, the impassioned scolia of Pindar. While they fail to reflect the ingenuous emotions of youth exulting in the Paradise of love without an afterthought, they no less fail to embody philosophy or chivalrous religion or the tragedy of passions in conflict. They are inspired by Aphrodité Pandemos, and the joys of which they tell are carnal.[48]

What has been said about the detached *Rispetti*, is true of those longer poems which consist of many octave stanzas strung together with a continuity of pleading rhetoric. The facility bordering on negligence of their construction is apparent. Verses that occur in one, reappear in others without alteration. All repeat the same arguments, the same enticements to a less than lawful love. The code of Florentine wooing may be conveniently studied in their rambling paragraphs, while the levity of their declarations and the fluency of their vows, doing the same service on different occasions, show them to be 'false as dicers' oaths,' mere verses of the moment, made to sway a yielding woman's heart.[49] Yet who can help enjoying them, when he connects their effusiveness of fervent language with the episodes of the 'Novelle,' illustrated by figures borrowed from contemporary frescoes? Those sinewy lads of Signorelli and Masuccio, in parti-coloured hose and tight jackets, climbing mulberry-tree or vine beneath their lady's window; those girls with the demure eyes of Lippo Lippi and Bandello, suspending rope-ladders from balconies to let their Romeo escape at daybreak; those lovers rushing, half clad in shirt or jerkin, from bower and bed-chamber to cross their swords with jealous husbands at street corners; rise before us and sing their love-songs in these verses of Poliziano, written for precisely such occasions to express the very feelings of these heroes of romance. After all, too, there is a certain sort of momentary sincerity in their light words of love.

Three lyrics of higher artistic intention and of very different calibre mark the zenith of Poliziano's achievement. These are the portraits of the country girl, *La brunettina mia*; the *canzone* to *La Bella Simonetta*, written for Giuliano de' Medici; and the magnificent imitation of Petrarch's manner, beginning *Monti, valli, antri e colli.*[50] They are three studies in pictorial poetry, transparent, limpid, of incomparable freshness. A woman has sat for the central figure of each, and the landscape round her is painted with the delicacy of a *quattrocento* Florentine. *La brunettina* is the simple village beauty, who bathes her face in the fountain, and crowns her blond hair with a wreath of wild flowers. She is

48 For translations of detached *Rispetti*, see my *Sketches and Studies in Italy*, p. 197;

49 I have translated one long *Rispetto Continuato* or *Lettera in Istrambotti*; see *Sketches and Studies in Italy*, pp. 198-201. It is probable that Poliziano wrote these love-poems for his young friends, which may excuse the frequent repetitions of the same thoughts and phrases.

50 In Carducci's edition, pp. 342, 355, 363. The first seems to me untranslatable. The second and third are translated by me in *Sketches and Studies*, &c., pp. 202-207.

a blossoming branch of thorn in spring. Her breasts are May roses, her lips are strawberries. The portrait is so ethereally tinted and so firmly modelled that we seem to be looking at a study painted by a lover from the life. Simonetta moves with nobler grace and a diviner majesty.[51]

> In lei sola raccolto
> Era quant' è d' onesto e bello al mondo.
> . . . . .
> Un' altra sia tra le belle la prima:
> Costei non prima chiamesi, ma sola;
> Chè 'l giglio e la viola
> Cedono e gli altri fior tutti alla rosa.
> Pendevon dalla testa luminosa
> Scherzando per la fronte e suoi crin d' oro,
> Mentre ella nel bel coro
> Movea ristretti al suono e dolci passi.

She is the lady of the 'Stanze,' whom Giuliano found among the fields that April morning:[52]

> Candida è ella, e candida la vesta,
> Ma pur di rose e fior dipinta e d' erba;
> Lo inanellato crin dall' aurea testa
> Scende in la fronte umilmente superba.
> Ridegli attorno tutta la foresta,
> E quanto può sue cure disacerba,
> Nell' atto regalmente è mansueta;
> E pur col ciglio le tempeste acqueta.
> . . . . .

[51] But she who gives my soul sorrow and mirth,
Seemed Pallas in her gait, and in her face
Venus; for every grace
And beauty of the world in her combined.
Merely to think, far more to tell my mind,
Of that most wondrous sight, confoundeth me;
For mid the maidens she
Who most resembled her was found most rare.
Call ye another first among the fair;
Not first, but sole before my lady set:
Lily and violet
And all the flowers below the rose must bow.
Down from her royal head and lustrous brow
The golden curls fell sportively unpent.
While through the choir she went
With feet well lessoned to the rhythmic sound.

[52] White is the maid, and white the robe around her,
With buds and roses and thin grasses pied;
Enwreathéd folds of golden tresses crowned her,
Shadowing her forehead fair with modest pride:
The wild wood smiled; the thicket, where he found her,
To ease his anguish, bloomed on every side:
Serene she sits, with gesture queenly mild,
And with her brow tempers the tempests wild.
. . . . .
Reclined he found her on the swarded grass

Ell' era assisa sopra la verdura
Allegra, e ghirlandetta avea contesta
Di quanti fior creasse mai natura,
De' quali era dipinta la sua vesta.
E come prima al giovan pose cura,
Alquanto paurosa alzò la testa;
Poi con la bianca man ripreso il lembo,
Levossi in piè con di fior pieno un grembo.

All the defined idealism, the sweetness and the purity of Tuscan portraiture are in these stanzas. Simonetta does not pass by with a salutation in a mist of spiritual glory like Beatrice. She is surrounded with no flames of sensual desire like the Griseida of Boccaccio. She sits for her portrait in a tranquil light, or moves across the canvas with the dignity of a great lady:

Lei fuor di guisa umana
Mosse con maestà l' andar celeste,
E con man sospendea l' ornata veste
Regale in atto e portamento altero.

It was a rare and fugitive moment in the history of art when Poliziano could paint La Simonetta in these verses, and Lippo Lippi showed her likeness on the cathedral walls of Prato. Different models of feminine beauty, different ideals of womanly grace served the painters and poets of a more developed age; Titian's Flora and Dosso Dossi's Circe illustrating the Alcina of Ariosto and the women of Guarini. Once more, it is the thought of Simonetta which pervades the landscape of the third canzone I have mentioned. Herself is absent; but, as in a lyric of Petrarch, her spirit is felt, and we are made to see her throned beneath the gnarled beech-branches or dipping her foot in the too happy rivulet. Something just short of perfection in the *staccato* exclamations of the final strophe reminds us of Poliziano's most serious defect. Amid so much tenderness of natural feeling, he fails to make us believe in the reality of his emotion. Not passion, not thought, but the refined sensuousness of a nature keenly alive to plastic beauty, educated in the schools of classical and Florentine art, and gifted with inexhaustible facility of language, is the dominant quality of Poliziano's Italian poetry. The same quality is found in his Latin and Greek verse—in the plaintive elegies for La Bella Simonetta and Albiera degli Albizzi, in the 'Violæ' and in that ode 'In puellam suam,'[53] which is the Latin sister of 'La brunettina.' The 'Sylvæ' add a new element of earnestness

In jocund mood; and garlands she had made
Of every flower that in the meadow was,
Or on her robe of many hues displayed;
But when she saw the youth before her pass,
Raising her timid head awhile she stayed;
Then with her white hand gathered up her dress,
And stood, lap full of flowers, in loveliness.

[53] Praised for their incomparable sweetness by Scaliger, and translated into softest Italian by Firenzuola.

to his style; for if Poliziano felt deep and passionate emotion, it was for Homer, Virgil and the poets praised in the 'Nutricia,' while the 'Rusticus' condenses in one picture of marvellous fulness the outgoings of genuine emotion stimulated by his love of the country.

> Hanc, o cœlicolæ magni, concedite vitam!
> Sic mihi delicias, sic blandimenta laborum,
> Sic faciles date semper opes; hac improba sunto
> Vota tenus. Nunquam certe, nunquam illa precabor,
> Splendeat ut rutilo frons invidiosa galero,
> Tergeminaque gravis surgat mihi mitra corona.

That is the heartfelt prayer of Poliziano. Give me the tranquil scholar's life among the pleasures of the fields; my books for serious thought in studious hours; the woods and fields for recreation; with moderate wealth well-gotten without toil; no bishop's mitre or triple tiara to vex my brows. It is the same ideal as Alberti's. From this background of the modest rural life emerge three splendid visions—the Golden Age, when all was plenitude and peace; Orpheus of the dulcet lyre, evoking harmony from discord in man's jarring life; and Venus rising from the waves to bless the world with beauty felt through art. Such was the programme of human life sketched by the representative mind of his century, in an age when the Italians were summoned to do battle with France, Germany and Spain invasive of their borders.

Poliziano died before the great catastrophe. He sank at the meridian of his fame, in the same month nearly as Pico, two years later than Lorenzo, a little earlier than Ficino, in the year 1494, so fatal to his country, the date that marks the boundary between two ages in Italian history.

CHAPTER VII

PULCI AND BOIARDO

The Romantic Epic—Its Plebeian Origin—The Popular Poet's Standpoint—The Pulci Family—The Carolingian Cycle—Turpin—'Chanson de Roland'—Historical Basis—Growth of the Myth of Roland—Causes of its Popularity in Italy—Burlesque Elements—The 'Morgante Maggiore'—Adventures in Paynimry—Roncesvalles—Episodes introduced by the Poet—Sources in older Poems—The Treason of Gano—Pulci's Characters—His Artistic Purpose—His Levity and Humour—Margutte—Astarotte—Pulci's bourgeois Spirit—Boiardo—His Life—Feudalism in Italy—Boiardo's Humour—His Enthusiasm for Knighthood—His Relation to Renaissance Art—Plot of the 'Orlando Innamorato'—Angelica—Mechanism of the Poem—Creation of Characters—Orlando and Rinaldo—Ruggiero—Lesser Heroes—The Women—Love—Friendship—Courtesy—Orlando and Agricane at Albracca—Natural Delineation of Passions—Speed of Narration—Style of Versification—Classical and Mediæval Legends—The Punishment of Rinaldo—The Tale of Narcissus—Treatment of Mythology—Treatment of Magic—Fate of the 'Orlando Innamorato.'

LORENZO DE' MEDICI and Angelo Poliziano reunited the two currents of Italian literature, plebeian and cultivated, by giving the form of refined art to popular lyrics of divers kinds, to the rustic idyll, and to the sacred drama. Another member of the Medicean circle, Luigi Pulci, aided the same work of restoration by taking up the rude tales of the *Cantori da Piazza* and producing the first romantic poem of the Renaissance.

Of all the numerous forms of literature, three seem to have been specially adapted to the Italians of this period. They were the *Novella*, the Romantic Epic, and the Idyll. With regard to the *Novella* and the Idyll, it is enough in this place to say that we may reckon them indigenous to modern Italy. They suited the temper of the people and the age; the *Novella* furnishing the fit artistic vehicle for Italian realism and objectivity; the Idyll presenting a point of contact with the literature of antiquity, and expressing that calm sensibility to natural beauty which was so marked a feature of the national character amid the distractions of the sixteenth century. The Idyll and the *Novella* formed, moreover, the most precious portion of Boccaccio's legacy.

Concerning the Romantic Epic it is necessary to speak at greater length. At first sight the material of the Carolingian Cycle, which formed the basis of the most considerable narrative poems of the Renaissance, seems uncongenial to the Italians. Feudalism had never taken a firm hold on the country. Chivalry was more a pastime of the upper classes, more consciously artificial than it had been in France or even England. The interest of the Italians in the Crusades was rather commercial than religious, and the people were not stirred to their centre by the impulse to recover the Holy Sepulchre. The enthusiasm of piety which animated the Northern myth of Charlemagne, was not characteristic of the race that earlier than the rest of Europe had indulged in speculative scepticism and sarcastic raillery; nor were the marvels of the legend congenial to their positive and practical imagination, turned ever to the beauties of the plastic arts. Charlemagne, again, was not a national hero. It seemed as though the great foreign epics, which had been transported into Italy during the thirteenth century, would find no permanent place in Southern literature after the close of the fourteenth. The cultivated classes in their eagerness to discover and appropriate the ancient authors lost sight of peer and paladin. Even Boccaccio alluded contemptuously to chivalrous romance, as fit reading only for idle women; and when he attempted an epical poem in octave stanzas, he chose a tale of ancient Greece. Still in spite of these apparent drawbacks, in spite of learned scorn and polished indifference, the Carolingian Cycle had taken a firm hold upon the popular fancy. We have seen how a special class of literary craftsmen reproduced its principal episodes in prose and verse for the multitudes gathered on the squares to hear their recitations, or for readers in the workshop and the country farm. Now, in the renascence of the native literature, poets of the highest rank were destined to receive the same material from the people and to give it a form appropriate to their own culture. This fact must not be forgotten by the student of Pulci, Boiardo, Berni, and Ariosto. The romantic epics of the golden age had a plebeian origin; and the masters of verse who devoted their best energies to that brilliant series of poems, were dealing with legends which had taken shape in the imagination of the people, before they applied their own inventive faculties to the task of beautifying them with art unrivalled for splendour and variety of fancy. This, and this alone, explains the anomalies of the Italian romantic epic—the mixture of burlesque with seriousness, the irony and sarcasm alternating with gravity and pathos, the wealth of comic episodes, the interweaving of extraneous incidents, the antithesis between the professed importance of the subject-matter and the spirit of the poet who plays with it as though he felt its puerility—all the startling contrasts, in a word, which have made this glittering Harlequin of art in the Renaissance so puzzling to modern critics. If we remember that the poets of the sixteenth century adopted their subjects from the people, finding them already impregnated with the plebeian instincts of *improvisatori*, who felt no real sympathy with knighthood, and whose one aim was to amuse and gratify an audience eager for excitement; if we further recollect that these poets approached their own task in the same spirit, adding yet another element of irony proper to men who stood aloof and laughed, and who desired to entertain the Courts of Italy with masterpieces of humour and fantastic beauty; we shall succeed in comprehending the peculiarities of their productions.

The romances of Orlando must be regarded as works of pure art, wrought by courtly singers from a previously existing popular literature, which in its turn had been fashioned from the Frankish legends to suit the tastes of a non-chivalrous, but humorous and marvel-loving multitude. In passing from the Song of Roland or Turpin's Chronicle to the 'Orlando Furioso' we can trace two separate processes of transmutation By the earlier process the *materia di Francia* was adapted to the Italian people; by the second the new material thus obtained was reconstructed for the Italian Courts. The final product is a masterpiece of refined art, retaining something of the French originals, something of the popular Italian *rifacimento*, but superadding the wisdom, the irony, and the poetry of one of the world's brightest geniuses. We might compare the growth of a romantic epic of the sixteenth century to the art of Calimala, whereby the rough stuffs of Flanders were wrought at Florence into finer cloths, and the finished fabric was tinted with the choicest dyes, and made fit for a king's chamber.

Hitherto I have spoken as though Pulci, Boiardo, Ariosto, Berni, and the lesser writers of romantic epics could be classed together in one sentence. The justification of so broad a treatment at the outset lies in this, that their relation to the popular romances they rehandled was substantially the same. But it will be the special purpose of the following pages to point out their essential differences, not only as poets, but also with regard to the spirit in which they viewed their common subject-matter.

Boccaccio, in his desire to fuse the classic and the mediæval modes of thought and style, not merely adapted the periods of Latin to Italian prose, but also sought to treat an antique subject in the popular measure of the octave stanza. His 'Teseide' is a narrative poem in which the Greek hero plays a prominent part, while all the chiefs of Theban and Athenian legend are brought upon the scene. Yet the main motive is a tale of love, and the language is as modern as need be. Writing to please the mistress of his heart, and emulous of epic fame, Boccaccio rejected the usual apostrophes and envoys of the *Cantori da Banca*, and constructed a poem divided into books. Poliziano approached the problem of fusing the antique and modern from a different point of view. He adorned a courtly theme of his own day with phrases and decorative details borrowed from the classic authors, presenting in a series of brilliant pictures an epitome of ancient art. It remained for Pulci to develop, without classical admixture, the elements of poetry existing in the popular Italian romances. The 'Morgante Maggiore' is therefore more thoroughly and purely Tuscan than any work of equal magnitude that had preceded it. This is its great merit, and this gives it a place apart among the hybrid productions of the Renaissance.

The Pulci were a noble family, reduced in circumstances and attached to the Casa Medici by ties of political and domestic dependency. Bernardo, the eldest of three brothers, distinguished himself in literature by his translations of Virgil's Eclogues, by his elegies on Cosimo de'

Medici, by a 'Sacra Rappresentazione' on the tale of Barlaam, and by a poem on the Passion of Christ which he composed at the instance of a devout nun. Luca wrote the stanzas on the Tournament of Lorenzo de' Medici above mentioned,[1] and took some part at least in the composition of an obscure poem called the 'Ciriffo Calvaneo.'[2] But the most famous of the brothers was Luigi, whose correspondence with Lorenzo de' Medici proves him to have been a kind of Court-poet in the Palace of the Via Larga, while the sonnets he exchanged with Matteo Franco breathe Burchiello's plebeian spirit.[3] He had a wild fantastic temperament, inclining to bold speculations on religious topics; tinctured with curiosity that took the form of magic art; bizarre in expression, yet withal so purely Florentine that his prose and verse are a precious mine of *quattrocento* idioms gathered from the jargon of the streets and squares. Of humanistic culture he seems to have possessed but little. Still the terms of familiar intercourse on which he lived with Angelo Poliziano, Matteo Palmieri, and Paolo Toscanelli enabled him to gather much of the learning then in vogue. The theological and scientific speculations of the age are transmitted to us in his comic stanzas with a vernacular raciness that renders them doubly precious.[4]

Before engaging with the 'Morgante Maggiore,' it is needful to inquire into the source of this and all the other Italian romantic poems, and to account for the fact that they were confined, so far as their subject went, within the circle of the Carolingian epic. In 1122 a prose history in monkish Latin, purporting to be the Chronicle of the last years of the reign of Charles the Great written by Turpin, Archbishop of Rheims, was admitted among the canonical books by Calixtus II., who in his Bull cursed those who should thenceforward listen to the 'lying songs of Jongleurs.' This Chronicle was merely a sanctimonious and prosaic version of the Songs of Roland and of Roncesvalles.[5] The

[1] See above p. 102.

[2] This poem relates the adventures of Ciriffo and Il Povero Avveduto, bastards of two noble ladies, and gives the history of a crusade of Louis against the Soldan of Egypt. It was published as the work, as far as the first Book, of Luca Pulci, completed and restored by Bernardo Giambullari. 'Il Ciriffo Calvaneo, diviso in iv Canti, col primo Libro di Luca Pulci, ed il resto riformato per Bernardo Giambullari' (Roma, Mazzocchio, 1514). Luigi Pulci claims a share in it, if not the whole, in the *Morgante*, xxviii. 118, 129.

[3] See *Lettere di Luigi Pulci a Lorenzo Il Magnifico*, Lucca, Giusti, 1868. *Sonetti di Matteo Franco e Luigi Pulci*, 1759. The sonnets are indescribably scurrilous, charged with Florentine slang, and loaded with the filthiest abuse. The point of humour is that Franco and Pulci undertook (it is said, for fun) to heap scandals on each other's heads, ransacking the language of the people for its vilest terms of invective. If they began in joke, they ended in earnest; and Lorenzo de' Medici, who had a low taste for buffoonery, enjoyed the scuffle of his Court-fools. It was a combat of humanists transferred from the arena of the schools to the market-place, where two men of parts degraded themselves by assuming the character of coal-heavers.

[4] The poetical talents of the Pulci family were hereditary. Cellini tells us of a Luigi of that name who improvised upon the market-place of Florence.

[5] Turpin's Chronicle consists of thirty-two chapters, relating the wars of Charlemain with the Spanish Moors, the treason of Ganelon, and Roland's death in Roncesvalles. The pagan knight, Ferraguto, and the Christian peers are mentioned by name,

object of the scribe who compiled it, and of the Pope who canonised it, was to give an ecclesiastical complexion to the martial chants which already possessed the ear of the public.[6] Accordingly, while he left untouched the tales of magic, the monstrous marvels and the unchristian ethics of the elder fable, this pseudo-Turpin interspersed prayers confessions, vows, miracles, homilies, and pulpit admonitions. In order to secure verisimilitude for his narrative, he reversed the old account of Roncesvalles, according to which Turpin perished on the field, anathematised all previous poets, and pretended that his Chronicle was written by the hands of the Archbishop.[7] What he effected for the Song of Roland, Geoffrey of Monmouth did, without a sacerdotal bias, for the romance of Arthur.

We possess a MS. of the 'Chanson de Roland' in Norman French. It was discovered in the Bodelian Library and published first in 1837 by M. Michel, afterwards in 1851 by M. Génin. The date of the MS. has been fixed by some critics as early as the eleventh, by others as late as the thirteenth, century. Purporting to be the work of one Turold, its most enthusiastic admirers claim it as the genuine production of Théroulde, tutor to William the Conqueror, which, after passing through the hands of Taillefer, the knightly bard of Senlac field, was deposited in his MS. chest by a second Théroulde, abbot of Peterborough.[8] Be that as it may, we can assume that the Bodleian MS. presents the ancient battle-song in nearly the same form as when the Normans followed Taillefer at Hastings, and heard him chanting of 'Charlemain and Roland and Oliver who died in Roncesvalles.' This song reverberated throughout mediæval Europe. Poggio in the 'Facetiæ' compares a man who weeps over the fall of Rome, to one who in Milan shed tears over Roland's death at Roncesvalles. Dante may have heard it on the lips of the *Cantores Francigenarum* in Lombard towns, or in the halls of Fosdinovo above the Tyrrhene Sea; for he writes with an energy of style scarcely inspired by the pseudo-Turpin:

> Dopo la dolorosa rotta, quando
> Carlo Magno perdè la santa gesta,
> Non sonò si terribilmente Orlando.

Orlando and Oliver (or Ogier) are carved upon the façade of the Duomo at Verona—Dietrich's town of Bern, where Northern traditions of chivalry long lingered.[9] Like the Spanish legend of the Cid, or the climax

proving that at the date of its compilation the whole Carolingian myth was tolerably perfect in the popular imagination.

[6] It has been conjectured by M. Génin, editor of the *Chant de Roland*, not without substantial grounds, that Gui de Bourgogne, bishop of Vienne, afterwards Pope Calixtus II., was himself the pseudo-Turpin.

[7] See *Chanson de Roland*, line 804, and compare *Morg. Magg.* xxvii. 79.

[8] See Ludlow's *Popular Epics of the Middle Ages*, vol. i. p. 412, and M. Génin's Introduction to the *Chanson de Roland*, Paris, 1851.

[9] See Génin (*op. cit.* pp. xxix, xxx) for the traces of the Roland myth in the Pyrenees, at Rolandseck, in England, and at Verona; also for gigantic statues in Germany called Rolands (*ib.* pp. xxi, xxii). At Spello, a little town of Umbria between Assisi

of the 'Niebelungenlied,' this Song of Roland, in dignity and strength of style, in tragic heroism and passionate simplicity, is worthy to be ranked with a Canto of the 'Iliad.' Like all mediæval romantic poetry, it is but a fragment—the portion of a cycle never wrought by intervention of a Homer into epical completeness. But its superiority over Turpin's Chronicle in all the qualities that could inspire a singer, is immeasurable.

Two questions have now to be asked. What historical basis can be found for the Carolingian myth? and how did it happen that the Italians preferred this legend of French Paladins to any other of the feudal romances? The history of Charlemagne and his peers—of Roland, Oliver, Ogier, Turpin, Ganilo the traitor, Pinabel, Marsilius the Moorish king of Spain, and all the rest, of whom we read in the Norman song, and who receive numerous additions from the Italian romancers—must not be sought in Eginhard. It is a Myth. But like all myths, it has some nucleus of reality, round which have crystallised the enthusiasms of a semi-barbarous age, the passionate memories of the people looking back to bygone greatness, the glowing fancies of poets intent on visions of the future. This nucleus of fact is little more than the name of Charles, the Frankish Emperor. All the legends of the cycle represent him as conducting a crusade, defeating the Saracens in mighty battles, besieged by them in Paris, betrayed by his own subject Ganilo, and bereft of his noblest paladins in the Pass of Roncesvalles. History knows nothing of these events. Nor can history account for the traditional character of the Emperor, who is feeble, credulous, browbeaten by lawless vassals, incapable of strenuous action, and yet respected as the conqueror of the world and the anointed of the Lord.[10] It is therefore clear that the myth has blent together divers incongruous elements, and that the spirit of the Crusades has been at work, giving a kind of unity to scarce remembered acts of the chief of Christendom. We hear from Eginhard that Charlemagne in 778 advanced as far as Saragossa into Spain, and during his retreat had his rear-guard cut off by the Basques.[11] Among the slain was 'Roland, prefect of the Breton Marches.' We read again in Eginhard (anno 824) how Louis le Debonair lost two of his counts, who were returning from Spain through the Pass of Roncesvalles. Furthermore, the Merovingian Chronicles tell us of a Pyrenean battle in the days of Dagobert, when twelve Frankish chiefs were surrounded in those passes and slain. These are sufficient data to account for the Pass of Roncesvalles becoming a valley dolorous, the

and Foligno, the people of the place showed me a dint in their ancient town wall, about breast-high, which passes for a mark made by Orlando's knee. There is learned tradition of a phallic monument named after Roland in that place; but I could find no trace of it in local memory.

[10] The *Song of Roland* does not give this portrait of Charlemagne's dotage. But it is an integral part of the Italian romances, a fixed point in all *rifacimenti* of the pseudo-Turpin.

[11] Ludlow (*op. cit.* i. 358) translates the Basque Song of Atta-biçar, which relates to some destruction of chivalrous forces by the Pyrenean mountaineers.

vale of the great woe. For the crusading exploits of Charlemagne we have to look to his predecessor, Charles Martel, who defeated the Saracens at Tours and stemmed the tide of Mussulman invasion. His successors, the feeble monarchs of the Frankish line, several of whom bore the name of Charles, explain the transformation of the Emperor into a vacillating monarch, infirm of purpose and incapable of keeping his peers in order; for the distinguishing surnames of history are later additions, and Chronicles, though written, were not popularly read. The bard, therefore, mixed his materials without care for criticism, and the myth produced a hybrid Charlemagne composed of many royal Karls. As for the traitor Gano, we hear of Lupus, Duke of Gascony, who dealt treasonably with Charlemagne, and of one Ganilo, Ganelon, or Wenelon, Archbishop of Sens, who played the same part toward Charles the Bald in 864.[12] This portion of the myth may possibly be referred to these dim facts. Yet it would be wiser not to insist upon them; for the endeavour to rationalise an entire legend is always hazardous, and it is enough to say that a traitor was needed for the fight of Roncesvalles no less than Mordred for the death of Arthur in the plain of Glastonbury. To explain the legendary siege of Paris by the Saracens, so important an incident in the Italian romances, it has been ingeniously remarked that, though the Moors never menaced the French capital, the Normans did so repeatedly, while both Saracens and Normans were Pagans.[13] It may also be remembered that Saracens had pillaged Rome, and that Saracen forays were a common incident of Italian experience. The gathering of great armies from the far East and the incursions of hideous barbarian hordes, which form an integral element of Boiardo's and Ariosto's scheme, can be referred to the memory of Tartar, Hun, and Turk; while the episodes of Christian knights enamoured of Pagan damsels are incidents drawn from actual history in the intercourse of Italy with the Levant. Allowing for this slight framework of fact, but not pressing even the few points that have been gathered by antiquarian research, it may be briefly said that the bulk of the Carolingian romance, with its numerous subordinate legends of knights and ladies, is purely mythical.

In the next place we have to consider what led the Italians to select the romances of Charlemagne for special development rather than those of Arthur, with which they were no less familiar.[14] We have seen that

[12] See Génin (*op. cit.* pp. xxv-xxviii).

[13] Introduction to Panizzi's edition of the *Orlando Innamorato* and *Orlando Furioso* (London, Pickering, 1830), vol. i. pp. 126-128.

[14] See Dante, *Inf.* xxxii. 61, v. 67, v. 128. Galeotto, Lancelot's go-between with Guinevere, gave his name to a pimp in Italy, as Pandarus to a pander in England. Boccaccio's *Novelliere* was called *Il Principe Galeotto*. Petrarch in the *Trionfi* and Boccaccio in the *Amorosa Visione* make frequent references to the knights of the Round Table. The latter in his *Corbaccio* mentions the tale of Tristram as a favourite book with idle women. The *Fiammetta* might be quoted with the same object of proving its widespread popularity. The lyrics of Folgore da San Gemignano and other *trecentisti* would furnish many illustrative allusions.

on the first introduction of the *materia di Francia* into Italy, the Arthurian Cycle became the property of the nobles, who found in it a mirror of the feudal manners they affected, whereas the people listened to *Chansons de Geste* upon the market-place.[15] When, therefore, the polite poets of the fifteenth century adopted the romantic epic from the popular rhymers, they found a mass of Carolingian tales in vogue to which they had themselves from infancy been used. But this preference of the multitude for Charlemagne and Roland requires further explanation. It must be remarked in the first place that the Empire exercised a fascination over the Italians in the middle ages, paralleled by no other power except the Papacy. They regarded it as their own, as their glory in the past, as their pride in the future, if only the inheritor of the Cæsars would do his duty and rule the world from Rome with equal justice. The pedigree of the Christian Emperors from Constantine to Charles the Great formed an integral part of the Carolingian romance as it took form in Italy.[16] It was something for the Italians that Charles had been crowned at Rome, a ceremony from time to time repeated by his German successors during the centuries which made his legend famous. Nor, though the people were but little influenced by the crusading fanaticism, was it of no importance that in the person of this Emperor Christendom had been imperilled by the infidels, and Christendom through him had triumphed. The Chronicle of Turpin, again, had received authoritative sanction. Add to it as the romancers chose, attribute nonsense to the Archbishop as they pleased, they always relied, in show at least, on his canonical veracity. Pulci, Bello, Boiardo, and Ariosto appeal to his authority with mock seriousness; and even the burlesque Berni, while turning Turpin into ridicule, adopts the style:

> Perchè egli era Arcivescovo, bisogna
> Credergli, ancor che dica la menzogna.[17]

The fashion lasted till the days of Folengo and Fortiguerra. It may further be mentioned that Orlando at an early date had been made a Roman by the popular Italian mythologists. They said that he was born at Sutri, and that Oliver was the son of the Roman prefect for

[15] See Vol. I. p. 852.

[16] The *Reali di Francia* sets forth this legendary genealogy at great length, and stops short at the coronation of Charles in Rome and the discovery of Roland. Considering the dryness of its subject-matter, it is significant that this should have survived all the prose romances of the fifteenth century. We may ascribe the fact perhaps to the tenacious Italian devotion to the Imperial idea.

[17] *Orl. Inn. Rifac.* i. 18, 26. Niccolò da Padova in the thirteenth century quoted Turpin as his authority for the history of Charlemagne which he composed in Northern French. This proves the antiquity of the custom. See Bartoli, *Storia della Lett. It.* vol. ii. p. 44. To believe in Turpin was not, however, an article of faith. Thus Bello in the *Mambriano*, c. viii.:

> Ma poi che 'l non è articolo di fede,
> Tenete quella parte che vi piace,
> Che l' autor libramente vel concede.

the Pope. The sentiment of the people for this strange *Senator Romanus* expressed itself touchingly and pithily in his supposed epitaph: 'One God, One Rome, One Roland.'[18] Orlando was so rooted in the popular consciousness as a hero, that to have substituted for him another epical character would have been impossible.

When we further investigate the naturalisation of Orlando in Italy, we find that all the romantic poems written on his legend inclined to the burlesque. The chivalrous element of love which pervades the Arthurian Cycle, had been extracted and treated after their own fashion by the lyrists of the fourteenth century. That was no immediate concern of the people, nor had the citizens any sympathy with the chivalry of arms. To deal as solemnly with mediæval romance as the Northern bards had done, was quite beside the purpose of the *improvisatori* who refashioned the *Chansons de Geste* for Italian townsfolk. When, therefore, Pulci undertook to amuse Lucrezia Tornabuoni, the mother of Lorenzo de' Medici, with a tale of Roland, he found his material already stripped of epical sobriety; nor was it hard for him to handle his theme in the spirit of Boccaccio, bent on exhausting every motive of amusement which it might suggest. He assumed the tone of a street-singer, opening each canto with the customary invocation to Madonna or a paraphrase of some Church collect, and dismissing his audience at the close with grateful thanks or brief good wishes. But Pulci was no mere *Cantastorie*. The popular style served but for a cloak to cover his subtle-witted satire and his mocking levity. Sarcastic Tuscan humour keeps up an *obbligato* accompaniment throughout the poem. Sometimes this humour is in harmony with the plebeian spirit of the old Italian romances; sometimes it turns aside and treats it as a theme of ridicule. In reading the 'Morgante,' we must bear in mind that it was written, canto by canto, to be recited in the Palace of the Via Larga, at the table where Poliziano and Ficino gathered with Michelangelo Buonarroti and Cristoforo Landino. Whatever topics may from time to time have occupied that brilliant circle, were reflected in its stanzas; and this alone suffices to account for its tender episodes and its burlesque extravagances, for the satiric picture of Margutte and the serious discourses of the devil Astarotte. The external looseness of construction, and the intellectual unity of the poem, are both attributable to these circumstances. Passing by rapid transitions from grave to gay, from pathos to cynicism, from theological speculations to ribaldry, it is at one and the same time a mirror of the popular taste which suggested the form, and also of the courtly wits who listened to it laughing. The 'Morgante' is no *naïve* production of a simple age, but the artistic plaything of a cultivated and critical society, entertaining its leisure with old-world stories, accepting some for their beauty's sake in seriousness, and turning others into nonsense for pure mirth.

A careful study of the 'Morgante Maggiore' reveals to the critic three

[18] 'Un Dio, uno Orlando, e una Roma.' *Morg. Magg.* xxvii. 220. Compare this with Arthur's 'Flos regum Arthurus, rex quondam rexque futurus.'

separate strains of style. To begin with, it is clear that we are dealing with two poems fused in one—the first ending with the twenty-third canto, the second consisting of the last five cantos. Between these two divisions a considerable period of time is supposed to have elapsed. The first poem consists of a series of romantic adventures in strange countries, whither Orlando, Uliviero, Rinaldo and Astolfo have been driven by the craft of Gano, and where they fight giants, liberate ladies, and fall in love with Pagan damsels, after the jovial fashion of knights errant. The second assumes a more heroic tone, and tells in truly thrilling verse the tale of Roncesvalles. But over and above this double material, different in matter and in manner, we trace throughout the whole romance a third element, which seems to be more essentially the poet's own than either his fantastic tissue of adventures or his serious narrative of Roland's death. This third element consists of half-ironical half-sober dissertations, reflective digressions, and brilliant interpolated incidents, among which we have to reckon the splendid episodes of Astarotte and Margutte. So much was clear to my mind when I first read the 'Morgante,' and attempted to comprehend the difficulties it presented to critics like Ginguenè and Hallam. Since then the truth of this view has been substantiated by the eminent Italian scholar, Pio Rajna, who has proved that the 'Morganté' is the *rifacimento* of two earlier popular poems, the first existing in MS. in the Laurentian Library, the second entitled 'La Spagna.'[19] Pulci availed himself freely of his popular models, at times repeating the old stanzas with no alteration, but oftener rehandling them and adding to their comic spirit, and interpolating passages of his own invention. Since the two originals differed in character, his *rifacimento* retained their divers peculiarities, notwithstanding those master-touches which betray the same hand in both of its main sections. But the most precious part of the poem remains Pulci's own. Nothing can deprive him of Margutte and Astarotte; nor without his clever transmutation of the old material would the bulk of the 'Morgante Maggiore' deserve more attention than many similar romances buried in condign oblivion. Between the two parts we may notice a considerable difference of literary merit. The second and shorter is by far the finer in poetic quality, earnestness, and power of treatment. The first is tedious to read. The second enthralls and carries us along.[20]

The poem takes its title from the comic hero Morgante, a giant captured and converted by Orlando in the first Canto.[21] He dies, however,

[19] See *Propugnatore* (Anni ii., iii., iv.). *La Spagna* was itself two popular compilations.

[20] This is only strictly true of Cantos xxiv., xxv., xxvi., xxvii. The last Canto, in fact the whole poem after the execution of Marsilio, is a dull historical epitome, brightened by Pulci's personal explanations at the ending.

[21] It is called *Morgante Maggiore* because the part relating to him was published separately under the title of *Morgante.* This character Pulci derived from the MS. poem called by Signor Rajna the *Orlando* to distinguish it. In the year 1500 we find one of the Baglioni called Morgante, which proves perhaps the popularity of this giant.

in the twentieth, and the narrative proceeds with no interruption. If we seek for epical unity, in a romance so loosely put together from so many diverse sources, we can find it in the treason of Gano. The action turns decisively and frequently upon this single point, returns to it from time to time for fresh motives, and reaches its conclusion in the execution of the traitor after the great deed of crime has been accomplished in the valley dolorous. An Italian of the fifteenth century could not have chosen a motive more suited to the temper and experience of his age, when conspiracies like that of the Pazzi at Florence and the Baglioni at Perugia were frightfully frequent, and when the successful massacre of Sinigaglia made Cesare Borgia the hero of historical romance. *Il tradimento*, *il traditore*, the kiss of Judas, the simile of the fox, recur with fatal resonance through all the Cantos of the poem. The style assumes a rugged grandeur of tragic realism, not unworthy of poets of the stamp of our own Webster or Marston, in the passage which describes the tempest by the well at Saragossa, where Gano met Marsilio to plan their fraud, and where the locust-tree let fall its fruit upon the traitor's head.[22] The 'Morgante' is, in truth, the epic of treason, and the character of Gano, as an accomplished yet not utterly abandoned Judas, is admirably sustained throughout. The powerful impression of his perversity is heightened by contrast with the loyalty of his son Baldovino. In the fight at Roncesvalles Baldovino carries a mantle given to Gano by the Saracen king, without knowing for what purpose his father made him wear it; and wherever he charges through the press of men, the foes avoid him. Orlando learns that he is protected by this ensign of fraud, and accuses him of partaking in Gano's treason. Then the youth flings the cloak from his shoulders, and plunges into the fight with an indignant repudiation of this shame upon his lips. The scene is not unworthy of the 'Iliad;'[23] and his last words, as he falls

[22] Canto xxv. 73-78. The locust-tree, according to the tradition of the South, served Judas when he hanged himself. Northern fancy reserved this honour for the elder, not perhaps without a poetic sense of the outcast existence of the plant and its worthlessness for any practical use. On the same locust-tree Marsilio was afterwards suspended (c. xxvii. 267). The description of the blasted pleasure-garden in the latter passage is also very striking. For the translation of these passages see Appendix.

[23] Canto xxvii. 5-7 and 47. Note in particular (translated in Appendix):

> Rispose Baldovin: Se il padre mio
> Ci ha qui condotti come traditore,
> S' io posso oggi campar, pel nostro Iddio,
> Con questa spada passerògli il core!
> Ma traditore, Orlando, non son io,
> Ch' io t' ho seguito con perfetto amore;
> Non mi potresti dir maggiore ingiuria!
> Poi si stracciò la vesta con gran furia,
> E disse: Io tornerò nella battaglia,
> Poi che tu m' hai per traditore scorto;
> Io non son traditor, se Dio mi vaglia,
> Non mi vedrai più oggi se non morto!
> E inverso l' oste de' Pagan si scaglia,

pierced in the breast with two lances, *Or non son io più traditore!* are dramatic.

Pulci deserves credit for strong delineation of character. Through all the apish tricks and fantastic arabesque-work of his style, the chief personages retain firmly marked types. Never since the 'Chanson de Roland' was first sung, has a more heroic portrait of Orlando, the God-fearing knight, obedient to his liege-lord, serene in his courage and gentle in his strength, courteous, pious and affectionate, been painted.[24] Close adherence to the popular conception of Orlando's character here stood Pulci in good stead; nor was he hampered with the difficulties which beset Boiardo and Ariosto, when they showed the champion of Christianity subdued to madness and to love. Thus one work at least of the Renaissance maintained for the Italians an ideal of chivalrous heroism, first conceived by Franco-Norman bards, and afterwards transmitted through the fancy of the people, who are ever ready to discern and to preserve the lineaments of greatness. Oliver the true friend and doughty warrior, Rinaldo the fiery foe and reckless lover, to whom the press of men was Paradise,[25] and Malagigi the magician, are drawn with no less skill. Charles is such as the traditions of the myth and the requirements of the plot obliged Pulci to make him. Yet in spite of the feebleness which exposes him to the treasonable arts of Gano, he is not deficient in a certain nobility. In the conduct of these characters, amid the windings of the poet's freakish fancy, we trace the solidity of his plan, his faculty for earnest art. But should there still be found critics who, after a careful study of Gano, Orlando, Uliviero, Rinaldo and Carlo, think that Pulci meant his poem for a mere burlesque, this opinion cannot but be shaken by a perusal of the twenty-fifth, twenty-sixth and twenth-seventh Cantos. The refusal of Orlando to blow his horn:

> Non sonerò perchè e' m' aiuti Carlo,
> Chè per viltà mai non volli sonarlo:

his address to the knights when rushing into desperate battle at impossible odds;[26] the scene of his death, so tender in its pathos, so quaint

> Dicendo sempre: Tu m' hai fatto torto!
> Orlando si pentea d' aver ciò detto,
> Chè disperato vide il giovinetto.

[24] Of all the Paladins only Orlando is uniformly courteous to Charlemagne. When Rinaldo dethrones the Emperor and flies to his cousin (c. xi. 114), Orlando makes him return to his obedience (*ibid.* 127). See, too, c. xxv. 100:

> Or oltre in Roncisvalle Orlando va,
> Per obbedir, com' e' fe' sempre, Carlo.

[25] Canto xxvi. 126:

> Rinaldo, quando e' fu nella battaglia,
> Gli parve esser in ciel tra' cherubini
> Tra suoni e canti.

[26] *Ibid.* 24-39. These two touches, out of many that are noble, might be chosen:

> Stasera in paradiso cenerete;

in its piety; the agony of Charles when he comes, too late, to find him slain, and receives his sword from the Paladin's dead hands; these passages must surely be enough to convince the most incredulous of doctrinaires.

It has been customary to explain the apparent contradictions of the 'Morgante Maggiore'—Pulci's brusque transitions from piety to ribaldry, from pathos to satire—by reference to the circumstances of Florence at the date of its composition. The republic was at war with Sixtus IV., who had taken part in the Pazzi conspiracy. To his Bull of excommunication the Signoria had retorted by terming it 'maledictam maledictionem damnatissimi judicis,' and had described the Pope himself as 'delirum senem,' 'leno matris suæ, adulterorum minister, diaboli vicarius.' It was not to be expected that even an orthodox Christian should be tender toward the vices of the clergy or careful in guarding his religious utterances at such a moment. Yet we need not go far afield to account for Pulci's profanity. The Italians of the age in which he lived, were freethinkers without ceasing to be Catholics. To begin a Canto with a prayer, and to end it with speculations on the destiny of the soul after death, was consistent with their intellectual temper. The schools and private coteries of Florence were the arena in which Platonism and Averroism waged war with orthodoxy, where questions of freewill and creation, the relation of man to God, and the essence of the human spirit, were being discussed with a philosophic indifference and warmth of curiosity that prepared the way for Pomponazzi's materialism. Criticism, the modern Hercules, was already in its cradle, strangling the serpents of sacerdotal authority: and as yet the Inquisition had not become a power of terror; the Council of Trent and the Spanish tyranny had not turned Italians into trembling bigots or sleek hypocrites. Externally they remained tenacious of their old beliefs; and from the point of view of art at least, they were desirous of adhering to tradition. For Pulci to have celebrated Orlando without assuming the customary style of the *cantastorie*, would have been beside his purpose. Therefore, the mixture of magic, theology, impiety, speculation and religious fervour which perplexes a reader of the present day in the 'Morgante,' corresponded to the mental attitude of the educated majority at Pulci's date. On the borderland between the middle ages and the modern world the keen Italian intellect loved to entertain itself with a perpetual *perhaps*, impartially including in the sphere of doubt old dogmas and novel hypotheses, and finding satisfaction in an insecurity that flattered it

> Come disse quel Greco anticamente
> Lieto a' suoi già, ma disse—Nello inferno:

and:

> La morte è da temere, o la partita,
> Quando l' anima e 'l corpo muore insieme;
> Ma se da cosa finita a infinita
> Si va qui in ciel fra tante diademe,
> Questo è cambiar la vita a miglior vita.

with the sense of disengagement from formulæ.[27] With some minds this volatile questioning was serious; with others it assumed a Rabelaisian joviality. Pulci ranked with those who made the problems of the world material for humorous debate.

A few instances of Pulci's peculiar levity might be selected from the last Cantos of the 'Morgante,' where no one can maintain that his intention was burlesque. We have just heard from the minstrel's lips how Roland died, recommending his soul to God and delivering his glove in sign of feudal fealty to Gabriel. The sound of his horn has startled Charlemagne from the sleep of false tranquillity, and the Emperor is on his way to Roncesvalles. But time is short. He prays Christ that as of old for Joshua, so now for him in his sore need, the sun may be stayed and the day be prolonged:[28]

> O crucifisso, il qual, già sendo in croce,
> Oscurasti quel sol contra natura;
> Io ti priego, Signor, con umil voce
> Infin ch' io giunga in quella valle oscura,
> Che tu raffreni il suo corso veloce.

The prayer is worthy, in its solemn tone, of this exordium; and the desired effect soon follows. But now Pulci changes his note from grave to gay:[29]

> E disse: Pazienzia, come Giobbe;
> Or oltre in Roncisvalle andar si vuole.
> Chè come savio il partito conobbe,
> *Per non tenere in disagio più il sole.*

A few lines further he describes the carnage in the dolorous valley, and finds this comic phrase to express the confusion of the field:[30]

> Chi mostra sanguinosa la percossa,
> Chi il capo avea quattro braccia discosto,
> *Da non trovarli in Giusaffà si tosto.*

Pulci's grotesque humour gives an air of false absurdity to many incidents which, together with his hearers, he undoubtedly took in good faith. During the slaughter of the Christians he wishes to impress the audience with the multitude of souls who crowded into Paradise. S.

[27] This pervasive doubt finds its noblest and deepest expression in some lines spoken by Orlando just before engaging in the fight at Roncesvalles (xxvi. 31):

> Tutte cose mortal vanno ad un segno;
> Mentre l' una sormonta, un' altra cade:
> Così fia forse di Cristianitade.

This is said not from the hero's but the author's point of view. Pomponazzi afterwards gave philosophical utterance to the same disbelief in the permanence of Christianity.

[28] Canto xxvii. 172.

[29] *Ibid.* 196.

[30] *Ibid.* 198.

Peter is tired to death with opening the door for them and deafened with their jubilations:[31]

> E così in ciel si faceva apparecchio
> D' ambrosia e nettar con celeste manna,
> E perchè Pietro alla porta è pur vecchio,
> Credo che molto quel giorno s' affanna;
> E converrà ch' abbi buono orecchio,
> Tanto gridavan quelle anime Osanna
> Ch' eran portate dagli angeli in cielo;
> Sicchè la barba gli sudava e 'l pelo.

In the same spirit is the picture of the fiends seated like hawks upon the bell-towers of a little chapel, waiting to pounce upon the souls of Pagans.[32]

Sometimes a flash of purely Bernesque humour appears in Pulci; as when he says that the Saracens

> Bestemmiavano Dio divotamente,

or when Oliver, after a pathetic love-lament, complains that it is impossible

> Celar per certo l' amore e la tossa.

According to modern notions his jokes not unfrequently savour of profanity. Rinaldo and Ricciardetto are feasting upon ortolans, and give this punning reason for their excellence:[33]

> Cioè che Cristo a Maddalena apparve
> In ortolan, che buon sozio gli parve.

On the same occasion Rinaldo is so pleased with his fare that he exclaims:

> Questi mi paion miracoli;
> Facciam qui sei non che tre tabernacoli.

Such expressions flash forth from mere Florentine sense of fun in passages by no means deliberately comic.

The most diverting character of the 'Morgante' is Margutte, an eccentric heteroclite creature, the prototype of Folengo's Cingar and Rabelais' Panurge, whom the giant met upon his wanderings and adopted for a comrade. It has been supposed with some reason that Pulci here intended to satirise the Greeks who flocked to Florence after the fall of Constantinople, and that either Marullo, the personal enemy of Poliziano, or Demetrius Chalcondylas, his rival in erudition, sat for Margutte's portrait. The character of the rogue, described by himself in thirty stanzas of fantastic humour, contains a complete epitome of the abuse which the scholars of those days used to vomit forth in their

[31] Canto xxvi. 91.
[32] Canto xxvi. 89.
[33] Canto xxv. 217, 218.

reciprocal invectives.[34] Part of the comic effect produced by his speech is due to this self-attribution of qualities which supplied the arsenals of humanistic combatants with poisoned arrows. But Margutte has far more than a merely ilustrative or temporary value. He is the first finished humoristic portrait sketched in modern literature, the first broadly conceived and jovially executed Rabelaisian study. Though it is very improbable that Pulci had any knowledge of Aristophanes, though he died eight years or thereabouts before the Curé of Meudon was born, his Margutte is cousin-german of the Sausage-seller and Panurge.[35] Margutte takes an impish pride in reckoning up his villanies and vices. When Morgante asks him whether he believes in Christ or Appollino, he replies:

A dirtel tosto,
Io non credo più al nero ch' all' azzurro,
Ma nel cappone, o lesso, o vuogli arrosto . . .
E credo nella torta e nel tortello,
L' una è la madre, e l' altro è il suo figliuolo;
Il vero paternostro è il fegatello,
E possono esser tre, e due, ed un solo,
E diriva dal fegato almen quello.

He explains his disengagement from all creeds by referring to his parentage:

Che nato son d' una monaca greca,
E d' un papasso in Bursia là in Turchia.

Beginning life by murdering his father, he next set out to seek adventures in the world:

E per compagni ne menai con meco
Tutt' i peccati o di turco o di greco,
Anzi quanti ne son giù nell' inferno:
Io n' ho settanta e sette de' mortali,
Che non mi lascian mai la state o 'l verno;
Pensa quanti io n' ho poi de' veniali!

Margutte's humour consists in the baboon-like self-contentment of his infamous confessions, and in the effect they produce upon Morgante, who feels that he has found in him a finished gentleman. After amusing his audience with this puppet for a while, Pulci flings him aside. Margutte, like Pietro Aretino, dies at last of immoderate laughter.[36]

Another of Pulci's own creations is Astarotte, the proud and courteous fiend, summoned by Malagigi to bring Rinaldo from Egypt to Roncesvalles. This feat he accomplishes in a few hours by entering the body of the horse Baiardo. The journey consists of a series of splendid leaps,

[34] Canto xviii. 114, *et seq.*

[35] I have placed in the Appendix a rough plaster cast rather than a true copy of Margutte's admirable comic autobiography. My stanzas cannot pretend to exactitude of rendering or interpretation. The *Morgante* has hitherto been very imperfectly edited; and there are many passages in this speech which would, I believe, puzzle a good Florentine scholar, and which, it is probable, I have misread.

[36] Canto xix. 148.

across lakes, rivers, mountains, seas and cities; and when the paladin hungers, Astarotte spreads a table for him in the wilderness or introduces him invisible into the company of queens at banquet in fair Saragossa. The humour and the fancy of this magic journey are both of a high order.[37] Yet Astarotte is made to serve a second purpose. Into his mouth Pulci places all his theological speculations, and makes him reason learnedly like Mephistophilis:

> Of Providence, foreknowledge, will, and fate,
> Fixed fate, free will, foreknowledge absolute.

He is introduced in these lines:[38]

> Uno spirto chiamato è Astarotte,
> Molto savio, terribil, molto fero,
> Questo si sta giù nell' infernal grotte;
> Non è spirto folletto, egli è più nero.

Of his noble descent from the highest of created intelligences Astarotte is well aware:[39]

> Io era Serafin de' principali . . .
> Io fui già Serafin più di te degno.

He is in earnest to prove that courtesy exists in Hell:[40]

> Chè gentilezza è bene anche in inferno . . .
> Non creder, nello inferno anche fra noi
> Gentilezza non sia.

When Malagigi questions him concerning divine foreknowledge and his own state in Hell, he replies with a complete theory of sin and punishment founded upon the doctrine of freewill.[41] The angels sinned with knowledge. Therefore for them there is no redemption. Adam sinned in ignorance. Therefore there is hope for all men, and a probability of final restitution for the whole human race:[42]

> Forse che 'l vero dopo lungo errore
> Adorerete tutti di concordia,
> E troverete ognum misericordia.

Astarotte's own torment in Hell causes him bitter anguish; but he recognises the justice of God, and knowing that the sentence of damnation

[37] Cantos xxv., xxvi.

[38] Canto xxv. 119. This distinction between the fallen angels and the *spiriti folletti* deserves to be noticed. The latter were light and tricksy spirits, on whom not even a magician could depend. Marsilio sent two of them in a magic mirror to Charlemagne (xxv. 92), and Astarotte warned Malagigi expressly against their vanity (xxv. 160, 161). Fairies, *feux follets*, and the lying spirits of modern spiritualists seem to be of this family. Translations from Astarotte's dialogue will be found in the Appendix.

[39] Canto xxv. 159, 208.

[40] *Ibid.* 161; xxvi. 83.

[41] Canto xxv. 141-158; translation in Appendix.

[42] *Ibid.* 233.

cannot be cancelled, he is too courageous to complain. When Rinaldo offers to intercede for him, he answers:[43]

> Il buon volero accetto;
> Per noi fien sempre perdute le chiavi,
> Maestà lesa, infinito è il difetto:
> O felici Cristian, voi par che lavi
> Una lacrima sol col pugno al petto,
> E dir: Signor, tibi soli peccavi;
> Noi peccammo una volta, e in sempiterno
> Rilegati siam tutti nello inferno.
> Chè pur se dopo un milione e mille
> Di secol noi sperassim rivedere
> Di quell' Amor le minime faville,
> Ancor sarebbe ogni peso leggiere:
> Ma che bisogna far queste postille?
> Se non si può, non si debbe volere;
> Ond' io ti priego, che tu sia contento
> Che noi mutiamo altro ragionamento.

There is great refinement in this momentary sadness of Astarotte, followed by his return to more cheerful topics. He is the Italian counterpart of Marlowe's fiend, that melancholy demon of the North, who tempts his victim by the fascination of mere horror.[44] Like Mephistophilis, again, Astarotte is ready to satisfy the curiosity of mortals, and condescends to amuse them with elfish tricks.[45] He explains to Rinaldo that it is quite a mistake to suppose that there are no inhabited lands beyond the Straits of Gibraltar. The earth, he says, is round, and can be circumnavigated; and cities full of people, worshipping our planets and our sun, are found in the antipodes. Hercules ought to blush for having fixed his pillars where he did.[46] The good understanding estab-

[43] Canto xxv. 284.

[44] *Doctor Faustus*, act i. Scene with Mephistophilis in a Franciscan's habit.

[45] The scene in the banquet-hall at Saragossa (xxv. 292-305) is very similar to some of the burlesque scenes in *Doctor Faustus*.

[46] Canto xxv. 228-231. Astarotte's discourses upon theology and physical geography are so learned that this part of the *Morgante* was by Tasso ascribed to Ficino. It is not improbable that Pulci derived some of the ideas from Ficino, but the style is entirely his own. The sonnets he exchanged with Franco prove, moreover, that he was familiar with the treatment of grave themes in a burlesque style. In acknowledging the help of Poliziano he is quite frank (xxv. 115-117, 169; xxviii. 138-149). What that help exactly was, we do not know. But there is nothing whatever to justify the tradition that Poliziano was the real author of the *Morgante*. Probably he directed Pulci's reading; and I think it not impossible, judging by one line in Canto xxv. (stanza 115, line 4), that he directed Pulci's attention to the second of the two poems out of which the narrative was wrought. If we were to ascribe all the passages in the *Morgante* that display curious knowledge to Pulci's friends, we might claim the discourse on the antipodes for Toscanelli and the debates on the angelic nature for Palmieri. Such criticism is, however, far fetched and laboriously hypothetical. Pulci lived in an intellectual atmosphere highly charged with speculation of all kinds, and his poem reflected the opinion of his age. His own methods of composition and the relation in which he stood to other poets of the age are explained in two passages of the *Morgante* (xxv. 117; xxviii. 138-149), where he disclaims all share of humanistic erudition, and expresses his indifference to the solemn academies of the learned. See translation in Appendix.

lished between Astarotte and Rinaldo on their journey is one of the prettiest incidents of this strange poem. When they part, the fiend and the paladin have become firm friends. Astarotte vows henceforth to serve Rinaldo for love; and Rinaldo promises to free him from Malagigi's power.[47]

Pulci dealt with the Carolingian Cycle in what may be termed a *bourgeois* spirit. Whether humorous or earnest, he maintained the tone of Florentine society; and his 'Morgante' reflects the peculiar conditions of the Medicean circle at the date of its composition. The second great poem on the same group of legends, Boiardo's 'Orlando Innamorato,' transports us into a very different social and intellectual atmosphere. The highborn Count of Scandiano, reciting his cantos in the huge square castle surrounded by its moat, which still survives to speak of mediæval Italy in the midst of Ferrara, had but little in common with Luigi Pulci, whose Tuscan fun and satire amused the merchant princes of the Via Larga. The value of the 'Orlando Innamorato' for the student of Italian development is principally this, that it is the most purely chivalrous poem of the Renaissance. Composed before the French invasion, and while the classical Revival was still unaccomplished, we find in it an echo of an earlier semi-feudal civility. Unlike the other literary performances of that age, which were produced for the most part by professional humanists, it was the work of a nobleman to whom feats of arms and the chase were familiar, who disdained the common folk (*popolaccio*, *canaglia*, as he always calls them), and whose ideal both of life and of art was contained in this couplet:[48]

> E raccontare il pregio e 'l grande onore
> Che donan l' armi giunte con l' amore.

Matteo Maria Boiardo was almost an exact contemporary of Pulci. He was born about 1434 at his hereditary fief of Scandiano, a village seven miles from Reggio, at the foot of the Apennines, celebrated for its excellent vineyards. His mother was Lucia Strozzi, a member of the Ferrarese house, connected by descent with the Strozzi of Florence. At the age of twenty-eight he married Taddea Gonzaga, daughter of the Count of Novellara. He lived until 1494, when he died at the same time as Pico and Poliziano, in the year of Charles VIII.'s invasion, two years after the death of Lorenzo de' Medici, and four years before

[47] Canto xxvi. 82-88. We may specially note these phrases:

> Astarotte, e' mi duole
> Il tuo partir, quanto fussi fratello;
> E nell' inferno ti credo che sia
> Gentilezza, amicizia e cortesia.
>
> . . . .
>
> Chè di servirti non mi fia fatica;
> E basta solo Astarotte tu dica,
> Ed io ti sentirò sin dello inferno.

[48] Book II. canto viii. 1. All references will be made to Panizzi's edition of the *Orlando Innamorato*, London, Pickering, 1830.

Ficino. These dates are not unimportant as fixing the exact epoch of Boiardo's literary activity. At the Court of Ferrara, where the Count of Scandiano enjoyed the friendship of Duke Borso and Duke Ercole, this bard of chivalry held a position worthy of his noble rank and his great talents. The princes of the House of Este employed him as ambassador in diplomatic missions of high trust and honour. He also administered for them the government of Reggio and Modena, their two chief subject cities. As a ruler, he was celebrated for his clemency and for his indifference to legal formalities. An enemy, Panciroli, wrote of him: 'He was a man of excessive kindness, more fit for writing poems than for punishing crimes.' He is even reported to have held that no offence deserved capital punishment—an opinion which at that period could only have been seriously entertained in Italy, and which even there was strangely at variance with the temper of the petty tyrants. Well versed in Greek and Latin literature, he translated Herodotus, parts of Xenophon, the 'Golden Ass' of Apuleius, and the 'Ass' of Lucian into Italian. He also versified Lucian's 'Timon' for the stage, and wrote Latin poems of fair merit. His lyrics addressed to Antonia Caprara prove that, like Lorenzo de' Medici, he was capable of following the path of Petrarch without falling into Petrarchistic mannerism.[49] But his literary fame depends less upon these minor works than on the 'Orlando Innamorato,' a masterpiece of inventive genius, which furnished Ariosto with the theme of the 'Orlando Furioso.' Without the 'Innamorato' the 'Furioso' is meaningless. The handling and structure of the romance, the characters of the heroes and heroines, the conception of Love and Arms as the double theme of romantic poetry, the interpolation of *Novelle* in the manner of Boccaccio, and the magic machinery by which the poem is conducted, are due to the originality of Boiardo. Ariosto adopted this plot, continued the story where he left it, and brought it to a close; so that, taken together, both poems form one gigantic narrative, of about 100,000 lines, which has for its main subject the love and the marriage of Ruggiero and Bradamante, mythical progenitors of the Estensi. Yet because the style of Boiardo is rough and provincial, while that of Ariosto is by all consent 'divine,' Boiardo has been almost forgotten by posterity.

Chivalry at no time took firm root in Italy, where the first act of the Communes upon their achievement of independence had been to suppress feudalism by forcing the nobles to reside as burghers within their walls. The true centres of national vitality were the towns. Here the Latin race assimilated to itself the Teutonic elements which might, if left to flourish in the country, have given a different direction to Italian

[49] *Sonetti e Canzone* [*sic*] *del poeta clarissimo Matteo Maria Boiardo Conte di Scandiano*, Milano, 1845. The descriptions of natural beauty, especially of daybreak and the morning star, of dewy meadows, and of flowers, in which these lyrics abound, are very charming and at all points worthy of the fresh delightful inspiration of Boiardo's epic verse. Nor are they deficient in metrical subtlety; notice especially the intricate rhyming structure of a long Canto, pp. 44-49.

development. During the fourteenth and fifteenth centuries the immense extension of mercantile activity, the formation of tyrannies, the secular importance of the Papacy, and the absorption of the cultivated classes in humanistic studies, removed the people ever further from feudal traditions. Even the new system of warfare, whereby the scions of noble families took pay from citizens and priests for the conduct of military enterprises, tended to destroy the stronghold of chivalrous feeling in a nation that grew to regard the profession of arms as another branch of commerce. Still Italy could not wholly separate herself from the rest of Europe, and there remained provinces where a kind of semi-feudalism flourished. The most important of these undoubtedly was the kingdom of Naples, subject to alternate influence from France and Spain, and governed by monarchs at frequent warfare with their barons. The second was Ferrara, where the House of Este had maintained unbroken lordship from the period when still the Empire was a power in Italy. Here the ancient Lombard traditions of chivalry, the customs of the Marca Amorosa, and the literature of the troubadours still lingered.[50] Externally at least, the manners of the Court were feudal, however far removed its princes may have been in spirit from the ideal of knighthood. In Ferrara, therefore, more than in Florence and Venice, those cities of financiers and traders, could the romance of chivalry be seriously treated by a poet who admired the knightly virtues, and looked back upon the days of Arthur and of Roland as a golden age of honour, far removed but real. While the Humanists of Florence indulged their fancy with dreams of Virgil's Saturnian reign, the baron of Ferrara refashioned a visionary world from the wrecks of old romance.[51]

Boiardo did not disdain to assume the style of a minstrel addressing his courtly audience with compliments and *congés* at the beginning and ending of each canto. The first opens with these words:

> Signori e cavalieri che v' adunati
> Per odir cose dilettose e nuove,
> State attenti, quieti, ed ascoltati
> La bella istoria che 'l mio canto muove.

But his spirit is always knightly, and he refrains from the quaint pietism of Pulci's preambles. He is no mere jongleur or *Cantatore da Banca*, but a new Sir Tristram, celebrating in heroic verse the valorous deeds and amorous emotions of which he had himself partaken. Nor does he, like Ariosto, appear before us as a courtier accomplished in the arts of flattery, or as a man of letters anxious above all things to refine his style. Neither the Court life of Italy nor the humanism of the revival had destroyed in him the spirit of old-world freedom and noble courtesy. At the same time he was so far imbued with the culture of the Renais-

[50] See Vol. I., p. 850.
[51] See the exordium to the Second Book, where it appears that the gentle poet caressed a vain hope that the peace of Italy in the second half of the fifteenth century was destined to revive chivalry.

sance as to appreciate the value of poetic unity and to combine certain elements of classic learning with the material of romance. Setting out with the aim of connecting all the Frankish legends in one poem, he made Orlando his hero; but he perceived that the element of love, which added so great a charm to the Arthurian Cycle, had hitherto been neglected by the minstrels of Charlemagne. He therefore resolved to tell a new tale of the mighty Roland; and the originality of his poem consisted in the fact that he treated the material of the *Chansons de Geste* in the spirit of the Breton legends.[52] Turpin, he asserts with a grave irony, had hidden away the secret of Orlando's love; but he will unfold the truth, believing that no knight was ever the less noble for his love. Accordingly the passion of Orlando for 'the fairest of her sex, Angelica,' like the wrath of Achilles in the 'Iliad,' is the mainspring of Boiardo's poem. To his genius we owe the creation of that fascinating princess of the East, as well as the invention of the fountains of Cupid and Merlin, which cause the alternate loves and hates of his heroes and heroines—the whole of that closely woven mesh of sentiment in which the adventures and the warlike achievements of Paladins and Saracens alike are involved.

In dealing with his subject Boiardo is serious—as serious, that is to say, as a writer of romance can be.[53] His belief in chivalry itself is earnest, though the presentation of knightly prowess runs into intentional extravagance. A dash of Italian merriment mingles with his enthusiasm; but he has none of Pulci's sceptical satiric humour, none of Ariosto's all-pervasive irony. The second thoughts of the burlesque poet or of the humorous philosopher do not cross the warp of his conception, and his exaggerations are romantic. Such a poem as the 'Orlando Innamorato' could not have been planned or executed in Italy at any other period or under any other circumstances. A few years after Boiardo's death Italy was plunged into the wars that led to her enslavement. Charles V. was born and Luther was beginning to shake Germany. The forces of the Renaissance were in full operation, destroying the faiths and fervours of the mediæval world, closing the old æon with laughter and lamentation, raising new ideals as yet imperfectly apprehended. Meanwhile Boiardo, whose life coincided with the final period of Italian independence, uttered the last note of the bygone age. His poem, chivalrous, free, joyous, with not one stain of Ariosto's servility or of Tasso's melancholy, corresponded to a brief and passing moment in the evolution of the national art. In the pure and vivid

[52] See the opening of Book II. Canto xviii. where Boiardo compares the Courts of Arthur and of Charlemagne.

[53] The acute and learned critic Pio Rajna, whose two massive works of scholarlike research, *I Reali di Francia* (Bologna, 1872), and *Le Fonti dell' Orlando Furioso* (Firenze, 1876), have thrown a flood of light upon Chivalrous Romance literature in Italy, is at pains to prove that the *Orlando Innamorato* contains a vein of conscious humour. See *Le Fonti*, &c., pp. 24-27. I agree with him that Boiardo treated his subject playfully. But it must be remembered that he was far from wishing to indulge a secret sarcasm like Ariosto, or to make open fun of chivalry like Fortiguerra.

beauty which distinguishes it, the sunset of chivalry and the sunrise of modern culture blend their colours, as in some far northern twilight of midsummer night. Joyousness pervades its cantos and is elemental to its inspiration—the joy of open nature, of sensual though steadfast love, of strong limbs and eventful living, of restless activity, of childlike security. Boiardo's style reminds us somewhat of Benozzo Gozzoli in painting, or of Piero di Cosimo, who used the skill of the Renaissance to express the cheerful *naïveté* of a less self-conscious time. It is sad to read the last stanza of the 'Innamorato,' cut short ere it was half completed by the entry of the French into Italy, and to know that so free and freshly tuned a 'native wood-note wild' would never sound again.[54] When Ariosto repieced the broken thread, the spirit of the times was changed. Servitude, adulation, irony, and the meridian splendour of Renaissance art had succeeded to independence, frankness, enthusiasm and the poetry of natural enjoyment. Far more magnificent is Ariosto's Muse; but we lack the spontaneity of the elder poet. And as the years advance, the change is more apparent toward decay. The genius of Boiardo might be compared to some high-born lad, bred in the country, pure-hearted, muscular, brave, fair to look upon. That of Ariosto is studious and accomplished with the smile of worldly sarcasm upon his lips. The elegances of Bembo and the Petrarchisti remind one of a hectic scented fop, emasculate and artificial. Aretino resembles his own *bardassonacci*, *paggi da taverna*, flaunting meretricious charms with brazen impudence. Tasso in the distance wears a hair shirt beneath his armour of parade; he is a Jesuit's pupil, crossing himself when he awakes from love-dreams and reveries of pleasure. It was probably the discord between Boiardo's spirit and the prevailing temper of the sixteenth century, far more than the roughness of his verse or the provinciality of his language, that caused him to be so strangely and completely forgotten. In the Italy of Machiavelli and the Borgias, of Michelangelo and Julius II., his aims, enthusiasms and artistic ideals found alike no sympathy. To class him with his own kind, we must go beyond the Alps and seek his brethren in France or England.

Boiardo's merit as a constructive artist can best be measured by the analysis of his plot. Crowded as the 'Orlando Innamorato' is with incidents and episodes, and inexhaustible as may be the luxuriance of the poet's fancy, the unity of his romance is complete. From the moment of Angelica's appearance in the first canto, the whole action depends upon her movements. She withdraws the Paladins to Albracca, and forces Charlemagne to bear the brunt of Marsilio's invasion alone. She restores Orlando to the French host before Montalbano. It is her ring which frees the fated Ruggiero from Atalante's charms. The na-

[54] Mentre che io canto, o Dio redentore,
Vedo l' Italia tutta a fiamma e foco
Per questi Galli, che con gran valore
Vengon, per disertar non so che loco.

Compare II. xxxi. 50; III. i. 2.

tions of the earth are in motion. East, West, and South and North send forth their countless hordes to combat; but these vast forces are controlled by one woman's caprice, and events are so handled by the poet as to make the fate of myriads waver in the balance of her passions. We might compare Boiardo's romance to an immense web, in which a variety of scenes and figures are depicted by the constant addition of new threads. None of the old threads is wasted; not one is merely superfluous. If one is dropped for a moment and lost to sight, it reappears again. The slightest incidents lead to the gravest results. Narratives of widely different character are so interwoven as to aid each other, introducing fresh agents, combining these with those whom we have learned to know, but leaving the grand outlines of the main design untouched.

The miscellaneous details which enliven a tale of chivalry, are grouped round four chief centres—Paris, where the poem opens with the tournament that introduces Angelica, and where, at the end of the second book, all the actors are assembled for the supreme struggle between Christendom and Islam; Albracca, where Angelica is besieged in the far East; Biserta, where the hosts of pagan Agramante muster, and the hero Ruggiero is brought upon the scene; Montalbano, where Charlemagne sustains defeat at the hands of Agramante, Rodamonte, Marsilio, and Ruggiero. In order to combine such distant places in one action, Boiardo was obliged to set geography and time at defiance. Between Tartary and Circassia, France and Spain, Africa and Hungary, the knights make marches and countermarches within the space of a few weeks or even days. All arrive at the same dangerous gates and passes, the same seductive lakes and gardens; for the magical machinery of the romance was more important to the poet's scheme than cosmographical conditions. His more than dramatic contempt for distance was indispensable in the conduct of a romance which admitted of no pause in the succession of attractive incidents, and was also pardonable in an age devoid of accurate geography. His chief aim was to secure novelty, excitement, variety, ideal unity.

Boiardo further showed his grasp of art by the emphatic presentation of the chief personages, whose action determined the salient features of his tale. It is impossible to forget Angelica after her first entrance on the scene at Paris. In like manner Marfisa at Albracca, Rodamonte in the council-chamber at Biserta, Ruggiero on the heights of Mount Carena, Orlando entering the combat before Albracca, Mandricardo passing forth unarmed and unattended to avenge his father's death, are brought so vividly before our eyes, that the earliest impression of each character remains with us in all their subsequent appearances. The inferior actors are introduced with less preparation and diminished emphasis, because they have to occupy subordinate positions, and to group themselves around the heroes; and thus the whole vast poem is like a piece of arras-work, where the strongest definition of form, and the most striking colours, serve to throw into relief the principal figures amid a multitude of minor shapes. Not less skill is manifested in the preservation of the types of character outlined in these first descriptions. To vary the specific qualities of all those knights engaged in the same pursuit of love and arms, was extremely difficult. Yet Boiardo, sometimes working on the lines laid down by earlier romancers, sometimes inventing wholly new conceptions (as in the case of Rodamonte, Ruggiero, Marfisa, Brandiamente), may be said to have succeeded in this master-stroke of art. The Homeric heroes are scarcely less firmly and subtly differentiated than his champions of chivalry.

Orlando is the ideal of Christian knighthood, fearless, indifferent to wealth, chaste, religious, respectful in his love, courteous toward women, swift to wrath, but generous even in his rage, exerting his strength only when the occasion is worthy of him.[55] His one weakness is the passion for Angelica. Twice he refuses for her sake to accompany Dudone to the help of his liege lord, and in the fight at Montalbano he is careless of Christendom so long as he can win his lady.[56] Studying Boiardo's delineation of love-lunacy in Orlando, we understand how Ariosto was led by it to the conception of the 'Furioso.' Rinaldo is cast in a somewhat inferior mould. Lion-hearted, fierce, rebellious against Charles, prone to love and hate excessively, he is the type of the feudal baron, turbulent and troublesome to his suzerain. Astolfo, slight, vain, garrulous, fond of finery and flirting, boastful, yet as fearless as the leopards on his shield, and winning hearts by his courtesy and grace, offers a spirited contrast to the massive vigour of Rinaldo. It was a master-stroke of humour to have provided this fop of a Paladin with the lance of Argalia, whereby his physical weakness is supplemented and his bravery becomes a match for the muscles of the doughtiest champions.[57] Brandimarte presents another aspect of the chivalrous ideal. Fidelity is his chief virtue—loyalty to his love, Fiordelisa, and his hero, Orlando, combined with a delightful frankness and the freshness of untainted youth. He is not wise, but boyish, amorous, of a simple, trustful soul; a kind of Italian Sir Bors. Ferraguto, on the contrary, is all fire and fury, as petulantly fierce in love as in arms, so hot in his temerity that even at times he can forget the laws of honour.[58] Mandricardo's distinctive quality (besides that of generous daring, displayed in his solitary and unarmed quest of Orlando, and in the achievement of Hector's armour) is singular good fortune. Ruggiero has for

[55] Orlando was not handsome (II. iii. 63):

avea folte le ciglia,
E l' un de gli occhi alquanto stralunava.

[56] See his prayer, II. xxix. 36, 37.

[57] See the description of him in the tournament (I. ii. 63, iii. 4), when he saves the honour of Christendom to the surprise of everybody including himself. Again (I. vii. 45-65), when he defies and overthrows Gradasso, and liberates Charles from prison. The irony of both situations reveals a master's hand.

[58] For instance, when he attacks Argalia with his sword, contrary to stipulation, after being unhorsed by him (I. i. 71-73). The fury of Ferraguto in this scene is one of Boiardo's most brilliant episodes.

his special mark victorious beauty, blent with a courtesy and loftiness of soul, that opens his heart to romantic love, and renders him peerless among youthful warriors. Boiardo has spared no pains to impress our imagination with the potency of his unrivalled comeliness.[59] He moves before our eyes like the angelic knight in Mantegna's 'Madonna of the Victory,' or like Giorgione's picture of the fair-haired and mail-clad donzel, born to conquer by the might of beauty. Agramante, the Eastern Emperor, whose council is composed of thirty-two crowned heads, enhances by his arrogance of youth the world-worn prudence of old Charlemagne. Marfisa, the Amazonian Indian Queen, who has the force of twenty knights, and is as cruel in her courage as a famished tigress, sets off the gentler prowess of Brandiamante, Rinaldo's heroic sister. Rodamonte is the blustering, atheistic, insolent young Ajax, standing alone against armies, and hurling defiance at heaven from the midst of a sinking navy.[60] Agricane is distinguished as the knight who loves fighting for its own sake, and disdains culture; Sacripante, as the gentle and fearless suitor of Angelica; Gradasso, as the hyperbolical champion of the Orient, inflamed with a romantic desire to gain Durlindana and Baiardo, the enchanted sword and horse. Gano and Truffaldino, among these paragons of honour, are notable traitors, the one brave when he chooses to abandon craft, the other cowardly. Brunello is the Thersites of the company, a perfect thief, misshapen, mischievous, consummate in his guile.[61] Malagise deals in magic, and has a swarm of demons at his back for all exigences. Turpin's chivalry is tempered with a subtle flavour of the priest, exposing him to Boiardo's mockery. Of Oliver and Ogier we hear, accidentally perhaps, but little. Such are some of Boiardo's personages. Not a few were given to him by the old romancers; but these he has new-fashioned to his needs.[62] Others he has moulded from his own imagination with such plastic force that they fall short in no respect of the time-honoured standard. It is no slight tribute to his creative power that we recognise a real fraternity between these puppets of his fancy and the mythic heroes with whom they are associated. As Boiardo left the actors in his drama, so Ariosto took them up and with but slight change treated them in his continuation of the tale.

Women, with the exception of Marfisa and Brandiamante, fare but

[59] His epithets are always *fiorito, fior di cortesia, di franchezza fiore,* &c For the effect of his beauty, see II. xxi. 49, 50. The education of Ruggiero by Atalante was probably suggested to Boiardo by the tale of Cheiron and Achilles. See II. i. 74, 75.

[60] See II. i. 56, for Rodamonte's first appearance; for his atheism, II. iii. 22:

> Che sol il mio buon brando e l' armatura
> E la mazza, ch' io porto, e 'l destrier mio
> E l' animo, ch' io ho, sono il mio Dio.

[61] II. iii. 40.

[62] In Bello's *Mambriano,* for instance, we have a very lively picture of the amorous and vain Astolfo. Pulci supplies us with even a more impressive Orlando than Boiardo's hero, while his Amazonian heroines, Meridiana and Antea, are at least rough sketches for Marfisa. It was Boiardo's merit to have grasped these characters and drawn them with a fulness of minute detail that enhances their vitality.

ill at Boiardo's hands. He seems to have conceived of female character as a compound of fickleness, infidelity, malice, falsehood, and light love. Angelica is little better than a seductive witch, who dotes on Rinaldo, and yet contrives to make use of Orlando, luring him to do her purpose by false promises.[63] Falerina and Dragontina are sorceresses, apt for all iniquity and guile. Morgana and Alcina display the capricious loves and inhuman spites of fairies. Origille is a subtle traitress, beautiful enough to deceive Orlando, but as poisonous as a serpent. Even the ladies who are intended to be amiable, show but a low standard of morality.[64] Leodilla, princess of the Far Isles, glories in adultery, and hates Orlando for his constancy to Angelica in absence.[65] Fiordelisa is false in thought to Brandimarte, when she sees Rinaldo sleeping in the twilight. The picture, however, of the slumbering warrior and the watchful maiden is so fresh and true to Boiardo's genius that it deserves quotation:[66]

Upon his steed forthwith hath sprung the knight,
And with the damsel rideth fast away;
Not far they fared, when slowly waned the light,
And forced them to dismount and there to stay.
Rinaldo 'neath a tree slept all the night;
Close at his side the lovely lady lay:
But the strong magic of wise Merlin's well
Had on the baron's temper cast a spell.

He now can sleep anigh that beauteous dame;
Nor of her neighbourhood have any care;
Erewhile a sea, a flood, a raging flame
Would not have stayed his quick desire, I swear:
To clasp so fair a creature without shame,
Walls, mountains, he'd have laid in ruins there;
Now side by side they sleep, and nought he recks;
While her, methinks, far other thoughts perplex.

The air, meanwhile, was growing bright around,
Although not yet the sun his face had shown;
Some stars the tranquil brows of heaven still crowned;
The birds upon the trees sang one by one:
Dark night had flown; bright day was not yet found:
Then toward Rinaldo turned the maid alone;
For she with morning light had cast off sleep,
While he upon the grass still slumbered deep.

Beauteous he was, and but a stripling then;
Strong-thewed and lithe, and with a lively face;
Broad in the chest, but in the haunches thin;
The lady gazed, smit with his manly grace:
His beard scarce budded upon cheek and chin:
Gazing, she almost fainted in that place,
And took such pleasure in so sweet a sight
That nought she heeds beyond this one delight.

[63] Her arts and their success are splendidly set forth, I. xxv. xxvi.

[64] In proem to II. xii., Boiardo makes an excuse, imitated by Ariosto, to his lady for this bad treatment of women.

[65] Leodilla's story is found in I. xxi. xxii. xxiv. 14-17, 44.

[66] I. iii. 47-50.

Love, as conceived by Boiardo, though a powerful and steadfast passion, is not spiritual. The knights love like centaurs, and fight like bulls for the privilege of paying suit to their ladies. Rinaldo and Orlando meet in deadly duel for Angelica; Rodamonte and Ferraguto dispute Doralice, though the latter does not care for her, and only asserts his right to dwell in thought upon her charms. Orlando and Agricane break their courteous discourse outside Albracca to fight till one of them is killed, merely because the name of Angelica has intervened. For Boiardo's descriptions of love returned, and crowned with full fruition, the reader may be referred to two magnificent passages in the episodes of Leodilla and Fiordelisa.[67] Poetically noble in spite of their indelicacy, these pictures of sensuous and natural enjoyment might be paralleled with the grand frankness of Venetian painting. It is to be regretted for Boiardo's credit as an artist in expression, that more than a bare reference to them is here impossible.

Boiardo's conception of friendship or fraternity in arms is finer. The delineation of affection generated by mutual courtesy under the most trying conditions of intercourse, which binds together the old rivals Iroldo and Prasildo, has something in it truly touching.[68] The same passion of comradeship finds noble expression in the stanzas uttered by Orlando, when he recognises Rinaldo's shield suspended by Aridano near Morgana's Lake.[69] It must be remembered that the cousins had recently parted as foes, after a fierce battle for Angelica before Albracca:

Hearing these dulcet words, the Count began
Little by little of his will to yield;
Backward already he withdrew a span,
When, gazing on the bridge and guarded field,
Force was that he the armour bright should scan
Which erst Rinaldo bore—broad sword and shield:
Then weeping, 'Who hath done me this despite?'
He cried: 'Oh, who hath slain my perfect knight?

'Here wast thou killed by foulest treachery
Of that false robber on this slippery bridge;
For all the world could not have conquered thee
In fair fight, front to front, and edge to edge:
Cousin, from heaven incline thine ear to me!
Where now thou reignest, list thy lord and liege!
Me who so loved thee, though my brief misprision,
Through too much love, wrought 'twixt our lives division.

'I crave thy pardon: pardon me, I pray,
If e'er I did thee wrong, sweet cousin mine!
I was thine ever, as I am alway,
Though false suspicion, or vain love malign,
And jealous blindness, on an evil day,
Brought me to cross my furious brand with thine:
Yet all the while I loved thee—love thee now;
Mine was the fault, and only mine, I vow.

[67] I. xxii. 24-27; I. xix. 60-65.
[68] I. xvii. 21, 22.
[69] II. vii. 50.

'What traitorous wolf ravening for blood was he
Who thus debarred us twain from kind return
To concord sweet and sweet tranquillity,
Sweet kisses, and sweet tears of souls that yearn?
This is the anguish keen that conquers me,
That now I may not to thy bosom turn,
And speak, and beg for pardon, ere I part;
This is the grief, the dole that breaks my heart!'

Scarcely less beautiful is the feeling which binds Brandimarte to the great Count, the inferior to the superior hero, making him ready to release his master from Manodante's prison at the price of his own liberty.[70] Boiardo devotes the exordium of the seventh Canto of the third Book to a panegyric of chivalrous friendship:

Far more than health, far more than strength is worth,
Nay more than pleasure, more than honour vain,
Is friendship tried alike in dole and mirth:
For when one love doth join the hearts of twain,
Their woes are halved, their joys give double birth
To joy, by interchange of grief and pain;
And when doubts rise, with free and open heart
Each calls his friend, who gladly bears a part.

What profit is there in much pearls and gold,
Or power, or proud estate, or royal reign?
Lacking a friend, mere wealth is frosty cold:
He who loves not, and is not loved again,
From him true joys their perfect grace withhold:
And this I say, since now across the main
Brave Brandimarte drives his flying ship
To help Orlando, drawn by comradeship.

Next to bravery the poet's favourite virtue is courtesy. It is enough to mention Orlando's gentle forbearance with Agricane at Albracca, their evening conversation in the midst of a bloody duel, and the hero's sorrow when he has wounded his opponent to the death.[71] Of the same quality is the courteous behaviour of Rinaldo and Gradasso before a deadly encounter, the aid afforded to Marfisa by Rinaldo in the midst of their duel, and the graceful sympathy of Astolfo for Brandimarte, whom he has unhorsed.[72] But the two passages which illustrate Boiardo's ideal of the chivalrous character, as blent of bravery and courtesy, of intelligence and love, are Orlando's discourse with Agricane and his speech to Morgana's maiden. In the first of these the Count and King have fought till nightfall. Then they agree to sleep together side by side, and to resume the combat at daybreak. Before they settle for the night, they talk:[73]

After the sun below the hills was laid
And with bright stars the sky began to glow,

[70] II. xii. 14, *et seq.*
[71] I. xvi. 36-44; xviii. 39-47; xix. 15, 16.
[72] I. v. 7-12; xix. 47; ix. 55-57.
[73] I. xviii. 39-47.

Unto the King these words Orlando said:
'What shall we do, now that the day is low?'
Then Agrican made answer, 'Make our bed
Together here, amid the herbs that grow;
And then to-morrow with the dawn of light
We can return and recommence the fight.'

No sooner said, than straight they were agreed:
Each tied his horse to trees that near them grew;
Then down they lay upon the grassy mead—
You might have thought they were old friends and true,
So close and careless couched they in the reed.
Orlando nigh unto the fountain drew,
And Agrican hard by the forest laid
His length beneath a mighty pine-tree's shade.

Herewith the twain began to hold debate
Of fitting things and meet for noble knights.
The Count looked up to heaven and cried, 'How great
And fair is yonder frame of glittering lights,
Which God, the mighty monarch, did create;
The silvery moon, and stars that gem our nights,
The light of day, yea, and the lustrous sun,
For us poor men God made them every one!'

But Agrican: 'Full well I apprehend
It is your wish toward faith our talk to turn;
Of science less than nought I comprehend;
Nay, when I was a boy, I would not learn,
But broke my master's head to make amend
For his much prating; no one since did yearn
To teach me book or writing, such the dread
Wherewith I filled them for my hardihead.

'And so I let my boyish days flow by,
In hunting, feats of arms, and horsemanship;
Nor is it meet, meseems, for chivalry
To pore the livelong day on scholarship.
True knights should strive to prove their skill, say I,
And strength of limb in noble fellowship;
Leave priests and teaching men from books to learn.
I know enough, thank God, to serve my turn.'

Then spake the Count: 'Thus far we both agree;
Arms are the chief prime honour of a knight.
Yet knowledge brings no shame that I can see,
But rather fame, as fields with flowers are bright;
More like an ox, a stock, a stone is he
Who never thinks of God's eternal light;
Nor without learning can we rightly dwell
On his high majesty adorable.'

Then Agrican, 'Small courtesy it were,
War with advantage so complete to wage!
My nature I have laid before you bare;
I know full well that you are learned and sage;
Therefore to answer you I do not care.
Sleep if you like; in sleep your soul assuage;
Or if you choose with me to hold discourse,
I look for talk of love, and deeds of force.

'Now, I beseech you, answer me the truth
Of what I ask, upon a brave man's faith:
Are you the great Orlando, in good sooth,
Whose name and fame the whole world echoeth?
Whence are you come, and why? And since your youth
Were you by love enthralled? For story saith
That any knight who loves not, though he seem
To sight alive, yet lives but in a dream.'

Then spake the Count: 'Orlando sure am I
Who both Almonte and his brother slew.
Imperious love hath lost me utterly,
And made me journey to strange lands and new;
And, for I fain would thus in amity
Prolong discourse, therefore I tell you true,
She who now lies within Albracca's wall,
Gallafron's daughter, holds my heart in thrall.'

This unlucky mention of Angelica stirs the rage of Agricane, and the two men fight in the moonlight beneath the forest trees till the young King is wounded to the death—a splendid subject for some imaginative painter's pencil. We may notice in this dialogue the modification of chivalry occasioned by Italian respect for culture. Boiardo exalts the courage of the educated gentleman above the valour of a man-at-arms. In the conversation between Orlando and Morgana's maiden he depicts another aspect of the knightly ideal. The fairy has made Orlando offer of inestimable treasures, but he answers that indifference to riches is the sign of a noble heart:[74]

Orlando smiling heard what she would say,
But scarce allowed her time her speech to end,
Seeing toward riches of the sort the fay
Proffered, his haughty soul he would not bend;
Wherefore he spake: 'It irked me not to-day
My very life unto the death to spend;
For only perils and great toils sustain
Honour of chivalry without a stain.

'But for the sake of gold or silver gear,
I would not once have drawn my brand so bright;
For he who holds mere gain of money dear
Hath set himself to labour infinite;
The more he gets the less his gains appear;
Nor can he ever sate his appetite;
They who most have, still care for more to spend,
Wherefore this way of life hath ne'er an end.'

Having seen the knights in their more generous moments, we ought to bear in mind that they are capable of blustering, boasting, and exchanging foul abuse like humanists. One reference will suffice. Orlando and Rinaldo quarrel at Albracca and defy each other to combat. Before fighting they indulge in elaborate caricatures and vilifications, from

[74] I. xxv. 13, 14.

which it would appear, to say the least, that these champions of Christendom were the subject of much scandalous gossip.[75]

Human nature, unsophisticated and unqualified, with the crude impulses and the contradictions proper to an unreflective age, has been studied by Boiardo for his men and women. His power of expressing the passions by natural signs might win for him the title of the Homer of Chivalry. The love-lamentations of Prasildo, the love-languors of Angelica, the frenzy of Marfisa, the wrath of Ferraguto, the truculency of Rodamonte, the impish craft of Brunello, Origille's cunning, Brandimarte's fervour, Ruggiero's impatience to try his strength in the tournament, and his sudden ecstasy of love for Brandiamante—these and a hundred other instances of vigorous dramatic presentation could be mentioned. In his pictures of scenery and descriptions Boiardo follows nature no less faithfully—and this, be it remembered, in an age which refined on nature and admitted into art only certain chosen phases of her loveliness. Of affectation and elaboration he has none. The freshness of authentic vision gives peculiar vividness to the storm that overtakes Rodamonte in mid-channel; to the garden of Falerina, where Orlando stuffs his casque with roses in order to stop his ears against a Siren's song; to the picture of Morgana combing Ziliante's hair in the midst of her enchanted meadows, and to the scene in which Angelica greets Orlando with a perfumed bath after the battle.[76] The charm of Boiardo's poetry consists in its firm grasp on truth and nature, the spontaneity and immediateness of its painting. He has none of Poliziano's richness, no Virgilian dignity or sweetness, no smooth and sparkling fluency like that of Ariosto. But all that he writes has in it the perfume of the soil, the freedom of the open air; the spirits of the woods and sea and stars are in it. Of his style the most striking merit is rapidity. Almost always unpolished, sometimes even coarse, but invariably spirited and masculine, his verse leaps onward like a greyhound in its swiftness. Story succeeds story with extraordinary speed; and whether of love or arms, they are equally well told. The pathetic novel of Tisbina, Rinaldo's wondrous combat with the griffins and the giants, the lion-hunt at Biserta, the mustering of Agramante's lieges, and the flux and reflux of battle before Montalbano tax the vivid and elastic vigour of Boiardo in five distinct species of rapid narration; and in all of them he proves himself more than adequate to the strain. For ornaments he cared but little, nor did he wait to elaborate similes. A lion at bay, a furious bull, a river foaming to the sea, a swollen torrent, two battling winds, a storm of hail, the clash of thunderclouds, an earthquake, are the figures he is apt to use. The descriptions of Rinaldo, Marfisa and Orlando, may be cited as favourable specimens of his illustrative metaphors.[77] Short phrases like *a guisa di leone*, *a guisa di colomba*, *a guisa di serpente*, *a guisa d' uno drago*, *a guisa di castello*,

[75] I. xxvii. 15-22: xxviii. 4-11.
[76] II. vi. 7-15, 28-42; II. iv. 24-39; II. xiii. 20-23; I. xxv. 38.
[77] I. xxiii. 38, 47; xxvi. 28.

indicate in outline images that aid the poet's thought. But nothing like the polish or minuteness of Ariosto's highly wrought comparisons can be found in the 'Innamorato.' Boiardo's study of the classics had not roused him to the emulation of their decorative beauties. Nor, again, did he attend to cadence in his versification. He would have wondered at the *limæ labor* of the poets who come after him. His own stanzas are forcible, swift, fiery, never pompous or voluptuous, liquid or sonorous. The changes wrought by Poliziano in the structure of *ottava rima*, his majesty and 'linked sweetness long drawn out,' were unknown to Boiardo. Yet those rugged octaves, in spite of their halting pauses at the end of the fifth line, in spite of their frequent repetitions and inequalities of volume, are better adapted to the spirit of his mediæval subject-matter than the sumptuous splendour of more polished versifiers. His diction, in like manner, judged by the standard of the *cinque cento*, is far from choice—loaded with Lombardisms, gaining energy and vividness at the expense of refinement and precision. Thus style and spirit alike removed him from the sympathies of the correct and classic age that followed.

For the student of the earlier Renaissance Boiardo's art has one commanding point of interest. In the romantic treatment of antique motives he is unique. It was the aim of Italian poets after Boccaccio to effect a fusion between the classical and modern styles, and to engraft the beauties of antique literature upon their own language. Boiardo, far more a child of nature than either Boccaccio or Poliziano, with deeper sympathy for feudal traditions and chivalrous modes of feeling, attacked this problem from a point of view directly opposite to theirs. His comprehensive study of Greek and Roman authors had stored his mind with legends which gave an impulse to the freedom of his own imagination. He did not imitate the ancients; but used the myths with so much novelty and delicate perception of their charm, that beneath his touch they assumed a fresh and fascinating quality. There is nothing grotesque in his presentation of Hellenic fancy, nothing corresponding to the mediæval transformation of deities into devils; and yet his spirit is not classical. His Sphinx, his Cyclops and his Circe-Dragontina, his Medusa, his Pegasus, his Centaur, his Atalanta, his Satyr, are living creatures of romantic wonderland, with just enough of classic gracefulness to remove them from the murky atmosphere of mediæval superstition into the serene ether of a neo-pagan mythology. Nothing can be more dissimilar from Ovid, more unlike the forms of Græco-Roman sculpture. With his firm grasp upon reality, Boiardo succeeded in naturalising these classic fancies. They are not copied, but drawn from the life of the poet's imagination. A good instance of this creative faculty is the description of the Faun, who haunts the woodland in the shade of leaves, and lives on fruits and drinks the stream, and weeps when the sky is fair, because he then fears bad weather, but laughs when it rains, because he knows the sun will shine again.[78] It is not

[78] I. xxiii. 6.

easy to find an exact analogue in the sister arts to this poetry, though some points in the work of Botticelli and Piero di Cosimo, some early engravings by Robeta and the Master of the Caduceus, some bas-reliefs of Amadeo or incrustations on the chapel-walls of S. Francesco at Rimini, a Circe by Dosso Dossi in the Borghese palace at Rome, an etching of Mantegna here or there, might be quoted in illustration of its spirit.[79] Better justice can be done to Boiardo's achievement by citation than by critical description. The following stanzas are a picture of Love, attended by the Graces, punishing Rinaldo for his rudeness near the Fount of Merlin:[80]

When to the leafy wood his feet were brought,
Towards Merlin's Fount at once he took his way;
Unto the fount that changes amorous thought
Journeyed the Paladin without delay;
But a new sight, the which he had not sought,
Caused him upon the path his feet to stay.
Within the wood there is a little close
Full of pink flowers, and white, and various:

And in the midst thereof a naked boy,
Singing, took solace with surpassing cheer;
Three ladies round him, as around their joy,
Danced naked in the light so soft and clear.
No sword, no shield, hath been his wonted toy;
Brown are his eyes; yellow his curls appear;
His downy beard hath scarce begun to grow:
One saith 'tis there, and one might answer, No!

With violets, roses, flowers of every dye,
Baskets they filled and eke their beauteous hands:
Then as they dance in joy and amity,
The Lord of Montalbano near them stands:
Whereat, 'Behold the traitor!' loud they cry,
Soon as they mark the foe within their bands;
'Behold the thief, the scorner of delight,
Caught in the trap at last in sorry plight!'

Then with their baskets all with one consent
Upon Rinaldo like a tempest bore:
One flings red roses, one with violets blent
Showers lilies, hyacinths, fast as she can pour:
Each flower in falling with strange pain hath rent
His heart and pricked his marrow to the core,
Lighting a flame in every smitten part,
As though the flowers concealed a fiery dart.

The boy who, naked, coursed along the sod,
Emptied his basket first, and then began,
Wielding a long-grown leafy lily rod,
To scourge the helmet of the tortured man:
No aid Rinaldo found against the god,
But fell to earth as helpless children can;
The youth who saw him fallen, by the feet
Seized him, and dragged him through the meadow sweet.

[79] Burne Jones, in his *Pan and Syrinx*, offers a parallel.
[80] II. xv. 43 *et seq.*

And those three dames had each a garland rare
Of roses; one was red and one was white:
These from their snowy brows and foreheads fair
They tore in haste, to beat the writhing knight:
In vain he cried and raised his hands in prayer;
For still they struck till they were tired quite:
And round about him on the sward they went,
Nor ceased from striking till the morn was spent.

Nor massy cuirass, nor stout plate of steel,
Could yield defence against those bitter blows:
His flesh was swollen with many a livid weal
Beneath his mail, and with such fiery woes
Inflamed as spirits damned in hell may feel;
Yet theirs, upon my troth, are fainter throes:
Wherefore that Baron, sore, and scant of breath,
For pain and fear was well-nigh brought to death.

Nor whether they were gods or men he knew;
Nor prayer, nor courage, nor defence availed,
Till suddenly upon their shoulders grew
And budded wings with gleaming gold engrailed,
Radiant with crimson, white, and azure blue;
And with a living eye each plume was tailed,
Not like a peacock's or a bird's, but bright
And tender as a girl's with love's delight.

Then after small delay their flight they took,
And one by one soared upward to the sky
Leaving Rinaldo sole beside the brook
Full bitterly that Baron 'gan to cry
For grief and dole so great his bosom shook
That still it seemed that he must surely die;
And in the end so fiercely raged his pain
That like a corpse he fell along the plain.

This is a fine painting in the style I have attempted to characterise—the imagery of the Greek mythology taking a new and natural form of fanciful romance. It is alien to anything in antique poetry or sculpture. Yet the poet's imagination had been touched to finest issues by the spirit of the Greeks before he wrote it. Incapable of transplanting the flowers of antiquity like delicate exotics into the conservatory of studied art, he acclimatised them to the air of thought and feeling in which his own romantic spirit breathed. This distinguishes him from Poliziano, whose stately poem, like the palm-house in Kew Gardens, contains specimens of all the fairest species gathered from the art of Greece and Rome. Even more exquisitely instinct with the first April freshness of Renaissance feeling is another episode, where Boiardo presents the old tale of Narcissus under a wholly new and original aspect. By what strange freak of fancy has he converted Echo into an Empress of the East and added the pathos of the fairy Silvanella, whose petulance amid her hopeless love throws magic on the well! We are far away indeed from the Pompeian frescoes here:[81]

[81] II. xvii. 49 *et seq.*

Beyond the bridge there was a little close
All round the marble of that fountain fair;
And in the midst a sepulchre arose,
Not made by mortal art, however rare:
Above in golden letters ran the glose,
Which said, 'That soul is vain beyond compare
That falls a-doting on his own sweet eyes.
Here in the tomb the boy Narcissus lies.'

Erewhile Narcissus was a damozel
So graceful, and of beauty so complete,
That no fair painted form adorable
Might with his perfect loveliness compete;
Yet not less fair than proud, as poets tell,
Seeing that arrogance and beauty meet
Most times, and thus full well with mickle woe
The laity of love is taught to know.

So that the Empress of the Orient
Doting upon Narcissus beyond measure,
And finding him on love so little bent,
So cruel and so careless of all pleasure,
Poor wretch, her dolorous days in weeping spent,
Craving from morn till eve of love the treasure,
Praying vain prayers of power from Heaven to turn
The very sun, and make him cease to burn.

Yet all these words she cast upon the wind;
For he, heart-hardened, would not hear her moan,
More than the asp, both death to charms and blind.
Wherefore by slow degrees more feeble grown,
Toward death she daily dwindling sank and pined;
But ere she died, to Love she cried alone,
Pouring sad sighs forth with her latest breath,
For vengeance for her undeservéd death.

And this Love granted: for beside the stream
Of which I spoke, Narcissus happed to stray
While hunting, and perceived its silvery gleam;
Then having chased the deer a weary way,
He leaned to drink, and saw as though in dream,
His face, ne'er seen by him until that day;
And as he gazed, such madness round him floated,
That with fond love on his fair self he doted.

Whoever heard so strange a story told?
Justice of Love! how true, how strong it is!
Now he stands sighing by the fountain cold
For what he hath, yet never can be his!
He that was erst so hard as stone of old,
Whom ladies like a god on bended knees
Devoutly wooed, imploring him for grace,
Now dies of vain desire for his own face.

Poring upon his perfect countenance,
Which on this earth hath ne'er a paragon,
He pined in deep desire's extravagance,
Little by little, like a lily blown,

Or like a cropped rose; till, poor boy, the glance
Of his black eyes, his cheek's vermilion,
His snowy whiteness, and his gleeful mirth
Death froze who freezes all things upon earth.

Then by sad misadventure through the glade
The fairy Silvanella took her way;
And on the spot where now this tomb is made,
Mid flowers the dead youth very beauteous lay:
She, marvelling at his fair face, wept and stayed
In sore discomfiture and cold dismay;
Nor could she quit the place, but slowly came
To pine and waste for him with amorous flame.

Yea, though the boy was dead, for him she burned;
Pity and grief her gentle soul o'erspread:
Beside him on the grass she lay and mourned,
Kissing his clay-cold lips and mouth and head.
But at the last her madness she discerned,
To love a corpse wherefrom the soul had fled:
Yet knows she not, poor wretch, her doom to shun;
She fain would love not, yet she must love on.

When all the night and all the following day
Were wasted in the torrent of her woes,
A comely tomb of marble fair the Fay
Built by enchantment in the flowery close;
Nor ever from that station would she stray,
But wept and mourned; till worn by weary throes,
Beside the fount within a little space
Like snow before the sun she pined apace.

Yet for relief, or that she might not rue
Alone the luckless doom which made her die,
E'en mid the pangs of love such charms she threw
Upon the fount in her malignity,
That all who passing toward the water drew
And gazed thereon, perchance with listless eye,
Must in the depth see maiden faces fair,
Graceful and soul-enthralling mirrored there.

They in their brows have beauty so entire
That he who gazes cannot turn to fly,
But in the end must fade of mere desire,
And in that field lay himself down to die.
Now it so chanced that by misfortune dire
A king, wise, gentle, ardent, passed thereby,
Together with his true and loving dame;
Larbin and Calidora, such their name.

In these stanzas the old vain passion of Narcissus for his own beauty lives again a new life of romantic poetry. That the enchantment of the boy's fascination, prolonged through Silvanella's mourning for his death, should linger for ever after in the fount that was his tomb, is a peculiarly modern touch of mysterious fancy. This part of the romance has little in common with the classic tale of Salmacis; it is far more fragile and refined. The Greeks did not carry their human sympathy with nature, deep and loyal as indeed it was, so far into the borderland of sensual and spiritual things. Haunted hills, like the Venusberg of Tannhäuser's legend; haunted waters, like Morgana's lake in Boiardo's poem; the charmed rivers and fountains of Naiads, where knights lose their memory and are enclosed in crystal prison-caves; these are essentially modern, the final flower and blossom of the mediæval fancy, unfolding stores of old mythology and half-forgotten emblems to the light of day in art.[82] For their perfection it was needful that the gods of Hellas should have died, and that the phantoms of old-world divinities should linger in dreams and reveries about the shores of young romance.

Boiardo's treatment of magic is complementary to his use of classical mythology. He does not employ this important element of mediæval art in its simplicity, but adapts it to the nature of his own imagination, adding, as it were, a new quality by the process of assimilation. Some of his machinery belongs, indeed, to the poems of his predecessors, or is framed in harmony with their spirit. The enchantment of Durlindana and Baiardo; the invulnerability of Orlando, Ferraguto, and other heroes; the wizardry of Malagise, Mambrino's helmet, Morgana's stag, the horse Rabicano, Argalia's lance, Angelica's ring, and the countless dragons and giants which Boiardo creates at pleasure, may be mentioned in this category. But it is otherwise with the gardens of Falerina and Dragontina, the sublacustrine domain of Fata Morgana, and the caverns of the Naiades. These, however much they may have once belonged to mediæval tradition, have been alchemised by the imagination of the poet of the Renaissance. They are glimpses into ideal fairyland, which Ariosto and Tasso could but refine upon and vary in their famous gardens of Alcina and Armida. Boiardo's use of the old tradition of Merlin's fountain, and the other well of Cupid feigned by him beside it, might again be chosen to illustrate his free poetic treatment of magical motives. When he trespasses on these enchanted regions, then and then only does he approach allegory. The quest of the tree guarded by Medusa in Tisbina's story; the achievement by Orlando of Morgana's garden, where Penitence and Fortune play their parts; and Rinaldo's encounter with Cupid in the forest of Ardennes, have obviously allegorical elements. Yet the hidden meaning is in each case less important than the adventure; and the same may be said about the highly tragic symbolism of the monster in the Rocca Crudele.[83] Boiardo had too vivid a sympathy with nature and humanity to appreciate the mysteries which allured the Northern poets of 'Parzival,' the 'Sangraal,' and the 'Faery Queen.' When he lapses into allegory, it is with him a sign of weakness. Akin, perhaps, to this disregard for parable is the freedom of his spirit from all superstition. The religion of his knights is bluff, simple, and sincere, in no sense savouring of the cloister and the cowl. A high sense of truth and personal honour, indifference to life

[82] See II. xxxi. xlv.; III. i. ii.

[83] See I. viii. 56 *et seq.* The whole tale of Grifone and Marchino in that Canto is horrible.

for life's sake, profound humility in danger, charity impelling men of power to succour the oppressed and feeble, are the fruits of their piety. But of penance for sins of the flesh, of ceremonial observances, of visions and fasts, of ascetic discipline and wonder-working images, of all the ecclesiastical trumpery with which the pseudo-Turpin is filled, and which contaminates even the 'Mort d'Arthur' of our heroic Mallory, we read nothing.

In taking up the thread of Boiardo's narrative, Ariosto made use of all his predecessor had invented. He adopted the machinery of the two fountains, the lance of Argalia, Angelica's ring, Rabicane, and the magic arts of Atalante. The characters of the 'Innamorato' reappear with slight but subtle changes and with somewhat softened names in the 'Furioso.'[84] Ariosto, again, followed Boiardo closely in his peculiar method of interweaving *Novelle* with the main narrative; of suspending one story to resume another at a critical moment; of prefacing his cantos with reflections, and of concluding them with a courteous license.[85] Lastly, Ariosto is at great pains, while connecting his poem with the 'Innamorato,' to make it intelligible by giving short abstracts at intervals of the previous action. Yet throughout this long laborious work of continuation he preserves a studied silence respecting the poet to whom he owed so much. Was this due to the desire of burying Boiardo's fame beneath his own? Did he so contrive that the contemporary repute of the 'Innamorato' should serve to float his 'Furioso' and then be forgotten by posterity? If so, he calculated wisely; for this is what almost immediately happened. Though the 'Orlando Innamorato' was printed four times before 1513—once at Venice in 1486, once at Scandiano in 1495, and again at Venice in 1506, 1511, and 1513—and though it continued to be reprinted at Venice through the first half of the sixteenth century, yet the sudden silence of the press after this period shows that the 'Furioso' had eclipsed Boiardo's fame. Still the integral connexion between the two poems could not be overlooked; and just about the period of Ariosto's death, Francesco Berni conceived the notion of rewriting Boiardo's epic with the expressed intention of correcting its diction and rendering it more equal in style to the 'Orlando Furioso.' This *rifacimento* was published in 1541, after his death. The

[84] On Ariosto's treatment of Boiardo's characters there is much excellent criticism in Pio Rajna's *Le Fonti dell' Orlando Furioso* (Firenze, Sansoni, 1876), pp. 43-53.

[85] I do not mean that other poets—Pulci and Bello, for example—had not interwoven episodical *Novelle*. The latter's poem of *Mambriano* owes all its interest to the episodes, and many of his introductory reflections are fair specimens of the discursive style. But the peculiarity of Boiardo, as followed by Ariosto, consisted in the art of subordinating these subsidiary motives to the main design. Neither Pulci nor Bello showed any true sense of poetical unity. It may here be parenthetically remarked that Francesco Bello, a native of Ferrara, called Il Cieco because of his blindness, recited his *Mambriano* at the Mantuan Court of the Gonzagas. It was not printed till after his death in 1509. This poem consists of a series of tales, loosely stitched together, each canto containing just enough to stimulate the attention of an idle audience. Rinaldo, Astolfo, and Mambriano, king of Bithynia, play prominent parts in the action.

mysterious circumstances that attended its publication, and the nature of the changes introduced by Berni into the substance of Boiardo's poem, will be touched upon when we arrive at this illustrious writer of burlesque verse. It is enough to mention here that Berni's version was printed twice between 1541 and 1545, and that then, like the original, it fell into comparative oblivion till the end of the last century. Meanwhile a second *rifacimento* by Domenichi appeared in 1545; and though this new issue was a mere piece of impudent book-making, it superseded Berni's masterpiece during the next two hundred years. The critics of the last century rediscovered Berni's *rifacimento*, and began to quote Boiardo s poem under his name, treating the real author as an ignorant and uncouth writer of a barbarous dialect. Thus one of the most original poets of the fifteenth century, to whom Italy owes the form and substance of the 'Furioso,' has been thrust aside and covered with contempt, by a curious irony of fortune, owing to the very qualities that ought to have ensured his immortality. Used by Ariosto as the ladder for ascending to Parnassus; by Berni as an exercising ground for the display of style; by Domenichi as the means of getting his name widely known, the 'Orlando Innamorato' served any purposes but that of its great author's fame. Panizzi, by reprinting the original poem along with the 'Orlando Furioso,' restored Boiardo at length to his right place in Italian literature. From that time forward it has been impossible to overlook his merits or to underestimate Ariosto's obligations to so gifted and original a master.

CHAPTER VIII

ARIOSTO

Ancestry and Birth of Ariosto—His Education—His Father's Death—Life at Reggio—Enters Ippolito d' Este's Service—Character of the Cardinal—Court Life—Composition and Publication of the 'Furioso'—Quiet Life at Ferrara—Comedies—Governorship of Garfagnana—His son Virginio—Last Eight Years—Death—Character and Habits—The Satires—Latin Elegies and Lyrics—Analysis of the Satires—Ippolito's Service—Choice of a Wife—Life at Court and Place-hunting—Miseries at Garfagnana—Virginio's Education—Autobiographical and Satirical Elements—Ariosto's Philosophy of Life—Minor Poems—Alessandra Benucci—Ovidian Elegies—Madrigals and Sonnets—Ariosto's Conception of Love.

ARIOSTO's family was ancient and of honourable station in the Duchy of Ferrara. His father, Nicolò, held offices of trust under Ercole I., and in the year 1472 was made Governor of Reggio, where he acquired property and married. His wife, Daria Maleguzzi, gave birth at Reggio in 1474 to their first-born, Lodovico, the poet. At Reggio the boy spent seven years of childhood, removing with his father in 1481 to Rovigo. His education appears to have been carried on at Ferrara, where he learned Latin but no Greek. This ignorance of Greek literature placed him, like Machiavelli, somewhat at a disadvantage among men of culture in an age that set great store upon the knowledge of both ancient languages. He was destined for a legal career; but, like Petrarch and Boccaccio, after spending some useless years in uncongenial studies, Ariosto prevailed upon his father to allow him to follow his strong bent for literature. In 1500 Nicolò Ariosto died, leaving a family of five sons and five daughters, with property sufficient for the honour of his house but scarcely adequate to the needs of his numerous children. Lodovico was the eldest. He therefore found himself at the age of twenty-six in the position of father to nine brothers and sisters, for whose education, start in life, and suitable settlement he was called on to arrange. The administration of his father's estate, and the cares thus early thrust upon him, made the poet an exact man of business, and brought him acquainted with real life under its most serious aspects. He discharged his duties with prudence and fidelity, managing by economy to provide portions for his sisters and honourable maintenance for his brothers out of their joint patrimony.

The first three years after his father's death were spent by Ariosto in the neighbourhood of Reggio, and to this period of his life we may perhaps refer some of the love affairs celebrated in his Latin poems. He held the Captaincy of Canossa, a small sinecure involving no important duties, since the Castle of Canossa was even in those days a ruin. In 1503 he entered the service of Cardinal Ippolito d' Este, with whom he remained until 1517. He was placed upon the list of the Cardinal's extraordinary servants, to be employed in matters of confidence and delicacy, involving frequent journeys to all parts of Italy and ceremonial embassies. His pay seems to have been fixed at 240 *lire marchesane*, corresponding to about 1,200 francs, charged upon the Archiepiscopal Chancery of Milan.[1] This salary, had it been regularly paid, would have sufficed to maintain the poet in decent comfort; but he had considerable difficulty from time to time in realising the sums due to him. Ippolito urged him to take orders, no doubt with a view of securing better emoluments from benefices that could only be conferred upon a member of the priesthood. But Ariosto refused to enter a state of life for which he felt no vocation.[2] The Cardinal Deacon of S. Lucia in Silice was one of those secular princes of the Church, addicted to worldly pleasures, profuse in personal expenditure, with more inclination for the camp and the hunting-field than for the duties of his station, who since the days of Sixtus IV. had played a prominent part in the society of the Italian Courts. He was of distinguished beauty; and his military courage, like that of the Cardinal Ippolito de' Medici, was displayed in the Hungarian campaign against the Turks. With regard to his character and temper, it may suffice to remind the reader how, in a fit of jealous passion, he hired assassins to put out his natural brother Giulio's eyes. That Ippolito d' Este did not share the prevailing enthusiasm of his age for literary culture, seems pretty clear; and he failed to discern the unique genius of the man whom he had chosen for his confidential agent. Ariosto camplains that he was turned into a common courier and forced to spend his days and nights upon the road by the master upon whom, at the expense of truth and reason, he conferred an immortality of fame in his great poem. Yet it would not be fair to echo the commonplace invectives against the Cardinal for illiberality and ingratitude. Ariosto knew the nature of his patron when he entered his service, and Ippolito did not hire a student but an active man of business for his work. It was an arrangement of convenience on both sides, to which the poet would never have stooped had his private means sufficed, or had the conditions of Italian society offered any decent career for a gentleman outside the circle of the Court. Moreover, it was not until after their final rupture, caused by Ariosto's refusal to undertake the Hungarian expedition in his master's train, that the true greatness of the author of the 'Furioso' was revealed. How should a dissolute and ill-conditioned Cardinal have discerned that a dreamy poem in MS. on the madness of Orlando would live as long as the 'Æneid,' or that the flattering lies invented by his courier would in after ages turn the fierce glare of criticism and celebrity upon the darkest

[1] See *Satire* i. 100-102; ii. 109-111.

[2] See *Satire* i. 113-123, for his reasons. He seems chiefly to have dreaded the loss of personal liberty if he took orders.

corners of his own history? The old legend about his brutal reception of the 'Orlando Furioso' has been now in part disproved.[3] We know that he defrayed the expenses of its publication, and secured the right and profits of its sale to Ariosto.[4] There is even an entry in his memoranda of expenditure proving that he bought a copy for the sum of one *lira marchesana*.[5] While deploring the waste of Ariosto's time and strength in the uncongenial service of this patron, we must acknowledge that his choice of Ippolito was a mistake for which he alone was responsible, and that the panegyrics showered on such a man are wholly inexcusable.[6] When all the circumstances of their connexion are taken into account, there is nothing but the extreme irritation caused by incompatibility of temper, and divergence of aims and interests, to condone the poet's private censure of the master whom publicly he loaded with praises.[7] The whole unhappy story illustrates the real conditions of that Court-life, so glowingly described by Castiglione, which proved the ruin of Tasso and the disgrace of Guarini. Could anything justify the brigandlike brutalities of Pietro Aretino, *il flagello de' Principi*, we might base his apology upon the dreary histories of these Italian poets, soured, impoverished, and broken because they had been forced to put their trust in princes. When there lay no choice between levying blackmail by menaces and coaxing crumbs by flatteries, it accorded better with the Italian ideal *virtù* to fatten upon the former kind of infamy than to starve upon the latter.

The 'Orlando Furioso' was conceived and begun in the year 1505. It was sent to press in 1515. Giovanni Mazzocchi del Bondeno published it in April 1516. A large portion of the poet's life was subsequently spent in correcting and improving it. In 1518, having freed himself from Ippolito's bondage, Ariosto entered the service of Duke Alfonso I. He was termed *cameriere* or *famigliare*, and his stipend was fixed at eighty-four golden crowns per annum, with maintenance for three servants and two horses, paid in kind.[8] He occupied his own house in Ferrara; and the Duke, who recognised his great literary qualities and appreciated the new lustre conferred upon his family by the publication of the 'Furioso,' left him in the undisturbed possession

[3] Ippolito is said to have asked the poet: 'Dove avete trovato, messer Lodovico, tante corbellerie?' That he did in effect say something of the kind is proved by *Satire* ii. 94-99.

[4] Campori, *Notizie per la Vita di L. Ariosto* (Modena, Vincenzi, 1871) pp. 55-58.

[5] *Ibid.* p. 58.

[6] He penned the following couplet in 1503, when it is to be hoped he had yet not learned to know his master's real qualities:

> Quis patre invicto gerit Hercule fortius arma,
> Mystica quis casto castius Hippolyto?

In another epigram, written on the death of the Cardinal, he pretends that Ippolito, hearing of Alfonso's illness, vowed his own life for his brother's and was accepted. See *Opere Minori*, i. 349.

[7] See *Satires* ii. vii.; *Capitoli* i. ii.

[8] Campori, *op. cit.* p. 59.

of his leisure.[9] The next four years were probably the happiest of Ariosto's life; for he had now at last secured independence and had entered upon the enjoyment of his fame. The Medici of Florence and Rome, and the ducal families of Urbino and Mantua, were pleased to number him among their intimate friends, and he received flattering acknowledgments of his poem from the most illustrious men of Italy. The few journeys he made at the request of Alfonso carried him to Florence, the headquarters of literary and artistic activity. At home the time he spared from the revision of the 'Furioso,' was partly devoted to the love-affairs he carried on with jealous secrecy, and partly to the superintendence of the ducal theatre. The criticism of Ariosto's comedies must be reserved for another chapter. It is enough to remark here that their composition amused him from his boyhood to his latest years. So early as 1493 he had accompanied Ercole I. to Pavia in order to play before Lodovico Sforza, and in the same year he witnessed the famous representation of the 'Menæchmi' at Ferrara. Some of his earliest essays in literature were translations of Latin comedies, now unfortunately lost. They were intended for representation; and, as exercises in the playwright's art, they strongly influenced his style. His own 'Cassaria' appeared for the first time at Ferrara in 1508; the 'Suppositi' followed in 1509, and was reproduced at the Vatican in 1519. It took Leo's fancy so much that he besought the author for another comedy. Ariosto, in compliance with this request, completed the 'Negromante,' which he had already had in hand during the previous ten years. The 'Lena' was first represented at Ferrara in 1528, and the 'Scolastica' was left unfinished at the poet's death. What part Ariosto took in the presentation of his comedies, is uncertain; but it is probable that he helped in their performance; besides directing the stage and reciting the prologue. He thus acquired a practical acquaintance with theatrical management, and it was by his advice, and on plans furnished by him, that Alfonso built the first permanent stage at Ferrara in 1532. On the last day of that year, not long after its erection, the theatre was burned down. These dates are important; since they prove that Ariosto's connexion with the stage, as actor, playwright, and manager, was continuous throughout his lifetime.

Ariosto's peaceful occupations at Ferrara were interrupted early in 1522 by what must be reckoned the strangest episode of his career. On February 7 in that year, he was nominated Ducal Commissary for the government of Garfagnana, a wild upland district stretching under Monte Pellegrino almost across the Apennines from the Lucchese to the Modenese frontiers. We find that the salary allowed him by Alfonso had never been very regularly paid, and that in 1521 the Duke, straitened in means by his warfare with the Papacy, was compelled to suspend it altogether.[10] At the same period the Communes forming what is known as Garfagnana (who had placed themselves beneath the Marquises of

[9] See *Satire* iv. 67-72.
[10] See *Satire* v. 172-204.

Ferrara in the first half of the fifteenth century, but had lately suffered from Florentine and Papal incursions) besought Alfonso to assert his suzerainty of their district and to take measures for securing its internal quiet. The emoluments of the Commissary amounted to about 930 *lire marchesane*, estimated at something like 2,300 francs of present value; and it was undoubtedly the pecuniary profits of the office which induced the Duke to offer it, and the poet to accept it.

We may think it strange that so acute a judge of men as Alfonso should have selected the author of the 'Furioso,' a confirmed student, almost a recluse in his habits, and already broken in health, for the governorship of a district half-ruined by foreign raids and domestic feuds, which had become the haunt of brigands and the asylum of bandits from surrounding provinces. Yet we must remember that Ariosto had already given ample proof of his good sense and business-like qualities, not only in the administration of his own affairs, but in numerous embassies undertaken for the Cardinal and Duke, his masters. At that epoch of Italian history the name and fame of an illustrious writer were themselves a power in politics; and it is said that during Ariosto's first journey into Garfagnana, he owed his liberation from the hands of brigands to the celebrity of the 'Orlando Furioso.'[11] Alfonso knew, moreover, that the poet was well qualified for negotiating with princes; and what was of grave practical importance, he stood in excellent personal relations to the Medici, from whom as the rulers of Florence the Garfagnana was menaced with invasion. These considerations are sufficient to explain Alfonso's choice. Nothing but necessity would probably have induced Ariosto to quit Ferrara for the intolerable seclusion of those barbarous mountains; where it was his duty to issue edicts against brigands, to hunt outlaws, to punish murderers and robbers, to exact fines for rape and infamous offences, to see that the hangman did his duty, and to sit in judgment daily upon suits that proved the savage immorality of the entire population. The hopelessness of the task might have been enough to break a sterner heart than Ariosto's, and his loathing of his life at Castelnovo found vent in the most powerful of his Satires. He managed to endure this uncongenial existence for three years, from February 20, 1522, till June, 1525, sustaining his spirits with correspondence and composition, and varying the monotony of his life by visits to Ferrara. It was during his Garfagnana residence in all probability that he composed the 'Cinque Canti.' The society of his dearly loved son, Virginio—whose education he superintended, and for whom he wrote the charming seventh Satire to Pietro Bembo—also served to diminish the dreariness of his exile from love, leisure, and the society of friends.

Virginio was Ariosto's natural son by a woman of Reggio. He collected the Latin poems after his father's death, and prepared the 'Cinque Canti' for Manuzio's press in 1545. He also helped his uncle Gabriele

[11] This is one of the pretty stories on which some doubt has lately been cast. See Campori, pp. 105-110, for a full discussion of its probable truth.

to finish 'La Scolastica,' and wrote a few brief recollections of his father. Ariosto had a second illegitimate son, named Giovanni Battista, who distinguished himself in a military career.

The last eight years of Ariosto's life were spent in great tranquillity at Ferrara. Soon after his return from Garfagnana he built his house in the Contrada Mirasol, and placed upon it the following characteristic inscription:[12]

Parva sed apta mihi sed nulli obnoxia sed non
Sordida parta meo sed tamen ære domus.

About this time, too, he married the lady to whom for many years he had been tenderly attached.[13] She was the Florentine Alessandra Benucci, widow of Tito Strozzi, whom he first saw at Florence in the year 1513. The marriage was kept strictly secret, probably because the poet did not choose to relinquish the income he derived from certain minor benefices. Nor did it prove fruitful of offspring, for Ariosto left no legitimate heirs. His life of tranquil study was varied only by short journeys to Venice, Abano, and Mantua. In 1531 he was sent to negotiate certain matters for his master in the camp of the Marquis del Vasto at Correggio. On this occasion he received from Alfonso Davalos a pension of one hundred golden ducats, by a deed which sets forth in its preamble the duty of princes to recompense poets who immortalise the acts of heroes. This is the only instance of reward bestowed on Ariosto for his purely literary merits. The poet repaid his benefactor by magnificent eulogies inserted in the last edition of the 'Furioso.'[14] Between the year 1525, when he left Garfagnana, and 1532, when his poem issued from the press, he devoted himself with unceasing labour to its revision and improvement. The edition of 1516 consisted of forty cantos. That of 1532 contained forty-six, and the whole text had been subjected in the interval to minute alterations.[15] Not long after the publication of the revised edition Ariosto's health gave way. His constitution had never been robust, for he suffered habitually from a catarrh of the lungs which made his old life as Ippolito d' Este's courier not only distasteful but dangerous.[16] Towards the close of 1532 this complaint took the form of a consumption, which ended his days on the sixth of June, 1533. Great pains have been bestowed by his biographers on proving that he died a good Catholic; nor is there any reason to suppose that he neglected the consolations of the Church in his last hours. He was by no means a man to break abruptly with tradition or to make an indecorous display of doubts that may have haunted him. Yet the

[12] 'Small, but suited to my needs, freehold, not mean, the fruit of my own earnings.' His son Virginio substituted another inscription which may still be seen upon the little house-front: *Sic domus hæc Areostea propitios habeat deos olim ut Pindarica*—'May this house of Ariosto have gods propitious as of old the house of Pindar.'

[13] The date is uncertain. It was not before 1522, perhaps even so late as 1527.

[14] xv. 28; xxxiii. 24.

[15] See Panizzi, *op. cit.* vol. vi. p. cxix, for a description of these verbal changes.

[16] See especially *Satire* ii. 28-51, and *Capitolo* i.

best Latin verses he ever penned were a half-humorous copy of hendecasyllables for his own epitaph, which seem to prove that he applied Montaigne's *peut-être* even to the grave.[17]

Of Ariosto's personal habits and opinions we know unfortunately but little, beyond what may be gathered from the incomparably transparent self-revelation of his Satires. His son Virginio, who might have amply satisfied our curiosity, confined himself to the fewest and briefest details in the notes transcribed and published by Barotti. Some of these, however, are so characteristic that it may not be inopportune to translate them. With regard to this method of composition, Virginio writes: 'He was never satisfied with his verses, but altered them again and again, so that he could not keep his lines in his memory, and consequently lost many of his compositions. . . . In horticulture he followed the same system as in composition, for he would not leave anything he planted for more than three months in one place; and if he sowed peaches or any kind of seed, he went so often to see if they were sprouting, that at last he broke the shoots. He had but small knowledge of herbs, and used to think that whatever grew near the things he had sown, were the plants themselves, and watched them diligently till his mistake was proved beyond all doubt. I remember once, when he had planted capers, he went every day to see them and was greatly delighted at their luxuriance. At last he discerned that they were but elders, and that the capers had not come up at all. . . . He was not much given to study, and cared to see but few books. Virgil gave him pleasure, and Tibullus for his diction; but he greatly commended Horace and Catullus; Propertius not much. . . . He ate fast and much, and made no distinction of food. So soon as he came home, if he found the bread set out, he would eat one piece walking, while the meats were being brought to table. When he saw them spread, he had water poured upon his hands and then began to eat whatever was nearest to him. . . . He was fond of turnips.'

From the bare details of Ariosto's biography it is satisfactory to turn to the living picture of the man himself revealed in his Satires. These compositions rank next to the 'Orlando Furioso' in the literary canon of his works, and have the highest value for the light they cast upon his temperament and mode of feeling. Though they are commonly called Satires, they rather deserve the name of Epistles; for while a satiric element gives a distinct flavour to each of the seven poems, this is subordinated to personal and familiar topics of correspondence. We learn from them what the great artist of the Golden Age thought and felt about the times in which he lived; what moved his indignation or aroused his sympathy; how he strove to meet the troubles of his chequered life; and where, amid the carnival of that mad century, he laid his finger upon hidden social maladies. Reading them, we come to know the man himself, and are better able to understand how, while Italy was distracted with wars and trampled on by foreign armies, he

[17] 'Ludovici Areosti humantur ossa,' &c., *Op. Min.* i. 365.

could withdraw himself from the tumult, and spend his years in polishing the stanzas of 'Orlando.' The Satires do not reveal a hero or a sage, a poet passionate like Dante with the sense of wrong, or like Petrarch aspiring after an impossible ideal. It is rather the type of Boccaccio's character, refined and purged of sensuality, with delicate touches of irony and a more fastidious taste, that meets us in this portrait of Ariosto painted by himself. His mental vision is more lucid, his judgment more acute, his philosophy less indulgent, and his ideal of art more exacting; yet he, too, might be nicknamed *Lodovico della Tranquillità.* With his head in Philiroe's lap beside a limpid rivulet, he basks away the summer hours, and cares not whether French or German get the upper hand in Italy.[18] Does it greatly signify, he asks Ercole Strozzi in one of his Latin poems, whether we serve a French or an Italian tyrant? Servitude is the same, if the despot be a barbarian only in manners, like our princelings, or in name too, like these foreigners.[19]

Left alone to study and to polish verses, Ariosto is content. He is content to flatter and confer immortality on the master he despises. He is content to rest in one place, turning his maps over when he fain would take a journey into foreign lands. Only let him be, and give him enough to live upon, and he will trouble no man, dispute no pretender's claims, raise no inconvenient questions of right and wrong, inflame the world with no far-reaching thoughts, but gild the refined gold of his purest phrases and paint the lilies of his loveliest thoughts, in placid ease. Italy has grown old, and Ariosto is the genius of a tired, world-weary, disillusioned age. What is there worth a struggle? At the same time he preserves his independence as a private gentleman. He passes free judgment upon society; and the patron he has praised officially in his epic, receives hard justice in his Satires. He is frank and honest,

[18] See the *Opere Minori*, vol. i. p. 336. Also Carducci's eloquent defence of these Horatian verses in his essay, *Delle Poesie Latine di L. Ariosto* (Bologna, Zanichelli, 1876), p. 82. The latter treatise is a learned criticism of Ariosto's Latin poetry from a point of view somewhat too indulgent to Ariosto as a poet and a man. Carducci, for example, calls the four Alcaic stanzas in question 'una cosellina quasi perfetta,' though they contain three third lines like these:

> Furore militis tremendo . . . . .
> Jacentem aquæ ad murmur cadentis . . . . .
> Mecumque cespite hoc recumbens.

Ariosto was but second-rate among the Latin versifiers of his century. It must, however, be added that his Latin poems were written in early manhood and only published after his death by Giambattista Pigna, in 1553.

[19] *Op. Min.* vol. i. p. 333:

> Quid nostra an Gallo regi an servire Latino,
> Si sit idem hinc atque hinc non leve servitium?
> Barbaricone esse est pejus sub nomine, quam sub
> Moribus? At ducibus, Dii, date digna malis.

What Ariosto thought about the Italian Despots finds full expression in the *Cinque Canti*, ii. 5, 6, where he protests that Caligula, Nero, Phalaris, Dionysius and Creon were surpassed by them in cruelty and crime.

free from hypocrisy and guile, genial and loyal toward his friends, upright in his dealings and manly in his instincts. We respect his candour, his contempt for worldly honours, and his love of liberty. We admire his intellectual sagacity, his deep and wise philosophy of life, the knowledge of the world so easily communicated, the irony so pungent yet so free from bitterness, which gives piquancy to these familiar discourses. Still both respect and admiration are tempered with some regret that the greatest poet of the sixteenth century should have been so easy-going. Such is the Ariosto revealed to us by the Satires—not a noble or sublime being: by no means the man to save the State if safety had been possible. Throughout the tragedy of Italy's last years of freedom he moves, an essentially comic character, only redeemed by genius and by *Weltweisheit* from the ridicule attaching to a man whose aims are commonplace, and whose complaints against the world are petty. He is not servile enough to accept the humiliations of a courtier's lot without a murmur. He is not proud enough to break his chains and live in haughty isolation. Hence in these incomparable records of his private opinion, we find him at once moment painting the discomforts of his position with a *naïveté* that provokes our laughter, at another analysing the vices of society with luminous acumen, then shrugging his shoulders and summoning philosophy to his aid with a final cry of *Pazienza!*

The motive of the first Epistle is a proposed journey to Rome.[20] The second enumerates the reasons why the poet will not accompany Ippolito d' Este to Hungary. The subject of the third is the choice of a wife. The fourth discusses the vanity of honours and wealth in comparison with a contended mind. The fifth describes the poet's isolation in the Garfagnana, and contains a confession of his love. In the sixth he explains why he does not wish to go to Rome and seek advancement from Clement VII. The seventh is devoted to the education of youth in the humanities, and contains a retrospect of his own early life. The satire of the first is directed against the ambition and avarice of priests, the pride of Roman prelates, and the nepotism of the Popes. The passage describing an ecclesiastic's levee is justly famous for its humour; and the diatribe on Papal vices for its force. The second shows how the dependents upon princes are forced to flatter, and how they exchange their freedom for the empty honour of sitting near great men at table. Ariosto takes occasion to describe the character of Ippolito

[20] I have followed the order of Lemonnier's edition, vol. i. of *Opere Minori*, Florence, 1857. But the dates of composition are uncertain, and it may be doubted whether Ariosto's own autograph can be taken as the basis of a chronological arrangement. Much obscurity rests upon these poems. We do not know, for instance, whether they were sent to the friends addressed in them by name, or whether the author intended them for publication. The student may profitably consult upon these points the lithographed facsimile of the autograph published at Bologna by Zanichelli in 1875. Meanwhile it is enough to mention that the first epistle was addressed to Messer Galasso Ariosto, the poet's brother, the second to Messer Alessandro Ariosto and Messer Lodovico da Bagno, the third and fourth to Messer Annibale Maleguccio, the fifth to Messer Sismondo Maleguccio, the sixth to Messer Buonaventura Pistofilo, and the seventh to Monsignore Pietro Bembo.

d' Este, who cared for his hawks and hounds more than for the Muses, and who paid his body-servants better than the poet of 'Orlando.'[21] 'I owe you nothing, Phœbus, nor you, holy college of the Muses! From you I never got enough to buy myself a cloak. "Indeed? your lord has given you . . . ." More than the price of several cloaks, I grant. But not for your sake, Muses, I am certain. He has told me, and I do not mind repeating it, that my verses are just worth the price of their waste-paper. He will not give a penny for my praises, but pays me for courier's service. His followers in the barge or villa, his *valet-de-chambre* and butler, his lacqueys who outwatch the night, get paid. But when I set his name with honour in my verse, he tells me I have whiled my time away in ease and pleasure—I had pleased him better by attendance on his person. If you remind me that I owe to him a third of the Chancery dues at Milan, I answer that he gave me this because I ply both spur and whip, change beasts and guides, and hurry over hills and precipices, risking my life upon his business.'

The third Epistle is a masterpiece of sound counsel and ripe knowledge of the world. Better rules could not be given about the precautions to be taken in selecting a wife, the qualities a man should seek in her, and the conduct he should use toward her after marriage. The satire consists in that poor opinion of female honesty which the author of the 'Furioso' had conceived, not without much experience of women, and after mature reflection upon social institutions. It is not envenomed like the invectives of the 'Corbaccio,' or exaggerated like the abuse in Alberti's dialogues. Leaning back in his armchair with an amused and quiet smile, the indulgent satirist enunciates truths that are biting only because they condense the wisdom of an observant lifetime. He never ceases to be kindly; and we feel, while listening to him, that his epigrams are double-edged. The poet who has learned this much of women, gives the measure of his limited capacity for noble feeling; for while he paints them as he finds them, he leaves an impression of his own emotional banality. After making due allowance for this defect in Ariosto's point of view, we may rank the third Epistle among the ripest products of his intellect. The fourth resumes the theme of Court-life and place-hunting. 'You ask me, friend Annibale, how I fare with Duke Alfonso, and whether I find his service lighter than the Cardinal's. To tell the truth, I do not like one burden better than the other; and were I rich enough, I certainly would be no man's servant. But I was not born an only son, and Mercury was never generous to my race. So I am forced to live at a patron's charge, and it is better to owe my maintenance to the Duke than to beg bread from door to door. I know that most people think it a grand thing to be a courtier, but I count Court-life as mere slavery. A nightingale is ill at ease in a cage, and a swallow dies after a day's imprisonment. If a man wants to be

[21] The first and second *Capitoli*, upon the irksome and exhausting service of the Cardinal, as dangerous to Ariosto's health as it was irritating to his temper, should be read side by side with this Epistle.

decorated with the spurs or the red hat, let him serve kings or popes. For my part, I care for neither; a turnip in my own house tastes sweeter to me than a banquet in a master's.[22] I would rather stretch my lazy limbs in my armchair than be able to boast that I had travelled over half the globe. I have seen Tuscany, Lombardy, Romagna, the Apennines and Alps, the Adriatic and the Mediterranean. That is enough for me. The rest of the world I can visit at my leisure with Ptolemy for guide. The Duke's service has this advantage, that it does not interrupt my studies, or take me far from Ferrara, where my heart is always. I think I hear you laughing at this point and saying that neither love of study nor of country, but a woman ties me to my home. Well: I will confess it frankly. But suppose I had gone to Rome to fish for benefices, says someone, I should certainly have netted more than one, especially as I was Leo's friend before his merits or his luck raised him to the highest earthly station. I knew him at Urbino when he cheered his exile with Castiglione and Bembo; and afterwards, when he returned to Florence, he bade me count upon him like a brother. All this is true; but listen to a fable I will tell you.[23] In time of drought, when there was no water to be had in all the country, a shepherd found a scanty spring. He drank of it first, and next his wife, and then his children, and afterwards his servants and his cattle. Last of all there came a magpie he had petted in old days; but the bird saw that she had no right to drink of the fountain, for she was neither wife nor child nor hind, nor could she bring wealth to the household.[24] It is just the same with me. Leo has all the Medici, and all his friends in exile, who risked their lives and fortunes for him, and all the priests who made him pope, to recompense. What is there left for me? It is true that he has not forgotten me. When I went to Rome and kissed his foot, he bent down from the holy seat, and took my hand and saluted me on both cheeks. Besides, he made me free of half the stamp-dues I was bound to pay; and then, breast-full of hope but soaked with rain and smirched with mud, I went and had my supper at the Ram![25] But supposing the Pope kept all his promises and put as many mitres on my head as Michelangelo's Jonah sees beneath him in the Sistine Chapel, what would this profit me? No amount of wealth can satisfy desire. Honours and riches do not bring tranquillity of mind. True

[22] See above, p. 160, for Ariosto's liking for turnips. He ate them with vinegar and wine sauce.

[23] Compare the apologue of the gourd and the pear-tree in the sixth Satire (55-114). It is to the same effect, but even plainer.

[24] The word I have translated 'magpie' is *gaza* in the autograph. This has been interpreted as a slip of the pen for *ganza*; but it may be a Lombardism for *gazza*. In the latter case we should translate it 'magpie,' in the former 'sweetheart.' I prefer to read *gazza*, as the ironical analogy between a magpie and a poet is characteristic of Ariosto.

[25] The irony of this passage is justly celebrated. After all his hopes and all the pontiff's promises, the poet gets a kiss, a trifling favour, and has to trudge down from the Vatican to his inn. The *mezza bolla* is supposed to refer to the fine for entrance on the little benefice of Sant' Agata, half of which Leo remitted.

honour is, to be esteemed an honest man, and to be this in good earnest; for if you are not really one, you will be detected. What is the advantage of wearing fine clothes and being bowed to in the market-place, if people point you out behind your back as thief and traitor? There are dignities which are notorious disgraces; and the richer and greater a man is who has gained his rank dishonourably, the more he calls attention to his shame.'

> Quante collane, quante cappe nove
> Per dignità si comprano, che sono
> Pubblici vituperi in Roma e altrove!

In the sixth Epistle written in the Garfagnana, Ariosto still further develops the same theme. His friend, Pistofilo, had advised him to go to Rome and seek preferment from Clement VII. 'What would be the use?' he argues. 'I have as much of worldly honour as I care for; and if Leo did not find it in his power to help me, I cannot expect anything from the other Medici. Nay, my friend, bait your hook with more enticing dainties: remind me of Bembo, Sadoleto, Giovio, Vida, Molza, Tibaldeo; in whose company I might wander over the seven hills: or speak to me about the libraries of Rome. Not even these allurements would move me; for if I had to live away from Ferrara, I should not be happy in the lap of Jove. Existence is only made endurable by occasional visits to the town I love; and if the Duke wishes to fulfil my desires, he must recall me to himself and make me stationary at Ferrara. Why do I cling so to that place, you ask me? I would as lief tell you as confess my worst crimes to a friar. I am forty-nine years of age, and too old to be the slave of love.' The conclusion of the sixth Epistle makes it clear that his residence at Castelnovo was irksome to the poet because it forced him to be absent from the woman he loved. But the fifth is even more explicit. 'This day completes the first year of my exile among these barbarous mountains, dead to the Muses, divided by snows, fells, forests, rivers, from the mistress of my soul![26] I am nearly fifty, and yet love rules me like a beardless boy. Well: this weakness is at least pardonable. I do not commit murder; I do not smite or stab, or vex my neighbours. I am not consumed with avarice, ambition, prodigality, or monstrous lust. But in this doleful place my heart fails me. I cannot write poetry as I used to do at Reggio when life was young. Imprisoned between the naked heights of Pania and Pellegrino's precipices, the wild steeps of these woody Apennines enclose me in a living grave. Here in the castle, or out there in the open air, my ears are deafened with continual law-suits, accusations, brawls. Theft, murder, hatred, vengeance, anger, furnish me with occupation day and night. My time is spent in threatening, punishing, persuading, or acquitting. I write despatches daily to the Duke for counsel or for

[26] The third elegy is a beautiful lamentation over his separation from his mistress. Written to ease his heart in solitude, it is more impassioned and less guarded than the epistle.

aid against the bandits that encompass me. The whole province is disorganised with brigandage, and its eighty-three villages are in a state of chronic discord. Is it likely then that Phœbus, when I call him, will quit Delphi for this den? You ask me why I left my mistress and my studies for so dolorous a cave of care. I was never greedy of money, and my stipend at Ferrara satisfied me, until the war stopped it altogether, as well as my profits from the Chancery at Milan. When I asked the Duke for help, it so happened that the Garfagnana wanted a Governor, and he sent me here with more regard for my necessities than for the needs of the people under my care. I am grateful to him for his good will; but though his gift is costly, it is not to my mind. So I am like the cock who found a jewel on his dung-heap, or like the Venetian who had a fine horse given him and could not ride it.'

The satirical passages in this Epistle can be separated from its autobiography, and furnish striking specimens of Ariosto's style. In order to show how ill the world judges of the faults and follies of great men, he draws a series of portraits with a few but telling touches. Though furnished with fictitious names, they suit the persons of the time to a nicety. This, for example, is Francesco Guicciardini, as Pitti represented him:

> Ermilian sì del denajo ardente
> Come di Alessio il Gianfa, e che lo brama
> Ogn' ora, in ogni loco, da ogni gente,
> Nè amico nè fratel nè sè stesso ama;
> Uomo d' industria, uomo di grande ingegno,
> Di gran governo e gran valor si chiama.

And here, without doubt, is the elder Lorenzo de' Medici:[27]

> Laurin si fa della sua patria capo,
> Ed in privato il pubblico converte;
> Tre ne confina, a sei ne taglia il capo;
> Comincia volpe, indi con forze aperte
> Esce leon, poi c' ha 'l popol sedutto
> Con licenze, con doni e con offerte.
> Gl' iniqui alzando, e deprimendo in lutto
> Gli buoni, acquista titolo di saggio,
> Di furti, stupri e d' omicidi brutto.

Autobiography and satire are mingled in the same unequal proportions in the seventh Epistle, which is perhaps the most interesting poem of the series. 'Bembo,' so begins the letter, 'I want my son Virginio to be well taught in the arts that elevate a man. You possess them all: I therefore ask you to recommend me a good Greek tutor at Venice or Padua, in whose house the youth may live and study. The Greek must be learned, but also of sound principles, for erudition without morality is worse than worthless. Unhappily, in these days it is diffi-

[27] It may be interesting to compare this scarcely disguised satire with the official flatteries of *Canzone* ii. and *Elegies* i., xiv., where Ariosto praises the Medici, and especially Lorenzo, as the saviours of Florence, the honour of Italy.

cult to find a teacher of this sort. Few humanists are free from the most infamous of vices, and intellectual vanity makes most of them sceptics also. Why is it that learning and infidelity go hand in hand? Why do our scholars latinise their names of baptism, changing Peter into Pierius, and John into Janus, or Jovianus? Plato was right when he expelled such poets from his State. Little have they in common with Phœbus and Amphion who taught civil life to barbarous races. For myself, it stings me to the quick when men of my own profession are proved thus vain and vicious. Find, then, an honest tutor to instruct Virginio in Greek. I have already taught him Latin; but the difficulties of my early manhood deprived me of Greek learning. My father drove me at the spear's point into legal studies. I wasted five years in that trifling, and it was not till I was twenty that I found a teacher in Gregorio da Spoleto. He began by grounding me in Latin; but before we had advanced to Greek, the good man was summoned to Milan. His pupil, Francesco Sforza, went with Il Moro, a prisoner, into France. Gregorio followed him, and died there. Then my father died and left me the charge of my younger brothers and sisters. I had to neglect study and become a strict economist. Next my dear relative Pandolfo Ariosto, the best and ablest of our house, died; and, as if these losses were not enough, I found myself beneath the yoke of Ippolito d' Este. All through the reign of Julius II. and for seven years of Leo's pontificate he kept me on the move from place to place, and made me courier instead of poet. Small chance had I of learning Greek or Hebrew on those mountain roads.'

These abstracts of Ariosto's so-called Satires will not be reckoned superfluous when we consider the clear light they cast upon his personal character and philosophy. The note of sincerity throughout is unmistakable. No one can read the pure and simple language of the poet without feeling that his mind was as transparent as his style, his character as ingenuous as his diction was perspicuous. When he tells us, for example, that he does not care for honours, that he prefers his study to the halls of princes, and that a turnip in his own house tastes better than the pheasants of a ducal table, we believe him. His confession of unseasonable love, and his acknowledgment that he has none of the qualities of judge or ruler, are a security for equal frankness when he professes himself free from avarice and the common vices of his age. His satire upon women, his picture of the Roman prelates, his portraits of great men, and his condemnation of the humanists are convincing by their very moderation. Like Horace, he plays about the heart instead of wielding the whip of Lucilius. This parsimony of expression adds weight to his censure, and renders these Epistles more decisive than the invectives in which contemporary authors indulged. We doubt the calumnies of Poggio and Filelfo until we read the well-considered passage of the seventh Epistle, which includes them all.[28] In like manner the last lines of the fourth Epistle confirm the Diaries of Burchard

[28] 22-69.

and Infessura, while the first contains an epitome of all that could be said of Alexander's nepotism. These familiar poems have, therefore, a singular value for the illustration of the Italian Renaissance in general no less than for that of Ariosto's own life. Furthermore, they are unique in the annals of Italian literature. The *terza rima* of Dante's vision has here become a vehicle for poetry separated by the narrowest interval from prose. It no longer lends itself to parody, as in the 'Beoni' of Lorenzo de' Medici. It is not contaminated by the foul frivolities of the Bernesque *Capitoli*. It takes with accuracy the impress of the writer's common thought and feeling. The metre designed to express a sublime belief, adapts itself to the discursive utterance of a man of sense and culture in a disillusioned age; and thus we might use the varying fortunes of *terza rima* to symbolise the passage from the *trecento* to the *cinque cento*, from Dante to Ariosto, from faith and inspiration to art and reflection.

Ariosto's minor poems, with but one or two exceptions, have direct reference to the circumstances of his life. They consist of Elegies, Capitoli, and an Eclogue composed in *terza rima*, with Canzoni, Sonnets, and Madrigals of the type made obligatory by Petrarch. The poet of the 'Orlando' was not great in lyric verse. These lesser compositions show his mastery of simple and perspicuous style; but the specific qualities of his best work, its colour and imagery and pointed humour, are absent. The language is sometimes pedestrian in directness, sometimes encumbered with conceits that anticipate the taste of the seventeenth century.[29] Where it is plainest, we lack the seasoning of epigram and illustration which enlivens the Satires; and though the sincere feeling and Ovidian fluency of the more ambitious lyrics render them delightful reading, we acknowledge that a wider channel of description or narrative or reflection was needed for the full tide of the poet's eloquence. The purely subjective style was hardly suited to his genius.

Only three *Canzoni* are admitted into the canon of Ariosto's works. The first relates the origin of his love for Alessandra Benucci, wife of Tito Strozzi, whom he admired as wife and married as widow. It was on S. John's Day in the year 1513 that he saw her at Florence among the gay crowd of the midsummer festival. She was dressed in black silk embroidered with two vines, her golden hair twisted into heavy braids, and her forehead overshadowed with a jewelled laurel-wreath. The brightness of the scene was blotted out for the poet, and swallowed in the intense lustre of her beauty:

> D' altro ch' io vidi, tenni
> Poco ricordo, e poco me ne cale:
> Sol mi restò immortale
> Memoria, ch' io non vidi in tutta quella
> Bella città, di voi cosa più bella.

[29] As when, for instance, he calls the sun in the first *Canzone*, 'l' omicida lucido d' Achille.' Several of the sonnets are artificial in their tropes.

How much he admired Florence, he tells us in the fourteenth Elegy, where this famous compliment occurs:

> Se dentro un mur, sotto un medesmo nome
> Fosser raccolti i tuoi palazzi sparsi,
> Non ti sarian da pareggiar due Rome.

The second *Canzone* is supposed to be spoken by the soul of Giuliano de' Medici, Duke of Nemours, to his widow, Filiberta of Savoy. Elevation of conception raises the language of this poem to occasional sublimity, as in the passage where he speaks of immortality:

> Di me t' incresca, ma non altrimente
> Che, s' io vivessi ancor, t' incresceria
> D' una partita mia
> Che tu avessi a seguir fra pochi giorni:
> E se qualche e qualch' anno anco soggiorni
> Col tuo mortale a patir caldo e verno,
> Lo dêi stimar per un momento breve,
> Verso quel altro, che mai non riceve
> Nè termine nè fin, viver eterno.

The undulation of rhythm obeying the thought renders these lines in a high sense musical.

Some of the Elegies have been already used in illustration of other poems. There remain a group apart, which seem to have been directly modelled upon Ovid. Of these the sixth, describing a night of love, and the seventh, when the lover dares not enter his lady's door in moonlight lest he should be seen, are among the finest. The ninth, upon fidelity in love, contains these noble lines:

> La fede mai non debbe esser corrotta,
> O data a un sol o data ancor a cento,
> Data in palese o data in una grotta.
> Per la vil plebe è fatto il giuramento;
> Ma tra gli spirti più elevati sono
> Le semplici promesse un sagramento.

The second is written on the famous black pen fringed with gold, which Ariosto adopted for his device and wore embroidered on his clothes. He declines to explain the meaning of this bearing; but it is commonly believed to have referred in some way to his love for Alessandra Strozzi. Baruffaldi conjectures that her black dress and golden hair suggested the two colours. But since this elegy threatens curious inquirers with Actæon's fate, we may leave his device to the obscurity he sought. Secrecy in respect to the great passion of his life was jealously maintained by Ariosto. His inkstand at Ferrara still bears a Cupid with one finger on his lip, as though to bid posterity observe the reticence adopted by the poet in his lifetime.

The Madrigals and Sonnets do not add much to our conception of Ariosto's genius. It has been well remarked that while his Latin love-poems echo the style of Horace, these are imitations of Petrarch's manner.[30] In the former he celebrates the facile attractions of Lydia and Megilla, or confesses that he is inconstant in everything except in always varying his loves.[31] In the latter he professes to admire a beautiful soul and eloquent lips more than physical charms, praises the spiritual excellences of his mistress, and writes complimentary sonnets on her golden hair.[32] In neither case is there any insincerity. Ariosto never pretended to be a platonic lover, nor did he credit women with great nobility of nature. Yet on the other hand it is certain that he was no less tenderly than passionately attached to Alessandra; and this serious love, of which the Sonnets are perhaps the record, triumphed over the volatility of his earlier affections.

It is enough in this chapter to have dealt with Ariosto's life and minor writings. The 'Orlando Furioso,' considered both as the masterpiece of his genius and also as the representative poem of the Italian Renaissance, must form the subject of a separate study.

[30] *De Sanctis*, ii.
[31] See especially the lines entitled *De suâ ipsius mobilitate.*
[32] See Sonnets xii. xi. xxvi. xxiii.

CHAPTER IX

THE 'ORLANDO FURIOSO'

'Orlando Furioso' and 'Divina Commedia'—Ariosto expresses the Renaissance as Dante the Middle Ages—Definition of Romantic, Heroic, Burlesque, Heroic-comic, and Satiric Poems—Ariosto's Bias toward Romance—Sense of Beauty in the Cinque Cento—Choice of Boiardo's unfinished Theme—The Propriety of this Choice—Ariosto's Irony and Humour—The Subject of the 'Furioso'—Siege of Paris—Orlando's Madness—Loves of Ruggiero and Bradamante—Flattery of the House of Este—The World of Chivalry—Ariosto's Delight in the Creatures of his Fancy—Close Structure of the Poem—Exaggeration of Motives—Power of Picture-painting—Faculty of Vision—Minute Description—Rhetorical Amplification—Rapidity of Movement—Solidity—Nicety of Ethical Analysis—The Introductions to the Cantos—Episodes and Novelle—Imitations of the Classics—Power of Appropriation and Transmutation—Irony—Astolfo's Journey to the Moon—Ariosto's Portrait—S. Michael in the Monastery—The Cave of Sleep—Humour—Pathos and Sublimity—Olimpia and Bireno—Conception of Female Character—The Heroines—Passion and Love—Ariosto's Morality—His Style—The Epithet of Divine—Exquisite Finish—Ariosto and Tasso—Little Landscape-painting—Similes—Realism—Adaptation of Homeric Images—Ariosto's Relation to his Age.

ARIOSTO's Satires make us know the man *intus et in cute*—to the very core. The Lyrics have a breadth and amplitude of style that mark no common master of the poet's craft. Yet neither the Satires nor the Lyrics reveal the author of the 'Furioso.' The artist in Ariosto was greater than the man; and the 'Furioso,' conceived and executed with no reference to the poet's personal experience, enthroned him as the Orpheus of his age. The 'Orlando Furioso' gave full and final expression to the *cinque cento*, just as the 'Divina Commedia' uttered the last word of the middle ages. The two supreme Italian singers stood in the same relation to their several epochs. Dante immortalised mediæval thoughts and aspirations at the moment when they were already losing their reality for the Italian people. Separated from him by a short interval of time, came Petrarch, who substituted the art of poetry for the prophetic inspiration; and while Petrarch was yet singing, Boccaccio anticipated in his multifarious literature the age of the Renaissance. Then the evolution of Italian literature was interrupted by the classical revival; and when Ariosto appeared, it was his duty to close the epoch which Petrarch had inaugurated and Boccaccio had determined, by a poem investing Boccaccio's world, the sensuous world of the Renaissance, with the refined artistic form of Petrarch. This he accomplished. But even while he was at work, Italy underwent those political and mental changes, in the wars of invasion, in the sack of Rome, in the siege of Florence, in the Spanish occupation, in the reconstruction of the Papacy beneath the pressure of Luther's schism, which ended the Renaissance and opened a new age with Tasso for its poet. Those, therefore, who would comprehend the spirit of Italy upon the point of transition from the middle ages, must study the 'Divine Comedy.' Those who would contemplate the genius of the Renaissance, consummated and conscious of its aim, upon the very verge of transmutation and eventual ruin, must turn to the 'Orlando Furioso.' It seems to be a law of intellectual development that the highest works of art can only be achieved when the forces which produced them are already doomed and in the act of disappearance.[1]

Italian critics have classified their narrative poems, of which the name is legion, into Romantic, Heroic, Burlesque, Heroic-comic, and Satiric.[2] The romantic poet is one who, having formed a purely imaginary world, deals with the figments of his fancy as though they were realities. His object is to astonish, fascinate, amuse and interest his readers. Nothing comes amiss to him, whether the nature of the material be comic or tragic, pathetic or satiric, miraculous or commonplace, impossible or natural, so long as it contributes grace and charm to the picture of adventurous existence he desires to paint. His aim is not instruction; nor does he seek to promote laughter. Putting all serious purposes aside, he creates a wonderland wherein the actions and passions of mankind shall be displayed, with truth to nature, under the strongly coloured light of the artistic phantasy. The burlesque poet enters the same enchanted region; but he deliberately degrades it below the level of common life, parodies the fanciful extravagances of romance, and seeks to raise a laugh at the expense of its most delicate illusions. The heroic poet has nothing to do with pure romance and pleasurable fiction. He deals with the truths of history, resolving to embellish them by art, to extract lessons of utility, to magnify the virtues and the valour of the noblest men, and to inflame his audience with the fire of lofty aspiration. His object, unlike that of the romancer, is essentially serious. He is less anxious to produce a work of pure beauty than to raise a monument of ideal and moralised sublimity. The heroic-comic poet adopts the tone, style, conduct and machinery of the heroic manner; but he employs his art on some trivial or absurd subject, making his ridicule of baseness and pettiness the more pungent by the mock-gravity of his treatment. Unlike the burlesque writer, he does not aim at mere scurrility. There is always method in his buffoonery, and a satiric purpose in his parody. The satirist strikes more directly; he

[1] Students who care to trace the thoughts and characters of this great poem to their sources, should read Pio Rajna's exhaustive essay, *Le Fonti dell' Orlando Furioso*, Firenze, Sansoni, 1876. The details of the *Orlando* are here investigated and referred with scientific patience to Greek, Latin, French, Italian, and other originals. If anything, Signor Rajna may seem to have overstrained the point of critical sagacity. It is hardly probable that Ariosto, reader of few books as Virginio says he was, should have drawn on stores so multifarious of erudition.

[2] See Ugo Foscolo's essay on the Narrative and Romantic Poems of Italy in the *Quarterly Review* for April 1819.

either attacks manners, customs, institutions, and persons without disguise, or he does so under a thin veil of parable. He differs from the heroic-comic poet chiefly in this, that he does not array himself in the epical panoply. Within the range of Italian literature we find ready examples of these several styles. Boiardo and Ariosto are romantic poets. The 'Morgante Maggiore' is a romance with considerable elements of burlesque and satire mingled.[3] Tasso's 'Gerusalemme Liberata' is a fair specimen of the heroic, and Tassoni's 'Secchia Raphita' of the heroic-comic species. The 'Ricciardetto' of Fortiguerri and Folengo's 'Orlandino' represent burlesque, while Casti's 'Animali Parlanti' is a narrative satire.

It may seem at first sight strange that Ariosto should have preferred the romantic to the heroic style of poetry, and that the epic of the Italian Renaissance should be a pure play of the fancy. Yet this was no less natural to the man revealed in his Epistles, than to the spirit of his century as we have learned to know it. The passions and convictions that give force to patriotism, to religion, and to morality, were extinct in Italy; nor was Ariosto an exception to the general temper of his age. Yet the heroic style demands some spiritual motive analogous to the enthusiasm for Rome which inspired Virgil, or to the faith that touched the lips of Milton with coals from the altar. An indolent and tranquil epicurean, indifferent to the world around him, desiring nothing better than a life among his books, with leisure for his loves and day-dreams, had not the fibre of a true heroic poet; and where in Italy could Ariosto have found a proper theme? Before he settled to the great work of his life, he began a poem in *terza rima* on the glories of the House of Este. That was meant to be heroic; but the fragment which remains, proves how frigid, how all unsuited to his genius and his times, this insincere and literary epic would have been.[4] Italy offered elements of greatness only to a prophet or a satirist. She found her prophet in Michelangelo. But what remained for a poet like Ariosto, without Dante's anger or Swift's indignation, without the humour of Cervantes or the fire of Juvenal, without Tasso's piety or Shakspere's England, yet equal as an artist to the greatest singers whom the world has known? The answer to this question is not far to seek. What really survived of noble and enthusiastic in the *cinque cento* was the sense of beauty, the adoration of form, the worship of art. The supreme artist of his age obeyed a right instinct when he undertook a work which required no sublime motive, and which left him free for the production of a masterpiece of beauty. In this sphere the defects of his nature were not felt, and he became the mouthpiece of his age in all that still remained of greatness to his country.

In like manner we can explain to ourselves Ariosto's choice of Boiardo's unfinished theme. He was not a poet with something irresistible to say, but an artist seeking a fit theatre for the exercise of his omnipotent

[3] Especially in Morgante and Margutte.
[4] See *Capitolo* iii.

skill. He did not feel impelled to create, but to embellish. Boiardo had constructed a vast hall in the style of the Renaissance, when it first usurped on Gothic; he had sketched a series of frescoes for the adornment of its walls and roof, and then had died, leaving his work incomplete. To enrich the remaining panels with pictures conceived in the same spirit, but executed in a freer and a grander manner, to adorn them with all that the most wealthy and fertile fancy could conceive, and to bestow upon them perfect finish, was a task for which Ariosto was eminently suited. Nor did he vary from the practice of the greatest masters in the other arts, who willingly lent their own genius to the continuation of designs begun by predecessors. Few craftsmen of the Renaissance thought as much of the purpose of their work or of its main motive as of execution in detail and richness of effect. They lacked the classic sense of unity, the mediæval sincerity and spontaneity of inspiration. Therefore Ariosto was contented to receive from Boiardo a theme he could embroider and make beautiful, with full employment of his rare inventive gifts upon a multitude of episodical inventions. It is vain to regret that a poet of his calibre should not have bent his faculties to the task of a truly original epic—to the re-awakening of prostrate Italy, to the scourging of her feebleness and folly, or even to the celebration of her former glories. Had he done either of these things, his poem would not have been so truly national, and we should have lacked the final product of a most brilliant though defective period of civilisation.

Ariosto's own temperament and the conditions of his age alike condemned him to the completion of a romance longer than the 'Iliad' and the 'Odyssey' together, which has for its sole serious aim, if serious aim it has of any sort, the glorification of an obscure family, and which, while it abounds in pathos, wisdom, wit, and poetry of dazzling brilliance, may at the same time be accused of levity, adulation, and licentiousness. To arraign Ariosto for these faults is tantamount to arraigning his whole century and nation. The greatest artist of the sixteenth century found no task worthier of his genius than to flatter the House of Este with false pedigrees and fulsome praises. He had no faith that could prevent him from laughing at all things human and divine, not, indeed, with the Titantic play of Aristophanes, whose merriment is but the obverse of profound seriousness, but with the indulgent nonchalance of an epicurean. No sentiment of sublimity raised him above the grosser atmosphere in which love is tainted with lust, luxurious images are sought for their own sake, and passion dwindles in the languor of voluptuousness. The decay of liberty, the relaxation of morals and the corruption of the Church had brought the Italians to this point, that their representative Renaissance poem is stained with flattery, contaminated with licentiousness, enfeebled with levity. Poetic beauty of the highest order it cannot claim. That implies more earnestness of purpose and an ideal of sublimer purity. Still, though the 'Furioso' misses the supreme beauty of the 'Iliad,' the 'Antigone' and the 'Paradise Lost,' it has in superfluity that secondary beauty which expressed itself less perfectly in Italian painting. In one respect it stands almost alone. The form reveals no inequalities or flaws. This artist's hand has never for a moment lost its cunning; this Homer never nods.

Pulci approached the romance of Charlemagne from a *bourgeois* point of view. He felt no sincere sympathy with the knightly or the religious sentiment of his originals. Boiardo treated similar material in a chivalrous spirit. The novelty of his poem consisted in the fusion of the Carolingian and Arthurian Cycles; for while he handled an episode of the former group, he felt sincere admiration for errant knighthood as figured in the tales of Lancelot and Tristram. Throughout the 'Orlando Innamorato' we trace the vivid influence of feudal ideals. Ariosto differed in his attitude from both of his predecessors. The irony that gives a special quality to his romance, is equally removed from the humour of Pulci and the frank enthusiasm of Boiardo. Ariosto was neither the citizen of a free burgh playing with the legends of a bygone age, nor yet the highborn noble in whose eyes the adventures of Orlando and his comrades formed a picture of existence as it ought to be. He was a courtier and a man of letters, and his poem is a masterpiece of courtly and literary art. Boiardo never flattered the princes of the House of Este. Ariosto took every occasion to interweave their panegyric with his verse. For Boiardo the days of chivalry were a glorious irrecoverable golden age. Ariosto contemplated this mythical past less with the regret of a man who had fallen upon worse days, than with the satisfaction of an artist who perceives the rare opportunities for poetic handling it afforded. He does not really believe in chivalry; where Boiardo is in earnest, Ariosto jests. It is not that, like Cervantes, he sought to satirise the absurdities of romance, or that he set himself, like Folengo, to burlesque the poems of his predecessors; but his philosophy inclined him to watch the doings of humanity with a genial half-smile, an all-pervasive irony that had no sting in it. A poet who stands thus aside and contemplates the comedy of the world with the dry light of a kindly and indulgent intellect, could not treat the tales of Paladins and giants seriously. He uses them as the machinery of a great work on human life, painting mankind, not as he thinks it ought to be, but as he finds it. This treatment of romance from the standpoint of good sense and quiet humour produces an apparent discrepancy between his practical knowledge of the world and his fanciful extravagance. In the artistic harmony effected by Ariosto between these opposite elements lies the secret of his irony. His worldly wisdom has the solidity of prose and embraces every circumstance of life. The creatures of his imagination belong to fairyland and exceed the wildest dreams in waywardness. He smiles to see them play their pranks; yet he never loses sight of reality, and moves his puppets by impulses and passions worthy of real men and women. Having granted the romantic elements of wonder and exaggeration for a basis, we find the superstructure to be natural. Never was sagacity of insight combined more perfectly with exuberance of fancy and a joyous lightheartedness than in this poem. Nowhere else have sound lessons in worldly wisdom been conveyed upon a stage of so much palpable impossibility.

We may here ask what is the main subject of the 'Orlando Furioso.' The poem has three chief sources of interest—the siege of Paris and the final rout of the Saracen army, the insanity of Orlando, and the loves of Ruggiero and Bradamante. The first serves merely as a groundwork for embroidery, a background for relieving more attractive incidents. Orlando's madness, though it gives its name to the romance, is subordinate to the principal action. It forms a proper development of the situation in the 'Orlando Innamorato;' and Ariosto intends it to be important, because he frequently laments that the Paladin's absence from the field injured the cause of Christendom. But Charlemagne, by help of Rinaldo, Bradamante, and Marfisa, conquers without Orlando's aid. Thus the hero's insanity is only operative in neutralising an influence that was not needed; and when he regains his wits, he performs no critical prodigies of valour. Finding the Saracens expelled from France, and Charlemagne at peace, Orlando fights a duel with a crownless king upon a desert island more for show than for real service. Far different is the remaining motive of the poem. If the 'Furioso' can be said to have constructive unity, the central subject is the love and marriage of Ruggiero. Ariosto found this solution of the plot foreshadowed in the 'Innamorato.' The pomp and ceremony with which the fourth book opens, the value attached to the co-operation of Ruggiero in the war with Charlemagne, and the romantic beginning of his love for Bradamante, make it clear that Boiardo would have crowned his poem, as Ariosto has done, with the union of the ancestors of Casa d' Este. Flattery, moreover, was Ariosto's serious purpose. Consequently, the love of Ruggiero and Bradamante, whose protracted disappointments furnished the occasion for renewed prophecies and promises of future glory for their descendants, formed the artistic centre of his romance. The growing importance of all that concerns this pair of characters, the accumulation of difficulties which interfere with their union, and the final honour reserved for Ruggiero of killing the dreadful Rodomonte in single combat, are so disposed and graduated as to make the marriage of the august couple the right and natural climax to one complete epic of some 80,000 lines. The fascinations of Angelica, the achievements of Orlando and Rinaldo, the barbaric chivalry of Rodomonte and Marfisa, even the shock of Christian and Pagan armies, sink into insignificance before the interest that environs Bradamante toward the poem's ending. Victorious art was needed for the achievement of this success. Like a pyramid, upon the top of which a sculptor places a gilded statue, up grows this voluminous romance, covering acres of the plain at first, but narrowing to a point whereon the poet sets his heroes of the House of Este.[5]

[5] Ariosto's method of introducing flattery is simple. He makes Merlin utter predictions from his tomb, Melissa prophesy to Bradamante and Atlante to Ruggiero;

Though the marriage of Ruggiero and Bradamante forms the consummation of the 'Furioso,' it would show want of sympathy with Ariosto's intention to imagine that he wrote his poem for this incident alone. The opening lines of the first canto are explicit:

> Le donne, i cavalier, l' arme, gli amori,
> Le cortesie, l' audaci imprese io canto
> Che furo al tempo che passaro i Mori
> D' Africa il mare, e in Francia nocquer tanto. . . .

'The ladies, the knights, the feats of arms, the loves, the courtesies, the bold adventures are my theme.' In one word, his purpose was to paint the world of chivalry. Agramante's expedition into France gives him the time; Orlando's madness is an episode; Ruggiero's marriage forms a fitting climax. But his true subject-matter is chivalry—the dream-world of love, honour, magic, marvel, courtesy, adventure, that afforded to his fancy scope for its most brilliant imaginings. In Ariosto's age chivalry was a thing of the past, even among the nations of the North. It is true that Francis I. was kneeling on the battlefield before Bayard to receive the honour of knighthood in the names of Oliver and Roland. It is true that Henry VIII. was challenging his Most Christian cousin to a kingly settlement of their disputed claims in a pitched field. But the spirit of the times was not in these picturesque incidents. Charles V., who incarnated modern diplomacy, dynastic despotism, and autocratic statecraft, was deciding the destinies of Europe. Gunpowder had already revolutionised the art of feudal war.[6] The order of the Golden Fleece, monarchical and pompous, had eclipsed the orders of the Temple and S. John. What remained of chivalry formed a splendid adjunct to Court-equipage; and the knight-errant, if he ever existed, was merged in the modern gentleman. Far less of real vitality had chivalry among the cities of the South, in the land of Popes like Sixtus, adventurers like Cesare Borgia, princes like Lodovico Sforza, commercial aristocracies like the Republic of S. Mark. A certain ideal of life, summed up in the word *cortesia*, existed in Italy; where numerous petty Courts had become the school of refined sentiment and manners. But this was not what we mean by chivalry, and even this was daily

or he displays magic frescoes, statues, and embroideries, where the future splendours of the Este family are figured; or, again, in the exordia of his cantos he directly addresses his patrons. Omitting lesser passages, we may reckon fifteen principal panegyrics of the Este house: canto iii. 16 to end, the fabulous pedigree; viii. 62, 63, praise of Ippolito; xiii. 57 and on, praises of the women of the family; xiv. beginning, the battle of Ravenna and Alfonso; xv. 2, 29, Alfonso's defeat of the Venetians; xviii. 1, 2, Alfonso's justice; xxxv. 4-9, prophecy of Ippolito; xxxvi. 1-9, Ippolito and the Venetians; xl. 1-5, defeat of the Venetians again; xli. 1-3, general adulation; xli. 62-67, pedigree again; xlii. 3, Alfonso wounded; xlii. 83-92, women of the family again; xliii. 54-62, praises of Ferrara; xlvii. 85-97, life of Ippolito. The most extravagant flatteries are lavished upon Ippolito and Lucrezia Borgia. When we remember who and what these Este princes were—how brutal in his cruelty Alfonso, how coarse and selfish and sensual Ippolito, how doubtful in her life Lucrezia—we cannot but feel these panegyrics to be sickening in their impudence.

[6] See the ending of the ninth and the beginning of the eleventh cantos of the *Furioso*.

falsified by the cynicism and corruption of the princes and their servants.[7] Castiglione's 'Cortegiano,' the handbook of that new ideal, must be read by the light of the Roman diaries and Machiavelli's speculative essays. The Renaissance was rapidly destroying the feudal fabric of ideas throughout Europe. Those ideas were always weak in Italy, and it was in Italy that the modern intellect first attained to self-consciousness. Therefore the magic and marvels of romance, the restless movement of knight-errantry, the love of peril and adventure for their own sake, the insane appetite for combat, the unpractical virtues no less than the capricious wilfulness of Paladins and Saracens, presented to the age and race of men like Guicciardini nothing but a mad unprofitable medley. *Dove avete trovato, messer Lodovico, tante minchionerie?* was no unpardonable question for a Cardinal to make, when he opened the 'Furioso' in the pontificate of Clement VII. Of all this Ariosto was doubtless well aware. Yet he recognised in the 'Orlando' a fit framework for the exercise of his unrivalled painter's power. He knew that the magic world he had evoked was but a plaything of the fancy, a glittering bubble blown by the imagination. This did not suggest an afterthought of hesitation or regret: for he could make the plaything beautiful. The serious problem of his life was to construct a miracle of art, organically complete, harmonious as a whole and lovely in the slightest details. Yet he never forgot that chivalry was a dream; and thus there is an airy unsubstantiality in his romantic world. His characters, though they are so much closer to us in time and sympathy, lack the real humanity of Achilles in the 'Iliad' or of Penelope in the 'Odyssey.' They do not live for us, because they were not living for the poet, but painted with perfection from an image in his brain. He stood aloof from the work of his own hands, and turned it round for his recreation, viewing it with a smile of conscious and delighted irony. Nowhere did he suffer himself to be immersed in his own visionary universe. That wonderland of love and laughter, magic and adventure, which so amused his fancy that once he walked from Carpi to Ferrara in slippers dreaming of it, was to him no more solid than the shapes of clouds we form, no more durable than the rime that melts before the sun to nothing. The smile with which he contemplates this fleeting image, is both tender and ironical. Sarcasm and pathos mingle on his lips and in his eyes; for while he knows it to be but a vision, he has used it as the form of all his thought and feeling, making of this dream a mirror for the world in which his days were spent.

Notwithstanding the difficulty of precisely ascertaining the main subject of the 'Orlando Furioso,' the unity of the poem is close, subtle, serried. But it is the unity of a vast piece of tapestry rather than of

[7] What Ariosto thought about contemporary Italy may be gathered from these lines (xvii. 76):

> O d' ogni vizio fetida sentina,
> Dormi, Italia imbriaca, e non ti pesa
> Ch' ora di questa gente, ora di quella,
> Che già serva ti fu, sei fatta ancella?

architecture. There is nothing massive in its structure, no simple and yet colossal design like that which forms the strength of the 'Iliad' or the 'Divine Comedy.' The delicacy of its connecting links, and the perpetual shifting of its scene, distinguish it as a romantic poem from the true epic. The threads by which the scheme is held together, are slight as gossamer; the principal figures are confounded with a multitude of subordinate characters; the interest is divided between a succession of episodical narratives. At no point are we aroused by the shock of a supreme sensation, such as that which the death of Patroclus in the 'Iliad' communicates. The rage of Rodomonte inside the walls of Paris has been cited as an instance of heroic grandeur. But the effect is exaggerated. Ariosto is too much amused with the extravagant situation for the blustering of his Pagan to arouse either terror or surprise. When we compare this episode with the appearance of Achilles in the trench, the elaborate similes and prolonged description of the Italian poet are as nothing side by side with the terrific shout of the Greek hero stung at last into activity. And what is true of Rodomonte may be said of all the studied situations in the 'Furioso.' Ariosto pushes every motive to the verge of the burlesque, heightening the passion of love till it becomes insanity, and the sense of honour till it passes over into whimsical punctiliousness, and the marvellous until the utmost bounds of credibility are passed. This is not done without profound artistic purpose. The finest comic effects in the poem are due to such exaggerations of the motives; and the ironic laughter of the poet is heard at moments when, if he preserved his gravity, we should accuse him of unpardonable childishness. Our chief difficulty in appreciating the 'Furioso' is to take the author's point of view, to comprehend the expenditure of so much genius and wisdom upon paradoxes, and to sympathise with the spirit of a masterpiece which, while it verges on the burlesque, is never meant to pass the limit.

In putting this dream-world of his phantasy upon the canvas, Ariosto showed the power of an accomplished painter. This is the secret of the 'Furioso's' greatness. This makes it in a deep sense the representative poem of the Italian Renaissance. All the affinities of its style are with the ruling art of Italy, rather than with sculpture or with architecture; and the poet is less a singer uttering his soul forth to the world in song, than an artist painting a multitude of images with words instead of colours. His power of delineation never fails him. Through the lucid medium of exquisitely chosen language we see the object as clearly as he saw it. We scarcely seem to see it with his eyes so much as with our own, for the poet stands aloof from his handiwork and is a spectator of his pictures like ourselves. So authentic is the vision that, while he is obliged by his subject to treat the same situations—in duels, battles, storms, love-passages—he never repeats himself. A fresh image has passed across the camera obscura of his brain, and has been copied in its salient features. For the whole of this pictured world is in movement, and the master has the art to seize those details which convey the very truth of life and motion. We sit in a dim theatre of thought, and watch the motley crowd of his fantastic personages glide across the stage. They group themselves for a moment ere they flit away; and then the scene is shifted, and a new procession enters; fresh *tableaux vivants* are arranged, and when we have enjoyed their melodies of form and colour, the spell is once more broken and new actors enter. The stage is never empty; scene melts into scene without breathing-space or interruption; but lest the show should weary by its continuity, the curtain is let down upon each canto's closing, and the wizard who evokes these phantoms for our pleasure, stands before it for a moment and discourses wit and wisdom to his audience.

It is this all-embracing universally illuminating faculty of vision that justifies Galileo's epithet of the DIVINE for Ariosto. This renders his title of the Italian Homer intelligible. But we must remember that these high-sounding compliments are paid him by a nation in whose genius the art of painting holds the highest rank; and it may well happen that critics less finely sensitive to pictorial delineation shall contest them both. As in Italian painting, so in Ariosto's poetry, deep thought and poignant passion are not suffered to interrupt the calm unfolding of a world where plastic beauty reigns supreme. No thrilling cry from the heart of humanity is heard; no dreadful insight into mortal woe disturbs the rhythmic dance. Tragedy is drowned and swallowed in a sea of images; and if the deeper chords of pathos are touched here and there, they are so finely modulated and blent with the pervading melody that a harsh note never jars upon our ears. A nation in whom the dramatic instinct is paramount, an audience attuned to 'Hamlet' or 'King Lear,' will feel that something essential to the highest poetry has been omitted. The same imperious pictorial faculty compels Ariosto to describe what more dramatic poets are contented to suggest. Where Dante conveys an image in one pregnant line, he employs an octave for the exhibition of a finished picture.[8] Thus our attention is withdrawn from the main object to a multitude of minor illustrations, each of which is offered to us with the same lucidity. The dædal labyrinth of exquisitely modelled forms begins to cloy, and in our tired ingratitude we wish the artist had left something to our own imagination. It is too much to be forced to contemplate a countless number of highly-wrought compositions. We long for something half-seen, indicated, shyly revealed by lightning flashes, and withdrawn before it has been fully shown. When Lessing in 'Laocoon' censured the famous portrait of Alcina, this was, in part at least, the truth of his complaint. She wearies us by the minuteness of the touches that present her to our gaze; and the elaboration of each detail prevents us from forming a complete conception of her beauty. But the Italians of the sixteenth

[8] Those who are curious may compare the three lines in which Dante likens Piero delle Vigne's voice issuing from his tree of torment to the hissing of sap in a green log upon the fire (*Inf.* xiii. 40) with the eight lines used by Ariosto to expand the same simile (*Orl. Fur.* vi. 27); or, again, Dante's picture of the sick woman on her bed of fever (*Purg.* vi. 149) with Ariosto's copy (*Orl. Fur.* xxviii. 90).

century, accustomed to painted forms in fresco and in oils, and educated in the descriptive traditions of Boccaccio's school, would not have recognised the soundness of this criticism. For them each studied phrase of Ariosto was the index to an image, summoned by memory from the works of their own masters, or from life. His method of delineation was analogous to that of figurative art. In a word, the defect pointed out by the German critic is the defect of Ariosto's greatest quality, the quality belonging to an age and race in which painting was supreme.

Closely allied to this pictorial method in the representation of all objects to our mental vision, was Ariosto's rhetorical amplification. He rarely allows a situation to be briefly indicated or a sentiment to be divined. The emotions of his characters are analysed at length; and their utterances, even at the fever-heat of passion, are expanded with a dazzling wealth of illustration. Many of the episodes in the 'Furioso' are eminently dramatic, and the impression left upon the memory is forcible enough. But they are not wrought out as a dramatist would handle them. The persons do not act before us, or express themselves by direct speech. The artist has seen them in motion, has understood what they are feeling; and by his manner of describing them he makes us see them also. But it is always a picture, always an image, that presents itself. Soul rarely speaks to soul without the intervention of interpretative art. This does not prevent Ariosto from being a master of the story-teller's craft. No poet of any nation knew better what to say and what to leave unsaid in managing a fable. The facility of his narration is perfect; and though the incidents of his tales are extremely complicated, there is no confusion. Each story is as limpid as each picture he invents. Nor, again, is there any languor in his poem. Its extraordinary swiftness can only be compared to the rush of a shining river, flowing so smoothly that we have to measure its speed by objects on the surface. The 'Furioso,' in spite of its accumulated images, in spite of its elaborated rhetoric, is in rapid onward movement from the first line to the last. It has an elasticity which is lacking to the monumental architecture of the 'Divine Comedy.' It is free from the stationary digressions that impede a student of 'Paradise Lost.'

The fairy-like fantastic structure of the 'Furioso' has a groundwork of philosophical solidity. Externally a child's story-book, it is internally a mine of deep world-wisdom, the product of a sane and vigorous intellect. Not that we have any right to seek for allegory in the substance of the poem. When Spenser fancied that Ariosto had 'ensampled a good governour and vertuous man' in Orlando—in the Orlando who went mad, neglected his liege-lord, and exposed Christendom to peril for Angelica's fair face—he was clearly on the wrong tack. For a man of Ariosto's temperament, in an age of violent contrast between moral corruption and mental activity, it was enough to observe human nature without creating ideals. His knowledge of the actions, motives, passions and characters of men is concrete; and his readings in the lessons of humanity are literal. The excellence of his delineation consists precisely in the nicety of *nuances*, the blending of vice and virtue, the correct analysis of motives. He paints men and women as he finds them, not without the irony of one who stands aloof from life and takes malicious pleasure in pointing out its misery and weakness. If I wished to indicate a single passage that displays this knowledge of the heart, I should not select the too transparent allegory of Logistilla[9]—though even here the contrast between Alcina's seductive charms and the permanent beauty of her sister is wrought with a magnificence of detail worthy of Spenser. I would rather point to the reflections which conclude the tale of Marganorre and his wicked sons.[10] In lucid exposition of fact lay the strength of Ariosto; and here it may be said that he proved his affinity to the profoundest spirits of his age in Italy—to Machiavelli and Guicciardini, the founders of analytical science for modern Europe. This intimate study of the laws which govern human action when it seems most wayward, is displayed in Grifone's subjection to the faithless Orrigille, in the conflict of passions which agitate the heroes of Agramante's camp, in the agony of Orlando when he finds Medoro's name coupled with Angelica's, in Bradamante's jealousy, in the conflict of courtesy between Leone and Ruggiero, in the delusive visions of Atlante's castle, in the pride of Rodomonte, and in the comic termination of Angelica's coquetries. The difference between Ariosto and Machiavelli is, that while the latter seems to have dissected human nature with a scalpel, the former has gained this wisdom by sympathy. The one exhibits his anatomical preparations with grim scientific gravity; the other makes his puppets move before us, and smiles sarcastically at their antics.

Sometimes he condenses his philosophy of life in short essays that form the prefaces to cantos, introducing us as through a shapely vestibule into the enchanted palace of his narrative. Among these the finest are the exordia on Love and Honour, on Jealousy, on Loyalty, on Avarice, on the fickleness of Fortune, on Hypocrisy in Courts, and on the pains of Love.[11] The merit of these discourses does not consist in their profundity so much as in their truth. They have been deeply felt, and are of universal applicability. What all men have experienced, what every age and race of men have known, the supreme poet expresses with his transparent style, his tender and caressing melody of phrase, his graceful blending of sympathy and satire. Tasso in the preface to 'Rinaldo' rebukes Ariosto for the introduction of these digressions. He says they are below the dignity of the heroic manner, and that a true poet should be able by example and the action of his characters to point the moral without disquisition. This may be true. Yet Ariosto was writing a romance, and we welcome these personal utterances as a relief from the perpetual movement of his figures. In like manner we should be loth to lose the lyrical inter-breathings of

[9] Canto x. 52 *et seq.*
[10] Canto xxxvii. 104 *et seq.*
[11] Cantos xxxviii. xxxi. xxi. xliii. xlv. xliv. xvi.

Euripidean choruses, or Portia's descant upon mercy, or Fielding's interpolated reflections, all of which are halting places for the mind to rest on in the rapid course of dramatic or narrative evolution. Still it is not in these detached passages that Ariosto shows his greatest wealth of observation. The *Novelle*, scattered with a lavish hand through all his cantos, combine the same sagacity with energy of action and pictorial effect. Whatever men are wont to do, feel, hope for, fear—what moves their wrath—what yields them pleasure, or inflicts upon them pain—that is the material of Ariosto's tales. He does not use this matter either as a satirist or a moralist, as a tragic poet to effect a purification of the passions, or, again, as a didactic poet to inculcate lessons. Like Plautus, he seems to say: 'Whatever be the hues of life, my words shall paint them.' Following the course of events without comment, his page reflects the masque of human joys and griefs which is played out before him. In the tale of Polinesso and Ginevra all the elements of pathos that can be extracted from the love of women and the treachery of men, are accumulated. The desertion of Olimpia by Bireno, after the sacrifices she has made for him, invests the myth of Ariadne with a wild romantic charm. Isabella's devotion to Zerbino through captivity and danger; the friendship of Cloridano for the beautiful Medoro, and their piety toward Dardinello's corpse; Angelica's doting on Medoro, and the idyll of their happiness among the shepherd folk; the death of Brandimarte, and Fiordeligi's agony of grief; Fiordespina's vain love for Bradamante, and her consolation in the arms of Ricciardetto; the wild legend of the Amazons, who suffered no male stranger to approach their city; Norandino's loyalty to Lucina in the cave of Orco; Lidia's cruel treatment of Alceste; the arts whereby Tanacro and Olindo, sons of Marganorre, work their wicked will in love; Gabrina's treachery toward husband and paramour; Giocondo's adventures with the king Astolfo; the ruse by which Argia justifies her infidelity to Anselmo; the sublime courtesies of Leone; the artful machinations of Melissa—these are the rubrics of tales and situations, so varied, so fertile in resource, that a hundred comedies and tragedies might be wrought from them. Ariosto, in his conduct of these stories, attempts no poetical justice. Virtue in distress, vice triumphant, one passion expelling another, nobler motives conquered by baser, loyalty undermined by avarice, feminine frailty made strong to suffer by the force of love; so runs the world, and so the poet paints it.

New and old, false and real, he mixes all together, and by the alchemy of his imagination makes the fusion true. The classics and the Italian poets, writers of history and romance, geographers and chroniclers, have been laid under contribution. But though the poem is composed of imitations, it is invariably original, because Ariosto has seen and felt whatever he described. Angelica on the horse going out to sea recalls Europa. The battle with the Orc is borrowed from the tale of Perseus. Astolfo in the myrtle grove comes straight from Virgil. Cloridano and Medoro are Nisus and Euryalus in modern dress. The shield of Atlante suggests Medusa's head. Pegasus was the parent of the Hippogriff, and Polyphemus of Orco. Rodomonte rages like Mezentius and dies like Turnus. Grifone on the bridge is a Renaissance study from Horatius Cocles. Senapo repeats the myth of Phineus and the Harpies. Yet throughout these plagiarisms Ariosto remains himself. He has assimilated his originals to his own genius, and has given every incident new life by the vividness of his humanity. If it were needful to cite an instance of his playful, practical, ironic treatment of old material, we might point to Lucinda's feminine delicacy in the cave of Orco. She refuses to smear herself with the old goat's fat, and fails to escape with Norandino and his comrades from the hands of this new Polyphemus. So comprehensive is the poet's fancy that it embraces the classic no less than the mediæval past. Both are blent in a third substance which takes life from his own experience and observation. In this respect the art of Ariosto corresponds to Raphael's—to the Stanza of the Segnatura or the Antinous-Jonah of the Chigi Chapel. It is the first emancipation of the modern spirit in a work of catholic beauty, preluding to the final emancipation of the reason in the sphere of criticism, thought, and science.

The quality which gives salt and savour to Ariosto's philosophy of life is irony, sometimes bordering on satire, sometimes running over into drollery and humour. Irony is implicit in the very substance of the 'Furioso.' The choice of a *mad* Orlando for hero reveals the poet's intention; and the recovery of his lost wits from the moon parodies the mediæval doctrine that only in the other world shall we find our true selves. The fate of Angelica, again, is supremely ironical. After flouting kings and Paladins, the noblest knights of the whole world, her lovers, she dotes upon a handsome country-lad and marries him in a shepherd's hut. Medro plucks the rose for which both Christendom and Paynimry had fought in furious rivalry; and wayward Love requites their insults with a by-blow from his dart. Such, smiles the poet, is the end of pride, ambition, passion, and the coquetries that placed the kingdoms of the East and West in peril. Angelica is the embodiment of mortal frailty. The vanity of human wishes, the vicissitudes which blind desire prepares for haughtiest souls, the paradoxes held in store by destiny, are symbolised and imaged in her fate.

Astolfo's journey to the moon, related in the thirty-fourth and thirty-fifth cantos, presents the Ariostean irony with all its gradations of satire, parody, and comic humour. This Duke of England in the Italian romances played the part of an adventurous vainglorious cavalier, eminent for courtesy and courage, who carried the wandering impulse of knight-errantry to the extreme verge of the ridiculous. We find him, at the opening of the thirty-fourth canto, in possession of Atlante's Hippogriff and Logistilla's marvellous horn. Mounting his winged horse, he flies through space, visits the sources of the Nile, and traverses the realm of Ethiopia. There he delivers King Senapo from a brood of

Harpies, whom he pursues to the mouth of a cavern whence issues dense smoke. This is the entrance into Hell:

> L' orecchie attente allo spiraglio tenne,
> E l' aria ne sentì percossa e rotta
> Da pianti e d' urli, e da lamento eterno;
> Segno evidente quivi esser lo 'nferno.

The Paladin's curiosity is roused, and he determines to advance:

> Di che debbo temer, dicea, s' io v' entro?
> Chè mi posso aiutar sempre col corno.
> Farò fuggir Plutone e Satanasso,
> E 'l can trifauce leverò dal passo.

This light-hearted reliance in a perfectly practical spirit upon his magic horn is wholly in keeping with Ariosto's genius. The terrible situation, the good sense of the adventurer, and the enchantment which protects him are so combined as to be prosaically natural. Astolfo gropes his way into the cavern, and is immediately suffocated by dense smoke. In the midst of it, above his head, he sees a body hanging and swinging to and fro like a corpse on a gibbet. He cuts at this object with his sword, and wakes the melancholy voice of Lidia, who tells him that in the smoke are punished obdurate and faithless lovers. The tale of her falseness to Alceste is very beautiful, and shows great knowledge of the heart. But it leads to nothing in the action of the poem, and Astolfo goes out of Hell as he came in—except that the smoke has befouled both face and armour, and he has to scrub himself in a fountain before he can get clean again. Meanwhile Ariosto has parodied the opening of Dante's 'Inferno' with its sublime:

> Mi mise dentro alle segrete cose.

Lidia is the inversion of Francesca; for her sin was, not compliance with the impulses of nature, but unkindness to her lover. This travesty is wrought with no deliberate purpose, but by a mere caprice of fancy, to entertain his audience with a novel while he flouts the faiths and fears of a more earnest age. For Ariosto, the child of the Renaissance, there remained nothing to affirm or to deny about the future of the soul. The Inferno of the middle ages had become a plaything of romance. Astolfo now pursues his journey, looks in on Prester John, and scales the mountain of the Earthly Paradise. There he finds a palace wrought of precious stones, and in the vestibule an ancient man with venerable beard and snowy hair. This is no other than S. John the Evangelist, who hastens to feed the knight's horse with good corn, and sets before him a table spread with fruits which make the sin of Adam seem excusable:

> Con accóglienza grata il cavaliero
> Fu dai santi alloggiato in una stanza:
> Fu provvisto in un' altra al suo destriero
> Di buona biada, che gli fu abbastanza.
> De' frutti a lui del paradiso diero,
> Di tal sapor, ch' a suo giudicio, sanza
> Scusa non sono i duo primi parenti,
> Se per quei fur sì poco ubbidienti!

S. John, delighted with his courteous guest, discourses many things about Orlando, his lost wits, and the moon where they have been stored with other rubbish. At the close of their conversation he remarks that it is a fine night for a journey to the moon; and orders out the fiery chariot which erewhile took Elijah up to heaven. It holds two passengers with comfort; and after a short voyage through the air, Astolfo and the Evangelist land upon the lunar shores. The stanzas which describe the valley of vain things and useless lumber lost to earth are justly famous for their satire and their pathos.[12] There are found the presents made to kings in hope of rich reward, the flatteries of poets, shameful loves, the services of courtiers, the false beauties of women, and bottles filled with the lost sense of men. The list is long; nor was Milton unmindful of it when he wrote his lines upon the Paradise of Fools.[13] The passage illustrates certain qualities in Ariosto's imagination. He has no dread of the prosaic and the simple. Inexhaustibly various alike in thought, in rhythm, in imagery, and in melody of phrase, he yet keeps close to reality, and passes without modulation from seriousness to extravagant fun, returning again to the sadness of profound reflection. His poetry is like the picture of his own face—a large and handsome man with sleepy eyes and epicurean mouth, over whose broad forehead and open features, ploughed by no wrinkles of old age or care, float subtle smiles and misty multitudes of thoughts half lost in dreams. Human life to Ariosto was a comedy such as Menander put upon the Attic stage; and the critic may ask of him, too, whether he or nature were the plagiarist.

Meanwhile S. John is waiting at Astolfo's elbow to point out the Fates, spinning their web of human destinies, and Time carrying the records of history to the river of oblivion. It is a sad picture, did not Ariosto enliven the most sombre matter with his incorrigible humour. By the river bank of Lethe wait cormorants and swans. The former aid Time in his labour of destruction. The latter, who symbolise great poets, save chosen names from undeserved neglect. This leads to a discourse on the services rendered by writers to their patrons, which is marked by Ariosto's levity. He has just been penning praises for Ippolito.[14] Yet here he frankly confesses that the eulogies of poets are distortions of the truth, that history is a lie, and that the whole pageant of humanity conceals a sorry sham. S. John is even made to hint that his good place in Paradise is the guerdon of a panegyric written on his Master:

> Gli scrittori amo, e fo il debito mio;
> Ch' al vostro mondo fui scrittore anch' io:
> E sopra tutti gli altri io feci acquisto
> Che non mi può levar tempo nè morte;
> E ben convenne al mio lodato Cristo
> Rendermi guidardon di sì gran sorte.

12 Canto xxxiv. 76-85.
13 *Par. Lost*, iii. 440.
14 Canto xxxv. 4-9.

The episode of Astolfo's journey to the moon abounds in satire upon human weakness in general. Another celebrated passage has satire of a more direct kind, and is, moreover, valuable for illustrating Ariosto's conduct of his poem. Paris is besieged by the assembled forces of the Saracens. The chief Paladins are absent, and Charlemagne in his sore need addresses a prayer to Heaven.[15] It is just such a prayer as the Israelites offer up in Rossini's 'Mosè in Egitto'—very resonant, very rhetorical, but without sincerity of feeling. Ariosto selects a number of decorous phrases redolent of Renaissance humanism, *tolte agl' inimici stigi*, *al maggior tempio*, *gli occhi al ciel supini*, and combines them with melodramatic effect. God accepts the Emperor's prayer, and sends Michael down to earth to find Discord and Silence, in order that the former may sow strife in the Saracen camp, and the latter lead reinforcements into Paris. Michael starts upon his errand:

> Dovunque drizza Michelangel l' ale,
> Fuggon le nubi, e torna il ciel sereno;
> Gli gira intorno un aureo cerchio, quale
> Veggiam di notte lampeggiar baleno.

He flies straight to a monastery, expecting to find Silence there. The choir, the parlour, the dormitory, the refectory are searched. Wherever he goes he sees *Silenzio* written up; but Silence cannot be found. Instead of him, Discord presents herself, and is recognised by her robe of many-coloured fluttering ribbons, dishevelled hair, and armful of law-papers. Fraud, too, accosts the angel with a gentle face like Gabriel's when he said *Ave!* To Michael's question after Silence, Fraud replies: he used to live in convents and the cells of sages; but now he goes by night with thieves, false coiners, and lovers, and you may find him in the houses of treason and homicide. Yet if you are very anxious to lay hands on him at once, haste to the haunt of Sleep. This cavern is described in stanzas that undoubtedly suggested Spenser's; but Ariosto has nothing so delicate as:

> A trickling stream from high rock tumbling down,
> And ever drizzling rain upon the loft,
> Mixed with a murmuring wind much like the sown
> Of swarming bees.

Instead, he paints, in his peculiar style of realistic imagery, the corpulent form of Ease, Sloth that cannot walk and scarce can stand, Forgetfulness who bars the door to messengers, and Silence walking round the cave with slippers of felt. Silence, summoned by the archangel, sets forth to meet Rinaldo. Discord also quits the convent with her comrade Pride, leaving Fraud and Hypocrisy to keep their places warm till they return. But Discord does her work inadequately; and the cries of Rodomonte's victims rise to heaven. This rouses Michael from his slumber of beatitude. He blushes, plumes his pinions, and shoots

[15] Canto xiv. 68-73.

down again to earth in search of Discord among the monks. He finds her sitting in a chapter convened for the election of officers, and makes her in a moment feel his presence:[16]

> Le man le pose l' Angelo nel crine,
> E pugna e calci le diè senza fine.
> Indi le roppe un manico di croce
> Per la testa, pel dosso e per le braccia.
> Mercè grida la misera a gran voce,
> E le ginocchia al divin nunzio abbraccia.

This is a good specimen both of Ariosto's peculiar levity and of the romantic style which in the most serious portion of his poem permitted such extravagance. The robust archangel tearing Discord's dishevelled hair, kicking her, pounding her with his fists, breaking a cross upon her back, and sending her about her business with a bee in her bonnet, presents a picture of drollery which is exceedingly absurd. Nor is there any impropriety in the picture from the poet's point of view. Michael and the Evangelist are scarcely serious beings. They both form part of his machinery, and help to make the action move.

Broad fun, untinctured by irony, seasons the 'Furioso'—as when Astolfo creates a fleet by throwing leaves into the sea, and mounts his Ethiopian cavalry on horses made of stone, and catches the wind in a bladder; all of which burlesque miracles are told with that keen relish of their practical utility which formed an element of Ariosto's sprightliness.[17] Ruggiero's pleasure-trip on Rabicane; Orlando's achievement of spitting six fat Dutchmen like frogs upon one spear; the index to Astolfo's magic book; the conceit of the knights who jousted with the golden lance, and ascribed its success to their own valour; Orlando's feats of prowess with the table in the robber's den—are other instances of Ariosto's light-heartedness, when he banters with his subject and takes his readers into confidence with his own sense of drollery.[18] The donkey race in armour between Marfisa and Zerbino for a cantankerous old hag, with its courteous ceremonies and chivalrous conclusion, might be cited as an example of more sustained humour.[19] And such, too, though in another region, is the novel of 'Jocondo.'

Ariosto's irony, no less than his romantic method, deprived the 'Furioso' of that sublimity which only belongs to works of greater seriousness and deeper conviction. Yet he sometimes touches the sublime by force of dramatic description or by pathetic intensity. The climax of Orlando's madness has commonly been cited as an instance of poetic grandeur. Yet I should be inclined to prefer the gathering of the storm of discord in Agramante's camp.[20] The whole of this elaborate scene, where the fiery characters and tempestuous passions of the

[16] Canto xxvii. 37.
[17] Canto xxxviii. 30, 33, 26.
[18] Canto x. 72; ix. 68; xxii. 16; xlv. 65; xiii. 36.
[19] Canto xx. 122.
[20] Canto xxvii.

Moslem chiefs, of Ruggiero, Rodomonte, Gradasso, Mandricardo, and Marfisa, are brought successively into play by impulses and motives natural to each and powerful to produce a clash of adverse claims and interests, is not only conceived and executed in a truly dramatic spirit, but is eminently important for the action of the poem. The thunder-clouds which had been mustering to break in ruin upon Christendom, rush together and spend their fury in mid air. Thus the moment is decisive, and nothing has been spared to dignify the passions that provoke the final crash. They go on accumulating in complexity, like a fugue of discords, till at last the hyperbole of this sonorous stanza seems justified:[21]

> Tremò Parigi, e turbidossi Senna
> All' alta voce, a quell' orribil grido;
> Rimbombò il suon fin alla selva Ardenna
> Sì che lasciâr tutte le fiere il nido.
> Udiron l' Alpi e il monte di Gebenna,
> Di Blaia e d' Arli e di Roano il lido;
> Rodano e Sonna udì, Garonna e il Reno:
> Si strinsero le madri i figli al seno.

His pathos also has its own sublimity. Imogen stretched lifeless on the corpse of Cloten; the Duchess of Malfi telling Cariola to see that her daughter says her prayers; Bellario describing his own sacrifice as a mere piece of boyhood flung away—these are instances from our own drama, in which the pathetic is sublime. Ariosto's method is different, and the effect is more rhetorical. Yet he can produce passages of almost equal poignancy, prolonged situations of overmastering emotion, worthy to be set side by side with the Euripidean pictures of Polyxena, Alcestis, or Iphigenia.[22] The death of Zerbino; the death of Brandimarte with half of Fiordeligi's name upon his lips; the constancy of Isabella offering her neck to Rodomonte's sword; the anguish of Olimpia upon the desert island—are instances of sublime poetry wrung from pathos by the force of highly-wrought impassioned oratory. Zerbino is one of the most sympathetic creations of the poet's fancy. Of him Ariosto wrote the famous line:[23]

> Natura il fece, e poi ruppe la stampa.

He is killed by the Tartar Mandricardo before his lady Isabella's eyes:[24]

> A questo la mestissima Isabella,
> Declinando la faccia acrimosa,
> E congiungendo la sua bocca a quella
> Di Zerbin, languidetta come rosa,
> Rosa non colta in sua stagion, sì ch' ella

[21] Canto xxvii. 101.

[22] The comparison of Ariosto and Euripides is not wholly fanciful. Both were supreme artists in an age of incipient decadence, lacking the convictions of their predecessors, and depending for effect upon rhetorical devices. Both were τραγικώτατοι in Aristotle's sense of the phrase, and both were romantic rather than heroic poets.

[23] Canto x. 84.

[24] The whole scene, with all its gradations of emotion, is too long to quote. But see xxiv. 74-87.

Impallidisca in su la siepe ombrosa,
Disse: Non vi pensate già, mia vita,
Far senza me quest' ultima partita.

With stanzas like this the poet cheats the sorrow he has stirred in us. Their imagery is too beautiful to admit of painful feeling while we read; and thus, though the passion of the scene is tragic, its anguish is brought by touches of pure art into harmony with the romantic tone of the whole poem. So also when Isabella, kneeling before Rodomonte's sword, like S. Catherine in Luini's fresco at Milan, has met her own death, Ariosto heals the wound he has inflicted on our sensibility by lines of exquisitely cadenced melody:[25]

Vattene in pace, alma beata e bella.
Così i miei versi avesson forza, come
Ben m' affaticherei con tutta quella
Arte che tanto il parlar orna e come,
Perchè mille e mill' anni, e più, novella
Sentisse il mondo del tuo chiaro nome.
Vattene in pace alla superna sede,
E lascia all' altre esempio di tua fede.

But it is in the situations, the elegiac lamentations, the unexpected vicissitudes, and the strong pictorial beauties of Olimpia's novel, that Ariosto strains his power over pathos to the utmost. Olimpia has lost her kingdom and spent her substance for her husband, Bireno. Orlando aids her in her sore distress, and frees Bireno from his prison. Bireno proves faithless, and deserts her on an island. She is taken by corsairs, exposed like Andromeda on a rock to a sea-monster, and is finally rescued by Orlando. Each of these touching incidents is developed with consummate skill; and the pathos reaches its height when Olimpia, who had risked all for her husband, wakes at dawn to find herself abandoned by him on a desolate sea-beach.[26] In this passage Ariosto comes into competition with two poets of a different stamp—with Catullus, who thus describes Ariadne:

Saxea ut effigies Bacchantis prospicit:

and with Fletcher, who makes Aspatia in the 'Maid's Tragedy' dramatise the situation. Catullus in a single felicitous simile, Fletcher by the agony of passionate declamation, surpass Ariosto's detailed picture. The one is more restrained, the other more tragic. But Ariosto goes straight to our heart by the natural touch of Olimpia feeling for Bireno in the darkness, and by the suggestion of pallid moonlight and a shivering dawn. The numerous prosaic details with which he has charged his picture, add to its reality, and enhance the Euripidean quality we admire in it.

In the case of a poet whose imagination was invariably balanced by practical sound sense, the personal experience he acquired of the female sex could not fail to influence his delineation of women. He was not a

[25] Canto xxix. 27.
[26] Canto x. 20-34.

man to cherish illusion, or to romance in verse about perfection he had never found in fact. He did not place a Beatrice or Laura on the pedestal of his heart; nor was it till he reached the age of forty-seven, when the 'Furioso' had lain for six years finished on his desk, that he married Alessandra Strozzi. His great poem, completed in 1515, must have been written under the influence of those more volatile amours he celebrated in his Latin verses. Therefore we are not surprised to find that the female characters of the 'Orlando' illustrate his epistle on the choice of a wife.[27] His highest ideal of woman is presented to us in Bradamante, whose virtues are a loyal attachment to Ruggiero and a modest submission to the will of her parents. Yet even in Bradamante he has painted a virago from whom the more delicate humanity of Shakspere would have recoiled. The scene in which she quarrels with Marfisa about Ruggiero degrades her in our eyes, and makes us feel that such a termagant might prove a sorry wife.[28] It was almost impossible to combine true feminine qualities with the blood-thirst of an Amazon. Consequently when, just before her marriage, she snuffs the carnage of the Saracens from afar, and regrets that she must withhold her hand from 'such rich spoil of slaughter in a spacious field,' a painful sense of incongruity is left upon our mind.[29] Marfisa, who remains a warrior to the last, and who in her first girlhood had preserved her virginity by slaughtering a palace-full of Pagans,[30] is artistically justified as a romantic heroine. But Bradamante, destined to become a mother, gentle in her home affections, obedient to her father's wishes, tremulous in her attachment to Ruggiero, cannot with any propriety be compared to a leopard loosed from the leash upon defenceless gazelles.[31] Between the Amazonian virgin and the mother of a race of kings to be, the outline of her character wavers.

After the more finished portrait of Bradamante, we find in Isabella and Fiordeligi, the lovers of Zerbino and Brandimarte, Ariosto's purest types of feminine affection. The cardinal virtue of woman in his eyes was self-devotion—loyalty to the death, unhesitating sacrifice of wealth, ease, reputation, life, to the one object of passionate attachment. And this self-devotion he has painted in Olimpia no less romantically than in Isabella and Fiordeligi. Still it must be remembered that Isabella had eloped with Zerbino from her father's palace, that Fiordeligi was only a wife in name, and that Olimpia murdered her first husband and consoled herself very rapidly for Bireno's loss in the arms of Oberto. The poet has not cared to interweave with either portrait such threads of piety and purity as harmonise the self-abandonment of Juliet. Fiordespina's ready credence of the absurd story by which Ricciardetto persuades her that he is Bradamante metamorphosed by a water-fairy to

[27] See above, p. 163.
[28] Canto xxxvi., especially stanza 50.
[29] Canto xxxix. 10-15; cp. *ib.* 67-72.
[30] Canto xxxvii. 15.
[31] Canto xxxix. 69.

a man, and her love-longings, so frankly confessed, so unblushingly indulged, illustrate the passion Ariosto delighted to describe. He feels a tender sympathy for feminine frailty, and in more than one exquisitely written passage claims for women a similar license in love to that of men.[32] Indeed, he never judges a woman severely, unless she adds to her want of chastity the spitefulness of Gabrina or the treachery of Orrigille or the cupidity of Argia or the heartlessness of Angelica. Angelica, who in the 'Innamorato' touches our feelings by her tenderness for Rinaldo, in the 'Furioso' becomes a mere coquette, and is well punished by her insane passion for the first pretty fellow that takes her fancy. The common faults with which Ariosto taxes women are cupidity, infidelity, and fraud.[33] The indulgence due to them from men is almost cynically illustrated by the story of Adonio and the magic virtues of Merlin's goblet.[34] In the preface to the fifth canto he condemns the brutality of husbands, and in the tenth he recommends ladies to be free of their favours to none but middle-aged lovers.[35]

Ariosto's morality was clearly on a level with that of the novelists from Boccaccio to Bandello; and his apology is that he was not inferior to the standard of his age. Still it is not much to his credit to plead that his cantos are less impure than the *Capitoli* of Monsignore La Casa or the prurient comedies of Aretino. Even allowing for the laxity of Renaissance manners, it must be conceded that he combined vulgar emotions and a coarse-fibred nature with the most refined artistic genius.[36] Our Elizabethan drama, in spite of moral crudity, contains nothing so cynical as Ariosto's novel of 'Jocondo.' The beauty of its style, the absence of tragedy in its situations or of passion in its characters, and the humorous smile with which the poet acts as showman to the secrets of the alcove, render this tale one of the most licentious in literature. Nor is this licentiousness balanced by any sublimer spiritual quality. His ideal of manliness is physical force and animal courage. Cruelty and bloodshed for the sake of slaughter stain his heroes.[37] The noblest conflict of emotion he portrays is the struggle between love and honour in Ruggiero,[38] and the contest of courtesy between Ruggiero and Leone.[39] In the few passages where he cele-

[32] See especially iv. 63-67.

[33] Introductions to cantos xliii. xxviii. xxix. xxii. xxvi.; cp. xxvii. 123.

[34] Canto xlii.

[35] Stanzas 6-9.

[36] If this seems overstated, I might refer the reader to the prologue of the *Suppositi*, where the worst vice of the Renaissance is treated with a flippant relish; or, again, to the prologue of the *Lena*, where the *double entendre* is worthy of the grossest *Capitolo*. The plots of all Ariosto's comedies are of a vulgar, obscene, *bourgeois* type.

[37] See xxxix. 10-72, xx. 113, xlvi. 137, and *passim*, for the carnage wrought by knights cased in enchanted armour with invulnerable bodies upon defenceless Saracens or unarmed peasants. It was partly this that made Shelley shrink with loathing from the *Furioso*.

[38] Cantos xxi. 1-3, xx. 143, xxxviii. introduction, xlv. 57, xxv. introduction.

[39] Cantos xliv. xlv.

brates the chivalrous ideal, he dwells chiefly on the scorn of gain and the contempt for ease which characterised the errant knighthood.[40]

The style of the 'Furioso' is said to have taught Galileo how to write Italian. This style won from him for Ariosto the title of *divine*. As the luminous and flowing octave stanzas pass before us, we are almost tempted to forget that they are products of deliberate art. The beauty of their form consists in its limpidity and naturalness. Ariosto has no mannerism. He always finds exactly the expression needed to give clearness to the object he presents. Whether the mood be elegiac or satiric, humorous or heroic, idyllic or rhetorical, this absolute sincerity and directness of language maintains him at an even level. In each case he has given the right, the best, the natural investiture to thought, and his phrases have the self-evidence of crystals. Just as he collected the materials of his poem from all sources, so he appropriated every word that seemed to serve his need. The vocabulary of Dante, Petrarch, and Boccaccio, the racy terms of popular poetry, together with Latinisms and Lombardisms, were alike laid under contribution. Yet these diverse elements were so fused together and brought into a common toning by his taste, that, though the language of his poem was new, it was at once accepted as classical. When we remember the difficulties which in his days beset Italian composition, when we call to mind the frigid experiments of Bembo in Tuscan diction, the meticulous proprieties of critics like Speron Speroni, and the warfare waged around the 'Gerusalemme Liberata,' we know not whether to wonder at Ariosto's happy audacities in language or at their still happier success. His triumph was not won without severe labour. He spent ten years in the composition of the 'Furioso' and sixteen in its polishing. The autograph at Ferrara shows page upon page of alteration, transposition, and refinement on the first draught, proving that the Homeric limpidity and ease we now admire, were gained by assiduous self-criticism. The result of this long toil is that there cannot be found a rough or languid or inharmonious passage in an epic of nigh on 40,000 lines. If we do not discern in Ariosto the inexhaustible freshness of Homer, the sublime music of Milton, the sculpturesque brevity of Dante, the purity of Petrarch, or the majestic sweetness of Virgilian cadences, it can fairly be said that no other poet is so varied. None mingles strength, sweetness, subtlety, rapidity, rhetoric, breadth of effect and delicacy of suggestion, in a harmony so perfect. None combines workmanship so artistic with a facility that precludes all weariness. Whether we read him simply to enjoy his story or to taste the most exquisite flavours of poetic diction, we shall be equally satisfied. Language in his hands is like a soft and yielding paste, which takes all forms beneath the moulder's hand, and then, when it has hardened, stays for ever sharp in outline, glittering as adamant.

While following the romantic method of Boiardo and borrowing the

[40] Canto vi. 80, vii. 41-44. The sentiments, though superficial, are exquisitely uttered.

polished numbers of Poliziano, Ariosto refined the stanzas of the former poet without losing rapidity, and avoided the stationary pomp of the latter without sacrificing richness. He thus effected a combination of the two chief currents of Italian versification, and brought the octave to its final perfection. When we study the passage which describes the entrance of Ruggiero into the island home of Alcina, we feel the advance in melody and movement that he made. We are reminded of the gardens of Morgana and Venus; but both are surpassed in their own qualities of beauty, while the fluidity that springs from complete command of the material, is added. Such touches as the following:[41]

> Pensier canuto nè molto nè poco
> Si può quivi albergare in alcun core:

are wholly beyond the scope of Boiardo's style. Again, this stanza, without the brocaded splendour of Poliziano, contains all that he derived from Claudian:[42]

> Per le cime dei pini e degli allori,
> Degli alti faggi e degli irsuti abeti,
> Volan scherzando i pargoletti Amori
> Di lor vittorie altri godendo lieti,
> Altri pigliando a saettare i cori
> La mira quindi, altri tendendo reti:
> Chi tempra dardi ad un ruscel più basso,
> E chi gli aguzza ad un volubil sasso.

Raphael, Correggio and Titian have succeeded to Botticelli and Mantegna; and as those supreme painters fused the several excellences of their predecessors in a fully developed work of art, so has Ariosto passed beyond his masters in the art of poetry. Nor was the process one of mere eclecticism. Intent upon similar aims, the final artists of the early sixteenth century brought the same profound sentiment for reality, the same firm grasp on truth, the same vivid imagination as their precursors to the task. But they possessed surer hands and a more accomplished method. They stood above their subject and surveyed it from the height of conscious power.

After the island of Alcinà, it only remained for Tasso to produce novelty in his description of Armida's gardens by pushing one of Ariosto's qualities to exaggeration. The *dolcezza*, which in Tasso is too sugared, has in Ariosto the fine flavour of wild honeycombs. In the tropical magnificence of Tasso's stanzas there is a sultry stupor which the fresh sunlight of the 'Furioso' never sheds. This wilding grace of the Ferrarese Homer is due to the lightness of his touch—to the blending of humorous with luxurious images in a style that passes swiftly over all it paints.[43] After a like fashion, the idyll of Angelica among the shepherds surpasses the celebrated episode of Erminia in the 'Gerusalemme.'

[41] Canto vi. 73.
[42] Canto vi. 75.
[43] Notice, for example, the irony of the seventh line in vi. 71, and of the third and fourth in the next stanza.

It is not that Tasso has not invented a new music and wrung a novel effect from the situation by the impassioned fervour of his sympathy and by the majestic languor of his cadences. But we feel that what Tasso relies on for his main effect, Ariosto had already suggested in combination with other and still subtler qualities. The one has the overpowering perfume of a hothouse jasmine; the other has the mingled scents of a garden where roses and carnations are in bloom.

Ariosto's pictorial faculty has already formed the topic of a paragraph, nor is it necessary to adduce instances of what determines the whole character of the 'Orlando Furioso.' Otherwise it would be easy to form a gallery of portraits and landscapes; to compare the double treatment of Andromeda exposed to the sea monster in the tenth and eleventh cantos,[44] to set a pageant in the style of Mantegna by the side of a Correggiesque vignette,[45] or to enlarge upon the beauty of those magical Renaissance buildings which the poet dreamed of in the midst of verdant lawns and flowery wildernesses.[46] True to the spirit of Italian art, he had no strong sentiment for nature except in connexion with humanity. Therefore we find but little of landscape-painting for its own sake and small sympathy with the wilder and uncultivated beauties of the world. His scenery recalls the backgrounds to Carpaccio's pictures or the idyllic gardens of the Giorgionesque school. Sometimes there is a magnificent drawing in the style of Titian's purple mountain ranges, and here and there we come upon minutely finished studies that imply deep feeling for the moods of nature. Of this sort is the description of autumn:[47]

> Tra il fin d' ottobre e il capo di novembre,
> Nella stagion che la frondosa vesta
> Vede levarsi, e discoprir le membre,
> Trepida pianta, finchè nuda resta,
> E van gli augelli a strette schiere insembre.

The illuminative force of his similes is quite extraordinary. He uses them not only as occasions for painting cabinet pictures of exquisite richness, but also for casting strong imaginative light upon the object under treatment. In the earlier part of the 'Furioso' he describes two battles with a huge sea monster. The Orc is a kind of romantic whale, such as Piero di Cosimo painted in his tale of Andromeda; and Ruggiero has to fight it first, while riding on the Hippogriff. It is therefore necessary for Ariosto to image forth a battle between behemoth and a mighty bird. He does so by elaborately painting the more familiar struggles of an eagle who has caught a snake, and of a mastiff snapping at a fly.[48]

[44] Canto x. 95, 96, xi. 65, 66. The one is Angelica, the other Olimpia.
[45] Canto vi. 62, 63, 75.
[46] Canto vi. 71, xxxiv. 51-53.
[47] Canto ix. 7.
[48] Canto x. 102-106.

At the same time he adds realistic touches like the following:

> L' orca, che vede sotto le grandi ale
> L' ombra di qua e di là correr su l' onda,
> Lascia la preda certa littorale,
> E quella vana segue furibonda.

Or, again, when Ruggiero is afraid of wetting his aerial courser's wings:

> Chè se lo sprazzo in tal modo ha a durare
> Teme sì l' ale innaffi all' Ippogrifo
> Che brami invano avere o zucca o schifo.

The mixture of imagery with prosaic detail brings the whole scene distinctly before our eyes. When Orlando engages the same monster, he is in a boat, and the conditions of the contest are altered. Accordingly we have a different set of similes. A cloud that fills a valley, rolling to and fro between the mountain sides, describes the movement of the Orc upon the waters; and when Orlando thrusts his anchor in between its jaws to keep them open, he is compared to miners propping up their galleries with beams in order that they may pursue their work in safety.[49] In this way we realise the formidable nature of the beast, and comprehend the stratagem that tames it to Orlando's will.

The same nice adaptation of images may be noticed in the similes showered on Rodomonte. The giant is alone inside the walls of Paris, and the poet is bound to make us feel that a whole city may have cause to tremble before a single man. Therefore he never leaves our fancy for a moment in repose. At one time it is a castle shaken by a storm; at another a lion retreating before the hunters; again, a tigress deprived of her cubs, or a bull that has broken from the baiting-pole, or the whelps of a lioness attacking a fierce young steer.[50] Image succeeds image with dazzling rapidity, all tending to render a strained situation possible.

Some of Ariosto's illustrations—like the ploughman and the thunderbolt, the two dogs fighting, the powder magazine struck by lightning, the house on fire at night, the leaves of autumn, the pine that braves a tempest, the forest bending beneath mighty winds, the April avalanche of suddenly dissolving snow—though wrought with energy and spirit, have not more than the usual excellences of carefully developed Homeric imitation.[51] Framed in single octave stanzas, they are pictures for the mind to rest on. Others illuminate the matter they are used to illustrate, with the radiance of subtle and remote fancy. Of this sort is the brief image by which the Paladins in Charlemagne's army are likened to jewels in a cloth of gold.[52]

[49] Canto xi. 34-38.
[50] Canto xviii. 11, 14, 19, 22, 35.
[51] Canto i. 65, ii. 5, ix. 78, xx. 89, xxi. 15, 16, xxiv. 63, xxxvi. 40.
[52] Canto xxxix. 17.

Ed hanno i paladin sparsi tra loro,
Come le gemme in un ricamo d' oro.

A common metaphor takes new beauty by its handling in this simile:[53]

Pallido come colto al mattutino
E da sera il ligustro o il molle acanto.

Homer had compared the wound of Menelaus to ivory stained by a Mæonian woman with crimson.[54] Ariosto refines on this conceit:[55]

Così talora un bel purpureo nastro
Ho veduto partir tela d' argento
Da quella bianca man più ch' alabastro,
Da cui partire il cor spesso mi sento.

Both Homer and Virgil likened their dying heroes to flowers cut down by the tempest or the plough. The following passage will bear comparison even with the death of Euphorbus:[56]

Come purpureo fior languendo muore,
Che 'l vomere al passar tagliato lassa,
O come carco di superchio umore
Il papaver nell' orto il capo abbassa:
Così, giù della faccia ogni colore
Cadendo, Dardinel di vita passa;
Passa di vita, e fa passar con lui
L' ardire e la virtù di tutti i sui.

One more example may be chosen where Ariosto has borrowed nothing from any model. He uses the perfume that clings to the hair or dress of youth or maiden, as a metaphor for the aroma of noble ancestry:[57]

L' odor ch' è sparso in ben notrita e bella
O chioma o barba o delicata vesta
Di giovene leggiadro o di donzella,
Ch' amor sovente sospirando desta;
Se spira, e fa sentir di sè novella,
E dopo molti giorni ancora resta,
Mostra con chiaro ed evidente effetto
Come a principio buono era e perfetto.

The unique importance of Ariosto in the history of Renaissance poetry justifies a lengthy examination of his masterpiece. In him the chief artistic forces of the age were so combined that he remains its best interpreter. Painting, the cardinal art of Italy, determined his method; and the tide of his narrative carried with it the idyll, the elegy, and the *Novella*. In these forms the genius of the Renaissance found fittest literary expression; for the epic and the drama lay beyond the scope of the Italians at this period. The defect of deep passion and

[53] Canto xliii. 169.
[54] *Iliad*, iv. 140.
[55] Canto xxiv. 66.
[56] Canto xviii. 153.
[57] Canto xli. 1.

serious thought, the absence of enthusiasm, combined with rare analytic powers and an acute insight into human nature, placed Ariosto in close relation to his age. Free from illusions, struggling after no high-set ideal, accepting the world as he found it, without the impulse to affirm or to deny, without hate, scorn, indignation or revolt, he represented the spirit of the sixteenth century in those qualities which were the source of moral and political decay to the Italians. But he also embodied the strong points of his epoch—especially that sustained pursuit of beauty in form, that width of intellectual sympathy, that urbanity of tone and delicacy of perception, which rendered Italy the mistress of the arts, the propagator of culture for the rest of Europe.

CHAPTER X

THE NOVELLIERI

Boccaccio's Legacy—Social Conditions of Literature in Italy—Importance of the Novella—Definition of the Novella—Method of the Novelists—Their Style—Materials used—Large Numbers of Novelle in Print—Lombard and Tuscan Species—Introductions to Il Lasca's 'Cene,' Parabosco's 'Diporti'—Bandello's Dedications—Life of Bandello—His Moral Attitude—Bandello as an Artist—Comparison of Bandello and Fletcher—The Tale of 'Gerardo and Elena'—'Romeo and Juliet'—The Tale of 'Nicuola'—The 'Countess of Salisbury'—Bandello's Apology for his Morals and his Style—Il Lasca—Mixture of Cruelty and Lust—Extravagant Situations—Treatment of the 'Parisina' Motive—The Florentine 'Burla'—Apology for Il Lasca's Repulsiveness—Firenzuola—His Life—His Satires on the Clergy—His Dialogue on Beauty—Novelettes and Poems—Doni's Career—His Bizarre Humour—Bohemian Life at Venice—The Pellegrini—His Novelle—Miscellaneous Works—The 'Marmi'—The Novelists of Siena—Their Specific Character—Sermini—Fortini—Bargagli's Description of the Siege of Siena—Illicini's Novel of 'Angelica'—The 'Proverbi' of Cornazano—The 'Notti Piacevoli' of Straparola—The Novel of 'Belphegor'—Straparola and Machiavelli—Giraldi Cinthio's 'Hecatommithi'—Description of the Sack of Rome—Plan of the Collection—The Legend of the Borgias—Comparison of Italian Novels and English Plays.

Of Boccaccio's legacy the most considerable portion, and the one that bore the richest fruit, was the 'Decameron.' During the sixteenth century the *Novella*, as he shaped it, continued to be a popular and widely practised form of literature. In Italy the keynote of the Renaissance was struck by the *Novella*, as in England by the Drama. Nor is this predominance of what must be reckoned a subordinate branch of fiction, altogether singular; for the *Novella* was in a special sense adapted to the public which during the Age of the Despots grew up in Italy. Since the fourteenth century the conditions of social life had undergone a thorough revolution. Under the influence of dynastic rulers stationed in great cities, merchants and manufacturers were confounded with the old nobility; and in commonwealths like Florence the *bourgeoisie* gave their tone to society. At the same time the community thus formed was separated from the people by the bar of humanistic culture. Literature felt this social transformation. Its products were shaped to suit the taste of the middle classes, and at the same time to amuse the leisure of the aristocracy. The *Novella* was the natural outcome of these circumstances. Its qualities and its defects alike betray the ascendency of the *bourgeois* element.

When a whole nation is addressed in drama or epic, it is necessary for the poet to strike a lofty and noble note. He appeals to collective humanity, and there is no room for aught that savours of the trivial and base. Homer and Sophocles, Dante and Shakspere, owed their grandeur in no slight measure to the audience for whom they laboured. The case is altered when a nation comes to be divided into orders, each of which has its own peculiar virtues and its own besetting sins. Limitations are of necessity introduced, and deflections from the canon of universality are welcomed. If the poet, for example, writes for the lowest classes of society, he can afford to be coarse, but he must be natural. An aristocracy, taken by itself, is apt, on the contrary, to demand from literature the refinements of fashionable vice and the subtleties of artificial sentiment. Under such influence we obtain the Arthurian legends of the later middle ages, which contrast unfavourably, in all points of simplicity and directness, with the earlier Niebelungen and Carolingian Cycles. The middle classes, for their part, delight in pictures of daily life, presented with realism, and flavoured with satire that touches on the points of their experience. Literature produced to please the *bourgeois*, must be sensible and positive; and its success will greatly depend upon the piquancy of its appeal to ordinary unidealised appetites. The Italians lacked such means of addressing the aggregated masses of the nation as the panhellenic festivals of Greece afforded. The public which gave its scale of grandeur and sincerity to the Attic and Elizabethan drama, was wanting. The literature of the *cinque cento*, though it owed much to the justice of perception and simple taste of the true people, was composed for the most part by men of middle rank for the amusement of citizens and nobles. It partook of those qualities which characterise the upper middle classes. It was deficient in the breadth, the magnitude, the purity, which an audience composed of the whole nation can alone communicate. We find it cynical, satirical, ingenious in sly appeals to appetite, and oftentimes superfluously naughty. Above all it was emphatically the literature of a society confined to cities.

It may be difficult to decide what special quality of the Italian temperament was satisfied with the *Novella*. Yet the fact remains that this species of composition largely governed their production, not only in the field of narrative, but also in the associated region of poetry and in the plastic arts. So powerful was the attraction it possessed, that even the legends of the saints assumed this character. A notable portion of the 'Sacre Rappresentazioni' were dramatised *Novelle*. The romantic poets interwove *Novelle* with their main theme, and the charm of the 'Orlando Furioso' is due in no small measure to such episodes. Popular poems of the type represented by 'Ginevra degli Almieri' were versified *Novelle*. Celebrated trials, like that of the Countess of Cellant, Vittoria Accoramboni, or the Cenci, were offered to the people in the form of *Novelle*. The humanists—Pontano, Poggio, Æneas Sylvius—wrote *Novelle* in Latin. The best serial pictures of the secondary painters —whether we select Benozzo Gozzoli's legend of S. Augustine at San Gemignano, or Carpaccio's legend of S. Ursula at Venice, or Sodoma's legend of S. Benedict at Monte Oliveto, or Lippo Lippi's legend of S. John at Prato—are executed in the spirit of the novelists. They are *Novelle* painted in their salient incidents for the laity to study on the walls of church and oratory.

The term *Novella* requires definition, lest the thing in question should be confounded with our modern novel. Although they bear the same name, these species have less in common than might be supposed. Both, indeed, are narratives; but while the novel is a history extending over a considerable space of time, embracing a complicated tissue of events, and necessitating a study of character, the *Novella* is invariably brief and sketchy. It does not aim at presenting a detailed picture of human life within certain artistically chosen limitations, but confines itself to a striking situation, or tells an anecdote illustrative of some moral quality. This is shown by the headings of the sections into which Italian *Novellieri* divided their collections. We read such rubrics as the following: 'On the magnanimity of princes;' 'Concerning those who have been fortunate in love;' 'Of sudden changes from prosperity to evil fortune;' 'The guiles of women practised on their husbands.' A theme is proposed, and the *Novelle* are intended to exemplify it. The *Novelle* were descended in a direct line from the anecdotes embedded in mediæval Treasuries, Bestiaries, and similar collections. The novel, on the other hand, as Cervantes, Richardson, and Fielding formed it for the modern nations, is an expansion and prose digest of the drama. It implies the drama as a previous condition of its being, and flourishes among races gifted with the dramatic faculty.

Furthermore, the *Novelle* were composed for the amusement of mixed companies, who met together and passed their time in conversation. All the *Novellieri* pretend that their stories were originally recited and then written down, nor is there the least doubt that in a large majority of cases they were really read aloud or improvised upon occasions similar to those invented by their authors. These circumstances determined the length and ruled the mechanism of the *Novella*. It was impossible within the short space of a spoken tale to attempt any minute analysis of character, or to weave the meshes of a complicated plot. The narrator went straight to his object, which was to arrest the attention, stimulate the curiosity, gratify the sensual instincts, excite the laughter, or stir the tender emotions of his audience by some fantastic, extraordinary, voluptuous, comic, or pathetic incident. He sketched his personages with a few swift touches, set forth their circumstances with pungent brevity, and expended his force upon the painting of the central motive. Sometimes he contented himself with a bare narrative, leaving its details to the fancy. Many *Novelle* are the mere skeletons of stories, short notes, and epitomes of tales. At another time he indulged in descriptive passages of great verbal beauty, when it was his purpose to delight the ideal audience with pictures, or to arouse their sympathy for his characters in a situation of peculiar vividness. Or he introduced digressions upon moral themes suggested by the passion of the moment, discoursing with the easy flow of one who raises points of casuistry in a drawing-room. Again, he heightened the effects of his anecdote by elaborate rhetorical development of the main emotions, placing carefully studied speeches into the mouth of heroine or hero, and using every artifice for appealing directly to the feelings of his hearers. Thus, while the several *Novellieri* pursue different methods at different times according to their purpose, their styles are all determined by the fact that recitation was essential to the species. All of them, moreover, have a common object in amusement. Though the *Novellieri* profess to teach morality by precept, and though some of them prefix prayers to their most impudent debauches of the fancy,[1] it is clear that entertainment was their one sole end in view. For their success they relied on the novelty and strangeness of their incidents; on obscenity, sometimes veiled beneath the innuendoes and suggestive metaphors of Italian convention, but more often unabashed and naked to the view; on startling horrors, acts of insane passion, or the ingenuities of diabolical cruelty. The humour of *beffe* and *burle*, jests played by rogues on simpletons, practical jokes, and the various devices whereby wives and lovers fooled confiding husbands, supplied abundant material for relieving the more tragic stories. Lastly, the wide realm of pathos, the spectacle of beauty in distress, young lovers overwhelmed by undeserved calamity, sudden reverses of fortune, and accidents of travel upon land and sea, provided the narrator with plentiful matter for working on the sympathy of his readers. Of moral purpose in any strict sense of the phrase the *Novelle* have none. This does not mean that they are invariably immoral; on the contrary, the theme of a considerable number is such that the tale can be agreeably told without violence to the most sensitive taste. But the novelist had no ethical intention; therefore he brought every motive into use that might amuse or stimulate, with business-like indifference. He felt no qualm of conscience at provoking the cruder animal instincts, at dragging the sanctities of domestic life in the mire of his buffoonery, or at playing on the appetite for monstrous vice, the thirst for abnormal sensations, in his audience. So long as he could excite attention, he was satisfied. We cannot but wonder at the customs of a society which derived its entertainment from these tales, when we know that noble ladies listened to them without blushing, and that bishops composed them as a graceful compliment to the daughter of a reigning duke.[2]

[1] See Bandello's Introduction to *Nov.* xxxv. of Part i., where a most disgusting story is ushered in with ethical reflections; and take this passage from the opening of one of Il Lasca's least presentable novels: 'Prima che al novellare di questa sera si dia principio, mi rivolgo a te. Dio ottimo e grandissimo che solo tutto sai e tutto puoi, pregandoti divotamente e di cuore, che per la tua infinita bontà e clemenza mi conceda, e a tutti questi altri che dopo me diranno, tanto del tuo ajuto e della tua grazia, che la mia lingua e la loro non dica cosa niuna, se non a tua lode e a nostra consolazione.'—*Le Cene* (Firenze, Lemonnier, 1857), p. 7.

[2] It may be mentioned that not *all* stories were recited before women. Bandello introduces one of his tales with the remark that in the absence of the ladies men may be less careful in their choice of themes (*Nov.* xxx. pt. i.). The exception is

In style the *Novelle* are, as might be expected, very unequal. Everybody tried his hand at them: some wrote sparkling Tuscan, others a dense Lombard dialect; some were witty, others dull. Yet all affected to be following Boccaccio. His artificial periods and rhetorical amplifications, ill-managed by men of imperfect literary training, who could not free themselves from local jargons, produced an awkward mixture of discordant faults. Yet the public expected little from the novelist in diction. What they required was movement, stimulus, excitement of their passions. So long as the tale-maker kept curiosity awake, it was a matter of comparative indifference what sort of words he used. The *Novella* was a literary no-man's-land, where the critic exercised a feeble sway, and amateurs or artists did what each found suited to his powers. It held its ground under conditions similar to those which determined the supply of plays among us in the seventeenth century, or of magazine novels in this.

In their material the *Novelle* embraced the whole of Italian society, furnishing pictures of its life and manners from the palaces of princes to the cottages of *contadini*. Every class is represented—the man of books, the soldier, the parish priest, the cardinal, the counter-jumper, the confessor, the peasant, the duke, the merchant, the noble lady, the village maiden, the serving-man, the artisan, the actor, the beggar, the courtesan, the cut-throat, the astrologer, the lawyer, the physician, the midwife, the thief, the preacher, the nun, the pander, the fop, the witch, the saint, the galley-slave, the friar—they move before us in a motley multitude like the masquerade figures of carnival time, jostling each other in a whirl of merriment and passion, mixing together in the frank democracy of vice. Though these pictures of life are brightly coloured and various beyond description, they are superficial. It is only the surface of existence that the *Novelliere* touches. He leaves its depths unanalysed, except when he plunges a sinister glance into some horrible abyss of cruelty or lust, or, stirred by gentler feeling, paints an innocent unhappy youthful love. The student of contemporary Italian customs will glean abundant information from these pages; the student of human nature gathers little except reflections on the morals of sixteenth-century society. It was perhaps this prodigal superfluity of striking incident, in combination with poverty of intellectual content, which made the *Novelle* so precious to our playwrights. The tales of Cinthio and Bandello supplied them with the outlines of tragedies, leaving the poet free to exercise his analytic and imaginative powers upon the creation of character and the elaboration of motive. But that, in spite of all their faults, the *Novelle* fascinate the fancy and stimulate the mental energies, will be admitted by all who have made them the subject of careful study.

To render an adequate account of the *Novellieri* and their works is

singular, as illustrating what was thought unfit for female ears. The *Novella* itself consists of a few jokes upon a disgusting subject; but it is less immodest than many which he dedicated to noble women.

very difficult.[3] The printing-press poured novels forth in every town in Italy, and authors of all districts vied with one another in their composition. At Florence Firenzuola penned stories with the golden fluency and dazzling wealth of phrase peculiar to him. Il Lasca's 'Cene' rank among the most considerable literary products of the age. At Florence, again, Machiavelli wrote 'Belphegor,' and Scipione Bargagli printed his 'Trattenimenti.' Gentile Sermini, Pietro Fortini and Giustiniano Nelli were the novelists of Siena; Masuccio and Antonio Mariconda, of Naples. At Rome the Modenese Francesco Maria Molza rivalled the purity of Tuscan in his 'Decamerone.' But it was chiefly in the North of Italy that novelists abounded. Giraldi's hundred tales, entitled 'Hecatommithi,' issued from Ferrara. They were heavy in style, and prosaic; yet their matter made them widely popular. Sabadino wrote his 'Porretane' at Bologna, and Francesco Straparola of Caravaggio published his 'Tredici piacevoli Notti' at Venice. There also appeared the 'Diporti' of Girolamo Parabosco, the 'Sei Giornate' of Sebastiano Erizzo, Celio Malespini's 'Ducento Novelle,' and the 'Proverbi' of Antonio Cornazano. Cademosto of Lodi, Monsignor Brevio of Venice, Ascanio de' Mori of Mantua, Luigi da Porto of Vicenza, and, last not least, the illustrious Matteo Bandello, proved how rich in this species of literature were the northern provinces. The Lombards displayed a special faculty for tales in which romance predominated. Venice, notorious for her pleasure-marts of luxury, became the emporium of publications which supplied her courtesans and rufflers with appropriate mental food. The Tuscans showed more comic humour, and, of course, a purer style. But in point of matter, intellectual and moral, there is not much to choose between the works of Florentine and Lombard authors.

Following the precedent of Boccaccio, it was usual for the *Novellieri* to invent a framework for their stories, making it appear that a polite society of men and women (called in Italy a *lieta brigata*) had by some chance accident been thrown upon their own resources in circumstances of piquant novelty. One of the party suggests that they should spend their time in telling tales, and a captain is chosen who sets the theme and determines the order of the story-tellers. These introductions are not unfrequently the most carefully written portion of the collection, and abound in charming sketches of Italian life. Thus Il Lasca at the opening of 'Le Cene' feigns that a company of young men and women went in winter-time to visit at a friend's house in Florence. It was snowing, and the youths amused themselves by a snow-ball match in the inner courtyard of the palace. The ladies watched them from a *loggia*, till it came into their heads to join the game. Snow was brought them from the roofs, and they began to pelt the young men from their balcony.[4] The fire was returned; and when the *brigata* had enough of

[3] *I Novellieri in Prosa*, by Giambattista Passano (Milano, Schiepatti, 1864), will be found an excellent dictionary of reference.

[4] This motive may have been suggested by Folgore da S. Gemignano's sonnet on the month of January.

this fun, they entered the house together, dried their clothes, and, sitting round a blazing hearth, formed a plan for telling stories at supper. Girolamo Parabosco places the scene of his 'Diporti' on the Venetian lagoons. A party of gentlemen have left the city to live in huts of wood and straw upon the islands, with the intention of fowling and fishing. The weather proves too bad for sport, and they while away the hours of idleness with anecdotes. Bandello follows a different method, which had been suggested by Masuccio. He dedicates his *Novelle* to the distinguished people of his acquaintance, in prefaces not devoid of flattery, but highly interesting to a student of those times. Princes, poets, warriors, men of state, illustrious women, and humanists pass before us in these dedications, proving that polite society in Italy, the society of the learned and the noble, was a republic of wit and culture. Alessandro Bentivoglio and Ippolita Sforza, the leaders of fashion and Bandello's special patrons, take the first rank.[5] Then we have the Gonzaga family of Mantua, Lancinus Curtius, Aldus Manutius, Machiavelli, Molsa, Guicciardini, Castiglione, the Duchess of Urbino, Giovanni de' Medici, Julius Cæsar Scaliger, Bernardo Tasso, Prospero Colonna, Julius II., Porcellio, Pontano, Berni, the Milanese Visconti, the Neapolitan Sanseverini, the Adorni of Genoa, the Foscari of Venice, the Estensi of Ferrara. Either directly addressed in prefaces or mentioned with familiar allusion in the course of the narratives, these historic names remind us that the author lived at the centre of civilisation, and that his *Novelle* were intended for the entertainment of the great world. What Castiglione presents abstractedly and in theory as a critique on noble society, is set before us by Bandello in the concrete form of every-day occurrence. Nor does the author forget that he is speaking to this company. His words are framed to suit their prejudices; his allusions have reference to their sentiments and predilections. The whole work of art breathes the air of good manners and is tuned to a certain pitch-note of fashionable tone. We may be astounded that ladies and gentlemen of the highest birth and breeding could tolerate the licenses of language and suggestion furnished by Bandello for their delectation. We may draw conclusions as to their corruption and essential coarseness in the midst of refined living and external gallantries.[6] Yet the fact remains that these *Novelle* were a customary adjunct to the courtly pleasures of the sixteenth century; and it was only through the printing-press that they passed into the taverns and the brothels, where perhaps they found their fittest audience.

Matteo Bandello was a member of the petty Lombard nobility, born at Castelnuovo in Tortona. His uncle was General of the Dominicans, and this circumstance determined Matteo's career. After spending some years of his youth at Rome, he entered the order of the Predicatori in

[5] These are the pair so nobly painted by Luini above the high altar of S. Maurizio at Milan. See my *Sketches and Studies in Italy*.

[6] What we know about manners at the Courts of our Elizabeth and James, and the gossip of the French Court in Brantôme's *Dames Galantes*, remind us that this blending of grossness and luxury was not peculiar to Italy.

the Convent delle Grazie at Milan. He was not, however, destined to the seclusion of a convent; for he attended his uncle, in the character apparently of a companion or familiar secretary, when the General visited the chief Dominican establishments of Italy, Spain, France and Germany. A considerable portion of Bandello's manhood was passed at Mantua, where he became the tutor and the platonic lover of Lucrezia Gonzaga. Before the date 1525, when French and Spaniards contested the Duchy of Milan, he had already formed a collection of *Novelle* in manuscript—the fruits of all that he had heard and seen upon his frequent travels. These were dispersed when the Spaniards entered Milan and pillaged the house of the Bandello family.[7] Matteo, after numerous adventures as an exile, succeeded in recovering a portion of his papers, and retired with Cesare Fregoso to the Court of France. He now set himself seriously to the task of preparing his *Novelle* for the press; nor was this occupation interrupted by the duties of the see of Agen, conferred upon him in 1550 by Henry II. The new bishop allowed his colleague of Grasse to administer the see, drawing enough of its emoluments for his private needs, and attending till his death, about the year 1560, to study and composition.

Bandello's life was itself a *novella*. The scion of a noble house, early dedicated to the order of S. Dominic, but with the General of that order for his uncle, he enjoyed rare opportunities of studying men and manners in all parts of Europe. His good abilities and active mind enabled him to master the essentials of scholarship, and introduced him as tutor to one of the most fascinating learned women of his age. These privileges he put to use by carrying on a courtly flirtation with his interesting pupil, at the same time that he penned his celebrated novels. The disasters of the Milanese Duchy deprived him of his literary collections and probably injured his fortune. But he found advancement on a foreign soil, and died a bishop at the moment when Europe was ringing with the scandals of his too licentious tales. These tales furnished the Reformers with a weapon in their war against the Church; nor would it have been easy to devise one better to their purpose. Even now it moves astonishment to think that a monk should have written, and a bishop should have published, the *facetiæ* with which Bandello's books are filled.

Bandello paints a society in dissolution, bound together by no monarchical or feudal principles, without patriotism, without piety, united by none of the common spiritual enthusiasms that make a people powerful. The word honour is on everybody's lips; but the thing is nowhere: and when the story-teller seeks to present its ideal image to his audience, he proves by the absurdity of his exaggeration that he has no clear conception of its meaning.[8] The virtues which inspired

[7] See Dedication to *Nov.* xi. of second part.

[8] Read, for example, the *Novella* of Zilia, who imposed silence on her lover because he kissed her, and the whole sequel to his preposterous obedience (iii. 17); or the tale of Don Giovanni Emmanuel in the lion's den (iii. 39); or the rambling story of Don Diego and Ginevra la Bionda (i. 27). The two latter have a touch of Spanish

an earlier and less corrupt civility, have become occasions for insipid rhetoric. The vice that formerly stirred indignation, is now the subject of mirth. There is no satire, because there is no moral sense. Bandello's revelations of clerical and monastic immorality supplied the enemies of Rome with a full brief; but it is obvious that Bandello and his audience regarded the monstrous tale of profligacy with amusement. His frankness upon the very eve of the Council of Trent has something at once cynical and sinister. It makes us feel that the hypocrisy engendered by the German Reformation, the *si non caste tamen caute* of the new ecclesiastical *régime*, was the last resort of a system so debased that vital regeneration had become impossible. This does not necessarily mean that the Italian Church had no worthy ministers in the sixteenth century. But when her dealing with the people ended in a humorous acceptance of such sin, we perceive that the rottenness had reached the core. To present the details of Bandello's clerical stories would be impossible in pages meant for modern readers. It is enough to say that he spares no rank or order of the Roman priesthood. The prelate, the parish curate, the abbot and the prioress, the monk and nun, are made the subject of impartial ribaldry.[9] The secrets of convents abandoned to debauchery are revealed with good-humoured candour, as though the scandal was too common to need special comment.[10] Sometimes Bandello extracts comedy from the contrast between the hypocritical pretensions of his clerical ruffians and their lawless conduct, as in the story of the priest who for his own ends persuaded his parishioners that the village was haunted by a griffin.[11] Sometimes he succeeds in drawing a satirical portrait, like that of the Franciscan friar who domesticated himself as chaplain in the castle of a noble Norman family.[12] But the majority of these tales are simply obscene, with no point but a coarse picture or a shockingly painful climax.[13]

The same judgment may be passed upon a large portion of the *Novelle* which deal with secular characters. They are indecent anecdotes, and do not illustrate any specific quality in the author or in the temper of his times.[14] The seasoning of horror only serves to render their licentiousness more loathsome. As Bandello lacked the indignation of Masuccio, so he failed to touch Masuccio's tragic chord. When he attempted it, as in the ghastly story of Violante, who revenged herself upon a faithless lover by tearing him to pieces with pincers, or in the

extravagance, but without the glowing Spanish passion. In quoting Bandello, I shall refer to *Part* and *Novel* by different numerals. References are made to the Milanese edition, *Novellieri Italiani*, 1813-1816.

[9] For instance, Parte ii. *Nov.* 14; ii. xlv.; iii. 2, 3, 4, 7, 20.

[10] See the description in ii. 36 (vol. v. p. 270); and again, iii. 61, ii. 45.

[11] ii. 2.

[12] ii. 24.

[13] See, for instance, ii. 20; ii. 7.

[14] I need not give any references to the *Novelle* of this grovelling type. But I may call attention to i. 35; ii. 11; iv. 34, 35. These tales are not exceptionally obscene; they illustrate to what extent mere filth of the Swiftian sort passed for fun in the Italy of Bembo and Castiglione.

disgusting novel of Pandora, or again in the tale of the husband who forced his wife to strangle her lover with her own hands, he only rouses physical repulsion.[15] He makes our flesh creep, and produces literature analogous to that of the 'Police Times.' Nor does he succeed better with subjects that require the handling of a profound psychologist. His Rosmunda and Tarquin, his Faustina and Seleucus, leave an impression of failure through defect of imaginative force;[16] while the incestuous theme of one tale, treated as it is with frigid levity, can claim no justification on the score of dramatic handling or high-wrought spiritual agony.[17]

It was not in this region of tragic terror that Bandello's genius moved with freedom. In describing the luxury of Milan or the manners of the Venetian courtesans, in bringing before us scenes from the *demimonde* of Rome or painting the life of a *grisette*, he shows acute knowledge of society, studied under its more superficial aspects, and produces pictures that are valuable for the antiquarian.[18] The same merit of freshness belongs to many minor anecdotes, like the romance of the girl who drowned herself in the Oglio to save her honour, or the pretty episode of Costantino Boccali who swam the Adige in winter at a thoughtless lady's behest.[19] Yet in Bandello's versions of contemporary histories which taxed the imaginative powers or demanded deeper insight into human passions, we miss the true dramatic ring. It was only when it fell into the hands of Webster, that his dull narrative of the Duchess of Amalfi revealed its capacities for artistic treatment.[20] Nor is the story of the Countess of Cellant, though full of striking details, so presented as to leave the impression of tragedy upon our minds.[21] We only feel what Webster, dealing with it as he dealt with Vittoria Corombona's crime, might have made out of this poor material.

It may be asked, if this is all, why anyone should take the pains to read through the two hundred and fourteen *Novelle* of Bandello, and, having done so, should think it worth his while to write about them? Ought they not rather to be left among the things the world would willingly let die? The answer to this question is twofold. In the first place they fairly represent the whole class of novels which were produced so abundantly in Italy that the historian of Renaissance literature cannot pass them by in silence. Secondly, Bandello at his best is a great artist in the story-teller's craft. The conditions under which he

[15] i. 42; iii. 21; iii. 52; ii. 12.
[16] ii. 18; ii. 21; i. 36; iii. 55.
[17] ii. 35; cp. i. 37.
[18] The pictures of Milanese luxury before the Spanish occupation are particularly interesting. See i. 9, and the beginning of ii. 8. It seems that then, as now, Milan was famous for her equipages and horses. The tale of the two fops who always dressed in white (iii. 11) brings that life before us. For the Venetian and Roman *demi-monde*, iii. 31; i. 19; i. 42; ii. 51, may be consulted. These passages have the value of authentic studies from contemporary life, and are told about persons whom the author knew at least by name.
[19] i. 8; i. 47.
[20] i. 26. [21] i. 108.

displayed his powers to true advantage, require some definition. Once only did he successfully handle a really comic situation. That was in his tale of the monkey who dressed himself up in a dead woman's clothes, and frightened her family when they returned from the funeral, by mimicking her movements.[22] He was never truly tragic. But in the intermediate region between tragedy and comedy, where situations of romantic beauty offer themselves to the sympathetic imagination—in that realm of pathos and adventure, where pictures of eventful living can be painted, and the conflicts of tender emotion have to be described, Bandello proved himself a master. It would make the orthodox Italian critics shudder in their graves to hear that he had been compared to Ariosto. Yet a foreigner, gifted with obtuser sensibility to the refinements of Italian diction, may venture the remark that Bandello was a kind of prose Ariosto—in the same sense as Heywood seemed a prose Shakspere to Charles Lamb. Judged by the high standard of Athenian or Elizabethan art, neither Ariosto nor Bandello was a first-rate dramatist. But both commanded the material of which romantic tragedies can be constructed. Bandello's best *Novelle* abound in the situations which delighted our playwrights of the Jacobean age—in the thrilling incidents and scenes of high-wrought passion we are wont to deem the special property of Fletcher. He puts them before us with a force of realistic colouring, and develops them with a warmth of feeling, that leave no doubt of his artistic skill. Composition and style may fail him, but his sympathy with the poetic situation, and his power to express it are unmistakable. In support of this opinion I might point to his vigorous but repulsive presentation of Parisina's legend, where the gradual yielding of a sensitive young man to the seductions of a sensual woman, is painted with touches of terrible veracity.[23] Or the tale of the Venetian lovers might be chosen.[24] Gerardo and Elena were secretly married; but in his absence on a voyage, she was plighted by her father to another husband. Before the consummation of this second marriage, Elena fell through misery into a death-like trance, and was taken by her kindred to be buried at Castello on the shores of the lagoons. At the moment when the funeral procession was crossing the waters by the light of many torches, the ship of Gerardo cast anchor in the port of Venice, and the young man heard that his wife was dead. Attended by a single friend, he went under cover of the night to where she had been laid in a sarcophagus outside the church. This he opened, and, frantic between grief and joy, bore the corpse of his beloved to his boat. He kissed her lips, and laid himself beside her lifeless body, wildly refusing to listen to his friend's expostulations. Then while the gondola rocked on the waves of the lagoons and the sea-wind freshened before daybreak, Elena awoke. It is needless to add that the story ends in happiness. This brief sketch conveys no notion of the pictur-

[22] iii. 65.
[23] i. 44.
[24] ii. 41.

esque beauty of the incidents described, or of the intimate acquaintance with Venetian customs displayed in the *Novella*. To one who knows Venice, it is full of delicate suggestions, and the reader illuminates the margin with illustrations in the manner of Carpaccio.

There is a point of Romeo and Juliet in the tale of Gerardo and Elena. Bandello's own treatment of the Veronese romance deserves comparison with Shakspere's.[25] The evolution of the tragedy is nearly the same in all its leading incidents; for we hear of Romeo's earlier love, and the friar who dealt in simples is there, and so are the nurse and apothecary. Bandello has anticipated Shakspere even in Juliet's soliloquy before she drinks the potion, when the dreadful thought occurs to her that she may wake too soon, and find herself alone among the dry bones of her ancestors, with Tybalt festering in his shroud. But the prose version exhibits one motive which Shakspere missed. When Romeo opens the tomb, he rouses Juliet from her slumber, and in his joy forgets that he has drunk the poison. For a while the lovers are in paradise together in that region of the dead; and it is only when the chill of coming death assails him, that Romeo remembers what he has done. He dies, and Juliet stabs herself with his sword. Had Shakspere chosen to develop this catastrophe, instead of making Romeo perish before the waking of Juliet, he might have wrought the most pathetically tragic scene in poetry. Reading the climax in Bandello, where it is overpoweringly affecting, we feel what we have lost.

Another *Novella* which provokes comparison with our dramatic literature—with the 'Twelfth Night' or with Fletcher's 'Philaster'—is the tale of Nicuola.[26] She and her brother Paolo were twins, so like in height and form and feature that it was difficult even for friends to know them apart. They were living with their father at Rome, when the siege of 1527 dispersed the family. Paolo was taken prisoner by Spaniards, and Nicuola went to dwell at Jesi. The *Novella* goes on to relate how she fell in love with a nobleman of Jesi, and entering his service disguised as a page, was sent by him to woo the lady of his heart; and how this lady loved her in her page's dress. Then her brother, Paolo, returned, attired like her in white, and recognitions were made, and both couples, Paolo and the lady, Nicuola and the nobleman, were happily married in the end. It will be seen that these situations, involving confusions of identity and sex, unexpected discoveries, and cross-play of passions, offered opportunities for rhetorical and picturesque development in the style of a modern Euripides; nor did Bandello fail to utilise them.

[25] ii. 37. It is clear that both followed the earlier version of Da Porto.

[26] ii. 36. This tale was fashionable in Italy. It forms the basis of that rare comedy, *Gli Ingannati*, performed by the Academy degli Intronati at Siena, and printed in 1538. The scene in this play is laid at Modena; the main plot is interwoven with two intrigues—between Isabella's father and Lelia, the heroine; and between Isabella's maid and a Spaniard. In spite of these complications the action is lucid, and the comedy is one of the best we possess. There is an excellent humorous scene of two innkeepers touting against each other for travellers (Act iii. 2). That Shakspere knew the *Novella* or the comedy before he wrote his *Twelfth Night* is more than probable.

Of a higher type is the *Novella* which narrates the love of Edward III. for the virtuous Alice of Salisbury.[27] Here the interest centres in four characters—the King, Alice, and her father and mother, the Earl and Countess of Salisbury. There is no action beyond the conflict of motives and emotions caused by Edward's passion, and its successive phases. But that conflict is so vigorously presented that attention never flags; and, though the tale is long, we are drawn without weariness by finely modulated transitions to the point where a felicitous catastrophe is not only natural but necessary. What is at first a mere desire in Edward, passes through graduated moods of confident, despairing, soul-absorbing love. The ordinary artifices of a seducer are replaced by the powerful compulsion of a monarch, who strives to corrupt the daughter by working on her father's ambition and her mother's weakness. Thwarted by the girl's constancy at every turn, he sinks into love-melancholy, then rouses himself with the furious resolve to attempt force, and lastly, yielding to his nobler nature, offers his crown to Alice. These several moments in the King's passion are exhibited with a descriptive wealth and exuberance of resource that remind us forcibly of our own stage. The contrasts between the girl's invincible honour and her lover's ungovernable impulse, between her firmness and her mother's feebler nature, and again between the sovereign's overbearing wilfulness and the Earl's stubborn but respectful resistance, suggest a series of highwrought situations, which only need to be versified and divided into acts to make a drama. Fletcher himself might have proudly owned the scene in which Edward discovers his love to the Earl, begs him to plead with his daughter, and has to hear his reproaches, so courteously and yet unflinchingly expressed. What follows is equally dramatic. The Earl explains to Alice his own ideal of honour; still he fairly sets before her the King's lawless offer, and then receives the assurance of her unconquerable chastity. Her mother, moved to feebler issues by the same pressure, attempts to break her daughter's resolve, and at last extorts a reluctant consent by her own physical agony. Finally, the girl, when left alone with her royal lover, demands from him or death or honour, and wins her cause by the nobility of her carriage in this hour of trial. The whole *Novella* in its choice of motives, method of treatment, and ethical tone, challenges comparison with Beaumont and Fletcher's serious plays. Nor is the style unlike theirs; for the situations are worked out in copious and coloured language, hasty and diffuse, but charged and surcharged with the passion of the thing to be portrayed. Bandello, like Fletcher, strikes out images at every turn, enlarges in rhetorical digressions, and pours forth floods of voluble eloquence.[28] The morality, though romantic, is above his usual level; for

[27] ii. 37. Historians will not look for accuracy in what is an Italian love-tale founded on an English legend.

[28] Take the description of the King's love-sickness (*Nov. It.* vol. v. p. 352), the incident of the King's offer to the Earl (pp. 353, 354), Edward's musings (p. 364), Alice alone in London (p. 376), the King's defiance of opinion (p. 379), the people's verdict against Alice (p. 380), Alice arming herself with the dagger (p. 398), the

while he paints a dissolute and wilful prince in Edward, he contrives to make us feel that the very force of passion, when purified to true love by the constancy of Alice, has brought the monarch to a knowledge of his better self. Nor is the type of honour in Alice and the Earl exaggerated. They act and speak as subjects, conscious of their duty to the King, but resolved to preserve their self-respect at any cost, should speak and act. The compliance of the Countess, who is willing to sacrifice her daughter's honour under the impulse of blind terror, cannot be called unnatural. The consequent struggle between a mother's frailty and a daughter's firmness, though painful enough, is not so disagreeably presented as in Tourneur's 'Revenger's Tragedy.' If all Bandello's novels had been conceived in the same spirit as this, he would have ranked among the best romantic writers of the modern age. As it is, we English may perhaps take credit to ourselves for the superior inspiration of the legend he here handled. The moral fibre of the tale is rather English than Italian.

Bandello was not unaware that his *Novelle* lay under censure for licentiousness. His apology deserves to be considered, since it places the Italian conscience on this point in a clear light. In the preface to the eleventh *Novella* of the second part, he attacks the question boldly.[29] 'They say that my stories are not honest. In this I am with them, if they rightly apprehend honesty. I do not deny that some are not only not honest, but I affirm and confess that they are most dishonest; for if I write that a maiden grants favours to a lover, I cannot pretend that the fact is not in the highest sense immoral. So also of many things I have narrated. No sane person will fail to blame incest, theft, homicide, and other vicious actions; and I concede that my *Novelle* set forth these and similar enormous crimes. But I do not admit that I deserve to be therefore blamed. The world ought to blame and stigmatise those who commit such crimes, and not the man who writes about them.' He then affirms that he has written his stories down as he heard them from the lips of the narrators, that he has clothed them in decent language, and that he has always been careful to condemn vice and to praise virtue. In the twenty-fourth novel of the same part he returns to the charge.[30] Hypocrites, he argues, complain that the 'Decameron' and similar collections corrupt the morality of women and teach vice; 'but I was always of opinion that to commit crimes rather than to know about them was vicious. Ignorance is never good, and it is better to be instructed in the wickedness of the world than to fall into error through defect of knowledge.' This apology, when read by the light of Bandello's own *Novelle*, is an impudent evasion of the

garden scene upon the Thames (p. 399). Then the discourses upon love and temperament (p. 325), on discreet conduct in love affairs (pp. 334-338), on real and false courtiers (pp. 382-388). Compare the descriptive passages on pp. 352, 354, 369, 393, 395, 398, with similar passages in Beaumont and Fletcher.

[29] *Nov. It.* vol. iv. p. 226. Compare the peroration of his Preface to the third part (vol. vii. p. 13).

[30] Vol. v. p. 38.

accusation. They are a school of profligacy; and the author was at pains to make his pictures of sensuality attractive. That he should plume himself upon the decorum of his language, is simply comic. Such simulation of a conscience was all that remained at an epoch when the sense of shame had been extinguished, while acquiescence in the doctrines of a corrupt Church had not ceased to be fashionable.

Bandello is more sensitive to strictures on his literary style, and makes a better defence. 'They say that I have no style. I grant it; nor do I profess to be a master of prose, believing that if those only wrote who were consummate in their art, very few would write at all. But I maintain that any history, composed in however rough and uncouth a language, will not fail to delight the reader; and these novels of mine (unless I am deceived by their narrators) are not fables but true histories.'[31] In another place he confesses that his manner is and always has been 'light and low and deficient in intellectual quality.'[32] Again, he meets the objection that his diction is not modelled on the purest Tuscan masterpieces, by arguing that even Petrarch wrote Italian and not Tuscan, and that if Livy smacked of Patavinity, he, a Lombard, does not shrink from Lombardisms in his style.[33] The line of defence is good; but, what is more, Bandello knew that he was popular. He cared to be read by all classes of the people rather than to be praised by pedants for the purity of his language. Therefore he snapped his fingers at Speron Sperone and Trifone, the so-called Socrates of his century. The *Novella* was not a branch of scholarly but of vulgar literature; and Bandello had far better right to class himself among Italian authors than Straparola or Giraldi, whose novels were none the less sought after with avidity and read with pleasure by thousands. It is true that he was not a master of the best Italian prose, and that his *Novelle* do not rank among the *Testi di Lingua*. He is at one and the same time prolix and involved, ornate and vulgar, coarse in phraseology and ambitious in rhetoric. He uses metaphors borrowed from the slang of the fashionable world to express gross thoughts or actions. He indulges in pompous digressions and overloads his narrative with illustrations. But, in spite of these defects, he is rarely dull. His energy and copiousness of diction never fail him. His style is penetrated with the passion of the subject, and he delights our imagination with wonderfully varied pictures drawn from life. It is probable that foreigners can render better justice to the merits of Bandello as a writer, than Italians, who are trained to criticise language from a highly refined and technical point of view. We recognise his vividness and force without being disgusted by his Lombardisms or the coarseness of his phrases. Yet even some Italian critics of no mean standing have been found to say a good

[31] Vol. iv. p. 226. Cp. vol. ix. p. 339.
[32] Vol. vi. p. 254.
[33] Vol. vii. p. 11.

word for his style. Among these may be reckoned the judicious Mazzuchelli.[34]

The author of 'Le Cene' presents a marked contrast to Bandello. Antonfrancesco Grazzini belonged to an ancient and honourable family of Staggia in Valdelsa.[35] Some of his ancestors held office in the Florentine republic, and many were registered in the Art of the Notaries. Born at Florence in 1503, he was matriculated into the Speziali, and followed the profession of a druggist. His literary career was closely connected with the academies of Gli Umidi and La Crusca.[36] The sobriquet Il Lasca, or The Roach, assumed by him as a member of the Umidi, is the name by which he is best known. Besides *Novelle*, he wrote comedies and poems, and made the renowned collection of *Canti Carnascialeschi*. He died in 1583 and was buried in S. Pier Maggiore. Thus while Bandello might claim to be a citizen of the great world, reared in the ecclesiastical purple and conversant with the noblest society of Northern Italy, Il Lasca began life and ended it as a Florentine burgher. For aught we know, he may not have travelled beyond the bounds of the republic. His stories are written in the raciest Tuscan idiom, and are redolent of the humour peculiar to Florence. If Bandello appropriated the romantic element in Boccaccio, Il Lasca chose his comic side for imitation. Nearly all his novels turn on *beffe* and *burle*, similar to those sketched in Sacchetti's anecdotes, or developed with greater detail by Pulci and the author of 'Il Grasso,' Legnaiuolo.[37] Three boon companions, Lo Scheggia, Il Monaco, and Il Pilucca are the heroes of his comedy; and the pranks they play, are described with farcical humour of the broadest and most powerful sort. Still the specific note of Il Lasca's novels is not pure fun. He combines obscenity with fierce carnal cruelty and inhuman jesting, in a mixture that speaks but ill for the taste of his time.[38] Neither Boccaccio nor the author of 'Il Grasso' struck a chord so vicious, though the latter carried his buffoonery to the utmost stretch of heartlessness. It needed the depravity of the sixteenth century to relish the lust, seasoned with physical torture and spiritual agony, which was so cunningly revealed, so coldly revelled in by Il Lasca.[39] A practical joke or an act of refined vengeance had peculiar attraction for the Florentines. But the men must have

[34] In the biography of Bandello he says, 'Lo stile è piuttosto colto e studiato, che che taluno n' abbia detto in contrario, non però in guisa che possa mettersi a confronto di quello del Boccaccio.'

[35] See Sonnet 79, *Rime* (ed. 1741).

[36] Founded respectively in 1540 and 1583. Grazzini quarrelled with them both.

[37] *Cena* i. *Nov.* 3, is in its main motive modelled on that novel.

[38] The contrast between the amiable manners of the young men and women described in the introduction to *Le Cene*, and the stories put into their mouths; between the profound immorality, frigid and repellent, of the tales and Ghiacinto's prayer at the beginning; need not be insisted on.

[39] As I shall not dilate upon these novels further in the text, I may support the above censure by reference to the practical joke played upon the pedagogue (i. 2), to the inhuman novel of *Il Berna* (ii. 2), to the cruel vengeance of a brother (ii. 7), and to the story of the priest (ii. 8).

been blunted in moral sensibility and surfeited with strange experiences, who could enjoy Pilucca's brutal tricks, or derive pleasure from the climax of a tale so ghastly as the fifth *Novella* of the second series.

This is a story of incest and a husband's vengeance. Substantially the same as Parisina's tragedy, Il Lasca has invented for it his own whimsically horrible conclusion. The husband surprises his wife and son. Then, having cut off their hands, feet, eyes and tongues, he leaves them to die together on the bed where he had found them. The rhetoric with which this catastrophe is embellished, and the purring sympathy expressed for the guilty couple, only serve to make its inhumanity more glaring. Incapable of understanding tragedy, these writers of a vitiated age sought excitement in monstrous situations. The work produced is a proper pendent to the filth of the burlesque *Capitoli*. Literature of this sort might have amused Caligula and his gladiators. Prefaced by an unctuous prayer to God, it realises the very superfluity of naughtiness.[40]

In favour of the Florentines, we might plead that these *Novelle* were accepted as pure fictions—debauches of the fancy, escapades of inventive wit. The ideal world they represented, claimed no contact with realities of life. The pranks of Lo Scheggia and Il Pilucca, which drove one man into exile, another to the hospital, and a third to his death, had no more actuality than the tricks of clown and pantaloon. A plea of this sort was advanced by Charles Lamb for the dramatists of the Restoration; and it carries, undoubtedly, its measure of conviction. Literature of convention, which begins by stimulating curiosity, must find novel combinations and fresh seasonings to pique the palate of the public. Thus the abominations of Il Lasca's stories would have to be regarded as the last desperate bids for popularity, as final hyperboles of exhausted rhetoric. Yet, after all, books remain the mirror of a people's taste. Whatever their quality may be, they are produced to satisfy some demand. And the wonderful vivacity of Il Lasca's colouring, the veracity of his art, preclude him from the benefit of a defence which presupposes that he stood in some unnatural relation to his age. While we read his tales, we cannot but remember the faces painted by Bronzino, or modelled by Cellini. The sixteenth-century Florentines were hard and cold as steel. Their temper had been brutalised by servitude, superficially polished by humanism, blunted by the extraordinary intellectual activity of three centuries. Compared with the voluptuous but sympathetic mood of the Lombard novelists, this cruelty means something special to the race.

Some of Il Lasca's stories, fortunately, need no such strained apology or explanation. The tale of Lisabetta's dream, though it lacks point, is free from his worse faults;[41] while the novel of Zoroaster is not only innocent, but highly humorous and charged with playful sarcasm.[42] It

[40] See above, p. 202, note.
[41] *Cena* ii. 3.
[42] *Cena* ii. 4.

contains a portrait of a knavish astrologer, worthy to be set beside the 'Negromante' of Ariosto or Ben Jonson's 'Alchemist.' When Jerome Cardan was coquetting with chiromancy and magic, when Cellini was raising fiends with the Sicilian necromancer in the Coliseum, a novelist found sufficient stuff for comedy and satire in the foibles of ghost-seekers and the tricks of philtre-mongers. The companion portrait of the dissolute monk, who sets his hand to any dirty work that has the spice of fun in it, is also executed with no little spirit.

Among the most graceful of the Tuscan novelists may be mentioned Agnolo Firenzuola. His family derived its name from a village at the foot of the Pistojan Apennines, and his father was a citizen of Florence. Agnolo spent his youth at Siena and Perugia, where he made the friendship of Pietro Aretino, leading the wild student life described in their correspondence.[43] That he subsequently entered the Vallombrosan order seems to be certain; but it is somewhat doubtful whether he attained the dignity of Abbot which his biographers ascribe to him.[44] Tiraboschi, unwilling to admit so great a scandal to the Church, has adduced reasons why we should suspend our judgment.[45] Yet the tradition rests on substantial authority. A monument erected by Firenzuola to his uncle Alessandro Braccio in the church of S. Prassede at Rome, describes him as *ædis hujus Abbas*. S. Maria di Spoleti and S. Salvator di Vaiano are supposed to have been his benefices. Some further collateral proof might be drawn from the opening of the dialogue 'Sopra le Bellezze delle Donne.' The scene of it is laid in the convent grounds of Grignano, and Celso is undoubtedly Firenzuola. A portion of his manhood was spent at Rome in friendship with Molza, Berni, and other brilliant literary men. While resident in Rome, he contracted a severe and tedious illness, which obliged him to retire to Prato, where he spent some of the happiest years of his life.[46] Nearly all his works contain frequent and affectionate recollections of this sunny little town, the beauty of whose women is enthusiastically celebrated by him. Firenzuola died before the middle of the sixteenth century at the age of about fifty. Neither his life nor his friendships nor yet his writings were consistent with his monastic profession and the dignity of Abbot. The charm of Firenzuola's *Novelle* is due in a large measure to his style, which has a wonderful transparency and ease, a wealth of the rarest Tuscan phrases, and a freshness of humour that renders them delightful reading. The storm at sea in the first tale, and the night scene in the streets of Florence in the third, are described with Ariostean brilliancy.[47] In point of subject-matter they do not greatly differ from the ordinary

[43] See the Letters of Aretino, vol. ii. p. 239.

[44] All my references are made to the *Opere di Messer Agnolo Firenzuola*, 5 vols. Milan, 1802.

[45] *Storia della Lett. It.* lib. iii. cap. 3, sect. 27.

[46] In a letter to Aretino, dated Prato, Oct. 5, 1541, he says he had been ill for eleven years. It seems probable that his illness was of the kind alluded to in his *Capitolo* 'In Lode del Legno Santo' (*Op. Volg.* iv. p. 204).

[47] *Op.* ii. pp. 94, 130.

novels of the day, and some of the tales reappear in the collections of other novelists.[48] Most of them turn upon the foibles and the vices of the clergy. The fourth *Novella*, which is perhaps the best of all in style and humour, presents a truly comic picture of the parish priest, while the fifth describes the interior of a dissolute convent at Perugia, and the tenth exposes the arts whereby confessors induced silly women to make wills in the favour of their convents. Don Giovanni, Suor Appellagia, and Fra Cherubino, the chief actors in these stories, might be selected as typical characters in the Italian comedy of clerical dissoluteness.

Firenzuola prefaced his novels with an elaborate introduction, describing the meeting of some friends at Celso's villa near Pazolatico, and their discourse on love.[49] From discussion they pass to telling amorous stories under the guidance of a Queen selected by the company.[50] The introductory conversation is full of a dreamy, sensualised, disintegrated Platonism. It parades conventional distinctions between earthly and heavenly love, between the beauty of the soul and the beauty of the body; and then we pass without modulation into the region of what is here called *accidenti amorosi*. The same insincere Platonism gives colour to Firenzuola's discourse on the Beauty of Women—one of the most important productions of the sixteenth century in illustration of popular and artistic taste.[51] The author imagines himself to have interrupted a bevy of fair ladies from Prato in the midst of a dispute about the beauty of Mona Amelia della Torre Nuova. Mona Amelia herself was present; and so were Mona Lampiada, Mona Amorrorisca, Mona Selvaggia, and Mona Verdespina.[52] Under these names it is clear that living persons of the town of Prato are designated; and all the examples of beauty given in the dialogue are chosen from well-known women of the district. The composition must therefore be reckoned as an elaborate compliment from Firenzuola to the fair sex of Prato.[53] Celso begins his exposition of beauty by declaring that 'it is God's highest gift to human nature, inasmuch as by its virtue we direct our soul to contemplation, and through contemplation to the desire of heavenly things.'[54] He then proceeds to define beauty as 'an ordered concord, or, as it were, a

[48] For example, *Nov.* iv. is the same as Bandello's II. xx.; *Nov.* vii. is the same as Il Lasca's ii. 10, and Fortini's xiv.

[49] Vol. ii. p. 28. The poem put into Celso's mouth, p. 39, is clearly autobiographical.

[50] There is the usual reference to Boccaccio, at p. 32. I may take this occasion for citing an allusion to Boccaccio from the Introduction to *Le Cene*, which shows how truly he was recognised as the patron saint of novelists. See *Le Cene* (Firenze, Lemonnier, 1857), p. 4.

[51] Vol. I. pp. 1-97. I may here allude to a still more copious and detailed treatise on the same theme by Federigo Luigino of Udine: *Il Libro della Bella Donna*, Milano, Daelli, 1863; a reprint from the Venetian edition of 1554. This book is a symphony of graceful images and delicately chosen phrases: it is a dithyramb in praise of feminine beauty, which owes its charm to the intense sympathy, sensual and æsthetic, of the author for his subject.

[52] Selvaggia was the lady of Firenzuola's *Rime*.

[53] See the *Elegia alle Donne Pratesi*, vol. iv. p. 41.

[54] Vol. i. p. 16. Compare the extraordinary paragraph about female beauty being

harmony inscrutably resulting from the composition, union, and commission of divers members, each of which shall in itself be well proportioned and in a certain sense beautiful, but which, before they combine to make one body, shall be different and discrepant among themselves.'[55] Having explained each clause of this definition, he passes to the appetite for beauty, and tells the myth invented for Aristophanes in Plato's 'Symposium.' This leads by natural transitions to the real business of the dialogue, which consists in analysing and defining every kind of loveliness in women, and minutely describing the proportions, qualities, and colours of each portion of the female body. The whole is carried through with the method of a philosopher, the enthusiasm of an artist, and the refinement of a well-bred gentleman. The articles upon *Leggiadria*, *Grazia*, *Vaghezza*, *Venustà*, *Aria*, *Maestà*, may even now be read with profit by those who desire to comprehend the nice gradations of meaning implied by these terms.[56] The discourses on the form and colour of the ear, and on the proper way of wearing ornamental flowers, bring incomparably graceful images before us;[57] and this, indeed, can be said about the whole dialogue, for there is hardly a sentence that does not reveal the delicate perceptions of an artistic nature.

Firenzuola's adaptation of the 'Golden Ass' may be reckoned among the triumphs of his style, and the fables contained in his 'Discorsi degli Animali' are so many minutely finished novelettes.[58] Both of these works belong to the proper subject of the present chapter. His comedies and his burlesque poems must be left for discussion under different headings. With regard to his serious verses, addressed to Mona Selvaggia, it will be enough to say that they are modelled upon Petrarch. Though limpid in style and musical, as all Firenzuola's writing never failed to be, they ring hollow. The true note of the man's feeling was sensual. The highest point it reached was the admiration for plastic beauty expressed in his dialogue on women. It had nothing in common with Petrarch's melancholy. Of these minor poems I admire the little ballad beginning 'O rozza pastorella,' and the wonderfully lucid version of Poliziano's *Violæ*—'O viole formose, o dolci viole'—more than any others.[59]

Except for the long illness which brought him to Prato, Firenzuola appears to have spent a happy and mirthful life; and if we may trust his introduction to the Novels, he was fairly wealthy. What we know about the biography of Antonfrancesco Doni, who also deserves a place among the Tuscan novelists, presents a striking contrast to this luxurious and amorous existence.[60] He was a Florentine, and, like Firenzuola,

an earnest of the beauties of Paradise (pp. 31, 32).

[55] *Ibid.* p. 21.

[56] *Ibid.* pp. 51-62.

[57] *Ibid.* pp. 75-80.

[58] Vol. iii. The *Golden Ass* begins with an autobiography (vol. i. p. 103).

[59] Vol. iv. pp. 19, 76.

[60] My principal authority is Doni's Life by S. Bongi prefixed to an edition of the *Novelle*, 1851, and reprinted in Fanfani's edition of *I Marmi*, Florence, 1863.

dedicated to religion. Born in 1513, he entered the Servite order in the cloister of the Annunziata. He began by teaching the boys entrusted to the monks for education. But about 1540 he was obliged to fly the monastery under the cloud of some grave charge connected with his pupils.[61] Doni turned his back on Florence; and after wandering from town to town in Northern Italy, settled at last in 1542 at Piacenza, where he seems for a short while to have applied himself with an unwilling mind to law-studies. At Piacenza he made the acquaintance of Lodovico Domenichi, who introduced him into the Accademia Ortolana. This was a semi-literary club of profligates with the Priapic emblems for its ensign. Doni's wild and capricious humour made him a chief ornament of the society; but the members so misconducted themselves in word and deed that it was soon found necessary to suppress their meetings. While amusing himself with poetry and music among his boon companions, Doni was on the look-out for a place at Court or in the household of a wealthy nobleman. His letters at this period show that he was willing to become anything from poet or musician down to fool or something worse. Failing in all his applications, he at last resolved to make what gains he could by literature. His friend Domenichi had already settled at Venice, when Doni joined him there in 1544. But his stay was of brief duration. We find him again at Piacenza, next at Rome, and then at Florence, where he established a printing-press. The principal event of this Florentine residence was a definite rupture with Domenichi. We do not know the causes of their quarrel; but both of them were such scamps that it is probable they took good care, while abusing one another in general terms, to guard the secrets of their respective crimes. During the rest of Doni's life he pursued his old friend with relentless animosity. His invectives deserve to be compared with those of the humanists in the preceding century; while Domenichi, who had succeeded in securing a position for himself at Florence, replied with no less hostility in the tone of injured virtue.

In 1547 Doni settled finally at Venice. The city of the lagoons was the only safe resort for a man who had offended the Church by abandoning his vows, and whose life and writings were a scandal even in that age of license. Everywhere else he would have been exposed to peril from the Inquisition. Though he had dropped the cowl, he could not throw aside the cassock, and his condition as priest proved not only irksome but perilous.[62] At Venice he lived a singular Bohemian existence, inhabiting a garret which overlooked one of the noisiest of the small canals, and scribbling for his daily bread. He was a rapid and prolific writer, sending his copy to the press before it was dry, and never caring for revision. To gain money was the sole object of his

[61] See Zilioli, quoted by Bongi, *I Marmi*, vol. i. p. xiv.

[62] How Doni hated his orders may be gathered from these extracts: 'La bestiai cosa che sia sopportare quattro corna in capo senza belare unquanco! Io ho un capriccio di farmi scomunicare per non cantare più *Domine labia*, e spretarmi per non essere a noia a tutte le persone.' 'L' esser colla chierica puzza a tutti.' His chief grievance was that he had made no money out of the Church.

labours. The versatility of his mind and his peculiar humour made his miscellanies popular; and like Aretino he wheedled or menaced ducats out of patrons. Indeed, Doni's life at Venice is the proper pendent to Aretino's, who was once his friend and afterwards his bitter foe. But while Aretino contrived to live like a prince, Doni, for many years at any rate, endured the miseries of Grub Street. They quarrelled about a present which the Duke of Urbino had promised Doni through his secretary. Aretino thought that this meant poaching on his manors. Accordingly he threatened his comrade with a thorough literary scourging. Doni replied by a pamphlet with this singular title: 'Terremoto del Doni fiorentino, con la rovina d' un gran Colosso bestiale Antichristo della nostra età.' His capricious nature and bizarre passions made Doni a bad friend; but he was an incomparably amusing companion. Accordingly we find that his society was sought by the literary circles of all cities where he lived. At Florence he had been appointed secretary to the Umidi. At Venice he became a member of the Pellegrini. This academy was founded before the League of Cambrai in a deserted villa near the lagoons.[63] Mystery hung over its origin and continued to involve its objects. Several wealthy noblemen of Venice supplied the club with ample funds. They had a good library, and employed two presses for the printing of their works. The members formed a kind of masonic body, bound together by strict mutual obligations, and sworn to maintain each other in peril or in want. They also exercised generosity toward needy men of letters, dowered poor girls, and practised many charities of a similar description. Their meetings took place in certain gardens at Murano or on the island of S. Giorgio Maggiore. The two Sansovini, Nardi, Titian, Dolce, and other eminent men belonged to the society; but Doni appears to have been its moving spirit on all occasions of convivial intercourse.

The last years of this Bohemian life were spent beneath the Euganean hills in a square castle, which, picturesquely draped with ivy, may still be seen towering above Monselice. That Doni had accumulated some capital by his incessant scribbling, is proved by the fact that he laid out the grounds about his fortress with considerable luxury. A passage quoted from the Venetian Zilioli serves to bring the man more vividly before us: 'At the summit of the hill above Monselice stands the house where Antonfrancesco Doni indulged his leisure with philosophy and poetry. He was a man of bizarre humour, who had but little patience with his neighbours. Retiring from society, he chose this abode in order to give full scope in his own way and without regard for anyone to his caprices, which were often very ludicrous. Who could have refrained from laughter, when he saw a man of mature age, with a beard down to his breast, going abroad at night barefooted and in his shirt, careering among the fields, singing his own songs and those of other

[63] The greater part of what we know about the Pellegrini occurs in Doni's *I Marmi*. See also a memoir by Giaxich, and the notices in Mutinelli's *Diari Urbani*.

poets; or else in daytime playing on a lute and dancing like a little boy?' Doni died at Venice in the autumn of 1574.

Doni's *Novelle* are rather detached scenes of life than stories with a plot or theme. Glowing and picturesque in style, sharply outlined, and smartly told, they have the point of epigrams. The fourth of the series might be chosen to illustrate the extravagant efforts after effect made by the Italian novelist with a view to stimulating the attention of his audience. It is a tale of two mortal enemies, one of whom kills the father and the brother of his foe. The injured man challenges and conquers him in single combat, when, having the ruffian at his mercy, he raises him from the ground, pardons him, and makes him his bosom friend. Likelihood and moral propriety are sacrificed in order that the *Novella* may end with a surprise.

Doni's *Novelle*, taken by themselves, would scarcely have justified the space allotted to him in this chapter. His biography has, however, the importance attaching to the history of a representative man, for much of the literature of amusement in the sixteenth century was supplied by Bohemians of Doni's type. To give a complete account of his miscellaneous works would be out of the question. Besides treatises on music and the arts of design and a catalogue of Italian books, which might be valuable if the author had not used it as a vehicle for his literary animosities, he published letters and poems, collections of proverbs and short tales under the title of 'La Zucca,' dialogues and dissertations on various topics with the name of 'I Mondi,' an essay on moral philosophy, an edition of Burchiello's poems illustrated by notes more difficult to understand than the text, an explanation of the Apocalypse proving Luther to be Antichrist, a libel upon Aretino, two commonplace books of sentences and maxims styled 'I Cancellieri,' a work on villa-building, a series of imaginary pictures, a comedy called 'Lo Stufaiuolo,' and many others which it would be tedious to catalogue. It is not probable that anyone has made a thorough study of Doni's writings; but those who know them best, report that they are all marked by the same sallies of capricious humour and wild fancy.[64]

A glance at the 'Marmi' will suffice to illustrate Doni's method in these miscellanies.[65] In his preface to the reader he says it often happens that, awaked from sleep, he spends the night hours in thinking of himself and of his neighbours—'not, however, as the common folk do, nor like men of learning, but following the whimsies of a teeming brain. I am at home, you see. I fly aloft into the air, above some city, and believe myself to be a huge bird, monstrous, monstrous, piercing with keen sight to everything that's going on below; and in the twinkling of an eye, the roofs fly off, and I behold each man, each woman at their several affairs. One is at home and weeping, another laughing; one giving birth to children, one begetting; this man reading,

[64] Those I am acquainted with are *I Marmi*, *I Mondi*, *Lo Stufaiuolo*, the *Novelle*, and two little burlesque caprices in prose, *La Mula* and *La Chiave*.
[65] *I Marmi*, per Fanfani e Bongi, Firenze, Barbèra, 1863, 2 vols.

that man writing; one eating, another praying. One is scolding his household, another playing; and see, yon fellow has fallen starved to earth, while that one vomits his superfluous food! What contrasts are there in one single city, at one single moment! Then I pass from land to land, and notice divers customs, with variety of speech and converse. In Naples, for example, the gentry are wont to ride abroad and take the evening freshness. In Rome they haunt cool vineyards, or seek their pleasure by artificial fountains. In Venice they roam the canals in dainty gondolas, or sweep the salt lagoons, with music, women, and such delights, putting to flight the day's annoyances and heat. But above all other pleasures in the cool, methinks the Florentines do best. Their way is this. They have the square of Santa Liberata, midway between the ancient shrine of Mars, now San Giovanni, and the marvellous modern Duomo. They have, I say, certain stairs of marble, and the topmost stair leads to a large space, where the young men come to rest in those great heats, seeing that a most refreshing wind is always blowing there, and a delicious breeze, and, besides, the fair white marbles for the most part keep their freshness. It is there I find my best amusements; for, as I sail through the air, invisibly I settle, soaring over them; and hear and see their talk and doings. And forasmuch as they are all fine wits and comely, they have a thousand lovely things to say—novels, stratagems and fables; they tell of intrigues, stories, jokes, tricks played off on men and women—all things sprightly, noble, noteworthy and fit for gentle ears.' Such is the exordium. What follows, consists of conversations, held at night upon these marble slabs by citizens of Florence. The dialogue is lively; the pictures tersely etched; the language racy; the matter almost always worthy of attention. One sustained dialogue on printing is particularly interesting, since it involves a review of contemporary literature from the standpoint of one who was himself exclusively employed in hack production for the press.[66] The whole book, however, abounds in excellent criticism and clever hints. 'See what the world is coming to,' says one of the speakers, 'when no one can read anything, full though it be of learning and goodness, without flinging it away at the end of three words! More artifice than patience goes nowadays to the writing of a book; more racking the brains to invent some whimsical title, which makes one take it up and read a word or two, than the composition of the whole book demands. Just try and tell people to touch a volume labelled "Doctrine of Good Living" or "The Spiritual Life!" God preserve you! Put upon the title page "An Invective against an Honest Man," or "New Pasquinade," or "Pimps Expounded," or "The Whore Lost," and all the world will grab at it. If our Gelli, when he wanted to teach a thousand fine things, full of philosophy and useful to a Christian, had not called them "The Cobbler's Caprices," there's not a soul would have so much as touched them. Had he christened his book "Instructions in Civil Conduct" or "Divine Discourses," it must have

[66] Parte ii. 'Della Stampa.'

fallen stillborn; but that "Cobbler," those "Caprices" make everyone cry out: "I'll see what sort of balderdash it is!" '

One might fancy that this passage had been written to satirise our own times rather than the sixteenth century. More than enough, however, remains from the popular literature of Doni's days to illustrate his observation. We have already seen how ingeniously he titillated public curiosity in the title of his invective against Aretino. 'The Earthquake of Doni, the Florentine, with the Ruin of a Great Bestial Colossus, the Antichrist of our Age,' is worthy to take rank among the most capricious pamphlets of the English Commonwealth. Meanwhile the Venetian press kept pouring out stores of miscellaneous information under bizarre titles; such as the 'Piazza,' which described all sorts of trades, including the most infamous, and 'Il Perchè,' which was a kind of vulgar cyclopædia, with special reference to physiology. Manuals of domestic medicine or directions for the toilette, like the curious 'Comare' on obstetrics, and Marinello's interesting 'Ornamenti delle Donne;' eccentricities in the style of the 'Hospidale de' Pazzi' or the 'Sinagoga degli Ignoranti;' might be cited through a dozen pages. It is impossible to do justice to this undergrowth of literature, which testifies to the extent of the plebeian reading public in Italy.

The Novelists of Siena form a separate group, and are distinguished by a certain air of delicate voluptuous grace.[67] Siena, though it wears so pensive an aspect now, was famous in the middle ages for the refinements of sensuality. It was here that the *godereccia brigata*, condemned to Hell by Dante, spent their substance in gay living. Folgore da San Gemignano's pleasure-seeking Company was Sienese. Beccadelli called the city *molles Senæ*, and Æneas Sylvius dedicated her groves and palaces to Venus—the Venus who appeared in dreams to Gentile Sermini.[68] The impress of luxury is stamped upon the works of her best novelists. They blend the *morbidezza* of the senses with a rare feeling for natural and artistic beauty. Descriptions of banquets and gardens, fountains and wayside thickets, form a delightful background to the never-ending festival of love. We wander through pleasant bypaths of Tuscan country, abloom in spring with acacia trees and resonant with song birds. Though indescribably licentious, these novelists are rarely coarse or vulgar. There is no Florentine blackguardism, no acerbity of scorn or stain of blood-lust on their pages. They are humorous; but they do not season humour with cruelty. Their tales, for the most part, are the lunes of wanton love, day dreams of erotic fancy, a free

[67] *Novelle di Autori Senesi*, edited by Gaetano Poggiali, Londra (Livorno), 1796. This collection, reprinted in the *Raccolta di Novellieri Italiani*, Milano, 1815, vols. xiv. and xv., contains Bernardo Illicini, Giustiniano Nelli, Scipione Bargagli, Gentile Sermini, Pietro Fortini, and others. Of Sermini's *Novelle* a complete edition appeared in 1874 at Livorno from the press of Francesco Vigo; and to this the student should now go. Romagnoli of Bologna in 1877 published three hitherto inedited novels of Fortini, together with the rubrics of all those which have not yet been printed. Their titles enable us to comprehend the scruples which prevented Poggiali from issuing the whole series.

[68] *Imbasciata di Venere*, Sermini, ed. cit. p. 117.

debauch of images, now laughable, now lewd, but all provocative of sensual desire. At the same time, their delight in landscape-painting, combined with a certain refinement of æsthetic taste, saves them from the brutalities of lust.

The foregoing remarks apply in their fullest extension to Sermini and Fortini. The best passages from the 'Ars Amandi' of these authors admit of no quotation. Attention may, however, be called to the graphic description by Sermini of the Sienese boxing-matches.[69] It is a masterpiece of vigorous dialogue and lively movement—a little drama in epitome or profile, bringing the excitement of the champions and their backers vividly before us by a series of exclamations and ejaculated sentences. Fortini does not offer the same advantage to a modest critic; yet his handling of a very comic situation in the fourteenth *Novella* may be conveniently compared with Firenzuola's and Il Lasca's treatment of the same theme.[70] Those, too, who are curious in such matters, may trace the correspondences between his twelfth *Novella* and many similar subjects in the 'Cent nouvelles Nouvelles.' The common material of a *fabliau* is here Italianised with an exquisite sense of plastic and landscape beauty; and the crude obscenity of the *motif* craves pardon for the sake of its rare setting.

Bargagli's tales are less offensive to modern notions of propriety than either Sermini's or Fortini's. They do not detach themselves from the average of such compositions by any peculiarly Sienese quality. But his 'Trattenimenti' are valuable for their introduction, which consists of a minute and pathetically simple narrative of the sufferings sustained by the Sienese during the siege of 1553. Boccaccio's description of the Plague at Florence was in Bargagli's mind, when he made this unaffected record of a city's agony the frontispiece to tales of mirth and passion. Though somewhat out of place, it has the interest which belongs to the faithful history of an eyewitness.

One beautiful story, borrowed from the annals of their own city, was treated by the two Sienese novelists, Illicini and Sermini. The palm of excellence, however, must be awarded to the elder of these authors. Of Bernardo Lapini, surnamed Illicini or Ollicino, very little is known, except that he served both Gian Galeazzo Visconti and Borso da Este in the capacity of physician, and composed a commentary on the 'Trionfi' of Petrarch. His *Novella* opens with a conversation between certain noble ladies of Siena, who agreed that the three most eminent virtues of a generous nature are courtesy, gratitude, and liberality. An ancient dame, who kept them company on that occasion, offered to relate a tale, which should illustrate these qualities and raise certain fine questions concerning their exercise in actual life. The two Sienese families De' Salimbeni and De' Montanini had long been on terms of coldness; and though their ancient feuds were passing into oblivion, no treaty of peace had yet been ratified between their houses, when Anselmo Salim-

[69] *Il Giuoco della pugna*, Sermini, ed. cit. p. 105.
[70] See *Le Cene*, pt. ii. *Nov.* 10, and Firenzuola's seventh *Novella*.

beni fell deeply in love with Angelica, the only sister of Carlo Montanini. Anselmo was wealthy; but to Carlo and his sister there only remained, of their vast ancestral possessions, one small estate, where they lived together in retirement. Delicacy thus prevented the rich Anselmo from declaring his affection, until an event happened which placed it in his power to be of signal service to the Montanini. A prosperous member of the Sienese government desired to purchase Carlo's house at the price of one thousand ducats. Carlo refused to sell this estate, seeing it was his sister's only support and future source of dowry. Thereupon the powerful man of state accused him falsely of treason to the commonwealth. He was cast into prison and condemned to death or the forfeit of one thousand ducats. Anselmo, the very night before Carlo's threatened execution, paid this fine, and sent the deed of release by the hands of a servant to the prison. When Carlo was once more at liberty, he made inquiries which proved beyond doubt that Anselmo, a man unknown to him, the member of a house at ancient feud with his, had done him this great courtesy. It then rushed across his mind that certain acts and gestures of Anselmo betrayed a secret liking for Angelica. This decided him upon the course he had to take. Having communicated the plan to his sister, he went alone with her at night to Salimbeni's castle, and, when he had expressed his gratitude, there left her in her lover's power, as the most precious thing he could bestow upon the saviour of his life. Carlo, not to be surpassed in this exchange of courtesies, delivered Angelica to the women of his household, and afterwards, attended by the train of his retainers, sought Anselmo in his home. There he made a public statement of what had passed between them, wedded Angelica with three rings, dowered her with the half of his estates, and by a formal deed of gift assigned the residue of his fortune to Carlo. This is a bare outline of the story, which Illicini has adorned in all its details with subtle analyses of feeling and reflections on the several situations. The problem proposed to the gentlewomen is to decide which of the two men, Anselmo and Carlo, showed the more perfect courtesy in their several circumstances. How they settled this knotty point, may be left to the readers of *Novelle* to discover.

Bandello more than adequately represents the Lombard group of novelists; and since his works have been already discussed, it will suffice to allude briefly to three collections which in their day were highly popular. These are 'I Proverbi' of Antonio Cornazano, 'Le Piacevoli Notti' of Straparola, and Giraldi's 'Hecatommithi.'[71] Cornazano was a copious writer both in Latin and Italian. He passed his life at the Courts of Francesco Sforza, Bartolommeo Colleoni, and Ercole I. of Ferrara. One of his earliest compositions was a Life of Christ. This fact is not insignificant, as a sign of the conditions under which litera-

[71] None of them is included in the *Milanese Novellieri Italiani*. The editions I shall use are *Proverbii di Messer Antonio Cornazano in Facetie*, Bologna, Romagnoli, 1865; *Le Piacevoli Notti*, in Vinegia per Comin da Trino di Monferrato, MDLI.; *Gli Hecatommithi di M. Giovanbattista Giraldi Cinthio, Nobile Ferrarese*, in Vinegia, MDLXVI., Girolamo Scotto, 2 vols.

ture was produced in the Renaissance. A man who had gained reputation by a learned or religious treatise ventured to extend it by jests of the broadest humour. The 'Proverbi,' by which alone Cornazano's name is now distinguished, are sixteen carefully wrought stories, very droll but very dirty. Each illustrates a common proverb, and pretends to relate the circumstances which gave it currency. The author opens one tale with a simple statement: 'From the deserts of the Thebaid came to us that trite and much used saying, *Better late than never;* and this was how it happened.' Having stated the theme, he enters on his narrative, diverts attention by a series of absurdities which lead to an unexpected climax. He concludes it thus: 'The abbot answered: "It is not this which makes me weep, but to think of my misfortune, who have been so long without discovering and commending so excellent an usage." "Father," said the monk, "*Better late than never.*"' There is considerable comic vigour in the working of this motive. Our sense of the ridiculous is stimulated by a studied disproportion between the universality of the proverb and the strangeness of the incidents invented to account for it.

Straparola breaks ground in a different direction. The majority of his novels bear traces of their origin in fairy stories or *Volksmärchen.* Much interest attaches to the 'Notti Piacevoli,' as the literary reproduction of a popular species which the Venetian Gozzi afterwards rendered famous. Students of folk-lore may compare them with the Sicilian fables recently committed to the press by Signor Pitrè.[72] The element of bizarre fancy is remarkable in all these tales; but the marvellous has been so mingled with the facts of common life as to give each narrative the true air of the conventional *Novella.* One in particular may be mentioned, since it is written on the same motive as Machiavelli's 'Belphegor.' The rubric runs as follows: 'The Devil, hearing the complaints of husbands against their wives, marries Silvia Ballastro, and takes Gasparino Boncio for gossip of the ring, and forasmuch as he finds it impossible to live with his wife, enters into the body of the Duke of Melphi, and Gasparino, his gossip, expels him thence.' Between Straparola's and Machiavelli's treatment of this subject, the resemblance is so close as to justify the opinion that the former tale was simply modelled on the latter, or that both were drawn from an original source. In each case it is the wife's pride which renders life unendurable to her demon husband, and in both he is expelled from the possessed person by mistaking a brass band in full play for the approach of his tumultuous consort. But Straparola's loose and careless style of narrative bears no comparison with the caustic satire of Machiavelli's meditated art.[73] The same theme was treated in Italian by

[72] *Fiabe, Novelle, Racconti,* Palermo, Lauriel, 1875, 4 vols. I may here take occasion to notice that one *Novella* by the Conte Lorenzo Magalotti (*Nov. It.* vol. xiii. p. 362), is the story of Whittington and his Cat, told of a certain Florentine, Ansaldo degli Ormanni, and the King of the Canary Islands.

[73] John Wilson's play of *Belphegor,* Dekker's *If it be not good the Diuell is in it,* and Ben Jonson's *The Devil is an Ass,* were more or less founded on Machiavelli's and Straparola's novels.

Giovanni Brevio; and since Machiavelli's novel first appeared in print in the year 1549, Straparola's seeing the light in 1550, and Brevio's in 1545, we may reasonably conclude that each version was an adaptation of some primitive monastic story.[74]

On the score of style alone, it would be difficult to explain the widespread popularity of Giraldi Cinthio's one hundred and ten tales.[75] The 'Hecatommithi' are written in a lumbering manner, and the stories are often lifeless. Compared with the brilliancy of the Tuscan *Novelle*, the point and sparkle of 'Le Cene,' the grace and gusto of Sermini, or Firenzuola's golden fluency, the diction of this noble Ferrarese is dull. Yet the 'Hecatommithi' were reprinted again and again, and translated into several languages. In England, through Painter's 'Palace of Pleasure,' they obtained wide circulation and supplied our best dramatists, including Shakspere and Fletcher, with hints for plays. It is probable that they owed their fame in no small measure to what we reckon their defects. Giraldi's language was more intelligible to ordinary readers of Italian than the racy Tuscan of the Sienese authors. His stories had less of a purely local flavour than those of the Florentines. They enjoyed, moreover, the singular advantage of diffusion through the press of Venice, which then commanded the book-market of Europe. But, if we put this point of style aside, the vogue of Cinthio in Italy and Europe becomes at once intelligible. There is a massive force and volume in his matter, which proclaims him an author to be reckoned with. The variety of scenes he represents, the tragic gravity of many of his motives, his intimate acquaintance with the manners and customs of a class that never fails to interest the vulgar, combined with great sagacity in selecting and multiplying instances of striking crime, stood him in the stead of finer art with the special public for whom *Novelle* were composed.[76] Compared even with Boccaccio, the prince of story-tellers, Cinthio holds his own, not as a great dramatic or descriptive writer, but as one who has studied, analysed, dissected, and digested the material of human action and passion in a vast variety of modes. His work is more solid and reflective than Bandello's: more moralised than Il Lasca's. The ethical tendency both of the tales and the discussions they occasion, is, for the most part, singularly wholesome. In spite, therefore, of the almost revolting frankness with which impurity, fraud, cruelty, violence, and bestial lust are exposed to view, one rises from the perusal of the 'Hecatommithi' with an unimpaired conscious-

[74] Dunlop in his *History of Fiction*, vol. ii. p. 411, speaks of a Latin MS. preserved in the library of S. Martin at Tours which contained the tale, but he also says that it was lost at 'the period of the civil wars in France.'

[75] The title leads us to expect one hundred tales; but counting the ten of the Introduction, there are one hundred and ten. When the book first circulated, it contained but seventy. The first edition is that of Monte Regale in Sicily, 1565. My copy of the Venetian edition of 1566 is complete.

[76] The ten novels of the Introduction deal exclusively with the manners of Italian prostitutes. Placed as a frontispiece to the whole repertory, they seem intended to attract the vulgar reader.

ness of good and evil. It is just the negation of this conscience which renders the mass of Italian *Novelle* worse than unprofitable.

The plan of the 'Hecatommithi' deserves a passing notice, if only because it illustrates the more than ordinary force of brain which Cinthio brought to bear upon his light material. He begins with an elaborate description of the Sack of Rome. A party of men and women take refuge from its horrors of rape, pestilence and tortures in one of the Colonna palaces. When affairs have been proved desperate, they set sail from Città Vecchia for Marseilles, and enliven their voyage with story-telling. A man of mature years opens the discussion with a long panegyric of wedded love, serving as introduction to the tales which treat of illicit passion. From this first day's debate the women of the party are absent. They intervene next day, and upon this and the following nine days one hundred stories are related by different members of the party upon subjects selected for illustration. Each novel is followed by a copious commentary in the form of dialogue, and songs are interspersed. Cinthio thus adhered, as closely as possible, to the model furnished by Boccaccio. But his framework, though ingeniously put together, lacks the grace and sweetness of the 'Decameron.' Not a few of the novels are founded upon facts of history. In the tenth tale of the ninth decade, for example, he repeats the legend of the Borgia family—the murder of the Duke of Gandia, Alexander's death by poison, and Cesare's escape. The names are changed; but the facts, as related by Guicciardini, can be clearly discerned through the transparent veil of fiction.

In concluding this chapter on the *Novelle*, it may be repeated that the species of narrative in question was, in its ultimate development, a peculiar Italian product. Originally derived through the French *fabliaux* from mediæval Latin stories, the *Novella* received in Italy more serious and more artistic treatment. It satisfied the craving of the race for such delineation of life and manners as a great literature demands; and it did this, for reasons which will be explained in the next chapter, with more originality, more adequacy to the special qualities of the Italian people, than even their comedies. What De Quincey wrote concerning our theatre in the age of Elizabeth and James, might almost be applied to the material which the *Novellieri* used: 'No literature, not excepting even that of Athens, has ever presented such a multiform theatre, such a carnival display, mask and anti-mask of impassioned life—breathing, moving, acting, suffering, laughing:

> Quicquid agunt homines—votum, timor, ira, voluptas,
> Gaudia, discursus.'

But, when we quit material to think of form, the parallel fails. De Quincey's further description of our dramas, 'scenically grouped, draped, and gorgeously coloured,' is highly inapplicable to the brief, careless, almost pedestrian prose of the *Novelle*. In spite of their indescribable wealth of subject-matter, in spite of those inexhaustible stores of plots and situations, characters and motives, which have made them a mine for playwrights in succeeding ages, they rarely rise to the height of poetry, nor are they ever dramas. The artistic limitations of the Italian *Novella* are among the most interesting phenomena presented by the history of literature.

CHAPTER XI

THE DRAMA

First Attempts at Secular Drama—The 'Orfeo' and 'Timone'—General Character of Italian Plays—Court Pageants and Comedies borrowed from the Latin—Conditions under which a National Drama is formed—Their Absence in Italy—Lack of Tragic Genius—Eminently Tragic Material in Italian History—The Use made of this by English Playwrights—The Ballad and the Drama—The Humanistic Bias in Italy—Parallels between Greek and Italian Life—Il Lasca's Critique of the Latinising Playwrights—The 'Sofonisba' of Trissino—Rucellai's 'Rosmunda'—Sperone's 'Canace'—Giraldi's 'Orbecche'—Dolce's 'Marianna'—Transcripts from the Greek Tragedians and Seneca—General Character of Italian Tragedies—Sources of their Failure—Influence of Plautus and Terence over Comedy—Latin Comedies acted at Florence, Rome, Ferrara—Translations of Latin Comedies—Manner of Representation at Court—Want of Permanent Theatres—Bibbiena's 'Calandra'—Leo X. and Comedy at Rome—Ariosto's Treatment of his Latin Models—The 'Cassaria,' 'Suppositi,' 'Lena,' 'Negromante,' 'Scolastica'—Qualities of Ariosto's Comedies—Machiavelli's Plays—The 'Commedia in Prosa'—Fra Alberigo and Margherita—The 'Clizia'—Its Humour—The 'Mandragola'—Its sinister Philosophy—Conditions under which it was composed—Aretino disengages Comedy from Latin Rules—His Point of View—The 'Cortegiana,' 'Marescalco,' 'Talanta'—Italy had innumerable Comedies, but no great Comic Art—General Character of the Commedia Erudita—Its fixed Personages—Gelli, Firenzuola, Cecchi, Ambra, Il Lasca—The Farsa—Conclusion on the Moral Aspects of Italian Comedy.

CONTEMPORANEOUSLY with the Romantic Epic, the Drama began to be a work of studied art in Italy. Boiardo by his 'Timone' and Poliziano by his 'Orfeo' gave the earliest specimens at Ferrara and Mantua of secular plays written in the vulgar tongue. The 'Timone' must have been composed before 1494, the date of Boiardo's death; and we have already seen that the 'Orfeo' was in all probability represented in 1472. It is significant that the two poets who were mainly instrumental in effecting a revival of Italian poetry should have tried their hands at two species of composition for the stage. In the 'Orfeo' we find a direct outgrowth from the 'Sacre Rappresentazioni.' The form of the Florentine religious show is adapted with very little alteration to a pagan story. In substance the 'Orfeo' is a pastoral melodrama with a tragic climax. Boiardo in the 'Timone' followed a different direction. The subject is borrowed from Lucian, who speaks the prologue, as Gower prologises in the 'Pericles' of Shakspere. The comedy aims at regularity of structure, and is written in *terza rima*. Yet the chief character leaves the stage before the end of the fifth act, and the conclusion is narrated by an allegorical personage, Lo Ausilio.[1]

These plays, though generally considered to have been the first attempts at secular Italian dramatic poetry, were by no means the earliest in date, if we admit the Latin plays of scholars.[2] Besides some tragedies, which will afterwards be mentioned, it is enough here to cite the 'Philogenia' of Ugolino Pisani (Parma, 1430), the 'Philodoxius' of Alberti, the 'Polissena' of Leonardo Bruni, and the 'Progne' of Gregorio Corrado. It is therefore a fact that, in addition to religious dramas in the mother tongue, the Italians from an early period turned their attention to dramatic composition. Still the drama never flourished at any time in Italy as a form of poetry indigenous and national. It did not succeed in freeing itself from classical imitation on the one hand, or on the other from the hampering adjuncts of Court-pageants and costly entertainments. Why the Italians failed to develop a national theatre, is a question easier to ask than to answer. The attempt to solve this problem will, however, serve to throw some light upon their intellectual conditions at the height of the Renaissance.

Plays in Italy at this period were either religious *Feste* of the kind peculiar to Florence, or Masques at Court, or Comedies and Tragedies imitated by men of learning from classical models, or, lastly, Pastorals combining the scenic attractions of the Masque with the action of a regular drama. None of these five species can be called in a true sense popular; nor were they addressed by their authors to the masses of the people. Performed in private by pious confraternities or erudite academies, or exhibited on state occasions in the halls of princely palaces, they were not an expression of the national genius but a highly-cultivated form of aristocratic luxury. When Heywood in his prologue to the 'Challenge for Beauty' wrote:

> Those [*i.e.* plays] that frequent are
> In Italy or France, *even in these days*,
> *Compared with ours*, are rather jigs than plays:

[1] 'Comedia de Timone per el Magnifico Conte Matheo Maria Boyardo Conte de Scandiano traducta de uno Dialogo de Luciano. Stampata in Venetia per Georgio di Rusconi Milanese, del MDXVIII. adì iii di Decembre.' From the play itself we learn that it must have been represented on a double stage, a lower one standing for earth and a higher one for heaven. The first three acts consist chiefly of soliloquies by Timon and conversations with celestial personages—Jove, Mercury, Wealth, Poverty. In the fourth act we are introduced to characters of Athenians—Gnatonide, Phylade, Demea, Trasycle, who serve to bring Timone's misanthropy into relief; and the fifth act brings two slaves, Syro and Parmeno, upon the scene, with a kind of underplot which is not solved at the close of the play. The whole piece must be regarded rather as a Morality than a Comedy, and the characters are allegories or types more than living persons.

[2] To determine the question of priority in such matters is neither easy nor important. Students who desire to follow the gradual steps in the development of Italian play-writing before the date of Ariosto and Machiavelli may be referred to D' Ancona's work on the *Origini del Teatro*.

when Marlowe in the first scene of 'Edward II.,' made Gaveston, thinking how he may divert the pleasure-loving king, exclaim:

> Therefore I'll have Italian masks by night,
> Sweet speeches, comedies, and pleasing shows:

both of these poets uttered a true criticism of the Italian theatre. Marlowe accurately describes the scenic exhibitions in vogue at the Courts of Ferrara, Mantua, Urbino, and Rome, where the stage was reckoned among the many instruments of wanton amusement. Heywood, by his scornful phrase, *jigs*, indicates their mixed nature between comedies and ballets, with interludes of pageantry and accompaniment of music. The words italicised show that the English playwrights were conscious of having developed a nobler type of the drama than had been produced in Italy. In order to complete the outline sketched by Heywood and Marlowe, we must bear in mind that comedies adapted from the Latin, like the 'Suppositi' of Ariosto, or constructed upon Latin principles, like Machiavelli's 'Mandragola' or the 'Calandra' of Bibbiena, were highly relished by a society educated in humanistic traditions. Such efforts of the scholarly muse approved themselves even in England to the taste of critics like Sir Philip Sidney, who shows in his 'Defence of Poesy' that he had failed to discern the future greatness of the national drama. But they had the fatal defect of being imitations and exotics. The stage, however learnedly adorned by men of scholarship and fancy, remained within the narrow sphere of courtly pastime. What was a mere *hors d'œuvre* in the Elizabethan age of England, formed the whole dramatic art of the Italians.

If tragedy and comedy sprang by a natural process of evolution from the mediæval Mystery, then the Florentines should have had a drama. We have seen how rich in the elements of both species were the 'Sacre Rappresentazioni;' and how men of culture like Lorenzo de' Medici and Bernardo Pulci deigned to compose them. But the 'Sacre Rappresentazioni' died a natural death, and left no heritage. They had no vital relation to the people, either as a source of amusement or as embodying the real thoughts and passions of the race. Designed for the edification of youth, their piety was too often hypocritical, and their extravagant monastic morality stood in glaring opposition to the ethics of society. We must go far deeper in our analysis, if we wish to comprehend this failure of the Italians to produce a drama.

Three conditions, enjoyed by Greece and England, but denied to Italy, seem necessary for the poetry of a nation to reach this final stage of artistic development. The first is a free and sympathetic public, not made up of courtiers and scholars, but of men of all classes—a public representative of the whole nation, with whom the playwright shall feel himself in close *rapport*. The second is, a centre of social life: an Athens, Paris or London: where the heart of the nation beats and where its brain is ever active. The third is a perturbation of the race in some great effort, like the Persian war or the struggle of the

Reformation, which unites the people in a common consciousness of heroism. Taken in combination, these three conditions explain the appearance of a drama fitted to express the very life and soul of a puissant nation, with the temper of the times impressed upon it, but with a truth and breadth that render it the heritage of every race and age. A national drama is the image created for itself in art by a people which has arrived at knowledge of its power, at the enjoyment of its faculties, after a period of successful action. Concentrated in a capital, gifted with a common instrument of self-expression, it projects itself in tragedies and comedies that bear the name of individual poets, but are in reality the spirit of the race made vocal.[3]

These conditions have only twice in the world's history existed—once in the Athens of Pericles, once in the London of Elizabeth. The measure of greatness to which the dramas of Paris and Madrid, though still not comparable with the Attic and the English, can lay claim, is due to the participation by the French and Spanish peoples in these privileges. But in Italy there was no public, no metropolis, no agitation of the people in successful combat with antagonistic force. The educated classes were, indeed, conscious of intellectual unity; but they had no meeting-point in any city, where they might have developed the theatre upon the only principles then possible, the principles of erudition. And, what was worse, there existed no enthusiasms, moral, religious or political, from which a drama could arise. A society without depth of thought or seriousness of passion, highly cultured, but devoid of energy and aspiration, had not the seed of tragedy within its loins. In those polite Italian Courts and pleasure-seeking coteries, the idyll, the *Novella*, and the vision of a golden age might entertain men weary with public calamities, indulgent to the vice and crime around them. From this soil the forest-trees of a great drama could not spring. But it yielded an abundant crop of comedies, an undergrowth of rankly sprouting vegetation. It was, moreover, well adapted to the one original production of the Italian stage. Pastoral comedy, attaining perfection in Tasso's 'Aminta' and Guarini's 'Pastor Fido,' and bearing the germs of the Opera in its voluptuous scenes, formed the climax of dramatic art in Italy.

Independently of these external drawbacks, we find in the nature of the Italian genius a reason why the drama never reached perfection. Tragedy, which is the soul of great dramatic poetry, was almost uniformly wanting after Dante. Petrarch, Boccaccio, Poliziano, Boiardo, Ariosto, Tasso are pathetic, graceful, polished, elevated, touching, witty, humorous, reflective, radiant, inventive, fanciful—everything but stern, impassioned, tragic in the true heroic sense. Even the Florentines, who dallied sometimes with the thoughts of Death and Judgment in bizarre pageants like the show of Hell recorded by Villani, or the Masque of

[3] I have enlarged on these points in my Essay on Euripides (*Greek Poets*, Series i.). I may take occasion here to say that until Sept. 1879, after this chapter was written, I had not met with Professor Hillebrand's *Etudes Italiennes* (Paris, Franck, 1868).

Penitence designed by Piero di Cosimo, or the burlesque festivals recorded in the life of Rustici by Giorgio Vasari—even the Florentines shrank in literature from what is terrible and charged with anguish of the soul. The horrors of the *Novelle* are used by them to stimulate a jaded appetite, to point the pleasures of the sense by contrast with the shambles and the charnel-house. We are never invited to the spectacle of human energies ravaged by passion, at war with destiny, yet superior to fate and fortune and internal tempest in the strength of will and dignity of herosim. It is not possible to imagine those *liete brigate* of young men and maidens responding to the fierce appeal of Marston's prologue:

> Therefore we proclaim,
> If any spirit breathes within this round,
> Uncapable of weighty passion—
> As from his birth being huggéd in the arms
> And nuzzled twixt the breasts of happiness—
> Who winks, and shuts his apprehension up
> From common sense of what men were, and are,
> Who would not know what men must be; let such
> Hurry amain from our black-visaged shows:
> We shall affright their eyes. But if a breast
> Nailed to the earth with grief, if any heart
> Pierced through with anguish pant within this ring,
> If there be any blood whose heat is choked
> And stifled with true sense of misery,
> If aught of these strains fill this consort up,
> They arrive most welcome.

Sterner, and it may be gloomier conditions of external life than those which the Italians enjoyed, were needed as a preparation of the public for such spectacles. It was not on these aspects of human existence that a race, accustomed to that genial climate and refined by the contemplation of all-golden art, loved to dwell in hours of recreation. The *Novella*, with its mixture of comedy and pathos, license and satire, gave the tone, as we have seen, to literature. The same quality of the Italian temperament may be illustrated from the painting of the sixteenth century, which rarely rises to the height of tragedy. If we except Michelangelo and Tintoretto, we find no masters of sublime and fervid genius, able to conceive with intensity and to express with force the thrilling moods of human passion. Raphael marks the height of national achievement, and even the more serious work of Raphael found no adequate interpreters among his pupils.

The absence of the tragic element in Italian art and literature is all the more remarkable because the essence of Italian history, whether political or domestic, was eminently dramatic. When we consider what the nation suffered during the civil wars of the thirteenth and fourteenth centuries, under the tyranny of monsters like Ezzelino, from plagues that swept away the population of great cities, and beneath the scourge of sinister religious revivals, it may well cause wonder that the Italian spirit should not have assumed a stern and tragic tone instead of that serenity and cheerfulness which from the first distinguished it. The Italians lived their tragedies in the dynasties of the Visconti and the Sforzas, in the contests of the Baglioni and Manfredi, in the persons of Pandolfo Sigismondo Malatesta and Cesare Borgia, in the murders, poisonings, rapes and treasons that form the staple of the annals of their noble houses. But it was the English and not the Italian poets who seized upon this tragic matter and placed it with the light of poetry upon the stage.[4] Our Elizabethan playwrights dramatised the legends of Othello and Juliet, the loves of Bianca Capello and Vittoria Accoramboni, the tragedies of the Duchess of Amalfi and the Duke of Milan. There is something even appalling in the tenacity with which poets of the stamp of Marlowe, Webster, Ford, Massinger and Tourneur clung to the episodes of blood and treachery furnished by Italian stories. Their darkest delineations of villainy, their subtlest analyses of evil motives, their most audacious pictures of vice, are all contained within the charmed circle of Italian history. A play could scarcely succeed in London unless the characters were furnished with Italian names.[5] Italy fascinated the Northern fancy, and the imagination of our dramatists found itself at home among her scenes of mingled pleasure and atrocity. Nowhere, therefore, can a truer study of Italian Court-intrigue be found than in the plays of Webster. His portraits, it may be allowed, are painted without relief or due gradation of tone. Flamineo and Bosola seem made to justify the proverb—*Inglese Italianato è un diavolo incarnato*. Yet after reading the secret history of the Borgias, or estimating the burden on Ferdinand's conscience when he quaked before the French advance on Naples, who can say that Webster has exaggerated the bare truth? He has but intensified it by the incubation of his intellect. Varchi's account of Lorenzino de' Medici, affecting profligacy and effeminancy in order to deceive Duke Alessandro, and forming to his purpose the ruffian Scoronconcolo from the dregs of the prisons, furnishes a complete justification for even Tourneur's plots. The snare this traitor laid for Alessandro, when he offered to bring his own aunt to the duke's lust, bears a close resemblance to Vendice's scheme in the 'Revenger's Tragedy;' while the inconsequence of his action after the crime tallies with the moral collapse of Duke Ferdinand before his strangled sister's corpse in the last act of the 'Duchess of Malfi.'

[4] Exception must be made in favour of some ancient quasi-tragedies, which seem to prove that before the influences of Boccaccio and the Renaissance had penetrated the nation, they were not deficient in the impulse to dramatise history. The *Eccerinis* of Albertino Mussato (*c.* 1300), half dialogue and half narration, upon the fate of Ezzelino da Romano, composed in the style of Seneca; the dialogue upon the destruction of Cesena (1377) falsely attributed to Petrarch; Giovanni Mangini della Motta's poem on the downfall of Antonio della Scala (1387), Lodovico da Vezzano's tragedy of Jacopo Piccinino; though far from popular in their character, and but partially dramatic, were such as under happier auspices might have fostered the beginnings of the tragic theatre. Later on we hear of the *Fall of Granada* being represented before Cardinal Riario at Rome, as well as the *Ferrandus Servatus* of Carlo Verradi (1492).

[5] See the first cast of Jonson's *Every Man in his Humour*.

The reality of these acted tragedies may have been a bar to their mimic presentation on the stage in Italy. When the Borgias were poisoning their victims in Rome; when Lodovico Sforza was compassing his nephew's death at Pavia; when the Venetians were decapitating Carmagnuola; when Sixtus was plotting the murder of the Medici in church, and Grifonetto Baglioni was executing *il gran tradimento*; could an Italian audience, in the Court or on the Piazza, have taken a keen pleasure in witnessing the scenic presentment of barbarities so close at hand? The sense of contrast between the world of fact and the work of art, which forms an essential element of æsthetic pleasure, would have been wanting. The poets turned from these crimes to comedy and romance, though the politicians analysed their motives with impartial curiosity. At the same time, we may question whether the Despots would have welcomed tragic shows which dramatised their deeds of violence; whether they would have suffered the patriotism of Brutus, the vengeance of Virginius, the plots of Catiline, or the downfall of Sejanus to be displayed with spirit-stirring pomp in theatres of Milan and Ferrara, when conspiracies like that of Olgiati were frequent. It was the freedom of the English public and the self-restraint of the English character, in combination with the profound appetite for tragic emotion inherent in our Northern blood, which rendered the Shaksperian drama possible and acceptable.

In connexion with this inaptitude of the Italians for tragedy, it is worth noticing that their popular poetry exhibits but rare examples of the ballad. It abounds in love-ditties and lyrics of the inner life. But references to history and the tragedies of noble families are comparatively scarce.[6] In Great Britain, on the contrary, while our popular poetry can show but few songs of sentiment, the Border and Robin Hood ballads record events in national history or episodes from actual domestic dramas, blent with the memories of old mythology. These poems prove in the unknown minstrels who produced them, a genuine appreciation of dramatic incident; and their manner is marked by vigorous objectivity. The minstrel loses himself in his subject and aims at creating in his audience a vivid sense of the action he has undertaken to set forth. The race which could produce such ballads, already contained the germs of Marlowe's tragedy. It would be interesting to pursue this subject further, and by examining the ballad-literature of the several European nations to trace how far the capacities which in a rude state of society were directed to this type of minstrelsy, found at a later period their true sphere of art in the drama.[7]

[6] See above, pp. 27, 28, where one ballad of the Border type is discussed.

[7] It is certainly significant that the Spanish share with the English the chief honours both of the ballad and the drama. The Scandinavian nations, rich in ballads, have been, through Danish poets, successful in dramatic composition. The Niebelungen Lied and the Song of Roland would, in the case of Germany and France, have to be set against the English ballads of action. But these Epics are different in character from the minstrelsy which turned passing events into poetry and bequeathed them in the form of spirit-stirring narratives to posterity. Long after the

The deficiency of the tragic instinct among the Italians seems to be further exhibited by their failure to produce novels of the higher type.[8] Though Boccaccio is the prince of story-tellers, his *Novelle* are tales, more interesting for their grace of manner and beautifully described situations, than for analysis of character or strength of plot. Recent Italian *romanzi* are histories rather than works of free fiction; and these novels were produced after the style of Sir Walter Scott had been acclimatised in every part of Europe. Meanwhile no Balzac or George Sand, no Thackeray or George Eliot, no Cervantes or Fielding, has appeared in Italy. The nearest approach to a great Italian novel of life and character is the autobiography of Cellini.[9] As the Italians lived instead of playing their tragedies, so they lived instead of imagining their novels.

If a national drama could have been produced in Italy, it might have appeared at Florence during the reign of Lorenzo de' Medici. In no other place and at no other period was the Italian genius more alive and centralised. But a city is not a nation, and the Compagnia di San Giovanni was not the Globe Theatre. The desires of the Florentines, so studiously gratified by their merchant prince, were bent on carnival shows and dances. In this modern Athens the fine arts failed to find their meeting-point and fulfilment on the stage, because the people lacked the spirit and the freedom necessary to the drama. Artists were satisfied with decorating masques and cars. Poets amused their patrons with romantic stories. Scholars were absorbed in the fervent passion for antiquity. Michelangelo carved and Lionardo painted the wonders of the modern world. Thus the Florentine genius found channels that led far afield from tragedy. At a later period, when culture had become more universally Italian, it might have been imagined that the bright spirit of Ariosto, the pregnant wit of Machiavelli, the genial humour of Bibbiena would have given birth to plays of fancy like Fletcher's or to original comedies of manners like Jonson's and Massinger's. But such was the respect of these Italian playwrights for their classic models, that the scenes of even the best Florentine comedies are crowded with spendthrifts, misers, courtesans, lovers and slaves, borrowed from the Latin authors. Plautus and Terence, Ariosto and Machiavelli, not nature, were their source of inspiration.[10] Mistakes between two brothers, con-

epical impulse had ceased and the British epic of Arthur had passed into the sphere of literature, the ballad minstrels continued to work with dramatic energy upon the substance of contemporary incidents.

[8] See above, p. 201, for the distinction between the Italian *Novella* and the modern novel.

[9] In the same way Alfieri's biography is a tragic and Goldoni's a comic novel. The Memoirs of Casanova, which I incline to accept as genuine, might rather be cited as a string of brilliantly written *Novelle*.

[10] Cantù quotes the prologue of a MS. play which goes so far as to apologise for the scene not being laid at Athens (*Lett. It.* p. 471):

Benchè l' usanza sia
Che ogni commedia
Si soglia fare a Atene,

fusions of sex, discoveries that poor girls are the lost daughters of princely parents, form the staple of their plots. The framework of comedy being thus antique, the playwright was reduced to narrow limits for that exhibition of 'truth's image, the ensample of manners, the mirror of life,' which Il Lasca rightly designated as the proper object of the comic art.

The similarity of conditions between late Greek and modern Italian life facilitated this custom of leaning on antique models, and deceived the poets into thinking they might safely apply Græco-Roman plots to the facts of fifteenth-century romance. With the Turk at Otranto, with the Cardinals of Este and Medici opposing his advance in Hungary, with the episodes of French invasion, with the confusions of the Sack of Rome, there was enough of social anarchy and public peril to justify dramatic intrigues based on kidnapping and anagnorisis. The playwrights, when they adapted comedies of Plautus and Terence, were fully alive to the advantage of these correspondences. Claudio in Ariosto's 'Suppositi' had his son stolen in the taking of Otranto. Bartolo in the 'Scolastica' lost sight of his intended wife at the moment of Lodovico Sforza's expulsion from Milan. Callimaco in Machiavelli's 'Mandragola' remained in Paris to avoid the troubles consequent on Charles VIII.'s invasion. Lidio and Santilla in Bibbiena's 'Calandra,' Blando's children in Aretino's 'Talanta,' were taken by the Turks. Fabrizio in the 'Ingannati' was lost in the Sack of Rome. Maestro Cornelio in Ambra's 'Furto' was captured by the German Lanzi. In the 'Cofanaria' of the same author there is a girl kidnapped in the Siege of Florence. Slavery itself was by no means obsolete in Italy upon the close of the middle ages; and the slave-merchant of Ariosto's 'Cassaria,' hardly distinguished from a common brothel-keeper, was not so anachronistic as to be impossible. The parasites of Latin comedy found their counterpart in the clients of rich families and the poorer courtiers of princes. The indispensable Davus was represented by the body servants of wealthy householders. The *miles gloriosus* reappeared in professional *bravi* and captains of mercenaries. Thus the personages of the Latin stage could easily be furnished with Italian masks. Still there remained an awkwardness in fitting these new masks to the old lay-figures; and when we read the genuine Italian comedies of Aretino, especially the 'Cortigiana' and the 'Marescalco,' we feel how much was lost to the nation by the close adherence of its greater playwrights, Ariosto and Machiavelli, to the conventions of the *Commedia erudita*.

The example of Ariosto and Machiavelli led even the best Florentine playwrights—Cecchi, Ambra, and Gelli—into a false path. The plays of these younger authors abound in reminiscences of the 'Suppositi' and 'Clizia,' adapted with incomparable skill and humour to contemporary customs, but suffering from too close adherence to models, which had

Non so donde si viene
Che questa non grecizza,
Anzi fiorentinizza.

been in their turn copied from the antique. It was not until the middle of the sixteenth century that criticism hit the vein of common sense. Il Lasca, who deserves great credit for his perspicacity, carried on an unremitting warfare against the comedy of *anagnorisis*. In the prologue to his 'Gelosia' he says:[11] 'All the comedies which have been exhibited in Florence since the Siege, end in discoveries of lost relatives. This has become so irksome to the audience that, when they hear in the argument how at the taking of this city or the sack of that, children have been lost or kidnapped, they know only too well what is coming, and would fain leave the room. . . . Authors of such comedies jumble up the new and the old, antique and modern together, making a hodgepodge and confusion, without rhyme or reason, head or tail. They lay their scenes in modern cities and depict the manners of to-day, but foist in obsolete customs and habits of remote antiquity. Then they excuse themselves by saying: Plautus did thus, and this was Menander's way and Terence's; never perceiving that in Florence, Pisa and Lucca people do not live as they used to do in Rome and Athens. For heaven's sake let these fellows take to translation, if they have no vein of invention, but leave off cobbling and spoiling the property of others and their own.' The prologue to the 'Spiritata' contains a similar polemic against 'quei ritrovamenti nei tempi nostri impossibili e sciocchi.'[12] In the prologue to the 'Strega,' after once more condemning 'quelle recognizioni deboli e sgarbate,' he proceeds to attack the authority of ancient critics on whom the pedantic school relied:[13] 'Aristotle and Horace knew their own times. But ours are wholly different. We have other manners, another religion, another way of life; and therefore our comedies ought to be composed after a different fashion. People do not live at Florence as they did in Rome and Athens. There are no slaves here; it is not customary to adopt children: our pimps do not put up girls for sale at auction; nor do the soldiers of the present century carry long-clothes babies off in the sack of cities, to educate them as their own daughters and give them dowries; nowadays they make as much booty as they can, and should girls or married women fall into their hands, they either look for a large ransom or rob them of their maidenhead and honour.'

This polemic of Il Lasca, and, indeed, all that he says about the art and aim of comedy, is very sensible. But at his date there was no hope for a great comedy of manners. What between the tyranny of the Medici and the pressure of the Inquisition, Spanish suspicion and Papal anxiety for a reform of manners, the liberty essential to a new development of the dramatic art had been extinguished. And even if external conditions had been favourable, the spirit of the race was spent. All intellectual energy was now losing itself in the quagmire of academical discussions and literary disputations upon verbal niceties.

[11] *Commedie di Antonfrancesco Grazzini* (Firenze, Lemonnier, 1859), p. 5.
[12] *Op. cit.* p. 109.
[13] *Op. cit.* p. 173.

Attention was turned backward to the study of Petrarch and Boccaccio. Authors aiming above all things at correctness, slavishly observant of rules and absurdly fearful of each other's ferrules, had not the stuff in them to create. What has been said of comedy, is still more true of tragedy. The tragic dramas of this period are stiff and lifeless, designed to illustrate critical principles rather than to stir and purify the passions. They have no relation to the spirit of the people or the times; and the blood spilt at their conclusion fails to distinguish them from moral lucubrations in the blankest verse.[14]

The first regular Italian tragedy was the 'Sofonisba' of Gian Giorgio Trissino, finished in 1515, and six times printed before the date of its first representation at Vicenza in 1562.[15] Trissino was a man of immense erudition and laborious intellect, who devoted himself to questions of grammatical and literary accuracy, studying the critics of antiquity with indefatigable diligence and seeking to establish canons for the regulation of correct Italian composition. He was by no means deficient in originality of aim, and professed himself the pioneer of novelties in poetry.[16] Thus, besides innovating in the minor matter of orthography, he set himself to supply the deficiencies of Italian literature by producing an epic in the heroic style and a tragedy that should compete with those of Athens. He had made a profound study of the 'Poetics' and believed that Aristotle's analyses of the epic and the drama might be used as recipes for manufacturing similar masterpieces in a modern tongue.[17] The 'Italia Liberata' and the 'Sofonisba,' meritorious but lifeless exercises which lacked nothing but the genius for poetry, were the results of these ambitious theories. Aristotle presided over both, while Homer served as the professed model for Trissino's heroic poem, and Sophocles was copied in his play. Of the 'Italia Liberata' this is not the place to speak. The 'Sofonisba' is founded on a famous episode in the Punic Wars, when the wife of Syphax was married by Massinissa contrary to the express will of Lælius and Scipio. She takes poison at her new husband's orders, and her death forms the catastrophe. There is some attempt to mark character in Lelio, Scipione, and Massinissa; but these persons do not act and react on one another,

[14] I have put into an Appendix some further notes upon the opinions recorded by the playwrights concerning the progress of the dramatic art.

[15] My references to Italian tragedies will be made to the *Teatro Italiano Antico*, 10 vols., Milano, 1809.

[16] This is shown by his device of a Golden Fleece, referring to the voyage of the Argonauts. To sail the ocean of antiquity as an explorer, and to bring back the spoils of their artistic method was his ambition.

[17] Compare what Giraldi says in the dedication of his *Orbecche* to Duke Ercole II.: 'Ancora che Aristotele ci dia il modo di comporle.' In the same passage he dwells on the difficulties of producing tragedies in the absence of dramatic instinct, with an ingenuousness that moves our pity: 'Quando altri si dà a scrivere in quella maniera de' Poemi, che sono stati per tanti secoli tralasciati, che appena di loro vi resta una lieve ombra.' It never occurred to him that great poetry comes neither by observation nor by imitation of predecessors. The same dedication contains the monstrous critical assertion that the Latin poets, *i.e.* Seneca, improved upon Greek tragedy—*assai più grave la fecero.*

nor is there real dramatic movement in the play. Sofonisba passes through it automatically, giving her hand to Massinissa without remorse for Syphax, drinking the poison like an obedient girl, and dying with decorous but ineffective pathos. Massinissa plays the part of an idiot by sending her the poison which he thinks, apparently, she will not take. His surprise and grief, no less than his previous impulse of passionate love, are stationary. In a word, Trissino selected a well-known story from Roman history, and forgot that, in order to dramatise it, he must present the circumstances, not as a narrated fable, but as a sequence of actions determined by powerful and convincing motives. The two essentials of dramatic art, action evolved before the eyes of the spectators, and what Goethe called the *motiviren* of each incident, are conspicuous by their absence. The would-be tragic poet was too mindful of rules—his unities, his diction, his connexion of scenes that should occupy the stage without interruption, his employment of the Chorus in harmony with antique precedent—to conceive intensely or to express vividly. In form the 'Sofonisba' is a fair imitation of Attic tragedy, and the good taste of its author secures a certain pale and frigid reflection of classical simplicity. Blank verse is judiciously mingled with lyric metres, which are only introduced at moments of high-wrought feeling. The Chorus plays an unobtrusive part in the dialogue, and utters appropriate odes in the right places. Consequently, the 'Sofonisba' was hailed as a triumph of skill by the learned audience to whom alone the author appealed. Its merits of ingenuity and scholarship were such as they could appreciate. Its lack of vitality and imaginative vigour did not strike men who were accustomed to judge of poetry by rule and precedent.

Numerous scholars entered the lists in competition with Trissino. Among these the first place must be given to Giovanni Rucellai, whose 'Rosmunda' was composed almost contemporaneously with the 'Sofonisba,' and was acted before Leo X. in the Rucellai Gardens upon the occasion of a Papal visit to Florence. The chief merit of 'Rosmunda' is brevity. But it has the fatal fault of being a story told in scenes and dialogues, not an action moving and expanding through a series of connected incidents. Rosmunda's father, Comundo, has been slain in battle with the Lombards under Albuino. Like Antigone, the princess goes by night to bury his corpse; and when the tyrant threatens her, she replies in language borrowed from Sophocles. Albuino decapitates Comundo and makes a wine-cup of his skull, from which, after his marriage to Rosmunda, he forces her to drink. This determines the catastrophe. Almachilde appears upon the scene and slaughters Albuino in his tent. We are left to conjecture the murderer's future marriage with the heroine. That the old tale of the *Donna Lombarda* is eminently fitted for tragic handling, admits of no doubt. But it is equally certain that Rucellai failed to dramatise it. Almachilde is not introduced until the fourth act, and he assassinates Albuino without any previous communication with Rosmunda. The horrible banquet scene and the incident of the murder are described by messengers, while the chief actors rarely come to speech together face to face. The business of the play is narrated in dialogues with servants. This abuse of the Messenger and of subordinate characters, introduced for the sole purpose of describing and relating what ought to be enacted, is not peculiar to the 'Rosmunda.' It weakens all the tragedies of the sixteenth century, reducing their scenes to vacant discussions, where one person tells another what the author has conceived but what he cannot bring before his audience. Afraid of straining his imaginative faculties by the display of characters in action, the poet studiously keeps the chief personages apart, supplying the hero and the heroine with a shadow or an echo, whose sympathetic utterances serve to elicit the plot without making any demand upon the dramatist's power of presentation. Unfortunately for the tragic poets, the precedent of Seneca seemed to justify this false method of dramatic composition. And Seneca's tragedies, we know, were written, not for action, but for recitation.

These defects culminate in Speron Sperone's 'Canace.' The tale is horrible. Eolo, god of the winds, has two children, Canace and Macareo, born at one birth by his wife Deiopea. Under the malign influence of Venus this unlucky couple love; and the fruit of their union is a baby, killed as soon as born. The brother and the sister commit suicide separately, after their father's anger has thrown the light of publicity upon their passion. In order to justify the exhibition of incest in this repulsive form, there should at least have been such scenes of self-abandonment to impulse as Ford has found for Giovanni and Annabella; or the poet might have suggested the operation of agencies beyond human control by treading in the footsteps of Euripides; or, again, he might have risen from the sordid facts of sin into the region of ideal passion by the presentation of commanding personality in his principal actors. Nothing of this kind redeems the dreary disgust of his plot. The first act consists of a dialogue between Eolo and his Grand Vizier; the second, of a dialogue between Canace and her nurse; the third, of dialogues between Deiopea and her servants; the fourth, of a Messenger's narrative; the fifth, of Macareo's dialogues with his valet and his father's henchman. This analysis of the situations shows how little of dramatic genius Sperone brought to bear upon the hideous theme he had selected. The *Canace* is a succession of conversations referring to events which happen off the stage, and which involve no play of character in the chief personages. It is written throughout in lyrical measures with an affected diction, where rhetorical conceits produce the same effect as artificial flowers and ribbons stuck upon a skeleton.

Giraldi, the author of the 'Hecatommithi,' fares little better in his 'Orbecche.'[18] It is a play founded on one of the poet's own *Novelle*.[19]

[18] This tragedy was acted at Ferrara in Giraldi's house before Ercole II., Duke of Ferrara, and a brilliant company of noble persons, in 1541. The music was composed by M. Alfonso dalla Viuola, the scenery by M. Girolamo Carpi.

[19] Giraldi, a prolific writer of plays, dramatised three other of his novels in the *Arrenopia*, the *Altile* and the *Antivalomeni*. He also composed a *Didone* and a *Cleopatra*.

Orbecche, the innocent child of Sulmone and Selina, has led her father to detect his wife's adultery with his own eldest son. Selina, killed together with her paramour, exercises a baleful influence from the world of ghosts over this daughter who unwittingly betrayed her sin. Orbecche privately marries the low-born Oronte, and has two sons by her husband. Sulmone, when he discovers this *mésalliance*, assassinates Oronte and his children in a secret place, and makes a present of his head and hands to his miserable daughter. Upon this, Orbecche stabs her father and then ends her own life. To horrors of extravagant passion and bloodshed we are accustomed in the works of our inferior playwrights. Nor would it perhaps be just to quarrel with Giraldi for having chosen a theme so morbid, if any excuse could have been pleaded on the score of stirring scenes or vivid incidents. Unluckily, the life of dramatic action and passion is wanting to his ponderous tragedy. Instead of it, we are treated to disquisitions in the style of Seneca, and to descriptions that would be harrowing but for their invincible frigidity. No amount of crime and bloodshed will atone for the stationary mechanism of this lucubration.

Lacking dramatic instinct, these Italian scholars might have redeemed their essential feebleness by acute analysis of character. Their tragedies might at least have contained versified studies of motives, metrical essays on the leading passions. But we look in vain for such compensations. Stock tyrants, conventional lovers, rhetorical pedants, form their *dramatis personæ*. The inherent vices of the *Novella*, expanded to excessive length and invested with the forms of antique art, neutralise the labours of the lamp and file that have been spent upon them.[20] If it were requisite to select one play in which a glimmer of dramatic light is visible, we could point to the 'Marianna' of Lodovico Dolce. Here the passion of love in a tyrant, dotingly affectionate but egotistic, roused to suspicion by the slightest hint, and jealous beyond Othello's lunacy, has been depicted with considerable skill. Herod is a fantastical Creon, who murders the fancied paramour of Marianna, and subsequently assassinates Marianna herself, his two sons by her, and her mother, in successive paroxysms of insane vindictiveness, waking up

[20] It may here be remarked that though the scholarly playwrights of the Renaissance paid great attention to Aristotle's *Poetics*, and made a conscientious study of some Greek plays, especially the *Antigone*, the *Œdipus Tyrannus*, the *Phœnissæ*, and the *Iphigenia in Tauris*, they held the uncritical opinion, openly expressed by Giraldi, that Seneca had improved the form of the Greek drama. Their worst faults of construction, interminable monologues, dialogues between heroines and confidantes, dry choric dissertations, and rhetorical declamations are due to the preference for Seneca. The more we study Italian literature in the sixteenth century, the more we are compelled to acknowledge that humanism and all its consequences were a revival of Latin culture, only slightly tinctured with the simpler and purer influences of the Greeks. Latin poetry had the fatal attraction of facility. It was, moreover, itself composite and derivatory, like the literature of the new age. We may profitably illustrate the attitude of the Italian critics by Sidney's eulogy of *Gorboduc*: 'full of stately speeches and well-sounding phrases, climbing to the height of Seneca his style, and as full of notable morality which it doth most delightfully teach and so obtain the very end of Poesy.'

too late from his dream of self-injury into ignoble remorse. Though his conviction that Marianna meant to poison him, and his persuasion of her adultery with Soemo are so ill prepared by reasonable motives as to be ridiculous, the operation of these beliefs upon his wild-beast nature leads to more real movement than is common in Italian tragedies. The inevitable Chorus is employed for the utterance of sententious commonplaces; and the part of the Messenger is abused for the detailed and disgusting description of executions that inspire no horror.

The tragedies hitherto discussed, though conforming to the type of the classical drama, were composed on original subjects. Yet the best plays of this pedantic school are those which closely follow some Attic model. Rucellai's 'Oreste,' produced in imitation of the 'Iphigenia in Tauris,' far surpasses the 'Rosmunda,' not only as a poem of action, but also for the richness and the beauty of its style. That Rucellai should spoil the plot of Euripides by his alterations, protracting the famous recognition scene till we are forced to suppose that Orestes and Iphigenia kept up a game of mutual misunderstanding out of consideration for the poet, and spinning out the contest between Orestes and Pylades to absurdity, was to be expected. A scholar in his study can scarcely hope to improve upon the work of a poet whose very blemishes were the defects of a dramatic quality. He fancies that expansion of striking situations will fortify them, and that the addition of ingenious rhetoric will render a simple action more effective. The reverse of this is true; and the best line open to such a poet is to produce a faithful version of his original. This was done by Luigi Alamanni, whose translation of the 'Antigone' though open to objections on the score of scholarship, is a brilliant and beautiful piece of Italian versification. Lodovico Dolce in his 'Giocasta' attempted to remodel the 'Phœnissæ' with very indifferent success; while Giovanni Andrea dell' Anguillara defaced the 'Œdipus Tyrannus' in his 'Edippo,' by adding a final act and interweaving episodical matter borrowed from Seneca. A more repulsive tragi-comedy than this *pasticcio* of Sophocles and Seneca can scarcely be imagined. Yet Quadrio and Tiraboschi mention it with cautious compliment, and it received the honour of public recitation at Vicenza in 1565, when Palladio erected a theatre for the purpose in the noble Palazzo della Ragione. We cannot contemplate these *rifacimenti* of standard-making masterpieces without mixed feelings of scorn and pity. Sprouting fungus-like upon the venerable limbs of august poetry, they lived their season of mildewy fame, and may now be reckoned among the things which the world would only too willingly let die. The ineptitude of such performance reached a climax in Lodovico Martelli's 'Tullia,' where the Roman legend of Lucius Tarquinius is violently altered to suit the plot of Sophocles' 'Electra.' Romulus appears at the conclusion of the play as a *deus ex machina*, and the insufferable tedium of the speeches may be imagined from the fact that one of them runs to the length of 211 lines.

These tragedies were the literary manufacture of scholars, writing in no relation of reciprocity with the world of action or the audience of busy cities. Applying rules of Aristotle and Horace, travestying Sophocles and Euripides, copying the worse faults of Seneca, patching, boggling, rehandling, misconceiving, devising petty traps instead of plots, mistaking bloodshed and brutality for terror, attending to niceties of diction, composing commonplace sentences for superfluous Choruses, intent on everything but the main points of passion, character, and action, they produced the dreariest *caput mortuum* of unintelligent industry which it is the melancholy duty of historians to chronicle. Their personages are shadows evoked in the camera obscura of a pedant's brain from figures that have crossed the orbit of his solitary studies. No breath or juice of life animates these formal marionettes. Their movements of passion are the spasms of machinery. No charm of poetry, no bursts of lyrical music, no resolutions of tragic solemnity into irony or sarcasm, afford relief from clumsy horrors and stale disquisitions, parcelled out by weight and measure in the leaden acts. An intolerable wordiness oppresses the reader, who wades through speeches reckoned by the hundred lines, wondering how any audience could endure the torment of their recitation. Each play is a flat and arid wilderness, piled with barrows of extinct sentences in Seneca's manner and with pyramids of reflection heaped up from the commonplace books of a pedagogue.

The failure of Italian tragedy was inseparable from its artificial origin. It was the conscious product of cultivated persons, who aimed at nothing nobler than the imitation of the ancients and the observance of inapplicable rules. The curse of intellectual barrenness weighed upon the starvelings of this system from the moment of their birth, and nothing better came of them than our own 'Gorboduc.' That tragedy, built upon the false Italian method, is indeed a sign of what we English might have suffered, if Sidney and the Court had gained their way with the Elizabethan Drama.

The humanistic influences of the fifteenth century were scarcely less unpropitious to national comedy at its outset than they had been to tragedy. Although the 'Sacre Rappresentazioni' contained the germ of vernacular farce, though interludes in dialect amused the folk of more than one Italian province, among which special reference may be made to the Neapolitan *Farse*, yet the playwrights of the Renaissance preferred Plautus and Terence to the indigenous growth of their own age and country.[21] We may note this fact with regret, since it helped to deprive the Italians of a national theatre. Still we must not forget that it was inevitable. Humanism embraced the several districts of Italy in a common culture, effacing the distinctions of dialect, and bringing the separate elements of the nation to a consciousness of intellectual unity. Divided as Venetians, as Florentines, as Neapolitans,

[21] D' Ancona (*Origini del Teatro*, vol. ii. sec. xxxix.) may be consulted upon the attempts to secularise the *Sacre Rappresentazioni* which preceded the revival of classical comedy.

as Lombards, and as Romans, the members of the Italian community recognised their identity in the spiritual city they had reconquered from the past. What the English translation of the Bible effected for us, the recovery of Latin and the humanistic education of the middle classes achieved for the Italians. For a Florentine scholar to have developed the comic elements existing in the *Feste*, for a Neapolitan to have refined the matter of the *Farse*, would have seemed the same in either case as self-restriction to the limits of a single province. But the whole nation possessed the Latin poets as a common heritage; and on the ground of Plautus, Florentines and Neapolitans could understand each other. It was therefore natural that the cultivated orders, brought into communion by the ancients, should look to these for models of an art they were intent on making national. Together with this imperious instinct, which impelled the Italians to create their literature in sympathy with the commanding spirit of the age, we must reckon the fashionable indifference toward vernacular and obscure forms of poetry. The princes and their courtiers strove alike to remodel modern customs in accordance with the classics. Illiterate mechanics might amuse themselves with farces.[22] Men who had once tasted the refined and pungent salt of Attic wit, could stomach nothing simpler than scenes from antique comedy.

We therefore find that, at the close of the fifteenth century, it was common to recite the plays of Plautus and Terence in their original language. Paolo Comparini at Florence in 1488 wrote a prologue to the 'Menæchmi,' which his pupils represented, much to the disgust of the elder religious Companies, who felt that the ruin of their *Feste* was involved in this revival of antiquity.[23] Pomponius Lætus at Rome, about the same time, encouraged the members of his Academy to rehearse Terence and Plautus in the palaces of nobles and prelates.[24] The company of youthful actors formed by him were employed by the Cardinal Raffaello Riario in the magnificent spectacles he provided for the amusement of the Papal Court. During the pontificate of Sixtus IV. and Innocent VIII., the mausoleum of Hadrian, not then transformed into a fortress, or else the squares of Rome were temporarily arranged as theatres for these exhibitions.[25] It was on this stage that Tommaso

[22] Leo X., with a Medici's true sympathy for plebeian literature, added to his own coarse sense of fun, patronised the farces of the Sienese Company called Rozzi. Had his influence lasted, had there been anyone to continue the traditions of his Court at Rome, it is not impossible that a more natural comedy, as distinguished from the *Commedia erudita*, might have been produced by this fashionable patronage of popular dramatic art.

[23] See D' Ancona, *Or. del Teatro*, vol. ii. p. 201.

[24] Sabellico, quoted by Tiraboschi, says of him: 'primorum antistitum atriis suo theatro usus, in quibus Plauti, Terentii, recentiorum etiam quædam agerentur fabulæ, quas ipse honestos adolescentes et docuit et agentibus præfuit.'

[25] See the letter of Sulpizio da Veroli to Raffaello Riario quoted by Tiraboschi: 'eamdemque, postquam in Hadriani mole Divo Innocentio spectante est acta, rursus inter tuos penates, tamquam in media Circi cavea, toto consessu umbraculis tecto,

Inghirami, by his brilliant acting in the 'Hippolytus' of Seneca, gained the surname of Phædra which clung to him through life. In the pontificate of Alexander we hear of similar shows, as when, upon the occasion of Lucrezia Borgia's espousal to the Duke of Ferrara in 1502, the 'Menæchmi' was represented at the Vatican.[26]

The Court which accomplished most for the resuscitation of Latin Comedy was that of the Estensi at Ferrara. Ercole I. had spent a delicate youth in humanistic studies, collecting manuscripts and encouraging his courtiers to make Italian translations of ancient authors. He took special interest in theatrical compositions, and spared no pains in putting Latin comedies with all the pomp of modern art upon the stage. Thus the Ferrarese diaries mention a representation of the 'Menæchmi' in 1486, which cost above 1000 ducats. In 1487 the courtyard of the castle was fitted up as a theatre for the exhibition of Nicolò da Correggio's Pastoral of 'Cefalo.'[27] Again, upon the occasion of Annibale de' Bentivogli's betrothal to a princess of the Este family, the 'Amphitryon' was performed; and in 1491, when Anna Sforza gave her hand to Alfonso d' Este, the same comedy was repeated. In 1493 Lodovico Sforza, on a visit to Ferrara, witnessed a representation of the 'Menæchmi,' which so delighted him that he begged Ercole to send his company to Milan. The Duke went thither in person, attended by his son Alfonso and by gentle actors of his Court, among whom Lodovico Ariosto played a part. Later on, in 1499, we again hear of Latin comedies at Ferrara. Bembo in a letter of that year mentions the 'Trinummus,' 'Pœnulus' and 'Eunuchus.'[28]

It is probable that Latin comedies were recited at Ferrara, as at Rome, in the original. At the same time we know that both Plautus and Terence were being translated into Italian for the amusement of an audience as yet but partially acquainted with ancient languages. Tiraboschi mentions the 'Anfitrione' of Pandolfo Collenuccio, the 'Cassina' and Mostellaria' versified in *terza rima* by Girolamo Berardo, and the 'Menæchmi' of Duke Ercole, among the earliest of these versions. Guarini and Ariosto followed on their path with translations from the Latin made for special occasions. It was thus that Italian comedy began to disengage itself from Latin. After the presentation of the original plays, came translation; and after translation, imitation. The

admisso populo, et pluribus tui ordinis spectatoribus honorifice excepisti. Tu etiam primus picturatæ scenæ faciem, quum Pomponiam comœdiam agerent, nostro sæculo ostendisti.'

[26] See *Lucrezia Borgia*, by Gregorovius (Stuttgart, 1874), vol. i. p. 201.

[27] Nicolò was a descendant of the princely house of Correggio. He married Cassandra, daughter of Bartolommeo Colleoni. His *Cefalo* was a mixed composition resembling the *Sacre Rappresentazioni* in structure. In the Prologue he says:

> Requiret autem nullus hic Comœdiæ
> Leges ut observentur, aut Tragœdiæ;
> Agenda nempe est historia, non fabula.

See D' Ancona, *op. cit.* ii. pp. 143-146, 155.

[28] *Ep. Fam.* i. 18, quoted by Tiraboschi.

further transition from imitation to freedom was never perfectly effected. The comic drama, determined in its form by the circumstances of its origin, remained emphatically a *commedia erudita*. Adapted to the conditions of modern life, it never lost dependence upon Latin models; and its most ingenious representations of manners were defaced by reminiscences which condemn them to a place among artistic hybrids. Ariosto, who did so much to stamp Italian comedy with the mark of his own genius, was educated, as we have already seen, in the traditions of Duke Ercole's Latin theatre; and Ariosto gave the law to his most genial successor, Cecchi. The Pegasus of the Italian drama, if I may venture on a burlesque metaphor, was a mule begotten by the sturdy ass of Latin on the fleet mare of the Italian spirit; and it had the sterility of the mule.

The year 1502, when Lucrezia Borgia came as Alfonso d' Este's bride to Ferrara, marks the climax of these Latin spectacles.[29] Ercole had arranged a theatre in the Palace of the Podestà (now called the Palazzo della Ragione), which was connected with the castle by a private gallery. His troupe, recruited from Ferrara, Rome, Siena, and Mantua, numbered one hundred and ten actors of both sexes. Accomplished singers, dancers, and scene-painters were summoned to add richness to the spectacle. We hear of musical interludes performed by six violins; while every comedy was diversified by morris-dances of Saracens, satyrs, gladiators, wild men, hunters, and allegorical personages.[30] The entertainment lasted over five nights, a comedy of Plautus forming the principal piece on each occasion. On the first evening the 'Epidicus' was given; on the second, the 'Bacchides;' on the third, the 'Miles Gloriosus;' on the fourth, the 'Asinaria;' on the fifth, the 'Casina.' From the reports of Cagnolo, Zambotto, and Isabella Gonzaga, we are led to believe that the unlettered audience judged the recitations of the Plautine comedies somewhat tedious. They were in the same position as unmusical people of the present day, condemned to listen to Bach's Passion Music, and afraid of expressing their dissatisfaction. Yet these more frivolous spectators found ample gratification in the ingenious ballets, accompanied with music, which relieved each act. The occasion was memorable. In those five evenings the Court of Ferrara presented to the fashionable world of Italy a carefully studied picture of Latin comedy framed in a setting of luxuriant modern arabesques. The simplicity of Plautus, executed with the fidelity born of reverence for antique art, was thrown into relief by extravagances borrowed from mediæval chivalry, tinctured with Oriental associations, enhanced by music and coloured with the glowing hues of Ferrarese imagination. The city of Boiardo, of Dossi, of Bello, of Ariosto, strained her resources to devise fantastic foils for the antique. It was as though

[29] Gregorovius in his book on *Lucrezia Borgia* (pp. 228-239) has condensed the authorities. See, too, Dennistoun, *Dukes of Urbino*, vol. i. pp. 441-448.

[30] The minute descriptions furnished by Sanudo of these festivals read like the prose letterpress accompanying the Masques of our Ben Jonson.

Cellini had been called to mount an onyx of Augustus in labyrinths of gold-work and enamel for the stomacher of a Grand-Duchess.

We may without exaggeration affirm that the practice of the Ferrarese stage, culminating in the marriage shows of 1502, determined the future of Italian comedy. The fashion of the Court of Ercole was followed by all patrons of dramatic art. When a play was written, the author planned it in connexion with subordinate exhibitions of dancing and music.[31] He wrote a poem in five acts upon the model of Plautus or Terence, understanding that his scenes of classical simplicity would be embedded in the grotesques of *cinque cento* allegory. The whole performance lasted some six hours; but the comedy itself was but a portion of the entertainment. For the majority of the audience the dances and the pageants formed the chief attraction.[32] It is therefore no marvel if the drama, considered as a branch of high poetic art, was suffocated by the growth of its mere accessories. Nor was this inconsistent with the ruling tendencies of the Renaissance. We have no reason to suppose that even Ariosto or Machiavelli grudged the participation of painters like Peruzzi, musicians like Dalla Viuola, architects like San Gallo, and dancers of ephemeral distinction, in the triumph of their plays.

The habit of regarding scenic exhibitions as the adjunct to extravagant Court luxury, prevented the development of a theatre in which the genius of poets might have shone with undimmed intellectual lustre. The want of permanent buildings, devoted to acting, in any great Italian town, may again be reckoned among the causes which checked the expansion of the drama. When a play had to be acted, a stage was erected at a great expense for the occasion.[33] It is true that Alfonso I. built a theatre after Ariosto's designs at Ferrara in 1528; but it was burnt down in 1532. According to Gregorovius, Leo X. fitted one up at Rome upon the Capitol in 1513,[34] capable of holding the two thousand spectators who witnessed a performance of the 'Suppositi.' This does not, however, seem to have been used continuously; nor was it until the second half of the sixteenth century that theatres

[31] Il Lasca in his prologue to the *Strega* (*ed. cit.* p. 171) says: 'Questa non è fatta da principi, nè da signori, nè in palazzi ducali e signorili; eperò non avrà quella pompa d' apparato, di prospettiva, e d' intermedj che ad alcune altre nei tempi nostris s' è veduto.'

[32] A fine example of the Italian Masque is furnished by *El Sacrificio*, played with great pomp by the Intronati of Siena in 1531 and printed in 1537. *El Sacrificio de gli Intronati celebrato ne i giuochi del Carnovale in Siena l' Anno MDXXXI*. Full particulars regarding the music, *mise en scène*, and ballets on such ceremonial occasions, will be found in two curious pamphlets, *Descrizione dell' Apparato fatto nel Tempio di S. Giov. di Fiorenza*, &c. (Giunti, 1568), and *Descrizione dell' Entrata della Serenissima Reina Giovanna d' Austria*, &c. (Giunti, 1566). They refer to a later period, but they abound in the most curious details.

[33] See the details brought together by Campori, *Notizie per la vita di Lodovico Ariosto*, p. 74, Castiglione's letter on the *Calandra* at Urbino, the private representation of the *Rosmunda* in the Rucellai gardens, of the *Orbecche* in Giraldi's house, of the *Sofonisba* at Vicenza of Gelli's *Errore* by the Fantastichi, &c.

[34] *Stadt Rom*, viii. 350.

began to form a part of the palatial residences of princes. One precious relic of those more permanent stages remains to show the style they then assumed. This is the Teatro Farnese at Parma, erected in 1618 by Ranuzio I. after the design of Galeotti Aleotti of Ferrara. It could accommodate seven thousand spectators; and, though now in ruins, it is still a stately and harmonious monument of architectural magnificence.[35] What, however, was always wanting in Italy was a theatre open to all classes and at all seasons of the year, where the people might have been the patrons of their playwrights.[36]

The transition from Latin to Italian comedy was effected almost simultaneously by three poets, Bernardo Dovizio, Lodovico Ariosto, and Niccolò Machiavelli. Dovizio was born at Bibbiena in 1470. He attached himself to the Cardinal Giovanni de' Medici, and received the scarlet from his master in 1513. We need not concern ourselves with his ecclesiastical career. It is enough to say that the 'Calandra,' which raised him to a foremost place among the literary men of Italy, was composed before his elevation to the dignity of Cardinal, and was first performed at Urbino some time between the dates 1504 and 1513, possibly in 1508. The reader will already have observed that the most popular Latin play, both at Ferrara and Rome, was the 'Menæchmi' of Plautus. In Dovizio's 'Calandra' the influence of this comedy is so noticeable that we may best describe it as an accommodation of the Latin form to Italian circumstance. The intrigue depends upon the close resemblance of a brother and sister, Lidio and Santilla, whose appearance by turns in male and female costume gives rise to a variety of farcical incidents. The name is derived from Calandro, a simpleton of Calandrino's type; and the interest of the plot is that of a *Novella*. The characters are very slightly sketched; but the movement is continuous, and the dialogue is always lively. The 'Calandra' achieved immediate success by reproducing both the humour of Boccaccio and the invention of Plautus in the wittiest vernacular.[37] A famous letter

[35] See the article 'Fornovo' in my *Sketches and Studies in Italy*.

[36] At this point, in illustration of what has been already stated, I take the opportunity of transcribing a passage which fairly represents the conditions of play-going in the *cinque cento*. Doni, in the *Marmi*, gives this description of two comedies performed in the Sala del Papa of the Palazzo Vecchio at Florence.* 'By my faith, in Florence never was there anything so fine: two stages, one at each end of the Hall: two wonderful scenes, the one by Francesco Salviati, the other by Bronzino: two most amusing comedies, and of the newest coinage; the *Mandragola* and the *Assiuolo*: when the first act of the one was over, there followed the first act of the other, and so forth, each play taking up the other, without interludes, in such wise that the one comedy served as interlude for the other. The music began at the opening, and ended with the close.'

[37] One of the chief merits of the *Calandra* in the eyes of contemporaries was the successful adaptation of Boccaccio's style to the stage. Though Italians alone have the right to pronounce judgment on such matters, I confess to preferring the limpid ease of Ariosto and the plebeian freshness of Gelli. The former has the merit of facile lucidity, the latter of native raciness. Bibbiena's somewhat pompous phraseology sits ill upon his farcical obscenities.

* Barbèra's edition, 1863, vol. i. p. 67.

of Baldassare Castiglione, describing its representation at Urbino, enlarges upon the splendour of the scenery and dresses, the masques of Jason, Venus, Love, Neptune and Juno, accompanied by morris-dances and concerts of stringed instruments, which were introduced as interludes.[38] From Urbino the comedy passed through all the Courts of Italy, finding the highest favour at Rome, where Leo more than once decreed its representation. One of these occasions was memorable. Wishing to entertain the Marchioness Isabella of Mantua (1514), he put the 'Calandra' with great pomp upon his private stage in the Vatican. Baldassare Peruzzi designed and painted the decorations, giving a new impulse to this species of art by the beauty of his inventions.[39]

Leo had an insatiable appetite for scenic shows. Comedies of the new Latinising style were his favourite recreation. But he also invited the Sienese Company of the Rozzi, who only played farces, every year to Rome; nor was he averse to even less artistic buffoonery, as may be gathered from many of the stories told about him.[40] In 1513 Leo opened a theatre upon the Capitol, and here in 1519, surrounded by two thousand spectators, he witnessed an exhibition of Ariosto's 'Suppositi.' We have a description of the scene from the pen of an eyewitness, who relates how the Pope sat at the entrance to the gallery leading into the theatre, and admitted with his benediction those whom he thought worthy of partaking in the night's amusements.[41] When the house was full, he took his throne in the orchestra, and sat, with eye-glass in hand, to watch the play. Raphael had painted the scenery, which is said to have been, and doubtless was, extremely beautiful. Leo's behaviour scandalised the foreign ambassadors, who thought it indecorous that a Pope should not only listen to the equivocal jests of the Prologue but also laugh immoderately at them.[42] As usual, the inter-acts consisted of vocal and instrumental concerts, with ballets on classical and allegorical subjects.

Enough has now been said concerning the mode of presenting comedies in vogue throughout Italy. The mention of Leo's entertainment in 1519 introduces the subject of Ariosto's plays. The 'Suppositi,' originally written in prose and afterwards versified by its author, first appeared in 1509 at Ferrara. In the preceding year Ariosto exhibited the 'Cassaria,' which, like the 'Suppositi,' was planned in prose and subsequently versified in *sdrucciolo* iambics.[43]

[38] See the translation in Dennistoun, vol. ii. p. 141.

[39] See Vasari, viii. 227.

[40] See D' Ancona, *op. cit.* vol. ii. p. 250, for the special nature of the *Farsa*. See also *ib.* p. 211, the description by Paolucci of Leo's buffooneries in the Vatican.

[41] See Campori, *Notizie Inedite di Raffaello di Urbino*, Modena, 1863, quoted by D' Ancona, *op. cit.* p. 212. The entertainment cost Leo 1,000 ducats.

[42] No doubt Paolucci refers to the obscene play upon the word *Suppositi*, and to the ironical epithet of *Santa* applied to *Roma* in a passage which does no honour to Ariosto.

[43] For the dates of Ariosto's dramatic composition, see above p. 157. The edition I shall refer to is that of Giovanni Tortoli (Firenze, Barbèra, 1856), which gives both the prose and verse redactions of the *Cassaria* and *Suppositi*. It may here be

In Ariosto's comedies the form of Roman art becomes a lay-figure, dressed according to various modes of the Italian Renaissance. The wire-work so to speak, of Plautus or of Terence can be everywhere detected; but this skeleton has been incarnated with modern flesh and blood, habited in Ferrarese costume, and taught the paces of contemporary fashion. Blent with the traditions of Plautine comedy, we find in each of the four plays an Italian *Novella.* The motive is invariably trivial. In the 'Cassaria' two young men are in love with two girls kept by a slave-merchant. The intrigue turns upon the arts of their valets, who cheat the pander and procure the girls for nothing for their masters. In the 'Suppositi' a young man of good family has assumed the part of servant, in order to seduce the daughter of his master. The devices by which he contrives to secure her hand in marriage, furnish the action of the play. The 'Lena' has even a simpler plan. A young man needs a few quiet hours for corrupting his neighbour's daughter. Lena, the chief actress, will not serve as a go-between without a sum of ready money paid down by the hero. The movement of the piece depends on the expedients whereby this money is raised, and the farcical obstacles which interrupt the lovers at the point of their felicity. In the 'Negromante' a young man has been secretly married to one woman, and openly to another. Cinthio loves his real wife, Lavinia, and feigns impotence in order to explain his want of affection for Emilia, who is the recognised mistress of his home. An astrologer, Iacchelino, holds the threads of the intrigue in his hands. Possessed of Cinthio's secret, paid by the parents of Emilia to restore Cinthio's virility, paid again by a lover of Emilia to advance his own suit, and seeking in the midst of these rival interests to make money out of the follies and ambitions of his clients, Iacchelino has the whole domestic company at his discretion. The comic point lies in the various passions which betray each dupe to the astrologer—Cinthio's wish to escape from Emilia, Camillo's eagerness to win her, the old folk's anxiety to cure Cinthio. Temolo, a servant, who is hoodwinked by no personal desire, sees that Iacchelino is an impostor; and the inordinate avarice of the astrologer undoes him. Thus the 'Negromante' presents a really fine comic web of humours at cross purposes and appetites that overreach themselves.

There is considerable similarity in Ariosto's plots. In all of them, except the 'Negromante,' we have a sub-plot which brings a tricksy valet into play. A sum of money is imperatively needed to effect the main scheme of the hero; and this has to be provided by the servant's ingenuity. Such direct satire as the poet thought fit to introduce, is common to them all. It concerns the costs, delays and frauds of legal procedure, favouritism at Court, the Ferrarese game-laws, and the

incidentally remarked that there are few thoroughly good editions of Italian plays. Descriptions of the *dramatis personæ,* stage directions, and illustrative notes are almost uniformly wanting. The reader is left to puzzle out an intricate action without help. All the slang, the local customs, and the passing allusions which give life to comedy and present so many difficulties to the student, are for the most part unexplained.

tyranny of custom-house officials. But satire of an indirect, indulgent species—the Horatian satire of Ariosto's own epistles—adds a pleasant pungency to his pictures of contemporary manners no less than to his occasional discourses. The prologue to the 'Cassaria,' on its reappearance as a versified play, might be quoted for the perfection of genial sarcasm, playing about the foibles of society without inflicting a serious wound. All the prologues, however, are not innocent. Those prefixed to the 'Lena' and the 'Suppositi' contain allusions so indecent, and veil obscenities under metaphors so flimsy, as to justify a belief in Ariosto's vulgarity of soul. Here the satirist borders too much on the sympathiser with a vice he professes to condemn.

It remains to speak of the 'Scolastica,' a comedy left incomplete at Ariosto's death, and finished by his brother Gabrielle, but bearing the unmistakable stamp of his ripest genius impressed upon the style no less than on the structure of the plot.[44] The scene is laid at Ferrara, where we find ourselves among the scholars of its famous university, and are made acquainted in the liveliest manner with their habits. The heroes are two young students, Claudio and Eurialo, firm friends, who have passed some years at Pavia reading with Messer Lazzaro, a doctor of laws. The disturbance of the country having driven both professors and pupils from Pavia,[45] a variety of accidents brings all the actors of the comedy to Ferrara, where Eurialo is living with his father, Bartolo. Of course the two lads are in love—Claudio with the daughter of his former tutor, and Eurialo with a fatherless girl in the service of a noble lady at Pavia. The intrigue is rather farcical than comic. It turns upon the difficulties encountered by Claudio and Eurialo in concealing their sweethearts from their respective fathers, the absurd mistakes they make in the hurry of the moment, and the misunderstandings which ensue between themselves and the old people. Ariosto has so cleverly complicated the threads of his plot and has developed them with such lucidity of method, that any analysis would fall short of the original in brevity and clearness. The *dênouement* is effected by the device of a recognition at the last moment. Eurialo's *innamorata* is found to be the lost ward of his father, Bartolo; and Claudio is happily married to his love, Flaminia. The merit of the play lies, however, less in the argument than the characters, which are ably conceived and sustained with more than even Ariosto's usual skill. The timid and perplexed Eurialo, trembling before his terrible father, seeking advice from every counsellor, despairing, resigning himself to fate, is admirably contrasted with the more passionate and impulsive Claudio, who takes rash steps with inconsiderate boldness, relies on his own address to extricate himself, and vibrates between the ecstasies of

[44] Gabrielle added the last two scenes of the fifth act. See his prologue. But whether he introduced any modifications into the body of the play, or filled up any gaps, does not appear.

[45] Poichè a Pavia levato era il salario
Alli dottor, nè più si facea studio
Per le guerre che più ogni dì augumentano.

love and the suspicions of an angry jealousy.[46] Bartolo, burdened in his conscience by an ancient act of broken faith, and punished in the disobedience of his son, forms an excellent pendant to the honest but pedantic Messer Lazzaro, who cannot bear to see his daughter suffer from an unrequited passion.[47] Each of the servants, too, has a well-marked physiognomy—the witty Accursio, picking up what learning he can from his master's books, and turning all he says to epigrams; the easy-going, Bacchanalian duenna; blunt Pistone; garrulous Stanna. But the most original of all the *dramatis personæ* is Bonifazio, that excellent keeper of lodgings for Ferrarese students, who identifies himself with their interests, sympathises in their love-affairs, takes side with them against their fathers, and puts his conscience in his pocket when required to pull them out of scrapes.[48] Each of these characters has been copied from the life. The taint of Latin comedy has been purged out of them.[49] They move, speak, act like living beings, true to themselves in every circumstance, and justifying the minutest details of the argument by the operation of their several qualities of head and heart. Viewed as a work of pure dramatic art, the 'Scolastica' is not only the most genial and sympathetic of Ariosto's comedies, but also the least fettered by his Latinising prepossessions, and the strongest in psychological analysis. Like the 'Lena,' it has the rare merit of making us at home in the Ferrara which he knew so well; but it does not, like that play, disgust us by the spectacle of abject profligacy.[50] There is a sunny, jovial freshness in this latest product of Ariosto's genius, which invigorates while it amuses and instructs.

The 'Scolastica' is not without an element of satire. I have said that Bartolo had a sin upon his conscience. In early manhood he

[46] Their opposite humours are admirably developed in the dialogues of act ii. sc. 5, act iii. sc. 5.

[47] Compare Bartolo's soliloquy in act iv. sc. 6, with Lazzaro's confidences to Bonifazio, whom he mistakes for Bartolo, in act v. sc. 3.

[48] His action in the comedy is admirably illustrated by the self-revelation of the following soliloquy (act iv. sc. 1):

> Io vuò a ogni modo aiutar questo giovane,
> E dir dieci bugie, perchè ad incorrere
> Non abbia con suo padre in rissa e in scandalo:
> E così ancor quest' altro mio, che all' ultima
> Disperazione è condotto da un credere
> Falso e da gelosia che a torto il stimola.
> Nè mi vergognerò d' ordire, o tessere
> Fallacie e giunti, *e far ciò ch' eran soliti*
> *Gli antichi servi già nelle commedie*:
> Chè veramente l' aiutare un povero
> Innamorato, non mi pare uffizio
> Servil, ma di gentil qualsivoglia animo.

[49] The process is well indicated in the lines I have italicised in Bonifazio's soliloquy. He is no longer a copy of the Latin slaves, but a free agent who emulates their qualities.

[50] With all admiration for the *Lena*, how can we appreciate the cynicism of the situation revealed in the first scene—the crudely exposed appetites of Flavio, the infamous conduct of Fazio, who places his daughter under the tutelage of his old mistress?

promised to adopt a friend's daughter, and to marry her in due course to his own Eurialo. But he neglected this duty, lost sight of the girl, and appropriated her heritage. He has reason to think that she may still be found in Naples; and the parish priest, to whom he confided his secret in confession, will not absolve him, unless he take the journey and do all he can to rectify the error of his past. Bartolo is disinclined to this long pilgrimage, with the probable loss of a fortune at the end of it. In his difficulty he has recourse to a Frate Predicatore, who professes to hold ample powers for dispensing with troublesome vows and pious obligations:[51]

> Voi potete veder la bolla, e leggere
> Le facultadi mie, che sono amplissime;
> E come, senza che pigliate, Bartolo
> Questo pellegrinaggio, io posso assolvere
> E commutar i voti; e maravigliomi
> Che essendo, com' io son, vostro amicissimo,
> Non m' abbiate richiesto; perchè, dandomi
> Quel solamente che potrestre spendere
> Voi col famiglio nel viaggio, assolvere
> Vi posso, e farvi schifar un grandissimo
> Disconcio, all' età vostra incomportabile:
> Oltra diversi infiniti pericoli,
> Che ponno a chi va per cammino occorrere.

The irony of this speech depends upon its plain and business-like statement of a simoniacal bargain, which will prove of mutual benefit to the parties concerned. Bartolo confides his case of conscience to the Friar, previously telling him that he has confessed it to the parson:

> Ma non mi sa decidere
> Questo caso, chè, come voi, teologo
> Non è; sa un poco di ragion canonica.

At the close of the communication, which is admirable for its lucid exposition of a domestic romance adapted to the circumstances of the sixteenth century, the Friar asks his penitent once more whether he would not willingly escape this pilgrimage. Who could doubt it? answers Bartolo. Well then:

> Ben si potrà commutare in qualche opera
> Pia. Non si trova al mondo sì forte obbligo,
> Che non si possa scior con l' elemosine.

Here again the sarcasm consists in the hypocritical adaptation of the old axiom that everything in this world can be got for money. On both sides the transaction is commercial. Bartolo, like a good man of business, wishes to examine the Frate's title-deeds before he engages

[51] Act iii. sc. 6.

in the purchase of his spiritual privileges. In other words he must be permitted to examine the Bull of Indulgence:[52]

> Porterollavi,
> E ve la lascerò vedere e leggere
> Siate pur certo che la bolla è amplissima,
> E che di tutti i casi, componendovi
> Meco, vi posso interamente assolvere,
> Non meno che potria 'l Papa medesimo.
> *Bartolo.* Vi credo; nondimeno, per iscarico
> Della mia coscienza, la desidero
> Veder, e farla anco vedere e leggere
> Al mio parrocchiano.
> *Frate.* Ora sia *in nomine*
> *Domini*, porterolla, e mostrerolla
> A chi vi pare.

We may further notice how the parish priest is here meant to play the part of solicitor in the bargain. He does not deal in these spiritual commodities; but he can give advice upon the point of validity. The episode of Bartolo and the Dominican reminds us that we are on the eve of the Reformation. While Rome and Ferrara laughed at the hypocrisies, credulities, and religious frauds implied in such transactions, Northern Europe broke into flame, and Luther opened the great schism.[53]

The artistic merit of Ariosto's comedies consists in the perfection of their structure. However involved the intrigues may be, we experience no difficulty in following them; so masterly is their development.[54] It may be objected that he too frequently resorts to the device of *anagnorisis*, in order to solve a problem which cannot find its issue in the action. This mechanical solution is so obviously employed to make things easy for the author that no interest attaches to the climax of his fables. Yet the characters are drawn with that ripe insight into

[52] Act. iv. sc. 4. In the last line but one, ought we not to read *mostreratela* or else *mostrerollavi*?

[53] Room must be found for a few of the sarcasms, uttered chiefly by Accursio, which enliven the *Scolastica*. Here are the humanists:

> questi umanisti, che cercano
> Medaglie, e di rovesci si dilettano.

Here is Rome:

> Roma, dove intendono
> Che 'l sangue degli Apostoli e de' Martiri
> È molto dolce, e a lor spese è un bel vivere.

Here is Ferrara:

> Ferrara, ove pur vedesi
> Che fino alli barbieri paion nobili.

Here are the Signori of Naples:

> da Napoli.
> Ho ben inteso che ve n' è piu copia
> Che a Ferrara di Conti; e credo ch' abbiano,
> Come questi contado, quei dominio.

[54] Cecchi noticed the lucid order, easy exposition and smooth conduct of Ariosto's plots, ranking him for these qualities above the Latin poets. See the passage from *Le Pellegrine* quoted below.

human nature which distinguished Ariosto. Machiavelli observed that, being a native of Ferrara, cautious in the handling of Tuscan idioms, and unwilling to use the dialect of his own city, Ariosto missed the salt of comedy.[55] There is truth in this criticism. Matched with the best Florentine dialogues, his language wants the raciness of the vernacular. The *sdrucciolo* verse, which he preferred, fatigues the ear and adds to the impression of formality. He frequently interrupts the action with tirades, talking, as it were, in his own person to the audience, instead of making his characters speak.[56] Yet foreigners, who study his comedies side by side with Plautus, at almost the same distance of unfamiliarity, will recognise the brilliance of his transcripts from contemporary life. These studies of Italian manners are eminent for good taste, passing at no point into extravagance, and only marred by a certain banality of moral instinct. The 'Lena' has the highest value as a picture of Ferrarese society. We have good reason to believe that it was founded on an actual incident. It deserves to rank with Machiavelli's 'Mandragola' and Aretino's 'Cortigiana' for the light it throws on sixteenth-century customs. And the light is far more natural, less lurid, less partial, than that which either Machiavelli or Aretino shed upon the vices of their century.

Of Machiavelli we have two genuine comedies in prose, the 'Mandragola' and the 'Clizia,' and two of doubtful authenticity, called respectively 'Commedia in Prosa' and 'Commedia in Versi,' besides a translation of the 'Andria.'[57] Judging by internal evidence alone, a cautious critic would reject the 'Commedia in Versi' from the canon of Machiavelli's works; and if the existence of a copy in his autograph has to be taken as conclusive evidence of its genuineness, we can only accept it as a crude and juvenile production. It is written in various measures, a graceless octave stanza rhyming only in the last couplet being used instead of blank verse, while many of the monologues are lyrical. The language is crabbed, uncertain, archaistic—in no point displaying the incisive brevity of Machiavelli's style. The scene is laid in ancient Rome, and the intrigue turns upon a confusion between two names, Catillo and Cammillo. The conventional parasite of antiquity and the inevitable slaves play prominent parts; while the plot is solved by a preposterous exchange of wives between the two chief characters. Thus the fabric of the comedy throughout is unnatural and false to the conditions of real life. Were it not for some piquant studies of Italian manners, scattered here and there in the descriptive passages, this 'Commedia in Versi' would scarcely deserve passing notice.[58]

[55] In an essay on the Italian language, included among Machiavelli's works, but ascribed to him on no very certain ground.

[56] Notice the long monologue of the *Cassaria* in which Lucramo describes the fashionable follies of Ferrara. Ariosto gradually outgrew this habit of tirade. The *Scolastica* is freer than any of his pieces from the fault.

[57] *Le Commedie di N. Machiavelli, con prefazione di F. Perfetti* Firenze, Barbèra, 1863.

[58] Take this picture of Virginia (act i. sc. 2):

Ap. Dilettasi ella dar prova a filare,
O tessere, o cucire, com' è usanza?

The 'Commedia in Prosa,' for which we might find a title in the name of the chief personage, Fra Alberigo, displays the spirit and the style of the 'Mandragola.' Critics who do not accept it for Machiavelli's own, must assume it to have been the work of a clever and obsequious imitator. It is a short piece in three acts written to expose the corruption of a Florentine household. Caterina, the heroine, is a young wife married to an old husband, Amerigo. Their maid-servant, Margherita, holds the threads of the intrigue in her hands. She has been solicited on the one side by Amerigo to help him in his amours with a neighbour's wife, and on the other by the friar, Alberigo, to win Caterina to his suit. The devices whereby Margherita brings her mistress and the monk together cheats Amerigo of his expected enjoyment, and so contrives that the despicable but injured husband should establish Fra Alberigo in the position of a favoured house-friend, constitute the argument. Short as the play is, it combines the chief points of the 'Clizia' and the 'Mandragola' in a single action, and may be regarded as the first sketch of two situations afterwards developed with more fulness by the author.[59] The language is coarse, and the picture of manners, executed with remorseless realism, would be revolting but for its strong workmanship.[60] The playwright expended his force on the servant-maid and the friar, those two instruments of domestic immorality. Fra Alberigo is a vulgar libertine, provided with pious phrases to cloak his vicious purpose, but casting off the mask when he has gained his object, well knowing from past experience that the appetites of the woman he seduces will secure his footing in her husband's home.[61] Margherita

Mis. No, chè far lassa tal cosa a sua madre.
Ap. Di che piglia piacer?
Mis. Delle finestre,
Dove la sta dal mattino alla sera,
E vaga è di novelle, suoni e canti,
E studia in lisci, e dorme, e cuce in guanti.

Or the picture of the lovers in church described by the servant, Doria (act iii. sc. 2), or Virginia's portrait of her jealous husband (act iii. sc. 5).

59 The scene between Caterina and Amerigo, when the latter is caught in flagrant adultery (act iii. 5), anticipates the catastrophe of the *Clizia.* The final scene between Caterina, Amerigo, and Fra Alberigo bears a close resemblance to the climax of the *Mandragola.* On the hypothesis that this comedy is not Machiavelli's but an imitator's, the playwright must have had both the *Clizia* and the *Mandragola* in his mind, and have designed a pithy combination of their most striking elements.

60 See especially the scenes between Caterina and Margherita (act i. 3; act ii. 1) where the advantages of taking a lover and of choosing a friar for this purpose are discussed. They abound in *gros mots*, as thus:

Cat. Odi, in quanto a cotesta parte tu di' la verità; ma quello odore, ch' egli hanno poi di salvaggiume, non ch' altro mi stomaca a pensarlo.

Marg. Eh! eh! poveretta voi! i frati, eh? Non si trova generazione più abile ai servigi delle donne. Voi dovete forse avere a pigliarvi piacere col naso? &c.

61 Compare his speech to Caterina (act ii. 5) with his dialogue with Margherita (act iii. 4) and his final discourse on charity and repentance (act iii. 6). The irony of these words, 'Certamente, Amerigo, che voi potete vantarvi d' aver la più saggia e casta giovane non vo' dir di Fiorenza ma di tutto 'l mondo,' pronounced before Caterina a couple of hours after her seduction, fixes the measure of Machiavelli's cynicism.

revels in the corruption she has aided. She delights in sin for its own sake, extracts handfuls of coppers from the friar, and counts on profiting by the secret of her mistress. Her speech and action display the animal appetites and gross phraseology of the proletariat, degraded by city vices and hardened to the spectacle of clerical hypocrisy.[62] One of her exclamations: 'I frati, ah! son più viziati che 'l fistolo!' taken in conjunction with her argument to Caterina: 'I frati, eh? Non si trova generazione più abile ai servigi delle donne!' points the satire intended by the playwright. Yet neither Caterina nor Amerigo yield a point of baseness to these servile agents. Plebeian coarseness is stamped alike upon their language and their desires. They have no delicacy of feeling, no redeeming passion, no self-respect. They speak of things unmentionable with a crudity that makes one shudder, and abuse each other in sarcasms borrowed from the rhetoric of the streets.[63] To a refined taste the calculations of Caterina are no less obnoxious and are far less funny than the rogueries of the friar.

This comedy of Fra Alberigo is a literal transcript from a cynical *Novella*, dramatised and put upon the stage to amuse an audience familiar with such arguments by their persual of Sacchetti and Boccaccio. Its freedom from Latinising conventionality renders it a striking example of the influence exercised by the *Novellieri* over the theatre. The same may be said about both the 'Clizia' and the 'Mandragola,' though the former owes a portion of its structure to the *Casina* of Plautus.[64] The 'Clizia' is a finished picture of Florentine home-life. Nicomaco and Sofronia are an elderly couple, who have educated a beautiful girl, Clizia, from childhood in their house. At the moment when the play opens, both Nicomaco and his son, Cleandro, are in love with Clizia. Nicomaco has determined to marry her to one of his servants, Pirro, having previously ascertained that the dissolute groom will not object to sharing his wife with his master. Sofronia's family pride opposes the marriage of her son and heir with Clizia; but she is aware of her husband's schemes, and seeks to frustrate them by giving the girl to an honest bailiff, Eustachio. In the contest that ensues, Nicomaco gains the victory. It is settled that Clizia is to be wedded to Pirro, and on the night of the marriage Nicomaco makes his way into the bridal chamber. But here Sofronia proves more than a match for her lord and master. Helped by Cleandro, she substitutes for Clizia a young man-servant disguised as a woman, who gives Nicomaco a warm reception, beats him within an inch of his life, and ex-

[62] The quite unquotable but characteristic monologue which opens the third act is an epitome of Margherita's character.

[63] Act iii. 5.

[64] From an allusion in act ii. sc. 3, it is clear that the *Clizia* was composed after the *Mandragola*. If we assign the latter comedy to a date later than 1512, the year of Machiavelli's disgrace, which seems implied in its prologue, the *Clizia* must be reckoned among the ripest products of his leisure. The author hints that both of these comedies were suggested to him by facts that had come under his notice in Florentine society.

poses him to the ridicule of the household.[65] Sofronia triumphs over her ashamed and miserable husband, who now consents to Clizia's marriage with Eustachio. But at this juncture the long-lost father of the heroine appears like a *deus ex machina*. He turns out to be a rich Neapolitan gentleman. There remains no obstacle to Cleandro's happiness, and the curtain falls upon a marriage in prospect between the hero and the heroine. The weakness of the play, considered as a work of art, is the mechanical solution of the plot. Its strength and beauty are the masterly delineation of a family interior. The *dramatis personæ* are vigorously sketched and act throughout consistently. Nothing can be finer than the portrait of a sober Florentine merchant, regular in his pursuits, punctual in the performance of his duties, exact in household discipline and watchful over his son's education, whose dignified severity of conduct has yielded to the lunacies of an immoderate passion.[66] For the time being Nicomaco forgets his old associates, abandons his business, and consorts with youthful libertines in taverns. His appetite so blinds him that he devises the odious scheme I have described, in order to gratify a senile whim.[67] The lifelong fabric of honesty and honour breaks down in him; and it is only when lessoned by the punishment inflicted on him by his wife and son, that he returns to his old self and sees the vileness of the situation his folly has created. Sofronia is a notable housewife, rude but respectable. The good understanding between her and her handsome son, Cleandro, whom she loves affectionately, but whom she will not indulge in his caprice for Clizia, is one of the best traits furnished by Italian comedy. Cleandro himself has less than usual of the selfishness and sensuality which degrade the Florentine *primo amoroso*. There is even something of enthusiasm in his passion for Clizia—a germ of sentiment which would have blossomed into romance under the more genial treatment of our drama.[68] Morally speaking, what is odious in this comedy is the willingness of everyone to sacrifice Clizia. Even Cleandro says of her: 'Io per me la torrei per moglie, per amica, e in tutti quei modi, che io la potessi avere.' Nicomaco, when he has failed in his plot to secure the girl, thinks only

[65] The *Clizia* furnished Dolce with the motive of his *Ragazzo* ('Il Ragazzo, commedia di M. Lodovico Dolce. Per Curtiode Navò e fratelli al Leone, MDXLI.'). An old man and his son love the same girl. A parasite promises to get the girl for the old man, but substitutes a page dressed up like a woman, while the son sleeps with the real girl. Readers of Ben Jonson will be reminded of *Epicœne*. But in Dolce's *Ragazzo* the situation is made to suggest impurity and lacks rare Ben's gigantic humour.

[66] See Sofronia's soliloquy, act ii. sc. 4.

[67] Cleandro understands the faint shadow of scruple that suggested this scheme: 'perchè tentare d' averla prima che maritata, gli debbe parere cosa impia e brutta' (act i. sc. 1). This sentence is extremely characteristic of Italian feeling.

[68] His observations on his father are, however, marked by more than ordinary coarseness. 'Come non ti vergogni tu ad avere ordinato, che si delicato viso sia da sì fetida bocca scombavato, sì delicate carni da sì tremanti mani, da sì grinze e puzzolenti membra tocche?' Then he mingles fears about Nicomaco's property with a lover's lamentations. 'Tu non mi potevi far la maggiore ingiuria, avendomi con questo colpo tolto ad un tratto e l' amata e la roba; perchè Nicomaco, se questo amor dura, è per lasciare delle sue sustanze più a Pirro che a me' (act iv. sc. 1).

of his own shame, and takes no account of the risk to which he has exposed her. Sofronia is merely anxious to get her decently established beyond her husband's reach.

Only long extracts could do justice to the sarcasm and irony with which the dialogue is seasoned. Still a few points may be selected.[69] Sofronia is rating Nicomaco for his unseasonable dissipation. He answers: 'Ah, moglie mia, non mi dire tanti mali a un tratto! Serba qualche cosa a domane.' Eustachio, in view of taking Clizia for his wife, reflects: 'In questa terra chi ha bella moglie non può essere povero, e del fuoco e della moglie si può essere liberale con ognuno, perchè quanto più ne dai, più te ne rimane.' When Pirro demurs to Nicomaco's proposals, on the score that he will make enemies of Sofronia and Cleandro, his master answers: 'Che importa a te? Sta' ben con Cristo e fàtti beffe de' santi.' A little lower down Nicomaco trusts the decision of Clizia's husband to lot:

Pirro. Se la sorte me venisse contro?
Nicom. Io ho speranza in Dio, che la non verrà.
Pirro. O vecchio impazzato! Vuole che Dio tenga le mani a queste sue disonesta.

Nor can criticism express the comic humour of the scenes, especially of those in which Nicomaco describes the hours of agony he spent in Siro's bed, and afterwards capitulates at discretion to Sofronia.[70] In spite of what is disagreeable in the argument and obscene in the catastrophe, the 'Clizia' leaves a wholesomer impression on the mind than is common with Florentine comedies. It has something of Ariosto's *bonhomie*, elsewhere unknown in Machiavelli.

Meanwhile the 'Mandragola' is claiming our attention. In that comedy, Machiavelli put forth all his strength. Sinister and repulsive as it may be to modern tastes, its power is indubitable. More than any plays of which mention has hitherto been made, more even than Ariosto's 'Lena' and 'Negromante,' it detaches itself from Latin precedents and offers an unsophisticated view of Florentine life from its author's terrible point of contemplation.

In order to appreciate the 'Mandragola,' it is necessary to know the plot. After spending his early manhood in Paris, Callimaco returns to Florence, bent on making the beautiful Lucrezia his mistress. He has only heard of her divine charms; but the bare report inflames his imagination, disturbs his sleep, and so distracts him that he feels forced 'to attempt some bold stroke, be it grave, dangerous, ruinous, dishonourable; death itself would be better than the life I lead.' Lucrezia is the faithful and obedient wife of Nicia, a doctor of laws, whose one wish in life is to get a son. The extreme gullibility of Nicia and his desire for an heir are the motives upon which Callimaco relies to work his schemes. He finds a parasite, Ligurio, ready to assist him. Ligurio is a friend of Nicia's family, well acquainted with the persons, and so utterly depraved that he would sell his soul for a good dinner. He

[69] Act iii. scs. 4, 5, 6.
[70] Acts v. scs. 2 and 3.

advises Callimaco to play the part of a physician who has studied the last secrets of his art in Paris, introduces him in this capacity to Nicia, and suggests that by his help the desired result may be obtained without the disagreeable necessity of leaving Florence for the baths of San Filippo. In their first interview Callimaco explains that a potion of mandragora administered to Lucrezia will remove her sterility, but that it has fatal consequences to the husband. He must perish unless he first substitutes another man, whose death will extinguish the poison and leave Lucrezia free to be the mother of a future family. Nicia revolts against this odious project, which makes him the destroyer of his own honour and a murderer. But Callimaco assures him that royal persons and great nobles of France have adopted this method with success. The argument has its due weight: 'I am satisfied,' says Nicia, 'since you tell me that a king and princes have done the like.' But the difficulty remains of persuading Lucrezia. Ligurio answers: that is simple enough; let us work upon her through her confessor and her mother. 'You, I, our money, our badness, and the badness of those priests will settle the confessor; and I know that, when the matter is explained, we shall have her mother on our side.' Thus we are introduced to Fra Timoteo, the chief agent of corruption. The monk, in a first interview, does not conceal his readiness to procure abortion and cover infanticide. For a consideration, he agrees to convince Lucrezia that the plot is for her good. He first demonstrates the utility of Callimaco's method to the mother Sostrata, and then by her help persuades Lucrezia that adultery and murder are not only venial, but commendable with so fair an end in view. His sophistries anticipate the darkest casuistry of Escobar. Lucrezia, with a woman's good sense, fastens on the brutal and unnatural loathsomeness of the proposed plan: 'Ma di tutte le cose che si sono tentate, questa mi pare la più strana; avere a sottomettere il corpo mio a questo vituperio, et essere cagione che un uomo muoia per vituperarmi: chè io non crederei, se io fussi sola rimasa nel mondo, e da me avesse a risurgere l' umana natura, che mi fusse simile partito concesso.' Timoteo replies: 'Qui è un bene certo, che voi ingraviderete, acquisterete un' anima a messer Domenedio. Il male incerto è, che colui che giacerà dopo la pozione con voi, si muoia; ma e' si truova anche di quelli che non muoiono. Ma perchè la cosa è dubbia, però è bene che messer Nicia non incorra in quel pericolo. Quanto all' atto che sia peccato, questo è una favola: perchè la volontà è quella che pecca, non il corpo; e la cagione del peccato è dispiacere al marito: e voi gli compiacete; pigliarne piacere: e voi ne avete dispiacere,' &c. Sostrata, accustomed to follow her confessor's orders, and not burdened with a conscience, clinches this reasoning: 'Di che hai tu paura, moccicona? E c' è cinquanta dame in questa terra che ne alzarebbero le mani al cielo.' Lucrezia gives way unwillingly: 'Io son contenta; ma non credo mai esser viva domattina.' Timoteo comforts her with a final touch of monkish irony: 'Non dubitare, figliuola mia, io pregherò Dio per te; io dirò l'orazione dell' Angiolo

Raffaello che t' accompagni. Andate in buon' ora, e preparatevi a questo misterio, che si fa sera.' What follows is the mere working of the plot, whereby Ligurio and Timoteo contrive to introduce Callimaco as the necessary victim into Lucrezia's bed-chamber. The silly Nicia plays the part of pander to his own shame; and when Lucrezia discovers the scheme by which her lover has attained his ends, she exclaims: 'Poi chè l' astuzia tua e la sciocchezza del mio marito, la semplicità di mia madre e la tristizia del mio confessore, m' hanno condotta a far quello che mai per me medesima avrei fatto, io voglio giudicare che e' venga da una celeste disposizione, che abbia voluto così. Però io ti prendo per signore, padrone e guida.' It must be remarked that Lucrezia omits from her reckoning the weakness which led her to consent.

My excuse for analysing a comedy so indecent as the 'Mandragola,' is the importance it has, not only as a product of Machiavelli's genius, but also as an illustration of contemporary modes of thought and feeling. In all points this play is worthy of the author of the 'Principe.' The 'Mandragola' is a microcosm of society as Machiavelli conceived it, and as it needs must be to justify his own philosophy. It is a study of stupidity and baseness acted on by roguery. Credulity and appetite supply the fulcrum needed by unscrupulous intelligence. The lover, aided by the husband's folly, the parasite's profligacy, the mother's familiarity with sin, the confessor's avarice, the wife's want of self-respect, achieves the triumph of making Nicia lead him naked to Lucrezia's chamber. Moving in the region of his fancy, the poet adds *Quod erat demonstrandum* to his theorem of vileness and gross folly used for selfish ends by craft. But we who read it, rise from the perusal with the certainty that it was only the corruption of the age which rendered such a libel upon human nature plausible—only the author's perverse and shallow view of life which sustained him in this reading of a problem he had failed to understand. Viewed as a critique upon life, the 'Mandragola' is feeble, because the premises are false; and these same false premises regarding the main forces of society, render the logic of the 'Principe' inconsequent. Men are not such fools as Nicia or such catspaws as Ligurio and Timoteo. Women are not such compliant instruments as Sostrata and Lucrezia. Human nature is not that tissue of disgusting meannesses and vices, by which Callimaco succeeds. Here lay Machiavelli's fallacy. He dreamed of action as the triumph of astuteness over folly. Virtue with him meant the management of immorality by bold intelligence. But while, on the one hand, he exaggerated the stupidity of dupes, on the other he underestimated the resistance which strongly rooted moral instincts offer to audacious villany. He left goodness out of his account. Therefore, though his reasoning, whether we examine the 'Mandragola' or the 'Principe,' seems irrefragable on the premises from which he starts, it is an unconvincing chain of sophisms. The world is not wholly bad; but in order to justify Machiavelli's conclusions, we have to assume that its essential forces are corrupt.

If we turn from the 'Mandragola' to the society of which it is a study, and which complacently accepted it as an agreeable work of art, we are filled with a sense of surprise bordering on horror. What must the people among whom Machiavelli lived, have been, to justify his delineation of a ruffian so vicious as Ligurio, a confessor so lost to sense of duty as Timoteo, a mother who scruples not to prostitute her daughter to the first comer, a lover so depraved as Callimaco, a wife so devoid of womanly feeling as Lucrezia? On first reflection, we are inclined to believe that the poet in this comedy was venting Swiftian indignation on the human nature which he misconceived and loathed. The very name Lucrezia seems chosen in irony—as though to hint that Rome's first martyr would have failed, if Tarquin had but used her mother and her priest to tame her. Yet, on a second reading, the 'Mandragola' reveals no scorn or anger. It is a piece of scientific anatomy, a demonstration of disease, executed without subjective feeling. The argument is so powerfully developed, with such simplicity of language, such consistency of character, such cold analysis of motives, that we cannot doubt the verisimilitude of the picture. No one, at the date of its appearance, resented it. Florentine audiences delighted in its comic flavour. Leo X. witnessed it with approval. His hatred of the monks found satisfaction in Timoteo. Society, far from rising in revolt against the poet who exposed its infamy with a pen of poisoned steel, thanked the man of genius for rendering vice amusing. Of satire or of moral purpose there is none in the 'Mandragola.' Machiavelli depicted human nature just as he had learned to know it. The sinister fruits of his studies made contemporaries laugh.

The 'Mandragola' was the work of an unhappy man. The prologue offers a curious mixture of haughtiness and fawning, only comparable to the dedication of the 'Principe' and the letter to Vettori.[71] A sense of his own intellectual greatness is combined with an uneasy feeling of failure:

> Non è componitor di molta fama.

As an apology for his application to trivialities, he pleads wretchedness and *ennui*:

> E se questa materia non è degna,
> Per esser più leggieri
> D' un uom che voglia parer saggio e grave,
> Scusatelo con questo, che s' ingegna
> Con questi vani pensieri
> Fare el suo tristo tempo più soave;
> Perchè altrove non ave
> Dove voltare el viso;
> Che gli è stato interciso
> Mostrar con altre imprese altra virtue,
> Non sendo premio alle fatiche sue.

[71] See Vol. I., *Age of the Despots*, pp. 159-162. Of the two strains of character so ill-blent in Machiavelli, the *Mandragola* represents the vulgar and the *Principe* the noble. The one corresponds to his days at Casciano, the other to his studious evenings.

These verses, indifferent as poetry, are poignant for their revelation of a disappointed life. Left without occupation, unable to display his powers upon a worthy platform, he casts the pearls of his philosophy before the pleasure-seeking swine. The sense of this degradation stings him and he turns upon society with threats. Let them not attempt to browbeat or intimidate him:

> Che sa dir male anch' egli,
> E come questa fu la sua prim' arte:
> E come in ogni parte
> Del mondo, ove il sì suona,
> Non istima persona,
> Ancor che faccia el sergiere a colui
> Che può portar miglior mantel di lui.

Throughout this prologue we hear the growl of a wounded lion, helpless in his lair, yet conscious that he still has strength to rend the fools and knaves around him.

Aretino completed the disengagement of Italian from Latin comedy. Ignoring the principles established by the Plautine mannerists, he liberated the elements of satire and of realism held in bondage by their rules. His reasoning was unanswerable. Why should he attend to the unities, or be careful to send the same person no more than five times on the stage in one piece? His people shall come and go as they think fit, or as the argument requires.[72] Why should he make Romans ape the style of Athens? His Romans shall be painted from life; his servants shall talk and act like Italian varlets, not mimicking the ways of Geta or Davus.[73] Why should he shackle his style with precedents from Petrarch and Boccaccio? He will seek the fittest words, the aptest phrases, the most biting repartees from ordinary language.[74] Why condescend to imitation, when his mother wit supplies him with material, and the world of men lies open like a book before his eyes?[75] Why follow in the footsteps of the pedants, who mistake their knowledge of grammar for genius, and whose commentaries are an insult to the poets they pretend to illustrate?[76]

[72] 'Se voi vedessi uscire i personaggi più di cinque volte in scena, non ve ne ridete, perchè le catene che tengono i molini sul fiume, non terrebbeno i pazzi d' oggidì' (Prologue to the *Cortigiana*).

[73] 'Non vi maravigliate se lo stil comico non s' osserva con l' ordine che si richiede, perchè si vive d' un' altra maniera a Roma che non si vivea in Atene' (*ibid.*).

[74] 'Io non mi son tolto dagli andari del Petrarca e del Boccaccio per ignoranza, chè pur so ciò che essi sono; ma per non perdere il tempo, la pazienza e ill nome nella pazzia di volermi trasformare in loro' (Prologue to the *Orazia*).

[75] 'Più pro fa il pane asciutto in casa propria che l' accompagnato con molte vivande su altrui tavola. Imita qua, imita là; tutto è fava, si può dire alle composizioni dei più . . . di chi imita, mi faccio beffe . . . posso giurare d' esser sempre me stesso, ed altri non mai' (*ibid.*).

[76] 'Io mi rido dei pedanti, i quali si credono che la dottrina consiste nella lingua greca, dando tutta la riputatione allo in *bus* in *bas* della grammatica' (Prologue to *Orazia*). 'I crocifissori del Petrarca, i quali gli fanno dir cose con i loro comenti, che non gliene fariano confessare diece tratti di corda. E bon per Dante che con le sue diavolerie fa star le bestie in dietro, che a questa ora saria in croce anch' egli' (Prologue to *Cortigiana*).

Conscious of his own defective education, and judging the puristic niceties of the age at their true value, Aretino thus flung the glove of defiance in the face of a learned public. It was a bold step; but the adventurer knew what he was doing. The originality of his 'Ars Poetica' took the world by surprise. His Italian audience delighted in the sparkle of a style that gave point to their common speech. Had Aretino been a writer of genius, Italy might now have owed to his audacity and self-reliance the starting-point of national dramatic art.[77] He was on the right path, but he lacked the skill to tread it. His comedies, loosely put together, with no constructive vigour in their plots and no grasp of psychology in their characters, are a series of powerfully written scenes, piquant dialogues, effective situations, rather than comedies in the higher sense of the word. We must not look for Ariosto's lucid order, for Machiavelli's disposition of parts, in these vagaries of a brilliant talent aiming at immediate success. We must be grateful for the filibustering bravado which made him dare to sketch contemporary manners from the life. The merit of these comedies is naturalness. Such affectation of antithesis or laboured epigram as mars their style, was part of Aretino's self. It reveals the man, and is not wearisome like the conceits of the pedantic school. What he had learned, seen or heard in his experience of the world—and Aretino saw, heard and learned the worst of the society in which he lived—is presented with vigour. The power to express is never shackled by a back-thought of reserve or delicacy. Each character stands outlined with a vividness none the less convincing because the study lacks depth. What Aretino cannot supply, is the nexus between these striking passages, the linking of these lively portraits into a coherent whole. Machiavelli's logic, perverse as it may be, produces by its stringent application a more impressive æsthetical effect. The doctrine of style for style's sake, derided by Aretino, satisfies at least our sense of harmony. In the insolence of freedom he spoils the form of his plays by discussions, sometimes dull, sometimes disgusting, in which he vents his spite or airs his sycophancy without regard for the exigencies of his subject. Still, in spite of these defects, Aretino's plays are a precious mine of information for one who desires to enter into direct communication with the men of the Renaissance.

Aretino's point of view is that of the successful adventurer. Unlike Machiavelli, he has no sourness and reveals no disappointment. He has never fallen from the high estate of an impersonal ambition. His report of human depravity is neither scientific nor indignant. He appreciates the vices of the world, by comprehending which, as means to ends, he has achieved celebrity. They are the instruments of his advance in life, the sources of his wealth, the wisdom he professes. Therefore, while he satirises, he treats them with complacence. Evil is

[77] His tragedy *Orazia* has just the same merits of boldness and dramatic movement in parts, the same defects of incoherence. It detaches itself favourably from the tragedies of the pedants.

good for its own sake also in his eyes. Having tasted all its fruits, he revels in recalling his sensations, just as Casanova took pleasure in recording his debaucheries. His knowledge of society is that of an upstart, who has risen from the lowest ranks by the arts of the bully, flatterer and pander. We never forget that he began life as a lacquey, and the most valuable quality of his comedies is that they depict the great world from the standpoint of the servants' hall. Aretino is too powerful and fashionable to be aware of this. He poses as the sage and satirist. But the revelation is none the less pungent because it is made unconsciously. The Court, idealised by Castiglione, censured by Guarini, inveighed against by La Casa, here shows its inner rottenness for our inspection, at the pleasure of a charlatan who thrives on this pollution. We hear how the valets of debauched prelates, the parasites of petty nobles, the pimps who battened on the vices of the rich, the flatterer who earned his bread by calumny and lies, viewed this world of fashion, how they discussed it among themselves, how they utilised its corruption. We shake hands with ruffians and cut-throats, enter the Roman brothels by their back-door, sit down in their kitchens, and become acquainted with the secrets of their trade. It may be suggested that the knowledge supplied by Aretino, if it concerns such details, is neither profitable nor valuable. No one, indeed, who is not specially curious to realise the manners of Renaissance Italy, should occupy his leisure with these comedies.

The 'Cortigiana' is a parody of Castiglione's 'Cortegiano.' A Sienese gentleman, simple and provincial, the lineal descendant of Pulci's Messer Goro, arrives in Rome to make his fortune.[78] He is bent on assuming the fine airs of the Court, and hopes to become at least a Cardinal before he returns home. On his first arrival Messer Maco falls into the clutches of a sharper, who introduces him to disreputable society, under colour of teaching him the art of courtiership. The satire of the piece consists in showing Rome to be the school of profligacy rather than of gentle customs.[79] Before he has spent more than a few days in the Eternal City, the country squire learns the slang of the *demi-monde* and swaggers among courtesans and rufflers. Maestro Andrea, who has undertaken his education, lectures him upon the virtues of the courtier in a scene of cynical irony:[80] 'La principa cosa, il cortigiano vuol sapere bestemmiare, vuole essere giuocatore, invidioso, puttaniere, eretico, adulatore, maldicente, sconoscente, ignorante, asino, vuol sapere frappare, far la ninfa, et essere agente e paziente.' Some of these qualities are understood at once by Messer Maco. Concerning others he asks for further information: 'Come si diventa eretico? questo è 'l caso.—Notate.—Io nuoto benissimo.—Quando alcuno vi dice che in Corte sia

[78] 'Egli è uno di quegli animali di tanti colori che il vostro avolo comperò in cambio d' un papagallo' (act i. sc. 1).

[79] Its most tedious episode is a panegyric of Venice at the expense of Rome (act iii. sc. 7).

[80] Act i. sc. 22.

bontà, discrezione, amore, o conoscenza, dite no 'l credo . . . . in somma a chi vi dice bene de la Corte, dite: tu sei un bugiardo.' Again, Messer Maco asks: 'Come si dice male?' The answer is prompt and characteristic of Aretino:[81] 'Dicendo il vero, dicendo il vero.' What Maestro Andrea teaches theoretically, is expounded as a fact of bitter experience by Valerio and Flamminio, the gentlemen in waiting on a fool of fortune named Parabolano.[82] These men, admitted to the secrets of a noble household, know its inner sordidness, and reckon on the vanity and passions of their patron. A still lower stage in the scale of debasement is revealed by the conversations of the lacqueys, Rosso and Cappa, who discuss the foibles of their master with the coarseness of the stables.[83] In so far as the 'Cortigiana' teaches any lesson, it is contained in the humiliation of Parabolano. His vices have made him the slave and creature of foul-minded serving-men, who laugh together over the disgusting details of his privacy, while they flatter him to his face in order to profit by his frivolities.[84] Aretino's own experience of life in Rome enabled him to make these pictures of the servants' hall and antechamber pungent.[85] The venom engendered by years of servitude and adulation is vented in his criticism of the Court as censured from a flunkey's point of view. Nor is he less at home in painting the pleasures of the class whom he has chosen for his critics of polite society. Cappa's soliloquy upon the paradise of the tavern, and Rosso's pranks, when he plays the gentleman in his master's fine clothes, owe the effect of humour to their realistic verve.[86] We feel them to be reminiscences of fact. These scenes constitute the salt of the comedy, supported by vivid sketches of town characters—the news-boy, the fisherman of the Tiber, and the superannuated prostitute.[87]

In the 'Cortigiana' it was Aretino's object to destroy illusions about Court-life by describing it in all the vileness of reality.[88] The 'Marescalco' is a study of the same conditions of society, with less malignity and far more geniality of humour.[89] A rich fool has been recommended by his lord and master, the Duke of Mantua, to take a wife. He loathes matrimony, and shrinks from spending several thousand ducats on the dower. But the parasites, buffoons and henchmen of the prince persuade and bully him into compliance. He is finally married to a page dressed as a woman, and his relief at discovering the sex of his supposed wife forms the climax of the plot. This play is conducted with so much

[81] He makes the same point in the prologue to *La Talenta*: 'Chi brama d' acquistarsi il nome del più scellerato uomo che viva, dica il vero.'

[82] Act i. sc. 9; act ii. sc. 6; act ii. sc. 10; act iii. sc. 7.

[83] See especially act i. sc. 7.

[84] Act iv. sc. 6.

[85] Notice the extraordinary virulence of his invective against the *tinello* or common room of servants in a noble household (act. v. sc. 15).

[86] Act ii. sc. 1; act i. scs. 11-18.

[87] Act i. sc. 4; act i. sc. 11; act ii. sc. 7.

[88] Act ii. sc. 6.

[89] Of all Aretino's plays the *Marescalco* is the simplest and the most artistically managed.

spirit that we may not be wrong in supposing Shakspere in 'Twelfth Night' and Ben Jonson in 'Epicœne' to have owed something to its humour. We look, however, in vain for such fine creatures of the fancy as Sir Toby Belch, or for a catastrophe so overwhelming as the *crescendo* of noise and bustle which subdues the obstinacy of Morose. On the other hand, the two companion scenes in which Marescalco's nurse enlarges on the luxuries of married life, while Ambrogio describes its miseries, are executed with fine sense of comic contrast.[90]

In the 'Talanta' we return to Roman society. This comedy is a study of courtesan life, analysed with thorough knowledge of its details. The character of Talanta, who plays her four lovers one against the other, extracting presents by various devices from each of them, displays the author's intimate acquaintance with his subject.[91] Talanta on the stage is a worthy pendant to Nanna in the 'Ragionamenti.' But the intrigue is confused, tedious and improbable; and after reading the first act, we have already seen the best of Aretino's invention. The same may be said about the 'Ipocrita' and the 'Filosofo,' two comedies in which Aretino attempted to portray a charlatan of Tartufe's type and a student helpless in his wife's hands. These characters are not ill-conceived, but they are too superficially executed to bear the weight of the plot laid upon them. In like manner the pedant in the 'Marescalco' and the swashbuckler in the 'Talanta' are rather silhouettes than finished portraits. Though well sketched, they lack substance. They have neither the life-like movement of Shakspere's minor persons, nor the impressive mechanism of Jonson's humours. Bobadil and Master Holofernes, though caricatures, move in a higher region of the comic art. The characters Aretino could imitate supremely well, were a page like Giannico in the 'Marescalco,' a footman like Rosso in the 'Cortigiana,' or a woman of the town like Talanta. His comedies are never wanting in bustle and variety of business; while the sarcasm of the author, flying at the best-established reputations, sneering at the most fashionable prejudices of society, renders them effective even now, when all the jealousies he flouted have long been buried in oblivion.[92]

Bibbiena's 'Calandra' is a farce, obscene but not malignant. Ariosto's comedies are studies of society from the standpoint of the middle class. If he is too indulgent to human frailty, too tolerant of vice, we never miss in him the wisdom of a genial observer. Machiavelli's 'Mandragola'

[90] Act i. sc. 6; act ii. sc. 5.

[91] Talanta's apology for her rapacity and want of heart (act i. sc. 1); the description of her by her lover Orfinio, who sees through her but cannot escape her fascination (act i. sc. 7); the critique of her by a sensible man (act i. sc. 12); her arts to bring her lover back to his allegiance and wheedle the most odious concessions (act i. sc. 13); her undisguised marauding (act i. sc. 14); these moments in the evolution of her character are set forth with the decision of a master's style.

[92] The Prologue to the *Cortigiana* passes all the literary celebrities of Italy in review with a ferocity of sarcasm veiled in irony that must have been extremely piquant. And take this equivocal compliment to Molza from the *Marescalco* (act v. sc. 3), 'il Molza Mutinense, che arresta con la sua fistola i torrenti.'

casts the dry light of the intellect on an abyss of evil. Nothing but the brilliance of the poet's wit reconciles us to his revelation of perversity. Aretino, by the animation of his sketches, by his prurient delight in what is vile, makes us comprehend that even the 'Mandragola' was possible. Machiavelli stands outside his subject, like Lucifer, fallen but disdainful. Aretino is the Belial who acknowledges corruption for his own domain. Ariosto and Machiavelli are artists each in his kind perfect. Aretino is an *improvvisatore*, clever with the pen he uses like a burin.

It would be difficult to render an account of the comedies produced by the Italians in the sixteenth century, or to catalogue their authors. A computation has been made which reckons the plays known to students at several thousands. In spite of this extraordinary richness in comic literature, Italy cannot boast of a great Comedy. No poet arose to carry the art onward from the point already reached when Aretino left the stage. The neglect that fell on those innumerable comedies, was not wholly undeserved. It is true that their scenes suggested brilliant episodes to French and English playwrights of celebrity. It is true that the historian of manners finds in them an almost inexhaustible store of matter. Still they are literary lucubrations rather than the spontaneous expression of a vivid nationality. Nor have they the subordinate merit of dealing in a scientific spirit with the cardinal vices and follies of society. We miss the original plots, the powerful modelling of character, the philosophical insight which would have reconciled us to a *Commedia erudita*.

When we examine the plays of Firenzuola, Cecchi, Ambra, Gelli, Il Lasca, Doni, Dolce, we find that a hybrid form of art had been established by the practice of the earlier playwrights. This hybrid implied Plautus and Terence as a necessary basis. It adopted the fusion of Latin arguments with Italian manners which was so ably realised by Ariosto and Machiavelli. It allowed something for the farce traditions which the Rozzi made fashionable at Rome. It assumed ingredients from the *Burle* and *Novelle* of the market-place, reproduced the language of the people, and made use of current scandals to give piquancy to its conventional plots. But notwithstanding the admixture of so many modern elements, the stereotyped Latinism of its form rendered this comedy unnatural. Ingenious *contaminatio*, to use a phrase in vogue among Roman critics, was always more apparent than creative instinct.

The *Commedia erudita* presented a framework ready-made to the playwright, and easily accepted on the strength of usage by the audience he sought to entertain. At the same time it left him free, within prescribed limits, to represent the manners of contemporary life. The main object of a great drama, 'to show the very age and body of the time his form and pressure,' is thrust into the second rank; and the most valuable portions of these clever works of skill are their episodes—such scenes, for example, as those which in the 'Aridosio' of Lorenzino de' Medici reveal the dissoluteness of conventual customs in a scholastic *rifacimento* of the 'Adelphi' and the 'Mostellaria.'[93] Had the fusion of classical and modern elements been complete as in the 'Epicœne' of Jonson, or had the character-drawing been masterly as in Molière's 'Avare,' we should have no cause for complaint. But these are just the qualities of success missed by the Italian playwrights. Their studies from nature are comparatively slight. Having exhibited them in the presentation of the subject or introduced them here and there by way of interludes, they work the play to its conclusion on the lines of Latinistic convention.[94]

Such being the form of *cinque cento* comedy, it follows that its details are monotonous. The characters are invariably drawn from the ranks of the rich burgher classes; and if we may trust the evidence furnished by the playwrights, the morality of these classes must have been of an almost inconceivable baseness. We survey a society separated from the larger interests that elevate humanity, without public ambition or the sense of national greatness, excluded from the career of arms, dead to honour, bent upon sensual enjoyment and petty intrigues. The motive which sustains the plot, is illicit love; but in its presentation there is no romance, nothing to cloak the animalism of an unchecked instinct. The young men who play the part of *primi amorosi*, are in debt or without money. It is their object to repair their fortunes by a rich marriage, to secure a maintenance from a neighbour's wife they have seduced, to satisfy the avarice of a greedy courtesan, or to conceal the results of an intrigue which has brought their mistress into difficulties. From the innumerable scenes devoted to these elegant and witty scapegraces, it would be difficult to glean a single sentence expressive of conscience, remorse, sense of loyalty or generous feeling. They submit to the most odious bargains and disreputable subterfuges, sacrificing the honour of their families or the good fame of the women who depend upon them, to the attainment of some momentary self-indulgence.[95] Without respect for age, they expend their ingenuity in robbing their parents and exposing their fathers to ridicule.[96] Nor is it possible to

[93] *Lorenzino de' Medici*, Daelli, Milano, 1862.

[94] The pseudo-classical hybrid I have attempted to describe is analogous in its fixity of outline to the conventional framework of the *Sacre Rappresentazioni*, which allowed a playwright the same subordinate liberty of action and saved him the trouble of invention to a like extent. It may here be noticed that the Italians in general adopted stereotyped forms for dramatic representation. Harlequin, Columbine, and Pantaloon, the Bolognese doctor, the Stenterello of Florence, the Meneghino of Milan, and many other dramatic types, recognised as stationary, yet admitting of infinite variety in treatment by author or actor, are notable examples. In estimating the dramatic genius of Italy this tendency to move within defined and conventional limits of art, whether popular or literary, must never be forgotten.

[95] Cinthio's conduct towards Emilia in the *Negromante* is a good instance.

[96] See above, p. 260, note, for Cleandro in the *Mandragola*; and compare Alamanno's conversation with his uncle Lapo, his robbery of his mother's money-box, and his reflections on the loss he should sustain by her re-marriage, in Gelli's *La Sporta* (act iii. 5; ii. 2). Camillo's allusions to his father's folly in Gelli's *Errore* (act iv. 2) are no less selfish and heartless. Alamanno's plot to raise a dower by fraud (*La Sporta*, iv. 1) may be compared with Fabio's trick upon his stepmother in Cecchi's *Martello*. In the latter his father takes a hand.

feel much sympathy for the elders, who are so brutally used. The old man of these comedies is either a superannuated libertine, who makes himself ridiculous by his intrigues with a neighbour's wife, or a parsimonious tyrant, or else an indulgent rake, who acts the pander for his good-for-nothing rascal of a son.[97] Mere simpletons like Machiavelli's Nicia, or Aretino's Messer Maco, furnish another type of irreverent age, unredeemed by the comic humour of Falstaff or the gigantic lusts of Sir Epicure Mammon. Between son and father the inevitable servant plays the part of clever rogue. It is he who weaves the meshes of the intrigue that shall cut the purse-strings of the stingy parent, blind the eyes of the husband to his wife's adultery, or cheat the creditor of his dues. Our sympathy is always enlisted on the side of the schemers; and however base their tricks may be, we are invited to applaud the success which crowns them. The girls are worthy of their lovers. Corrupted by nurses; exposed to the contaminating influences of the convent; courted by grooms and servants in their father's household; tampered with by infamous duennas; betrayed by their own mothers or entrusted by their fathers to notorious prostitutes; they accept the first husband proposed to them by their parents, confident in the hope of continuing clandestine intrigues with the neighbour's son who has seduced them.[98] The wives are such as the *Novelle* paint them, yielding to the barest impulses of wantonness, and covering their debauchery with craft that raises a laugh against the husbands they have cozened. Such are the main actors, the conventional personages of this domestic comedy. The subordinate characters consist of parasites and flatterers; ignorant pedants and swaggering *bravi*; priests who ply the trade of pimps; astrologers who thrive upon the folly of their clients; doctors who conceal births; prostitutes and their attendant bullies; compliant go-betweens and rapacious bawds; pages, street urchins, and officers of justice. The adulterous intrigue required such minor persons as instruments; and it often happens that scenes of vivid comic humour, dialogues of the most brilliant Tuscan idiom, are suggested by the interaction of these puppets, whose wires the clever valet and the *primo amoroso* pull.

The point of interest for contemporary audiences was the *burla*—the joke played off by a wife upon her husband, by rogues upon a simpleton, by a son upon his father, by a servant on his master's creditors, by a pupil on his pedantic tutor. Accepting the conditions of a comedy so constructed, and eliminating ethical considerations, we readily admit that these jokes are infinitely amusing. The scene in Gelli's 'Sporta' where Ghirigoro de' Macci receives the confidences of the youth who has seduced his daughter, under the impression that he is talking about

[97] Ghirigoro in Gelli's *Sporta,* Gherardo in Gelli's *Errore,* Girolamo in Cecchi's *Martello.* It is needless to multiply examples. The analyses of Machiavelli's comedies will suffice.

[98] It would be easy to illustrate each of these points from the comedies of Ariosto, Cecchi, Machiavelli, Lorenzino de' Medici; to which the reader may be referred *passim* for proof.

his money-box, is not unworthy of Molière's 'Avare.' Two scenes in Gelli's 'Errore' where Gherardo Amieri, disguised as an old woman, is tormented by a street urchin whom his son has sent to tease him, and afterwards confronted by his angry wife, might have adorned the 'Merry Wives of Windsor.'[99] Cecchi's comedies in like manner abound in comical absurdities involving exquisitely realistic pictures of Florentine manners.[100] For the student of language, no less than for the student of Renaissance life, they are invaluable. But the similarity of form which marks the comedies of the *cinque cento*, renders it impossible to do justice to their details in the present work. I must content myself with the foregoing sketch of their structure derived from the perusal of such plays as were accessible in print, and with the further observation that each of these eminent dramatists developed some side of the common heritage transmitted by their common predecessors. Thus Firenzuola continued the Latin tradition with singular tenacity, adapting classical arguments in his 'Lucidi' and 'Trinuzia' to modern themes with the same inimitable transparency of style he had displayed in his *rifacimento* of the 'Golden Ass.'[101] Gelli adapted the 'Aulularia' in his 'Sporta,' and closely followed the 'Clizia' in his 'Errore.' The devotion professed for Machiavelli by this playwright, was yielded by Cecchi to Ariosto: and thus we notice two divergent strains of tradition within the circle of Florentine art.[102] Cecchi was a voluminous dramatic writer. Besides his comedies in *sdrucciolo* and *piano* verse, he composed 'Sacre Rappresentazioni' and plays of a mixed kind derived from a free handling of that elder form.[103] While Gelli and Cecchi severally followed the example of Machiavelli and Ariosto, Il Lasca attempted to free the Italian drama from the fetters of erudite convention.[104] His comedies are exceedingly witty versions of *Novelle* forming dramatic pendants to his narratives in that style. Yet though he strove to make

[99] *Opere di Gio. Battista Gelli* (Milano, 1807), vol. iii.

[100] *Commedie di Giovan Maria Cecchi*, 2 vols. Lemonnier.

[101] *Opere di Messer Agnolo Firenzuola* (Milano, 1802), vol. v.

[102] E 'l divino Ariosto anco, a chi cedono
Greci, Latini e Toscan, tutti i comici.

Prologue to *I Rivali*.

Ma che dirò di te, spirito illustre,
Ariosto gentil, qual lode fia
Uguale al tuo gran merto, al tuo valore?
Cede a te nella comica palestra
Ogni Greco e Latin, perchè tu solo
Hai veramente dimostrato come
Esser deve il principio, il mezzo e 'l fine
Delle comedie, etc.

Le Pellegrine, Intermedio Sesto, published by Barbèra, 1855.

[103] See the 'Esaltazione della Croce,' *Sacre Rappresentazioni*, Lemonnier, vol. iii. Compare those curious hybrid plays, *Il Figliuolo Prodigo*, *La Morte del Re Acab*, *La Conversione della Scozia*, in his collected plays (Lemonnier, 1856). *Lo Sviato* may be mentioned as another of his comedies derived from the *Sacre Rappresentazioni* with a distinctly didactic and moral purpose.

[104] See Prologue to *La Strega*, and above, p. 239.

the stage a mirror of contemporary customs, he could not wholly escape from the mannerism into which the dramatic art had fallen. Nor was it possible, now that the last gleam of liberty had expired in Italy, when even Florence accepted her fate, and the Inquisition was jealously watching every new birth of the press, to create what the earlier freedom of the Renaissance had missed. The drama was condemned to trivialities which only too faithfully reflected the political stagnation, and the literary trifling of a decadent civilisation.[105]

It is worthy of notice, as a final remark upon the history of the comic stage, that at this very moment of its ultimate frustration there existed the germ of a drama analogous to that of England, only waiting to be developed by some master spirit. That was the *Farsa*, which Cecchi, the most prolific, original and popular of Florentine playwrights, deigned to cultivate.[106] He describes it thus: 'The *Farsa* is a new third species between tragedy and comedy. It enjoys the liberties of both, and shuns their limitations; for it receives into its ample boundaries great lords and princes, which comedy does not, and, like a hospital or inn, welcomes the vilest and most plebeian of the people, to whom Dame Tragedy has never stooped. It is not restricted to certain motives; for it accepts all subjects—grave and gay, profane and sacred, urbane and rude, sad and pleasant. It does not care for time or place. The scene may be laid in a church, or a public square, or where you will; and if one day is not long enough, two or three may be employed. What, indeed, does it matter to the *Farsa*? In a word, this modern mistress of the stage is the most amusing, the most convenient, the sweetest, prettiest country-lass that can be found upon our earth.'[107] He then goes on to describe the liberty of language allowed in the *Farsa*, rounding off a picture which exactly applies to our Elizabethan drama. The *Farsa*, in the form it had assumed when Cecchi used it, was, in fact, the survival of an ancient, obscure species of dramatic art, which had descended from the period of classical antiquity, and which recently had blent with the traditions of the 'Sacre Rappresentazioni.' Had circumstances been favourable to the development of a national drama in Italy, the popular elements of the Pagan farce and the mediæval Mystery would have naturally issued through the *Farsa* in a modern form of art analogous to that produced in England. But the Italians had, as we have seen, no public to demand the rehabilitation of the *Farsa*; nor was Cecchi a Shakspere, or even a Marlowe, to prove, in the face of Latinising playwrights, that the national stage lay in its cradle here. It remained for the poets of a far-off island, who disdained Italian *jigs* and owed nothing to the *Farse* of either Florentine or Neapolitan contemporaries, acting by instinct and in concert with the sympathies of a great nation,

[105] I reserve for another chapter the treatment of the Pastoral, which eventually proved the most original and perfect product of the Italian stage.

[106] The titles of his *Farse* given by D' Ancona are *I Malandrini*, *Pittura*, *Andazzo*, *Sciotta*, *Romanesca*.

[107] Prologue to the *Romanesca*, Firenze, Cenniniana, 1874.

to take this 'sweetest, prettiest country-lass' by the hand and place her side by side with Attic Tragedy and Comedy upon the supreme throne of art.

The Italian comedies offer an even more startling picture of social vice than the *Novelle*.[108] To estimate how far they represent a general truth, is difficult; especially when we remember that they were written in a conventional style, to amuse princes, academicians, and prelates.[109] Comparing their testimony with that of private letters and biographical literature (the correspondence, for example, of Alessandra degli Strozzi, Alberti's treatise on the Family, and statements gleaned from memoirs and *Ricordi*), we are justified in believing that a considerable difference existed at the commencement of this epoch between public and domestic manners in Italy; between the Court and the home, the piazza and the fireside, the diversions of fashionable coteries and the conversation of friends and kinsmen. The family still retained some of its antique simplicity. And it was not as yet vitiated by the institution of Cicisbeism. But the great world was incredibly corrupt. Each Court formed a nucleus of dissolute living. Rome, stigmatised successively by men so different as Lorenzo de' Medici, Pietro Aretino, Gian-Giorgio Trissino, and Messer Guidiccioni, poisoned the whole Italian nation. Venice entertained a multitude of prostitutes, and called them *benemeritæ* in public acts. Since, therefore, these centres of aristocratic and literary life drew recruits from the burgher and rural classes, the strongholds of patriarchal purity were continually being sapped by contact with fashionable uncleanliness. And thus in the sixteenth century a common standard of immorality had been substituted for earlier severity of manners. The convulsions of that disastrous epoch, following upon a period of tranquillity, during which the people had become accustomed to luxury, submerged whole families in vice. 'Wars, famines, and the badness of the times,' wrote Aretino, 'inclining men to give themselves amusement, have so debauched all Italy (*imputtanita tutta Italia*), that cousins and kinsfolk of both sexes, brothers and sisters, mingle together without shame, without a shadow of conscience.'[110] Though it is preposterous to see Aretino posing as a censor of morals, his acuteness was indubitable; nor need we suppose that his acquaintance with the disease rendered him less sagacious in detecting its causes. What Corio tells

[108] Dolce in the Prologue to his *Ragazzo* says that, immodest as a comedy may be, it would be impossible for any play to reproduce the actual depravity of manners.

[109] What I have already observed with regard to the *Novelle*—namely, that Italy lacked the purifying and ennobling influences of a real public, embracing all classes, and stimulating the production of a largely designed, broadly executed literature of human nature—is emphatically true also of her stage. The people demand greatness from their authors—simplicity, truth, nobleness. They do not shrink from grossness; they tolerate what is coarse. But these elements must be kept in proper subordination. Princes, petty coteries, academies, drawing-room patrons, the audience of the antechamber and the boudoir, delight in subtleties, *doubles entendre*, scandalous tales, Divorce Court arguments. The people evokes Shakspere: the provincial Court breeds Bibbiena.

[110] *Cortigiana* act ii. sc. 10.

us about Lodovico Sforza's capital, what we read about the excess of luxury into which the nobles of Vicenza and Milan plunged, amid the horrors of the French and Spanish occupation, confirms his testimony.[111] After the Black Death, described by Matteo Villani, the Florentines consoled themselves for previous sufferings by an outburst of profligate and reckless living. So now they sought distraction in unbridled sensuality. Society was in dissolution, and men lived for the moment, careless of consequences. The immorality of the theatre was at once a sign and a source of this corruption. 'O times! O manners!' exclaims Lilius Giraldus[112]: 'the obscenities of the stage return in all their foulness. Plays are acted in every city, which the common consent of Christendom had banned because of their depravity. Now the very prelates of the faith, our nobles, our princes, bring them back among us, and cause them to be publicly presented. Nay, priests themselves are eagerly ambitious of the infamous title of actors, in order to bring themselves into notoriety, and to enrich themselves with benefices.'

It must not be supposed that the immorality of the comic stage consists in the license of language, incident or plot. Had this been all, we should hardly be justified in drawing a distinction between the Italians of the Renaissance and our own Elizabethan playwrights. It lies far deeper, in the vicious philosophy of life paraded by the authors, in the absence of any didactic or satirical aim. Molière, while exposing evil, teaches by example. A canon of goodness is implied, from which the deformities of sin and folly are deflections. But Machiavelli and Aretino paint humanity as simply bad. The palm of success is awarded to unscrupulous villainy. An incapacity for understanding the immutable power of moral beauty was the main disease of Italy. If we seek the cause of this internal cancer, we must trace the history of Italian thought and feeling back to the age of Boccaccio; and we shall probably form an opinion that misdirected humanism, blending with the impieties of a secularised Papacy, the self-indulgence of the despots, and the coarse tastes of the *bourgeoisie*, had sapped the conscience of society.

[111] See Corio, quoted in Vol. I., *Age of the Despots*, p. 275, note 10. For Milanese luxury, Bandello, vol. i. pp. 219 *et seq.*; vol. iv. p. 115 (Milan edition, 1814). For Vicenza, Morsolin's *Trissino*, p. 291.

[112] *De Poet. Hist.* Dial. 8. Giraldi may have had men like Inghirami, surnamed 'Phædra' and Cardinal Bibbiena in view.

CHAPTER XII

PASTORAL AND DIDACTIC POETRY

The Idyllic Ideal—Golden Age—Arcadia—Sannazzaro—His Life—The Art of the 'Arcadia'—Picture-painting—Pontano's Poetry—The Neapolitan Genius—Baiæ and Eridanus—Eclogues—The Play of 'Cefalo'—Castiglione's 'Tirsi'—Rustic Romances—Molza's Biography—The 'Ninfa Tiberina'—Progress of Didactic Poetry—Rucellai's 'Api'—Alamanni's 'Coltivazione'—His Life—His Satires—Pastoral Dramatic Poetry—The 'Aminta'—The 'Pastor Fido'—Climax of Renaissance Art.

THE transition from the middle ages to the Renaissance was marked by the formation of a new ideal, which in no slight measure determined the type of Italian literature. The faiths and aspirations of Catholicism, whereof the 'Divine Comedy' remains the monument in art, began to lose their hold on the imagination. The world beyond the grave grew dim to mental vision, in proportion as this world, through humanism rediscovered, claimed daily more attention. Poliziano's contemporaries were as far removed from Dante's apprehension of a future life as modern Evangelicals from Bunyan's vivid sense of sin and salvation. This parallel, though it may seem strained, is close enough to be serviceable. As the need of conversion is taken for granted among Protestants, so the other world was then assumed to be real. Yet neither the expectation of heavenly bliss nor the fear of purgatorial pain was felt with that intense sincerity which inspired Dante's cantos and Orcagna's frescoes. On both emotions the new culture, appearing at one moment as a solvent through philosophical speculation, at another as a corrosive in the sceptical and critical activity it stimulated, was acting with destructive energy. The present offered a distracting tumult of antagonistic passions, harmonised by no great hope. The future, to those inexperienced pioneers of modern thought, was dim, although the haze, through which the vision came to them, seemed golden. Thus it happened that the sensibilities of men, athirst for some consoling fancy, took refuge in the dream of a past happy age. Virgil's description of Saturn's reign:

> Aureus hanc vitam in terris Saturnus agebat,
> Necdum etiam audierant inflari classica, necdum
> Impositos duris crepitare incudibus enses:

fascinated their imagination, and they amused themselves with the fiction of a primal state of innocence. Hesiod and the 'Metamorphoses' of Ovid, the Idylls of Theocritus and Virgil's Eclogues, legends of early

Greek civility, and romances of late Greek literature, contributed their several elements to this conception of a pastoral ideal. It blent with Biblical reminiscences of Eden, with mediæval stories of the Earthly Paradise. It helped that transfusion of Christian fancy into classic shape, for which the age was always striving.[1] On one side the ideal was purely literary, reflecting the artistic instincts of a people enthusiastic for form, and affording scope for their imitative activity. But on the other side it corresponded to a deep and genuine Italian feeling. That sympathy with rustic life, that love of nature humanised by industry, that delight in the villa, the garden, the vineyard, and the grove, which modern Italians inherited from their Roman ancestors, gave reality to what might otherwise have been but artificial. Vespasiano's anecdote of Cosimo de' Medici pruning his own fruit-trees; Ficino's description of the village feasts at Montevecchio; Flamminio's picture of his Latin farm; Alberti's tenderness in gazing at the autumn fields—all these have the ring of genuine emotion. For men who felt thus, the Age of Gold was no mere fiction, and Arcady a land of possibilities.

What has been well called *la voluttà idillica*—the sensuous sensibility to beauty, finding fit expression in the Idyll—formed a marked characteristic of Renaissance art and literature. Boccaccio developed this idyllic motive in all his works which dealt with the origins of society. Poliziano and Lorenzo devoted their best poetry to the praise of rural bliss, the happiness of shepherd folk anterior to life in cities. The same theme recurs in the Latin poems of the humanists, from the sonorous hexameters of the 'Rusticus' down to the delicate hendecasyllables of the later Lombard school. It pervades the elegy, the ode, the sonnet, and takes to itself the chiefest honours of the drama. The vision of a Golden Age idealised man's actual enjoyment of the country, and hallowed, as with inexplicable pathos, the details of ordinary rustic life. Weary with Courts and worldly pleasures, in moments of revolt against the passions and ambitions that wasted their best energies, the poets of that century, who were nearly always also men of state and public office, sighed for the good old times, when honour was an unknown name, and truth was spoken, and love sincere, and steel lay hidden in the earth, and ships sailed not the sea, and old age led the way to death unterrified by coming doom. As time advanced, their ideal took form and substance. There rose into existence, for the rhymesters to wander in, and for the readers of romance to dream about, a region called Arcadia, where all that was imagined of the Golden Age was found in combination with refined society and manners proper to the civil state. A literary Eldorado had been discovered, which was destined to attract explorers through the next three centuries. Arcadia became the wonder-world of noble youths and maidens, at Madrid no less than at Ferrara, in Elizabeth's London and in Marie Antoinette's Versailles. After engaging the genius of Tasso and Guarini,

[1] See above, Vol. I. p. 936, for the Golden Age in the *Quadriregio*.

Spenser and Sidney, it degenerated into quaint conventionality. Companions of Turenne and Marlborough told tales of pastoral love to maids of honour near the throne. Frederick's and Maria Theresa's courtiers simpered and sighed like Dresden-china swains and shepherdesses. Crooked sticks with ribbons at the top were a fashionable appendage to red-heeled shoes and powdered perukes. Few phenomena in history are more curious than the prolonged prosperity and widespread fascination of this Arcadian romance.

To Sannazzaro belongs the glory of having first explored Arcadia, mapped out its borders, and called it after his own name. He is the Columbus of this visionary hemisphere. Jacopo Sannazzaro has more than once above been mentioned in the chapters devoted to Latin poetry. But the events of his life have not yet been touched upon.[2] His ancestors claimed to have been originally Spaniards, settled in a village of Pavia called S. Nazzaro, whence they took their name. The poet's immediate forefather was said to have followed Charles of Durazzo in 1380 to the south of Italy, where he received fiefs and lands in the Basilicata. Jacopo was born at Naples in 1458, and was brought up in his boyhood by his mother at S. Cipriano.[3] He studied at Naples under the grammarian Junianus Maius,[4] and made such rapid progress in both Greek and Latin scholarship as soon to be found worthy of a place in Pontano's Academy. In that society he assumed the pseudonym of Actius Sincerus. The friendship between Pontano and Sannazzaro lasted without interruption till the former's death in 1503. Their Latin poems abound in passages which testify to a strong mutual regard, and the life size effigies of both may still be seen together in the church of Monte Oliveto at Naples.[5] Distinction in scholarship was, after the days of Alfonso the Magnanimous, a sure title to consideration at the Neapolitan Court. Sannazzaro attached himself to the person of Frederick, the second son of Ferdinand I.; and when this prince succeeded to the throne, he conferred upon the poet a pension of 600 ducats and the pleasant villa of Mergoglino between the city and Posilippo.[6] This recompense for past service was considerably below the poet's expectations and deserts; nor did he receive any post of state importance. Yet Sannazzaro remained faithful through his lifetime to the Aragonese dynasty. He attended the princes on their campaigns; espoused their quarrels in his fierce and potent series of epigrams against the Rovere and Borgia Pontiffs; and when Frederick retired to France in 1501, he

[2] The chief sources of Sannazzaro's biography are a section of his *Arcadia* (Prosa, vii.), and his Latin poems. The Sannazzari of Pavia had the honour of mention in Dante's *Convito*. Among the poet's Latin odes are several addressed to the patron saint of his race. See *Sannazarii op. omn. Lat. scripta* (Aldus, 1535), pp. 16, 53, 56, 59.

[3] Elegy, 'Quod pueritiam egerit in Picentinis,' *op. cit.* p. 27.

[4] Elegy, 'Ad Junianum Maium Præceptorem,' *op. cit.* p. 20.

[5] I may refer in particular to Sannazzaro's beautiful elegy, 'De Studiis suis et Libris Joviani Pontani' among his Latin poems, *op. cit.* p. 10. For their terra-cotta portraits, see Vol. I., *Revival of Learning*, p. 496.

[6] Sannazzaro's two odes on 'Villa Mergellina' and 'Fons Mergellines' (*op. cit.* pp. 31, 53) are among his purest and most charming Latin compositions.

journeyed into exile with his royal master, only returning to Naples after the ex-king's death. There Sannazzaro continued to reside until his own death in 1530. His later years were embittered by the destruction of his Villa Mergellina during the occupation of Naples by the imperial troops under the Prince of Orange. But with the exception of this misfortune, he appears to have passed a quiet and honourable old age, devoting himself to piety, contributing to charitable works and church-building, and employing his leisure in study and the society of a beloved lady, Cassandra Marchesa.

In his early youth Sannazzaro formed a romantic attachment for a girl of noble birth, called Carmosina Bonifacia. This love made him first a poet; and the majority of his Italian verses may be referred to its influence. They consist of sonnets and *canzoni*, modelled upon Petrarch, but marked by independence of treatment, and spontaneity of feeling. The puristic revival had not yet set in, and Sannazzaro's style shows no servile imitation of his model. It may not be out of place to give a specimen in translation of these early *Rime*. I have chosen a sonnet upon Jealousy, which La Casa afterwards found worthy of rehandling:

Horrible curb of lovers, Jealousy,
That with one force doth check and sway my will;
Sister of loathed and impious Death, that still
With thy grim face troublest the tranquil sky;
Thou snake concealed in laughing flowers which lie
Rocked on earth's lap; thou that my hope dost kill;
Amid fair fortunes thou malignant ill;
Venom mid viands which men taste and die!
From what infernal valley didst thou soar,
O ruthless monster, plague of mortals, thou
That darkenest all my days with misery o'er?
Hence, double not these griefs that cloud my brow!
Accurséd fear, why camest thou? Was more
Needed than Love's keen shafts to make me bow?

About the reality of Sannazzaro's passion for Carmosina there can be no doubt. The most directly powerful passages in the 'Arcadia' are those in which he refers to it.[7] His Southern temperament exposed him to the fiercest pangs of jealousy; and when he found that love disturbed his rest and preyed upon his health he resolved to seek relief in travel. For this purpose he went to France; but he could not long endure the exile from his native country, and on his return he found his Carmosina dead. The elegies in which he recorded his grief, are not the least poetical of his compositions both in Latin and Italian.[8]

[7] She is described in Prosa iv., and frequently mentioned under the name of *Arancio* or *Amaranta*.

[8] See the Epitaph 'Hic Amarantha jacet,' the last Eclogue of *Arcadia*, and the Latin Eclogue 'Mirabar vicina Mycon,' in which Carmosina is celebrated under the name of Phyllis. I may here call attention to Pontano's elegy beginning 'Harmosyne jacet hic' in the *Tumuli*, lib. ii. (*Joannis Joviani Pontani Amorum Libri, &c.*, Aldus, 1518, p. 87).

After establishing himself once more at Naples, Sannazzaro began the composition of the 'Eclogæ Piscatoriæ,' in which he has been said to have brought the pastoral Muses down to the seashore. The novelty of these poems secured for them no slight celebrity. Nor are they without real artistic merit. The charm of the sea is nowhere felt more vividly than on the bay of Naples, and nowhere else are the habits of a fishing population more picturesque. Nereids and Sirens, Proteus and Nisa, Cymothoe and Triton, are not out of place in modern verses, which can commemorate Naples, Ischia and Procida, under the titles of Parthenope, Inarime and Prochyte. Happy indeed is the poet, if he must needs write Latin elegies, whose home suggests such harmonies and cadences, for whom Baiæ and Cumæ and the Lucrine Lake, Puteoli and Capreæ and Stabiæ, are household words, and who looks from his study windows daily on scenes which realise the mythology still lingering in names and memories around them by beauty ever-present, inexpressible.

The second mistress of Sannazzaro's heart was a noble lady, Cassandra Marchesa. He paid his addresses to her *more Platonico*, and chose her for the object of refined compliments in classical and modern verse. The Latin elegies and epigrams are full of her praises; and one of the Eclogues, 'Pharmaceutria,' is inscribed with her name. It would scarcely have been necessary to mention this courtly attachment, but for the pleasant light it casts upon Sannazzaro's character. The lady whom he had celebrated and defended in his manhood, was the friend of his old age. He is said to have died in her house.

The 'Arcadia' was begun at Nocera in Sannazzaro's youth, continued during his first residence in France, and finished on his return to Naples. So much can be gathered from its personal references. The book blends autobiography and fable in a narrative of very languid interest. The poet's circumstances and emotions in exile are described at one moment in plain language, at another are presented with the indirectness of an allegory. Arcadia in some passage stands for a semi-savage country-district in France; in others it is the dream-world of poetry and pastoral simplicity. But in either case its scenery is drawn from Sannazzaro's own Italian home. The inhabitants are shepherds such as Virgil fancied, with even more of personal refinement. Through their lips the poet tells the tale of his own love, and paints his Neapolitan mistress among the nymphs of Mount Parthenion. Throughout, we note an awkward interminglement of subjective and objective points of view. Realism merges into fancy. Experience of life assumes the garb of myth or legend. Neither as an autobiographical romance nor again as a work of pure invention has the 'Arcadia' surpassing merit. Loose in construction and uncertain in aim, it lacks the clearness and consistency of perfect art. And yet it is a masterpiece; because its author, led by prescient instinct, contrived to make it reflect one of the deepest and most permanent emotions of his time. The whole pastoral ideal—the yearning after a golden age, the beauty and pathos of the country, the felicity of simple folk, the details of rustic life, the charm of woods and gardens, the mythology of Pan and Satyrs, Nymphs and Fauns—all this is expressed in a series of pictures, idyllically graceful, artistically felt. It is not for its story that we read 'Arcadia,' but for the Feast of Pales, the games at Massilia's shrine, the Sacrifice to Pan, Androgeo's tomb, the group of girls a-maying, the carved work of the beechen cup, the passion of Carino, the gardens with their flowers, and the bands of youths and maidens meeting under shadowy trees to dance and play. Pictures like these are presented with a scrupulous and loving sincerity, an anxious accuracy of studied style, which proves how serious was the author. His heart, as an artist, is in the realisation of his dream-world; and his touch is firm and dry and delicate as Mantegna's. Indeed, we are constantly reminded of the Mantegnesque manner, and one reference justifies the belief that Sannazzaro strove to reproduce its effect.[9] The sensuousness of the Italian feeling for mere beauty is tempered with reticence and something of the coldness of Greek marbles. In point of diction, Boccaccio has been obviously imitated. But Boccaccio's style is not revived, as Masuccio strove to revive it, with the fire and energy of Southern passion substituted for its Tuscan irony and delicacy. On the contrary, the periods are still more artificial, the turns of phrase more tortured. Sannazzaro writes with difficulty in a somewhat unfamiliar language, rendered all the more stubborn by his endeavours to add classical refinements. Boccaccio's humour is gone; his sensuality is purged by contact with antique examples; the waving groves of the 'Filocopo' are clipped and tutored like box-hedges in an academic garden. If there is less of natural raciness than came unsummoned to Boccaccio's aid, there is more of Virgil and Theocritus than he chose to appropriate. The slow deliberate expansion of each picture, stroke by stroke and touch by touch, reminds us of the *quattrocento* painters; while the *précieuseté* of the phrasing has affinity to the manner of a late Greek stylist, especially perhaps, though almost certainly unconsciously, to that of Philostratus. This close correspondence of the 'Arcadia' to the main artistic sympathies of the Renaissance, rendered it indescribably popular in its own age, and causes it still to rank as one of the representative masterpieces of the epoch. Through its peculiar blending of classical and modern strains—the feasts of Pales and of Pan taking colour from Capo di Monte superstitions; the nymphs of wood and river modelled after girls from Massa and Sorrento; the yellow-haired shepherds of Mount Mænalus singing love-laments for Neapolitan Carmosina—we are enabled more nearly than in almost any other literary essay to appreciate the spirit of the classical revival as it touched Italian art. A little earlier, there was more of spontaneity and *naïveté*. A little later, there was more of conscious erudition and consummate skill. The 'Arcadia' comes midway between the 'Filocopo' and the 'Pastor Fido.'

[9] In Prosa xi. he mentions a vase painted by the 'Padoano Mantegna, artefice sovra tutti gli altri accorto ed ingegnosissimo.'

It is time to turn from dissertation, and to detach, almost at haphazard, some of those descriptions which render the 'Arcadia' a storehouse of illustrations to the pictures of the fifteenth century. I will first select the frescoes on the front of Pales' chapel, endeavouring so far as possible to reproduce the intricacies and quaint affectations of the style.[10] The constant abuse of epithets, and the structure of the period by means of relatives, pegging its clauses down and keeping them in their places, will be noticed as part of the Boccaccesque tradition. 'Intending now to ratify with souls devout the vows which had been made in former times of need, upon the smoking altars, all together in company we went unto the sacred temple along whose frontal, raised upon a few ascending steps, we found above the doorway painted certain woods and hills of most delightful beauty, full of leafy trees and of a thousand sorts of flowers, among the which were seen many herds that went a-pasture, wending at pleasure through green fields, with peradventure ten dogs to guard them, the footsteps of the which upon the dust were traced most natural to the view. Of the shepherds, some were milking, some shearing wool, others playing on pipes, and there were there a few, who, as it seemed, were singing and endeavouring to keep in tune with these. But that which pleased me to regard with most attention were certain naked Nymphs, the which behind a chestnut bole stayed, as it were, half-hidden, laughing at a ram, who, in his eagerness to gnaw a wreath of oak that hung before his eyes, forgot to feed upon the grass around him. In that while came four Satyrs, with horns upon their heads and goats' feet, stealing through a shrubbery of lentisks, softly, softly, to take the maidens from behind. Whereof when they were ware, they took to flight through the dense grove, shunning nor thorns nor aught else that might annoy them; and of these one, nimbler than the rest, was clinging to a hornbeam's branches, and thence, with a long bough in her hands, defending herself. The others had cast themselves through fright into a river, where through they fled a-swimming; and the clear water hid little or but nothing of their snow-white flesh. But whenas they saw themselves escaped, they sat them down upon the further bank, fordone with toil and panting, drying their soaked hair, and thence with word and gesture seemed to mock at those who had not shown the power to capture them. And in one of the sides there was Apollo, with the yellowest hair, leaning upon a wand of wild olive, and watching Admetus' herds beside a river-bed; and thus, intently gazing on two sinewy bulls which jousted with their horns, he was not ware of wily Mercury, who in a shepherd's habit, with a kid-skin girded under his left shoulder, stole the cows away from him. And in that same space stood Battus, the bewrayer of the theft, transformed into a stone, stretching his finger forth in act of one who pointed. A little lower, Mercury was seen again, seated upon a large stone, and playing with swollen cheeks upon a rustic pipe, while his eyes were turned to mark a white calf close beside him, and with most

[10] Prosa iii.

cunning arts he strove to cozen Argus of the many eyes. On the other side, at the foot of an exceeding high oak-tree, was stretched a shepherd asleep among his goats; and a dog stayed near him, smelling at his pouch, which lay beneath his head; and he, forasmuch as the moon gazed at him with glad eyes, methought must be Endymion. Next to him was Paris, who with his sickle had begun to carve *Œnone* on an elm-tree's bark, and being called to judge between the naked goddesses that stood before him, had not yet been able to complete his work. But what was not less subtle in the thought than pleasant in the seeing was the shrewdness of the wary painter, who, having made Juno and Minerva of such extreme beauty that to surpass them was impossible, and doubting of his power to make Venus so lovely as the tale demanded, had painted her with back turned, covering the defect of art by ingenuity of invention. And many other things right charming and most beautiful to look upon, of the which I now have but a faulty memory, I saw there painted upon divers places.' It is clear that Sannazzaro had not read Lessing's 'Laocoon' or noted the distinctions between poetry and painting. Yet in this he was true to the spirit of his age; for actions no less continuous than some of those described by him, may be found represented in the frescoes of Gozzoli or Lippo Lippi.

The finished portrait of Sannazzaro's mistress Carmosina shall supply my next quotation.[11] The exile is listening to shepherds singing, and one of them has mentioned Amaranta. He knows that she is present, and resolves to choose her by her gestures from the rest. 'With wary glance, watching now one and now another, I saw among the maidens one who seemed to me the loveliest. Her hair was covered with a very thin veil, beneath which two eyes, lovely and most brilliant, sparkled not otherwise than the clear stars are wont to shine in a serene and limpid sky; and her face, inclining somewhat to the oval more than the round, of fair shape, with a pallor that was not unpleasing, but tempered, as it were toward dark complexion turning, and relieved therewith by vermeil and gracious hues, filled with joy of love the eyes that gazed on her. Her lips were of the sort that surpass the morning roses; between the which, each time she spoke or smiled, she showed some portion of her teeth, of such rare and marvellous grace that I could not have compared them to aught else but orient pearls. Thence passing down to her marble and delicate throat, I saw upon that tender bosom the slight and youthful breasts, which, like two rounded apples, thrust her robe of finest texture somewhat forward; and in the midst of them I could discern the fairest little way, exceeding pleasant to the sight, the which, because it ended and escaped the view, was reason why I dwelt thereon with greater force of thought. And she, with most delicate gait and a gentle and aspiring stature, went through the fair fields, with her white hand plucking tender flowers. With the which when she had filled her lap, no sooner had the singing youth within her hearing mentioned Amaranta, than, dropping her hands and

[11] Prosa iv.

gathered robe, and as it were lost to her own recollection, without her knowing what befell, they all slid from her grasp, sowing the earth with peradventure twenty sorts of colours. Which, as though suddenly brought to herself, when she perceived, she blushed not otherwise than sometimes reddens the enchanted moon with rosy aspect, or as, upon the issuing of the sun, the red Aurora shows herself to mortal gaze. Whereupon she, not for any need methinks compelling her thereto, but haply hoping better thus to hide the blushes that came over her, begotten by a woman's modesty, bent toward earth again to pick them up, as though she cared for only that, choosing the white flowers from the crimson and the dark blue from the violet blossoms.' Amaranta makes a pretty picture, but one which is too elaborate in detail. Her sisterhood is described with touches more negligent, and therefore the more artful.[12] 'Some wore garlands of privet with yellow buds and certain crimson intermingled; others had white lilies and purple mixed with a few most verdant orange leaves between; one went starred with roses, and yon other whitened with jasmines. So that each by herself and all together were more like to divine spirits than to human creatures. Whereupon many men there present cried with wonder: O blessed the possessor of such beauties!' The young swains are hardly less attractive than their nymphs.[13] 'Logisto and Elpino, shepherds, comely of person and in years within the bounds of earliest youth: Elpino guardian of goats, Logisto of the woolly sheep: both with hair yellower than ripe ears of corn; both of Arcadia; both fit alike to sing and to make answer.'

Sannazzaro's touch upon inanimate nature is equally precise. Here is a description of the evening sky.[14] 'It was the hour when sunset embroidered all the west with a thousand varieties of clouds; some violet, some darkly blue, and certain crimson; others between yellow and black, and a few so burning with the fire of backward-beaten rays that they seemed as though of polished and finest gold.' Here is a garden:[15] 'Moved by sympathy for Ergasto, many shepherds had moreover wrought the place about with high hedges, not of thorns or briars, but of junipers, roses and jasmines, and had delved therein with their mattocks a pastoral seat, and at even spaces certain towers of rosemary and myrtles interwoven with the most incomparable art.' Here are flowers:[16] 'There were lilies, there privets, there violets toned to amorous pallor, and in large abundance the slumberous poppies with their leaning heads, and the ruddy spikes of the immortal amaranth, most comely of coronals mid winter's rudeness.'

The same research of phrase marks the exhibition of emotion. Carino, the shepherd, tells how, overwhelmed with grief, he lay upon the ground and seemed lost to life:[17] 'Came the oxherds, came the herdsmen of the sheep and goats, together with the peasants of the neighbouring farms, deeming me distraught, as of a truth indeed I was; and all with deepest pity asked the reason of my woe. Unto whom I made no

[12] Prosa iv. [13] *Ibid.* [14] Prosa v.
[15] Prosa x. [16] *Ibid.* [17] Prosa viii.

answer, but, minding my own weeping, thus with lamentable voice exclaimed: You of Arcady shall sing among your mountains of my death! You of Arcady, who only have the art of song, you of my death shall sing amid your mountains!' His complaint extends to a length which defies quotation. But here is an extract from it:[18] 'O gods of heaven and earth, and whosoe'er ye are who have regard for wretched lovers, lend, I pray, your ears of pity to my lamentation, and listen to the dolent cries my tortured spirit sendeth forth! O Naiads, dwellers in the running water brooks! O Napean nymphs, most gracious haunters of far places and of liquid founts, lift up your yellow tresses but a little from the crystal waves, and receive these my last cries before I perish! O you, O fairest Oreads, who naked on the hanging cliffs are wont to go a-chase, leave now your lofty mountain realm, and in my misery visit me, for I am sure to win your sorrow by what brings my cruel maid delight! Come forth from your trees, O pitying Hamadryads, ye anxious guardians over them, and turn your thoughts a little toward the martyrdom these hands of mine prepare for me! And you, O Dryads, most beauteous damsels of the woods profound, ye who not once but many and many a time have watched our shepherds at the fall of even in circle dancing neath the shadow of cool walnut trees, with yellowish curls a-ripple down their snow-white necks, cause now I pray, if you are not with my too changeful fortune changed, that mid these shades my death may not be mute, but ever grow from day to day through centuries to come, so that the tale of years life lacks, may go to lengthen out my fame!'

For English students the 'Arcadia' has a special interest, since it begot the longer and more ambitious work of Sir Philip Sidney. Hitherto I have spoken only of its prose; but the book blends prose and verse in alternating sections. The verse consists of mingled *terza rima*, *canzoni* and sestines. Not less artificial and decidedly less original than the prose, Sannazzaro's lyrics and eclogues do not demand particular attention. He put needless restraint upon himself by affecting the awkwardness of *sdrucciolo* rhymes;[19] and he lacked the roseate fluency, the winning ease, the unaffected graces of Poliziano. One sestine, sung by himself among the shepherds of Arcady, I have translated, because it paints the actual conditions of life which drove Sannazzaro into his first exile.[20] But the singularly charmless form adopted, which even Petrarch hardly rendered tolerable, seems to check the poet's spontaneity of feeling.

> Even as a bird of night that loathes the sun,
> I wander, woe is me, through places dark,
> The while refulgent day doth shine on earth;

[18] *Ibid.*
[19] Even in this Sidney tried to follow him, with an effect the clumsiness of which can only be conceived by those who have read his triple-rhyming English *terza rima*.
[20] Egloga vii.

Then when upon the world descendeth eve,
I cannot, like all creatures, sink in sleep,
But wake to roam and weep among the fields.

If peradventure amid woods and fields,
Where shines not with his radiance the sun,
Mine eyes, o'er-tired with weeping, close in sleep,
Harsh dreams and wandering visions, vain and dark,
Affright me so that still I shrink at eve,
For fear of sleep, from resting on the earth.

O universal mother, kindly earth,
Shall 't ever be that, stretched on verdant fields,
In slumber deep, upon that latest eve,
I ne'er shall wake again, until the sun
Rise to reveal his light to eyelids dark,
And stir my soul again from that long sleep?

From that first moment when I banished sleep,
And left my bed to lay myself on earth,
The cloudless days for me were drear and dark,
And turned to stubbly straw the flowery fields;
So that when morn to men brings back the sun,
It darkens round mine eyes in shadowy eve.

My lady, of her kindness, came one eve,
Joyous and very fair, to me in sleep,
And gladdened all my heart, even as the sun,
When rains are past, is wont to clear the earth;
And said to me: Come, gather from my fields
Some flow'ret; cease to haunt those caverns dark.

Fly hence, fly hence, ye tedious thoughts and dark,
That have obscured me in so long an eve!
For I'll go seek the sunny smiling fields,
Taking upon their herbage honeyed sleep:
Full well I know that ne'er man made of earth
More blest than now I am beheld the sun!

Song, in mid eve thou'lt see the orient sun,
And me neath earth among those regions dark,
Or e'er on yonder fields I take my sleep.

Whether the distinctively Neapolitan note can be discerned in Sannazzaro, seems more than doubtful. As in his Sapphic Odes and Piscatory Eclogues, so also in his 'Arcadia' we detect the working of a talent self-restrained within the limits of finely tempered taste. The case is very different with Pontano's Latin elegies and lyrics.[21] They breathe the sensuality and self-abandonment to impulse of a Southern tempera-

[21] From my chapter on Latin poetry in Vol. I., *Revival of Learning*, I purposely omitted more than a general notice of Pontano's erotic verses, intending to treat of them thereafter, when it should be necessary to discuss the Neapolitan contribution to Italian literature. The lyrics and elegies I shall now refer to, are found in two volumes of *Pontani Opera*, published by Aldus, 1513 and 1518. These volumes I shall quote together, using the minor titles of *Amorum*, *Hendecasyllabi*, and so forth, and mentioning the page. I am sorry that I have not a uniform edition of his Latin poetry (if that, indeed, exists, of which I doubt) before me.

ment. They reflect the profuseness of nature in a region where men scarcely know what winter means, her somewhat too nakedly voluptuous beauties, her volcanic energies and interminglement of living fire with barren scoriæ. For this reason, and because there is some danger of neglecting the special part played by the Southern Province in Italian literary history, I am induced to digress from the main topic of this chapter in the direction of Pontano's poetry.

Though a native of Cerreto in Umbria, Pontano passed his life at Naples, and became, if we may trust the evidence of his lyrics, more Neapolitan than the Neapolitans. In him the Southern peoples found a voice, which, though it uttered a dead language, expressed their sentiments. It is unlucky that Pontano, who deserves to be reckoned as the greatest poet of Naples, should have made this important contribution to Italian literature in Latin. Whether at that moment he could have spoken so freely in the vulgar tongue is more than doubtful. But be that as it may, we must have recourse to his Latin poems, in order to supply a needed link in the chain of Italian melody. Carducci acutely remarked that, more than any other poems of the century, they embody 'the æsthetic and learned reaction against the mystical idealism of Christianity in a preceding age.' They do so better than Beccadelli's, because, where the 'Hermaphroditus' is obscene, the 'Eridanus,' 'Baiæ,' 'Amor Conjugalis,' 'Pompæ,' 'Næniæ' of Pontano are only sensual. The cardinal point in Pontano is the breadth of his feeling. He touches the whole scale of natural emotions with equal passion and sincerity. The love of the young man for his sweetheart, the love of the husband for his bride, the love of a father for his offspring, the love of a nurse for her infant charge, find in his verse the same full sensuous expression. In Pontano there is no more of Teutonic *Schwärmerei* than of Dantesque transcendentalism. He does not make us marvel how the young man, who has embroidered odes upon the theme of 'Alma Pellegrina,' or who has woven violet and moonshine into some 'Du bist wie eine Blume,' can submit to light the hymeneal torch and face the prose of matrimony. Within the limits of unsophisticated instinct he is perfectly complete and rounded to a flawless whole. He does not say one thing and leave another to be understood—a contradiction that imports some radical unreality into the Platonic or sentimental modes of sexual expression. He expects woman to weigh but little less than man in scales of natural appetite. And yet his Muse is no mere vagrant Venus. She is a respectable if not, according to our present views, an altogether decent Juno. The final truth about her is that she revealed to her uniquely gifted bard, on earth and in the shrine of home, that poetry of love, which Milton afterwards mythologised in Eden. The note of unadulterated humanity sounds with a clearness that demands commemoration in this poetry of passion. It is, if not the highest, yet the frankest and most decided utterance of mutual, legitimate desire. As such, it occupies an enviable place in the history of Italian love—equally apart from *trecento* sickliness and *cinque cento* corruption: unrefined perchance, but healthy; doing justice to the proletariat of Naples whence it sprang.

Pontano paints all primitive affections in a way to justify his want of reticence. His Fannia, Focilla, Stella, Ariadne, Cinnama—mistress or wife, we need not stop to question—are the very opposite of Dante's or of Petrarch's loves.[22] Liberal of their charms, rejoicing like the waves of the Chiaja in the laughter of the open day, they think it no shame to unbare their beauties to their lover's eyes, or to respond with ardour to his caresses. Christian modesty, mediæval asceticism, the strife between the spirit and the flesh, the aspiration after mystic modes of feeling, have been as much forgotten in their portraits, as though the world had never undergone reaction against paganism. And yet they differ from the women of the Roman elegiac poets. They are less artificial than Corinna. Though 'The sweet witty soul of Ovid' passed over these honeyed elegies, the Neapolitan poet remains a *bourgeois* of the fifteenth century. His passion is unreservedly sensual and at the same time tenderly affectionate. Its motive force is sexual desire; its depth and strength are in the love a husband and a father feels. Given the verses upon Fannia alone, we should be justified in calling Pontano a lascivious poet. The three books 'De Amore Conjugali' show him in a different light. He there expounds the duties and relations of the family with the same robust and unaffected force of feeling he had shown in the description of a wanton. After painting his Stella with the gusto of an Italian Rubens, he can turn to shed tears almost sublime in their pathos over the tomb of Lucia, his daughter, or to write a cradle-song for his son Luciolus.[23] The carnal appetites which are legitimated by matrimony and hallowed in domestic relations, but which it is the custom of civilised humanity to veil, assume a tone of almost Bacchic rapture in this fluent Latin verse. This constitutes Pontano's originality. Such a combination has never been presented to the world before or since. The genial bed, from which he draws his inspiration, found few poets to appreciate it in ancient days, and fewer who have dared to celebrate it so unblushingly among the moderns.[24]

[22] Fannia is the most attractive of these women. See *Amorum*, lib. i. pp. 4, 5, 13. Stella, the heroine of the *Eridani*, is touched with greater delicacy. Cinnama seems to have been a girl of the people. Pontano borrows for her the language of popular poetry (*Amorum*, i. 19).

> Ipsa tibi dicat, mea lux, mea vita, meus flos,
> Liliolumque meum, basiolumque meum.
> Carior et gemmis, et caro carior auro,
> Tu rosa, tu violæ, tu mihi lævis onyx.

[23] Among the most touching of his elegiac verses is the lament addressed to his dead wife upon the death of their son Lucius, *Eridanorum*, lib. ii. p. 134. The collection of epitaphs called *Tumuli* bears witness to the depth and sincerity of his sorrow for the dead, to the all-embracing sympathy he felt for human grief. The very original series of lullabies, entitled *Næniæ*, illustrate the warmth of his paternal feeling. The nursery has never before or since been celebrated with such exuberance of fancy—and in the purest Ovidian elegiacs! It may, however, be objected that there is too much about wet-nurses in these songs.

[24] Pontano revels in Epithalamials and pictures of the joys of wedlock. See the series of elegies on Stella, *Eridanorum*, lib. i. pp. 108, 111, 113, 115; the congratulation

The same series of Pontano's poems may be read with no less profit for their pictures of Neapolitan life.[25] He brings the baths of Baiæ, unspoiled as yet by the eruption from Monte Nuovo, vividly before us; the myrtle-groves and gardens by the bay; the sailors stretched along the shore; the youths and maidens flirting as they bathe or drink the waters, their evening walks, their little dinners, their assignations; all the round of pleasure in a place and climate made for love. Or we watch the people at their games, crowded together on those high-built carts, rattling the tambourine and dancing the tarantella—as near to fauns and nymphs in shape as humanity well may be.[26] Each mountain and each stream is personified; the genii of the villages, the Oreads of the copses, the Tritons of the waves, come forth to play with men:[27]

> Claudicat hinc heros Capimontius, et de summo
> Colle ruunt misti juvenes mistæque puellæ;
> Omnis amat chorus, et juncti glomerantur amantes.
> Is lento incedit passu, baculoque tuetur
> Infirmum femur, et choreis dat signa movendis,
> Assuetus choreæ ludisque assuetus amantum.

Nor are these personifications merely frigid fictions. The landscape of Naples lends itself to mythology, not only because it is so beautiful, but because human life and nature interpenetrate, as nowhere else in Europe, on that bay. Pontano has a tale to tell of every river and every grove—how Adonis lives again in the orange trees of Sorrento, how the Sebeto was a boy beloved by one of Nereus' daughters and slain by him in anger.[28] His tendency to personification was irresistible. Not content, like Sannazzaro, with singing the praises of his villa, he feigns a Nympha Antiniana, whom he invokes as the Muse of neo-Latin lyric rapture.[29] In the melodious series of love-poems entitled 'Eridanus,' he exercises the same imaginative faculty on Lombard scenery. After closing this little book, we seem to be no less familiar with the 'king of rivers,' Phaethon, and the Heliades, than with the living Stella, to frame whose beauty in a fitting wreath these fancies have been woven.[30] Even the Elegy, which he used so freely and with

addressed to Alfonso, Duke of Calabria, *Hendecasyllaborum*, lib. i. p. 194; and two among the many Epithalamial hymns, *Hendec.* lib. i. p. 195; *Lepidina*, Pompa 7, p. 172, with its reiterated 'Dicimus o hymenæe Io hymen hymenæe.' The sensuality of these compositions will be too frank and fulsome for a chastened taste; but there is nothing in them extra or infra-human.

[25] *Hendecasyllaborum*, lib. i. and ii. pp. 186-218. If one of these lyrics should be chosen from the rest, I should point to 'Invitantur pueri et puellæ ad audiendum Charitas,' p. 209. It begins 'Ad myrtum juvenes venite, myrti.'

[26] For such glimpses into actual life, see *Lepidina*, pp. 160-174, in which a man and woman of Naples discourse of their first loves and wedlock. The Eclogues abound in similar material.

[27] *Lepidina*, p. 168. Capimontius is easily recognised as Capo di Monte.

[28] See *De Hortis Hesperidum*, p. 139, and *Amorum*, lib. ii. p. 33.

[29] *Versus Lyrici*, pp. 91-94.

[30] See, for example, the elegy 'De Venere lavante se in Eridano et quiescente,' *Erid.* lib. i. p. 118.

so complete a pleasure in its movement, becomes for him a woman, with specific form and habit, and a love-tale taken from some Propertian memory of the poet's Umbrian home. To quote Pontano is neither easy nor desirable. Yet I cannot resist the inclination to present Dame Elegia in her Ionian garb in part at least before a modern audience.[31]

> Huc ades, et nitidum myrto compesce capillum,
> Huc ades ornatis o Elegia comis.
> Inque novam venias cultu prædivite formam,
> Laxa fluat niveos vestis adusque pedes.
> Quaque moves, Arabum spires mollissima nardum,
> Lenis et Assyrio sudet odore liquor.
> Tecum etiam Charites veniant, tua cura, puellæ,
> Et juvet insolita ducere ab arte choros.
> Tu puerum Veneris primis lasciva sub annis
> Instruis, et studio perficis usque tuo.
> Hinc tibi perpetuæ tribuit Cytherea juventæ
> Tempora, neu formæ sint mala damna tuæ;
> Ergo ades, et cape, diva, lyram, sed pectine molli,
> Sed moveas dulci lenia fila sono.
> Quinetiam tu experta novos, ni fallor, amores,
> Dulcia supposito gramine furta probas.
> Namque ferunt, patrios vectam quandoque per Umbros,
> Clitumni liquidis accubuisse vadis:
> Hic juvenem vidisse, atque incaluisse natantem,
> Et cupisse ulnas inter habere tuas.
> Quid tibi lascivis, puer o formose, sub undis?
> Deliciis mage sunt commoda prata tuis.
> Hic potes e molli viola junxisse coronam,
> Et flavam vario flore ligare comam;
> Hic potes et gelida somnum quæsisse sub umbra,
> Et lassum viridi ponere corpus humo;
> Hic et adesse choris Dryadum, et saluisse per herbas,
> Molliaque ad teneros membra movere modos.
> Hic juvenis succensus amor, formamque secutus
> Et facilem cantum, quo capis ipsa deos,

[31] *De Amore Conjugali*, lib. i. p. 35. 'Hither, and bind with myrtle thy shining hair! O hither, Elegia, with the woven tresses! Take a new form of sumptuous grace, and let thy loose robe flutter to thy snow-white feet. And where thou movest, breathe Arabian nard, and blandest perfume of Assyrian unguents. Let the girl Graces come, thy charge, with thee, and take their joy in dances woven with unwonted arts. Thou in his earliest years dost teach the boy of Venus, and instruct him in thy lore. Wherefore Cytherea gives thee perpetual youth, that never may thy beauty suffer decrease. Come hither, then, and take, O goddess, thy lyre, but with a gentle quill, and move the soft strings to a dulcet sound, Nay, thou thyself hast tried new pleasures, and knowest the sweet thefts of lovers laid on meadow grass. For they say that, wandering once in Umbria, my home, thou didst lie down beside Clitumnus' liquid pools; and there didst see a youth, and dote upon him while he swam, and long to hold him in thine arms. What dost thou, beauteous boy, beneath the wanton waves? These fields are better suited to thy joys! Here canst thou weave a violet wreath, and bind thy yellow hair with flowers of many a hue! Here canst thou sleep beneath cool shade, and rest thy body on the verdant ground! Here join the dances of the Dryads, and leap along the sward, and move thy supple limbs to tender music! The youth inflamed with this, and eager for the beauty and the facile song, wherewith thou captivatest gods, with thee among the willows, under a vine-mantled elm, joined his white limbs upon a grassy bed, and both enjoyed the bliss of love.'

Tecum inter salices, sub amicata vitibus ulmo,
In molli junxit candida membra toro;
Inter et amplexus lassi jacuistis uterque,
Et repetita venus dulce peregit opus.

That this poet was no servile imitator of Tibullus or Ovid is clear. That he had not risen to their height of diction is also manifest. But in Pontano, as in Poliziano, Latin verse lived again with new and genuine vitality.

If it were needful to seek a formal return from this digression to the subject of my chapter, there would be no lack of opportunity. Pontano's Eclogues, the description of his gardens, his vision of the golden age and his long discourse on the cultivation of orange trees, justify our placing him among the strictly pastoral poets.[32] In treating of the country he displays his usual warmth and sensuous realism. He mythologises; but his myths are the substantial forms of genuine emotion and experience. The Fauns he talks of, are such lads as even now may be seen upon the Ischian slopes of Monte Epomeo, with startled eyes, brown skin, and tangled tresses tossed adown their sinewy shoulders. The Bacchus of his vintage has walked, red from the wine-press, crowned with real ivy and vine, and sat down at the poet's elbow, to pledge him in a cup of foaming must.

While Sannazzaro was exploring Arcadia at Naples, Poliziano had already transferred pastoral poetry to the theatre at Mantua. Of the 'Orfeo' and its place in Italian literature, I have spoken sufficiently elsewhere. It is enough to remember, in the present connexion, that, while Arcady became the local dreamland of the new ideal, Orpheus took the place of its hero. As the institutor of civil society in the midst of a rude population, he personified for our Italian poets the spirit of their own renascent culture. Arcadia represented the realm of art and song, unstirred by warfare or unworthy passions. Orpheus attuned the simple souls who dwelt in it, to music with his ravishing lyre.

Pastoral representations soon became fashionable. Niccolò da Correggio put the tale of Cephalus and Procris on the stage at Ferrara, with choruses of nymphs, vows to Diana, eclogues between Corydon and Thyrsis, a malignant Faun, and a *dea ex machinâ* to close the scene.[33] At Urbino in the carnival of 1506 Baldassare Castiglione and his friend Cesare Gonzaga recited amœbean stanzas, attired in pastoral dress, before the Court. This eclogue, entitled 'Tirsi,' deserves notice, less perhaps for its intrinsic merits, though these, judged by the standard of bucolic poetry, are not slight, than because it illustrates the worst vices of the rustic style in its adaptation to fashionable usage.[34] The dialogue opens with the customary lament of one love-lorn shepherd to another, and turns upon time-honoured bucolic themes, until the

[32] I will only refer in detail to the elegy entitled 'Lætatur in villa et hortis suis constitutis' (*De Amore Conjugali*, lib. ii. p. 52). The two books *De Hortis Hesperidum* (Aldus, 1513, pp. 138-159) compose a typical didactic poem.

[33] It was printed in 1486.

[34] See the *Poesie Volgari e Latine del Conte B. Castiglione* (Roma, 1760), pp. 7-26.

mention of Metaurus reminds us that we are not really in Arcadia but at Urbino. The goddess who strays among her nymphs along its bank, is no other than the Duchess, attended by Emilia Pia and the other ladies of her Court. 'The good shepherd, who rules these happy fields and holy lands,' is Duke Guidubaldo. Then follow compliments to all the interlocutors of the 'Cortegiano.' Bembo is the shepherd, 'who hither came from the bosom of Hadria.' The 'ancient shepherd, honoured by all, who wears a wreath of sacred laurel,' is Morello da Ortona. The Tuscan shepherd, 'wise and learned in all arts,' must either be Bernardo Accolti or else Giuliano de' Medici. And yonder shepherd from the Mincio is Lodovico da Canossa. A chorus of shepherds and a morris-dance relieved the recitation, which was also enlivened by the introduction of one solo, sung by Iola. Thus in this early specimen of the pastoral masque we observe that confusion of things real and things ideal, of past and present, of imaginary rustics and living courtiers, which was destined to prove the bane of the species and to render it a literary plague in every European capital. The radical fault existed in Virgil's treatment of the Syracusan idyll. But each remove from its source rendered the falsehood more obnoxious. In Spenser's Eclogues the awkwardness is greater than in Castiglione's. Before Teresa Maria the absurdity was more apparent than before Elizabeth. At last the common sense of the public could no longer tolerate the sham, and Arcadia, with its make-believe and flattery and allegory, became synonymous with affectation.

It is no part of my programme to follow the development of the pastoral drama through all its stages in Italy.[35] For the end of this chapter I reserve certain necessary remarks upon its masterpieces, the 'Aminta' and the 'Pastor Fido.' At present it will suffice to indicate the fact that, on the stage, as in the eclogue, bucolic poetry followed two distinct directions—the one Arcadian and artificial, the other national and closely modelled on popular forms. The 'Nencia da Barberino' and 'Beca da Dicomano' of Lorenzo de' Medici and Luigi Pulci belong to the latter class of eclogues.[36] Their corresponding forms in dramatic verse are Berni's 'Catrina' and 'Mogliazzo,' together with the 'Tancia' and 'Fiera' of Michelangelo Buonarroti the younger.[37] If it is impossible to render any adequate account of pastoral drama, to do this for bucolic idylls would be no less difficult. Their name in Latin

[35] To do so would be almost impossible within lesser limits than those of a bulky volume. Anyone who wishes to form a conception of the multitudes of pastoral plays written and printed in Italy, may consult the catalogues. I have before me one list, which I do not believe to be complete, in the *Teatro Italiano*, vol. x. It occupies twenty-seven closely printed pages, and is devoted solely to rural scenes of actual life. The Arcadian masques and plays are omitted. Mutinelli, in the *Annali Urbani di Venezia*, p. 541, gives a list of the shows performed at Doges' banquets between 1574 and 1605. The large majority are pastoral; and it is noticeable that, as years go on, the pastorals drive all other forms of drama out of the field.

[36] See above, pp. 88, 89.

[37] For Berni, see Barbèra's small edition, Florence, 1863. For Buonarroti, Lemonnier's edition in two volumes, 1860.

and Italian is legion. Poets so different in all things else as were Girolamo Benivieni, Antonio Tebaldeo, Speron Sperone, Bernardino Baldi, Benedetto Varchi, and Luigi Tansillo—to mention only men of some distinction—brought Mopsus and Tityrus, Menalcas and Melibæus, Amaryllis and Cydippe, from Virgil's Arcadia, and made them talk interminably of their loves and sheep in delicate Italian.[38] Folengo's sharp satiric wit, as we shall remark in another chapter, finally pursued them with the shafts of ridicule in 'Baldus' and 'Zanitonella.' Thus pastoral poetry completed the whole cycle of Italian literature—expressed itself through dialogue in the drama, adhered to Virgilian precedent in the Latinists and their Italian followers, adopted the forms of popular poetry, and finally submitted to the degradation of Maccaronic burlesque.

We can well afford to turn in silence from the common crowd of eclogue-writers. Yet one poet emerges from the rank and file, and deserves particular attention. Francesco Maria Molza stood foremost in his own day among scholars of ripe erudition and literary artists of accomplished skill. His high birth, his genial conversation, his loves and his misfortunes rendered him alike illustrious; and his 'Ninfa Tiberina' is still the sweetest pastoral of the golden age. Molza was born in 1489 at Modena. Since his parents were among the richest and noblest people of that city, it is probable that he acquired the Greek and Latin scholarship, for which he was in after-life distinguished, under tutors at home. At the age of sixteen he went to Rome in order to learn Hebrew, and was at once recognised as a youth of more than ordinary promise by men like Marcantonio Flamminio and Lilio Giraldi. In 1512 he returned to Modena, where he married according to his rank. His wife brought him four children, and he passed a few years at this period with his family. But Molza soon wearied of domestic and provincial retirement. In 1516 he left home again and plunged into the dissipations of Roman life. From this date forward till his death in 1544 he must be reckoned among those Italians for whom Rome was dearer than their native cities. The brilliance of his literary fame and the affection felt for him by men of note in every part of Italy will not distract attention from the ignobility of his career. Faithless to his wife, neglectful of his children, continually begging money from his father, he passed his manhood in a series of amours. Some of these were respectable, but most of them disreputable. A certain Furnia, a low-born Beatrice Paregia, and the notorious Faustina Mancina are to be mentioned among the women who from time to time enslaved him. In the course of his intrigue with Beatrice he received a stab in the back from some obscure rival, which put him in peril of his life. For Faustina he composed the 'Ninfa Tiberina.' She was a Roman courtesan, so famous for her beauty and fine breeding as to attract the sympathy of even severe natures. When she died, the town went

[38] See *Poesie Pastorali e Rusticali* (Milano, *Classici Italiani*, 1808), for a fairly representative collection of these authors.

into mourning, and the streets echoed with elegiac lamentations. It is curious that among Michelangelo's sonnets should be found one—not, however, of the best—written upon this occasion. While seeking amusement with the Imperias, who took Aspasia's place in Papal Rome, Molza formed a temporary attachment for a more illustrious lady—the beautiful and witty Camilla Gonzaga. He passed two years, between 1523 and 1525, in her society at Bologna. After his return to Rome, Molza witnessed the miseries of the sack, which made so doleful an impression on his mind that, saddened for a moment, he retired like the prodigal to Modena. Rome, however, although not destined to regain the splendour she had lost, shook off the dust and blood of 1527; and there were competent observers who, like Aretino, thought her still more reckless in vice than she had been before. Molza could not long resist the attractions of the Papal city. In 1529 we find him once more in Rome, attached to the person of Ippolito de' Medici, and delighting the Academies with his wit. Two years afterwards, his father and mother died on successive days of August. Molza celebrated their death in one of the most lovely of his many sonnets. But his ill life and obstinate refusal to settle at Modena had disinherited him; and henceforth he lived upon his son Camillo's bounty. To follow his literary biography at this period would be tantamount to writing the history of the two famous Academies *delle Virtù* and *de' Vignaiuoli*. Of both he was a most distinguished member. He amused them with his conversation, recited before them his *Capitoli*, and charmed them with the softness and the sweetness of his manners. Numbers of his sonnets commemorate the friendships he made in those urbane circles.

From the interchange, indeed, of occasional poems between such men as Molza, Soranzo, Gandolfo, Caro, Varchi, Guidiccioni, and La Casa, the materials for forming a just conception of the inner life of men of letters at that epoch must be drawn. They breathe a spirit of gentle urbanity, enlivened by jests, and saddened by a sense, rather uneasy than oppressive, of Italian disaster. The moral tone is pensive and relaxed; and in spite of frequent references to a corrupt Church and a lost nation, scarcely one spark of rage or passion flashes from the dreamy eyes that gaze at us. Leave us alone, they seem to say; it is true that Florence has been enslaved, and the shadow of disgrace rests upon our Rome; but what have we to do with it? And then they turn to indite sonnets on Faustina's hair or elegies upon her modesty;[39] and when they are tired with these recreations, meet together to invent ingenious obscenities.[40] It was in the midst of such trifling that the great misfortune of Molza's life befell him. The disease of the Renaissance, not the least of Italy's scourges in those latter days of heedlessness and dissolute living, overtook him in some haunt of pleasure. After 1539 he languished miserably under the infliction, and died of it, having first

[39] Of Molza's many sonnets upon this woman and her death, see especially Nos. cxi. cxii.

[40] In the chapter on Burlesque Poetry I shall have to justify this remark.

suffered a kind of slow paralysis, in February 1544. During the last months of his illness his thoughts turned to the home and children he had deserted. The exquisitely beautiful Latin elegy, in which he recorded the misery of slow decay, speaks touchingly, if such a late and valueless repentance can be touching, of his yearning for them.[41] In the autumn of 1543, accordingly, he managed to crawl back to Modena; and it was there he breathed his last, offering to the world, as his biographer is careful to assure us, a rare example of Christian resignation and devotion.[42] All the men of the Renaissance died in the odour of piety; and Molza, as many of his sonnets prove, had true religious feeling. He was not a bad man, though a weak one. In the flaccidity of his moral fibre, his intellectual and æsthetical serenity, his confused and yet contented conscience, he fairly represents his age.

It would be difficult to choose between Molza's Latin and Italian poems, were it necessary to award the palm of elegance to either. Both are marked by the same *morbidezza*, the same pliancy, as of acanthus leaves that feather round the marble of some Roman ruin. Both are languid alike and somewhat tiresome, in spite of a peculiar fragrance. I have sought through upwards of 350 sonnets contained in two collections of his Italian works, for one with the ring of true virility, or for one sufficiently perfect in form to bear transplantation. It is not difficult to understand their popularity during the poet's lifetime. None is deficient in touches of delicate beauty, spontaneous images, and sentiments expressed with much lucidity. And their rhythms are invariably melodious. Reading them, we might seem to be hearing flutes a short way from us played beside a rippling stream. And yet—or rather, perhaps, for this very reason—our attention is not rivetted. The most distinctly interesting note in them is sounded when the poet speaks of Rome. He felt the charm of the seven hills, and his melancholy was at home among their ruins. Yet even upon this congenial topic it would be difficult to select a single poem of commanding power.

The 'Ninfa Tiberina' is a monody of eighty-one octave stanzas, addressed by the poet, feigning himself a shepherd, to Faustina, whom he feigns a nymph. It has nothing real but the sense of beauty that inspired it, the beauty, exquisite but soulless, that informs its faultless pictures and mellifluous rhythms. We are in a dream-world of fictitous feelings and conventional images, where only art remains sincere and unaffected. The proper point of view from which to judge these stanzas, is the simply æsthetic. He who would submit to their influence and comprehend the poet's aim, must come to the reading of them attuned by contemplation of contemporary art. The arabesques of the Loggie, the metal-work of Cellini, the stucchi of the Palazzo del Te, Sansovino's bas-reliefs of fruits and garlands, Albano's cupids, supply the necessary

[41] See Vol. I., *Revival of Learning*, p. 555.

[42] The best Life of Molza is that written by Pierantonio Serassi, Bergamo, 1747. It is republished, with Molza's Italian poems, in the series of *Classici Italiani*, Milano, 1808.

analogues. Poliziano's 'Giostra' demanded a similar initiation. But between the 'Giostra' and the 'Ninfa Tiberina' Italian art had completed her cycle from early Florence to late Rome, from Boticelli and Donatello to Giulio Romano and Cellini. The freshness of the dawn has been lost in fervour of noonday. Faustina succeeds to the fair Simonetta. Molza cannot 'recapture the first fine careless rapture' of Poliziano's morning song—so exuberant and yet so delicate, so full of movement, so tender in its sentiment of art. The *voluttà idillica*, which opened like a rosebud in the 'Giostra,' expands full petals in the 'Ninfa Tiberina;' we dare not shake them, lest they fall. And these changes are indicated even by the verse. It has the glory of Poliziano to have discovered the various harmonies, of which the octave, artistically treated, is capable, and to have made each stanza a miniature masterpiece. Under Molza's treatment the verse is heavier and languid, not by reason of relapse into the negligence of Boccaccio, but because he aims at full development of its resources. He weaves intricate periods, and sustains a single sentence, with parentheses and involutions, from the opening of the stanza to its close. Given these conditions, the 'Ninfa Tiberina' is all nectar and all gold.

After an exordium, which introduces

> La bella Ninfa mia, che al Tebro infiora
> Col piè le sponde,

Molza calls upon the shepherds to transfer their vows to her from Pales. She shall be made the goddess of the spring, and claim an altar by Pomona's. Here let the rustic folk play, dance, and strive in song. Hither let them bring their gifts.[43]

> Io dieci pomi di fin oro eletto,
> Ch' a te pendevan con soave odore,
> Simil a quel, che dal tuo vago petto
> Spira sovente, onde si nutre amore,
> Ti sacro umil; e se n' avrai diletto,
> Doman col novo giorno uscendo fuore,
> Per soddisfar in parte al gran disio,
> Altrettanti cogliendo a te gl' invio.
> E d' ulivo una tazza, ch' ancor serba
> Quel puro odor, che già le diede il torno,
> Nel mezzo a cui si vede in vista acerba
> Portar smarrito un giovinetto il giorno,
> E sì 'l carro guidar che accende l' erba,
> E sin al fondo i fiumi arde d' intorno.
> Stolto che mal tener seppe il viaggio,
> E il consiglio seguir fedele e saggio!

[43] Ten apples of fine gold, elect and rare,
Which hung for thee, and softest perfume shed,
Like unto that which from thy bosom fair
Doth often breathe, whence Love is nourishéd,
Humbly I offer; and if thou shalt care,
To-morrow with the dawn yon fields I'll tread,
My great desire some little to requite,
Plucking another ten for thy delight.

The description of the olive cup is carried over the next five stanzas, when the poet turns to complain that Faustina does not care for his piping. And yet Pan joined the rustic reeds; and Amphion breathed through them such melody as held the hills attentive; and Silenus taught how earth was made, and how the seasons come and go, with his sweet pipings. Even yet, perchance, she will incline and listen, if only he can find for her some powerful charm. Come forth, he cries, repeating the address to Galatea, leave Tiber to chafe within his banks and hurry toward the sea. Come to my fields and caves:[44]

> A te di bei corimbi un antro ingombra,
> E folto indora d' elicrisi nembo
> L' edera bianca, e sparge sì dolce ombra,
> Che tosto tolta a le verd' erbe in grembo
> D' ogni grave pensier te n' andrai sgombra;
> E sparso in terra il bel ceruleo lembo,
> Potrai con l' aura, ch' alberga il colle,
> Seguir securo sonno dolce e molle.

It is perilous for thee to roam the shores where Mars met Ilia. O Father Tiber, deal gently with so fair a maiden. It was thou who erewhile saved the infant hope of Rome, whom the she-wolf suckled near thine overflow! But such themes soar too high for shepherd's pipings. I turn to Caro and to Varchi. Both are shepherds, who know how to stir the streams of Mincius and Arethuse. Even the gods have lived in forest wild, among the woods, and there Anchises by the side of Venus pressed the flowers. What gifts shall I find for my Faustina? Daphnis and Mœris are richer far than I. How can I contend with them in presents to the fair? And yet she heeds them not:

> Tanto d' ogni altrui dono poco si cura
> Questa vaga angioletta umile e pura.

My passion weighs upon me as love weighed on Aristæus. He forgot his flocks, his herds, his gardens, even his beehives for Eurydice. His

> Also an olive cup, where still doth cling
> That pure perfume it borrowed from the lathe,
> Where in the midst a fair youth ruining
> Conducts the day, and with such woeful scathe
> Doth guide his car, that to their deepest spring
> The rivers burn, and burn the grasses rathe;
> Ah fool, who knew not how to hold his way,
> Nor by that counsel leal and wise to stay!

[44] White ivy with pale corymbs loads for thee
That cave, and with thick folds of helichryse
Gildeth the arch it shades so lovingly;
Here lapped in the green grass which round it lies,
Thou shalt dismiss grave thoughts, and fancy-free
Spread wide thy skirt of fair cerulean dyes,
And with the wholesome airs that haunt the hill,
Welcome sweet soothing sleep, secure from ill.

heartache made him mad, and he pursued her over field and forest. She fled before him, but he followed:[45]

> La sottil gonna in preda a i venti resta,
> E col crine ondeggiando addietro torna:
> Ella più ch' aura, o più che strale, presta
> Per l' odorata selva non soggiorna;
> Tanto che il lito prende snella e mesta,
> Fatta per paura assai più adorna:
> Fende Aristeo la vagha selva anch' egli,
> E la man parle aver entro i capegli.
>
> Tre volte innanzi la man destra spinse
> Per pigliar de le chiome il largo invito;
> Tre volte il vento solamente strinse,
> E restò lasso senza fin schernito:
> Nè stanchezza però tardollo o vinse,
> Perchè tornasse il pensier suo fallito;
> Anzi quanto mendico più si sente,
> Tanto s' affretta, non che il corso allente.

The story of Eurydice occupies twenty-nine stanzas, and with it the poem ends abruptly. It is full of carefully wrought pictures, excessively smooth and sugared, recalling the superficial manner of the later Roman painters. Even in the passage that describes Eurydice's agony, just quoted, the forest is *odorata* or *vagha*. Fear and flight make the maiden more *adorna*. The ruffian Aristæus gets tired in the chase. He, too, must be presented in a form of elegance. Not the action, but how the action might be made a groundwork for embroidery of beauty, is the poet's care. We quit the 'Ninfa Tiberina' with senses swooning under superfluity of sweetness—as though we had inhaled the breath of hyacinths in a heated chamber.

Closely allied to bucolic stands didactic poetry. The 'Works and Days' of Hesiod and the 'Georgics' of Virgil—the latter far more effectually, however, than the former—determined this style for the Italians. We have already seen to what extent the neo-Latin poets cultivated a form of verse that, more than any other, requires the skill of a great

[45] Her rippling raiment, to the winds a prey,
Waves backward with her wavering tresses light;
Faster than air or arrow, without stay
She through the perfumed wood pursues her flight;
Then takes the river-bed, nor heeds delay,
Made even yet more beautiful by fright;
Threads Aristæus, too, the forest fair,
And seems to have his hands within her hair.

Three times he thrust his right hand forth to clasp
The abundance of her curls that lured him on;
Three times the wind alone deceived his grasp,
Leaving him scorned, with all his hopes undone;
Yet not the toil that made him faint and gasp,
Could turn him from his purpose still unwon;
Nay, all the while, the more his strength is spent,
The more he hurries on the course intent.

artist and the inspiration of true poetry, if it is to shun intolerable tedium.[46] The best didactic poems written in Latin by an Italian are undoubtedly Poliziano's 'Sylvæ,' and of these the most refined is the 'Rusticus.'[47] But Poliziano, in composing them, struck out a new line. He did not follow his Virgilian models closely. He chose the form of declamation to an audience, in preference to the time-honoured usage of apostrophising a patron. This relieves the 'Sylvæ' from the absurdity of the poet's feigning to instruct a Memmius or Augustus, a Francis I. or Charles V., in matters about which those warriors and rulers can have felt but a frigid interest. Pontano's 'Urania' and 'De Hortis Hesperidum' are almost free from the same blemish. The former is addressed to his son Lucius, but in words so brief and simple that we recognise the propriety of a father giving this instruction to his child.[48] The latter is dedicated to Francesco Gonzaga, Marquis of Mantua, who receives complimentary panegyrics in the exordium and peroration, but does not interfere with the structure of the poem. Its chief honours are reserved, as is right and due, for Virgil:—[49]

> Dryades dum munera vati
> Annua, dum magno texunt nova serta Maroni,
> E molli violâ et ferrugineis hyacinthis,
> Quasque fovent teneras Sebethi flumina myrtos.

Pontano's greatness, here as elsewhere, is shown in his mytho-poetic faculty. The lengthy dissertation on the heavens and the lighter discourse on orange-cultivation are adorned and enlivened with innumerable legends suggested to his fertile fancy by the beauty of Neapolitan scenery. When we reach the age of Vida and Fracastoro, we find ourselves in the full tide of Virgilian imitation;[50] and it is just at this point in our inquiry that the transition from Latin to Italian didactic poetry should be effected.

Giovanni Rucellai, the son of that Bernardo, who opened his famous Florentine gardens to the Platonic Academy, was born in 1475. As the author of 'Rosmunda,' he has already appeared in this book. When he died, in 1526, he bequeathed a little poem on Bees to his brother Palla and his friend Gian Giorgio Trissino. Trissino and Rucellai had been intimate at Florence and in Rome. They wrote the 'Sofonisba' and 'Rosmunda' in generous rivalry, meeting from time to time to compare notes of progress and to recite their verses. An eye-witness related to Scipione Ammirato how 'These two dearest friends, when they

[46] Vol. I., *Revival of Learning*, chap. viii.

[47] *Ibid.* pp. 536-541.

[48] Tu vero nate ingentes accingere ad orsus
Et mecum illustres cœli spatiare per oras,
Namque aderit tibi Mercurius, cui cœlifer Atlas
Est avus, et notas puerum puer instruet artes.
Ed. Aldus (1513), p. 2.

[49] *Ibid.* p. 138.

[50] See Vol. I., *Revival of Learning*, pp. 546-551, for notices of the *Poetica*, *Bombyces*, *Scacchia* and *Syphilis*.

were together in a room, would jump upon a bench and declaim pieces of their tragedies, calling upon the audience to decide between them on the merits of the plays.'[51] Trissino received the MS. of his friend's posthumous poem at Padua, and undertook to see it through the press. The 'Api' was published at Venice in 1539.[52] What remained to be said or sung about bees after the Fourth Georgic? Very little indeed, it must be granted. Yet the 'Api' is no mere translation from Virgil; and though the higher qualities of variety, invention and imagination were denied to Rucellai, though he can show no passages of pathos to compete with the 'Corycius senex,' of humour to approach the battle of the hives, no episode, it need be hardly said, to match with 'Pastor Aristæus,' still his modest poem is a monument of pure taste and classical correctness. It is the work of a ripe scholar and melodious versifier, if not of a great singer; and its diction belongs to the best period of polite Italian.

The same moderate praise might be awarded to the more ambitious poem of Luigi Alamanni, entitled 'Coltivazione,' but for its immoderate prolixity.[53] Alamanni resolved to combine the precepts of Hesiod, Virgil and Varro, together with the pastoral passages of Lucretius, in one work, adapting them to modern usage, and producing a comprehensive treatise upon farming. With this object he divided his poem into six books, the first four devoted to the labours of the several seasons, the fifth to gardens, and the sixth to lucky and unlucky days. On a rough computation, the whole six contain some 5,500 lines. 'La Coltivazione' is dedicated to Francis I., and is marred by inordinate flatteries of the French people and their king. Students who have the heart to peruse its always chaste and limpidly flowing blank verse, will be rewarded from time to time with passages like the following, in which the sad circumstances of the poet and the pathos of his regrets for Italy raise the style to more than usual energy and dignity:[54]

> Ma qual paese è quello ove oggi possa,
> Glorioso Francesco, in questa guisa
> Il rustico cultor goderse in pace
> L' alte fatiche sue sicuro e lieto?
> Non già il bel nido ond' io mi sto lontano,
> Non già l' Italia mia; che poichè lunge
> Ebbe, altissimo Re, le vostre insegne,
> Altro non ebbe mai che pianto e guerra.
> I colti campi suoi son fatti boschi,
> Son fatti albergo di selvagge fere,
> Lasciati in abbandono a gente iniqua.
> Il bifolco e 'l pastor non puote appena
> In mezzo alle città viver sicuro
> Nel grembo al suo signor; chè di lui stesso

[51] See Morsolin's *Giangiorgio Trissino* (Vicenza, 1878), p. 92.

[52] *Ibid.* p. 245.

[53] See *Versi e Prose di Luigi Alamanni*, 2 vols. Lemonnier, Firenze, 1859. This edition is prefaced by a Life written by Pietro Raffaelli.

[54] *Op. cit.* vol. ii. p. 210. It is the opening of the peroration to Book i.

Che 'l devria vendicar, divien rapina . . .
Fuggasi lunge omai dal seggio antico
L' italico villan; trapassi l' alpi;
Truove il gallico sen; sicuro posi
Sotto l' ali, Signor, del vostro impero.
E se quì non avrà, come ebbe altrove,
Così tepido il sol, sì chiaro il cielo,
Se non vedrà, quei verdi colli toschi,
Ove ha il nido più bello Palla e Pomona;
Se non vedrà quei cetri, lauri e mirti,
Che del Partenopeo veston le piagge;
Se del Benaco e di mill' altri insieme
Non saprà quì trovar le rive e l' onde;
Se non l' ombra, gli odor, gli scogli ameni
Che 'l bel liguro mar circonda e bagna;
Se non l' ampie pianure e i verdi prati
Che 'l Po, l' Adda e 'l Tesin rigando infiora,
Quì vedrà le campagne aperte e liete,
Che senza fine aver vincon lo sguardo, &c.[55]

Luigi Alamanni was a member of a noble Florentine family, who for several generations had been devoted to the Medicean cause. He was born in 1495, and early joined the band of patriots and scholars who assembled in the Rucellai gardens to hear Machiavelli read his notes on Livy. After the discovery of the conspiracy against Cardinal Giulio de' Medici in which Machiavelli was implicated, and which cost his cousin Luigi di Tommaso Alamanni and his friend Jacopo del Diacceto their lives, Luigi escaped across the mountains by Borgo San Sepolcro to Urbino. Finally, after running many risks, and being imprisoned for a while at Brescia by Giulio's emissaries, he made good his flight to France. His wife and three children had been left at Florence. He was poor and miserable, suffering as only exiles suffer when their home is such a paradise as Italy. In 1527, after the expulsion of the Medici, Luigi returned to Florence, and took an active part in the preparations for the siege as well as in the diplomatic negotiations which followed the fall of the city. Alessandro de' Medici declared him a rebel; and he was forced to avail himself again of French protection. With the

[55] 'But what land is that where now, O glorious Francis, the husbandman may thus enjoy his labours with gladness and tranquillity in peace? Not the fair nest, from which I dwell so far away; nay, not my Italy! She since your ensigns, mighty king, withdrew from her, hath had nought else but tears and war. Her tilled fields have become wild woods, the haunts of beasts, abandoned to lawless men. Herdsman or shepherd can scarce dwell secure within the city beneath their master's mantle; for those who should defend them, make the country folk their prey . . . . Let Italy's husbandman fly far from his own home, pass the Alpine barrier, seek out the breast of Gaul, repose, great lord, beneath thy empire's pinions! And though he shall not have the sun so warm, the skies so clear, as he was wont to have; though he shall not gaze upon those green Tuscan hills, where Pallas and Pomona make their fairest dwelling; though he shall not see those groves of orange, laurel, myrtle, which clothe the slopes of Parthenope; though he shall seek in vain the banks and waves of Garda and a hundred other lakes; the shade, the perfume, and the pleasant crags, which Liguria's laughing sea surrounds and bathes; the ample plains and verdant meadows which flower beneath the waters of Po, Adda, and Ticino; yet shall he behold glad fields and open, spreading too far for eyes to follow!'

exception of a few years passed in Italy between 1537 and 1540, the rest of his life was spent as a French courtier. Both Francis I. and Henri II. treated him with distinction and bounty. Catherine de Medici made him her master of the household; and his son received the bishopric of Macon. In 1556 he died at Amboise following the Court.

Luigi Alamanni was the greatest Italian poet of whose services Francis I. could boast, as Cellini was the greatest Italian artist. His works are numerous, and all are marked by the same qualities of limpid facility, tending to prolixity and feebleness. Sonnets and *Canzoni*, satires, romantic epics, eclogues, translations, comedies, he tried them all. His translation of the 'Antigone' deserves commendation for its style. His 'Flora' is curious for its attempt to reproduce the comic iambic of the Latin poets. If his satires dealt less in generalities, they might aspire to comparison with Ariosto's. As it is, the poet's bile vents itself in abstract invectives, of which the following verses upon Rome may stand for a fair specimen:[56]

> Or chi vedesse il ver, vedrebbe come
> Più disnor tu, che 'l tuo Luter Martino,
> Porti a te stessa, e più gravose some.
> Non la Germania, no, ma l' ozio e 'l vino,
> Avarizia, ambizion, lussuria, e gola
> Ti mena al fin, che già veggiam vicino.
> Non pur questo dico io, non Francia sola,
> Non pur la Spagna, tutta Italia ancora
> Che ti tien d' eresia, di vizi scola.
> E chi nol crede, ne dimandi ognora
> Urbin, Ferrara, l' Orso, e la Colonna,
> La Marca, il Romagnuol, ma più chi plora
> Per te servendo, che fu d' altri donna.

Alamanni is said to have been an admirable improvisatore; and this we can readily believe, for his verses, even when they are most polished, flow with a placidity of movement that betrays excessive ease.

We have traced the pastoral ideal from its commencement in Boccaccio, through the 'Arcadia' of Sannazzaro, Poliziano's 'Orfeo,' and the didactic poets, up to the point when it was destined soon to find its perfect form in the 'Aminta' and the 'Pastor Fido.' Both Tasso and Guarini lived beyond the chronological limits assigned to this work. The Renaissance was finished; and Italy had passed into a new phase of existence, under the ecclesiastical reaction which is called the Counter-Reformation. It is no part of my programme to enter with particularity into the history of the second half of the sixteenth century. And yet

[56] Vol. i. p. 251. It is the end of the third satire. 'He who saw truly, would perceive that thyself brings on thee more dishonour than thy Martin Luther, and heavier burdens too. Not Germany, no, but sloth and wine, avarice, ambition, sensuality, and gluttony, are bringing thee to thy now near approaching end. It is not I who say this, not France alone, nor yet Spain, but all Italy, which holds thee for the school of heresy and vice. He who believes it not, let him inquire of Urbino, Ferrara, the Bear and the Column, the Marches and Romagna, yet more of her who weeps because thou makest her serve, who was once mistress over nations.'

the subject of this and the preceding chapter would be incomplete were I not to notice the two poems which combined the drama and the pastoral in a work of art no less characteristic of the people and the age than fruitful of results for European literature. Great tragedy and great comedy were denied to the Italians. But they produced a novel species in the pastoral drama, which testified to their artistic originality, and led by natural transitions to the opera. Poetry was on the point of expiring; but music was rising to take her place. And the imaginative medium prepared by the lyrical scenes of the Arcadian play, afforded just that generality and aloofness from actual conditions of life, which were needed by the new art in its first dramatic essays.

It would be a mistake to suppose that because the form of the Arcadian romance was artificial, it could not lend itself to the presentation of real passion when adapted to the theatre. The study of the 'Aminta' and the 'Pastor Fido' is sufficient to remove this misconception. Though the latter is the more carefully constructed of the two, the plot in either case presents a series of emotional situations, developed with refined art and expressed with lyrical abundance. The rustic fable is but a veil, through which the everlasting lineaments of love are shown. Arcadia, stripped of pedantry and affectation, has become the ideal world of sentiment. Like amber, it encloses in its glittering transparency the hopes and fears, the pains and joys, which flit from heart to heart of men and women when they love. The very conventionality of the pastoral style assists the lyrical utterance of real feeling. For it must be borne in mind that both 'Aminta' and the 'Pastor Fido' are essentially lyrical. The salt and savour of each play are in their choruses and monologues. The dialogue, the fable and the characters serve to supply the poet with motives for emotion that finds vent in song. This being conceded, it will be understood how from their scenes a whole world of melodrama issued. Whatever may have been the subject of an opera before the days of Gluck, it drew its life-blood from these pastorals.

The central motive of 'Aminta' and the 'Pastor Fido' is the contrast between the actual world of ambition, treachery and sordid strife, and the ideal world of pleasure, loyalty and tranquil ease. Nature is placed in opposition to civil society, the laws of honour to the laws of love, the manners of Arcadia to the manners of Italy. This cardinal motive finds its highest utterance in Tasso's chorus on the Age of Gold:

O bella età dell' oro,
Non già perchè di latte
Sen corse il fiume, e stillò mele il bosco;
Non perchè i frutti loro
Dier dall' aratro intatte
Le terre, e gli angui erràr senz' ira o tosco;
Non perchè nuvol fosco
Non spiegò allor suo velo,
Ma in primavera eterna,
Ch' ora s' accende, e verna,
Rise di luce e di sereno il cielo;

Nè portò peregrino
O guerra, o merce agli altrui lidi il pino:
Ma sol perchè quel vano
Nome senza oggetto,
Quell' idolo d' errori, idol d' inganno,
Quel che dal volgo insano
Onor poscia fu detto,
Che di nostra natura 'l feo tiranno,
Non mischiava il suo affanno
Fra le liete dolcezze
Dell' amoroso gregge;
Nè fu sua dura legge
Nota a quell' alme in libertate avvezze:
Ma legge aurea e felice,
Che Natura scolpì, 'S' ei piace, ei lice.'

The last phrase, *S' ei piace, ei lice*, might be written on the frontispiece of both dramas, together with Dafne's sigh: *Il mondo invecchia, E invecchiando intristisce.* Of what use is life unless we love?

Amiam, che 'l sol si muore, e poi rinasce;
A noi sua breve luce
S' asconde, e 'l sonno eterna notte adduce.

The girl who wastes her youth in proud virginity, prepares a sad old age of vain regret:

Cangia, cangia consiglio,
Pazzarella che sei;
Che 'l pentirsi da sezzo nulla giova.

It is the old cry of the Florentine *Canti* and *Ballate*, 'Gather ye rosebuds while ye may!' *Di doman non c' è certezza.* And the stories of 'Aminta' and 'Pastor Fido' teach the same lesson, that nature's laws cannot be violated, that even fate and the most stubborn bosoms bow to love.

Of the music and beauty of these two dramas, I find it difficult to speak. Before some masterpieces criticism bends in silence. We cannot describe what must be felt. All the melodies that had been growing through two centuries in Italy, are concentrated in their songs. The idyllic voluptuousness, which permeated literature and art, steeps their pictures in a golden glow. It is easy enough to object that their apparent simplicity conceals seduction, that their sentimentalism is unmanly, and their suggestions of physical beauty effeminating:

Ma come Silvia il riconobbe, e vide
Le belle guance tenere d' Aminta
Iscolorite in sì leggiadri modi,
Che viola non è che impallidisca
Sì dolcemente, e lui languir sì fatto,
Che parea già negli ultimi sospiri
Esalar l' alma; in guisa di Baccante,
Gridando e percotendosi il bel petto,
Lasciò cadersi in sul giacente corpo;
E giunse viso a viso, e bocca a bocca.

This passage warns us that an age of *cicisbei* and *castrati* has begun, and that the Italian sensuousness has reached its final dissolution. Silvia's kisses in 'Aminta,' Mirtillo's kisses in 'Pastor Fido,' introduce a new refinement of enervation. Marino with his 'Adone' is not distant. But, while we recognise in both these poems—the one perfumed and delicate like flowers of spring, the other sculptured in pure forms of classic grace—evident signs of a civilisation sinking to decay; though we almost loathe the beauty which relaxes every chord of manhood in the soul that feels it; we are bound to confess that to this goal the Italian genius had been steadily advancing since the publication of the 'Filocopo.' The negation of chivalry, mysticism, asceticism, is accomplished. After traversing the cycle of comedy, romance, satire, burlesque poetry, the plastic arts, and invading every province of human thought, the Italian reaction against the middle ages assumes a final shape of hitherto unapprehended loveliness in the 'Aminta' and the 'Pastor Fido.' They complete and close the Renaissance, bequeathing in a new species of art its form and pressure to succeeding generations.

CHAPTER XIII

THE PURISTS

The Italians lose their Language—Prejudice against the Mother-tongue—Problem of the Dialects—Want of a Metropolis—The Tuscan Classics—Petrarch and Boccaccio—Dante Rejected—False Attitude of the Petrarchisti—Renaissance Sense of Beauty unexpressed in Lyric—False Attitude of Boccaccio's Followers—Ornamental Prose—Speron Sperone—The Dictator Bembo—His Conception of the Problem—The 'Asolani'—Grammatical Essay—Treatise on the Language—Poems—Letters—Bembo's Place in the 'Cortegiano'—Castiglione on Italian Style—His Good Sense—Controversies on the Language—Academical Spirit—Innumerable Poetasters—La Casa—His Life—'Il Forno'—Peculiar Melancholy—His Sonnets—Guidiccioni's Poems on Italy—Court Life—Caro and Castelvetro—Their Controversies—Castelvetro accused of Heresy—Literary Ladies—Veronica Gambara—Vittoria Colonna—Her Life—Her Friendship for Michelangelo—Life of Bernardo Tasso—His 'Amadigi' and other Works—Life of Giangiorgio Trissino—His Quarrel with his son Giulio—His Critical Works—The 'Italia Liberata.'

It was the misfortune of the Italians that, when culture had become national and the revival of the vulgar literature had been effected, they found themselves in nearly the same relation to their own language as to Latin. After more than a hundred years absorbed in humanistic studies, the authors of the fourteenth century were hardly less remote than the Augustan classics; and to all but Tuscans their diction was almost foreign. At the beginning of the *cinque cento*, the living mother-tongue of Italy which Dante sought—the *Vulgare, quod superius venabamur, quod in qualibet redolet civitate, nec cubat in ulla*—was still to seek. Since the composition of Dante's essay 'De Vulgari Eloquio,' the literary activity of the nation had, indeed, created a desire for some fixed standard of style in modern speech. But the experiments of the *quattro cento* had not far advanced the matter. They only proved that Tuscan was the dialect to imitate, and that success in the future must depend on adherence to the Tuscan authors. Hence it happened that Petrarch and Boccaccio came to be studied with the same diligence, the same obsequious reverence, as Cicero and Virgil. Italian was written with no less effort after formal purity, no less minute observance of rules, than if it had been a dead language. At the same time, as a consequence of this system, the vices of the humanistic style—its tendency to servile imitation, emptiness, rhetorical verbosity, and preference of form to matter—were imported into the vernacular literature.

While noting these drawbacks, which attended the resurgence of Italian at an epoch when the whole nation began to demand a common language, we must give due credit to the sagacity displayed by scholars at that epoch in grappling with the problem before them. The main points at issue were, *firstly*, to overcome the prejudice against the mother-tongue, which still lingered among educated people; *secondly*, to adjust Italian to the standards of taste established by the humanistic movement; and, *thirdly*, to decide whether Tuscan should reign supreme, or be merged in a speech more representative of the Italians as a nation. Early in the century, the battle of Italian against Latin was practically won. There remained no obstinate antagonism to a purely national and modern literature. Still the type to which this literature should conform, the laws by which it should be regulated, were as yet unsettled. These questions had to be decided by intelligence rather than by instinct; for the Italians possessed no common medium of conversation, no common opportunities of forensic or parliamentary debate. That insensible process whereby French style has been modelled on the usages of conversation, and English style has been adapted to the tone of oratory, had to be performed, so far as this was possible, by conscious analysis. The Italians were aware that they lacked a language, and they set themselves deliberately to remedy this defect. These peculiar circumstances gave a pedantic tone to the discussion of the problem. Yet the problem itself was neither puerile nor pedantic. It concerned nothing less than the formation of an instrument of self-expression for a people, who had reached the highest grade of artistic skill in the exercise of the dead languages, and who, though intellectually raised to an equality of culture, were divided by tenacious local differences.

That Petrarch and Boccaccio should have been chosen as models of classical Italian style, was not only natural but inevitable. Writers, trained in the method of the humanists, required the guidance of authoritative masters. Just as they used Cicero and Virgil for the correction of mediæval Latin, so Petrarch and Boccaccio were needed for the castigation of homespun dialects. Dante, had he been comprehended by such men, would not have satisfied ears educated in the niceties of Latin versification; nor could the builders of Ciceronian perorations have revived the simple prose of the Villani. Petrarch contented their sense of polish; Boccaccio supplied them with intricate periods and cadences of numerous prose. Yet the choice was in either case unfortunate, though for somewhat different reasons.

It was impossible for poets of the sixteenth century to follow Petrarch to the very letter of his diction, without borrowing his tone. Consequently these versifiers affected to languish and adore, wove conceits and complained of cruelty, in the fashion of Vaucluse. Their facile mistresses became Lauras; or else they draped a lay-figure, and wrote sonnets to its painted eyebrows. The confusion between literary ceremony and practical experience of passion wrought an ineradicable discord. Authors of indecent burlesques penned Platonic odes. Bembo, who was answerable for the 'Menta' in its Latin form, praised his mistress Morosina in polished sonnets and elegiac threnodies. Firenzuola published the poems to Selvaggia and the 'Capitolo' in praise of a specific against infamous diseases. La Casa gratified the same Academies with his panegyric of the Oven and his scholastic exercises in a metaphysical emotion. Reading these diverse compositions side by side, we wake to the conviction that the Petrarchistic counterfeits, however excellent in form, have precisely the same mediocrity as Sannazzaro's epic, while the Bernesque effusions express the crudest temper of the men who wrote them. The one class of poems is redolent of affectation, the other of coarse realism. The middle term between these opposites is wanting. Nor could it well be otherwise. The conditions of society in the sixteenth century rendered Petrarch's sentiment impossible. His melancholy, engendered by the contest between passion and religious duty, had become a thing of the far past. The license of the times rendered this halting between two impulses ridiculous, when no man was found to question the divine right of natural appetite. Even the reverential attitude assumed by Petrarch as a lover, was out of date; and when his imitators aped it, their insincerity was patent. The highest enthusiasm of the Renaissance revealed itself through the plastic arts in admiration for corporeal beauty. This feeling, while it easily degenerated into sensuality, had no point of contact with Petrarch's mediæval Platonism. Therefore the tone of the Petrarchisti was hypocritical, and the love they professed a sham.

We have a further reason for resenting this devotion to a poet with whose habitual mood the men of that age could not sympathise. We know that they had much to say which remained buried beneath their fourteenth-century disguises. The sincerity of feeling, the fervid passion of poets like Bembo, Molza, or La Casa, cannot be denied. But their emotion found no natural channel of expression. It is not without irritation that we deplore the intellectual conditions of an age, which forced these artists to give forth what they felt in one of two equally artificial forms. Between transcription from the Latin elegists and reproduction of Petrarch there lay for them no choice. Consequently, the Renaissance lacked its full development upon the side of lyric poetry. The secret of the times remained unspoken—a something analogous to Venetian painting, a something indicated in Firenzuola's and Luigini's dialogues on female beauty, a something indirectly presented in Ariosto's episodes, which ought to have been uttered from the heart in song by men who felt the loveliness of plastic form. Instead of this lyrical expression of a ruling passion, we have to content ourselves with pseudoplatonic rhymes and with the fervid sensualities of Pontano's elegiacs. The sensibility to corporeal beauty, which was abundantly represented by Titian, Lionardo, Raphael, Corregio, Michelangelo in art, in literature was either shorn of its essential freedom by the limitations of conventional Platonism, or exaggerated on the side of animalism by imitation of erotic Latin poets. Furthermore, we have some right to regard the burlesque obscenity of academical literature as a partial reaction against the hypocritical refinements of the Petrarchistic mannerism.

Thus the deepest instinct of the epoch, that which gave its splendour to the painting of the golden age, found no spontaneous utterance in lyric verse.

The academical study of Boccaccio proved disastrous for a different reason. In this case there was no division between the master and his pupils; for we have seen already that the author of the 'Decameron' anticipated the Renaissance in the scope and tenor of his work. But he supplied students with a false standard. His Latinising periods, his involved construction of sentences and oratorical amplification of motives encouraged the worst qualities of humanistic style. Boccaccio prevented the Italians from forming a masculine prose manner. Each writer, whatever might be the subject of his work, aimed at ornate diction. Cumbrous and circuitous phrases were admired for their own sake. The simplicity of the Chronicles was abandoned for ponderous verbosity, and Machiavelli's virile force found no successors in the crowd of academicians who dissected the 'Decameron' for flowers of rhetoric.

Thus the efforts of the purists took a false direction from the outset both in prose and verse. The literature which aimed at being national, began with archaistic exercises; and Italy, at the moment of attaining self-consciousness, found herself, without a living language, forced to follow in the steps of antiquated authors. The industry and earnestness of the disciples made their failure the more notable; for while they pursued a track that could not lead to aught but mannerism, they plumed themselves upon the soundness of their method. In order to illustrate the spirit of this movement, I will select a passage from the works of Speron Sperone, who was by no means the least successful stylist of the period. He is describing his earlier essays in the art of writing and the steps by which he arrived at what he clearly thought to be perfection:[1]

'Being in all truth desirous beyond measure from my earliest years to speak and to write my thoughts in our mother tongue, and that not so much with a view to being understood, which lies within the scope of every unlettered person, as with the object of placing my name upon the roll of famous men, I neglected every other interest, and gave my whole attention to the reading of Petrarch and the hundred Novels; in which studies having exercised myself for many months with little profit and without a guide, under the inspiration of God I finally betook me to our revered Master Trifone Gabrielli;[2] by whose

[1] *I Dialoghi di Messer Speron Sperone* (Aldus, Venice, 1542), p. 146. The passage is taken from a Dialogue on Rhetoric. I have tried to preserve the clauses of the original periods.

[2] Trifone Gabrielli was a Venetian, celebrated for his excellent morals no less than for his learning. He gained the epithet of the Socrates of his age, and died in 1549. His personal influence seems to have been very great. Bembo makes frequent and respectful references to him in his letters, and Giasone de Nores wrote a magnificent panegyric of him in the preface to his commentary on Horace's *Ars Poetica*, which he professed to have derived orally from Trifone.

kindly assistance I arrived at perfect comprehension of those authors, whom, through ignorance of what I ought to notice, I had frequently before misunderstood. This excellent man and true father of ours first bade me observe the vocables, then gave me rules for knowing the declension and conjugation of nouns and verbs in Tuscan, and lastly explained to me articles, pronouns, participles, adverbs, and other parts of speech; so that, collecting all that I had learned, I composed a grammar for myself, by following the which while writing I so controlled my style that in a short space of time the world held me for a man of erudition, and still considers me as such. When it seemed to me that I had taken rank as a grammarian, I set myself, with the utmost expectation of everyone who knew me, to the making of verses; and then, my head full of rhythms, sentences and words from Petrarch and Boccaccio, for a few years, I produced things that appeared wonderful to my judgment; but afterwards, thinking that my vein was beginning to dry up (inasmuch as words frequently failed me, and, not finding what to say in different sonnets, it occurred to me to rehandle the same thoughts), I had recourse to that which all the world does now;[3] for, using the greatest diligence, I composed a rhyming dictionary or vocabulary of Italian phrases; in the which I classed by the alphabet every word those two authors had used; moreover I collected in another book their divers ways of describing things, as day, night, anger, peace, hate, love, fear, hope, beauty, in such wise that not a single word or thought came from me which had not its precedent in their sonnets and novels.' At this point Sperone frankly admits that his practice was too slavish. He then proceeds to tell how he compared Petrarch's Latin with his vulgar style in order to discover the correct rules of Italian versification. 'Conquered by the arguments and experiments I have described, I returned to my earlier studies; and then, in addition to continual self-exercise in the reading of Petrarch (which by itself and without any other artifice may procure great benefit), by fixing my mind more diligently than before upon his modes of diction, I observed (as I believed) certain qualities pertaining in an eminent degree to the poet and also the orator; which, since you desire it, I will briefly expound. In the first place, while numbering and weighing his words one by one, I became aware that I discovered none common and none base, few harsh, all clear, all elegant; and all, moreover, so adapted to common use that one might have supposed he had selected and accumulated them with the concurrence of all Italy in conclave. Among the which (like stars amid the limpid space of midnight) some few shone out with special lustre; for some part ancient words, but not unpleasing through their age, as *uopo*, *unquanco*, *sovente*; for some part beautiful and very graceful words, which, like jewels that delight the

[3] Sperone probably alludes to works like Minerbi's Vocabulary of words used by Boccaccio (Venice, 1535); Luna's *Vocabolario di cinque mila vocaboli toschi del Furioso Petrarca Boccaccio e Dante* (Naples, 1536); Accarigi's dictionary to Boccaccio entitled *Ricchezze della lingua volgare* (Venice, 1543); and so forth.

eyes of all men, are only used by gentle and high intellects, such as *gioia*, *speme*, *rai*, *disio*, *soggiorno*, *beltà*, and others of like quality, the which no learned tongue would utter, nor hand write, unless the ear consented. Time would fail to tell in detail of the verbs, adverbs, and other parts of speech, which make his verses noble; but one thing I will not pass in silence, namely that, when speaking of his lady, now of her person, now of her soul, now of her tears, now of her smile, now of her movement, now of her taking rest, now of her anger, now of her pity, and now of her age, in a word when describing and magnifying her alive or dead, he generally avoids the proper name of things, and by some wonderful art adorns each thing by words appropriate to others, calling her head fine gold and roof of gold, her eyes suns, stars, sapphires, nest and home of love, her cheeks now snow and roses, now milk and fire, rubies her lips, pearls her teeth, her throat and breast now ivory now alabaster.' Halfway up this 'Gradus ad Parnassum' we are forced to stop and take deep breath. Sperone has launched the theory of 'poetic diction,' and advances boldly to its extreme consequences. We need not follow his analysis further into particulars. He carries it through the several topics of tautology, periphrasis, antithesis, and proportion of syllables in words of different length; after which the subject of prosody proper is discussed. Having finished with Petrarch, he then proceeds to render the same account of his studies in Boccaccio, observing the variety and choice of his phrases, but calling special attention to the numbers of his periods, and winding up with this sonorous sentence on prose architecture. 'But you must know that as the composition of prose is a marshalling of the sounds of words in proper order, so its numbers are certain orders in their syllables; pleasing the ear wherewith, the art of oratory opens, continues and finishes a period: forasmuch as every clause has not only a beginning but also a middle and an end; at the beginning it puts itself in motion and ascends; in the middle, as though weary with exertion, it rests upon its feet awhile; then it descends, and flies to the conclusion for repose.'[4]

What is admirable, in spite of pedantry and servility, in this lengthy diatribe is the sense of art as art, the devotion to form for its own sake, the effort to grapple with the problems of style, the writer's single-hearted seeking after perfection. Nothing but a highly developed artistic instinct in the nation could have produced students of this type. At the same time we feel an absence of spontaneity, and the tendency to aim at decorative writing is apparent. When the glow of discovery, which impelled Sperone and his fellow-pioneers to open a way across the continent of literature, had failed; when the practice of their school had passed into precepts, and their inventions had been formulated as canons of style; nothing remained for travellers upon this path but

[4] It should be mentioned that the passage I have paraphrased is put into the lips of Antonio Broccardo, a Venetian poet, whose *Rime* were published in 1538. He attacked Bembo's works, and brought down upon himself such a storm of fury from the pedants of Padua and Venice that he took to his bed and died of grief.

frigid repetition, precise observance of conventional limitations, and exercises in sonorous oratory. The rhetoric of the seventeenth century was a necessary outgrowth of pedantic purism. The conceits of Marini and his imitators followed inevitably from a rigorous application of rules that denied to poetry the right of natural expression. It may be urged that for a nation so highly sensitive to form as the Italians, without a metropolis to mould the language in the process of development, and without a spoken dialect of good society, there existed no common school of style but the recognised classics of Tuscany.[5] When each district habitually used a different speech for private and public utterance, men could not write as they talked, and they were therefore forced to write by rule. There is force in these arguments. Yet the consequences of a too minute and fastidious study of the Tuscan authors proved none the less fatal to the freedom of Italian literature; and, what is more, sagacious critics foresaw the danger, though they were unable to avert it.

The leader in this movement, acknowledged throughout Italy for more than half a century as dictator in the republic of letters, 'foster-father of the language' (*balio della lingua*), 'guide and master of our tongue' (*guida e maestro di questa lingua*), was Pietro Bembo.[6] Though only sixteen years junior to Angelo Poliziano, whom he had himself saluted as 'ruler of the Ausonian lyre,' Bembo outlived his master for the space of fifty-one years, and swayed the literary world at a period when Italian succeeded to the honours of Latin scholarship.[7] He was a Venetian. This fact is not insignificant, since it clearly marks the change that had come over the nation, when the sceptre of learning was transferred to the northern provinces, and the exclusive privilege of correct Italian composition was shared with Tuscans by men of other dialects.[8] In his early youth Bembo had the good sense to perceive that the mother-tongue was no less worthy of cultivation than Greek

[5] The difficulty is well put by one of the interlocutors in Castiglione's dialogue upon the courtier (ed. Lemonnier, p. 41): 'Oltre a questo, le consuetudini sono molto varie, nè è città nobile in Italia che non abbia diversa maniera di parlar da tutte l' altre. Però non vi ristringendo voi a dichiarar qual sia la migliore, potrebbe l' uomo attaccarsi alla bergamasca così come alla fiorentina.' Messer Federigo Fregoso of Genoa is speaking, and he draws the conclusion which practically triumphed in Italy: 'Parmi adunque, che a chi vuol fuggir ogni dubio ed esser ben sicuro, sia necessario proporsi ad imitar uno, il quale di consentimento di tutti sia estimato buono . . . e questo (nel volgar dico), non penso che abbia da esser altro che il Petrarca e 'l Boccaccio; e chi da questi dui si discosta, va tentoni, come chi cammina per le tenebre e spesso erra la strada.'

[6] In the famous passage of the *Furioso* where Ariosto pronounces the eulogy of the poets of his day, he mentions Bembo thus (*Orl. Fur.* xlvi. 15):

Pietro
Bembo, che 'l puro e dolce idioma nostro,
Levato fuor del volgar uso tetro,
Quale esser dee, ci ha co 'l suo esempio mostro.

[7] See Bembo's elegy on Poliziano quoted by me in Vol. I., *Revival of Learning*, p. 553.

[8] See Vol. I., *Revival of Learning*, p. 564, for the transference of scholarship to Lombardy.

and Latin. The arguments advanced by Dante, by Alberti, by Lorenzo de' Medici, recurred with fresh force to his mind. He therefore made himself the champion of Italian against those exclusive students who, like Ercole Strozzi, still contended that the dead languages were alone worthy of attention.[9] He also saw that it was necessary to create a standard of correct style for writers who were not fortunate enough to have been born within the bounds of Tuscany. Accordingly, he devoted himself to the precise and formal study of fourteenth-century literature, polishing his own Italian compositions with a diligence that, while it secured transparent purity of diction, deprived them of originality and impulse. It is said that he passed each of his works through forty successive revisions, keeping as many portfolios to represent the stages at which they had arrived.

Having already sketched the life of Bembo, I shall here restrict myself to remarks upon those of his works which were influential in reviving the practice of Italian composition.[10] Among these the first place must be awarded to 'Gli Asolani,' a dialogue on Love, written in his early manhood and dedicated to Lucrezia Borgia. The beauty of its language and the interest of the theme discussed rendered this treatise widely fashionable. Yet it is not possible to study it with pleasure now. Those Platonic conversations, in which the refined society of the Italian Courts delighted, have lost their attraction for us. Nothing but the charming description of Asolo, where the Queen of Cyprus had her garden, surrounded by trimmed laurels and divided crosswise with a leafy *pergola* of vines, retains its freshness. That picture, animated by the figures of the six novitiates of Love, now sauntering through shade and sunlight under the vine-branches, now seated on the grass to hear a lute or viol deftly touched, is in the best idyllic style of the Venetian masters. At the Court of Urbino, where Bembo was residing when his book appeared, it was received with acclamation, as a triumph of divine genius. The illustrious circle celebrated by Castiglione in his 'Cortegiano' perused it with avidity, and there is no doubt that the publication gave a powerful impulse to Italian studies. These were still further fostered by Bembo's Defence of the Vulgar Tongue.[11] He had secured the hearing of the world by his 'Asolani.' Women and the leaders of fashionable society were with him; and he pushed his arguments home against the Latinising humanists. 'To abandon our own language for another,' he reminded them, 'is the same as withdrawing supplies from our mother to support a strange woman.' This phrase is almost identical with what Dante had written on the same topic two centuries earlier. But Bembo's standing-ground was

[9] See the Latin hendecasyllables quoted by me in Vol. I., *Revival of Learning*, p. 519, and the Defence of Italian in the treatise 'Della volgare Lingua' (Bembo, *Opere*, Milan, *Class. It.* x. 28). Carducci in his essay *Delle Poesie Latine di Ludovico Ariosto*, pp. 179-181, gives some interesting notices of Ercole Strozzi's conversion to the vulgar tongue.

[10] See Vol. I., *Revival of Learning*, pp. 517-519, 551-553.

[11] *Opere del Cardinale Bembo* (*Class. It.* Milano, 1808, vol. x.).

different from Dante's. The poet of the fourteenth century felt called to create a language for his nation. The student of the sixteenth, imbued with the assimilative principles of scholarship, too fastidious to risk a rough note in his style, too feeble to attempt a new act of creation, was content to 'affect the fame of an imitator.'[12] His piety toward the mother-tongue was generous; his method of rehabilitation was almost servile.

With the view of illustrating his practice by precepts, Bembo published a short Italian grammar, or compendium of *Regole Grammaticali.* It went through fourteen editions, and formed the text-book for future discussions of linguistic problems. Though welcomed with enthusiasm, this first attempt to reduce Italian to system was severely criticised, especially by Sannazzaro, Caro, Castelvetro and the Florentine Academy.

I have already had occasion to observe that, as a Latin poet, Bembo succeeded best with memorial verses. The same may be said about his Italian poems. The *Canzoni* on the death of his brother, and that on the death of his mistress Morosina, are justly celebrated for their perfection of form; nor are they so wanting in spontaneous emotion as many of his Petrarchistic exercises. Bembo was tenderly attached to this Morosina, whom he first met at Rome, and with whom he lived till her death at Padua in 1525. She was the mother of his three children, Lucilio, Torquato and Elena. The *Canzone* in question, beginning:

Donna, de' cui begli occhi alto diletto:

was written so late as 1539, three months after Bembo had been raised to the dignity of Cardinal.[13] As a specimen of the conceits which he tolerated in poetry, I have thought it worth while to present the following translation of a sonnet:[14]

Ah me, at one same moment forced to cry
And hush, to hope and fear, rejoice and grieve,
The service of one master seek and leave,
Over my loss laugh equally and sigh!
My guide I govern; without wings I fly;
With favouring winds, to rocks and sandbanks cleave;
Hate haughtiness, yet meekness misbelieve;
Mistrust all men, nor on myself rely.
I strive to stay the sun, set snows on fire;
Yearn after freedom, run to take the yoke;
Defend myself without, but bleed within;
Fall when there's none to lift me from the mire;
Complain, when plaints are vain, of fortune's stroke;
And power, being powerless, from impuissance win.

In the sixteenth century verses of this stamp passed for masterpieces of incomparable elegance. The same high value was set on Bembo's familiar letters. He wrote them with a view to publication, and they

[12] See his Latin treatise *De Imitatione.* It is in the form of an epistle.
[13] See Panizzi, *Boiardo ed Ariosto*, vi. lxxxi.
[14] Sonnet xxxvi. of his collected poems.

were frequently reprinted during the course of the next fifty years.[15] These may still be read with profit by students for the light they cast upon Italian society during the first half of the *cinque cento*, and with pleasure by all who can appreciate the courtesies of refined breeding expressed in language of fastidious delicacy. The chief men of the day, whether Popes, princes, Cardinals or poets, and all the illustrious ladies, including Lucrezia Borgia, Veronica Gambara, and Vittoria Colonna, are addressed with a mingled freedom and ceremony, nicely graduated according to their rank or degree of intimacy, which proves the exquisite tact developed by the intercourse of Courts in men like Bembo.

Since the composition and publication of such letters formed a main branch of literary industry in the period we have reached,[16] it will be well to offer some examples of Bembo's epistolary style; and for this purpose, the correspondence with Lucrezia Borgia may be chosen, not only because of the interest attaching to her friendship with the author, but also because the topics treated display the refinement of his nature in a very agreeable light.[17] In one of these, written upon the occasion of her father's death, he calls Alexander VI. 'quel vostro così gran padre.' In a second, touched with the deepest personal feeling, he announces the death of his own brother Carlo, 'mio solo e caro fratello, unico sostegno e sollazzo della vita mia.'[18] In a third he thanks her for her letters of condolence: 'Le lagrime alle quali mi scrivete essere stata constretta leggendo nelle mie lettere la morte del mio caro e amato fratello M. Carlo, sono dolcissimo refrigerio stato al mio dolore, se cosa dolce alcuna m' e potuta venire a questo tempo.' In a fourth he turns this graceful compliment: 'Pregherei eziandio il cielo, che ogni giorno v' accrescerebbe la bellezza; ma considero che non vi se ne può aggiungere.' In a fifth he congratulates Lucrezia upon the birth of a son and heir, and in a sixth condoles with her upon his early death. Then another boy is born, just when the Duke of Urbino dies; and Bembo mingles courtly tears with ceremonious protestations of his joy. It would be impossible to pen more scholarly exercises upon similar occasions; and through the style of the professed epistolographer we seem to feel that Bembo had real interest in the events he illustrates so elegantly. The fatal defect of his letters is, that he is always thinking more of his manner than of his matter. Like the humanists from whom he drew his mental lineage, he laboured for posterity without

[15] My edition is in four volumes, Gualtero Scotto, Vinegia, MDLII. They are collected with copious additions in the *Classici Italiani*.

[16] It will be impossible to do more than make general reference to the vast masses of Italian letters printed in the sixteenth century. I must, therefore, content myself here with mentioning the collections of La Casa, Caro, Bernardo, and Torquato Tasso, Aretino, Guidiccioni, together with the miscellanies published under the titles of *Lettere Scritte al Signor Pietro Aretino*, the *Lettere Diverse* in three books (Aldus, 1567), and the *Lettere di Tredici Uomini Illustri* (Venetia, 1554).

[17] *Lettere*, ed. cit. vol. iv. pp. 1-31.

[18] Another letter, dated Venice, August 1, 1504, is fuller in particulars about this dearly loved brother.

reckoning on the actual demands posterity would make. Success crowned his efforts in the pleasure he afforded to the public of his day; but this was a success comparable with that of Bernardo Accolti or Tibaldeo of Ferrara, whom he scorned. He little thought that future students would rate an annalist of Corio's stamp, for the sake of his material, at a higher value than the polished author of the 'Lettere.' Yet such is the irony of fame that we could willingly exchange Bembo's nicely turned phrases for a few solid facts, a few spontaneous effusions.

Bembo was a power in literature, the exact force of which it is difficult to estimate without taking his personal influence into consideration. Distinguished by great physical beauty, gifted with a noble presence, cultivated in the commerce of the best society, he added to his insight and his mental energy all the charm that belongs to a man of fashion and persuasive eloquence in conversation. He was untiring in his literary industry, unfailing in his courtesy to scholars, punctual in correspondence, and generous in the use he made of his considerable wealth. At Urbino, at Venice, at Rome, and at Padua, his study was the meeting-place of learned men, who found the graces of the highest aristocracy combined in him with genial enthusiasm for the common interests of letters. Thus the man did even more than the author to promote the revolution he had at heart. This is brought home to us with force when we consider the place assigned to him in Castiglione's 'Cortegiano' —a masterpiece of composition transcending, in my opinion, all the efforts made by Bembo to conquer the difficulties of style. Castiglione is no less correct than the dictator strove to be; but at the same time he is far more natural. He treats the same topics with greater ease, and with a warmth of feeling and conviction which endears him to the heart of those who read his golden periods. Yet Castiglione gives the honours of his dialogue to the author of the 'Asolani,' when he puts into the mouth of Bembo that glowing panegyric of Platonic love, which forms the close and climax of his dialogue upon the qualities of a true gentleman.[19]

The crowning merit of the 'Cortegiano' is an air of good breeding and disengagement from pedantic prejudices. This urbanity renders it a book to read with profit and instruction through all time. Castiglione's culture was the result of a large experience of men and books, ripened by intercourse with good society in all its forms. His sense and breadth of view are peculiarly valuable when he discusses a subject like that which forms the topic of the present chapter. There is one passage in his book, relating to the problem of Italian style, which, had it been treated with the attention it deserved, might have saved his fellow-countrymen from the rigours of pedagogical depsotism.[20]

[19] *Il Cortegiano* (ed. Lemonnier, Firenze, 1854), pp. 296-303. I have already spoken at some length about this essay in Vol. I., *Age of the Despots*, pp. 93-96, and have narrated the principal events of Castiglione's life in Vol. I., *Revival of Learning*, pp. 521-522. For his Latin poems see *ib.* pp. 556-559.

[20] Ed. cit. pp. 39-53.

Starting from his cardinal axiom that good manners demand freedom from all affectation, he deprecates the use in speech or writing of those antiquated Tuscan words the purists loved. As usual, he hits the very centre of the subject in his comments on this theme. 'It seems to me, therefore, exceedingly strange to employ words in writing which we avoid in all the common usages of conversation. Writing is nothing but a form of speaking, which continues to exist after a man has spoken, and is, as it were, an image or rather the life of the words he utters. Therefore in speech, which, as soon as the voice has issued from the mouth, is lost, some things may be tolerated that are not admissible in composition, because writing preserves the words, subjects them to the criticism of the reader, and allows time for their mature consideration. It is consequently reasonable to use greater diligence with a view to making what we write more polished and correct, yet not to do this so that the written words shall differ from the spoken, but only so that the best in spoken use shall be selected for our composition.' After touching on the need of lucidity, he proceeds: 'I therefore should approve of a man's not only avoiding antiquated Tuscan phrases, but also being careful to employ such as are in present use in Tuscany and other parts of Italy, provided they have a certain grace and harmony.'[21] At this point another interlocutor in the dialogue observes that Italy possesses no common language. In the difficulty of knowing whether to follow the custom of Florence or of Bergamo, it is desirable to recognise a classical standard of style. Petrarch and Boccaccio should be selected as models. To refuse to imitate them is mere presumption. Here Castiglione states the position of the school he combats. In his answer to their argument he makes Giuliano de' Medici, one of the company, declare that he, a Tuscan of the Tuscans as he is, should never think of employing any words of Petrarch or Boccaccio which were obsolete in good society. Then the thread of exposition is resumed. The Italian language, in spite of its long past, may still be called young and unformed. When the Roman Empire decayed, spoken Latin suffered from the corruptions introduced by barbarian invaders. It retained greater purity in Tuscany than elsewhere. Yet other districts of Italy preserved certain elements of the ancient language that have a right to be incorporated with the living tongue; nor is it reasonable to suppose that a modern dialect should at a certain moment have reached perfection any more than Latin did. The true rule to follow is to see that a man has something good to say. 'Making a division between thoughts and words is much the same as separating soul and body. In order, therefore, to speak or write well, our courtier must have knowledge; for he who has none, and whose mind is void of matter worthy to be apprehended, has nought to say or write.' He must be careful to clothe his thoughts in select and fitting words, but above all things to use such 'as are still upon the lips of the people.' He need not shun foreign phrases, if there be a special force in them above their

[21] Ariosto's style was formed on precisely these principles.

synonyms in his own language. Nor is there cause to fear lest the vulgar tongue should prove deficient in resources when examined by grammarians and stylists. 'Even though it be not ancient Tuscan of the purest water, it will be Italian, common to the nation, copious and varied, like a delicious garden full of divers fruits and flowers.' Here Castiglione quotes the precedent of Greek, showing that each of its dialects contributed something to the common stock, though Attic was recognised as sovereign for its polish. Among the Romans likewise, Livy was not tabooed because of his patavinity, nor Virgil because the Romans recognised a something in him of rusticity. 'We, meanwhile, far more severe than the ancients, impose upon ourselves certain new-fangled laws that have no true relation to the object. With a beaten track before our eyes, we try to walk in bypaths. We take a wilful pleasure in obscurity, though our language, like all others, is only meant to express our thoughts with force and clearness. While we call it the popular speech, we plume ourselves on using phrases that are not only unknown to the people, but unintelligible to men of birth and learning, and which have fallen out of conversation in every district of the land.' If Petrarch and Boccaccio were living at our epoch, they would certainly omit words that have fallen out of fashion since their days; and it is mere impertinence for a purist to tell me that I ought to say *Campidoglio* instead of *Capitolio* and so forth, because some elder Tuscan author wrote it, or the peasants of the Tuscan district speak it so. You argue that only pride prevents our imitating Petrarch and Boccaccio. But pray inform me whom they imitated? To model Latin poems upon Virgil or Catullus is necessary, because Latin is a dead language. But since Italian is alive and spoken, let us write it as we use it, with due attention to artistic elegance. 'The final master of style is genius, and the ultimate guide is a sound natural judgment.' Do we require all our painters to follow one precedent? Lionardo, Mantegna, Raphael, Michelangelo, Giorgione have struck out different paths of excellence in art. Writers should claim the same liberty of choice, the same spontaneity of inspiration. 'I cannot comprehend how it should be right, instead of enriching Italian and giving it spirit, dignity and lustre, to make it poor, attenuated, humble and obscure, and so to pen it up within fixed limits as that everyone should have to copy Petrarch and Boccaccio. Why should we, for example, not put equal faith in Poliziano, Lorenzo de' Medici, Francesco Diaceto, and others who are Tuscan too, and possibly of no less learning and discretion than were Petrarch and Boccaccio? However, there are certain scrupulous persons abroad nowadays, who make a religion and ineffable mystery of their Tuscan tongue, frightening those who listen to them, to the length of preventing many noble and lettered men from opening their lips, and forcing them to admit they do not know how to talk the language they learned from their nurses in the cradle.'[22]

[22] The preface to the *Cortegiano* may be compared with this passage. When it appeared, the critics complained that Castiglione had not imitated Boccaccio. His

If the Italians could have accepted Castiglione's principles, and approached the problem of their language in his liberal spirit, the nation would have been spared its wearisome, perpetually recurrent quarrel about words. But the matter had already got into the hands of theorists; and local jealousies were inflamed. The municipal wars of the middle ages were resuscitated on the ground of rhetoric and grammar. Unluckily, the quarrel is not over; *adhuc sub judice lis est*, and there is no judge to decide it. But in the nineteenth century it no longer rages with the violence that made it a matter of duels, assassinations and lifelong hatreds in the sixteenth. The Italians have recently secured for the first time in their history the external conditions which are necessary to a natural settlement of the dispute by the formation of a common speech through common usage. The parliament, the army, the newspapers of United Italy are rapidly creating a language adequate to all the needs of modern life; and though purists may still be found, who maintain that Passavanti's 'Specchio' is a model of style for leading articles in 'Fanfulla,' yet the nation, having passed into a new phase of existence, must be congratulated on having exchanged the 'golden simplicity of the *trecento*' for a powerful and variously coloured instrument of self-expression.

To stir the dust of those obsolete controversies on the language of Italy—to make extracts from Varchi's, Sperone's or Bembo's treatises upon the Tongues—to set Tolommei's claims for Tuscan priority in the balance against Muzio's more modest pleas in favour of Italian[23]—to describe how one set of scholars argued that the vernacular ought to be called Tuscan, how another dubbed it Florentine or Sienese, and how a third, more sensible, voted for Italian[24]—to enumerate the blasts and counterblasts of criticism blown about each sentence in Boccaccio and Petrarch[25]—to resuscitate the orthographical encounters between Trissino and Firenzuola on the matter of the letter K—is no part of my present purpose. It must suffice to have noted that these problems occupied the serious attention of the literary world, and to have indicated by extracts from Sperone and Castiglione the extreme limits of pedantry and sound sense between which the opinion of the learned vibrated. The details of the quarrel may be left to the obscurity of treatises, long since doomed to 'dust and an endless darkness.'

answer is marked by good sense and manly logic: see pp. 3, 4. With Castiglione, Aretino joined hands, the ruffian with the gentleman, in this matter of revolt against the purists. See the chapter in this volume upon Aretino.

[23] Varchi's *Ercolano* or *Dialogo delle Lingue*; Sperone's dialogue *Delle Lingue*; Claudio Tolommei's *Cesano*; Girolamo Muzio's *Battaglie*.

[24] Varchi called it *Fiorentina*, Tolommei and Salviati *Toscana*, Bargagli *Senese*, Trissino and Muzio *Italiana*. Castiglione and Bembo agreed in aiming at Italian rather than pure Tuscan, but differed in their proposed method of cultivating style. Bembo preferred to call the language *Volgare*, as it was the common property of the *Volgo*. Castiglione suggested the title *Cortigiana*, as it was refined and settled by the usage of Courts. Yet Castiglione was more liberal than Bembo in acknowledging the claims of local dialects.

[25] For a list of commentators upon Petrarch at this period, see Tiraboschi, lib. iii. cap. iii. section 1. Common sense found at last sarcastic utterance in Tassoni.

Much unprofitable expenditure of time and thought upon verbal questions of no vital interest was encouraged by the Academies, which now began to sprout like mushrooms in all towns of Italy.[26] The old humanistic societies, founded by Cosimo de' Medici, Pomponius Lætus, Pontano, and Aldo for the promotion of classical studies, had done their work and died away. Their successors, the Umidi of Florence, the Pellegrini of Venice, the Eterei of Padua, the Vignaiuoli of Rome, professed to follow the same objects, with special attention to the reformation of Italian literature. Yet their very titles indicate a certain triviality and want of manly purpose. They were clubs combining conviviality with the pursuit of study; and it too frequently happened that the spirit of their jovial meetings extended itself to the *dicerie*, *cicalate* and *capitoli* recited by their members, when the cloth was drawn and the society sat down to intellectual banquets. At the same time the Academies were so fashionable and so universal that they gave the tone to literature. It was the ambition of all rising students to be numbered with the more illustrious bodies; and when a writer of promise joined one of these, he naturally felt the influence of his companions. Member vied with member in producing sonnets and rhetorical effusions on the slenderest themes; for it was less an object to probe weighty matters or to discover truth, than to make a display of ingenuity by clothing trifles in sonorous language. Surrounded by a crowd of empty-pated but censorious critics, exercised in the minutiæ of style and armed with precedents from Petrarch, the poet read his verses to the company. They were approved or rejected according as they satisfied the sense of correctness, or fell below the conventional standard of imitative diction. To think profoundly, to feel intensely, to imagine boldly, to invent novelties, to be original in any line, was perilous. The wealth of the Academies, the interest of the public in purely literary questions, and the activity of the press encouraged the publication and circulation of these pedantic exercises. Time would fail to tell of all the poems and orations poured forth at the expense of these societies and greedily devoured by friends prepared to eulogise, or rival bodies eager to dissect and criticise. Students who are desirous of forming some conception of the multitudes of poets at this period, must be referred to the pages of Quadrio with a warning that Tiraboschi is inclined to think that even Quadrio's lists are incomplete. All ranks and conditions both of men and women joined in the pursuit. Princes and plebeians, scholars and worldlings, noble ladies and leaders of the *demi-monde*, high-placed ecclesiastics and penniless Bohemians aspired to the same honours; and the one idol of the motley crowd was Petrarch. There is no doubt that the final result of their labours was the attainment of a certain grace and the diffusion of literary elegance. Yet these gains carried with them a false feeling about poetry in general, a wrong conception of its purpose and its scope. The Italian purists could scarcely have comprehended the drift of Milton's excur-

[26] See Vol. I., *Revival of Learning*, pp. 496-497.

sion, in his 'Reason of Church Government urged against Prelaty,' upon the high vocation of the prophet-bard. They would have been no less puzzled by Sidney's definition of poetry, and have felt Shelley's last word upon the poetic office, 'Poets are the unacknowledged legislators of the world,' to be no better than a piece of pardonable lunacy.

In this thick-spreading undergrowth of verse, where, as Tiraboschi aptly remarks, 'beneath the green and ample foliage we seek in vain for fruit,' it is difficult to see the wood by reason of the trees. Poet so closely resembles poet in the mediocrity of similar attainment, that we are forced to sigh for the energy of Michelangelo's unfinished sonnets, or the crudities of Campanella's muse. Yet it is possible to make a representative selection of writers, who, while they belonged to the school of the purists and were associated with the chief Academies of the day, distinguished themselves by some originality of style or by enduring qualities of literary excellence. Foremost among these may be placed Monsignore Giovanni della Casa. He was born in 1503 of noble Florentine parents, his mother being a member of the Tornabuoni family. Educated at Bologna, he entered the service of the Church, and already in 1538 had reached the dignity of Apostolic Clerk. Rome was still what Lorenzo de' Medici had called it, 'a sink of all the vices,' and very few ecclesiastics escaped its immoralities. La Casa formed some permanent connexion, the fruit of which was his acknowledged son Quirino.[27] In 1540 he was sent on a special mission to Florence with the title of Apostolic Commissary; and in 1544 he was raised to the Archbishopric of Benevento, and soon afterwards appointed Nuncio at Venice. During the pontificate of Julius III., finding himself out of favour with the Vatican, he continued to reside at Venice, employing his leisure in literary occupations. Paul IV. recalled him to Rome, and made him Secretary of State. But though he seemed upon the point of touching the highest ecclesiastical dignity, La Casa was never promoted to the Cardinalate. It is difficult to find a reason for this omission, unless we accept the traditional belief that the scandal of his 'Capitolo del Forno' barred La Casa's entrance to the Sacred College.[28] This burlesque poem, at any rate, supplied the Protestants with a weapon which they used against the Church. The legend based

[27] Quirino is mentioned as 'legitimatum, seu forsitan legitimandum,' in La Casa's will (*Opp.* Venezia, Pasinelli, 1752, vol. i. p. lxxvii.). From his name and his age at La Casa's death we ought perhaps to refer this fruit of his amours to the Venetian period of his life and his intimacy with the Quirino family. His biographer, Casotti, says that he discovered nothing about the mother's name (*loc. cit.* p. lxxiii.).

[28] La Casa received a special commission at Venice in 1546, to prosecute Pier Paolo Vergerio for heresy. When Vergerio went into exile, he did his best to blacken La Casa's character, and used his writings to point the picture he drew in Protestant circles of ecclesiastical profligacy. The whole subject of La Casa's exclusion from the College is treated by his editor, Casotti (*Opp.* vol. i. pp. xlv.-xlviii.). That the Bishop of Benevento was stung to the quick by Vergerio's invectives may be seen in his savage answer 'Adversus Paulum Vergerium' (*Opp.* iii. 103), and in the hendecasyllables 'Ad Germanos' (*Opp.* i. 295), both of which discuss the *Forno* and attempt to apologise for it.

upon its audacious obscenities was credited by Bayle, and in part refuted by the 'Antibaillet' of Ménage. Though by no means more offensive to good taste than scores of similar compositions, the high rank of its author and the offices of trust he had discharged for the Papal Curia, emphasised its infamy, and caused La Casa to be chosen as the scapegoat for his comrades. He died in 1556.

La Casa's name is best known in modern literature by his treatise on the manners of the finished gentleman. In this short essay, entitled 'Galateo,' he discussed the particulars of social conduct, descending to rules about the proper use of the drinking-glass at table, the employment of the napkin, the dressing of the hair, and the treatment of immodest topics by polite periphrases.[29] Galateo is recommended not to breathe hard in the face of the persons he is speaking to, not to swear at his servants in company, not to trim his nails in public, not to tell indecent anecdotes to girls, and so forth. He is shown how to dress with proper pomp, what ceremonies to observe, and which to omit as servile or superfluous, how to choose his words, and how to behave at dinner. The book is an elaborate discourse on etiquette; and while it never goes far below the surface, it is full of useful precepts based upon the principles of mutual respect and tolerance which govern good society. We might accept it as a sequel to the 'Courtier;' for while Castiglione drew the portrait of a gentleman, La Casa explained how this gentleman should conduct himself among his equals. The chief curiosity about the book is, that a man of its author's distinction should have thought it worthy of his pains to formulate so many rules of simple decency. From the introduction it is clear that La Casa meant the 'Galateo' to be a handbook for young men entering upon the world. That it fulfilled this purpose, seems proved by the fact that its title passed into a proverb. 'To teach the Galateo' is synonymous in Italian with to teach good manners.

One whole volume of La Casa's collected works is devoted to his official and familiar correspondence, composed in choice but colourless Italian.[30] Another contains his Italian and Latin poems. No poet of the century expressed his inner self more plainly than La Casa in his verse. The spectacle is stern and grave. From the vocabulary of the Tuscan classics he seems to have chosen the gloomiest phrases, to adumbrate some unknown terror of the soul.[31] Sometimes his sonnets,

[29] *Opp.* vol. i. pp. 237-306. Galateo is said to have been a certain Galeazzo Florimonte of Sessa.

[30] Vol. ii. of the Venetian edition, 1752.

[31] Take for instance this outburst from a complimentary sonnet (No. 40, vol. i. p. 70);

> O tempestosa, o torbida procella,
> Che 'n mar sì crudo la mia vita giri!
> Donna amar, ch' Amor odia e i suoi desiri,
> Che sdegno e feritate onor appella.

Or this opening of the sonnet on Court-honours (No. 26):

> Mentre fra valli paludose ed ime
> Ritengon me larve turbate, e mostri,

in their vivid but polished grandeur, rise even to sublimity, as when he compares himself to a leafless wood in winter, beaten by fiercer storms, with days more cold and short in front, and with a longer night to follow.[32] It is a cheerless prospect of old age and death, uncomforted by hope unvisited, by human love. The same shadow, intensified by even a deeper horror of some coming doom, rests upon another sonnet in which he deplores his wasted life.[33] It drapes, as with a funeral pall, the long majestic ode describing his early errors and the vanity of worldly pomp.[34] It adds despair to his lines on Jealousy, intensity to his satire on Court-life, and incommunicable sadness to the poems of his love.[35] Very judicious were the Italian critics who pronounced his style too stern for the erotic muse. We find something at once sinister and solemn in his mood. The darkness that envelops him, issues from the depth of his own heart. The world around is bright with beautiful women and goodly men; but he is alone, shut up with fear and self-reproach. Such a voice befits the age, as we learn to know it in our books of history, far better than the light effusions of contemporary rhymesters. It suits the black-robed personages painted by Moroni, whose calm pale eyes seem gazing on a world made desolate, they know not why. Its accents are all the more melancholy because La Casa yielded to no impulses of rage. He remained sober, cold, sedate; but by some fatal instinct shunned the light and sought the shade. The gloom that envelops him is only broken by the baleful fires of his *Capitoli*. That those burlesque verses, of which I shall speak in another place, were written in his early manhood, and that the *Rime* were perhaps the composition of his age, need not prevent us from connecting them together. The dreariness of La Casa's later years may well have been engendered by the follies of his youth. It is the despondency of exhaustion following on ill-expended energy, the *tædium vitæ* which fell on Italy when she awoke from laughter.

In illustration of the foregoing remarks I have translated six of La Casa's sonnets, which I shall here insert without further comment.[36]

Che tra le gemme, lasso, e l' auro, e gli ostri
Copron venen, che 'l cor mi roda e lima.

Or this from a *Canzone* on his love (No. 2):

Qual chiuso albergo in solitario bosco
Pien di sospetto suol pregar talora
Corrier di notte traviato e lasso;
Tal io per entro il tuo dubbioso, e fosco,
E duro calle, Amor, corro e trapasso.

[32] Sonnet 58, vol. i. 154.
[33] No. 52, *ib.* p. 136.
[34] *Canzone* 4, *ib.* p. 102.
[35] Sonnets 8, 26, 40, *ib.* pp. 12, 39, 70; *Canzone* 2, *ib.* p. 79.
[36] They are Nos. 58, 50, 25, 26, 8. The sixth, on Jealousy, may be compared with Sannazzaro's, above, p. 280.

In point of form, Italian literature can show few masterpieces superior to the first and second.

Sweet woodland solitude, that art so dear
  To my dark soul lost in doubt's dreadful maze,
  Now that the North-wind, these short sullen days,
  Wraps earth and air in winter's mantle drear,
And thy green ancient shadowy locks are sere,
  White as my own, above the frosty ways,
  Where summer flowers once basked beneath heaven's rays,
  But rigid ice now reigns and snows austere;
Pondering upon that brief and cloudy light
  That's left for me, I walk, and feel my mind
  And members, like thy branches, frozen too;
Yet me, within, without, worse frost doth bind,
  My winter brings a fiercer East-wind's blight,
  A longer darkness, days more cold, more few.

O Sleep, O tranquil son of noiseless Night,
  Of humid, shadowy Night; O dear repose
  For wearied men, forgetfulness of woes
  Grievous enough the bloom of life to blight!
Succour this heart that hath outworn delight,
  And knows no rest; these tired limbs compose;
  Fly to me, Sleep; thy dusky vans disclose
  Over my languid eyes, then cease thy flight.
Where, where is Silence, that avoids the day?
  Where the light dreams, that with a wavering tread
  And unsubstantial footing follow thee?
Alas! in vain I call thee; and these grey,
  These frigid shades flatter in vain. O bed,
  How rough with thorns! O nights, how harsh to me!

It was my wont by day to seek the grove
  Or grot or fount, soothing my soul with song,
  Weaving sweet woes in rhyme, and all night long
  To watch the stars with Phœbus and with Love;
Nor, Bernard, did I fear with thee to rove
  That sacred mount where now few poets throng:
  Till like sea-billows, uncontrollably strong,
  Me too the vulgar usage earthward drove;
And bound me down to tears and bitter life,
  Where founts are not, nor laurel boughs, nor shade,
  But false and empty honour stirs vain strife.
Now, not unmixed with envious regret,
  I watch thee scale yon far-off heights, where yet
  No footstep on the sward was ever laid.

While mid low-lying dells and swampy vales
  Those troubled ghosts and dreams my feet delay,
  Which hide neath gems and gold and proud array
  The barb of poison that my heart impales;
Thou on the heights that virtue rarely scales,
  By paths untrodden and a trackless way,
  Wrestling for fame with thine own soul, dost stray,
  Free o'er yon hills no earth-born cloud assails.

Whence I take shame and sorrow, when I think
  How with the crowd in this low net accursed
  I fell, and how 'tis doomed that I shall die.
O happy thou! Thou hast assuaged thy thirst!
  Not Phœbus but grief dwells with me, and I
  Must wait to purge my woes on Lethe's brink.

Now pomps and purple, now clear stream or field
  Seeking, I've brought my day to evensong,
  Profitless, like dry fern or tares, the throng
  Of luckless herbs that no fair fruitage yield.
Wherefore my heart, false guide on this vain quest,
  More than a smitten flint strikes spark and flame;
  So dulled a spirit must she bring with shame
  To Him who placed it bright within my breast.
Poor heart! She well deserves to chafe and burn
  Since her so precious and so noble freight,
  Ill-governed, she to loss and woe doth turn!
Nor neath the North-wind do the branches quake
  On yonder bristling oak-trees, as I shake
  Fearing that even repentance comes too late.

Heart-ache, that drawest nutriment from fear,
  And still through growing fear dost gather power;
  That mingling ice with flame, confusion drear
  And fell disaster on love's realm dost shower!
Forth from my breast, since all thy bitter cheer
  With my life's sweet thou'st blent in one brief hour!
  Hence to Cocytus! Where hell drinks each tear
  Of tortured souls, self-plagued, self-loathing, cower!
There without rest thy dolorous days drag out,
  Thy dark nights without slumber! Smart thy worst
  No less with felt pangs than fictitious doubt!
Avaunt! Why fiercer now than at the first,
  Now when thy venom runs my veins throughout,
  Bring'st thou on those black wings new dreams accurst?

The vicissitudes of Italy during the first half of the sixteenth century were so tragic, and her ruin was so near at hand, that we naturally seek some echo of this anguish in the verses of her poets. Nothing, however, is rarer than to find direct allusion to the troubles of the times, or apprehension of impending danger expressed in sonnet or *canzone*. While following Petrarch to the letter, the purists neglected his odes to Rienzi and the Princes of Italy. His passionate outcry, *Italia mia*, found no response in their rhetoric. Those sublime outpourings of eloquence, palpitating with alternate hopes and fears, might have taught the poets how to write at least the threnody of Rome or Florence. Had they studied this side of their master's style, the gravity of the matter supplied them by the miseries of their country, might have immortalised their purity of style. As it was, they preferred the 'Rime in Vita e Morte di Madonna Laura,' and sang of sentiments they had not felt, while Italy was dying. Only here and there, as in the sombre rhymes of La Casa, the spirit of the age found utterance unconsciously. But for the mass of versifiers it was enough to escape from the real agonies of the moment into academical Arcadia, to forget the Spaniard and the Frenchman in Philiroe's lap with Ariosto, or to sigh for a past age of gold:[37]

> O rivi, o fonti, o fiumi, o faggi, o querce,
> Onde il mondo novello ebbe suo cibo
> In quei tranquilli secoli dell' oro:
> Deh come ha il folle poi cangiando l' esca,
> Cangiato il gusto! e come son questi anni
> Da quei diversi in povertate e 'n guerra!

This makes the occasional treatment of political subjects the more valuable; and we hail the patriotic poems of Giovanni Guidiccioni as a relief from the limpid nonsense of the amorists. Born at Lucca in 1500, he was made Bishop of Fossombrone by Paul III., and died in 1541. Contemporaries praised him for the grandeur of his conceptions and the severity of his diction, while they censured the obscurity that veiled his unfamiliar thoughts. 'In those songs,' wrotes Lilius Giraldus, 'which he composed upon the woes and miseries of Italy, he set before his readers ample proofs of his illustrious style.'[38] One sonnet might be chosen from these rhymes, reproving the Italians for their slavery and shame, and pointing to the cause, now irremediable, of their downfall:[39]

> From deep and slothful slumber, where till now
> Entombed thou liest, waken, breathe, arise!
> Look on those wounds with anger in thine eyes,
> Italia, self-enslaved in folly's slough!
> The diadem of freedom from thy brow
> Torn through thine own misdoing, seek with sighs;
> Turn to the path, that straight before thee lies,
> From yonder crooked furrow thou dost plough.
> Think on thine ancient memories! Thou shalt see
> That those who once thy triumphs did adorn,
> Have chained thee to their yoke with fetters bound.
> Foe to thyself, thine own iniquity,
> With fame for them, for thee fierce grief and scorn,
> To this vile end hath forced thee, Queen discrowned!

Such appeals were impotent. Yet they proved a consciousness of the situation, an unextinguished sense of duty, in the man who penned them.[40]

The Court-life followed by professional men of letters made it difficult for them to utter their real feelings in an age of bitter political jeal-

[37] La Casa, *Canzone* 4 (*Opp.* i. 151).

[38] *De Poetis*, Dial. ii.

[39] *Opere di Messer G. Guidiccioni* (Firenze, Barbèra, 1867), vol. i. p. 12.

[40] We might parallel Guidiccioni's lamentations with several passages from the Latin elegies of the period, and with some of the obscurer compositions of Italian poetasters. See, for example, the extracts from Carieto of Naples, Tibaldeo of Ferrara and Cammelli of Pistoja on the passage of Charles VIII. quoted by Carducci, *Delle Poesie Latine di Ludovico Ariosto*, pp. 83-86. But the most touching expression of sympathy with Italy's disaster is the sudden silence of Boiardo in the middle of a canto of *Orlando*. See above, p. 136.

ousies. They either held their tongues, or kept within the safer regions of compliment and fancy. The biographies of Annibale Caro and Lodovico Castelvetro illustrate the ordinary conditions as well as the exceptional vicissitudes of the literary career at this epoch. Annibale Caro was born in 1507 at Civitanuova in the March of Ancona. Being poor and of humble origin, he entered the family of Luigi Gaddi at Florence, in the quality of tutor to his children. This patron died in 1541, and Caro then took service under Pier Luigi Farnese, one of the worst princelings of the period. When the Duke was murdered in 1547, he transferred himself to Parma, still following the fortunes of the Farnesi. Employed as secretary by the Cardinal Ranuccio and afterwards by the Cardinal Alessandro of that house, he lived at ease until his death in 1566. Caro's letters, written for his patrons, and his correspondence with the famous scholars of the day, pass for models of Italian epistolography. Less rigid than La Casa's, less manneristic than Bembo's, his style is distinguished by a natural grace and elegance of diction. He formed his manner by translation from the Greek, especially by a version of 'Daphnis and Chloe,' which may be compared with Firenzuola's 'Asino d' Oro' for classic beauty and facility of phrase. But the great achievement of his life was a transcription of the 'Æneid' into blank verse. Though Caro's poem exceeds the original by about 5,500 lines, and therefore cannot pass for an exact copy of Virgil's form, Italians still reckon it the standard translation of their national epic. The charm of Caro's prose was communicated to his *versi sciolti*, always easy, always flowing, with varied cadence and sustained melody of rhythm. A 'Diceria de' Nasi,' or discourse on noses, and a dissertation called 'Ficheide,' commenting on Molza's 'Fichi,' prove that Caro lent himself with pleasure to the academical follies of his contemporaries. It seems incredible that a learned man, who had spent the best years of his maturity in diplomatic missions to the Courts of princes, should have employed the leisure of his age in polishing these trifles. Yet such was the temper of the times that this frivolity passed for a commendable exercise of ingenuity.

Caro's original poems have not much to recommend them beyond limpidity of language. The sonnets to an imaginary mistress repeat conventional antitheses and complimentary *concetti*.[41] The adulatory odes are stiff and laboured, as, indeed, they might be, when we consider that they were made to order upon Charles V., the Casa Farnese, and the lilies of France, by a plebeian scholar from Ancona.[42] The last-named of these flatteries, 'Venite all' ombra de' gran gigli d' oro,' is a masterpiece of prize poetry, produced with labour, filed to superficial smoothness, and overloaded with conceits. On its appearance it was hailed with acclamation as the final triumph of Italian writing.

[41] See, for example, 'Donna, qual mi foss' io,' and 'In voi mi trasformai,' or 'Eran l' aer tranquillo e l' onde chiare.'

[42] See 'Carlo il Quinto fu questi;' 'Nell' apparir del giorno;' and 'Venite all' ombra de' gran gigli d' oro.'

The Farnesi, who had recently placed themselves under the protection of France, and who bore her lilies on their scutcheon, used all their influence to get their servant's work applauded. The Academies were delighted with a display of consummate artifice and mechanical ability. One only voice was raised in criticism. Aurelio Bellincini, a gentleman of Modena, had sent a copy of the ode to Lodovico Castelvetro, with a request that he should pronounce upon its merits. Castelvetro, who was wayward and independent beyond the usual prudence of his class, replied with a free censure of the 'plebeian diction, empty phrases, strange digressions, purple patches, poverty of argument, and absence of sentiment or inspiration,' he detected in its stanzas. At the same time he begged his friend to keep this criticism to himself. Bellincini was indiscreet, and the letter found its way to Caro. Then arose a literary quarrel, which held all Italy in suspense, and equalled in ferocity the combats of the humanists.

Lodovico Castelvetro was born in 1505 at Modena. He studied successively at Bologna, Ferrara, Padua and Siena. Thence he passed to Rome, where strong pressure was put upon him to enter orders. His uncle, Giovanni Maria della Porta, promised, if he did so, to procure for him the bishopric of Gubbio. But Castelvetro had no mind to become a priest. He escaped clandestinely from Rome, and, after a brief sojourn at Siena, returned to Modena. Here in 1542 he subscribed the Formulary of Faith dictated by Cardinal Contarini, and thereby fell under suspicion of heresy. Though he escaped inquisitorial censure at the moment, the charges of Lutheranism were revived in 1554, when Caro declared open war against him. Invectives, apologies, censures and replies were briskly interchanged between the principals, while half the scholars of Italy allowed themselves to be drawn into the fray—Varchi and Molza siding with Caro, Gian Maria Barbieri and other friends of Castelvetro taking up the cudgels for the opposite champion.[43] The bitterness of the contending parties may be gathered from the fact that Castelvetro was accused of having murdered a friend of Caro's, and Caro of having hired assassins to take Castelvetro's life.[44] It seems tolerably certain that either Caro or one of his supporters denounced their enemy to the Inquisition. He was summoned to Rome, and in 1560, was confined in the convent of S. Maria in Via to await his trial. After undergoing some preliminary examinations, Castelvetro became persuaded that his life was in peril. He contrived to escape by night from Rome, and, after a journey of much anxiety and danger, took refuge in Chiavenna, at that time a city of the Grisons. The Holy Office condemned him as a contumacious heretic in his absence

[43] Among the liveliest missiles used in this squabble are Bronzino's *Saltarelli*, recently reprinted by Romagnoli, Bologna, 1863.

[44] Alberigo Longo was in fact murdered in 1555, and a servant of Castelvetro's was tried for the offence. But he was acquitted. Caro, on his side, gave occasion to the worst reports by writing in May 1560 to Varchi: 'E credo che all' ultimo sarò sforzato a finirla, per ogni altra via, e vengane ciò che vuole.' See Tiraboschi, Part 3, lib. iii. chap. 3, sec. 13.

Wandering from Chiavenna to Lyons and Geneva, and back again to Chiavenna, he spent the rest of his life in exile, and died at the last place in 1571.

Castelvetro's publications do not correspond to his fame; for though he gave signs of an acute wit and a biting pen in his debate with Caro, he left but little highly finished work to posterity. In addition to critical annotations upon Bembo's prose, published in his lifetime, he wrote a treatise upon Rhetoric, which was printed at Modena in 1653, and sent an Italian version of Aristotle's 'Poetics' to the press in 1570. This book was the idol of his later years. It is said that, while residing at Lyons, his house took fire, and Castelvetro, careless of all else, kept crying out 'The "Poetics," the "Poetics!" Save me my "Poetics!"' He may be fairly reckoned among the men who did solid service in the cause of graver studies. Yet, but for the vicissitudes of his career, he could hardly claim a foremost place in literary history.

The ladies who cultivated poetry and maintained relations with illustrious men of letters at this epoch, were almost as numerous as the songsters of the other sex. Lodovico Domenichi in the year 1559 published the poems of no less than fifty authoresses in his 'Rime di alcune nobilissime e virtuosissime Donne.' Subjected to the same intellectual training as men, they felt the same influences, and passed at the same moment from humanism to renascent Italian literature.[45] Many of these Viragos,[46] as it was the fashion of the age approvingly and with no touch of sarcasm to call them, were dames of high degree and leaders of society. Some, like *la bella Imperia*, were better known in the resorts of pleasure. All were distinguished by intercourse with artists and writers of eminence. It is impossible to render an account of their literary labours. But the names of a few, interesting alike for their talents and their amours, may here be recorded. Tullia di Aragona, the mistress of Girolamo Muzio, who ruled society in Rome, and lived in infamy at Venice[47]—Vittoria Accoramboni, whose tragedy thrilled Italy, and gave a masterpiece to our Elizabethan stage—Tarquinia Molza, grand-daughter of the poet, and maid of honour at Ferrara in Guarini's brilliant days—Laura Terracina, with whose marriage and murder romance employed itself at the expense of probability—Veronica Franco, who entertained Montaigne in her Venetian home in 1580—Ersilia Cortese, the natural daughter of a humanist and wife of a Pope's nephew—Gaspara Stampa, 'sweet songstress and most excellent musician:'—such were the women, to whom Bembo and Aretino addressed letters, and whose drawing-rooms were the resort of Bandello's heroes.

[45] The identity of male and female education in Italy is an important feature of this epoch. The history of Vittorino da Feltre's school at Mantua given by his biographer, Rosmini, supplies valuable information upon this point. Students may consult Burckhardt, *Cultur der Renaissance*, sec. 5, ed. 2, p. 312; Gregorovius, *Lucrezia Borgia*, book i. sec. 4; Janitschek, *Gesellschaft der Renaissance*, Lecture 3.

[46] See Vulgate, Gen. ii. 23: 'Hæc vocabitur Virago,' &c.

[47] In a rare tract called *Tariffa delle puttane, &c.* Tullia d' Aragona is catalogued among the courtesans of Venice. See Passano, *Novellieri in Verso*, p. 118.

Two poetesses have to be distinguished from the common herd. These are Veronica Gambara and Vittoria Colonna. Veronica was the daughter of Count Gianfrancesco Gambara and his wife Alda Pia of Carpi, whose name recalls the fervid days of humanism at its noon.[48] She was born in 1485, and was therefore contemporary with the restorers of Italian literature. Bembo was the guide of her youth, and Vittoria Colonna the friend of her maturer years. In 1509 she married Giberto, lord of Correggio, by whom she had two sons, Ippolito and Girolamo. Her husband died after nine years of matrimony, and she was left to educate her children for the State and Church. She discharged her duties as a mother with praiseworthy diligence, and died in 1550, respected by all Italy, the type of what a noble woman should be in an age when virtue shone by contrast with especial lustre. Her letters and her poems were collected and published in 1759 at Brescia, the city of her birth. Except for the purity of their sentiments and the sincerity of their expression, her verses do not rise far above mediocrity. Like literary ladies of the French metropolis, she owed her fame to personal rather than to literary excellence. 'The house of Veronica,' writes a biographer of the sixteenth century, 'was an Academy, where every day she gathered round her for discourse on noble questions Bembo and Cappello, Molza and Mauro, and all the famous men of Europe who followed the Italian Courts.'[49]

Fabrizio, the father of Vittoria Colonna, was Grand Constable of Naples. He married Agnesina di Montefeltro, daughter of Duke Federigo of Urbino. Their child Vittoria was born at Mariano, a feud of the Colonna family, in the year 1490. At the age of four she was betrothed to Ferrante Francesco D' Avalos, a boy of the same age, the only son of the Marchese di Pescara. His father died while he was still a child; and in their nineteenth year the affianced couple were married at Ischia, the residence of the house of D' Avalos. The splendour of two princely families, alike distinguished in the annals of Spanish and Italian history and illustrious by their military honours, conferred unusual lustre upon this marriage. It was, moreover, on the bride's side at least, a love-match. Vittoria was beautiful and cultivated; the young Marquis of Pescara chivalrous and brave. She was tenderly attached to him, and he had not as yet revealed the darker side of his mixed character. Yet their happiness proved of very short duration. In 1512 he was wounded and made prisoner at the battle of Ravenna; and though he returned to his wife for a short interval, his duties again called him to the field of war in Lombardy in 1515. Vittoria never saw him after this date; and before his death the honour of her hero was tarnished by one of the darkest deeds of treason recorded in Italian history. Acting as general for the Spanish emperor, the Marquis entered Milan immediately after the battle of Pavia in 1525. He there and then began his intrigues with Girolamo Morone,

48 See Vol. I., *Revival of Learning*, pp. 500-501.

49 Rinaldo Corso, quoted by Tiraboschi.

Grand Chancellor of Francesco Sforza's duchy. Morone had formed a plan for reinstating his master in Milan by the help of an Italian coalition. With the view of securing the Marquis of Pescara, by which bold stroke he would have paralysed the Spanish military power, Morone offered the young general the crown of Naples, if he would consent to join the league. D' Avalos turned a not unwilling ear to these proposals; but while the plot was hatching, he saw good reason to doubt of its success, and determined to clear himself with Charles V. by revealing the conspiracy. Accordingly, he made his lieutenant, Antonio de Leyva, assist at a privy conference between Morone and himself. Concealed behind the arras, this Spanish officer heard enough to be able afterwards to deliver direct testimony against the conspirators, while the Marquis averred that he had led them on designedly to this end. It may be difficult to estimate the precise amount of Pescara's guilt. But whether he was deceiving Morone from the first, or whether, as seems more probable, he entered the negotiation resolved to side with Charles or with the League as best might suit his purpose, there can be no doubt that he played an odious part in this transaction. He did not long survive the treason; for his constitution had been ruined by wounds received at Pavia. It was also rumoured that Charles accelerated his death by poison. He died on November 25, 1525, execrated by the Italians, and handed down by their historians to perpetual infamy. Something of national jealousy mingled undoubtedly in their resentment. D' Avalos was a Spaniard, and made no concealment of his contempt for the Italian character. Finally, it must be admitted that if he really was acting throughout in his master's interest, his betrayal of Morone was but a bold stroke of policy which Machiavelli might have approved. The game was a dangerous one; but it was thoroughly consistent with statecraft as then understood.[50]

No suspicion of her husband's guilt seems to have crossed Vittoria Colonna's mind. Though left so young a widow, beautiful and illustrious by her high rank and education, she determined to consecrate her whole life to his memory and to religion. She survived him two-and-twenty years, which were spent partly in retirement at Ischia, partly in convents at Orvieto and Viterbo, partly in a semi-monastic seclusion at Rome. While still a girl and during her husband's absence in the field, she had amused her leisure with study. This now became her chief resource in the hours she spared from pious exercises. There was no man of great name in the world of letters who did not set his pride on being thought her friend. The collections of letters and poems belonging to that period abound in allusions to her genius, her holiness, and her great beauty. But her chief associates were the group of earnest thinkers who felt the influences of the Reformation without ceasing to be children of the Church. With Vittoria Colonna's name are inseparably connected those of Gasparo Contarini, Reginald Pole, Giovanni

[50] See *Ricordi Inediti di Gerolamo Morone*, pubblicati dal C. Tullio Dandolo, Milano, 1855.

Morone, Jacopo Sadoleto, Marcantonio Flamminio, Pietro Carnesecchi, and Fra Bernardino Ochino. The last of these avowed his Lutheran principles; and Carnesecchi was burned for heresy; but Vittoria never adopted Protestantism in any of its dogmatic aspects. She remained an orthodox Catholic to the last, although it seems tolerably certain that she was by no means ignorant of the new doctrines nor unsympathetic to their spirit.[51] Her attitude was probably the same as that of many Italians who, before the opening of the Council of Trent, desired a reformation from within the Church. To bring it back to purer morals and an evangelical sincerity of faith, was their aim. Like Savonarola, they shrank from heresy, and failed to comprehend that a radical renovation of religion was inseparable, in the changed conditions of modern thought, from a metamorphosis of dogma and a new freedom accorded to the individual conscience. While the Teutonic world struck boldly for the liberation of the reason, the Italians dreamed of an impossible harmony between Catholicism and philosophy. Their compromises led to ethical hypocrisies and to that dogmatic despotism which was confirmed by the Tridentine Council.

A pleasant glimpse into Vittoria's life at Rome is given by the Portuguese artist, Francesco d' Olanda, who visited her about the year 1548. 'Madonna Vittoria Colonna,' he says, 'Marchioness of Pescara and sister to the Lord Antonio Colonna, is one of the most excellent and famous women of Europe—that is, of the whole civilised world. Not less chaste than beautiful, learned in Latin literature and full of genius, she possesses all the qualities and virtues that are praiseworthy in woman. After the death of her hero husband, she now leads a modest and retired life. Tired with the splendour and grandeur of her former state, she gives her whole affections to Christ and to serious studies. To the poor she is beneficent, and is a model of true Catholic devotion.' He then proceeds to describe a conversation held with her, in which Michelangelo Buonarroti took a part.[52]

Vittoria Colonna's *Rime* consist for the most part of sonnets on the death of her husband, and on sacred and moral subjects. Penetrated by genuine feeling and almost wholly free from literary affectation, they have that dignity and sweetness which belong to the spontaneous utterance of a noble heart. Like the poets of an earlier and simpler age, Vittoria listens to the voice of Love, and when he speaks, records the thoughts dictated by his inspiration.[53] That the object of her

[51] The most recent investigations tend rather to confirm the tradition of Vittoria's Lutheran leanings. See Giuseppe Campori's *Vittoria Colonna* (Modena, 1878), and the fine article upon it by Ernesto Masi in the *Rassegna Settimanale*, January 29, 1879. Karl Benrath's *Ueber die Quellen der italienischen Reformationsgeschichte* (Bonn, 1876) is a valuable contribution to the history of Lutheran opinion in the South.

[52] The whole document may be seen in the *Archivio Storico*, nuov. ser. tom. v. part. 2, p. 139, or in Grimm's Life of Michelangelo.

[53] The first lines of the introductory sonnet are strictly true:

Scrivo sol per sfogar l' interna doglia,
Di che si pasce il cor, ch' altro non vole,
E non per giunger lume al mio bel sole,
Che lasciò in terra si onorata spoglia.

lifelong regret was unworthy of her, does not offend our sense of fitness.[54] It is manifest that her own feeling for the Marquis of Pescara, *il mio bel sole, mio lume eterno*, as she loves to call him with pathetic iteration of the chosen metaphor, had satisfied her unsuspecting nature.[55] Death consecrates her husband for Vittoria, as death canonised Laura for Petrarch. He has become divine, and her sole desire is to rejoin him in a world where parting is impossible.[56] The blending of the hero with the saint, of earthly fame with everlasting glory, in this half Christian half Pagan apotheosis, is characteristic of the Renaissance. Michelangelo strikes the same note in the *Capitolo* upon his father's death: 'Or sei tu del morir morto e fatto divo.' It is said that, in her first grief, Vittoria thought of suicide as the means of escaping from this world. But she triumphed over the temptation, and in Bembo's words proved herself *vincitrice di se stessa*. We seem to trace the anguish of that struggle in a sonnet which may possibly have suggested Bembo's phrase.[57]

The religious sonnets are distinguished in general by the same simplicity and sincerity of style.[58] While Vittoria proves herself a Catholic by her invocation of Madonna and S. Francis,[59] it is to the cross of Christ that she turns with the deepest outgoings of pious feeling.[60] Her cry is for lively faith, for evangelical purity of conviction. There is nothing in these meditations that a Christian of any communion may not read with profit, as the heartfelt utterances of a soul athirst for God and nourished on the study of the Gospel.

The memory of Vittoria Colonna is inseparable from that of Michelangelo Buonarroti, who was her intimate companion during the closing years of her life. Of that famous friendship this is not the place to speak at length. It may be enough to report Condivi's words about Michelangelo's grief when he had lost her. 'I remember having heard him say that nothing caused him so much sorrow as that, when he went to visit her upon her passage from this life, he had not kissed her

[54] The last biographer of Vittoria Colonna, G. Campori, has shown that her husband was by no means faithful to his marriage vows.

[55] The close of the twenty-second sonnet is touching by reason of its allusion to the past. Vittoria had no children.

> Sterili i corpi fur, l' alme feconde,
> Chè il suo valor lasciò raggio si chiaro,
> Che sarà lume ancor del nome mio.
> Se d' altre grazie mi fu il ciel avaro,
> E se il mio caro ben morte m' asconde,
> Pur con lui vivo; ed è quanto disio.

[56] See, for instance, *Rime Varie*, Sonetto li. and lxxi. xc.

[57] It is No. 31 of the *Rime Varie* (Florence, Barbèra, 1860).

[58] The introductory Sonnet has, however, these ugly *concetti*:

> I santi chiodi ormai sian le mie penne,
> E puro inchiostro il prezioso sangue;
> Purgata carta il sacro corpo esangue,
> Sì ch' io scriva nel cor quel ch' ei sostenne.

[59] *Rime Sacre*, 119, 120, 86, 87.

[60] *Ibid.* 75, 80, 81.

forehead and face, even as he kissed her hand. Her death left him oftentimes astonied and, as it were, deprived of reason.' Some of Michelangelo's best sonnets were composed for Vittoria Colonna in her lifetime. Others record his sorrow for her loss. Those again which give expression to his religious feelings, are animated by her spirit of genuine piety. It is clear that her influence affected him profoundly.

To include any notice of Michelangelo's poetry in a chapter devoted to the purists, may seem paradoxical.[61] His verses are remarkable for the imperfection of their style, and the rugged elevation of their thoughts. With the school of Bembo he has nothing in common except that Platonism which the versifiers of the time affected as a fashion, but which had a real meaning for his creative genius. In the second half of the sixteenth century Michelangelo's sonnets upon the divine idea, lifting the soul by contemplation to her heavenly home, reach our ears like utterances from some other and far distant age. Both in form and in spirit they are alien to the *cinque cento*. Yet the precisians of the time admired these uncouth verses for the philosophic depth of thought they found in them. Benedetto Varchi composed a learned treatise on the sonnet 'Non ha l' ottimo artista;' and when the poems were printed, Mario Guidicci delivered two lectures on them before the Florentine Academy.[62]

There is no sort of impropriety in placing Bernardo Tasso and Giangiorgio Trissino upon the list of literary purists. The biographies of these two men, more interesting for the share they took in public life than for their poetical achievements, shall close a chapter which has been, almost of necessity, rambling. Bernardo Tasso was a member of the noble and ancient Bergamasque family Dei Tassi.[63] He was born at Venice in 1493. Left an orphan in his early childhood, an uncle on his father's side, the Bishop of Recanati, took charge of him. But this good man was murdered in 1520, at the time when Bernardo had just begun a brilliant career in the University of Padua. The loss of his father and his uncle threw the young student on the world, and he was glad to take service as secretary with the Count Guido Rangone. At this epoch the Rangoni stood high among the first nobility of Italy, and Count Guido was Captain-General of the Church. He employed Bernardo in a mission to Paris in 1528, on the occasion of Ercole d' Este's marriage to Renée, daughter of Louis XII. Tasso went to France as servant of the Rangoni. He returned to Italy in the employment of the Estensi. But he did not long remain at the Court of Ferrara. About the year 1532, we find him with Ferrante Sanseverino, Prince of Salerno, whom he accompanied in 1535 on the expedition to Tunis. It cannot have been much later than this date that he married

[61] For a brief account of Michelangelo's *Rime*, see Vol. I., *Fine Arts*, Appendix ii.; also the introduction to my translation of the sonnets, *The Sonnets of Michael Angelo Buonarroti and Tommaso Campanella*, Smith & Elder, 1878.

[62] Varchi's and Guidicci's *Lezioni* will be found in Guasti's edition of the *Rime*.

[63] I use the Life prefixed by G. Campori to his *Lettere Inedite di Bernardo Tasso* (Bologna, Romagnoli, 1869).

the beautiful Porzia de' Rossi, who was the mother of his illustrious son, Torquato. But though this marriage was in all respects a happy one, in none more fortunate than in the birth of Italy's fourth sovran poet, Bernardo was not destined to lead a life of tranquil domesticity. His master, whom he followed whithersoever military service called him, fell out of favour with the Spanish Court in 1547. Maddened by the injustice of his treatment, the Prince deserted from Charles V. to his rival, Francis, was declared a rebel and deprived of his vast domains. Bernardo resolved to share his fortunes, and in return for this act of loyalty, found himself involved in the ruin of the Sanseverini. Henceforth he lived a wandering life, away from Porzia and his family, and ill-contented with the pittance which his patron could afford. In 1556, at Duke Guidubaldo's invitation, he joined the Court of Urbino; and again in 1563 he entered the service of the Duke of Mantua. He died in 1569 at Ostiglia.

It will be seen from this brief sketch that Bernardo Tasso spent his life in mixed employments, as courtier, diplomatist, and military secretary. His career was analogous to that of many nobly born Italians, for whom there existed no sphere outside the service of a prince. Yet he found time, amid his journeys, campaigns and miscellaneous Court duties, to practise literature. The seven books of his collected poems—sonnets, odes and epithalamial hymns—placed him among the foremost lyrists of the century; while his letters displayed the merits which were usual in that species of composition. Had this been all, he would have deserved honourable mention by the side of Caro, on a somewhat lower level than Bembo. But he was also ambitious of giving a new kind of epic to Italian literature. With this view, he versified the Spanish romance of Amadis of Gaul in octave stanzas. The 'Amadigi' is a chivalrous poem in the style of the 'Orlando,' but without the irony of Ariosto.[64] It cannot be reckoned a success; for though written with fertile fancy and a flowing vein, its prolixity is tedious. Tasso lacked the art of sustaining his reader's attention. His attempt to treat the ideal of feudalism seriously, without the faith and freshness of the chivalrous epoch, deprived his work of that peculiar charm which belongs to the Italian romantic epic. While still in MS., he submitted his poem to literary friends, and read it at the Court of Urbino. The acclamation it received from men whose literary principles coincided with his own, raised Tasso's expectations high. He imagined that the world would welcome 'Amadigi' as a masterpiece, combining the interest of 'Orlando' with the dignity and purity of a classic. When it appeared, however, the public received it coldly, and on this occasion the verdict of the people was indubitably right. Another mortification awaited the author. He had dedicated his epic to Philip II. and filled its cantos with adulation of the Spanish race. But the king took no notice of the gift; and two years after the publication of 'Amadigi,' it appeared that

[64] The *Amadigi* was printed by Giolito at Venice in 1560 under the author's own supervision. The book is a splendid specimen of florid typography.

Tasso's agents at the Spanish Court had not taken the trouble to present him with a copy.[65]

Bernardo Tasso is the representative of a class which was common in Renaissance Italy, when courtiers and men of affairs devoted their leisure to study and composed poetry upon scholastic principles. His epic failed precisely through the qualities for which he prized it. Less the product of inspiration than pedantic choice, it bore the taint of languor and unpardonable dulness. Giangiorgio Trissino, in the circumstances of his life no less than in the nature of his literary work, bears a striking resemblance to the author of the 'Amadigi.' The main difference between the two men is that Trissino adopted by preference the career of diplomacy into which poverty drove Tasso.[66] He was born at Vicenza in 1478 of wealthy and noble ancestors, from whom he inherited vast estates. His mother was Cecilia, of the Bevilacqua family. During his boyhood Trissino enjoyed fewer opportunities of study than usually fell to the lot of young Italian nobles. He spent his time in active exercises; and it was only in 1506 that he began his education in earnest. At this date he had been married nine years, and had already lost his wife, the mother of two surviving children, Francesco and Giulio.[67]

Trissino's inclination towards literature induced him to settle at Milan, where he became a pupil of the veteran Demetrius Chalcondylas. He cultivated the society of learned men, collected MSS., and devoted himself to the study of Greek philosophy. From the first, he showed the decided partiality for erudition which was destined to rule his future career. But scholars at that epoch, even though they might be men of princely fortune, had little chance of uninterrupted leisure. Trissino's estates gave him for a while as much trouble as poverty had brought on Tasso. Vicenza was allotted to the Empire in 1509; and afterwards, when the city gave itself to the Venetian Republic, Trissino's adherence to Maximilian's party cost him some months of exile in Germany and the temporary confiscation of his property. Between 1510 and 1514, after his return from Germany, but before he made his peace with Venice, Trissino visited Ferrara, Florence and Rome. These years determined his life as a man of letters. The tragedy of 'Sofonisba,' which was written before 1515, won for its author a place among the foremost poets of the time.[68] The same period decided his future as a courtier. Leo X. sent him on a mission to Bavaria, and upon his return procured his pardon from the Republic of S. Mark. There is not much to be gained by following the intricate details of Trissino's public career. After Leo's death, he was employed by Clement VII. and Paul III. He assisted at the coronation of Charles V., and

[65] Besides the *Amadigi*, Bernardo Tasso composed a second narrative poem, the *Floridante*, which his son, Torquato, retouched and published at Mantua in 1587.

[66] *Giangiorgio Trissino*, by Bernardo Morsolin (Vicenza, 1878), is a copious biography and careful study of this poet's times.

[67] Francesco died in 1514.

[68] See above, pp. 240-241.

on this occasion was made Knight and Count. Gradually he assumed the style of a finished courtier; and though he never took pay from his Papal or princely masters, no poet carried the art of adulation further.[69]

This self-subjection to the annoyances and indignities of Court-life is all the more remarkable because Trissino continued to live like a great noble. When he travelled, he was followed by a retinue of servants. A chaplain attended him for the celebration of Mass. His litter was furnished with silver plate, and with all the conveniences of a magnificent household. His own cook went before, with couriers, to prepare his table; and the equipage included a train of sumpter mules and serving men in livery.[70] At home, in his palace at Vicenza or among his numerous villas, he showed no less magnificence. Upon the building of one country-house at Cricoli, which he designed himself and surrounded with the loveliest Italian gardens, enormous sums were spent; and when the structure was completed, he opened it to noble friends, who lived with him at large and formed an Academy called after him La Trissiniana.[71] Trissino was, moreover, a diligent student and a lover of solitude. He spent many years of his life upon the island of Murano, in a villa secluded from the world, and open to none but a few guests of similar tastes.[72] Yet in spite of the advantages which fortune gave him, in spite of his studious habits, he could not resist the attraction which Courts at that epoch exercised over men of birth and breeding throughout Europe. He was for ever returning to Rome, although he expressed the deepest horror for the corruptions of that sinful city.[73] No sooner had he established himself in quiet among the woods and streams of the Vicentine lowlands or upon the breast of the Venetian lagoons, than the hankering to shine before a Prince came over him, and he resumed his march to Ferrara, or made his bow once more in the Vatican.

The end of Trissino's life was troubled by a quarrel with his son Giulio, in which it is difficult to decide whether the father or the son was more to blame. Some years after the death of his first wife, he married a cousin, Bianca Trissino, by whom he had another son, Ciro. Giulio was sickly, and had taken to the ecclesiastical career. His father's preference for Ciro was decided, and he openly expressed it. That Bianca was not entirely responsible for the ensuing quarrel, is certain from the fact that Trissino separated from this second wife in 1535. But it appears that Giulio opened hostilities by behaving with brutal rudeness to his stepmother. Trissino refused to receive him, and cut off his allowance. Giulio then went to law with his father. A hollow peace was patched up, and, after Bianca's death in 1540, Giulio was appointed steward of the family estates. His management of Trissino's

[69] See Morsolin, *op. cit.* p. 360, for Trissino's own emphatic statement that his services had been unpaid. *Ibid.* p. 344, for a list of the personages he complimented.

[70] *Ibid.* p. 323.

[71] *Ibid.* pp. 219-235.

[72] *Ibid.* p. 301.

[73] *Op. cit.* p. 366.

property led to new disputes, and new acts of violence. On one occasion the son broke into his father's palace at Vicenza, and tried to turn him by armed force into the streets upon a bitter night of Christmas. Meanwhile fresh lawsuits were on foot, and Giulio's cause triumphed in the courts of Venice, whither the case had been removed on appeal from Vicenza. Infuriated by what he deemed a maladministration of justice, the old poet hurled sonnets and invectives against both cities, execrating their infamy in the strongest verse he ever penned.[74] But he could not gain redress against the son he hated. At the age of seventy-two, in the midst of these private troubles, Trissino undertook his last journey to Rome. There he died in 1550, and was buried near John Lascaris in the church of S. Agata in Suburra.

Whatever may have been the crimes of Giulio against his father, Trissino used a cruel and unpardonable revenge upon his eldest son. Not content with blackening his character under the name of Agrilupo in the 'Italia Liberata,'[75] he wrote a codicil to his will, in which he brought against Giulio the most dangerous charge it was then possible to make. He disinherited him with a curse, and accused him of Lutheran heresy.[76] It was clearly the father's intention to hand his son down to an immortality of shame in his great poem, to ruin him in his temporal affairs, and to deprive him of his ecclesiastical privileges. Posterity has defeated his first purpose; for few indeed are the readers of Trissino's 'Italia Liberata.' In his second and his third objects, he was completely successful. Giulio was prosecuted for heresy in 1551, cited before the Inquisition of Bologna in 1553, excommunicated by the Roman Holy Office in 1554, condemned as a contumacious heretic in 1556, driven into hiding at Venice, attacked in bed and half murdered there in 1568, and finally thrown into prison in 1573. He died in prison in 1576, without having shown any signs of repentance, a martyr to his Lutheran opinions.[77] Ciro Trissino, the third actor in this domestic tragedy, had already been strangled in his villa at Cornedo in the year 1574.

Trissino's literary labours bring us back to the specific subject of this chapter. He made it the aim of his life to apply the methods of the ancients to the practice of Italian poetry, and to settle the vexed questions of the language on rational principles. Conscious of the novelty and ambitious nature of his designs, he adopted the Golden Fleece of Jason for an emblem, signifying that his voyages in literature led far beyond the ordinary track, with an inestimable prize in view.[78] Had

[74] *Op. cit.* p. 385.

[75] *Ibid.* p. 413.

[76] *Ibid.* p. 414.

[77] The whole of this extraordinary sequel to Trissino's biography will be read with interest in the last chapter of Signor Morsolin's monograph. It leaves upon my mind the impression that Giulio, though unpardonably ill-tempered, and possibly as ill-conducted in his private life as his foes asserted, was the victim of an almost diabolical persecution.

[78] See Morsolin, *op. cit.* p. 197. This device was imprinted as early as 1529, upon the books published for Trissino at Verona by Janicolo of Brescia.

his genius been equal to his enterprise, he might have effected a decisive revolution. But Trissino was a man of sterling parts and sound judgment rather than a poet; a formulator of rules and precepts rather than a creator. His bent of mind was critical; and in this field he owed his success more to coincidence with prevalent opinion than to originality. Though he fixed the type of Italian tragedy by his 'Sofonisba,' and tied comedy down to Latin models by his 'Simillimi,' we cannot rate his talents as a playwright very high. The 'Poetica,' in which he reduced Horace and Aristotle to Italian prose, and laid down laws for adapting modern literature to antique system, had a wide and lasting influence.[79] We may trace the canon of dramatic unities, which through Italian determined French practice, up to this source; but had not Trissino's precepts been concordant with the tendencies of his age, it is probable that even this treatise would have carried little weight. When he attempted to reform Italian orthography on similar principles, he met with derision and resistance.[80] The world was bent on aping the classics; it did not care about adopting the Greek Kappa, Zeta, Phi, &c. Trissino intervened with more effect in the dispute on language. He pleaded that the vernacular, being the common property of the whole nation, should be called Italian and cultivated with a wise tolerance of local diction. Having discovered a copy of Dante's 'De Eloquio,' he communicated this treatise to the learned world in support of his own views, and had a translation of it printed.[81] This publication embittered the strife which was then raging. Some Florentine scholars, led by Martelli, impugned its genuineness. But the 'De Eloquio' survived antagonistic criticism, and opened a new stage in the discussion.

In his attempt to add the heroic species of the epic to Italian literature, Trissino was even less successful than in his dramatic experiments. Disgusted with Ariosto's success in what he regarded as a barbarous style of art, he set himself to make an epic on the model of Homer, with scrupulous obedience to Aristotle's rules. For his subject he chose an episode from Italian history, and used blank verse instead of the attractive octave stanza. The 'Italia Liberata' cost its author twenty years of labour.[82] It was a masterpiece of erudition, displaying profound acquaintance with Roman tactics, and a competent knowledge of Roman topography. But in spite of its characters *plaqués* upon those of the 'Iliad,' in spite of its learnedly constructed episodes, in spite of its fidelity to Aristotle, the 'Italia Liberata' was not a poem. The

[79] The *Poetica* was printed in 1529; but it had been composed some years earlier.

[80] His grammatical and orthographical treatises were published under the titles of *Epistola a Clemente VII.*, *Grammatichetta*, *Dialogo Castellano*, *Dubbi Grammaticali*. Firenzuola made Trissino's new letters famous and ridiculous by the burlesque sonnets he wrote upon them.

[81] Vicenza, Tolomeo Janicolo, 1529.

[82] Nine books were first printed at Rome in 1547 by Valerio and Luigi Dorici. The whole, consisting of twenty-seven books, was published at Venice in 1548 by Tolomeo Janicolo of Brescia. This Janicolo was Trissino's favourite publisher.

good sense of the nation refused it. Tasso returned to the romantic method and the meretricious charms of the *ottava rima*. Only Gravina among critics spoke a good word for it. The subject lacked real grandeur. Italy delivered from the Goths, was only Italy delivered to the Lombards. The unity of the poem was not the unity of an epic, but of a chapter from a mediæval Chronicle. The machinery of angels, travestied with classic titles, was ridiculous. The Norcian Sibyl, introduced in rivalry with Virgil's Sibyl of Avernus, was out of place. And though Trissino expunged what made the old romantic poems charming, he retained their faults. Intricate underplots and flatteries of noble families were consistent with a species which had its origin in feudal minstrelsy. They were wholly out of character with a professed transcription from the Greek. Neither style nor metre rose to the heroic level. The blank verse was pedestrian and prolix. The language was charged with Lombardisms. Thus the 'Italia Liberata' proved at all points that Trissino could make rules, but that he could not apply them to any purpose. It is curious to compare his failure with Milton's success in a not entirely dissimilar endeavour. The poet achieves a triumph where the pedant only suffers a defeat; and yet the aim of both was almost identical. So different is genius guided by principles from the mechanical carpentry of imitative talent.

CHAPTER XIV

BURLESQUE POETRY AND SATIRE

Relation of Satiric to Serious Literature—Italy has more Parody and Caricature than Satire or Comedy—Life of Folengo—His 'Orlandino'—Critique of Previous Romances—Lutheran Doctrines—Orlando's Boyhood—Griffarosto—Invective against Friars—Maccaronic Poetry—The Travesty of Humanism—Pedantesque Poetry—Glottogrysio Ludimagistro—Tifi Odassi of Padua—The Pedant Vigonça—Evangelista Fossa—Giorgio Alione—Folengo employs the Maccaronic Style for an Epic—His Address to the Muses—His Hero Baldus—Boyhood and Youth—Cingar—The Travels of the Barons—Gulfora—Witchcraft in Italy—Folengo's Conception of Witchcraft—Entrance into Hell—The Zany and the Pumpkin—Nature of Folengo's Satire—His Relation to Rabelais—The 'Moscheis'—The 'Zanitonella'—Maccaronic Poetry was Lombard—Another and Tuscan Type of Burlesque—Capitoli—Their Popular Growth—Berni—His Life—His Mysterious Death—His Character and Style—Three Classes of Capitoli—The pure Bernesque Manner—Berni's Imitators—The Indecency of this Burlesque—Such Humour was Indigenous—Terza Rima—Berni's Satires on Adrian VI. and Clement VII.—His Caricatures—His Sonnet on Aretino—The 'Rifacimento' of Boiardo's 'Orlando'—The Mystery of its Publication—Albicante and Aretino—The Publishers Giunta and Calvi—Berni's Protestant Opinions—Eighteen Stanzas of the 'Rifacimento' printed by Vergerio—Hypothesis respecting the Mutilation of the 'Rifacimento'—Satire in Italy.

In all classical epochs of literature comedy and satire have presented their antithesis to ideal poetry, by setting the actual against the imagined world, or by travestying the forms of serious art. Thus the Titanic farce of Aristophanes was counterposed to Æschylean tragedy; and Molière portrayed men as they are, before an audience which welcomed Racine's pictures of men as the age conceived they ought to be. It is the mark of really great literature when both thesis and antithesis, the aspiration after the ideal and the critique of actual existence, exhibit an equality of scale. The comic and satiric species of poetry attain to grandeur only by contact with impassioned art of a high quality, or else by contrast with a natural greatness in the nation that produces them. Both masque and anti-masque reveal the mental stature of the people. Both issue from the conscience of society, and bear its impress.

If so much be admitted, we can easily understand why burlesque poetry formed the inevitable pendant to polite literature in Italy. There was no national tragedy; therefore there could be no great comedy. The best work of the age, typified by Ariosto's epic, was so steeped in irony that it offered no vantage-ground for humorous counterpoise. There was nothing left but to exaggerate its salient qualities, and to caricature its form. Such exaggeration was burlesque; such caricature was parody. In like manner, satire found no adequate sphere. The nation's life was not on so grand a scale as to evolve the elements of satire from the contrast between faculties and foibles. Nor again could a society, corrupt and satisfied with corruption, anxious to live and let live, apply the lash with earnestness to its own shoulders. *Facit indignatio versus*, was Juvenal's motto; and indignation tore the heart of Swift. But in Italy there was no indignation. All men were agreed to tolerate, condone, and compromise. When vices come to be laughingly admitted, when discords between practice and profession furnish themes for tales and epigrams, the moral conscience is extinct. But without an appeal to conscience the satirist has no *locus standi*. Therefore, in Italy there was no great satire, as in Italy there was no great comedy.

The burlesque rhymesters portrayed their own and their neighours' immorality with self-complacent humour, calling upon the public to make merry over the spectacle. This poetry, obscene, equivocal, frivolous, horribly sincere, supplied a natural antithesis to the pseudo-platonic, pedantic, artificial mannerism of the purists. In point of intrinsic value, there is not much to choose between the Petrarchistic and the burlesque styles. Many burlesque poets piqued themselves with justice on their elegance, and clothed gross thoughts in diction of elaborate polish. Meanwhile they laid the affectations, conventions and ideals of the age impartially under contribution. The sonnetteers suggested parodies to Aretino, who celebrated vice and deformity in women with hyperboles adapted from the sentimental school.[1] The age of gold was ridiculed by Romolo Bertini.[2] The idyll found its travesty in Berni's pictures of crude village loves and in Folengo's 'Zanitonella.' Chivalry became absurd by the simple process of enforcing the prosaic elements in Ariosto, reducing his heroes to the level of plebeian life, and exaggerating the extravagance of his romance. The ironical smile which played upon his lips, expands into broad grins and horse-laughter. Yet though the burlesque poets turned everything they touched into ridicule, these buffoons were not unfrequently possessed of excellent good sense. Not a few of them, as we shall see, were among the freest thinkers of their age. Like Court jesters they dared to utter truths which would have sent a serious writer to the stake. Lucidity of intellectual vision was granted at this time in Italy to none but positive and materialistic thinkers—to analysts like Machiavelli and Pomponazzi, critics like Pietro Aretino, poets with feet firmly planted on the earth like Berni and Folengo. The two last-named artists in the burlesque style may be selected as the leaders of two different but cognate schools, the one flourishing in Lombardy, the other in Florence.

Girolamo Folengo was born in 1491 of noble parents at Cipada, a village of the Mantuan district. He made his first studies under his father's roof, and in due time proceeded to Bologna. Here he attended the lectures of Pomponazzi, and threw himself with ardour into the pleasures and perils of the academical career. Francesco Gonzaga, a

[1] See the Madrigals in *Opere Burlesche*, vol. iii. pp. 36-38.
[2] *Ibid*. p. 290.

fantastical and high-spirited libertine from Mantùa, was the recognised leader of the students at that moment. Duels, challenges, intrigues and street-quarrels formed the staple of their life. It was an exciting and romantic round of gaiety and danger, of which the novelists have left us many an animated picture. Folengo by his extravagant conduct soon exhausted the easy patience of the university authorities. He was obliged to quit Bologna, and his father refused to receive him. In this emergency he took refuge in a Benedictine convent at Brescia. When he made himself a monk, Folengo changed his Christian name to Teofilo, by which he is now best known in literature. But he did not long endure the confinement of a cloister. After six years spent among the Benedictines, he threw the cowl aside, and ran off with a woman, Girolama Dieda, for whom he had conceived an insane passion.[3] This was in the year 1515. During the next eleven years he gave himself to the composition of burlesque poetry. His 'Maccaronea' appeared at Venice in 1519, and his 'Orlandino' in 1526. The former was published under the pseudonym of Merlinus Cocaius, compounded of a slang word in the Mantuan dialect, and of the famous wizard's title of romance.[4] The latter bore the *nom de plume* of *Limerno Pitocco*—an anagram of Merlino, with the addition of an epithet pointing to the poet's indigence. These works brought Folengo fame but little wealth, and he was fain to return at last to his old refuge.[5] Resuming the cowl, he now retired to a monastery in the kingdom of Naples, visited Sicily, and died at last near Padua, in the convent of S. Croce di Campese. This was in 1544. The last years of his life had been devoted to religious poetry, which is not read with the same curiosity as his burlesque productions.

Teofilo Folengo, or Merlinus Cocaius, or Limerno Pitocco, was, when he wrote his burlesque poems, what the French would call a *déclassé*. He had compromised his character in early youth and had been refused the shelter of his father's home. He had taken monastic vows in a moment of pique, or with the baser object of getting daily bread in idleness. His elopement from the convent with a paramour had brought scandal on religion. Each of these steps contributed to place him beyond the pale of respectability. Driven to bay and forced to earn his living, he now turned round upon society; and spoke his mind out

[3] In *Mac.* xx. (p. 152 of Mantuan edition, 1771), he darkly alludes to this episode of his early life, where he makes an exposed witch exclaim:

> Nocentina vocor magicis tam dedita chartis,
> Decepique mea juvenem cum fraude Folengum.

[4] I cannot find sufficient authority for the story of Folengo's having had a grammar-master named Cocaius, from whom he borrowed part of his pseudonym. The explanation given by his Mantuan editor, which I have adopted in the text, seems the more probable. *Coeáj* in Mantuan dialect means a cork for a bottle; and the phrase *ch' al fà di cocaj* is used to indicate some extravagant absurdity or blunder.

[5] There seems good reason, from many passages in his *Maccaronea*, to believe that his repentance was sincere. I may here take occasion to remark that, though his poems are gross in the extreme, their moral tone is not unhealthy. He never makes obscenity or vice attractive.

with a freedom born of bile and cynical indifference. If he had learned nothing else at Bologna, he had imbibed the materialistic philosophy of Pomponazzi together with Gonzaga's lessons in libertinage. Brutalised, degraded in his own eyes, rejected by the world of honest or decorous citizens, but with a keen sense of the follies, vices and hypocrisies of his age, he resolved to retaliate by a work of art that should attract attention and force the public to listen to his comments on their shame. In his humorous poetry there is, therefore, a deliberate if not a very dignified intention. He does not merely laugh, but mixes satire with ribaldry, and points buffoonery with biting sarcasm. Since the burlesque style had by its nature to be parasitical and needed an external motive, Folengo chose for the subject of his parody the romance of 'Orlando,' which was fashionable to the point of extravagance in Italy after the appearance of the 'Furioso.' But he was not satisfied with turning a tale of Paladins to ridicule. He used it as the shield behind which he knew that he might safely shoot his arrows at the clergy and the princes of his native land, attack the fortresses of orthodoxy, and vent his spleen upon society by dragging its depraved ideals in the mire of his own powerful but vulgar scorn.

Folengo has told us that the 'Orlandino' was conceived and written before the 'Maccaronea,' though it was published some years later. It is probable that the rude form and plebeian language of this burlesque romance found but little favour with a public educated in the niceties of style. They were ready to accept the bastard Latin dialect invented for his second venture, because it offended no puristic sensibilities. But the coarse Italian of the 'Orlandino' could not be relished by academicians, who had been pampered with the refinements of Berni's wanton Muse.[6] Only eight cantos appeared; nor is there reason to suppose that any more were written, for it may be assumed that the fragment had fulfilled its author's purpose.[7] That purpose was to satirise the vice, hypocrisy and superstition of the clergy, and more particularly of the begging friars. In form the 'Orlandino' pretends to be a romance of chivalry, and it bears the same relation to the 'Orlando' of Boiardo and Ariosto as the 'Secchia Rapita' to the heroic poems of Tasso's school. It begins with a burlesque invocation to Federigo Gonzaga, Marquis of Mantua, in which the poet bluntly describes his poverty

[6] Part of Folengo's satire is directed against the purists. See Canto i. 7-9. He confesses himself a Lombard, and shrugs his shoulders at their solemn criticisms:

> Non però, se non nacqui Tosco, i' piango;
> Chè ancora il ciacco gode nel suo fango.

To the reproach of 'turnip-eating Lombard' he retorts, 'Tuscan chatter-box.' Compare vi. 1, 2, on his own style:

> Oscuri sensi ed affettate rime,
> Qual' è chi dica mai compor Limerno?

[7] The first line of the elegy placed upon the edition of 1526 runs thus:

> Mensibus istud opus tribus *indignatio fecit*.

Folengo claims for himself a satiric purpose. The edition used by me is Molini's Londra, 1775.

and begs for largess. Then Folengo passes to an account of his authorities and to the criticism of his predecessors in romantic poetry He had recourse, he says, to a witch of Val Camonica, who mounted him upon a ram, and bore him to the country of the Goths. There he found forty decades of Turpin's history among the rubbish of old books stolen from Italy. Of these, three decades had already been discovered and translated by Boiardo; but after versifying a large portion of the second, the poet left the rest of it to Ariosto. The sixth was stolen from him by Francesco Bello. The last he gave with his own hands to Poliziano, who put it into rhyme and allowed Pulci to have the credit of his labours.[8] Folengo himself took a portion of the first decade, and thus obtained material for treating of the birth and boyhood of Orlando. This exordium is chiefly valuable as a piece of contemporary criticism:

Queste tre Deche dunque sin quà trovo
Esser dal fonte di Turpin cavate;
Ma *Trebisonda*, *Amcroia*, *Spagna*, e *Bovo*
Coll' altro resto al foco sian donate:
Apocrife son tutte, e le riprovo
Come nemiche d' ogni veritate;
Boiardo, l'Ariosto, Pulsi, e 'l Cieco
Autenticati sono, ed io con seco.

If we may accept this stanza as expressing the opinion of Italians in the sixteenth century relative to their romantic poets, we find that it almost exactly agrees with that of posterity. Only the 'Mambriano' of Bello has failed to maintain its place beside the 'Morgante' and 'Orlando.'

Embarking upon the subject of his tale, Folengo describes the Court of Charlemagne, and passes the Paladins in review, intermingling comic touches with exaggerated imitations of the romantic style. The peers of France preserve their well-known features through the distorting medium of caricature; while humorous couplets, detonating here and there like crackers, break the mock-heroical monotony. Gano, for example, is still the arch-traitor of the tribe of Judas:

Figliuol non d' uomo, nè da Dio creato,
Ma il gran Diavol ebbelo cacato.

The effect of parody is thus obtained by emphasising the style of elder poets and suddenly breaking off into a different vein. Next comes the description of Berta's passion for Milone, with a singularly coarse and out-spoken invective against love.[9] Meanwhile Charlemagne has pro-

[8] See above, p. 131 *note* 46, for the belief that Poliziano was the real author of the *Morgante Maggiore*.

[9] Canto i. 64, 65; ii. 1-4.

Ed io dico ch' Amor è un bardassola
Più che sua madre non fu mai puttana, &c.

Folengo, of course, has a mistress, to whom he turns at the proper moments of his narrative. This *mia diva Caritunga* is a caricature of the fashionable Laura. See v. i. 2:

O donna mia, ch' hai gli occhi, ch' hai l' orecchie,
Quelli di pipistrel, queste di bracco, &c.

claimed a tournament. The peers array themselves, and the Court is in a state of feverish expectation. *Parturiunt montes*: instead of mailed warriors careering upon fiery chargers, the knights crawl into the lists on limping mules and lean asses, with a ludicrous array of kitchen-gear for armour. The description of this donkey-tournament is one of Folengo's triumphs.[10] When Milone comes upon the scene and jousts beneath his lady's balcony, the style is heightened to the tone of true romance, and, but for the roughness of the language, we might fancy that a page of the 'Orlando' were beneath our eyes. A banquet follows, after which we are regaled with a Court-ball, and then ensues the comic chain of incidents which bring Milone and Berta to the fruition of their love. They elope, take ship, and are separated by a series of mishaps upon the open sea. Berta is cast ashore alone in Italy, and begs her way to Sutri, where she gives birth to Orlando in a shepherd's cabin. During the course of these adventures, Folengo diverts his readers with many brilliant passages and bits of satire, at one time inveighing against the license of balls, at another describing the mixed company on board a ship of passage; now breaking off into burlesque pedigrees, and then again putting into Berta's mouth a string of Lutheran opinions. Though the personages are romantic, the incidents are copied with realistic fidelity from actual life. We are moving among Italian *bourgeois* in the masquerade of heroes and princesses.

Berta's prayer, when she found herself alone upon the waters in an open boat, is so characteristic of Folengo's serious intention that it deserves more than a passing comment.[11] She addresses herself to God instead of to any Saints:

> A te ricorro, non a Piero, o Andrea,
> Chè l' altrui mezzo non mi fa mestiero:
> Ben tengo a mente che la Cananea
> Non supplicò nè a Giacomo nè a Piero.

It is the hypocrisy of friars, Folengo says, who sacrifice to Moloch, while they use the name of Mary to cloak their crimes—it is this damnable hypocrisy which has blinded simple folk into trusting the invocation of Saints. Avarice is the motive of these false priests; and lust moves them to preach the duty of confession:

> E quì trovo ben spesso un Confessore
> Essere più ruffiano che Dottore.

Therefore, cries Berta, I make my confession to God alone and from Him seek salvation, and vow that, if I escape the fury of the sea, I will no more lend belief to men who sell indulgences for gold. So far

[10] Canto ii. 9-42.
[11] Canto vi. 40-46. I have placed a translation of this passage in an Appendix to this chapter.

the poet is apparently sincere. In the next stanza he resumes his comic vein:

> Cotal preghiere carche d' eresia
> Berta facea, mercè ch' era Tedesca;
> Perhèc in quel tempo la Teologia
> Era fatta Romana e fiandresca;
> Ma dubito ch' alfin nella Turchia
> Si troverà vivendo alla Moresca;
> Perchè di Cristo l' inconsutil vesta
> Squarciata è sì che più non ve ne resta.

The blending of buffoonery and earnestness in Folengo's style might be illustrated by the bizarre myth of the making of peasants, where he introduces Christ and the Apostles:[12]

> *Transibat Jesus* per un gran villaggio
> Con Pietro, Andrea, Giovanni, e con Taddeo;
> Trovan ch' un asinello in sul rivaggio
> Molte pallotte del suo sterco feo.
> Disse allor Piero al suo Maestro saggio:
> *En, Domine, fac homines ex eo.*
> *Surge, Villane,* disse Cristo allora;
> E 'l villan di que' stronzi saltò fora.

His fantastic humour, half-serious, half-flippant, spares nothing sacred or profane. Even the Last Judgment receives an inconceivably droll treatment on the slender occasion of an allusion to the disasters of Milan.[13] Folengo has just been saying that Italy well deserves her title of *barbarorum sepultura.*[14]

> Chè veramente in quell' orribil giorno
> Che in Giosafatto suonerà la tromba,
> Facendosi sentire al mondo intorno,
> E i morti salteran fuor d' ogni tomba,
> Non sarà pozzo, cacatojo, o forno,
> Che mentre il tararan del ciel ribomba,
> Non getti fuora Svizzeri, Francesi,
> Tedeschi, Ispani, e d' altri assai paesi;

[12] Canto v. 56-58. The contempt for country folk seems unaffected.

[13] Canto vi. 55-57. This passage is a caricature of Pulci's burlesque description of the Last Day. See above, p. 127. Folengo's loathing of the strangers who devoured Italy is clear here, as also in i. 43, ii. 4, 59. But there is no force in his invectives or laments.

> L'Italia non più Italia appello,
> Ma d' ogni strana gente un bel bordello.
>
> . . . .
>
> Che 'l cancaro mangiasse il Taliano,
> Il quale, o ricco, i povero che sia,
> Desidra in nostre stanze il Tramontano.
>
> . . . .
>
> Chè se non fosser le gran parti in quella,
> Dominerebbe il mondo Italia bella.

[14] For verily on that most dreadful day,
When in the Valley of Jehosaphat
The trump shall sound, and thrill this globe of clay,
And dead folk shuddering leave their tombs thereat,

E vederassi una mirabil guerra,
Fra loro combattendo gli ossi suoi:
Chi un braccio, chi una man, chi un piede afferra;
Ma vien chi dice—questi non son tuoi—
Anzi son miei—non sono; e sulla terra
Molti di loro avran gambe di buoi,
Testi di muli, e d' asini le schiene,
Siccome all' opre di ciascum conviene.

The birth of Orlando gives occasion for a mock-heroic passage, in which Pulci is parodied to the letter.[15] All the more amusing for the assumption of the pompous style, is the ensuing account of the hero's boyhood among the street-urchins of Sutri. When he is tall enough to bestride a broomstick, Orlandino proves his valour by careering through the town and laughing at the falls he gets. At seven he shows the strength of twelve:

Urta, fracassa, rompe, quassa, e smembra:
Orsi, leoni, tigri non paventa,
Ma contro loro intrepido s' avventa.

The octave stanzas become a cataract of verbs and nouns to paint his tempestuous childhood. It is a spirited comic picture of the Italian *enfant terrible*, stone-throwing, boxing, scuffling, and swearing like a pickpocket. At the same time the boy grows in cunning, and supports his mother by begging from one and bullying another of the citizens of Sutri:

Io v' addimando per l' amor di Dio
Un pane solo ed un boccal di vino;
Officio non fu mai più santo e pio
Che se pascete il pover pellegrino:
Se non men date, vi prometto ch' io,
Quantunque sia di membra si piccino,
Ne prenderò da me senza riguardo:
Chè salsa non vogl' io di San Bernardo.
Cancar vi mangi, datemi a mangiare,
Se non, vi butterò le porte giuso;
Per debolezza sentomi mancare,

No well, sewer, privy shall be found, I say,
Which, while the angels roar their rat-tat-tat,
Shall not disgorge its Spaniards, Frenchmen, Swiss,
Germans, and rogues of every race that is.

Then shall we see a wonderful dispute,
As each with each they wrangle, bone for bone;
One grasps an arm, one grabs a hand, a foot;
Comes one who says, 'These are not yours, you loon!'
'They're mine!' 'They're not!' While many a limb of brute
Joined to their human bodies shall be shown,
Mule's heads, bull's legs, cruppers and ears of asses,
As each man' life on earth his spirit classes.

[15] Canto vi. 8-11:

Quì nacque Orlando, l' inclito Barone;
Quì nacque Orlando, Senator Romano, &c.

E le budella vannomi a riffuso.
Gente devota, e voi persone care
Che vi leccate di buon rosto il muso,
Mandatemi, per Dio, qualche minestra,
O me la trate giù dalla finestra.

In the course of these adventures Orlandino meets Oliver, the son of Rainero, the governor, and breaks his crown in a quarrel. This brings about the catastrophe; for the young hero pours forth such a torrent of voluble slang, mixed with imprecations and menaces, that Rainero is forced to acknowledge the presence of a superior genius.[16] But before the curtain falls upon the discovery of Orlandino's parentage and his reception into the company of peers, Folengo devotes a canto to the episodical history of the Prelate Griffarosto.[17] The name of this Rabelaisian ecclesiastic—Claw-the-roast—sufficiently indicates the line of the poet's satire.

Whatever appeared in the market of Sutri fit for the table, fell into his clutches, or was transferred to the great bag he wore beneath his scapulary. His library consisted of cookery books; and all the tongues he knew, were tongues of swine and oxen.[18] Orlandino met this Griffarosto fat as a stalled ox, one morning after he had purchased a huge sturgeon:

La Reverenzia vostra non si parta;
Statemi alquanto, prego, ad ascoltare.
Nimis sollicita es, o Marta, Marta,
Circa substantiam Christi devorare.
Dammi poltron, quel pesce, ch' io 'l disquarta,
Per poterlo *in communi* dispensare,
Nassa d' anguille che tu sei, lurcone;
E ciò dicendo dagli col bastone.

The priest was compelled to disgorge his prey, and the fame of the boy's achievement went abroad through Sutri. Rainero thereupon sent for Griffarosto, and treated the Abbot to such a compendious abuse of monks in general as would have delighted a Lutheran.[19] Griffarosto essayed to answer him with a ludicrous jumble of dog Latin; but the Governor requested him to defer his apology for the morrow. The description of Griffarosto's study in the monastery, where wine and victuals fill the place of books, his oratory consecrated to Bacchus, the conversation with his cook, and the *ruse* by which the cook gets chosen Prior in his master's place, carry on the satire through fifty stanzas of

[16] Canto vii. 61-65.

[17] He has been identified on sufficiently plausible grounds with Ignazio Squarcialupo, the prior of Folengo's convent. In the *Maccaronea* this burlesque personage reappears as the keeper of a tavern in hell, who feeds hungry souls on the most hideous messes of carrion and vermin (Book xxiii. p. 217). There is sufficient rancour in Griffarosto's portrait to justify the belief that Folengo meant in it to gratify a private thirst for vengeance.

[18] In the play on the word *lingue* there is a side-thrust at the Purists.

[19] Canto viii. 23-32.

slashing sarcasm. The whole episode is a pendent picture to Pulci's Margutte. Then, by a brusque change from buffoonery to seriousness, Folengo plunges into a confession of faith, attributed to Rainero, but presumably his own.[20] It includes the essential points of Catholic orthodoxy, abjuring the impostures of priests and friars, and taking final station on the Lutheran doctrine of salvation by faith and repentance. Idle as a dream, says Folengo, are the endeavours made by friars to force scholastic conclusions on the conscience in support of theses S. Paul would have rejected. What they preach, they do not comprehend. Their ignorance is only equal to their insolent pretension. They are worse than Judas in their treason to Christ, worse than Herod, Anna, Caiaphas, or Pilate. They are only fit to consort with usurers and slaves. They use the names of saints and the altar of the Virgin as the means of glutting their avarice with the gold of superstitious folk. They abuse confession to gratify their lusts. Their priories are dens of dogs, hawks, and reprobate women. They revel in soft beds, drink to intoxication, and stuff themselves with unctuous food. And still the laity entrust their souls to these rogues, and there are found many who defraud their kith and kin in order to enrich a convent![21]

It would not be easy to compose an invective more suited to degrade the objects of a satirist's anger by the copiousness and the tenacity of the dirt flung at them. Yet the 'Orlandino' was written by a monk, who, though he had left his convent, was on the point of returning ot it; and the poem was openly printed during the pontificate of Clement VII. That Folengo should have escaped inquisitorial censure is remarkable. That he should have been readmitted to the Benedictine order after this outburst of bile and bold diffusion of heretical opinion, is only explicable by the hatred which subsisted in Italy between the rules of S. Francis and S. Benedict. While attacking the former, he gratified the spite and jealousy of the latter. But the fact is that his auditors, whether lay or clerical, were too accustomed to similar charges and too frankly conscious of their truth, to care about them. Folengo stirred no indignation in the people, who had laughed at ecclesiastical corruption since the golden days of the 'Decameron.' He roused no shame in the clergy, for, till Luther frightened the Church into that pseudo-reformation which Sarpi styled a deformation of manners, the authorities of Rome were nonchalantly careless what was said about them.[22] An atrabilious monk in his garret vented his spleen with more than usual acrimony, and the world applauded. *Ha fatto un bel libro!* That was all. Conversely, it is not strange that the weighty truths about religion uttered by Folengo should have had but little influence. He was a scribbler, famous for scurrility, notoriously profligate in private

[20] Canto viii. 73-84. This passage I have also translated and placed in an Appendix to this chapter, where the chief Lutheran utterances of the burlesque poets will be found together.

[21] In addition to the eighth Canto, I have drawn on iii. 4, 20; iv. 13; vi. 44, for this list.

[22] Leo X.'s complacent acceptance of the *Mandragola* proves this.

life. Free thought in Italy found itself too often thus in company with immorality. The names of heretic and Lutheran carried with them at that time a reproach more pungent and more reasonable than is usual with the epithets of theological hatred.[23]

In the 'Orlandino,' Ariosto's irony is degraded to buffoonery. The prosaic details he mingled with his poetry are made the material of a new and vulgar comedy of manners. The satire he veiled in allegory or polite discussion, bursts into open virulence. His licentiousness yields to gross obscenity. The chivalrous epic, as employed for purposes of art in Italy, contained within itself the germs of this burlesque. It was only necessary to develop certain motives at the expense of general harmony, to suppress the noble and pathetic elements, and to lower the literary key of utterance, in order to produce a parody. Ariosto had strained the semi-seriousness of romance to the utmost limits of endurance. For his successors nothing was left but imitation, caricature, or divergence upon a different track. Of these alternatives, Folengo and Berni, Aretino and Fortiguerra, chose the second; Tasso took the third, and provided Tassoni with the occasion of a new burlesque.

While the romantic epic lent itself thus easily to parody, another form of humorous poetry took root and flourished on the mass of Latin literature produced by the Revival. Latin never became a wholly dead language in Italy: and at the height of the Renaissance a public had been formed whose appreciation of classic style ensured a welcome for its travesty. To depreciate the humanistic currency by an alloy of plebeian phrases, borrowed from various base dialects; to ape Virgilian mannerism while treating of the lowest themes suggested by boisterous mirth or satiric wit; was the method of the so-called Maccaronic poets. It is matter for debate who first invented this style, and who created the title *Maccaronea*. So far back as the thirteenth century, we notice a blending of Latin with French and German in certain portions of the 'Carmina Burana.'[24] But the two elements of language here lie side by side, without interpenetration. This imperfect fusion is not sufficient to constitute the genuine Maccaronic manner. The jargon known as Maccaronic must consist of the vernacular, suited with Latin terminations, and freely mingled with classical Latin words. Nothing should meet the ear or eye, which does not sound or look like Latin; but, upon inspection, it must be discovered that a half or third is simple slang and common speech tricked out with the endings of Latin declen-

[23] The curious history of Giulio Trissino, told by Bernardo Morsolin in the last chapters of his *Giangiorgio Trissino* (Vicenza, 1878), reveals the manner of men who adopted Lutheranism in Italy in the sixteenth century. See above, p. 339. I shall support the above remarks lower down in this chapter by reference to Berni's Lutheran opinions.

[24] The political and ecclesiastical satires known in England as the work of Walter Mapes, abound in pseudo-Maccaronic passages. Compare Du Méril, *Poésies Populaires Latines antérieures au xiime Siècle*, p. 142, &c., for further specimens of undeveloped Maccaronic poetry of the middle ages.

sions and conjugations.[25] In Italy, where the modern tongue retained close similarity to Latin, this amalgamation was easy; and we find that in the fifteenth century the hybrid had already assumed finished form. The name by which it was then known, indicates its composition. As maccaroni is dressed with cheese and butter, so the maccaronic poet mixed colloquial expressions of the people with classical Latin, serving up a dish that satisfied the appetite by rarity and richness of concoction. At the same time, since maccaroni was the special delicacy of the proletariat, and since a stupid fellow was called a *Maccherone*, the ineptitude and the vulgarity of the species are indicated by its title. Among the Maccaronic poets we invariably find ourselves in low Bohemian company. No Phœbus sends them inspiration; nor do they slake their thirst at the Castalian spring. The muses they invoke are tavern-wenches and scullions, haunting the slums and stews of Lombard cities.[26] Their mistresses are of the same type as Villon's Margot. Mountains of cheese, rivers of fat broth, are their Helicon and Hippocrene. Their pictures of manners demand a coarser brush than Hogarth's to do them justice.

Before engaging in the criticism of this Maccaronic literature, it is necessary to interpolate some notice of a kindred style, called *pedantesco*. This was the exact converse of the Maccaronic manner. Instead of adapting Italian to the rules of Latin, the parodist now treated Latin according to the grammatical usages and metrical laws of Italian. A good deal of the 'Hypnerotomachia Poliphili' is written in *lingua pedantesca*. But the recognised masterpiece of the species is a book called 'I Cantici di Fidentio Glottogrysio Ludimagistro.' The author's real name was Camillo Scrofa, a humanist and schoolmaster of Vicenza. Though more than once reprinted, together with similar compositions by equally obscure craftsmen, his verses are exceedingly rare.[27] They owe their neglect partly to the absurdity of their language, partly to the undisguised immorality of their subject matter. Of the *stilo pedantesco*

[25] Those who are curious to study this subject further, should consult the two exhaustive works of Octave Delepierre, *Macaronéana* (Paris, 1852), and *Macaronéana Andra* (Londres, Trübner, 1862). These two publications contain a history of Maccaronic verse, with reprints of the scarcer poems in this style. The second gives the best text of Odassi, Fossa, and the *Virgiliana*. The *Maccheronee di Cinque Poeti Italiani* (Milano, Daelli, 1864) is a useful little book, since it reproduces Delepierre's collections in a cheap and convenient form. In the uncertainty which attends the spelling of this word, I have adopted the form *Maccaronic*.

[26] Take one example, from the induction to Odassi's poems (*Mac. Andr.* p. 63):

> O putanarum putanissima, vacca vaccarum,
> O potifarum potissima pota potaza . . .
> Tu Phrosina mihi foveas, mea sola voluptas;
> Nulla mihi poterit melius succurrere Musa,
> Nullus Apollo magis.

[27] The book was first printed at Vicenza. The copy I have studied is the Florentine edition of 1574. Scrofa's verses, detached from the collection, may be found in the *Parnaso Italiano*, vol. xxv.

the following specimen may suffice. It describes a hostelry of boors and peasants:[28]

Pur pedetentim giunsi ad un cubiculo,
Sordido, inelegante, ove molti hospiti
Facean corona a un semimortuo igniculo.
Salvete, dissi, et Giove lieti e sospiti
Vi riconduca a i vostri dolci hospitii!
Ma responso non hebbi; o rudi, o inhospiti!
Io che tra veri equestri e tra patritii
Soglio seder, mi vedi alhor negligere
Da quegli huomini novi et adventitii.
Non sapea quasi indignabundo eligere
Partito; pur al fin fu necessario
Tra lor per calefarmi un scanno erigere.
Che colloquio, O Dii boni, empio e nefario
Pervenne a l' aure nostre purgatissime,
Da muover nausea a un lenone, a un sicario!

One of the most famous and earliest, if not absolutely the first among the authors of Maccaronic verse, was Tifi Odassi, a Paduan, whose poems were given to the press after his death, in at least two editions earlier than the close of the fifteenth century.[29] He chose a commonplace *Novella* for his theme; but the interest of his tale consists less in its argument than in its vivid descriptions of low town-life. Odassi's portraits of plebeian characters are executed with masterly realism, and the novelty of the vehicle gives them a singularly trenchant force. It is unfortunately impossible to bring either the cookshop-keeper or his female servant, the mountebank or the glutton, before modern readers. These pictures are too Rabelaisian.[30] I must content myself with a passage taken from the description of a bad painter, which, though it is inferior in comic power, contains nothing unpardonably gross.[31]

Quodsi forte aliquem voluit depingere gallum,
Quicunque aspiciat poterit jurare cigognam;
Depinxitque semel canes in caza currentes,
Omnes credebant natantes in æquore luzos;
Sive hominem pingit, poteris tu credere lignum
In quo sartores ponunt sine capite vestes;
Seu nudos facit multo sudore putinos,
Tu caput a culo poteris dignoscere nunquam;
Sive facit gremio Christum retinere Mariam,
Non licet a filio sanctam dignoscere matrem;

[28] *Op. cit.* p. 23.

[29] Bernardino Scardeone in his work *De antiquitate urbis Patavii*, &c. (Basileæ, 1560), speaks of Odassi as the inventor of Maccaronic poetry: 'adinvenit enim primus ridiculum carminis genus, nunquam prius a quopiam excogitatum, quod Macaronæum nuncupavit, multis farcitum salibus, et satyrica mordacitate respersum.' He adds that Odassi desired on his deathbed that the book should be burned. In spite of this wish, it was frequently reprinted during Scardeone's lifetime.

[30] It is with great regret that I omit Bertapalia, the charlatan—a portrait executed with inimitable verve. Students of Italian life in its lowest and liveliest details should seek him out. *Mac. Andr.* pp. 68-71.

[31] *Ibid.* p. 71. I have altered spelling and punctuation.

Pro gardelinis depingit sepe gallinas,
Et pro gallinis depingit sepe caballos:
Blasfemat, jurat, culpam dicit esse penelli,
Quos spazzaturas poteris jurare de bruscho;
Tam bene depingit pictorum pessimus iste,
Nec tamen inferior se cogitat esse Bellino.

It will be seen from this specimen that Italian and Latin are confounded without regard to either prosody or propriety of diction. The style, far from being even pedestrian, is reptile, and the inspiration is worthy of the source imagined by the poet.[32] As Odassi remarks in his induction:

Aspices, lector, Prisciani vulnera mille
Gramaticamque novam, quam nos docuere putane.

The note struck by Odassi was sustained by his immediate imitators. Another Paduan author used this parody of humanistic verse to caricature a humanist, whom he called Vigonça.[33] Like Odassi, he invoked Venus Volgivaga; and like Odassi's, very little of his verse is quotable. The following extracts may be found acceptable for their humorous account of a Professor's inaugural lecture in the University of Padua.[34] Vigonça announces the opening of his course:

Ipse ante totis facit asavere piacis,
Et totis scolis mandat bolletina bidelis,
Quæ bolletina portabant talia verba:
'Comes magnificus cavalerius ille Vigonça,
Patricius Patavus comesque ab origine longa,
Vos rogat ad primam veniatis quisque legendam;
Qui veniet, magnum fructum portabit a casa.'
Omnes venturos sese dixere libenter;
Promissit comes, capitaneus atque potestas,
Et paduani vechi juvenesque politi.
Lux promissa aderat, qua se smatare Vigonça
Debebat, atque suam cunctis monstrare matieram.
Ille tamen totam facit conçare la scolam,
De nigro totam facit conzare cathedram,
In qua debebat matus sprologare Vigonça;
Cetera fulgebant banchalis atque thapetis,
Et decem in brochis dicit spendidisse duchatos.

After narrating how the whole town responded to Vigonça's invitation, and how the folk assembled to hear his first address, the poet thus describes the great occasion:[35]

[32] Cognosces in me quantum tua numina possunt,
Quæque tua veniunt stilantia carmina pota.

[33] This anonymous poet has been variously identified with Odassi and with Fossa of Cremona. The frequent occurrence of Paduan idioms seems to point to a Paduan rather than a Cremonese author; and though there is no authoritative reason for referring the poem to Odassi, it resembles his style sufficiently to render the hypothesis of his authorship very plausible. The name of the hero, Vigonça, is probably the Italian *Bigoǹcia*, which meant in one sense a pulpit or a reading-desk, in its ordinary sense a tub.

[34] Daelli, *Maccheronee di Cinque Poeti Italiani* (Milano, 1864), p. 50: cp. *Mac. Andr.* p. 19.

[35] Daelli, *op. cit.* pp. 52, 54.

Sed neque bastabat ingens intrantibus ussus;
Rumpebat cupos parietes atque fenestras,
Inque ipso multos busos fecere parete.
Tunc ibi bidelus cunctos ratione pregavit,
Et sibi cavavit nigrum Vigonça biretum,
Et manicas alzans dedit hic sua verba de mato,
Et començavit sanctam faciendo la crucem.
'Magnifice pretor, pariter generose prefecte,
Tu facunde comes auri portando colanam,
Magnus philosophus, lingua in utraque poeta,
Tu primicerius, Venete spes alma paludis,
Et vos doctores, celeberrima fama per orbem,
Vos cavalerii multum sperone dorati,
Vosque scolares, cives, charique sodales!
Non ego perdivi tempus futuendo putanas,
Non ego zugando, non per bordella vagando;
Non ego cum canibus lepores seguendo veloces,
Non cum sparveris, non cum falconibus ipse;
Non ego cum dadis tabulam lissando per ullam;
Non ego cum chartis volui dissipare dinaros,
Qualiter in Padue faciunt de nocte scolares.
Quum jocant alii, stabat in casa Vigonça
Et studiabat guardando volumina longa.'

This Paduan caricature may be reckoned among the most valuable documents we possess for the illustration of the professorial system in Italy during the ascendency of humanism. Some material of the same kind is supplied by the 'Virgiliana' of Evangelista Fossa, a Cremonese gentleman, who versified a Venetian *Burla* in mock-heroic Latin. He, too, painted the portrait of a pedant, Priscianus:[36]

Est mirandus homo; nam sunt miracula in illo,
Omnes virtutes habet hic in testa fichatas . . .
Nam quicquid dicit, semper per littera parlat,
Atque habet in boccham pulchra hæc proverbia semper. . . .
Est letrutus nam multum, studiavit in omni
Arte, fuit Padoe, fuit in la citta de Perosa,
Bononie multum mansit de senno robando.

But Fossa's 'Virgiliana,' while aiming at a more subtle sort of parody than the purely maccaronic poems, misses their peculiar salt, and, except for the Hudibrastic description of the author on horseback,[37] offers nothing of great interest.

Brief notice also may be taken of Giovan Giorgio Alione's satire on the Lombards. Alione was a native of Asti, and seasoned his maccaroni with the base French of his birthplace. For Asti, trans erred to the House of Orleans by Gian Galeazzo Visconti, was more than half a French city, and its inhabitants spoke the Gallic dialect common to Piedmont.[38] Alione is proud of this subjection, and twits the Lombards of Milan and Pavia with being unworthy of their ancient origin no less

[36] *Ibid.* p. 112; *Mac. Andr.* p. 32.
[37] 'De fossa compositore quando venit patavio' (*Mac. Andr.* p. 39.)
[38] Alione says:

Cum nos Astenses reputemur undique Galli.

than of their modern masters.[39] Unlike the ordinary run of burlesque poems, his 'Macharonea' is virulently satirical. Animated by a real rage against the North Italians, Alione paints them as effeminate cowards, devoid of the sense of honour and debased by the vices of ill-bred *parvenus*. The opening of a *Novella* he relates, may be cited as a fair specimen of his style:[40]

> Quidam Franzosus, volens tornare Parisum,
> Certum Milaneysum scontravit extra viglianam
> Sine capello docheti testa bagnatum:
> Et cum ignoraret Gallicus hic unde fuisset
> Dixit vulgariter *estes vous moglie mon amicus?*
> Ille qui intelligit a la rebusa, respondit
> *Sy sy mi che ho mogle Milani et anca fiolos.*
> Gallus tunc cernens Lombardum fore loquela,
> Et recordatus quod tempore guerre Salucis
> Alixandrini fecerant pagare menestram
> Scutumque sibi sgrafignarant de gibesera,
> Sfodravit ensem dicens *o tretre ribalde*
> *Rendez moy sa mon escu*, sy non a la morte spazat.

The end of the story is far too crude to quote, and it is probable that even the most curious readers will already have had enough of Alione's peculiar gibberish.

The maccaronic style had reached this point when Folengo took possession of it, stamped it with his own genius, and employed it for one of the most important poems of the century. He is said to have begun a serious Latin epic in his early manhood, and to have laid this aside because he foresaw the impossibility of wresting the laurels from Virgil. This story is probably a legend; but it contains at least an element of truth. Folengo aimed at originality; he chose to be the first of burlesque Latin poets rather than to claim the name and fame of a Virgilian imitator.[41] In the proemium to his 'Moscheis' he professes to have found the orthodox Apollo deaf to his prayers:

> Illius heu frustra doctas captare sorores
> Speravi ac multa laude tenere polos.

[39] See the passage beginning 'O Longobardi frapatores,' and ending with these lines:

> Tunc baratasti Gal orum nobile nomen
> Cum Longobardo, &c.

Daelli, *op. cit.* p. 94.

[40] Daelli, p. 93.

[41] In the first book of the *Moscheis*, line 7, he says:

> Gens ceratana sinat vecchias cantare batajas,
> Squarzet Virgilios turba pedanta suos.

The end of the *Maccaronea* sets forth the impossibility of modern bards contending with the great poet of antiquity. Pontanus, Sannazzarius, all the best Latin writers of the age, pale before Virgil:

> Non tamen æquatur vati quem protulit Andes,
> Namque vetusta nocet laus nobis sæpe modernis.

This refrain he repeats for each poet with whimsical reiteration. Folengo's own ambition to take the first place among burlesque writers appears in the final lines of *Mac.* book iii.:

The reason of the god's anger was that his votary had sullied the clear springs of Hippocrene:

> Nescio quas reperi musas, turpesve sorores,
> Nescio quas turpi carmina voce canunt.
> Limpida Pegasidium vitiavi stagna profanus,
> Totaque sunt limo dedecorata meo.

The exordium to the 'Maccaronea' introduces us to these vulgar Muses, *grossæ Camœnæ*, who fill their neophytes with maccaronic inspiration:

> Jam nec Melpomene, Clio, nec magna Thalia,
> Nec Phœbus grattando lyram mihi carmina dictet,
> Qui tantos olim doctos fecere poetas;
> Verum cara mihi foveat solummodo Berta,
> Gosaque, Togna simul, Mafelina, Pedrala, Comina.
> Veridicæ Musæ sunt hæ, doctæque sorellæ;
> Quarum non multis habitatio nota poetis.

The holy hill of Folengo's Muses is a mountain of cheese and maccaroni, with lakes of broth and rivers of unctuous sauces:

> Stant ipsæ Musæ super altum montis acumen,
> Formajum gratulis durum retridando foratis.

Here he seeks them, and here they deign to crown him poet:[42]

> Ergo macaronicas illic cattavimus artes,
> Et me grossiloquum vatem statuere sorores.

We have seen already that the maccaronic style involved a free use of plebeian Italian, embedded in a mixed mass of classical and mediæval Latinity. Folengo refined the usage of his predecessors, by improving the versification, adopting a more uniformly heroic tone, and introducing scraps of Mantuan dialect at unexpected intervals, so that each lapse into Italian has the force of a surprise—what the Greeks called παρὰ προσδοκίαν. The comic effect is produced by a sustained epical inflation, breaking irregularly into the coarsest and least pardonable freaks of vulgarity. It is as though the poet were improvising, emulous of Virgil; but the tide of inspiration fails him, he falls short of classical phrases to express his thoughts, and is forced in the hurry of the moment to avail himself of words and images that lie more close at hand. His Pegasus is a showy hack, who ambles on the bypaths of Parnassus, dropping now and then a spavined hock and stumbling back into his paces with a snort. His war-trumpet utters a sonorous fanfaronnade;

> Mantua Virgilio gaudet, Verona Catullo,
> Dante suo florens urbs Tusca, Cipada Cocajo:
> Dicor ego superans alios levitate poetas,
> Ut Maro medesimos superans gravitate poetas.

The induction to the *Moscheis* points to a serious heroic poem on Mantua, which he abandoned for want of inspiration. We have in these references enough to account for the myth above mentioned.

[42] Compare *Mac.* vii. p. 195.

> Nil nisi crassiloquas dicor scrivisse camœnas,
> Crassiloquis igitur dicamus magna camœnis.

This *great theme* is nothing less than monasticism in its vilest aspects.

but the blower loses breath, and breaks his note, or suffers it to lapse into a lamentable quaver.

Tifi Odassi, who may be regarded as Folengo's master in this species of verse, confined the Maccaronic Muse to quaintly finished sketches in the Dutch style.[43] His pupil raised her to the dignity of Clio and composed an epic in twenty-five books. The length of this poem and the strangeness of the manner render it unpalatable to all but serious students at the present time. Its humour has evaporated, and the form itself strikes us as rococo. We experience some difficulty in sympathising with those readers of the sixteenth century, who, perfectly acquainted with Latin poetry and accustomed to derive intellectual pleasure from its practice, found exquisite amusement in so cleverly constructed a parody. Nor is it possible for Englishmen to appreciate the more delicate irony of the vulgarisms, which Folengo adopted from one of the coarsest Italian dialects, and cemented with subtle skill upon the stately structure of his hexameters. Still we may remember that the 'Maccaronea' was read with profit by Rabelais, and that much of Butler's humour betrays a strong affinity to this antiquated burlesque.

In substance the 'Maccaronea' begins with a rehandling of the 'Orlandino.' Guido, peerless among Paladins, wins the love of his king's daughter, Baldovina of France. They fly together into Italy, and she dies in giving birth to a son at Cipada, near Mantua. Guido disappears, and the boy, Baldus, is brought up by a couple of peasants. He believes himself to be their child, and recognises the rustic boor, Zambellus, for his brother. Still the hero's nature reveals itself in the village urchin; and, like the young Orlando, Baldus performs prodigies of valour in his boyhood:

> Non it post vaccas, at sæpe caminat ad urbem,
> Ac ad Panadæ dispectum praticat illam;
> In villam semper tornabat vespere facto,
> Portabatque caput fractum gambasque macatas.

When he goes to school, he begins by learning his letters with great readiness. But he soon turns away from grammar to books of chivalry:

> Sed mox Orlandi nasare volumina cœpit:
> Non vacat ultra deponentia discere verba,
> Non species, numeros, non casus atque figuras,
> Non Doctrinalis versamina tradere menti:
> Fecit de norma scartazzos mille Donati
> Inque Perotinum librum salcicia coxit.
> Orlandi solum, nec non fera bella Rinaldi
> Aggradant; animum faciebat talibus altum:
> Legerat Ancrojam, Tribisondam, gesta Danesi,
> Antonæque Bovum, mox tota Realea Francæ,
> Innamoramentum Carlonis et Asperamontem,
> Spagnam, Altobellum, Morgantis facta gigantis

[43] At the end of the *Maccaronea* I think there may be an allusion to Odassi conveyed in these words, *Tifi Caroloque futuris*.

And so forth through the whole list of chivalrous romances, down to the 'Orlando Furioso' and the 'Orlandino.' The boy's heart is set on deeds of daring. He makes himself the captain of a band of rogues who turn the village of Cipada upside down. Three of these deserve especial notice—Fracassus, Cingar, and Falchettus; since they became the henchmen of our hero in all his subsequent exploits. Fracassus was descended in the direct line from Morgante:

> Primus erat quidam Fracassus prole gigantis,
> Cujus stirps olim Morganto venit ab illo,
> Qui bachiocconem campanæ ferre solebat
> Cum quo mille hominum colpo sfracasset in uno.

Cingar in like manner drew his blood from Pulci's Margutte:

> Alter erat Baldi compagnus, nomine Cingar,
> Accortus, ladro, semper truffare paratus;
> Scarnus enim facie, reliquo sed corpore nervis
> Plenus, compressus, picolinus, brunus, et atrox,
> Semper habens nudam testam, rizzutus et asper.
> Iste suam traxit Marguti a sanguine razzam,
> Qui ad calcagnos sperones ut gallus habebat
> Et nimio risu simia cagante morivit.

Falchettus boasted a still stranger origin:[44]

> Sed quidnam de te, Falchette stupende, canemus?
> Tu quoque pro Baldo bramasti prendere mortem.
> Forsitan, o lector, quæ dico, dura videntur,
> Namque Pulicano Falchettus venit ab illo
> Quem scripsere virum medium, mediumque catellum;
> Quapropter sic sic moster Falchettus habebat
> Anteriora viri, sed posteriora canina.

It would be too long to relate how Baldus received knightly education from a nobleman who admired his daring; how, ignorant of his illustrious blood, he married the village beauty Berta; and how he made himself the petty tyrant of Cipada. The exploits of his youth are a satire on the violence of local magnates, whose manners differed little from those of the peasants they oppressed. In course of time Baldus fell under the displeasure of a despot stronger than himself, and was shut up in prison.[45] In the absence of his hero from the scene, the poet now devotes himself to the exploits of Cingar among the peasants of Cipada. Without lowering his epic tone, Folengo fills five books with whimsical adventures, painting the manners of the country in their coarsest colours, and introducing passages of stinging satire on the

[44] I do not recognise Pulicanus, who is said to be the ancestor of Falchettus. Is it a misprint for Fulicanus? Fulicano is a giant in Bello's *Mambriano*, one of Folengo's favourite poems of romance.

[45] *Mac.* iii. The edition I quote from is that of Mantua (?) under name of Amsterdam, 1769 and 1771, 2 vols. 4to. See vol. i. p. 117, for a satire on the frauds and injustice of a country law-court, followed by a mock heroic panegyric of the Casa Gonzaga. The description of their celebrated stud and breed of horses may be read with interest.

monks he hated.[46] Cingar, finding himself on one occasion in a convent, gives vent to a long soliloquy which expresses Folengo's own contempt for the monastic institutions that filled Italy with rogues:

> Quo diavol, ait, tanti venere capuzzi?
> Nil nisi per mundum video portare capuzzos:
> Quisquam vult fieri Frater, vult quisque capuzzum.
> Postquam giocarunt nummos, tascasque vodarunt,
> Postquam pane caret cophinum, celaria vino,
> In Fratres properant, datur his extemplo capuzzus.
> Undique sunt isti Fratres, istique capuzzi.
> Qui sint nescimus; discernere nemo valeret
> Tantas vestitum foggias, tantosque colores:
> Sunt pars turchini, pars nigri, parsque morelli,
> Pars albi, russi, pars gialdi, parsque bretini.
> Si per iter vado telluris, cerno capuzzos;
> Si per iter pelagi, non mancum cerno capuzzos;
> Quando per armatos eo campos, cerno capuzzos;
> Sive forum subeo, sive barcam, sive tabernam,
> Protinus ante oculos aliquem mihi cerno capuzzum.

There will soon be no one left to bear arms, till the fields, or ply the common handicrafts. All the villeins make themselves monks, aspiring to ecclesiastical honours and seeking the grade of superiority denied them by their birth. It is ambition that fills the convents:

> Illic nobilitas sub rusticitate laborat,
> Ambitio quoniam villanos unica brancat.

This tirade is followed by the portrait of Prae Jacopinus, a village parson whose stupidity is only equalled by his vices. Jacopino's education in the alphabet is a masterpiece of Rabelaisian humour, and the following passage on his celebration of the Mass brings all the sordidness of rustic ceremonial before our eyes:[47]

> Præterea Missam foggia dicebat in una,
> Nec crucis in fronte signum formare sciebat.
> Inter Confiteor parvum discrimen et Amen
> Semper erat, jam jam meditans adjungere finem;
> Incipiebat enim nec adhuc in nomine Patris,
> Quod tribus in saltis veniebat ad Ite misestum.

From generalities Folengo passes to particulars in the following description of a village Mass:[48]

[46] The episode of Berta's battle with her sister Laena (*Mac.* iv. p. 144), the apostrophe to old age (*Mac.* v. p. 152), the village ball (*ibid.* p. 163), the tricks played by Cingar on Zambellus (*ibid.* p. 168, and *Mac.* vi.), the description of the convent of Motella (*Mac.* vii. 196), the portrait of the ignorant parish-priest (*Mac.* vii. p. 202), the Carnival Mass (*Mac.* viii. p. 212), followed by a drunken *Ker Mess* (*ibid.* p. 214), are all executed in the broad style of a Dutch painter, and abound in realistic sketches of Lombard country-life.

[47] *Mac.* vii. p. 204.

[48] *Mac.* vii. p. 212. Folengo seems to have been fond of music. See the whimsical description of four-part singing, *Mac.* xx. p. 139, followed by the panegyric of Music and the malediction of her detractors.

Inde Jacopinus, chiamatis undique Pretis,
Cœperat in gorga Missam cantare stupendam;
Subsequitant alii, magnisque cridoribus instant.
Protinus Introitum spazzant talqualiter omnem,
Ad Chyrios veniunt, quos miro dicere sentis
Cum contrappunto, veluti si cantor adesset
Master Adrianus, Constantius atque Jachettus.
Hic per dolcezzam scorlabant corda vilani
Quando de quintis terzisque calabat in unam
Musicus octavam noster Jacopinus et ipsas
Providus octavas longa cum voce tirabat.
Gloria in excelsis passat, jam Credo propinquat;
Oh si Josquinus Cantorum splendor adesset!

Meanwhile Baldus has been left in prison, and it is time for Cingar to undertake his rescue. He effects this feat, by stripping two Franciscan monks, and dressing himself up in the frock he has just filched from one of them, while he coaxes the unfortunate Zambellus to assume the other. Then he persuades the people of Mantua that he has seen himself assassinated on the high road; gains access to Baldus in the dungeon, on the plea of hearing his confession; and contrives to leave Zambellus there in the clothes of Baldus after disguising his friend in one of the friars' tunics. The story is too intricate for repetition here.[49] Suffice it to say that Baldus escapes and meets a knight errant, Leonardus, at the city gate, who has ridden all the way from Rome to meet so valorous a Paladin. They swear eternal friendship. The three henchmen of the hero muster round the new comrades in arms; and the party thus formed set forth upon a series of adventures in the style of Astolfo's journey to the moon.

This part of the epic is a close copy of the chivalrous romances in their more fantastic details. The journey of the Barons, as they are now invariably styled, is performed in a great ship. They encounter storms and pirates, land on marvellous islands, enter fairy palaces, and from time to time recruit their forces with notable rogues and drunkards whom they find upon their way. The parody consists in the similarity of their achievements to those of knight-errantry, while they are themselves in all points unlike the champions of chivalry. One of their most cherished companions, for example, is Boccalus, a Bergamasque buffoon, who distinguishes himself by presence of mind in a great storm:[50]

Ille galantus homo, qui nuper in æquora bruttam
Jecerat uxorem, dicens non esse fagottum
Fardellumque homini plus laidum, plusque pesentum
Quam sibi mojeram lateri mirare tacatam
Quæ sit oca ingenio, quæ vultu spazzacaminus.

[49] This episode of Cingar's triumph over the enemies of Baldus, his craft, his rhetoric, his ready wit, his infinite powers of persuasion, his monkey tricks and fox-like cunning, is executed with an energy of humour and breadth of conception, that place it upon a level with the choicest passages in Rabelais.

[50] *Mac.* xii. p. 296.

The tale of adventures is diversified, after the manner of the romantic poets, by digressions, sometimes pathetic, sometimes dissertational. Among these the most amusing is Cingar's lecture on astronomy, in which the planetary theories of the middle ages are burlesqued with considerable irony.[51] The most affecting is the death of Leonardus, who chooses to be torn in piece by bears rather than yield his virginity to a vile woman. This episode suggests one of the finest satiric passages in the whole poem. Having exhibited the temptress Muselina, the poet breaks off with this exclamation:[52]

> Heu quantis noster Muselinis orbis abundat!

He then enumerates their arts of seduction, and winds up with a powerful dramatic picture, painted from the life, of a *mezzana* engaged in corrupting a young man's mind during Mass-time:

> Dum Missæ celebrantur, amant cantonibus esse,
> Postque tenebrosos mussant chiachiarantque pilastros;
> Ah miserelle puer, dicunt, male nate, quod ullam
> Non habes, ut juvenes bisognat habere, morosam! . . .
> Numquid vix fieri Frater Monachusve, remotis
> Delitiis Veneris, Bacchi, Martisque, Jovisque,
> Quos vel simplicitas, vel desperatio traxit? . . .
> Nemo super terram sanctus; stant æthere sancti:
> Nos carnem natura facit, quo carne fruamur.

As the epic approaches its conclusion, Baldus discovers his true father, Guido, under the form of a holy hermit, and learns that it is reserved for him by destiny, first to extirpate the sect of witches under their queen Smirna Gulfora, and afterwards to penetrate the realms of death and hell. The last five books of the 'Maccaronea' are devoted to these crowning exploits. Merlin appears, and undertakes the guidance of the Barons on their journey to Avernus.[53] But first he requires full confession of their sins from each; and this humorous act of penitence forms one of the absurdest episodes, as may be easily imagined, in the poem. Absolved and furnished with heroic armour, the Barons march to the conquest of Gulfora and the destruction of her magic palace. Folengo has placed it appropriately on the road to hell; for under Gulfora he allegorises witchcraft. The space allotted to Smirna Gulfora and the importance attached to her overthrow by Baldus and his Barons, call

[51] In the course of this oration Folengo introduces an extraordinarily venomous invective against *contadini*, which may be paralleled with his allegory in the *Orlandino*. It begins (*Mac.* xiii. p. 11):

> Progenies maledicta quidem villana vocatur,

and extends through forty lines of condensed abuse.

[52] *Mac.* xvi. p. 66.

[53] *Mac.* xx. p. 152. From this point onward the poet and Merlin are one person:

> Nomine Merlinus dicor, de sanguine Mantus,
> Est mihi cognomen Cocajus Maccaronensis.

attention to the prevalence of magic in Italy at this epoch.[54] It may not, therefore, be out of place, before engaging in this portion of the analysis, to give some account of Italian witchcraft drawn from other sources, in order to estimate the truth of the satire upon which Folengo expended his force.

'Beautiful and humane Italy,' as Bandello calls his country in the preface to one of his most horrible *Novelle*, was, in spite of her enlightenment, but little in advance of Europe on the common points of mediæval superstition. The teaching of the Church encouraged a belief in demons; and the common people saw on every chapel wall the fresco of some saint expelling devils from the bodies of possessed persons, or exorcising domestic utensils which had been bewitched.[55] Thus the laity grew up in the confirmed opinion that earth, air, and ocean swarmed with supernatural beings, whom they distinguished as fiends from hell or inferior sprites of the elements, called *spiriti folletti*.[56] While the evil spirits of both degrees were supposed to lie beneath the ban of ecclesiastical malediction, they lent their aid to necromancers, witches and wizards, who, defying the interdictions of the Church, had the audacity to use them as their slaves by the employment of powerful spells and rites of conjuration. There was a way, it was believed, of taming both the demons and the elves, of making them the instruments of human avarice, ambition, jealousy and passion. Since all forms of superstition in Italy lent themselves to utilitarian purposes, the necromancer and the witch, having acquired this powerful over supernatural agents, became the servants of popular lusts. They sold their authority to the highest bidders, undertaking to blast the vines or to poison the flocks of an enemy; to force young men and maidens to become the victims of inordinate appetites; to ruin inconvenient husbands by slowly-wasting diseases; to procure abortion by spells and potions; to confer wealth and power upon aspirants after luxury; to sow the seeds of discord in families—in a word, to open a free path for the indulgence of the vain desires that plague ill-regulated egotisms. A class of impostors, half dupes of their own pretensions, half rogues relying on the folly of their employers, sprang into existence, who combined the Locusta of ancient Rome with the witch of mediæval Germany. Such was the Italian *strega*—a loathsome creature who studied the chemistry of poisons, philtres, and abortion-hastening drugs, and while she pretended to work her miracles by the help of devils, played upon the common

[54] The *Novella* of Luca Philippus, who kept a tavern at the door of Paradise, and had no custom, since no one came that way so long as Gulfora ruled on earth, forms a significant preface to her episode. See *Mac.* xxi. p. 180. The altercation between this host and Peter at the rusty gate of heaven is written in the purest Italian style of pious parody.

[55] Aretino's *Cortigiana* contains a very humorous exorcism inflicted by way of a practical joke upon a fisherman.

[56] See above, p. 130, note 38, for the distinction between the fiends and the sprites drawn by Pulci.

passions and credulities of human kind.[57] By her side stood her masculine counterpart, the *stregone*, *negromante* or *alchimista*, who plays so prominent a part in the Italian comedies and novels.

Witchcraft was localised in two chief centres—the mountains of Norcia, and the Lombard valleys of the Alps.[58] In the former we find a remnant of antique superstition. The witches of this district, whether male or female, had something of the classical Sibyl in their composition and played upon the terrors of their clients. Like their Roman predecessors, they plied the trades of poisoner, quack-doctor and bawd. In Lombardy witchcraft assumed a more Teutonic complexion. The witch was less the instrument of fashionable vices, trading in them as a lucrative branch of industry, than the hysterical subject of a spiritual disease. Lust itself inflamed the victims of this superstition, who were burned by hundreds in the towns, and who were supposed to hold their revels in the villages of Val Camonica. Like the hags of northern Europe, these Lombard *streghe* had recourse to the black art in the delirious hope of satisfying their own inordinate ambitions, their own indescribable desires. The disease spread so wildly at the close of the fifteenth century that Innocent VIII., by his bull of 1484, issued special injunctions to the Dominican monks of Brescia, Bergamo and Cremona, authorising them to stamp it out with fire and torture.[59] The result was a crusade against witchcraft, which seems to have increased the evil by fascinating the imagination of the people. They believed all the more blindly in the supernatural powers to be obtained by magic arts, inasmuch as this traffic had become the object of a bloody persecution. When the Church recognised that men and women might command the fiends of hell, it followed as a logical consequence that wretches, maddened by misery and intoxicated with ungovernable lusts, were tempted to tamper with the forbidden thing at the risk of life and honour in this world and with the certainty of damnation in the other. After this fashion the confused conscience of illiterate people bred a formidable extension of this spiritual malady throughout the northern provinces of

[57] See Lasca's *Novella* of *Zoroastro*; Bandello's novels of witchcraft (Part iii. 29 and 52); Cellini's celebrated conjuration in the Coliseum; and Ariosto's comedy of the *Negromante*. These sources may be illustrated from the evidence given by Virginia Maria Lezia before her judges, and the trial of witches at Nogaredo, both of which are printed in Dandolo's *Signora di Monza* (Milano, 1855). Compare the curious details about Lombard witchcraft in Cantù's *Diocesi di Como*.

[58] It may be remembered that the necromancer in Cellini sent his book to be enchanted in the Apennines of Norcia. Folengo alludes to this superstition:

> Qualiter ad stagnum Nursæ sacrare quadernos.

With regard to Val Camonica, see the actual state of that district as reported by Cantù. Folengo in the *Orlandino* mentions its witches. Bandello (iii. 52) speaks of it thus: 'Val Camonica, ove si dice essere di molte streghe.'

[59] Witchcraft in Italy grew the more formidable the closer it approached the German frontier. It seems to have assumed the features of an epidemic at the close of the fifteenth century. Up to that date little is heard of it, and little heed was paid to it. The exacerbation of the malady portended and accompanied the dissolution of mediæval beliefs in a population vexed by war, famine and pestilence, and vitiated by ecclesiastical corruption.

Italy. Some were led by morbid curiosity; others by a vain desire to satisfy their appetites, or to escape the consequences of their crimes. A more dangerous class used the superstition to acquire power over their neighbours and to make money out of popular credulity.

Born and bred in Lombardy at the epoch when witchcraft had attained the height of popular insanity, Folengo was keenly alive to the hideousness of a superstition which, rightly or wrongly, he regarded as a widespread plague embracing all classes of society. It may be questioned whether he did not exaggerate its importance. But there is no mistaking the verisimilitude of the picture he drew. All the uncleanliness of a diseased imagination, all the extravagances of wanton desire, all the consequences of domestic unchastity—incest, infanticide, secret assassination, concealment of births—are traced to this one cause and identified by him with witchcraft. The palace of the queen Gulfora is a pandemonium of lawless vice:

> Quales hic reperit strepitus, qualemque tumultum,
> Quales mollities turpes, actusque salaces,
> Utile nil scribi posset, si scribere vellem.

Her courts are crowded with devils who have taken human shape to gratify the lusts of her votaries:

> Leggiadros juvenes, bellos, facieque venustos,
> Stringatos, agiles, quos judicat esse diablos,
> Humanum piliasse caput moresque decentes,
> Conspicit, innumeras circum scherzare puellas,
> Quæ gestant vestes auri brettasque veluti.

The multitude is made up of all nations, sexes, ages, classes:

> Obstupet innumeros illic retrovare striones,
> Innumerasque strias vecchias, modicasque puellas.
> Non ea medesimo generatur schiatta paeso;
> At sunt Italici, Græci, Gallique, Spagnoles,
> Magnates, poveri, laici, fratresque, pretesque,
> Matronæ, moniglæ per forzam claustra colentes.

Some of them are engaged in preparing love-potions and poisonous draughts from the most disgusting and noxious ingredients. Others compound unguents to be used in the metamorphosis of themselves on their nocturnal jaunts. Among these are found poets, orators, physicians, lawyers, governors, for whose sins a handful of poor old women play the part of scapegoats before the public:

> Sed quia respectu legis prævertitur ordo,
> Namque solent grossi pisces mangiare minutos,
> Desventuratæ quædam solummodo vecchiæ
> Sunt quæ supra asinos plebi spectacula fiunt,
> Sunt quæ primatum multorum crimina celant,
> Sunt quæ sparagnant madonnis pluribus ignem.

Some again are discovered compiling books of spells:

> Quomodo adulterium uxoris vir noscere possit,
> Quomodo virgineæ cogantur amare puellæ,
> Quomodo non tumeat mulier cornando maritum,
> Quomodo si tumuit fantinum mingat abortum,
> Quomodo vix natos vitient sua fascina puttos,
> Quomodo desiccent odiati membra mariti.

The elder witches keep a school for the younger, and instruct them in the secrets of their craft. Among these Baldus recognises his own wife, together with the principal ladies of his native land.

It is clear that under the allegory of witchcraft, in which at the same time he seems to have believed firmly, Folengo meant to satirise the secret corruption of society. When Gulfora herself appears, she holds her court like an Italian duchess:

> Longa sequit series hominum muschiata zibettis,
> Qui cortesanos se vantant esse tilatos,
> Quorum si videas mores rationis ochialo,
> Non homines maschios sed dicas esse bagassas.

The terrible friar then breaks into a tirade against the courtiers of his day, comparing them with Arthur's knights:

> Tempore sed nostro, proh dii, sæcloque dadessum,
> Non nisi perfumis variis et odore zibetti,
> Non nisi, seu sazaræ petenentur sive tosentur,
> Brettis velluti, nec non scufiotibus auri,
> Auri cordiculis, impresis, atque medallis,
> Millibus et frappis per calzas perque giupones,
> Cercamus carum merdosi germen amoris.

Baldus exterminates the whole vile multitude, while Fracassus pulls Gulfora's palace about her ears. After this, the Barons pursue their way to Acheron, and call upon Charon to ferry them across. He refuses to take so burdensome a party into his boat; but by the strength of Fracassus and the craft of Cingar they effect a passage. Their entry into hell furnishes Folengo with opportunities for new tirades against the vices of Italy. Tisiphone boasts how Rome, through her machinations, has kept Christendom in discord. Alecto exults in her offspring, the Guelph and Ghibelline factions:

> Unde fides Christi paulatim lapsa ruinet,
> Dum gentes Italæ bastantes vincere mundum
> Se se in se stessos discordant, seque medesmos
> Vassallos faciunt, servos, vilesque famejos
> His qui vassalli, servi, vilesque fameji
> Tempore passato nobis per forza fuere.

After passing the Furies, and entering the very jaws of Hades, Baldus encounters the phantasies of grammarians and humanists, the idle nonsense of the schoolmen, all the lumber of mediæval philosophy mixed with the trifles of the Renaissance.[60] He fights his way through

[60] His sunt Grammaticæ populi, gentesque reductæ,

the thick-crowding swarm of follies, and reaches the hell of lovers, where a mountebank starts forward and offers to be his guide. Led by this zany, the hero and his comrades enter an enormous gourd, the bulk of which is compared to the mountains of Val Camonica. Within its spacious caverns dwell the sages of antiquity, with astrologers, physicians, wizards, and false poets. But, having brought his Barons to this place, Merlinus Cocajus can advance no further.

He is destined to inhabit the great gourd himself. Beyond it he has no knowledge; and here, therefore, he leaves the figments of his fancy without a word of farewell:

> Nec Merlinus ego, laus, gloria, fama Cipadæ,
> Quamvis fautrices habui Tognamque Gosamque,
> Quamvis implevi totum macaronibus orbem,
> Quamvis promerui Baldi cantare batajas,
> Non tamen hanc zuccam potui schifare decentem,
> In qua me tantos opus est nunc perdere dentes,
> Tot, quot in immenso posui mendacia libro.

With this grotesque invention of the infernal pumpkin, where lying bards are punished by the extraction of teeth which never cease to grow again, Folengo breaks abruptly off. His epic ends with a Rabelaisian peal of laughter, in which we can detect a growl of discontent and anger.

Laying the book down, we ask ourselves whether the author had a serious object, or whether he meant merely to indulge a vein of wayward drollery. The virulent invectives which abound in the 'Maccaronea,' seem to warrant the former conclusion; nor might it be wholly impossible to regard the poem as an allegory, in which Baldus should play the part of the reason, unconscious at first of its noble origin, consorting with the passions and the senses, but finally arriving at the knowledge of its high destiny and defeating the powers of evil.[61] Yet when we attempt to press this theory and to explain the allegory in detail, the thread snaps in our hands. Like the romances of chivalry which it parodies, the 'Maccaronea' is a bizarre mixture of heterogene-

> Huc, illus, istuc, reliqua seguitante fameja:
> Argumenta volant dialectica, mille sophistæ
> Adsunt bajanæ, pro, contra, non, ita, lyque:
> Adsunt Errores, adsunt mendacia, bollæ,
> Atque solecismi, fallacia, fictio vatum . . .
> Omnes altandem tanto rumore volutant
> Ethicen et Physicen, Animam, centumque novellas,
> Ut sibi stornito Baldus stopparet orecchias.
> Squarnazzam Scoti Fracassus repperit illic,
> Quam vestit, gabbatque Deum, pugnatque Thomistas.
> Alberti magni Lironus somnia zaffat.

[61] This hypothesis receives support from the passage in which Baldus compares his new love for Crispis, the paragon of all virtues, with his old infatuation for Berta, who is the personification of vulgar appetite, unrefined natural instinct. See the end of Book xxiii.

ous elements, loosely put together to amuse an idle public and excite curiosity. If its author has used it also as the vehicle for satire which embraces all the popular superstitions, vices and hypocrisies of his century; if, as he approaches the conclusion, he assumes a tone of sarcasm more sinister than befits the broad burlesque of the commencement; we must rest contented with the assumption that his choleric humour led him from the path of comedy, while the fury of a soul divided against itself inspired his muses of the cookshop with loftier strains than they had promised at the outset.[62] Should students in the future devote the same minute attention to Folengo that has been paid to Rabelais, it is not improbable that the question here raised may receive solution. The poet is not unworthy of such pains. Regarded merely as the precursor of Rabelais, Folengo deserves careful perusal. He was the creator of a style, which, when we read his epic, forces us to think of the seventeenth century; so strongly did it influence the form of humorous burlesque in Europe for at least two hundred years. On this account, the historian of modern literature cannot afford to neglect him. For the student of Italian manners in Lombardy during the height of the Renaissance, the huge amorphous undigested mass of the 'Maccaronea' is one of the most valuable and instructive documents that we possess. I do not hesitate, from this point of view, to rank it with the masterpieces of the age, with the 'Orlando' of Ariosto, with Machiavelli's comedies, and with the novels of Bandello.

Folengo used the maccaronic style in two other considerable compositions. The one entitled 'Moscheis' is an elegant parody of the 'Batrachomyomachia,' relating the wars of ants and flies in elegiac verse. The other, called 'Zanitonella,' celebrates the rustic loves of Zanina and Tonello in a long series of elegies, odes and eclogues. This collection furnishes a complete epitome of parodies modelled on the pastorals in vogue. The hero appears upon the scene in the following *Sonolegia*, under which title we detect a blending of the Sonnet and the Elegy:[63]

> Solus solettus stabam colegatus in umbra,
>   Pascebamque meas virda per arva capras.
> Nulla travajabant animum pensiria nostrum,
>   Cercabam quoniam tempus habere bonum.
> Quando bolzoniger puer, o mea corda forasti;
>   Nec dedit in fallum dardus alhora tuus.
> Immo fracassasti rationis vincula, quæ tunc
>   Circa coradam bastio fortis erat.

The lament is spun out to the orthodox length of fourteen verses, and

[62] The rage of a man who knows that he has chosen the lower while he might have trodden the higher paths of life and art, flames out at intervals through this burlesque. Take this example, the last five lines of Book xxiii.:

> Sic ego Macronicum penitus volo linquere carmen
> Cum mihi tempus erit, quod erit, si celsa voluntas
> Flectitur et nostris lachrymis et supplice voto.
> Heu heu! quod volui misero mihi? floribus Austrum
> Perditus et liquidis immisi fontibus aprum.

[63] *Zanitonella*, p. 3.

concludes with a pretty point. Who the *bolzoniger puer* was, is more openly revealed in another *Sonolegia*:[64]

> Nemo super terram mangiat mihi credite panem,
> Seu contadinus, seu citadinus erit,
> Quem non attrapolet Veneris bastardulus iste,
> Qui volat instar avis, cæcus, et absque braga.

To follow the poet through all his burlesques of Petrarchistic and elegiac literature, Italian or Latin, would be superfluous. It is enough to say that he leaves none of their accustomed themes untouched with parody. The masterpiece of his art in this style is the sixth Eclogue, consisting of a dialogue between two drunken bumpkins—*interloquutores Tonellus et Pedralus, qui ambo inebriantur.*[65]

The maccaronic style was a product of North Italy, cultivated by writers of the Lombard towns, who versified comic or satiric subjects in parodies of humanistic poetry. The branch of burlesque literature we have next to examine, belonged to Tuscany, and took its origin from the equivocal carnival and dance songs raised to the dignity of art by Lorenzo de' Medici. Its conventional metre was *terza rima*, handled with exquisite sense of rhythm, but degraded to low comedy by the treatment of trivial or vulgar motives. The author of these *Capitoli*, as they were called, chose some common object—a paint-brush, salad, a sausage, peaches, figs, eels, radishes—to celebrate; affected to be inspired by the grandeur of his subject; developed the drollest tropes, metaphors and illustrations; and almost invariably conveyed an obscene meaning under the form of innuendoes appropriate to his professed theme. Though some exceptions can be pointed out, the *Capitoli* in general may be regarded as a species of Priapic literature, fashioned to suit the taste of Florentines, who had been accustomed for many generations to semi-disguised obscenity in their vernacular town poetry.[66] Taken from the streets and squares, adopted by the fashionable rhymesters of academies and courtly coteries, the rude Fescennine verse lost none of its license, while it assumed the polish of urbane art. Were it not for this antiquity and popularity of origin, which suggests a plausible excuse for the learned writers of *Capitoli*, and warns us to regard their indecency as in some measure conventional, it would be difficult to approach the three volumes which contain a selection of their poems, without horror.[67] So deep, universal, unblushing is the vice revealed in them.

[64] *Ibid.* p. 2. Compare *Sonolegia* xiii *ib.* p. 40.

[65] *Op. cit.* p. 42.

[66] We may ascend to the very sources of popular Tuscan poetry, and we shall find this literature of *double entendre* in the *Canzoni* of the *Nicchio* and *Ugellino,* noticed above, p. 863. Besides the *Canti Carnascialeschi* edited by Il Lasca, we have a collection of *Canzoni a Ballo*, printed at Florence in 1569, which proves that the raw material of the *Capitoli* lay ready to the hand of the burlesque poets in plebian literature.

[67] My references are made to *Opere Burlesche*, 3 vols. 1723, with the names of of Londra and Firenze. Gregorovius says of them: 'Wenn man diese "scherzenden"

To Francesco Berni belongs the merit, such as it is, of having invented the burlesque *Capitolo*. He gave his name to it, and the term Bernesque has passed into the critical phraseology of Europe. The unique place of this rare poet in the history of Italian literature, will justify a somewhat lengthy account of his life and works. Studying him, we study the ecclesiastical and literary society of Rome in the age of Leo X. and Clement VII.

Francesco Berni was born at Lamporecchio, in the Val di Nievole, about the end of the fifteenth century.[68] His parents were poor; but they were connected with the family of the Cardinal Bibbiena, who, after the boy's education at Florence, took him at the age of nineteen to Rome. Upon the death of this patron in 1520, Berni remained in the service of Bibbiena's nephew, Agnolo Dovizio. Receiving no advancement from these kinsmen, he next transferred himself, in the quality of secretary, to the household of Giammatteo Giberti, Bishop of Verona, who was a distinguished Mecænas of literary men. This change involved his taking orders. Berni now resided partly at Rome and partly at Verona, tempering the irksome duties of his office by the writing of humorous poetry, which he recited in the then celebrated Academy of the Vignajuoli. This society, which numbered Molza, Mauro, La Casa, Lelio Capilupi, Firenzuola, and Francesco Bini among its members, gave the tone to polite literature at the Courts of Leo and Clement.

Berni survived the sack of 1527, which proved so disastrous to Italian scholars; but he lost everything he possessed.[69] Monsignor Giberti employed him on various missions of minor importance, involving journeys to Venice, Padua, Nice, Florence, and the Abruzzi. After sixteen years of Court-life, Berni grew weary of the petty duties, which must have been peculiarly odious to a man of his lazy temperament, if it is true, as he informs us, that the Archbishop kept him dancing attendance till daylight, while he played primiera with his friends. Accordingly, he retired to Florence, where he held a canonry in the cathedral. There, after a quiet life of literary ease, he died suddenly in 1535. It was rumoured that he had been poisoned; and the most recent investigations into the circumstances of his death tend rather to confirm this report. All that is known, however, for certain, is that he spent the evening of May 25 with his friends the Marchionesse di Massa in the Palazzo Pazzi, and that next morning he breathed his last. His mysterious and unexplained decease was ascribed to one of the two Medicean princes then resident in Florence. A sonnet in Berni's best style, containing a vehement invective against Alessandro de' Medici, is extant. The hatred

Gedichte liest, muss man entweder über die Nichtigkeit ihrer Gegenstände staunen, oder vor dem Abgrund der Unsittlichkeit erschrecken, den sie frech entschleiern.' *Stadt Rom*, vol. viii. p. 345.

[68] The probable date is 1496.

[69] *Orl. Inn. rifatto da Fr. Berni*, i. 14, 23-28, makes it clear that Berni was an eyewitness of the Sack of Rome. Panizzi's reference to this passage (*Boiardo ed Ariosto*, London, 1830, vol. ii. p. cxi) involves what seems to me a confusion.

expressed in this poem may have occasioned the rumour (which certainly acquired a certain degree of currency) that Cardinal Ippolito de' Medici attempted to use the poet for the secret poisoning of his cousin, and on his refusal had him murdered. Other accounts of the supposed assassination ascribe a like intention to the Duke, who is said to have suggested the poisoning of the Cardinal to Berni. Both stories agree in representing his tragic end as the price paid for refusal to play the part of an assassin. The matter remains obscure; but enough suspicion rests upon the manner of his death to render this characteristic double legend plausible; especially when we remember what the customs of Florence with respect to poisoning were, and how the Cardinal de' Medici ended his own life.[70]

Such is the uneventful record of Berni's career. He was distinguished among all the poets of the century for his genial vein of humour and amiable personal qualities. That he was known to be stained with vices which it is not easy to describe, but which he frankly acknowledged in his poetical epistles, did not injure his reputation in that age of mutual indulgence.[71] Willing to live and let live, with a never-failing fund of drollery, and with a sincere dislike for work of any sort, he lounged through existence, an agreeable, genial and witty member of society. If this were all, we should not need to write about him now. But with this easy-going temperament he combined a genius for poetry so peculiar and delicate, that his few works mark an epoch in Italian literature.

The best description of Berni is contained in the burlesque portrait of himself, which forms part of his 'Boiardo Innamorato.'[72] This has been so well translated by an English scholar, the late W. S. Rose, that I cannot do better than refer the student to his stanzas. They convey as accurate a notion of the Bernesque manner as can be derived from any version in a foreign language.[73] The character he there has given to himself for laziness is corroborated by his extant epistles in prose. Berni represents himself as an incurably bad correspondent, pleased to get letters, but overcome with mortal terror when he is obliged to answer them.[74] He confides to his friend Francesco Bini

[70] The matter is fully discussed by Mazzuchelli in his biography of Berni. He, relying on the hypothesis of Berni having lived till 1536, if not till 1543, points out the impossibility of his having been murdered by the Cardinal, who died himself in July 1535. This difficulty has recently been removed by Signor Antonio Virgili's demonstration of the real date of Berni's death in May 1535. See *Rassegna Settimanale*, February 23, 1879, a paper of great importance for students of Berni's life and works, to which I shall frequently refer.

[71] It is enough to mention the *Capitoli* 'Delle Pesche,' 'A. M. Antonio da Bibbiena,' 'Sopra un Garzone,' 'Lamentazion d'Amore.' References are made to the *Rime e Lettere di Fr. Berni*, Firenze, Barbèra, 1865. For the *Rifacimento* of the *Orlando Innamorato* I shall use the Milan reprint in 5 vols. 1806, which also contains the *Rime*.

[72] Book III. canto vii. (canto 67 of the *Rifacimento*, vol. iv. p. 266).

[73] This translation will be found in Panizzi's edition of the *Orlando Innamorato* (London, Pickering, 1830), vol. ii. p. cxiv.

[74] Letter vi. to Messer Giamb. Montebuona.

that the great affair in life is to be gay and to write as little as possible:[75] 'A vivere avemo sino alla morte a dispetto di chi non vuole, e il vantaggio è vivere allegramente, come conforto a far voi, attendando a frequentar quelli banchetti che si fanno per Roma, e scrivendo sopra tutto manco che potete. *Quia hæc est victoria, quæ vincit mundum.*' The curse has been laid upon him of having to drive his quill without ceasing:[76] '*O ego lævus*, che scrivo d' ogni tempo, e scrivo ora che ho una gamba al collo, che ieri tornando dalla Certosa mi ruppe la mia cavalla, cascandomivi sopra. Sono pure un gran coglione!' So his pen runs on. The man writes just as he spoke, without affectation, mixing his phrases of Latin with the idiom of common life. The whole presents an agreeable contrast to the stilted style of Bembo, La Casa's studied periods, and the ambitious epistolary efforts of Aretino. Sometimes he breaks into doggerel:[77] 'S' io avessi l' ingenio del Burchiello, Io vi farei volentier un sonetto, Che non ebbi giammai tema e subietto, Più dolce, più piacevol, nè più bello.' When his friends insist upon his writing to them, rhyme comes to his aid, and he affects a comic fit of rage:[78]

> Perchè m' ammazzi con le tue querele,
> Priuli mio, perchè ti duole a torto,
> Che sai che t' amo più che l' orso il miele, &c.

Importuned to publish the poëms he recited with so much effect in private circles, he at last consents because he cannot help it:[79] 'Compare, io non ho potuto tanto schermirmi che pure m' è bisognato dar fuori questo benedetto Capitolo e Comento della Primiera; e siate certo che l' ho fatto, non perchè mi consumassi d' andare in stampa, nè per immortalarmi come il cavalier Casio, ma per fuggire la fatica mia, è la malevolenza di molti che domandandomelo e non lo avendo mi volevano mal di morte.' Nor were these the ordinary excuses of an author eager to conceal his vanity. The *Capitolo* upon the game of primiera was the only poem which appeared with his consent.[80] He intended his burlesque verses for recitation, and is even said to have preserved no copies of them, so that many of his compositions, piratically published in his lifetime, were with difficulty restored to a right text by Il Lasca in 1548. This indifference to public fame did not imply any carelessness of style. Mazzuchelli, who had seen some of his rough copies, asserts that they bore signs of the minutest pains bestowed upon them. The melody of versification, richness of allusion, refinement of phrase, equality and flowing smoothness, which distinguish Berni's work from that of his imitators, confirm the belief that his *Capitoli* and sonnets,

[75] Letter xvii.
[76] Letter xxiv.
[77] Letter to Ippolito de' Medici (ed. Milan, vol. v. p. 227).
[78] Letter ix.
[79] Letter vii. Compare the sonnet 'In nome di M. Prinzivalle da Pontremoli' (ed. Milan, vol. v. p. 3).
[80] It was published at Rome by Calvo in 1526, with the comment of M. Pietro Paolo da S. Chirico.

in spite of their apparent ease, were produced with the conscientious industry of a real artist.

Berni's theory of poetry revealed a common-sense and insight which were no less rare than commendable in that age of artificial literature. He refused to write at command, pleading that spontaneity of inspiration is essential to art, and quoting Vida's dictum:

> Nec jussa canas, nisi forte coactus
> Magnorum imperio regum.

Notwithstanding his avoidance of publication and parsimony of production, Berni won an almost unique reputation during his lifetime, and after his death was worshipped as a saint by the lovers of burlesque.[81] In one of his drollest sonnets he complains that poets were wont to steal their neighbours' verses, but that he is compelled to take the credit of more than he ever wrote:[82]

> A me quei d' altri son per forza dati,
> E dicon tu gli arai, vuoi o non vuoi.

A piece of comic prose or verse cannot appear but that it is at once ascribed to him:

> E la gente faceta
> Mi vuole pure impiastrar di prose e carmi,
> Come s' io fussi di razza di marmi:
> Non posso ripararmi;
> Come si vede fuor qualche sonetto,
> Il Berni l' ha composto a suo dispetto.
> E fanvi su un guazzetto
> Di chiose e di sensi, che rinnieghi il cielo,
> Se Luter fa più stracci del Vangelo.

One of the glosses referred to in this *coda*, lies before me as I write. It was composed by Gianmaria Cecchi on Berni's sonnet which begins 'Cancheri e beccafichi.' The sonnet is an amusing imprecation upon

[81] Il Lasca prefixed a sonnet to his edition of 1548, in which he speaks of 'Il Berni nostro dabbene e gentile,' calls him 'primo e vero trovatore, Maestro e padre del burlesco stile,' says that it is possible to envy but impossible to imitate him, and compares him thus with Burchiello:

> Non sia chi mi ragioni di Burchiello,
> Che saria proprio come comparare
> Caron Dimonio all' Agnol Gabriello.

In another sonnet he climbs a further height of panegyric:

> Quanti mai fur poeti al mondo e sono,
> Volete in Greco, in Ebreo, o in Latino,
> A petto a lui non vagliono un lupino,
> Tant' è dotto, faceto, bello e buono:

and winds up with the strange assurance that:

> da lui si sente
> Anzi s' impara con gioja infinita
> Come viver si debbe in questa vita.

[82] Sonnet xxvii.

matrimony, written in one paragraph, and containing the sting of the epigram in its short *coda* of three lines.[83] But it did not need a commentary, and Cecchi's voluminous annotations justify the poet's comic anger.

Berni's *Capitoli* may be broadly divided into three classes. The first includes his poetical epistles, addressed to Fracastoro, Sebastian del Piombo, Ippolito de' Medici, Marco Veneziano, and other friends. Except for the peculiar humour, which elevates the trivial accidents of life to comedy, except for the consummate style, which dignifies the details of familiar correspondence and renders fugitive effusions classical, these letters in verse would scarcely detach themselves from a mass of similar compositions. As it is, Berni's personality renders them worthy companions of Ariosto's masterpieces in a similar but nicely differentiated branch of literature. It remains for the amateurs of autobiographical poetry to choose between the self-revelation of the philosophising Ferrarese poet and the brilliant trifling of the Florentine. The second class embrances a number of occasional poems—the 'Complaint against Love,' the 'Deluge in Mugello,' the 'Satire upon Adrian VI.,' the 'Lamentation of Nardino'—descriptive or sarcastic pieces, where the poet chooses a theme and develops it with rhetorical abundance. The third class may be regarded as the special source and fountain of the Bernesque manner, as afterwards adopted and elaborated by Berni's imitators. Omitting personal or occasional motives, he sings the praises of the Plague, of Primiera, of Aristotle, of Peaches, of Debt, of Eels, of the Urinal, of Thistles, and of other trifling subjects. Here his burlesque genius takes the most fantastic flight, soaring to the ether of absurdity and sinking to the nadir of obscenity, combining heterogeneous elements of fun and farce, yet never transgressing the limits of refined taste. These *Capitoli* revealed a new vehicle of artistic expression to his contemporaries. Penetrated with their author's individuality, they caught the spirit of the age and met its sense of humour. Consequently they became the touchstones of burlesque inspiration, the models which tempted men of feebler force and more uncertain tact to hopeless tasks of emulation. We still possess La Casa's *Capitolo* on the Oven; Molza's on Salad and the Fig; Firenzuola's on the Sausage and the Legno Santo; Bronzino's on the Paint-brush and the Radish; Aretino's on the Quartan Fever; Franzesi's on Carrots and Chestnuts; Varchi's on Hard Eggs and Fennel; Mauro's on Beans and Priapus; Dolce's on Spittle and Noses; Bini's on the *Mal Franzese*; Lori's on Apples; Ruscelli's on the Spindle—not to speak of many authors, the obscurity of whose names and the obscenity of the themes they celebrated condemn them to condign oblivion. Not without reason did Gregorovius stigmatise these poems as a moral syphilis, invading Italian literature and penetrating to the remotest fibres of its organism. After their publication in academical circles and their further diffusion through the press, simple terms which had been used to cloak their improprieties,

[83] Sonnet ix.

became the bywords of pornographic pamphleteers and poets. Figs, beans, peaches, apples, chestnuts acquired a new and scandalous significance. Sins secluded from the light of day by a modest instinct of humanity, flaunted their loathsomeness without shame beneath the ensigns of these literary allegories. The corruption of society, hypocritically veiled or cynically half-revealed in coteries, expressed itself too plainly through the phraseology invented by a set of sensual poets. The most distinguished members of society, Cardinals like Bembo, prelates like La Casa, painters like Bronzino, critics like Varchi, scholars like Molza, lent the prestige of their position and their talents to the diffusion of this leprosy, which still remains the final most convincing testimony to the demoralisation of Italy in the Renaissance.[84]

To what extent, it may be asked, was Berni responsible for these consequences? He brought the indecencies of the piazza, where they were the comparatively innocuous expression of coarse instincts, into the close atmosphere of the study and the academical circle, refined their vulgarisms, and made their viciousness attractive by the charm of his incomparable style. This transition from the *Canto Carnascialesco* to the *Capitolo* may be observed in Berni's 'Caccia di Amore,' a very licentious poem dedicated to 'noble and gentle ladies.' It is a Carnival Song or *Canzone a Ballo* rewritten in octave stanzas of roseate fluency and seductive softness. A band of youthful huntsmen pay their court in it to women, and the *double entendre* exactly reproduces the style of innuendo rendered fashionable by Lorenzo de' Medici. Yet, though Berni is unquestionably answerable for the obscene *Capitoli* of the sixteenth century, it must not be forgotten that he only gave form to material already sufficiently appropriated by the literary classes. With him, the grossness which formed the staple of Mauro's, Molza's, Bini's, La Casa's and Bronzino's poems, the depravities of appetite which poisoned the very substance of their compositions, were but accidental. The poet stood above them and in some measure aloof from them, employing these ingredients in the concoction of his burlesque, but never losing the main object of his art in their development. A bizarre literary effect, rather than the indulgence of a sensual imagination, was the aim he had in view. Therefore, while we regret that his example gave occasion to coarser debaucheries of talent, we are bound to acknowledge that the jests to which he condescended, do not represent his most essential self. This, however, is but a feeble apology. That, without the excuse of passion, without satirical motive or overmastering personal proclivity, he should have penned the 'Capitolo a M. Antonio

[84] The scholars of the day were not content with writing burlesque *Capitoli*. They must needs annotate them. See Caro's Commentary on the *Ficheide* of Molza (Romagnoli, *Scelta di Curiosità Letterarie*, Dispensa vii. Bologna, 1862) for the most celebrated example. There is not a sentence in this long and witty composition, read before the Accademia delle Virtù, which does not contain a grossly obscene allusion, scarcely a paragraph which does not refer to an unmentionable vice.

da Bibbiena,' and have joked about giving and taking his metaphorical peaches, remains an ineradicable blot upon his nature.[85]

The Bernesque *Capitoli* were invariably written in *terza rima*, which at this epoch became the recognised metre of epistolary, satirical, and dissertational poetry throughout Italy.[86] Thus the rhythm of the 'Divine Comedy' received final development by lending itself to the expression of whims, fancies, personal invectives and scurrilities. To quote from Berni's masterpieces in this style would be impossible. Each poem of about one hundred lines is a perfect and connected unity, which admits of no mutilation by the detachment of separate passages. Still readers may be referred to the 'Capitolo a Fracastoro' and the two 'Capitoli della Peste' as representative of the poet's humour in its purest form, without the moral deformities of the still more celebrated 'Pesche' or the uncleanliness of the 'Orinale.'

At the close of the *Capitolo* written on the occasion of Adrian VI.'s election to the Papacy, Berni declared that it had never been his custom to speak ill of people:

L' usanza mia non fu mai di dir mael;
E che sia il ver, leggi le cose mie,
Leggi l' Anguille, leggi l' Orinale,
Le Pesche, i Cardi e l' altre fantasie:
Tutte sono inni, salmi, laudi ed ode.

We have reason to believe this declaration. Genial good humour is a characteristic note of his literary temperament.

At the same time he was no mean master of caricature and epigram. The *Capitolo* in question is a sustained tirade against the Fleming, who had come to break the peace of polished Rome—a shriek of angry lamentation over altered times, intolerable insults, odious innovations. The amazement and discomfiture of the poet, contrasted with his burlesque utterance, render his composition comic in a double sense. Its satire cuts both ways, against the author and the object of his rage. Yet when Adrian gave place to Giulio de' Medici, and Berni discovered what kind of man the new Pope was, he vented nobler scorn in verse of far more pungent criticism. His sonnet on Clement is remarkable for exactly expressing the verdict posterity has formed after cool and mature inquiry into this Pope's actions. Clement's weakness and irresolution must end, the poet says, by making even Adrian seem a saint:[87]

Un Papato composto di rispetti,
Di considerazioni e di discorsi,

[85] The six opening lines of the *Lamentazion d' Amore* prevent our regarding Berni's jests as wholly separate from his experience and practice.

[86] A familiar illustration is Cellini's *Capitolo del Carcere*. Curious examples of these occasional poems, written for the popular taste, are furnished by Mutinelli in his *Annali Urbani di Venezia*. See Vol. I., p. 937, Vol. II., p. 168, for the vicissitudes of *terza rima* after the close of the fourteenth century.

[87] A Papacy composed of compliment,
Debate, consideration, complaisance,
Of furthermore, then, but, yes, well, perchance,

Di più, di poi, di ma, di sì, di forsi,
Di pur, di assai parole senza effetti;
Di pensier, di consigli, di concetti,
Di congetture magre per apporsi
D' intratternerti, purchè non si sborsi,
Con audienze, risposte, e bei detti:
Di piè di piombo e di neutralità,
Di pazienza, di dimostrazione,
Di Fede, di Speranza e Carità,
D' innocenza, di buona intenzione;
Ch' è quasi come dir, semplicità,
Per non le dare altra interpretazione,
Sia con sopportazione,
Lo dirò pur, vedrete che pian piano
Farà conanizzar Papa Adriano.

The insight into Clement's character displayed in this sonnet, the invective against Adrian, and the acerbity of another sonnet against Alessandro de' Medici:

Empio Signor, che de la roba altrui
Lieto ti vai godendo, e del sudore:

would gain in cogency, could we attach more value to the manliness of Berni's utterances. But when we know that, while he was showering curses on the Duke of Cività di Penna, he frequented the Medicean Court and wrote a humorous *Capitolo* upon Gradasso, a dwarf of Cardinal Ippolito, we feel forced to place these epigrammatic effusions among the ebullitions of personal rather than political animosity. There was nothing of the patriot in Berni, not even so much as in Machiavelli, who himself avowed his readiness to roll stones for the Signori Medici.

As a satirist, Berni appears to better advantage in his caricatures of private or domestic personages. The portrait of his housekeeper, who combined in her single person all the antiquities of all the viragos of romance:

Io ho per cameriera mia l' Ancroja
Madre di Ferraù, zia di Morgante,
Arcavola maggior dell' Amostante,
Balia del Turco e suocera del Boja:

Haply, and such-like terms inconsequent;
Of thought, conjecture, counsel, argument,
Starveling surmise to summon countenance,
Negotiations, audiences, romance,
Fine words and shifts, disbursement to prevent;
Of feet of lead, of tame neutrality,
Of patience and parade to outer view,
Of fawning Faith, of Hope and Charity,
Of Innocence and good intentions too,
Which it were well to dub simplicity,
Uglier interpretations to eschew;
With your permission, you,
To speak the plain truth out, shall live to see
Pope Adrian sainted through this Papacy.

Alcionio upon his mule:

> Quella che per superchio digiunare
> Tra l' anime celesti benedette
> Come un corpo diafano traspare:

Ser Cecco who could never be severed from the Court, nor the Court from Ser Cecco:

> Perch' ambedue son la Corte e ser Cecco:

the pompous doctor:

> l'ambasciador del Boja,
> Un medico, maestro Guazzaletto:

Domenico d' Ancona, the memory of whose beard, shorn by some Vandal of a barber, draws tears from every sympathetic soul:

> Or hai dato, barbier, l' ultimo crollo
> Ad una barba la più singolare
> Che mai fosse descritta in verso o 'n prosa:

these form a gallery of comic likenesses, drawn from the life and communicated with the force of reality to the reader. Each is perfect in style, clearly cut like some antique chalcedony, bringing the object of the poet's mirth before us with the exact measure of ridicule he sought to inflict.[88]

This satiric power culminates in the sonnet on Pietro Aretino.[89] The tartness of Berni's more good-humoured pasquinades is concentrated to vitriol by unadulterated loathing. He flings this biting acid in the face of one whom he has found a scoundrel. The sonnet starts at a white heat of fury:

> Tu ne dirai e farai tante e tante,
> Lingua fracida, marcia, senza sale.

It proceeds with execration; and when the required fourteen lines have been terminated, it foams over into rage more voluble and still more voluble, unwinding the folds of an interminable *Coda* with ever-increasing *crescendo* of vituperation, as though the passion of the writer could not be appeased. The whole has to be read at one breath. No quotation can render a conception of its rhetorical art. Every word strikes home, because every word contains a truth expressed in language of malignant, undiluted, heart-felt hate. That most difficult of literary triumphs, to render abuse sublime, to sustain a single note of fierce invective without relaxing or weakening the several grades that lead to the catastrophe,

[88] Sonnets xi. xvi. xiv. iii. xx. The same vivid picturesqueness is displayed in the desecrated Abbey (Sonnet xvii.), which deserves to be called an etching in words.

[89] Sonnet xix. In the *Capitolo* to Ippolito de' Medici, Berni thus alludes to Aretino:

> Com' ha fatto non so chi mio vicino,
> Che veste d' oro, e più non degna il panno,
> E dassi del messere e del divino.

has been accomplished. This achievement is no doubt due in some measure to the exact correspondence between what we know of Pietro Aretino and what Berni has written of him. Yet its blunt fidelity to fact does not detract from the skill displayed in the handling of those triple series of rhymes, each one of which descends like a lash upon the writhing back beneath:

> Ch' ormai ogni paese
> Hai ammorbato, ogn' uom, ogn' animale,
> Il ciel e Dio e 'l diavol ti vuol male.
> Quelle veste ducale,
> O ducali accattate e furfantate,
> Che ti piangono addosso sventurate,
> A suon di bastonate
> Ti saran tratte, prima che tu muoja,
> Dal reverendo padre messer boja,
> Che l' anima di noja,
> Mediante un capestro, caveratti,
> E per maggior favore squarteratti;
> E quei tuoi leccapiatti,
> Bardassonacci, paggi da taverna,
> Ti canteranno il requiem eterna.
> Or vivi e ti governa,
> Bench' un pugnale, un cesso, overo un nodo
> Ti faranno star cheto in ogni modo.

From this conclusion the rest may be divined. Berni paid dearly for the satisfaction of thus venting his spleen. Aretino had found more than his match. Though himself a master in the art of throwing dirt, he could not, like Berni, sling his missiles with the certainty of gaining for himself by the same act an immortality of glory. This privilege is reserved for the genius of style, and style alone. Therefore he had to shrink in silence under Berni's scourge. But Aretino was not the man to forego revenge if only an opportunity for inflicting injury upon his antagonist, full and effectual, and without peril to himself, was offered. The occasion came after Berni's death; and how he availed himself of it, will appear in the next paragraphs.

Though the *Capitolo* and sonnets won for their author the high place he occupies among Italian poets, Berni is also famous for his *rifacimento* or remodelling of the 'Orlando Innamorato.' He undertook this task after the publication of the 'Furioso;' and though part was written at Verona, we know from references to contemporary events contained in the *rifacimento*, that Berni was at work upon it in the last years of his life at Florence. It was not published until some time after his death. Berni subjected the whole of Boiardo's poem to minute revision, eliminating obsolete words and Lombard phrases, polishing the verse, and softening the roughness of the elder poet's style. He omitted a few passages, introduced digressions, connected the episodes by links and references, and opened each canto with a dissertation in the manner of Ariosto. Opinions may vary as to the value of the changes wrought by Berni. But there can be no doubt that his work was executed with artistic accuracy, and that his purpose was a right one. He aimed at nothing less than rendering a noble poem adequate to the measure of literary excellence attained by the Italians since Boiardo's death. The 'Innamorato' was to be made worthy of the 'Furioso.' The nation was to possess a continuous epic of Orlando, complete in all its parts and uniformly pure in style. Had Berni lived to see his own work through the press, it is probable that this result would have been attained. As it happened, the malignity of fortune or the malice of a concealed enemy defeated his intention. We only possess a deformed version of his *rifacimento*. The history, or rather the tragedy, of its publication involves some complicated questions of conjecture. Yet the side-lights thrown upon the conditions of literature at that time in Italy, as well as on the mystery of Berni's death, are sufficiently interesting to justify the requisite expenditure of space and time.

The *rifacimento* appeared in a mutilated form at Venice in 1541, from the press of the Giunti, and again in 1542 at Milan from that of Francesco Calvo. These two issues are identical, except in the title and tail pages. The same batch of sheets was in fact divided by the two publishers. In 1545 another issue, called *Edizione Seconda*, saw the light at Venice, in which Giunta introduced a very significant note, pointing out that certain stanzas were not the work of 'M. Francesco Berni, but of one who presumptuously willed to do him so great an injury.'[90] This edition, differing in many respects from those of 1541 and 1542, was on the whole an improvement. It would seem that the publishers, in the interval between 1541 and 1545, regretted that Berni's copy had been tampered with, and did their best, in the absence of the original, to restore a correct text. Still, as Giunta acknowledged, the *rifacimento* had been irretrievably damaged by some private foe.[91] The introductory dedication to Isabella Gonzaga, where we might have expected an allusion to Boiardo, is certainly not Berni's; and the two lines,

> Nè ti sdegnar veder quel ch' altri volse
> Forse a te dedicar, ma morte il tolse,

must be understood to refer to Berni's and not to Boiardo's death.

[90] 'Di chi presuntuosamente gli ha voluto fare tanta ingiuria.' This note occurs at Stanza 83 of Canto 1.

[91] In some cases the readings of the second edition are inferior to those of the first, while both fall short of Boiardo. Boiardo wrote in his description of Astolfo (Canto i. 60):

> Quel solea dir ch' egli era per sciagura,
> E tornava a cader senza paura.

In the *rifacimento* of 1541 we have:

> E alle volte cadeva per sciagura,
> E si levava poi senza paura.

In that of 1545:

> Un sol dispetto avea: dice Turpino
> Che nel cader alquanto era latino.

I take these instances from Panizzi.

Comparison of the two editions makes it, moreover, clear that Berni's MS. had been garbled, and the autograph probably put out of the way before the publication of the poem.

Who is to be held responsible for this fraud? Who was the presumptuous enemy who did such injury to Berni? Panizzi, so far back as 1830, pointed out that Giovanni Alberto Albicante took some part in preparing the edition of 1541-2. This man prefixed sonnets written by himself to the *rifacimento*; 'whence we might conclude that he was the editor.'[92] Signor Virgili, to whose researches attention has already been directed, proved further by references to Pietro Aretino's correspondence that this old enemy of Berni had a hand in the same work. Writing to Francesco Calvo from Venice on February 16, 1540, Aretino approaches the subject of the *rifacimento* in these words:[93] 'Our friend Albicante informs me, with reference to the printing of "Orlando" defamed by Berni, that you are good enough to meet my wishes, for which I thank you. . . . You will see that, for the sake of your own modesty, you are bound either not to issue the book at all, or else to purge it of all evil-speaking.' He then states that it had been his own intention 'to emend the Count of Scandiano's "Innamoramento," a thing in its kind of heroic beauty, but executed in a trivial style, and expressed with phrases at once plebeian and obsolete.' This task he renounced upon reflection that it would bring him no fame to assume the mask of a dead man's labours. In another letter to the same Calvo, dated February 17, 1542, Aretino resumes the subject. Sbernia (so he chooses to call Berni) has been 'overwhelmed beneath the ruins he pulled down upon himself by his undoing of the "Innamoramento."'[94] Now, it is certain that the ruin proclaimed by Aretino did really fall on Berni's labours. In 1545 Lodovico Domenichi published a second *rifacimento*, far inferior in style to that of Berni, and executed with the slovenliness of a literary hack. But this was several times reprinted, whereas Berni's remained neglected on the shelves of the librarians until the year 1725, when it was republished and welcomed with a storm of exaggerated enthusiasm.

We have therefore reached this conclusion, that Aretino, aided by Albicante, both of them notable literary brigands, contrived to send a mutilated version of the *rifacimento* to press, with the view of doing irreparable mischief to Berni's reputation.[95] We have also seen that

[92] *Boiardo ed Ariosto*, vol. ii. p. cxxxiv.

[93] *Lettere*, Book ii. p. 121.

[94] *Ibid.* p. 249. We might quote a parallel passage from the Prologue to the *Ipocrita,* which Aretino published in 1542, just after accomplishing his revenge on Berni: 'Io non ho pensato al gastigo che io darei a quegli che pongono il lor nome nei libri che essi guastano nella foggia che un non so chi ha guasto il Boiardo, per non mi credere che si trovasse cotanta temerità nella presunzione del mondo.' The hypocrisy of this is worthy of the play's title.

[95] Mazzuchelli (*Scrittori d' Italia*: Albicante, Giov. Alberto) may be consulted about the relations between these two ruffians, who alternately praised and abused each other in print.

there was something dangerous in Berni's work, described by Aretino as *maldicentia*, which he held as a threat over the Milanese publisher. Lastly, Giunta recognised too late that he had made himself the party to some act of malice by issuing a garbled copy. Aretino had, we know, a private grudge to satisfy. He could not forget the castigation he received at Berni's hands, in the sonnet which has been already described. The hatred subsisting between the two men, had been further exasperated by the different parts they took in a literary duel. Antonio Broccardo, a young Venetian scholar, attacked Pietro Bembo's fame at Padua in 1530, and attempted to raise allies against the great dictator. Aretino took up the cudgels for Bembo, and assailed Broccardo with vehement abuse and calumny. Berni ranged himself upon Broccardo's side. The quarrel ended in Broccardo's death under suspicious circumstances in 1531 at Padua. He was, indeed, said to have been killed by Aretino.[96] Berni died mysteriously at Florence four years later, and Aretino caused his *rifacimento*, 'purged of evil-speaking,' to be simultaneously published at Venice and Milan.

The question still remains to be asked how Aretino, Berni's avowed enemy, obtained possession of the MS. Berni had many literary friends. Yet none of them came forward to avert the catastrophe. None of them undertook the publication of his remains. His last work was produced, not at Florence, where he lived and died, but at Venice; and Albicante, Aretino's tool, was editor. In the present state of our knowledge it is impossible to answer this question authoritatively. Considerable light, however, is thrown upon the mystery by a pamphlet published in 1554 by the heretic Vergerio. He states that Berni undertook his *rifacimento* with the view of diffusing Protestant doctrines in a popular and unobtrusive form; but that the craft of the devil, or in other words the policy of the Church, effected its suppression at the very moment when it was finished and all but printed.[97] Here, then, we seem to find some missing links in the dark chain of intrigue. Aretino's phrase *maldicentia* is explained; his menace to Francesco Calvo becomes intelligible; the silence of Berni's friends can be accounted for; and the agency by which the MS. was placed in Albicante's hands, can be at least conjectured.

[96] See Mazzuchelli, *op. cit.* under 'Brocardo, Antonio.' The spelling of the name varies. Bembo, six years afterwards, told Varchi that Aretino drove Broccardo for him into an early grave. See *Lettere all' Aretino*, vol. ii. p. 186, ed. Romagnoli. The probability is that Broccardo died of fever aggravated by the annoyance caused him by Aretino's calumnies. There is no valid suspicion of poison.

[97] This curious pamphlet was reprinted from a unique copy by Panizzi, *op. cit.* vol iii. p. 361. In the introduction, Vergerio gives an interesting account of Berni. He represents him as a man of worldly life, addicted to gross pleasures and indecent literature until within a few years of his death. Having been converted to evangelical faith in Christ, Berni then resolved to use the *Orlando* as a vehicle for Lutheran opinions; and his *rifacimento* was already almost printed, when the devil found means to suppress it. Vergerio is emphatic in his statement that the poem was finished and nearly printed. If this was indeed the case, we must suppose that Albicante worked upon the sheets, cancelling some and leaving others, and that the book thus treated was afterwards shared by Giunta and Calvo.

As a specimen of Berni's Lutheran propaganda, Vergerio subjoins eighteen stanzas, written in the poet's purest style, which were addressed to Battista Sanga, and which formed the induction to the twentieth Canto. This induction, as it stands in Berni's 'Innamorato,' is reduced to seven stanzas, grossly garbled and deformed in diction. Very few of the original lines have been retained, and those substituted are full of vulgarisms.[98] From a comparison of the original supplied by Vergerio with the mutilated version, the full measure of the mischief practised upon Berni's posthumous work can be gauged. Furthermore, it must be noticed that these compromising eighteen stanzas contained the names of several men alive in Italy, all of whom were therefore interested in their suppression, or precluded from exposing the fraud.

The inference I am inclined to draw from Signor Virgili's researches, combined with Vergerio's pamphlet, is that the Church interfered to prevent the publication of Berni's heretical additions to Boiardo's poem. Berni's sudden death, throwing his affairs into confusion at the moment when he was upon the point of finishing the business, afforded an excellent occasion to his ecclesiastical and personal opponents, who seem to have put some pressure on his kinsmen to obtain the MS. or the sheets they meant to mutilate.[99] The obnoxious passages may have been denounced by Aretino; for we know that he was intimate with Vergerio, and it is more than probable that the verses to Sanga were already in circulation.[100] Aretino, strange to say, was regarded in clerical quarters as a pillar of the Church. He therefore found it in his power to wreak his vengeance on an enemy at the same time that he posed as a defender of the faith. That he was allowed to control the publication, appears from his letters to Calvo; and he confided the literary part of the business to Albicante. His threats to Calvo have reference to Berni's heresy, and the *maldicentia* may possibly have been the eighteen stanzas addressed to Sanga. The terror of the Inquisition reduced Berni's friends to silence. Aretino, even if he had not denounced Berni to the Church, had now identified himself with the crusade against his poem, and he was capable of ruining opponents in this unequal contest by charges they would have found it impossible to refute. The eighteen stanzas were addressed to a secretary of Clement VII.; and men of note like Molza, Flamminio, Navagero, Fondulo, Fregoso.

[98] I shall print a translation of the eighteen stanzas in an Appendix to this volume. Lines like the following:

Arrandellarsi come un salsicciuolo,

which are common in the mangled version, would never have passed Berni's censure.

[99] This appears from a reference in Aretino's second letter to Calvo, where he talks of Berni's 'friends and relatives.' It might be going too far to suggest that Berni was murdered by his ecclesiastical enemies, who feared the scandal which would be caused by the publication of his opinions.

[100] Vergerio may have communicated the eighteen stanzas to Aretino; or conversely he may have received them from him. I have read through the letters exchanged between him and Aretino—and they are numerous—without, however, finding any passage that throws light on this transaction. Aretino published both series of letters. He had therefore opportunity to suppress inconvenient allusions.

were distinctly named in them. If, then, there is any cogency in the conclusions I have drawn from various sources, Berni's poem, and perhaps his life, was sacrificed to theological hatred in combination with Aretino's personal malice. The unaccountable inactivity of his friends is explained by their dread of being entangled in a charge of heresy.[101]

Enough has been already said about Berni's imitators in the burlesque style. Of satire in the strict sense of the term, the poets of the sixteenth century produced nothing that is worth consideration. The epistolary form introduced by Ariosto, and the comic caprices rendered fashionable by Berni, determined the compositions of Pietro Aretino, of Ercole Bentivoglio, of Luigi Alamanni, of Antonio Vinciguerra, of Giovanni Andrea dell' Anguillara, of Cesare Caporali, and of the minor versifiers whose occasional poems in *terza rima*, seasoned with more or less satirical intention, are usually reckoned among the satires of the golden age.[102] Personal vituperation, poured forth in the heat of literary quarrels, scarcely deserves the name of satire. Else it might be necessary in this place to mention Niccolò Franco's sonnets on Pietro Aretino, or the far more elegant compositions of Annibale Caro directed against his enemy Castelvetro.[103] Models for this species of poetical abuse had been already furnished by the sonnets exchanged between Luigi Pulci and Matteo Franco in a more masculine age of Italian literature.[104] It is not, however, incumbent upon the historian to resuscitate the memory of those forgotten and now unimportant duels. The present allusion to them may suffice to corroborate the opinion already stated that, while the Italians of the Renaissance were ingenious in burlesque, and virulent in personal invective, they lacked the earnestness of moral conviction, the indignation, and the philosophic force that generate real satire.

[101] We may note the dates and fates of the chief actors in this tragedy. Broccardo died of grief in 1531. Berni died, under suspicion of poison, in 1535. Cardinal Ippolito de' Medici was poisoned a few months later, in 1535. Alessandro de' Medici was murdered by Lorenzino in 1537. Pietro Paolo Vergerio was deprived of his see and accused of heresy in 1544. Berni's old friend, the author of *Il Forno*, M. La Casa, conducted his trial, as Papal Nuncio at Venice. Aretino, who had assumed the part of inquisitor and mutilator to gratify his private spite, survived triumphant.

[102] See the *Raccolta di Poesie Satiriche*, Milano, 1808.

[103] See, for the latter series, *Poesie Satiriche*, pp. 138-156.

[104] See *Sonetti di Matteo Franco e di Luigi Pulci*, 1759. Cp. above, p. 117.

CHAPTER XV

PIETRO ARETINO

Aretino's Place in Italian Literature and Society—His Birth and Boyhood—Goes to Rome—In the Service of Agostino Chigi—At Mantua—Gradual Emergence into Celebrity—The Incident of Guilio Romano's Postures—Giovanni delle Bande Nere—Aretino settles at Venice—The Mystery of his Influence—Discerns the Power of the Press—Satire on the Courts—Magnificent Life—Aretino's Wealth—His Tributary Princes—Bullying and Flattery—The Divine Aretino—His Letter to Vittoria Colonna—To Michelangelo—His Admiration of Artists—Relations with Men of Letters—Epistle to Bernardo Tasso—His Lack of Learning—Disengagement from Puristic Prejudices—Belief in his own Powers—Rapidity of Composition—His Style—Originality and Independence—Prologue to 'Talanta'—Bohemian Comrades—Niccolò Franco—Quarrel with Doni—Aretino's Literary Influence—His Death—The Anomaly of the Renaissance—Estimate of Aretino's Character.

PIETRO ARETINO, as I have already had occasion to observe, is a representative name in the history of Italian literature. It is almost as impossible to slur him over with a passing notice as it would be to dwell but casually upon Machiavelli, or Ariosto, Cellini or Poliziano, in reviewing the Renaissance. Base in character, coarse in mental fibre, unworthy to rank among real artists, notwithstanding his undoubted genius, Aretino was the typical ruffian of an age which brought ruffiansim to perfection, welcomed it when successful, bowed to its insolence, and viewed it with complacent toleration in the highest places of Church, State, and letters. He was the *condottiere* of the pen in a society which truckled to the Borgias. He embodied the infamy and cowardice which lurked beneath the braveries of Italian Court-life—the coarseness of speech which contradicted literary purism—the cynicism and gross strength of appetite for which convention was a flimsy veil.[1] The man himself incarnated the dissolution of Italian culture. His works, for the student of that period, are an anti-masque to the brilliant display of Ariosto's or of Tasso's puppets. It is the condemnation of Italy that we are forced to give this prominence to Aretino. If we place Poliziano or Guicciardini, Bembo or La Casa, Bandello or Firenzuola, Cellini or Berni, Paolo Giovio or Lodovico Dolce—typical men of letters chosen from the poets, journalists, historians, thinkers, artists, novel-writers of

[1] The best source of information regarding Pietro Aretino is his own correspondence published in six volumes (Paris, 1609), and the two volumes of letters written to him by eminent personages, which are indeed a rich mine of details regarding Italian society and manners in the sixteenth century. Mazzuchelli's *Vita di Pietro Aretino* (Padua, 1741) is a conscientious, sober, and laborious piece of work, on which all subsequent notices have been based.

the age—under the critical microscope, we find in each and all of them a tincture of Aretino. It is because he emphasises and brings into relief one master element of the Renaissance, that he deserves the rank assigned to him. In Athens Aristophanes is named together with Sophocles, Thucydides, and Plato, because, with genius equal to theirs, he represented the comic antithesis to tragedy, philosophy and history. In Italy Aretino is classed with Machiavelli and Ariosto for a different reason. His lower nature expressed, not an antithesis, but a quality, which, in spite of intellectual and moral superiority, they possessed in common with him, which he exhibited in arrogant abundance, and which cannot be omitted from the survey of his century. The alloy of cynicism in Machiavelli, his sordid private pleasures, his perverse admiration for Cesare Borgia, his failure to recognise the power of goodness in the world, condemn him to the company of this triumvir. The profligacy of genius in Ariosto, his waste of divine gifts upon trifles, his lack of noble sentiment, his easy acquiescence in conditions of society against which he should have uttered powerful protest, consign him, however undeservedly, to the same association.[2]

Pietro was born at Arezzo in 1492. His reputed father was a nobleman of that city, named Luigi Bacci. His mother, Tita, was a woman of the town, whose portrait, painted as the Virgin of the Annunciation, adorned the church-door of S. Pietro. The boy, 'born,' as he afterwards boasted, 'in a hospital with the spirit of a king,' passed his childhood at Arezzo with his mother. He had no education but what he may have picked up among the men who frequented Tita's house, or the artists who employed her as a model. Of Greek and Latin he learned nothing either now or afterwards. Before growing to man's estate, he had to quit his native city—according to one account because he composed and uttered a ribald sonnet on indulgences, according to another because he robbed his mother. He escaped to Perugia, and gained his livelihood by binding books. Here he made acquaintance with Firenzuola, as appears from a letter of the year 1541, in which he alludes to their youthful pranks together at the University. One of Aretino's exploits at Perugia became famous. 'Having noticed in a place of much resort upon the public square a picture, in which the Magdalen was represented at the feet of Christ, with extended arms and in an attitude of passionate grief, he went privily and painted in a lute between her hands.' From Perugia he trudged on foot to Rome, and entered the service of Agostino Chigi, under whose patronage he made himself useful to the Medici, remaining in the retinue of both Leo X. and Clement VII. between 1517 and 1524. This period of seven years formed the man's character; and it would be interesting to know for certain what his employment was. Judging by the graphic descriptions

[2] It may be mentioned that Ariosto has immortalised this bully in the *Orlando* (xlvi. 14), among the most illustrious men and women of his age:

ecco il flagello
De' principi, il divin Pietro Aretino.

he has left us of the Roman Court in his comedy of the 'Cortigiana' and his dialogue 'De le Corti,' and also by his humble condition in Perugia, we have reason to believe that he occupied at first the post of lacquey, rising gradually by flattery and baser arts to the position of a confidential domestic, half favourite, half servant.[3] That he possessed extraordinary social qualities, and knew how to render himself agreeable by witty conversation and boon companionship, is obvious from the whole course of his subsequent history. It is no less certain that he allowed neither honour nor self-respect to interfere with his advancement by means which cannot be described in detail, but which opened the readiest way to favour in that profligate society of Rome. His own enormous appetite for sensual enjoyment, his cynicism, and his familiarity with low life in all its forms, rendered him the congenial associate of a great man's secret pleasures, the convenient link of communication between the palace and the stews.[4]

Yet though Pietro resided at this time principally in Rome, he had by no means a fixed occupation, and his life was interrupted by frequent wanderings. He is said to have left Agostino Chigi's service, because he stole a silver cup. He is also said to have taken the cowl in a Capuchin convent at Ravenna, and to have thrown his frock to the nettles on the occasion of Leo's election to the Papacy. We hear of him parading in the Courts of Lombardy, always on the look out for patronage, supporting himself by what means is unapparent, but gradually pushing his way to fame and fashion, loudly asserting his own claims to notice, and boasting of each new favour he received. Here is a characteristic glimpse into his nomadic mode of life:[5] 'I am now in Mantua with the Marquis, and am held by him in so high favour that he leaves off

[3] Aretino's comedies, letters, and occasional poems are our best sources for acquaintance with the actual conditions of palace-life. The *Dialogo de le Corti* opens with a truly terrible description of the debauchery and degradation to which a youth was exposed on his first entrance into the service of a Roman noble. It may have been drawn from the author's own experience. The nauseous picture of the *tinello*, or upper-servants' hall, which occurs in the comedy *Cortigiana* (act. v. sc. 15), proves intimate familiarity with the most revolting details of domestic drudgery. The dirt of these places made an ineffaceable impression on Aretino's memory. In his burlesque *Orlandino*, when he wishes to call up a disgusting image, he writes:

Odorava la sala come odora
Un gran tinel d' un Monsignor Francese,
O come quel d' un Cardinal ancora
Quando Febo riscalda un bestial mese.

[4] Aretino's correspondence and the comedy above mentioned throw sufficient light upon these features of Roman society. It will, for the rest, suffice to quote a passage from Monsignore Guidiccioni's letter to Giambattista Bernardi (*Opere di M. Giov. Guidiccioni*, Barbèra, 1867, vol. i. p. 195): 'Non solamente *da questi illustri per ricchezze* non si può avere, ma non si puote ancora sperare premio che sia di lunghe fatiche o di rischio di morte, se *l' uomo non si rivolge ad acquisitarlo per vie disoneste.* Perciocchè essi non carezzano e non esaltano se non adulatori, e *quelli che sanno per alfabeto le abitazioni, le practiche e le qualità delle cortigiane.*' The whole letter should be read by those who would understand Roman society of the Renaissance. The italics are mine.

[5] Quoted by Philarète Chasles from Gamurrini, *Ist. Gen. delle famiglie nobili Toscane ed Umbre*, iii. 332. I do not know exactly to what period the letter refers.

sleeping and eating to converse with me, and says he has no other pleasure in life; and he has written to the Cardinal about me things that will not fail to help me greatly to my credit. I have also received a present of 300 crowns. He has assigned to me the very same apartment which Francesco Maria, Duke of Urbino, occupied when he was in exile; and has appointed a steward to preside over my table, where I always have some nobleman of rank. In a word, more could not be done for the entertainment of the greatest prince. Besides, the whole Court worships me. Happy are they who can boast of having got a verse from me. My Lord has had all the poems ever writ by me copied, and I have made some in his praise. So I pass my life here, and every day get some gift, grand things which you shall see at Arezzo. But it was at Bologna they began to make me presents. The Bishop of Pisa had a robe of black satin embroidered with gold cut for me; nothing could be handsomer. So I came like a prince to Mantua. Everybody calls me "Messere" and "Signore." I think this Easter we shall be at Loreto, where the Marquis goes to perform a vow; and on this journey I shall be able to satisfy the Dukes of Ferrara and Urbino, both of whom have expressed the desire to make my acquaintance.'

On the election of Clement VII., Pietro returned to Rome with a complimentary sonnet in his pocket for the new Pope. He had now acquired an Italian reputation, and was able to keep the state of an independent gentleman, surrounded by a band of disreputable hangers-on, the *bardassonacci*, *paggi da taverna*, of Berni's satirical sonnet. But a misfortune obliged him suddenly to decamp. Giulio Romano had designed a series of obscene figures, which Marcantonio Raimondi engraved, and Aretino illustrated by sixteen sonnets, describing and commenting upon the lewdness of each picture. Put in circulation, these works of immodest art roused the indignation of the Roman prelates, who, though they complacently listened to Berni's 'Pesche' or La Casa's 'Forno' behind the closed doors of a literary club, disliked the scandal of publicity. Raimondi was imprisoned; Giulio Romano went in the service of the Marquis of Mantua to build the famous Palazzo del Te: and Aretino discreetly retired from Rome for a season. Of the three accomplices in this act of high treason against art, Aretino was undoubtedly the guiltiest. Yet he had the impudence to defend his sonnets in 1537, and to address them with a letter of dedication, unmatched for its parade of shamelessness, to Messer Battista Zatti of Brescia.[6] In this epistle he takes credit to himself for having procured the engraver's pardon and liberation from Clement VII. However this may be, he fell in 1524 under the special ban of Monsignor Giberti's displeasure, and had to take refuge with Giovanni de' Medici delle Bande Nere.[7] This famous general was a wild free-liver. He conceived a real affection for Aretino, made him the sharer in his debaucheries, gave him a place

[6] *Lettere*, vol. i. p. 258.

[7] It may be remembered that Giberti, Bishop of Verona, was Berni's patron. This helps to account for the animosity between Berni and Aretino.

even in his own bed, and listened with rapture to his indecent improvisations. Aretino's fortune was secured. It was discovered that he had the art of pleasing princes. He knew exactly how to season his servility with freedom, how to flatter the great man by pandering to his passions and tickling his vanity, while he added the pungent sauce of satire and affected bluntness. *Il gran Diavolo*, as Giovanni de' Medici was called, introduced Aretino to Francis I., and promised, if fortune favoured him, to make the adventurer master of his native town, Arezzo.[8]

Aretino's intercourse with these powerful protectors was broken by a short visit to Rome, where he seems to have made peace with the prelates. It was probably inconvenient to protract hostilities against a man who had gained the friendship of a King of France and of the greatest Italian *condottiere* of his age. But fortune had ceased to smile on our hero in Rome. It so happened that he wrote a ribald sonnet on a scullion-wench in the service of Monsignor Giberti, to whom a certain Achille della Volta was at the same time paying his addresses. The *bravo* avenged this insult to his mistress by waylaying Aretino in the Trastevere and stabbing him several times in the breast and hands. When Aretino recovered from his wounds, he endeavoured in vain to get justice against Achille. The Pope and his Datary refused to inferfere in this ignoble quarrel. Aretino once more retired from Rome, vowing vengeance against Clement, whom he defamed to the best of his ability in scurrilous libels and calumnious conversation.[9]

He now remained with Giovanni de' Medici until that general's death in 1526. The great captain died in Aretino's arms at Mantua from the effect of a wound inflicted by an unknown harquebuss in Frundsperg's army.[10] This accident decided Aretino to place no further reliance on princely patronage. He was thirty-two years of age, and had acquired a singular reputation throughout Italy for social humour, pungent wit and literary ability. Though deficient in personal courage, as the affair of Achille della Volta proved, he contrived to render himself formidable by reckless evil-speaking; and while he had no learning and no style, he managed to pass for a writer of distinction. How he attained this position in an age of purists, remains a puzzle; we possess nothing which

[8] *Op. Burl.* ii. p. 11:

Sotto Milano dieci volte, non ch' una,
Mi disse: Pietro, se di questa guerra
Mi scampa Dio e la buona fortuna,
Ti voglio impadronir della tua terra.

Giovanni de' Medici wrote to him thus: 'Vieni presto. . . . Il re a buon proposito si dolse che non ti aveva menato al solito, onde io diedi la colpa al piacerti più lo stare in Corte che in Campo . . . non so vivere senza l' Aretino.'—*Lettere scritte all' Aretino*, i. 6.

[9] The sonnet by Berni quoted above, p. 379, was written to meet these libels of Aretino. It contains an allusion to Achille della Volta's poignard.

[10] See Aretino's Letters, vol. i. pp. 8, 10, for very interesting details concerning the death of Giovanni de' Medici. He here used the interest of his old master to secure the favour of Duke Cosimo.

explains the importance attached to his compositions at this early period. His sonnets had made what the French call a success of scandal; and the libertines who protected him, were less particular about literary elegance than eager to be amused. If we inquire minutely into the circumstances of Aretino's career, we find that he had worked himself into favour with a set of princes—the Marquis of Mantua, the Dukes of Ferrara and Urbino, Giovanni de' Medici, and the King of France—who were powerful enough to confer fashion upon an adventurer, and to place him in a position where it would be perilous to contest his claims, but who were not eminent for literary taste. In the Court of the two Medici at Rome, who exacted more scholarship and refinement than Aretino possessed, he never gained firm footing; and this was perhaps the chief reason of his animosity against Clement. He had in fact become the foremost parasite, the wittiest and most brilliant companion of debauch, in the less cultivated Italian Courts. This reputation he now resolved to use for his own profit. From the moment when he retired to Venice in 1527, resolved to support himself by literary work, until his death, in 1557, he enjoyed a princely income, levying tribute on kings and nobles, living with prodigal magnificence, corresponding with the most illustrious men of all nations, and dictating his own terms to the society he alternately flattered and insulted. The history of these last thirty years, which may be clearly read in the six bulky volumes of his published correspondence, and in the four volumes of letters written to him, is one of the most extraordinary instances on record of celebrity and power acquired by calculated imposture and audacious brigandism.[11]

Aretino showed prudence in the choice of Venice for his fixed abode. In Venice there was greater liberty both of life and speech than elsewhere at that time in Italy. So long as a man refrained from politics and offered no cause of suspicion to the State, he might do and publish pretty much what he chose, without fear of interference and without any serious peril from the Inquisition. For a filibuster of Aretino's type, Venice offered precisely the most advantageous harbour, whence he could make sallies and predatory excursions, and whither he might always return to rest at ease beneath the rampart of a proud political indifference. His greatness consisted in the accurate measure he had taken of the society upon which he now intended to live by literary speculation. His acute common sense enabled him to comprehend the power of the press, which had not as yet been deliberately used as a weapon of offence and an instrument of extortion. We have seen in another portion of this book how important a branch of literature the invectives of the humanists had been, how widely they were read, and what an impression they produced upon society. The diatribes of Poggio

[11] The edition of Aretino's own letters which I shall use is that of Paris, 1609, in six books. The edition of the *Lettere scritte all' Aretino* is Romagnoli's reprint, *Scelta di Curiosità*, Bologna, 1873-1876, Dispensa cxxxii., two books divided into four volumes; to these, for convenience sake, I shall refer as 1, 2, 3, 4.

and Filelfo circulated in manuscript; but now the press was in full working order, and Aretino perceived that he might make a livelihood by printing threats and libels mixed with eulogies and personal panegyrics. The unwieldy three-decker of the invective should be reduced to the manageable form of the epistolary torpedo and gunboat. To propagate calumnies and to render them imperishable by printing was the menace he addressed to society. He calculated wisely on the uneasiness which the occasional appearance of stinging pamphlets, fully charged with personalities, would produce among the Italians, who were nothing if not a nation of readers at this epoch. At the same time he took measures to secure his own safety. Professing himself a good Christian, he liberally seasoned his compositions with sacred names; and, though he had no more real religion than Fra Timoteo in Machiavelli's 'Mandragola,' he published pious romances under the titles of 'I tre libri della Humanità di Christo,' 'I Sette Salmi de la penitentia di David,' 'Il Genesi di Pietro Aretino,' 'La Vita di Catherina Vergine,' 'La Vita di Maria Vergine,' 'La Vita di S. Tommaso Signor d' Aquino.' These books, proceeding from the same pen as the 'Sonetti lussuriosi' and the pornographic 'Ragionamenti,' were an insult to piety. Still they served their author for a shield, behind which he shot the arrows of his calumnies, and carried on the more congenial game of making money by pandering to the licentiousness or working on the cowardice of the wealthy.[12]

Aretino, who was able to boast that he had just refused a flattering invitation from the Marquis of Montferrat, was received with honour by the State of Venice. Soon after his arrival he wrote thus to the Doge Andrea Gritti:[13] 'I, who, in the liberty of so great and virtuous a commonwealth, have now learned what it is to be free, reject Courts henceforth for ever, and here make my abiding tabernacle for the years that yet remain to me; for here there is no place for treason, here favour cannot injure right, here the cruelty of prostitutes exerts no sway, here the insolence of the effeminate is powerless to command, here there is no robbing, no violence to the person, no assassination. Wherefore I, who have stricken terror into kings, I, who have restored confidence to virtuous men, give myself to you, fathers of your people, brothers of your servants, sons of truth, friends of virtue, companions of the stranger, pillars of religion, observers of your word, executors of justice, treasuries of charity, and subjects of clemency.' Then follows a long tirade in the same stilted style upon the majesty of Venice. The Doge took Aretino by the hand, reconciled him with Clement and the Bishop of Verona, and assured him of protection, so long as the illustrious author chose to make the city of the lagoons his home. Luigi Gritti, the

[12] It is clear from a perusal of the *Lettere all' Aretino* that his reputation depended in a great measure upon these pious romances. The panegyrics heaped on them are too lengthy and too copious to be quoted. They are curiously mixed with no less fervent praises of the *Dialoghi*.

[13] *Lettere*, vol. i. p. 3.

Doge's son, assigned him a pension; and though invitations came from foreign Courts, Aretino made his mind up to remain at Venice. He knew that the very singularity of his resolve, in an age when men of letters sought the patronage of princely houses, would enable him to play the game he had in view. Nor could he forget the degradation he had previously undergone in courtly service. 'Only let me draw breath outside that hell! Ah! your Court! your Court! To my mind a gondolier here is better off than a chamberlain there. Look you at yonder poor waiting man, tortured by the cold, consumed by the heat, standing at his master's pleasure—where is the fire to warm him? where is the water to refresh him? When he falls ill, what chamber, what stable, what hospital will take him in? Rain, snow, mud! Faugh, it murders a man to ride in such weather with his patron or upon his errands. Think how cruel it is to have to show a beard grown in the service of mere boys, how abject are white hairs, when youth and manhood have been spent in idling around tables, antechamber doors, and privies? Here I sit when I am tired; when I am hungry, eat; when I feel the inclination, sleep; and all the hours are obedient to my will.'[14] He revels in the sense of his own freedom. 'My sincerity, and my virtue, which never could stomach the lies that bolster up the Court of Rome, nor the vices that reign in it, have found favour in the eyes of all the princes of the world. Emperors, thank God, are not Popes, nor Kings Cardinals! Therefore I enjoy their generosity, instead of courting that hypocrisy of priests, which acts the bawd and pander to our souls. Look at Chieti, the parasite of penitence! Look at Verona, the buffoon of piety! They at least have solved the doubts in which their ambitious dissimulation held those who believed that the one would not accept the hat, and the other was not scheming for it. I meanwhile praise God for being what I am. The hatred of slaves, the rancours of ambition no longer hem me round. I rob no man's time. I take no delight in seeing my neighbours go naked through the world. Nay, I share with them the very shirts off my back, the crust of bread upon my plate. My servant-girls are my daughters, my lacqueys are my brothers. Peace is the pomp of my chambers, and liberty the majordomo of my palace. I feast daily off bread and gladness; and, wishing not to be of more importance than I am, live by the sweat of my ink, the lustre of which has never been extinguished by the blasts of malignity or the mists of envy.'[15] At another time he breaks into jubilant descriptions of his own magnificence and popularity. 'I swear to you by the wings of Pegasus that, much as may have reached your ears, you have not heard one half the hymn of my celebrity. Medals are coined in my honour; medals of gold, of silver, of brass, of lead, of stucco. My features are carved along the fronts of palaces. My portrait is stamped upon comb-cases, engraved on mirror-handles, painted on majolica. I am a second Alexander, Cæsar, Scipio. Nay more: I tell you that some

[14] *Lettere* i. 204.
[15] *Lettere,* ii. 58.

kinds of glasses they make at Murano, are called Aretines. Aretine is the name given to a breed of cobs—after one Pope Clement sent me and I gave to Duke Frederick. They have christened the little canal that runs beside my house upon the Canalozzo, Rio Aretino. And, to make the pedants burst with rage, besides talking of the Aretine style, three wenches of my household, who have left me and become ladies, will have themselves known only as the Aretines.'[16]

These self-congratulations were no idle vaunts. His palace on the Grand Canal was crowded with male and female servants, thronged with visitors, crammed with costly works of art and presents received from every part of Italy and Europe. The choicest wines and the most exquisite viands—rare birds, delicate fruits, and vegetables out of season—arrived by special messengers to furnish forth his banquets. Here he kept open house, enjoying the society of his two bosom friends, Titian and Sansovino, entertaining the magnificent Venetian prostitutes, and welcoming the men of fashion or of learning who made long journeys to visit him.[17] 'If I only spent in composition one third of the time I fling away, the printers would do nothing but attend to the issuing of my works. And yet I could not write so much if I would; so enormous is the multitude which comes incessantly to see me. I am often forced to fly from my own house, and leave the concourse to take care of itself.'[18] 'So many lords and gentlemen are eternally breaking in upon me with their importunities, that my stairs are worn by their feet like the Capitol with wheels of triumphal chariots. Turks, Jews, Indians, Frenchmen, Germans, Spaniards, flock to see me. You can fancy how many Italians come! I say nothing about the common folk. You could not find me without a flock of friars and priests. I have come to be the Oracle of Truth, the Secretary of the Universe: everybody brings me the tale of his injury by this prince or that prelate.'[19] This sumptuous train of life demanded a long purse, and Aretino had nothing but his brains to live by. Yet, by the sale of his books and the contributions levied on great folk, he accumulated a yearly income sufficient to his needs. 'Thanks to their Majesties of Spain and France, with the addition of a hundred crowns of pension allowed me by the

[16] *Lettere*, iii. 145; cp. iii. 89. The whole of the passage translated above is an abstract of a letter professedly written to Aretino by Doni (*Lett. all' Ar.* vol. iv. p. 395), which may be read with profit as an instance of flattery. The occurrence of the same phrases in both series of epistles raises a doubt whether Aretino did not tamper with the text of the correspondence he published, penning panegyrics of himself and printing them under fictitious names as advertisements. Doni was a man who might have lent himself to such imposture on the public.

[17] See *Lettere all.' Ar.* vol. iv. p. 352, for a vivid description, written by Francesco Marcolini, of Aretino's train of living and prodigal hospitality. It realises the vast banquetting-pictures of Veronese.

[18] *Lettere*, iii. 72.

[19] *Lettere*, i. 206. This passage occurs also in a letter addressed to Aretino by one Alessandro Andrea (*Lett. all' Ar.* vol. iii. p. 178); whence Mazzuchelli argues that Aretino tampered with the letters written to him, and interpolated passages before he sent them to the press. See note 16, above.

Marquis of Vasto, and the same amount paid by the prince of Salerno, I have six hundred crowns of fixed income, besides the thousand or thereabouts I make yearly with a quire of paper and a bottle of ink.'[20] In another place he says that in the course of eighteen years 'the alchemy of his pen had drawn over twenty-five thousand crowns from the entrails of various princes.'[21] It was computed that, during his lifetime, he levied blackmail to the extent of about 70,000 crowns, or considerably more than a million of francs, without counting his strictly professional earnings. All this wealth he spent as soon as he laid hands upon it, boasting loudly of his prodigality, as though it were a virtue. He dressed splendidly, and denied himself no sensual indulgence. His house contained a harem of women, devoted to his personal pleasures and those, apparently, of his familiar friends. He had many illegitimate daughters, whom he dowered. Moreover, he was liberal to poor people; and while squandering money first upon his vices, he paid due attention to his reputation for generosity.[22] The bastard of Arezzo vaunted he had been born in a hospital with the soul of a king.[23] Yet he understood nothing of real magnanimity; his charity was part of an open-handed recklessness, which made him fling the goods of fortune to the wind as soon as gained—part of the character of *grand seigneur* he aspired to assume.[24]

It would fatigue the patience of the reader to furnish forth a complete list of the presents made to Aretino and acknowledged by him in his correspondence. Chains, jewels, horses, pictures, costly stuffs, cups, mirrors, delicacies of the table, wines—nothing came amiss to him; and the more he received the more he cried continually, Give, give, give! There was hardly a reigning prince in Europe, hardly a noble of distinction in Italy, who had not sent some offering to his shrine. The Sultan Soliman, the pirate Barbarossa, the Pope, the Emperor, were among his tributaries.[25] The Empress gave him a golden collar worth three hundred crowns. Philip, Infante of Spain, presented him with another worth four hundred. Francis I. bestowed on him a still more costly chain, wrought of pure gold, from which hung a row of red enamelled tongues, bearing the inscription *Lingua ejus loquetur mendacium.* Aretino received these presents from the hands of ambassadors, and wore them when he sat to Titian or to Tintoretto for his portrait. Instead of resenting the equivocal compliment of the French king's motto, he gloried in it. Lies, no less than flattery, were among the openly-avowed weapons of his armoury.[26] Upon the medals struck in his

[20] *Lettere*, ii. 213.
[21] *Lettere*, iii. 70.
[22] See *Lettere*, ii. 257; iii. 340; v. 251.
[23] See the *Capitolo al Duca di Fiorenza.*
[24] Marcolini's letter (*Lettere all' Aretino*, vol. iv. p. 352), and some letters from obscure scholars (for example, *ib.* vol. ii. pp. 118-121), seem to prove that he was really open-handed in cases of distress.
[25] There is a letter from Barbarossa to Aretino in the *Lettere all' Ar.* vol. iii. p. 269.
[26] See the frank admissions in *Lettere*, ii. 52; iv. 168; i. 19, 30, 142.

honour he styled himself *Divus P. Aretinus Flagellum Principum*, the Divine Pietro Aretino, Scourge of Princes. Another inscription ran as follows: *I Principi tributati dai popoli il Servo loro tributano*—Princes who levy tribute from their people, bring tribute to their servant. And there is Aretino seated on a throne, with noble clients laying golden vases at his feet.[27]

It is incredible that arrogance so palpable should have been tolerated, inconceivable how such a braggart exercised this fascination. What had Emperors and Kings to gain or lose by Aretino's pen? What was the secret of his power? No satisfactory answer has yet been given to these questions. The enigma does not, indeed, admit of solution. We have to deal in Aretino's case with a blind movement among 'the better vulgar,' expressing itself as fashion; and nothing is more difficult to fathom than the fashion of a bygone age.[28] The prestige which attached itself to people like Cagliostro or S. Germains or Beau Nash is quite incalculable. Yet some account may be rendered of what seems to have been Aretino's method. He assiduously cultivated a reputation for reckless freedom of speech. He loudly trumpeted his intention of speaking evil when and where it pleased him. He proclaimed himself the champion of veracity, asserted that nothing was so damnatory as the truths he had to tell, and announced himself the 'Censor of the world,' the foe of vice, the defender of virtue. Having occupied the ear of society by these preliminary fanfaronnades, he proceeded to satirise the courts in general, and to vilify the manners of princes, without mentioning any in particular.[29] It thus came to be believed that Aretino was a dangerous person, a writer it would be wiser to have upon one's side, and who, if he were not coaxed into good humour, might say something eminently disagreeable.[30] There was pungency

[27] See the plates prefixed to Mazzuchelli's Life of Aretino. Compare a passage in his Letters, vi. 115, and the headings of the Letters addressed to him, *passim*.

[28] After studying the *Lettere scritte all' Aretino*—epistles, it must be remembered, from foreign kings and princes, from cardinals and bishops, from Italian dukes and noblemen, from illustrious ladies and great artists and from the most distinguished men of letters of his day—I am quite at a loss to comprehend the *furore* of fashion which accompanied this man through his career. One and all praise him as the most powerful, the most virtuous, the bravest, the wittiest, the wisest, or, to use their favorite phrase, the *divinest* man of his century. Was all this a mere convention? Was it evoked by fear and desire of being flattered in return? Or, after all, had Aretino some now occult splendour, some real, but now unintelligible, utility for his contemporaries?

[29] The Papal Court was attacked by him; but none other that I can discover. The only Prince who felt the rough side of his tongue was the Farnese:

> Impara tu, Pierluigi ammorbato,
> Impara, Ducarel da sei quattrini,
> Il costume d' un Rè si onorato.

Cardinal Gaddi and the Bishop of Verona were pretty roughly treated. So was Clement VII. But all these personages made their peace with Aretino, and paid him homage.

[30] See the curious epistle written to Messer Pompeo Pace by the Conte di Monte Labbate, and included among the *Lettere all' Aretino*, vol. iv. p. 385. Speaking of Aretino's singular worth and excellent qualities, it discusses the question of the terror

enough in his epigrams, in the slashing, coarse, incisive brutality of his style, to make his attack formidable. People shrank from it, as they now shrink from articles in certain libellous weekly papers. Aretino was recognised as a Cerberus, to whom sops should be thrown. Accordingly, the custom began of making him presents and conferring on him pensions. Then it was discovered that if he used a pen dipped in vitriol for his enemies, he had a reserve pen of gold for his patrons, from which the gross mud-honey of flatteries incessantly trickled.[31] To send him a heavy fee was the sure way of receiving an adulatory epistle, in which the Scourge of Princes raised his benefactor of the moment to the skies. In a word, Aretino's art consisted in making each patron believe that the vigilant satirist of other people's vices bestowed just eulogy on him alone, and that his praises were wrung from the mouth of truth by singular and exceptional merit. The fact is that though Aretino corresponded with all the princes of Europe and with at least thirty Cardinals, his letters are nothing but a series of the grossest flatteries. There is a hint here and there that the benefactor had better loosen his purse strings, if he wishes the stream of sycophancy to continue. When Cerberus has been barking long without a sop, we hear an angry growl, a menace, a curt and vicious snarl for gold.[32] But no sooner has the gift been sent, than the fawning process recommences. In this way, by terrorism and toad-eating, by wheedling and bullying, by impudent demands for money and no less impudent assertions of his power to confer disgrace or fame, the rascal held society at his disposal. He boasted, and not without reason, that from his study in Venice he could move the world by a few lines scribbled on a piece of paper with his pen. What remains inconceivable, is that any value should have been attached to his invectives or his panegyrics—that persons of distinction should have paid him for the latter, and have stooped to deprecate the former. But it had become the fashion to be afraid of

he inspired, which the author attributes to a kind of justifiable *chantage*. That Aretino was the inventor of literary *chantage* is certain; but that it was justifiable, does not appear.

[31] Aretino made no secret of his artificial method of flattery. In a letter to Bembo (*Lettere*, ii. 52), he openly boasts that his literary skill enables him to 'swell the pride of grandees with exorbitant praises, keeping them aloft in the skies upon the wings of hyperboles.' 'It is my business,' he adds, 'to transform digressions, metaphors, and pedagogeries of all sorts into capstans for moving and pincers for opening. I must so work that the voice of my writings shall break the sleep of avarice; and baptize that conceit or that phrase which shall bring me crowns of gold, not laurels.'

[32] As a sample of his begging style, we may extract the following passage from a letter (1537), referring to the king of France (*Lettere*, i. 111): 'I was and ever shall be the servant of his Majesty, of whom I preached and published what appears in all my utterances and in all my works. But since it is my wonted habit not to live by dreams, and since certain persons take no care for me, I have with glory to myself made myself esteemed and sought by those who are really liberal. The chain was three years delayed, and four have gone without so much as a courtesy to me from the King's quarter. Therefore I have turned to one who gives without promising—I speak of the emperor. I adored Francis; but never to get money from the stirring of his liberality, is enough to cool the furnaces of Murano.'

Aretino, the fashion to court his goodwill, the fashion to parade his praises. Francis I. and Charles V. led this vogue. The other princes followed suit. Charles wished to knight Aretino; but the adventurer refused a barren honour. Julius III. made him knight of S. Peter with a small pension. Henry VIII. sent him a purse of 300 crowns for a dedicatory epistle.[33] It was even talked of elevating him to the rank of Cardinal, and engrossing his talents for the service of the Church.[34] Nobody thought of addressing him without the prefix of *Divino*.[35] And yet, all this while, it was known to everyone in Italy that Aretino was a pander, a coward, a liar, a debauchee, who had wallowed in every lust, sold himself to work all wickedness, and speculated on the grossest passions, the basest curiosities, the vilest vices of his age.[36]

Sometimes he met with men stout enough to treat him as he deserved. The English ambassador at Venice cudgelled him within an inch of his life. Pietro Strozzi threatened to assassinate him if he showed his face abroad, and Aretino kept close so long as the *condottiere* remained in Venice. Tintoretto offered to paint his portrait; and when he had got the fellow inside his studio, grimly took his measure with a cutlass. Aretino never resented these insults. Bully as he was he bowed to blows, and kissed the hand that dared to strike him. We have already seen how he waited till Berni's death before he took revenge for the famous sonnet. All this makes the general adulation of society for the 'divine Aretino' the more unintelligible. We can only compare the treatment he received with the mingled contempt and

[33] See Cromwell's letter, in the *Lettere all' Aretino*, vol. ii. p. 15.

[34] *Lettere all' Aretino*, vol. i. p. 245; vol. iv. pp. 281, 289, 300, contain allusions to this project, which is said to have originated with the Duke of Parma. The first citation is a letter of Titian's.

[35] 'Divino,' 'Divinissimo,' 'Precellentissimo,' 'Unichissimo,' 'Onnipotente,' are a few of the epithets culled from the common language of his flatterers.

[36] I will translate passages from two letters, which, by their very blasphemies, emphasise this contradiction. 'One might well say that you, most divine Signor Pietro, are neither Prophet nor Sibyl, but rather the very Son of God, seeing that God is highest truth in heaven, and you are truth on earth; nor is any city but Venice fit to give you harbourage, who are the jewel of the earth, the treasure of the sea, the pride of heaven; and that rare cloth of gold, bedecked with gems, they place upon the altar of S. Mark's, is nought but you' (*Lettere scritte a P. Aretino*, vol. iii. p. 176). The next is more extraordinary, since it professes to be written by a monk: 'In this our age you are a column, lantern, torch, and splendour of Holy Church, who, could she speak, would give to you the revenues of Chieti, Farnese, Santa Fiore, and all those other idlers, crying out—Let them be awarded to the Lord Pietro, who distinguishes, exalts and honours me, in whom unite the subtlety of Augustine, the moral force of Gregory, Jerome's profundity of meaning, the weighty style of Ambrose. It is not I but the whole world that says you are another Paul, who have borne the name of the Son of God into the presence of kings, potentates, princes of the universe; another Baptist, who with boldness, fearing nought, have reproved, chastised, exposed iniquities, malice, hypocrisy before the whole world; another John the Evangelist, for exhorting, entreating, exalting, honouring the good, the righteous, and the virtuous. Verily he who first called you Divine, can claim the words Christ spake to Peter: Beatus es, quia caro et sanguis non revelavit tibi, sed Pater noster qui in cœlis est' (*Ibid.* p. 142).

flattery, the canings and the invitations, showered at the present time on editors of scandal-mongering journals.

The miracle of Aretino's dictatorship is further enhanced by the fact that he played with cards upon the table. His epistles were continually being printed—in fact, were sent to the press as soon as written. Here all the world could see the workings of his mind, his hypocrisies, his contradictions, the clamorousness of his demands for gold, the grossness and universality of his flatteries, his cynical obscenity, his simulation of a superficial and disgusting piety. Yet the more he published of his correspondence, the louder was the acclamation of society. The charlatan of genius knew his public, and won their favour by effronteries that would have ruined a more cautious impostor. Some of his letters are masterpieces of infernal malice. The Marchioness of Pescara had besought him to change his mode of life, and to dedicate his talents only to religion.[37] This is how he answers her:[38] 'It gives me pleasure, most modest lady, that the religious pieces I have written do not displease the taste of your good judgment. Your doubt, whether to praise me or to dispraise me for expending my talents on aught else than sacred studies, is prompted by that most excellent spirit which moves you to desire that every thought and every word should turn toward God, forasmuch as He is the giver of virtue and of intellectual power. I confess that I am less useful to the world, and less acceptable to Christ, when I exhaust my studious energies on lying trifles, and not on the eternal verities. But all this evil is caused by the pleasure of others, and by my own necessities; for if the princes were as truly pious as I am indigent, I would employ my pen on nothing else but Misereres. Excellent my lady, all men are not gifted with the graces of divine inspiration. *They* are ever burning with lustful desires, while *you* are every hour inflamed with angelic fire. For *you* the services of the Church and sermons are what music and comedies are for *them*. *You* would not turn your eyes to look at Hercules upon his pyre, nor yet on Marsyas without his skin: while *they* would hardly keep a S. Lawrence on the gridiron or a flayed Bartholomew in their bedrooom. There's my bosom friend Bruciolo; five years ago he dedicated his Bible to the King, who calls himself Most Christian, and yet he has not had an answer. Perhaps the book was neither well translated nor well bound. On this account my "Cortigiana," which drew from his Majesty the famous chain of gold, abstained from laughing at his "Old Testament;" for this would be indecent. So you see I ought to be excused if I compose jests for my livelihood and not for evil purpose. Anyhow, may Jesus inspire you with the thought of paying me through M. Sebastiano of Pesaro—from whom I received your thirty crowns—the rest, which I owe, upon my word and honour. From Venice. The 9th of January, 1537.'

This letter, one long tissue of sneers, taunts and hypocritical sar-

[37] Her letter may be read in the *Lettere all' Aretino*, vol. iii. p. 28.
[38] *Lettere*, ii. 9.

casms, gives the complete measure of Aretino's arrogance. Yet the illustrious and pious lady to whom it was addressed, suffered the writer—such was this man's unaccountable prestige—to remain her correspondent. The collection of his letters contains several addressed to Vittoria Colonna, of which the date is subsequent to 1537.[39] Not less remarkable were Aretino's dealings with the proud, resentful solitary Michelangelo. Professing the highest admiration for Buonarroti's genius, averring that 'the world has many kings but one only Michelangelo,' Aretino wrote demanding drawings from the mighty sculptor, and giving him advice about his pictures in the Sistine. Instead of treating these impertinent advances with silence or sending a well-merited rebuff, we have a letter from Michelangelo addressed to 'M. Pietro, my lord and brother,' requesting the dictator to write something concerning him:[40] 'Not only do I hold this dear, but I implore you to do so, since kings and emperors regard it as the height of favour to be mentioned by your pen.' Was this the depth of humility, or the acme of irony, or was it the acquiescence of a noble nature in a fashion too prevalent to be examined by the light of reason? Let those decide who have read a portion of Aretino's letters to his 'singularly divine Buonaruoto.' For my own part, in spite of their strange but characteristic fusion of bullying and servility, I find in these epistles a trace of Aretino's most respectable quality—his worship of art, and his personal attachment to great artists. It may be said in passing that he never shows so well as in the epistles to Sansovino and Titian, men from whom he could gain but indirectly, and to whom he clung by an instinct of what was truest and sincerest in his nature. It is, therefore, not improbable that Michelangelo gave him credit for sincerity, and, instead of resenting his importunity, was willing to accept his advances in a kindly spirit.[41]

Thus far we have been dealing with Aretino's relation to sovereigns, ladies, and people of importance in the world of art. That he should have imposed upon them is singular. But his position in the republic of letters offers still stranger food for reflection. In an age of literary refinement and classical erudition, this untaught child of the people arrogated to himself the fame of a prominent author, and had his claims acknowledged by men like Bembo, Varchi, Molza, Sperone.[42] All the

[39] She wrote to him again in 1539; see *Lettere all' Aretino*, vol. iii. p. 30. The series of letters from the virtuous Veronica Gambara are equally astonishing (*ib.* vol. i. pp. 318-333).

[40] *Lettere all' Aretino*, vol. ii. p. 335.

[41] Giorgio Vasari, the common friend of Pietro Aretino and M. A. Buonarroti, had no doubt something to do with the acquiescent courtesy of the latter.

[42] The adulation with which all the chief literary men of Italy greeted Aretino, is quite incredible. One must read their letters in the *Lettere all' Aretino* to have any conception of it. See in particular those of Varchi (*ib.* vol. ii. p. 186-202), of Dolce (vol. ii. pp. 277-295), of Paolo Giovio (vol. iii. pp. 59-64), of Niccolò Martelli (vol. iii. pp. 116-125), of Annibale Caro (*ib.* p. 163), of Sperone (*ib.* pp. 324-330), of Firenzuola (*ib.* p. 345), of Doni (vol. iv. p. 395). Molza, terrified by one of Aretino's threats, cringes before him (vol. i. p. 340). Doni signs himself 'Il Doni dell' Aretino,' and Vergerio, Bishop of Capo d' Istria, 'Il Vescovo dell' Aretino.' Even the excellent Bishop

Academies in Italy made him their member with extraordinary honours, and he corresponded with every writer of distinction. He treated the scholars of his day as he treated the princes of Italy, abusing them collectively for pedantry, and showering the epithets of *divino*, *divinissimo*, upon them individually. With his usual sagacity, Aretino saw how to command the public by running counter to the prejudices of his century, and proclaiming his independence of its principles. He resolved to win celebrity by contrast, by piquancy of style, by the assertion of his individual character, by what Machiavelli termed *virtù*. As he had boasted of the baseness of his origin, so now he piqued himself upon his ignorance. He made a parade of knowing neither Latin nor Greek, derided the puristic veneration for Petrarch and Boccaccio then in vogue, and asserted that his mother-wit was the best source of inspiration. This audacity proved successful. While the stylists of the day were polishing their laboured periods to smoothness, he expressed such thoughts as occurred to him in the words which came first to hand, seeking only vivacity, relief and salience. He wrote as he talked; and the result was that he acquired a well-won reputation for freshness, wit, originality and vigour. This is how he dictates the terms of epistolary style to Bernardo Tasso:[43] 'I, who am more your brother in benevolence than you show yourself to be my friend in honour, did not believe that the serenity of my mind would ever again be dimmed by those clouds, which, after thunders and lightnings, burst in the bolt that sent Antonio Broccardo beneath the earth. Pride and vanity, for certain, prompted you to tell the excellent and illustrious Annibale Caro that no writer of letters is worthy to be imitated at the present day, sagaciously hinting at yourself as the right man to be imitated. Without doubt, your inordinate self-love, combined with your inattention to the claims of others, brought your judgment to this pass. I published letters before you, and you borrowed your style, in so far as it is worth anything, from me. Yet you cannot produce even a counterfeit of my manner. My sentences and similes are made to live; yours issue stillborn from your mind. It is time that you copy a few of my familiar phrases, word by word. What else can you do? Your own taste is rather inclined to the scent of flowers than the savour of fruits. You have the graces of a certain celestial style, fit for epithalamial odes and hymns. But all that sweetness is out of place in epistles, where we want the salience of invention, not the illuminated arabesques of artifice. I am not going to sing my own praises, nor to tell you that men of merit ought to mark my birthday with white chalk—I, who without

of Fossombrone pays him courtly compliments (vol. ii. pp. 61-67). The pitch attained by these flatteries may be understood from this opening of a letter: 'Bella armonia, e soave concento, dovea essere nel cielo, Signor Pietro divino, e fra le stelle amiche, il dì, che Iddio e la Natura di voi fece altero dono a questa nostra etade,' &c. *ad inf.* (vol. iv. p. 269). Here is another fragment: 'Manifestamente si vede e si conosce che da Iddio per conservazione de la sua gloria e per utilità del mondo v' abbi fra tanti avversari,' &c. (vol. iv. p. 398).

[43] *Lettere*, v. 184. The above is only a condensed paraphrase of a very long tirade.

scouring the post-roads, without following Courts, without stirring from my study, have made every living duke, prince, sovereign, tributary to my virtue—I, who hold fame at my discretion through the universe—I, whose portrait is revered, whose name is honoured in Persia and the Indies. To end this letter, I salute you with the assurance that nobody, so far as your epistles go, blames you for envy's sake, while many, very many, praise you through compassion for your having written them.' There was no limit to his literary self-confidence.[44] 'Of the three opinions current respecting the talents which keep my name alive, time has refuted that, which, hearing I had no erudition, judged my compositions to be nonsense, together with that other, which, finding in them some gust of genius, affirmed they were not mine. Whence it follows that only one remains, the opinion, to wit, that I, who never had a tutor, am complete in every branch of knowledge. All this comes from the poverty of art, which ever envies the wealth of nature, from whom I borrow my conceptions. Wherefore, if you are of the number of those who, in order to deprive me of nature's favour, attribute to me the learning that comes from study, you deceive yourself, for I swear by God I hardly understand my mother tongue.' Meanwhile his tirades against the purists are full of excellent good sense. 'O mistaken multitude, I tell you again, and yet again, that poetry is a caprice of nature in her moments of gladness; it depends on a man's own inspiration, and if this fails, a poet's singing is but a tambourine without rattles, a bell-tower without bells. He who attempts to write verses without the gift is like the alchemists, who, for all their industry and eager avarice, never yet made gold, while nature, without labour, turns it out in plenty, pure and beautiful. Take lessons from that painter, who, when he was asked whom he imitated, pointed to a crowd of living men, meaning that he borrowed his examples from life and reality. This is what I do, when I write or talk. Nature herself, of whose simplicity I am the secretary, dictates that which I set down.'[45] And again: 'I laugh at those pedants, who think that learning consists in Greek and Latin, laying down the law that one who does not understand these languages, cannot open his mouth. It is not because I do not know them, that I have departed from Petrarch's and Boccaccio's precedents; but because I care not to lose time, patience, reputation, in the mad attempt to convert myself into their persons. The true aim of writing is to condense into the space of half a page, the length of histories, the tedium of orations; and this my letters clearly show that I have done.' 'It is far better to drink out of one's own wooden cup than another's golden goblet; and a man makes a finer show in his own rags than in stolen velvets. What have we to do with other people's property?'[46] 'What have we to do with words which, however once in

[44] *Lettere*, ii. 242.
[45] *Lettere*, i. 123.
[46] *Lettere*, ii. 182.

common use, have now passed out of fashion?'[47] At times he bursts into a fury of invective against erudition: 'Those pedants, the asses of other people's books, who, after massacring the dead, rest not till they have crucified the living! It was pedantry that murdered Duke Alessandro, pedantry that flung the Cardinal of Ravenna into prison, and, what is worse, stirred up heresy against our faith through the mouth of that arch-pedant Luther.'[48] This is admirable. It plunges to the very root of the matter. Sharpened by his hostility to the learning he did not share, and the puerile aspects of which he justly satirised, this acute and clairvoyant critic is enabled to perceive that both Italian tyrannicide and German Reformation had their origin in the humanistic movement of the fifteenth century. He is equally averse to either consequence. Erudition spoils sport, stiffens style, breaks in upon the pastimes of the principalities and papacies, which breed the lusts on which an Aretino lives.

It was Aretino's boast that he composed as fast as the pen would move across the paper, and that his study contained no books of reference—nothing but the quire of paper and the bottle of ink, which were necessary to immortalise the thick-crowding fancies of his brain. His comedy of the 'Filosofo' was written in ten mornings; the 'Talanta' and the 'Ipocrita' in 'the hours robbed from sleep during perhaps twenty nights.'[49] Referring to his earlier fertility in 1537, he says:[50] 'Old age begins to stupefy my brains, and love, which ought to wake them up, now sends them off to sleep. I used to turn out forty stanzas in a morning; now I can with difficulty produce one. It took me only seven mornings to compose the "Psalms;" ten for the "Cortigiana" and the "Marescalco;" forty-eight for the two "Dialogues;" thirty for the "Life of Christ." ' The necessary consequences of this haste are discernible in all his compositions. Aretino left nothing artistically finished, nothing to which it is now possible to point in justification of his extraordinary celebrity. His sonnets are below contempt. Frigid, inharmonious, pompous, strained, affected, they exhibit the worst vices to which this species of poetry is liable. His *Capitoli*, though he compared them to 'colossal statues of gold or silver, where I have carved the forms of Julius, a Pope, Charles, an Emperor, Catherine, a Queen, Francesco Maria, a Duke, with such art that the outlines of their inner nature are brought into relief, the muscles of their will and purpose are shown in play, the profiles of their emotions are thrown into salience'[51]—these *Capitoli* will not bear comparison for one moment with Berni's. They are coarse and strident in style, threadbare in sentiment, commonplace in conception, with only one eminent quality, a certain gross prolific force, a brazen clash and clangour of antithesis, to compensate for their

[47] *Lettere*, i. 210.
[48] *Lettere*, i. 143.
[49] *Lettere*, iii. 84. Letter at the end of the *Talanta*.
[50] *Lettere*, i. 99.
[51] *Lettere*, vi. 4.

vulgarity. Yet, such as they are, the *Capitoli* must be reckoned the best of his compositions in verse. Of his comedies I have already spoken. These will always be valuable for their lively sketches of contemporary manners, their free satiric vein of humour. The 'Dialoghi,' although it is scarcely possible to mention them in a decent book of history, are distinguished by the same qualities of veracity, acumen, prolific vigour, animal spirits, and outspokenness. Aretino's religious works, it need hardly be said, are worthless or worse. Impudent romances, penned by one of the most unscrupulous of men, frankly acknowledged by their author to be a tissue of 'poetical lies,' we are left to marvel how they could have deceived the judgment and perverted the taste of really elevated natures.[52] That the Marchioness of Pescara should have hailed the coarse fictions of the Life of S. Catherine, which Aretino confessed to have written out of his own head, as a work of efficient piety, remains one of the wonders of that extraordinary age.

What then, it may finally be asked, was Aretino's merit as an author? Why do we allude to him at all in writing the history of sixteenth-century literature? The answer can be given in two words—originality and independence. It was no vain boast of Aretino that he trusted only to nature and mother wit. His intellectual distinction consisted precisely in this confidence and self-reliance, at a moment when the literary world was given over to pedantic scruples and the formalities of academical prescription. Writing without the fear of pedagogues before his eyes—seeking, as he says, relief, expression, force, and brilliancy of phrase, he produced a manner at once singular and attractive, which turned to ridicule the pretensions of the purists. He had the courage of his personality, and stamped upon his style the very form and pressure of himself. As a writer, he exhibited what Machiavelli demanded from the man of action—*virtù*, or the virility of self-reliance. That was the secret of his success. The same audacity and independence characterise all his utterances of opinion—his criticisms of art and literature—his appreciation of natural beauty. In some of the letters written to painters and sculptors, and in a description of a Venetian sunset already quoted in this book, we trace the dawnings of a true and natural school of criticism, a forecast of the spontaneity of Diderot and Henri Beyle. This naturalness of expression did not save Aretino from glaring bad taste. His letters and his dedicatory introductions abound in confused metaphors, extravagant *concetti*, and artificial ornaments. It seems impossible for him to put pen to paper without inventing monstrous and ridiculous periphrases. Still the literary impropriety, which would have been affectation in anyone else, and which became affectation in his imitators, was true to the man's nature. He could not be true to himself without falseness of utterance, because there was in him an inherent insincerity, and this was veiled by no scholastic accuracy or studied purity of phrase.

Much of the bad taste of the later Renaissance (the tropes of Marini

[52] See *Lettere*, ii. 168, iii. 169, for his method of composing these books.

and the absurdities of *seicentismo*) may be ascribed to the fascination exercised by this strange combination of artificiality and naturalness in a style remarkable for vigour. Who, for instance, does not feel that the mannerism of our euphuistic prosaists is shadowed forth in the following passage from the introduction to the 'Talanta'?[53] The Prologue, on the drawing of the curtain, takes the audience into his confidence, and tells them that he long had hesitated which of the Immortal Gods to personate. Mars, Jupiter, Phœbus, Venus, Mercury, and all the Pantheon in succession were rejected, for different appropriate reasons, till the God of Love appeared. 'When at last it came to Cupid's turn, I immediately said Yes! and having so assented, I felt wings growing at my shoulders, the quiver at my side, the bow within my hands. In a moment I became all steel, all fire; and eager to be ware what things are done in love, I cast a glance upon the crowd of lovers; whence I soon could see who has the rendezvous, who is sent about his business, who prowls around his mistress' house, who enters by the door, who clambers up the walls, who scales the rope, who jumps from the window, who hides himself within a tub, who takes the cudgel, who gets a gelding for his pains, who is stowed away by the chambermaid, who is kicked out by the serving-man, who goes mad with anxiety, who bursts with passion, who wastes away in gazing, who cuts snooks at hope, who lets himself be hoodwinked, who spends a fortune on his mistress to look grand, who robs her for a freak, who saps her chastity with threats, who conjures her with prayers, who blabs of his success, who hides his luck, who bolsters up his vaunt with lies, who dissembles the truth, who extols the flame that burns him, who curses the cause of his heart's conflagration, who cannot eat for grief, who cannot sleep for joy, who compiles sonnets, who scribbles billets-doux, who dabbles in enchantments, who renews assaults, who takes counsel with bawds, who ties a favour on his arm, who mumbles at a flower the wench has touched, who twangles the lute, who hums a glee, who thrusts his rival through the body, who gets killed by his competitors, who eats his heart out for a mylady, who dies of longing for a strumpet. When I understood the things aforesaid, I turned round to these female firebrands, and saw how the devil (to chastise them for the perverse ways they use toward men who serve them, praise them, and adore them) gives them up, easy victims, to a pedant, a plebeian, a simpleton, a loon, a groom, a graceless clown, and to a certain mange that catches them.'

Aretino congregated round him a whole class of literary Bohemians, drawing forth the peccant humours of more than one Italian city, and locating these greedy adventurers in Venice as his satellites. It is enough to mention Niccolò Franco, Giovanni Alberto Albicante, Lorenzo Veniero, Doni, Lodovico Dolce. They were, most of them, hack writers, who gained a scanty livelihood by miscellaneous work for the book-

[53] I have purposely chosen an extract where the style is keen and mobile. Had I taken examples from the Letters, I could have produced a far closer parallel to Lilly's rhetoric.

sellers and by selling dedications to patrons. More or less successfully, they carried on the trade invented and developed by Aretino; remaining on terms of intimacy with him, at first as friends or secretaries, afterwards as enemies and rivals. We have already seen what use was made of Albicante for the mutilation of Berni's 'Innamoramento.' This poetaster was a native of Milan, who published a history of the war in Piedmont, which Aretino chose to ridicule in one of his *Capitoli*.[54] Albicante replied with another poem in *terza rima*, and Aretino seems to have perceived that he had met a worthy adversary. It was Albicante's glory to be called *furibondo* and *bestiale*. He affected an utter indifference to consequences, an absolute recklessness concerning what he did and said. Whether Aretino was really afraid of him, or whether he wished to employ him in the matter of Berni's 'Innamoramento,' is not certain. At any rate, he made advances to Albicante in a letter which begins: 'My brother, the rage of poets is but a frenzy of stupidity.' The antagonists were reconciled, and the Academy of the Intronati at Siena thought this event worthy of commemoration in a volume: 'Combattimento poetico del divino Aretino e del bestiale Albicante occorso sopra la Guerra di Piemonte, e la pace loro celebrata nella Accademia de gli Intronati a Siena.'

Niccolò Franco was a native of Benevento, whom Aretino took into his service as a kind of secretary.[55] Being deficient in scholarship, he needed a man capable of supplying him with Greek and Latin quotations, and who could veneer his coarse work with a show of humanistic erudition. Franco undertook the office; and it is probable that some of Aretino's earlier works of piety and learning—the 'Genesis,' for instance—issued from this unequal collaboration. But their good accord did not last long. Franco proved to be a ruffian of even fiercer type than his master. If Aretino kept a literary poignard in the scabbard, ready to strike when his utility demanded, Franco went about the world with unsheathed dagger, stabbing for the pleasure of the sport. 'I would rather lose a dinner,' he writes, 'than omit to fire my pen off when the fancy takes me.' The two men could not dwell together in union. When Aretino published the first series of his letters, Franco issued a rival volume, in the last epistle of which, addressed to Envy, he made an attack on his patron. Ambrogio degli Eusebi, an *âme damneé* of the Aretine, about whom many scurrilous stories were told, stabbed Franco, while Aretino published invective after invective against him in the form of letters. Franco left Venice, established himself for a while at Casale in the lordship of Montferrat, opened a school at Mantua, and ran a thousand infamous adventures, pouring forth satirical sonnets all the while at Aretino. In the course of his wanderings, he completed a Latin commentary on the 'Priapea.' These two works together—the centuries of sonnets against Aretino, and the Priapic

[54] See the article on Albicante in Mazzuchelli's *Scrittori Italiani*, vol. i.
[55] For what follows see Tiraboschi, tom. vii. part 3, lib. iii.

lucubrations—obtained a wide celebrity. Speaking of the book, Tiraboschi is compelled to say that 'few works exist which so dishonour human nature. The grossest obscenities, the most licentious evil-speaking, the boldest contempt of princes, Popes, Fathers of the Council, and other weighty personages, are the gems with which he adorned his monument of perverse industry.' Franco proved so obnoxious to polite society that he was at last taken and summarily hanged in 1569. The curious point about this condemnation of a cur is, that he was in no whit worse than many other scribblers of the day. But he made more noise; he had not the art to rule society like Aretino; he committed the mistake of trusting himself to the perilous climates of Lombardy and Rome. His old master drove him out of Venice, and the unlucky reprobate paid the penalty of his misdeeds by becoming the scapegoat for men whom he detested.

Doni began his Venetian career as a friend of Aretino, whose companion he was in the famous Academy of the Pellegrini. They quarrelled over a present sent to Doni by the Duke of Urbino, and the bizarre Florentine passed over to the ranks of Aretino's bitterest enemies. In 1556 he declared war, with a book entitled 'Terremoto del Doni Fiorentino.' The preface was addressed to 'the infamous and vicious Pietro Aretino, the source and fountain of all evil, the stinking limb of public falsehood, and true Antichrist of our century.' Soon after the appearance of this volume, followed Aretino's death. But Doni pursued his animosity beyond the grave, and was instrumental in causing his rival's writings to be subjected to ecclesiastical interdiction.

We tire of these low literary quarrels. Yet they form an integral part of the history of Italian civilisation; and the language of invective used in them, originating with Aretino and improved upon by Doni and Franco, became the model of vituperative style in Europe. Doni's 'Earthquake, with the Ruin of a great Bestial Colossus, the Antichrist of our age,' brings to mind a score of pamphlets, published in Europe during the conflict of the Church with Reformation. We find an echo of its strained metaphors in the polemical writings of Bruno and Campanella. The grotesque manner of the seventeenth century begins with Aretino and his satellites, just as its far-fetched conceits may be traced in the clear language of Guarini. Gongora, Marini, Euphues, and the *Précieuses Ridicules* of the Hôtel Rambouillet are contained, as it were, in germ among this little knot of refugees at Venice, who set their wits against the academical traditions of pure Italian taste.

A characteristic legend is told of Aretino's death. Two of his sisters kept, it is said, a house of ill fame; and the story runs that he died of immoderate laughter, flinging himself backward in his chair and breaking his neck, on hearing some foul jest reported by them. It is difficult to believe that this tale has any foundation in fact. We must take it as a scurrilous invention, proving the revolution of public opinion, which, since his books had been put upon the Index in 1559, undoubtedly took place. Of like tenor is the epitaph which was never really placed upon his grave:[56]

> Qui giace l' Aretin poeta tosco,
> Che disse mal d' ognun fuorchè di Cristo,
> Scusandosi col dir: non lo conosco.

His features, though formed upon a large and not ignoble type, bore in later life a mixed expression of the wolf and the fox; nor was it without oblique satire that the engraver of his portrait, Giuseppe Patrini, surrounded the medallion with a wolf's hide, the grinning snarl and slanting eyes of the brute mimicking the man's physiognomy. It was a handsome face, no doubt, in youth, when, richly attired in the satin mantle cut for him by a bishop, and mounted on his white charger, he scoured the streets of Reggio at Giovanni de' Medici's side, curling his blue-black beard, and fixing his bold bright eyes upon the venal beauties they courted in company. But the thick lips and open sensual mouth, the distended nostrils, and the wicked puckers of the wrinkles round his eyes and nose, show that the beast of prey and appetite had been encouraged through a life of self-indulgence, until the likeness of humanity yielded to victorious animalism. The same face, at once handsome and bestial, never to be forgotten after a first acquaintance, leans out, in the company of Sansovino and Titian, from the bronze door of the Sacristy in S. Mark's Church.[57] The high relief is full of life and movement, one of Sansovino's masterpieces. And yet it strikes one here with even greater strangeness than the myths of Ganymede and Leda on the portals of S. Peter's at Rome.

Aretino is, in truth, not the least of the anomalies which meet us everywhere in the Italian Renaissance. Was he worse, was he not even in some respects better than his age? How much of the repulsion he inspires can be ascribed to altered taste and feeling? To what extent was the legend of the man, so far as this is separable from the testimony of his writings, made black by posthumous malevolence and envy? These are the questions which rise in our mind when we reflect upon the incidents of his extraordinary career, and calmly estimate his credit

[56] These lines have been, without authority, ascribed to Giovio; they may thus be rendered:

> Here lieth Aretine, in prose and poem
> Who spake such ill of all the world but Christ,
> Pleading for this neglect, I do not know him.

Giovio, we may remember, styled Aretino *divino, divinissimo, unichissimo, precellentissimo*, in his letters.

[57] Among the many flatteries addressed to Aretino none is more laughable than a letter (*Lettere all' Aretino*, vol. iii. p. 175) which praises his physical beauty in most extravagant terms: 'Most divine Lord Peter, if, among the many and so lovely creatures that swinish Nature sends into this worst of worlds, you alone are of such beauty and incomparable grace that you combine all qualities the human frame can boast of: for the which cause there is no need to wonder that Titian, when he seeks to paint a face that has in it true beauty, uses his skilled brush in only drawing you,' &c. &c. The period is too long to finish.

with contemporaries. The contradictions of the epoch were concentrated in his character. He was a professed Christian of the type formed by Rome before the Counter-Reformation. He helped the needy, tended the sick, dowered orphans, and kept open house for beggars. He was the devoted friend of men like Titian, a sincere lover of natural and artistic beauty, an acute and enthusiastic critic. At the same time he did his best to corrupt youth by painting vice in piquant colours. He led a life of open and voluptuous debauchery. He was a liar, a bully, a braggart, venomous in the pursuit of private animosities, and the remorseless foe of weaker men who met with his displeasure. From the conditions of society which produced Cesare and Lucrezia Borgia, Pier Luigi Farnese and Gianpaola Baglioni, it was no wonder that a writer resolved on turning those conditions to account, should have arisen. The credit of originality, independence, self-reliant character—of what Machiavelli called *virtù*—does certainly belong to him. It is true that he extracted the means of a luxurious existence from patrons upon whom he fawned. Yet he was superior to the common herd of courtiers, in so far as he attached himself to no master, and all his adulation masked a battery of menaces. The social diseases which emasculated men of weaker fibre, he turned to the account of his rapacious appetites. His force consisted in the clear notion he had formed of his own aim in life, and the sagacity with which he used the most efficient means for attaining it. The future, whether of reputation or of literary fame, had no influence over his imagination. He resolved to enjoy the present, and he succeeded beyond expectation. Corruption is itself a kind of superiority, when it is consummate, cynical, self-conscious. It carries with it its own clairvoyance, its own philosophy of life, its own good sense. More than this, it imposes on opinion and fascinates society. Aretino did not suffer from a divided will. He never halted between two courses, but realised the ideal of the *perfettamente tristo*. He lived up to Guicciardini's conception of the final motive, which may be described as the cult of self. Sneering at all men less complete in purpose than himself, he disengaged his conduct from contemporary rules of fashion; dictated laws to his betters in birth, position, breeding, learning, morals, taste; and vindicated his virility by unimpeded indulgence of his personal proclivities. He was the last, the most perfect, if also the most vitiated product of Renaissance manners. In the second half of the sixteenth century, when hypocrisy descended like a cloud upon the ineradicable faults of Italy, there was no longer any possibility for the formation of a hero after Aretino's type.

Thus at the close of any estimate of Aretino, we are forced to do justice to the man's vigour. It is not for nothing that even a debased society bows to a dictatorship so autocratic; nor can eminence be secured, even among the products of a decadent civilisation, by undiluted defects. Aretino owed his influence to genuine qualities—to the independence which underlay his arrogance, to the acute commonsense which almost justified his vanity, to the outspokenness which made him satirise the vices that he shared and illustrated.[58] We have abundant and incontrovertible testimony to the fact that his 'Dialoghi,' when they were first published, passed for powerful and drastic antidotes to social poisons;[59] and it is clear that even his religious works were accepted by the pious world as edifying. The majority of his contemporaries seem to have beheld in him the fearless denouncer of ecclesiastical and civil tyrants, the humble man's friend, and the relentless detective of vice. The indescribable nastiness of the 'Dialoghi,' the false feeling of the 'Vita di S. Catherina,' which makes us turn with loathing from their pages, did not offend the taste of his century. While, therefore, he comprehended and expressed his age in its ruffianism and dissoluteness, he stood outside it and above it, dealing haughtily and like a potentate with evils which subdued less hardened spirits, and with personages before whom his equals grovelled. We must not suffer our hatred of his mendacity, uncleanliness, brutality, and arrogance to blind us to the elements of strength and freedom which can be discerned in him.[60]

[58] I should not be surprised to see an attempt soon made to whitewash Aretino. Balzac, in his *Catherine de Médicis*, has already indicated the line to be followed: 'L'Arétin, l'ami de Titien et le Voltaire de son siècle, a, de nos jours, un renom en complète opposition avec ses œuvres, avec son caractère, et que lui vaut une débauche d'esprit en harmonie avec les écrits de ce siècle, où le drolatique était en honneur, où les reines et les cardinaux écrivaient des contes, dits aujourd'hui licentieux.'

[59] I will only refer to a very curious epistle (*Lettere a P. Aretino*, vol. iii. p. 193), which appears to me genuine, in which Aretino is indicated as the poor man's friend against princely tyrants; and another from Daniello Barbaro (*ibid.* p. 217), in which the Dialogue on Courts is praised as a handbook for the warning and instruction of would-be courtiers. The Pornographic Dialogues made upon society the same impression as Zola's *Nana* is now making, although it is clear to us that they were written with a licentious, and not an even ostensibly scientific intention.

[60] While these sheets are passing through the press, I see announced a forthcoming work by Antonio Virgili, *Francesco Berni con nuovi documenti*. We may expect from this book more light upon Aretino's relation to the Tuscan poet. [Signor Virgili's book appeared in 1881, and deals at great length with the relations between Berni and Aretino, with especial reference to the *Rifacimento*, the author's theory being that the book as published does not represent the original, but was a garbled version prepared by Aretino.]

CHAPTER XVI

HISTORY AND PHILOSOPHY

Frivolity of Renaissance Literature—The Contrast presented by Machiavelli—His Sober Style—Positive Spirit—The Connexion of his Works—Two Men in Machiavelli—His Political Philosophy—The Patria—Place of Religion and Ethics in his System—Practical Object of his Writings—Machiavellism—His Conception of Nationality—His Relation to the Renaissance—Contrast between Machiavelli and Guicciardini—Guicciardini's Doctrine of Self-Interest—The Code of Italian Corruption—The Connexion between these Historians and the Philosophers—General Character of Italian Philosophy—The Middle Ages in Dissolution—Transition to Modern Thought and Science—Humanism counterposed to Scholasticism—Petrarch—Pico—Dialogues on Ethics—Importance of Greek and Latin Studies—Classical substituted for Ecclesiastical Authority—Platonism at Florence—Ficino—Translations—New Interest in the Problem of Life—Valla's Hedonism—The Dialogue 'Du Voluptate'—Aristotle at Padua and Bologna—Arabian and Greek Commentators—Life of Pietro Pomponazzi—His Book on Immortality—His Controversies—Pomponazzi's Standpoint—Unlimited Belief in Aristotle—Retrospect over the Aristotelian Doctrine of God, the World, the Human Soul—Three Problems in the Aristotelian System—Universals—The First Period of Scholastic Speculation—Individuality—The Second Period of Scholasticism—Thomas Aquinas—The Nature of the Soul—New Impulse given to Speculation by the Renaissance—Averroism—The Lateran Council—Is the Soul Immortal?—Pomponazzi reconstructs Aristotle's Doctrine by help of Alexander Aphrodisius—The Soul is Material and Mortal—Man's Place in Nature—Virtue is the End of Man—Pomponazzi on Miracles and Spirits—His Distinction between the Philosopher and the Christian—The Book on Fate—Pomponazzi the Precursor—Coarse Materialism—The School of Cosenza—Aristotle's Authority Rejected—Telesio—Campanella—Bruno—The Church stifles Philosophy in Italy—Italian Positivism.

THE literature which has occupied us during the last nine chapters, is a literature of form and entertainment. Whether treating chivalrous romance, or the Arcadian ideal, or the conditions of contemporary life, these poets, playwrights and novelists had but one serious object—the perfection of their art, the richness and variety of their pictures. In the conscious pursuit of beautiful form, Poliziano and Ariosto, Bembo and Berni, Castiglione and Firenzuola, Il Lasca and Molza, were alike earnest. For the rest, they sought to occupy their own leisure, and to give polite society the pastime of refined amusement. The content of this miscellaneous literature was of far less moment to the authors and their audience than its mode of presentation. Even when they undertook some theme involving the realities of life, they dwelt by preference upon externals. In the 'Cortegiano' and 'Galateo,' for example, conduct is studied from an æsthetical far more than from a moral point of view. The questions which stirred and divided literary coteries, were questions of scholarship, style, language. Matter is everywhere subordinated to expression; the writer's interest in actuality is slight; the power or the inclination to think is inferior to the faculty for harmonious construction. These characteristics of literature in general render the exceptions noticeable, and force me, at some risk of repetition, to devote a chapter to those men in whom the speculative vigour of the race was concentrated. These were the historians and a small band of metaphysicians, who may be fitly represented by a single philosopher, Pietro Pomponazzi. Of the Florentine historiographers, from Villani to Guicciardini, I have already treated at some length in a previous portion of this work.[1] I shall therefore confine myself to resuming those points in which Machiavelli and Guicciardini uttered the reflections of their age on statecraft and the laws that govern political life.

When we compare Machiavelli with his contemporaries, we are struck by his want of sympathy with the prevalent artistic enthusiasms. Far from being preoccupied with problems of diction, he wrote with the sole object of making what he had to say plain. The result is that, without thinking about expression, Machiavelli created Italian prose anew, and was the first to form a monumental modern style. Language became, beneath his treatment, a transparent and colourless medium for presenting thoughts to the reader's mind; and his thoughts were always removed as little as possible from the facts which suggested them. He says himself that he preferred in all cases the essential reality of a fact to its modification by fancy or by theory.[2] His style is, therefore, the reverse of that which the purists cultivated. They uttered generalities in ornamented and sonorous phrases. Machiavelli scorned ornament, and ignored the cadence of the period. His boldest abstractions are presented with the hard outline and relief of concrete things. Each sentence is a crystal, formed of few but precise words by a spontaneous process in his mind. It takes shape from the thought; not from any preconceived type of rhythm, to which the thought must be accommodated. It is perfect or imperfect according as the thinking process has been completely or incompletely victorious over the difficulties of language. It is figurative only when the fact to be enforced derives new energy from the imagination. Beauty is never sought, but comes unbidden as upon the limbs and muscles of an athlete, whose aim has been to gain agility and strength. These qualities render Machiavelli's prose a model worthy of imitation by all who study scientific accuracy.

The style is the man; and Machiavelli's style was the mirror of his mind and character. While the literary world echoed to the cry of Art for Art, he followed Science for the sake of Science. Occupied with practical problems, smiling at the supra-mundane aspirations of the Middle Ages, scorning the æsthetical ideals of the Renaissance, he

[1] Vol. I., *Age of the Despots*, chaps. v. and vi.

[2] 'Mi è parso più conveniente andare dietro alla verità effettuale della cosa che all' immaginazione di essa' (*Principe*, cap. xv.).

made the political action of man, *l'homme politique*, the object of exclusive study. His resolute elimination of what he considered irrelevant or distracting circumstances from his chosen field of research, justifies our placing him among the founders or precursors of the modern scientific method. We may judge his premises insufficient, his conclusions false; but we cannot mistake the positive quality of his mind in the midst of a rhetorical and artistic generation.

There is a strict link of connexion between Machiavelli's works. These may be divided into four classes—official, historical, speculative and literary. To the first belongs his correspondence with the Florentine Government; to the second, his Florentine History and several minor studies, the 'Vita di Castruccio,' the 'Ritratti,' and the 'Metodo tenuto dal Duca Valentino;' to the third, his 'Discorsi,' 'Principe,' 'Arte della Guerra' and 'Discorso sopra la Riforma di Firenze;' to the fourth, his comedies, poems, novel of 'Belfagor,' and 'Descrizione della Peste.' The familiar letters should be used as a key to the more intimate understanding of his character. They illustrate some points in his political philosophy, explain his personal motives, and throw much light upon his purely literary compositions. We learn from them to know him as a friend, the father of a family, the member of a little social circle, and finally as the ever-restless aspirant after public employment. Valuable as these letters are for the student of Machiavelli's writings, his private reputation would have gained by their destruction. They show that the man was inferior to the thinker. In spite of his logical consistency of intellect, we become convinced, while reading them, that there were two persons in Machiavelli. The one was a faithful servant of the State, a student of books and human nature, the inaugurator of political philosophy for modern Europe. The other was a boon companion, stooping to low pleasures, and soiling his correspondence with gossip which breathes the tainted atmosphere of Florentine vice. These letters force us to reject the theory that he wrote his comedies with any profound ethical purpose, or that he personally abhorred the moral corruption of which he pointed out the weakening results for Italy. The famous epistle from San Casciano paints the man in his two aspects—at one moment in a leathern jerkin, playing games of hazard with the butcher, or scouring the streets of Florence with a Giuliano Brancaccio; at another, attired in senatorial robes, conversing with princes, approaching the writers of antiquity on equal terms, and penning works which place him on a level with Ariosto and Galileo. The second of these Machiavellis claims our exclusive attention at the present moment. Yet it is needful to remember that the former existed, and was no less real. Only by keeping this in mind can we avoid the errors of those panegyrists who credit the 'Mandragola' with a didactic purpose, and refuse to recognise the moral bluntness betrayed in Machiavelli's theorisation of human conduct. The man who thought and felt in private what his familiar letters disclose, was no right censor of the principles that rule society. We cannot trust his moral tact or taste.

Machiavelli was not a metaphysician. He started with the conception of the State as understood in Italy. His familiarity with the Latin classics, and his acquaintance with the newly-formed monarchies of Europe, caused him, indeed, to modify the current notion. But he did not inquire into the final cause of political communities, or present to his own mind a clear definition of what was meant by the phrase *patria*. We are aware of a certain hesitancy between the ideas of the Commune and the race, the State and the Government, which might have been removed by a more careful preliminary analysis. Between the Roman Republic, on the one hand, and the modern nation, on the other, we always find an Italian city. From this point of view, it is to be regretted that he did not appropriate Plato's 'Republic' or Aristotle's 'Politics.'[3] He might by such a course of study have avoided the severance of politics from ethics, which renders his philosophy unnatural. We must, however, remember that he did not propose to plan a scientific system. His works have a practical aim in view. They are directed toward the grand end of Italy's restoration from weakness and degeneracy to a place among the powerful peoples of the world. This purpose modifies them in the most minute particulars. It is ever present to Machiavelli's mind. It makes his philosophy assume the form of a critique. It explains the apparent discord between the 'Discorsi' and the 'Principe.' It enables us to comprehend the nature of a patriotism which subordinates the interest of the individual to the body politic, even though the State were in the hands of an unscrupulous autocrat. The salvation of Italy, rather than any metaphysical principle, is the animating motive of Machiavelli's political writings. Yet we may note that if he had laid a more solid philosophical basis, if he had striven more vigorously to work out his own conception of the *patria*, and to understand the laws of national health, instead of trusting to such occasional remedies as the almost desperate state of Italy afforded, he would have deserved better of his country and more adequately fulfilled his own end.

Though Machiavelli had not worked out the conception of a nation as an organic whole, he was penetrated with the thought, familiar to his age, that all human institutions, like men, have a youth, a manhood, and a period of decline. Looking round him, he perceived that Italy, of all the European nations, had advanced farthest on the path of dissolution. He calls the Italians the reproach and corruption of the world—*la corruttela, il vituperio del mondo*. When he inquires into the causes of this ruin, he is led to assign (i) the moral debasement of his country to the Roman Church; (ii) her sloth and inefficiency in warfare to the despots and the mercenaries; (iii) her inability to cope with

[3] The section on the types of commonwealths in the *Discorsi* (cap. ii.) comes straight from Polybius. But I am not aware of any signs in Machiavelli of a direct study of the elder Greek philosophical writings.

greater nations to the want of one controlling power in the peninsula. A nation, he argues, cannot be a nation while divided into independent and antagonistic States. It needs to be united under a monarch like France, reduced beneath the sway of a presiding commonwealth like ancient Rome, or connected in a federation like the Swiss. This doctrine of the nation, or, to use his own phrase, of the *patria*, as distinguished from the Commune and the Empire, was highly original in Italy at the time when Machiavelli gave it utterance. It contained the first logically reasoned aspiration after that independence in unity, which the Italians were destined to realise between the years 1858 and 1871. He may be said to have formed it by meditating on the Roman historians, and by comparing Italy with the nascent modern nations. The notion of ethnology did not enter into it so much as the notion of political and social cohesion. Yet nationality was not excluded; for he conceived of no power, whether Empire or Church, above the people who had strength to define themselves against their neighbours. To secure for the population of the Italian peninsula that unity which he rightly considered essential to the *patria*, and the want of which constituted their main inferiority, was the object of all his speculations.

The word *patria* sounds the keynote of his political theory, and a patriot is synonymous for him with a completely virtuous man. All energies, public and private, are only valuable in so far as they build up the fabric of the commonwealth. Religion is good because it sustains the moral fibre of the people. It is a powerful instrument in the hands of a wise governor; and the best religion is that which develops hardy and law-loving qualities. He criticises Christianity for exalting contemplative virtues above the energies of practical life, and for encouraging a spirit of humility. He sternly condemns the Church because she has been unfaithful even to the tame ideal of her saints, and has set an example of licentious living. Religion is needed as the basis of morality; and morality itself must be encouraged as the safeguard of that discipline which constitutes a nation's vigour. A moralised race is stronger than a corrupt one, because it has a higher respect for law and social order, because it accepts public burdens more cheerfully, because it is more obedient to military ordinances. Thus both religion and morality are means to the grand end of human existence, which is strenuous life in a united nation. I need hardly point out how this conception runs counter to the transcendentalism of the Middle Ages.

Machiavelli admires the Germans for their discipline and sobriety, which he ascribes to the soundness of their religious instincts. France and Spain, he says, have been contaminated by the same corrupting influence as Italy; but they owe their present superiority to the fact of their monarchical allegiance. This opens a second indictment against the Church. Not only has the Church demoralised the people; but it is chiefly due to the ambition of the Popes that Italy has never passed beyond the stage of conflict and disunion.

An important element in this conception of the *patria* is that it should be militant. Races that have ceased from war, are on the road to ruin; and only those are powerful which train the native population to arms. The feebleness of Italy can be traced to the mercenary system, introduced by despots, adopted by commercial republics, and favoured by ecclesiastics. If the Italians desire to recover freedom, they must form a national militia; and this can best be done by adapting the principles of the Roman army to modern requirements. The 'Art of War' is a development of this theme. At its close, Machiavelli promises the sceptre of Italy, together with the glory of creating Italian nationality, to any State clear-sighted and self-denying enough to arm its citizens and take the lead in the peninsula. That State, he says, shall play the part of Macedon. Reading the peroration of the 'Art of War' by the light of recent history, its paragraphs sound like a prophecy. What Machiavelli there promised, has been achieved, much in the way he indicated, by Piedmont, the Macedon of United Italy.

When Machiavelli discusses the forms of constitutions, he is clearly thinking of cities rather than of nations as we understand them. He has no conception of representative government, but bases all his observations on the principle of burghership. There is no sound intermediate, he says, between a commonwealth and a principality. In the former, the burghers have equal rights. In the latter there will be a hierarchy of classes. Though his sympathies are with the former (since he holds that the equality of the citizens is the best safeguard for the liberties and law-abiding virtues of the State), he is yet by no means unfavourable to despotism. The decadence of Italy, indeed, had gone so far that her best chance of restoration depended on a prince. Therefore, while he suggests measures for converting despotic States into republics by crushing the aristocracy, and for creating principalities out of free commonwealths by instituting an order of nobles, he regards the latter as the easier task of the two. Upon such topics we must always bear in mind that what he says is partly speculative, and partly meant to meet the actual conditions of Italian politics. The point of view is never simply philosophical nor yet simply practical. So long as the great end could be achieved, and a strong military power could rise in Italy, he is indifferent to the means employed. The peroration of the 'Art of War' is an appeal to either prince or republic. The peroration of the 'Riforma di Firenze' is an appeal to a patriotic Nomothetes. He there says to Clement: You have one of those singular opportunities offered to you, which confer undying glory on a mortal: you may make Florence free, and, by wise regulations, render her the bulwark of renascent Italy. The peroration of the 'Principe' is an appeal to an ambitious autocrat. Follow the suggestions of ancient and contemporary history, which all point to the formation of a native army. Comprehend the magnitude of the task, and use the right means for executing it; and you will earn the fame of restoring your country to her place among the nations.

The case of Italy is almost desperate. Yet there is still hope. A prudent lawgiver may infuse life into the decaying commonwealth of Florence. A spirited despot may succeed in bringing the whole peninsula by force of arms beneath his sway. Machiavelli will not scrutinise the nature of the remedy too closely. He is ready to sacrifice his republican sympathies, and to welcome the saviour who comes even in the guise of Cesare Borgia. When the salvation of the *patria* is at stake, none but precisians can hesitate about the choice of instruments.

This indifference to means, provided the end be secured, is characteristic of the man. Machiavelli's Machiavellism consists in regarding politics as a game of skill, where all ways are justified, and fixity of purpose wins. He does not believe in Fortune, though he admits the favourable circumstances which smoothed the way for men like Cesare. With Juvenal, he says: *Nos te, nos facimus, Fortuna, deam.* Again, he does not believe in Providence. Though a prophet speak with the voice of God, he will not succeed unless, like Moses, he be provided with a sword to ratify his revelation. History is a logical sequence of events, the sole intelligible nexus between its several links being the human will. Virtue is decision of character, accompanied by intellectual sagacity; it is the strong man's subordination of his passions, prejudices, predilections, energies, to the chosen aim. We all admit that it is better to be good than bad. Yet morality has little to do with political success. What lies in the way of really great achievement, is the mediocrity of human nature. Men will not be completely bad or perfectly good. They spoil their best endeavours by vacillation and incompetence to guide their action with regard to the sole end in view.

Enough has been said in different portions of this book about the morality of Machiavelli's political essays. Yet this much may be here repeated. Those who wish to understand it, must not forget the mediæval background of the despots—Ezzelini, Visconti, Scaligeri, Estensi, Carreresi—which lay behind Machiavelli. The sinfulness, treason, masterful personality, Thyestean tragedies, enormous vices and intolerable mischief of the Renaissance—all this was but a pale reflex of the Middle Ages. In those earlier tyrants, the Centaur progenitors of feebler broods, through generations in which men gradually discriminated the twy-formed nature of their ancestry, the lust and luxury of sin had been at their last apogee. *In istis peccandi voluptas erat summa.* What followed in Machiavelli's age, was reflection succeeding to action—evil philosophised in place of evil energetic.

Though Machiavelli perceived that the decadence of Italy was due to bad education, corrupt customs, and a habit of irreligion, he did not insist on the necessity of reformation. He was satisfied with invoking a Dictator, and he counselled this Dictator to meet the badness of his age with fraud and violence. Thus he based his hope of national regeneration upon those very vices which he indicated as the cause of national degeneracy. Whether we ascribe this error to the spirit of the times in which he lived, or to something defective in his own character, it is clear he had not grasped the fundamental principle of righteousness, as that which can alone be safely trusted by a people or its princes. Perhaps he thought that, for practical purposes, the method of radical reformation was too tardy. Perhaps he despaired of seeing it attempted. Of all Italian institutions, the Church, in his opinion, was the most corrupted. Yet the Church held religious monopoly, and controlled education. And the Church had severed morality from religion, religion from the State; making both the private concern of individuals between their conscience and their God.

Just as Machiavelli proved himself incapable of transcending the corruption of his age, though he denounced it; so, while he grasped the notion of a *patria* superior to the commune, he was not able to disengage his mind from the associations of Italian diplomacy. He perceived that the *dêbris* of mediæval society in Italy—the Papacy, the nobles, the *condottieri*—afforded no foundation for the State he dreamed of building. He relied on the masses of the people as the only sound constituent of his ideal *patria*. He foresaw a united nation, to which the individual should devote himself, and which should absorb the dispersed forces of the race. And yet he had not conceived of the nation as a living whole, obeying its own laws of evolution and expansion. He regarded the State as a mechanical or artificial product, to be moulded by the will of a firm ruler. In his theory there is always a Nomothetes, a Dictator, the intervenient skill of a constructor, whom he imagines capable of altering the conditions of political existence by a *coup d'état* or by a readjustment of conflicting rights and interests. Even while praising the French monarchy for its stability, in words that show a just appreciation of constitutional government, he hypothesises a lawgiver in the past. *Chi ordino quello stato, volle che quelli rè*—he who organised that State, willed that those kings, &c. The *ordinò* and *volle* are both characteristic of his habitual point of view. Probably this faith in manipulation arose from his lifelong habit of regarding small political communities, where change was easily effected. In his works we do not gain any broad prospect from the vantage-ground of comprehensive principles, but a minutely analytical discussion of statecraft based in the last resort upon the observation of decadent Italian cities. The question always presents itself: How, given certain circumstances, ought a republic or a prince to use them to the best advantage? The deeper problem, how a nation stirred by some impulse, which combines all classes in a common heroism or a common animosity, must act, hardly occurs to his mind. England, with forces intellectual, emotional and practical at fullest strain, in combat with the Spanish tyranny, adopting a course of conduct which reveals the nation to itself by the act of its instinctive will—such a phase of the larger, more magnetic life of peoples, which Milton compared to the new youth of the eagle, had not been observed by Machiavelli. The German Reformation, the French Revolution, the American War of Independence, might have taught him to understand that conception of the modern nation which he had divined, but which the conditions of his experience prevented his appropriating. Had he fully grasped it, we can scarcely believe that the 'Principe' would have been written. The good faith of that essay depends upon a misconception.

In like manner Machiavelli discerned the weaknesses of the Renaissance without escaping from its enthusiasms. He despised the æsthetical ideal of his age. He was willing to sacrifice form, beauty, rhythm, the arts of culture and learned leisure, to stern matters of fact and stringent discipline. Yet he believed as firmly as any humanist, that the regeneration of his country must proceed from a revival of the past. It is the loss of antique virtues that has enervated our character, he cries. It is the neglect of historical lessons that renders our policy so suicidal. We need to recover the Roman military system, the Roman craft of conquest, the Roman pride and poverty, the Roman subordination of the individual to the State. What we want is a dictator or a lawgiver after the Roman fashion—a Romulus, a Numa, a Camillus, a Coriolanus. The *patria*, as he imagines it, is less the modern nation than the Roman Commonwealth before the epoch of the Empire. This unquestioning belief in the efficacy of classical revival finds vent, at the close of the 'Arte della Guerra,' in a sentence highly characteristic of the Renaissance. 'This province, Italy,' he says, 'seems made to give new birth to things dead, as we have seen in poetry, in painting, and in sculpture.' Hence, he argues, it may be her vocation to bring back the military system and supremacy of ancient Rome.

Thus, to resume what has been said, Machiavelli ascribed the weakness of the Italians to their loss of morality; but he was not logical enough to insist that their regeneration must begin with a religious revolution. He foresaw the modern nation; but he attempted to construct it on the outlines of antiquity. Believing that States might be formed or reformed by ingenious manipulation of machinery, he acquired no true notion of constitutional development or national evolution. His neglect to base his speculations on a thoroughgoing definition of the State and its relation to man as a social being, caused him to assume a severance between ethics and politics, which no sound philosophy of human life will warrant.

On what, then, if these criticisms are just, is founded his claim to rank among the inaugurators of historical and political science? The answer has been already given. It was not so much what he taught, as the spirit in which he approached the problems of his inquiry, which was scientific in the modern sense. Practical, sincere and positive, Machiavelli never raises points deficient in actuality. He does not invite us to sympathise with the emotions of a visionary, or to follow the vagaries of a dreamer. All that he presents is hard, tangible fact, wrought into precise uncompromising argument, expressed in unmistakably plain language. Not only do his works cast floods of light upon Italian history; but they suggest questions of vital importance, which can still be discussed upon the ground selected by their author. They are, moreover, so penetrated with the passion of a patriot, however mistaken in his plan of national reconstitution, that our first sense of repulsion yields to a warmer feeling of admiration for the man who, from the depths of despair, could thus hope on against hope for his country.

Studying Guicciardini, we remain within the same sphere of conceptions, limited by the conditions of Italian politics in the beginning of the sixteenth century. There is no less stringency of minute analysis, an even sharper insight into motives, an equal purity and precision of language.[4] But the moral atmosphere is different. The corruption which Machiavelli perceived and criticised, is now accepted. In the place of desperate remedies suggested by the dread of certain ruin, Guicciardini has nothing to offer but indifference and self-adjustment to the exigencies of the moment. Machiavelli was a visionary and an idealist in spite of his positive bias. Guicciardini is a practical diplomatist, bent on saving his own State and fortune from the wreck which he contemplated. What gives grandeur to Machiavelli's speculation is the conception of the *patria*, superior to the individual, demanding unlimited self-sacrifice, and repaying the devotion of the citizens by strength in union. This idea has disappeared in Guicciardini's writings. In its stead he offers us self-interested egotism. Where Machiavelli wrote *patria*, he substituted *il particolare.* It follows from this cold acquiescence in a base theory of public conduct, adapted to a recognised state of social anarchy, that Guicciardini's philosophy is far more immoral than Machiavelli's. The 'Ricordi,' in which, under the form of aphorisms, he condensed the results of his experience and observation, have been well described as the 'code of Italian corruption.' Resistance has to be abandoned. Remedies are hopeless. Let us sit down and calmly criticise the process of decay. A wise man will seek to turn the worst circumstances to his own profit; and what remains for political sagacity is the accumulation of wealth, honours, offices of power on the ambitious individual.

Machiavelli and Guicciardini had this in common, that their mental attitude was analytical, positive, critically scientific. It negatived the *a priori* idealism of mediæval political philosophy, and introduced a just conception of the method of inquiry. This quality connects them on the one hand with the practical politicians of their age, and on the other with its representative thinkers in the field of metaphysics.

It is no part of my plan to attempt a general history of Italian philosophy during the Renaissance period, or even to indicate its leading moments. On the scale of my present work, any such endeavour would of necessity be incomplete; for the material to be dealt with is obscure, and the threads of thought to be interwoven are scattered, requiring no little patience and no slight expenditure of exposition on the part of one who seeks to place them in their proper relations. Of philosophy,

[4] I refer to the *Opere Inedite*. In the *Istoria d' Italia*, Guicciardini's style is inferior to Machiavelli's.

in the strict sense of the term, the Italian Renaissance had not much to offer. We do not revert to that epoch, expecting to meet with systematic theories of the universe, plausible analyses of the laws of thought, or ingenious speculations upon the nature of being. It is well known that the thinkers of the fifteenth and sixteenth centuries can scarcely claim to have done more than lead the revolt of reason against scholastic tyranny and obsolete authorities, appealing with often misdirected enthusiasm to original sources, and suggesting theories and methods which, in the hands of abler speculators, at a more fortunate epoch, generated the philosophies of modern Europe. Yet even so the movement of thought in Italy was of no slight moment, and the work accomplished deserves to be recorded with more honour than it has hitherto received from the historians of philosophy.

The Renaissance in general may be called the Middle Ages in dissolution. That the period was transitional in its chief aspects, has often already been insisted on. The massive fabrics of feudalism and the Church were breaking up. The vast edifice of scholastic theology was being undermined by men who had the energy to free themselves from orthodox tradition, but scarcely force enough or opportunity to mould the thought of the new age. The Italians who occupied themselves with philosophical problems, from Petrarch to Campanella, hold an intermediate place between the schoolmen and the founders of modern metaphysics. They accomplish the transition from S. Thomas and Occam to Bacon, Descartes and Spinoza. It is possible to mark three phases in this process of transition, each of which was necessary in the progress of the mind from theological ontology to science and free speculation. The thinkers of the first stage began by questioning the authority of dogma. Those of the second stage accepted the authority of the ancients. Those of the third appealed to Nature against ecclesiastical and classical authority alike. Humanism was thus intermediate between scholasticism and what, for want of a more definite phrase, may be termed rationalism. Succeeding to the schoolmen, the scholars cleared the groundwork of philosophy of old encumbrances, and reappropriated antique systems of thought. After them, the schools of Lower Italy, including Telesio, Campanella and Bruno, prepared the path to be immediately followed; with what profit is apparent to the dullest intellect. Clearly, and beyond the possibility of question, they propounded the main problems which have agitated all the scientific schools of modern Europe. To them belongs the credit of having first speculated knowledge and reality from no external standpoint, but from the immediate consciousness. The *Interrogatio Naturæ* and the *Cogito ergo sum*, which became the watchwords of modern empiricism and rationalism, are theirs. But, at the very moment when the Italians of the Revival had performed their pioneering task-work, all vital vigour in the nation was extinguished or suspended by the deadly influences of

Spanish domination and Papal terrorism.[5] It was left for other races to enter on the promised land which they had conquered.

Upon its first appearance, it was clear that humanism would run counter to both currents of mediæval thought, the orthodox and the heretical, the Thomistic and Averroistic. Dante designed his epic in accordance with the fixed outlines of Thomistic theology. The free-thinkers of the Lombard universities expressed a not uncertain adhesion to the materialistic doctrines which passed for Averroism. But Petrarch, the hero of the coming age, pronounced his contempt for scholastic quibbles, and at the same time waged war against the tenets of Averroes. He introduced a new spirit into philosophical discussion, a new style of treatment, literary rather than scientific, which tended to substitute humane culture for logical pedantry. The departure from mediæval lines of thought, thus signalised by Petrarch, was followed by the students of the next two centuries. Questions which had agitated Europe since the days of Roscelin, now seemed to lose the interest of actuality. The distinctions of Nominalism and Realism retained no attraction for men who were engaged in discovering manuscripts, learning to write correct Latin, acquiring Greek, and striving to penetrate the secret of antiquity. The very style of the schoolmen became a byword for ineptitude and barbarism. It required no little courage and a prestige as brilliant as Pico's to sustain the cause of Albertus Magnus or Johannes Scotus.[6] Scholars of the type of Poggio and Filelfo, Beccadelli and Poliziano, abhorred their ponderous metaphysics, as though they were grotesque chimeras generated by the indigestion of half-starved intellectual stomachs. Orpheus had reappeared. He bade the world thenceforward move to music and melodious rhythms both of thought and language. The barbarians might harbour Mercury within their hearts, to quote Pico's apology; they might display wisdom in unvarnished plainness; but what were these claims worth in an age that required the lips rather than the soul to be eloquent, and when a decorated fiction found more favour than a naked truth? No more decided antithesis than that of scholastic philosophy to the new classical ideal is conceivable.

Thus the first movement of the Revival implied an uncompromising abandonment of mediæval thought as worse than worthless. If men educated by the humanistic method were to speculate, they would do

[5] I cannot refrain from translating a paragraph in Spaventa's Essay upon Bruno, which, no less truly than passionately, states the pith of this Italian tragedy. 'The sixteenth century was the epoch in which the human spirit burst the chains that up to then had bound it, and was free. There is no more glorious age for Italy. The heroes of thought and freedom, who then fought for truth, were almost all her sons. They were persecuted, and extinguished with sword and fire. Would that the liberty of thought, the autonomy of the reason, they gave to the other nations of Europe, had borne fruit in Italy! From that time forward we remained as though cut off from the universal life; it seemed as if the spirit which inspired the world and pushed it onward, had abandoned us' (*Saggi di Critica*, Napoli, 1867, p. 140).

[6] *Epistolæ Angeli Poliziani*, lib. ix. p. 269 (ed. Gryphius, 1533).

so upon lines different from those suggested by the schoolmen. Cicero and Seneca became their models; and the rhetorical treatment of moral topics passed muster with them for philosophy. A garrulous colloquial skimming in fair Latin over the well-trodden ground of ethics supplanted the endeavour to think strictly upon difficult subjects. Much of this literature—the dialogues of Alberti, for example, and Landino's 'Camaldolese Disputations'—can still be read with profit. But regarded from the point of view of systematic thought, it has slight importance. We value it principally for the light it casts upon contemporary manners and modes of opinion.

The study of Greek and Latin texts revealed a world to the Italians far wider than the regions where the mediæval mind had moved in narrow limits. The immediate effect of this discovery was not, however, wholly salutary. The ancients began to exercise a kind of despotism; and a new authority, no less stringent than that of dogma, bound the scholars of the Revival beneath the tyranny of classical names. It was impossible for the intellect to free itself from fetters at a single leap. This second servitude seemed destined to be even more pernicious than the first; for as yet there was no criticism, and the superincumbent masses of antique literature, extending from the earliest dawn of Greek history to the latest commentators of Byzantium and Ravenna, underwent but little process of sifting. It was enough for the Italians of that epoch to assimilate. Nothing which bore the stamp of antiquity came amiss to their omnivorous appetite. Compilations from second or third sources were valued as equally precious with original texts. The testimony of hearsay reporters passed for conclusive evidence in matters of history. Masters in philosophy were confounded with expositors, who flourished at the distance of some centuries. Athens and Alexandria, Rome and Constantinople, were indiscriminately regarded as a single Holy Land of wisdom.

While this fermentation of assimilative erudition was still at its height, Gemistos Plethon preached his Neo-platonic mysticism at Florence; and the first attempt at a new philosophy for Western Europe, independent of the schoolmen, uninfluenced by orthodoxy, proceeded from the Medicean academy. The Platonism of Ficino and Pico, we now know, was of a very mixed and ill-determined quality. Uncontrolled by critical insight, and paralysed by the prestige attaching to antiquity, the Florentine school produced little better than an unintelligent eclecticism. Their so-called philosophical writings were commonplace books of citations, anthologies of ill-digested abstracts, in which Greek and Asiatic and Christian opinions issued in an incoherent theosophy. It must be reckoned a great misfortune for Italian thought that the Platonists were able to approach the masterpieces of their Attic teacher through a medium of Alexandrian and Byzantine enthusiasm. Had they been forced to attack the 'Republic' without the intervention of Plotinus and Gemistos, they might have started on some fruitful line of speculation. They would at least have perceived that Plato's theology formed a background to his psychological, ethical, educational and political theories, instead of fastening upon those visionary systems which his later Greek expositors extracted from the least important portions of his works. At the same time, this Neo-platonic mysticism was only too sympathetic to the feebler pietism of the Middle Ages for men who had discovered it, to doubt its inspiration.

What was finally accomplished for sound scholarship by Ficino, lay in the direction, not of metaphysics or of history, but of translation. The enduring value of Pico's work is due, not to his Quixotic quest of an accord between Pagan, Hebrew and Christian traditions, but to the noble spirit of confidence and humane sympathy with all great movements of the mind, which penetrates it. If we cannot rate the positive achievements of the Florentines in philosophy at a high value, still the discussion of Platonic and Aristotelian doctrines which their investigations originated, caused the text of the Greek philosophers to be accurately examined for the first time in Western Europe. Their theories, though devoid of originality and clogged at every point with slavish reverence for classical authority, marked a momentous deviation from the traditional methods of mediæval speculation.

Thus a vast and tolerably accurate acquaintance with the chief thinkers of antiquity, reinforced by the translation of their principal works, was the main outcome of the Platonic revival at Florence. Uncritically, and with many a blundering divergence into the uncongenial provinces of Oriental thought, the Italian intellect appropriated Greek philosophy. A groundwork was laid down for the discussion of fundamental problems in the forms under which they had presented themselves to the ancient world. But while the Platonists were wrangling with the Aristotelians about the superiority of their respective masters; while the scholars were translating from the original languages; while the mystics were building castles in the air, composed of fragments from Neo-platonic and Neo-pythagorean systems, cementing them with the mortar of Christianity and adding quaint outbuildings of cabalistic and astrological delusions; the writers of ethical treatises pursued another line of inquiry, which was no less characteristic of the age and no less fruitful of results. During the Middle Ages thought of every kind had been concentrated on the world beyond this life. The question of how to live here was answered with reference to eternal interests solely. Human existence had no meaning except as the prelude to heaven or hell. But contact with antiquity introduced a new class of problems. Men began once more to ask themselves how they ought to live in this world, not with the view of avoiding misery and securing happiness in the next, but with the aim of making their terrestrial home most comfortable and their sojourn in it most effective for themselves and their companions. The discussion of the fundamental question how to live to best advantage, without regard for the next world and unbiassed by the belief in a rigid scheme of salvation, occupies an important place in the philosophical essays of the time.

Landino, for example, in his 'Camaldolese Disputations,' raises the question whether the contemplative or the practical life offers superior attractions to a man desirous of perfecting self-culture. Alberti touches the same topic in his minor dialogues, while he subjects the organism of the Family in all its relations to a searching analysis in his most important essay.

Valla, in the famous dialogue 'De Voluptate,' attacks the problem of conduct from another point of view.[7] Contrasting the Stoical with the Epicurean ideals, asceticism with hedonism, he asks which of the two fulfils the true end of human life. His treatise on Pleasure is, indeed, a disputation between renascent paganism, naturalism, and humanism on the one side, and the mediæval scheme of ethics on the other. Man according to nature contends with man according to grace; the soul, obeying the desires of the flesh, defends her cause against the spirit, whose life is hid with a crucified Christ in God. Thus the two points of view between which the Renaissance wavered, are placed in powerful contrast; and nowhere has their antagonism been more ably stated. For the champion of hedonism Valla appropriately chose the poet Beccadelli, while he committed the defence of asceticism to Niccolò Niccoli. Though at the close of the argument he awarded the palm of victory to the latter,[8] it is clear that his sympathies lay with the former, and all the strength of his reasoning faculty is employed in the statement and support of Beccadelli's thesis. The first and far the longest part of the dialogue, where we detect a true note of sincerity, is a remorseless onslaught upon monasticism under the name of Stoicism, resulting in a no less uncompromising defence of physical appetite. Some of the utterances upon sexual morality are penetrated with the rancour of rebellion.[9] It is the revolt of the will against unnatural restrictions, the reassertion of natural liberty, emboldened by the study of classical literature, embittered by long centuries of ecclesiastical oppression. Underlying the extravagances of an argument which owes its crudity and coarseness to the contradictions of the century, we find one central thought of permanent importance. Nature can do nothing wrong; and that must be wrong which violates nature.[10] It is man's duty, by interrogation of nature, to discover the laws of his own being and to obey those. In other words, Valla, though in no sense a man of science,

[7] *Laurentius Valla*: *Opera omnia*, Basileæ, 1465. The 'De Voluptate' begins at p. 896 of this edition.

[8] 'Uterque pro se de laudibus Voluptatis suavissime quidem quasi cantare visus est; sed Antonius hirundini, Nicolaus philomelæ (quam lusciniam nominant) magis comparandus (*ib.* lib. iii. p. 697).

[9] 'Meâ quidem sententiâ odiosus est si quis in mœchos, si rerum naturam intueri volumus, invehat' (*ib.* lib. i. cap. 38). 'Quisquis virgines sanctimoniales primus invenit, abominandum atque in ultimas terras exterminandum morem in civitatem induxisse. . . . Melius merentur scorta et postribula quam sanctimoniales virgines ac continentes' (*ib.* lib. i. cap. 43).

[10] 'Quod natura finxit atque formavit id nisi sanctum laudabileque esse non posse' (*ib.* lib. i. cap. 9).

proclaims the fundamental principle of science, and inaugurates a new criterion of ethics.

Three main points may be discriminated in the intellectual movement briefly surveyed in the preceding paragraphs. The first is an abrupt breach with scholasticism. The whole method of philosophy has been changed, and the canon of authority has altered. The second is the acquisition of classical thought, and the endeavour, especially at Florence, among the Platonists, to appropriate it and adapt it to Christianity. The third is the introduction of a new problem into philosophical discussion. How to make the best of human life, is substituted for the question how to ensure salvation in the world beyond the grave. It will be observed that each of these three points implies departure from the prescribed ground of mediæval speculation which always moved within the limits of theology. Theology, except in the mysticism of the Platonists, except in occasional and perfunctory allusions of the rhetoricians, has no place in this medley of scholarship, citation, superstition, and frank handling of practical ideals.

While the Florentine Platonists were evolving an eclectic mysticism from the materials furnished by their Greek and Oriental studies; while the Ciceronian humanists were discussing the fundamental principles which underlie the various forms of human life; the Universities of Lombardy continued their exposition of Aristotle upon the lines laid down by Thomistic and Averroistic schoolmen. Padua and Bologna extended the methods of the Middle Ages into the Renaissance. Their professors adhered to the formal definitions and distinctions of an earlier epoch, accumulating comment upon comment, and darkening the text of their originals with glosses. Yet the light shed by the Revival penetrated even to the lecture-rooms of men like Achillini. Humanism had established the principle of basing erudition on the study of authentic documents. The text of Aristotle in the Greek or in first-hand translations, had become the common property of theologians and philosophers. It was from these universities that the first dim light of veritable science was to issue. And here the part played by one man in the preparation of a new epoch for modern thought is so important that I may be allowed to introduce him with some prolixity of biographical details.[11]

Pietro Pomponazzi was born of noble lineage at Mantua in 1462. He completed his studies at Padua, where he graduated in 1487 as laureate of medicine. It may be remarked incidentally that teachers of philosophy at this era held the degree of physicians. This point is not unimportant, since it fixes our attention on the fact that philosophy, as distinguished from theology, had not yet won a recognised position.

[11] For the following sketch of Pomponazzi's life, and for help in the study of his philosophy, I am indebted to Francesco Fiorentino's *Pietro Pomponazzi*, Firenze, Lemonnier, 1868, 1 vol. I may here take occasion to mention a work by the same author, *Bernardino Telesio*, *ibid.* 1872, 2 vols. Together, these two books form an important contribution to the history of Italian philosophy.

Logic formed a separate part of the educational curriculum. Rhetoric was classed with humanistic literature. Philosophy counted as a branch of Physics. At Florence, in the schools of the Platonists, metaphysical inquiries assumed a certain hue of mysticism. At Padua and Bologna, in the schools of the physicians, they assimilated something of materialism. During the Middle Ages they had always flourished in connexion with theology. But that association had been broken; and as yet a proper place had not been assigned to the science of the human mind. A new department of knowledge was in progress of formation, distinct from theology, distinct from physics, distinct from literature. But at the epoch of which we are now treating, it had not been correctly marked off from either of these provinces, and in the schools of Lombardy it was confounded with physical science.

In 1488 Pomponazzi, soon after taking his degree as a physician, was appointed Professor Extraordinary of Philosophy at Padua. He taught in concurrence with the veteran Achillini, who was celebrated for his old-world erudition and his leaning toward the doctrines of Averroes. Pomponazzi signalised his *début* in the professorial career, by adopting a new method of instruction. Less distinguished for learning than acuteness, he confined himself to brilliant elucidations of his author's text. For glosses, citations and hair-splitting distinctions, he substituted lucid and precise analysis. It is probable that he was a poor Greek scholar. Paolo Giovio goes so far, indeed, as to assert that, of the two classical languages, he only knew Latin; nor is there anything in his own writings to demonstrate that he had studied Greek philosophy in the original. But he proved himself a child of the new era by his style of exposition, no less than by a strict adherence to Alexander of Aphrodisias, the Greek commentator of Aristotle. What that divergence from the system of his rival, Achillini, who still adhered to the commentaries of Averroes, implied, I shall endeavour to make clear in the sequel. For the present, we must follow his career as a professor. Before the year 1495 he had been appointed to the ordinary chair of Natural Philosophy at Padua; and there he resided until 1509, when the schools of Padua were closed. He spent this period chiefly in lecturing on Aristotle's Physics, for the sake presumably of the medical students who crowded that university. Forced by circumstances to leave Padua, Pomponazzi found a home in Ferrara, where he began to expound Aristotle's treatise 'De Animâ.' Unlike Padua, the University of Ferrara had a literary bias; and we may therefore conclude that Pomponazzi availed himself of this first favourable opportunity to pursue the studies in Aristotelian psychology for which he had a decided personal preference. In 1512 he was invited to Bologna, where he remained until his death, in the capacity of Professor of Natural and Moral Philosophy. His stipend, increased gradually through a series of engagements, varied from a little over 200 to 600 golden ducats. Bologna, like Ferrara, was not distinguished for its school of medicine. Consequently, we find that from the date of his first settlement in that city, Pomponazzi devoted himself to psychological and ethical investigations. All the books on which his fame are founded were written at Bologna. In the autumn of 1516 he published his treatise 'De Immortalitate Animæ.' It was dedicated to Marcantonio Flavio Contarini; and, finding its way to Venice, it was immediately burned in public because of its heretical opinions. A long and fierce controversy followed this first publication. Contarini, Agostino Nifo, Ambrogio Fiandino, and Bartolommeo di Spina issued treatises, in which they strove to combat the Aristotelian materialism of Pomponazzi with arguments based on Thomistic theology or Averroistic mysticism. He replied with an 'Apologia' and a 'Defensorium,' avowing his submission to the Church in all matters of faith, but stubbornly upholding a philosophical disagreement with the doctrine of the immortality of the human soul.

During this discussion Pomponazzi ran some risk of being held accountable for his opinions. The friars and preachers of all colours were loud in their denunciations; and it is said that Bembo's intercession with Pope Leo in behalf of his old master was needed to secure Pomponazzi from ecclesiastical procedure. During the last years of his life the professor of Bologna completed two important treatises, 'De Incantationibus,' and 'De Fato.' They were finished in 1520 but not published until after his death, when they appeared in the Basle edition of his collected works. He died in 1525, and was buried at Mantua. Pomponazzi had been thrice married. He left behind him an unsullied reputation for virtuous conduct and sweet temper. He was, physically, a little man, and owed to this circumstance the *sobriquet* of 'Peretto.' We gain a glimpse of him in one of Bandello's novels. But, with this exception, the man is undiscernible through the mists of three intervening centuries. With the author the case is different. In his books Pomponazzi presents a powerful and unmistakable personality. What remains to be said about him and his influence over Italian thought must be derived from an examination of the three treatises already mentioned.

In order to make Pomponazzi's position intelligible, it will be needful to review the main outlines of Aristotelian thought, as it was transmitted through the Middle Ages to the men of the Renaissance. Pomponazzi claimed to be no more than an expositor of Aristotle's system. If he diverged from the paths of orthodox philosophy, it was because he recognised a discrepancy upon vital points between Thomas of Aquino and the Peripatetic writings. If he rejected some fashionable theories of the freethinkers who preceded him, it was because he saw that Averroes had misinterpreted their common master. He aimed at stating once again the precise doctrine of the Greek philosopher. He believed that if he could but grasp Aristotle's real opinion, he should by that mental act arrive at truth. The authority of the Stagirite in all matters of human knowledge lay for him beyond the possibility of question; or, what amounted to nearly the same thing, his interest in speculative questions was confined to making Aristotle's view intelligible. Thus, under the humble garb of a commentator, one of the boldest and in some respects the most original thinkers of his age stepped forth to wage war with superstition and ecclesiastical despotism. The Church, since the date of Thomas Aquinas, had so committed herself to Aristotle that proving a discrepancy between her dogma and the Aristotelian text upon any vital point, was much the same as attacking the dogma itself. This must be kept steadily in mind if we wish to appreciate Pomponazzi.[12] His attitude cannot easily be understood at the present day, when science has discarded authority, and the *ipse dixit* of a dead man carries no weight outside religious or quasi-religious circles. This renders the prefatory remarks I have to make necessary.

In the Platonic system it was impossible to explain the connexion between ideas, conceived as sole realities, and phenomena, regarded as distinct from that ideal world to which they owed their qualities of relative substantiality and cognisability. Aristotle attempted to solve Plato's problem by his theory of form and matter, activity and passivity, energy and potentiality, inseparable in the reality of the individual. He represented the intelligible world as a scale of existences, beginning with form and matter coherent in the simplest object, and ending in God. God was the form of forms, the thought of thoughts, independent of matter, immoveable and unchangeable, although the cause of movement and variety. The forms resumed in God, as species are included in the Summum Genus, were disseminated through the universe in a hierarchy of substances, from the most complex immediately below God, to the most simple immediately above the groundwork given by incognisable matter. In this hierarchy matter was conceived as the mere base; necessary, indeed, to every individual but God; an essential element of reality; but beyond the reach of knowledge. The form or universal alone was intelligible. It may already be perceived that in this system, if the individual, composed of form and matter, alone is substantial and concrete, while the universal alone is cognisable, Aristotle admitted a division between reality and truth. The former attribute belongs to the individual, the latter to the universal. The place of God, too, in the system is doubtful. Is He meant to be immanent in the universe, or separated from it? Aristotle uses language which supports each of these views. Again, God is immaterial, universal, the highest form; and yet at the same time He is an individual substance; whereas, by the fundamental conception of the whole scheme, the coherence of form and matter in the individual is necessary to reality. It might seem possible to escape from these difficulties by regarding Aristotle's Deity as the Idea of the Universe, and each inferior form in the ascending series of existences as the material of its immediate superior, until the final and inclusive form is reached in God. But what, then, becomes of matter in itself, which, though recognised as unintelligible, is postulated as the necessary base of individual substances?

[12] It will be remembered that in the controversy between Galileo and the Inquisition, the latter condemned Copernicus on the score that he contradicted Aristotle and S. Thomas of Aquino.

In Aristotle's theory of life there is a similar ascending scale. The soul (ψυχὴ) is defined as the form of the body. Its vegetative, motive, sensitive, appetitive faculties (ψυχὴ θρεπτικὴ, κινητικὴ, αἰσθητικὴ, ὀρεκτικὴ), are subordinated to the passive intellect (νοῦς παθητικὸς), which receives their reports; and this in its turn is subordinated to the active intellect (νοῦς ποιητικὸς), which possesses the content of the passive intellect as thought. The intellect (νοῦς) is man's peculiar property: and Aristotle in plain words asserts that it is separate from the soul (ψυχὴ). But he has not explained whether it is separate as the highest series of an evolution may be called distinct from the lower, or as something alien and communicated from without is separate. The passive intellect, being a receptacle for images and phantasms furnished by the senses, perishes with the soul, which, upon the dissolution of the body, whereof it is the form, ceases to exist. But the active intellect is immortal and eternal, being pure thought, and identifiable in the last resort with God. So much Aristotle seems to have laid down about the immortality of the intellect. It is tempting to infer that he maintained a theory of man's participation in the divine Idea—that is to say, in the complex of the categories which render the universe intelligible and distinguish it as a cosmos. But, just as Aristotle failed to explain the connexion of God with the world, so he failed to render his opinion regarding the relation of God to the human intellect, and of the immortal to the perishable part of the soul, manifest. It can, however, be safely asserted that he laid himself open to a denial of the immortality of each individual person. This, at any rate, would follow from the assumption that he believed us to be persons by reasons of physical existence, of the soul's faculties, and of that blending of the reason with the orectic soul which we call will. As the universe culminates in God, so man culminates in thought, which is the definition of God; and this thought is eternal, the same for all and for ever. It does not, however, follow that each man who has shared the divine thought, should survive the dissolution of his body. The person is a complex, and this complex perishes. The active intellect is imperishable, but it is impersonal. In like manner the whole hierarchy of substances between the ground of matter and the form of forms is in perpetual process of combination and dissolution. But the supreme Idea endures, in isolation from that flux and reflux of the individuals it causes. Whether we regard the ontological or the psychological series, only the world of pure thought, the Idea, is indissoluble, subject to no process of becoming, and superior to all change. The supreme place assigned to Thought in either hierarchy is clear enough. But the nexus between (i) God and the universe, (ii) God and the active intellect, (iii) the active intellect, or pure thought, and the inferior faculties of the soul, which supply it with material for thought, is unexplained.

Three distinct but interpenetrating problems were presented by the Aristotelian system. One concerns the theory of the Universal. Are universals or particulars prior? Do we collect the former from the latter; or do the latter owe their value as approximate realities to the former? The second concerns the theory of the Individual. Assuming that the Individual is a complex of form and matter, are we to regard the matter or the form as its essential substratum? The third concerns the theory of the human Soul. Is it perishable with the body, or immortal? If it is immortal, does the incorruptible quality perpetuate the person who has lived upon this globe; or is it the common property of all persons, surviving their decease, but not ensuring the prolongation of each several consciousness? The first of these problems formed the battle-field of Nominalists, Realists and Conceptualists in the first period of mediæval thought. It was waged upon the data supplied by Porphyry's abstract of the Aristotelian doctrine of the predicaments. The second problem occupied the encyclopædic thinkers of the second period, Albertus Magnus, Duns Scotus and Thomas of Aquino. Their contest was fought out over the Metaphysics of Aristotle. The third problem arrested the attention of speculators in the age of the Renaissance. The text which they disputed was Aristotle's essay 'De Animâ.' This movement of mediæval thought from point to point was not unnatural nor unnecessitated. In the first period Aristotle was unknown; but the creeds of Christianity supplied a very definite body of conceptions to be dealt with. About the personality of God, the immortality of the soul, and the concrete reality of the human individual, there was then no doubt. Theology was paramount; and the contention of the schoolmen at this epoch regarded the right interpretation of the Universal. Was it a simple conception of the mind, or an external and substantial reality? Was it a name or an entity? The Nominalists, who adopted the former of these two alternatives, fell necessarily beneath the ban of ecclesiastical censure and suspicion; not because their philosophical conclusions were unwarranted, but because these ran counter to the prevailing spirit of the Christian belief. Their definitions sapped the basis of that transcendentalism on which the whole fabric of mediæval thought reposed. Nevertheless, at the end of the battle, the Nominalists virtually gained the day. Abelard's Conceptualism was an attempt to harmonise antagonistic points of view by emphasising the abstractive faculty of the human subject. In the course of this warfare the problem of the Individual had been neglected. The reciprocity of form and matter had not been expressly made a topic of dispute. Meanwhile a flood of new light was being cast upon philosophical questions by the introduction into Europe of Latin texts translated by Jewish scholars from the Arabic versions of Aristotle, as well as by the commentaries of Averroes. This re-discovery of Aristotle forced the schoolmen of the second period to consider the fundamental relation of matter to form. The master had postulated the conjunction of these two constituents in the individual. Thomas of Aquino and Duns Scotus advanced opposing theories to explain the ground and process of individualisation. With regard to the elder problem of the Universal, S. Thomas declared himself for modified Conceptualism.

With regard to the second problem, he pronounced matter to be the substratum of individuals—matter stamped as with a seal by the form impressed upon it. Thus he adhered as closely as was possible for a theologian to the Peripatetic doctrines. For a student of philosophy to advance opinions without reckoning with Aristotle was now impossible. The great Dominican Doctor achieved the task of bringing Aristotle into satisfactory accord with Christian dogma. Nor was this so difficult as it appears. Aristotle, as we have seen, did not define his views about the soul and God. Moreover, he had written no treatise on theology proper. Whether he ascribed personality or conscious thought to God was more than doubtful. His God stood at the apex of the world's pyramid, inert, abstract, empty and devoid of life. Christendom, meanwhile, was provided with a robust set of theological opinions, based on revelation and held as matters of faith. To transfer these to the account of the Aristotelian Deity, to fill out the vacuous and formal outline, and to theosophise the whole system was the work of S. Thomas. To the fixed dogmas of the Latin Church he adjusted the more favourable of Aristotle's various definitions, and interpreted his dubious utterances by the light of ecclesiastical orthodoxy.

Up to this point the doctrine of personal immortality had been accepted by all Christians as requiring no investigation. Human life was only studied in relation to the world beyond the grave, where each man and woman was destined to endure for all eternity. To traverse this fundamental postulate, was to proclaim the grossest heresy; and though Epicureans, as Dante calls them, of that type were found, they had not formulated their opinions regarding the soul's corruptibility in any scientific theory, nor based them on the authority of Aristotle. S. Thomas viewed the soul as the essential form of the human body; he further affirmed its separate existence in each person, and its separate immortality. The soul, he thought, although defined as the form of a physical body, acquired a habit of existence in the body, which sufficed for its independent and perpetual survival. These determinations were clearly in accordance with the Christian faith. But the time was approaching when the problem of the soul itself should be narrowly considered. Averroes had interpreted Aristotle to mean that the active intellect alone, which he regarded as common to all human beings, was immortal. This was tantamount to denying the immortality of the individual. Men live and die, but the species is eternal. The active intellect arrives continually at human consciousness in persons, who participate in it and perish. Knowledge is indestructible for the race, transitory for each separate soul. At one end of the universal hierarchy is matter; at the other end is God. Between God and man in the descending scale are the intelligences of the several spheres. From the lowest or lunar sphere humanity derives the active intellect. This active intellect is a substantial entity, separate no less from God than from the human soul on which it rains the knowledge of a lifetime. It is not necessary to point out how much of mystical and Oriental material

Averroes engrafted on Aristotle's system. His doctrine, though vehemently repudiated by orthodox schoolmen, found wide acceptance: and there were other heretics who asserted the perishable nature of the human soul, without distinction of its faculties. These heterodoxies gained ground so rapidly through the first two centuries of the Italian revival (1300-1500), that in December 1513 it was judged needful to condemn them, and to reassert the Thomistic doctrine by a Council of the Lateran over which Leo X. presided.[13]

If we consider the intellectual conditions of the Renaissance, it becomes clear why the problem of Immortality acquired this importance, and why heretical opinions spread so widely as to necessitate a confirmation of the orthodox dogma. Mediæval speculation had a perpetual tendency to transcend the sphere of this earth. The other world gave reality and meaning to human life. All eyes were fixed on the Beyond, at first with an immediate expectation of the Judgment, afterwards with a continued looking forward to Paradise or Punishment. This attitude toward eternity was an absorbing preoccupation. But with the dawn of the new age our life on earth acquired a deeper significance; and the question was not unnaturally posed—This soul, whose immortality has been postulated, on whose ultimate destiny so many anticipations of weal and woe have been based, what is it? Are we justified in assuming its existence as an incorruptible and everlasting self? What did Aristotle really think about it? The age inclined with overmastering bias toward a practical materialism. Men were eager to enjoy their lives and to indulge their appetites. They tired of the restrictions imposed upon their nature by the prospect of futurity. They found in their cherished classics, whose authority had triumphed over Church and Council, but vague and visionary hints of immortality. Even in the highest ecclesiastical quarters it was fashionable to speak lightly of the fundamental dogmas of the Christian creed. Leo X., who presided over the Lateran Council of 1513, did not disguise his doubts concerning the very doctrine it had reinforced. The time had come for a reconsideration *ab initio* of a theory which the Middle Ages had accepted as an axiom. The battle was fought out on the ground of Aristotle's treatise on the soul. Independent research had not yet asserted its claims against authority; and the problem which now presented itself to the professors and students of Italy, was not: Is the soul immortal? but: Did Aristotle maintain the immortality of the soul? The philosopher of Stagira, having been treated on his first appearance as a foe of the faith and then accepted as its bulwark, was now to be used as an efficient battering ram against the castles of orthodox opinion.

There were two ways of regarding Aristotle's doctrine of the active

[13] These are the words: 'Hoc sacro approbante Concilio damnamus et reprobamus omnes asserentes *animam intellectivam mortalem esse*, aut *unicam in cunctis hominibus*, et hæc in dubium vertentes, cum illa non solum vere per se et essentialiter humani corporis forma existat . . . verum et immortalis, et pro corporum quibus infunditur multitudine, singulariter multiplicabilis et multiplicata et multiplicanda sit.'

intellect. The one was to view the Nous as a development from the soul, which in its turn should be conceived as a development from the senses. The other was to recognise it as separate from the soul and imported from without. Each claimed substantial support in various dicta of the master. The latter found able exposition at the hands of his Arabic commentator Averroes. The former was maintained by the fullest and latest of the Greek peripatetics, Alexander of Aphrodisias. In the later Middle Ages free thought, combating the Thomistic system, inclined to Averroism. Pomponazzi, the chief Aristotelian of the Renaissance, declared for Alexander. His great work, 'De Immortalitate Animæ,' is little more than an attempt to reconstruct the doctrine of Aristotle by the help of Alexander. Pomponazzi starts by laying down the double nature of the human soul. It is both sensitive and intelligent. On this point philosophers are agreed; the questions at issue relate to the mode of connexion between the two portions, and the prospect of immortality for both or either. He next proceeds to state the opinions of Averroes, the Platonists, and Thomas of Aquino, meeting their several arguments, and showing how and where they diverge from Aristotle, and endeavouring to prove the superiority of his master's doctrine. Pomponazzi agrees with S. Thomas as to the division of the soul and its relation to the body. He differs with him on the point of immortality, declaring with sufficient clearness that no portion of the human soul can be other than perishable. If we admit that the soul in general is the act or form of the body, the intelligent portion of the soul is included in this definition. It cannot dispense with the body, at least as the object of its intelligent activity. But if it be thus intimately bound up with the body, it must suffer corruption with the body; or even should we suppose it to survive, it will have no images or phantasms furnished by the senses, which are the necessary pabulum of its thinking faculty.[14] The order of nature admits of no interruption. It will not do to say that the soul thinks in one way during life on earth, and in another way after death. This contradicts the first principle of continuity. Man occupies a middle place between imperishable and perishable things.[15] He has a certain odour of immateriality, a mere shadow of intellect, because he stands upon the confine between

[14] Cap. viii. 'Cum et Aristoteles dicat, necesse esse intelligentem phantasma aliquod speculari.' Again, *ibid.*: 'Ergo in omni suo intelligere indiget phantasia, sed si six est, ipsa est materialis; ergo anima intellectiva est materialis.' Again, *ibid.*: 'Humanus intellectus corpus habet caducum, quare vel corrupto corpore ipse non esset, quod positioni repugnat, vel si esset, sine opere esset, cum sine phantasmate per positionem intelligere non posset et sic otiaretur.'

[15] Cap. ix. 'Et sic medio modo humanus intellectus inter materialia et immaterialia est actus corporis organici.' Again, *ibid.*: 'Ipse igitur intellectus sic medius existens inter materialia et immaterialia.' Again, *ibid.*: 'Homo est medius inter Deos et bestias, quare sicut pallidum comparatum nigro dicitur album, sic homo, comparatus bestiis, dici potest Deus et immortalis, sed non vere et simpliciter.'

these regions.[16] But his very conduct shows how vain and unsubstantial is his claim to pure reason. If we see a few men elevate themselves toward God, there are thousands who descend toward the brutes; and of those who spend their lives in clarifying their intelligence, none can boast of more than an obscure and cloudy vision.[17] In the hierarchy of souls we can broadly distinguish three grades: the pure intelligences of the astral spheres, who have no need of physical organs; the souls of brutes, immersed in matter, and no better than a mode of it; the souls of men, which occupy a middle place, requiring matter as the object of their thought, but rising by speculation above it. Even so within the mind of man we may discern a triple series: the factive, practical, and speculative intellects. The first subserves utility; man shares it with the brutes. The third enables him to lift himself toward God. The second is essentially human; he uses it in moral action, and performs his duty by obeying it. Both the sensitive soul and the intellect are material in the full sense of extension.[18] To conceive of them otherwise is contradictory to reason and to Aristotle. It is therefore impossible to hold that either soul or intellect, although the latter has certain affinities to imperishable intelligence, should survive the body. The senses supply the object of thought; the phantasms dealt with by the intellect depend upon the physical organs: abstract these, and where is the cogitative faculty? Having thus attempted to demonstrate the mortality of the human soul, Pomponazzi feels bound to attack the problem of the final end of human beings. Hitherto, throughout the ages of Christianity, men had lived on this world with eternity in view. That was their aim and goal. He has removed this object; and he anticipates hostile argument by affirming that virtue itself is the proper end of man on earth. The practical intellect is the attribute of humanity as distinguished both from the brutes and from the separate intelligences of the spheres. To act in accordance with the nature of this specific quality—in other words, to follow virtue—is the end of man. Virtue is her own reward, as vice is its own punishment.[19] The question whether the soul be mortal or immortal, whether we have a right to expect future judgment or not, has really nothing to do with

[16] Cap. viii. 'Vixque sit umbra intellectûs.' Again, cap. ix.: 'Cum ipsa sit materialium nobilissima, in confinioque immaterialium, aliquid immaterialitatis odorat, sed non simpliciter.'

[17] See (cap. viii.) the passage which begins 'Secundò quia cum in ista essentia.'

[18] See the passages quoted above; and compare *De Nutritione*, lib. i. cap. 11, which contains Pomponazzi's most mature opinion on the material extension of the soul, which he calls, in all its faculties, *realiter extensa*.

[19] *De Immortalitate*, cap. xiv. After demonstrating that the *intellectus practicus*, as distinguished from the *speculativus* and the *factivus*, is the special property of man, and that consequently in Ethics we have the true science of humanity, he lays down and tries to demonstrate the two positions that (1) 'præmium essentiale virtutis est ipsamet virtus quæ hominem felicem facit;' (2) 'pœna vitiosi est ipsum vitium, quo nihil miserius, nihil infelicius esse potest.'

the matter.[20] With this ethical conclusion Pomponazzi terminates his argument. He is careful, however, to note that though he disbelieves in the immortality of the soul as a philosopher, he accepts it in the fullest sense as a Christian.[21] It has been suggested that the orthodox doctrine of the resurrection of the body might have supplied Pomponazzi with a link between science and faith.[22] However, he did not avail himself of it; and his philosophy stands in abrupt and open conflict with his creed.

The treatise 'De Incantatione' presents the same antithesis between Peripatetic science and Christian faith. Pomponazzi composed it at the instance of a physician, his friend, who begged him to offer an explanation of some apparently supernatural phenomena. It is, in fact, an essay upon demons and miracles. As a philosopher, Pomponazzi stoutly rejects both. The order of nature cannot be interrupted. Angels and devils only exist in the popular imagination. Miracles are but imperfectly comprehended manifestations of natural forces, which the vulgar ascribe to the intervention of God or spirits.[23] Each religion has its own miracles and its own saints, to whom the common folk attribute supernatural power.[24] But Moses, Mahomet and Christ stand upon the same level; the thaumaturgists of every creed are equally unable to alter the universal order.[25] Credulity and ignorance ascribe to all of them faculties they cannot possess. Having, as a philosopher, expressed these revolutionary ideas, as a Christian, he briefly and summarily states his belief in all that he has just denied.[26]

Basing his argument upon the ground of reason, which, for him, was no other than the Aristotelian doctrine of the Cosmos, Pomponazzi recognises no agency that interrupts the sequence of cause and effect in nature. But the astral intelligences are realities, and their operation has been as clearly ascertained as that of any other natural force. Therefore Pomponazzi refers to the planets many extraordinary exhibitions of apparently abnormal power, conceding upon this point as much as could have been desired by the most superstitious of his contemporaries. Not only are the lives of men subject to planetary influence; but all human institutions rise, flourish and decay in obedience to the same superior laws. Even religions have their day of inevitable decline, and Christianity is no exception to the general rule. At the present moment, says Pomponazzi, we may discern signs of approaching dissolution in the fabric of our creed.[27] He is careful to add, as

[20] For this argument he refers to Plato in cap. xiv.: 'Sive animus mortalis sit, sive immortalis, nihilominus contemnenda est mors, neque alio pacto declinandum est a virtute quicquid accidat post mortem.'

[21] See especially the exordium to cap. viii.

[22] Ritter, *Geschichte der christlichen Philosophie*, part v. p. 426, quoted by Fiorentino, *op. cit.*

[23] *De Incant.* cap. 3.

[24] *Ibid.* cap. 4.

[25] *Ibid.* cap. 12.

[26] Peroration of *De Incant.*

[27] *De Incant.* cap. 12.

usual, that he holds this doctrine as a philosopher; but that, as a Christian, he believes in the permanence of revealed religion. Faith and reason could not be brought into more glaring antagonism, nor is it possible to affirm contradictory propositions with less attempt at reconciliation. Pomponazzi seems determined to act out by anticipation Pascal's axiom, *Il faut être Pyrrhonniste accompli et Chrétien soumis.* What the real state of his mind was, and whether the antithesis which seems to us so untenable did not present itself to him as an anomaly, hardly admits of explanation. A similar unresolved discord may be traced in nearly all the thinkers of this epoch.

It remains to mention one more treatise of Pomponazzi, the 'Book on Fate.' Here he raises the question of human freedom face to face with God and the unbroken order of the Universe. The conclusions at which he arrives are vacillating and unsatisfactory; nor is there much in his method of handling this ancient problem to arrest attention. The essay, however, contains one sentence which deserves to be recorded. 'A very Prometheus,' he says, 'is the philosopher. Seeking to penetrate the secret things of God, he is consumed with ceaseless cares and cogitations; he forgets to thirst, to hunger, to eat, to sleep, to spit: he is derided of all men, and held for a fool and sacrilegious person: he is persecuted by inquisitors; he becomes a gazing-stock to the common folk. These, then, are the gains of the philosophers; these are their guerdons.'[28] Not only were these words spoken from the man's own heart, smarting under the attacks to which his treatise on the soul had exposed him; but they were in a profound sense prophetic. While reading them, we think of Campanella's lifelong imprisonment and sevenfold tortures; of Bruno's death by fire, and Vanini's tongue torn out before his execution; of Galileo's recantation and disgrace; of Carnesecchi, Paleario and Montalcino burned or strangled. A whole procession of Italian martyrs to free thought and bold avowal of opinion passes before our eyes.

Reviewing Pomponazzi's work, we find that, though he occupied for the most part the modest place of a commentator and expositor, he valiantly asserted the rights of reason face to face with ecclesiastical authority. Under the ægis of the formula *salvâ fide*, he attacked the popular belief, disputed the fiats of Church Councils, denied miracles, rejected supernatural causes, and proclaimed that science must be based upon the axiom of an unalterable permanence in the order of the universe. The controversy which his treatise on immortality inflamed in Italy, popularised the two conceptions of God's immanence in nature and of the evolution of the human soul from corporeal organs. In other words it struck a powerful blow at transcendental, extra-mundane speculation, and prepared the way for sounder physical investigations. The positive spirit appeared in Pomponazzi, never thenceforward to be set at rest until the cycle of modern scientific illumination shall be accomplished.

[28] *De Fato*, lib. iii. cap. 7.

The deep impression produced by this controversy on the mind of the Italians, may be illustrated by a little story. Pomponazzi's disciple, Simone Porzio, when invited to lecture at Pisa, opened Aristotle's meteorological treatises at the commencement of his course. The assembly, composed of students and people of the town, who had assembled, as was then the custom, to gaze upon the new professor and to judge his manner,[29] cried in a loud voice: '*Quid de animâ*? Speak to us about the soul!' He had to close his book, and take up the 'De Animâ.' This Porzio frankly professed his belief that the human soul differed in no essential point from the soul of a lion or a plant, and that those who thought otherwise, were prompted by a generous pity for our mean estate.[30] Materialism of the purest water became fashionable, and expressed itself in pithy sentences, which, though devoid of historical accuracy, sufficiently paint the temper of the folk who gave them currency. Of this type is the apocryphal epitaph of Cesare Cremonini, one of the latest of the Italian peripateticians. He died in 1631, and on his grave was said to have been written at his own request: *Hic jacet Cremoninus totus*. To the same Cremonini is ascribed the Jesuitical motto *Foris ut moris, intus ut libet*, which may be regarded as a cynical version of Pomponazzi's oft-repeated protestation of belief in dogmas he had demonstrated contrary to reason.[31] Had it been possible for the Church to continue her tolerance of Leo's age, or had the Counter-Reformation taken a direction less inimical to free inquiry, the studied hypocrisy of this epigram, so painfully characteristic of the age that gave it birth, might have been avoided. The men who uttered it and acted by it, were the same of whom Milton spoke in 'Areopagitica:' 'I have sat among their learned men (for that honour I had), and been counted happy to be born in such a place of philosophic freedom as they supposed England was, while themselves did nothing but bemoan the servile condition into which learning amongst them was brought; that this was it which had damped the glory of Italian wits; that nothing had been written now these many years but flattery and fustian.'

Central and Northern Italy performed the first two stages of Renaissance thought. Florence, true to the destiny which made her artful and form-giving, attempted to restore Platonic philosophy in accordance with the conditions determined by the Middle Ages. Bologna, gifted with a personality no less substantial, adhered to scholastic traditions, but accommodated their rigid subject-matter to the spirit breathed upon them by more liberal scholarship. It remained for the

[29] An interesting description of a humanist opening his course at Padua, and of the excitement in the town about it, is furnished by the anonymous Maccaronic poet who sang the burlesque praises of *Vigonça*. See Delepierre, *Macaronéana Andra*, London, 1862. Above, p. 355.

[30] He makes these assertions in a treatise *De Mente Humanâ*.

[31] In the peroration of his treatise on Incantation, Pomponazzi says: 'Habes itaque, compater charissime, quæ, ut mea fert opinio, Peripatetici ad ea quæ quæsivisti, dicere verisimiliter haberent. Habes et quæ veritati et Christianæ religioni consona sunt.'

South of Italy to complete the work, and to supply the fulcrum needed for the first true effort of modern science. Hitherto, whether at Florence or Bologna, philosophy had recognised authority. Discarding the yoke of the Church, both Platonists and Aristotelians recognised masters, whose words they were contented to interpret. Reason dared not declare herself, except beneath the mask of some great teacher—Plato or Plotinus, Aristotle or Alexander or Averroes. The school of Cosenza cut itself adrift from authority, ecclesiastical or classical. This is the import of the first sonnet in Campanella's series, preserved for us by the fortunate mediation of his disciple, the German with the Italianised patronymic, Tobia Adami:[32]

Born of God's Wisdom and Philosophy,
Keen lover of true beauty and true good,
I call the vain self-traitorous multitude
Back to my mother's milk; for it is she,
Faithful to God her spouse, who nourished me,
Making me quick and active to intrude
Within the inmost veil, where I have viewed
And handled all things in eternity.
If the whole world's our home where we may run,
Up, friends, forsake those secondary schools
Which give grains, units, inches for the whole!
If facts surpass mere words, melt pride of soul,
And pain, and ignorance that hardens fools,
Here in the fire I've stolen from the Sun!

Campanella calls the students of truth back to Nature from the 'secondary schools' of the philosophers, Plato, Aristotle, Thomas of Aquino, or Averroes; who imposed upon their reason by the word 'authority.' In his fifth sonnet he enforces the same theme:[33]

The world's the book where the eternal sense
Wrote his own thoughts; the living temple where,
Painting his very self, with figures fair
He filled the whole immense circumference.
Here then should each man read, and gazing find
Both how to live and govern, and beware
Of godlessness; and, seeing God all-where,
Be bold to grasp the universal mind.
But we tied down to books and temples dead,
Copied with countless errors from the life,—
These nobler than that school sublime we call.
O may our senseless souls at length be led
To truth by pain, grief, anguish, trouble, strife!
Turn we to read the one original!

Tyrants, hypocrites and sophists—that is to say, the triple band of State and Church oppressors, of interested ecclesiastics, and of subtle logicians—have drawn their threefold veil between the human intelligence and the universe, from which alone, as their proper home and

[32] From my *Sonnets of Michael Angelo and Campanella*, p. 119.
[33] *Ibid*. p. 123.

milieu, men must derive the knowledge that belongs to them. Campanella, with the sincerity of one to whom the truth is dearer than his own reputation, yields the *spolia opima* of this latest victory over the strongholds of authority to his master—the master whom he never knew in life, but over whose bier he wept and prayed in secret, hiding the fire of modern freedom and modern science beneath the black cowl of a Dominican friar:[34]

> Telesius, the arrow from thy bow
> Midmost his band of sophists slays that high
> Tyrant of souls that think; he cannot fly:
> While Truth soars free, loosed by the self-same blow.
> Proud lyres with thine immortal praises glow,
> Smitten by bards elate with victory:
> Lo, thine own Cavalcante, stormfully
> Lightning, still strikes the fortress of the foe!
> Good Gaieta bedecks our saint serene
> With robes translucent, light-irradiate,
> Restoring her to all her natural sheen;
> The while my tocsin at the temple-gate
> Of the wide universe proclaims her queen,
> Pythia of first and last ordained by fate.

In these verses, the saint and queen proclaimed by Campanella is Nature. During the Middle Ages truth had seemed to descend as by a sort of inspiration upon man from an extra-mundane God. During the first and second periods of the Renaissance the human intellect repudiated this transcendentalism, but yielded itself, a willing victim, to the authority of books, Plato or Aristotle, and their commentators. Now the mind of man stands face to face with nature, and knows that there, and there alone, is inspiration. The great Baconian secret, the Interrogation of Nature, has been revealed. It is now acknowledged on all sides that not what Telesio or Campanella, or their famous disciple, Bacon, achieved in actual discovery, was noteworthy. But the spirit communicated from Telesio and Campanella to Bacon, is the spirit of modern science. Meanwhile, another native of South Italy, Giordano Bruno, proclaimed the immanence of God in the world, the identification of the universe with God in thought, the impossibility of escaping from God in nature, because nature, realising God for the human soul, is divine. The central conception of the third age of Italian thought, underlying the apparently divergent systems of Campanella and Bruno—the conception, namely, of a real and indestructible correlation between the human spirit and the actual universe, and the consequent reliance of the human consciousness upon its own testimony in the search for truth—contained the germ of all that has, in very various regions, been subsequently achieved by French, Dutch, English, and German speculators. Telesio and Campanella, long before Bacon, founded empirical science. Campanella and Bruno, long before Descartes, established the principle of idealistic philosophy in the self-

[34] *Ibid.* p. 174.

conscious thinking faculty of man. The sensualism of Telesio, the spiritualism of Bruno, and Campanella's dualism, foreshadow all possible sects of empiricists, rationalists and eclectics, which have since divided the field of modern speculation. It is easy enough now to look down either from the height of full-blown transcendental metaphysics or from the more modest eminence of solid physical science upon the intellectual abortions generated by this potent conception in its earliest fusion with mediæval theology. Yet it is impossible to neglect the negative importance of the work effected by men who declared their independence of ecclesiastical and classical authority in an age when the Church and antiquity contended for the empire of the human reason. Still less possible is it to deny the place of Galileo, Descartes, Bacon, Spinoza, among the offspring begotten of the movement which Pomponazzi, Telesio, Campanella and Bruno inaugurated and developed.

Thus, therefore, by the substitution of human for revealed authority; by the suggestion of new and real topics of inquiry, and finally by the repudiation of all authority except that of nature's ascertained laws; by the rending of all veils between the human reason and the universe, the Italian philosophers of the Renaissance effected for Europe the transition from the Middle Ages to the modern era.

What is the link of connexion between Machiavelli and Pomponazzi, the two leaders of Italian thought at the height of the Renaissance? It may be expressed in one formula—a vivid sense of man and the world as they are; or, in other words, positivism. Machiavelli dispenses with Providence, smiles incredulously at Fortune, explains all social and historical problems by reference to the will and thought of men in action. He studies human nature as he finds it, not as it ought to be according to some ideal standard. Pomponazzi shatters transcendentalism at a blow. He proves that there is no convincing argument for immortality. He demonstrates that the end of man is to be found in conduct. He treats religions without exception as transitory institutions, subject to the universal laws of birth and corruption, useful to society in their day of vigour, but destined to succeed each other with the waxing and the waning of the influences that control our globe and all that it contains. On this point Machiavelli and Pomponazzi are in complete accord. Both of them interpret the spirit of their century.

As Machiavellism existed in Italian politics before Machiavelli theorised it, so materialism leavened society before Pomponazzi gave it the consistency of demonstration. The Middle Ages with their political and theological idealism were at an end. Machiavelli and Pomponazzi contemporaneously philosophised the realism on which science was destined to be founded. They were the deicides of elder faiths; the hierophants of a new revelation, as yet but dimly apprehended; the Columbus and Vespucci of an intellectual hemisphere which it remained for their posterity to colonise. The conditions of public and private life in the Italian cities—the decline of religious feeling, the corruption of morality, the paganising tendencies of humanism, the extinction of political activity, the decay of freedom, the survival of the Church and Commune when their work was ended—rendered any such movement as that of the German Reformation wholly impossible. The people lacked the spiritual stuff for it. We have seen that it was chiefly men like Berni and Folengo who gave open utterance to Lutheran opinions; and from sources like those no pure or vivifying waters could be drawn. Italy's work lay in another direction. Those very conditions which unfitted her for a religious revival, enabled her to perform her true mission. It was no slight achievement to have set up the pillars of Hercules for transcendentalism, and at the same time to have discovered the continent of positive science. For the fruits and recognition of her labours she has had to wait. Her history since the date of Machiavelli's death has been obscure until the middle of this century, and in the race of the nations she has been left behind.[35] But the perturbation of the intellectual current caused by the Reformation is now nearly over, and the spirit of modern science still finds itself in harmony with that of the Italian thinkers who gave it earliest expression.

[35] It may be worth reminding the reader that Pomponazzi died in 1525, andMachiavelli in 1527—the year of Rome's disaster. Their births also were nearly synchronous. Pomponazzi was born in 1462, Machiavelli in 1469.

CHAPTER XVII

CONCLUSION

Retrospect—Meaning of the Renaissance—Modern Science and Democracy—The Preparation of an Intellectual Medium for Europe—The Precocity of Italy—Servitude and Corruption—Antiquity and Art—The Italian Provinces—Florence—Lombardy and Venice—The March of Ancona, Urbino, Umbria—Perugia—Rome—Sicily and Naples—Italian Ethnology—Italians Independent of the Empire and the Church—Persistence of the Old Italic Stocks—The New Nation—Its Relation to the Old—The Revival of Learning was a National Movement—Its Effect on Art—On Literature—Resumption of the Latin Language—Affinities between the Latin and Italian Genius—Renascence of Italian Literature combined with Humanism—Greek Studies comparatively Uninfluential—The Modern Italians inherited Roman Qualities—Roman Defects—Elimination of Roman Satire—Decay of Roman Vigour—Italian Realism—Positivism—Sensuousness—Want of Mystery, Suggestion, Romance—The Intellectual Atmosphere—A Literature of Form and Diversion—Absence of Commanding Genius—Lack of Earnestness—Lack of Piety—Materialism and Negation—Idyllic Beauty—The Men of the Golden Age—The Cult of Form—Italy's Gift to Europe—The Renaissance is not to be Imitated—Its Importance in Human Development—Feudalism, Renaissance, Reformation, Revolution.

AT the end of a long journey it is natural to review the stages of the way that has been traversed. We resume the impressions made upon our mind, and extract that element of generality from recollection, which the rapid succession of scenes, incidents and interests denied to the experience of travel. In like manner, those who have been engaged in some historical inquiry, after examining each province of the subject separately, seek a vantage-ground of contemplation, whence the conclusions they have reached can be surveyed in their relation to each other.

What we call, for want of a better name, the Renaissance, was a period of transition from the Middle Ages to the first phase of modern life. It was a step which had to be made, at unequal distances of time and under varying influences, by all the peoples of the European community. Its accomplishment brought the several members of that community into international relationship, and formed a confederation of reciprocally balanced powers out of the Occidental races who shared the inheritance of imperial Rome. At the commencement of this period, the modern nations acquired consistency and fixity of type. Mutually repelled by the principle of nationality, which made of each a separate organism, obeying its own laws of growth according to peculiarities of climate, blood and social institutions, they were at the same time drawn and knit together by a common bond of intellectual activities and interests. The creation of this international consciousness or spirit, which, after the lapse of four centuries, justifies us in regarding the past history of Europe as the history of a single family, and encourages us to expect from the future a still closer interaction of the Western nations, can be ascribed in a great measure to the Renaissance. One distinctive feature of that epoch was, reaction against the main forces of the Middle Ages. And since reaction implies a vivid principle of vitality, we find, in the further progress of this movement, the new ideas of democracy and science counterposed to feudalism and the Church. So vast a revolution as the reconstruction of society upon new bases, could not be effected by any simple or continuously progressive process. The nations educated by the Church and disciplined by feudalism, could not pass into a new phase of being without checks, hesitations, retrogressions, hindrances innumerable. Nor was it to be expected that the advance of each member in the European community should proceed upon an exactly similar method, or with equally felicitous results. It was inevitable that both feudalism and the Church should long remain in liquidation, resisting the impact of scepticism inherent in the Reformation; opposing stubborn resistance to republican energy liberated by the Revolution; crystallising the counter-movement of the modern spirit at one point in monarchical absolutism, at another in Protestant establishments; receding from this rebellious province to fortify and garrison that loyal stronghold; tolerating no compromise here, and there achieving a temporary triumph by transaction with the steadily advancing forces ranged against them. The battle even now is being waged with varying success over the wide field of Europe; and whatever may be our conviction as to the ultimate issue of the struggle, it is impossible to foresee a definite end, or to assign even probable limits to the extent and the duration of the conflict.

Although we may hold the opinion that science and democracy constitute the fundamental points in modern as distinguished from mediæval history, it would be paradoxical to assert that they emerged into prominence during the initial stage of the Renaissance. A common intellectual atmosphere had first to be prepared for Europe. The sense of human freedom had to be acquired by studies and discoveries which made man master of himself and of the world around him. His attention had to be diverted from the life beyond the grave to his life upon this planet. The culture, which formed the great achievement of the Italian Renaissance and which was diffused through Europe, uniting men of all races and all creeds in speculative and literary activity, evoking sympathies and stimulating antagonisms upon vital questions of universal import, was necessary for the evolution of the modern world as we now know it. In many senses we have already transcended the original conditions of that culture. But we owe to it our spiritual solidarity, our feeling of intellectual identity, our habit of pouring convergent contributions from divers quarters into the stock of indestructible experience.

Quickened to livelier consciousness by contact with the masterpieces of antiquity, in the dawn of that new age, the reason rapidly engaged in exploratory expeditions. Both human nature and the material universe presented themselves with altered aspects to thought and senses, which had lain dormant during centuries of incubation. At first, like the blind man of the miracle, the awakening intelligence saw confusedly. It is easy with our clearer vision to despise the hybrid fancies of a time when things old and new were so romantically blent—'the men as trees, walking,' of that inexperienced intuition, the childish science and the scarce-fledged criticism of discoverers, who, while they reached forth to the future, still retained the hold of custom and long reverence on the past. A note of imperfection, vacillation, tentative endeavour, can be traced in all the productions of the Renaissance—everywhere, in fact, but in the fine arts, where a simpler insight and more unimpeded faculties were exercised at that period than the last three centuries have boasted. In another important department the men of that age proved themselves more than merely precocious and immature. The humanistic system of mental training has survived with little alteration to the present day, and still forms the basis of what is called a liberal education.

This transition from the Middle Ages to the modern era, which we designate by the metaphor of Renascence or new birth, made itself first powerfully felt in Italy. Of all the European nations, the Italians alone can boast of a great and uninterrupted history, extending over the twenty-five centuries which are known to us by tolerably trustworthy records. They first gave the civilisation of republican and imperial Rome to the Western world. They formed the Latin Church, and extended the organisation of ecclesiastical Rome to European Christendom. This was their double work in what we call the ancient and mediæval periods. At the close of the latter, they inaugurated the age of culture, science and associated intellectual endeavour, in which we are now living. In Italy the people preserved unbroken memories of their classical past; and, as we have seen throughout these volumes, the point of departure for modern reconstruction was a renewed and vital interest in antiquity. Here, too, the characteristic institutions of feudalism had taken but slight hold, while the secularisation of the Papacy had undermined the spiritual prestige of the Church. Thus the forces to be overcome were feebler in Italy than elsewhere, while the current of fresh energy was stronger.

The conditions under which the Italians performed their task in the Renaissance were such as seem at first sight unfavourable to any great achievement. Yet it is probable that, the end in view being the stimulation of mental activity, no better circumstances than they enjoyed could have been provided. Owing to a series of adverse accidents, and owing also to their own instinctive preference for local institutions, they failed to obtain the coherence and the centralised organisation which are necessary to a nation as we understand that word. Their dismemberment among rival communities proved a fatal source of political and military weakness, but it developed all their intellectual energies by competition to the utmost.

At the middle of the fifteenth century their communes had lost political liberty, and were ruled by despots. Martial spirit declined. Wars were carried on by mercenaries; and the people found itself in a state of practical disarmament, when the neighbouring nations quarrelled for the prize of those rich provinces. At the same time society underwent a rapid moral deterioration. When Machiavelli called Italy 'the corruption of the world,' he did not speak rhetorically. An impure and worldly clergy; an irreligious, though superstitious, laity; a self-indulgent and materialistic middle class; an idle aristocracy, excluded from politics and unused to arms; a public given up to pleasure and money-getting; a multitude of scholars, devoted to trifles, and vitiated by studies which clashed with the ideals of Christianity—from such elements in the nation proceeded a widely-spread and ever-increasing degeneracy. Public energy, exhausted by the civil wars and debilitated by the arts of the tyrants, sank deep and deeper into the lassitude of acquiescent lethargy. Religion expired in laughter, irony and license. Domestic simplicity yielded to vice, whereof the records are precise and unmistakable. The virile virtues disappeared. What survived of courage assumed the forms of ruffianism, ferocity and treasonable daring. Still, simultaneously with this decline in all the moral qualities which constitute a powerful people, the Italians brought their arts and some departments of their literature to a perfection that can only be paralleled by ancient Greece. The anomaly implied in this statement is striking; but it is revealed to us by evidence too overwhelming to be rejected. We must be careful not to insist on any casual link of connexion between the moral and intellectual conditions of Italian society at this epoch. Still we are forced to admit that servitude and corruption are the commanding features of the age in which Italy for the third time in her history won and held the hegemony of the world. In politics, in religion, in ethics, she seemed to have been left devoid of guiding principles; and tragic interest is added to the climax of her greatness by the long series of disasters, culminating in Spanish enslavement and ecclesiastical tyranny, which proved her internal rottenness and put an end to her unrivalled intellectual triumphs.

It has been my object in this work to review the part played by the Italians at the beginning of modern history, subjecting each department of their activity to separate examination. In the first of these volumes I described the social and political conditions under which the renascence of the race took place. In the second I treated of that retrogressive movement toward antiquity, which constitutes the most important factor in the problem offered by that age. The third volume was devoted to the Fine Arts, wherein the main originality of modern Italy emerged. It was through art that the creative instincts of the people found their true and adequate channel of expression. Paramount over all other manifestations of the epoch, fundamental beneath all, penetrative to the core of all, is the artistic impulse. The slowly self-consolidating life of a great kingdom, concentrating all elements of national existence by the centripetal force of organic unity, was wanting. Commonwealths and despotisms, representing a more imperfect stage of political growth, achieved completion and decayed. But art survived this disintegration of the mediæval fabric; and in art the Italians found the cohesion denied them as a nation. While speaking thus of art, it is necessary to give a wide extension to that word. It must be understood to include literature. Nor, in the case of Italy, does this imply an undue strain upon its meaning. The last portion of my work has been devoted to the stages whereby vernacular literature absorbed into itself the elements of scholarship, and gave form to the predominating thoughts and feelings of the people. This process of form-giving was controlled, more or less consciously throughout, by the artistic instincts of which I have been speaking. Thus we are justified in regarding the literary masterpieces of the sixteenth century as the fullest and most representative expression of the Italian temperament at the climax of its growth. The literature of the golden age implies humanism, implies painting. It will be seen that the logic of the whole subject necessitated the reservation of this department for final treatment, and justified a more minute investigation than had been accorded to the rest.

It is not only possible but right to speak of Italy collectively when we review her work in the Renaissance. Yet it should not be forgotten that Italy at this time was a federation, presenting upon a miniature scale the same diversities in her component parts as the nations of Europe do now. If for this reason alone, we may profitably survey the different shares claimed by her several communities in the general achievement.

At the beginning of such a review, we cannot fail to be struck with the predominance of Florence. The superiority of the Tuscans was threefold. In the first place, they determined the development of art in all its branches. In the second place, they gave a language to Italy, which, without obliterating the local dialects, superseded them in literature when the right moment for intellectual community arrived. That moment, in the third place, was rendered possible by the humanistic movement, which began at Florence. The humanists prepared the needful literary medium by introducing classical studies into every town of the peninsula. Without this discipline, Tuscan could not so speedily have produced Italian, or have been so readily accepted by North and South. It may, indeed, be affirmed without exaggeration that, prior to the close of the fifteenth century, what we call the Italian genius was, in truth, the genius of Florence.

What the Lombards and Venetians produced in fine art and literature was of a later birth.[1] Yet the novelists of Lombardy, the Latin lyrists of Garda, the school of romantic and dramatic poets at Ferrara, the

[1] I need hardly guard this paragraph by saying that I speak within the limits of the Renaissance.

group of sculptors and painters assembled in Milan by the Sforza dynasty, the maccaronic Muse of Mantua, the unrivalled magnificence of painting at Venice, the transient splendour of the Parmese masters, the wit of Modena, the learning of the princes of Mirandola and Carpi, must be catalogued among the most brilliant and characteristic manifestations of Italian genius. In pure literature Venice contributed but little, though she sent forth a dictator, Pietro Bembo, to rule the republic of letters at the moment when the sceptre was about to pass from Florence. Her place, as the home of Aldo's Greek press, and as the refuge for adventurers like Aretino and Folengo, when the rest of Italy was yielding to reactionary despotism, has to be commemorated. Of the northern universities, Padua preserved the tradition of physical studies, and Bologna that of legal erudition, onward from the Middle Ages. Both became headquarters of materialistic philosophy in the sixteenth century. The school of Vicenza had flourished in humane letters at the commencement of the epoch. But it declined early; while that of Ferrara, on the contrary, succeeded to the honours of Florence and Pisa. Genoa was almost excluded from the current of Italian culture. Her sumptuous palaces and churches, her sensual unsympathetic painting, belong to the last days of Italian energy. Her few great scholars owed their fame to correspondence and connexion with the students of more favoured districts.

From Romagna, the Marches of Ancona, and the Umbrian cities, more captains of adventure than men of letters or artists swelled the muster-roll of Italian worthies. We must not, however, forget the unique place which Urbino, with its refined society, pure Court, and concourse of accomplished men and women, occupies in the history of Italian civilisation. The position of Perugia, again, is not a little singular. Situated upon the borders of Tuscany and Umbria, sharing something of the spirit of both districts, overshadowed by Papal Rome, yet harbouring such broods of *bravi* as the Baglioni, conferring a tyranny on Braccio and the honour of her name on Pietro Vannucci, this city offers a succession of picturesque and perplexing contradictions. Perugia was the centre of the most religious school of painting which flourished in the fifteenth century, and also the cradle of the religious drama. For the student of Italian psychology, very much of serious moment is contained in this statement.

Rome continued to be rather cosmopolitan than Italian. The power, wealth, and prestige of the Popes made their Court a centre; and men who settled in the Eternal City, caught something of its greatness. There is, however, no reason to recapitulate the benefits conferred by ecclesiastical patronage at various times on fine arts, scholarship, and literature. Rather must it be borne in mind that the Romans who advanced Italian culture, were singularly few. The work of Rome was done almost exclusively by aliens, drawn for the most part from Tuscany and Lombardy.

After Frederick II.'s brilliant reign, the Sicilians shared but little in the intellectual activity of the nation. That this was not due to want of capacity in the people, seems proved by their aptitude for poetry first shown at Frederick's Court, and next by the unrivalled richness of their dialectical literature, both popular and cultivated. Whether the semi-feudalism which oppressed the Southern provinces, checked the free expansion of mental faculty, admits of question. But it is certainly remarkable that, during the Renaissance, the wide districts of the Regno produced so little. Antonio Beccadelli was, indeed, a native of Palermo; but Pontano owned Cerreto for his birthplace. Valla claimed to be a Roman, and Sannazzaro traced his ancestry through Piacenza into Spain. These are the four greatest names of the period when Naples formed a literary centre under the Aragonese dynasty. We have already seen that Naples, though not prolific of native genius, gave specific tone of warmth and liberty to literature. This may be ascribed partly to the free manners, bordering on license, of the South, and partly to the permanent jealousy subsisting between the Kingdom and the Papacy. The *Novella* produced humorous pictures of society at Florence, facetiæ in Rome, but bitter satires on the clergy at Naples. The scandals of the Church provoked the frigid animosity of Florentines like Machiavelli and Guicciardini: in Naples they led to Valla's ponderous critique and Sannazzaro's envenomed epigrams. The sensuousness of Poliziano assumed voluptuous fervour in Pontano's lyrics. Lastly, the Platonic mysticism of Florence, and the Peripatetic materialism of Bologna, ended in the new philosophy of the Calabrian school. This crowning contribution of the South to Italy, this special glory of the sixteenth century, came less from Naples than from minor cities of Calabria. Telesio of Cosenza, Bruno of Nola, Campanella of Stilo, showed that something of the old Greek speculative genius—the spirit of Parmenides and Pythagoras—still lingered round the shores of Magna Græcia. Just as the Hellenic colonists at Elea and Tarentum anticipated the dawn of Attic philosophy, so did those robust and innovating thinkers shoot the arrows of their speculation forward at the mark of modern science.

It is tempting to pass from this review of the Italian provinces to meditations on a further problem. How far may the qualities of each district have endured from remote antiquity? To what extent may they have determined the specific character of Italian production in the modern age? Did the population of Calabria, we ponder, really inherit philosophical capacity from their Greek ancestors? Dare we connect the Tuscan aptitude for art with that mysterious race who built their cities on Etrurian hill-tops? Can the primitive ethnology of the Ligurian and Iapygian stocks be used to explain the silence of the Genoese Riviera and the Apulian champaign? Is a Teutonic strain discernible in the gross humour of the Mantuan Muse, or in the ballads of Montferrat? It would be easy to multiply these questions. But the whole subject of national development is still too obscure to admit of satisfactory answers.[2] All we can affirm without liability to error, amounts to this; that Rome never completely fused the divers races of the Italian peninsula, nor obliterated their characteristic differences. After the dissolution of her empire, we find the Italian provinces presenting local types in language, manners, sentiments, and intellectual proclivities. It is not unreasonable therefore, to conjecture that certain of these differences sprang from the persistence of ethnological qualities, and others from the infusion of fresh blood from without.

The decisive fact of Italian history in all its branches at this epoch is the resurgence of the Latin, or shall we rather say, of the Italic spirit? The national consciousness survived, though dimly, through the Middle Ages; nor had the people suffered shipwreck in the break-up of the Roman power. This was due in no small measure to the fact that the Empire was the creation of this people, and that consequently they were in a sense superior to its fall. Roman civilisation, Roman organisation, Roman institutions, Roman law, were the products of the Italian genius; and when the Roman State declined, the home province suffered a less thorough-going transformation than, to take an instance, either Gaul or Spain. It would be paradoxical to maintain that the imperial despotism exercised a more controlling authority over the outlying provinces than over Italy proper. Yet something of this kind might be advanced, when we reflect upon the self-indulgent majesty of Rome herself; upon the sovereign privileges accorded to the chief Italian cities; upon the prosperity and vastness of Mediolanum, Aquileia and Ravenna. Local ties and local institutions kept a lasting hold upon the ancient no less than the mediæval Italian; and long after Rome became the *colluvies omnium gentium* so bitterly described by Juvenal, the country towns, especially in the valley of the Po, retained a vigorous personality. In this respect the relation in which men of state and letters, like the Plinies, stood on one side to the capital and on the other to their birthplace, is both interesting and instructive. The citizens of the provincial *municipia* gloried in the might of Rome. Rome was for them the fulcrum of a lever which set the habitable globe in movement at their touch. Still the Empire existed for the world, while each Italian city claimed the duty and affection of its own inhabitants. When Rome failed, the cosmopolitan authority of the Empire was extended to the Church, or, rather, fell into abeyance between the Church and the resuscitated Empire. Just as the *municipia* flour-

[2] Those who are curious in such matters, may be referred to the following works by Giustiniano Nicolucci: *La Stirpe Ligure in Italia*, Napoli, 1864; *Sulla Stirpe Iapigica* Napoli, 1866; *Sull' Antropologia della Grecia*, Napoli, 1867; *Antropologia dell' Etruria*, Napoli, 1869; *Antropologia del Lazio*, Napoli, 1873. Also to Luigi Calori's *Del Tipo Brachicefalo negli Italiani odierni*, Bologna, 1868, and a learned article upon this work by J. Barnard Davis in the *Journal of the Anthropological Institute*, Jan. July, 1871. Nicolucci's and Calori's researches lead to opposite results regarding the distribution of brachycephalic skulls in Italy. Nicolucci adopts in its entirety the theory of an Aryan immigration from the North; Barnard Davis rejects it. It seems to me impossible in our present state of knowledge to draw conclusions from the extremely varied and interesting observations recorded in the treatises cited above.

ished beneath the shadow of old Rome, so now the Communes grew beneath the Church and the new Empire. These two creations of the earlier Middle Ages, though formulated and legalised in Italy, weighed less heavily there than on some other parts of Europe. The Italians resisted imperial authority, and preserved their own local independence. The Northern Emperors were never really strong below the Alps except on sufferance and by the aid of faction. In like manner the Italian burghers tolerated ecclesiastical despotism only in so far as they found it convenient to do so. In spite of Gothic, Lombard, Frankish and German attempts at solidification, the cities succeeded in asserting their autonomy. The Italic stock absorbed the several foreign elements that mingled with it. Vernacular Latin, surviving the decay of literature, repelling the influence of alien dialects, prevailed and was the language of the people.

Notwithstanding this persistence of the antique type, the Italian nation, between the ages of Constantine and Frederick Barbarossa, was intellectually and actually remade. It was not a new nation like the English, French or Germans; for its life had continued without cessation on the same soil from a period antecedent to the birth of Rome. It had no fund of myth and legend, embodying its memories in popular epical poetry. Instead of Siegfried, Arthur or Roland, it looked back to the Virgilian Æneas.[3] Still it underwent, together with the rest of Europe, the transformation from Paganism to Christianity. It felt the influences of feudalism, while repelling them with obstinate and finally victorious jealousy. It owed something to chivalry, though the instincts of the race were rather practical and positive than romantic. It suffered the eclipse of antique culture, and borrowed from its conquerors a tincture of their style in art and literature. When these new Italians found a voice, they spoke in tones which lacked the ring of Roman eloquence. The massy fabric of the Roman syntax was dismembered. And yet their speech had more affinity to Roman style than that of any Northern people. The greatest jurists, ecclesiastics and statesmen of the Middle Ages, the interpreters of Roman law, the fabricators of solid theological edifices, the founders of the Catholic Church, the champions of the Imperial idea, were Italians, proving by their grasp of practical affairs and by the positive turn they gave to speculative inquiries, a participation in the ancient Latin spirit.[4] Even when it is least classical, the mediæval work of the Italian genius betrays this ancestry—in Lombard no less than in Tuscan architecture, in the monumental structure of the 'Divine Comedy,' in the comprehensive digest of the 'Summa,' in the rejection of sentimentalism from the

[3] That the *Æneid* was still the Italian Epos is proved by the many local legends which connected the foundation of cities with the Trojan wars.

[4] It is enough to mention a few names—Gregory the Great, Lanfranc, S. Anselm, Peter the Lombard, Hildebrand, S. Thomas Aquinas, Accursius, Bartolus—to prove how strong in construction, as opposed to criticism, were the Italian thinkers of the Middle Ages.

tradition of Provençal poetry, in Petrarch's conception of scholarship, in the sensuous realism of Boccaccio.

The Revival of Learning was the acquisition of complete self-consciousness by this new race, which still retained so much of its old temperament. Ill at ease among the customs and ideals of Teutonic tribes; stubbornly refusing to merge their local independence in a kingdom; struggling against feudalism; accepting Chivalry and Gothic architecture as exotics; without national legends; without crusading enthusiasms; the Italians were scarcely themselves until they regained the right use of their energies by contact with the classics. This makes the Revival of Learning a national, a patriotic, a dramatic movement. This gives life and passion to a process which in any other country, upon any other soil, might have possessed but little more than antiquarian interest. This, and this alone, explains the extraordinary fervour with which the Italians threw themselves into the search, abandoning the new-gained laurels of their modern tongue, absorbing the intellectual faculties of at least three generations in the labour of erudition, and emerging from the libraries of the humanists with a fresh sense of national unity. At the same moment, and by the same series of discoveries, they found themselves and found for Europe the civilisation of the modern world.

It is only by remembering that the Italic races, clogged by the ruins of the Roman Empire, and tardily receptive of Teutonic influences, resumed their natural activity and recognised their vocation in the Revival of Learning, that we can comprehend the radical revolution effected in all departments of thought by this event. In Architecture, the Gothic style, which had been adopted as it were with repugnance and imperfectly assimilated, was at once abandoned. Brunelleschi, Alberti, Bramante, San Gallo, Michelangelo, Palladio, strove, one and all, to effect a right adjustment of the antique style to modern requirements. Foreign elsewhere, the so-called Palladian manner is at home and national in Italy. Sculpture, even earlier than architecture, took and followed the same hint. What chiefly distinguishes the work of the Pisan school from contemporary work of French or German craftsmen is, that here the manner of Græco-Roman art has been felt and partly comprehended. Painting, though more closely connected with Christianity, more perfectly related to conditions of contemporary life, owed strength and vigour in great measure to the same conditions. During the fifteenth century classical influences continued increasingly to modify the practice of the strongest masters. In literature, the effect of the Revival was so decisive as to demand a somewhat closer investigation.

The awakened consciousness of the Italic people showed itself first in the creation of a learned literature, imitating as closely as possible in a dead language the models recovered from ancient Rome. It was not enough to appropriate the matter of the Latin authors. Their form had to be assimilated and reproduced. These pioneers in scholarship believed that the vulgar tongue, with its divergent dialects, had ever been and still remained incapable of higher culture. The refined diction of Cicero and Virgil was for them a separate and superior speech, consecrated by infallible precedent, and no less serviceable for modern than it formerly had been for antique usage. Recovering the style of the Augustan age, they thought they should possess an instrument of utterance adapted to their present needs, and correlated to the living language of the people as it had been in the age of Roman greatness. They attacked the easier branches of composition first. Epistolography and rhetoric assumed the Roman habit. Then the metres of Horace, Ovid, and Virgil were analysed and copied. In the inevitable compromise between classical modes of expression and modern necessities of thought, concessions were always made to the advantage of the former. The Persons of the Trinity, the saints and martyrs of the Church, pranked themselves in phrases borrowed from an obsolete mythology. Christ figured as a hero. The councils of each petty Commune arrogated the style of Senate and People. *Condottieri* masqueraded as Scipio, Hannibal, and Fabius Cunctator. Cecco and Tonino assumed the graceful garb of Lycidas and Thyrsis. So fervid was the sense of national resurgence that these literary conventions imposed on men who ruled the politics of Italy—on statesmen with subtle insight into practical affairs; on generals with egotistic schemes to be developed from the play and counter-play of living interests. When Poliziano ruled the republic of letters, this acclimatisation of the Latin classics was complete. Innumerable poems, reproducing the epic, elegiac and lyric measures of the Romans, poured from the press. Moralists draped themselves in the Hortensian toga. Orators fulminated copious floods of Ciceronian rhetoric. Critics aped Quintilian. Historians stuffed their chapters with speeches and descriptions modelled upon Livy. Pastoral and didactic poets made centos from Virgil. The drama flourished under the auspices of Plautus, Terence and Seneca. Preachers were more scrupulous to turn their sentences in florid style than to clinch a theological argument. Upon the lips of Popes the God of Sinai or Calvary was Jupiter Optimus Maximus. Even envoys and ambassadors won causes for their States by paragraphs, citations, perorations in the manner of the ancients.

This humanistic ardour at first effected a division between the lettered and unlettered classes. The people clung to their dialects. Educated folks despised all forms of speech but Latin. It seemed as though the national literature might henceforth follow two separate and divergent courses. But with the cessation of the first enthusiasm for antique culture, the claims of vernacular Italian came to be recognised. No other modern nation had produced masterpieces equal to Dante's, Petrarch's, and Boccaccio's. The self-esteem of the Italians could not suffer the exclusion of the 'Divine Comedy,' the 'Canzoniere' and the 'Decameron' from the rank of classics. Men of delicate perception, like Alberti and Lorenzo de' Medici, felt that the honours of posterity would fall to the share of those who cultivated and improved their mother tongue. Thus the earlier position of the humanists was recognised as false. Could not their recent acquisitions be carried over to the account and profit of the vernacular? A common Italian language, based upon the Tuscan, but modified for general usage, was now practised in accordance with the rules and objects of the scholars. Upon the briar of the popular literature were grafted the highly cultivated roses of the classic gardens. It was thus that the masterpieces of *cinque cento* literature came into being—the 'Orlando' and the comedies of Ariosto, Machiavelli's histories and Sannazzaro's 'Arcadia'—Tasso's 'Gerusalemme,' and Guarini's 'Pastor Fido,' together with the multitudinous and multifarious work of lesser craftsmen in prose and verse.

Steeped in classical allusion and reminiscence, the form of this new literature was modern; but its spirit was in a true sense Latin. The Italic people had found their proper mode of self-expression, and proclaimed their hereditary affinities to the makers of Roman art. In the history of the Italian Renaissance Greek studies form but an episode. The Platonic school of Florence, the Venetian labours of Aldus, exercised a partial and imperfect influence over Italian culture. They proved more important for Europe at large than for the peninsula, more valuable in their remote than their immediate consequences. With the whole of classic literature to choose from, this instinctive preference of Latin illustrates the point I am engaged in demonstrating—namely, that in Italy the Revival of Learning was a resurgence of the Italic genius modified and formed by Roman influence. True to their ancestry, the Italians assimilated Roman types, and left the Greek aside.

If we pause to consider the qualities of the Roman spirit in art and literature, we shall see in how real a sense the modern people reproduced them and remained within their limits. Compared with the Hellenic and Teutonic races, the Romans were not myth-making, nor in the sincerest sense poetical. In like manner the Italians are deficient on the side of legend and romance. This defect has been insisted on in the preceding volumes, where the practical and positive quality of Italian poetry, its leaning to realism and abstinence from visionary flights of the imagination, have more than once been pointed out. Roman literature was composite and cultured, rather than simple or spontaneous. The Roman Epic was literary; based on antecedent models, and confined within the sphere of polished imitation. The Roman Comedy and Tragedy were copies of the Greek. In these highest departments of art the Roman poets gave new form to foreign matter, and infused their national spirit into works that might be almost ranked with free translations. The same is true of their lyrics. Even the metres in all these species are appropriated. The Italians in like manner invented but little. They borrowed from every source—from the Arthurian and Carolingian romances, from Provençal love-poetry, and lastly in copious quantities from Roman literature. But they stamped their own genius on the materials adopted, retouched the form, and modified the sentiment, converting all they took to their own genuine uses. In this respect the Italians, though apparently so uncreative, may be called more original than the Romans. Their metrical systems, to begin with—the sonnet, the octave stanza, and *terza rima*—are their own. Their touch upon Teutonic legend is more characteristic than the Roman touch on Greek mythology. Dante and Petrarch deal more freely with Provençal poetry than Horace or Catullus with the lyrics of their predecessors. In the matter of dramatic composition, the Italians stand in much the same relation to the Romans as the Romans to the Greeks; and this may be repeated with reference to elegiac and pastoral poetry, and some minor species. The Italic race, in its later as in its earlier development, seems here, also, satisfied with form-giving and delicacy of execution.

If we turn to the indigenous and characteristic qualities of Roman literary genius, we find these reappearing with the force of spontaneity among the Italians. First of all may be reckoned the strong love of country-life which lends undying freshness to Catullus, Horace, and the poetical episodes of Lucretius. This is a no less marked feature of Italian literature. The very best poetry of the humanists is that which deals with villa-life among the Tuscan hills, beside the Bay of Naples, or on the shores of Garda. The purest passages in the *Novelle*, the least intolerable descriptions in the treatises of the essayists, are those which celebrate the joys of field and wood and garden. The most original products of the Italian stage are the 'Aminta' and the 'Pastor Fido,' penetrated through and through with a real love of the country—not with any feeling for Nature in her sublimer and wilder aspects, but with the old Saturnian pathos and fresh clinging loveliness of nature made the friend of man and humanised by labour. The tears shed by Alberti over the rich fields of autumn, as he gazed upon them from some Tuscan summit, seem to have fallen like a dew of real emotion upon the driest places of a pastoral literature which is too often conventional.

Resuming the main thread of the argument, it may be said that the Italians also shared the Roman partiality for didactic poetry. The Latin poems of Poliziano, Vida, and Fracastoro, together with the Italian work of Alamanni, Rucellai, and other authors, sufficiently prove this. Nor does it seem to me that we need suppose these essays in a style of inevitable weariness to have been merely formal imitations of the ancients. The delight with which they were first received and even now sometimes are read in Italy, and the high reputation they have won for their authors, show that there is something in the Italian genius sympathetic to their spirit. One department of their Roman heritage was left uncultivated by the Italians. They produced no really great satire; but, on the other hand, that indigenous satiric humour, inclining to caricature and obscenity, which found vent in the fescennine songs of Roman festivals and triumphs, endured without material change through all modifications of the national life. The earliest monuments of the vernacular literature afford instances of its popularity throughout the Middle Ages. It gave a special quality to the Florentine Carnival; it assumed high literary form in Lorenzo's *Canti* and Berni's burlesque *Capitoli*; it flourished on the quays of Naples, and sheltered at Rome under the protection of Pasquino.

Leaving pure literature aside, we may trace the Latin ancestry of the Italians in their strong forensic bias. Just as the Forum was the centre of Roman, so was the Piazza the centre of Italian life. The declamatory emphasis that spoils much Latin prose and verse for Northern ears, sounds throughout Italian literature. Their writers too easily assume a rhetorical tone, and substitute sonorousness of verbiage for solid matter or sound feeling. The recitations of the Romans find an analogue in the Italian Academies. The colloquial taint of Roman philosophical discussion is repeated in the moral diatribes of the humanists. But with equal justice we might urge that the practical and legal qualities of the Latin race, and its powerful organising faculty, survived, and found expression in the modern nation. The Italians, as we have already said, were the greatest Churchmen, Statesmen, and Jurists of mediæval Europe. They created the Papacy. They formulated the conception of the Empire. They preserved, explained, and taught Roman law. But this element was already worked out and exhausted at the close of the mediæval period. We find it in abeyance during the Renaissance. The political vigour, the martial energy, the cohesive force, the indomitable will of the Romans, have clearly deserted their Italian inheritors. There is a massive architecture, as of masonry, in Roman writing, which Italian almost always misses.

If it were permissible to venture here upon a somewhat bold hypothesis, we might ask whether the Italic races now displayed themselves as they might have been without the centralising and controlling genius of Rome? In the history of the Italian peninsula, can we regard the ascendency of Rome as a gigantic episode? Rome bound the various tribes together in a common system, formed one language, and used Italy as the throne of world-wide empire. But Rome's empire passed, and the tribes remained—indelibly stamped, it is true, with her mark, and subsequently modified by a succession of intrusive incidents—yet yielding to the world in a new form a second crop of flowers and fruitage similar to that which they had borne for Rome. It will not do to press these speculations. They suggest themselves when we observe that, what the Italians lacked in the Renaissance was precisely what Rome, or the Latin confederacy, gave to Italy in the ancient days of her supremacy. It is as though the great Saturnian mother, exhausted by the production of Rome and all that Rome implied through Empire and through Papacy for Europe, had little force left but for amenities and subtleties in modern literature. To the masonry of Rome succeeds the filigree work of the *cinque cento*.

There is no mistaking the positive, materialistic quality possessed by the Italians in common with their Latin ancestors. This, after all is said, constitutes the true note of their art and literature. Realism, preferring the tangible and concrete to the visionary and abstract, the defined to the indefinite, the sensuous to the ideal, determines the character of their genius in all its manifestations. We find it even in the 'Divine Comedy.' Dante's pictures appeal to our eyes; his songs of angels and cries of damned souls reach our ears; he makes us shrink with physical loathing from the abominations of Malebolge, and feel upon our foreheads the cool morning wind of Purgatory. His imaginary world can be mapped out; his journey through it has been traced and measured, inch by inch, and hour by hour. The same realism determined the speculation of the Italians, deflecting it from metaphysics to problems of practical life. Again it leavened their religion. We find it in S. Catherine's visions, in the stigmata of S. Francis, in the miracle of Bolsena. Under its influence the dogmas of the Church assumed a kind of palpability. It was against Italian sensuousness that the finer spiritual perceptions of the Teutonic races rose in revolt; and the Italians, who had transmitted their own religious forms to Europe, could not understand the point at issue. Feeble or insufficient as we may judge this realism in the regions of pure thought or pious feeling, it was supremely powerful in art. It enabled the Italians so to apprehend the mysteries of the faith, and so to assimilate the classic myths, as to find for both a form of beauty in sculpture and in painting. Had they inclined more to the abstract or to the visionary, Christian art would have remained impossible. Had they been less simply sensuous, they might perhaps have shrunk from pagan legends, or have failed to touch them with the right sincerity. How ill these legends fared at the hands of contemporary Teutonic artists, is notorious. In the realm of literature the same quality gave to Petrarch's treatment of chivalrous love a new substantiality. It animated Boccaccio, and through his influence created a literature of fiction, indescribably rich in objective realism and spontaneous passion. Ariosto owed to it the incomparable brilliance of his pictures. And, since such sensuousness has perforce its evil side, we find it, in the last resort, no longer clothing unsubstantial thoughts with forms of beauty, lending reality to the poet's visions, or humanising the austerities of faith, but frankly and simply subordinating its powers to a debased imagination. The Italian sensuousness too often degenerates into mere sensuality in the period of our inquiry. Nor is this the only defect of the quality. When we complain that the Italians are deficient in the highest tragic imagination, that their feeling for nature lacks romance, or that none but their rarest works of art attain sublimity, we are but insisting on the realistic bias which inclined them to things tangible, palpable, experienced, compassable by the senses. How much of tragedy is due to horror the soul alone can gauge; how much of romance depends upon a sense of mystery and unexplored capacities in natural things; how much of the sublime consists of incorporeal vagueness, need not here be insisted on. The sensuousness of the Italians, simpler and less finely tempered with spiritual substance than that of the Greeks, while it gave them so much of serene beauty and intelligible form, denied them those high and rare touches which the less evenly balanced genius of the Northern races can command at will. The poverty of imaginative suggestion in their lyrical and dramatic poetry has been already indicated. We feel this even in their music. The most adorable melodies, poured forth like nightingale songs in the great schools of the eighteenth century, owe their perfection to purity of outline; their magic depends on a direct appeal to sensibility. There is not in them 'more than the ear discovers.' They are not, to quote Sir Thomas Browne again, 'a hieroglyphical and shadowed lesson of the whole world and creatures of God.' Palestrina and Stradella, Pergolese and Salvator Rosa, move in a region less mystical and pregnant with accumulated meaning than that which belongs to Bach and Beethoven.

The intellectual medium formed in Italy upon the dissolution of the Middle Ages was irreligious and indifferent; highly refined and highly cultivated; instinctively æsthetic and superbly gifted, but devoid of moral earnestness or patriotic enthusiasm, of spiritual passion or political energy. Society, enslaved, disfranchised, and unwarlike, was composed of peasants and artisans, sleek citizens, effeminated nobles, courtiers and scholars of a hundred types, monks and clergy of manifold variety and almost incalculable multitude, despots more or less successful in their arts of imposition and seduction, and the countless dependents on the wants and whims and vices of this motley population. Among the last may be reckoned artists of all but the first rank, men of letters, parasites and captains of adventure, courtesans and abbés, pamphleteers and *bravi*, orators and secretaries. Outside the universities, the factories and the market-place, there were few callings that could be reckoned honourable or honest, independent or respectable. Over the rest hung the shadow of servitude and corruption, of ecclesiastical depravity and private debauchery, of political stagnation and haughty patronage. Still the qualities of intellectual sagacity, determined volition, and a certain æsthetical good taste, were all but universal. We find them in such works as Cellini's biography, Lorenzino de' Medici's apology, and the memoirs of his murderer—to mention only documents where the last-named quality might well have been absent. Even the lowest instruments of public or private profligacy maintained an independence face to face with art, and recognised a higher law than their employer's in the duties imposed upon them by the ideal after which they strove as men of letters, painters, or the like. We trace this loyal service and artistic freedom even in Pietro Aretino.

A literature, corresponding to this medium, of necessity arose. It was a literature of form and style, of pleasure and diversion, without intensity of passion, earnestness of purpose, or profundity of thought. It could boast no Shakspere, no Pindar, no Dante, no Descartes. The prevailing types which it developed, were idyllic, descriptive, melodramatic, narrative, elegiac, sentimental, burlesque, and licentious. Poliziano, Sannazzaro, Lorenzo de' Medici, Pulci, the writers of sonnets and *Capitoli*, the novelists and the satirists, are each and all of them related by no superficial tie to Boccaccio. He is the morning star of this multifarious and brilliant band of artist-authors, until the moment when Ariosto rises above the horizon, and the *cinque cento* finds adequate expression in the 'Orlando Furioso.' In that poem the qualities by which the age is characterised, are concentrated, and the advance in artistic faculty and feeling since the period of the 'Decameron' is manifested. Amid the many writers of the century we seek in vain a true philosopher. We have, instead, to content ourselves with the ethical dissertations of the humanists; with sketches like the 'Cortegiano,' the 'Galateo,' the 'Governo della Famiglia;' with erudite fancies like the speculations of Ficino, or the scholastic triflings of Pico della Mirandola. Yet out of the very indifferentism of the age philosophy will spring. Pomponazzi formulates the current materialism. It remains for Telesio, Campanella, Bruno, Galileo to found the modern scientific method. Meanwhile, the political agitations of despotisms and republics alike, and the diplomatic relations of so many petty States, have stimulated observation and developed the powers of analysis. Therefore the most vigorous and virile product of this literature is such work as the 'Pricipe' and 'Discorsi' of Machiavelli, the 'Ricordi' of Guicciardini, together with the histories and reflective treatises on statecraft published by the statists of their school.

The absence of seriousness in the literature of the golden age is striking to a Northern student. It seems to have been produced for and by men who had lost their ethical and political conscience, and had enthroned an æsthetical conscience in its room. Their religious indiffence is deadlier than atheism. Their levity is worse than sarcasm. They fulfil the epigram of Tacitus, who wrote: *corrumpere et corrumpi sæculum vocant.* Yet no one has the vigour to be angry. It is difficult to detect the true note of satire in their criticism of society. Ariosto is playful, Aretino scurrilous, Alamanni peevish, Folengo atrabilious. The purely religious compositions of the period lack simplicity and sincerity. The 'Sacre Rappresentazioni' are sentimental and romantic. The Christian epics of the Latin poets are indescribably frigid. The 'Laudi' are either literary like Lorenzo's, or hysterical like Benivieni's praise of Christian madness. The impertinent biographies of Aretino pass muster for genuinely pious work with Vittoria Colonna. It is only in some heart-felt utterance of the aged Michelangelo, in the holy life of a S. Antonino, or the charity of Luca della Robbia's mission to young Boscoli, or the fervour of Savonarola's sermons, that here and there the chord of real religious feeling vibrates. Philosophy entrenches herself, where she is strongest, in negation—in Valla's negation of any ethical standard superior to sensuous hedonism, in Pomponazzi's negation of immortality, in Machiavelli's negation of Providence. So complete an antithesis to the mediæval ground of thought was necessary; and its results for the future of science are incontestable. But at the moment it meant a withdrawal from spiritual interests, an insistence on the material side of human life, which was correlated to religious indifference and social dissolution.

The drama abounds in comedies and masques, of wonderful variety and great artistic beauty. But there is no tragedy worthy of the name. And the tragic element, as distinguished from romance and pathos, is conspicuous by its absence in the novels of the period. Lyrical poets prefer the conscious shams of Petrarchism to any genuine utterance of emotion. The gravity of La Casa's sonnets, wrenched from an uneasy and unwilling conscience, the sublimity of Michelangelo's Platonic mysticism, the patriotic indignation of Guidiccioni's laments for Italy enslaved and sunk in sensual sloth, must rank as luminous exceptions. In the romantic epic, chivalry, the ideal of an earlier age, is turned to gentle ridicule. Honour is sneered at or misunderstood. The absurd, the marvellous, the licentious are mingled in a form of incomparable artistic suavity. Tasso's graver epic belongs to another epoch. Trissino's heroic poem is unreadable. Like the tragedies of the scholars, it lacks life and stands in no relation to the spirit of the age.

Over the whole art and literature of the epoch is shed an agreeable light of quietude and acquiescence, a glow of contentment and well-being, which contrasts strangely with the tragic circumstances of a nation crumbling into an abyss of ruin. It is not precisely the *bourgeois* felicity of Boccaccio, but a tranquillity that finds choicest expression in the painted idylls of Giorgione and the written idylls of Sannazzaro. Its ultimate ideal is the Golden Age, when no restraints were placed on natural inclination, and no ambition ruffled the spirit rocked in halcyon ease. This prevailing mood of artists and writers was capable of sensuous depth, as in the 'Baiæ' of Pontano. It was capable of refined irony, as in the smile of Ariosto. It was capable of broad laughter, as in the farce of Bibbiena. It was capable of tenderness, as in the *ballate* of Poliziano. It was capable of cynical licentiousness, as in Aretino's 'Ragionamenti,' and the Florentine *Capitoli*. But it was incapable of tragic passion, lyrical rapture, intensity, sublimity, heroism. What ears would there have been in Italy for Marston's prologue to 'Antonio and Mellida' or for Milton's definition of the poet's calling? The men who made this literature and those with whom they lived, for whom they wrote, were well-bred, satisfied with inactivity, open at all pores to pleasure, delighting in the refinements of tact and taste, but at the same time addicted to gross sensuality of word and deed. The world was over for them. The arenas of energy were closed. About the future life they entertained a suave and genial scepticism, a delicate *peut-être* of blended affirmation and negation, lightly worn, which did not interrupt the observance of ceremonial piety. They loved their villa, like Flamminio, Ficino, Bembo, all the poets of Benacus. They spent their leisure between a grove of laurels and a study. They met in courtly circles for polite discourse and trifling dissertation, with no influencing passion, no speculative enthusiasm, no insight into mysteries deeper than the subtleties of poetry and art. Not one of them, amid the crash and conflict of three nations on their soil, exlaimed in darkness, *Imus, imus præcipites!* When the woes of Italy touched them with a shade of melancholy, they sought relief in pastimes or in study. Cinthio, prefacing his novels with the horrors of the Sack of Rome, Bargagli using Siena's agony as introduction to his love-romances, are parables of what was happening in the world of fact and feeling. The portrait of Castiglione, clear-browed, sedate, intelligent, humane, expresses the best men of the best moment in that age. The 'Aminta' is their dream-world, modelled on reality. Vida's apostrophe to *pulcherrima Roma* utters their sentiment of nationality.

There is a beautiful side to all this. It is the idyllic ideal of life, revealed in Titian's picture of the 'Three Ages of Man,' the ideal which results in golden and consummate art, tranquillised to euthanasia, purged of all purpose more earnest than may be found in melodies played beside a fountain in the fields by boys to listening girls, on flute or viol. For this ideal a great future was in store, when the animating motive of idyllic melody expressed itself in the opera music of the eighteenth century, and Italy gave the last of her imperishable gifts, a new and perfect art of song, to Europe. But there is also an ugly side to all this. The ultimate corruption of the age—in its absence of energy, its avoidance of serious endeavour, its courtly adulation, its ruffianism, servility, cynicism and hypocrisy—is incarnated in Aretino. Here the vices of the Italian Renaissance show their cloven hoofs. Through the orange and laurel bowers, flooded with Tintoretto's golden sunlight, grins a bestial all-devouring satyr, a satyr far less innocent or gentle than Greek poets feigned, with a wolf's jaws as well as a goat's legs. And in Aretino is already foreshadowed Baffo, the prurient and porcine Caliban of verse, more barbarously bestial than Venetian Casanova. Meanwhile amid apparent civility of manner, the violent crimes of a corrupt and servile race were frequent. Poisoning and secret assassination, acts of personal vengeance and the employment of hired cut-throats, rendered life unsafe in that idyllic Italy.

The historian of this epoch, though he feels its splendour and would fain bless, finds himself forced to insist upon the darker details of the subject. The triumphal pæan of his opening pages ends, too often for his sympathy, in dissonance and wailing echoes. Yet it would be unjust and unscientific to close on any note of lamentation, when the achievements of the eldest-born of Europe's daughters stand arrayed before him. It has often been said that the Renaissance presents an insoluble problem. Twy-natured and indeterminate, the spirit of the age has been likened to the Sphinx, whose riddle finds no Œdipus. But this language is at best rhetorical. The anomalies and contradictions of a period to which we owe so much of our spiritual and intellectual force, are due to its transitional character. The Middle Ages were closed. The modern world was scarcely formed. This interval was chosen for the re-birth of the Italian spirit. On the Italians fell the complicated and perplexing task of modulating from the one phase to the other.

And, as I have attempted to explain, the Italians were a peculiar people. They had resisted the Teutonic impact of the mediæval past; but they had failed to prepare themselves for the drama of violence and bloodshed which the feudal races played out on the plains of Lombardy. When we say that it was their duty to have formed themselves into a nation like the French, we are criticising their conduct from a modern point of view. Experience proved that their policy of municipal independence was a kind of suicide. But the instincts of clanship, slowly transmuted through feudal institutions into a monarchical system, had from time immemorial been absent in Italy. Rome herself had never gathered the Italian cities into what we call a nation. And when Rome, the world's head, fell, the municipalities of Italy remained, and the Italian people sprang to life again by contact with their irrecoverable past.[5] Then, though the Church swayed Europe from Italian soil, she had nowhere less devoted subjects than in Italy. Proud as the Italians had been of the Empire, proud as they now were of the Church, still neither the Roman Empire nor the Roman Church imposed on the Italian character. Pondering on the unique circumstances of this new nation, unorganised like her sisters, conscious of an immense past and a persistent vitality, shrewdly apathetic to the religious enthusiasms of the younger races, yet obliged to temporise and acquiesce and cloak indifference with hypocrisy, we are brought to feel, though we may not fully explain, the inevitableness of many distracting discords in what was still an incomplete phase of national existence.

As a final consideration, after reviewing the anomalies of Italian society upon the dissolution of the Middle Ages, we are fully justified in maintaining that the race which had produced Machiavelli and Columbus, Campanella and Galileo—that is to say, the firmest pioneers and freest speculators of the dawning modern age—was capable, left but alone, of solving its own moral contradictions by some virile effort. Pioneering energy, speculative boldness, virility of effort (however masked by pedantry and purism, by the urbanities and amenities of polite culture, by the baseness of egotism and the immorality of social decadence), were the deepest notes of the bewildering age which forms our theme. But this freedom from interference, this luck of being left alone, was just what the Italians could never get. The catastrophes of several successive invasions, followed by the petrifying stagnation of political and ecclesiastical tyranny, checked their natural evolution and suspended their intellectual life, before the fruit-time had succeeded to the flower-time of the Renaissance. The magnificent audacity of their impulse fell checked in mid-career. Their achievement might be likened to an arch ascending bravely from two mighty piers, whereon the keystone of completion was not set.

When all her deities were decayed or broken, Italy still worshipped beauty in fine art and literary form. When all her energies seemed

[5] 'Roma, caput mundi,' is a significant phrase. It marks the defect of Italian nationality as distinguished from cosmopolitan empire.

paralysed, she still pursued her intellectual development with unremitting ardour. This is the true greatness of those fifty years of glorious achievement and pitiful humiliation, during which the Italians, like Archimedes in his Syracusan watch-tower, turned deaf ears to combatant and conqueror, intent on problems that involved the future destinies of man. The light of the classics had fallen on their pathway at the close of the Middle Ages. The leading of that light they still pursued, as though they had been consecrated to the service of a god before unknown in modern Europe. Their first and foremost gift to nations who had scourged and slain them, was a new and radiant conception of humanity. This conception externalised itself in the creation of a common mental atmosphere, in the expression of the modern spirit by fine art and literature, in the diffusion of all that is contained for us in culture. They wrought, thought, painted, carved and built with the antique ideal as a guiding and illuminative principle in view. This principle enabled them to elevate and harmonise, to humanise and beautify the coarser elements existing in the world around them. What they sought and clung to in the heritage of the ancients, was the divinity of form—the form that gives grace, loveliness, sublimity to common flesh and blood in art; style to poetry and prose; urbanity to social manners; richness and elegance to reflections upon history and statecraft and the problems of still infantine science. Lastly, whatsoever is implied in the double formula of the discovery of man and of the world—the resuscitation of learning by scholars: the positive study of human motives and action by historians; the new philosophy prepared by speculators of the Southern school; the revival of mathematical and astronomical researches after a sound method; the endeavour to base physical science on experiment and observation; the exploration of the western hemisphere by navigators—all this we owe to the Italians of the fifteenth and sixteenth centuries.

We may allow that their execution of a task so arduous and beneficial was accomplished under conditions of social corruption and political apathy, which somewhat dimmed the lustre of their triumph. It may be admitted that they failed, even in their own domains of art and poetry, to realise the highest possible ideals; and we may ascribe this failure partly to their moral feebleness, which contradicts our sense of manhood. Still these are no reasons why we should not pay the homage due to their achievement. The deepest interest in the Italian Renaissance, the warmest recognition of its services to modern Europe, are compatible with a just conviction that the tone of that epoch is not to be imitated. Such imitation would, in point of fact, be not merely anachronistic but impossible. To insist on anything so obvious would be impertinent to common sense, were we not from time to time admonished from the chair of criticism that a new Gospel, founded on the principles of the Renaissance, has been or is being preached in England. Criticism, however, is fallible; and in this matter its mistake is due to the English incapacity for understanding that scientific curiosity may be engaged, without didactic objects, on moral and historical problems. We cannot extract from the Renaissance a body of ethical teaching, an ideal of conduct, or a discipline of manners, applicable to the altered conditions of the nineteenth century. But we can exercise our ingenuity upon the complex questions which it offers; we can satisfy the passion of inquiry, which prompts men to examine, analyse, reflect upon, and reappropriate the past. We can attempt to depict the period, as we recover a phase of our own youth by recollection, extenuating nothing, setting nothing down in malice, using the results of our researches for no purposes of propaganda, but aiming, in so far as our capacity sustains us, at the simple truth about it.

For a student animated with this passion of curiosity, the Italian Renaissance, independently of any sympathies he may have formed for the Italian people, or any fascination which an age and race so picturesque may exercise, must be a subject worthy of most patient contemplation. As we grow in knowledge, corroborating and confirming those views about the world and man which originated with the new direction given to inquiry in the fifteenth century, we learn with ever stronger certainty, that as there is no interruption in the order of nature, so the history of civilisation is continuous and undivided. In the sequence of events, in the growth of human character, no arbitrary freaks, no flaws of chance, are recognisable. Age succeeds to age; nations rise and perish; new elements are introduced at intervals into the common stock; the drama is not played out with one set of actors. But, in spite of all change, and though we cannot as yet demonstrate the law of evolution in details, we are reasonably convinced that the development of human energy and intellectual consciousness has been carried on without cessation from the earliest times until the present moment, and is destined to unbroken progress through the centuries before us. History, under the influence of this conception, is rapidly ceasing to be the record of external incidents, of isolated moments, or of brilliant episodes in the epic of humanity. We have learned to look upon it as the biography of man. To trace the continuity of civilisation through the labyrinths of chance and error and suspended energy, apparent to a superficial glance or partial knowledge, but on closer observation and a wider sweep of vision found to disappear, is the highest aim of the historian. The germ of this new notion of man's life upon our planet was contained in the cardinal intuition of the Renaissance, when the ancient and the modern worlds were recognised as one. It assumed the dignity of organised speculation in the German philosophies of history, and in the positive philosophy of Auguste Comte. It has received its most powerful corroboration from recent physical discoveries, and has acquired firmer consistency in the Darwinian speculation. Whether we approach the problem from a theological, a positive, or a purely scientific point of view, the force of the hypothesis remains unaltered. We are obliged to think of civilised humanity as one.

In this unbroken sequence of events, a place of prime importance must be assigned to the Renaissance; and the Italian race at that moment must be regarded, for a short while at least, as the protagonist of the universal drama. The first stage of civilisation is by common consent assigned to the Eastern empires of remote antiquity; the second to the Hellenic system of civic liberty and intellectual energy; the third to Roman organisation. During the third period a new spiritual force was evolved in Christianity, and new factors were introduced into Europe by the immigration of the Northern races. The fourth historical period is occupied by the Church and feudalism, the first inheriting Roman organisation, the second helping to constitute the immigrant races into new nationalities. The fifth great epoch is the emancipation of modern Europe from mediæval influences. We may be said to live in it; for though the work of liberation has in large measure been accomplished, no new social principle or comprehensive system has yet supervened. Three movements in the process can, however, be discerned; and these are respectively known by the names of Renaissance, Reformation, Revolution. It was in the first of these three stages that Italy determined the course of civilisation. To neglect the work achieved by Italy, before the other nations of Europe had emerged from feudalism, is tantamount to dropping a link indispensable to the strength and cohesion of the whole chain.

Accustomed to regard the Church as a political member of their own confederation, and withdrawn from the feudal system by the action of their communes, the Italians were specially fitted to perform their task. The conditions under which they lived as the inheritors of Rome, obliged them to look backward instead of forward; and from this necessity emerged the Revival of Learning, which not only restored the interrupted consciousness of human unity, but supplied the needful starting-point for a new period of intellectual growth. The connexion between the study of classical literature, scientific investigation, and Biblical criticism, has been already insisted on in this work. From the Renaissance sprang the Reformation, veiling the same spirit in another form, before the Church bethought herself of quenching the new light in Italy. Without the sceptical and critical industry of the Italians; without their bold explorations in the fields of philosophy, theology and political science; without their digging round the roots of human knowledge; without their frank disavowal of past mediæval transcendentalism; neither the German Reformation nor the advance of speculative thought in France, Holland and England, would have been possible.

To pursue the subject further is not necessary. How the Revolution was linked to the Reformation by the intermediate action of Holland, England and America; and how the European peoples, educated after the type designed by Italian humanists, formed their literatures, built up philosophies, and based positive inquiry on solid foundations, are matters too well known and have too often been already noted to need illustration. It is enough for a student of the Renaissance to have suggested that the peculiar circumstances and sympathies of the Italians, at a certain moment of this modern evolution, forced and enabled them to do what was imperatively demanded for its after progress. That they led the van of liberation; that, like the Jews and Greeks, their predecessors, they sacrificed their independence in the very triumph of achievement; are claims upon our everlasting gratitude. This lends the interest of romance or drama to the doleful tale of depredation and enslavement which concludes the history of the Italian Renaissance.

APPENDICES

APPENDIX I

Note on Italian Heroic Verse

(See Vol. I., p. 855)

THE Italian hendecasyllable is an accentual iambic line of five feet with one unaccented syllable over and included in the rhyme. Thus the first line of the 'Inferno' may be divided:—

Nel mez|zo del | cammin | di nos|tra vita.

When the verse is so constructed, it is said to be *piano*, the rhyme being what in English we call double. When the rhyme is single, the verse is *tronco*, and the rhythm corresponds to that of our heroic, as in the following instance ('Par.' xxv. 102):

Il ver|no avreb|be un me|se d' un | sol dì.

When the rhyme is treble, the verse is *sdrucciolo*, of which form this is a specimen ('Par.' xxvi. 78):

Che ri|fulge|va più | di mil|le milia.

It is clear that the quality of the verse is not affected by the number of syllables in the rhyme; and the line is called hendecasyllabic because *versi piani* are immeasurably more frequent and more agreeable to the ear than either *versi tronchi* or *sdruccioli*.

If we inquire into the origin of the metre, the first remark we have to make is that lines of similar construction were used by poets of Provence. Dante, for example, quotes ('De Vulg. Eloq.' ii. 2) from Bertram:

Non puesc mudar q' un chantar non esparja.

This fact will seem to many minds conclusive on the point in question. But, following the investigations of recent scholars, we find this form of verse pretty generally referred to the watch-song of the Modenese soldiers. Thus Professor Adolfo Bartoli, after quoting two lines of that song,

O tu qui servas armis ista moenia,
Noli dormire, moneo, sed vigila,

adds: 'quì apparisce per la prima volta il nostro verso endecasillabo, regolarmente accentato.' If this, which is the view accepted by Italian critics, be right, he ought to have added that each line of the Modenese watch-song is a *sdrucciolo* verse. Otherwise, the rhythm bears the appearance of a six-foot accentual iambic, an appearance which is confirmed by the recurrence of a single rhyme or assonance in *a* throughout the poem. Still the strong accent on the antepenultimate syllable of every verse is sufficient to justify us in regarding the metre as *endecasillabo sdrucciolo*.

Going further back than the Modenese watch-song (date about 924), the next question is whether any of the classic metres supplied its precedent. By reading either Horatian Sapphics or Catullian hendecasyllables without attention to quantity, we may succeed in marking the beat of the *endecasillabo piano*.[1] Thus:

Cui do|no lep|idum | novum | libellum?

and:

Serus | in cœ|lum red|eas, | diuque
Lætus | inter|sis po|pulo | Quirini.

When these lines are translated into literal Italian, the metamorphosis is complete. Thus:

Cui don|o il lep|ido | nuovo | libretto?

and:

Tardo in | ciel ried|i e di|utur|no serba
Fausto il | tuo aspet|to al pop|ol di | Quirino.

Even Alcaics, unceremoniously handled by a shifting of the accent, which is violent disregard of quantity, yield like results. Thus:

Atqui | scie|bat quæ | sibi | barbarus.

Or in Italian:

Eppur | conob|be ciò | ch' il man|igoldo.

The accentual Sapphics of the Middle Ages throw some curious light upon these transmutations of metre. In a lament for Aquileia (tenth century) we find these lines:

Bella sublimis inclyta divitiis,
Olim fuisti celsa ædificiis.

Here, instead of the Latin Sapphic, we get a loose *sdrucciolo* rhythm. The metre of the Serventese seems built upon this mediæval Sapphic model. Here is an example:[2]

O Jeso Cristo, padre onipotente,
Aprestame lo core con la mente
Che rasonare possa certamente
Un servientese.

[1] See Ermolao Rubieri, *Storia della Poesia Popolare Italiana*, p. 45.
[2] Carducci, *Intorno ad alcune Rime*, p 107.

When the humanistic Italians tried to write Italian Sapphics, they produced a metre not very dissimilar. Thus in the 'Certamen Coronarium':[3]

> Eccomi, i' son qui Dea degli amici,
> Quella qual tutti li omini solete
> Mordere, e falso fuggitiva dirli
> Or la volete

What seems tolerably certain is that the modern Italian hendecasyllable was suggested by one of the Latin eleven-syllabled metres, but that, in the decay of quantitative prosody, an iambic rhythm asserted itself. It has no exact correspondence in any classic metre; but it was early developed out of the accentual Latin measures which replaced quantitative metre in the Middle Ages. Signor Rubieri points out that there may be traces of it in the verses of Etruscan inscriptions.[4] Nor is it impossible that the rhythm was indigenous, persisting through a long period of Græco-Roman culture, to reappear when the rustic language threw out a modern idiom.

[3] *Opere Volgari di L. B. Alberti*, vol. i. p. ccxxv.
[4] See passage referred to above, p. 468, note 1.

APPENDIX II

Ten Sonnets translated from Folgore da San Gemignano

(See Vol. I., p. 871)

ON THE ARMING OF A KNIGHT

I

This morn a young squire shall be made a knight;
  Whereof he fain would be right worthy found,
  And therefore pledgeth lands and castles round
  To furnish all that fits a man of might.
Meat, bread and wine he gives to many a wight;
  Capons and pheasants on his board abound,
  Where serving men and pages march around;
  Choice chambers, torches, and wax-candle light.
Barbed steeds, a multitude, are in his thought,
  Mailed men at arms and noble company,
  Spears, pennants, housing-cloths, bells richly wrought.
Musicians following with great barony
  And jesters through the land his state have brought,
  With dames and damsels whereso rideth he.

II

Lo Prowess, who despoileth him straightway,
  And saith: 'Friend, now beseems it thee to strip;
  For I will see men naked, thigh and hip,
  And thou my will must know and eke obey;
And leave what was thy wont until this day,
  And for new toil, new sweat, thy strength equip;
  This do, and thou shalt join my fellowship,
  If of fair deeds thou tire not nor cry nay.'
And when she sees his comely body bare,
  Forthwith within her arms she him doth take,
  And saith: 'These limbs thou yieldest to my prayer;
I do accept thee, and this gift thee make,
  So that thy deeds may shine for ever fair,
  My lips shall never more thy praise forsake.'

III

Humility to him doth gently go,
  And saith: 'I would in no wise weary thee;
  Yet must I cleanse and wash thee thoroughly,
  And I will make thee whiter than the snow.
Hear what I tell thee in few words, for so
  Fain am I of thy heart to hold the key;
  Now must thou sail henceforward after me;
  And I will guide thee as myself do go.

But one thing would I have thee straightway leave:
  Well knowest thou mine enemy is pride;
  Let her no more unto thy spirit cleave:
So leal a friend with thee will I abide
  That favour from all folk thou shalt receive
  This grace hath he who keepeth on my side.

IV

Then did Discretion to the squire draw near,
  And drieth him with a fair cloth and clean,
  And straightway putteth him the sheets between,
  Silk, linen, counterpane, and minevere.
Think now of this! Until the day was clear,
  With songs and music and delight the queen,
  And with new knights, fair fellows well-beseen,
  To make him perfect, gave him goodly cheer.
Then saith she: 'Rise forthwith, for now 'tis due,
  Thou shouldst be born into the world again;
  Keep well the order thou dost take in view.'
Unfathomable thoughts with him remain
  Of that great bond he may no more eschew;
  Nor can he say, 'I'll hide me from this chain.'

V

Comes Blithesomeness with mirth and merriment,
  All decked in flowers she seemeth a rose-tree;
  Of linen, silk, cloth, fur, now beareth she
  To the new knight a rich habiliment;
Head-gear and cap and garland flower-besprent,
  So brave they were, Maybloom he seemed to be;
  With such a rout, so many and such glee,
  That the floor shook. Then to her work she went;
And stood him on his feet in hose and shoon;
  And purse and gilded girdle neath the fur
  That drapes his goodly limbs, she buckles on;
Then bids the singers and sweet music stir,
  And showeth him to ladies for a boon
  And all who in that following went with her.

THE CRY FOR COURTESY

Courtesy! Courtesy! Courtesy! I call:
  But from no quarter comes there a reply.
  They who should show her, hide her; wherefore I
  And whoso needs her, ill must us befall.
Greed with his hook hath ta'en men one and all,
  And murdered every grace that dumb doth lie:
  Whence, if I grieve, I know the reason why;
  From you, great men, to God I make my call:
For you my mother Courtesy have cast
  So low beneath your feet she there must bleed;
  Your gold remains, but you're not made to last:
Of Eve and Adam we are all the seed:
  Able to give and spend, you hold wealth fast:
  Ill is the nature that rears such a breed!

ON THE GHIBELLINE VICTORIES

I praise thee not, O God, nor give thee glory,
Nor yield thee any thanks, nor bow the knee,
Nor pay thee service; for this irketh me
More than the souls to stand in purgatory;
Since thou hast made us Guelphs a jest and story
Unto the Ghibellines for all to see:
And if Uguccion claimed tax of thee,
Thou'dst pay it without interrogatory.
Ah, well I wot they know thee! and have stolen
St. Martin from thee, Altopascio,
St. Michael, and the treasure thou hast lost;
And thou that rotten rabble so hast swollen
That pride now counts for tribute; even so
Thou'st made their heart stone-hard to thine own cost.

TO THE PISANS

Ye are more silky-sleek than ermines are,
Ye Pisan counts, knights, damozels, and squires,
Who think by combing out your hair like wires
To drive the men of Florence from their car.
Ye make the Ghibellines free near and far,
Here, there, in cities, castles, buts, and byres,
Seeing how gallant in your brave attires,
How bold you look, true paladins of war.
Stout-hearted are ye as a hare in chase,
To meet the sails of Genoa on the sea;
And men of Lucca never saw your face.
Dogs with a bone for courtesy are ye:
Could Folgore but gain a special grace,
He'd have you banded 'gainst all men that be.

ON DISCRETION

Dear friend, not every herb puts forth a flower;
Nor every flower that blossoms, fruit doth bear;
Nor hath each spoken word a virtue rare;
Nor every stone in earth its healing power:
This thing is good when mellow, that when sour;
One seems to grieve, within doth rest from care;
Nor every torch is brave that flaunts in air;
There is what dead doth seem, yet flame doth shower.
Wherefore it ill behoveth a wise man
His truss of every grass that grows to bind,
Or pile his back with every stone he can,
Or counsel from each word to seek to find,
Or take his walks abroad with Dick and Dan:
Not without cause I'm moved to speak my mind.

ON DISORDERED WILL

What time desire hath o'er the soul such sway
That reason finds nor place nor puissance here,
Men oft do laugh at what should claim a tear,
And over grievous dole are seeming gay.

He sure would travel far from sense astray
 Who should take frigid ice for fire; and near
 Unto this plight are those who make glad cheer
 For what should rather cause their soul dismay.
But more at heart might he feel heavy pain
 Who made his reason subject to mere will,
 And followed wandering impulse without rein;
Seeing no lordship is so rich as still
 One's upright self unswerving to sustain,
 To follow worth, to flee things vain and ill.

APPENDIX III

Translations from Alesso Donati

(See Vol. I., p. 928)

THE NUN

The knotted cord, dark veil and tunic grey,
I'll fling aside, and eke this scapulary,
Which keeps me here a nun immured alway:
And then with thee, dressed like a gallant gay,
With girded loins and limber gait and free,
I'll roam the world, where chance us twain may carry.
I am content slave, scullion-wench to be;
That will not irk me as this irketh me!

THE LOVERS

Nay, get thee gone now, but so quietly,
By God, so gently go, my love,
That yon damned villain may hear nought thereof!
He's quick of hearing: if he hears but me
Turn myself round in bed,
He clasps me tight for fear I may be sped.
God curse whoever joined me to this hind,
Or hopes in churls good merchandise to find!

THE GIRL

In dole I dree the days all lonely here,
A young girl by her mother shut from life,
Who guardeth me with jealousy and strife:
But by the cross of God I swear to her,
If still she keeps me pent up thus to pine,
I'll say: 'Aroint thee, thou fell hag malign!'
And fling yon wheel and distaff to the wall,
And fly to thee, my love, who art mine all!

APPENDIX IV

Jacopone's Presepio, Corrotto, and Cantico dell' Amore Superardente, Translated into English Verse

(See above, pp. 35 *et seq.*)

THREE POEMS ATTRIBUTED TO JACOPONE DA TODI

Though judging it impossible to preserve the least part of Jacopone's charm in a translation, I have made versions of the Christmas Carol, the Passion Poem, and the Hymn of Divine Love, alluded to in Chapter V., pp. 35-40. The metrical structure of the first is confused in the original; but I have adopted a stanza which follows the scheme pretty closely, and reproduces the exact number of the lines. In the second I have forced myself to repeat the same rhyme at the close of each of the thirty-four strophes, which in the Italian has a very fine effect—the sound being *ato*. No English equivalent can do it justice. The third poem I admit to be really untranslatable. The recurrences of strong vowelled endings in *ore, are, ezza, ate* cannot be imitated.

THE PRESEPIO

By thy great and glorious merit,
Mary, Mother, Maid!
In thy firstling, new-born child
All our life is laid.

That sweet smiling infant child,
Born for us, I wis;
That majestic baby mild,
Yield him to our kiss!
Clasping and embracing him,
We shall drink of bliss.
Who could crave a deeper joy?—
Purer none was made.

For thy beauteous baby boy
We a-hungered burn;
Yea, with heart and soul of grace
Long for him and yearn.
Grant us then this prayer; his face
Toward our bosom turn:
Let him keep us in his care,
On his bosom stayed!

Mary in the manger where
Thou hast strewn his nest,
With thy darling baby we
Fain would dwell at rest.
Those who cannot take him, see,
Place him on their breast!
Who shall be so rude and wild
As to spurn thee, Maid?

Come and look upon her child
Nestling in the hay!
See his fair arms opened wide,
On her lap to play!
And she tucks him by her side,
Cloaks him as she may;
Gives her paps unto his mouth,
Where his lips are laid.

For the little babe had drouth,
Sucked the breast she gave;
All he sought was that sweet breast,
Broth he did not crave;
With his tiny mouth he pressed,
Tiny mouth that clave:
Ah, the tiny baby thing,
Mouth to bosom laid!

She with left hand cradling
Rocked and hushed her boy,
And with holy lullabies
Quieted her toy.
Who so churlish but would rise
To behold heaven's joy
Sleeping?—In what darkness drowned
Dead and renegade?—

Little angels all around
Danced, and carols flung;
Making verselets sweet and true,
Still of love they sung;
Calling saints and sinners too
With love's tender tongue;
Now that heaven's high glory is
On this earth displayed.

Choose we gentle courtesies,
Churlish ways forswear
Let us one and all behold
Jesus sleeping there.
Earth, air, heaven he will unfold,
Flowering, laughing fair;
Such a sweetness, such a grace
From his eyes hath rayed.

O poor humble human race,
How uplift art thou!
With the divine dignity
Re-united now!
Even the Virgin Mary, she
All amazed doth bow;
And to us who sin inherit,
Seems as though she prayed.

By thy great and glorious merit,
Mary, Mother, Maid!
In thy firstling, new-born child
All our life is laid.

THE CORROTTO

Messenger. Lady of Paradise, woe's me,
Thy son is taken, even he,
Christ Jesus, that saint blessed!
Run, Lady, look amain
How the folk him constrain:
Methinks they him have slain,
Sore scourged, with rods opprest.

Mary. Nay, how could this thing be?
To folly ne'er turned he,
Jesus, the hope of me:
How did they him arrest?

Messenger. Lady, he was betrayed;
Judas sold him, and bade
Those thirty crowns be paid—
Poor gain, where bad is best.

Mary. Ho, succour! Magdalen!
The storm is on me: men
My own son, Christ, have ta'en!
This news hath pierced my breast.

Messenger. Aid, Lady! Up and run!
They spit upon thy son,
And hale him through the town;
To Pilate they him wrest.

Mary. O Pilate, do not let
My son to pain be set!
That he is guiltless, yet
With proofs I can protest.

The Jews. Crucify! Crucify!
Who would be King, must die.
He spurns the Senate by
Our laws, as these attest.
We'll see if, stanch of state,
He can abide this fate
Die shall he at the gate,
And Barab be redressed.

Mary. I pray thee, hear my prayer!
Think on my pain and care!
Perchance thou then wilt bear
New thoughts and change thy quest.

The Jews. Bring forth the thieves, for they
Shall walk with him this day:
Crown him with thorns, and say
He was made king in jest.

Mary. O Son, Son, Son, dear Son!
O Son, my lovely Son!
Son, who shall shed upon
My anguished bosom rest?

O jocund eyes, sweet Son!
Why art Thou silent? Son!
Son, wherefore dost Thou shun
This thy own mother's breast?

Messenger. Lady, behold the tree!
The people bring it, see
Where the true Light must be
Lift up at man's behest!

Mary. O cross, what wilt thou do?
Wilt thou my Son undo?
Him will they fix on you,
Him who hath ne'er transgressed?

Messenger. Up, full of grief and bale!
They strip thy son, and rail;
The folk are fain to nail
Him on yon cross they've dressed.

Mary. If ye his raiment strip,
I'll see him, breast and hip!
Lo, how the cruel whip
Hath bloodied back and chest!

Messenger. Lady, his hand outspread
Unto the cross is laid:
'Tis pierced; the huge nail's head
Down to the wood they've pressed.

They seize his other hand,
And on the tree expand:
His pangs are doubled and
Too keen to be expressed!

Lady, his feet they take,
And pin them to the stake,
Rack every joint, and make
Each sinew manifest!

Mary. I now the dirge commence.
Son, my life's sole defence!
Son, who hath torn thee hence?
Sweet Son, my Son caressed!

Far better done had they
My heart to pluck away,
Than by thy cross to lay
Of thee thus dispossessed!

Christ. Mother, why weepst thou so?
Thou dealest me death's blow.
To watch thy tears, thy woe
Unstinted, tears my breast.

Mary. Son, who hath twinned us two?
Son, father, husband true!
Son, who thy body slew?
Son, who hath thee suppressed?

Christ. Mother, why wail and chide?
I will thou shouldst abide,
And serve those comrades tried
I saved amid the rest.

Mary. Son, say not this to me!
Fain would I hang with thee
Pierced on the cross, and be
By thy side dying blessed!
One grave should hold us twain,
Son of thy mother's pain!
Mother and Son remain
By one same doom oppressed!

Christ. Mother, heart-full of woe,
I bid thee rise and go
To John, my chosen!—so
Is he thy son confessed.
John, this my mother see:
Take her in charity:
Cherish her piteously:
The sword hath pierced her breast.

Mary. Son! Ah, thy soul hath flown!
Son of the woman lone!
Son of the overthrown!
Son, poisoned by sin's pest!
Son of white ruddy cheer!
Son without mate or peer!
Son, who shall help me here,
Son, left by thee, distressed!
Son, white and fair of face!
Son of pure jocund grace!
Son, why did this wild place,
This world, Son, thee detest?
Son, sweet and pleasant Son!
Son of the sorrowing one!
Son, why hath thee undone
To death this folk unblessed?
John, my new son, behold
Thy brother he is cold!
I feel the sword foretold,
Which prophecies attest.
Lo, Son and mother slain!
Dour death hath seized the twain:
Mother and Son, they strain
Upon one cross embraced.

Here the miserable translation ends. But I would that I could summon from the deeps of memory some echo of the voice I heard at Perugia, one dark Good Friday evening, singing Penitential Psalms. This made me feel of what sort was the 'Corrotto,' chaunted by the confraternities of Umbria. The psalms were sung on that occasion to a monotonous rhythm of melodiously simple outline by three solo voices in turn—soprano, tenor, and bass. At the ending of each psalm a candle before the high-altar was extinguished, until all light and hope and spiritual life went out for the damned soul. The soprano, who sustained the part of pathos, had the fulness of a powerful man's chest and larynx, with the pitch of a woman's and the timbre of a boy's voice. He seemed able to do what he chose in prolonging and sustaining notes, with wonderful effects of *crescendo* and *diminuendo*, passing from the wildest and most piercing *forte* to the tenderest *pianissimo*. He was hidden in the organ-loft: and as he sang, the organist sustained his cry with long-drawn shuddering chords and deep groans of the diapason. The whole church throbbed with the vibrations of the rising, falling melody; and the emotional thrill was as though Christ's or Mary's soul were speaking through the darkness to our hearts. I never elsewhere heard a soprano of this sort sing in tune so perfect or with so pure an intonation. The dramatic effect produced by the contrast between this soprano and the bass and tenor was simple but exceedingly striking. Englishmen, familiar with cathedral music, may have derived a somewhat similar impression from the more complex Motett of Mendelssohn upon Psalm xxii. I think that when the Umbrian Laud began to be dramatic, the parts in such a hymn as Jacopone's 'Corrotto' must have been distributed after the manner of these Perugian Good Friday services. Mary's was undoubtedly given to the soprano; that of the Jews, possibly, to the bass; Christ's, and perhaps the messenger's also, to the tenor. And it is possible that the rhythm was almost identical with what I heard; for that had every mark of venerable antiquity and popular sincerity.

I now pass to the Hymn of Divine Love, which Tresatti entitles 'Cantico dell' Amore Superardente' (Book vi. 16). It consists of three hundred and seventy lines, all of which I have translated, though I content myself here with some extracts:

O Love of Charity!
Why didst thou so wound me?
Why breaks my heart through thee,
My heart which burns with Love?

It burns and glows and finds no place to stay;
It cannot fly, for it is bound so tight;
It melts like wax before the flame away;
Living, it dies; swoons, faints, dissolves outright;
Prays for the force to fly some little way;
Finds itself in the furnace fiery-white;
Ah me, in this sore plight,
Who, what consumes my breath?
Ah, thus to live is death!
So swell the flames of Love.

Or ere I tasted Jesus, I besought
To love him, dreaming pure delights to prove,
And dwell at peace 'mid sweet things honey-fraught,
Far from all pain on those pure heights above:
Now find I torment other than I sought;
I knew not that my heart would break for love!
There is no image of
The semblance of my plight!
I die, drowned in delight,
And live heart-lost in Love!

Lost is my heart and all my reason gone,
My will, my liking, and all sentiment;
Beauty is mere vile mud for eyes to shun;
Soft cheer and wealth are nought but detriment;
One tree of love, laden with fruit, but one,
Fixed in my heart, supplies me nourishment:
Hourly therefrom are sent,
With force that never tires
But varies still, desires,
Strength, sense, the gifts of Love.

. . . . . .

Let none rebuke me then, none reprehend,
If love so great to madness driveth me!
What heart from love her fortress shall defend?
So thralled, what heart from love shall hope to flee?
Think, how could any heart not break and rend,
Or bear this furnace-flame's intensity?—
Could I but only be
Blest with some soul that knows,
Pities and feels the woes
Which whelm my heart with Love!

Lo, heaven, lo, earth cries out, cries out for aye,
And all things cry that I must love even thus!
Each calls:—With all thy heart to that Love fly,
Loving, who strove to clasp thee, amorous;
That Love who for thy love did seek and sigh,
To draw thee up to him, He fashioned us!—
Such beauty luminous,
Such goodness, such delight,
Flows from that holy light,
Beams on my soul from Love!

. . . . . .

For thee, O Love, I waste, swooning away!
I wander calling loud with thee to be!
When thou departest, I die day by day;
I groan and weep to have thee close to me:
When thou returnest, my heart swells; I pray
To be transmuted utterly in thee!
Delay not then!—Ah me!
Love deigns to bring me grace!
Binds me in his embrace,
Consumes my heart with Love!

. . . . . .

Love, Love, thou hast me smitten, wounded sore!
No speech but Love, Love, Love! can I deliver!
Love, I am one with thee, to part no more!
Love, Love, thee only shall I clasp for ever!
Love, Love, strong Love, thou forcest me to soar
Heavenward! my heart expands; with love I quiver;
For thee I swoon and shiver,
Love, pant with thee to dwell!
Love, if thou lovest me well,
Oh, make me die of Love!

Love, Love Love, Jesus, I have scaped the seas!
Love Love, Love, Jesus, thou hast guided me!
Love, Love, Love, Jesus, give me rest and peace!
Love, Love, Love, Jesus, I'm inflamed by thee!
Love, Love, Love, Jesus! From wild waves release!
Make me, Love, dwell for ever clasped with thee!
And be transformed in thee,
In truest charity,
In highest verity,
Of pure transmuted Love!

Love, Love, Love, Love, the worlds exclaim and cry!
Love, Love, Love, Love each thing this cry returns!
Love, Love, Love, Love, thou art so deep, so high;
Whoso clasps thee, for thee more madly yearns!
Love, Love, thou art a circle like the sky;
Who enters, with thy love for ever burns!
Web, woof, art thou; he learns,
Who clothes himself with thee,
Such sweetness, suavity,
That still he shouts, Love, Love.

Love, Love, Love, Love, thou giv'st me such strong pain!
Love, Love, Love, Love, how shall I bear this ache?
Love, Love, Love, Love, thou fill'st my heart amain!
Love, Love, Love, Love, I feel my heart must break!
Love, Love, Love, Love thou dost me so constrain!
Love, Love, Love, Love, absorb me for Love's sake!
Love-languor, sweet to take!
Love, my Love amorous!
Love, my delicious!
Swallow my soul in Love!

Love, Love, Love, Love, my heart it is so riven!
Love, Love, Love, Love, what wounds I feel, what bliss!
Love, Love, Love, Love, I'm drawn and rapt to heaven!
Love, Love, I'm ravished by thy beauteousness!
Love, Love, life's nought, for less than nothing given!
Love, Love, the other life is one with this!
Thy love the soul's life is!
To leave thee were death's anguish!
Thou mak'st her swoon and languish,
Clasped, overwhelmed in Love!

Love, Love, Love, Love, O Jesus amorous!
Love, Love, fain would I die embracing Thee!
Love, Love, Love, Love, O Jesus my soul's Spouse!
Love, Love, Love, Love, death I demand of thee!
Love, Love, Love, Love, Jesus, my lover, thus
Resume me, let me be transformed in thee!
Where am I? Love! Ah me!
Jesus, my hope! in thee
Engulf me, whelm in Love!

APPENDIX V

Passages translated from the Morgante Maggiore of Pulci

(See above, p. 124 *et seq.*) Morgante xviii. 115

Answered Margutte: 'Friend, I never boasted:
I don't believe in black more than in blue,
But in fat capons, boiled, or may be roasted;
And I believe sometimes in butter too,
In beer and must, where bobs a pippin toasted;
Sharp liquor more than sweet I reckon true;
But mostly to old wine my faith I pin,
And hold him saved who firmly trusts therein.

'I believe in the tartlet and the tart;
One is the mother, t'other is her son:
The perfect paternoster is a part
Of liver, fried in slips, three, two, or one;
Which also from the primal liver start:
And since I'm dry, and fain would swill a tun,
If Mahomet forbids the juice of grape,
I reckon him a nightmare, phantom, ape.

'Apollo's nought but a delirious vision,
And Trivigant perchance a midnight spectre:
Faith, like the itch, is catching; what revision
This sentence needs, you'll make, nor ask the rector:
To waste no words, you may without misprision.
Dub me as rank a heretic as Hector:
I don't disgrace my lineage, nor indeed
Am I the cabbage-ground for any creed.

'Faith's as man gets it, this, that, or another!
See then what sort of creed I'm bound to follow:
For you must know a Greek nun was my mother,
My sire at Brusa, 'mid the Turks, a mollah;
I played the rebeck first, and made a pother
About the Trojan war, flattered Apollo,
Praised up Achilles, Hector, Helen fair,
Not once, but twenty thousand times, I swear.

'Next, growing weary of my light guitar,
I donned a military bow and quiver;
One day within the mosque I went to war,
And shot my grave old daddy through the liver:
Then to my loins I girt this scimitar,
And journeyed forth o'er sea, land, town, and river,
Taking for comrades in each holy work
The congregated sins of Greek and Turk.

'That's much the same as all the sins of hell!
I've seventy-seven at least about me, mortal;
Summer and winter in my breast they swell:
Guess now how many venial crowd the portal!
'Twere quite impossible, I know full well,
If the world never ended, to report all
The crimes I've done in this one life alone;
Each item too is catalogued and known.

'I pray you listen for one little minute;
The skein shall be unravelled in a trice:—
When I've got cash, I'm gay as any linnet,
Cast with who calls, cut cards, and fling the dice;
All times, all places, or the devil's in it,
Serve me for play; I've spent on this one vice
Fame, fortune—staked my coat, my shirt, my breeches;
I hope this specimen will meet your wishes.

'Don't ask what juggler's tricks I teach the boxes!
Or whether sizes serve me when I call,
Or jumps an ace up!—Foxes pair with foxes;
The same pitch tars our fingers, one and all!—
Perhaps I don't know how to fleece the doxies?
Perhaps I can't cheat, cozen, swindle, bawl?
Perhaps I never learned to patter slang?—
I know each trick, each turn, and lead the gang.

'Gluttony after gambling 's my prime pleasure.
Here it behoves one to be learned and wise,
To gauge the merits and the virtues measure
Of pheasant, partridge, fowl; with practised eyes
Noting each part of every dish at leisure,
Seeking where tender slice or morsel lies;
And since I've touched upon this point, I'll tell ye
How best to grease your jaws and stuff your belly.

'If I could only show you how I baste,
If you could see me turn the spit and ladle,
You'd swear I had a most consummate taste!—
Of what ingredients are black-puddings made all?
Not to be burned, and not to run to waste,
Not over-hot nor frozen in the cradle,
Done to a turn, juicy, not bathed in butter,
Smooth, plump and swelling!—Don't you hear 'em sputter?

'About fried liver now receive my say:
It wants five pieces—count them on your fingers;
It must be round—keep this in mind, I pray!—
Fire on this side or that the frying injures!
Be careful not to brush the fat away,
Which keeps the stew soft while it drops and lingers;
You must divide it in two parts, and see
That each part is apportioned equally.

'It should not be too large; but there's a saw—
Stint not your bag-pudding of hose and jacket:
Now mark me, for I'm laying down the law—
Don't overcook the morsel in the packet;
It ought to melt, midway twixt done and raw,

Like a ripe autumn fig, when you attack it:
Serve it up hissing, and then sound the tabors
With spice and orange peel, to end your labours!

'I've got a hundred hints to give the wary!
But take it on my word, ragouts and pies
Are the true test of science culinary:
A lamprey now—you'd scarce believe your eyes
To see its stews and salmis, how they vary!
Yet all are known and numbered by the wise.—
True gourmandise hath seventy-two divisions,
Besides a few that are my own additions:

'If one be missed, the cooking's spoiled, that's granted:
Not heaven itself can save a ruined platter!—
From now till noon I'd hold your sense enchanted
With secrets of my art, if I dared chatter!—
I kept an inn at Corinth once, and wanted
To argue publicly upon the matter.—
But we must leave this point, for 'twill divert you
To hear about another cardinal virtue.

'Only to F these confidences carry;
Just think what 'twill be when we come to R!
I plough (no nonsense) with ass, cassiowary,
Ox, camel—any other beast bizarre.
A thousand bonfires, prisons, by Lord Harry,
My tricks have earned, and something uglier far:
Where my head will not pass, I stick my tail in,
And what I like 's to hear the good folk railing.

'Take me to balls, to banquets, for an airing;
I'll do my duty there with hands and feet:
I'm rude, importunate, a bore, and daring;
On friends no less than foes I'll take a seat:
To shame I've said farewell, nor am I sparing
Of fawning like a cur when kicks I meet,
But tell my tale and swagger up and down,
And with a thousand fibs each exploit crown.

'No need to ask if I've kept geese at grass,
Purveyed stewed prunes, taught kittens how to play.
Suppose a thousand—widow, wife, and lass:
That's just about my figure, I dare say.
When mid the women by mishap I pass,
Six out of every five become my prey;
I make the pretty dears so deucéd cunning,
They beat nurse, maid, duenna out of running.

'Three of my moral qualities are these—
Gluttony dicing, as I said, and drinking:
But, since we'll drain the barrel to the lees,
Hear now the fourth and foremost to my thinking.
No need of hooks or ladders, crows or keys,
I promise, where my hands are! Without blinking
I've worn the cross and mitre on my forehead—
No pope's nor priest's, but something much more horrid!

'Screws, files and jemmies are my stock in trade,
Springs, picklocks, of more sorts than I could mention;
Rope and wood ladders, levers, slippers made
Of noiseless felt—my patented invention—
Drowsing all ears, where'er my feet are laid;
I fashioned them to take my mind's intention;
Fire too that by itself no light delivers,
But when I spit on it, springs up and quivers.

'See me but in a church alone and frisky!
I'm keener on the robbing of an altar
Than gaugers when they scent a keg of whisky;
Then to the alms-box off I fly, nor falter:
Sacristies are my passion; though 'tis risky,
With cross and sacring cup I never palter,
But pull the crucifixes down and stow 'em—
Virgins and saints and effigies, you know 'em!

'I've swept, may-be, a hen-roost in my day;
And if you'd seen me loot a lot of washing,
You'd swear that never maid or housewife gay
Could clear it in a style so smart and dashing!
If nought, Morgante, 's left but blooming May
To strip, I steal it—I can't keep from flashing!
I ne'er drew difference twixt thine and mine:
All things, to start with, were effects divine.

'But ere I learned to thieve thus on the sly,
I ran the highway rig as bold as any;
I would have robbed the biggest saint on high—
If there *are* saints above us—for a penny;
But loving peace and fair tranquillity,
I left assassination to the many:
Not that my will was weak—I'd rather say,
Because theft mixed with murder does not pay.

'My virtues theological now smile on!
God knows if I can forge or falsify:
I'll turn an H into a Greek Upsilon—
You could not write a neater, prettier Y!
I gut the pages of a book, and pile on
New rubrics for new chapters, change the die,
Change title, cover, index, name—the poet
Who wrote the verse I counterfeit, won't know it.

'False oaths and perjuries come trickling down
Out of my mouth as smooth and sweet as honey,
Ripe figs, or macaroni nicely brown,
Or anything that's natural and funny:
Suppose they brain some guileless count or clown;
All's one; ware heads, I cry, and pouch my money!
I've set on foot full many a strife and wrangle,
And left 'em in inextricable tangle.

'With ready coin I always square a scandal:
Of oaths I've got a perfect stock in trade;
Each saint supplies my speech with some choice handle;
I run them off in rows from A to Z:
In lying no man holds to me a candle;

Truth's always the reverse of what I've said:—
I'd like to see more fire than land or water,
In heaven and earth nought but plague, famine, slaughter.

'Don't fancy that in fasting, prayer and prate,
Or charities my spare time I employ!
Not to seem stiff, I beg from gate to gate,
And always utter something to annoy;
Proud, envious, tiresome and importunate—
This character I've cherished from a boy;
For the seven deadly sins and all the other
Vices have brought me up to be their brother!

'So that I'd roam the world, cross ban and border,
Hood-winked, nor ever fear to miss my way;
As sweet and clean as any lump of ordure,
I leave my trail like slugs where'er I stray,
Nor seek to hide that slimy self-recorder:
Creeds, customs, friends I slough from day to day;
Change skin and climate, as it suits me best,
For I was evil even in the nest.

'I've left a whole long chapter undiscussed
Of countless peccadilloes in a jumble:
Were I to catalogue each crime and lust,
The medley of my sins might make you grumble:
'Twould take from now to June to lay the dust,
If in this mud-heap we began to tumble;
One only point I'd have you still perpend—
I never in my life betrayed a friend.'

MORGANTE XXV. 119

There is a spirit, Astarotte hight,
Wise, terrible, and fierce exceedingly;
In Hell's dark caves profound he hides from sight:
No goblin, but a fiend far blacker he.—
Malgigi summoned him one deep midnight,
And cried: 'How fares Rinaldo, tell to me!
Then will I say what more I'd have thee work;
But look not on me with a face so mirk!

'If thou wilt do this bidding, I declare
I'll never call nor conjure thee by force,
But burn upon my death yon book, I swear,
Which can alone compel thee in due course:
So shalt thou live thenceforward free as air.'—
Thereat the fiend swaggered, and had recourse
To threatening wiles, and would not yield an inch
If haply he could make the master flinch.

But when he saw Malgigi's blood was stirred,
In act to flash the ring of his dread art,
And hurl him to some tomb by book and word,
He threw his cards up with a sudden start,
And cried: 'Of your will yet I've nothing heard.'
Then Malgigi answered: 'In what part
Are Ricciardetto and Rinaldo now?
Tell all the truth or you'll repent, I vow!'

MORGANTE XXV. 135

Said Astarot: 'This point remains obscure,
Unless I thought the whole night through thereon;
Nor would my best of judgments be secure;—
The paths of heaven for us are all undone,
Our sight of things to be is no more sure
Than that of sages gazing on the sun;
For neither man nor beast would 'scape from Hell,
Had not our wings been shortened when we fell.

'Of the Old Testament I've much to teach,
And of what happened in the days gone by;
But all things do not come within our reach:
One only Power there is, who sees on high,
As in a glass before Him, all and each,
Past, present, and remote futurity:
He who made all that is alone knows all,
Nor doth the Son well know what shall befall.

'Therefore I could not without thought intense
Tell thee the destined fate of Charlemain:—
Know that the air around us now is dense
With spirits; in their hands I see them strain
Astrolabe, almanac, and tablet, whence
To read yon signs in heaven of strife and bane—
The blood and treason, overthrow and war,
Menaced by Mars in Scorpio angular.

'And for thy better understanding, he
Is joined with Saturn in the ascendant, so
Charged with all-powerful malignity
That e'en the wars of Turnus had less woe.
Slaughters of many peoples we shall see,
With dire disasters in confusion flow,
And change of states and mighty realms; for I
Know that these signs were never wont to lie.

'I know not whether thou hast fixed thy thought
Upon those comets which appeared of late,
Veru and Dominus and Ascon, brought
Treasons and wars and strife to indicate,
With deaths of princes and great nobles fraught?
These, too, ne'er falsified the word of fate.
So that it seems from what I learn and see,
That what I say, and worse, is like to be.

'What Gano with Marsilio planned before,
I know not, since I did not think thereon:
But he's the same, methinks, he was of yore;
Wherefore this needs no divination:
A seat is waiting for him at hell's core;
And if his life's book I correctly con,
That evil soul will very shortly go
To weep his sins in everlasting woe.'

Then spake Malgigi: 'Something thou hast said
Which holds my sense and reason still in doubt,

That some things even from the Son are hid;
This thy dark saying I can fathom not.'
Then Astarotte: 'Thou, it seems, hast read
But ill thy Bible, or its words forgot;
For when the Son was asked of that great day,
Only the Father knows, He then did say.

'Mark my words, Malagigi! Thou shalt hear,
Now if thou wilt, the fiends' theology:
Then to thy churchmen go, and make it clear.
You say: Three Persons in one entity,
One substance; and to this we, too, adhere:
One flawless, pure, unmixed activity:—
Wherefore it follows from what went before,
That this alone is what you all adore.

'One Mover, whence all movement is impelled;
One order, whence all order hath its rise;
One cause, whereby all causes are compelled;
One power, whence flow all powers and energies;
One fire, wherein all radiances are held;
One principle, which every truth implies;
One knowledge, whence all wisdom hath been given;
One Good, which made all good in earth and heaven.

'This is that Father and that ancient King,
Who hath made all things and can all things know,
But cannot change His own wise ordering,
Else heaven and earth to ruin both would go.
Having lost His friendship, I no more may wing
My flight unto the mirror, where our woe
Perchance e'en now is clearly shown to view;
Albeit futurity I never knew.

'If Lucifer had known the doom to be,
He had not brought those fruits of rashness forth;
Nor had he ruined for eternity,
Seeking his princely station in the North;
But being impotent all things to see,
He and we all were damned 'neath heaven and earth
And since he was the first to sin, he first
Fell to Giudecca, and still fares the worst.

'Nor had we vainly tempted all the blest,
Who now sit crowned with stars in Paradise,
If, as I said, a veil by God's behest
Had not been drawn before our mental eyes;
Nor would that Saint, of Saints the first and best,
Been tempted, as your Gospel testifies,
And borne by Satan to the pinnacle
Where at the last he saw His miracle.

'And forasmuch as He makes nothing ill,
And all hath circumscribed by fixed decrees,
And what He made is present with Him still,
Being established on just premises,
Know that this Lord repents not of His will;
Nay, if one saith that change hath been, he sees
Falsehood for truth, in sense and judgment blind
For what is now, was in the primal mind.'

'Tell me,' then answered Malagigi, 'more,
Since thou'rt an angel sage and rational!
If that first Mover, whom we all adore,
Within His secret soul foreknew your fall,
If time and hour were both foreseen before,
His sentence must be found tyrannical,
Lacking both justice and true charity;
Since, while creating, and while damning, He

'Foreknew you to be frail and formed in sin;
Nathless you call Him just and piteous,
Nor was there room, you say, pardon to win:—
This makes our God the partisan of those
Angels who stayed the gates of heaven within,
Who knew the true from false, discerning thus
Which side would prosper, which would lose the day,
Nor went, like you, with Lucifer astray.'

Astarot, like the devil, raged with pain;
Then cried: 'That just Sabaoth loved no more
Michael than Lucifer; nor made He Cain
More apt than Abel to shed brother's gore:
If one than Nimrod was more proud and vain,
If the other, all unlike to Gabriel, swore
He'd not repent nor bellow psalms to heaven,
It was free-will condemned both unforgiven.

'That was the single cause that damned us all:
His clemency, moreover, gave full time,
Wherein 'twas granted us to shun the fall,
And by repentance to compound our crime;
But now we've fallen from grace beyond recall:
Just was our sentence from that Judge sublime;
His foresight shortened not our day of grace,
For timely penitence aye finds a place.

'Just is the Father, Son, and just the Word!
His justice with great mercy was combined:
Through pride no more than thanklessness we erred:
That was our sin malignant and unkind:
Nor hath remorse our stubborn purpose stirred,
Seeing that evil nourished in the mind
And will of those who knew the good, and were
Untempted, never yet was changed to fair.

'Adam knew not the nature of his sin;
Therefore his primal error was forgiven,
Because the tempter took him in a gin:
Only his disobedience angered heaven;
Therefore, though cast from Eden, he might win
Grace, when repentance from his heart had driven
The wicked will, with peace to end his strife
And mercy also in eternal life.

'But the angelic nature, once debased,
Can never more to purity return:
It sinned with science and corrupted taste:
Whence in despair incurable we burn.
Now, if that wise one answered not, nor raised

His voice, when Pilate asked of Him to learn
What was the truth, the truth was at His side;
This ignorance was therefore justified.

'Pilate was lost, because in doing well
He persevered not when he washed his hand;
And Judas, too, beyond redemption fell,
Because, though penitent at last, he banned
Hope, without which no soul escapes from hell:
His doom no Origen shall countermand,
Nor who to Judas give what's meant for Judah—
In diebus illis salvabitur Juda.

'Thus there is one first Power in heaven who knew
All things, by whom all things were also made:
Making and damning us, He still was true;
On Truth and Justice all His work is laid:
Future and past are present to His view;
For it must follow, as I elsewhere said,
That the whole world before His face should lie
From whom proceeds force, virtue, energy.

'But now that thou hast bound me to relate,
My master thou, the cause of our mischance,
Thou fain would'st hear why He who rules o'er fate,
And of our fall foresaw each circumstance,
Laboured in vain, and made us reprobate?—
Sealed is that rubric, closed from every glance,
Reserved for Him, the Lord victorious:
I know not, I can only answer thus!

'Nor speak I this to put thy mind to proof;
But forasmuch as I discern that men
Weave on this warp of doubts a misty woof,
Seeking to learn; albeit they cannot ken
Whence flows the Nile—the Danube's not enough!
Assure thy soul, nor ask the how and when,
That heaven's high Master, as the Psalmist taught
Is just and true in all that He hath wrought.

'The things whereof I speak are known not by
Poet or prophet, moralist or sage:
Yet mortal men in their presumption try
To rank the hierarchies, stage over stage!
A chieftain among Seraphim was I;
Yet knew not what in many a learnéd page
Denys and Gregory wrote!—Full surely they
Who paint heaven after earth will go astray!

'But above all things see thou art not led
By elves and wandering sprites, a tricksy kind,
Who never speak one word of truth, but shed
Doubt and suspicion on the hearer's mind;
Their aim is injury toward fools ill-sped:
And, mark this well, they ne'er have been confined
To glass or water, but reside in air,
Playing their pranks here, there, and everywhere.

'From ear to ear they pass, and 'tis their vaunt
Ever to make things seem that are not so:
For one delights in horseplay, jeer and jaunt;
One deals in science; one pretends to show
Where treasures lurk in some forgotten haunt:
Others, more grave, futurity foreknow:—
But now I've given thee hints enough, to tell
That courtesy can even be found in Hell!'

MORGANTE XXV. 282

And when Rinaldo had learned all his need,
'Astarot,' he cried, 'thou art a perfect friend,
And I am bound to thee henceforth indeed!
This I say truly: if God's will should bend,
If grace divine should e'er so much concede
As to reverse heaven's ordinance, amend
Its statutes, sentences, or high decrees,
I will remember these thy services.

'More at the present time I cannot give:
The soul returns to Him from whom it flew:
The rest of us, thou knowest, will not live!
O love supreme, rare courtesy and new.'—
I have no doubt that all my friends believe
This verse belongs to Petrarch; yet 'tis true
Rinaldo spoke it very long ago:
But who robs not, is called a rogue, you know.—

Said Astarotte: 'Thanks for your good will!
Yet shall those keys be lost for us for ever:
High treason was our crime, measureless ill.
Thrice happy Christians! One small tear can sever
Your bonds!—One sigh, sent from the contrite will:
Lord, to Thee only did I sin!—But never
Shall *we* find grace: we sinned once; now we lie
Sentenced to Hell for all eternity.

'If after, say, some thousand million ages
We might have hope yet once to see again
The least spark of that Love, this pang that rages
Here at the core, could scarce be reckoned pain!—
But wherefore annotate such dreary pages?
To wish for what can never be, is vain.
Therefore I mean with your kind approbation
To change the subject of our conversation.'

MORGANTE XXV. 73

What God ordains is no chance miracle.
Next prodigies and signs in heaven were seen;
For the sun suddenly turned ghastly pale,
And clouds with rain o'erladen flew between,
Muttering low prelude to their thunder-knell,
As when Jove shakes the world with awful spleen:
Next wind and fury, hail and tempest, hiss
O'er earth and skies—Good God, what doom is this?

Then while they cowered together dumb with dread,
Lightning flashed forth and hurtled at their side,
Which struck a laurel's leaf-embowered head

And burned it; cleft unto the earth, it died.
O Phœbus! yon fair curls of gold outspread!
How could'st thou bear to see thy love, thy pride,
Thus thunder-smitten? Hath thy sacred bay
Lost her inviolable rights to-day?

Marsilio cries: 'Mahound! What can it mean!
What doleful mystery lies hid beneath?
O Bianciardino, to our State, I ween,
This omen brings some threat of change or death!
But, while he spoke, an earthquake shook the scene,
Nay, shook both hemispheres with blustering breath:
Falseron's face changed hue, grew cold and hot,
And even Bianciardino liked it not.

Yet none for very fear dared move a limb,
The while above their heads a sudden flush
Spread like live fire, that made the daylight dim;
And from the fount they saw the water gush
In gouts and crimson eddies from the brim;
And what it sprinkled, with a livid flush
Burned: yea, the grass flared up on every side;
For the well boiled, a fierce and sanguine tide.

Above the fountain rose a locust-tree,
The tree where Judas hanged himself, 'tis said;
This turned the heart of Gano sick to see,
For now it ran with ruddy sweat and bled,
Then dried both trunk and branches suddenly,
Moulting its scattered leaves by hundreds dead;
And on his pate a bean came tumbling down,
Which made the hairs all bristle on his crown.

The beasts who roamed at will within the park,
Set up a dismal howl and wail of woe;
Then turned and rushed amuck with yelp and bark,
Butting their horns and charging to and fro:
Marsilio and his comrades in the dark
Watched all dismayed to see how things would go;
And none knew well what he should say or do,
So dreadful was heaven's wrath upon the crew.

MORGANTE XXV. 115

I had it in my mind once to curtail
This story, knowing not how I should bring
Rinaldo all that way to Roncesvale,
Until an angel straight from heaven did wing,
And showed me Arnald to recruit my tale:
He cries, 'Hold, Louis! Wherefore cease to sing?
Perchance Rinaldo will turn up in time!'
So, just as he narrates, I'll trim my rhyme.

I must ride straight as any arrow flies,
Nor mix a fib with all the truths I say;
This is no story to be stuffed with lies!
If I diverge a hand's breadth from the way,
One croaks, one scolds, while everybody cries,
'Ware madman!' when he sees me trip or stray.

I've made my mind up to a hermit's life,
So irksome are the crowd and all their strife.

Erewhile my Academe and my Gymnasia
Were in the solitary woods I love,
Whence I can see at will Afric or Asia;
There nymphs with baskets tripping through the grove,
Shower jonquils at my feet or colocasia:
Far from the town's vexations there I'd rove,
Haunting no more your Areopagi,
Where folk delight in calumny and lie.

MORGANTE XXVII. 6

Then answered Baldwin: 'If my sire in sooth
Hath brought us here by treason, as you say,
Should I survive this battle, by God's truth,
With this good sword I will my father slay!—
But, Roland, I'm no traitor—I forsooth,
Who followed thee with love as clear as day!—
How could'st thou fling worse insult on thy friend?'
Then with fierce force the mantle he did rend,

And cried: 'I will return into the fight,
Since thou hast branded me with treason, thou!
I am no traitor! May God give me might,
As living thou shalt see me ne'er from now!'
Straight toward the Paynim battle spurs the knight,
Still shouting, 'Thou hast done me wrong, I vow!'
Roland repents him of the words he spake,
When the youth, mad with passion, from him brake.

MORGANTE XXVIII. 138

I ask not for that wreath of bay or laurel
Which on Greek brows or Roman proudly shone:
With this plain quill and style I do not quarrel,
Nor have I sought to sing of Helicon:
My Pegasus is but a rustic sorrel;
Untutored mid the groves I still pipe on:
Leave me to chat with Corydon and Thyrsis;
I'm no good shepherd, and can't mend my verses.

Indeed I'm not a rash intrusive claimant,
Like the mad piper of those ancient days,
From whom Apollo stripped his living raiment,
Nor quite the Satyr that my face bewrays.
A nobler bard shall rise and win the payment
Fame showers on loftier style and worthier lays:
While I mid beech-woods and plain herdsmen dwell,
Who love the rural muse of Pulci well.

I'll tempt the waters in my little wherry,
Seeking safe shallows where a skiff may swim:
My only care is how to make men merry
With these thick-crowding thoughts that take my whim:
'Tis right that all things in this world should vary;—
Various are wits and faces, stout and slim,
One dotes on white, while one dubs black sublime,
And subjects vary both in prose and rhyme.

APPENDIX VI

Translations of Elegiac Verses by Girolamo Benivieni and Michelangelo Buonarroti

(See above p. 53)

The heavenly sound is hushed, from earth is riven
    The harmony of that delightful lyre,
    Which leaves the world in grief, to gladden heaven.
Yea, even as our sobs from earth aspire,
    Mourning his loss, so ring the jocund skies
    With those new songs, and dance the angelic choir.
Ah happy he, who from this vale of sighs,
    Poisonous and dark, heavenward hath flown, and lost
    Only the vesture, frail and weak, that dies!
Freed from the world, freed from the tempest-tossed
    Warfare of sin, his splendour now doth gaze
    Full on the face of God through endless days.

Thou'rt dead of dying, and art made divine;
    Nor need'st thou fear to change or life or will;
    Wherefore my soul well-nigh doth envy thine.
Fortune and time across thy threshold still
    Shall dare not pass, the which mid us below
    Bring doubtful joyance blent with certain ill.
Clouds are there none to dim for thee heaven's glow;
    The measured hours compel not thee at all;
    Chance or necessity thou canst not know.
Thy splendour wanes not when our night doth fall,
    Nor waxes with day's light however clear,
    Nor when our suns the season's warmth recall.

APPENDIX VII

(See above, Chapter XI.)

Italian Comic Prologues

THE current of opinion represented by the prologues to Italian comedies deserves some further illustration.

Bibbiena, in the 'Calandra,' starts with what is tantamount to an apology for the modern style of his play. 'Voi sarete oggi spettatori d' una nuova commedia intitolata Calandra, in prosa non in versi, moderna non antica, volgare non latina.' He then explains why he has chosen the language of his age and nation, taking great pains to combat learned prejudices in favour of pure Latin. At the close he defends himself from the charge of having robbed from Plautus, confessing at the same time that he has done so, and thus restricting his earlier boast of novelty to the bare point of diction.

In the prose 'Cassaria,' which was contemporaneous with the 'Calandra,' Ariosto takes the same line:

> Nuova commedia v' appresento, piena
> Di vari giuochi; che nè mai latine
> Nè greche lingue recitarno in scena.
> Parmi vedere che la più parte incline
> A riprenderla, subito ch' ho detto
> Nuova, senza ascoltarne mezzo o fine:
> Chè tale impresa non gli par suggetto
> Delli moderni ingegni, e solo stima
> Quel, che gli antiqui han detto, esser perfetto.

He then proceeds to defend his own audacity, which really consists in no more than the attempt to remodel a Latin play. In the prologue to the prose 'Suppositi' Ariosto follows a different course, apologising for his *contaminatio* of Plautus and Terence by the argument that they borrowed from Menander and Apollodorus.

Machiavelli in the prologue to the 'Clizia' says that history repeats itself. What happened at Athens, happened yesterday at Florence. He has, therefore, laid his scene at Florence: 'perchè Atene è rovinata, le vie, le piazze, i luoghi non vi si riconoscono.' He thus justifies the modern *rifacimento* of an ancient comedy conducted upon classical principles.

Gelli in the 'Sporta' reproduces Ariosto's defence for the 'Suppositi.' If he has borrowed from Plautus and Terence, they borrowed from Menander. Then follows an acute description of comedy as it should be: 'La commedia, per non essere elleno altro ch' uno specchio di costumi della vita privata e civile sotto una imaginazione di verità, non tratto da altro che di cose, che tutto 'l giorno accaggiono al viver nostro, non ci vedrete riconoscimenti di giovani o di fanciulle che oggidì non ne occorre.'

Cecchi in the 'Martello' says he has followed the 'Asinaria:'

> Rimbustata a suo dosso, e su compostovi
> (Aggiungendo e levando, come meglio
> Gli è parso; e ciò, non per corregger Plauto,
> Ma per accomodarsi ai tempi e agli uomini
> Che ci sono oggidì) questa sua favola.

In the 'Moglie' and the 'Dissimili' he makes similar statements, preferring 'la opinione di quelli maestri migliori' (probably Ariosto and Machiavelli), and also:

> perchè il medesimo
> Ved' egli che hanno fatto li più nobili
> Comici che vi sieno.

Lorenzino de' Medici in his prologue to the 'Aridosio' tells the audience they must not be angry if they see the usual lover, miser, and crafty servant, 'e simil cose delle quali non può uscire chi vuol fare commedie.'

These quotations may suffice. If we analyse them, it is clear that at first the comic playwrights felt bound to apologise for writing in Italian; next, that they had to defend themselves against the charge of plagiarism; and in the third place that, when the public became accustomed to Latinising comedies in the vulgar tongue, they undertook the more difficult task of justifying the usage which introduced so many obsolete, monotonous, and anachronistic elements into dramatic literature. At first they were afraid to innovate even to the slight extent of adaptation. At last they were driven to vindicate their artificial forms of art on the score of prescribed usage. But when Cecchi and Lorenzino de' Medici advanced these pleas, which seem to indicate a desire on the part of their public for a more original and modern comedy, the form was too fixed to be altered. Aretino, boldly breaking with tradition, had effected nothing. Il Lasca, laughing at the learned unrealities of his contemporaries, was not strong enough to burst their fetters. Nothing was left for the playwrights but to go on cutting down the old clothes of Plautus and Terence to fit their own backs —as Cecchi puts it.

APPENDIX VIII

(See above, Chapter XIV.)

Passages translated from Folengo and Berni, which illustrate the Lutheran opinions of the Burlesque Poets

ORLANDINO VI. 41

'To Thee, and not to any Saint I go;
How should their mediation here succeed?
The Canaanitish woman, well I know,
Prayed not to James or Peter in her need:
She had recourse to only Thee; and so,
Alone with Thee alone, I hope and plead.
Thou know'st my weal and woe; make plain the way,
Thou, Lord, for to none other dare I pray.

'Nor will I wander with the common kind,
Who, clogged with falsehood and credulity,
Make vows to Gothard or to Roch, and mind
I know not what Saint Bovo more than Thee;
Because some friar, as cunning as they're blind,
Offering to Moloch, his dark deity,
Causes Thy Mother, up in heaven, a Queen,
To load with spoil his sacrifice obscene.

'Beneath the husk of piety these friars
Make a huge harvest for themselves to hold;
The alms on Mary's altar quench the fires
Of impious greed in priests who burn for gold:
Another of their odious laws requires
That year by year my faults should still be told
To a monk's ears:—I who am young and fair!—
He hears, and straightway flogs his shoulders bare:

'He flogs himself because he feels the sting
My words, impregnate with lasciviousness,
Send to his heart; so sharp are they, and wring
His lust so nearly, that, in sore distress,
With wiles and wheedling ways, he seeks to bring
Me in his secret will to acquiesce;
And here confessors oft are shown to be
More learned in pimping than divinity.

'Therefore, O Lord, that know'st the heart of man,
And seest Thy Church in these same friars' grasp,
To Thee with contrite soul, as sinners can,
Who hope their faults forgiven, my hands I clasp;

And if, my God, from this mad ocean
Thou'lt save me, now, as at my latest gasp,
I vow that never more will I trust any
Who grant indulgences for pound or penny.'

Such prayers, chock-full of rankest heresy,
Prayed Berta; for she was a German wench:
In those days, you must know, theology
Had changed herself to Roman, Flemish, French;
But I've my doubts that in the end she'll be
Found squatting *à la* Moor on some Turk's bench,
Because Christ's seamless coat has so been tattered
Its rags have long since to the winds been scattered.

ORLANDINO VIII. 22

'I do not marvel much,' Rainero cried,
'If the lambs suffer scandals and the fold
Be ruined by these wolves of lust and pride,
Foemen to God beneath God's flag enrolled:
But for the present need I'll soon provide—
Ho! to my presence drag yon Prior bold!'
Sharp were the words; the sheriff in a skurry,
He and his serjeants to the convent hurry,

Drag forth that *monstr' horrendum* from his lair,
And lead him straight to Rayner on his throne;
Folk run together at the brute to stare,
You never saw an ox so overgrown;
And not a man but stops his nostrils there
From the foul stench of wine, sweat, filth unknown;
One calls him Bacchus, and Silenus one,
Or hog, or bag of beastliness, or tun.

'Stand forth before my face,' Rainero cries,
'Thou man of God, prophet most reverend!
I know that thou in all the lore art wise,
Of things divine, and what the stars portend;
With thee the freedom of S. Peter lies,
Great freedom though but little pelf to spend!
Stand forth, I say, before me, Father blest;
There are some doubts I'd fain have put to rest.

'Truly thou know'st e'en better how much tripe
Must go to stuff the cupboard of thy prog:
'Tis there are stowed more fish, flesh, onions ripe,
Than there be leaves in forest, field, or bog:
Thy scores of partridge, pheasant, woodcock, snipe,
Outnumber the sea sands, thou gorging dog!
Therefore I honour thee no more nor less
Than a beast filled with filth, a stinking cess.

'Bundle of guts, hast thou no shame to show
Thy visage to the eyes of living wight?
Think'st thou that 'tis for nothing thou dost owe
Thy calling to Christ's sheepfold? By this light,
Judas the traitor did no worse, I know,
Than thou what time he sold his Lord at night;
Caiaphas, Annas, Herod, Pilate, all
Helped Pluto less than thou man's soul to thrall.

'Think'st thou the Benedicts, Pauls, Anthonies,
Gave rules like thine unto their neophytes?
They fed on lentils, beans, peas, cabbages,
Curbing their own rebellious appetites,
Not merely preaching how the spirit flees
From Satan's fraud and his accursèd rites;
They slept on sand and marble cold, and sang
Psalms that through night and day unceasing rang.

'Quiet within their cells they stayed, nor dealt
On street or square with idle loitering bands;
Kindly to wayfarers and meek, they knelt
To wash their feet, and not, like you, their hands;
And when they left the cloisters where they dwelt,
To traverse hills or plains in foreign lands,
A staff or crutch upon their pilgrimage
Sufficed to prop the faltering steps of age.

'That frugal diet of plain herb and root
You've changed to-day for quails and partridges;
Some miracle has turned to flesh their fruit,
Their acorns, brambles, and wild strawberries;
The straw they slept on, hath grown dissolute
With down and cushions; their lean visages
Are swathed in fat, with double, treble chins,
Red as the sun's face when the day begins.

'Their staves and crutches, O rare miracle
Wrought by these living Saints! are steeds of price;
Their reed-built cot, refectory or cell,
Soar into palaces that flout the skies;
In many an Abbey now lewd strumpets dwell,
Hounds, hawks, the instruments of pride and vice:—
Fools, madmen, idiots, maniacs are ye,
Who've left to priests or friars your wealth in fee!

'What could be worse impiety than thus
To rob your lawful kindred of their own,
And squander it on those obstreperous
Bell-ringing monks, who let one voice alone
Speak in the Church for twenty?—All that fuss
In praise of poverty is only shown
To bait beneath the shadow of their cowl
Some gudgeon, or birdlime some silly fowl!'

Such things and others full of angry spite
Said Rayner, contrary to sober reason;
For if a man should lose his temper quite,
Sense leaves him, he can't speak one word in season:
But when Church rights and wrongs their wrath excite
I've noticed that your great men often seize on
Some crazy fad; they fancy, O how silly!
That friars should feed on acorns, willy-nilly.

Then spake the Prior: 'Noble Lord and Sir!
With your forbearance I'll speak with precision.
Ecclesia Dei ne'er was known to err;
You may have read in Tully this decision:

The Stagyrite, our sole interpreter
Of Gospel text, confirms this definition—
Quod merum Laicus non det judicare
Clericam Preti et Fratris scapulare.

'There is a gloss which lays down, *quod Prelatum*
Non est subjectus legi Constantina,
Affirmans eo quod nullum peccatum,
Accidit in persona et re divina.
Et hoc deinceps fuit roboratum
In capite, Ne agro a Clementina.
Et princeps, qui de Ecclesia se impazzabit,
Scomunicatus cito publicabit.

'Saith *Thomas* in a text on which I've pored,
Second distinction of his Chapter *quo*,
Quod unde Spirtus Sanctum hath been stored,
Possibile non est for sin to accrue:
My life hath naught to hide, illustrious Lord,
In visu verbo et opera from you;
For Christ himself our Saviour teaches that,
Speaking to all, *lux vestra luceat.*

'Behold and see how next my skin I wear
A shirt of wool instead of linen fine!
By hair-cloth of this texture you may swear
I circumspectly walk in duty's line.
Look now a little lower!'—Free and fair
Laughed Rayner, when the excellent divine
Shows all he's got—an illustration purer
Than e'er occurred to Saint Bonaventura.

ORLANDINO VIII. 73

I am no heretic, as to my shame
Before the common folk you christen me!
Perchance your lofty Reverence will claim
Me for a cut-throat, come from Saxony,
To wreak my violence on Rome's dread name!
Yet you are wrong: for, look you, Burgundy
Trusts less in German Bishops, or in French,
Or Spanish, than the mighty Roman Bench.

Far more I trust in the high Trinity,
In Father, Son, and eke the Spirit blest;
In Mary's undefiled virginity,
Since God from her derived his fleshly vest;
I trust in that inscrutable potency
Granted from God to man, by which behest
He dares, if his enormities be great,
Call himself, not God, but God's delegate.

It is my creed that the good Jesus wrought
All that He came to witness here below;
I hold that the predicted sword he brought,
Came to bring peace on earth and also woe;
I hold that a thief's tear, repentance-fraught,

Shuts Hell and opens Heaven; and this I know
That the firm truth of what the Gospel saith,
Is nought but pure and uncorrupted Faith.

I hold that He was fair without one flaw,
Wore beard and locks around his shoulder sprent;
I hold the Lamb's blood abrogates the law
And every type of that old Testament;
Wherefore I hold there differs not a straw
Betwixt the tonsure and the hair unshent;
But I believe the clergy still were known
For rebels to His work and will alone.

I hold that on the motion of a lewd
Pope of that year, with certain Pharisees,
Pilate did nail Him to the cruel wood
Between two thieves with fierce indignities;
I hold that thence for men a pledge accrued,
And memory so sweet that still it frees
Us from God's righteous anger, and discloses
The veil that clung before the eyes of Moses.

I speak of His dire passion, and the boon
Most wondrous of His body and His blood,
Eating the which all persons late or soon
May quit those quails and grouse, their desert food;
I hold that Christ seeks not for eyes that swoon,
Wry necks, and faces set to solemn mood,
But for the heart alone: this is my creed;
If it be wrong, I waste vain breath indeed.

I hold that Hell exists, and Purgatory,
Beyond this world; and here I prove it too:
Wherefore, in concert with S. Paul, I glory
In having passed those many trials through,
Not by my might but that great adjutory,
Who calls aloud with ringing voice and true;
Perils mid hills and robbers, storms and fires,
Perils at sea, and perils from false friars!

My Saviour in the flesh I trust to see,
And hope for ever to enjoy His sight:—
But here the force of faith abandons me;
Help then, thou Bishop, Great Albertus hight!
Son of Nichomachus, I turn to thee,
Dubbed Doctor of the Church by Thomas wight,
Without whose Metaphysic, as I've read,
The *Verbum Dei* were but ill bestead.

I hold that a lay sinner can repent;
That Churchmen never are what they pretend—
I speak of bad ones:—d'you mistake my bent,
And in God's house defy me to contend?—
Pray softly, softly! It was never meant,
Good servants of our Lord, *your* fame to rend:
Nay, *you* I honour, since you please God duly;
Places I'd change with *you* really and truly:

Gainst scapular and cord I've nought to tell,
Gainst cowl or tassel, breviary or book;
That superstition need not choke you, well
I know; you may be pious as you look:
I swear to all that no man here should smell
Disparagement to monks, from prior to cook;
I'm aiming at those wolves and hirelings fairly,
Who give large orders and perform them sparely.

ORLANDO INNAMORATO, CANTO XX. THE SUPPRESSED INDUCTION

A brand-new story now compels my song,
To make the twentieth canto bright and clear,
Whence all the world shall plainly learn ere long
Some saints are not such saints as they appear;
For cowls, grey, blue or black, a motley throng,
With dangling breviaries and brows severe,
And often naming on the lips our Lord,
While the heart's cold, no sanctity afford.

A cupping-glass upon your skull, a leech,
A blister, or a tonsure, are all one;
It will not help you though you gird your breech
With several braces or with one alone;
Or wear straight vestments, long and lank, that reach
Like coachmen's great-coats to your heels, or drone
Gibberish and Paternosters:—Sainthood needs
More than fair words for foul and filthy deeds.

The hands are where true charity begins;
Not the mouth, face, or clothes: be mild, humane,
Reticent, sorry for your neighbour's sins,
Pitiful to his suffering and his pain:
Christians need wear no masks; who wears them, wins
A backway to the fold, and brings it bane,
Scaling the wall by craft—a traitor he,
A thief and knave, who deals in subtlety.

These be that tribe of rogues and rascals whom
Our good Lord hates, the race on whom alone
In wrath he uttered that tremendous doom,
Though every other fault he could condone:
Ye whited sepulchres, ye living tomb,
Fire on the surface, in the soul a stone!
Why will ye wash the outside of the platter?
First cleanse your heart—that is the graver matter!

'Tis said by some that by-and-by the good
Pope and his Prelates will reform their ways:
I tell you that a turnip has no blood,
Nor sick folk health, nor can you hope to raise
Syrup from vinegar to sauce your food:
The Church will be reformed when summer days
Come without gad-flies, when a butcher's store
Has neither bones nor dogs about the door.

Sanga, this lewd age is an age of lead,
Whence Truth is banished both in deed and word:
You're called a fool, poor-spirited, ill-bred,
If you but name S. Peter and our Lord:
Where'er you walk, where'er you turn your head,
Some rascal hypocrite, with scowl abhorred,
Snarls twixt his teeth 'Freethinker! Lutheran!'—
And Lutheran means, you know, good Christian.

Those grasping priests have thrown a net full wide:
With bells and anthems, altar-cloth and cope,
They lift their well-decked shrines on every side,
Bent upon life eternal—sorry hope!
This wooden image is the sailor's pride,
That plastered face the soldier's; piss-pots slope
In rows to Cosmo and S. Damian;
The pox belongs to stout Sebastian.

Baron S. Anthony hides fire in heart,
Thoughts of the donkey and the swine in head;
Whence comes it that all monks in every part
Stuff paunch and wallet with flesh, wine, and bread:
Yon Abbot, like Silenus, fills a cart;
Yon Cardinal's a Bacchus overfed;
The Pope through Europe sells, a second Mars,
Bulls and indulgences to feed his wars.

The Word of God, aroused from its long trance,
Runs like life fire abroad through Germany;
The work continues, as the days advance,
Unmasking that close cloaked iniquity,
Which with a false and fraudulent countenance
So long imposed on France, Spain, Italy:
Now by the grace of God we've learned in sooth
What means the words Church, Charity, Hope, Truth.

O the great goodness of our heavenly Sire!
Behold, his Son once more appears on high,
Treads under foot the proud rebellious ire
Of faithless Churchmen, who by threat and lie
Strove to conceal the Love that did inspire
The mighty Maker of earth, sea, and sky,
What time he served, and bore our flesh, and trod
With blood the path that leads men back to God.

None speaks in this lost land of his pure blood,
That sinless blood of Christ, both God and man,
Which quelled the serpent's stiff and venomous brood,
The powers malign that reigned where Lethe ran!
In his fair bleeding limbs he slew the lewd
Old Adam from whose sin our woes began,
Appeased his Father's wrath, and on the door
Of impious Hell set bars for evermore.

This is that seed thrice holy and thrice blest,
Promised to our first parents, which doth bring
Unto the stairs of heaven our hope oppressed!
This is that puissant and victorious king,

Whose foot treads man's misjudgment on the crest!
This is that calm clear light, whose sunbeams fling
Shade on the souls and darkness o'er the eyes
Of fools in this world's knowledge vainly wise!

O Christians, with the hearts of Hebrews! Ye
Who make a mortal man your chief and head,
Of these new Pharisees first Pharisee!
Your soaring and immortal pinions spread
For that starred shrine, where, through eternity,
The Lamb of God is Pope, whose heart once bled
That men, blind men, from yon pure fount on high
Might seek indulgence full and free for aye!

Yet that cooked crayfish hath the face to pray,
Kneeling in chapel opposite that crow,
That Antichrist, upon some holy day—
'Thou art our sail, our rudder!'—when we know
The simple truth requires that he should say
'Thou art the God of ruin and of woe,
Father of infinite hypocrisies,
Of evil customs and all heresies!'—

O Sanga, for our lord Verona's sake,
Put by your Virgil, lay Lucretius down,
Ovid, and him in whom such joy you take,
Tully, of Latin eloquence the crown!
With arms out-spread, our heart's arms, let us make
To Him petition, who, without our own
Merit or diligence or works, can place
Our souls in heaven, made worthy by his grace

And prithee see that Molza is aware,
And Navagero, and Flaminio too,
That here far other things should be our care
Than Janus, Flora, Thetis, and the crew
Of Homer's gods, who paint their page so fair!
Here we experience the false and true;
Here find that Sun, which shows, without, within,
That man by nature is compact of sin.

O good Fregoso, who hast shut thine ear
To all those siren songs of Poesy,
Abiding by the mirror keen and clear,
In joyance of divine Philosophy,
Both Testaments, Old, New, to thee are dear!
Thou hast outworn that ancient phantasy
Which led thee once with Fondulo to call
Plato the link twixt Peter and S. Paul!—

But now Gradasso calls me; I am bid
Back to the follies of my Paladins—
&c. &c.

APPENDIX IX

On Palmieri's 'Città di Vita. (*To illustrate Vol. I, p. 936*)

In the first part of this sketch of Italian literary history ('Renaissance in Italy,' Vol. I., p. 936, note 56) I promised, if possible, to give some further notice of Palmieri's poem entitled the 'Città di Vita.' This promise I was unable to fulfil in the proper place. But while my book was going through the press, I obtained the necessary materials for such a study of Palmieri's work through the courtesy of a Florentine scholar, Signor A. Gherardi, who sent me extracts from a MS. existing in the Laurentian Library. This MS., which is an illuminated parchment codex, contains, besides the poem, the commentary of Lionardo Dati, with his Life of the author and two of his letters addressed to Palmieri. Whether or not the codex is an autograph, remains uncertain. But it has this singular interest, that Matteo Palmieri himself presented it to the Art of the Notaries in Florence, sealed and under the express condition that it should not be opened so long as he lived imprisoned in his body—'ut non aperiatur dum in suo religatus corpusculo vivat.' After his death, the Republic decreed a public funeral to their honoured magistrate and servant; and the MS. in question was placed upon his breast in the church of S. Pier Maggiore, where he was interred in the family chapel of the Palmieri. Alamanno Rinuccini pronounced the panegyrical oration on this occasion; and in his speech he alluded to 'this bulky volume which lies upon his breast, a poem in *terza rima*, called by him the City of Life.'

It would appear, from the circumstance of the volume having been presented under seal to the Art of the Notaries, that Palmieri, while wishing to secure the safety of his poem, was aware of its liability to censure. What he may have dreaded, happened after his decease; for his opinions were condemned as heretical, and the picture Botticelli painted for him in illustration of his views, was removed from its place in the Palmieri Chapel of S. Pier Maggiore. This picture is now in the possession of the Duke of Hamilton.

The MS. of the 'Città di Vita' passed from the Art of the Notaries into the Laurentian Library. Since the biographical notices from the pen of Palmieri's friend, Lionardo Dati, which this MS. contains, form our most trustworthy source of information about the poet's life, it may be well to preface the account of his poem with an abstract of their contents. Matteo Palmieri was a member of an honourable Florentine family. Born in 1405, he received his first education in grammar from Sozomeno of Pistoja. Afterwards he studied Greek and Latin letters in the schools of Carlo Aretino and Ambrogio Traversari. In early manhood he entered public life, and passed through the various Florentine magistracies to the dignity of Gonfalonier of Justice. The Signory employed him upon embassies to Calixtus III., Frederick III., Alfonso the Magnanimous, and Paul II. Matteo devoted his leisure to study and composition. The treatise 'Della Vita Civile,' which he wrote in Italian, was a work of his adolescence. Then followed, in Latin, a life of Niccolò Acciaiolo, a narrative of the successful war with Pisa, and a Universal History, which was subsequently continued by Mattia Palmieri—a Pisan, who, though he bore the same name, was in no wise related to our author. The 'Città di Vita' was a work of his mature age. He died probably in 1478.

Matteo told Lionardo Dati that on the first of August 1451, while he was living at Pescia as Governor of the Val di Nievole, he dreamed that his dead friend Cipriano Rucellai appeared to him, and invited him to the yearly festival which was celebrated on that day in a monastery, called Il Paradiso, near Florence. In his dream, Matteo accompanied the ghost of Cipriano, conversing on the way about the state of spirits after death—where they dwell, and how they are permitted to revisit their living friends. Cipriano, moreover, revealed to him weighty matters concerning the nature of the human soul. He told him how God first made angels in innumerable hosts. These angels separated into three companies. The one band followed Lucifer, when he rebelled. The second held with Michael and abode firm in their allegiance. The third decided neither for God nor for the Devil. After Lucifer's defeat, these angels of the third class were relegated to the Elysian fields, which extend at all points over the extreme periphery of the highest sphere; and God, wishing to give them a final chance of determining for good or evil, ordained that they should, one by one, be sent to dwell in human bodies. There, attended by a good and a bad spirit, they have the choice of lives, and after their death in the body, are drafted into the trains of Lucifer or Michael according to their conduct. Having communicated this doctrine, Cipriano vanished from his friend's sight with these words upon his lips:

> Misero ad noi quanto mal segno
> Rizoron quelli che si fer ribelli
> Per porre in aquilon loco più degno.

Palmieri forgot or neglected the import of his dream until the year 1455, when he was at Alfonso's Court in Naples. There Cipriano appeared to him again, rebuked him for his carelessness, and bade him write a poem in *terza rima*, after Dante's method, on the subject of their former discourse. He also recommended him three books, which would assist him in the labour. When Palmieri returned to Florence, he obtained these helps and set about the composition of his poem. It must have been completed in 1464; for in this year Dati received a copy, which he styled *opus pæne divinum*, and began to annotate. In

1466 Dati wrote again to Palmieri, thanking him for an emended copy of the work, which the author had sent him from Florence to Rome. Palmieri's own letter accompanying the gift, refers to the poem as already published. This proves (as would, indeed, appear from the title given him by Ficino of *Poeta Theologicus*) that, whatever may have been his dread of a prosecution for heresy, he had at least divulged the 'Città di Vita' to the learned.

The poem consists of three books, divided, like Dante's 'Commedia,' into one hundred Cantos; but the extra Canto has by Palmieri been assigned to the last instead of the first Cantica. The title 'Città di Vita' was given to it, because Palmieri designed to bring the universe into consideration under the aspect of spiritual existence. The universe, as he conceived it, is the burgh in which all souls live. His object was to show how free-will is innate in men, who have the choice of good and evil, of salvation or perdition, in this life. The origin of evil he relegates to that prehistoric moment of Lucifer's revolt, when the third class of angels refused to side with either God or Devil. In the first book, then, he describes how these angels are transmitted from the Elysian fields to earth, in order that they may become men, and in their mortal body be forced to exercise their faculty of election. In the second book he treats of the way of perdition. In the third book he deals with the way of salvation. Following Dante's precedent in the choice of Virgil, he takes the Sibyl for his guide upon the beginning of this visionary journey.

The heretical portions of the 'Città di Vita' are Cantos v. ix. x. xi. of the first Cantica. These deal with the original creation of angelic essences, and with the transit of the indeterminate angels to our earth. Regarding the universe from the Ptolemaic point of view, Palmieri conceives that these angels, who inhabit the Elysian fields beyond the utmost verge of the stellar spheres, proceed on their earthward journey through the several planets, till they reach our globe, which is the centre of the whole. On their way, they gradually submit to animal impressions and prepare themselves for incarnation, according to that conception which made the human soul itself in a certain sense corporeal. It is here that Palmieri adjusts the theory of planetary influences to his theory of free-will. For he supposes that the angels assimilate the qualities of the planetary spheres as they pass through them, being attracted by curiosity to one planet rather than another. At the same time they undergo the action of the three superior elements, which fits them for their final reception into an earthy habitation. After this wise he ingeniously combined his theories of the Creation, the Fall, and Free-will, with Averroistic doctrines of intermediate intelligences and speculations collected from Platonistic writings.

The path of the descending angels is, to quote the words of Dati, 'in a straight line beneath the first point of Cancer to the cave of earth, in which line there are ten gates, for each of the planets to wit, and for the three super-terrestrial elements each his gate. The whole of this vast body of the universe is by our poet called the City of Life, forasmuch as in this universe all creatures live. And this journey of the souls from Elysium to their bodies is performed in one year.' It will be observed that Palmieri affected the precision of his master Dante. Having thus conducted the soul to earth, he is no less definite in his description of the two ways, which severally lead to damnation and salvation. In the second Cantica, he employs the space of a whole year compressed into one night, in passing through the eighteen mansions of the passions of the flesh, fortune and the mind. For this journey he has the guidance of an evil spirit. Afterwards, in the third Cantica, he employs the same space of one year compressed into a single day, in traversing the twelve mansions of civil virtue and purgation, through which the soul arrives at beatific life. In this voyage he is guided by a good angel. It is not necessary to enter further into the calculations whereby Palmieri adjusts the chronology and cosmography of his vision to the Ptolemaic theory of the universe.

Though the material of the poem is thus curious, and the structure thus ingenious, it does not rise in style above the level of the works of Frezzi and Uberti (see above, Vol. I., p. 935 *et seq*). In order to give the reader a specimen of its composition, I will extract a passage from Cantica I. Canto v., which concerns the Divine Being and the Creation of Angels:

Sopra ogn' altro potere è questo tale,
 che come e' vuole in tutto può giovare,
 sanza potenza di voler far male.
Tal carità volendo ad altri dare
 la gloria in sè, (?) di se stesso godeva,
 degnò co' cieli ancor la terra fare.
Et perche cosa far non si poteva
 che eterno bene in ciel sempre godesse,
 se sempre quel goder non intendeva;
Intelligenza bisognò facesse
 con lume di ragione et immortale,
 ad chi l' eterno ben tutto si desse.
Creatura fè per questo rationale,
 l' angelo et l' huomo acciò che 'l sommo bene
 godessono intendendo quel che e' vale.
Da 'ntenderlo et amar di ragion vene
 volerlo possedere, et con letitia
 per sempre usar sanza timor di pene.
Ad questo Idio creò la gran militia
 del celestiale exercitio et felice,
 che 'n parte cadde per la sua malitia.

THE CATHOLIC REACTION

'Deh! per Dio, donna,
Se romper si potria quelle grandi ale!
. . . .
Tu piangi e taci; e questo meglio parmi'

SAVONAROLA: *De Ruina Ecclesiae*

'Il mondo invecchia
E invecchiando intristisce'

TASSO: *Aminta*, Act 2, sc. 2

PREFACE[1]

At the end of the second volume of my 'Renaissance in Italy' I indulged the hope that I might live to describe the phase of culture which closed that brilliant epoch. It was in truth demanded that a work pretending to display the manifold activity of the Italian genius during the fifteenth century and the first quarter of the sixteenth, should also deal with the causes which interrupted its further development upon the same lines.

This study, forming a logically necessitated supplement to the five former volumes of 'Renaissance in Italy,' I have been permitted to complete. The results are now offered to the public in these two parts.

So far as it was possible, I have conducted my treatment of the Catholic Revival on a method analogous to that adopted for the Renaissance. I found it, however, needful to enter more minutely into details regarding facts and institutions connected with the main theme of national culture.

The Catholic Revival was by its nature reactionary. In order to explain its influences, I have been compelled to analyse the position of Spain in the Italian peninsula, the conduct of the Tridentine Council, the specific organisation of the Holy Office and the Company of Jesus, and the state of society upon which those forces were brought to bear.

In the list of books which follows these prefatory remarks, I have indicated the most important of the sources used by me. Special references will be made in their proper places to works of a subordinate value for the purposes of my inquiry.

Davos Platz: *July* 1886.

[1] To the original edition of this volume.

WORKS COMMONLY REFERRED TO IN THE CATHOLIC REACTION

SISMONDI.—Histoire des Républiques Italiennes du Moyen-Age.
RANKE.—History of the Popes. 3 vols. English edition: Bohn.
CREIGHTON.—History of the Papacy during the Reformation. 2 vols. Macmillan.
BOTTA.—Storia d'Italia. Continuata da quella del Guicciardini sino al 1789.
FERRARI.—Rivoluzioni d' Italia. 3 vols.
QUINET.—Les Révolutions d'Italie.
GALLUZZI.—Storia del Granducato di Toscana.
PALLAVICINI.—Storia del Concilio Tridentino.
SARPI.—Storia del Concilio. Vols. 1 and 2 of Sarpi's Opere.
DENNISTOUN'S Dukes of Urbino. 3 vols.
ALBERI.—Relazioni degli Ambasciatori Veneti.
MUTINELLI.—Storia Arcana ed Aneddotica d' Italia. Raccontata dai Veneti Ambasciatori. 4 vols. Venice. 1858.
MUTINELLI.—Annali Urbani di Venezia.
LITTA.—Famiglie Celebri Italiane.
PHILIPPSON.—La Contre-Révolution Religieuse au XVIme Siècle. Bruxelles. 1884.
DEJOB.—De l'Influence du Concile de Trente. Paris. 1884.
GIORDANI.—Della Venuta e Dimora in Bologna del Sommo Pontefice Clemente VII. per la Coronazione di Carlo V., Imperatore. Bologna. 1832.
BALBI.—Sommario della Storia d'Italia.
CANTÙ.—Gli Eretici d' Italia. 3 vols. Torino. 1866.
LLORENTE.—Histoire Critique de l'Inquisition d'Espagne. 4 vols. Paris. 1818.
LAVALLÈE.—Histoire des Inquisitions Religieuses. 2 vols. Paris. 1808.
MCCRIE.—History of the Reformation in Italy. Edinburgh. 1827.
TIRABOSCHI.—Storia della Letteratura Italiana.
DE SANCTIS.—Storia della Letteratura Italiana. 2 vols.
SETTEMBRINI.—Storia della Letteratura Italiana. 3 vols.
CANTÙ.—Storia della Letteratura Italiana.
Decreta, &c., Societatis Jesu. Avignon. 1827.
CANTÙ.—Storia della Diocesi di Como. 2 vols.
DANDOLO.—La Signora di Monza e le Streghe del Tirolo. Milano. 1855.
BONGHI.—Storia di Lucrezia Buonvisi. Lucca. 1864.
Archivio Storico Italiano.
Bandi Lucchesi.—Bologna: Romagnoli. 1863.
BERTOLOTTI.—Francesco Cenci e la sua Famiglia. Firenze. 1877.
GNOLI.—Vittoria Accoramboni. Firenze: Le Monnier. 1870.
DAELLI.—Lorenzino de' Medici. Milano. 1862.
DE STENDHAL.—Chroniques et Nouvelles. Paris. 1855.
GIORDANO BRUNO.—Opere Italiane (Wagner). 2 vols. Leipzig. 1830.
JORDANUS BRUNUS.—Opera Latina. 2 vols. Neapoli. 1879.
BRUNO.—Scripta Latina (Gförer). Stuttgart. 1836.
BERTI.—Vita di Giordano Bruno. Firenze, Torino, Milano. 1868.
BRUNNHOFER.—Giordano Bruno's Weltanschauung und Verhängniss. Leipzig. 1882.
PAOLO SARPI.—Opere. 6 vols. Helmstat. 1765.
FRA FULGENZIO MICANZI.—Vita del Sarpi.
BIANCHI GIOVINI.—Biografia di Fra Paolo Sarpi. 2 vols. Bruxelles. 1836.
Lettere di Fra Paolo Sarpi. 2 vols. Firenze. 1863.
CAMPBELL.—Life of Fra Paolo Sarpi. London: Molini and Green. 1869.
DEJOB.—Marc-Antoine Muret. Paris: Thorin. 1881.

Christie.—Etienne Dolet. London: Macmillan. 1880.
Renouard.—Imprimerie des Aldes.
Torquato Tasso.—Opere. Ed. Rosini. 33 vols. Pisa. 1822 and on.
Tasso.—Le Lettere. Ed. Guasti. 5 vols. Firenze. 1855.
Cecchi.—T. Tasso, e la Vita Italiana. Firenze. 1877.
Cecchi.—T. Tasso. Il Pensiero e le Belle Lettere, &c. Firenze. 1877.
D' Ovidio.—Saggi Critici. Napoli. 1878.
Manso.—Vita di T. Tasso, in Rosini's edition, vol. 33.
Rosini.—Saggio sugli Amori di T. Tasso, in edition cited above, vol. 33.
Guarini.—Il Pastor Fido. Ed. Casella. Firenze: Barbèra. 1866.
Marino.—Adone, &c. Napoli. 1861.
Chiabrera.—Ed. Polidori. Firenze: Barbèra. 1865.
Tassoni.—La Secchia Rapita. Ed. Carducci. Firenze: Barbèra. 1861.
Il Parnaso Italiano.
Baini.—Vita di G. P. L. Palestrina.
Felsina Pittrice.—2 vols. Bologna. 1841.
Lanzi.—History of Painting in Italy. English Edition. London: Bohn. Vol. 3.

CHAPTER I

THE SPANISH HEGEMONY

Italy in the Renaissance.—The Five Great Powers—The Kingdom of Naples—The Papacy—The Duchy of Milan—Venice—The Florentine Republic—Wars of Invasion closed by the Sack of Rome in 1527—Concordat between Clement VII. and Charles V.—Treaty of Barcelona and Paix des Dames—Charles lands at Genoa—His Journey to Bologna—Entrance into Bologna and Reception by Clement—Mustering of Italian Princes—Francesco Sforza replaced in the Duchy of Milan—Venetian Embassy—Italian League signed on Christmas Eve 1529—Florence alone excluded—The Siege of Florence pressed by the Prince of Orange—Charles's Coronation as King of Italy and Holy Roman Emperor—The Significance of this Ceremony at Bologna—Ceremony in S. Petronio—Settlement of the Duchy of Ferrara—Men of Letters and Arts at Bologna—The Emperor's Use of the Spanish Habit—Charles and Clement leave Bologna in March 1530—Review of the Settlement of Italy effected by Emperor and Pope—Extinction of Republics—Subsequent Absorption of Ferrara and Urbino into the Papal States—Savoy becomes an Italian Power—Period between Charles's Coronation and the Peace of Cateau Cambresis in 1559—Economical and Social Condition of the Italians under Spanish Hegemony—The Nation still exists in Separate Communities—Intellectual Conditions—Predominance of Spain and Rome—Both Cosmopolitan Powers—Levelling down of the Component Portions of the Nation in a Common Servitude—The Evils of Spanish Rule.

In the first section of this work on 'Renaissance in Italy' I attempted to set forth the political and social phases through which the Italians passed before their principal States fell into the hands of despots, and to explain the conditions of mutual jealousy and military feebleness which exposed those States to the assaults of foreign armies at the close of the fifteenth century.

In the year 1494, when Charles VIII. of France, at Lodovico Sforza's invitation, crossed the Alps to make good his claim on Naples, the peninsula was independent. Internal peace had prevailed for a period of nearly fifty years. An equilibrium had been established between the five great native Powers, which secured the advantages of confederation and diplomatic interaction.

While using the word confederation I do not of course imply that anything similar to the federal union of Switzerland or of North America existed in Italy. The contrary is proved by patent facts. On a miniature scale, Italy then displayed political conditions analogous to those which now prevail in Europe. The parcels of the nation adopted different forms of self-government, sought divers foreign alliances, and owed no allegiance to any central legislative or administrative body. I therefore speak of the Italian confederation only in the same sense as Europe may now be called a confederation of kindred races.

In the year 1530, when Charles V. (of Austria and Spain) was crowned Emperor at Bologna, this national independence had been irretrievably lost by the Italians. This confederation of evenly balanced Powers was now exchanged for servitude beneath a foreign monarchy, and for subjection to a cosmopolitan elective priesthood.

The history of social, intellectual, and moral conditions in Italy during the seventy years of the sixteenth century which followed Charles's coronation at Bologna, forms the subject of this work; but before entering upon these topics it will be well to devote one chapter to considering with due brevity the partition of Italy into five States in 1494, the dislocation of this order by the wars between Spain and France for supremacy, the position in which the same States found themselves respectively at the termination of those wars in 1527, and the new settlement of the peninsula effected by Charles V. in 1529-30.

The five members of the Italian federation in 1494 were the Kingdom of Naples, the Papacy, the Duchy of Milan, and the Republics of Venice and Florence. Round them, in various relations of amity or hostility, were grouped these minor Powers: the Republics of Genoa, Lucca, Siena; the Duchy of Ferrara, including Modena and Reggio; the Marquisates of Mantua and Montferrat; and the Duchy of Urbino. For our immediate purpose it is not worth taking separate account of the Republic of Pisa, which was practically though not thoroughly enslaved by Florence; or of the Despots in the cities of Romagna, the March, Umbria, and the Patrimony of S. Peter, who were being gradually absorbed into the Papal sovereignty. Nor need we at present notice Savoy, Piemonte, and Saluzzo. Although these north-western provinces were all-important through the period of Franco-Spanish wars, inasmuch as they opened the gate of Italy to French armies and supplied those armies with a base for military operations, the Duchy of Savoy had not yet become an exclusively Italian Power.

The kingdom of Naples, on the death of Alfonso the Magnanimous in 1458, had been separated from Sicily, and passed by testamentary appointment to his natural son Ferdinand. The bastard Aragonese dynasty was Italian in its tastes and interests, though unpopular both with the barons of the realm and with the people, who in their restlessness were ready to welcome any foreign deliverer from its oppressive yoke. This state of general discontent rendered the revival of the old Angevine party, and their resort to French aid, a source of peril to the monarchy. It also served as a convenient fulcrum for the ambitious schemes of conquest which the princes of the House of Aragon in Spain began to entertain. In territorial extent the kingdom of Naples was the most considerable parcel of the Italian community. It embraced the whole of Calabria, Apulia, the Abruzzi, and the Terra di Lavoro; marching on its northern boundary with the Papal States, and having no other neighbours. But though so large and so compact a State, the semi-feudal system of government which had obtained in Naples since the first conquest of the country by the Normans, the nature of its population, and the savage dynastic wars to which it had been constantly exposed, rendered it more backward in civilisation than the northern and central provinces.

The Papacy, after the ending of the schism and the settlement of Nicholas V. at Rome in 1447, gradually tended to become an Italian sovereignty. During the residence of the Popes at Avignon, and the weakness of the Papal See which followed in the period of the Councils (Pisa, Constance, and Basel), it had lost its hold not only on the immediate neighbourhood of Rome, but also on its outlying possessions in Umbria, the Marches of Ancona, and the Exarchate of Ravenna. The great Houses of Colonna and Orsini asserted independence in their principalities. Bologna and Perugia pretended to republican government under the shadow of noble families; Bentivogli, Bracci, Baglioni. Imola, Faenza, Forli, Rimini, Pesaro, Urbino, Camerino, Città di Castello, obeyed the rule of tyrants, who were practically lords of these cities though they bore the title of Papal vicars, and who maintained themselves in wealth and power by exercising the profession of *condottieri*. It was the chief object of the Popes, after they were freed from the pressing perils of General Councils, and were once more settled in their capital and recognised as sovereigns by the European Powers, to subdue their vassals and consolidate their provinces into a homogeneous kingdom. This plan was conceived and carried out by a succession of vigorous and unscrupulous Pontiffs—Sixtus IV., Alexander VI., Julius II., and Leo X.—throughout the period of distracting foreign wars which agitated Italy. They followed for the most part one line of policy, which was to place the wealth and authority of the Holy See at the disposal of their relatives, Riarios, Della Roveres, Borgias, and Medici. Their military delegates, among whom the most efficient captain was the terrible Cesare Borgia, had full power to crush the liberties of cities, exterminate the dynasties of despots, and reduce refractory districts to the Papal sway. For these services they were rewarded with ducal and princely titles, with the administration of their conquests, and with the investiture of fiefs as vassals of the Church. The system had its obvious disadvantages. It tended to indecent nepotism; and as Pope succeeded Pope at intervals of a few years, each bent on aggrandising his own family at the expense of those of his predecessors and the Church, the ecclesiastical States were kept in a continual ferment of expropriation and internal revolution. Yet it is difficult to conceive how a spiritual Power like the Papacy could have solved the problem set before it of becoming a substantial secular sovereignty, without recourse to this ruinous method. The Pope, a lonely man upon an ill-established throne, surrounded by rivals whom his elevation had disappointed, was compelled to rely on the strong arm of adventurers with whose interests his own were indissolubly connected. The profits of all these schemes of egotistical rapacity eventually accrued, not to the relatives of the Pontiffs (none of whom except the Della Roveres in Urbino founded a permanent dynasty at this period), but to the Holy See. Julius II., for example, on his election in 1503, entered into possession of all that Cesare Borgia had attempted to grasp for his own use. He found the Orsini and Colonna humbled, Romagna reduced to submission; and he carried on the policy of conquest by trampling out the liberties of Bologna and Perugia, recovering the cities held by Venice on the coast of Ravenna, and extending his sway over Emilia. The martial energy of Julius added Parma and Piacenza to the States of the Church, and detached Modena and Reggio from the Duchy of Ferrara. These new cities were gained by force; but Julius pretended that they formed part of the Exarchate of Ravenna, which had been granted to his predecessors by Pepin and Charles the Great. He pursued the Papal line of conquest in a nobler spirit than his predecessors, not seeking to advance his relatives so much as to reinstate the Church in her dominions. But he was reckless in the means employed to secure this object. Italy was devastated by wars stirred up, and by foreign armies introduced, in order that the Pope might win a point in the great game of ecclesiastical aggrandisement. That his successor, Leo X., reverted to the former plan of carving principalities for his relatives out of the possessions of their neighbours and the Church, may be counted among the most important causes of the final ruin of Italian independence.

Of the Duchy of Milan it is not necessary to speak at any great length, although the wars between France and Spain were chiefly carried on for its possession. It had been formed into a compact domain, of comparatively small extent, but of vast commercial and agricultural resources, by the two dynasties of Visconti and Sforza. In 1494 Lodovico Sforza, surnamed Il Moro, ruled Milan for his nephew, the titular Duke, whom he kept in gilded captivity, and whom he eventually murdered. In order to secure his usurped authority, this would-be Machiavelli thought it prudent to invite Charles VIII. into Italy. Charles was to assert his right to the throne of Naples. Lodovico was to be established in the Duchy of Milan. All his subsequent troubles arose from this transaction. Charles came, conquered, and returned to France, disturbing the political equilibrium of the Italian States and founding a disastrous precedent for future foreign interference. His successor in the French kingdom, Louis XII., believed he had a title to the Duchy of Milan through his grandmother Valentina, daughter of Gian Galeazzo Visconti. The claim was not a legal one; for in the investiture of the Duchy females were excluded. It sufficed, however, to inflame the cupidity of Louis; and while he was still but Duke of Orleans, with no sure prospect of inheriting the crown of France, he seems to have indulged the fancy of annexing Milan. No sooner had he ascended the French throne than he began to act upon this ambition. He descended into Lombardy, overran the Milanese, sent Lodovico Sforza to die in a French prison, and initiated the duel between Spain and France for mastery, which ended with the capture of Francis I. at Pavia and his final cession of all rights over Italy to Charles V. by the Treaty of Cambray (Paix des Dames).

Of all the republics which had conferred lustre upon Italy in its mediæval period of prosperity Venice alone remained independent. She never submitted to a tyrant; and her government, though growing yearly more closely oligarchical, was acknowledged to be just and liberal. During the centuries of her greatest power Venice hardly ranked among Italian States. It had been her policy to confine herself to the lagoons and to the extension of her dominion over the Levant. In the fifteenth century, however, this policy was abandoned. Venice first possessed herself of Padua, by exterminating the despotic House of Carrara; next of Verona, by destroying the Scala dynasty. Subsequently, during the long dogeship of Francesco Foscari (1423-1457), she devoted herself in good earnest to the acquisition of territory upon the mainland. Then she entered as a Power of the first magnitude into the system of purely Italian politics. The Republic of S. Mark owned the sea coast of the Adriatic from Aquileia to the mouths of the Po; and her Lombard dependencies stretched as far as Bergamo westward. Her Italian neighbours were, therefore, the Duchy of Milan, the little Marquisate of Mantua, and the Duchy of Ferrara. When Constantinople fell in 1453, Venice was still more tempted to pursue this new policy of Italian aggrandisement. Meanwhile her growing empire seemed to menace the independence of less wealthy neighbours. The jealousy thus created and the cupidity which brought her into collision with Julius II. in 1508, exposed Venice to the crushing blow inflicted on her power by the combined forces of Europe in the war of the League of Cambray. From this blow, as well as from the simultaneous decline of their Oriental and Levantine commerce, the Venetians never recovered.

When we turn to the Florentines, we find that at the same epoch, 1494, their ancient republican constitution had been fatally undermined by the advances of the family of Medici towards despotism. Lorenzo de' Medici, who enjoyed the credit of maintaining the equilibrium of Italy by wise diplomacy, had lately died. He left his son Piero, a hot-headed and rash young man, to control the affairs of the commonwealth, as he had previously controlled them, with a show of burgherlike equality, but with the reality of princely power. Another of his sons, Giovanni, received the honour of the Cardinalship. The one was destined to compromise the ascendency of his family in Florence for a period of eighteen years; the other was destined to re-establish that ascendency on a new and more despotic basis. Piero had not his father's prudence, and could not maintain himself in the delicate position of a commerical and civil tyrant. During the disturbances caused by the invasion of Charles VIII. he was driven with all his relatives into exile. The Medici were restored in 1512, after the battle of Ravenna, by Spanish troops, at the petition of the Cardinal Giovanni. The elevation of this man to the Papacy in 1513 enabled him to plant two of his nephews, as rulers, in Florence, and to pave the way whereby a third eventually rose to the dignity of the tiara. Clement VII. finally succeeded in rendering Florence subject to the Medici, by extinguishing the last sparks of republican opposition, and by so modifying the dynastic protectorate of his family that it was easily converted into a titular Grand Duchy.

The federation of these five Powers had been artificially maintained during the half-century of Italy's highest intellectual activity. That was the epoch when the Italians nearly attained to coherence as a nation, through common interests in art and humanism, and by the complicated machinery of diplomatic relations. The federation perished when foreign Powers chose Lombardy and Naples for their fields of battle. The disasters of the next thirty-three years (1494-1527) began in earnest on the day when Louis XII. claimed Milan and the Regno. He committed his first mistake by inviting Ferdinand the Catholic to share in the partition of Naples. That province was easily conquered; but Ferdinand retained the whole spoils for himself, securing a large Italian dependency and a magnificent basis of operations for the Spanish crown. Then Louis made a second mistake by proposing to the visionary Emperor Maximilian that he should aid France in subjugating Venice. We have few instances on record of short-sighted diplomacy to match the Treaties of Granada and Blois (1501 and 1504), through which this monarch, acting rather as a Duke of Milan than a King of France, complicated his Italian schemes by the introduction of two such dangerous allies as the Austrian Emperor and the Spanish sovereign, while the heir of both was in his cradle—that fatal child of fortune, Charles.

The stage of Italy was now prepared for a conflict which in no wise interested her prosperous cities and industrious population. Spain, France, Germany, with their Swiss auxiliaries, had been summoned upon various pretexts to partake of the rich prey she offered. Patriots like Machiavelli perceived too late the suicidal self-indulgence which, by substituting mercenary troops for national militia, and by accustoming selfish tyrants to rely on foreign aid, had exposed the Italians defenceless to the inroads of their warlike neighbours. Whatever parts the Powers of Italy might play, the game was really in the hands of French, Spanish, and German invaders. Meanwhile the mutual jealousies and hatreds of those Powers, kept in check by no tie stronger than diplomacy, prevented them from forming any scheme of common action. One great province (Naples) had fallen into Spanish hands; another (Milan) lay open through the passes of the Alps to France. The Papacy, in the centre, manipulated these two hostile foreign forces with some advantage to itself, but with ever-deepening disaster for the race. As in the days of Guelf and Ghibelline, so now again the nation was bisected. The contest between French and Spanish factions became cruel. Personal interests were substituted for principles; cross-combinations perplexed the real issues of dispute; while one sole fact emerged into distinctness—that, whatever happened, Italy must be the spoil of the victorious duellist.

The practical termination of this state of things arrived in the battle of Pavia, when Francis was removed as a prisoner to Madrid, and in the Sack of Rome, when the Pope was imprisoned in the Castle of S. Angelo. It was then found that the laurels and the profit of the bloody contest remained with the King of Spain. What the people suffered from the marching and countermarching of armies, from the military occupation of towns, from the desolation of rural districts, from ruinous campaigns and sanguinary battles, from the pillage of cities and the massacres of their inhabitants, can best be read in Burigozzo's 'Chronicle of Milan,' in the details of the siege of Brescia and the destruction of Pavia, in the 'Chronicle of Prato' and in the several annals of the Sack of Rome. The exhaustion of the country seemed complete; the spirit of the people was broken. But what soon afterwards became apparent, and what in 1527 might have been thought incredible, was that the single member of the Italian union which profited by these apocalyptic sufferings of the nation, was the Papacy. Clement VII., imprisoned in the Castle of S. Angelo, forced day and night to gaze upon his capital in flames and hear the groans of tortured Romans, emerged the only vigorous survivor of the five great Powers on whose concert Italian independence had been founded. Instead of being impaired, the position of the Papacy had been immeasurably improved. Owing to the prostration of Italy, there was now no resistance to the Pope's secular supremacy within the limits of his authorised dominion. The defeat of France and the accession of a Spanish monarch to the Empire guaranteed peace. No foreign force could levy armies or foment uprisings in the name of independence. Venice had been stunned and mutilated by the League of Cambray. Florence had been enslaved after the battle of Ravenna. Milan had been relinquished, outworn and depopulated, to the nominal ascendency of an impotent Sforza. Naples was a province of the Spanish monarchy. The feudal vassals and the subject cities of the Holy See had been ground and churned together by a series of revolutions unexampled even in the mediæval history of the Italian communes. If, therefore, the Pope could come to terms with the King of Spain for the partition of supreme authority in the peninsula, they might henceforward share the mangled remains of the Italian prey at peace together. This is precisely what they resolved on doing. The basis of their agreement was laid in the Treaty of Barcelona in 1529. It was ratified and secured by the Treaty of Cambray in the same year. By the former of these compacts Charles and Clement swore friendship. Clement promised the Imperial crown and the investiture of Naples to the King of Spain. Charles agreed to reinstate the Pope in Emilia, which had been seized from Ferrara by Julius II.; to procure the restoration of Ravenna and Cervia by the Venetians; to subdue Florence to the House of Medici; and to bestow the hand of his natural daughter Margaret of Austria on Clement's bastard nephew Alessandro, who was already designated ruler of the city. By the treaty of Cambray Francis I. relinquished his claims on Italy and abandoned his Italian supporters without conditions, receiving in exchange the possession of Burgundy. The French allies who were sacrificed on this occasion by the Most Christian to the Most Catholic monarch consisted of the Republics of Venice and Florence, the Dukes of Milan and Ferrara, the princely Houses of Orsini and Fregosi in Rome and Genoa, together with the Angevine nobles in the realm of Naples. The Paix des Dames, as this act of capitulation was called (since it had been drawn up in private conclave by Louise of Savoy and Margaret of Austria, the mother and the aunt of the two signatories), was a virtual acknowledgment of the fact that French influence in Italy was at an end.[1]

The surrender of Italy by Francis made it necessary that Charles V. should put order in the vast estates to which he now succeeded as sole master. He was, moreover, Emperor elect; and he judged this occasion good for assuming the two crowns according to antique custom. Consequently in July 1529 he caused Andrea Doria to meet him at Barcelona, crossed the Mediterranean in a rough passage of fourteen days, landed at Genoa on August 12, and proceeded by Piacenza, Parma and Modena to Bologna, where Clement VII. was already awaiting him. The meeting of Charles and Clement at Bologna was so solemn an event in Italian history, and its results were so important for the several provinces of the peninsula, that I may be excused for enlarging at some length upon this episode. With pomp and pageantry it closed an age of unrivalled intellectual splendour and of unexampled sufferings through war. By diplomacy and debate it prescribed laws for a new age of unexpected ecclesiastical energy and of national peace procured at the price of slavery. Illustrious survivors from the period of the Pagan Renaissance met here with young men destined to inaugurate the Catholic Revival. The compact struck between Emperor and Pope in private conferences, laid a basis for that firm alliance between Spain and Rome which seriously influenced the destinies of Europe. Finally, this was the last occasion upon which a modern Cæsar received the iron and the golden crowns in Italy from the hands of a Roman Pontiff. The fortunate inheritor of Spain, the Two Sicilies, Austria and the Low Countries, who then assumed them both at the age of twenty-nine, was not only the last who wielded the Imperial insignia with imperial authority, but was also a far more formidable potentate in Italy than any of his predecessors since Charles the Great had been.[2]

That Charles should have employed the galleys of Doria for the transshipment of his person, suite, and military escort from Barcelona, deserves a word of comment. Andrea Doria had been bred in the service of the French crown, upon which Genoa was in his youth dependent. He formed a navy of decisive preponderance in the Western Mediterranean, and in return for services rendered to Francis in the Neapolitan campaign of 1528, he demanded the liberation of his native city. When this was refused, Doria transferred his allegiance to the Spaniard, surprised Genoa and reinstated the republic, magnanimously refusing to secure its tyranny for himself or even to set the ducal cap upon his head. Charles invested him with the principality of Melfi and made him a Grandee of Spain. By this series of events Genoa was prepared to accept

[1] It is significant for the future of Italy that both the ladies who drew up this agreement were connected with Savoy. Louise, Duchess of Angoulême, was a daughter of the house. Margaret, daughter of Maximilian, was Duchess Dowager of Savoy.

[2] In what follows regarding Charles V. at Bologna I am greatly indebted to Giordani's laboriously compiled volume: *Della Venuta e Dimora in Bologna del Sommo Pont. Clemente VII.* &c. (Bologna, 1832.)

the yoke of Spanish influence and customs, which pressed so heavily in the succeeding century on Italy.

Charles had a body of 2,000 Spaniards already quartered at Genoa, as well as strong garrisons in the Milanese, and a force of about 7,000 troops collected by the Prince of Orange from the *dêbris* of the army which had plundered Rome. While he was on his road from Genoa to Bologna, this force was already moving upon Florence. He brought with him as escort some 10,000 men, counting horse and infantry. The total of the troops which obeyed his word in Italy might be computed at about 27,000 including Spanish cavalry and foot-soldiers, German lansknechts, and Italian mercenaries. This large army, partly stationed in important posts of defence, partly in movement, was sufficient to make every word of his a law. The French were in no position to interfere with his arrangements. His brother Ferdinand, King of Bohemia and Hungary, was engaged in a doubtful contest with Soliman before the gates of Vienna. He was himself the most considerable potentate in Germany, then distracted by the struggles of the Reformation. Italy lay crushed and prostrate, trampled down by armies, exhausted by imposts and exactions, terrorised by brutal violence. That Charles had come to speak his will and be obeyed was obvious.

To greet the King on his arrival at Genoa, Clement deputed two ambassadors, the Cardinals Ercole Gonzaga and Monsignor Gianmatteo Giberti, Bishop of Verona. Gonzaga was destined to play a part of critical importance in the Tridentine Council. Giberti had made himself illustrious in the Church by the administration of his diocese on a system which anticipated the coming ecclesiastical reforms, and was already famous in the world of letters by his generous familiarity with students.[3] Three other men of high distinction and of fateful future waited on their imperial master. Of these the first was Cardinal Alessandro Farnese, who succeeded Clement in the Papacy, opened the Tridentine Council, and added a new reigning family to the Italian princes. The others were the Pope's nephews, Alessandro de' Medici, Duke of Florence designate, and his cousin the Cardinal Ippolito de' Medici. Six years later, Ippolito died at Itri, poisoned by his cousin Alessandro, who was himself murdered at Florence in 1537 by another cousin, Lorenzino de' Medici.

It had been intended that Charles should travel to Bologna from Parma through Mantua, where the Marquis Federigo Gonzaga had made great preparations for his reception. But the route by Reggio and Modena was more direct; and, yielding to the solicitations of Alfonso, Duke of Ferrara, he selected this instead. One of the stipulations of the Treaty of Barcelona, it will be remembered, had been that the Emperor should restore Emilia—that is to say, the cities and territories of Modena, Reggio, and Rubbiera—to the Papacy. Clement regarded Alfonso as a contumacious vassal, although his own right to that province only rested on the force of arms by which Julius II. had detached it from the Duchy of Ferrara. It was therefore somewhat difficult for Charles to accept the

[3] See Vol. I., *Italian Literature*, p. 371.

duke's hospitality. But when he had once done so, Alfonso knew how to ingratiate himself so well with the arbiter of Italy, that on taking leave of his guest upon the confines of Bologna, he had already secured the success of his own cause.

Great preparations, meanwhile, were being made in Bologna. The misery and destitution of the country rendered money scarce, and cast a gloom over the people. It was noticed that when Clement entered the city on October 24, none of the common folk responded to the shouts of his attendants, *Viva Papa Clemente!* The Pope and his Court, too, were in mourning. They had but recently escaped from the horrors of the Sack of Rome, and were under a vow to wear their beards unshorn in memory of their past sufferings. Yet the municipality and nobles of Bologna exerted their utmost in these bad times to render the reception of the Emperor worthy of the lustre which his residence and coronation would confer upon them. Gallant guests began to flock into the city. Among these may be mentioned the brilliant Isabelle d' Este, sister of Duke Alfonso, and mother of the reigning Marquis of Mantua. She arrived on November 1 with a glittering train of beautiful women, and took up her residence in the Palazzo Manzoli. Her quarters obtained no good fame in the following months; for the ladies of her suite were liberal of favours. Jousts, masquerades, street-brawls and duels were of frequent occurrence beneath her windows—Spaniards and Italians disputing the honour of those light amours. On November 3 came Andrea Doria with his relative, the Cardinal Girolamo of that name. About the same time, Cardinal Lorenzo Campeggi, Bishop of Bologna, returned from his legation to England, where (as students of our history are well aware) he had been engaged upon the question of Henry VIII.'s divorce from Katherine of Aragon. Next day Charles arrived outside the gate, and took up his quarters in the rich convent of Certosa, which now forms the Campo Santo.

He was surrounded by a multitude of ambassadors and delegates from the Bolognese magistracy, by Cardinals and ecclesiastics of all ranks, some of whom had attended him from the frontier, while others were drawn up to receive him. November 5 was a Friday, and this day was reckoned lucky by Charles. He therefore passed the night of the 4th at the Certosa, and on the following morning made his solemn entry into the city. A bodyguard of Germans, Burgundians, Spaniards, halberdiers, lansknechts, men at arms and cannoneers, preceded him. High above these was borne the captain-general of the imperial force in Italy, the fierce and cruel Antonio de Leyva, under whose oppression Milan had been groaning. This ruthless tyrant was a martyr to gout and rheumatism. He could not ride or walk; and though he retained the whole vigour of his intellect and will, it was with difficulty that he moved his hands or head. He advanced in a litter of purple velvet, supported on the shoulders of his slaves. Among the splendid crowd of Spanish grandees who followed the troops, it is enough to mention the Grand Marshal, Don Alvaro Osorio, Marquis of Astorga, who carried a naked sword aloft.

He was armed, on horseback; and his mantle of cloth of gold blazed with dolphins worked in pearls and precious stones. Next came Charles, mounted on a bay jennet, armed at all points, and holding in his hand the sceptre. Twenty-four pages, chosen from the nobles of Bologna, waited on his bridle and stirrups. The train was brought up by a multitude of secular and ecclesiastical princes too numerous to record in detail. Conspicuous among them for the historian were the Count of Nassau, Albert of Brandenburg, and the Marquis Bonifazio of Montferrat, the scion of the Eastern Paleologi. As this procession defiled through the streets of Bologna, it was remarked that Charles, with true Spanish haughtiness, made no response to the acclamations of the people, except once when, passing beneath a balcony of noble ladies, he acknowledged their salute by lifting the cap from his head.

Clement, surrounded by a troop of prelates, was seated to receive him on a platform raised before the Church of San Petronio in the great piazza. The king dismounted opposite the Papal throne, ascended the steps beneath his canopy of gold and crimson, and knelt to kiss the Pontiff's feet. When their eyes first met, it was observed that both turned pale; for the memory of outraged Rome was in the minds of both; and Cæsar, while he paid this homage to Christ's vicar, had the load of those long months of suffering and insult on his conscience. Clement bent down, and with streaming eyes saluted him upon the cheek. Then, while Charles was still upon his knees, they exchanged a few set words referring to the purpose of their meeting and their common desire for the pacification of Christendom. After this the Emperor elect arose, seated himself for a while beside the Pope, and next, at his invitation, escorted him to the great portal of the church. On the way, he inquired after Clement's health; to which the Pope replied somewhat significantly that, after leaving Rome, it had steadily improved. He tempered this allusion to his captivity, however, by adding that his eagerness to greet his Majesty had inspired him with more than wonted strength and courage. At the doorway they parted; and the Emperor, having paid his devotions to the Sacrament and kissed the altar, was conducted to the apartments prepared for him in the Palazzo Pubblico. These were adjacent to the Pope's lodgings in the same palace, and were so arranged that the two potentates could confer in private at all times. It is worthy of remark that the negotiations for the settlement of Italy which took place during the next six months in those rooms, were conducted personally by the high contracting parties, and that none of their deliberations transpired until the result of each was made public.

The whole of November 5 had been occupied in these ceremonies. It was late evening when the Emperor gained his lodgings. The next few days were ostensibly occupied in receiving visitors. Among the first of these was the unfortunate ex-queen of Naples, Isabella, widow of Frederick of Aragon, the last king of the bastard dynasty founded by Alfonso. She was living in poverty at Ferrara, under the protection of her relatives, the Este family. On the 13th came the Prince of Orange and Don

Ferrante Gonzaga, from the camp before Florence. The siege had begun, but had not yet been prosecuted with the strictest vigour. During the whole time of Charles's residence at Bologna, it must be borne in mind that the siege of Florence was being pressed. Superfluous troops detached from garrison duty in the Lombard towns were drafted across the hills to Tuscany. Whatever else the Emperor might decide for his Italian subjects, this at least was certain: Florence should be restored to the Medicean tyrants, as compensation to the Pope for Roman sufferings. The Prince of Orange came to explain the state of things at Florence, where government and people seemed prepared to resist to the death. Gonzaga had private business of his own to conduct, touching his engagement to the Pope's ward, Isabella, daughter and heiress of the wealthy Vespasiano Colonna.

Meanwhile, ambassadors from all the States and lordships of Italy flocked to Bologna. Great nobles from the South—Ascanio Colonna, Grand Constable of Naples; Alfonso d' Avalos, Marquis of Vasto; Giovanni Luigi Caraffa, Prince of Stigliano—took up their quarters in adjacent houses, or in the upper story of the Public Palace. The Marquis of Vasto arrests our gaze for a moment. He was nephew to the Marquis of Pescara (husband of Vittoria Colonna), who had the glory of taking Francis prisoner at Pavia, and afterwards the infamy of betraying the unfortunate Girolamo Morone and his master the Duke of Milan to the resentment of the Spanish monarch. What part Pescara actually played in that dark passage of plot and counterplot remains obscure. But there is no doubt that he employed treachery, single if not double, for his own advantage. His arrogance and avowed hostility to the Italians caused his very name to be execrated; nor did his nephew, the Marquis of Vasto, differ in these respects from the more famous chief of his house. This man was also destined to obtain an evil reputation when he succeeded in 1532 to the government of Milan. Here too may be noticed the presence at Bologna of Girolamo Morone's son, who had been created Bishop of Modena in 1529. For him a remarkable fate was waiting. Condemned to the dungeons of the Inquisition as a heretic by Paul IV., rescued by Pius IV., and taken into highest favour at that Pontiff's Court, he successfully manipulated the closing of the Tridentine Council to the profit of the Papal See.

Negotiations for the settlement of Italian affairs were proceeding without noise, but with continual progress, through this month. The lodgings of ambassadors and lords were so arranged in the Palazzo Pubblico that they, like their Imperial and Papal masters, could confer at all times and seasons. Every day brought some new illustrious visitor. On the 22nd arrived Federigo Gonzaga, Marquis of Mantua, who took up his quarters in immediate proximity to Charles and Clement. His business required but little management. The House of Gonzaga was already well affected to the Spanish cause, and counted several captains in the imperial army. Charles showed his favour by raising Mantua to the rank of a Duchy. It was different with the Republic of Venice and the Duke of Milan. The Emperor elect had reasons to be strongly prejudiced against them both—against Venice, as the most formidable of the French allies in the last war; against Francesco Maria Sforza, as having been implicated, though obscurely, in Morone's conspiracy to drive the Spaniards from Italy and place the crown of Naples on Pescara's head. Clement took both under his protection. He had sufficient reasons to believe that the Venetians would purchase peace by the cession of their recent acquisitions on the Adriatic coast, and he knew that the pacification of Italy could not be accomplished without their aid. In effect, the Republic agreed to relinquish Cervia and Ravenna to the Pope, and their Apulian ports to Charles, engaging at the same time to pay a sum of 300,000 ducats and stipulating for an amnesty to all their agents and dependents. It is not so clear why Clement warmly espoused the cause of Sforza. That he did so is certain. He obtained a safe-conduct for the duke, and made it a point of personal favour that he should be received into the Emperor's grace. This stipulation appears to have been taken into account when the affairs of Ferrara were decided at a later date against the Papal interests.

Francesco Maria Sforza appeared in Bologna on the 22nd. This unfortunate bearer of one of the most coveted titles in Europe had lately lived a prisoner in his own Castello, while the city at his doors and the fertile country round it were being subjected to cruellest outrage and oppression from Spanish, French, Swiss, and German mercenaries. He was a man ruined in health as well as fortune. Six years before this date, one of his chamberlains, Bonifazio Visconti, had given him a slight wound in the shoulder with a poisoned dagger. From this wound he never recovered; and it was pitiable to behold the broken man, unable to move or stand without support, dragging himself upon his knees to Cæsar's footstool. Charles appears to have discerned that he had nothing to fear and much to gain, if he showed clemency to so powerless a suitor. Francesco was the last of his line. His health rendered it impossible that he should expect heirs; and although he subsequently married a princess of the House of Denmark, he died childless in the autumn of 1535. It was therefore determined, in compliance with the Pope's request, that Sforza should be confirmed in the Duchy of Milan. Pavia, however, was detached and given to the terrible Antonio de Leyva for his lifetime. The garrisons of Milan and Como were left in Spanish hands; and the duke promised to wring 400,000 ducats as the price of his investiture, with an additional sum of 500,000 ducats to be paid in ten yearly instalments, from his already blood-sucked people. It will be observed that money figured largely in all these high political transactions. Charles, though lord of many lands, was, even at this early stage of his career, distressed for want of cash. He rarely paid his troops, but commissioned the captains in his service to levy contributions on the provinces they occupied. The funds thus raised did not always reach the pockets of the soldiers, who subsisted as best they could by marauding. Having made these terms, Francesco Maria Sforza was received into the Imperial favour.

He returned to Milan, in no sense less a prisoner than he had previously been, and with the heartrending necessity of extorting money from his subjects at the point of Spanish swords. In exchange for the ducal title, he thus had made himself a tax-collector for his natural enemies. Secluded in the dreary chambers of his castle, assailed by the execrations of the Milanese, he may well have groaned, like Marlowe's Edward—

> But what are Kings, when regiment is gone,
> But perfect shadows in a sunshine day?
> My foemen rule; I bear the name of King;
> I wear the crown; but am controlled by them.

When he died he bequeathed his duchy to the crown of Spain. It was detached from the Empire, and became the private property of Charles and of his son, Philip II.

During the month of December negotiations for the terms of peace in Italy went briskly forward. On the part of Venice, two men of the highest distinction arrived as orators. These were Pietro Bembo and Gasparo Contarini, both of whom received the honours of the Cardinalate from Paul III. on his accession. Of Bembo's place in Italian society, as the dictator of literature at this epoch, I have already sufficiently spoken in another part of my work on the Renaissance. Contarini will more than once arrest our notice in the course of this volume. Of all the Italians of the time, he was perhaps the greatest, wisest, and most sympathetic. Had it been possible to avert the breach between Catholicism and Protestantism, to curb the intolerance of Inquisitors and the ambition of Jesuits, and to guide the reform of the Church by principles of moderation and liberal piety, Contarini was the man who might have restored unity to the Church in Europe. Once, indeed, at Regensburg in 1541, he seemed upon the very point of effecting a reconciliation between the parties that were tearing Christendom asunder. But his failure was even more conspicuous than his momentary semblance of success. It was not in the temper of the times to accept a Concordat founded on however philosophical, however politic considerations. Contarini will be remembered as a 'beautiful soul,' born out of the due moment, and by no means adequate to cope with the fierce passions that raged round him. Among Protestants he was a Catholic, and they regarded his half-measures with contempt. Among Catholics he passed for a suspected Lutheran, and his writings were only tolerated after they had been subjected to rigorous castration at the hands of Papal Inquisitors.[4]

On Christmas eve the ambassadors and representatives of the Italian Powers met together in the chambers of Cardinal Gattinara, Grand Chancellor of the Empire, to subscribe the terms of a confederation and perpetual league for the maintenance of peace. From this important document the Florentines were excluded, as open rebels to the will of Charles and Clement. There was no justice in the rigour with which Florence was now treated. Her republican independence had hitherto

[4] See Ranke, vol. i. p. 153, note.

been recognised, although her own internal discords exposed her to a virtual despotism. But Clement stipulated and Charles conceded, as a *sine qua non* in the project of pacification, that Florence should be converted into a Medicean duchy. For the Duke of Ferrara, whom the Pope regarded as a contumacious vassal, and whose affairs were still the subject of debate, a place was specially reserved in the treaty. He, as I have already observed, had been taken under the Imperial protection; and a satisfactory settlement of his claims was now a mere question of time. On the evening of the same day, the Pope bestowed on Charles the Sword of the Spirit, which it was the wont of Rome to confer on the best-beloved of her secular sons at this festival. The peace was publicly proclaimed, amid universal plaudits, on the last day of the year 1529.

The chief affairs to be decided in the new year were the reduction of Florence to submission and the coronation of the Emperor. The month of January was passed in jousts and pastimes; ceremonial privileges were conferred on the University of Bologna; magnificent embassies from the Republic of S. Mark, glowing in senatorial robes of crimson silk, were entertained; and a singular deputation from the African Court of Prester John obtained audience of the Roman Pontiff. Amid these festivities there arrived, on January 16, three delegates from Florence, who spent some weeks in fruitless efforts to obtain a hearing from the arbiters of Italy. Clement refused to deal with them, because their commonwealth was still refractory. Charles repelled them, because he wished to gratify the Pope, and knew that Florence remained staunch in her devotion to the French crown. The old proverb 'Lilies with lilies,' the white lily of Florence united with the golden fleur-de-lys of France, had still political significance in this day of Italian degradation. Meanwhile Francis I. treated his faithful allies with lukewarm tolerance. The smaller fry of Italian potentates, worshippers of the rising sun of Spain, curried favour with their masters by insulting the republic's representatives. On their return to Florence, the ambassadors had to report a total diplomatic failure. But this, far from breaking the untamable spirit of the Signory and people, prompted them in February to new efforts of resistance and to edicts of outlawry against citizens whom they regarded as traitors to the State. Among the proscribed were Francesco Guicciardini, Roberto Acciaiuoli, Francesco Vettori, and Baccio Valori. Of these men Francesco Guicciardini, Francesco Vettori, and Baccio Valori were attendant at Bologna upon the Pope. They all adhered with fidelity to the Medicean party at this crisis of their country's fate, and all paid dearly for their loyalty. When Cosimo I., by their efforts, was established in the duchy, he made it one of his first cares to rid himself of these too faithful servants. Baccio Valori was beheaded after the battle of Montemurlo in 1537 for practice with the exiles of Filippo Strozzi's party. Francesco Guicciardini, Francesco Vettori, and Roberto Acciaiuoli died in disgrace before the year 1543—their only crime being that they had made themselves the ladder whereby a Medici had climbed into his throne, and which it was his business to upset when firmly seated. For the heroism of Florence at this moment it would be difficult to find fit words of panegyric. The republic stood alone, abandoned by France to the hot rage of Clement and the cold contempt of Charles, deserted by the Powers of Italy, betrayed by lying captains, deluged on all sides with the scum of armies pouring into Tuscany from the Lombard pandemonium of war. The situation was one of impracticable difficulty. Florence could not but fall. Yet every generous heart will throb with sympathy while reading the story of that final stand for independence, in which a handful of burghers persisted, though congregated princes licked the dust from feet of Emperor and Pontiff.

Charles had come to assume the iron and the golden crowns in Italy. He ought to have journeyed to Monza or to S. Ambrogio at Milan for the first and to the Lateran in Rome for the second of these investitures. An Emperor of the Swabian House would have been compelled by precedent and superstition to observe this form. It is true that the coronation of a German prince as the successor of Lombard kings and Roman Augusti, had always been a symbolic ceremony rather than a rite which ratified genuine Imperial authority. Still the ceremomy connoted many mediæval aspirations. It was the outward sign of theories that had once exerted an ideal influence. To dissociate the twofold sacrament from Milan and from Rome was the same as robbing it of its main virtue, the virtue of a mystical conception. It was tantamount to a demonstration that the belief in Universal Monarchy had passed away. By breaking the old rules of his investiture, Charles notified the disappearance of the mediæval order, and proclaimed new political ideals to the world. When asked whether he would not follow custom and seek the Lombard crown in Monza, he brutally replied that he was not wont to run after crowns, but to have crowns running after him. He trampled no less on that still more venerable *religio loci* which attached imperial rights to Rome. Together with this ancient piety, he swept the Holy Roman Empire into the dust-heap of archaic curiosities. By declaring his will to be crowned where he chose, he emphasised the modern state motto of *L'état, c'est moi*, and prepared the way for a Pope's closing of a General Council by the phrase *L'Eglise, c'est moi.* Charles had sufficient reasons for acting as he did. The Holy Roman Empire ever since the first event of Charles the Great's coronation, when it justified itself as a diplomatical expedient for unifying Western Christendom, had existed more or less as a shadow. Charles violated the duties which alone gave the semblance of a substance to that shadow. As King of Italy, he had desolated the Lombard realm of which he sought the title. As Emperor elect, he had ravished his bride, the Eternal City. As suitor to the Pope for both of his expected crowns, he stood responsible for the multiplied insults to which Clement had been so recently exposed. No Emperor had been more powerful since Charles the Great than this Charles V., the last who took his crowns in Italy. It was significant that the man in whose name Rome had suffered outrage, and who was about to detach Lombardy from the Empire, was by his own will invested at Bologna. The citizens of Monza were accordingly bidden to send the iron crown to Bologna. It arrived on February 20, and on the 22nd Charles received it from the hands of Clement in the chapel of the palace. The Cardinal who preformed the ceremony of unction was a Fleming, William Hencheneor, who in the Sack of Rome had bought his freedom for the large sum of 40,000 crowns. On this auspicious occasion he cut off half the beard which he still wore in sign of mourning!

The Duke and Duchess of Urbino made their entrance into Bologna on the same day. Francesco Maria della Rovere, Duke of Urbino, Prefect of Rome, and Captain General of the armies of the Church, was one of the most noted warriors of that time. Yet victory had rarely crowned his brows with laurels. Imitating the cautious tactics of Braccio, and emulating the fame of Fabius Cunctator, he reduced the art of war to a system of manœuvres, and rarely risked his fortune in the field. It was chiefly due to his dilatory movements that the disaster of the Sack of Rome was not averted. He had been expelled by Leo X. from his duchy to make room for Lorenzo de' Medici, and report ran that a secret desire to witness the humiliation of a Medicean Pontiff caused him to withhold his forces from attacking the tumultuary troops of Bourbon. Francesco Maria was a man of violent temper; nineteen years before, he had murdered the Pope's Legate, Cardinal Francesco Alidosi, with his dagger, in the open streets of Bologna. His wife, Eleanora Ippolita Gonzaga, presided with grace over that brilliant and cultivated Court which Castiglione made famous by his 'Cortegiano.' The duke and duchess survive to posterity in two masterpieces of portraiture by the hand of Titian which now adorn the gallery of the Uffizzi.

February 24, which was the anniversary of Charles's birthday, had been fixed for his coronation as Emperor in San Petronio. This church is one of the largest Gothic buildings in Italy. Its façade occupies the southern side of the piazza. The western side, on the left of the church, is taken up by the Palazzo Pubblico. In order to facilitate the passage of the Pope and Emperor with their Courts and train of princes from the palace to the cathedral, a wooden bridge wide enough to take six men abreast was constructed from an opening in the Hall of the Ancients. The bridge descended by a gradual line to the piazza, broadened out into a platform before the front of San Petronio, and then again ascended through the nave to the high altar. It was covered with blue draperies, and so arranged that the vast multitudes assembled in the square and church to see the ceremony had free access to it on all sides. On the morning of the 24th, the solemn procession issued from the palace, and defiled in order down the gangway. Clement was borne aloft by Pontifical grooms in their red liveries. He wore the tiara and a cope of state fastened by Cellini's famous stud, in which blazed the Burgundian diamond of Charles the Bold. Charles walked in royal robes attended by the Count of Nassau and Don Pietro di Toledo, the Viceroy of Naples, who afterwards gave his name to the chief street in that city. Before him went the Marquis of Montferrat, bearing the sceptre; Philip, Duke of

Bavaria, carrying the golden orb; the Duke of Urbino, with the sword; and the Duke of Savoy, holding the imperial diadem. This Duke of Savoy was uncle to Francis I. and brother-in-law to Charles—his wife, Beatrice, being a sister of the Empress, and his sister, Louise, mother of the French king. This double relationship made his position during the late wars a difficult one. Yet his territory had been regarded as neutral, and in the pacification of Italy he judged it wise to adhere without reserve to the victorious King of Spain. It was noticed that Ferrante di Sanseverino, Prince of Salerno, though known to be in Bologna, occupied no post of distinction in the Imperial train. He was closely related to the Emperor by his mother, Maria of Aragon, and had done good service in the recent campaigns against Lautrec. The reason for this neglect does not appear. But it may be mentioned that some years later he espoused the French cause, and was deprived of his vast hereditary fiefs. In his ruin the poet Bernardo, father of Torquato Tasso, was involved.

To enumerate all the nobles of Spain, Italy and Germany, with the ambassadors from England, France, Scotland, Hungary, Bohemia and Portugal, who swelled the Imperial *cortège*; to describe the series of ceremonies by which Charles was first consecrated as a deacon, anointed, dressed and undressed, and finally conducted to the Pope for coronation; to narrate the breaking of the bridge at one point, and the squabbles between the Genoese and Sienese delegates for precedence, would be superfluously tedious. The day was well-nigh over when at length Charles received the Imperial insignia from the Pope's hands. *Accipe gladium sanctum, Accipe virgam, Accipe pomum, Accipe signum gloriæ!* As Clement pronounced these sentences, he gave the sword, the sceptre, the globe, and the diadem in succession to the Emperor, who kelt before him. Charles bent and kissed the Papal feet. He then rose and took his throne beside the Pope. It was placed two steps lower than that of Clement. The ceremony of coronation and inthronisation being now complete, Charles was proclaimed: *Romanorum Imperator semper augustus, mundi totius Dominus, universis Dominis, universis Principibus et Populis semper venerandus.* When Mass was over, Pope and Emperor shook hands. At the church-door, Charles held Clement's stirrup, and when the Pope had mounted, he led his palfrey for some paces, in sign of filial submission.

The month of March was distinguished by the arrival of illustrious visitors. The Duchess of Savoy, with an escort of eighteen lovely maids of honour, made her pompous entry on the 4th, and took up her quarters in the Palazzo Pepoli. On the 6th came the Duke of Ferrara, for whom Charles had procured a safe-conduct from the Pope. During the Emperor's stay at Bologna, Alfonso d' Este had been assiduous in paying him and his Court small attentions, sending excellent provisions for the household and furnishing the royal table with game and every kind of delicacy. The settlement of his dispute with the Holy See was the only important business that remained to be transacted. Charles prevailed upon both Clement and Alfonso to state their cases in writing and to place them in the hands of jurisconsults to report upon. There is little doubt that his own mind was already made up in favor of the duke; but he did not pass sentence until the following December, nor was the decision published before April in the year 1531. The substance of the final agreement was as follows. Modena, Reggio and Rubbiera were declared fiefs of the Empire, seeing that they had not been included in Pepin's gift of the Exarchate. Charles confirmed their investiture to Alfonso, in return for a considerable payment to the Imperial Chancery. He had previously conferred the town of Carpi, forfeited by Alberto Pio as a French adherent, on the duke. Ferrara remained a fief of the Church, and Clement consented to acknowledge Alfonso's tenure, upon his disbursement of 100,000 ducats. This decision saved Modena to the bastard line of Este, when Pope Clement VIII. seized Ferrara as a lapsed fief in 1598. In the sixty-seven years which passed between the date of Charles's coronation and the extinction of the duchy, Ferrara enjoyed the fame of the most brilliant Court in Italy, and shone with the lustre conferred on it by men like Tasso and Guarini.

The few weeks which now remained before Charles left Bologna were spent for the most part in jousts and tournaments, visits to churches, and social entertainments. Veronica Gambara threw her apartments open to the numerous men of letters who crowded from all parts of Italy to witness the ceremony of Charles's coronation. This lady was widow to the late lord of Correggio, and one of the two most illustrious women of her time.[5] She dwelt with princely state in a palace of the Marsili; and here might be seen the poets Bembo, Mauro, and Molza in conversation with witty Berni, learned Vida, stately Trissino, and noblehearted Marcantonio Flaminio. Paolo Giovio and Francesco Guicciardini, the chief historians of their time, were also to be found there, together with a host of literary and diplomatic worthies attached to the Courts of Urbino and Ferrara or attendant on the train of cardinals, who, like Ippolito de' Medici, made a display of culture. Meanwhile the Dowager Marchioness of Mantua and the Duchess of Savoy entertained Italian and Spanish nobles with masqued balls and carnival processions in the Manzoli and Pepoli palaces. Frequent quarrels between hot-blooded youths of the rival nations added a spice of chivalrous romance to love-adventures in which the ladies of these Courts played a too conspicuous part. What still remained to Italy of Renaissance splendour, wit, and fashion, after the Sack of Rome and the prostration of her wealthiest cities, was concentrated in this sunset blaze of sumptuous festivity at Bologna. Nor were the arts without illustrious representatives. Francesco Mazzola, surnamed Il Parmigianino, before whose altar-piece in his Roman studio the rough soldiers of Bourbon's army were said to have lately knelt in adoration, commemorated the hero of the day by painting Charles attended by Fame who crowned his forehead, and an infant Hercules who handed him the globe. Titian, too, was there, and received the honour

[5] See Vol. I., *Italian Literature,* p. 331.

of several sittings from the Emperor. His life-sized portrait of Charles in full armour, seated on a white war-horse, has perished. But it gave such satisfaction at the moment that the fortunate master was created knight and count palatine, and appointed painter to the Emperor with a fixed pension. Titian also painted portraits of Antonio de Leyva and Alfonso d' Avalos, but whether upon this occasion or in 1532, when he was again summoned to the Imperial Court at Bologna, is not certain. From this assemblage of eminent personages we notice the absence of Pietro Aretino. He was at the moment out of favour with Clement VII. But independently of this obstacle, he may well have thought it imprudent to quit his Venetian retreat and expose himself to the resentment of so many princes whom he had alternately loaded with false praises and bemired with loathsome libels.

People observed that the Emperor in his excursions through the streets of Bologna usually wore the Spanish habit. He was dressed in black velvet, with black silk stockings, black shoes, and a black velvet cap adorned with black feathers. This sombre costume received some relief from jewels used for buttons; and the collar of the Golden Fleece shone upon the monarch's breast. So slight a circumstance would scarcely deserve attention, were it not that in a short space of time it became the fashion throughout Italy to adopt the subdued tone of Spanish clothing. The upper classes consented to exchange the varied and brilliant dresses which gave gaiety to the earlier Renaissance for the dismal severity conspicuous in Morone's masterpieces, in the magnificent gloom of the Genoese Brignoli, and in the portraits of Roman Inquisitors. It is as though the whole race had put on mourning for its loss of liberty, its servitude to foreign tyrants and ecclesiastical hypocrites. Nor is it fanciful to detect a note of moral sadness and mental depression corresponding to these black garments in the faces of that later generation. How different is Tasso's melancholy grace from Ariosto's gentle joyousness; the dried-up precision of Baroccio's Francesco Maria della Rovere from the sanguine joviality of Titian's first duke of that name! One of the most acutely critical of contemporary poets felt the change which I have indicated, and ascribed it to the same cause. Campanella wrote as follows:

> Black robes befit our age. Once they were white;
> Next many-hued; now dark as Afric's Moor,
> Night-black, infernal, traitorous, obscure,
> Horrid with ignorance and sick with fright.
> For very shame we shun all colours bright,
> Who mourn our end—the tyrants we endure,
> The chains, the noose, the lead, the snares, the lure—
> Our dismal heroes, our souls sunk in night.

In the midst of this mirth-making there arrived on March 20 an embassy from England, announcing Henry VIII.'s resolve to divorce himself at any cost from Katherine of Aragon. This may well have recalled both Pope and Emperor to a sense of the gravity of European affairs. The schism of England was now imminent. Germany was distracted by Protestant revolution. The armies of Cæsar were largely composed of mutinous Lutherans. Some of these soldiers had even dared to overthrow a colossal statue of Clement VII. and grind it into powder at Bologna; and this outrage, as it appears, went unpunished. The very troops employed in reducing rebellious Florence were commanded by a Lutheran general; and Clement began to fear that, after Charles's departure, the Prince of Orange might cross the Apennines and expose the Papal person to the insults of another captivity in Bologna. Nor were the gathering forces of revolutionary Protestants alone ominous. Though Soliman had been repulsed before Vienna, the Turks were still advancing on the eastern borders of the Empire. Their fleets swept the Levantine waters, while the pirate dynasties of Tunis and Algiers threatened the whole Mediterranean coast with ruin. Charles, still uncertain what part he should take in the disputes of Germany, left Bologna for the Tyrol on March 23. Clement, on the last day of the month, took his journey by Loreto to Rome.

It will be useful, at this point, to recapitulate the net results of Charles's administration of Italian affairs in 1530. The kingdom of the Two Sicilies, with the island of Sardinia and the Duchy of Milan, became Spanish provinces, and were ruled henceforth by viceroys. The House of Este was confirmed in the Duchy of Ferrara, including Modena and Reggio. The Duchies of Savoy and Mantua and the Marquisate of Montferrat, which had espoused the Spanish cause, were undisturbed. Genoa and Siena, both of them avowed allies of Spain, the former under Spanish protection, the latter subject to Spanish coercion, remained with the name and empty privileges of republics. Venice had made her peace with Spain, and though she was still strong enough to pursue an independent policy, she showed as yet no inclination, and had, indeed, no power, to stir up enemies against the Spanish autocrat. The Duchy of Urbino, recognised by Rome and subservient to Spanish influence, was permitted to exist. The Papacy once more assumed a haughty tone, relying on the firm alliance struck with Spain. This league, as years went by, was destined to grow still closer, still more fruitful of results.

Florence alone had been excepted from the articles of peace. It was still enduring the horrors of the memorable siege when Clement left Bologna at the end of May. The last hero of the republic, Francesco Ferrucci, fell fighting at Gavignana on August 2. Their general, Malatesta Baglioni, broke his faith with the citizens. Finally, on August 12, the town capitulated. Alessandro de' Medici, who had received the title of Duke of Florence from Charles at Bologna, took up his residence there in July 1531, and held the State by help of Spanish mercenaries under the command of Alessandro Vitelli. When he was murdered by his cousin in 1537, Cosimo de' Medici, the scion of another branch of the ruling family, was appointed Duke. Charles V. recognised his title and Cosimo soon showed that he determined to be master in his own duchy. He crushed the exiled party of Filippo Strozzi, who attempted a revolution of the State, exterminated its leaders, and contrived to rid himself of the powerful adherents who had placed him on the throne. But he remained a subservient though not very willing ally of Spain; and when he expelled Alessandro Vitelli from the fortress that commanded Florence, he admitted a Spaniard, Don Juan de Luna, in his stead. During the petty wars of 1552-56 which Henri II. carried on with Charles V. in Italy, Siena attempted to shake off the yoke of a Spanish garrison established there in 1547 under the command of Don Hurtado de Mendoza. The citizens appealed to France, who sent them the great Marshal, Piero Strozzi, brother of Cosimo's vanquished enemy Filippo. Cosimo through these years supported the Spanish cause with troops and money, hoping to guide events in his own interest. At length, by the aid of Gian Giacomo Medici, sprung from an obscure Milanese family, who had been trained in the Spanish methods of warfare, he succeeded in subduing Siena. He now reaped the fruits of his Spanish policy. In 1557 Philip II. conceded the Sienese territory, reserving only its forts, to the Duke of Florence, who in 1569 obtained the title of Grand Duke of Tuscany from Pope Pius V. This title was confirmed by the Empire in 1575 to his son Francesco.

Thus the republics of Florence and Siena were extinguished. The Grand Duchy of Tuscany was created. It became an Italian power of the first magnitude, devoted to the absolutist principles of Spanish and Papal sovereignty. The further changes which took place in Italy after the year 1530, turned equally to the profit of Spain and Rome. These were principally the creation of the Duchy of Parma for the Farnesi (1545-1559), of which I shall have to speak in the next chapter; the resumption of Ferrara by the Papacy in 1597, which reduced the House of Este to the smaller fiefs of Modena and Reggio; the acquisition of Montferrat by Mantua in 1536; the cession of Saluzzo to Savoy in 1598, and the absorption of Urbino into the Papal domains in 1631.

It was hoped when Charles and Clement proclaimed the pacification of Italy at Bologna on the last day of 1529, that the peninsula would no longer be the theatre of wars for supremacy between the French and Spaniards. This expectation proved delusive; for the struggle soon broke out again. The people, however, suffered less extensively than in former years; because the Spanish party, supported by Papal authority, was decidedly predominant. The Italian princes, whether they like it or not, were compelled to follow in the main a Spanish policy. At length, in 1559, by the Peace of Cateau Cambresis signed between Henri II. and Philip II., the French claims were finally abandoned, and the Spanish hegemony was formally acknowledged. The later treaty of Vervins, in 1598, ceded Saluzzo to the Duchy of Savoy, and shut the gates of Italy to French interference.

Though the people endured far less misery from foreign armies in the period between 1530 and 1600 than they had done in the period from 1494 to 1527, yet the state of the country grew ever more and more deplorable. This was due in the first instance to the insane methods of taxation adopted by the Spanish viceroys, who held monopolies of corn and other necessary commodities in their hands, and who invented imposts for the meanest articles of consumption. Their example was followed by the Pope and petty princes. Alfonso II. of Ferrara, for instance, levied a tenth on all produce which passed his city gates, and on the capital engaged in every contract. He monopolised the sale of salt, flour, bread; and imposed a heavy tax on oil. Sixtus V. by exactions of a like description and by the sale of numberless offices, accumulated a vast sum of money, much of which bore heavy interest. He was so ignorant of the first principle of political economy as to lock up the accruing treasure in the Castle of S. Angelo. The rising of Masaniello in Naples was simply due to the exasperation of the common folk at having even fruit and vegetables taxed. In addition to such financial blunders, we must take into account the policy pursued by all princes at this epoch, of discouraging commerce and manufactures. Thus Cosimo I. of Tuscany induced the old Florentine families to withdraw their capital from trade, sink it in land, create entails in perpetuity on eldest sons, and array themselves with gimcrack titles which he liberally supplied. Even Venice showed at this epoch a contempt for the commerce which had brought her into a position of unrivalled splendour. This wilful depression of industry was partly the result of Spanish aristocratic habits, which now invaded Italian society. But it was also deliberately chosen as a means of extinguishing freedom. Finally, if war proved now less burdensome, the exhaustion of Italy and the decay of military spirit rendered the people liable to the scourge of piracy. The whole seacoast was systematically plundered by the navies of Barbarossa and Dragut. The inhabitants of the ports and inland villages were carried off into slavery, and many of the Italians themselves drove a brisk trade in the sale of their compatriots. Brigandage, following in the wake of agricultural depression and excessive taxation, depopulated the central provinces. All these miseries were exacerbated by frequent recurrences of plagues and famines.

It is characteristic of the whole tenor of Italian history that, in spite of the virtual hegemony which the Spaniards now exercised in the peninsula, the nation continued to exist in separate parcels, each of which retained a certain individuality. That Italy could not have been treated as a single province by the Spanish autocrat will be manifest, when we consider the European jealousy to which so summary an exhibition of force would have given rise. It is also certain that the Papacy, which had to be respected, would have resisted an openly declared Spanish despotism. But more powerful, I think, than all these considerations together, was the past prestige of the Italian States. Europe was not prepared to regard that brilliant and hitherto respected constellation of commonwealths, from which all intellectual culture, arts of life, methods of commerce, and theories of political existence had been diffused, as a single province of the Spanish monarchy. The Spaniards themselves were scarcely in a position to entertain the thought of reducing the peninsula to bondage, *vi et armis*. And if they had attempted any measure tending to this result, they would undoubtedly have been resisted by an alliance of the European Powers. What they sought, and what they gained, was a preponderating influence in each of the parcels which they recognised as nominally independent.

The intellectual and social life of the Italians, though much reduced in vigour, was therefore still, as formerly, concentrated in cities marked by distinct local qualities, and boastful of their ancient glories. The Courts of Ferrara and Urbino continued to form centres for literary and artistic coteries. Venice remained the stronghold of mental unrestraint and moral license, where thinkers uttered their thoughts with tolerable freedom, and libertines indulged their tastes unhindered. Rome early assumed novel airs of piety, and external conformity to austere patterns became the fashion here. Yet the Papal capital did not wholly cease to be the resort of students and of artists. The universities maintained themselves in a respectable position—far different, indeed, from that which they had held in the last century, yet not ignoble. Much was being learned on many lines of study divergent from those prescribed by earlier humanists. Padua, in particular, distinguished itself for medical researches. This was the flourishing time, moreover, of Academies, in which, notwithstanding nonsense talked and foolish tastes indulged, some solid work was done for literature and science. The names of the Cimento, Della Crusca, and Palazzo Vernio at Florence, remind us of not unimportant labours in physics, in the analysis of language, and in the formation of a new dramatic style of music. At the same time the resurgence of popular literature and the creation of popular theatrical types deserve to be particularly noticed. It is as though the Italian nation at this epoch, suffocated by Spanish etiquette, and poisoned by Jesuitical hypocrisy, sought to expand healthy lungs in free spaces of open air, indulging in dialectical niceties and immortalising street-jokes by the genius of masqued comedy.

This most ancient and intensely vital race had given Europe the Roman Republic, the Roman Empire, the system of Roman law, the Romance languages, Latin Christianity, the Papacy, and, lastly, all that is included in the art and culture of the Renaissance. It was time, perhaps, that it should go to rest a century or so, and watch uprising nations—the Spanish, English, French, and so forth—stir their stalwart limbs in common strife and novel paths of pioneering industry.

After such fashion let us, then, if we can contrive to do so, regard the Italians during their subjection to the Church and Austria. Were it not for these consolatory reflections, and for the present reappearance of the nation in a new and previously unapprehended form of unity, the history of the Counter-Reformation period would be almost too painful for investigation. What the Italians actually accomplished during this period in art, learning, science, and literature, was indeed more than enough to have conferred undying lustre on such races as the Dutch or Germans at the same epoch. But it would be ridiculous to compare Italians with either Dutchmen or Germans at a time when Italy was still so incalculably superior. Compared with their own standard, compared with what they might have achieved under more favourable conditions of national independence, the products of this age are saddening. The tragic elements of my present theme are summed up in the fact that Italy during the Counter-Reformation was inferior to Italy during the Renaissance, and that this inferiority was due to the interruption of vital and organic processes by reactionary forces.

It would not be just to condemn Spain and the Papacy because, being reactionary powers, they quenched for three centuries the genial light of Italy. We must rather bear in mind that both Spain and the Papacy were at that time cosmopolitan factors of the first magnitude, with perplexing world-problems confronting them. Charles bore upon his shoulders the concerns of the Empire, the burden of the German revolution, and the distracting anxiety of a duel with Islam. When his son bowed to the yoke of government, he had to meet the same perplexities, complicated with Netherlands in revolt, England in antagonism, and France in dubious ferment. A succession of Popes were hampered by painful European questions, which the instinct of self-preservation taught them to regard as paramount. They were fighting for existence; for the Catholic creed; for their own theocratic sovereignty. They held strong cards. But against them were drawn up the battalions of heresy, free thought, political insurgence in the modern world. The *Zeitgeist* that has made us what we are, had begun to organise stern opposition to the Church. It was natural enough that both the Spanish autocrat and the successor of S. Peter should at this crisis have regarded Italian affairs as subordinate in importance to wider matters which demanded their attention. Yet if we shift our point of view from this high vantage-ground of Imperial and Papal anxieties, and place ourselves in the centre of Italy as our post of observation, it will be apparent that nothing more ruinous for the prosperity of the Italian people could have been devised than the joint autocracy accorded at Bologna to two cosmopolitan but non-national forces in their midst. An alien monarchy greedy for gold, a panic-stricken hierarchy in terror for its life, warped the tendencies and throttled the energies of the most artistically sensitive, the most heroically innovating of the existing races. However we may judge the merits of the Spaniards, they were assuredly not those which had brought Italy into the first rank of European nations. The events of a single century proved that, far from being able to govern other peoples, Spain was incapable of self-government on any rational principle. Whatever may have been the policy thrust upon the chief of Latin Christianity in the desperate struggle with militant rationalism, the repressive measures which it felt bound to adopt were eminently pernicious to a race like the Italians, who showed no disposition for religious regeneration, and who were yet submitted to the tyranny of ecclesiastical discipline and intellectual intolerance at every point.

The settlement made by Charles V. in 1530, and the various changes which took place in the duchies between that date and the end of the century, had then the effect of rendering the Papacy and Spain omnipotent in Italy. These kindred autocrats were joined in firm alliance, except during the brief period of Paul IV.'s French policy, which ended in the Pope's complete discomfiture by Alva in 1557. They used their aggregated forces for the riveting of spiritual, political, and social chains upon the modern world. What they only partially effected in Europe at large, by means of S. Bartholomew massacres, exterminations of Jews in Toledo and of Mussulmans in Granada, holocausts of victims in the Low Countries, wars against French Huguenots and German Lutherans, naval expeditions and plots against the state of England, assassinations of heretic princes, and occasional burning of free-thinkers, they achieved with plenary success in Italy. The centre of the peninsula, from Ferrara to Terracina, lay at the discretion of the Pope. The Two Sicilies, Sardinia and the Duchy of Milan were absolute dependencies of the Spanish crown. Tuscany was linked by ties of interest, and by the stronger bonds of terrorism, to Spain. The insignificant principalities of Mantua, Modena, Parma could not do otherwise than submit to the same predominant authority. It is not worth while to take into account the tiny republics of Genoa and Lucca. Their history through this period, though not so uneventful, is scarcely less insignificant than that of San Marino. Venice alone stood independent, still powerful enough to extinguish Bedmar's Spanish conspiracy in silence, still proud enough to resist the encroachments of Paul V. with spirit, yet sensible of her decline and spending her last energies on warfare with the Turk.

At the close of the century, by the Peace of Vervins in 1598 and two subsequent treaties, Spain and France settled their long dispute. France was finally excluded from Italy by the cession of Saluzzo to Savoy, while Savoy at the same moment, through the loss of its Burgundian provinces, became an Italian power. The old antagonism which, dating from the Guelf and Ghibelline contentions of the thirteenth century, had taken a new form after the Papal investiture of Charles of Anjou with the kingdoms of Sicily and Naples, now ceased. That antique antagonism of parties, alien to the home interests of Italy, had been exasperated by the rivalry of Angevine and Aragonese princes; had assumed formidable intensity after the invasion of Charles VIII. in 1494; and had expanded under the reigns of Louis XII. and Francis I. into an open struggle between France and Spain for the supremacy of Italy. It now was finally terminated by the exclusion of the French and the acknowledged overlordship of the Spaniard. But though peace seemed to be secured to a nation tortured by so many desolating wars of foreign armies, the Italians regarded the cession of Saluzzo with despondency. The partisans of national independence and political freedom had become, however illogically, accustomed to consider France as their ally.[6] They now beheld the gates of Italy closed against the French; they saw the extinction of their ancient Guelf policy of calling French arms into Italy. They felt that rest from strife was dearly bought at the price of prostrate servitude

[6] See, for instance, temp. Henri IV., Sarpi's *Letters*, vol. i. p. 233.

beneath Spanish and Austrian Hapsburgs, Spanish Bourbons, and mongrel princelings bred by crossing these stocks with decaying scions of Italian nobility. As a matter of fact, this was the destiny which lay before them for nearly two centuries after the signing of the Peace of Vervins.

Yet the cession of Saluzzo was really the first dawn of hope for Italy. It determined the House of Savoy as an Italian dynasty, and brought for the first time into the sphere of purely Italian interests that province from which the future salvation of the nation was to come. From 1598 until 1870 the destinies of Italy were bound up with the advance of Savoy from a duchy to a kingdom, with its growth in wealth, military resources and political self-consciousness, and with its ultimate acceptance of the task, accomplished in our days, of freeing Italy from foreign tyranny and forming a single nation out of many component elements. Those component elements by their diversity had conferred lustre on the race in the Middle Ages, by their jealousies had wrecked its independence in the Renaissance, and by their weakness had left it at the period of the Counter-Reformation a helpless prey to Papal and Spanish despotism.

The levelling down of the component elements of the Italian race beneath a common despotism, which began in the period I have chosen for this work, was necessary perhaps before Italy could take her place as a united nation gifted with constitutional self-government and independence. Except, therefore, for the sufferings and the humiliations inflicted on her people; except for their servitude beneath the most degrading forms of ecclesiastical and temporal tyranny; except for the annihilation of their beautiful Renaissance culture; except for the depression of arts, learning, science, and literature, together with the enfeeblement of political energy and domestic morality; except for the loathsome domination of hypocrites and persecutors and informers; except for the Jesuitical encouragement of every secret vice and every servile superstition which might emasculate the race and render it subservient to authority—except for these appalling evils, we have no right perhaps to deplore the settlement of Italy by Charles V. in 1530, or the course of subsequent events. For it is tolerably certain that some such levelling down as then commenced was needed to bring the constituent States of Italy into accord; and it is indubitable, as I have had occasion to point out, that the political force which eventually introduced Italy into the European system of federated nations, was determined in its character, if not created, then. None the less, the history of this period (1530-1600) in Italy is a prolonged, a solemn, an inexpressibly heartrending tragedy.

It is the tragic history of the eldest and most beautiful, the noblest and most venerable, the freest and most gifted of Europe's daughters, delivered over to the devilry that issued from the most incompetent and arrogantly stupid of the European sisterhood, and to the cruelty, inspired by panic, of an impious theocracy. When we use these terms to designate the Papacy of the Counter-Reformation, it is not that we forget how many of those Popes were men of blameless private life and serious views for Catholic Christendom. When we use these terms to designate the Spanish race in the sixteenth century, it is not that we are ignorant of Spanish chivalry and colonising enterprise, of Spanish romance, or of the fact that Spain produced great painters, great dramatists, and one great novelist in the brief period of her glory. We use them deliberately, however, in both cases; because the Papacy at this period committed itself to a policy of immoral, retrograde, and cowardly repression of the most generous of human impulses under the pressure of selfish terror; because the Spaniards abandoned themselves to a dark fiend of religious fanaticism; because they were merciless in their conquests and unintelligent in their administration of subjugated provinces; because they glutted their lusts of avarice and hatred on industrious folk of other creeds within their borders; because they cultivated barren pride and self-conceit in social life; because at the great epoch of Europe's reawakening they chose the wrong side and adhered to it with fatal obstinacy. This obstinacy was disastrous to their neighbours and ruinous to themselves. During the short period of three reigns (between 1598 and 1700) they sank from the first to the third grade in Europe, and saw the sceptre passing in the New World from their hands to those of more normally constituted races. That the self-abandonment to sterilising passions and ignoble persecutions which marked Spain out for decay in the second half of the sixteenth century, and rendered her the curse of her dependencies, can in part be ascribed to the enthusiasm aroused in previous generations by the heroic conflict with advancing Islam, is a thesis capable of demonstration. Yet none the less is it true that her action at that period was calamitous to herself and little short of destructive to Italy.

After the year 1530 seven Spanish devils entered Italy. These were the devil of the Inquisition, with stake and torture-room, and war declared against the will and soul and heart and intellect of man; the devil of Jesuitry, with its sham learning, shameless lying, and casuistical economy of sins; the devil of vice-royal rule, with its life-draining monopolies and gross incapacity for government; the devil of an insolent soldiery, quartered on the people, clamorous for pay, outrageous in their lusts and violences; the devil of fantastical taxation, levying tolls upon the bare necessities of life, and drying up the founts of national well-being at their sources; the devil of petty-princedom, wallowing in sloth and cruelty upon a pinchbeck throne; the devil of effeminate hidalgoism, ruinous in expenditure, mean and grasping, corrupt in private life, in public ostentatious, vain of titles, cringing to its masters, arrogant to its inferiors. In their train these brought with them seven other devils, their pernicious offspring: idleness, disease, brigandage, destitution, ignorance, superstition, hypocritically sanctioned vice. These fourteen devils were welcomed, entertained, and voluptuously lodged in all the fairest provinces of Italy. The Popes opened wide for them the gates of outraged and depopulated Rome. Dukes and marquises fell down and worshipped the golden image of the Spanish Belial-Moloch—that hideous idol whose face was blackened with soot from burning human flesh, and whose skirts were dabbled with the blood of thousands slain in wars of persecution. After a tranquil sojourn of some years in Italy, these devils had everywhere spread desolation and corruption. Broad regions, like the Patrimony of S. Peter and Calabria, were given over to marauding bandits; wide tracts of fertile country, like the Sienese Maremma, were abandoned to malaria; wolves prowled through empty villages round Milan; in every city the pestilence swept off its hundreds daily; manufactures, commerce, agriculture, the industries of town and rural district, ceased; the Courts swarmed with petty nobles, who vaunted paltry titles, and resigned their wives to cicisbei and their sons to sloth; art and learning languished; there was not a man who ventured to speak out his thought or write the truth; and over the Dead Sea of social putrefaction floated the sickening oil of Jesuitical hypocrisy.

CHAPTER II

THE PAPACY AND THE TRIDENTINE COUNCIL

The Counter-Reformation—Its Intellectual and Moral Character—Causes of the Gradual Extinction of Renaissance Energy—Transition from the Renaissance to the Catholic Revival—New Religious Spirit in Italy—Attitude of Italians toward German Reformation—Oratory of Divine Love—Gasparo Contarini and the Moderate Reformers—New Religious Orders—Paul III.—His early History and Education—Political Attitude between France and Spain—Creation of the Duchy of Parma—Imminence of a General Council—Review of previous Councils—Paul's Uneasiness—Opens a Council at Trent in 1542—Protestants virtually excluded, and Catholic Dogmas confirmed in the first Sessions—Death of Paul in 1549—Julius III.—Paul IV.—Character and Ruling Passions of G. P. Caraffa—His Futile Opposition to Spain—Tyranny of his Nephews—Their Downfall—Paul devotes himself to Church Reform and the Inquisition—Pius IV.—His Minister Morone—Diplomatic Temper of this Pope—His Management of the Council—Assistance rendered by his Nephew Carlo Borromeo—Alarming State of Northern Europe—The Council reopened at Trent in 1562—Subsequent History of the Council—It closes with a complete Papal Triumph in 1563—Place of Pius IV. in History—Pius V.—The Inquisitor Pope—Population of Rome—Social Corruption—Sale of Offices and Justice—Tridentine Reforms depress Wealth—Ascetic Purity of Manners becomes fashionable—Piety—The Catholic Reaction generates the Counter-Reformation—Battle of Lepanto—Gregory XIII.—His Relatives—Policy of Enriching the Church at Expense of the Barons—Brigandage in States of the Church—Sixtus V.—His Stern Justice—Rigid Economy—Great Public Works—Taxation—The City of Rome assumes its present Form—Nepotism in the Counter-Reformation Period—Various Estimates of the Wealth accumulated by Papal Nephews—Rise of Princely Roman Families.

It is not easy to define the intellectual and moral changes which passed over Italy in the period of the Counter-Reformation;[1] it is still less easy to refer those changes to distinct causes. Yet some analysis tending toward such definition is demanded from a writer who has undertaken to treat of Italian culture and manners between the years 1530 and 1600.

In the last chapter I attempted to describe the depth of servitude to which the States of Italy were severally reduced at the end of the wars between France and Spain. The desolation of the country, the loss of national independence, and the dominance of an alien race, can be counted among the most important of those influences which produced the changes in question. Whatever opinions we may hold regarding the

[1] I may here state that I intend to use this term Counter-Reformation to denote the reform of the Catholic Church, which was stimulated by the German Reformation, and which, when the Council of Trent had fixed the dogmas and discipline of Latin Christianity, enabled the Papacy to assume a militant policy in Europe, whereby it regained a large portion of the provinces that had previously lapsed to Lutheran and Calvinistic dissent.

connexion between political autonomy and mental vigour in a people, it can hardly be disputed that a sudden and universal extinction of liberty must be injurious to arts and studies that have grown up under free institutions.

But there were other causes at work. Among these a prominent place should be given to an alteration in the intellectual interests of the Italians themselves. The original impulses of the Renaissance, in scholarship, painting, sculpture, architecture, and vernacular poetry, had been exhausted. Humanism, after recovering the classics and forming a new ideal of culture, was sinking into pedantry and academic erudition. Painting and sculpture, having culminated in the great work of Michelangelo, tended toward a kind of empty mannerism. Architecture settled down into the types fixed by Palladio and Barozzi. Poetry seemed to have reached its highest point of development in Ariosto. The main motives supplied to art by mediæval traditions and humanistic enthusiasm were worked out. Nor was this all. The Renaissance had created a critical spirit which penetrated every branch of art and letters. It was not possible to advance further on the old lines; yet painters, sculptors, architects, and poets of the rising generation had before their eyes the masterpieces of their predecessors, in their minds the precepts of the learned. All alike were rendered awkward and self-conscious by the sense of labouring at a disadvantage, and by the dread of academical censorship.

In truth, this critical spirit, which was the final product of the Renaissance in Italy, favoured the development of new powers in the nation: it hampered workers in the elder spheres of art, literature, and scholarship; but it set thinkers upon the track of those investigations which we call scientific. I shall endeavour, in a future chapter, to show how the Italians were now upon the point of carrying the ardour of the Renaissance into fresh fields of physical discovery and speculation, when their evolution was suspended by the Catholic Reaction. But here it must suffice to observe that formalism had succeeded by the operation of natural influences to the vigour and inventiveness of the national genius in the main departments of literature and fine art.

If we study the development of other European races, we shall find that each of them in turn, at its due season, passed through similar phases. The mediæval period ends in the efflorescence of a new delightful energy, which gives a Rabelais, a Shakspere, a Cervantes to the world. The Renaissance riots itself away in Marinism, Gongorism, Euphuism, and the affectations of the Hôtel Rambouillet. This age is succeeded by a colder, more critical, more formal age of obedience to fixed canons, during which scholarly efforts are made to purify style and impose laws on taste. The ensuing period of sense is also marked by profounder inquiries into nature and more exact analysis of mental operations. The correct school of poets, culminating in Dryden and Pope, hold sway in England; while Newton, Locke, and Bentley extend the sphere of science. In France the age of Rabelais and Montaigne yields place to the age of Racine and

Descartes. Germany was so distracted by religious wars, Spain was sc downtrodden by the Inquisition, that they do not offer equally luminous examples.[2] It may be added that in all these nations the end of the eighteenth and the beginning of the nineteenth centuries are marked by a similar revolt against formality and common sense, to which we give the name of the Romantic movement.

Quitting this sphere of speculation, we may next point out that the European system had undergone an incalculable process of transformation. Powerful nationalities were in existence, who, having received their education from Italy, were now beginning to think and express thought with marked originality. The Italians stood no longer in a relation of uncontested intellectual superiority to these peoples, while they met them under decided disadvantages at all points of political efficiency. The Mediterranean had ceased to be the high road of commercial enterprise and naval energy. Charles V.'s famous device of the two columns, with its motto *Plus Ultra*, indicated that illimitable horizons had been opened, that an age had begun in which Spain, England and Holland should dispute the sovereignty of the Atlantic and Pacific Oceans. Italy was left, with diminished forces of resistance, to bear the brunt of Turk and Arab depredations. The point of gravity in the civilised world had shifted. The Occidental nations looked no longer toward the South of Europe.

While these various causes were in operation, Catholic Christianity showed signs of re-awakening. The Reformation called forth a new and sincere spirit in the Latin Church; new antagonisms were evoked, and new efforts after self-preservation had to be made by the Papal hierarchy. The centre of the world-wide movement which is termed the Counter-Reformation was naturally Rome. Events had brought the Holy See once more into a position of prominence. It was more powerful as an Italian State now, through the support of Spain and the extinction of national independence, than at any previous period of history. In Catholic Christendom its prestige was immensely augmented by the Council of Trent. At the same epoch, the foreigners who dominated Italy, threw themselves with the enthusiasm of fanaticism into this Revival. Spain furnished Rome with the militia of the Jesuits and with the engines of the Inquisition. The Papacy was thus able to secure successes in Italy which were elsewhere only partially achieved. It followed that the moral, social, political and intellectual activities of the Italians at this period were controlled and coloured by influences hostile to the earlier Renaissance. Italy underwent a metamorphosis, prescribed by the Papacy and enforced by Spanish rule. In the process of this transformation the people submitted to rigid ecclesiastical discipline, and adopted without assimilating the customs of a foreign troop of despots.

At first sight we may wonder that the race which had shone with such incomparable lustre from Dante to Ariosto, and which had done so much

[2] With regard to Germany, see Mr. T. E. Perry's acute and philosophical study, entitled *From Opitz to Lessing* (Boston).

to create modern culture for Europe, should so quietly have accepted a retrogressive revolution. Yet, when we look closer, this is not surprising. The Italians were fatigued with creation, bewildered by the complexity of their discoveries, uncertain as to the immediate course before them. The Renaissance had been mainly the work of a select few. It had transformed society without permeating the masses of the people. Was it strange that the majority should reflect that, after all, the old ways are the best? This led them to approve the Catholic Revival. Was it strange that, after long, distracting, aimless wars, they should hail peace at any price? This lent popular sanction to the Spanish hegemony, in spite of its obvious drawbacks.

These may be reckoned the main conditions which gave a peculiar but not easily definable complexion of languor, melancholy, and dwindling vitality to nearly every manifestation of Italian genius in the second half of the sixteenth century, and which well-nigh sterilised that genius during the two succeeding centuries. In common with the rest of Europe, and in consequence of an inevitable alteration of their mental bias, they had lost the blithe spontaneity of the Renaissance. But they were at the same time suffering from grievous exhaustion, humiliated by the tyranny of foreign despotism, and terrorised by ecclesiastical intolerance. In their case, therefore, a sort of moral and intellectual atrophy becomes gradually more and more perceptible. The clear artistic sense of rightness and of beauty yields to doubtful taste. The frank audacity of the Renaissance is superseded by cringing timidity, lumbering dulness, somnolent and stagnant acquiescence in accepted formulæ. At first the best minds of the nation fret and rebel, and meet with the dungeon or the stake as the reward of contumacy. In the end everybody seems to be indifferent, satisfied with vacuity, enamoured of insipidity. The brightest episode in this dreary period is the emergence of modern music with incomparable sweetness and lucidity.

It must not be supposed that the change which I have adumbrated, passed rapidly over the Italian spirit. When Paul III. succeeded Clement on the Papal throne in 1534, some of the giants of the Renaissance still survived, and much of their great work was yet to be accomplished. Michelangelo had neither painted the Last Judgment nor planned the cupola which crowns S. Peter's. Cellini had not cast his Perseus for the Loggia de' Lanzi, nor had Palladio raised San Giorgio from the sea at Venice. Pietro Aretino still swaggered in lordly insolence; and though Machiavelli was dead, the 'silver histories' of Guicciardini remained to be written. Bandello, Giraldi and Il Lasca had not published their *Novelle*, nor had Cecchi given the last touch to Florentine comedy. It was chiefly at Venice, which preserved the ancient forms of her oligarchical independence, that the grand style of the Renaissance continued to flourish. Titian was in his prime; the stars of Tintoretto and Veronese had scarcely risen above the horizon. Sansovino was still producing masterpieces of picturesque beauty in architecture.

In order to understand the transition of Italy from the Renaissance to the Counter-Reformation manner, it will be well to concentrate attention on the history of the Papacy during the eight reigns of Paul III., Julius III., Paul IV., Pius IV., Pius V., Gregory XIII., Sixtus V., and Clement VIII.[3] In the first of these reigns we hardly notice that the Renaissance has passed away. In the last we are aware of a completely altered Italy. And we perceive that this alteration has been chiefly due to the ecclesiastical policy which brought the Council of Trent to a successful issue in the reign of Pius IV.

Before engaging in this review of Papal history, I must give some brief account of the more serious religious spirit which had been developed within the Italian Church; since the determination of this spirit toward rigid Catholicism in the second half of the sixteenth century decided the character of Italian manners and culture. Protestantism in the strict sense of the term took but little hold upon Italian society. It is true that the minds of some philosophical students were deeply stirred by the audacious discussion of theological principles in Germany. Such men had been rendered receptive of new impressions by the Platonising speculations of Ficino and Pico della Mirandola, as well as by the criticism of the Bible in its original languages which formed a subordinate branch of humanistic education. They had, furthermore, been powerfully affected by the tribulations of Rome at the time of Bourbon's occupation, and had grown to regard these as a divine chastisement inflicted on the Church for its corruption and ungodliness. Lutheranism so far influenced their opinions that they became convinced of the necessity of a return to the simpler elements of Christianity in creed and conduct. They considered a thoroughgoing reform of the hierarchy and of all Catholic institutions to be indispensable. They leant, moreover, with partiality to some of the essential tenets of the Reformation, notably to the doctrines of justification by faith and salvation by the merits of Christ, and also to the principle that Scripture is the sole authority in matters of belief and discipline. Thus both the Cardinals Morone and Contarini, the poet Flaminio, and the nobles of the Colonna family in Naples who imbibed the teaching of Valdes, fell under the suspicion of heterodoxy on these points. But it was characteristic of the members of this school that they had no will to withhold allegiance from the Pope as chief of Christendom. They shrank with horror from the thought of encouraging a schism or of severing themselves from the communion of Catholics. The essential difference between Italian and Teutonic thinkers on such subjects at this epoch seems to have been this: Italians could not cease to be Catholics without at the same time ceasing to be Christians. They could not accommodate their faith to any of the compromises suggested by the Reformation. Even when they left their country in a spirit of rebellion, they felt ill at ease both with Lutherans and Calvinists. Like Bernardino Ochino and the Anti-Trinitarians of the Socinian sect, they wandered restlessly through Europe, incapable of settling down in communion with any one of the established forms of Pro-

[3] These eight reigns cover a space of time from 1534 to 1605.

testantism. Calvin at Geneva instituted a real crusade against Italian thinkers, who differed from his views. He drove Valentino Gentile to death on the scaffold; and expelled Gribaldi, Simone, Biandrata, Alciati, Negro. Most of these men found refuge in Poland, Transylvania, even Turkey.[4]

There were bold speculators in Italy enough, who had practically abandoned the Catholic faith. But the majority of these did not think it worth their while to make an open rupture with the Church. Theological hair-splitting reminded them only of the mediæval scholasticism from which they had been emancipated by classical culture. They were less interested in questions touching the salvation of the individual or the exact nature of the sacraments than in metaphysical problems suggested by the study of antique philosophers, or new theories of the material universe. The indifference of these men in religion rendered it easy for them to conform in all external points to custom. Their fundamental axiom was that a scientific thinker could hold one set of opinions as a philosopher, and another set as a Christian. Their motto was the celebrated *Foris ut moris, intus ut libet.*[5] Nor were ecclesiastical authorities dissatisfied with this attitude during the ascendency of humanistic culture. It was, indeed, the attitude of Popes like Leo, Cardinals like Bembo. And it only revealed its essential weakness when the tide of general opinion, under the blast of Teutonic revolutionary ideas, turned violently in favour of formal orthodoxy. Then indeed it became dangerous to adopt the position of a Pomponazzo.

The mental attitude of such men is so well illustrated by a letter written by Celio Calcagnini to Peregrino Morato, that I shall not hesitate to transcribe it here. It seems that Morato had sent his correspondent some treatise on the theological questions then in dispute; and Calcagnini replies:

'I have read the book relating to the controversies so much agitated at present. I have thought on its contents, and weighed them in the balance of reason. I find in it nothing which may not be approved and defended, but some things which, as mysteries, it is safer to suppress and conceal than to bring before the common people, inasmuch as they pertained to the primitive and infant state of the Church. Now, when the decrees of the Fathers and long usage have introduced other modes, what necessity is there for reviving antiquated practices which have long fallen into desuetude, especially as neither piety nor the salvation of the soul is concerned with them? Let us then, I pray you, allow these things to rest. Not that I disapprove of their being embraced by scholars and lovers of antiquity; but I would not have them communicated to the common people and those who are fond of innovations, lest they give occasion to strife and sedition. There are unlearned and unqualified persons who having, after long ignorance, read or heard certain new opinions respecting baptism, the marriage of the clergy, ordination, the distinction

[4] See Berti's *Vita di G. Bruno*, pp. 105-108.
[5] This maxim is ascribed to the materialistic philosopher Cremonini.

of days and food, and public penitence, instantly conceive that these things are to be stiffly maintained and observed. Wherefore, in my opinion, the discussion of these points ought to be confined to the initiated, that so the seamless coat of our Lord may not be rent and torn. . . . Seeing it is dangerous to treat such things before the multitude and in public discourses, I must deem it safest to "speak with the many and think with the few," and to keep in mind the advice of Paul, "Hast thou faith? Have it to thyself before God." '[6]

The new religious spirit which I have attempted to characterise as tinctured by Protestant opinions but disinclined for severance from Rome, manifested itself about the same time in several groups. One of them was at Rome, where a society named the Oratory of Divine Love, including from fifty to sixty members, began to meet as early as the reign of Leo X., in the Trastevere. This pious association included men of very various kinds. Sadoleto, Giberto, and Contarini were here in close intimacy with Gaetano di Thiene, the sainted founder of the Theatines, and with his friend Caraffa, the founder of the Roman Inquisition. Venice was the centre of another group, among whom may be mentioned Reginald Pole, Gasparo Contarini, Luigi Priuli, and Antonio Bruccioli, the translator of the Bible from the original tongues into Italian. The poet Marcantonio Flaminio became a member of both societies; and was furthermore the personal friend of the Genoese Cardinals Sauli and Fregoso, whom we have a right to count among thinkers of the same class. Flaminio, though he died in the Catholic communion, was so far suspected of heresy that his works were placed upon the Index of 1559. In Naples Juan Valdes made himself the leader of a similar set of men. His views, embodied in the work of a disciple, and revised by Marcantonio Flaminio, 'On the Benefits of Christ's Death,' revealed strong Lutheran tendencies, which at a later period would certainly have condemned him to perpetual imprisonment or exile. This book had a wide circulation in Italy, and was influential in directing the minds of thoughtful Christians to the problems of Justification. It was ascribed to Aonio Paleario, who suffered martyrdom at Rome for maintaining doctrines similar to those of Valdes.[7] Round him gathered several members of the Great Colonna family, notably Vespasiano, Duke of Palliano, and his wife, the star of Italian beauty, Giulia Gonzaga. Vittoria Colonna, Marchioness of Pescara, imbibed the new doctrines in the same circle; and so did Bernardino Ochino. Modena could boast another association, which met in the house of Grillenzone; while Ferrara became the headquarters of a still more pronounced reforming party under the patronage of the Duchess, Renée of France, daughter of Louis XII. These various so-

[6] *C. Calcagnini Opera*, p. 195. I am indebted for the above version to McCrie's *Reformation in Italy*, p. 183.

[7] Though as many as 40,000 copies were published, this book was so successfully stamped out that it seemed to be irrecoverably lost. The library of St. John's College at Cambridge, however, contains two Italian copies and one French copy. That of Laibach possesses an Italian and a Croat version. Cantù, *Gli Eretici*, vol. i. p. 360.

cieties and coteries were bound together by ties of friendship and literary correspondence, and were indirectly connected with less fortunate reforming theologians, with Aonio Paleario, Bernardino Ochino, Antonio dei Pagliaricci, Carnesecchi, and others, whose tragic history will form a part of my chapter on the Inquisition.

It does not fall within the province of this chapter to write an account of what has, not very appropriately, been called the Reformation in Italy. My purpose in the present book is, not to follow the fortunes of Protestantism, but to trace the sequel of the Renaissance, the merging of its impulse in new phases of European development. I shall therefore content myself with pointing out that at the opening of Paul III.'s reign, there was widely diffused throughout the chief Italian cities a novel spirit of religious earnestness and enthusiasm, which as yet had taken no determinate direction. This spirit burned most highly in Gasparo Contarini, who in 1541 was commissioned by the Pope to attend a conference at Rechensburg for the discussion of terms of reconciliation with the Lutherans. He succeeded in drawing up satisfactory articles on the main theological points regarding human nature, original sin, redemption, and justification. These were accepted by the Protestant theologians at Rechensburg and might possibly have been ratified in Rome, had not the Congress been broken up by Contarini's total failure to accommodate differences touching the Pope's supremacy and the conciliar principle.[8] He made concessions to the Reformers, which roused the fury of the Roman Curia. At the same time political intrigues were set on foot in France and Germany to avert a reconciliation which would have immeasurably strengthened the Emperor's position. The moderate sections of both parties, Lutheran and Catholic, failed at Rechensburg. Indeed, it was inevitable that they should fail; for the breach between the Roman Church and the Reformation was not of a nature to be healed over at this date. Principles were involved which could not now be harmonised, and both parties in the dispute were on the point of developing their own forces with fresh internal vigour.

The Italians who desired reform of the Church were now thrown back upon the attempt to secure this object within the bosom of Catholicism. At the request of Paul III. they presented a memorial on ecclesiastical abuses, which was signed by Contarini, Caraffa, Sadoleto, Pole, Fregoso, Giberto, Cortese and Aleander. These Cardinals did not spare plain speech upon the burning problem of Papal misgovernment.

Meanwhile, the new spirit began to manifest itself in the foundation of orders and institutions tending to purification of Church discipline. The most notable of these was the order of Theatines established by Thiene and Caraffa. Its object was to improve the secular priesthood, with a view to which end seminaries were opened for the education of priests, who took monastic vows and devoted themselves to special observance of their clerical duties, as preachers, administrators of the sacraments, visitors of the poor and sick.

[8] It should be observed, however, that Luther rejected the article on justification, and that Caraffa in Rome used his influence to prevent its acceptance by Paul III.

A Venetian, Girolamo Miani, at the same period founded a congregation, called the Somascan, for the education of the destitute and orphaned, and for the reception of the sick and infirm into hospitals. The terrible state in which Lombardy had been left by war rendered this institution highly valuable. Of a similar type was the order of the Barnabites, who were first incorporated at Milan, charged with the performance of acts of mercy, education, preaching, and other forms of Christian ministration. It may be finally added that the Camaldolese and Franciscan orders had been in part reformed by a spontaneous movement within their bodies.

If we compare the spirit indicated by these efforts in the first half of the sixteenth century with that of the earlier Renaissance, it will be evident that the Italians were ready for religious change. They sink, however, into insignificance beside two Spanish institutions which about the same period added their weight and influence to the Catholic revival. I mean, of course, the Inquisition and the Jesuit order. Paul III. empowered Caraffa in 1542 to re-establish the Inquisition in Rome upon a new basis resembling that of the Spanish Holy Office. The same Pope sanctioned and confirmed the Company of Jesus between the years 1540 and 1543. The establishment of the Inquisition gave vast disciplinary powers to the Church at the moment when the Council of Trent fixed her dogmas and proclaimed the absolute authority of the Popes. At the same time the Jesuits, devoted by their founder in blind obedience—*perinde ac cadaver*—to the service of the Papacy, penetrated Italy, Spain, France, Germany, and the transatlantic colonies.

The Pope who succeeded Clement VII. in 1534 was in all ways fitted to represent the transition which I have indicated. Alessandro Farnese sprang from an ancient but decayed family in the neighbourhood of Bolsena, several of whose members had played a foremost part in the mediæval revolutions of Orvieto. While still a young man of twenty-five, he was raised to the Cardinalate by Alexander VI. This advancement he owed to the influence of his sister Giulia, surnamed La Bella, who was then the Borgia's mistress. It is characteristic of an epoch during which the bold traditions of the fifteenth century still lingered, that the undraped statue of this Giulia (representing Vanity) was carved for the basement of Paul III.'s monument in the choir of S. Peter's. The old stock of the Farnesi, once planted in the soil of Papal corruption at its most licentious period, struck firm roots and flourished. Alessandro was born in 1468, and received a humanistic education according to the methods of the earlier Renaissance. He studied literature with Pomponius Laetus in the Roman Academy, and frequented the gardens of Lorenzo de' Medici at Florence. His character and intellect were thus formed under the influences of the classical revival and of the Pontifical Curia, at a time when pagan morality and secular policy had obliterated the ideal of Catholic Christianity. His sister was the Du Barry of the Borgian Court. He was himself the father of several illegitimate children, whom he acknowledged, and on whose advancement by the old system of Papal nepotism he spent the best years of his reign. Both as a patron of the arts and as an elegant scholar in the Latin and Italian languages, Alessandro showed throughout his life the effects of this early training. He piqued himself on choice expression, whenever he was called upon to use the pen in studied documents, or to answer ambassadors in public audiences. To his taste and love of splendour Rome owes the Farnese palace. He employed Cellini, and forced Michelangelo to paint the Last Judgment. On ascending the Papal throne he complained that this mighty genius had been too long occupied for Della Roveres and Medici. When the fresco was finished, he set the old artist upon his last great task of completing S. Peter's.

So far there was nothing to distinguish Alessandro Farnese from other ecclesiastics of the Renaissance. As Cardinal he seemed destined, should he ever attain the Papal dignity, to combine the qualities of the Borgian and Medicean Pontiffs. But before his elevation to that supreme height, he lived through the reigns of Julius II., Leo X., Adrian VI., and Clement VII. Herein lies the peculiarity of his position as Paul III. The pupil of Pomponius Laetus, the creature of Roderigo Borgia, the representative of Italian manners and culture before the age of foreign invasion had changed the face of Italy, Paul III. was called at the age of sixty-six to steer the ship of the Church through troubled waters and in very altered circumstances. He had witnessed the rise and progress of Protestant revolt in Germany. He had observed the stirrings of a new and sincere spirit of religious gravity, an earnest desire for ecclesiastical reform in his own country. He had watched the duel between France and Spain, during the course of which his predecessors Alexander V. and Julius II. restored the secular authority of Rome. He had seen that authority humbled to the dust in 1527, and miraculously rehabilitated at Bologna in 1530. He had learned by the example of the Borgias how difficult it was for any Papal family to found a substantial principality; and the vicissitudes of Florence and Urbino had confirmed this lesson. Finally, he had assisted at the coronation of Charles V.; and when he took the reins of power into his hands, he was well aware with what a formidable force he had to cope in the great Emperor.

Paul III. knew that the old Papal game of pitting France against Spain in the peninsula could not be played on the same grand scale as formerly. This policy had been pursued with results ruinous to Italy but favourable to the Church by Julius. It had enabled Leo and Clement to advance their families at the hazard of more important interests. But in the reign of the latter Pope it had all but involved the Papacy itself in the general confusion and desolation of the country. Moreover, France was no longer an effective match for Spain; and though their struggle was renewed, the issue was hardly doubtful. Spain had got too firm a grip upon the land to be cast off.

Yet Paul was a man of the elder generation. It could not be expected that a Pope of the Renaissance should suddenly abandon the mediæval policy of Papal hostility to the Empire, especially when the Empire was in the hands of so omnipotent a master as Charles. It could not be expected that he should recognise the wisdom of confining Papal ambition to ecclesiastical interests, and of forming a defensive and offensive alliance with Catholic sovereigns for the maintenance of absolutism. It could not be expected that he should forego the pleasures and apparent profits of creating duchies for his bastards whereby to dignify his family and strengthen his personal authority as a temporal sovereign. It is true that the experience of the last half century had pointed in the direction of all these changes; and it is certain that the series of events connected with the Council of Trent, which began in Paul III.'s reign, rendered them both natural and necessary. Yet Paul, as a man of the elder generation, filling the Papal throne for fifteen years during a period of transition, adhered in the main to the policy of his predecessors. It was fortunate for him and for the Holy See that the basis of his character was caution combined with tough tenacity of purpose, capacity for dilatory action, diplomatic shiftiness and a political versatility that can best be described by the word trimming. These qualities enabled him to pass with safety through perils that might have ruined a bolder, a hastier, or a franker Pope, and to achieve the object of his heart's desire, where stronger men had failed, in the foundation of a solid duchy for his heirs.

Paul's jealousy of the Spanish ascendency in Italian affairs caused him to waver between the Papal and Imperial, Guelf and Ghibelline, parties. These names had lost much of their significance; but the habit of distinction into two camps was so rooted in Italian manners that each city counted its antagonistic factions, maintained by various forms of local organisation and headed by the leading families.[9] Burigozzo, under the year 1517, tells how the whole population of Milan was divided between Guelfs and Ghibellines, wearing different costumes; and it is not uncommon to read of petty nobles in the country at this period, who were styled Captains of one or the other party. The wars between France and Spain revived the almost obsolete dispute, which the despots of the fifteenth century and the diplomatic confederation of the five great powers had tended in large measure to erase. The Guelfs and Ghibellines were now partisans of France and Spain respectively. Thus a true political importance was regained for the time-honoured factions; and in the distracted state of Italy they were further intensified by the antagonism between exiles and the ruling families in cities. If Cosimo de' Medici, for example, was a Ghibelline or Spanish partisan, it followed as a matter of course that Filippo Strozzi was a Guelf and stood for France. Paul III. managed to maintain himself by manipulating these factions and holding the balance between them for the advantage of his family and of the Church.

He thus succeeded in creating the Duchy of Parma and Piacenza for his son, Pier Luigi Farnese, that outrageous representative of the worst vices and worst violences of the Renaissance. It will be remembered

[9] See Bruno's *Cena delle Ceneri*, ed. Wagner, vol. i. p. 133, for a humorous story illustrative of the state of things ensuing among the lower Italian classes.

that Julius had detached these two cities from the Duchy of Milan, and annexed them to the Papal States, on the plea that they formed part of the old Exarchate of Ravenna. When Charles decided against this plea in the matter of Modena and Reggio, he left the Church in occupation of Parma and Piacenza. Paul created his son Duke of Nepi and Castro in 1537, and afterwards conferred the Duchy of Camerino on his grandson, Ottavio, who was then married to Margaret of Austria, daughter of Charles V., and widow of the murdered Alessandro de' Medici. The usual system of massacre, exile, and confiscation had reduced the signorial family of the Varani at Camerino to extremities. The fief reverted to the Church, and Paul induced the Cardinals to sanction his investiture of Ottavio Farnese with its rights and honours. He subsequently explained to them that it would be more profitable for the Holy See to retain Camerino and to relinquish Parma and Piacenza to the Farnesi in exchange. There was sense in this arrangement; for Camerino formed an integral part of the Papal States, while Parma and Piacenza were held under a more than doubtful title. Pier Luigi did not long survive his elevation to the dukedom of Parma. He was murdered by his exasperated subjects in 1547. His son, Ottavio, with some difficulty, maintained his hold upon this principality, until in 1559 he established himself and his heirs, with the approval of Philip II., in its perpetual enjoyment. The Farnesi repaid Spanish patronage by constant service, Alessandro, Prince of Parma, and son of Ottavio, being illustrious in the annals of the Netherlands. It would not have been worth while to enlarge on this foundation of the Duchy of Parma, had it not furnished an excellent example of my theme. By this act Paul III. proved himself a true and able inheritor of those political traditions by which all Pontiffs from Sixtus IV. to Clement VII. had sought to establish their relatives in secular princedoms. It was the last eminent exhibition of that policy, the last and the most brilliant display of nepotistical ambition in a Pope. A new age had opened, in which such schemes became impossible —when Popes could no longer dare to acknowledge and legitimise their bastards, and when they had to administer their dominions exclusively for the temporal and ecclesiastical aggrandisement of the tiara.

Nevertheless, Paul was living under the conditions which brought this modern attitude of the Papacy into potent actuality. He was surrounded by intellectual and moral forces of recent growth but of incalculable potency. One of the first acts of his reign was to advance six members of the moderate reforming party—Sadoleto, Pole, Giberto, Federigo Fregoso, Gasparo Contarini, and G. M. Caraffa—to the Cardinalate. By this exercise of power he showed his willingness to recognise new elements of very various qualities in the Catholic hierarchy. Five of these men represented opinions which at the moment of their elevation to the purple had a fair prospect of ultimate success. Imbued with a profound sense of the need for ecclesiastical reform, and tinctured more or less deeply with so-called Protestant opinions, they desired nothing more intensely than a reconstitution of the Catholic Church upon a basis which might render reconciliation with the Lutherans practicable. They had their opportunity during the pontificate of Paul III. It was a splendid one; and, as I have already shown, the Conference of Rechensburg only just failed in securing the end they so profoundly desired. But the Papacy was not prepared to concede so much as they were anxious to grant; the German Reformers proved intractable; they were themselves impeded by their loyalty to antique Catholic traditions, and by their dread of a schism; finally, the militant expansive force of Spanish orthodoxy, expressing itself already in the concentrated energy of the Jesuit order, rendered attempts at fusion impossible. The victory in Rome remained with the faction of *intransigeant* Catholics; and this was represented, in Paul III.'s first creation of Cardinals, by Caraffa. Caraffa was destined to play a singular part in the transition period of Papal history which I am reviewing. He belonged as essentially to the future as Alessandro Farnese belonged to the past. He embodied the spirit of the Inquisition, and upheld the principles of ecclesiastical reform upon the narrow basis of Papal absolutism. He openly signalised his disapproval of Paul's nepotism; and when his time for ruling came, he displayed a remorseless spirit of justice without mercy in dealing with his own family. Yet he hated the Spanish ascendency with a hatred far more fierce and bitter than that of Paul III. His ineffectual efforts to shake off the yoke of Philip II. was the last spasm of the older Papal policy of resistance to temporal sovereigns, the last appeal made in pursuance of that policy to France by an Italian Pontiff.[10]

The object of this excursion into the coming period is to show in how deep a sense Paul III. may be regarded as the beginner of a new era, while he was at the same time the last continuator of the old. The Cardinals whom he promoted on his accession included the chief of those men who strove in vain for a concordat between Rome and Reformation; it also included the man who stamped Rome with the impress of the Counter-Reformation. Yet Caraffa would not have had the fulcrum needed for this decisive exertion of power, had it not been for another act of Paul's reign. This was the convening of a Council at Trent. Paul's attitude toward the Council, which he summoned with reluctance, which he frustrated as far as in him lay, and the final outcome of which he was far from anticipating, illustrates in a most decisive manner his destiny as Pope of the transition.

The very name of a Council was an abomination to the Papacy. This will be apparent if we consider the previous history of the Church during the first half of the fifteenth century, when the conciliar authority was again invoked to regulate the Papal See and to check Papal encroachments on the realms and Churches of the Western nations. The removal of the Papal Court to Avignon, the great schism which resulted from this

[10] Paul IV. as Pope was feeble compared with his predecessors, Julius II. and Leo X.; the Guises, on whom he relied for resuscitating the old French party in the South, were but half-successful adventurers, mere shadows of the Angevine invaders whom they professed to represent.

measure, and the dissent which spread from England to Bohemia at the close of the fourteenth century, rendered it necessary that the representative powers of Christendom should combine for the purpose of restoring order in the Church. Four main points lay before the powers of Europe, thus brought for the first time into deliberative and confederated congress to settle questions that vitally concerned them. The most immediately urgent was the termination of the schism, and the appointment of one Pope, who should represent the mediæval idea of ecclesiastical face to face with imperial unity. The second was the definition of the indeterminate and ever-widening authority which the Popes asserted over the kingdoms and the Churches of the West. The third was the eradication of heresies which were rending Christendom asunder and threatening to destroy that ideal of unity in creed to which the Middle Ages clung with not unreasonable passion. The fourth was a reform of the Church, considered as a vital element of Western Christendom, in its head and in its members.

The programme, very indistinctly formulated by the most advanced thinkers of the age, and only gradually developed by practice into actuality, was a vast one. It involved the embitterment of national jealousies, the accentuation of national characteristics, and the complication of antagonistic principles regarding secular and ecclesiastical government, which rendered a complete and satisfactory solution well-nigh impracticable. The effort to solve these problems had, however, important influence in creating conditions under which the politico-religious struggles of the sixteenth and seventeenth centuries were conducted.[11]

The first Council, opened at Pisa in 1409, was a congress of prelates summoned by Cardinals for the conclusion of the schism. It deposed two Popes, who still continued to assert their titles; it elected a third, Alexander V., who had no real authority. For the rest, it effected no reform, and cannot be said to have done much more than to give effect to those aspirations after Church-government by means of Councils which had been slowly forming during the continuance of the schism.

The second Council, opened at Constance in 1414, was a Council not convened by Cardinals, but by the universal demand of Europe that the advances of the Papacy toward tyranny should be checked, and that the innumerable abuses of the Church and Papal Curia should be reformed. It received a different complexion from that of Pisa, through the presidency of the Emperor and the attendance of representatives from the chief nations. At Constance the Papacy and the Roman Curia stood together, exposed to the hostile criticism of Europe. The authority of a General Council was, after a sharp conflict, decreed superior to that of the Bishop of Rome. Three Popes were forced to abdicate: and a fourth, Martin V., was elected. The Council further undertook to deal with heresy and with the reform of the Church. It discharged the first of these offices by condemning Hus and Jerome of Prague to the stake. It

[11] The best account of the Councils will be found in Professor Creighton's admirable *History of the Papacy during the Reformation* (2 vols. Longmans).

left the second practically untouched. Yet the question of reform had been gravely raised, largely discussed, and fundamentally examined. Two methods were posed at Constance for the future consideration of earnest thinkers throughout Europe. One was the way suggested by John Hus; that the Church should be reconstituted, after a searching analysis of the real bases of Christian conduct, an appeal to Scripture as the final authority, and a loyal endeavour to satisfy the spiritual requirements of individual souls and consciences. The second plan was that of inquiry into the existing order of the Church and detailed amendment of its flagrant faults, with preservation of the main system. The Council adopted satisfactory measures of reform on neither of these methods. It contented itself with stipulations and concordats, guaranteeing special privileges to the Churches of the several nations. But in the following century it became manifest that the Teutonic races had declared for the method suggested by Hus; while the Latin races, in the Council of Trent, undertook a purgation of the Church upon the second of the two plans. The Reformation was the visible outcome of the one, the Counter-Reformation of the other method.

The Council of Constance was thus important in causing the recognition of a single Pope, and in ventilating the divergent theories upon which the question of reform was afterwards to be disputed. But perhaps the most significant fact it brought into relief was the new phase of political existence into which the European races had entered. Nationality, as the main principle of modern history, was now established; and the diplomatic relations of sovereigns as the representatives of peoples were shown to be of overwhelming weight. The visionary mediæval polity of Emperor and Pope faded away before the vivid actuality of full-formed individual nations, federally connected, controlled by common but reciprocally hostile interests.[12]

The Council of Basel, opened in 1431, was in appearance a continuation of the Council of Constance. But its method of procedure ran counter to the new direction which had been communicated to European federacy by the action of the Constance congress. There the votes had been taken by nations. At Basel they were taken by men, after the questions to be decided had been previously discussed by special congregations and committees deputed for preliminary deliberations. It soon appeared that the fathers of the Basel Council aimed at opposing a lawfully elected Pope, and sought to assume the administration of the Church into their own hands. Their struggle with Eugenius IV., their election of an antipope, Felix V., and their manifest tendency to substitute oligarchical for Papal tyranny in the Church, had the effect of bringing the conciliar principle itself into disfavour with the European powers. The first symptom of this repudiation of the Council by Europe was shown in the neutrality proclaimed by Germany. The attitude of other Courts and nations proved that the Western races were for the moment prepared

[12] See above, p. 517, for the special sense in which I apply the word federation to Italy before 1530, and to Europe at large in the modern period.

to leave the Papal question open on the basis supplied by the Council of Constance.

The result of this failure of the conciliar principle at Basel was that Nicholas V. inaugurated a new age for the Papacy in Rome. I have already described the chief features of the Papal government from his election to the death of Clement VII. It was a period of unexampled splendour for the Holy See, and of substantial temporal conquests. The second Council of Pisa, which began its sittings in 1511 under French sanction and support, exercised no disastrous influence over the restored powers and prestige of the Papacy. On the contrary, it gave occasion for a counter-council, held at the Lateran under the auspices of Julius II. and Leo X., in which the Popes established several points of ecclesiastical discipline that were not without value to their successors. But the leaven which had been scattered by Wyclif and Hus, of which the Council of Constance had taken cognisance, but which had not been extirpated, was spreading in Germany throughout this period. The Popes themselves were doing all in their power to propagate dissent and discontent. Well aware of the fierce light cast by the new learning they had helped to disseminate, upon the dark places of their own ecclesiastical administration, they still continued to raise money by the sale of pardons and indulgences, to bleed their Christian flock by monstrous engines of taxation, and to offend the conscience of an intelligent generation by their example of ungodly living. The Reformation ran like wild-fire through the North. It grew daily more obvious that a new Council must be summoned for carrying out measures of internal reform and for coping with the forces of belligerent Protestantism. When things had reached this point, Charles V. declared his earnest desire that the Pope should summon a General Council. Paul III. now showed in how true a sense he was the man of a transitional epoch. So long as possible he resisted, remembering to what straits his predecessors had been reduced by previous Councils, and being deeply conscious of scandals in his own domestic affairs which might expose him to the fate of a John XXIII. Reviewing the whole series of events which have next to be recorded, we are aware that Paul had no great cause for agitation. The Council he so much dreaded was destined to exalt his office, and to recombine the forces of Catholic Christendom under the absolute supremacy of his successors. The Inquisition and the Company of Jesus, both of which he sanctioned at this juncture, were to guard, extend, and corroborate that supreme authority. But this was by no means apparent in 1540. It is a character of all transitional periods that in them the cautious men regard past precedents of peril rather than sanguine expectations based on present chances. A hero, in such passes, goes to meet the danger, armed with his own cause and courage. A genius divines the future, and interprets it, and through interpretation tries to govern it. Paul was neither a hero nor a man of genius. Yet he did as much as either could have done; and he did it in a temper which perhaps the hero and the genius could not have commanded. He sent Legates to publish the opening of a Council at Trent in the spring of 1545; and he resolved to work this Council on the principles of diplomatical conservatism, reserving for himself the power of watching events and of enlarging or restricting its efficiency as might seem best to him.[13]

It is singular that the Council thus reluctantly conceded by Paul III. should, during its first sessions and while he yet reigned, have confirmed the dogmatic foundations of modern Catholicism, made reconciliation with the Teutonic Reformers impossible, and committed the secular powers which held with Rome to a policy that rendered the Papal supremacy incontestable.[14] Face to face with the burning question of the Protestant rebellion, the Tridentine fathers hastened to confirm the following articles. First, they declared that divine revelation was continuous in the Church of which the Pope was head; and that the chief written depository of this revelation—namely, the Scriptures—had no authority except in the version of the Vulgate. Secondly, they condemned the doctrine of Justification by Faith, adding such theological qualifications and reservations as need not, at this distance of time, and on a point devoid of present actuality, be scrupulously entertained. Thirdly, they confirmed the efficacy and the binding authority of the Seven Sacraments. It is thus clear that, on points of dogma, the Council convened by Pope and Emperor committed Latin Christianity to a definite repudiation of the main articles for which Luther had contended. Each of these points they successively traversed, foreclosing every loophole for escape into accommodation. It was in large measure due to Caraffa's energy and ability that these results were attained.

The method of procedure adopted by the Council, and the temper in

[13] The first official opening of the Council at Trent was in November 1542, by Cardinals Pole and Morone as Legates. It was adjourned in July 1543, on account of insufficient attendance. When it again opened in 1545, Pole reappeared as Legate. With him were associated two future Popes, Giov. Maria del Monte (Julius III.), and Marcello Cervini (Marcellus II.). The first session of the Council took place in December 1545, four Cardinals, four Archbishops, twenty-one Bishops, and five Generals of Orders attending. Among these were only five Spanish and two French prelates; no German, unless we count Cristoforo Madrazzo, the Cardinal Bishop of Trent, as one. No Protestants appeared; for Paul III. had successfully opposed their ultimatum, which demanded that final appeal on all debated points should be made to the sole authority of Holy Scripture.

[14] Throughout the sessions of the Council, Spanish, French, and German representatives, whether fathers or ambassadors, maintained the theory of Papal subjection to conciliar authority. The Spanish and French were unanimous in zeal for episcopal independence. The French and German were united in a wish to favour Protestants by reasonable concessions. Thus the Papal supremacy had to face serious antagonism, which it eventually conquered by the numerical preponderance of the Italian prelates, by the energy of the Jesuits, by diplomatic intrigues, and by manipulation of discords in the opposition. Though the Spanish fathers held with the French and German on the points of episcopal independence and conciliar authority, they disagreed whenever it became a question of compromise with Protestants upon details of dogma or ritual. The Papal Court persuaded the Catholic sovereigns of Spain and France and the Emperor that episcopal independence would be dangerous to their own prerogatives; and at every inconvenient turn in affairs, it was made clear that Catholic sovereigns, threatened by the Protestant revolution, could not afford to separate their cause from that of the Pope.

which its business was conducted, were no less favourable to the Papacy than the authoritative sanction which it gave to dogmas. From the first, the presidency and right of initiative in its sessions were conceded to the Papal Legates; and it soon became customary to refer decrees, before they were promulgated, to his Holiness in Rome for approval. The decrees themselves were elaborated in three congregations, one appointed for theological questions, the second for reforms, the third for supervision and ratification. They were then proposed for discussion and acceptance in general sessions of the Council. Here each vote told; and as there was a standing majority of Italian prelates, it required but little dexterity to secure the passing of any measure upon which the Court of Rome insisted. The most formidable opposition to the Papal prerogatives during these manœuvres proceeded from the Spanish bishops, who urged the introduction of reforms securing the independence of the episcopacy.

We find a remarkable demonstration of Paul III.'s difficulties as Pope of the transition, in the fact that while the Council of Trent was waging this uncompromising war against Reformers, his dread of Charles V. compelled him to suspend its sessions, transfer it to Bologna, and declare himself the political ally of German Protestants. This transference took place in 1547. His Legates received orders to invent some decent excuse for a step which would certainly be resisted, since Bologna was a city altogether subject to the Holy See. The Legates, by the connivance of the physicians in Trent, managed to create a panic of contagious epidemic.[15] Charles had won victories which seemed to place Germany at his discretion. His preponderance in Italy was thereby dangerously augmented. Paul, following the precedents of policy in which he had been bred, thought it at this crisis necessary to subordinate ecclesiastical to temporal interests. He interrupted the proceedings of the Council in order to hamper the Emperor in Germany. He encouraged the Northern Protestants in order that he might maintain an open issue in the loins of his Spanish rival. Nothing could more delicately illustrate the complications of European politics than the inverted attitude assumed by the Roman Pontiff in his dealings with a Catholic Emperor at this moment of time.[16]

The opposition of the Farnesi to Paul's scheme for restoring Parma to the Holy See in 1549, broke Paul III.'s health and spirits. He died on November 10, and was succeeded by the Cardinal Giovanni Maria del Monte, of whose reign little need be said. Julius III. removed the Council from Bologna to Trent in 1551, where it made some progress in questions touching the Eucharist and the administration of episcopal sees; but in the next year its sessions were suspended, owing to the disturbed

[15] See Sarpi, p. 249.

[16] Charles, at this juncture, was checkmated by Paul through his own inability to dispense with the Pope's co-operation as chief of the Catholic Church. So long as he opposed the Reformation it was impossible for him to assume an attitude of violent hostility to Rome.

state of Southern Germany and the presence of a Protestant army under Maurice of Saxony in the Tyrol.[17] This Pope passed his time agreeably and innocently enough in the villa which he built near the Porta del Popolo. His relatives were invested with several petty fiefs—that of their birthplace, Monte Sansovino, by Cosimo de' Medici; that of Novara by the Emperor, and that of Camerino by the Church. The old methods of Papal nepotism were not as yet abandoned. His successor, Marcello II., survived his elevation only three weeks; and in May 1555, Giovanni Pietro Caraffa was elected, with the title of Paul IV. We have already made the acquaintance of this Pope as a member of the Oratory of Divine Love, as a co-founder of the Theatines, as the Organiser of the Roman Inquisition, and as a leader in the first sessions of the Tridentine Council. Paul IV. sprang from a high and puissant family of Naples. He was a man of fierce, impulsive and uncompromising temper, animated by two ruling passions—burning hatred for the Spaniards who were trampling on his native land, and ecclesiastical ambition intensified by rigid Catholic orthodoxy. The first act of his reign was a vain effort to expel the Spaniards from Italy by resorting to the old device of French assistance. The abdication of Charles V. had placed Philip II. on the throne of Spain, and the settlement whereby the Imperial crown passed to his brother Ferdinand had substituted a feeble for a powerful Emperor. But Philip's disengagement from the cares of Germany left him more at liberty to maintain his preponderance in Southern Europe. It was fortunate for Paul IV. that Philip was a bigoted Catholic and a superstitiously obedient son of the Church. These two potentates, who began to reign in the same year, were destined, after the settlement of their early quarrel, to lead and organise the Catholic Counter-Reformation. The Duke of Guise at the Pope's request marched a French army into Italy. Paul raised a body of mercenaries, who were chiefly German Protestants;[18] and opened negotiations with Soliman, entreating the Turk to make a descent on Sicily by sea. Into such a fantastically false position was the Chief of the Church, the most Catholic of all her Pontiffs, driven by his jealous patriotism. We seem to be transported back into the times of a Sixtus IV. or an Alexander VI. And in truth, Paul's reversion to the antiquated Guelf policy of his predecessors was an anachronism. That policy ceased to be efficient when Francis I. signed the Treaty of Cambray; the Church, too, had gradually assumed such a position that armed interference in the affairs of secular sovereigns was suicidal. This became so manifest that Paul's futile attack on Philip in 1556 may be reckoned the last war raised by a Pope. From it we date the commencement of a new system of Papal co-operation with Catholic powers.

[17] During the brief and unimportant sessions at Bologna, Jesuit influences began to make themselves decidedly felt in the Council, where Lainez and Salmeron attended as Theologians of the Papal See. Up to this time the Dominicans had shaped decrees. Dogmatic orthodoxy was secured by their means. Now the Jesuits were to fight and win the battle of Papal Supremacy.

[18] Sarpi, quoted in his Life by Fra Fulgenzio, p. 83, says Paul called his Grisons mercenaries 'Angels sent from Heaven.'

The Duke of Alva put the forces at his disposal in the Two Sicilies into motion, and advanced to meet the Duke of Guise. But while the campaign dragged on, Philip won the decisive battle of S. Quentin. The Guise hurried back to France, and Alva marched unresisted upon Rome. There was no reason why the Eternal City should not have been subjected to another siege and sack. The will was certainly not wanting in Alva to humiliate the Pope, who never spoke of Spaniards but as renegade Jews, Marrani, heretics, and personifications of pride. Philip, however, wrote reminding his general that the date of his birth (1527) was that of Rome's calamity, and vowing that he would not signalise the first year of his reign by inflicting fresh miseries upon the capital of Christendom. Alva was ordered to make peace on terms both honourable and advantageous to his Holiness; since the King of Spain preferred to lose the rights of his own crown rather than to impair those of the Holy See in the least particular. Consequently, when Alva entered Rome in peaceful pomp, he did homage for his master to the Pope, who was generously willing to absolve him for his past offences. Paul IV. publicly exulted in the abasement of his conquerors, declaring that it would teach kings in future the obedience they owed to the Chief of the Church. But Alva did not conceal his discontent. It would have been better, he said, to have sent the Pope to sue for peace and pardon at Brussels, than to allow him to obtain the one and grant the other on these terms.

Paul's ambition to expel the Spaniards from Italy exposed him to the worst abuses of that Papal nepotism which he had denounced in others. He judged it necessary to surround himself with trusty and powerful agents of his own kindred.[19] With that view he raised one of his nephews, Carlo, to the Cardinalate, and bestowed on two others the principal fiefs of the Colonna family. The Colonnas were by tradition Ghibelline. This sufficed for depriving them of Palliano and Montebello. Carlo Caraffa, who obtained the scarlet, had lived a disreputable life which notoriously unfitted him for any ecclesiastical dignity. In the days of Sixtus and Alexander this would have been no bar to his promotion. But the Church was rapidly undergoing a change; and Carlo, complying with the hypocritical spirit of his age, found it convenient to affect a thorough reformation, and to make open show of penitence. Rome now presented the singular spectacle of an inquisitorial Pope, unimpeachable in moral conduct and zealous for Church reform, surrounded by nephews who were little better than Borgias. The Caraffas began to dream of principalities and sceptres. It was their ambition to lay hold on Florence, where Cosimo de' Medici, as a pronounced ally of Spain, had gained the bitter hatred of their uncle. But their various misdoings, acts of violence and oppression, avarice and sensuality, gradually reached the ears of the Pope. In an assembly of the Inquisition, held in January

[19] New men—and Popes were always *novi homines*—are compelled to take this course, and suffer when they take it. We might compare their difficulties with those which hampered Napoleon when he aspired to the Imperial tyranny over French conquests in Europe.

1559, he cried aloud, 'Reform! reform! reform!' Cardinal Pacheco, a determined foe of the Caraffeschi, raised his voice, and said, 'Holy Father! reform must first begin with us.' Pallavicini adds the remark that Paul understood well who was meant by *us*. He immediately retired to his apartments, instituted a searching inquiry into the conduct of his nephews, and, before the month was out, deprived them of all their offices and honours, and banished them from Rome. He would not hear a word in their defence; and when Cardinal Farnese endeavoured to procure a mitigation of their sentence, he brutally replied, 'If Paul III. had shown the same justice, your father would not have been murdered and mutilated in the streets of Piacenza.' In open consistory, before the Cardinals and high officials of his realm, with tears streaming from his eyes, he exposed the evil life of his relatives, declared his abhorrence of them, and protested that he had dwelt in perfect ignorance of their crimes until that time. This scene recalls a similar occasion, when Alexander VI. bewailed himself aloud before his Cardinals after the murder of the Duke of Gandia by Cesare. But Alexander's repentance was momentary; his grief was that of a father for Absalom; his indignation gave way to paternal weakness for the fratricide. Paul, though his love for his relatives seems to have been fervent, never relaxed his first severity against them. They were buried in oblivion; no one uttered their names in the Pope's presence. The whole secular administration of the Papal States was changed; not an official kept his place. For the first time Rome was governed by ministers in no way related to the Holy Father.

Paul now turned his attention, with the fiery passion that distinguished him, to the reformation of ecclesiastical abuses. On his accession he had published a Bull declaring that this would be a principal object of his reign. Nor had he in the midst of other occupations forgotten his engagement. A Congregation specially appointed for examining, classifying, and remedying such abuses had been established. It was divided into three committees, consisting of eight Cardinals, fifteen prelates, and fifty men of learning. At the same time the Inquisition was rigorously maintained. Paul extended its jurisdiction, empowered it to use torture, and was constant in his attendance on its meetings and 'acts of faith.'[20] But now that his plans for the expulsion of the Spaniards had failed, and his nephews had been hurled from their high station into the dust, there remained no other interest to distract his mind. Every day witnessed the promulgation of some new edict touching monastic discipline, simony, sale of offices, collation to benefices, church ritual, performance of clerical duties, and appointment to ecclesiastical dignities. It was his favourite boast that there would be no need of a Council to restore the Church to

[20] Pallavicini, in his history of the Council of Trent (Lib. xiv. ix. 5), specially commends Paul's zeal for the Holy Office. Speaking of his other pious institutions, he says: 'Fra esse d' eterna lode lo fa degno il tribunal dell' inquisizione, che dal zelo di lui e prima in autorità di consigliero e poscia in podestà di principe riconosce il presente suo vigor nell' Italia, e dal quale riconosce l' Italia la sua conservata integrità della fede: e per quest' opera salutare egli rimane ora tanto più benemerito ed onorabile quanto più allora ne fu mal rimeritato e disonorato.'

purity, since he was doing it.[21] And indeed his measures formed the nucleus of the Tridentine decrees upon this topic in the final sessions of the Council. Under this government Rome assumed an air of exemplary behavior which struck foreigners with mute astonishment. Cardinals were compelled to preach in their basilicas. The Pope himself, who was vain of his eloquence, preached. Gravity of manners, external signs of piety, a composed and contrite face, ostentation of orthodoxy by frequent confession and attendance at the Mass, became fashionable; and the Court adopted for its motto the *Si non caste tamen caute* of the Counter-Reformation.[22] Aretino, with his usual blackguardly pointedness of expression, has given a hint of what the new *régime* implied in the following satiric lines:—

> Caraffa, ipocrita infingardo,
> Che tien per coscienza spirituale
> Quando si mette del pepe in sul cardo.

Paul IV. brought the first period of the transition to an end. There were no attempts at dislodging the Spaniard, no Papal wars, no tyranny of Papal nephews converted into feudal princes, after his days. He stamped Roman society with his own austere and bigoted religion. That he was in any sense a hypocrite is wholly out of the question. But he made Rome hypocritical, and by establishing the Inquisition on a firm basis, he introduced a reign of spiritual terror into Italy. At his death the people rose in revolt, broke into the dungeons of the Inquisition, rereleased the prisoners, and destroyed the archives. The Holy Office was restored, however; and its higher posts of trust soon came to be regarded as stepping-stones to the Pontifical dignity.

The successor of Paul IV. was a man of very different quality and antecedents. Giovanni Angelo Medici sprang, not from the Florentine house of Medici, but from an obscure Lombard stem. His father acquired some wealth by farming the customs in Milan; and his eldest brother, Gian Giacomo, pushed his way to fame, fortune and a title by piracy upon the Lake of Como.[23] Gian Giacomo established himself so securely in his robber fortress of Musso that he soon became a power to reckon with. He then entered the Imperial service, was created Marquis of Marginano by the Duke of Milan, and married a lady of the Orsini house, a sister of the Duchess of Parma. At a subsequent period he succeeded in subduing Siena to the rule of Cosimo de' Medici, who then acknowledged a pretended consanguinity between the two families.[24] The younger brother, Giovanni Angelo, had meanwhile been studying law, practising as a jurist, and following the Court at Rome in the place

[21] See Luigi Mocenigo in *Rel. degli Amb. Veneti*, vol. x. p. 25.

[22] 'Roma a paragone delli tempi degli altri pontefici si poteva riputar come un onesto monasterio di religiosi' (*op. cit.* p. 41).

[23] In my *Sketches and Studies in Italy* I have narrated the romantic history of this filibuster.

[24] Soranzo: Alberi, vol. x. p. 67. Pius IV. adopted the arms of the Florentine Medici, and spent 30,000 scudi on carving them about through Rome. See P. Tiepolo, *ib.* p. 174.

of protonotary, which, as the custom then was, he purchased in 1527. Paul III. observed him, took him early into favour, and on the marriage of Gian Giacomo, advanced him to the Cardinalate. This was the man who assumed the title of Pius IV. on his election to the Papacy in 1559.

Paul IV. hated Cardinal Medici, and drove him away from Rome. It is probable that this antipathy contributed something to Giovanni Angelo's elevation. Of humble Lombard blood, a jurist and a worldling, pacific in his policy, devoted to Spanish interests, cautious and conciliatory in the conduct of affairs, ignorant of theology and indifferent to niceties of discipline, Pius IV. was at all points the exact opposite of the fiery Neapolitan noble, the Inquisitor and fanatic, the haughty trampler upon kings, the armed antagonist of Alva, the brusque impulsive autocrat, the purist of orthodoxy, who preceded him upon the Papal throne.[25] His trusted counsellor was Cardinal Morone, whom Paul had thrown into the dungeons of the Inquisition on a charge of favouring Lutheran opinions, and who was liberated by the rabble in their fury.[26] This in itself was significant of the new *régime* which now began in Rome. Morone, like his master, understood that the Church could best be guided by diplomacy and arts of peace. The two together brought the Council of Trent to that conclusion which left an undisputed sovereignty in theological and ecclesiastical affairs to the Papacy. It would have been impossible for a man of Caraffa's stamp to achieve what these sagacious temporisers and adroit managers effected.

Without advancing the same arrogant claims to spiritual supremacy as Paul had made, Pius was by no means a feeble Pontiff. He knew that the temper of the times demanded wise concessions; but he also knew how to win through these concessions the reality of power. It was he who initiated and firmly followed the policy of alliance between the Papacy and the Catholic sovereigns.[27] Instead of asserting the interests of the Church in antagonism to secular potentates, he undertook to prove

[25] 'Veramente quasi in ogni parte si può chiamare il rovescio dell' altro' (*op. cit.* p. 50).

[26] Luigi Mocenigo says of him that Pius 'averlo per un angelo di paradiso, e adoperandolo per consiglio in tutte le sue cose importanti.' Alberi, vol. x. p. 40. The case made out against Morone during the pontificate of Paul IV. may be studied in Cantù, *op. cit.* vol. ii. pp. 171-192, together with his defence in full. It turned mainly on these articles:—unsound opinions regarding justification by faith, salvation by Christ's blood, good works, invocation of saints, reliques; dissemination of the famous book on the *Benefits of Christ's Death*; practice with heretics. He was imprisoned in the Castle of S. Angelo from June 1557 till August 1559. Suspicions no doubt fell on him through his friendship with several of the moderate reformers, and from the fact that his diocese of Modena was a nest of liberal thinkers—the Grillenzoni, Castelvetro, Filippo Valentini, Faloppio, Camillo Molza, Francesco da Porto, Egidio Foscarari, and others, all of whom are described by Cantù, *op. cit.* Disc. xxviii. The charges brought against these persons prove at once the mainly speculative and innocuous character of Italian heresy, and the implacable enmity which a Pope of Caraffa's stamp exercised against the slightest shadow of heterodoxy.

[27] Soranzo, *op. cit.* p. 75, says: 'Con li principi tiene modo affatto contrario al suo predecessore; perchè mentre quello usava dire, il grado dei pontefici esser per mettersi sotto i piedi gl' imperatori e i re, questo dice che senza l'autorità dei principi non si può conservare quella dei pontefici.'

that their interests were identical. Militant Protestantism threatened the civil no less than the ecclesiastical order. The episcopacy attempted to liberate itself from monarchical and pontifical authority alike. Pius proposed to the autocrats of Europe a compact for mutual defence, divesting the Holy See of some of its privileges, but requiring in return the recognition of its ecclesiastical absolutism. In all difficult negotiations he was wont to depend upon himself; treating his counsellors as agents rather than as peers, and holding the threads of diplomacy in his own hands. Thus he was able to transact business as a sovereign with sovereigns, and came to terms with them by means of personal correspondence. The reconstruction of Catholic Christendom, which took visible shape in the decrees of the Tridentine Council, was actually settled in the Courts of Spain, Austria, France, and Rome. The Fathers of the Council were the mouthpieces of royal and Papal cabinets. The Holy Ghost, to quote a profane satire of the time, reached Trent in the despatch-bags of couriers, and in the sealed instructions issued to ambassadors and legates.

We observe throughout the negotiations which crowned the policy of this Pope with success, the operation not only of a pacific and far-seeing character, but also of the temper of a lawyer. Pius drew up the Tridentine decrees as an able conveyancer draws up a complicated deed, involving many trusts, recognising conflicting rights, providing for distant contingencies. It was in fact the marriage contract of ecclesiastical and secular absolutism, by which the estates of Catholic Christendom were put in trust and settlement for posterity. In formulating its terms the Pope granted points to which an obstinate or warlike predecessor, a Julius II. or a Paul IV., would never have subscribed his signature. In purely theological matters, such as the concession of the chalice to the laity and the marriage of the clergy, he was even willing to yield more for the sake of peace than his Court and clergy would agree to. But for each point he gave, he demanded a substantial equivalent, and showed such address in bargaining, that Rome gained far more than it relinquished. When the contract had been drafted, he ratified it by a full and ready recognition, and lawyer-like was punctual in executing all the terms to which he pledged himself.

We must credit Pius IV. with keen insight into the new conditions of Catholic Europe, and recognise him as the real founder of the modern as distinguished from the mediæval Papacy. That transition which I have been describing in the present chapter remained uncertain in its issue up to his pontificate. Before his death the salvation of Catholicism, the integrity of the Catholic Church, the solidity of the Roman hierarchy, and the possibility of a vigorous Counter-Reformation were placed beyond all doubt.

It is noticeable that these substantial successes were achieved, not by a religious fanatic, but by a jurist; not by a saint, but by a genial man of the world; not by force of intellect and will, but by adroitness; not by masterful authority, but by pliant diplomacy; not by forcing, but by following the current of events. Since Gregory VII., no Pope had done so much as Pius IV. for bracing the ancient fabric of the Church and confirming the Papal prerogative. But what a difference there is between a Hildebrand and a Giovanni Angelo Medici! How Europe had changed, when a man of the latter's stamp was the right instrument of destiny for starting the weather-beaten ship of the Church upon a new and prosperous voyage.

Pius IV. was greatly assisted in his work by circumstances, of which he knew how to avail himself. Had it not been for the renewed spiritual activity of Catholicism to which I have alluded in this chapter, he might not have been able to carry that work through. He took no interest in theology, and felt no sympathy for the Inquisition.[28] But he prudently left that institution alone to pursue its function of policing the ecclesiastical realm. The Jesuits rendered him important assistance by propagating their doctrine of passive obedience to Rome. Spain supported him with the massive strength of a nation Catholic to the core; and when the Spanish prelates gave him trouble, he could rely for aid upon the Spanish crown. His own independence, as a prudent man of business, uninfluenced by bigoted prejudices or partialities for any sect, enabled him to manipulate all resources at his disposal for the main object of uniting Catholicism and securing Papal supremacy. He was also fortunate in his family relations, having no occasion to complicate his policy by nepotism. One of the first acts of his reign had been to condemn four of the Caraffeschi—Cardinal Caraffa, the Duke of Palliano, Count Aliffe and Leonardo di Cardine—to death; and this act of justice ended for ever the old forms of domestic ambition which had hampered the Popes of the Renaissance in their ecclesiastical designs. His brother, the Marquis of Marignano, died in 1555; and this event opened for him the path to the Papacy, which he would never have attained in the lifetime of so grasping and ambitious a man.[29] With his next brother, Augusto, who succeeded to the marquisate, he felt no sympathy.[30] His nephew Federigo Borromeo died in youth. His other nephew, Carlo Borromeo, the sainted Archbishop of Milan, remained close to his person in Rome.[31] But Carlo Borromeo was a man who personified the new spirit of Catholicism. Sincerely pious, zealous for the faith, immaculate in conduct, unwearied in the discharge of diocesan duties, charitable to the poor, devoted to the sick, he summed up all the virtues of the Counter-Reformation. Nor had he any of the virtues of the Renaissance. A Venetian Ambassador described him as cold of political temperament, little versed in worldly affairs, and perplexed when he attempted to handle matters of grave moment.[32] His presence at the Papal Court, so far from being perilous, as that of an ambitious Cardinal Nipote would have been, or scandalous, as that of former Riarios, Borgias and Caraffas

[28] Soranzo, *op. cit.* p. 74.

[29] Soranzo, *op. cit.* p. 71, says: 'Il marchese suo fratello con la moglie gli diedi il cappello, e con la morte il papato.'

[30] Mocenigo, *op. cit.* p. 52. Soranzo, *op. cit.* p. 93.

[31] Margherita Medici, sister of the Pope, had married Gilberto Borromeo.

[32] See Mocenigo, *op. cit.* p. 53. Soranzo, *op. cit.* p. 91.

had undoubtedly been, was a source of strength to Pius. It imported into his immediate surroundings just what he himself lacked, and saved him from the imputations of worldliness which in the altered temper of the Church might have proved inconvenient.[33] Truly, among all Pontiffs who have occupied S. Peter's Chair, Pius IV. deserved in the close of his life to be called fortunate. He had risen from obscurity, had entered Rome in humble office at the moment of Rome's deepest degradation. He had lived through troubled times, and for some years had felt the whole weight of Catholic concerns upon his shoulders. At the last, he was conscious of having opened a new era for the Church, and of being able to transmit a sceptre of undisputed authority to his successors. His death-bed was troubled with no remorse, with no ingratitude of relatives, with no political complications produced by family ambition or by the sacrifice of his official duties to personal aggrandisement.

Soon after the election of Pope Pius IV. the state of Europe made the calling of a General Council indispensable. Paul's impolitic pretensions had finally alienated England from the Roman Church. Scotland was upon the point of declaring herself Protestant. The Huguenots were growing stronger every year in France, the Queen Mother, Catherine de' Medici, being at that time inclined to favour them. The Confession of Augsburg had long been recognised in Germany. The whole of Scandinavia, with Denmark, was lost to Catholicism. The Low Countries, in spite of Philip, Alva, and the Inquisition, remained intractable. Bohemia, Hungary, and Poland were alienated, ripe for open schism. The tenets of Zwingli had taken root in German Switzerland. Calvin was gaining ground in the French cantons. Geneva had become a stationary fortress, the stronghold of belligerent reformers, whence heresy sent forth its missionaries and promulgated subversive doctrines through the medium of an ever-active press. Transformed by Calvin from its earlier condition of a pleasure-loving and commercial city, it was now what Deceleia under Spartan discipline had been to Athens in the Peloponnesian war—a permanent ἐπιτειχισμός, perpetually garrisoned and on guard to harry the flanks of Catholics. Faithful to the Roman See in a strict sense of the term, there remained only Spain, Portugal, and Italy. As the events of the next century proved, the disaffected nations still offered rallying-points for the Catholic cause, from which the tide of conquest was rolled back upon the Reformation. But in 1559 the outlook for the Church was very gloomy; no one could predict whether a General Council might not increase her difficulties by weakening the Papal power and sowing further seeds of discord among her few faithful adherents. Yet Pius, after an attempt to combine the Catholic nations in a crusade against Geneva, which was frustrated by the jealousy of Spain, the internal weakness of France and the respect inspired by Switzerland,[34] determined to cast his fortunes on the Council. He had several

[33] Gia. Soranzo (*op. cit.* p. 133) says of Carlo Borromeo, 'ch' egli solo faccia più profitto nella Corte di Roma che tutti i decreti del Concilio insieme.'

[34] See Sarpi, vol. ii. pp. 43, 44.

strong points in his favour. The reigning Emperor, Ferdinand, wielded a power insignificant when compared with that of Charles V. The Protestants, though formally invited, were certain not to attend a Council which had already condemned the articles of their Confession. The cardinal dogmas of Catholicism had been confirmed in the sessions of 1545-1552. It was to be hoped that, with skilful management, existing differences of opinion with regard to doctrine, church-management, and reformation of abuses, might be settled to the satisfaction of the Catholic powers.

The Pope accordingly sent five Legates, the Cardinals Gonzaga, Seripando, Simoneta, Hosius, and Puteo, to Trent, who opened the Council on January 15, 1562.[35] As had been anticipated, the Protestants showed strong disinclination to attend. The French prelates were unable to appear, pending negotiations with the Huguenots at Poissy and Pontoise. The German prelates intimated their reluctance to take part in the proceedings. The Court of France demanded that the chalice for the laity and the use of the vulgar tongue in religious services should be conceded. The Emperor also insisted on these points, making a further demand for the marriage of the clergy. Circumstances both in France and Germany seemed to render these conditions imperative, if the rapid spread of Protestant dissent were to be checked and the remnant of the Catholic population to be kept in obedience. Of ecclesiastics, only Spaniards and Italians, the latter in a large majority, appeared at Trent. The Courts of other nations were represented by ambassadors, who took no part in the deliberations of the Council.[36]

In spite of this inauspicious commencement, Pius declared the Council a General Council, and further decreed that it should be recognised as a continuation of that Council which had begun at Trent in 1545. This rendered the co-operation of Protestants impossible, since they would have been compelled to accept the earlier dogmatic resolutions of the Fathers. It was decided that no proxies should be allowed to absentees; that the questions of doctrine and reform should be prepared for discussion in two separate congregations, and should be taken into consideration in full sessions simultaneously; finally that the Papal Legates should alone have the privilege of proposing resolutions to the fathers. This last point, by which the Court of Rome reserved to itself the control of all proceedings in the Council, was carried by a clever ruse. Until too late the Spanish prelates do not seem to have been aware of the immense power they had conferred on Rome by passing the words *Legatis proponentibus*.[37] The principle involved in this phrase continued to be hotly

[35] Cardinal Puteo was soon replaced by a Papal nephew, the Cardinal d'Altemps (Mark of Hohen Ems).

[36] At the first session there were five Cardinals, one hundred and four prelates, including Patriarchs, Archbishops and Bishops, four Abbots, and four Generals of Orders. These were all Italians, Spaniards, and Portuguese. And yet this Conciliabulum called itself a General Council, inspired by the Holy Ghost to legislate for the whole of Latin and Teutonic Christianity.

[37] See Sarpi, vol. ii. p. 87.

disputed all through the sessions of the Council. But Pius knew that so long as he stuck fast to it he always held the ace of trumps, and nothing would induce him to relinquish it.

Fortified in this position of superiority, Pius now proceeded to organise his forces and display his tactics. All through the sessions of the Council they remained the same; and as the method resulted in his final victory, it deserves to be briefly described. At any cost he determined to secure a numerical majority in the Synod. This was effected by drafting Italian prelates, as occasion required, to Trent. Many of the poorer sort were subsidised, and placed under the supervision of Cardinal Simoneta, who gave them orders how to vote. A small squadron of witty bishops was told off to throw ridicule on inconvenient speakers by satirical interpolations, or to hamper them by sophistical arguments. Spies were introduced into the opposite camps, who kept the Legates informed of what the French or Spaniards deliberated in their private meetings. The Legates meanwhile established a daily post of couriers, who carried the minutest details of the Council to the Vatican. When the resolutions of the congregations on which decrees were to be framed had been drawn up, they referred them to his Holiness. Without his sanction they did not propose them in a general session. In this fashion, by means of his standing majority, the exclusive right of his Legates to propose resolutions, and the previous reference of these resolutions to himself, Pius was enabled to direct the affairs of the Council. It soon became manifest that while the fathers were talking at Trent their final decisions were arranged in Rome. This not unnaturally caused much discontent. It began to be murmured that the Holy Ghost was sent from Rome to Trent in carpet-bags. A man of more imperious nature than Pius might, by straining his prerogatives, have produced an irreconcilable rupture. But he was aware that the very existence of the Papacy depended on circumspection. He therefore used all his advantages with caution, and resolved to win the day by diplomacy. With this object in view he introduced the further system of negotiating with the Catholic Courts through special agents. Instead of framing the decrees upon the information furnished by his Legates, he in his turn submitted them to Philip, Catherine de' Medici, and Ferdinand, agreed on terms of mutual concession, persuaded the princes that their interests were identical with his own, and then returned such measures to the Council as could be safely passed. In course of time the Holy Ghost was not packed up at Rome for Trent in carpet-bags before he had gone the round of Europe and made his bow in all the cabinets.

It must not, however, be thought that matters went smoothly for the Pope at first, or that so novel a method as that which I have described, whereby the faith and discipline of Christendom were settled by negotiations between sovereigns, came suddenly into existence. In its first sessions the Council, to quote the Pope's own words, resembled the Tower of Babel rather than a Synod of Fathers. The Spanish prelates contended fiercely for two principles touching the episcopacy: one was that the residence of bishops in their dioceses had been divinely commanded; the other, that their authority is derived from Christ immediately. The first struck at the Pope's power to dispense from the duty of residence; and if it had been established without qualification, it would have ruined his capital. The second would have rendered the episcopacy independent of Rome, and have made the Holy Father one of a numerous oligarchy instead of the absolute chief of a hierarchy. Pius was able to show Philip that the independence of the bishops must inflict deep injuries on the crown of Spain. Philip therefore wrote to forbid insistence on this point. But the Spanish prelates, though coerced, were not silenced, and the storm which they had raised went grumbling on.

Difficulties of a no less serious nature arose when the French and Imperial ambassadors arrived at Trent in the spring. They demanded, as I have already stated, that the chalice should be conceded to the laity; nor is it easy to understand why this point might not have been granted. Pius himself was ready to make the concession; and the only valid argument against it was that it imperilled the uniformity of ritual throughout all Catholic countries. The Germans further stipulated for the marriage of the clergy, which the Pope was also disposed to entertain, until he reflected that celibacy alone retained the clergy faithful to his interests and regardless of those of their own nations. At this juncture of affairs the Roman Court, which was strongly opposed to both concessions, received material aid from the dissensions of the Council. The Spaniards would hear nothing of the Eucharist under both forms. The marriage of the clergy was opposed by French and Spaniards alike. On the point of episcopal independence, the French supported the Spaniards; but Pius used the same arguments in France which he had used in Spain, with similar success. Thus there was no agreement on any of the disputed questions between Spaniards, Frenchmen and Germans; and since the ambassadors could neither propose nor vote, and the Italian prelates were in a permanent majority, Pius was able to defer and temporise at leisure

Nevertheless, he began to feel the gravity of the situation. He saw that the embassies constituted dangerous centres of intrigue and national organisation at Trent. He was not entirely satisfied with his own Legate, the Cardinal Gonzaga, who supported the divine right of the episcopacy and quarrelled with his colleagues. The Spaniards, infuriated at having sacrificed the right of proposing measures, began to talk openly about the reform of the Papacy. Disagreeable messages reached Rome from France and Spain and Germany, complaining of the Pope's absolutism in Council, and demanding that the reform of the Church should be taken into serious and instant consideration. His devoted adherent, Lainez, General of the Jesuits, embittered opposition by passionately preaching the doctrine of passive obedience. Two dangers lay before him. One was that the Council should break up in confusion, with discredit to Rome and anarchy for the Catholic Church. The other was that it should be prolonged in its dissensions by the princes, with a view of depressing and enfeebling the Papal authority. Other perils of an incalculable kind threatened him in the announced approach of the mighty Cardinal of Lorraine, brother to the Duke of Guise, with a retinue of French bishops released from the Conference at Poissy. Though he kept on packing the Council with fresh relays of Italians, it was much to be apprehended that they might be unable to oppose a coalition between French and Spanish prelates, should that be now effected.

Pius, at this crisis, resolved on two important lines of policy, the energetic pursuit of which speedily brought the Council of Trent to a peaceful termination. The first was to meet the demand for a searching reformation of the Church with cheerful acquiescence; but to oppose a counter-demand that the secular States in all their ecclesiastical relations should at the same time be reformed. This implied a threat of alienating patronage and revenue for the princes; it also indicated plainly that the tiara and the crowns had interests in common. The second was to develop the diplomatic system upon which he had already tentatively entered.

The events of the spring, 1563, hastened the adoption of these measures by the Pope. Cardinal Lorraine had arrived with his French bishops;[38] and the Papal Legates found themselves involved at once in intricate disputes on questions touching the Huguenots and the interests of the Gallican Church. The Italians were driven in despair to epigrams: *Dalla scabie Spagnuola siamo caduti nel mal Francese.* Somewhat later, the Emperor despatched a bulky and verbose letter, announcing his intention to play the part which Sigismund had assumed at the Council of Constance. He complained roundly of the evils caused by the reference of all resolutions to Rome, by the exclusive rights of the Legates to propose decrees, and by the intrigues of the Italian majority in the Synod. He wound up by declaring that the reformation of the Church must be accomplished in Trent, not left to the judgment of the Papal Curia; and threatened to arrive from Innsbruck by the Brenner. Though Ferdinand was in a position of ecclesiastical and political weakness, such an Imperial rescript could not be altogether contemned; especially as Cardinal Lorraine, soon after his arrival, had made the journey to Innsbruck on purpose to confer with the Emperor. It therefore behoved the Pope to act with decision; and an important event happened in the first days of March, which materially assisted him in doing so. This was the death of Cardinal Gonzaga, whom Pius determined to replace by the moderate and circumspect Morone.[39]

Through Ippolito d' Este, Cardinal of Ferrara, he opened negotiations with the French Court, showing that the wishes of the prelates in the Council on the question of episcopacy were no less opposed to the crown

[38] He reached Trent, November 13, 1562, with eighteen Bishops and three Abbots of France, charged by Charles IX. to demand purified ritual, reformed discipline of clergy, use of vernacular in church services, and finally, if possible, the marriage of the clergy.

[39] The confusion at Trent in the spring of 1563 is thus described by the Bishop of Alife: 'Methinks Antichrist has come, so greatly confounded are the perturbations of the Holy Fathers here.' Phillipson, p. 525.

than to his own interests. Cardinal Simoneta urged the same point on the Marquis of Pescara, who governed Milan for Philip, and was well inclined to the Papal party. Cardinal Morone was sent on a special embassy to the Emperor.[40] By wise concessions, in which the prerogatives of the Imperial ambassadors at Trent were considerably enlarged, and a searching reformation of the Church was promised, Morone succeeded in establishing a good working basis for the future. It came to be understood that while the Pope would allow no further freedom to the bishops, he was well disposed to let his Legates admit the envoys of the Catholic powers into their counsels. From this time forward the Synod may be said to have existed only as a mouthpiece for uttering the terms agreed on by the Pope and potentates. Morone returned to Trent, and the Emperor withdrew from Innsbruck toward the north.

The difficulty with regard to France and Germany consisted in this, that politics forced both King and Emperor to consider the attitude of their Protestant subjects. Yet both alike were unable to maintain their position as Catholic sovereigns, if they came to open rupture with the Papacy. Ferdinand, as we have just seen, had expressed himself contented with the situation of affairs at Trent. But the French prelates still remained in opposition, and the French Court was undecided. Cardinal Morone, upon his arrival at Trent, began to flatter the Cardinal of Lorraine, affecting to take no measures of importance without consulting him. This conduct, together with timely compliments to several Frenchmen of importance, smoothed the way for future agreement; while the couriers who arrived from France, brought the assurance that Ippolito de' Este's representations had not been fruitless. Pius, meanwhile, was playing the same conciliatory game in Rome, where Don Luigi d' Avila arrived as a special envoy from Philip. The ambassador obtained a lodging in the Vatican, and was seen in daily social intercourse with his Holiness.[41] But the climax of this policy was reached when Lorraine accepted the Pope's invitation, and undertook a journey to Rome. This happened in September. The French Cardinal was pompously received, entertained in the palace, and honoured with personal visits in his lodgings by the Pope. Weary of Trent and the tiresome intrigues of the Council, this unscrupulous prelate was still further inclined to negotiation after the murder of his brother, Duke of Guise. It must be remembered that the Guises in France were after all but a potent faction of semi-royal adventurers, who had risen to eminence by an alliance with Diane de Poitiers. The murder of the Duke shook the foundations of their power; and the Cardinal was naturally anxious to be back again in France. For the moment he basked in the indolent atmosphere of Rome,

[40] When Morone set out, he told the Venetian envoy in Rome that he was going on a forlorn hope. 'L' ill^mo Morone, quando partì per il Concilio, mi disse che andava a cura disperata e che *nulla spes erat* della religione Cattolica' (Soranzo, *op. cit.* p. 82). The Jesuit Canisius, by his influence with Ferdinand, secured the success of Morone's diplomacy.

[41] Sarpi says that Don Luigi resided in the lodgings of Count Federigo Borromeo, a deceased nephew of the Pope.

surrounded by those treasures of antique and Renaissance luxury which still remained after the Sack of 1527. Pius held out flattering visions of succession to the Papacy, and proved convincingly that nothing could sustain the House of Guise or base the Catholic faith in France except alliance with the Papal See. Lorraine, who had probably seen enough of episcopal *canaillerie* in the Council, and felt his inner self expand in the rich climate of pontifical Rome, allowed his ambition to be caressed, confessed himself convinced, and returned to Trent intoxicated with his visit, the devoted friend of Rome.

Menaces, meanwhile, had been astutely mingled with cajoleries. The French and the Imperial Courts were growing anxious on the subject of reform in secular establishments. Pius had threatened to raise the whole question of national Churches and the monarch's right of interfering in their administration. This was tantamount to flinging a burning torch into the powder-magazine of Huguenot and Lutheran grievances. In order to save themselves from the disaster of explosion, they urged harmonious action with the Papacy upon their envoys. The Spanish Court, through Pescara, De Luna, and D'Avalos, wrote despatches of like tenor. It was now debated whether a congress of crowned heads should not be held to terminate the Council in accordance with the Papal programme. This would have suited Pius. It was the point to which his policy had led. Yet no such measure could be lightly hazarded. A congress, while the Council was yet sitting, would have been too palpable and cynical a declaration of the Papal game. As events showed, it was not even necessary. When Lorraine returned to Trent, the French opposition came to an end. The Spanish had been already neutralised by the firm persistent exhibition of Philip's will to work for Roman absolutism.[42] There was nothing left but to settle details, to formulate the terms of ecclesiastical reform, and to close the Council of Trent with a unanimous vote of confidence in his Holiness. The main outlines of dogma and discipline were quickly drawn. Numerous details were referred to the Pope for definition. The Council terminated in December with an act of submission, which placed all its decrees at the pleasure of the Papal sanction. Pius was wise enough to pass and ratify the decrees of the Tridentine fathers by a Bull dated on December 26, 1563, reserving to the Papal sovereign the sole right of interpreting them in doubtful or disputed cases. This he could well afford to do; for not an article had been penned without his concurrence, and not a stipulation had been made without a previous understanding with the Catholic powers. The very terms, moreover, by which his ratification was conveyed, secured his supremacy, and conferred upon his successors and himself the privileges of a court of ultimate appeal. At no previous period in the history of the Church had so wide, so undefined, and so unlimited an authority been

[42] Yet the Spanish bishops fought to the end, under the leadership of their chief Guerrero, for the principle of conciliar independence and the episcopal prerogatives. 'We had better not have come here, than be forced to stand by as witnesses,' says the Bishop of Orense. Phillipson, p. 577.

accorded to the See of Rome. Thus Pius IV. was triumphant in obtaining conciliar sanction for Pontifical absolutism, and in maintaining the fabric of the Roman hierarchy unimpaired, the cardinal dogmas of Latin Christianity unimpeached and after formal inquisition reasserted in precise definitions. A formidable armoury had been placed at the disposal of the Popes, who were fully empowered to use it, and who had two mighty engines for its application ready in the Holy Office and the Company of Jesus.[43]

After the termination of the Council there was nothing left for Pius but to die. He stood upon a pinnacle which might well have made him nervous—lest haply the Solonian maxim, 'Call no man fortunate until his death,' should be verified in his person. During the two years of peace and retirement which he had still to pass, the unsuccessful conspiracy of Benedetto Accolti and Antonio Canossa against his life gave point to this warning. But otherwise, withdrawn from cares of state, which he committed to his nephew, Carlo Borromeo, he enjoyed the tranquillity that follows successful labour, and sank with undiminished prestige into his grave at the end of 1565. Those who believe in masterful and potent leaders of humanity may be puzzled to account for the triumph achieved by this commonplace arbiter of destiny. Not by strength but by pliancy of character he accomplished the transition from the mediæval to the modern epoch of Catholicism. He was no Cromwell, Frederick the Great, or Bismarck; only a politic old man, contriving by adroit avoidance to steer the ship of the Church clear through innumerable perils. This scion of the Italian middle class, this moral mediocrity, placed his successors in S. Peter's Chair upon a throne of such supremacy that they began immediately to claim jurisdiction over kins and nations. Thirty-eight years before his death, when Clement VII. was shut up in S. Angelo, it seemed as though the Papal power might be

[43] The vague reference of all decrees passed by the Tridentine Council to the Pope for interpretation enabled him and his successors to manipulate them as they chose. It therefore happened, as Sarpi says ('Tratt. delle Mat. Ben.' *Opere*, vol. iv. p. 161), that no reform, with regard to the tenure of benefices, residence, pluralism, &c., which the Council had decided, was adopted without qualifying expedients which neutralised its spirit. If the continuance of benefices *in commendam* ceased, the device of *pensions* upon benefices was substituted; and a thousand pretexts put colossal fortunes extracted from Church property, now as before, into the hands of Papal nephews. Witness the contrivances whereby Cardinal Scipione Borghese enriched himself in the Papacy of Paul V. The Council had decreed the residence of bishops in their sees; but it had reserved to the Pope a power of dispensation; so that those whom he chose to exile from Rome were bound to reside, and those whom he desired to have about him were released from this obligation. On each and all delicate points the Papacy was more autocratic after than before the Council.One of Sarpi's letters (vol. i. p. 371) to Jacques Leschassier, dated December 22, 1609, should be studied by those who wish to penetrate the '*reserve ed altre arcane arti*,' the '*renunzie*,' '*pensioni*' and '*altri stratagemmi*,' by means of which the Papal Curia, during the half-century after the Tridentine Council, managed to evade its decrees, and to get such control over Church property in Italy that 'out of 500 benefices not one is conferred legally.' Compare the passage in the 'Trattato delle Materie Beneficiarie,' p. 163. There Sarpi says that five-sixths of Italian benefices are at the Pope's disposal, and that there is good reason to suppose that he will acquire the remaining sixth.

abolished. Forty-five years after his death, Sarpi, writing to a friend in 1610, expressed his firm opinion that the one, the burning question for Europe was the Papal power.[44] Through him, poor product as he was of ordinary Italian circumstances, elected to be Pope because of his easy-going mildness by prelates worn to death in fiery Caraffa's reign, it happened that the flood of Catholic reaction was rolled over Europe. In a certain sense we may therefore regard him as a veritable *Flagellum Dei*, wielded by inscrutable fate. It seems that at momentous epochs of world-history no hero is needed to effect the purpose of the Time-Spirit. A Gian Angelo Medici, agreeable, diplomatic, benevolent, and pleasure-loving, sufficed to initiate a series of events which kept the Occidental races in perturbation through two centuries.

A great step had been taken in the Pontificate of Pius IV. That reform of the Church, which the success of Protestantism rendered necessary, and which the Catholic powers demanded, had been decreed by the Council of Trent. Pius showed no unwillingness to give effect to the Council's regulations; and the task was facilitated for him by his nephew, Carlo Borromeo, and the Jesuits. It still remained, however, to be seen whether a new Pope might not reverse the policy on which the Counter-Reformation had been founded, and impede the beneficial inner movement which was leading the Roman hierarchy into paths of sobriety. Should this have happened, it would have been impossible for Romanism to assume a warlike attitude of resistance toward the Protestants in Europe, or to have rallied its own spiritual forces. The next election was therefore a matter of grave import.

Nothing is more remarkable in the history of the Papacy at this epoch than the singular contrast offered by each Pontiff in succession to his predecessor. The conclave was practically uncontrolled in its choice by any external force of the first magnitude. Though a Duke of Florence might now, by intrigue, determine the nomination of a Pius IV., no commanding Emperor or King of France, as in the times of Otto the Great or Philip le Bel, could designate his own candidate. There was no strife, so open as in the Renaissance period, between Cardinals subsidised by Spain or Austria or France.[45] The result was that the deliberations of the conclave were determined by motives of petty interests, personal jealousies, and local considerations, to such an extent that the election seemed finally to be the result of chance or inspiration. We find the most unlikely candidates, Caraffa and Peretti, attributing their elevation to the direct influence of the Holy Ghost, in the consciousness that they had slipped into S. Peter's Chair by the maladroitness of conflicting factions. The upshot, however, of these uninfluenced elections generally was to promote a man antagonistic to his predecessor. The clash of

[44] *Lettere*, vol. ii. p. 167.

[45] This does not mean that the Spanish crown had not a powerful voice in the elections. See the history of the conclaves which elected Urban VII., Gregory XIV., Innocent IV., Clement VIII., in Ranke, vol. ii. pp. 31-39. Yet it was noticed by those close observers, the Venetian envoys, that France and Spain had abandoned their former policy of subsidising the Cardinals who adhered to their respective factions.

parties and the numerical majority of independent Cardinals excluded the creatures of the last reign, and selected for advancement one who owed his position to the favour of an antecedent Pontiff. This result was further secured by the natural desire of all concerned in the election to nominate an old man, since it was for the general advantage that a pontificate should, if possible, not exceed five years.

The personal qualities of Carlo Borromeo were of grave importance in the election of a successor to his uncle. He had ruled the Church during the last years of Pius IV.; and the newly appointed Cardinals were his dependents. Had he attempted to exert his power for his own election, he might have met with opposition. He chose to use it for what he considered the deepest Catholic interests. This unselfishness led to the selection of a man, Michele Ghislieri, whose antecedents rendered him formidable to the still corrupt members of the Roman hierarchy, but whose character was precisely of the stamp required for giving solidity to the new phase on which the Church had entered. As Pius IV. had been the exact opposite of Paul IV., so Pius V. was a complete contrast to Pius IV. He had passed the best years of his life as chief of the Inquisition. Devoted to theology and to religious exercises, he lacked the legal and mundane faculties of his predecessor. But these were no longer necessary. They had done their duty in bringing the Council to a favourable close, and in establishing the Catholic concordat. What was now required was a Pope who should, by personal example and rigid discipline, impress Rome with the principles of orthodoxy and reform. Carlo Borromeo, self-conscious, perhaps, of the political incapacity which others noticed in him, and fervently zealous for the Catholic Revival, devolved this duty on Michele Ghislieri, who completed the work of his two predecessors.

Paul IV. had laid a basis for the modern Roman Church by strengthening the Inquisition and setting internal reforms on foot. Pius IV., externally, by his settlement of theTridentine Council, and by the establishment of the Catholic concordat, built upon this basis an edifice which was not as yet massive. Carlo Borromeo and the Jesuits during the last pontificate prepared the way for a Pope who should cement and gird that building, so that it should be capable of resisting the inroads of time and should serve as a fortress of attack on heresy. That Pope was Michele Ghislieri, who assumed the title of Pius V. in 1566.

Before entering on the matter of his reign, it will be necessary to review the state of Rome at this moment in the epoch of transition, when the mediæval and Renaissance phases were fast merging into the phase of the Counter-Reformation. Old abuses which have once struck a deep root in any institution, die slowly. It is therefore desirable to survey the position in which the Papal Sovereign of the Holy City, as constituted by the Council of Trent, held sway there.

The population of Rome was singularly fluctuating. Being principally composed of ecclesiastics with their households and dependents; foreigners resident in the city as suitors or ambassadors; merchants, tradespeople and artists attracted by the hope of gain; it rose or fell according to the qualities of the reigning Pope and the greater or less train of life which happened to be fashionable. Noble families were rather conspicuous by their absence than by their presence; for those of the first rank, Colonna and Orsini, dwelt upon their fiefs and visited the capital only as occasion served. The minor aristocracy which gave solidity to social relations in towns like Florence and Bologna, never attained the rank of a substantial oligarchy in Rome. Nor was there an established dynasty round which a circle of peers might gather in permanent alliance with the Court. On the other hand, the frequent succession of Pontiffs chosen from various districts encouraged the growth of an ephemeral nobility who battened for a while upon the favour of their Papal kinsmen, flooded the city with retainers from their province, and disappeared upon the election of a new Pope, to make room for another flying squadron. Instead of a group of ancient Houses, intermarrying and transmitting hereditary rights and honours to their posterity, Rome presented the spectacle of numerous celibate establishments, displaying great pomp, it is true, but dispersing and disappearing upon the decease of the patrons who assembled them. The households of wealthy Cardinals were formed upon the scale of princely Courts. Yet no one, whether he depended on the mightiest or the feeblest prelate, could reckon on the tenure of his place beyond the lifetime of his master. Many reasons, again—among which may be reckoned the hostility of reigning Pontiffs to the creatures of their predecessors or to their old rivals in the conclave—caused the residence of the chief ecclesiastics in Rome to be precarious. Thus the upper stratum of society was always in a state of flux, its elements shifting according to laws of chronic uncertainty. Beneath it spread a rabble of inferior and dubious gentlefolk, living in idleness upon the favour of the Court, serving the Cardinals and bishops in immoral and dishonest offices, selling their wives, their daughters and themselves, all eager to rise by indirect means to places of emolument.[46] Lower down, existed the *bourgeoisie* of artists, bankers, builders, shopkeepers and artisans; and at the bottom of the scale came hordes of beggars. Rome, like all Holy Cities, entertained multitudes of eleemosynary paupers. Gregory XIII. is praised for having spent more than 200,000 crowns a year on works of charity, and for having assigned the district of San Sisto (in the neighbourhood of Trinità del Monte, one of the best quarters of the present city) to the beggars.[47]

Such being the social conditions of Rome, it is not surprising to learn that during the reign of so harsh a Pontiff as Paul IV., the population sank to a number estimated at between 40,000 and 50,000. It rose rapidly to 70,000, and touched 80,000 in the reign of Pius IV. Afterwards it gradually ascended to 90,000, and during the popular pontificate of Gregory XIII. it is said to have reached the high figure of 140,000. These calculations are based upon the reports of the Venetian ambassa-

[46] See Mocenigo, *op. cit.* p. 35; Aretino's *Dialogo della Corte di Roma*; and the private history of the Farnesi.

[47] Giov. Carraro and Lor. Priuli, *op. cit.* pp. 275,306.

dors, and can be considered as impartial, although they may not be statistically exact.[48]

What rendered Roman society rotten to the core was universal pecuniary corruption. In Rome nothing could be had without payment; but men with money in their purse obtained whatever they desired. The office of the Datario alone brought from ten to fourteen thousand crowns a month into the Papal treasury in 1560.[49] This large sum accrued from the composition of benefices and the sale of vacant offices. The Camera Apostolica, or Chamber of Justice, was no less venal. A price was set on every crime, for which its punishment could be commuted into cash-payment. Even so severe a Pope as Paul IV. committed to his nephew, by published and printed edict, the privilege of compounding with criminals by fines.[50] One consequence of this vile system, rightly called by the Venetian envoy 'the very strangest that could be witnessed or heard of in such matters,' was that wealthy sinners indulged their appetites at the expense of their families, and that innocent people became the prey of sharpers and informers.[51] Rome had organised a vast system of *chantage*. Another consequence was that acts of violence were frightfully common. Men could be hired to commit murders at sums varying from ten to four scudi; and on the death of Paul IV., when anarchy prevailed for a short while in Rome, an eyewitness asserts that several hundred assassinations were committed within the walls in a few days.[52]

It was not to be expected that a population so corrupt, accustomed for generations to fatten upon the venality and vices of the hierarchy, should welcome those radical reforms which were the best fruits of the Tridentine Council. They specially disliked the decrees which enforced the residence of prelates, and the limitation of benefices held by a single ecclesiastic. These regulations implied the withdrawal of wealthy patrons from Rome, together with an incalculable reduction in the amount of foreign money spent there. Nor were the measures for abolishing a simoniacal sale of offices, and the growing demand for decency in the administration of justice, less unpopular. The one struck at the root of private speculation in lucrative posts, and deprived the Court of revenues which had to be replaced by taxes. The other destroyed the arts of informers, checked lawlessness and license in the rich, and had the same lamentable effect of impoverishing the Papal treasury. In proportion as the Curia ceased to subsist upon the profits of simony, superstition, and sin, it was forced to maintain itself by imposts on the people, and by resuming, as Gregory XIII. attempted to do, its obsolete rights over fiefs and lands accorded on easy terms or held by doubtful titles. Meanwhile the retrenchment rendered necessary in all households of the hierarchy,

[48] Alberi, vol. x. pp. 35, 83, 277.
[49] Mocenigo's computation, *op. cit.* p. 29.
[50] *Ibid.* p. 31.
[51] The true history of the Cenci, as written by Bertolotti, throws light upon these points.
[52] Mocenigo, *op. cit.* p. 38.

and the introduction of severer manners, threatened many minor branches of industry with extinction.

These changes began to manifest themselves during the pontificate of Pius IV. The Pope himself was inclined to a liberal and joyous scale of living. But he was not remarkable for generosity; and the new severity of manners made itself felt by the example of his nephew Carlo Borromeo—a man who, while living in the purple, practised austerities that were apparent in his emaciated countenance. The Jesuits ruled him; and, through him, their influence was felt in every quarter of the city.[53] 'The Court of Rome,' says the Venetian envoy in the year 1565, 'is no longer what it used to be either in the quality or the numbers of the courtiers. This is principally due to the poverty of the Cardinals and the parsimony of the Popes. In the old days, when they gave away more liberally, men of ability flocked from all quarters. This reduction of the Court dates from the Council; for the bishops and beneficed clergy being now obliged to retire to their residences, the larger portion of the Court has left Rome. To the same cause may be ascribed a diminution in the numbers of those who serve the Pontiff, seeing that since only one benefice can now be given, and that involves residence, there are few who care to follow the Court at their own expense and inconvenience without hope of greater reward. The poverty of the Cardinals springs from two causes. The first is that they cannot now obtain benefices of the first class, as was the case when England, Germany, and other provinces were subject to the Holy See, and when moreover they could hold three or four bishoprics apiece together with other places of emolument, whereas they now can only have one apiece. The second cause is that the number of the Cardinals has been increased to seventy-five, and that the foreign powers have ceased to compliment them with large presents and benefices, as was the wont of Charles V. and the French crown.' In the last of these clauses we find clearly indicated one of the main results of the concordat established between the Papacy and the Catholic sovereigns by the policy of Pius IV. It secured Papal absolutism at the expense of the College. Soranzo proceeds to describe the changes visible in Roman society. 'The train of life at Court is therefore mean, partly through poverty, but also owing to the good example of Cardinal Borromeo, seeing that people are wont to follow the manners of their princes. The Cardinal holds in his hands all the threads of the administration; and living religiously in the retirement I have noticed, indulging in liberalities to none but persons of his own stamp, there is neither Cardinal nor courtier who can expect any favour from him unless he conform in fact or in appearance to his mode of life. Consequently one observes that they have altogether withdrawn, in public at any rate, from every sort of pleasures. One sees no longer Cardinals in masquerade or on horseback, nor driving with women about Rome for pastime, as the custom was of late; but the utmost they do is to go alone in close coaches. Banquets, diversions, hunting parties, splendid liveries and all the other signs of outward luxury have been abolished; the

[53] Giac. Soranzo, *op. cit.* pp. 131-136.

more so that now there is at Court no layman of high quality, as formerly when the Pope had many of his relatives or dependents around him. The clergy always wear their robes, so that the reform of the Church is manifested in their appearance. This state of things, on the other hand, has been the ruin of the artisans and merchants, since no money circulates. And while all offices and magistracies are in the hands of Milanese, grasping and illiberal persons, very few indeed can be still called satisfied with the present reign.'[54]

One chief defect of Pius IV., judged by the standard of the new party in the Church, had been his coldness in religious exercises. Paolo Tiepolo remarks that during the last seven months of his life he never once attended service in his chapel.[55] This indifference was combined with lukewarmness in the prosecution of reforms. The Datatario still enriched itself by the composition of benefices, and the Camera by the composition of crimes. Pius V., on the contrary, embodied in himself those ascetic virtues which Carlo Borromeo and the Jesuits were determined to propagate through the Catholic world. He never missed a day's attendance on the prescribed services of the Church, said frequent Masses, fasted at regular intervals, and continued to wear the coarse woollen shirt which formed a part of his friar's costume. In his piety there was no hypocrisy. The people saw streams of tears pouring from the eyes of the Pontiff bowed in ecstasy before the Host. A rigid reformation of the churches, monasteries and clergy was immediately set on foot throughout the Papal States. Monks and nuns complained, not without cause, that austerities were expected from them which were not included in the rules to which they vowed obedience. The severity of the Inquisition was augmented, and the Index Expurgatorius began to exercise a stricter jurisdiction over books. The Pope spent half his time at the Holy Office, inquiring into cases of heresy of ten or twenty years' standing. From Florence he caused Carnesecchi to be dragged to Rome and burned; from Venice the refugee Guido Zanetti of Fano was delivered over to his tender mercies; and the excellent Carranza, Archbishop of Toledo, was sent from Spain to be condemned to death before the Roman tribunal. Criminal justice, meanwhile, was administered with greater purity, and the composition of crimes for money, if not wholly abolished, was moderated. In the collation to bishoprics and other benefices the same spirit of equity appeared; for Pius inquired scrupulously into the character and fitness of aspirants after office.

The zeal manifested by Pius V. for a thoroughgoing reform of manners may be illustrated by a curious circumstance related by the Venetian ambassador in the first year of the pontificate.[56] On July 26, 1566, an edict was issued, compelling all prostitutes to leave Rome within six days, and to evacuate the States of the Church within twelve days. The exodus began. But it was estimated that about 25,000 persons, counting

[54] Soranzo, *op. cit.* pp. 136-138.
[55] *Op. cit.* p. 171.
[56] Mutinelli, *Storia Arcana*, &c. vol. i. pp. 51-54.

the women themselves with their hangers-on and dependents, would have to quit the city if the edict were enforced.[57] The farmers of the customs calculated that they would lose some 20,000 ducats a year in consequence, and prayed the Pope for compensation. Meanwhile the roads across the Campagna began to be thronged by caravans, which were exposed to the attacks of robbers. The confusion became so great, and the public discontent was so openly expressed, that on August 17 Pius repealed his edict and permitted the prostitutes to reside in certain quarters of the city.

Pius IV. had wasted the greater part of his later life in bed, neglecting business, entertaining his leisure with buffoons and good companions, eating much and drinking more. Pius V., on the contrary, carried the habits of the convent with him into the Vatican, and bestowed the time he spared from devotion upon the transaction of affairs. He was of choleric complexion, adust, lean, wasted, with sunken eyes and snow-white hair, looking ten years older than he really was.

Such a Pope changed the face of Rome, or rather stereotyped the change which had been instituted by Cardinal Borromeo. 'People, even if they are not really better, seem at least to be so,' says the Venetian envoy, who has supplied me with the details I have condensed.[58] Retrenchments in the Papal establishment were introduced; money was scarce; the Court grew meaner in appearance; and nepotism may be said to have been extinct in the days of Pius V. He did indeed advance one nephew, Michele Bonelli, to the Cardinalate; but he showed no inclination to enrich or favour him beyond due measure. A worn man, without ears, marked by the bastonado, frequented the palace, and stood near the person of the Pope, as Captain of the Guard. This was Paolo Ghislieri, a somewhat distant relative of Pius, who had passed his life in servitude to Barbary corsairs and had been ransomed by a merchant upon the election of his kinsman. No other members of the Papal family were invited to Rome.

Pius V., while living this exemplary monastic life upon the Papal throne, ruled Catholic Christendom more absolutely than any of his predecessors. As the Papacy recognised its dependence on the sovereigns, so the sovereigns in their turn perceived that religious conformity was the best safeguard of their secular authority. Therefore the Catholic States subscribed, one after the other, to the Tridentine Profession of Faith, and adopted one system in matters of Church discipline. A new Breviary and a new Missal were published with the Papal sanction. Seminaries were established for the education of ecclesiastics, and the Jesuits laboured in their propaganda. The Inquisition and the Congregation of the Index redoubled their efforts to stamp out heresy by fire and iron, and by the suppression or mutilation of books. A rigid uniformity was impressed

[57] Assuming the population of Rome to have been about 90,000 at that date, this number appears incredible. Yet we have it on the best of all evidences, that of a resident Venetian envoy.

[58] Tiepolo, *op. cit.* p. 172.

on Catholicism. The Pope, to whom such power had been committed by the Council, stood at the head of each section and department of the new organisation. To his approval every measure in the Church was referred, and the Jesuits executed his instructions with punctual exactness.

It is not, therefore, to be wondered that Pius V. should have opened the era of active hostilities against Protestantism. Firmly allied with Philip II., he advocated attacks upon the Huguenots in France, the Protestants in Flanders, and the English crown. There is no evidence that he was active in promoting the Massacre of S. Bartholomew, which took place three months after his death; and the expedition of the Invincible Armada against England was not equipped until another period of fifteen years had elapsed. Yet the negotiations in which he was engaged with Spain, involving enterprises to the detriment of the English realm and the French Reformation, leave no doubt that both S. Bartholomew and the Armada would have met with his hearty approval. One glorious victory gave lustre to the reign of Pius V. In 1571 the navies of Spain, Venice and Rome inflicted a paralysing blow upon the Turkish power at Lepanto; and this success was potent in fanning the flame of Catholic enthusiasm.

The pontificates of Paul IV., Pius IV., and Pius V., differing as they did in very important details, had achieved a solid triumph for reformed Catholicism, of which both the diplomatical and the ascetic parties in the Church, Jesuits and Theatines, were eager to take advantage. A new spirit in the Roman polity prevailed, upon the reality of which its future force depended; and the men who embodied this spirit had no mind to relax their hold on its administration. After the death of Pius V. they had to deal with a Pope who resembled his penultimate predecessor, Pius IV., more than the last Pontiff. Ugo Buoncompagno, the scion of a *bourgeois* family settled in Bologna, began his career as a jurist. He took orders in middle life, was promoted to the Cardinalate, and attained the supreme honour of the Holy See in 1572. The man responded to his name. He was a good companion, easy of access, genial in manners, remarkable for the facility with which he cast off care and gave himself to sanguine expectations.[59] In an earlier period of Church history he might have reproduced the Papacy of Paul II. or Innocent VIII. As it was Gregory XIII. fell at once under the potent influence of Jesuit di-directors. His confessor, the Spanish Francesco da Toledo, impressed upon him the necessity of following the footsteps of Paul IV. and Pius V. It was made plain that he must conform to the new tendencies of the Catholic Church; and in his neophyte's zeal he determined to outdo his predecessors. The example of Pius V. was not only imitated, but surpassed. Gregory XIII. celebrated three Masses a week, built churches, and enforced parochial obedience throughout his capital. The Jesuits in his reign attained to the maximum of their wealth and influence. Rome, 'abandoning her ancient license, displayed a moderate and

[59] Paolo Tiepolo, *op. cit.* p. 312.

Christian mode of living; and in so far as the external observance of religion was concerned, she showed herself not far removed from such perfection as human frailties allow.'[60]

While he was yet a layman, Gregory became the father of one son, Giacomo. Born out of wedlock, he was yet acknowledged as a member of the Buoncompagno family, and admitted under this name into the Venetian nobility.[61] The Pope manifested paternal weakness in favour of his offspring. He brought the young man to Rome, and made him Governatore di Santa Chiesa with a salary of 10,000 ducats. The Jesuits and other spiritual persons scented danger. They persuaded the Holy Father that conscience and honour required the alienation of his bastard from the sacred city. Giacomo was relegated to honourable exile in Ancona. But he suffered so severely from this rebuff, that terms of accommodation were agreed on. Giacomo received a lady of the Sforza family in marriage, and was established at the Papal Court with a revenue amounting to about 25,000 crowns.[62] The ecclesiastical party, now predominant in Rome, took care that he should not acquire more than honorary importance in the government. Two of the Pope's nephews were promoted to the Cardinalate with provisions of about 10,000 crowns apiece. His old brother abode in retirement at Bologna under strict orders not to seek fortune or to perplex the Papal purity of rule in Rome.[63]

I have introduced this sketch of Gregory's relations in order to show how a Pope of his previous habits and personal proclivities was now obliged to follow the new order of the Church. It was noticed that the mode of life in Rome during his reign struck a just balance between license and austerity, and that general satisfaction pervaded society.[64] Outside the city this contentment did not prevail. Gregory threw his States into disorder by reviving obsolete rights of the Church over lands mortgaged or granted with obscure titles. The petty barons rose in revolt, armed their peasants, fomented factions in the country towns, and filled the land with brigands. Under the leadership of men like Alfonso Piccolomini and Roberto Malatesta, these marauding bands assumed the proportion of armies. The neighbouring Italian States—Tuscany, Venice, Naples, Parma, all of whom had found the Pope arbitrary and aggressive in his dealings with them—encouraged the bandits by offering them an asylum and refusing to co-operate with Gregory for their reduction.

His successor, Sixtus V., found the whole Papal dominion in confusion. It was impossible to collect the taxes. Life and property were nowhere safe. By a series of savage enactments and stern acts of justice Sixtus

[60] *Id.*, *op. cit.* p. 214.

[61] The Venetians, when they inscribed his name upon the Libro d'Oro, called him 'a near relative of his Holiness.'

[62] This lady was a sister of the Count of Santa Fiora. For a detailed account of the wedding, see Mutinelli, *Stor. Arc.* vol. i. p. 112.

[63] Tiepolo, *op. cit.* pp. 213, 219-221, 263, 266.

[64] Giov. Corraro, *op. cit.* p. 277.

swept the brigands from his States. He then applied his powerful will to the collection of money and the improvement of his provinces. In the four years which followed his election he succeeded in accumulating a round sum of four million crowns, which he stored up in the Castle of S. Angelo. The total revenues of the Papacy at this epoch were roughly estimated at 750,000 crowns, which in former reigns had been absorbed in current costs and the pontifical establishment. By rigorous economy and retrenchments of all kinds Sixtus reduced these annual expenses to a sum of 250,000, thus making a clear profit of 500,000 crowns.[65] At the same time he had already spent about a million and a half on works of public utility, including the famous Acqua Felice, which brought excellent water into Rome. Roads and bridges throughout the States of the Church were repaired. The Chiana of Orvieto and the Pontine Marsh were drained. Encouragement was extended, not only to agriculture, but also to industries and manufactures. The country towns obtained wise financial concessions, and the unpopular resumption of lapsed lands and fiefs were discontinued. Rome meanwhile began to assume her present aspect as a city, by the extensive architectural undertakings which Sixtus set on foot. He loved building; but he was no lover of antiquity. For pagan monuments of art he showed a monastic animosity, dispersing or mutilating the statues of the Vatican and Capitol; turning a Minerva into an image of the Faith by putting a cross in her hand; surmounting the columns of Trajan and Antonine with figures of Peter and Paul; destroying the Septizonium of Severus, and wishing to lay sacrilegious hands on Caecilia Metella's tomb. To mediæval relics he was hardly less indifferent. The old buildings of the Lateran were thrown down to make room for the heavy modern palace. But, to atone in some measure for these acts of vandalism, Sixtus placed the cupola upon S. Peter's and raised the obelisk in the great piazza which was destined to be circled with Bernini's colonnades. This obelisk he topped with a cross. Christian inscriptions, signalising the triumph of the Pontiff over infidel emperors, the victory of Calvary over Olympus, the superiority of Rome's saints and martyrs to Rome's old deities and heroes, left no doubt that what remained of the imperial city had been subdued to Christ and purged of paganism. Wandering through Rome at the present time, we feel in every part the spirit of the Catholic Revival, and murmur to ourselves those lines of Clough:

> O ye mighty and strange, ye ancient divine ones of Hellas!
> Are ye Christian too? To convert and redeem and renew you,
> Will the brief form have sufficed, that a Pope has set up on the apex
> Of the Egyptian stone that o'ertops you, the Christian symbol?
> And ye, silent, supreme in serene and victorious marble,
> Ye that encircle the walls of the stately Vatican chambers,
> Are ye also baptized; are ye of the Kingdom of Heaven?
> Utter, O some one, the word that shall reconcile Ancient and Modern.

Nothing was more absent from the mind of Sixtus than any attempt to

[65] See Giov. Gritti, *op. cit.* p. 333.

reconcile Ancient and Modern. He was bent on proclaiming the ultimate triumph of Catholicism, not only over antiquity, but also over the Renaissance. His inscriptions, crosses, and images of saints are the enduring badges of serfdom set upon the monuments of ancient and renascent Italy, bearing which they were permitted by the now absolute Pontiff to remain as testimonies to his power.

Retrenchment alone could not have sufficed for the accumulation of so much idle capital, and for so extensive an expenditure on works of public utility. Sixtus therefore had recourse to new taxation, new loans, and the creation of new offices for sale. The Venetian envoy mentions eighteen imposts levied in his reign; a sum of 600,000 crowns accruing to the Camera by the sale of places; and extensive loans, or Monti, which were principally financed by the Genoese.[66] It was necessary for the Papacy, now that it had relinquished the larger part of its revenues derived from Europe, to live upon the proceeds of the Papal States. The complicated financial expedients on which successive Popes relied for developing their exchequer, have been elaborately explained by Ranke.[67] They were materially assisted in their efforts to support the Papal dignity upon the resources of their realm, by the new system of nepotism which now began to prevail. Since the Council of Trent, it was impossible for a Pope to acknowledge his sons, and few, if any, of the Popes after Pius IV. had sons to acknowledge.[68] The tendencies of the Church rendered it also incompatible with the Papal position that near relatives of the Pontiff should be advanced, as formerly, to the dignity of independent princes. The custom was to create one nephew Cardinal, with such wealth derived from office as should enable him to benefit the Papal family at large. Another nephew was usually ennobled, endowed with capital in the public funds for the purchase of lands, and provided with lucrative places in the secular administration. He then married into a Roman family of wealth and founded one of the aristocratic houses of the Roman State. We possess some details respecting the incomes of the Papal nephews at this period, which may be of interest.[69] Carlo Borromeo was reasonably believed to enjoy revenues amounting to 50,000 scudi. Giacomo Buoncompagno's whole estate was estimated at 120,000 scudi; while the two Cardinal nephews of Gregory XIII. had each about 10,000 a year. At the same epoch Paolo Giordano Orsini, Duke of Bracciano, enjoyed an income of some 25,000, his estate being worth 60,000,

[66] Giov. Gritti, *op. cit.* p. 337.
[67] *History of the Popes*, Book IV. section I.
[68] Giacomo Buoncompagno was born while Gregory XIII. was still a layman and a lawyer.
[69] Sarpi writes: 'In my times Pius V., during five years, accumulated 25,000 ducats for the Cardinal nephew; Gregory XIII., in thirteen years, 30,000 for one nephew, and 20,000 for another; Sixtus V., for his only nephew, 9,000; Clement VIII., in thirteen years, for one nephew, 8,000, and for the other, 3,000; and this Pope, Paul V., in four years, for one nephew alone, 40,000. To what depths are we destined to fall in the future?' (*Lettere*, vol. i. p. 281). This final question was justified by the event; for, after the Borghesi, came the Ludovisi and Barberini, whose accumulations equalled, if they did not surpass, those of any antecedent Papal families.

but being heavily encumbered. These figures are taken from the Reports of the Venetian envoys. If we may trust them as accurate, it will appear by a comparison of them with the details furnished by Ranke, that Gregory's successors treated their relatives with greater generosity.[70] Sixtus V. enriched the Cardinal Montalto with an ecclesiastical income of 100,000 scudi. Clement VIII. bestowed on two nephews—one Cardinal, the other layman—revenues of about 60,000 apiece in 1599. He is computed to have hoarded altogether for his family a round sum of 1,000,000 scudi. Paul V. was believed to have given to his Borghese relatives nearly 700,000 scudi in cash, 24,600 scudi in funds, and 268,000 in the worth of offices.[71] The Cardinal Ludovico Lodovisi, nephew of Gregory XV., had a reputed income of 200,000 scudi; and the Ludovisi family obtained 800,000 in *luoghi di monte* or funds. Three nephews of Urban VIII., the brothers Barberini, were said to have enjoyed joint revenues amounting to half a million scudi, and their total gains from the pontificate touched the enormous sum of 105,000,000. These are the families, sprung from obscurity or mediocre station, whose palaces and villas adorn Rome, and who now rank, though of such recent origin, with the aristocracy of Europe.

Sixtus V. died in 1590. To follow the history of his successors would be superfluous for the purpose of this book. The change in the Church which began in the reign of Paul III. was completed in his pontificate. About half a century, embracing seven tenures of the Holy Chair, had sufficed to develop the new phase of the Papacy as an absolute sovereignty, representing the modern European principle of Absolutism, both as the acknowledged Head of Catholic Christendom, and also as a petty Italian power.

[70] The details may be examined in Ranke, vol. ii. pp. 303-311.

[71] Sarpi's Letters supply some details relating to Paul V.'s nepotism. He describes the pleasure which this Pope took on one day of each week in washing his hands in the gold of the Datatario and the Camera (vol. i. p. 281), and says of him, 'attende solo a far danari' (vol. ii. p. 237). When Paul gave his nephew Scipione the Abbey of Vangadizza, with 12,000 ducats a year, Sarpi computed that the Cardinal held about 100,000 ducats of ecclesiastical benefices (vol. i. p. 219). When the Archbishopric of Bologna, worth over 16,000 ducats a year, fell vacant in 1610, Paul gave this to Scipione, who held it a short time without residence, and then abandoned it to Alessandro Ludovisi, retaining all its revenues, with the exception of 2,000 ducats, for himself as a *pension* (vol. ii. pp. 158, 300). In the year 1610 Sarpi notices the purchase of Sulmona and other fiefs by Paul for his family, at the expenditure of 160,000 ducats (vol. ii. p. 70). In another place he speaks of another sum of 100,000 spent upon the same object (vol. i. p. 249, note). Well might he exclaim, 'Il pontefice è atteso ad arrachir la sua casa' (vol. i. p. 294).

CHAPTER III

THE INQUISITION AND THE INDEX

Different Spirit in the Holy Office and the Company of Jesus—Both needed by the Counter-Reformation—Heresy in the Early Church—First Origins of the Inquisition in 1203—S. Dominic—The Holy Office becomes a Dominican Institution—Recognised by the Empire—Its early Organisation—The Spanish Inquisition—Founded in 1484—How it differed from the earlier Apostolical Inquisition—Jews, Moors, New Christians—Organisation and History of the Holy Office in Spain—Torquemada and his Successors—The Spanish Inquisition never introduced into Italy—How the Roman Inquisition organised by Caraffa differed from it—Autos da fe in Rome—Proscription of suspected Lutherans—The Calabrian Waldenses—Protestants at Locarno and Venice—Digression on the Venetian Holy Office—Persecution of Free Thought in Literature—Growth of the Index Librorum Prohibitorum—Sanction given to it by the Council of Trent—The Roman Congregation of the Index—Final Form of the Censorship of Books under Clement VIII.—Analysis of its Regulations—Proscription of Heretical Books—Corrections of Texts—Purgation and Castration—Inquisitorial and Episcopal Licences—Working of the System of this Censorship in Italy—Its long Delays—Hostility to Sound Learning—Ignorance of the Censors—Interference with Scholars in their Work—Terrorism of Booksellers—Vatican Scheme for the Restoration of Christian Erudition—Frustrated by the Tyranny of the Index—Dishonesty of the Vatican Scholars—Biblical Studies rendered nugatory by the Tridentine Decree on the Vulgate—Decline of Learning in Universities—Miserable Servitude of Professors—Greek dies out—Muretus and Manutius in Rome—The Index and its Treatment of Political Works—Machiavelli—Ratio Status—Encouragement of Literature on Papal Absolutism—Sarpi's Attitude—Comparative Indifference of Rome to Books of Obscene or Immoral Tendency—Bandello and Boccaccio—Papal Attempts to control Intercourse of Italians with Heretics.

In pursuing the plan of this book, which aims at showing how the spirit of the Catholic Revival penetrated every sphere of intellectual activity in Italy, it will now be needful to consider the two agents, both of Spanish origin, on whose assistance the Church relied in her crusade against liberties of thought, speech and action. These were the Inquisition and the Company of Jesus. The one worked by extirpation and forcible repression; the other by mental enfeeblement and moral corruption. The one used fire, torture, imprisonment, confiscation of goods, the proscription of learning, the destruction or emasculation of books. The other employed subtle means to fill the vacuum thus created with spurious erudition, sophistries, casuistical abominations and false doctrines profitable to the Papal absolutism. Opposed in temper and in method, the one fierce and rigid, the other saccharine and pliant, these two bad angels of Rome contributed in almost equal measure to the triumph of Catholicism.

In the earlier ages of the Church, the definition of heresy had been committed to episcopal authority. But the cognisance of heretics and the determination of their punishment remained in the hands of secular magistrates. At the end of the twelfth century the wide diffusion of the Albigensian heterodoxy through Languedoc and Northern Italy alarmed the chiefs of Christendom, and furnished the Papacy with a good pretext for extending its prerogatives. Innocent III. in 1203 empowered two French Cistercians, Pierre de Castelnau and Raoul, to preach against the heretics of Provence. In the following year he ratified this commission by a Bull, which censured the negligence and coldness of the bishops, appointed the Abbot of Citeaux Papal delegate in matters of heresy, and gave him authority to judge and punish misbelievers. This was the first germ of the Holy Office as a separate Tribunal. In order to comprehend the facility with which the Pope established so anomalous an institution, we must bear in mind the intense horror which heresy inspired in the Middle Ages. Being a distinct encroachment of the Papacy upon the episcopal jurisdiction and prerogatives, the Inquisition met at first with some opposition from the bishops. The people for whose persecution it was designed, and at whose expense it carried on its work, broke into rebellion; the first years of its annals were rendered illustrious by the murder of one of its founders, Pierre de Castelnau. He was canonised, and became the first Saint of the Inquisition. Two other Peters obtained the like honour through their zeal for the Catholic faith: Peter of Verona, commonly called Peter Martyr, the Italian saint of the Dominican order; and Peter Arbues, the Spanish saint, who sealed with his blood the charter of the Holy Office in Aragon.

In spite of opposition the Papal institution took root and flourished. Philip Augustus responded to the appeals of Innocent; and a crusade began against the Albigenses, in which Simon de Montfort won his sinister celebrity. During those bloody wars, the Inquisition developed itself as a force of formidable expansive energy. Material assistance to the cause was rendered by a Spanish monk of the Augustine order, who settled in Provence on his way back from Rome in 1206. Domenigo de Guzman, known to universal history as S. Dominic, organised a new militia for the service of the orthodox Church between the years 1215 and 1219. His order, called the Order of the Preachers, was originally designed to repress heresy and confirm the faith by diffusing Catholic doctrine and maintaining the creed in its purity. It consisted of three sections: the Preaching Friars; nuns living in conventual retreat; and laymen, entitled the Third Order of Penitence or the Militia of Christ, who in after years were merged with the congregation of S. Peter Martyr, and corresponded to the familiars of the Inquisition. Since the Dominicans were established in the heat and passion of a crusade against heresy, by a rigid Spaniard who employed his energies in persecuting misbelievers, they assumed at the outset a belligerent and inquisitorial attitude. Yet it is not strictly accurate to represent S. Dominic himself as the first Grand Inquisitor. The Papacy proceeded with caution in its design of forming a tribunal dependent on the Holy See and independent of the bishops. Papal Legates with plenipotentiary authority were sent to Languedoc, and decrees were issued against the heretics, in which the Inquisition was rather implied than directly named; nor can I find that S. Dominic, though he continued to be the soul of the new institution until his death in 1221, obtained the title of Inquisitor.

Notwithstanding this vagueness, the Holy Office may be said to have been founded by S. Dominic; and it soon became apparent that the order he had formed was destined to monopolise its functions. The Emperor Frederick II. on his coronation, in 1221, declared his willingness to support a separate Apostolical tribunal for the suppression of heresy. He sanctioned the penalty of death by fire for obstinate heretics, and perpetual imprisonment for penitents—forms of punishment which became stereotyped in the proceedings of the Holy Office.[1] The tribunal, now recognised as a Dominican institution, derived its authority from the Pope. The bishops were suffered to sit with the Inquisitors, but only in such subordinate capacity as left to them a bare title of authority.[2] The secular magistracy was represented by an assessor, who, being nominated by the Inquisitor, became his servile instrument. The expenses of the Court in prosecuting, punishing and imprisoning heretics, together with the maintenance of the Inquisitors and their guards, were thrown upon the communes which they visited. Such was the organisation which the Popes, aided by S. Dominic, and availing themselves of the fanatical passions aroused in the Provençal wars, succeeded in creating for their own aggrandisement. It is strange to think that its ratification by the supreme secular power was obtained from an Emperor who died in contumacy, excommunicated and persecuted as an arch-heretic by the priests he had supported.

This Apostolical Inquisition was at once introduced into Lombardy, Romagna and the Marches of Treviso. The extreme rigour of its proceedings, the extortions of monks, and the violent resistance offered by the communes, led to some relaxation of its original constitution. More authority had to be conceded to the bishops; and the right of the Inquisitors to levy taxes on the people was modified. Yet it retained its true form of a Papal organ, superseding the episcopal prerogatives, and overriding the secular magistrates, who were bound to execute its biddings. As such it was admitted into Tuscany, and established in Aragon. Venice received it in 1289, with certain reservations that placed its pro-

[1] See Cantù, *Gli Eretici d' Italia*, vol. i. Discorso 5, and the notes appended to it, for Frederick's edicts and letters to Gregory IX. upon this matter of heresy. The Emperor treats of *Heretica Pravitas* as a crime against society, and such, indeed, it then appeared according to the mediæval ideal of Christendom united under Church and Empire. Yet Frederick himself, it will be remembered, died under the ban of the Church and was placed by Dante among the heresiarchs in the tenth circle of Hell. We now regard him justly as one of the precursors of the Renaissance. But at the beginning of his reign, in his peculiar attitude of Holy Roman Emperor, he had to proceed with rigour against free-thinkers in religion. They were foes to the mediæval order, of which he was the secular head.

[2] Sarpi, 'Discorso dell' Origine,' &c. *Opere*, vol. iv. p. 6.

ceedings under the control of Doge and Council. In Languedoc, the country of its birth, it remained rooted at Toulouse and Carcassonne; but the Inquisition did not extend its authority over central and northern France.[3] In Paris its functions were performed by the Sorbonne. Nor did it obtain a footing in England, although the statute 'De Haeretico Comburendo,' passed in 1401 at the instance of the higher clergy, sanctioned the principles on which it existed.

The wide and ready acceptance of so terrible an engine of oppression enables us to estimate the profound horror which heresy inspired in the Middle Ages.[4] On the whole, the Inquisition performed the work for which it had been instituted. Those spreading sects, known as Waldenses, Albigenses, Cathari and Paterines, whom it was commissioned to extirpate, died away into obscurity during the fourteenth century; and through the period of the Renaissance the Inquisition had little scope for the display of energy in Italy. Though dormant, it was by no means extinct, however; and the spirit which created it, needed only external cause and circumstance to bring it once more into powerful operation. Meanwhile the Popes throughout the Renaissance used the imputation of heresy, which never lost its blighting stigma, in the prosecution of their secular ambition. As Sarpi has pointed out, there were few of the Italian princes with whom they came into political collision, who were not made the subject of such accusation.

The revival of the Holy Office on a new and far more murderous basis, took place in 1484. We have seen that hitherto there had been two types of inquisition into heresy. The first, which remained in force up to the year 1203, may be called the episcopal. The second was the Apostolical or Dominican; it transferred this jurisdiction from the bishops to the Papacy, who employed the order of S. Dominic for the special service of the tribunal instituted by the Imperial decrees of Frederick II. The third deserves no other name than Spanish, though, after it had taken shape in Spain, it was transferred to Portugal, applied in all the Spanish and Portuguese colonies, and communicated with some modifications to Italy and the Netherlands.[5] Both the second and the third types of

[3] See Christie's *Etienne Dolet*, chap. 21.

[4] Visitors to Milan must have been struck with the equestrian statue to the Podestà Oldrado da Trezzeno in the Piazza de' Mercanti. Underneath it runs an epitaph containing among the praises of this man: *Catharos ut debuit ussit*. An Archbishop of Milan of the same period (middle of the thirteenth century), Enrico di Settala, is also praised upon his epitaph because *jugulavit haereses*. See Cantù, *Gli Eretici d' Italia*, vol. i. p. 108.

[5] Sarpi estimates the number of victims in the Netherlands during the reign of Charles V. at 50,000; Grotius at 100,000. In the reign of Philip II. perhaps another 25,000 were sacrificed. Motley (*Rise of the Dutch Republic*, vol. ii. p. 155) tells how in February 1568 a sentence of the Holy Office, confirmed by royal proclamation, condemned all the inhabitants of the Netherlands, some three millions of souls, with a few specially excepted persons, to death. It was customary to burn the men and bury the women alive. In considering this institution as a whole, we must bear in mind that it was extended to Mexico, Lima, Carthagena, the Indies, Sicily, Sardinia, Oran, Malta. Of the working of the Holy Office in the Spanish and Portuguese colonies we possess but few authentic records. The *Histoire des Inquisitions* of Joseph Lavallèe

inquisition into heresy were Spanish inventions, patented by the Roman Pontiffs and monopolised by the Dominican order. But the third and final form of the Holy Office in Spain distinguished itself by emancipation from Papal and Royal control, and by a specific organisation which rendered it the most formidable of irresponsible engines in the annals of religious institutions.

The crimes of which the second or Dominican Inquisition had taken cognisance were designated under the generic name of heresy. Heretics were either patent by profession of some heterodox cult or doctrine; or they were suspected. The suspected included witches, sorcerers, and blasphemers who invoked the devil's aid; Catholics abstaining from confession and absolution; harbourers of avowed heretics; legal defenders of the cause of heretics; priests who gave Christian burial to heretics; magistrates who showed lukewarmness in pursuit of heretics; the corpses of dead heretics, and books that might be taxed with heretical opinions. All ranks in the social hierarchy, except the Pope, his Legates and Nuncios, and the bishops, were amenable to this Inquisition. The Inquisitors could only be arraigned and judged by their peers. In order to bring the machinery of imprisonment, torture and final sentence into effect, it was needful that the credentials of the Inquisitor should be approved by the sovereign, and that his procedure should be recognised by the bishop. These limitations of the Inquisitorial authority safeguarded the crown and the episcopacy in a legal sense. But since both crown and episcopacy concurred in the object for which the Papacy had established the tribunal, the Inquisitor was practically unimpeded in his functions. Furnished with royal or princely letters patent, he travelled from town to town, attended by his guards and notaries, defraying current expenses at the cost of provinces and towns through which he passed. Where he pitched his camp, he summoned the local magistrates, swore them to obedience, and obtained assurance of their willingness to execute such sentences as he might pronounce. Spies and informers gathered round him, pledged to secrecy and guaranteed by promises of State protection. The court opened; witnesses were examined; the accused were acquitted or condemned. Then sentence was pronounced, to which the bishop or his delegate, often an Inquisitor, gave a formal sanction. Finally, the heretic was handed over to the secular arm for the execution of justice. The extraordinary expenses of the tribunal were defrayed by confiscation of goods, a certain portion being paid to the district in which the crime had occurred, the rest being reserved for the maintenance of the Holy Office.

Such, roughly speaking, was the method of the Inquisition before 1484; and it did not materially differ in Italy and Spain. Castile had hitherto been free from the pest. But the conditions of that kingdom

(Paris, 1809) may, however, be consulted. In vol. ii. pp. 5-9 of this work there is a brief account of the Inquisition at Goa written by one Pyrard; and pp. 45-157 extend the singularly detailed narrative of a Frenchman, Dellon, imprisoned in its dungeons. Some curious circumstances respecting delation, prison life, and *autos da fe* are here minutely recorded.

offered a good occasion for its introduction at the date which I have named. During the Middle Ages the Jews of Castile acquired vast wealth and influence. Few families but felt the burden of their bonds and mortgages. Religious fanaticism, social jealousy, and pecuniary distress exasperated the Christian population; and as early as the year 1391, more than 5,000 Jews were massacred in one popular uprising. The Jews, in fear, adopted Christianity. It is said that in the fifteenth century the population counted some million of converts—called New Christians, or, in contempt, Marranos; a word which may probably be derived from the Hebrew Maranatha. These converted Jews, by their ability and wealth, crept into high offices of state, obtained titles of aristocracy, and founded noble houses. Their daughters were married with large dowers into the best Spanish families; and their younger sons aspired to the honours of the Church. Castilian society was being penetrated with Jews, many of whom had undoubtedly conformed to Christianity in externals only. Meanwhile a large section of the Hebrew race remained faithful to their old traditions; and a mixed posterity grew up, which hardly knew whether it was Christian or Jewish, and had opportunity for joining either party.

A fertile field was now opened for Inquisitorial energy. The orthodox Dominicans saw Christ's flock contaminated. Not without reason did earnest Catholics dread that the Church in Castile would suffer from this blending of the Jewish with the Spanish breed. But they had a fiery Catholic enthusiasm to rely upon in the main body of the nation. And in the crown they knew that there were passions of fear and cupidity, which might be used with overmastering effect. It sufficed to point out to Ferdinand that a persecution of the New Christians would flood his coffers with gold extorted from suspected misbelievers. No merely fabled El Dorado lay in the broad lands and costly merchandise of these imperfect converts to the faith. It sufficed to insist upon the peril to the state if an element so ill-assimilated to the nation were allowed to increase unchecked. At the same time, the Papacy was nothing loth to help them in their undertaking. Sixtus IV., one of the worst of Pontiffs, sat then on S. Peter's Chair. He readily discerned that a considerable portion of the booty might be indirectly drawn into his exchequer; and he knew that any establishment of the Inquisition on an energetic basis would strengthen the Papacy in its combat with national and episcopal prerogatives. The Dominicans on their side can scarcely be credited with a pure zeal for the faith. They had personal interests to serve by spiritual aggrandisement, by the elevation of their order, and by the exercise of an illimitable domination.

It was a Sicilian Inquisitor, Philip Barberis, who suggested to Ferdinand the Catholic the advantage he might secure by extending the Holy Office to Castile. Ferdinand avowed his willingness; and Sixtus IV. gave the project his approval in 1478. But it met with opposition from the gentler-natured Isabella. She refused at first to sanction the introduction of so sinister an engine into her hereditary dominions. The clergy now contrived to raise a popular agitation against the Jews, reviving old calumnies of impossible crimes, and accusing them of being treasonable subjects. Then Isabella yielded; and in 1481 the Holy Office was founded at Seville. It began its work by publishing a comprehensive edict against all New Christians suspected of Judaising, which offence was so constructed as to cover the most innocent observance of national customs. Resting from labour on Saturday; performing ablutions at stated times; refusing to eat pork or puddings made of blood; and abstaining from wine, sufficed to colour accusations of heresy. Men who had joined the Catholic communion after the habits of a lifetime had been formed, thus found themselves exposed to peril of death by the retention of mere sanitary rules.[6]

Upon the publication of this edict, there was an exodus of Jews by thousands into the fiefs of independent vassals of the crown—the Duke of Medina Sidonia, the Marquis of Cadiz, and the Count of Arcos. All emigrants were *ipso facto* declared heretics by the Holy Office. During the first year after its foundation, Seville beheld 298 persons burned alive, and 79 condemned to perpetual imprisonment. A large square stage of stone, called the Quemadero, was erected for the execution of those multitudes who were destined to suffer death by hanging or by flame. In the same year, 2,000 were burned and 17,000 condemned to public penitence, while even a larger number were burned in effigy, in other parts of the kingdom.

While estimating the importance of these punishments, we must remember that they implied confiscation of property. Thus whole families were orphaned and consigned to penury. Penitence in public carried with it social infamy, loss of civil rights and honours, intolerable conditions of ecclesiastical surveillance, and heavy pecuniary fines. Penitents who had been reconciled, returned to society in a far more degraded condition than convicts released on ticket of leave. The stigma attached in perpetuity to the posterity of the condemned, whose names were conspicuously emblazoned upon church-walls as foemen to Christ and to the state.

It is not strange that the New Christians, wealthy as they were and allied with some of the best blood in Spain, should have sought to avert the storm descending on them by appeals to Rome. In person or by procurators, they carried their complaints to the Papal Curia, imploring the relief of private reconciliation with the Church, special exemption

[6] See Lavallèe, *Histoire des Inquisitions*, vol. ii. pp. 341-361, for the translation of a process instituted in 1570 against a Mauresque female slave. Suspected of being a disguised infidel, she was exposed to the temptations of a Moorish spy, and convicted mainly on the evidence furnished by certain Mussulman habits to which she adhered. Llorente reports a similar specimen case, vol. i. p. 442. The culprit was a tinker aged 71, accused in 1528 of abstaining from pork and wine, and using certain ablutions. He defended himself by pleading that, having been converted at the age of 45, it did not suit his taste to eat pork or drink wine, and that his trade obliged him to maintain cleanliness by frequent washing. He was finally condemned to carry a candle at an *auto da fe* in sign of penitence, and to pay four ducats, the costs of his trial. His detention lasted from September 1529 till December 18, 1530.

from the jurisdiction of the Holy Office, rehabilitation after the loss of civil rights and honours, dispensation from humiliating penances, and avocation of causes tried by the Inquisition to less prejudiced tribunals. The object of these petitions was to avoid perpetual infamy, to recover social status, and to obtain an impartial hearing in doubtful cases. The Papal Curia had anticipated the profits to be derived from such appeals. Sixtus IV. was liberal in briefs of indulgence, absolution and exemption, to all comers who paid largely. But when his suitors returned to Spain, they found their dearly purchased parchments of no more value than waste paper. The Holy Office laughed Papal Bulls of Privilege to scorn, and the Pope was too indifferent to exert such authority as he might have possessed.

Meanwhile, the Inquisition rapidly took shape. In 1483 Thomas of Torquemada was nominated Inquisitor General for Castile and Aragon. Under his rule a Supreme Council was established, over which he presided for life. The crown sent three assessors to this board; and the Inquisitors were strengthened in their functions by a council of jurists. Seville, Cordova, Jaen, Toledo became the four subordinate centres of the Holy Office, each with its own tribunal and its own right of performing acts of faith. Commission was sent out to all Dominicans, enjoining on them the prosecution of their task in every diocese.

In 1484 a General Council was held, and the constitution of the Inquisition was established by articles. In these articles four main points seem to have been held in view. The first related to the system of confiscation, fines, civil disabilities, losses of office, property, honours, rights, inheritances, which formed a part of the penitentiary procedure, and by which the crown and Holy Office made pecuniary gains. The second secured secrecy in the action of the tribunal, whereby a door was opened to delation, and accused persons were rendered incapable of rational defence. The third elaborated the judicial method, so as to leave no loophole of escape even for those who showed a wish to be converted, empowering the use of torture, precluding the accused from choosing their own counsel, and excluding the bishops from active participation in the sentence. The fourth multiplied the charges under which suspected heretics, even after their death, might be treated as impenitent or relapsed, so as to increase the number of victims and augment the booty.

The two most formidable features of the Inquisition as thus constituted were the exclusion of the bishops from its tribunal and the secrecy of its procedure. The accused was delivered over to a court that had no mercy, no common human sympathies, no administrative interest in the population. He knew nothing of his accusers; and when he died or disappeared from view no record of his case survived him.

The Inquisition rested on the double basis of ecclesiastical fanaticism and protected delation. The court was *prima facie* hostile to the accused; and the accused could never hope to confront the detectives upon whose testimony he was arraigned before it. Lives and reputations lay thus at the mercy of professional informers, private enemies, malicious calumniators. The denunciation was sometimes anonymous, sometimes signed, with names of two corroborative witnesses. These witnesses were examined, under a strict seal of secrecy, by the Inquisitors, who drew up a form of accusation, which they submitted to theologians called Qualificators. The qualificators were not informed of the names of the accused, the delator, or the witnesses. It was their business to qualify the case of heresy as light, grave, or violent. Having placed it in one of these categories, they returned it to the Inquisitors, who now arrested the accused and flung him into the secret prisons of the Holy Office. After some lapse of time he was summoned for a preliminary examination. Having first been cautioned to tell the truth, he had to recite the Paternoster, Credo, Ten Commandments, and a kind of catechism. His pedigree was also investigated, in the expectation that some traces of Jewish or Moorish descent might serve to incriminate him. If he failed in repeating the Christian shibboleths, or if he was discovered to have infidel ancestry, there existed already a good case to proceed upon. Finally, he was questioned upon the several heads of accusation condensed from the first delation and the deposition of the witnesses. If needful at this point, he was put to the torture, again and yet again.[7] He never heard the names of his accusers, nor was he furnished with a full bill of the charges against him in writing. At this stage he was usually remanded, and the judicial proceedings were deliberately lengthened out with a view of crushing his spirit and bringing him to abject submission. For his defence he might select one advocate, but only from a list furnished by his judges; and this advocate in no case saw the original documents of the impeachment. It rarely happened, upon this one-sided method of trial, that an accused person was acquitted altogether. If he escaped burning or perpetual incarceration, he was almost certainly exposed to the public ceremony of penitence, with its attendant infamy, fines, civil disabilities, and future discipline. Sentence was not passed upon condemned persons until they appeared, dressed up in a San Benito, at the place of punishment. This costume was a sort of sack, travestying a monk's frock, made of coarse yellow stuff, and worked over with crosses, flames, and devils, in glaring red. It differed in details according to the destination of the victim: for some ornaments symbolised eternal hell, and others the milder fires of purgatory. If sufficiently versed in the infernal heraldry of the Holy Office, a condemned man might read his doom before he reached the platform of the *auto*. There he heard whether he was sentenced to relaxation—in other words, to burning at the hands of the hangman—or to reconciliation by means of penitence. At the last moment, he might by confession *in extremis* obtain the commutation of a death sentence into life-imprisonment, or receive the favour of being strangled before he was burned. A relapsed heretic, however—that is, one who after being reconciled had once again apostatised, was never exempted from the

[7] The Supreme Council forbade the repetition of torture; but this hypocritical law was evaded in practice by declaring that the torture had been suspended. Llorente, vol. i. p. 307.

penalty of burning. To make these holocausts of human beings more ghastly, the pageant was enhanced by processions of exhumed corpses and heretics in effigy. Artificial dolls and decomposed bodies, with grinning lips and mouldy foreheads, were hauled to the huge bonfire, side by side with living men, women, and children. All of them alike—*fantoccini*, skeletons, and quick folk—were enveloped in the same grotesquely ghastly San Benito, with the same hideous yellow mitres on their pasteboard, worm-eaten, or palpitating foreheads. The procession presented an ingeniously picturesque discord of ugly shapes, an artistically loathsome dissonance of red and yellow hues, as it defiled, to the infernal music of growled psalms and screams and moanings, beneath the torrid blaze of Spanish sunlight.

Spaniards—such is the barbarism of the Latinised Iberian nature—delighted in these shows as they did and do in bull-fights. Butcheries of heretics formed the choicest spectacles at royal christenings and bridals.

At Seville the Quemadero was adorned with four colossal statues of prophets, to which some of the condemned were bound, so that they might burn to death in the flames arising from the human sacrifice between them.

In the autumn of 1484 the Inquisition was introduced into Aragon; and Saragossa became its headquarters in that State. Though the Aragonese were accustomed to the institution in its earlier and milder form, they regarded the new Holy Office with just horror. The Marranos counted at that Epoch the Home Secretary, the Grand Treasurer, a Protonotary, and a Vice-Chancellor of the realm among their members; and they were allied by marriage with the purest aristocracy. It is not, therefore, marvellous that a conspiracy was formed to assassinate the Chief Inquisitor, Peter Arbues. In spite of a coat-of-mail and an iron skullcap worn beneath his monk's dress, Arbues was murdered one evening while at prayer in church. But the revolt, notwithstanding this murder, flashed like an ill-loaded pistol in the pan. Jealousies between the old and new Christians prevented any common action; and the Inquisition took a bloody vengeance upon all concerned. It even laid its hand on Don James of Navarre, the Infant of Tudela.

The Spanish Inquisition was now firmly grounded. Directed by Torquemada, it began to encroach upon the crown, to insult the episcopacy, to defy the Papacy, to grind the Commons, and to outrage by its insolence the aristocracy. Ferdinand's avarice had overreached itself by creating an ecclesiastical power dangerous to the best interests of the realm, but which fascinated a fanatically pious people, and the yoke of which could not be thrown off. The Holy Office grew every year in pride, pretensions, and exactions. It arrogated to its tribunal crimes of usury, bigamy, blasphemous swearing, and unnatural vice, which appertained by right to the secular courts. It depopulated Spain by the extermination and banishment of at least three million industrious subjects during the first 139 years of its existence. It attacked princes of the blood, archbishops, fathers of the Tridentine Council.[8] It filled every city in the kingdom, the convents of the religious, and the palaces of the nobility, with spies. The Familiars, or lay brethren devoted to its service, lived as charges of the communes, and debauched society by crimes of rapine, lust and violence.[9] Ignorant and bloodthirsty monks composed its provincial tribunals, who, like the horrible Lucero el Tenebroso, at Cordova, paralysed whole provinces with a veritable reign of terror.[10] Hated and worshipped, its officers swept through the realm in the guise of powerful *condottieri*. The Grand Inquisitor maintained a bodyguard of fifty mounted Familiars and two hundred infantry; his subordinates were allowed ten horsemen and fifty archers apiece. Where these black guards appeared, city gates were opened; magistrates swore fealty to masters of more puissance than the king; the resources of flourishing districts were placed at their disposal. Their arbitrary acts remained unquestioned, their mysterious sentences irreversible. Shrouded in secrecy, amenable to no jurisdiction but their own, they revelled in the license of irresponsible dominion. Spain gradually fell beneath the charm of their dark fascination. A brave though cruel nation drank delirium from the poison-cup of these vile medicine-men, whose Moloch-worship would have disgusted cannibals.

Torquemada was the genius of evil who created and presided over this foul instrument of human crime and folly. During his eighteen years of administration, reckoning from 1480 to 1498, he sacrificed, according to Llorente's calculation, above 114,000 victims, of whom 10,220 were burned alive, 6,860 burned in effigy, and 97,000 condemned to perpetual imprisonment or public penitence.[11] He, too, it was who in 1492 compelled Ferdinand to drive the Jews from his dominions. They offered 30,000 ducats for the war against Granada, and promised to abide in Spain under heavy social disabilities, if only they might be spared this act of national extermination. Then Torquemada appeared before the king, and, raising his crucifix on high, cried: 'Judas sold Christ for thirty pieces of silver. Look ye to it, if ye do the like!' The edict of expulsion was issued on the last of March. Before the last of July all Jews were sentenced to depart, carrying no gold or silver with them. They disposed of their lands, houses, and goods for next to nothing, and went forth to die by thousands on the shores of Africa and Italy. Twelve who were found concealed at Malaga in August were condemned to be pricked to death by pointed reeds.[12]

The exodus of the Jews was followed in 1502 by a similar exodus of Moors from Castile, and in 1524 by an exodus of Mauresques from Ara-

[8] Llorente, in his Introduction to the *History of the Inquisition*, gives a long list of illustrious Spanish victims.

[9] See Llorente, vol. i. p. 349, for their outrages on women.

[10] For the history of Lucero's tyranny, read Llorente, vol. i. pp. 345-353. When at last he had to be deposed, it was not to a dungeon or the scaffold, but to his bishopric of Almeria that this miscreant was relegated.

[11] Llorente, vol. i. p. 229. The basis for these and following calculations is explained *ib.* pp. 272-281.

[12] Llorente, vol. i. p. 263.

gon. To compute the loss of wealth and population inflicted upon Spain by these mad edicts, would be impossible. We may wonder whether the followers of Cortes, when they trod the teocallis of Mexico and gazed with loathing on the gory elf-locks of the Aztec priests, were not reminded of the Torquemada they had left at home. His cruelty became so intolerable that even Alexander VI. was moved to horror. In 1494 the Borgia appointed four assessors, with equal powers, to restrain the bloodthirst of the fanatic.

After Torquemada, Diego Deza reigned as second Inquisitor General from 1498 to 1507. In these years, according to the same calculation, 2,592 were burned alive, 896 burned in effigy, 34,952 condemned to prison or public penitence.[13] Cardinal Ximenez de Cisneros followed between 1507 and 1517. The victims of this decade were 3,564 burned alive, 1,232 burned in effigy, 48,059 condemned to prison or public penitence.[14] Adrian, Bishop of Tortosa, tutor to Charles V. and afterwards Pope, was Inquisitor General between 1516 and 1525. Castile, Aragon, and Catalonia, at this epoch, simultaneously demanded a reform of the Holy Office from their youthful sovereign. But Charles refused, and the tale of Adrian's administration was 1,620 burned alive, 560 burned in effigy, 21,845 condemned to prison or public penitence.[15] The total, during forty-three years, between 1481 and 1525, amounted to 234,526, including all descriptions of condemned heretics.[16] These figures are of necessity vague, for the Holy Office left but meagre records of its proceedings. The vast numbers of cases brought before the Inquisitors rendered their method of procedure almost as summary as that of Fouquier-Tinville, while policy induced them to bury the memory of their victims in oblivion.[17]

Sometimes, while reading the history of the Holy Office in Spain, we are tempted to imagine that the whole is but a grim unwholesome nightmare, or the fable of malignant calumny. That such is not the case, however, is proved by a jubilant inscription on the palace of the Holy Office at Seville, which records the triumphs of Torquemada. Of late

[13] Llorente, vol. i. p. 341.

[14] *Ib.* p. 360.

[15] *Ib.* p. 406.

[16] *Ib.* p. 407.

[17] I know that Llorente's calculations have been disputed: as, for instance, in some minor details by Prescott (*Ferd. and Isab.* vol. iii. p. 492). The truth is that no data now exist for forming a correct census of the victims of the Spanish Moloch; and Llorente, though he writes with the moderation of evident sincerity, and though he had access to the archives of the Inquisition, does not profess to do more than give an estimate based upon certain fixed data. However, it signifies but little whether we reckon by thousands or by fifteen hundreds. That foul monster spawned in the unholy embracements of perverted religion with purblind despotism cannot be defended by discounting five or even ten per cent. Let its apologists write for every 1,000 of Llorente 100 and for every 100 of Llorente 10, and our position will remain unaltered. The Jesuit historian of Spain, Mariana, records the burning of 2,000 persons in Andalusia alone in 1482. Bernaldez mentions 700 burned in the one town of Seville between 1482 and 1489. An inscription carved above the portals of the Holy Office in Seville stated that about 1,000 had been burned between 1492 and 1524.

years, too, the earth herself has disgorged some secrets of the Inquisition. 'A most curious discovery,' writes Lord Malmesbury in his Memoirs,[18] 'has been made at Madrid. Just at the time when the question of religious liberty was being discussed in the Cortes, Serrano had ordered a piece of ground to be levelled, in order to build on it, and the workmen came upon large quantities of human bones, skulls, lumps of blackening flesh, pieces of chains, and braids of hair. It was then recollected that the *autos da fe* used to take place at that spot in former days. Crowds of people rushed to the place, and the investigation was continued. They found layer upon layer of human remains, showing that hundreds had been inhumanly sacrificed. The excitement and indignation this produced among the people was tremendous, and the party for religious freedom taking advantage of it, a Bill on the subject was passed by an enormous majority.' Let modern Spain remember that a similar Aceldama lies hidden in the precincts of each of her chief towns!

I have enlarged upon the details of the Spanish Inquisition for two reasons. In the first place it strikingly illustrates the character of the people who now had the upper hand in Italy. In the second place, its success induced Paul III., acting upon the advice of Giov. Paolo Caraffa, to remodel the Roman office on a similar type in 1542. It may at once be said that the real Spanish Inquisition was never introduced into Italy.[19] Such an institution, claiming independent jurisdiction and flaunting its cruelties in the light of day, would not have suited the Papal policy. As temporal and spiritual autocrats, the Popes could not permit a tribunal of which they were not the supreme authority. It was their interest to consult their pecuniary advantage rather than to indulge insane fanaticism; to repress liberty of thought by cautious surveillance rather than by public terrorism and open acts of cruelty. The Italian temperament was, moreover, more humane than the Spanish; nor had the refining culture of the Renaissance left no traces in the nation. Furthermore, the necessity for so Draconian an institution was not felt. Catholicism in Italy had not to contend with Jews and Moors, Marranos and Moriscoes. It was, indeed, alarmed by the spread of Lutheran opinions. Caraffa complained to Paul III. that 'the whole of Italy is infected with the Lutheran heresy, which has been embraced not only by statesmen but also by many ecclesiastics.'[20] Pius V. was so panic-stricken by the prevalence of heresy in Faenza that he seriously meditated destroying the town and dispersing its inhabitants.[21] Yet, after a few years of active persecution, this peril proved to be unreal. The Reformation had not taken root so deep and wide in Italy that it could not be eradicated. When, therefore, the Spanish viceroys sought to establish their national Inquisition in Naples and Milan, the rebellious people received protection

[18] Vol. ii. p. 399.

[19] Naples and Milan passionately and successfully opposed its introduction by the Spanish viceroys. But it ruled in Sicily and Sardinia.

[20] McCrie, p. 186.

[21] Mutinelli, *Storia Arcana*, vol. i. p. 79.

and support from the Papacy; and the Holy Office, as remodelled in Rome, became a far less awful engine of oppression than that of Seville.

It was sufficiently severe, however. 'At Rome,' writes a resident in 1568, 'some are daily burned, hanged, or beheaded; the prisons and places of confinement are filled, and they are obliged to build new ones.'[22] This general statement may be checked by extracts from the dispatches of Venetian ambassadors in Rome, which, though they are not continuous, and cannot be supposed to give an exhaustive list of the victims of the Inquisition, enable us to judge with some degree of accuracy what the frequency of executions may have been.[23] On September 27, 1567, a session of the Holy Office was held at S. Maria sopra Minerva. Seventeen heretics were condemned. Fifteen of these were sentenced to perpetual imprisonment, the galleys for life, fines or temporary imprisonment, according to the nature of their offences. Two were reserved for capital punishment—namely, Carnesecchi and a friar from Cividale di Belluno. They were beheaded and burned upon the bridge of S. Angelo on October 4. On May 28, 1569, there was an Act of the Inquisition at the Minerva, twenty Cardinals attending. Four impenitent heretics were condemned to the stake. Ten penitents were sentenced to various punishments of less severity. On August 2, 1578, occurred a singular scandal touching some Spaniards and Portuguese of evil manners, all of whom were burned with the exception of those who contrived to escape in time. On August 5, 1581, an English Protestant was burned for grossly insulting the Host. On February 20, 1582, after an Act of the Inquisition in due form, seventeen heretics were sentenced, three to death, and the rest to imprisonment &c. We must bear in mind that Mutinelli, who published the extracts from the Venetian despatches which contain these details, does not profess to aim at completeness. Gaps of several years occur between the documents of one envoy and those of his successor. Nor does it appear that the writers themselves took notice of more than solemn and ceremonial proceedings, in which the Acts of the Inquisition were published with Pontifical and Curial pomp.[24] Still, when these considerations have been weighed, it will appear that the victims of the Inquisition, in Rome, could be counted, not by hundreds, but by units. After illustrious examples, like those of Aonio Paleario, Pietro Carnesecchi, Giordano Bruno, who were burned for Protestant or Atheistical opinions, the names of distinguished sufferers are few. Wary heretics, a Celio Secundo Curio, a Galeazzo Caracciolo, a Bernardino Ochino, a Pietro Martire Vermigli, a Pietro Paolo Vergerio, a Lelio Socino, escaped betimes to Switzerland and carried on their warfare with the Church by means of writings.[25] Others, tainted with heresy, like Marco Antonio

[22] McCrie, p. 272.

[23] Mutinelli's *Storia Arcana*, &c. vol. i., is the source from which I have drawn the details given above.

[24] It is singular that only one contemporary writes from Rome about Bruno's execution in 1600; whence, I think, we may infer that such events were too common to excite much attention.

[25] The main facts about these men may be found in Cantù's *Gli Eretici d' Italia*, vol.

Flaminio, managed to satisfy the Inquisition by timely concessions. The Protestant Churches, which had sprung up in Venice, Lucca, Modena, Ferrara, Faenza, Vicenza, Bologna, Naples, and Siena, were easily dispersed.[26] Their pastors fled or submitted. The flocks conformed to Catholic orthodoxy. Only in a few cases was extreme rigour displayed. A memorable massacre took place in the year 1561 in Calabria within the province of Cosenza. Here at the end of the fourteenth century a colony of Waldensians had settled in some villages upon the coast. They preserved their peculiar beliefs and ritual, and after three centuries numbered about 4,000 souls. Nearly the whole of these, it seems, were exterminated by sword, fire, famine, torture, noisome imprisonment, and hurling from the summits of high cliffs.[27] A few of the survivors were sent to work upon the Spanish galleys. Some women and children were sold into slavery. At Locarno, on the Lago Maggiore, a Protestant community of nearly 300 persons was driven into exile in 1555: and at Venice, in 1560-7, a small sect, holding reformed opinions, suffered punishment of a peculiar kind. We read of five persons by name, who, after being condemned by the Holy Office, were taken at night from their dungeons to the Porto del Lido beyond the Due Castelli, and there set upon a plank between two gondolas. The gondolas rowed asunder: and one by one the martyrs fell and perished in the waters.[28]

ii. This work is written in no spirit of sympathy with Reformers. But it is superior in learning and impartiality to McCrie's.

[26] For the repressive measures used at Lucca, see *Archivio Storico*, vol. x. pp. 162-185. They include the prohibition of books, regulation of the religious observances of Lucchese citizens abroad in France or Flanders, and proscription of certain heretics, with whom all intercourse was forbidden.

[27] An eye-witness gives a heart-rending account of these persecutions; sixty thrown from the tower of Guardia, eighty-eight butchered like beasts in one day at Montalto, seven burned alive, one hundred old women tortured and then slaughtered. *Arch. Stor.* vol. ix. pp. 193-195.

[28] McCrie, *op. cit.* pp. 232-236. The five men were Giulio Gherlandi of Spresiano, near Treviso (executed in 1562), Antonio Rizzetto of Vicenza (in 1566), Francesco Sega of Rovigo (sentenced in 1566), Francesco Spinola of Milan (in 1567), and Fra Baldo Lupatino (1556). McCrie bases his report upon the *Histoire des Martyrs* (Genéve, 1597), and De Porta's *Historia Reformationis Rhœticarum Ecclesiarum*. Thinking these sources somewhat suspicious, I applied to my friend Mr. H. F. Brown, whose researches in the Venetian archives are becoming known to students of Italian history. He tells me that all the above cases, except that of Spinola, exist in the Frari. Lupatino was condemned as a Lutheran; the others as Anabaptists. In passing sentence on Lupatino, the Chief Inquisitor remarked that he could not condemn him to death by fire in Venice, but must consign him to a watery grave. This is characteristic of Venetian state policy. It appears that, of the above-named persons, Sega, though sentenced to death by drowning, recanted at the last moment, saying, 'Non voglio esser negato, ma voglio redirmi et morir buon Christiano.' Mr. Brown adds that there is nothing in the archives to prove that he was executed; but there is also nothing to show that his sentence was commuted. Two other persons involved in this trial, viz. Nic. Bucello of Padua and Alessio of Bellinzona, upon recantation, were subjected to public penances and confessions for different terms of years. Sega's fate must, therefore, be considered doubtful; since the fact that no commutation of sentence is on record lends some weight to the hypothesis that he withdrew his recantation, and submitted to martyrdom. I will close this note by expressing my hope that Mr. Brown, who is already engaged upon the papers of the Venetian Holy Office, will make them shortly the subject of a special

The position of the Holy Office in Venice was so far peculiar as to justify a digression upon its special constitution. Always jealous of ecclesiastical interference, the Republic insisted on the Inquisition being made dependent on the State. Three nobles of senatorial rank were chosen to act as Assessors of the Holy Office in the capital; and in the subject cities this function was assigned to the Rectors, or lieutenants of S. Mark. It was the duty of these lay members to see that justice was impartially dealt by the ecclesiastical tribunal, to defend the State against clerical encroachments, and to refer dubious cases to the Doge in Council. They were forbidden to swear oaths of allegiance or of secrecy to the Holy Office, and were bound to be present at all trials, even in the case of ecclesiastical offenders. No causes could be avocated to Rome, and no crimes except heresy were held to lie within the jurisdiction of the court. The State reserved to itself witchcraft, profane swearing, bigamy and usury; allowed no interference with Jews, infidels, and Greeks; forbade the confiscation of goods in which the heirs of condemned persons had interest; and made separate stipulations with regard to the Index of Prohibited Books. It precluded the Inquisition from extending its authority in any way, direct or indirect, over trades, arts, guilds, magistrates and communal officials.[29] The tenor of this system was to repress ecclesiastical encroachments on the State prerogatives, and to secure equity in the proceedings of the Holy Office. Had practice answered to theory in the Venetian Inquisition, by far the worst abuses of the institution would have been avoided. But as a matter of fact, causes were not unfrequently transferred to Rome; confiscations were permitted; and the lists of the condemned include Mussulmans, witches, conjurers, men of scandalous life, &c., showing that the jurisdiction of the Holy Office extended beyond heresy in Venice.[30]

The truth is that the Venetians, though they were willing to risk an open rupture with Rome, remained at heart sound Churchmen devoted to the principles of the Catholic Reaction. The Republic conceded the fact of the Inquisitorial authority, while it reserved the letter of State-supervision. Venetian decadence was marked by this hypocrisy of pride; and so long as appearances were saved, the Holy Office exercised its functions freely. The nobles who acted as assessors had no sympathy with religious toleration, being themselves under the influence of confessors and directors.

How little the subjects of S. Mark at this epoch trusted the good faith of laws securing liberty of thought in Venice, may be gathered from what

publication. Considering how rare are the full and authentic records of any Inquisition, this would be of incalculable value for students of history. The series of trials in the Frari extends from 1541 to 1794, embracing 1,562 *processi* for the sixteenth century, 1,469 for the seventeenth, 541 for the eighteenth, and 25 of no date. Nearly all the towns and districts of the Venetian State are involved.

[29] See Sarpi's 'Discourse on the Inquisition.' *Opere*, vol. iv.

[30] I owe to Mr. H. F. Brown details about the register of criminals condemned by the Holy office, which substantiate my statement regarding the various types of cases in its jurisdiction.

happened immediately after the publication of the Index Expurgatorius in 1596. From an official report upon the decline of the printing trade in Venice, it appears that within the space of a few months the number of presses fell from 125 to 40.[31] Printers were afraid to undertake either old or new works, and the trade languished for lack of books to publish. Yet an edict had been issued announcing that by the terms of the Concordat with Clement VIII., the Venetian press would only be subject to State control and not to the Roman tribunals.[32] The truth is that, in regard both to the Holy Office and to the Index, Venice was never strong enough to maintain the independence which she boasted. By cunning use of the confessional and by unscrupulous control of opinion, the Church succeeded in doing there much the same as in any other Italian city. Successive Popes made, indeed, a show of respecting the liberties of the Republic. On material points, touching revenue and State administration, they felt it wise to concede even more than complimentary privileges; and when Paul V. encroached upon these privileges, the Venetians were ready to resist him. Yet the quarrels between the Vatican and San Marco were, after all, but family disputes. The Venetians at the close of the sixteenth century proved themselves no better friends to spiritual freedom than were the Grand Dukes of Tuscany. Their political jealousies, commercial anxieties, and feints of maintaining a power that was rapidly decaying, denoted no partiality for the opponents of Rome—unless, like Sarpi, these wore the livery of the State and defended with the pen its secular prerogatives. Therefore, when the Signory published Clement VIII.'s Index, when copies of that Index were sown broadcast, while only an edition of sixty was granted to the Concordat, authors and publishers felt, and felt rightly, that their day had passed. The art of printing sank at once to less than a third of its productivity. The city where it had flourished so long, and where it had effected so much of enduring value for European culture, was gagged in scarcely a less degree than Rome. We have full right to insist upon these facts, and to draw from them a stringent corollary. If Venice allowed the trade in books, which had brought her so much profit and such honour in the past, to be paralysed by Clement's Index, what must have happened in other Italian towns? The blow which maimed Venetian literature, was mortal elsewhere; and the finest works of genius in the first half of the seventeenth century had to find their publishers in Paris.[33] But these reflections have led me to anticipate the proper development of the subject of this chapter.

In Italy at large the forces of the Inquisition were directed, not as in Spain against heretics in masses, but against the leaders of heretical opinion, and less against personalities than against ideas. Italy during the Renaissance had been the workshop of ideas for Europe. It was the

[31] The document in question, prepared for the use of the Signoria, exists in MS. in the Marcian Library, Misc. Eccl. et Civ. Class. VII. Cod. MDCCLXI.

[32] This edict is dated August 24, 1596.

[33] This will be apparent when I come to treat of Marino and Tassoni.

business of the Counter-Reformation to check the industry of that *officina scientiarum*, to numb the nervous centres which had previously emitted thought of pregnant import for the modern world, and to prevent the reflux of ideas, elaborated by the northern races in fresh forms, upon the intelligence which had evolved them. To do so now was comparatively easy. It only needed to put the engine of the Index Librorum Prohibitorum into working order in concert with the Inquisition.

Throughout the Middle Ages it had been customary to burn heretical writings. The bishops, the universities, and the Dominican Inquisitors exercised this privilege; and by their means, in the age of manuscripts, the life of a book was soon extinguished. Whole libraries were sometimes sacrificed at one fell swoop, as in the case of the 6,000 volumes destroyed at Salamanca in 1490 by Torquemada, on a charge of sorcery.[34] After the invention of printing it became more difficult to carry on this warfare against literature, while the rapid diffusion of Protestant opinions through the press rendered the need for their extermination urgent. Sixtus IV. laid a basis for the Index by prohibiting the publication of any books which had not previously been licensed by ecclesiastical authority. Alexander VI. by a brief of 1501 confirmed this measure, and placed books under the censorship of the episcopacy and the Inquisition. Finally, the Lateran Council, in its tenth session, held under the auspices of Leo X., gave solemn ecumenical sanction to these regulations.

The censorship having been thus established, the next step was to form a list of books prohibited by the Inquisitors appointed for that purpose. The Sorbonne in Paris drew one up for their own use, and even presented a petition to Francis I. that publication through the press should be forbidden altogether.[35] A royal edict to this effect was actually promulgated in 1535. Charles V. commissioned the University of Louvain in 1539 to furnish a similar catalogue, proclaiming at the same time the penalty of death for all who read or owned the works of Luther in his realms.[36] The University printed their catalogue with Papal approval in 1549. These lists of the Sorbonne and Louvain formed the nucleus of the Apostolic Index, which, after the close of the Council of Trent, became binding upon Catholics. When the Inquisition had been established in Rome, Caraffa, who was then at its head, obtained the sanction of Paul III. for submitting all books, old or new, printed or in manuscript, to the supervision of the Holy Office. He also contrived to place booksellers, public and private libraries, colporteurs and officers of customs, under the same authority; so that from 1543 forward it was a penal offence to print, sell, own, convey or import any literature, of which the Inquisition had not first been informed, and for the diffusion or possession of which it had not given its permission. Giovanni della Casa, who was sent in 1546 to Venice with commission to prosecute P. Paolo Vergerio for heresy, drew up a list of about seventy prohibited volumes, which was printed in

[34] Llorente, vol. i. p. 281.
[35] Christie's *Etienne Dolet*, pp. 220-224.
[36] Llorente, vol. i. p. 463.

that city.[37] Other lists appeared, at Florence in 1552, and at Milan in 1554. Philip II. at last, in 1558, issued a royal edict commanding the publication of one catalogue which should form the standard for such Indices throughout his States.[38] These lists, revised, collated, and confirmed by Papal authority, were reprinted, in the form which ever afterwards obtained, at Rome by command of Paul IV. in 1559. The Tridentine Council ratified the regulations of the Inquisition and the Index concerning prohibited books, and referred the execution of them in detail to the Papacy. A congregation was appointed at Rome, which, though technically independent of the Holy Office, worked in concert with it. This Congregation of the Index brought the Tridentine decrees into harmony with the practice that had been developed by Caraffa as Inquisitor and Pope. Their list was published in 1564 with the authority of Pius IV. Finally, in 1595, the decrees embodying the statutes of the Church upon this topic were issued in print, together with a largely augmented catalogue of interdicted books. This document will form the basis of what I have to say with regard to the Catholic crusade against literature.

Not without reason did Aonio Paleario call this engine of the Index 'a dagger drawn from the scabbard to assassinate letters'—*sica districta in omnes scriptores*.[39] Not without reason did Sarpi describe it as 'the finest secret which has ever been discovered for applying religion to the purpose of making men idiotic.'[40] Paul IV. designated in his Index Expurgatorius sixty-one printing firms by name, all of whose publications were without exception prohibited, adding a similar prohibition for the books edited by any printer who had published the writings of any heretic; so that in fine, as Sarpi says, 'there was not a book left to read.' Truly he might well exclaim in another passage that the Church was doing its best to extinguish sound learning altogether.[41]

In order to gain a clear conception of the warfare carried on by Rome against free literature, it will be well to consider first the rules for the Index of Prohibited Books, sketched out by the fathers delegated by the Tridentine Council, published by Pius IV., augmented by Sixtus V., and reduced to their final form by Clement VIII. in 1595.[42] Afterwards I shall proceed to explain the operation of the system, and to illustrate by details the injury inflicted upon learning and enlightenment.

[37] In the year 1548. The MS. cited above (p. 607) mentions another Index of the Venetian Holy Office published in 1554.

[38] Sarpi, *Ist. del Conc. Trid.* vol. ii. p. 90.

[39] In his *Oratio pro se ipso ad Senenses*. Printed by Gryphius at Lyons in 1552.

[40] *Ist. del Conc. Trid.* vol. ii. p. 91. The passage deserves to be transcribed. 'Sotto colore di fede e religione sono vietati con la medesima severità e dannati gli autori de' libri da' quali l' autorità del principe e magistrati temporali è difesa dalle usurpazioni ecclesiastiche; dove l' autorità de' Concilj e de' Vescovi è difesa dalle usurpazioni della Corte Romana; dove le ipocrisie o tirannidi con le quali sotto pretesto di religione il popolo è ingannato o violentato sonon manifestate. In somma non fu mai trovato più bell' arcano per adoperare la religione a far gli uomini insensati.'

[41] *Discorso sopra l' Inq.* vol. iv. p. 54.

[42] These rules form the Preface to modern editions of the Index. The one I use is dated Naples, 1862. They are also printed in vol. iv of Sarpi's works.

The preambles to this document recite the circumstances under which the necessity for digesting an Index or Catalogue of Prohibited Books arose. These were the diffusion of heretical opinions at the epoch of the Lutheran schism, and their propagation through the press. The Council of Trent decreed that a list of writings 'heretical, or suspected of heretical pravity, or injurious to manners and piety,' should be drawn up. This charge they committed to prelates chosen from all nations, who, when the catalogue had been completed, referred it for sanction and approval to the Pope. He nominated a congregation of eminent ecclesiastics, by whose care the catalogue was perfected, and rules were framed, defining the use that should be made of it in future. It was issued officially, as I have already stated, in 1564, the fifth year of the pontificate of Pius IV. with warning to all universities and civil and ecclesiastical authorities that any person of what grade or condition soever, whether clerk or layman, who should read or possess one or more of the proscribed volumes, would be accounted *ipso jure* excommunicate, and liable to prosesution by the Inquisition on a charge of heresy.[43] Booksellers, printers, merchants, and custom-house officials received admonition that the threat of excommunication and prosecution concerned them specially.

The first rules deal with the acknowledged writings of Protestant heresiarchs. Those of Luther, Zwingli, and Calvin, whether in their original languages or translated, are condemned absolutely and without exception. Next follow regulations for securing the monopoly of the Vulgate, considered as the sole authorised version of the Holy Scriptures. Translations of portions of the Bible made by learned men in Latin may be used by scholars with permission of a bishop, provided it be understood that they are never appealed to as the inspired text. Translations into any vernacular idiom are strictly excluded from public use and circulation, but may, under exceptional circumstances, be allowed to students who have received license from a bishop or Inquisitor at the recommendation of their parish priest or confessor. Compilations made by heretics, in the form of dictionaries, concordances, &c., are to be prohibited until they have been purged and revised by censors of the press. The same regulation extends to polemical and controversial works touching on matters of doctrine in dispute between Catholics and Protestants. Next follow regulations concerning books containing lascivious or obscene matter, which are to be rigidly suppressed. Exception is made in favour of the classics, on account of their style; with the proviso that they are on no account to be given to boys to read. Treatises dealing professedly with occult arts, magic, sorcery, predictions of future events, incantation of spirits, and so forth, are to be proscribed; due reservation being made in favour of scientific observations touching navigation, agriculture, and the healing art, in which the prognostics may be useful to mankind. Having thus broadly defined the literature which has to be suppressed or subjected to supervision, rules are laid down for the exercise of censure. Books, whereof the general tendency is good, but which contain passages

[43] Paulus Manutius Aldus printed this Index at Venice in 1564.

savouring of heresy, superstition or divination, shall be reserved for the consideration of Catholic theologians appointed by the Inquisition; and this shall hold good also of prefaces, summaries, or annotations. All writings printed in Rome must be submitted to the judgment of the Vicar of the Pope, the Master of the Sacred Palace, or a person nominated by the Pontiff. In other cities the bishop, or his delegate, and the Inquisitor of the district shall be responsible for examining printed or manuscript works previous to publication; and without their license it shall be illegal to circulate them. Inquisitorial visits shall from time to time be made, under the authority of the bishop and the Holy Office, in bookshops or printing-houses, for the removal and destruction of prohibited works. Colporteurs of books across the frontiers, heirs and executors who have become depositaries of books, collectors of private libraries, as well as editors and booksellers, shall be liable to the same jurisdiction, bound to declare their property by catalogue, and to show license for the use, transmission, sale, or possession of the same.

With regard to the correction of books, it is provided that this duty shall fall conjointly on bishops and Inquisitors, who must appoint three men distinguished for learning and piety to examine the text and make the necessary changes in it. Upon the report of these censors, the bishops and Inquisitors shall give license of publication, provided they are satisfied that the work of emendation has been duly performed. The censor must submit not only the body of a book to scrupulous analysis; but he must also investigate the notes, summaries, marginal remarks, indexes, prefaces, and dedicatory epistles, lest haply pestilent opinions lurk there in ambush. He must keep a sharp look-out for heretical propositions, and arguments savouring of heresy; insinuations against the established order of the sacraments, ceremonies, usages and ritual of the Roman Church; new turns of phrase insidiously employed by heretics, with dubious and ambiguous expressions that may mislead the unwary; plausible citations of Scripture, or passages of holy writ extracted from heretical translations; quotations from the authorised text, which have been adduced in an unorthodox sense; epithets in honour of heretics, and anything that may redound to the praise of such persons; opinions savouring of sorcery and superstition; theories that involve the subjection of the human will to fate, fortune, and fallacious portents, or that imply paganism; aspersions upon ecclesiastics and princes; impugnments of the liberties, immunities, and jurisdiction of the Church; political doctrines in favour of antique virtues, despotic government, and the so-called Reason of State, which are in opposition to the evangelical and Christian law; satires on ecclesiastical rites, religious orders, and the state, dignity, and persons of the clergy; ribaldries or stories offensive and prejudicial to the fame and estimation of one's neighbours, together with lubricities, lascivious remarks, lewd pictures, and capital letters adorned with obscene images. All such peccant passages are to be expunged, obliterated, removed or radically altered, before the license for publication be accorded by the ordinary.

No book shall be printed without the author's name in full, together with his nationality, upon the title-page. If there be sufficient reason for giving an anonymous work to the world, the censor's name shall stand for that of the author. Compilations of words, sentences, excerpts, &c., shall pass under the name of the compiler. Publishers and booksellers are to take care that the printed work agrees with the MS. copy as licensed, and to see that all rules with regard to the author's name and his authority to publish have been observed. They are, moreover, to take an oath before the Master of the Sacred Palace in Rome, or before the bishop and Inquisitor in other places, that they will scrupulously follow the regulations of the Index. The bishops and Inquisitors are held responsible for selecting as censors men of approved piety and learning, whose good faith and integrity they shall guarantee, and who shall be such as will obey no promptings of private hatred or of favour, but will do all for the glory of God and the advantage of the faithful. The approbation of such censors, together with the license of the bishop and Inquisitor, shall be printed at the opening of every published book. Finally, if any work composed by a condemned author shall be licensed after due purgation and castration, it shall bear his name upon the title-page, together with the note of condemnation, to the end that, though the book itself be accepted, the author be understood to be rejected. Thus, for example, the title shall run as follows: 'The Library, by Conrad Gesner, a writer condemned for his opinions, which work was formerly published and proscribed, but is now expurgated and licensed by superior authority.'

The Holy Office was made virtually responsible for the censorship of books. But, as I have already stated, there existed a Congregation of prelates in Rome to whom the final verdict upon this matter was reserved. If an author in some provincial town composed a volume, he was bound in the first instance to submit the MS. to the censor appointed by the bishop and Inquisitor of his district. This man took time to weigh the general matter of the work before him, to scrutinise its propositions, verify quotations, and deliberate upon its tendency. When the license of the ordinary had been obtained, it was referred to the Roman Congregation of the Index, who might withhold or grant their sanction. So complicated was the machinery, and so vast the pressure upon the officials who were held responsible for the expurgation of every book imprinted or reprinted in all the Catholic presses, that even writers of conspicuous orthodoxy had to suffer grievous delays. An archbishop writes to Cardinal Sirleto about a book which had been examined thrice, at Rome, at Venice and again at Rome, and had obtained the Pope's approval, and yet the licence for reprinting it is never issued.[44] The censors were not paid; and in addition to being overworked and overburdened with responsibility, they were rarely men of adequate learning. In a letter from Bartolommeo de Valverde, chaplain to Philip II., under date 1584,

[44] Dejob, *De l'Influence*, &c. p. 60.

we read plain-spoken complaints against these subordinates.[45] 'Unacquainted with literature, they discharge the function of condemning books they cannot understand. Without knowledge of Greek or Hebrew, and animated by a prejudiced hostility against authors, they take the easy course of proscribing what they feel incapable of judging. In this way the works of many sainted writers and the useful commentaries made by Jews have been suppressed.' A memorial to Sirleto, presented by Cardinal Gabriele Paleotti points out the negligence of the Index-makers and their superficial discharge of onerous duties, praying that in future men of learning and honesty should be employed, and that they should receive payment for their labours.[46] These are the expostulations addressed by faithful Catholics, engaged in literary work demanded by the Vatican, to a Cardinal who was the soul and mover of the Congregation. They do not question the salutary nature of the Index, but only call attention to the incapacity and ignorance of its unpaid officials. Meanwhile, it was no easy matter to appoint responsible and learned scholars to the post. The inefficient censors proceeded with their work of destruction and suppression. A commentator on a Greek Father or the Psalms was corrected by an ignoramus who knew neither Greek nor Hebrew, anxious to discover petty collisions with the Vulgate, and eager to create annoyances for the author. Latino Latini, one of the students employed by the Vatican, refused his name to an edition of Cyprian which he had carefully prepared with far more than the average erudition, because it had been changed throughout by the substitution of bad readings for good, in defiance of MS. authority, with a view of preserving a literal agreement with the Vulgate.[47] Sigonius, another of the Vatican students, was instructed to prepare certain text-books by Cardinal Paleotti. These were an Ecclesiastical History, a treatise on the Hebrew Commonwealth, and an edition of Sulpicius Severus. The MSS. were returned to him, accused of unsound doctrine, and scrawled over with such remarks as 'false,' 'absurd.'[48] In addition to the intolerable delays of the Censure, and the arrogant inadequacy of its officials, learned men suffered from the pettiest persecution at the hands of informers. The Inquisitors themselves were often spies and persons of base origin. 'The Roman Court,' says Sarpi, 'being anxious that the office of the Inquisition should not suffer through negligence in its ministers, has confided these affairs to individuals without occupation, and whose mean estate renders them proud of their official position.'[49] It was not to be expected that such people should discharge their duties with intelligence and scrupulous equity. Pius V., himself an incorruptible Inquisitor, had to condemn one of his lieutenants for corruption or extortion of money by menaces.[50] There was still another source of peril and annoyance to which scholars

[45] *Id. op. cit.* p. 76.
[46] Dejob, *op. cit.* p. 78.
[47] *Id. op. cit.* p. 74.
[48] Dejob, *op. cit.* p. 54.
[49] 'Discorso dell' Origine, &c. dell' Inquisizione.' *Opp.* vol. iv. p. 34.
[50] Mutinelli, *Storia Arcana*, vol. i. p. 277.

were exposed. Their comrades, engaged in similar pursuits, not unfrequently wreaked private spite by denouncing them to the Congregation.[51] Van Linden indicated heresies in Osorius, Giovius, Albertus Pighius. The Jesuit Francesco Torres accused Maës, and threatened Latini. Sigonius obtained a license for his 'History of Bologna,' but could not print it, owing to the delation of secret enemies. Baronius, when he had finished his 'Martyrology,' found that a cabal had raised insuperable obstacles in the way of its publication. I have been careful to select only examples of notoriously Catholic authors, men who were in the pay and under the special protection of the Vatican. How it fared with less-favoured scholars, may be left to the imagination. We are not astonished to find a man like Latini writing thus from Rome to Maës during the pontificate of Paul IV.:[52] 'Have you not heard of the peril which threatens the very existence of books? What are you dreaming of, when now that almost every published book is interdicted, you still think of making new ones? Here, as I imagine, there is no one who for many years to come will dare to write except on business or to distant friends. An Index has been issued of the works which none may possess under pain of excommunication; and the number of them is so great that very few indeed are left to us, especially of those which have been published in Germany. This shipwreck, this holocaust of books will stop the production of them in your country also, if I do not err, and will teach editors to be upon their guard. As you love me and yourself, sit and look at your bookcases without opening their doors, and beware lest the very cracks let emanations come to you from those forbidden fruits of learning.' This letter was written in 1559, when Paul proscribed sixty-one presses, and prohibited the perusal of any work that issued from them. He afterwards withdrew this interdict. But the Index did not stop its work of extirpation.

Another embarrassment which afflicted men of learning, was the danger of possessing books by heretics and the difficulty of procuring them.[53] Yet they could not carry on their Biblical studies without reference to such authors as, for example, Erasmus or Reuchlin. The universities loudly demanded that books of sound erudition by heretics should at least be expurgated and republished. Yet the process of disfiguring their arguments, effacing the names of authors, expunging the praises of heretics, altering quotations and retouching them all over, involved so much labour that the demand was never satisfied. The strict search instituted at the frontiers stopped the importation of books,[54] and carriers refused

[51] Dejob, *op. cit.* pp. 53-57.

[52] Dejob, *op. cit.* p. 75.

[53] Sarpi's Letters abound in useful information on this topic. Writing to French correspondents, he complains weekly of the impossibility even in Venice of obtaining books. See, for instance, *Lettere*, vol. i. pp. 286, 287, 360, vol. ii. p. 13. In one passage he says that the importation of books into Italy is impeded at Innsbruck, Trento, and throughout the Tyrolese frontiers (vol. i. p. 74). In another he warns his friends not to send them concealed in merchandise, since they will fall under so many eyes in the custom-houses and lazzaretti (vol. i. p. 303).

[54] It was usual at this epoch to send Protestant publications from beyond the Alps in

to transmit them. In their dread of the Inquisition, these folk found it safer to abstain from book traffic altogether. Public libraries were exposed to intermittent raids, nor were private collections safe from such inspection. The not uncommon occurrence of old books in which precious and interesting passages have been erased with printer's ink, or pasted over with slips of opaque paper, testifies to the frequency of these inquisitorial visitations.[55] Any casual acquaintance, on leaving a man's house, might denounce him as the possessor of a proscribed volume; and everybody who owned a bookcase was bound to furnish the Inquisitors with a copy of his catalogue. Bookstalls lay open to the malevolence of informers. We possess an insolent letter of Antonio Possevino to Cardinal Sirleto, telling him that he had noticed a forbidden book by Filiarchi on a binder's counter, and bidding him to do his duty by suppressing it.[56] When this Cardinal's library was exposed for sale after his death, the curious observed that it contained 1,872 MSS. in Greek and Latin, 530 volumes of printed Greek books, and 3,939 volumes of Latin, among which 39 were on the Index. But charity suggested that the Cardinal had retained these last for censure.

During the period of the Counter-Reformation it was the cherished object of the Popes to restore ecclesiastical and theological learning. They gathered men of erudition round them in the Vatican, and established a press for the purpose of printing the Fathers and diffusing Catholic literature. But they were met in the pursuance of this project by very serious difficulties. Their own policy tended to stifle knowledge and suppress criticism. The scholars whom they chose as champions of the faith worked with tied hands. Baronio knew no Greek; Latini knew hardly any; Bellarmino is thought to have known but little. And yet these were the apostles of Catholic enlightenment, the defenders of the infallible Church against students of the calibre of Erasmus, Casaubon, Sarpi! An insuperable obstacle to sacred studies of a permanently useful kind was the Tridentine decree which had declared the Vulgate inviolable. No codex of age or authority which displayed a reading at variance with the inspired Latin version might be cited. Sirleto, custodian of the Vatican Library, refused lections from its MSS. to learned men, on the ground that they might seem to impugn the Vulgate.[57] For the same reason, the critical labours of all previous students, from Valla to Erasmus, on the text of the Bible were suppressed, and the best MSS. of the Fathers were ruthlessly garbled, in order to bring their quotations into accordance with Jerome's translation. Galesini takes credit to himself in a letter to Sirleto for having withheld a clearly right reading in his edition of the Psalms, because it explained a mistake in the Vulgate.[58] We have seen

bales of cotton or other goods. This appears from the Lucchese proclamations against heresy published in *Arch. Stor.* vol. x.

[55] I may mention that having occasion to consult Savonarola's works in the Public Library of Perugia, which has a fairly good collection of them, I found them useless for purposes of study by reason of these erasures and Burke-plasters.

[56] Dejob, *op. cit.* p. 43. [57] Dejob, *op. cit.* p. 50. Also his *Muret*, pp. 223-227.

[58] Dejob, *De l'Influence*, p. 49.

how Latini's 'Cyprian' suffered from the censure; and there is a lamentable history of the Vatican edition of Ambrose, which was so mutilated that the Index had to protect it from confrontation with the original codices.[59] This dishonest dealing not only discouraged students and paralysed the energy of critical investigation, but it also involved the closing of public libraries to scholars. The Vatican could not afford to let the light of science in upon its workshop of forgeries and sophistications. A voice of reasonable remonstrance was sometimes raised by even the most incorruptible children of the Church. Thus Bellarmino writes to Cardinal Sirleto, suggesting a doubt whether it is obligatory to adhere to the letter of the Tridentine decree upon the Vulgate.[60] Is it rational, he asks, to maintain that every sentence in the Latin text is impeccable? Must we reject those readings in the Hebrew and the Greek which elucidate the meaning of the Scriptures, in cases where Jerome has followed a different and possibly a corrupt authority? Would it not be more sensible to regard the Vulgate as the sole authorised version for use in universities, pulpits, and divine service, while admitting that it is not an infallible rendering of the inspired original? He also touches, in a similar strain of scholar-like liberality, upon the Septuagint, pointing out that this version cannot have been the work of seventy men in unity, since the translator of Job seems to have been better acquainted with Greek than Hebrew, while the reverse is true of the translator of Solomon. Such remonstrances were not, however, destined to make themselves effectively heard. Instead of relaxing its severity after the pontificate of Pius IV., the Congregation of the Index grew, as we have seen, more rigid, until, in the rules digested by Clement VIII., it enforced the strictest letter of the law regarding the Vulgate, and ratified all the hypocrisies and subterfuges which that implied.

Under the conditions which I have attempted to describe, it was impossible that Italy should hold her place among the nations which encouraged liberal studies. Rome had one object in view—to gag the revolutionary free voice of the Renaissance, to protect conservative principles, to establish her own supremacy, and to secure the triumph of the Counter-Reformation. In pursuance of this policy, she had to react against the learning and the culture of the classical revival; and her views were seconded not only by the overwhelming political force of Spain in the Peninsula, but also by the petty princes who felt that their existence was imperilled.

Independence of judgment was rigorously proscribed in all academies and seats of erudition. New methods of education and new text-books were forbidden. Professors found themselves hampered in their choice of antique authors. Only those classics which were sanctioned by the Congregation of the Index could be used in lecture rooms. On the one hand, the great republican advocates of independence had incurred suspicion.

[59] *Id. op. cit.* pp. 96-98.

[60] This very interesting and valuable letter is printed by Dejob in the work I have so often cited, p. 391.

On the other hand, the poets were prohibited as redolent of paganism. To mingle philosophy with rhetoric was counted a crime. Thomas Aquinas had set up Pillars of Hercules beyond which the reason might not seek to travel. Roman law had to be treated from the orthodox scholastic standpoint. Woe to the audacious jurist who made the Pandects serve for disquisitions on the rights of men and nations! Scholars like Sigonius found themselves tied down in their class-rooms to a weariful routine of Cicero and Aristotle. Aonio Paleario complained that a professor was no better than a donkey working in a mill; nothing remained for him but to dole out commonplaces, avoiding every point of contact between the authors he interpreted and the burning questions of modern life. Muretus, who brought with him to Italy from France a ruined moral reputation with a fervid zeal for literature, who sold his soul to praise the Massacre of S. Bartholomew and purge by fulsome panegyrics of great public crimes the taint of heresy that clung around him, found his efforts to extend the course of studies in Rome thwarted.[61] He was forbidden to lecture on Plato, forbidden to touch jurisprudence, forbidden to consult a copy of Eunapius in the Vatican Library. It cost him days and weeks of pleading to obtain permission to read Tacitus to his classes. Greek, the literature of high thoughts, noble enthusiasms, and virile sciences was viewed with suspicion. As the monks of the Middle Ages had written on the margins of their MSS.: *Græca sunt, ergo non legenda*, so these new obscurantists exclaimed: *Græca sunt, periculosa sunt, ergo non legenda*. 'I am forced,' he cries in this extremity, 'to occupy myself with Latin and to abstain entirely from Greek.' And yet he knew that 'if the men of our age advance one step further in their neglect of Greek, doom and destruction are impending over all sound arts and sciences.' 'It is my misery,' he groans, 'to behold the gradual extinction and total decay of Greek letters, in whose train I see the whole body of refined learning on the point of vanishing away.'[62]

A vigorous passage from one of Sarpi's letters directly bearing on these points may here be cited (vol. i. p. 170): 'The revival of polite learning undermined the foundations of Papal monarchy. Nor was this to be wondered at. This monarchy began and grew in barbarism; the cessation of barbarism naturally curtailed an threatened it with extinction. This we already see in Germany and France; but Spain and Italy are still subject to barbarism. Legal studies sink daily from bad to worse. The Roman Curia opposes every branch of learning which savours of polite literature, while it defends its barbarism with tooth and nail. How can it do otherwise? Abolish those books on Papal Supremacy, and where shall they find that the Pope is another God, that he is almighty, that all rights and laws are closed within the cabinet of his breast, that he can shut up folk in hell, in a word that he has power to square the circle? Destroy that false jurisprudence, and this tyranny will vanish; but the two are reciprocally supporting, and we shall not do away with the for-

[61] See Dejob's Life of Muret, pp. 231, 238, 274, 320.
[62] *Id. op. cit.* pp. 262, 481.

mer until the latter falls, which will only happen at God's good pleasure.'

The jealousy with which liberal studies were regarded by the Church bred a contempt for them in the minds of students. Benci, a professor of humane letters at Rome, says that his pupils walked about the class-room during his lectures. With grim humour he adds that he does not object to their sleeping, so long as they abstain from snoring.[63] But it is impossible, he goes on to complain, 'that I should any longer look upon the place in which I do my daily work as an academy of learning; I go to it rather as to a mill in which I must grind out my tale of worthless grain.' Muretus, when he had laboured twenty years in the chair of rhetoric at Rome, begged for dismissal. His memorial to the authorities presents a lamentable picture of the insubordination and indifference from which he had suffered.[64] 'I have borne immeasurable indignities from the continued insolence of these students, who interrupt me with cries, whistlings, hisses, insults, and such opprobrious remarks that I sometimes scarcely know whether I am standing on my head or heels.' 'They come to the lecture-room armed with poignards, and when I reprove them for their indecencies, they threaten over and over again to cut my face open if I do not hold my tongue.' The walls, he adds, are scrawled over with obscene emblems and disgusting epigrams, so that this haunt of learning presents the aspect of the lowest brothel; and the professor's chair has become a more intolerable seat than the pillory, owing to the missiles flung at him and the ribaldry with which he is assailed. The manners and conversation of the students must have been disgusting beyond measure, to judge by a letter of complaint from a father detailing the contamination to which his son was exposed in the Roman class-rooms, and the immunity with which the lewdest songs were publicly recited there.[65] But the total degradation of learning at this epoch in Rome is best described in one paragraph of Vittorio de' Rossi, setting forth the neglect endured by Aldo Manuzio, the younger. This scion of an illustrious family succeeded to the professorship of Muretus in 1588. 'Then,' says Rossi, 'might one marvel at, or rather mourn over, the abject and down-trodden state of the liberal arts. Then might one perceive with tears how those treasures of humane letters, which our fathers exalted to the heavens, were degraded in the estimation of youth. In the good old days men crossed the seas, undertook long journeys, traversed the cities of Greece and Asia, in order to obtain the palm of eloquence and salute the

[63] Dejob, *Marc Antoine Muret*, p. 349.

[64] The original is printed by Dejob, *Marc Antoine Muret*, pp. 487-489.

[65] The original letter, printed by Dejob, *op. cit.* p. 491, is signed by Giustiniano Finetti, who seems to have been a professor of medicine in the Roman University. His son, a youth of sixteen, complained that the students had demanded and obtained leave to recite a certain 'lettione che era carnavalesca d' ano et de priapo,' adding that they were in the habit of holding debates upon the thesis that 'res sod[cæ] erant praeferendae veneri naturali, et reprobabant rem veneream cum feminis ac laudabant masturbationem.' The dialogue which the students obtained leave publicly to recite was probably similar to one that might still be heard some years ago in spring upon the quays of Naples, and which appeared to have descended from immemorial antiquity.

masters of languages and learning, at whose feet they sat entranced by noble words. But now these fellows poured scorn upon an unrivalled teacher of both Greek and Latin eloquence, whose services were theirs for the asking, theirs without the fatigue of travel, without expense, without exertion. Though he freely offered them his abundance of erudition in both learned literatures, they shut their ears against him. At the hours when his lecture-room should have been thronged with multitudes of eager pupils you might see him, abandoned by the crowd, pacing the pavement before the door of the academy with one, or may be two, for his companions.'[66]

To accuse the Church solely and wholly for this decay of humanistic learning in Italy would be uncritical and unjust. We must remember that after a period of feverish energy there comes a time of languor in all epochs of great intellectual excitement. Nor was it to be expected that the enthusiasm of the fifteenth century for classical studies should have been prolonged into the second half of the sixteenth century. But we are justified in blaming the ecclesiastical and civil authorities of the Counter-Reformation for their determined opposition to the new direction which that old enthusiasm for the classics was now manifesting. They strove to force the stream of learning backward into scholastic and linguistic channels, when it was already ploughing for itself a fresh course in the fields of philosophical and scientific discovery. They made study odious, because they attempted to restrain it to the outworn husks of pedantry and rhetoric. These, they thought, were innocuous. But what the intellectual appetite then craved, the pabulum that it required to satisfy its yearning, was rigidly denied it. Speculations concerning the nature of man and of the world, metaphysical explorations into the regions of dimly apprehended mysteries, physics, political problems, religious questions touching the great matters in dispute through Europe, all the storm and stress of modern life, the ferment of the modern mind and will and conscience, were excluded from the schools, because they were antagonistic to the Counter-Reformation. Italy was starved and demoralised in order to avert a revolution; and learning was asphyxiated by confinement to a narrow chamber filled with vitiated and exhausted air.[67]

Similar deductions may be drawn from the life of Paolo Manuzio in Rome. He left Venice in 1561 at the invitation of Pius IV., who proposed to establish a press 'for the publication of books printed with the finest type and the utmost accuracy, and more especially of works bearing upon sacred and ecclesiastical literature.'[68] Paolo's engagement was for twelve years; his appointments were fixed at 300 ducats for travelling expenses, 500 ducats of yearly salary, a press maintained at the Pontifical expense, and a pension secured upon his son's life. The scheme was a noble one. Paolo was to print all the Greek and Latin Fathers, and to furnish the

[66] The Latin text is printed in Renouard's *Imprimerie des Aldes*, p. 473.

[67] As Sarpi says: 'Of a truth the extraordinary rigour with which books are hunted out for extirpation, shows how vigorous is the light of that lantern which they have resolved to extinguish.' *Lettere*, vol. i. p. 328.

[68] See Renouard, *op. cit.* pp. 442-459, for Paulus Manutius's life at Rome.

Catholic world with an arsenal of orthodox learning. Yet, during his residence in Rome, no Greek book issued from his press.[69] Of the Latin Fathers he gave the Epistles of Jerome, Salvian, and Cyprian to the world. For the rest, he published the decrees of the Tridentine Council ten times, the Tridentine Catechism eight times, the 'Breviarium Romanum' four times, and spent the greater part of his leisure in editing minor translations, commentaries, and polemical or educational treatises. The result was miserable, and the man was ruined.

It remains to notice the action of the Index with regard to secular books in the modern languages. I will first repeat a significant passage in its statutes touching upon political philosophy and the so-called *Ratio Status*: 'Item, let all propositions, drawn from the digests, manners, and examples of the Gentiles, which foster a tyrannical polity and encourage what they falsely call the reason of state, in opposition to the law of Christ and of the Gospel, be expunged.' This, says Sarpi in his 'Discourse on Printing,' is aimed in general against any doctrine which impugns ecclesiastical jurisdiction over the civil sphere of princes and magistrates and the economy of the family.[70] Theories drawn from whatever source to combat Papal and ecclesiastical encroachments and to defend the rights of the sovereign in his monarchy or of the father in his household, are denominated and denounced as *Ratio Status*. The impugner of Papal absolutism in civil as well as ecclesiastical affairs is accounted *ipso facto* a heretic.[71] It would appear at first sight as though the clause in question had been specially framed to condemn Machiavelli and his school. The works of Machiavelli were placed upon the Index in 1559, and a certain Cesare of Pisa who had them in his library was put to the torture on this account in 1610. It was afterwards proposed to correct and edit them without his name; but his heirs very properly refused to sanction this proceeding, knowing that he would be made to utter the very reverse of what he meant in all that touched upon the Roman Church. This paragraph in the statutes of the Index had, however, a further and far more ambitious purpose than the suppression of Machiavelli, Guicciardini, and Sarpi. By assuming to condemn all political writings of which she disapproved, and by forbidding the secular authorities to proscribe any works which had received her sanction, the Church obtained a monopoly of popular instruction in theories of government. She interdicted every treatise that exposed her own ambitious interference in civil affairs or which maintained the rights of temporal rulers.[72] She protected and propagated the works of her servile minis-

[69] *Op. cit.* pp. 184-216.

[70] Sarpi's Works, vol. iv. p. 4.

[71] Sarpi, *Discorso*, vol. iv. p. 25, on Bellarmino's doctrine. Sarpi's *Letters*, vol. i. pp. 138, 243. Sarpi says that he and Gillot had both had their portraits painted in a picture of Hell and shown to the common folk as foredoomed to eternal fire, because they opposed doctrines of Papal omnipotence. *Ibid*. p. 151.

[72] On this point, again, Sarpi's *Letters* furnish valuable details. He frequently remarks that a general order had been issued by the Congregation of the Index to suppress all books against the writings of Baronius, who was treated as a saint (vol. i.

ters, who proclaimed that the ecclesiastical was superior in all points to the civil power; that nations owed their first allegiance to the Pope, who was divinely appointed to rule over them, and their second only to the Prince, who was a delegate from their own body; and that tyrannicide itself was justifiable when employed against a contumacious or heretical sovereign. Such were the theories of the Jesuits—of Allen and Parsons in England, Bellarmino in Italy, Suarez and Mariana in Spain, Boucher in France. In his critique of this monstrous unfairness Sarpi says: 'There are not wanting men in Italy, pious and of sound learning, who hold the truth upon such topics; but these can neither write nor send their writings to the press.'[73] The best years and the best energies of Sarpi's life were spent, as is well known, in combating the arrogance of Rome and in founding the relations of State to Church upon a basis of sound common sense and equity. More than once he narrowly escaped martyrdom as the reward of his temerity; and when the poignard of an assassin struck him, his legend relates that he uttered the celebrated epigram: *Agnosco stilum Curiæ Romanæ.*

Sarpi protested, not without good reason, that Rome was doing her best to extinguish sound learning in Italy. But how did she deal with that rank growth of licentious literature which had sprung up during the Renaissance period? This is the question which should next engage us. We have seen that the Council of Trent provided amply for the extirpation of lewd and obscene publications. Accordingly, as though to satisfy the sense of decency, some of the most flagrantly immoral books, including the 'Decameron,' the 'Priapeia,' the collected works of Aretino, and certain mediæval romances, were placed upon the Index. Berni was proscribed in 1559; but the interdict lasted only a short time, probably because it was discovered that his poems, though licentious, were free from the heresies which Pier Paolo Vergerio had sought to fix upon him. Meanwhile no notice was taken of the 'Orlando Furioso' and a multitude of novelists, of Beccadelli's and Pontano's verses, of Molza and Firenzuola, of the whole mass of mundane writers in short who had done so much to reveal the corruption of Italian manners. It seemed as though the Church cared less to ban obscenity than to burke those authors who had spoken freely of her vices. When we come to examine the expurgated editions of notorious authors, we shall see that this was literally the case. A castrated version of Bandello, revised by Ascanio Centorio degli Ortensi, was published in 1560.[74] It omitted the dedications and

pp. 3, 147, ii. p. 35). He relates how the Jesuits had procured the destruction of a book written to uphold aristocracy in states, without touching upon ecclesiastical questions, as being unfavourable to their theories of absolution (vol. i. p. 122). He tells the story of a confessor who refused the sacraments to a nobleman, because he owned a treatise written by Quirino in defence of the Venetian prerogatives (vol. i. p. 113). He refers to the suppression of James I.'s *Apologia* and De Thou's *Histories* (vol. i. pp. 286, 287, 383).

[73] In the Treatise on the Inquisition, *Opere*, vol. iv. p. 53. Sarpi, in a passage of his *Letters* (vol. ii. p. 163), points out why the secular authorities were ill fitted to retaliate in kind upon these Papal proscriptions.

[74] See Dejob, *De l'Influence*, &c. chapter iii.

preambles, suppressed some disquisitions which palliated vicious conduct, expunged the novels that brought monks or priests into ridicule, but left the impurities of the rest untouched. A reformed version of Folengo's 'Baldus' appeared in 1561. The satires on religious orders had been erased. Zambellus was cuckolded by a layman instead of a priest. Otherwise the filth of the original received no cleansing treatment. When Cosimo de' Medici requested that a revised edition of the 'Decameron' might be licensed, Pius V. entrusted the affair to Thomas Manrique, Master of the Sacred Palace. It was published by the Giunti in 1573 under the auspices of Gregory XIII., with the approval of the Holy Office and the Florentine Inquisition, fortified by privileges from Spanish and French kings, dukes of Tuscany, Ferrara, and so forth. The changes which Boccaccio's masterpiece had undergone were these; passages savouring of doubtful dogma, sarcasms on monks and clergy, the names of saints, allusions to the devil and hell, had disappeared. Ecclesiastical sinners were transformed into students and professors, nuns and abbesses into citizens' wives. Immorality in short was secularised. But the book still offered the same allurements to a prurient mind. Sixtus V. expressed his disapproval of this recension, and new editions were licensed in 1582 and 1588 under the revision of Lionardo Salviati and Luigi Groto. Both preserved the obscenities of the 'Decameron,' while they displayed more rigour with regard to satires on ecclesiastical corruption. It may be added, in justice to the Roman Church, that the 'Decameron' stands still upon the Index with the annotation *donec expurgetur*.[75] Therefore we must presume that the work of purification is not yet accomplished, though the Jesuits have used parts of it as a text-book in their schools, while Panigarola quoted it in his lectures on sacred eloquence.

It would weary the reader to enlarge upon this process of stupid or hypocritical purgation, whereby the writings of men like Doni and Straparola were stripped of their reflections on the clergy, while their indecencies remained untouched; or to show how Ariosto's Comedies were sanctioned, when his Satires, owing to their free speech upon the Papal Court, received the stigma.[76] But I may refer to the grotesque attempts which were made in this age to cast the mantle of spirituality over profane literature. Thus Hieronimo Malipieri rewrote the 'Canzoniere' of Petrarch, giving it a pious turn throughout; and the 'Orlando Furioso' was converted by several hands into a religious allegory.[77]

The action of Rome under the influence of the Counter-Reformation was clearly guided by two objects: to preserve Catholic dogma in its integrity, and to maintain the supremacy of the Church. She was eager to extinguish learning and to paralyse intellectual energy. But she show-

[75] *Index*, Naples, Pelella, 1862, p. 87.

[76] This treatment of Ariosto is typical. Men of not over-scrupulous nicety may question whether his Comedies are altogether wholesome reading. But not even a Puritan could find fault with his Satires on the score of their morality. Yet Rome sanctioned the Comedies and forbade the Satires.

[77] Curious details on this topic are supplied by Dejob, *op. cit.* pp. 179-181, and p. 184.

ed no unwillingness to tolerate those pleasant vices which enervate a nation. Compared with unsound doctrine and audacious speculation, immorality appeared in her eyes a venial weakness. It was true that she made serious efforts to reform the manners of her ministers, and was fully alive to the necessity of enforcing decency and decorum. Yet a radical purification of society seemed of less importance to her than the conservation of Catholic orthodoxy and the inculcation of obedience to ecclesiastical authority. When we analyse the Jesuits' system of education, and their method of conducting the care of souls, we shall see to what extent the deeply seated hypocrisy of the Counter-Reformation had penetrated the most vital parts of the Catholic system. It will suffice, at the close of this chapter, to touch upon one other repressive measure adopted by the Church in its panic. Magistrates received strict injunctions to impede the journeys of Italian subjects into foreign countries where heresies were known to be rife, or where the rites of the Roman Church were not regularly administered.[78] In 1595 Clement VIII. reduced these admonitions to Pontifical law in a Bull, whereby he forbade Italians to travel without permission from the Holy Office, or to reside abroad without annually remitting a certificate of confession and communion to the Inquisitors. To ensure obedience to this statute would have been impossible without the co-operation of the Jesuits. They were, however, diffused throughout the nations of North, East, South, and West. When an Italian arrived, the Jesuit Fathers paid him a visit, and unless they received satisfactory answers with regard to his license of travel and his willingness to accept their spiritual direction, these serfs of Rome sent a delation to the central Holy Office, upon the ground of which the Inquisitors of his province instituted an action against him in his absence. Merchants, who neglected these rules, found themselves exposed to serious impediments in their trading operations and to the peril of prosecution involving confiscation of property at home. Sarpi, who composed a vigorous critique of this abuse, points out what injury was done to commerce by this system.[79] We may still further censure it as an intolerable interference with the liberty of the individual; as an odious exercise of spiritual tyranny on the part of an ambitious ecclesiastical power which aimed at nothing less than universal domination.

[78] Any correspondence with heretics was accounted sufficient to implicate an Italian in the charge of heresy. Sarpi's *Letters* are full of matter on this point. He always used cypher, which he frequently changed, addressed his letters under feigned names, and finally resolved on writing in his own hand to no heretic. See *Lettere*, vol. ii. pp. 2, 151, 242, 248, 437. See also what Dejob relates about the timidity of Muretus, *Muret*, pp. 229, 231.

[79] 'Treatise on the Inquisition,' *Opere*, vol. iv. p. 45.

CHAPTER IV

THE COMPANY OF JESUS

Vast Importance of the Jesuits in the Counter-Reformation—Ignatius Loyola—His Youth—Retreat at Manresa—Journey to Jerusalem—Studies in Spain and Paris—First Formation of his Order at Sainte Barbe—Sojourn at Venice—Settlement at Rome—Papal Recognition of the Order—Its Military Character—Absolutism of the General—Devotion to the Roman Church—Choice of Members—Practical and Positive Aims of the Founder—Exclusion of the Ascetic, Acceptance of the Worldly Spirit—Review of the Order's Rapid Extension over Europe—Loyola's Dealings with his Chief Lieutenants—Propaganda—The Virtue of Obedience—The 'Exercitia Spiritualia'—Materialistic Imagination—Intensity and Superficiality of Religious Training—The Status of the Novice—Temporal Coadjutors—Scholastics—Professed of the Three Vows—Professed of the Four Vows—The General—Control exercised over him by his Assistants—His Relation to the General Congregation—Espionage a Part of the Jesuit System—Advantageous Position of a Contented Jesuit—The Vow of Poverty—Houses of the Professed and Colleges—The Constitutions and Declarations—Problem of the Monita Secreta—Reciprocal Relations of Rome and the Company—Characteristics of Jesuit Education—Direction of Consciences—Moral Laxity—Sarpi's Critique—Casuistry—Interference in Affairs of State—Instigation to Regicide and Political Conspiracy—Theories of Church Supremacy—Insurgence of the European Nations against the Company.

We have seen in the preceding chapters how Spain became dominant in Italy, superseding the rivalry of confederated states by the monotony of servitude, and lending its weight to Papal Rome. The internal changes effected in the Church by the Tridentine Council, and the external power conferred on it, were due in no small measure to Spanish influence or sanction. A Spanish institution, the Inquisition, modified to suit Italian requirements, lent revived Catholicism weapons of repression and attack. We have now to learn by what means a partial vigour was communicated to the failing body of Catholic beliefs, how the Tridentine creed was propagated, the spiritual realm of the Roman Pontiff policed, and his secular authority augmented. A Spanish Order rose at the right moment to supply that intellectual and moral element of vitality without which the Catholic Revival might have remained as inert as a stillborn child. The devotion of the Jesuits to the Papacy was in reality the masterful Spanish spirit of that epoch masking its world-grasping ambition under the guise of obedience to Rome. This does not mean that the founders and first organisers of the Company of Jesus consciously pursued one object while they pretended to have another in view. The impulse which moved Loyola was spontaneous and romantic. The world has seen few examples of disinterested self-devotion equal to that of Xavier.

Yet the fact remains that Jesuitry, taking its germ and root in the Spanish character, persisting as an organism within the Church but separate from the ecclesiastical hierarchy, devised the doctrine of Papal absolutism, and became the prime agent of that Catholic policy in Europe which passed for Papal during the Counter-Reformation. The indissoluble connexion between Rome, Spain, and the Jesuits, was apparent to all unprejudiced observers. For this triad of reactionary and belligerent forces Sarpi invented the name of the Diacatholicon, alluding under the metaphor of a drug to the virus which was being instilled in his days into all the States of Europe.[1]

The founder of the Jesuit order was the thirteenth child of a Spanish noble, born in 1491 at his father's castle of Loyola in the Basque province of Guipuzcoa.[2] His full name was Iñigo Lopez de Recalde; but he is better known to history as Saint Ignatius Loyola. Ignatius spent his boyhood as page in the service of King Ferdinand the Catholic, whence he passed into that of the Duke of Najara, who was the hereditary friend and patron of his family. At this time he thought of nothing but feats of arms, military glory, and romantic adventures. He could boast but little education; and his favourite reading was in 'Amadis of Gaul.' That romance appeared during the boy's earliest childhood, and Spain was now devouring its high-flown rhapsodies with rapture. The peculiar admixture of mystical piety, Catholic enthusiasm, and chivalrous passion, which distinguishes 'Amadis,' exactly corresponded to the spirit of the Spaniards at an epoch when they had terminated their age-long struggle with the Moors, and were combining propagandist zeal with martial fervour in the conquest of the New World. Its pages inflamed the imagination of Ignatius. He began to compose a romance in honour of S. Peter, and chose a princess of blood royal for his Oriana. Thus, in the first days of youth, while his heart was still set on love and warfare, he revealed the three leading features of his character—soaring ambition, the piety of a devotee, and the tendency to view religion from the point of fiction.

Ignatius was thirty years of age when the events happened which determined the future of his life and so powerfully affected the destinies of Catholic Christendom. The French were invading Navarre; and he was

[1] For Sarpi's use of this phrase see his *Lettere*, vol. ii. pp. 72, 80, 92. He clearly recognised the solidarity between the Jesuits and Spain. 'The Jesuit is no more separable from the Spaniard than the accident from the substance.' 'The Spaniard without the Jesuit is not worth more than lettuce without oil.' 'For the Jesuits to deceive Spain, would be tantamount to deceiving themselves.' *Ibid.* vol. i. pp. 203, 384, vol. ii. p. 48. Compare passages in vol. i. pp. 184, 189. He only perceived a difference in the degrees of their noxiousness to Europe. Thus 'the worst Spaniard is better than the least bad of the Jesuits' (vol. i. p. 212).

[2] Study of the Jesuits must be founded on *Institutum Societatis Jesu*, 7 vols. Avenione; Orlandino, *Hist. Soc. Jesu*; Crétineau-Joly, *Histoire de la Compagnie de Jésus*; Ribadaneira, *Vita Ignatii*; Genelli's Life of Ignatius in German or the French translation; the Jesuit work, *Imago Primi Sæculi;* Ranke's account in his *History of the Popes*, and the three chapters assigned to this subject in Philippson's *La Contre-Révolution Religieuse*. The latter will be found a most valuable summary.

engaged in the defence of its capital, Pampeluna. On May 20, 1521, a bullet shattered his right leg, while his left foot was injured by a fragment of stone detached from a breach in the bastion. Transported to his father's castle, he suffered protracted anguish under the hands of unskilled medical attendants. The badly set bone in his right leg had twice to be broken; and when at last it joined, the young knight found himself a cripple. This limb was shorter than the other; the surgeons endeavoured to elongate it by machines of iron, which put him to exquisite pain. After months of torture, he remained lame for life.

During his illness Ignatius read such books as the castle of Loyola contained. These were a 'Life of Christ' and the 'Flowers of the Saints' in Spanish. His mind, prepared by chivalrous romance, and strongly inclined to devotion, felt a special fascination in the tales of Dominic and Francis. Their heroism suggested new paths which the aspirant after fame might tread with honour. Military glory and the love of women had to be renounced; for so ambitious a man could not content himself with the successes of a cripple in these spheres of action. But the legends of saints and martyrs pointed out careers no less noble, no less useful, and even more enticing to the fancy. He would become the spiritual Knight of Christ and Our Lady. To S. Peter, his chosen protector, he prayed fervently; and when at length he rose from the bed of sickness, he firmly believed that his life had been saved by the intercession of this patron, and that it must be henceforth consecrated to the service of the faith. The world should be abandoned. Instead of warring with the enemies of Christ on earth, he would carry on a crusade against the powers of darkness. They were first to be met and fought in his own heart. Afterwards, he would form and lead a militia of like-hearted champions against the strongholds of evil in human nature.

It must not be thought that the scheme of founding a Society had so early entered into the mind of Ignatius. What we have at the present stage to notice is that he owed his adoption of the religious life to romantic fancy and fervid ambition, combined with a devotion to Peter, the saint of orthodoxy and the Church. Animated by this new enthusiasm, he managed to escape from home in the spring of 1522. His friends opposed themselves to his vocation; but he gave them the slip, took vows of chastity and abstinence, and began a pilgrimage to our Lady of Montserrat near Barcelona. On the road he scourged himself daily. When he reached the shrine he hung his arms up as a votive offering, and performed the vigil which chivalrous custom exacted from a squire before the morning of his being dubbed a knight. This ceremony was observed point by point, according to the ritual he had read in 'Amadis of Gaul.' Next day he gave his raiment to a beggar, and assumed the garb of a mendicant pilgrim. By self-dedication he had now made himself the Knight of Holy Church.

His first intention was to set sail for Palestine, with the object of preaching to the infidels. But the plague prevented him from leaving port; and he retired to a Dominican convent at Manresa, a little town of Catalonia, north-west of Barcelona. Here he abandoned himself to the cruellest self-discipline. Feeding upon bread and water, kneeling for seven hours together rapt in prayer, scourging his flesh thrice daily, and reducing sleep to the barest minimum, Ignatius sought by austerity to snatch that crown of sainthood which he felt to be his due. Outraged nature soon warned him that he was upon a path which led to failure. Despair took possession of his soul, sometimes prompting him to end his life by suicide, sometimes plaguing him with hideous visions. At last he fell dangerously ill. Enlightened by the expectation of early death, he then became convinced that his fanatical asceticism was a folly. The despair, the dreadful phantoms which had haunted him, were ascribed immediately to the devil. In those rarer visitings of brighter visions, which sometimes brought consolation, bidding him repose upon God's mercy, he recognised angels sent to lead him on the pathway of salvation. God's hand appeared in these dealings; and he resolved to dedciate his body as well as his soul to God's service, respecting both as instruments of the divine will, and entertaining both in efficiency for the work required of them.

The experiences of Manresa proved eminently fruitful for the future method of Ignatius. It was here that he began to regard self-discipline and self-examination as the needful prelude to a consecrated life. It was here that he learned to condemn the asceticism of anchorites as pernicious or unprofitable to a militant Christian. It was here that, while studying the manual of devotion written by Garcia de Cisneros, he laid foundations for those famous 'Exercitia,' which became his instrument for rapidly passing neophytes through spiritual training similar to his own. It was here that he first distinguished two kinds of visions, infernal and celestial. Here also he grew familiar with the uses of concrete imagination; and understood how the faculty of sensuous realisation might be made a powerful engine for presenting the past of sacred history or the dogmas of orthodox theology under shapes of fancy to the mind. Finally, in all the experiences of Manresa, he tried the temper of his own character, which was really not that of a poet or a mystic, but of a sagacious man of action, preparing a system calculated to subjugate the intelligence and will of millions. Tested by self-imposed sufferings and by diseased hallucinations, his sound sense, the sense of one destined to control men, gathered energy and grew in solid strength: yet enough remained of his fanaticism to operate as a motive force in the scheme which he afterwards developed; enough survived from the ascetic phase he had surmounted, to make him comprehend that some such agony as he had suffered should form the vestibule to a devoted life. We may compare the throes of Ignatius at Manresa with the contemporary struggles of Luther at Wittenberg and in the Wartzburg. Our imagination will dwell upon the different issues to which two heroes distinguished by practical ability were led through their contention with the powers of spiritual evil. Protagonists respectively of Reformation and Counter-Reformation, they arrived at opposite conclusions; the one championing the cause of spiritual freedom in the modern world, the other consecrating his genius to the maintenance of Catholic orthodoxy by spiritual despotism. Yet each alike fulfilled his mission by having conquered mysticism at the outset of his world-historical career.

Ignatius remained for the space of ten months at Manresa. He then found means to realise his cherished journey to the Holy Land. In Palestine he was treated with coldness as an ignorant enthusiast, capable of subverting the existing order of things, but too feeble to be counted on for permanent support. His motive ideas were still visionary; he could not cope with conservatism and frigidity established in comfortable places of emolument. It was necessary that he should learn the wisdom of compromise. Accordingly he returned to Spain, and put himself to school. Two years spent in preparatory studies at Barcelona, another period at Alcala, and another at Salamanca, introduced him to languages, grammar, philosophy, and theology. This man of noble blood and vast ambition, past the age of thirty, sat with boys upon the common benches. This self-consecrated saint imbibed the commonplaces of scholastic logic. It was a further stage in the evolution of his iron character from romance and mysticism into political and practical sagacity. It was a further education of his stubborn will to pliant temper. But he could not divest himself of his mission as a founder and apostle. He taught disciples, preached, and formed a sect of devotees. Then the Holy Office attacked him. He was imprisoned, once at Alcala for forty-two days, once at Salamanca for three weeks, upon charges of heresy. Ignatius proved his innocence. The Inquisitors released him with certificates of acquittal; but they sentenced him to four years' study of theology before he should presume to preach. These years he resolved to spend at Paris. Accordingly he performed the journey on foot, and arrived in the capital of France upon February 2, 1528. He was then thirty-seven years old.

At Paris he had to go to school again from the beginning. The alms of well-wishers, chiefly devout women at Barcelona, amply provided him with funds. These he employed not only in advancing his own studies, but also in securing the attachment of adherents to his cause. At this epoch he visited the towns of Belgium and London during his vacations. But the main outcome of his residence at Paris was the formation of the Company of Jesus. Those long years of his novitiate and wandering were not without their uses now. They had taught him, while clinging stubbornly to the main projects of his life, prudence in the choice of means, temperance in expectation, sagacity in the manipulation of fellow-workers selected for the still romantic ends he had in view. His first two disciples were a Savoyard, Peter Faber or Le Fèvre, and Francis Xavier of Pampeluna. Faber was a poor student, whom Ignatius helped with money. Xavier sprang from a noble stock, famous in arms through generations, for which he was eager to win the additional honours of science and the Church. Ignatius assisted him by bringing students to his lectures. Under the personal influence of their friend and benefactor, both of these men determined to leave all and follow the new light. Visionary as the object yet was, the firm will, fervent confidence, and saintly life of Loyola inspired them with absolute trust. That the Christian faith, as they understood it, remained exposed to grievous dangers from without and from within, that millions of souls were perishing through ignorance, that tens of thousands were falling away through incredulity and heresy, was certain. The realm of Christ on earth needed champions, soldiers devoted to a crusade against Satan and his hosts. And here was a leader, a man among men, a man whose words were as a fire, and whose method of spiritual discipline was salutary and illuminative; and this man bade them join him in the Holy War. He gained them in a hundred ways, by kindness, by precept, by patience, by persuasion, by attention to their physical and spiritual needs, by words of warmth and wisdom, by the direction of their conscience, by profound and intense sympathy with souls struggling after the higher life. The means he had employed to gain Faber and Xavier were used with equal success in the case of seven other disciples. The names of these men deserve to be recorded; for some of them played a part of importance in European history, while all of them contributed to the foundation of the Jesuits. They were James Lainez, Alfonzo Salmeron, and Nicholas Bobadilla, three Spaniards; Simon Rodriguez d'Azevedo, a Portuguese; two Frenchmen, Jean Codure and Brouet; and Claude le Jay, a Savoyard. All these neophytes were subjected by Ignatius to rigid discipline, based upon his 'Exercitia.' They met together for prayer, meditation, and discussion, in his chamber at the College of S. Barbe. Here he unfolded to them his own plans, and poured out on them his spirit. At length, upon August 15, 1534, the ten together took the vows of chastity and poverty in the church of S. Mary at Montmartre, and bound themselves to conduct a missionary crusade in Palestine, or, if this should prove impracticable, to place themselves as devoted instruments, without conditions and without remuneration, in the hands of the Sovereign Pontiff.

The society was thus established, although its purpose remained indecisive. The founder's romantic dream of a crusade in Holy Land, though never realised, gave an object of immediate interest to the associated friends. Meanwhile two main features of its historical manifestation, the propaganda of the Catholic faith and unqualified devotion to the cause of the Roman See, had been clearly indicated. Nothing proves the mastery which Ignatius had now acquired over his own enthusiasm, or the insight he had gained into the right method of dealing with men, more than the use he made of his authority in this first instance. The society was bound to grow and to expand; and it was fated to receive the lasting impress of his genius. But, as though inspired by some prophetic vision of its future greatness, he refrained from circumscribing the still tender embryo within definite limits which might have been pernicious to its development.

The associates completed their studies at Paris, and in 1535 they separated, after agreeing to meet at Venice in the first months of 1537. Ignatius meanwhile travelled to Spain, where he settled his affairs by bestowing such property as he possessed on charitable institutions. He also resumed preaching with a zeal that aroused enthusiasm and extended his personal influence. At the appointed time the ten came together at Venice, ostensibly bent on carrying out their project of visiting Palestine. But war was now declared between the Turks and the Republic of S. Mark. Ignatius found himself once more accused of heresy, and had some trouble in clearing himself before the Inquisition. It was resolved in these circumstances to abandon the mission to Holy Land as impracticable for the moment, and to remain in Venice waiting for more favourable opportunities. We may believe that the romance of a crusade among the infidels of Syria had already begun to fade from the imagination of the founder, in whose career nothing is more striking than his gradual abandonment of visionary for tangible ends, and his progressive substitution of real for shadowy objects of ambition.

Loyola's first contact with Italian society during this residence in Venice exercised decisive influence over his plans. He seems to have perceived with the acute scent of an eagle that here lay the quarry he had sought so long. Italy, the fountain-head of intellectual enlightenment for Europe, was the realm which he must win. Italy alone offered the fulcrum needed by his firm and limitless desire of domination over souls. It was with Caraffa and the Theatines that Ignatius obtained a home. They were now established in the States of S. Mark through the beneficence of a rich Venetian noble, Girolamo Miani, who had opened religious houses and placed these at their disposition. Under the direction of their founder, they carried on their designed function of training a higher class of clergy for the duties of preaching and the priesthood, and for the repression of heresy by educational means. Caraffa's scheme was too limited to suit Ignatius; and the characters of both men were ill adapted for co-operation. One zeal for the faith inspired both. Here they agreed. But Ignatius was a Spaniard; and the second passion in Caraffa's breast was a Neapolitan's hatred for that nation. Ignatius, moreover, contemplated a vastly more expansive and elastic machinery for his workers in the vineyard of the faith than the future Pope's coercive temper could have tolerated. These two leaders of the Counter-Reformation, equally ambitious, equally intolerant of opposition, equally bent upon a vast dominion, had to separate. The one was destined to organise the Inquisition and the Index. The other evolved what is historically known as Jesuitry. Nevertheless we know that Ignatius learned much from Caraffa. The subsequent organisation of his Order showed that the Theatines suggested many practical points in the method he eventually adopted for effecting his designs.

Some of his companions, meanwhile, journeyed to Rome. There they obtained from Paul III. permission to visit Palestine upon a missionary enterprise, together with special privileges for their entrance into sacerdotal orders. Those of the ten friends who were not yet priests were ordained at Venice in June 1537. They then began to preach in public, roaming the streets with faces emaciated by abstinence, clad in ragged clothes, and using a language strangely compounded of Italian and Spanish. Their obvious enthusiasm, and the holy lives they were known to lead, brought them rapidly into high reputation of sanctity. Both the secular and the religious clergy of Italy could show but few men at that epoch equal to these brethren. It was settled in the autumn that they should all revisit Rome, travelling by different routes, and meditating on the form which the Order should assume. Palestine had now been definitely, if tacitly, abandoned. As might have been expected, it was Loyola who baptised his Order and impressed a character upon the infant institution. He determined to call it the Company of Jesus, with direct reference to those Companies of Advénture which had given irregular organisation to restless military spirits in the past. The new Company was to be a 'cohort or century combined for combat against spiritual foes; men-at-arms devoted, body and soul, to our Lord Jesus Christ and to His true and lawful Vicar upon earth.'[3] An Englishman of the present day may pause to meditate upon the grotesque parallel between the nascent Order of the Jesuits and the Salvation Army, and can draw such conclusions from it as may seem profitable.

Loyola's withdrawal from all participation in the nominal honour of his institution, his enrolment of the militia he had levied under the name of Jesus, and the combative functions which he ascribed to it, were very decided marks of originality. It stamped the body with impersonality from the outset, and indicated the belligerent attitude it was destined to assume. There was nothing exactly similar to its dominant conception in any of the previous religious orders. These had usually received their title from the founder, had aimed at a life retired from the world, had studied the sanctification of their individual members, and had only contemplated an indirect operation upon society. Ignatius, on the contrary, placed his community under the protection of Christ, and defined it at the outset as a militant and movable legion of auxiliaries, dedicated, not to retirement or to the pursuit of salvation, but to freely avowed and active combat in defence of their Master's vicegerent upon earth. It was as though he had divined the deficiencies of Catholicism at that epoch, and had determined to supplement them by the creation of a novel and a special weapon of attack. Some institutions of mediæval chivalry, the Knights of the Temple and S. John, for instance, furnished the closest analogy to his foundation. Their spirit he transferred from the sphere of physical combat with visible forces, infidel and Mussulman, to the sphere of intellectual warfare against heresy, unbelief, insubordination in the Church. He had refined upon the crude enthusiasm of romance which inspired him at Montserrat. Without losing its intensity, this had become a motive force of actual and political gravity.

The Company of Jesus was far from obtaining the immediate approval of the Church. Paul III. indeed, perceived its utility, and showed marked favour to the associates when they arrived in Rome about the end of 1537. The people, too, welcomed their ministration gladly, and

[3] These phrases occur in the *Deliberatio primorum patrum*.

recognised the zeal which they displayed in acts of charity and their exemplary behaviour. But the Curia and higher clergy organised an opposition against them. They were accused of heresy and attempts to seduce the common folk. Ignatius demanded full and public inquiry, which was at first refused him. He then addressed the Pope in person, who ordered a trial, out of which the brethren came with full acquittal. After this success, they obtained a hold upon religious instruction in many schools of Rome. Adherents flocked around them; and they saw that it was time to give the society a defined organisation and to demand its official recognition as an Order. It was resolved to add the vow of obedience to their former vows of chastity and poverty. Obedience had always been a prime virtue in monastic institutions; but Ignatius conceived of it in a new and military spirit. The obedience of the Jesuits was to be absolute, extending even to the duty of committing sins at a superior's orders. The General, instead of holding office for a term of years, was to be elected for life, with unlimited command over the whole Order in its several degrees. He was to be regarded as Christ present and personified. This autocracy of the General might have seemed to menace the overlordship of the Holy See, but for a fourth vow which the Company determined to adopt. It ran as follows: 'That the members will consecrate their lives to the continual service of Christ and of the Popes, will fight under the banner of the Cross, and will serve the Lord and the Roman Pontiff as God's vicar upon earth, in such wise that they shall be bound to execute immediately and without hesitation or excuse all that the reigning Pope or his successors may enjoin upon them for the profit of souls or for the propagation of the faith, and shall do so in all provinces whithersoever he may send them, among Turks or any other infidels, to furthest Ind, as well as in the region of heretics, schismatics, or believers of any kind.'

Loyola himself drew up these constitutions in five chapters, and had them introduced to Paul III., with the petition that they might be confirmed. This was in September 1539, and it is singular that the man selected to bring them under the Pope's notice should have been Cardinal Contarini. Paul had no difficulty in recognising the support which this new Order would bring to the Papacy in its conflict with Reformers and its diplomatic embarrassments with Charles V. He is even reported to have said, 'The finger of God is there!' Yet he could not confirm the constitutions without the previous approval of three Cardinals appointed to report on them. This committee condemned Loyola's scheme; and nearly a year passed in negotiations with foreign princes and powerful prelates, before a reluctant consent was yielded to the Pope's avowed inclination. At length the Bull of Sept. 27, 1540, 'Regimini militantis Ecclesiae,' launched the Society of Jesus on the world. Ignatius became the first General of the Order; and the rest of his life, a period of sixteen years, was spent in perfecting the machinery and extending the growth of this institution, which in all essentials was the emanation of his own mind.

It may be well at this point to sketch the oranisation of the Jesuits, and to describe the progress of the Society during its founder's lifetime, in order that a correct conception may be gained of Loyola's share in its creation. Many historians of eminence, and among them so acute an observer as Paolo Sarpi, have been of the opinion that Jesuitry in its later developments was a deflection from the spirit and intention of Ignatius. It is affirmed that Lainez and Salmeron, rather than Loyola, gave that complexion to the Order which has rendered it a mark for the hatred and disgust of Europe. Aquaviva, the fifth General, has been credited with its policy of interference in affairs of states and nations. Yet I think it can be shown that the Society, as it appeared in the seventeenth century, was a logical and necessary development of the Society as Ignatius framed it in the sixteenth.[4] Lainez, who succeeded the founder as General, digested the constitutions and supplied them with a commentary or Directorium. He defined, formulated, and stereotyped the system; but the essential qualities of Jesuitry, its concentration upon political objects, its unscrupulousness in choice of means to ends, the worldliness which lurked beneath the famous motto *Ad Majorem Dei Gloriam*, were implicit in Loyola's express words and in his actual administration. The framework of the Order, as he fixed it, was so firmly traced and so cunningly devised for practical efficiency, that it admitted of no alteration except in the direction of more rigid definition. Lainez may, indeed, have emphasised its tendency to become a political machine, and may have weakened its religious tone, by his rules for the interpretation of the constitutions; but we have seen that the development of Loyola's own ideas ran in this direction. The real strength as well as the worst vices of Jesuitry were inherent in the system from the first; and in it we have perhaps the most remarkable instance on record of the evolution of a cosmopolitan and world-important organism from the embryo of one man's conception.

The Bull 'Regimini militantis Ecclesiae' restricted the number of the Jesuits to sixty. If Ignatius did not himself propose this limit, the restriction may perhaps have suggested his policy of reserving the full privileges of the Society for a small band of selected members—the very essence of the body, extracted by processes which will be afterwards described. Anyhow, it is certain that, though the Papal limitation was removed in 1543, and though candidates flowed on the tide of fashion toward the Order, yet the representative and responsible Fathers remained few in numbers. These were distributed as the General thought fit. He stayed in Rome; for Rome was the chosen headquarters of the Society, the nucleus of their growth, and the fulcrum of their energy. From Rome, as from a centre, Ignatius moved his men about the field of Europe. We might compare him under one metaphor to a chess-player

[4] Sarpi, though he expressed an opinion that the Jesuits of his day had departed from the spirit of their founders, spoke thus of Loyola's worldly aims (*Lettere*, vol. i. p. 224): 'Even Father Ignatius, Founder of the Company, as his biography attests, based himself in such wise upon human interest as though there were none divine to think about.'

directing his pieces upon the squares of the political and ecclesiastical chessboard: under another, to a spider spinning his web so as to net the greatest number of profitable partisans. The fathers were kept in perpetual motion. To shift them from place to place, to exclude them from their native soil, to render them cosmopolitan and pliant was the first care of the founder. He forbade the follies of ascetic piety, inculcated the study of languages and exact knowledge, and above all things recommended the acquisition of those social arts which find favour with princes and folk of high condition. 'Prudence of an exquisite quality,' he said, 'combined with average sanctity, is more valuable than eminent sanctity and less of prudence.' Also he bade them keep their eyes open for neophytes 'less marked by pure goodness than by firmness of character and ability in conduct of affairs, since men who are not apt for public business do not suit the requirements of the Company.' Orlandino tells us that though Ignatius felt drawn to men who showed eminent gifts for erudition, he preferred, in the difficulties of the Church, to choose such as knew the world well and were distinguished by their social station. The fathers were to seek out youths 'of good natural parts, adapted to the acquisition of knowledge and to practical works of utility.' Their pupils were, if possible, to have physical advantages and manners that should render them agreeable. These points had more of practical value than a bare vocation for piety. In their dealings with tender consciences, they were to act like 'good fishers of souls, passing over many things in silence as though these had not been observed, until the time came when the will was gained, and the character could be directed as they thought best.'[5] Loyola's dislike for the common forms of monasticism appears in his choice of the ordinary secular priest's cassock for their dress, and in his emancipation of the members from devotional exercises and attendance in the choir. The aversion he felt for ascetic discipline is evinced in a letter he addressed to Francis Borgia in 1548. It is better, he writes, to strengthen your stomach and other faculties, than to impair the body and enfeeble the intellect by fasting. God needs both our physical and mental powers for His service; and every drop of blood you shed in flagellation is a loss. The end in view was to serve the Church by penetrating European society, taking possession of its leaders in rank and hereditary influence, directing education, assuming the control of the confessional, and preaching the faith in forms adapted to the foibles and the fancies of the age. The interests of the Church were paramount: 'If she teaches that what seems to us white is black, we must declare it to be black upon the spot.' There were other precepts added. These, for instance, seem worth commemoration: 'The workers in the Lord's vineyard should have but one foot on earth, the other should be raised to travel forward.' 'The abnegation of our own will is of more value than if one should bring the dead to life again.' 'No storm is so pernicious as a calm, and no enemy is so dangerous as having none.' It will be seen that what is known as Jesuitry, in its mundane force and in its personal devotion to a cause,

[5] See Philippson, *op. cit.* pp. 61, 62.

emerges from the precepts of Ignatius. We may wonder how the romances of the mountain-keep of Loyola, the mysticism of Montserrat, and the struggles of Manresa should have brought the founder of the Jesuits to these results. Yet, if we analyse the problem, it will yield a probable solution. What survived from that first period was the spirit of enthusiastic service to the Church, the vast ambition of a man who felt himself a destined instrument for shoring up the crumbling walls of Catholicity, the martial instinct of a warrior fighting at fearful odds with nations ruining toward infidelity. He had no doubt where the right lay. He was a Spaniard, a servant of S. Peter; and for him the creed enounced by Rome was all in all. But his commerce with the world, his astute Basque nature, and his judgment of the European situation, taught him that he must use other means than those which Francis and Dominic had employed. He had to make his Company, that forlorn hope of Catholicism, the exponent of a decadent and rotten faith. He had to adapt it to the necessities of Christendom in dissolution, to constitute it by a guileful and sagacious method. He had to render it wise in the wisdom of the world, in order that he might catch the powers of this world by their interests and vices for the Church. He was like Machiavelli, endeavouring to save a corrupt state by utilising corruption for ends acknowledged sound. And, like Machiavelli, he was mistaken, because it will not profit man to trust in craft or the manipulation of evil. Luther was stronger in his weakness than the creator of the Jesuit machinery, wiser in his simplicity than the deviser of that subtle engine. But Luther had the onward forces of humanity upon his side. Ignatius could but retard them by his ingenuity. We may be therefore excused if we admire Ignatius for the virile effort which he made in a failing cause, and for the splendid gifts of organising prudence which he devoted to a misplaced object.

Under his direction, the members of the Society spread themselves over Europe, and always with similar results. Wherever they went, hundreds of adherents joined the Order. Paul III. and Julius III. heaped privileges upon it, seeing what a power it had become in warfare with heresy. Ignatius spared no pains to secure his position in Rome, paying court to cardinals and prelates, visiting ambassadors and princes, soliciting their favours and offering the service of his brethren in return. Profitable negotiations were opened with the King of Spain and the Duke of Bavaria, which, under cover of reforming convents, led to a partition of ecclesiastical property between the Jesuits and the State. Good reasons seemed to justify such acts of spoliation; for the old Orders were sunk in sloth and immorality beyond redemption, while the Company kept alive all that was sound in Catholic discipline, preaching, and instruction. In Italy the Jesuits made rapid progress from the first. Lainez occupied the Venetian territory, opposing Protestant opinions in Venice itself, at Brescia, and among the mountains of the Valtelline. Le Jay combated the forces of Calvin and Renée of France at Ferrara. Salmeron took possession of Naples and Sicily. Piacenza, Modena, Faenza, Bologna, and Montepulciano received the fathers with open arms. The Farnesi welcomed them in Parma. Wherever they went, they secured the good will of noble women, and gained some hold on universities. Colleges were founded in the chief cities of the peninsula, where they not only taught gratis, but used methods superior to those previously in vogue. Rome, however, remained the stronghold of the Company. Here Ignatius founded its first house in 1550. This was the Collegium Romanum; and in 1555 some hundred pupils, who had followed a course of studies in Greek, Latin, Hebrew, and theology, issued from its walls. In 1557 he purchased the palace Salviati, on the site of which now stands the vast establishment of the Gesù. In 1552 he started a separate institution, Collegium Germanicum, for the special training of young Germans. There was also a subordinate institution for the education of the sons of nobles. These colleges afforded models for similar schools throughout Europe: some of them intended to supply the Society with members, and some to impress the laity with Catholic principles. Uniformity was an object which the Jesuits always held in view.

They did not meet at first with like success in all Catholic countries. In Spain, Charles V. treated them with suspicion as the sworn men of the Papacy; and the Dominican Order, so powerful through its hold upon the Inquisition, regarded them justly as rivals. Though working for the same end, the means employed by Jesuits and Dominicans were too diverse for these champions of orthodoxy to work harmoniously together. The Jesuits belonged to the future, to the party of accommodation and control by subterfuge. The Dominicans were rooted in the past; their dogmatism admitted of no compromise; they strove to rule by force. There was therefore, at the outset, war between the kennels of the elder and the younger dogs of God in Spain. Yet Jesuitism gained ground. It had the advantage of being a native and a recent product. It was powerful by its appeals to the sensuous imagination and carnal superstitions of that Iberian-Latin people. It was seductive by its mitigation of oppressive orthodoxy and inflexible prescriptive law. Where the Dominican was steel, the Jesuit was reed; where the Dominican breathed fire and faggots, the Jesuit suggested casuistical distinctions; where the Dominican raised difficulties, the Jesuit solved scruples; where the Dominican presented theological abstractions, the Jesuit offered stimulative or agreeable images; where the Dominican preached dogma, the Jesuit retailed romance. It only needed one illustrious convert to plant the Jesuits in Spain. Him they found in Francis Borgia, Duke of Gandia, Viceroy of Catalonia, and subsequently the third General of the Order and a saint. This man placed the university, which he had founded, in their hands; and about the same time they gained a footing in the University of Salamanca. Still they continued to retain their strongest hold upon the people, who regarded them as saviours from the tyranny and ennui of the established Dominican hierarchy.

Portugal was won at a blow. Xavier and Rodriguez planted the Company there under the affectionate protection of King John III.

When Xavier started on his mission to the Indies in 1541, Rodriguez took the affairs of the realm into his hands, controlled the cabinet, and formed the heir-apparent to their will.

With France they had more trouble. Both the University and the Parliament of Paris opposed their settlement. The Sorbonne even declared them 'dangerous in matters of the faith, fit to disturb the peace of the Church, and to reverse the order of monastic life; more adapted to destroy than to build.' The Gallican Church scented danger in these bondsmen of the Papacy; and it was only when they helped to organise the League that the influence of the Guises gave them a foothold in the kingdom. Even then their seminaries at Reims, Douai, and S. Omer must be rather regarded as outposts (ἐπιτειχισμοὶ)—against England and Flanders than as nationally French establishments. In France they long remained a seditious and belligerent faction.[6]

They had the same partial and clandestine success in the Low Countries, where their position was at first equivocal, though they early gained some practical hold upon the University of Louvain. We are perhaps justified in attributing the evil fame of Reims, Douai, S. Omer, and Louvain to the incomplete sympathy which existed between the Jesuits and the countries where they made these settlements. Not perfectly at home, surrounded by discontent and jealousy, upon the borderlands of the heresies they were bound to combat, their system assumed its darkest colours in those hotbeds of intrigue and feverish fanaticism. In time, however, the Jesuits fixed their talons firmly upon the Netherlands, through the favour of Anne of Austria; and the year 1562 saw them comfortably ensconced at Antwerp, Louvain, Brussels, and Lille, in spite of the previous antipathy of the population. Here, as elsewhere, they pushed their way by gaining women and people of birth to their cause, and by showily meritorious services to education. Faber achieved ephemeral success as lecturer at Louvain.

To take firm hold on Germany had been the cherished wish of Ignatius, 'for there,' to use his own words, 'the pest of heresy exposed men to graver dangers than elsewhere.' The Society had scarcely been founded when Faber, Le Jay, and Bobadilla were sent north. Faber made small progress, and was removed to Spain. But Bobadilla secured the confidence of William, Duke of Bavaria; while Le Jay won that of Ferdinand of Austria. In both provinces they avowed their intention of working at the reformation of the clergy and the improvement of popular education—ends, which in the disorganised condition of Germany, seemed of highest importance to those princes. Through the influence of Bavaria, Bobadilla succeeded in rendering the Interim proclaimed by Charles V. nugatory; while Le Jay founded the college of the Order at Vienna. In this important post he was soon succeeded by Canisius, Ferdinand's confessor, through whose co-operation Cardinal Morone afterwards brought this Emperor into harmony with the Papal plan for winding up the Council of

[6] It was not till the epoch of Maria de' Medici's Regency that the Jesuits obtained firm hold on France.

Trent. It should be added that Ingolstadt in Bavaria became the second headquarters of the Jesuit propaganda in Germany.

The methods adopted by Ignatius in dealing with his three lieutenants, Bobadilla, Le Jay, and Canisius, are so characteristic of Jesuit policy that they demand particular attention. Checkmated by Bobadilla in the matter of the Interim, Charles V. manifested his resentment. He was already ill-affected toward the Society, and its founder felt the need of humouring him. The highest grade of the Order was therefore ostentatiously refused to Bobadilla, until such time as the Emperor's attention was distracted from the cause of his disappointment. With Le Jay and Canisius the case stood differently. Ferdinand wished to make the former Bishop of Trieste and the latter Archbishop of Vienna. Ignatius opposed both projects, alleging that the Company of Jesus could not afford to part with its best servants, and that their vows of obedience and poverty were inconsistent with high office in the Church. He discerned the necessity of reducing each member of the Society to absolute dependence on the General, which would have been impracticable if any one of them attained to the position of a prelate. A law was therefore passed declaring it mortal sin for Jesuits to accept bishoprics or other posts of honour in the Church. Instead of assuming the mitre, Canisius was permitted to administer the See of Vienna without usufruct of its revenues. To the world this manifested the disinterested zeal of the Jesuits in a seductive light; while the integrity of the Society, as an independent self-sufficing body, exacting the servitude of absolute devotion from its members, was secured. Another instance of the same adroitness may be mentioned. The Emperor in 1552 offered a Cardinal's hat to Francis Borgia, who was by birth the most illustrious of living Jesuits. Ignatius refrained from rebuffing the Emperor and insulting the Duke of Gandia by an open prohibition; but he told the former to expect the Duke's refusal, while he wrote to the latter expressing his own earnest hope that he would renounce an honour injurious to the Society. This diplomacy elicited a grateful but firm answer of *Nolo Episcopari* from the Duke, who thus took the responsibility of offending Charles V. upon himself. Meanwhile the missionary objects of the Company were not neglected. Xavier left Portugal in 1541 for that famous journey through India and China, the facts of which may be compared for their romantic interest with Cortes' or Pizarro's exploits. Brazil, the transatlantic Portugal, was abandoned to the Jesuits, and they began to feel their way in Mexico. In the year of Loyola's death, 1556, thirty-two members of the Society were resident in South America; one hundred in India, China, and Japan; and a mission was established in Ethiopia. Even Ireland had been explored by a couple of fathers, who returned without success, after undergoing terrible hardships. At this epoch the Society counted in round numbers one thousand men. It was divided in Europe into thirteen provinces: seven of these were Portuguese and Spanish; three were Italian (namely, Rome, Upper Italy, and Sicily); one was French; two were German. Castile contained ten colleges of the Order; Aragon, five; Andalusia, five. Portugal was penetrated through and through with Jesuits. Rome displayed the central Roman and Teutonic colleges. Upper Italy had ten colleges. France could show only one college. In Upper Germany the Company held firm hold on Vienna, Prag, Munich, and Ingolstadt. The province of Lower Germany, including the Netherlands, was still undetermined. This expansion of the Order during the first sixteen years of its existence enables us to form some conception of the intellectual vigour and commanding will of Ignatius. He lived, as no founder of an Order, as few founders of religions, ever lived, to see his work accomplished and the impress of his genius stereotyped exactly in the forms he had designed upon the most formidable social and political organisation of modern Europe.

In his administration of the Order, Ignatius was absolute and autocratic. We have seen how he dealt with aspirants after ecclesiastical honours, and how he shifted his subordinates, as he thought best, from point to point upon the surface of the globe. The least attempt at independence on the part of his most trusted lieutenants was summarily checked by him. Simon Rodriguez, one of the earliest disciples of the College of S. Barbe at Paris, ruled the kingdom of Portugal through the ascendency which he had gained over John III. Elated by the vastness of his victory, Rodriguez arrogated to himself the right of private judgment, and introduced that ascetic discipline into the houses of his province which Ignatius had forbidden as inexpedient. Without loss of time, the General superseded him in his command; and, after a sharp struggle, Rodriguez was compelled to spend the rest of his days under strict surveillance at Rome. Lainez, in like manner, while acting as Provincial of Upper Italy, thought fit to complain that his best coadjutors were drawn from the colleges under his control to Rome. Ignatius wrote to this old friend, the man who best understood the spirit of its institution, and who was destined to succeed him in his headship, a cold and terrible epistle. 'Reflect upon your conduct. Let me know whether you acknowledge your sin, and tell me at the same time what punishment you are ready to undergo for this dereliction of duty.' Lainez expressed immediate submission in the most abject terms; he was ready to resign his post, abstain from preaching, confine his studies to the Breviary, walk as a beggar to Rome, and there teach grammar to children or perform menial offices. This was all Ignatius wanted. If he were the Christ of the Society, he well knew that Lainez was its S. Paul. He could not prevent him from being his successor, and he probably was well aware that Lainez would complete and supplement what he must leave unfinished in his life-work. The grovelling apology of such an eminent apostle, dictated as it was by hypocrisy and cunning, sufficed to procure his pardon, and remained among the archives of the Jesuits as a model for the spirit in which obedience should be manifested by them.

Obedience was, in fact, the cardinal and dominant quality of the Jesuit Order. To call it a virtue, in the sense in which Ignatius understood it, is impossible. The *Exercitia*, the Constitutions, and the letter to the Portuguese Jesuits, all of which undoubtedly explain Loyola's views, reveal to us the essence of historical Jesuitry, the *fons et origo* of that long-continued evil which impested modern society. Let us examine some of his precepts on this topic. 'I ought to desire to be ruled by a superior who endeavours to subjugate my judgment and subdue my understanding.'—'When it seems to me that I am commanded by my superior to do a thing against which my conscience revolts as sinful, and my superior judges otherwise, it is my duty to yield my doubts to him, unless I am constrained by evident reasons.'—'I ought not to be my own, but His who created me, and his too through whom God governs me.'—'I ought to be like a corpse which has neither will nor understanding, like a crucifix that is turned about by him that holds it, like a staff in the hands of an old man who uses it at will for his assistance or pleasure.'—'In our Company the person who commands must never be regarded in his own capacity, but as Jesus Christ in him.'—'I desire that you strive and exercise yourselves to recognise Christ our Lord in every Superior.'—'He who wishes to offer himself wholly up to God, must make the sacrifice not only of his will but of his intelligence.'—'In order to secure the faithful and successful execution of a Superior's orders, all private judgment must be yielded up.'—'A sin, whether venial or mortal, must be committed, if it is commanded by the Superior in the name of our Lord Jesus Christ or in virtue of obedience.' Of such nature was the virtue of obedience within the Order.[7] It rendered every member a tool in the hands of his immediate Superior, and the whole body one instrument in the hand of the General. The General's responsibility for the oblique acts and evasions of moral law, committed in the name of this virtue, was covered by the sounding phrase, 'Unto the greater glory of God.' He had also his own duty of obedience, which was to Holy Church. 'In making the sacrifice of our own judgment, the mind must keep itself ever whole and ready for obedience to the spouse of Christ, our Holy Mother, the Church orthodox, apostolic and hierarchical.'[8] Not a portion of the Catholic creed, of Catholic habits, of Catholic institutions, of Catholic superstitions, but must be valiantly defended. 'It is our duty loudly to uphold reliques, the cult of saints, stations, pilgrimages, indulgences, jubilees, the candles which are lighted before altars.' To criticise the clergy, even though notoriously corrupt, is a sin. The philosophy of the Church, as expressed by S. Thomas Aquinas, S. Bonaventura, and others, must be recognised as equal in authority with Holy Writ. It follows that just as a subordinate was enjoined to sin, if sin were ordered by his Superior, so the whole Company were bound to lie, and do the things they disapproved, and preach the mummeries in which they disbelieved, in virtue

[7] The letter addressed by Ignatius to the Portuguese Jesuits, March 22, 1553, on the virtue of obedience, the Constitutions and the glosses on them called Declarations, and the last chapter of the *Exercitia*, furnish the above sentences. See, too, Philippson, *op. cit.* pp. 60, 120-124.

[8] Read in the *Exercitia* (*Inst. Soc. Jesu*, vol. iv. pp. 167-173) the Rules for right accord with the Orthodox Church. What follows above is taken from that chapter.

of obedience to the Church. They may not even trust their senses; for 'If the Church pronounces a thing which seems to us white to be black, we must immediately say that it is black.[9] The Jesuits were enrolled as an army, in an hour of grave peril for the Church, to undertake her defence. They pledged themselves, by this vow of obedience, to perform that duty with their eyes shut. It was not their mission to reform or purify or revivify Catholicism, but to maintain it intact with all its intellectual anachronisms. How well they succeeded may be judged from the issue of the Council of Trent, in which Lainez and Salmeron played so prominent a part. That rigid enforcement of every jot and tittle in the Catholic hierarchical organisation, in Catholic ritual, in the Catholic cult of saints and images, in the Catholic interpretation of Sacraments, in Catholic tradition as of equal value with the Bible, and lastly in the theory of Papal Supremacy, which was the astounding result of a Council convened to alter and reform the Church, can be attributed in no small measure to Jesuit persistency.

Ignatius attained his object. Obedience, blind, servile, unquestioning, unscrupulous, became the distinguishing feature of the Jesuits. But he condemned his Order to mediocrity. No really great man in any department of human knowledge or activity has arisen in the Company of Jesus. In course of time it became obvious to anyone of independent character and original intellect that their ranks were not the place for him. And if youths of real eminence entered it before they perceived this truth, their spirit was crushed. The machine was powerful enough for good and evil; but it remained an aggregate of individual inferiorities. Its merit and its perfection lay in this, that so complex an instrument could be moved by a single finger of the General in Rome. He consistently employed its delicate system of wheels and pulleys for the aggrandisement of the Order in the first place, in the second place for the control of the Catholic Church, and always for the subjugation and cretinisation of the mind of Europe.

The training of a Jesuit began with study of the *Exercitia Spiritualia*.[10] This manual had been composed by Loyola himself at intervals between 1522 and 1548, when it received the imprimatur of Pope Paul III. He based it on his own experiences at Manresa, and meant it to serve as a perpetual introduction to the mysteries of the religious life. It was used under the direction of a father, who prescribed a portion of its text for each day's meditation, employing various means to concentrate attention and enforce effect. The whole course of this spiritual drill extended over four weeks, during which the pupil remained in solitude. Light and sound and all distractions of the outer world were carefully excluded from his chamber. He was bidden to direct his soul inward upon itself and

[9] *Exercitia*, ibid. p. 171. In this spirit a Jesuit of the present century writing on astronomy develops the heliocentric theory while he professes his submission to the geocentric theory as maintained by the Church.

[10] *Inst. Soc. Jesu*, vol. iv. The same volume contains the Directorium or rules for the use of the *Exercitia*.

God, and was led by graduated stages to realise in the most vivid way the torments of the damned and the scheme of man's salvation. The first week was occupied in an examination of the conscience; the second in contemplation of Christ's Kingdom upon earth; the third in meditation on the Passion; the fourth in an ascent to the glory of the risen Lord. Materialism of the crudest type mingled with the indulgence of a reverie in this long spiritual journey. At every step the neophyte employed his five senses in the effort of intellectual realisation. Prostrate upon the ground, gazing with closed eyelids in the twilight of his cell upon the mirror of imagination, he had to *see* the boundless flames of hell and souls encased in burning bodies, to *hear* the shrieks and blasphemies, to *smell* their sulphur and intolerable stench, to *taste* the bitterness of tears, and *feel* the stings of ineffectual remorse. He had to localise each object in the camera obscura of the brain. If the Garden of Gethsemane, for instance, were the subject of his meditation, he was bound to place Christ here and the sleeping apostles there, and to form an accurate image of the angel and the cup. He gazed and gazed until he was able to handle the raiment of the Saviour, to watch the drops of bloody sweat beading his forehead and trickling down his cheeks, to grasp the chalice with the fingers of the soul. As each carefully chosen and sagaciously suggested scene was presented, he had to identify his very being, soul, will, intellect, and senses, with the mental vision. He lived again, so far as this was possible through fancy, the facts of sacred history. If the director judged it advisable, symbolic objects were placed before him in the cell; at one time skulls and bones, at another fresh sweet-smelling flowers. Fasting and flagellation, peculiar postures of the body, groanings and weepings, were prescribed as mechanical aids in cases where the soul seemed sluggish. The sphere traversed in these exercises was a narrow one. The drill aimed at intensity of discipline, at a concentrated and concrete impression, not at width of education or at intellectual enlightenment. Speculation upon the fundamental principles of religion was excluded. God's dealings with mankind revealed in the Old Testament found no place in this theory of salvation. Attention was riveted upon a very few points in the life of Christ and Mary, such as every Catholic child might be supposed to be familiar with. But it was fixed in such a way as to bring the terrors and raptures of the mystics, of a S. Catherine or a S. Teresa, within the reach of all; to place spiritual experience *à la portée de tout le monde*. The vulgarity is only equalled by the ingenuity and psychological adroitness of the method. The soul inspired with carnal dread of the doom impending over it, passed into almost physical contact with the incarnate Saviour. The designed effect was to induce a vivid and varied hypnotic dream of thirty days, from the influence of which a man should never wholly free himself. The end at which he arrived upon this path of self-scrutiny and materialistic realisation, was the conclusion that his highest hope, his most imperative duty, lay in the resignation of his intellect and will to spiritual guidance, and in blind obedience to the Church. Thousands and thousands of souls in the modern world have passed through this discipline; and those who responded to it best, have ever been selected, when this was possible, as novices of the Order. The director had ample opportunity of observing at each turn in the process whether his neophyte displayed a likely disposition.

When the 'Exercitia' had been performed, there was an end of asceticism. Ignatius, as we have seen, dreaded nothing more than the intrusion of that dark spirit into his Company; he aimed at nothing more earnestly than at securing agreeable manners, a cheerful temper, and ability for worldly business in its members.

The novice, when first received into one of the Jesuit houses, was separated so far as possible for two years from his family, and placed under the control of a master, who inspected his correspondence and undertook the full surveillance of his life. He received cautiously restricted information on the constitutions of the Society, and was recommended, instead of renouncing his worldly possessions, to reserve his legal rights and make oblation of them when he took the vows. It was not then made clear to him that what he gave would never under any circumstances be restored, although the Society might send him forth at will a penniless wanderer into the world. Yet this was the hard condition of a Jesuit's existence. After entering the Order he owned nothing, and he had no power to depart if he repented. But the General could cashier him by a stroke of the pen, condemning him to destitution in every land where Jesuits held sway, and to suspicion in every land where Jesuits were loathed. Before the end of two years, the novice generally signed an obligation to assume the vows. He was then drafted into the secular or spiritual service. Some novices became what is called Temporal Coadjutors; their duty was to administer the property of the Society, to superintend its houses, to distribute alms, to work in hospitals, to cook, garden, wash, and act as porters. They took the three vows of poverty, chastity, and obedience. Those, on the other hand, who showed some aptitude for learning, were classified as Scholastics, and were distributed among the colleges of the Order. They studied languages, sciences, and theology, for a period of five years; after which they taught in schools for another period of five or six years; and when they reached the age of about thirty, they might be ordained priests with the title of Spiritual Coadjutors. From this body the Society drew the rectors and professors of its colleges, its preachers, confessors, and teachers in schools for the laity. They were not yet full members, though they had taken the three vows and were irrevocably devoted to the service of the Order. The final stage of initiation was reached toward the age of forty-five, after long and various trials. Then the Jesuit received the title of Professed. He was either a professed of the three vows, or a professed of the four vows; having in the latter case dedicated his life to the special service of the Papacy in missions or in any other cause. The professed of four vows constituted the veritable Company of Jesus, the kernel of the organisation. They were never numerous. At Loyola's death they numbered thirty-five out of a thousand; and it has been calculated that their average proportion to the whole body is as two to a hundred.[11] Even these had no indefeasible tenure of their place in the Society. They might be dismissed by the General without indemnification.

The General was chosen for life from the professed of four vows by the General Congregation, which consisted of the provincials and two members of each province. He held the whole Society at his discretion; for he could deal at pleasure with each part of its machinery. The constitutions, strict as they appeared, imposed no barriers upon his will; for almost unlimited power was surrended to him of dispensing with formalities, freeing from obligations, shortening or lengthening the periods of initiation, retarding or advancing a member in his career. Ideal fixity of type, qualified by the utmost elasticity in practice, formed the essence of the system. And we shall see that this principle pervaded the Jesuit treatment of morality. The General resided at Rome, consecrated solely to the government of the Society, holding the threads of all its complicated affairs in his hands, studying the personal history of each of its members in the minute reports which he constantly received from every province, and acting precisely as he chose with the highest as well as the lowest of his subordinates. Contrary to all precedents of previous religious orders, Ignatius framed the Company of Jesus upon the lines of a close aristocracy with autocratic authority confided to an elected chief. Yet the General of the Jesuits, like the Doge of Venice, had his hands tied by subtly powerful though almost invisible fetters. He was subjected at every hour of the day and night to the surveillance of five sworn spies, especially appointed to prevent him from altering the type or neglecting the concerns of the Order. The first of these functionaries, named the Administrator, who was frequently also the confessor of the General, exhorted him to obedience, and reminded him that he must do all things for the glory of God. Obedience and the glory of God, in Jesuit phraseology, meant the maintenance of the Company. The other four were styled Assistants. They had under their charge the affairs of the chief provinces; one overseeing the Indies, another Portugal and Spain, a third France and Germany, a fourth Italy and Sicily. Together with the Administrator, the Assistants were nominated by the General Congregation and could not be removed or replaced without its sanction. It was their duty to regulate the daily life of the General, to control his private expenditure on the scale which they determined, to prescribe what he should eat and drink, and to appoint his hours for sleep, and religious exercises, and the transaction of public business. If they saw grave reasons for his deposition, they were bound to convene the General Congregation for that purpose. And since the Founder knew that guardians need to be guarded, he provided that the Provincials might convene this assembly to call in question the acts of the Assistants. The General himself had no power to oppose its convocation.

The Company of Jesus was thus based upon a system of mutual and

[11] Philippson, *op. cit.* p. 142.

pervasive espionage. The novice on first entering had all his acts, habits, and personal qualities registered. As he advanced in his career, he was surrounded by jealous brethren, who felt it their duty to report his slightest weakness to a superior. The superiors were watched by one another and by their inferiors. Masses of secret intelligence poured into the central cabinet of the General; and the General himself ate, slept, prayed, worked, and moved about the world beneath the fixed gaze of ten vigilant eyes. Men accustomed to domesticity and freedom may wonder that life should have been tolerable upon these terms. Yet we must remember that from the moment when a youth had undergone the 'Exercitia' and taken the vows, he became no less in fact than in spirit *perinde ac cadaver* in the hands of his superior. The Company replaced for him both family and state; and in spite of the fourth vow, it is very evident that the Black Pope, as the General came to be nicknamed, owned more of his allegiance than the White Pope, who filled the chair of S. Peter. He could, indeed, at any moment be expelled and ruined. But if he served the Order well, he belonged to a vast, incalculably potent organism, of which he might naturally, after such training as he had received, be proud. The sacrifice of his personal volition and intelligence made him part of an indestructible corporation, which seemed capable of breaking all resistance by its continuity of will and effecting all purposes by its condensed sagacity. Nor was he in the hands of rigid disciplinarians. His peccadilloes were condoned, unless the credit of the Order came in question. His natural abilities obtained free scope for their employment; for it suited the interest of the Company to make the most of each member's special gifts. He had no tedious duties of the regular monastic routine to follow. He was encouraged to become a man of the world, and to mix freely with society. And thus, while he resigned himself, he lived the large life of a complex microcosm. Nor were men of resolute ambition without the prospect of eventually swaying an authority beyond that possessed by princes; for anyone of the professed might rise to the supreme power in the Order.

Something must be said about Loyola's interpretation of the vow of poverty. During his lifetime the Company acquired considerable wealth; and after his death it became a large owner of estates in Europe. How was this consistent with the observance of that vow, so strictly inculcated by the Founder on his first disciples, and so pompously proclaimed in their constitutions? The professed and all their houses, as well as their churches, were bound to subsist on alms; they preached, administered the sacraments of the Church, and educated gratis. They could inherit nothing, and were not allowed to receive money for their journeys. But here appeared the wisdom of restricting the numbers of the professed to a small percentage of the whole Society. The same rigid prohibition with regard to property was not imposed upon the houses of novices, colleges, and other educational establishments of the Jesuits; while the secular coadjutors were specially appointed for the administration of wealth which the professed might use but could not own.[12] In like manner, as they lived on alms, there was no objection to a priest of the Order receiving valuable gifts in cash or kind from grateful recipients of his spiritual bounty. A separate article of the constitutions furthermore reserved for the General the right of accepting any donation whatsoever made in favour of the whole Company, and of assigning capital or revenue as he judged wisest. Scholastics, even after they had taken the vow of poverty, were not obliged to relinquish their private possessions. Sooner or later, it was hoped that these would become the property of the order. In a word, the principle of this solemn obligation was so manipulated as to facilitate the acquisition and accumulation of wealth by the Jesuit like any other corporation. Only no individual Jesuit owned anything. He was rich or poor, he wore the clothes of princes or the rags of a mendicant, he lived sumptuously or begged in the street, he travelled with a following of servants or he walked on foot, according as it seemed good to his superiors. The vow of poverty, thus interpreted in practice, meant a total disengagement from temporalities on the part of every member, an absolute dependence of each subordinate upon his superiority in the hierarchy.

Having thus far treated the organisation of the Jesuits as implicit in Loyola's own conception and administration, I ought to add that it received definite form from his successor, Lainez. The founder pronounced the Constitutions in 1553. But they were thoroughly revised after his death in 1558, at which date they first issued from the press. Lainez, again, supplemented these laws with a perpetual commentary which is styled the Declarations. These contain the bulk of those easements and indulgent interpretations, whereby the strictness of the original rules was explained away, and an almost unbounded elasticity was communicated to the system.

It would be rash to pronounce a decided opinion upon the much disputed question, whether, in addition to their Constitutions and Declarations, the Jesuits were provided with an esoteric code of rules known as 'Monita Secreta.'[13] The existence of such a manual, which was supposed to contain the very pith of Jesuitical policy, has been confidently asserted and no less confidently denied. In the absence of direct evidence, it may be worth quoting two passages from Sarpi's Letters, which prove that this keen-sighted observer believed the Society to be governed in its practice by statutes inaccessible to all but its most trusted members. 'I have always admired the policy of the Jesuits,' he writes in 1608, 'and their method of maintaining secrecy. Their Constitutions are in print, and yet one cannot set eyes upon a copy. I do not mean their Rules, which are published at Lyons, for those are mere puerilities, but the digest of laws

[12] Quinet calculates that at the close of the sixteenth century there were twenty-one houses of the professed (incapable of owning property) to 293 colleges (free from this inability).

[13] A book with this title was published in 1612 at Cracow. It was delcared a forgery at Rome by a congregation of Cardinals.

which guide their conduct of the Order, and which they keep concealed. Every day many members leave, or are expelled from the Company; and yet their artifices are not exposed to view.'[14] In another letter, of the date 1610, Sarpi returns to the same point. 'The Jesuits before this Aquaviva was elected General were saints in comparison with what they afterwards became. Formerly they had not mixed in affairs of state or thought of governing cities. Since then they have indulged a hope of controlling the whole world. And I am sure that the least part of their Cabala is in the Ordinances and Constitutions of 1570. All the same, I am very glad to possess even these. Their true Cabala they never communicate to any but men who have been well tested and proved by every species of trial; nor is it possible for those who have been initiated into it, to think of retiring from the Order, since the congregation, through their excellent management of its machinery, know how to procure the immediate death of any such initiated member who may wish to leave their ranks.'[15] Probably the mistake which Sarpi and the world made, was in supposing that the Jesuits needed a written code for their most vital action. Being a potent and life-penetrated organism, the secret of their policy was not such as could be reduced to rule. It was not such as, if reduced to rule, could have been plastic in the affairs of public importance which the Company sought to control. Better than rule or statute, it was biological function. The supreme deliberative bodies of the Order created, transmitted, and continuously modified its tradition of policy. This tradition some member, partially initiated into their counsels, may have reduced to precepts in the published 'Monita Secreta' of 1612. But the quintessential flame which breathed a breath of life into the fabric of the Jesuits through two centuries of organic activity, was far too vivid and too spiritual to be condensed in any charter. A friar and a jurist, like Sarpi, expected to discover some controlling code. The public, grossly ignorant of evolutionary laws in the formation of social organisms, could not comprehend the non-existence of this code. Adventurers supplied the demand from their knowledge of the ruling policy. But like the 'Liber Trium Impostorum' we may regard the 'Monita Secreta' of the Jesuits as an *ex post facto* fabrication.

There is no need to trace the further history of the Jesuits. Their part in the Counter-Reformation has rather been exaggerated than insufficiently recognised. Though it was incontestably considerable, we cannot, now concede, as Macaulay in his random way conceded to this Company, the *spolia opima* of down-beaten Protestantism. Without the ecclesiastical reform which originated in the Tridentine Council; without the gold and sword of Spain; without the stakes and prisons of the Inquisition; without the warfare against thought conducted by the Congregation of the Index; the Jesuits alone could not have masterfully governed the Catholic revival. That revival was a movement of world-historical importance, in which they participated. It was their fortune to find

[14] *Lettere*, vol. i. p. 100.
[15] *Lettere*, vol. ii. p. 174.

forces in the world which they partially understood; it was their merit to know how to manipulate those forces; it was their misfortune and their demerit that they proved themselves incapable of diverting those forces to any wholesome end. In Italy a succession of worldly Popes, Paul III., Julius III., Pius IV., and Gregory XIII., heaped favours and showered wealth upon the Order. The Jesuits incarnated the political spirit of the Papacy at this epoch; they lent it a potency for good and evil which the decrepit but still vigorous institution arrogated to itself. They adapted its anachronisms with singular adroitness to the needs of modern society. They transfused their throbbing blood into its flaccid veins, until it became doubtful whether the Papacy had been absorbed into the Jesuits, or whether the Jesuits had remodelled the Papacy for contemporary uses. But this tendency in the aspiring Order to identify itself with Rome, this ambition to command the prestige of Rome as leverage for carrying out its own designs, stirred the resentment of haughty and *intransigeant* Pontiffs. The Jesuits were not beloved by Paul IV., Pius V., and Sixtus V.

It remains, however, to inquire in what the originality, the effective operation, and the modifying influence of the Jesuit Society consisted during the period with which we are concerned. It was their object to gain control over Europe by preaching, education, the direction of souls, and the management of public affairs. In each of these departments their immediate success was startling; for they laboured with zeal, and they adapted their methods to the requirements of the age. Yet, in the long run, art, science, literature, religion, morality and politics, all suffered from their interference. By preferring artifice to reality, affectation to sincerity, shams and subterfuges to plain principle and candour, they confused the conscience and enfeebled the intellect of Catholic Europe. When we speak of the Jesuit style in architecture, rhetoric and poetry, of Jesuit learning and scholarship, of Jesuit casuistry and of Jesuit diplomacy, it is either with languid contempt for bad taste and insipidity, or with the burning indignation which systematic falsehood and corruption inspire in honourable minds.

In education, the Jesuits, if they did not precisely innovate, improved upon the methods of the grammarians which had persisted from the Middle Ages through the Renaissance. They spared no pains in training a large and competent body of professors, men of extensive culture, formed upon one uniform pattern, and exercised in the art of popularising knowledge. These teachers were distributed over the Jesuit colleges; and in every country their system was the same. New catechisms, grammars, primers, manuals of history, enabled their pupils to learn with facility in a few months what it had cost years of painful labour to acquire under pompous pedants of the old *régime*. The mental and physical aptitudes of youths committed to their charge were carefully observed; and classes were adapted to various ages and degrees of capacity. Hours of recreation alternated with hours of study, so that the effort of learning should be neither irksome nor injurious to health. Nor was religious education neglected. Attendance upon daily Mass, monthly confession, and instruction in the articles of the faith, formed an indispensable part of the system. When we remember that these advantages were offered gratuitously to the public, it is not surprising that people of all ranks and conditions should have sent their boys to the Jesuit colleges. Even Protestants availed themselves of what appeared so excellent a method; and the Jesuits obtained the reputation of being the best instructors of youth.[16] It soon became the mark of a good Catholic to have frequented Jesuit schools; and in after life a pupil who had studied creditably in their colleges, found himself everywhere at home. Yet the Society took but little interest in elementary or popular education. Their object was to gain possession of the nobility, gentry, and upper middle class. The proletariat might remain ignorant; it was the destiny of such folk to be passive instruments in the hands of spiritual and temporal rulers. Nor were they always scrupulous in the means employed for taking hold on young men of distinction. One instance of the animosity they aroused even in Italy at an early period of their activity will suffice. Tuscany was thrown into commotion by the discovery of their designs upon the boys they undertook to teach. 'They were so madly bent,' says Galluzzi, 'upon filling the ranks of their Company with individuals of wealth and birth that in 1584, in the single city of Siena, under the pretence of devotion, they seduced thirty youths of the noblest and richest houses, not without great injury to their families and grief to their parents. The most notorious of these cases was that of two sons of Pandolfo Petrucci, whose name indicates his high position in the aristocracy of Siena. These young men they got into their power by inducing them to commit a theft, and then compelled them to pledge fealty to the Society. Escaping by night in the direction of Rome, the lads were arrested by the city guards, and confessed that they had agreed to meet two Jesuits who were waiting to conduct them on their journey.'[17] It was, indeed, not the propagation of sound principles or liberal learning, but the aggrandisement of the Order and the enforcement of Catholic usages, at which the Jesuits aimed in their scheme of education. This was noticeable in their attitude toward literature and science. Michelet has described their method in a brilliant and exact metaphor, as the attempt to counteract the poison of free thought and stimulative studies by means of vaccination. They taught the classics in expurgated editions, history in drugged epitomes, science in popular lectures. Instead of banning what M. Renan is wont to style *études fortes*, they undertook to emasculate these and render them innocuous. While Bruno was burned by the Inquisition for proclaiming what the Copernican discovery involved for faith and metaphysic, Father Koster at Cologne vulgarised it into something pretty and agreeable. While Scaliger and Casaubon used the humanities as a propædeutic of the virile reason, the Jesuits contrived to sterilise and mech-

[16] See Sarpi's *Letters*, vol. i. p. 352, for Protestant pupils of Jesuits. Sarpi's *Memorial to the Signory of Venice on the Collegio de' Greci in Rome* exposes the fallacy of their being reputed the best teachers of youth, by pointing out how their aim is to withdraw their pupils' allegiance from the nation, the government and the family, to themselves.

[17] *Storia del Granducato di Toscana*, vol. iv. p. 275.

anise their influences by insipid rhetoric. Everywhere through Europe, by the side of stalwart thinkers, crept plausible Jesuit professors, following the light of learning like its shadow, mimicking the accent of the gods like parrots, and mocking their gestures like apes. Their adroit admixture of falsehood with truth in all departments of knowledge, their substitution of veneer for solid timber, and of pinchbeck for sterling metal, was more profitable to the end they had in view than the torture-chamber of the Inquisition or the quarantine of the Index. Mediocrities and respectabilities of every description—that is to say, the majority of the influential classes—were delighted with their method. What could be better than to see sons growing up, good Catholics in all external observances, devoted to the order of society and Mother Church, and at the same time showy Latinists, furnished with a cyclopædia of current knowledge, glib at speechifying, ingenious in the construction of an epigram or compliment? If some of the more sensible sort grumbled that Jesuit learning was shallow and Jesuit morality of base alloy, the reply, like that of an Italian draper selling palpable shoddy for broadcloth, came easily and cynically to the surface: *Imita bene!* The stuff is a good match enough! What more do you want? To produce plausible imitations, to save appearances, to amuse the mind with tricks, was the last resort of Catholicism in its warfare against rationalism. And such is the banality of human nature as a whole, that the Jesuits, those monopolists of Brummagem manufactures, achieved eminent success. Their hideous churches, daubed with plaster painted to resemble costly marbles, encrusted with stucco polished to deceive the eye, loaded with gewgaws and tinsel and superfluous ornament and frescoes turning flat surfaces into cupolas and arcades, passed for masterpieces of architectonic beauty. The conceits of their pulpit oratory, its artificial cadences and flowery verbiage, its theatrical appeals to gross sensations, wrought miracles and converted thousands. Their sickly Ciceronian style, their sentimental books of piety, 'the worse for being warm,' the execrable taste of their poetry, their flimsy philosophy and disingenuous history, infected the taste of Catholic Europe like a slow seductive poison, flattering and accelerating the diseases of mental decadence. Sound learning died down beneath the tyranny of the Inquisition, the Index, the Council of Trent, Spain and the Papacy. A rank growth of unwholesome culture arose and flourished on its tomb under the forcing-frames of Jesuitry. But if we peruse the records of literature and science during the last three centuries, few indeed are the eminences even of a second order which can be claimed by the Company of Jesus.

The same critique applies to Jesuit morality. It was the Company's aim to control the conscience by direction and confession, and especially the conscience of princes, women, youths in high position. To do so by plain speaking and honest dealing was clearly dangerous. The world had had enough of Dominican austerity and dogmatism. To do so by open toleration and avowed cynicism did not suit the temper of the time. A reform of the monastic orders and the regular clergy had been undertaken by the Church. Pardoners, palmers, indulgence-mongers, jolly Franciscan confessors, and such-like folk were out of date. But the Jesuits were equal to the exigencies of the moment. We have seen how Ignatius recommended fishers of souls to humour queasy consciences. His successors expanded and applied the hint.—You must not begin by talking about spiritual things to people immersed in worldly interests. That is as simple as trying to fish without bait. On the contrary, you must insinuate yourself into their confidence by studying their habits, and spying out their propensities. You must appear to notice little at the first, and show yourself a good companion. When you become acquainted with the bosom sins and pleasant vices of folk in high position, you can lead them on the path of virtue at your pleasure. You must certainly tell them then that indulgence in sensuality, falsehood, fraud, violence, covetousness and tyrannical oppression is unconditionally wrong. Make no show of compromise with evil in the gross; but refine away the evil by distinctions, reservations, hypothetical conditions, until it disappears. Explain how hard it is to know whether a sin be venial or mortal, and how many chances there are against its being in any strict sense a sin at all. Do not leave folk to their own blunt sense of right and wrong, but let them admire the finer edge of your scalpel, while you shred up evil into morsels they can hardly see. A ready way may thus be opened for the satisfaction of every human desire without falling into theological faults. The advantages are manifest. You will be able to absolve with a clear conscience. Your penitent will abound in gratitude and open out his heart to you. You will fulfil your function as confessor and counsellor. He will be secured for the sacred ends of our Society, and will contribute to the greater glory of God.—It was thus that the Jesuit labyrinth of casuistry, with its windings, turnings, secret chambers, whispering galleries, blind alleys, issues of evasion, came into existence; the whole vicious and monstrous edifice being crowned with the saving virtue of obedience and the theory of ends justifying means. After the irony of Pascal, the condensed rage of La Chalotais, and the grave verdict of the Parlement of Paris (1762), it is not necessary now to refute the errors or to expose the abominations of this casuistry in detail.[18] Yet it cannot be

[18] Having mentioned the names of these illustrious Frenchmen, I feel bound to point out how accurately their criticism of the Jesuits was anticipated by Paolo Sarpi. His correspondence between the years 1608 and 1622 demonstrates that this body of Social corrupters had been early recognised by him in their true light. Sarpi calls them 'sottilissimi maestri in mal fare,' 'donde esce ogni falsità e bestemmia,' 'il vero morbo Gallico,' 'peste pubblica,' 'peste del mondo' (*Letters*, vol. i. pp. 142, 183, 245, ii. 82, 109). He says that they 'hanno messo l' ultima mano a stabilire una corruzione universale' (*ib.* vol. i. p. 304). By their equivocations and mental reservations 'fanno essi prova di gabbare Iddio' (*ib.* vol. ii. p. 82). 'La menzogna non iscusano soltanto ma lodano' (*ib.* vol. ii. p. 106). So far, the utterances which I have quoted might pass for the rhetoric of mere spite. But the portrait gradually becomes more definite in details limned from life. 'The Jesuits have so many loopholes for escape, pretexts, colours of insinuation, that they are more changeful than the Sophist of Plato; and when one thinks to have caught them between thumb and finger, they wriggle out and vanish' (*ib.* vol. i. p. 230). 'The Jesuit fathers have methods of acquiring in this world, and making their neophytes acquire, heaven without diminution, or rather with augmen-

wholly passed in silence here; for its application materially favoured the influence of Jesuits in modern Europe.

The working of the Company, as we have seen, depended upon a skilful

tation, of this life's indulgences' (*ib.* vol. i. p. 313). 'The Jesuit fathers used to confer Paradise; they now have become dispensers of fame in this world' (*ibid.* p. 363). 'When they seek entrance into any place, they do not hesitate to make what promises may be demanded of them, possessing as they do the art of escape by lying with equivocations and mental reservations' (*ib.* vol. ii. p. 147). 'The Jesuit is a man of every colour; he repeats the marvel of the chameleon' (*ibid.* p. 105). 'When they play a losing game, they yet rise winners from the table. For it is their habit to insinuate themselves upon any condition demanded, having arts enough whereby to make themselves masters of those who bind them by prescribed rules. They are glad to enter in the guise of galley-slaves with irons on their ankles; since, when they have got in, they will find no difficulty in loosing their own bonds and binding others' (*ibid.* p. 134). 'They command two arts: the one of escaping from the bonds and obligations of any vow or promise they shall have made, by means of equivocation, tacit reservation, and mental restriction; the other of insinuating, like the hedgehog, into the narrowest recesses, being well aware that when they unfold their piercing bristles, they will obtain the full possession of the dwelling and exclude its master' (*ibid.* p. 144). 'Everybody in Italy is well aware how they have wrought confession into an art. They never receive confidences under that seal without disclosing all particulars in the conferences of their Society; and that with the view of using confession to the advantage of their Order and the Church. At the same time they preach the doctrine that the seal of the confessional precludes a penitent from disclosing what the confessor may have said to him, albeit his utterances have had no reference to sins or to the safety of the soul' (*ib.* vol. ii. p. 108). 'Should the Jesuits in France get hold of education, they will dominate the university, and eradicate sound letters. Yet why do I speak of healthy literature? I ought to have said good and wholesome doctrine, the which is verily mortal to that Company' (*ibid.* p. 162). 'Every species of vice finds its patronage in them. The avaricious trust their maxims, for trafficking in spiritual commodities; the superstitious, for substituting kisses upon images for the exercise of Christian virtues; the base fry of ambitious upstarts, for cloaking every act of scoundreldom with a veil of holiness. The indifferent find in them a palliative for their spiritual deadness; and whoso fears no God has a visible God ready made for him, whom he may worship with merit to his soul. In fine, there is nor perjury, nor sacrilege, nor parricide, nor incest, nor rapine, nor fraud, nor treason, which cannot be masked as meritorious beneath the mantle of their dispensation' (*ibid.* p. 330). 'I apprehend the difficulty of attacking their teachings; seeing that they merge their own interests with those of the Papacy, and that not only in the article of Pontifical authority, but in all points. At present they stand for themselves upon the ground of equivocations. But believe me, they will adjust this also, and that speedily; forasmuch as they are omnipotent in the Roman Court, and the Pope himself fears them' (*ibid.* p. 333). 'Had S. Peter known the creed of the Jesuits, he could have found a way to deny our Lord without sinning' (*ibid.* p. 353). 'The Roman Court will never condemn Jesuit doctrine; for this is the secret of its empire—a secret of the highest and most capital importance, whereby those who openly refuse to worship it are excommunicated, and those who would do so if they dared are held in check' (*ibid.* p.105). The object of this lengthy note is to vindicate for Sarpi a prominent and early place among those candid analysts of Jesuitry who now are lost in the great light of Pascal's genius. Sarpi's *Familiar Letters* have for my mind even more weight than the famous *Lettres Provinciales* of Pascal. They were written with no polemical or literary bias, at a period when Jesuitry was in its prime; and their force as evidence is strengthened by their obvious spontaneity. A book of some utility was published in 1703 at Salzburg (?), under the title of *Artes Jesuiticae* by Christianus Aletophilus. This contains a compendium of those passages in casuistical writings on which Pascal based his brilliant satires. Paul Bert's modern work, *La Morale des Jesuites* (Paris: Charpentier, 1881), is intended to prove that recent casuistical treatises of the school repeat those ancient perversions of sound morals.

manipulation of apparently hard-and-fast principles. The Declarations explained away the Constitutions; and an infinite number of minute exceptions and distinctions volatilised vows and obligations into ether. Transferring the same method to the sphere of ethics, they so wrought upon the precepts of the moral law, whether expressed in holy writ, in the ecclesiastical decrees, or in civil jurisprudence, as to deprive them of their binding force. The subtlest elasticity had been gained for the machinery of the order by casuistical interpretation. A like elasticity was secured for the control and government of souls by an identical process. It was no wonder that the Jesuits became rapidly fashionable as confessors. The plainest prohibitions were as wax in their hands. The Decalogue laid down as rules for conduct: 'Thou shalt not steal;' 'Thou shalt not kill;' 'Thou shalt not commit adultery.' Christ spiritualised these rules into their essence: 'Thou shalt love thy neighbour as thyself;' 'Whosoever looketh on a woman to lust after her hath committed adultery already with her in his heart.' It is manifest that both the old and the new covenant, upon which modern Christianity is supposed to rest, suffered no transactions in matters so clear to the human conscience. Jesus himself refined upon the legality of the Mosaic code by defining sin as egotism or concupiscence. But the Company of Jesus took pains in their casuistry to provide attenuating circumstances for every sin in detail. By their doctrines of the invincible erroneous conscience, of occult compensation, of equivocation, of mental reservation, of probabilism, and of philosophical sin, they afforded loopholes for the gratification of every passion and for the commission of every crime. Instead of maintaining that any injury done to a neighbour is wrong, they multiplied instances in which a neighbour may be injured. Instead of holding firm to Christ's verdict that sexual vice is implicit in licentious desire, they analysed the sensual modes of crude voluptuousness, taxed each in turn at arbitrary values, and provided plausible excuses for indulgence. Instead of laying it down as a broad principle that men must keep their word, they taught them how to lie with spiritual impunity and with credit to their reputation as sons of the Church. Thus the inventive genius of the casuist, bent on dissecting immorality and reducing it to classes; the interrogative ingenuity of the confessor, pruriently inquisitive into private experience; the apologetic subtlety of the director, eager to supply his penitent with salves and anodynes; were all alike and all together applied to anti-social contamination in matters of lubricity, and to anti-social corruption in matters of dishonesty, fraud, falsehoods, illegality and violence. The single doctrine of probabilism, as Pascal abundantly proved, facilitates the commission of crime; for there is no perverse act which some casuist of note has not plausibly excused.

It may be urged that confession and direction, as adopted by the Catholic Church, bring the abominations of casuistry logically in their train. Priests who have to absolve sinners must be familiar with sin in all its branches. In the confessional they will be forced to listen to recitals, the exact bearings of which they cannot understand unless they are previously instructed. Therefore the writings of Sanchez, Diana, Liguori, Burchard, Billuard, Rousselot, Gordon, Gaisson, are put into their hands at an early age—works which reveal more secrets of impudicity than Aretino has described, or Commodus can have practised—works which recommend more craft and treachery and fraud and falsehood than Machiavelli accorded to his misbegotten Saviour of Society. In these writings men vowed to celibacy probe the foulest labyrinths of sexual impurity; men claiming to stand outside the civil order and the state imbibe false theories upon property and probity and public duty.

The root of the matter is wrong indubitably. It is contrary to good government that a sacerdotal class, by means of confession and direction, should be placed in a position of deciding upon conduct. It is revolting to human dignity that this same class, without national allegiance and without domestic ties, should have the opportunity of infecting young minds by unhealthy questionings and dishonourable suggestions. But this wrong, which is inherent in the modern Catholic system, becomes an atrocity when it is employed, as the Jesuits employed it, as an instrument for moulding and controlling society in their own interest.

While the Jesuits rendered themselves obnoxious to criticism by their treatment of the individual in his private and social capacity, they speedily became what Hallam cautiously styles 'rather dangerous supporters of the See of Rome' in public and political affairs. The ultimate failure of their diplomacy and intrigue over the whole field of modern statecraft inclines historians of the present epoch to underrate their mechanics of obstruction, and to underestimate the many occasions on which they did successfully retard the progress of civil government and intellectual freedom. It were wiser to regard them in the same light as fanatics laying stones upon a railway, or of dynamiters blowing up an emperor or a corner of Westminster Hall. The final end of the nefarious traffic may not be attained. But credit can be claimed by those who took their part in it, for the wreck of express trains, the perturbation of cities, and the mourning of peaceable families. And thus it was with the Jesuits. Though the results of their political intrigues have not corresponded to their hopes, they yet worked appreciable mischief by the organisation of the League in France, and the Thirty Years' War in Germany, and by their revolutionary theories which infected Europe with conspiracy and murder. Their method was not original. Machiavelli had expounded the doctrines they put in practice. He taught that in a desperate state of the nation men may have recourse to treachery and violence. The nation of the Jesuits was a hybrid between their Order and Catholicism. The peril to the Church was imminent; its decadence demanded desperate remedies. They invoked regicide, revolt, and treason, to effect an impossible cure.

The political theory of the Jesuits was deduced from their fundamental principle of obedience to the Church. They maintained that the ecclesiastical is *jure divino* superior to the secular power. The Pope through God's commission and appointment sways the Church; the Church takes rank above the State, as the soul above the body. Consequently, the first allegiance of a Christian nation, together with its secular rulers, belongs of right to the Supreme Pontiff. The people is the real sovereign; and kings are delegates from the people, with authority which they can only justly exercise so long as they remain in obedience to Rome. It follows from these positions that every nation must refuse fealty to an irreligious or contumacious ruler. In the last resort they may lawfully remove him by murder; and they are *ipso facto* in a state of mortal sin if they elect or recognise a heretic as sovereign. This theory sprang from the writings of the English Jesuits, Allen and Parsons. It was elaborated in Rome by Cardinal Bellarmino, applied in Spain by Suarez and Mariana, and openly preached in France by Jean Boucher. The best energies of Paolo Sarpi were devoted to combating the main position of ecclesiastical supremacy. His works had a salutary effect by delimiting the relations of the Church to the State, and by demonstrating even to Catholics the pernicious results of acknowledging a Papal overlordship in temporal affairs. At the same time the boldly democratic principle of the sovereignty of the people, which the Jesuits advanced in order to establish their doctrine of ecclesiastical superiority, provoked opposition. It led to the contrary hypothesis of the Divine Right of sovereigns, which found favour in Protestant kingdoms and especially in England under the Stuart dynasty. When the French Catholics resolved to terminate the discords of their country by the recognition of Henri IV., they had recourse to this argument for justifying their obedience to a heretic. It was felt by all sound thinkers and by every Patriot in Europe that the Papal prerogatives claimed by the Jesuits were too inconsistent with national liberties to be tolerated. The zeal of the Society had clearly outrun its discretion; and the free discussion of the theory of government which their insolent assumptions stimulated, weakened the cause they sought to strengthen. Their ingenuity overreached itself.

This, however, was as nothing compared with the hostility evoked by their unscrupulous application of these principles in practice. There was hardly a plot against established rule in Protestant countries with which they were not known or believed to be connected. The invasion of Ireland in 1579, the judicial murder of the Regent Morton in Scotland, and Babington's conspiracy against Elizabeth, emanated from their councils. They were held responsible for the attempted murder of the Prince of Orange in 1580, and for his actual murder in 1584. They loudly applauded Jacques Clément, the assassin of Henri III. in 1589, as 'the eternal glory of France.'[19] Numerous unsuccessful attacks upon the life of Henri IV., culminating in that of Jean Chastel in 1594, caused their expulsion from France. When they returned in 1603, they set to work again[20]; and the assassin Ravaillac, who succeeded in removing the obnoxious champion of European independence in 1610, was probably in-

[19] See Mariana, *De Rege*, lib. i. cap. 6. This book, be it remembered, was written for the instruction of the heir-apparent, afterwards Philip III.

[20] Henri IV. let them return to France in mere dread of their machinations against him. See Sully, vol. v. p. 113.

spired by their doctrine.[21] They had a hand in the Gunpowder Plot of 1605, and were thought by some to have instigated the Massacre of S. Bartholomew. They fomented the League of the Guises, which had for its object a change in the French dynasty. They organised the Thirty Years' War, and they procured the revocation of the Edict of Nantes. If it is not possible to connect them immediately with all and each of the criminal acts laid to their charge, the fact that a Jesuit in every case was lurking in the background, counts by the force of cumulative evidence heavily against them, and explains the universal suspicion with which they came to be regarded as factious intermeddlers in the concerns of nations. Moreover, their written words accuse them; for the tyrannicide of heretics was plainly advocated in their treatises on government. So profound was the conviction of their guilt, that the death of Sixtus V. in 1590, predicted by Bellarmino, the sudden death of Urban VII. in the same year, and the death of Clement VIII. in 605, also predicted by Bellarmino—these three Popes being ill-affected toward the Order—were popularly ascribed to their agency. But of their practical intervention there is no proof. Old age and fever must be credited, in these as in other cases, with the decease of Roman Pontiffs supposed to have been poisoned.

It is not, however, to be wondered that sooner or later the Jesuits made themselves insupportable by their intrigues in all the countries where they were established.[22] Even to the Papacy itself they proved too irksome to be borne. The Company showed plainly that what they meant by obedience to Rome was obedience to a Rome controlled and fashioned by themselves. It was their ambition to stand in the same relation to the Pope as the Shogun to the Mikado of Japan. Nor does the analysis of their opinions fail to justify the condemnation passed upon them by the Parlement of Paris in 1762. 'These doctrines tend to destroy the natural law, that rule of manners which God Himself has imprinted on the hearts of men, and in consequence to sever all the bonds of civil society, by the authorisation of theft, falsehood, perjury, the most culpable impurity, and in a word each passion and each crime of human weakness; to obliterate all sentiments of humanity by favouring homicide and parricide; and to annihilate the authority of sovereigns in the State.'

Great psychological and pathological interest attaches to the study of the Jesuit Order. To withhold our admiration from the zeal, energy, self-devotion and constructive ability of its founders, would be impos-

[21] Sarpi, who was living at the time of Henri's murder, and who saw his best hopes for Italy and the Church of God extinguished by that crime, at first credited the Jesuits with the deliberate instigation of Ravaillac. He gradually came to the conclusion that, though they were not directly responsible, their doctrine of regicide had inflamed the fanatic's imagination. See, in succession, *Letters*, vol. ii. pp. 78, 79, 81, 83, 86, 91, 105, 121, 170, 181, 192.

[22] Expelled from Venice in 1606, from Bohemia in 1618, from Naples and the Netherlands in 1622, from Russia in 1676, from Portugal in 1759, from Spain in 1767, from France in 1764. Suppressed by the Bull of Clement XIV. in 1773. Restored in 1814, as an instrument against the Revolution.

sible. Equally futile would it be to affect indifference before the sinister spectacle of so world-embracing an organism, persistently maintained in action for an anti-social end. There is something Roman in the colossal proportions of Loyola's idea, something Roman in the durability of the structure which perpetuates it. Yet the philosopher cannot but agree with the vulgar in his final judgment on the odiousness of these sacerdotal despots, these unflinching foes not merely to the heroes of the human intellect and to the champions of right conduct, but also to the very angels of Christianity. That the Jesuits should claim to have been founded by Him who preached the Sermon on the Mount, that they should flaunt their motto, A.M.D.G., in the sight of Him who spake from Sinai, is one of those practical paradoxes in which the history of decrepit religions abounds.

CHAPTER V

SOCIAL AND DOMESTIC MORALS: PART I

How did the Catholic Revival affect Italian Society?—Difficulty of Answering this Question—Frequency of Private Crimes of Violence—Homicides and Bandits—Savage Criminal Justice—Paid Assassins—Toleration of Outlaws—Honourable Murder—Example of the Lucchese Army—State of the Convents—The History of Virginia de Leyva—Lucrezia Buonvisi—The True Tale of the Cenci—The Brothers of the House of Massimo—Vittoria Accoramboni—The Duchess of Palliano—Wife-Murders—The Family of Medici.

We are naturally led to inquire what discernible effect the Catholic Revival and the Counter-Reformation had upon the manners and morals of the Italians as a nation. Much has been said about the contrast between intellectual refinement and almost savage license which marked the Renaissance. Yet it can with justice be maintained that, while ferocity and brutal sensuality survived from the Middle Ages, humanism, by means of the new ideal it introduced, tended to civilise and educate the race. Now, however, the Church was stifling culture and attempting to restore that ecclesiastical conception of human life which the Renaissance had superseded. Did, then, her resuscitated Catholicism succeed in permeating the Italians with the spirit of Christ and of the Gospel? Were the nobles more quiet in their demeanour, less quarrelsome and haughty, more law-abiding and less given to acts of violence, than they had been in the previous period? Were the people more contented and less torn by factions, happier in their homes, less abandoned to the insanities of baleful superstitions?

It is obviously difficult to answer these questions with either completeness or accuracy. In the first place, we have no right to expect that the religious revival, signalised by the Tridentine Council, should have made itself immediately felt in the sphere of national conduct. In the second place, it was not, like the German Reformation, a renewal of Christianity at its sources, but a resuscitation of mediæval Catholicity, in direct antagonism to the intellectual tendencies of the age. The new learning among northern races disintegrated that system of ideas upon which mediæval society rested; but it also introduced religious and moral conceptions more vital than those ideas in their decadence. In Italy the disintegrating process had been no less thorough, nay far more subtle and pervasive. Yet the new learning had not led the nation to attempt a reconstruction of primitive Christianity. The Catholic Revival gave nothing vital or enthusiastic to the conscience of the race. It brought the old creeds, old cult, old superstitions, old abuses back, with stricter discipline and under a *régime* of terror. Meanwhile, it resolutely ranged its forces in opposition to what had been salutary and life-giving in the mental movement of the Renaissance. It compelled people who had watched the dawning of a new light, to shut their eyes upon that dayspring. It extinguished the studies of the Classical Revival; bade philosophers return to Thomas of Aquino; threatened thinkers with the dungeon or the stake who should presume to pass the Pillars of Hercules, when a whole Atlantic of knowledge had been opened to their curiosity. Under these circumstances it was impossible that a revolution, so retrograde in its nature, checking the tide of national energy in full flow, should have exercised a healthy influence over the Italian temperament at large. We have a right to expect, what in fact we find, the advent of hypocrisy and ceremonial observances, but little actual amendment in manners. In the third place, the question is still further complicated by the Catholic Revival having been effected concurrently with the establishment of the Spanish Hegemony. At the end of the first chapter of this volume I pointed out the evils brought on Italy by her servitude to a foreign and unsympathetic despot: the decline of commercial activity, the multiplication of slothful lordlings, the depression of industry, the diminution of wealth, and the suffering of the lower classes from pirates, bandits, and tax-gatherers. These conditions were sufficient to demoralise a people. And mediæval Catholicism, restored by edict, enforced by the Inquisition, propagated by Jesuits, was not of the fine enthusiastic quality to counteract them. Servile in its conception, it sufficed to bridle and benumb a race of serfs, but not to soften or to purify their brutal instincts.[1]

In this chapter I shall not attempt a general survey of Italian society.[2] I shall content myself with supplying materials for the formation of a judgment by narrating some of the most remarkable domestic tragedies of the second half of the sixteenth century, choosing those only which rest upon well-sifted documentary evidence, and which bring the social conditions of the country into strong relief. Before engaging in these historical romances, it will be well to preface them with a few general remarks upon the state of manners they will illustrate.

The first thing which strikes a student of Italy between 1530 and 1600 is that crimes of violence, committed by private individuals for personal ends, continued steadily upon the increase.[3] Compared with the later

[1] The last section of Loyola's *Exercitia* is an epitome of post-Tridentine Catholicism, though penned before the opening of the Council. In its last paragraph it inculcates the fear of God: 'neque porro is timor solum, quem filialem appellamus, qui pius est ac sanctus maxime; verum etiam alter, servilis dictus' (*Inst. Soc. Jesu.* vol. iv. p. 173).

[2] An interesting survey of this wider kind has been attempted by U. A. Canello for the whole sixteenth century in his *Storia della Lett. It. nel Secolo XVI.* (Milano Vallardi, 1880). He tries to demonstrate that, in the sphere of private life, Italian society gradually refined the brutal lusts of the Middle Ages, and passed through fornication to a true conception of woman as man's companion in the family. The theme is bold; and the author seems to have based it upon too slight acquaintance with the real conditions of the Middle Ages.

[3] Galluzzi, in his *Storia del Granducato di Toscana*, vol. iv. p. 34, estimates the murders committed in Florence alone during the eighteen months which followed the death of Cosimo I., at 186.

Middle Ages, compared with the Renaissance, this period is distinguished by extraordinary ferocity of temper and by an almost unparalleled facility of bloodshed.[4] The broad political and religious contests which had torn the country in the first years of the sixteenth century, were pacified. Foreign armies had ceased to dispute the provinces of Italy. The victorious powers of Spain, the Church, and the protected principalities, seemed secure in the possession of their gains. But those international quarrels which kept the nation in unrest through a long period of municipal wars, ending in the horrors of successive invasions, were now succeeded by an almost universal discord between families and persons. Each province, each city, each village became the theatre of private feuds and assassinations. Each household was the scene of homicide and empoisonment. Italy presented the spectacle of a nation armed against itself, not to decide the issue of antagonistic political principles by civil strife, but to gratify lawless passions—cupidity, revenge, resentment—by deeds of personal high-handedness. Among the common people of the country and the towns, crimes of brutality and bloodshed were of daily occurrence; every man bore weapons for self-defence and for attack upon his neighbour. The aristocracy and the upper classes of the *bourgeoisie* lived in a perpetual state of mutual mistrust, ready upon the slightest occasion of fancied affront to blaze forth into murder. Much of this savagery was due to the false ideas of honour and punctilio which the Spaniards introduced. Quarrels arose concerning a salute, a title, a question of precedence, a seat in church, a place in the prince's antechamber, a meeting in the public streets. Noblemen were ushered on their way by servants, who measured distances and took the height of daïs or of bench, before their master committed his dignity by advancing a step beyond the minimum that was due. Love-affairs and the code of honour with regard to women opened endless sources of implacable jealousies, irreconcileable hatreds, and offences that could only be wiped out with blood. On each and all of these occasions, the sword was ready to the right hand; and where this generous weapon would not reach, the harquebuss and knife of paid assassins were employed without compunction.[5] We must not, however, ascribe this condition of society wholly or chiefly to Spanish influences. It was in fact a survival of mediæval habits under altered circumstances. During the municipal wars of the thirteenth century, and afterwards during the struggle of the despots for ascendency, the nation had become accustomed to internecine contests which set party against party, household against household, man against

[4] In drawing up these paragraphs I am greatly indebted to a vigorous passage by Signor Salvatore Bonghi in his *Storia di Lucrezia Buonvisi*, pp. 7-9, of which I have made free use, translating his words when they served my purpose, and interpolating such further details as might render the picture more complete.

[5] The lax indulgence accorded by the Jesuit casuists to every kind of homicide appears in the extracts from those writers collected in *Artes Jesuiticae* (Salisburgi, 1703, pp. 75-83). Tamburinus went so far as to hold that if a man mixed poison for his enemy, and a friend came in and drank it up before his eyes, he was not bound to warn his friend, nor was he guilty of his friend's death (*ib.* p. 135, Art. 651).

man. These humours in the cities, as Italian historians were wont to call them, had been partially suppressed by the confederation of the five great Powers at the close of the fifteenth century, and also by a prevalent urbanity of manners. At that epoch, moreover, they were systematised and controlled by the methods of *condottiere* warfare, which offered a legitimate outlet to the passions of turbulent young men. But when Italy sank into the sloth of pacification after the settlement of Charles V. at Bologna in 1530, when there were no longer *condottieri* to levy troops in rival armies, when political parties ceased in the cities, the old humours broke out again under the aspect of private and personal feuds. Though the names of Guelf and Ghibelline had lost their meaning, these factions reappeared, and divided Milan, the towns of Romagna, the villages of the Campagna. In the place of *condottieri* arose brigand chiefs, who, like Piccolomini and Sciarra, placed themselves at the head of regiments and swept the country on marauding expeditions. Instead of exiles driven by victorious parties in the state to seek precarious living on a foreign soil, bandits proscribed for acts of violence abounded. Thus the habits which had been created through centuries of political ferment, subsisted when the nation was at rest in servitude, assuming baser and more selfish forms of ferocity. The end of the sixteenth century witnessed the final degeneration and corruption of a mediæval state of warfare, which the Renaissance had checked, but which the miseries of foreign invasions had resuscitated by brutalising the population, and which now threatened to disintegrate society in aimless anarchy and private lawlessness.

It must not be imagined that governments and magistracies were slack in their pursuit of criminals. Repressive statutes, proclamations of outlawry, and elaborate prosecutions succeeded one another with unwearied conscientiousness. The revenues of states were taxed to furnish blood-money and to support spies. Large sums were invariably offered for the capture or assassination of escaped delinquents; and woe to the wretches who became involved in criminal proceedings! Witnesses were tortured with infernal cruelty. Convicted culprits suffered horrible agonies before their death, or were condemned to languish out a miserable life in pestilential dungeons. But the very inhumanity of this judicial method, without mercy for the innocent from whom evidence could be extorted, and frequently inequitable in the punishments assigned to criminals of varying degrees of guilt, taught the people to defy justice and encouraged them in brutality. They found it more tolerable to join the bands of brigands who preyed upon their fields and villages, than to assist rulers who governed so unequally and cruelly. We know, for instance, that a robber chief, Marianazzo, refused the Pope's pardon, alleging that the profession of brigandage was more lucrative and offered greater security of life than any trade within the walls of Rome. Thus the bandits of that generation occupied the specious attitude of opposition to oppressive governments. There were, moreover, many favourable chances for a homicide. The Church was jealous of her rights of sanctuary. Whatever may have been her zeal for orthodoxy, she showed herself an indulgent mother to culprits who demanded an asylum. Feudal nobles prided themselves on protecting refugees within their fiefs and castles. There were innumerable petty domains left, which carried privileges of signorial courts and local justice. Cardinals, ambassadors, and powerful princes claimed immunity from common jurisdiction in their palaces, the courts and basements of which soon became the resort of escaped criminals. No extradition treaties subsisted between the several and numerous states into which Italy was then divided, so that it was only necessary to cross a frontier in order to gain safety from the law. The position of an outlaw in that case was tolerably secure, except against private vengeance or the cupidity of professional cutthroats, who gained an honest livelihood by murdering bandits with a good price on their heads. Condemned for the most part in their absence, these homicides entered a recognised and not dishonourable class. They were tolerated, received, and even favoured by neighbouring princes, who generally had some grudge against the state from which the outlaws fled. After obtaining letters of safe-conduct and protection, they enrolled themselves in the militia of their adopted country, while the worst of them became spies or secret agents of police. No government seems to have regarded crimes of violence with severity, provided these had been committed on a foreign soil. Murders for the sake of robbery or rape were indeed esteemed ignoble. But a man who had killed an avowed enemy, or had shed blood in the heat of a quarrel, or had avenged his honour by the assassination of a sister convicted of light love, only established a reputation for bravery which stood him in good stead. He was likely to make a stout soldier, and he had done nothing socially discreditable. On the contrary, if he had been useful in ridding the world of an outlaw some prince wished to kill, this murder made him a hero. In addition to the blood-money, he not unfrequently received lucrative office or a pension for life.

A very curious state of things resulted from these customs. States depended in large measure for the execution of their judicial sentences in cases of manslaughter and treason, upon foreign murderers and traitors. Towns were full of outlaws, each with a price upon his head, mutually suspicious, individually desirous of killing some fellow-criminal and thereby enriching his own treasury. If he were successful, he received a fair sum of money, with privileges and immunities from the state which had advertised the outlaw; and not unfrequently he obtained the further right of releasing one or more bandits from penalties of death or prison. It may be imagined at what cross-purposes the outlaws dwelt together, with crimes in many states accumulated on their shoulders; and what peril might ensue to society should they combine together, as indeed they tried to do in Bedmar's conspiracy against Venice. Meanwhile, the states kept this floating population of criminals in check by various political and social contrivances, which grew up from the exigencies and the habits of the moment. Instead of recruiting soldiers from the stationary population, it became usual, when a war was imminent, to enrol outlaws. Thus, when Lucca had to make an inroad into Garfagnana in 1613, the Republic issued a proclamation promising pardon and pay to those of its own bandits who should join its standard. Men to the number of 591 answered this call, and the little war which followed was conducted with more than customary fierceness.[6] Even the ordinary police and guards of cities were composed of fugitives from other states, care being taken to select by preference those who came stained only with honourable bloodshed. In 1593 the guard of the palace of Lucca was reinforced by the addition of forty-three men, among whom four were bandits for wounds inflicted upon enemies in open fight; twelve for homicide in duel sword to sword; five for the murder of more than one person in similar encounters; one for the murder of a sister and the wounding of her seducer; two for mutilating an enemy in the face; one for unlawful recruiting; one for wounding; one for countenancing bandits; and sixteen simple refugees.[7] The phrases employed to describe these men in the official report are sufficiently illustrative of contemporary moral standards. Thus we read 'Banditi per omicidi semplici *da buono a buono*, a sangue caldo, da spada a spada, *o di nemici*.' 'Per omicidio d' una sorella *per causa d' onore*.' To murder an enemy or a sister who had misbehaved herself was accounted excusable.

The prevalence of lawlessness encouraged a domestic custom which soon grew into a system. This was the maintenance of so-called *bravi* by nobles and folk rich enough to afford so expensive a luxury. The outlaws found their advantage in the bargain which they drew with their employers; for besides being lodged, fed, clothed and armed, they obtained a certain protection from the spies and professional murderers who were always on the watch to kill them. Their masters used them to defend their persons when a feud was being carried on, or directed them against private enemies whom they wished to injure. It is not uncommon in the annals of these times to read: 'Messer So-and-so, having received an affront from the Count of V, employed the services of three *bravi*, valiant fellows up to any mischief, with whom he retired to his country house.' Or again: 'The Marquis, perceiving that his neighbour had a grudge against him on account of the Signora Lucrezia, thought it prudent to increase his body-guard, and therefore added Pepi and Lo Scarabone, bandits from Tuscany for murders of a priest and a citizen, to his household.' Or again: 'During the vacation of the Holy See the Baron X had, as usual, engaged men-at-arms for the protection of his palace.'

It course of time it became the mark of birth and wealth to lodge a rabble of such rascals. They lived on terms of familiarity with their employer, shared his secrets, served him in his amours, and executed any devil's job he chose to command. Apartments in the basement of the palace were assigned to them, so that a nobleman's house continued to resemble the castle of a mediæval baron. But the *bravi*, unlike soldiery, were rarely employed in honourable business. They formed a permanent element of treachery and violence within the social organism. Not a

[6] See Salvatore Bonghi, *op. cit.* p. 159.
[7] Bonghi, *op. cit.* p. 159, note.

little singular were the relations thus established. The community of crime, involving common interests and common perils, established a peculiar bond between the noble and his *bravo*. This was complexioned by a certain sense of 'honour rooted in dishonour,' and by a faint reflection from elder retainership. The compact struck between landowner and bandit parodied that which drew feudal lord and wandering squire together. There was something ignobly noble in it, corresponding to the confused conscience and perilous conditions of the epoch.

While studying this organised and half-tolerated system of social violence, we are surprised to observe how largely it was countenanced and how frequently it was set in motion by the Church. In a previous chapter on the Jesuits I have adverted to their encouragement of assassination for ends which they considered sacred. In a coming chapter upon Sarpi I shall show to what extent the Roman prelacy was implicated in more than one attempt to take away his life. The chiefs of the Church, then, instead of protesting against this vice of corrupt civilisation in Italy, lent the weight of their encouragement to what strikes us now, not only as eminently unchristian, but also as pernicious to healthy national conditions of existence. We may draw two conclusions from these observations: first, that religions, except in the first fervour of their growth and forward progress, recognise the moral conventions of the society which they pretend to regulate; secondly, that it is well-nigh impossible for men of one century to sympathise with the ethics of a past and different epoch. We cannot comprehend the regicidal theories of the Jesuits or the murderous intrigues of a Borghese Pontiff's Court, without admitting that priests, specially dedicated to the service of Christ and to the propagation of His gospel, felt themselves justified in employing the immoral and unchristian means which social custom placed at their disposal for ridding themselves of inconvenient enemies. This is at the same time their defence as human beings in the sixteenth century and their indictment as self-styled and professed successors of the Founder who rebuked Peter in the Garden of Gethsemane.

To make general remarks upon the state of sexual morality at this epoch, is hardly needful. Yet there are some peculiar circumstances which deserve to be noticed, in order to render the typical stories which I mean to relate intelligible. We have already seen that society condoned the murder of a sister by a brother, if she brought dishonour on her family; and the same privilege was extended to a husband in the case of a notoriously faithless wife. Such homicides did not escape judicial sentence, but they shared in the conventional toleration which was extended to murders in hot blood or in the prosecution of a feud. The state of the Italian convents at this period gave occasion to crimes in which women played a prominent part. After the Council of Trent reforms were instituted in religious houses. But they could not be immediately carried out; and, meanwhile, the economical changes which were taking place in the commercial aristocracy, filled nunneries with girls who had no vocation for a secluded life. Less money was yearly made in trade; merchants became nobles, investing their capital in land, and securing their estates on their eldest sons by entails. It followed that they could not afford to marry all their daughters with dowries befitting the station they aspired to assume. A large percentage of well-born women, accustomed to luxury and vitiated by bad examples in their homes, were thus thrown on a monastic life. Signor Bonghi reckons that at the end of the sixteenth century, more than five hundred girls, who had become superfluous in noble families, crowded the convents in the single little town of Luca. At a later epoch there would have been no special peril in this circumstance. But at the time with which we are now occupied, an objectionable license still survived from earlier ages. The nunneries obtained evil notoriety as houses of licentious pleasure, to which soldiers and youths of dissolute habits resorted by preference.[8] There appears to have been a specific profligate fanaticism, a well-marked morbid partiality for these amours with cloistered virgins. The young men who prosecuted them, obtained a nickname indicative of their absorbing passion.[9] The attraction of mystery and danger had something, no doubt, to do with this infatuation; and the fascination that sacrilege has for depraved natures, may also be reckoned into the account. To enjoy a lawless amour was not enough; but to possess a woman who alternated between transports of passion and torments of remorse, added zest to guilty pleasure. For men who habitually tampered with magic arts and believed firmly in the devil, this raised romance to rapture. It was a common thing for debauchees to seek what they called *peripetezie di nuova idea*, or novel and exciting adventures stimulative of a jaded appetite, in consecrated places. At any rate, as will appear in the sequel of this chapter, convent intrigues occupied a large space in the criminal annals of the day.

The Lady of Monza

VIRGINIA MARIA DE LEYVA was a descendant of Charles V.'s general, Antonio de Leyva, who through many years administered the Duchy of

[8] In support of this assertion I translate a letter addressed (Milan, September 15, 1622) by Cardinal Federigo Borromeo to the Prioress of the Convent of S. Margherita at Monza (Dandolo, *Signora di Monza*, p. 132). 'Experience of similar cases has shown how dangerous to your holy state is the vicinity of soldiers, owing to the correspondence which young and idle soldiers continually try to entertain with monasteries, sometimes even under fair and honourable pretexts . . . . Wherefore we have heard with much displeasure that in those places of our diocese where there are convents of nuns and congregations of virgins, ordinary lodgings for the soldiery have been established, called lonely houses (*case erme*), where they are suffered or obliged to dwell through long periods.' The Bishop commands the Prioress to admit no soldier, on any plea of piety, devotion or family relationship, into her convent; to receive no servant or emissary of a soldier; to forbid special services being performed in the chapel at the instance of a soldier; and, finally, to institute a more rigorous system of watch and ward than had been formerly practised.

[9] In Venice, for example, they were called *Monachini*. But the name varied in various provinces.

Milan and died loaded with wealth and honours.[10] For his military service he was rewarded with the principality of Ascoli, the feudal lordship of the town of Monza, and the life-tenure of the city of Pavia. Virginia's father was named Martino, and upon his death her cousin succeeded to the titles of the house. She, for family reasons, entered the convent of S. Margherita at Monza, about the year 1595. Here she occupied a place of considerable importance, being the daughter of the Lord of Monza, of princely blood, wealthy, and allied to the great houses of the Milanese. S. Margherita was a convent of the Umiliate, dedicated to the education of noble girls, in which, therefore, considerable laxity of discipline prevailed.[11] Sister Virginia dwelt at ease within its walls, holding a kind of little court, and exercising an undefined authority in petty affairs which was conceded to her rank. Among her favourite companions at the time of the events I am about to narrate, were numbered the Sisters Ottavia Ricci, Benedetta Homata, Candida Brancolina, and Silvia Casata; she was waited on by a converse sister, Caterina da Meda. Adjoining the convent stood the house and garden of a certain Gianpaolo Osio, who plays the principal part in Virginia's tragedy. He must have been a young man of distinguished appearance; for when Virginia first set eyes upon him from a window overlooking his grounds, she exclaimed: 'Is it possible that one could ever gaze on anything more beautiful?' He attracted her notice as early as the year 1599 or 1600, under circumstances not very favourable to the plan he had in view. His hands were red with the blood of Virginia's bailiff, Giuseppe Molteno, whom he had murdered for some cause unknown to us. During their first interview (Virginia leaning from the window of her friend Candida's cell, and Osio standing on his garden-plot beneath), the young man courteously excused himself for this act of violence, adding that he would serve her even more devotedly than the dead Molteno, and begging to be allowed to write her a letter. When the letter came, it was couched in terms expressive of a lawless passion. Virginia's noble blood rebelled against the insult, and she sent an answer back, rebuffing her audacious suitor. The go-betweens in the correspondence which ensued were the two nuns Ottavia and Benedetta, and a certain Giuseppe Pesen, who served as letter-carrier. Osio did not allow himself to be discouraged by a first refusal, but took the hazardous step of opening his mind to the confessor of the convent, Paolo Arrigone, a priest of San Maurizio in Milan. Arrigone at once lent himself to the intrigue, and taught Osio what kind of letters he should write Virginia. They were to be courteous, respectful, blending pious rhetoric with mystical suggestions of romantic passion. It seems that the confessor composed these documents himself, and advised his fair penitent that there was no sin in perusing them. From correspondence, Osio

[10] The following abstract of the history of Virginia Maria de Leyva is based on Dandolo's *Signora di Monza* (Milano, 1855). Readers of Manzoni's *I Promessi Sposi*, and of Rosini's tiresome novel, *La Signora di Monza*, will be already familiar with her in romance under the name of Gertrude.

[11] Carlo Borromeo found it necessary to suppress the Umiliati. But he left the the female establishment of S. Margherita untouched.

next passed to interviews. By the aid of Arrigone he gained access to the parlour of the convent, where he conversed with Virginia through the bars. In their earlier meetings the lover did not venture beyond compliments and modest protestations of devotion. But as time went on, he advanced to kisses and caresses, and once he made Virginia take a little jewel into her mouth. This was a white loadstone, blessed by Arrigone, and intended to operate like a love-charm. The girl, in fact, began to feel the influence of her seducer. In the final confession which she made, she relates how she fought against temptation. 'Some diabolical force compelled me to go to the window overlooking his garden; and one day when Sister Ottavia told me that Osio was standing there, I fainted from the effort to restrain myself. This happened several times. At one moment I flew into a rage and prayed to God to help me; at another I felt lifted from the ground and forced to go and gaze on him. Sometimes when the fit was on me, I tore my hair; I even thought of killing myself.' Virginia was surrounded by persons who had an interest in helping Osio. Not only the confessor, who was a man of infamous character, but her friends among the nuns, themselves accustomed to intrigue of a like nature, led her down the path to ruin. False keys were made, and one or other of the faithless sisters introduced the young man into the convent at night. When Virginia resisted and enlarged upon the sacrilege of breaking cloister, Arrigone supplied her with a printed book of casuistry, in which it was written that, though it might be sinful for a nun to leave her convent, there was no sin in a man entering it. At last she fell; and for seven years she lived in close intimacy with her lover, passing the nights with him, either in his own house or in one of the cells of S. Margherita. On one occasion, when he had to fly from justice, the girls concealed him in their rooms for fifteen days. The first fruit of this amour was a stillborn child; after giving birth to which Virginia sold all the silver she possessed, and sent a votive tablet to Our Lady of Loreto, on which she had portrayed a nun and baby, kneeling and weeping. 'Twice again I sent the same memorial to our Lady, imploring the grace of liberation from this passion. But the sorceries with which I was surrounded, prevailed. In my bed were found the bones of the dead, hooks of iron, and many other things of which the nuns were well informed. Nay, I would fain have given up my life to save my soul; and so great were my afflictions that in despair I went to throw myself into the well, but was restrained by the image of the Virgin at the bottom of the garden, for which I had a special devotion.' In course of time she gave birth to a little girl, named Francesca, who frequented the convent, and whom Osio legitimated as his child.

It was impossible that a connexion of long standing, known to several accomplices, and corroborated by the presence of the child Francesca, should remain hidden from the world. People began to speak about the fact in Monza. A druggist, named Reinaro Soncini, gossiped somewhat too openly. Osio had him shot one night by a servant in his pay. And now the lovers were engaged in a career of crime, which brought them finally to justice. Virginia's waiting-woman Caterina fell into disgrace with her mistress, and was shut up in a kind of prison by her orders. The girl declared that she would bring the whole bad affair before the superior authorities, and would do so immediately, seeing that Monsignor Barca, the visitor of S. Margherita, was about to make one of his official tours of inspection. This threat cost Caterina her life. About midnight, while a thunderstorm was raging, Virginia, accompanied by her usual associates, Ottavia, Benedetta, Silvia, and Candida, entered the room where the girl was confined. They were followed by Osio, holding in his hand a heavy instrument of wood and iron, called *piede di bicocca*, which he had snatched up in the convent outhouse. He found Caterina lying face downward on the bed, and smashed her skull with a single blow. The body was conveyed by him and the nuns into the fowlhouse of the sisters, whence he removed it on the following night, by the aid of Benedetta, into his own dwelling. From evidence which afterwards transpired, Osio decapitated the corpse, concealed the body in a sort of cellar, and flung the head into an empty well at Velate.

The disappearance of Caterina just before the visitation of Monsignor Barca, roused suspicion; and, though a murder was not immediately apprehended, the guilty associates felt that the cord of fate was being drawn around them. In the autumn of 1607 the tempest broke upon their heads. Virginia was removed from Monza to the convent called Del Bocchetto at Milan; and on November 27 the depositions of the abbess, prioress, and other members of S. Margherita were taken regarding Osio's intrigues, the assassination of Soncini, and the disappearance of Caterina. Among the nuns who had abetted Osio, the two most criminally implicated were Ottavia and Benedetta. Their evidence, if closely scrutinised, must reveal each secret of the past. It was much to Osio's interest, therefore, that they should not fall into the hands of justice; nor had he any difficulty in persuading them to rely on his assistance for contriving their escape to some convent in the Bergamasque territory. We may wonder, by the way, what sort of discipline was then maintained in nunneries, if two so guilty sisters counted upon safe entrance into an asylum, provided only they could leave the diocese of Milan for another.[12] On the night of Thursday, November 30, 1607, Osio came to the wall of the convent garden, and began to break a hole in it, through which Ottavia and Benedetta crept. The three then prowled along the city wall of Monza, till they found a breach wide enough for exit. Afterwards they took a path beside the river Lambro, and stopped for a while at the church of the Madonna delle Grazie. Here the sisters prayed for assistance from our Lady in their journey, and recited the 'Salve Regina' seven times. Then they resumed their walk along the Lambro, and at a certain point Ottavia fell into the river. In her dying depositions she accused Osio of having pushed her in; and there seems little doubt that he did so; for while she

[12] In ecclesiastical affairs the diocese of Milan exercised jurisdiction over that of Bergamo, although Bergamo was subject in civil affairs to Venice. This makes the matter more puzzling.

was struggling in the water, he disengaged his harquebuss from his mantle and struck her several blows upon the head and hands. She pretended to be dead, and was carried down the stream to a place where she contrived to crawl to land. Some peasants came by, whose assistance she implored. But they, observing that she was a nun of S. Margherita by her dress, refused to house her for the rest of the night. They gave her a staff to lean on, and after a painful journey she regained the church of the Grazie at early dawn. Ottavia's wounds upon the head, face, and right hand, inflicted by the stock of Osio's gun, were so serious that, after making a clean breast to her judges, she died of them upon December 26, 1607.

When Osio had pushed Ottavia into the Lambro, and had tried to smash her brains out with his harquebuss, he resumed his midnight journey with Sister Benedetta. They reached an uninhabited house in the country about five or six miles distant from Monza. Here Osio shut Benedetta up in an empty room with a stone bench running along the wall. She remained there all Friday, visited once by her dreaded companion, who brought her bread, cheese, and wine. She abstained from touching any of this food, in fear of poison. About nine in the evening he returned, and bade her prepare to march. They set out again together in the dark; and after walking about three miles they came to a well, down which Osio threw her. The well was deep and had no water in it. Benedetta injured her left side in the fall; and when she had reached the bottom, her would-be murderer flung a big stone on her, which broke her right leg. She contrived to protect her head by gathering stones around it, and lay without moaning or moving, in the fear that Osio would attempt fresh violence unless he thought her dead. From the middle of Friday night until Sunday morning she remained thus, exploring with her eyes the surface of her dungeon. It was dry and strewn with bones. In one corner lay a round black object which bore the aspect of a human skull. As it eventually turned out, this was the head of Caterina, whom Benedetta herself had helped to murder, and which Osio had thrown there. On Sunday, during Mass, the men of the village of Velate were in church, when they heard a voice from outside calling out, 'Help, help! I am at the bottom of this well!' The well, as it happened, was distant some dozen paces from the church door, and Benedetta had timed her call for assistance at a lucky moment. The villagers ran to the spot, and drew her out by means of a man who went down with a rope. She was then taken to the house of a gentleman, Signor Alberico degli Alberici, who, when no one else was charitable enough to receive her, opened his doors to the exhausted victim of that murderous outrage. It may be remarked that the same surgeon who had been employed to report on Ottavia's wounds, now appeared to examine Benedetta. His name was Ambrogio Vimercati. Benedetta was taken to the convent of S. Orsola, where her friend Ottavia lay dying; and after making a full confession, she eventually recovered her health and suffered life-long incarceration in her old convent.

Osio was still at large. On December 20, he addressed a long letter to the Cardinal Federigo Borromeo, in which he vainly attempted to defend himself and throw the blame on his associates. It is a loathsome document, blending fulsome protestations and fawning phrases with brutal denouncements of his victims and treacherous insinuations. One passage deserves notice. 'Who was it,' he says, 'who suggested my correspondence with Virginia? The priest Paolo Arrigone, that ruin of the monastery! The Canon Pisnato, who is now confessor to the nuns of Meda; in his house you will find what will never be discovered in mine, presents from nuns, incitements to amours, and other such things. The priest Giacomo Bertola, confessor of the nuns of S. Margharita; who was his devotee? Sacha!—and he stayed there all the day through. These men, being priests, are not prosecuted; they are protected by their cloth, forsooth! It is only of poor Osio that folk talk. Only he is persecuted, only he is a malefactor, only he is the traitor!' Arrigone, as a matter of fact, was tried, and condemned to two years' labour at the galleys, after the expiration of which term he was not to return to Monza or its territory. This seems a slight sentence; for the judges found him guilty, not only of promoting Osio's intrigue with Virginia by conducting the correspondence and watching the door during their interviews in the parlour, but also of pursuing the Signora herself with infamous proposals.

In his absence Osio was condemned to death on the gibbet. His goods were confiscated to the State. His house in Monza was destroyed, and a pillar of infamy recording his crimes was erected on its site. A proclamation of outlawry was issued on April 5, 1608, under the seal of Don Pietro de Acevedo, Count of Fuentes, and governor of the State of Milan, which offered 'to any person not himself an outlaw, or to any commune, that shall consign Gianpaolo Osio to the hands of justice, the reward of a thousand scudi from the royal ducal treasury, together with the right to free four bandits condemned for similar or less offences; and in case of his being delivered dead, even though he shall be slain in foreign parts, then the half of the aforesaid sum of money, and the freedom of two bandits as above. And if the person who shall consign him alive be himself an outlaw for similar or less offences he shall receive, besides the freedom of himself and two other bandits, the half of the aforesaid sum of money; and in the case of his consignment after death, the freedom of himself and of two other bandits as aforesaid.' I have recited this *Bando*, because it is a good instance of the procedure in use under like conditions. Justice preferred to obtain the culprit alive, and desired to receive him at honest hands. But there was an expectation of getting hold of him through less reputable agents. Therefore they offered free pardon to a bandit and a couple of accomplices, who might undertake the capture or the murder of the proscribed outlaw in concert, and in the event of his being produced alive a sum of money down. Osio, apparently, spent some years in exile, changing place and name and dress, living as he could from hand to mouth, until the rumour spread abroad that he was dead. He then returned to his country, and begged for sanctuary from an old friend. That friend betrayed him, had his throat cut in a cellar, and exposed his head upon the public market place.

Virginia was sentenced to perpetual incarceration in the convent of S. Valeria at Milan. She was to be 'inclosed within a little dungeon, the door of which shall be walled up with stones and mortar, so that the said Virginia Maria shall abide there for the term of her natural life, immured both day and night, never to issue thence, but shall receive food and other necessaries through a small hole in the wall of the said chamber, and light and air through an aperture or other opening.' This sentence was carried into effect. But at the expiration of many years, her behaviour justified some mitigation of the penalty. She was set at large, and allowed to occupy a more wholesome apartment, where the charity of Cardinal Borromeo supplied her with comforts befitting her station and the reputation she acquired for sanctity. Her own family cherished implacable sentiments of resentment against the woman who had brought disgrace upon them. Ripamonte, the historian of Milan, says that in his own time she was still alive: 'a bent old woman, tall of stature, dried and fleshless, but venerable in her aspect, whom no one could believe to have been once a charming and immodest beauty.' Her associates in guilt, the nuns of S. Margherita, were consigned to punishments resembling hers. Sisters Benedetta, Silvia, and Candida suffered the same close incarceration.

Lucrezia Buonvisi.

The tale of Lucrezia Buonvisi presents some points of similarity to that of the Signora di Monza.[13] Her father was a Lucchese gentleman, named Vincenzo Malpigli, who passed the better portion of his life at Ferrara as treasurer to Duke Alfonso II. He had four children; one son, Giovan Lorenzo, and three daughters, of whom Lucrezia, born at Lucca in 1572, was probably the youngest. Vincenzo's wife sprang from the noble Lucchese family of Buonvisi, at that time by their wealth and alliances the most powerful house of the Republic. Lucrezia spent some years of her girlhood at Ferrara, where she formed a romantic friendship for a nobleman of Lucca named Massimiliano Arnolfine. This early attachment was not countenanced by her parents. They destined her to be the wife of one of Paolo Buonvisi's numerous sons, her relatives upon the mother's side. In consequence of this determination, she was first affianced to an heir of that house, who died; again to another, who also died; and in the third place to their brother, called Lelio, whom she eventually married in the year 1591. Lelio was then twenty-five years of age, and Lucrezia nineteen. Her beauty was so distinguished that in poems written on the ladies of Lucca it received this celebration in a madrigal:—

Like the young maiden rose
Which at the opening of the dawn,
Still sprinkled with heaven's gracious dew,

[13] *Storia di Lucrezia Buonvisi*, by Salvatore Bonghi, Lucca 1864. This is an admirably written historical monograph, based on accurate studies and wide researches, containing a mine of valuable information for a student of those times.

Her beauty and her bosom on the lawn
Doth charmingly disclose,
For nymphs and amorous swains with love to view;
So delicate, so fair, Lucrezia yields
New pearls, new purple to our homely fields,
While Cupid plays and Flora laughs in her fresh hue.

Less than a year after her marriage with Lelio Buonvisi, Lucrezia resumed her former intimacy with Massimiliano Arnolfini. He was scarcely two years her elder, and they had already exchanged vows of fidelity in Ferrara. Massimiliano's temper inclined him to extreme courses; he was quick and fervent in all the disputes of his age, ready to back his quarrels with the sword, and impatient of delay in any matter he had undertaken. Owing to a feud which then subsisted between the families of Arnolfini and Boccella, he kept certain *bravi* in his service, upon whose devotion he relied. This young man soon found means to open a correspondence with Lucrezia, and arranged meetings with her in the house of some poor weavers who lived opposite the palace of the Buonvisi. Nothing passed between them that exceeded the limits of respectful courtship. But the situation became irksome to a lover so hot of blood as Massimiliano was. On the evening of June 5, in 1593, his men attacked Lelio Buonvisi, while returning with Lucrezia from prayers in an adjacent church. Lelio fell, stabbed with nineteen thrusts of the poignard, and was carried lifeless to his house. Lucrezia made her way back alone; and when her husband's corpse was brought into the palace, she requested that it should be laid out in the basement. A solitary witness of this act of violence, Vincenzo di Coreglia, deposed to having raised the dying man from the ground, put earth into his mouth by way of Sacrament, and urged him to forgive his enemies before he breathed his last. The weather had been very bad that day, and at nightfall it was thundering incessantly.

Inquisition was made immediately into the causes of Lelio's death. According to Lucrezia's account, her husband had reproved some men upon the road for singing obscene songs, whereupon they turned and murdered him. The corpse was exposed in the Church of the Servi, where multitudes of people gathered round it; and there an ancient dame of the Buonvisi house, flinging herself upon her nephew's body, vowed vengeance, after the old custom of the *Vocero*, against his murderers. Other members of the family indicated Massimiliano as the probable assassin; but he meantime had escaped, with three of his retainers, to a villa of his mother's at S. Pancrazio, whence he managed to take the open country and place himself in temporary safety.

During this while the judicial authorities of Lucca were not idle. The Podestà issued a proclamation inviting evidence under the menace of decapitation and confiscation of goods for whomsoever should be found to have withheld information. To this call a certain Orazio Carli, most imprudently, responded. He confessed to having been aware that Massimiliano was plotting the assassination of somebody—not Lelio; and said that he had himself facilitated the flight of the assassins by preparing a ladder, which he placed in the hands of a *bravo* called Ottavio da Trapani. This revelation delivered him over, bound hand and foot, to the judicial authorities, who at the same time imprisoned Vincenzo da Coreglia, the soldier present at the murder.

Massimiliano and his men meanwhile had made their way across the frontier to Garfagnana. Their flight and the suspicions which attached to them, rendered it tolerably certain that they were the authors of the crime. But justice demanded more circumstantial information, and the Podestà decided to work upon the two men already in his clutches. On June 4 Carli was submitted to the torture. The rack elicited nothing new from him, but had the result of dislocating his arms. He was then placed upon an instrument called the 'she-goat,' a sharp wooden trestle, to which the man was bound with weights attached to his feet, and where he sat for nearly four hours. In the course of this painful exercise, he deposed that Massimiliano and Lucrezia had been in the habit of meeting in the house of Vincenzo del Zoppo and Pollonia his wife, where the *bravi* also congregated and kept their arms. Grave suspicion was thus cast on Lucrezia. Had she perchance connived at her husband's murder? Was she an accomplice in the tragedy?

Lucrezia's peril now became imminent. Her brother, Giovan Lorenzo Malpigli, who remained her friend throughout, thought it best for her to retire as secretly as possible into a convent. The house chosen was that of S. Chiara in the town of Lucca. On June 5, she assumed the habit of S. Francis, cut her hair, changed her name from Lucrezia to Umilia, and offered two thousand crowns of dower to this monastery. Only four days had elapsed since her husband's assassination. But she, at all events, was safe from immediate peril; for the Church must now be dealt with; and the Church neither relinquished its suppliants, nor disgorged the wealth they poured into its coffers. The Podestà, when news of this occurrence reached him, sent at once to make inquiries. His messenger, Ser Vincenzo Petrucci, was informed by the Abbess that Lucrezia had just arrived and was having her hair shorn. At his request, the novice herself appeared—'a young woman, tall and pale, dressed in a nun's habit, with a crown upon her head.' She declared herself to be 'Madonna Lucretiina Malpigli, widow of Lelio Buonvisi.' The priest who had conducted her reception affirmed that 'the gentle lady, immediately upon her husband's death, conceived this good prompting of the spirit, and obeyed it on the spot.'

For the moment Lucrezia, whom in future we must call Sister Umilia, had to be left unmolested. The judges returned to the interrogation of their prisoners. Vincenzo del Zoppo and his wife Pollonia, in whose house the lovers used to meet, were tortured; but nothing that implied a criminal correspondence transpired from their evidence. Then the unlucky Carli was once more put to the strappado. He fell into a deep swoon, and was with difficulty brought to life again. Next his son, a youth of sixteen years, was racked with similar results. On June 7, they resolved to have another try at Vincenzo da Coreglia. This soldier had been kept on low diet in his prison during the last week, and was therefore ripe, according to the judicial theories of those times, for salutary torments. Having been strung up by his hands, he was jerked and shaken in the customary fashion until he declared his willingness to make a full confession. He had been informed, he said, that Massimiliano intended to assassinate Lelio by means of his three bravi, Pietro da Castelnuovo, Ottavio da Trapani, and Niccolo da Pariano. He engaged to stand by and cover the retreat of these men. It was Carli, and not Massimiliano, who had made overtures to him. On being once more tortured, he only confirmed this confession. Carli was again summoned, and set upon the 'she-goat,' with heavy weights attached to his feet. The poor wretch sat for two hours on this infernal machine, the sharp edges and spikes of which were so contrived as to press slowly and deeply upon the tenderest portions of his body.[14] But he endured this agony without uttering a word, until the judges perceived that he was at the point of death. Next day, the 8th of June, Coreglia was again summoned to the justice-chamber. Terrified by the prospect of future torments, and wearied out with importunities, he at last made a clean breast of all he knew. It was not Carli, but Massimiliano himself, who had engaged him; and he had assisted at the murder of Lelio, which was accomplished by two of the *bravi*, Ottavio and Pietro. Coreglia said nothing to implicate Sister Umilia. On the contrary, he asserted that she seemed to lose her senses when she saw her husband fall.

The General Council, to whom the results of these proceedings were communicated, published an edict of outlawry against Massimiliano and his three *bravi*. A price of 500 crowns was put upon the head of each, wherever he should be killed; and 1,000 crowns were offered to anyone who should kill Massimiliano within the city or state of Lucca. At the same time they sent an envoy to Rome, requesting the Pope's permission to arrest Umilia, on the ground that she was gravely suspected of being privy to the murder and of entering the convent to escape justice. A few days afterwards, the miserable witnesses, Carli and Coreglia, were beheaded in their prison.

The Chancellor, Vincenzo Petrucci, left Lucca on June 12, and reached Rome on the 14th. He obtained an audience from Clement VIII. upon the 15th. When the Pope had read the letter of the Republic, he struck his palm down on his chair, and cried: 'Jesus! This is a grave case! It seems hardly possible that a woman of her birth should have been induced to take share in the murder of her husband.' After some conversation with the envoy, he added: 'It is certainly an ugly business. But what can we do now that she has taken the veil?' Then he promised to deliberate upon the matter and return an answer later. Petrucci soon

[14] Campanella, who was tortured in this way at Naples, says that on one occasion a pound and a half of his flesh was macerated, and ten pounds of his blood shed. 'Perduravi horis quadraginta, funiculis arctissimis ossa usque secantibus ligatus, pendens manibus retro contortis de fune super acutissimum lignum qui (?) carnis setertium (?) in posterioribus mihi devoravit et decem sanguinis libras tellus ebebit.' Preface to *Atheismus Triumphatus*.

perceived that the Church did not mean to relinquish its privileges, and that Umilia was supported by powerful friends at court. Cardinal Castrucci remarked in casual conversation: 'She is surely punished enough for her sins by the life of the cloister.' A second interview with Clement on June 21, confirmed him in the opinion that the Republic would not obtain the dispensation they requested. Meanwhile the Signory of Lucca prepared a schedule of the suspicions against Umilia, grounded upon her confused evidence, her correspondence with Massimiliano, the fact that she had done nothing to rescue Lelio by calling out, and her sudden resort to the convent. This paper reached the Pope, who, on July 8, expressed his view that the Republic ought to be content with leaving Umilia immured in her monastery; and again, upon the 23rd, he pronounced his final decision that 'the lady, being a nun and tonsured, and prepared for the perfect life, is not within the jurisdiction of your Signory. It is further clear that, finding herself exposed to the calumnies of those two witnesses and injured in her reputation, she took the veil to screen her honour.' On August 13, Petrucci returned to Lucca.

Clement conceded one point. He gave commission to the Bishop of Lucca to inquire into Umilia's conduct within the precincts of the monastery. But the Council refused this intervention, for they were on bad terms with the Bishop and resented ecclesiastical interference in secular causes. Moreover, they judged that such an inquisition, without torture used and in a place of safety, would prove worse than useless. Thus the affair dropped.

Meanwhile we may relate what happened to Massimiliano and his *bravi*. They escaped, through Garfagnana and Massa, into the territory of Alfonso Malaspina, Marquis of Villafranca and Tresana. This nobleman, who delighted in protecting outlaws, placed the four men in security in his stronghold of Tresana. Pietro da Castelnuovo was an outlaw from Tuscany for the murder of a Carmelite friar, which he had committed at Pietrasanta a few days before the assassination of Lelio. Seventeen years after these events he was still alive and wanted for grave crimes committed in the Duchy of Modena. History knows no more about him, except that he had a wife and family. Of Niccolo da Pariana nothing has to be related. Ottavio da Trapani was caught at Milan, brought back to Lucca, and hanged there on June 13, 1604, after being torn with pincers. Massimiliano is said to have made his way to Flanders, where the Lucchese enjoyed many privileges, and where his family had probably hereditary connexions.[15] Like all outlaws, he lived in perpetual peril of assassination. Remorse and shame invaded him, especially when news arrived that the mistress, for whom he had risked all, was turning to a dissolute life (as we shall shortly read) in her monastery. His reason gave way; and, after twenty-two years of wandering, he returned to Lucca, and was caught. Instead of executing the capital sentence which had been pronounced upon him, the Signory consigned

[15] I may here allude to a portrait in our National Gallery of a Lucchese Arnolfini and his wife, painted by Van Eyck.

him to perpetual prison in the tower of Viareggio, which was then an insalubrious and fever-stricken village on the coast. Here, walled up in a little room, alone, deprived of light and air and physical decency, he remained forgotten for ten years from 1615 to 1625. At the latter date report was made that he had refused food for three days and was suffering from a dangerous hemorrhage. When the authorities proposed to break the wall of his dungeon and send a priest and surgeon to relieve him, he declared that he would kill himself if they intruded on his misery. Nothing more was heard of him until 1629, when he was again reported to be at the point of death. This time he requested the assistance of a priest; and it is probable that he then died at the age of sixty-nine, having survived the other actors in this tragedy and expiated the passion of his youth by life-long sufferings.

When we return to Sister Umilia, and inquire how the years had worn with her, a new chapter in the story opens. In 1606 she was still cloistered in S. Chiara, which indeed remained her home until her death. She had now reached the age of thirty-four. Suspicion meanwhile fell upon the conduct of the nuns of S. Chiara; and on January 9, in that year, a rope-ladder was discovered hanging from the garden wall of the convent. Upon inquiry, it appeared that certain men were in the habit of entering the house and holding secret correspondence with the sisters. Among these the most notorious were Piero Passari, a painter, infamous for vulgar profligacy, and a young nobleman of Lucca, Tommaso Samminiati. Both of them contrived to evade justice, and were proclaimed, as usual, outlaws. In the further course of investigation the strongest proofs were brought to light, from which it appeared that the chief promoter of these scandals was a man of high position in the state, advanced in years, married to a second wife, and holding office of trust as Protector of the Nunnery of S. Chiara. He was named Giovanbattista Dati, and represented an ancient Lucchese family mentioned by Dante. While Dati carried on his own intrigue with Sister Cherubina Mei, he did his best to encourage the painter in promiscuous debauchery, and to foster the passion which Samminiati entertained for Sister Umilia Malpigli. Dati was taken prisoner and banished for life to the island of Sardinia; but his papers fell into the hands of the Signory, who extracted from them the evidence which follows touching Umilia and Samminiati. This young man was ten years her junior; yet the quiet life of the cloister had preserved Umilia's beauty, and she was still capable of inspiring enthusiastic adoration. This transpires in the letters which Samminiati addressed to her through Dati from his asylum in Venice. They reveal, says Signor Bonghi, a strange confusion of madness, crime, and love.[16] Their style is that of a delirious rhetorician. One might fancy they had been composed as exercises, except for certain traits which mark the frenzy of genuine exaltation. Threats, imprecations, and blasphemies alternate with prayers, vows of fidelity and reminiscences of past delights in love.

[16] Here again I have very closely followed the text of Signor Bonghi's monograph, pp. 112-115.

Samminiati bends before 'his lady' in an attitude of respectful homage, offering upon his knees the service of awe-struck devotion. At one time he calls her 'his most beauteous angel,' at another 'his most lovely and adored enchantress.' He does not conceal his firm belief that she has laid him under some spell of sorcery; but entreats her to have mercy and to liberate him, reminding her how a certain Florentine lady restored Giovan Lorenzo Malpigli to health after keeping him in magic bondage till his life was in danger.[17] Then he swears unalterable fealty; heaven and fortune shall not change his love. It is untrue that at Florence or at Venice he has cast one glance on any other woman. Let lightning strike him, if he deserts Umilia. But she has caused him jealousy by stooping to a base amour. To this point he returns with some persistence. Then he entreats her to send him her portrait, painted in the character of S. Ursula. At another time he gossips about the nuns, forwarding messages, alluding to their several love-affairs, and condoling with them on the loss of a compliant confessor. This was a priest, who, when the indescribable corruptions of S. Chiara had been clearly proved, calmly remarked that there was no reason to make such a fuss—they were only affairs of gentlefolk, *cose di gentil uomini*. The rival of whom Samminiati was jealous seems to have been the painter Pietro, who held the key to all the scandals of the convent in his hand. Umilia, Dati and Samminiati at last agreed 'to rid their neighbourhood of that pest.' The man had escaped to Rovigo, whither Samminiati repaired from Venice, 'attended by two good fellows thoroughly acquainted with the district.' But Pietro got away to Ferrara, his enemy following and again missing him. Samminiati writes that he is resolved to hunt 'that rascal' out, and make an end of him. Meanwhile Umilia is commissioned to do for Calidonia Burlamacchi, a nun who had withdrawn from the company of her guilty sisters and knew too many of their secrets. Samminiati sends a white powder and a little phial containing a liquid, both of which, he informs Umilia, are potent poisons, with instructions how to use them and how to get Calidonia to swallow the ingredients. Then 'if the devil does not help her, she will pass from this life in half a night's time and without the slightest sign of violence.'

It may be imagined what disturbance was caused in the General Council by the reading of this correspondence. Nearly all the noble families of Lucca were connected by ties of blood or marriage with one or other of the culprits; and when the relatives of the accused had been excluded from the session, only sixty members were left to debate on further measures. I will briefly relate what happened to the three outlaws. Venice refused to give up Samminiati at the request of the Lucchese, saying that 'the Republic of S. Mark would not initiate a course of action prejudicial to the hospitality which every sort of person was wont to enjoy there.' But the young man was banished to Candia, whither he obediently retired. Pietro, the painter, was eventually permitted to return to the territory

[17] It appears that violent passion for a person was commonly attributed at that epoch to enchantment. See above, the confession of the Lady of Monza, p. 667.

but not the town of Lucca. Dati surrounded himself with armed men, as was the custom of rich criminals on whose head a price was set. After wandering some time, he submitted and took up his abode in Sardinia, whence he afterwards removed, by permission of the Signory, to France. There he died. With regard to the nuns, it seemed at first that the ends of justice would be defeated through the jealousies which divided the civil and ecclesiastical authorities in Lucca. The Bishop was absent, and his Vicar refused to institute a criminal process. Umilia remained at large in the convent, and even began a new intrigue with one Simo Menocchi. At last, in 1609, the Vicar prepared his indictment against the guilty nuns, and forwarded it to Rome. Their sentence was as follows: Sister Orizia condemned to incarceration for life and loss of all her privileges; Sister Umilia, to the same penalties for a term of seven years; Sisters Paola, Cherubina, and Dionea, received a lighter punishment. Orizia, it may be mentioned, had written a letter with her own blood to some lover; but nothing leads us to suppose that she was equally guilty with Umilia, who had entered into the plot to poison Sister Calidonia.

Umilia was duly immured, and bore her punishment until the year 1616, at which time the sentence expired. But she was not released for another two years; for she persistently refused to humble herself, or to request that liberation as a grace which was her due in justice. Nor would she submit to the shame of being seen about the convent without her monastic habit. Finally, in 1618, she obtained freedom and restoration to her privileges as a nun of S. Chiara. It may be added, as a last remark, that, when the convent was being set to rights, Umilia's portrait in the character of S. Ursula was ordered to be destroyed or rendered fit for devout uses by alterations. Any nun who kept it in her cell incurred the penalty of excommunication. In what year Umilia died remains unknown.

The Cenci.

Shifting the scene to Rome, we light upon a group of notable misdeeds enacted in the last half of the sixteenth century, each of which is well calculated to illustrate the conditions of society and manners at that epoch. It may be well to begin with the Cenci tragedy. In Shelley's powerful drama, in Guerazzi's tedious novel and Scolari's digest, the legend of Beatrice Cenci has long appealed to modern sympathy. The real facts, extracted from legal documents and public registers, reduce its poetry of horror to comparatively squalid prose.[18] Yet, shorn of romantic glamour, the bare history speaks significantly to a student of Italian customs. Monsignore Cristoforo Cenci, who died about the year 1562, was in holy orders, yet not a priest. One of the clerks of the Apostolic Camera, a Canon of S. Peter's, the titular incumbent of a Roman parish, and an occupant of minor offices about the Papal Court and Curia, he represented an epicene species, neither churchman nor

[18] *Francesco Cenci e la sua Famiglia.* Per A. Bertolotti, Firenze, 1877.

layman, which the circumstances of ecclesiastical sovereignty rendered indispensable. Cristoforo belonged to a good family among that secondary Roman aristocracy which ranked beneath the princely feudatories and the Papal bastards. He accumulated large sums of money by maladministration of his official trusts, inherited the estates of two uncles, and bequeathed a colossal fortune to his son Francesco. This youth was the offspring of an illicit connexion carried on between Monsignore Cenci and Beatrice Amias during the lifetime of that lady's husband. Upon the death of the husband the Monsignore obtained dispensation from his orders, married Beatrice, and legitimated his son, the inheritor of so much wealth. Francesco was born in 1549, and had therefore reached the age of thirteen when his father died. His mother Beatrice soon contracted a third matrimonial union; but during her guardianship of the boy she appeared before the courts accused of having stolen clothing from his tutor's wardrobe.

Francesco Cenci disbursed a sum of 33,000 crowns to various public offices, in order to be allowed to enter unmolested into the enjoyment of his father's gains: 3,800 crowns of this sum went to the Chapter of S. Peter's.[19] He showed a certain precocity; for at the age of fourteen he owned an illegitimate child, and was accused of violence to domestics. In 1563 his family married him to Ersilia, a daughter of the noble Santa Croce house, who brought him a fair dowry. Francesco lived for twenty-one years with this lady, by whom he had twelve children. Upon her death he remained a widower for nine years, and in 1593 he married Lucrezia Petroni, widow of a Roman called Velli. Francesco's conduct during his first marriage was not without blame. Twice at least he had to pay fines for acts of brutality to servants; and once he was prosecuted for an attempt to murder a cousin, also named Francesco Cenci. On another occasion we find him outlawed from the States of the Church. Yet these offences were but peccadilloes in a wealthy Roman baron; and Francesco used to boast that, with money in his purse, he had no dread of justice. After the death of his wife Ersilia, his behaviour grew more irregular. Three times between 1591 and 1594 he was sued for violent attacks on servants; and in February of the latter year he remained six months in prison on multiplied charges of unnatural vice. There was nothing even here to single Francesco Cenci out from other nobles of his age.[20] Scarce-

[19] He was afterwards forced, in 1590, to disgorge a second sum of 25,000 crowns.

[20] Prospero Farinaccio, the advocate of Cenci's murderers, was himself tried for this crime (Bertolotti, *op. cit.* p. 104). The curious story of the Spanish soldiers alluded to above will be found in Mutinelli, *Stor. Arc.* vol. i. p. 121. See the same work of Mutinelli, vol. i. p. 48, for a similar prosecution in Rome, 1566; and vol. iv. p. 152 for another involving some hundred people of condition at Milan in 1679, Compare what Sarpi says about the Florentine merchants and Roman *cinedi* in his *Letters*, date 1609, vol. i. p. 288. For the manners of the Neapolitans, *Vita di D. Pietro di Toledo* (*Arch. Stor. It.* vol. ix. p. 23). The most scandalous example of such vice in high quarters was given by Pietro de' Medici, one of Duke Cosimo's sons. Galluzzi, vol. v. p. 174, and Litta's pedigree of the Medici. The *Bandi Lucchese*, ed. S. Bonghi, Bologna, 1863, pp. 377-381, treats the subject in full; and it has been discussed by Canello, *op. cit.* pp. 20-23. The *Artes Jesuiticæ*,op. cit. Articles 62, 120, illustrate casuistry on the topic.

ly a week passed in Rome without some affair of the sort, involving outrage, being brought before the judges. Cardinals, prelates, princes, professional men and people of the lowest rank were alike implicated. The only difference between the culprits was that the rich bought themselves off, while the destitute were burned. Eleven poor Spaniards and Portuguese were sent to the stake in 1578 for an offence which Francesco Cenci compounded in 1594 by the payment of 100,000 crowns. After this warning and the loss of so much money, he grew more circumspect, married his second wife Lucrezia, and settled down to rule his family. His sons caused him considerable anxiety. Giacomo, the eldest, married against his father's will, and supported himself by forging obligations and raising money. Francesco's displeasure showed itself in several law-suits, one of which accused Giacomo of having plotted against his life. The second son, Cristoforo, was assassinated by Paolo Bruno, a Corsican, in the prosecution of a love affair with the wife of a Trasteverine fisherman. The third son, Rocco, spent his time in street adventures, and on one occasion laid his hands on all the plate and portable property that he could carry off from his father's house. This young ruffian, less than twenty years of age, found a devoted friend in Monsignore Querro, a cousin of the family well placed at court, who assisted him in the burglary of the Cenci palace. Rocco was killed by Amilcare Orsini, a bastard of the Count of Pitigliano, in a brawl at night. The young men met, Cenci attended by three armed servants, Orsini by two. A single pass of rapiers, in which Rocco was pierced through the right eye, ended the affair.

In addition to his vindictive persecution of his worthless eldest son, Francesco Cenci behaved with undue strictness to the younger, allowing them less money than befitted their station and treating them with a severity which contrasted comically with his own loose habits. The legend which represents him as an exceptionally wicked man, cruel for cruelty's sake and devoid of natural affection, receives some colour from the facts. Yet these alone are not sufficient to justify its darker hues, while they amply prove that Francesco's children gave him grievous provocation. The discontents of this ill-governed family matured into rebellion; and in 1598 it was decided on removing the old Cenci by murder. His second wife Lucrezia, his eldest son Giacomo, his daughter Beatrice, and a younger son Bernardo, were implicated in the crime. It was successfully carried out at the Rocca di Petrella in the Abruzzi on the night of September 9. Two hired *bravi*, Olimpio Calvetti and Marzio Catalani, entered the old man's bedroom, drove a nail into his head, and flung the corpse out from a gallery, whence it was alleged that he had fallen by accident. Six days after this assassination Giacomo and his brothers took out letters both at Rome and in the realm of Naples for the administration of their father's property; nor does suspicion seem for some time to have fallen upon them. It awoke at Petrella in November, the feudatory of which fief, Marzio Colonna, informed the government of Naples that proceedings ought to be taken against the Cenci and their cut-throats. Accordingly, on December 10, a ban was published against Olimpio and Marzio. Olimpio met his death at an inn door in a little village called Cantalice. Three desperate fellows, at the instigation of Giacomo de' Cenci and Monsignore Querro, surprised him there. But Marzio fell into the hands of justice, and his evidence caused the immediate arrest of the Cenci. It appears that they were tortured and that none of them denied the accusation; so that their advocates could only plead extenuating circumstances. To this fact may possibly be due the legend of Beatrice. In order to mitigate the guilt of parricide, Prospero Farinaccio, who conducted her defence, established a theory of enormous cruelty and unspeakable outrages committed on her person by her father. With the same object in view, he tried to make out that Bernardo was half-witted. There is quite sufficient extant evidence to show that Bernardo was a young man of average intelligence; and with regard to Beatrice, nothing now remains to corroborate Farinaccio's hypothesis of incest. She was not a girl of sixteen, as the legend runs, but a woman of twenty-two;[21] and the codicils to her will render it nearly certain that she had given birth to an illegitimate son, for whose maintenance she made elaborate and secret provisions. That the picture ascribed to Guido Reni in the Barberini palace is not a portrait of Beatrice in prison, appears sufficiently proved. Guido did not come to Rome until 1608, nine years after her death; and catalogues of the Barberini gallery, compiled in 1604 and 1623, contain no mention either of a painting by Guido or of Beatrice's portrait. The Cenci were lodged successively in the prisons of Torre di Nona, Savelli, and S. Angelo. They occupied wholesome apartments and were allowed the attendance of their own domestics. That their food was no scanty dungeon fare appears from the *menus* of dinners and suppers supplied to them, which include fish, flesh, fruit, salad, and snow to cool the water. In spite of powerful influence at court, Clement VIII. at last resolved to exercise strict justice on the Cenci. He was brought to this decision by a matricide perpetrated in cold blood at Subiaco, on September 5, 1599. Paolo di S. Croce, a relative of the Cenci, murdered his mother Costanza in her bed, with the view of obtaining property over which she had control. The sentence issued a few days after this event. Giacomo was condemned to be torn to pieces by red-hot pincers, and finished with a *coup de grâce* from the hangman's hammer. Lucrezia and Beatrice received the slighter sentence of decapitation; while Bernardo, in consideration of his youth, was let off with the penalty of being present at the execution of his kinsfolk, after which he was to be imprisoned for a year and then sent to the galleys for life. Their property was confiscated to the Camera Apostolica. These punishments were carried out.[22] But Bernardo, after working at Cività Vecchia until 1606, obtained release and lived in banishment till his death in 1627. Monsignor Querro, for his connivance in the whole affair, was banished

[21] De Stendhal's MS. authority says she was sixteen, Shelley's that she was twenty.
[22] De Stendhal's MS. describes how Giacomo was torn by pincers; Shelley's says that this part of the sentence was remitted.

to the island of Malta, whence he returned at some date before the year 1633 to Rome, having expiated his guilt by long and painful exile. In this abstract of the Cenci tragedy, I have followed the documents published by Signor Bertolotti. They are at many points in startling contradiction to the legend, which is founded on MS. accounts compiled at no distant period after the events. One of these was employed by Shelley; another, differing in some particulars, was translated by De Stendhal. Both agree in painting that lurid portrait of Francesco Cenci which Shelley has animated with the force of a great dramatist.[23] Unluckily, no copy of the legal instructions upon which the trial was conducted is now extant. In the absence of this all-important source of information, it would be unsafe to adopt Bertolotti's argument, that the legend calumniates Francesco in order to exculpate Beatrice, without some reservation. There is room for the belief that facts adduced in evidence may have partly justified the prevalent opinion of Beatrice's infamous persecution by her father.

The Massimi.

The tragedy of the Cenci, about which so much has been written in consequence of the supposed part taken in it by Beatrice, seems to me commonplace compared with that of the Massimi.[24] Whether this family really descended from the Roman Fabii matters but little. In the sixteenth century they ranked, as they still rank, among the proudest nobles of the Eternal City. Lelio, the head of the house, had six stalwart sons by his first wife, Girolama Savelli. They were conspicuous for their gigantic stature and herculean strength. After their mother's death in 1571, their father became enamoured of a woman inferior at all points, in birth, breeding, and antecedents, to a person of his quality. She was a certain Eufrosina, who had been married to a man called Corberio. The great Marc Antonio Colonna murdered this husband, and brought the wife to Rome as his own mistress. Lelio Massimo committed the grand error of so loving her, after she had served Colonna's purpose, that he married her. This was an insult to the honour of the house, which his sons could not or would not bear. On the night of her wedding, in 1585, they refused to pay her their respects; and on the next morning, five of them entered her apartments and shot her dead. Only one of the six sons, Pompeo Massimo, bore no share in this assassination. Him, the father, Lelio, blessed; but he solemnly cursed the other five. After the lapse of a few weeks, he followed his wife to the grave with a broken heart, leaving this imprecation unrecalled. Pompeo grew up to continue the great line of Massimo. But disaster fell on each of his five brothers, the flower of Roman youth, exulting in their blood, and insolence, and vigour.—The first of them, Ottavio, was killed by a cannon ball at sea

[23] The author of De Stendhal's MS. professes to have known the old Cenci, and gives a definite description of his personal appearance.

[24] Litta supplies the facts related above.

in honourable combat with the Turk. Another, Girolamo, who sought refuge in France, was shot down in an ambuscade while pursuing his amours with a gentle lady. A third, Alessandro, died under arms before Paris while serving in the troops of General Farnese. A fourth, Luca, was imprisoned at Rome for his share of the stepmother's murder, but was released on the plea that he had avenged the wounded honour of his race. He died, however, poisoned by his own brother, Marcantonio, in 1599.[25] Marcantonio was arrested on suspicion and imprisoned in Torre di Nona, where he confessed his guilt. He was shortly afterwards beheaded on the little square before the bridge of S. Angelo.

Vittoria Accoramboni.

Next in order, I shall take the story of Vittoria Accoramboni. It has been often told already,[26] yet it combines so many points of interest bearing upon the social life of the Italians in my period, that to omit it would be to sacrifice the most important document bearing on the matter of this chapter. As the Signora di Monza and Lucrezia Buonvisi help us to understand the secret history of families and convents, so Vittoria Accoramboni introduces us to that of courts. It will be noticed how the same machinery of lawless nobles and profligate *bravi*, acting in concert with bold women, is brought into play throughout the tragedies which form the substance of our present inquiry.

Vittoria was born in 1557, of a noble but impoverished family, at Gubbio among the hills of Umbria. Her biographers are rapturous in their praises of her beauty, grace, and exceeding charm of manner. Not only was her person most lovely, but her mind shone at first with all the amiable lustre of a modest, innocent, and winning youth. Her father, Claudio Accoramboni, removed to Rome, where his numerous children were brought up under the care of their mother, Tarquinia, an ambitious woman, bent on rehabilitating the decayed honours of her house. Here Vittoria in early girlhood soon became the fashion. She exercised an irresistible influence over all who saw her, and many were the offers of marriage she refused. At length a suitor appeared whose condition and connexion with the Roman ecclesiastical nobility rendered him acceptable in the eyes of the Accoramboni. Francesco Peretti was welcomed as the successful candidate for Vittoria's hand. His mother, Camilla, was sister to Felice, Cardinal of Montalto; and her son, Francesco Mignucci, had changed both of his names to Felice Peretti in compliment to this illustrious relative.[27]

[25] This fratricide, concurring with the matricide of S. Croce, contributed to the rigour with which the Cenci parricide was punished in that year of Roman crimes.

[26] *The White Devil*, a tragedy by John Webster, London, 1612; De Stendhal's *Chroniques et Nouvelles*, Vittoria Accoramboni, Paris, 1855; *Vittoria Accoramboni*, D. Gnoli, Firenze, 1870; *Italian Byways*, by J. A. Symonds, London, 1883. The greater part of what follows above is extracted from my *Italian Byways*.

[27] I find a Felice Peretti mentioned in the will of Giacomo Cenci condemned in 1597. But this was after the death of this Peretti, whom I shall continue to call Francesco.

It was the nephew, then, of the future Sixtus V., that Vittoria Accoramboni married on June 28, 1573. For a short while the young couple lived happily together. According to some accounts of their married life, the bride secured the favour of her powerful uncle-in-law, who indulged her costly fancies to the full. It is, however, more probable that the Cardinal Montalto treated her follies with a grudging parsimony; for we soon find the Peretti household hopelessly involved in debt. Discord, too, arose between Vittoria and her husband on the score of levity in her behaviour; and it was rumoured that even during the brief space of their union she had proved a faithless wife. Yet she contrived to keep Francesco's confidence, and it is certain that her family profited by their connexion with the Peretti. Of her six brothers, Mario, the eldest, was a favourite courtier of the great Cardinal d' Este. Ottavio was in orders, and through Montalto's influence obtained the See of Fossombrone. The same eminent protector placed Scipione in the service of the Cardinal Sforza. Camillo, famous for his beauty and his courage, followed the fortunes of Filibert of Savoy, and died in France. Flaminio was still a boy, dependent, as the sequel of this story shows, upon his sister's destiny. Of Marcello, the second in age and most important in the action of this tragedy, it is needful to speak with more particularity. He was young, and, like the rest of his breed, singularly handsome—so handsome, indeed, that he is said to have gained an infamous ascendency over the great Duke of Bracciano, whose privy chamberlain he had become. Marcello was an outlaw for the murder of Matteo Pallavicino, the brother of the Cardinal of that name. This did not, however, prevent the chief of the Orsini house from making him his favourite and confidential friend. Marcello, who seems to have realised in actual life the worst vices of those Roman courtiers described for us by Aretino, very soon conceived the plan of exalting his own fortune by trading on his sister's beauty. He worked upon the Duke of Bracciano's mind so cleverly that he brought this haughty prince to the point of an insane passion for Peretti's young wife; and meanwhile he so contrived to inflame the ambition of Vittoria and her mother, Tarquini, that both were prepared to dare the worst of crimes in expectation of a dukedom. The game was a difficult one to play. Not only had Francesco Peretti first to be murdered, but the inequality of birth and wealth and station between Vittoria and the Duke Bracciano rendered a marriage almost impossible. It was also an affair of delicacy to stimulate without satisfying the Duke's passion. Yet Marcello did not despair. The stakes were high enough to justify great risks; and all he put in peril was his sister's honour, the fame of the Accoramboni, and the favour of Montalto. Vittoria, for her part, trusted in her power to ensnare and secure the noble prey both had in view.

Paolo Giordano Orsini, born about the year 1537, was reigning Duke of Bracciano. Among Italian princes he ranked almost upon a par with the Dukes of Urbino; and his family, by its alliances, was more illustrious than any of that time in Italy. He was a man of gigantic stature, prodigious corpulence, and marked personal daring; agreeable in manners, but subject to uncontrollable fits of passion, and incapable of self-restraint when crossed in any whim or fancy. Upon the habit of his body it is needful to insist, in order that the part he played in this tragedy of intrigue, crime, and passion may be well defined. He found it difficult to procure a charger equal to his weight, and he was so fat that a special dispensation relieved him from the duty of genuflexion in the Papal presence. Though lord of a large territory, yielding princely revenues, he laboured under heavy debts; for no great noble of the period lived more splendidly, with less regard for his finances. In the politics of that age and country, Paolo Giordano leaned towards France. Yet he was a grandee of Spain, and had played a distinguished part in the battle of Lepanto. Now, the Duke of Bracciano was a widower. He had been married in 1553 to Isabella de' Medici, daughter of the Grand Duke Cosimo, sister of Francesco, Bianca Capello's lover, and of the Cardinal Ferdinando. Suspicion of adultery with Troilo Orsini had fallen on Isabella; and her husband, with the full concurrence of her brothers, removed her in 1576 from this world by his own hand.[28] No one thought the worse of Bracciano for this murder of his wife. In those days of abandoned vice and intricate villainy, certain points of honour were maintained with scrupulous fidelity. A wife's adultery was enough to justify the most savage and licentious husband in an act of semi-judicial vengeance; and the shame she brought upon his head was shared by the members of her own house, so that they stood by, consenting to her death. Isabella, it may be said, left one son, Virginio, who became, in due time, Duke of Bracciano.

It appears that in the year 1581, eight years after Vittoria's marriage, the Duke of Bracciano satisfied Marcello of his intention to make her his wife, and of his willingness to countenance Francesco Peretti's murder. Marcello, feeling sure of his game, now introduced the Duke in private to his sister, and induced her to overcome any natural repugnance she may have felt for the unwieldy and gross lover. Having reached this point, it was imperative to push matters quickly on toward matrimony.

But how should the unfortunate Francesco be entrapped? They caught him in a snare of peculiar atrocity, by working on the kindly feelings which his love for Vittoria had caused him to extend to all the Accoramboni. Marcello, the outlaw, was her favourite brother, and Marcello at that time lay in hiding, under the suspicion of more than ordinary crime, beyond the walls of Rome. Late in the evening of April 16, while the Peretti family were retiring to bed, a messenger from Marcello arrived, entreating Francesco to repair at once to Monte Cavallo. Marcello had affairs of the utmost importance to communicate, and begged his brother-in-law not to fail him at a grievous pinch. The letter containing this request was borne by one Dominico d' Aquaviva, *alias* Il Mancino, a confederate of Vittoria's waiting-maid. This fellow, like

[28] The balance of probability leans against Isabella in this affair. At the licentious court of the Medici she lived with unpardonable freedom. Troilo Orsini was himself assassinated in Paris by Bracciano's orders a few years afterwards.

Marcello, was an outlaw; but when he ventured into Rome he frequented Peretti's house, and he had made himself familiar with its master as a trusty *bravo*. Neither in the message, therefore, nor in the messenger was there much to rouse suspicion. The time, indeed, was oddly chosen, and Marcello had never made a similar appeal on any previous occasion. Yet his necessities might surely have obliged him to demand some more than ordinary favour from a brother. Francesco immediately made himself ready to start out, armed only with his sword and attended by a single servant. It was in vain that his wife and his mother reminded him of the dangers of the night, the loneliness of Monte Cavallo, its ruinous palaces and robber-haunted caves. He was resolved to undertake the adventure, and went forth, never to return. As he ascended the hill, he fell to earth, shot with three harquebusses. His body was afterwards found on Monte Cavallo, stabbed through and through, without a trace that could identify the murderers. Only, in the course of subsequent investigations, Il Mancino (February 24, 1582) made the following statements:—That Vittoria's mother, assisted by the waiting-woman, had planned the trap; that Marchionne of Gubbio and Paolo Barca of Bracciano, two of the Duke's men, had despatched the victim. Marcello, himself, it seems, had come from Bracciano to conduct the whole affair. Suspicion fell immediately upon Vittoria and her kindred, together with the Duke of Bracciano; nor was this diminished when the Accoramboni, fearing the pursuit of justice, took refuge in a villa of the Duke's at Magnanapoli a few days after the murder.

A cardinal's nephew, even in those troublous times, was not killed without some noise being made about the matter. Accordingly, Pope Gregory XIII. began to take measures for discovering the authors of the crime. Strange to say, however, the Cardinal Montalto, notwithstanding the great love he was known to bear his nephew, begged that the investigation might be dropped. The coolness with which he first received the news of Francesco Peretti's death, the dissimulation with which he met the Pope's expression of sympathy in a full consistory, his reserve while greeting friends on ceremonial visits of condolence, and, more than all, the self-restraint he showed in the presence of the Duke of Bracciano, impressed the society of Rome with the belief that he was of a singularly moderate and patient temper. It was thought that the man who could so tamely submit to his nephew's murder, and suspend the arm of justice when already raised for vengeance, must prove a mild and indulgent ruler. When, therefore, in the fifth year after this event, Montalto was elected Pope, men ascribed his elevation in no small measure to his conduct at the present crisis. Some, indeed, attributed his extraordinary moderation and self-control to the right cause. '*Veramente costui è un gran frate!*' was Gregory's remark at the close of the consistory when Montalto begged him to let the matter of Peretti's murder rest. '*Of a truth, that fellow is a consummate hypocrite!*' How accurate this judgment was, appeared when Sixtus V. assumed the reins of power. The priest who, as monk and cardinal, had smiled on Bracciano, though he knew him to be his nephew's assassin, now, as Pontiff and sovereign, bade the chief of the Orsini purge his palace and dominions of the scoundrels he was wont to harbour, adding significantly, that if the Cardinal Felice Peretti forgave what had been done against him in a private station, the same man would exact uttermost vengeance for disobedience to the will of Sixtus. The Duke of Bracciano judged it best, after that warning, to withdraw from Rome.

Francesco Peretti had been murdered on April 16, 1581. Sixtus V. was proclaimed on April 24, 1585. In this interval Vittoria underwent a series of extraordinary perils and adventures. First of all, she had been secretly married to the Duke in his gardens of Magnanapoli at the end of April 1581. That is to say, Marcello and she secured their prize, as well as they were able, the moment after Francesco had been removed by murder. But no sooner had the marriage become known, than the Pope, moved by the scandal it created no less than by the urgent instance of the Orsini and Medici, declared it void. After some while spent in vain resistance, Bracciano submitted, and sent Vittoria back to her father's house. By an order issued under Gregory's own hand, she was next removed to the prison of Corte Savella, thence to the monastery of S. Cecilia in Trastevere, and finally to the Castle of S. Angelo. Here, at the end of December 1581, she was put on her trial for the murder of her first husband. In prison she seems to have borne herself bravely, arraying her beautiful person in delicate attire, entertaining visitors, exacting from her friends the honours due to a duchess, and sustaining the frequent examinations to which she was submitted with a bold, proud front. In the middle of the month of July her constancy was sorely tried by the receipt of a letter in the Duke's own handwriting, formally renouncing his marriage. It was only by a lucky accident that she was prevented on this occasion from committing suicide. The Papal court meanwhile kept urging her either to retire to a monastery or to accept another husband. She firmly refused to embrace the religious life, and declared that she was already lawfully united to a living husband, the Duke of Bracciano. It seemed impossible to deal with her; and at last, on November 8, she was released from prison under the condition of retirement to Gubbio. The Duke had lulled his enemies to rest by the pretence of yielding to their wishes. But Marcello was continually beside him at Bracciano, where we read of a mysterious Greek enchantress whom he hired to brew love-philtres for the furtherance of his ambitious plots. Whether Bracciano was stimulated by the brother's arguments or by the witch's potions need not be too curiously questioned. But it seems in any case certain that absence inflamed his passion instead of cooling it.

Accordingly, in September 1583, under the excuse of a pilgrimage to Loreto, he contrived to meet Vittoria at Trevi, whence he carried her in triumph to Bracciano. Here he openly acknowledged her as his wife, installing her with all the splendour due to a sovereign duchess. On October 10 following, he once more performed the marriage ceremony in the principal church of his fief; and in the January of 1584 he brought her openly to Rome. This act of contumacy to the Pope, both as feudal superior and as Supreme Pontiff, roused all the former opposition to his marriage. Once more it was declared invalid. Once more the Duke pretended to give way. But at this juncture Gregory died; and while the conclave was sitting for the election of the new Pope, he resolved to take the law into his own hands, and to ratify his union with Vittoria by a third and public marriage in Rome. On the morning of April 24, 1585, their nuptials were accordingly once more solemnised in the Orsini palace. Just one hour after the ceremony, as appears from the marriage register, the news arrived of Cardinal Montalto's election to the Papacy. Vittoria lost no time in paying her respects to Camilla, sister of the new Pope, her former mother-in-law. The Duke visited Sixtus V. in state to compliment him on his elevation. But the reception which both received proved that Rome was no safe place for them to live in. They consequently made up their minds for flight.

A chronic illness from which Bracciano had lately suffered furnished a sufficient pretext. This seems to have been something of the nature of a cancerous ulcer, which had to be treated by the application of raw meat to open sores. Such details are only excusable in the present narrative on the ground that Bracciano's disease considerably affects our moral judgment of the woman who could marry a man thus physically tainted, and with her husband's blood upon his hands. At any rate, the Duke's *lupa* justified his trying what change of air, together with the sulphur waters of Abano, would do for him.

The Duke and Duchess arrived in safety at Venice, where they had engaged the Dandolo palace on the Zueca. There they only stayed a few days, removing to Padua, where they had hired palaces of the Foscari in the Arena and a house called De' Cavalli. At Salò, also, on the Lake of Garda, they provided themselves with fit dwellings for their princely state and their large retinues, intending to divide their time between the pleasures which the capital of luxury afforded and the simpler enjoyments of the most beautiful of the Italian lakes. But *la gioia dei profani è un fumo passaggier*. Paolo Giordano Orsini, Duke of Bracciano, died suddenly at Salò on November 10, 1585, leaving the young and beautiful Vittoria helpless among enemies. What was the cause of his death? It is not possible to give a clear and certain answer. We have seen that he suffered from a horrible and voracious disease, which after his removal from Rome seems to have made progress. Yet, though this malady may well have cut his life short, suspicion of poison was not, in the circumstances, quite unreasonable. The Grand Duke of Tuscany, the Pope, and the Orsini family were all interested in his death. Anyhow, he had time to make a will in Vittoria's favour, leaving her large sums of money, jewels, goods, and houses—enough, in fact, to support her ducal dignity with splendour. His hereditary fiefs and honours passed by right to his only son, Virginio.

Vittoria, accompanied by her brother, Marcello, and the whole court of Bracciano, repaired at once to Padua, where she was soon after joined by

Flaminio, and by the Prince Lodovico Orsini. Lodovico Orsini assumed the duty of settling Vittoria's affairs under her dead husband's will. In life he had been the Duke's ally as well as relative. His family pride was deeply wounded by what seemed to him an ignoble, as it was certainly an unequal, marriage. He now showed himself the relentless enemy of the Duchess. Disputes arose between them as to certain details, which seem to have been legally decided in the widow's favour. On the night of December 22, however, forty men, disguised in black and fantastically tricked out to elude detection, surrounded her palace. Through the long galleries and chambers hung with arras, eight of them went bearing torches, in search of Vittoria and her brothers. Marcello escaped, having fled the house under suspicion of the murder of one of his own followers. Flaminio, the innocent and young, was playing on his lute and singing 'Miserere' in the great hall of the palace. The murderers surprised him with a shot from one of their harquebusses. He ran, wounded in the shoulder, to his sister's room. She, it is said, was telling her beads before retiring for the night. When three of the assassins entered, she knelt before the crucifix, and there they stabbed her in the left breast, turning the poignard in the wound, and asking her with savage insults if her heart was pierced. Her last words were, 'Jesus, I pardon you.' Then they turned to Flaminio, and left him pierced with seventy-four stiletto wounds.

The authorities of Padua identified the bodies of Vittoria and Flaminio, and sent at once for further instructions to Venice. Meanwhile it appears that both corpses were laid out in one open coffin for the people to contemplate. The palace and the church of the Eremitani, to which they had been removed, were crowded all through the following day with a vast concourse of the Paduans. Vittoria's dead body, pale yet sweet to look upon, the golden hair flowing around her marble shoulders, the red wound in her breast uncovered, the stately limbs arrayed in satin as she died, maddened the populace with its surpassing loveliness. '*Dentibus fremebant*,' says the chronicler, when they beheld that gracious lady stiff in death. And of a truth, if her corpse was actually exposed in the chapel of the Eremitani, as we have some right to assume, the spectacle must have been impressive. Those grim gaunt frescoes of Mantegna looked down on her as she lay stretched upon her bier, solemn and calm, and, but for pallor, beautiful as though in life. No wonder that the folk forgot her first husband's murder, her less than comely marriage to the second. It was enough for them that this flower of surpassing loveliness had been cropped by villains in its bloom. Gathering in knots around the torches placed beside the corpse, they vowed vengeance against the Orsini; for suspicion, not unnaturally, fell on Prince Lodovico.

The Prince was arrested and interrogated before the court of Padua. He entered their hall attended by forty armed men, responded haughtily to their questions, and demanded free passage for his courier to Virginio Orsini, then at Florence. To this demand the court acceded; but the precaution of waylaying the courier and searching his person was very wisely taken. Besides some formal despatches which announced Vittoria's assassination, they found in this man's boot a compromising letter, declaring Virginio a party to the crime, and asserting that Lodovico had with his own poignard killed their victim. Padua placed itself in a state of defence, and prepared to besiege the palace of Prince Lodovico, who also got himself in readiness for battle. Engines, culverins, and firebrands were directed against the barricades which he had raised. The militia was called out and the Brenta was strongly guarded. Meanwhile the Senate of S. Mark had despatched the Avogadore, Aloisio Bragadin, with full power, to the scene of action. Lodovico Orsini, it may be mentioned, was in their service; and had not this affair intervened, he would in a few weeks have entered on his duties as Governor for Venice of Corfu.

The bombardment of Orsini's palace began on Christmas Day. Three of the Prince's men were killed in the first assault; and since the artillery brought to bear upon him threatened speedy ruin to the house and its inhabitants, he made up his mind to surrender. 'The Prince Luigi,' writes one chronicler of these events, 'walked attired in brown, his poignard at his side, and his cloak slung elegantly under his arm. The weapon being taken from him he leaned upon a balustrade, and began to trim his nails with a little pair of scissors he happened to find there.' On the 27th he was strangled in prison by order of the Venetian Republic. His body was carried to be buried, according to his own will, in the church of S. Maria dell' Orto at Venice. Two of his followers were hanged next day. Fifteen were executed on the following Monday; two of these were quartered alive; one of them, the Conte Paganello, who confessed to having slain Vittoria, had his left side probed with his own cruel dagger. Eight were condemned to the galleys, six to prison, and eleven were acquitted. Thus ended this terrible affair, which brought, it is said, good credit and renown to the lords of Venice through all nations of the civilised world. It only remains to be added that Marcello Accoramboni was surrendered to the Pope's vengeance and beheaded at Ancona, where also his mysterious accomplice, the Greek sorceress, perished.

The Duchess of Palliano.

It was the custom of Italians in the sixteenth and seventeenth centuries to compose and circulate narratives of tragic or pathetic incidents in real life. They were intended to satisfy curiosity in an age when newspapers and law reports did not exist, and also to suit the taste of ladies and gentlemen versed in Boccaccio and Bandello. Resembling the London letters of our ancestors, they passed from hand to hand, rarely found their way into the printing office, and when they had performed their task were left to moulder in the dust of bookcases. The private archives of noble families abound in volumes of such tales, and some may still be found upon the shelves of public libraries. These MS. collections furnish a mine of inexhaustible riches to the student of manners. When checked by legal documents, they frequently reveal carelessness, inaccuracy, or even wilful distortion of facts. The genius of the *Novella*, so paramount in popular Italian literature of that epoch, presided over their composition, adding *intreccio* to disconnected facts, heightening sympathy by the suggestion of romantic motives, turning the heroes or the heroines of their adventures into saints, and blackening the faces of the villains. Yet these stories, pretending to be veracious and aiming at information no less than entertainment, present us with even a more vivid picture of customs than the *Novelle*. By their truthful touches of landscape and incident painting, by their unconscious revelation of contemporary sentiment in dialogue and ethical analysis of motives, they enable us to give form and substance to the drier details of the law courts. One of these narratives I propose to condense from the transcript made by Henri Beyle, for the sake of the light it throws upon the tragedy of the Caraffa family.[29] It opens with an account of Paul IV.'s ascent to power and a description of his nephews. Don Giovanni, the eldest son of the Count of Montorio, was married to Violante de Cardona, sister of the Count Aliffe. Paul invested him with the Duchy of Palliano, which he wrested from Marc Antonio Colonna. Don Carlo, the second son, who had passed his life as a soldier, entered the Sacred College; and Don Antonio, the third, was created Marquis of Montebello. The Cardinal, as prime minister, assumed the reins of government in Rome. The Duke of Palliano disposed of the Papal soldiery. The Marquis of Montebello, commanding the guard of the palace, excluded or admitted persons at his pleasure. Surrounded by these nephews, Paul saw only with their eyes, heard only what they whispered to him, and unwittingly lent his authority to their lawlessness. They exercised an unlimited tyranny in Rome, laying hands on property and abusing their position to gratify their lusts. No woman who had the misfortune to please them was safe; and the cells of convents were as little respected as the palaces of gentlefolk. To arrive at justice was impossible; for the three brothers commanded all avenues, civil, ecclesiastical, and military, by which the Pope could be approached.

Violante, Duchess of Palliano, was a young woman distinguished for her beauty no less than for her Spanish pride. She had received a thoroughly Italian education; could recite the sonnets of Petrarch and the stanzas of Ariosto by heart, and repeated the tales of Ser Giovanni and other novelists with an originality that lent new charm to their style.[30] Her court was a splendid one, frequented by noble youths and gentlewomen of the best blood in Naples. Two of these require particular notice: Diana Brancaccio, a relative of the Marchioness of Montebello; and Marcello Capecce, a young man of exceptional beauty. Diana was a woman of thirty years, hot-tempered, tawny-haired, devotedly in love with Dominiziano Fornari, a squire of the Marchese di Montebello's household. Marcello had conceived one of those bizarre passions for

29 'La Duchesse de Palliano,' in *Chroniques et Nouvelles*, De Stendhal (Henri Beyle).

30 This touch shows what were then considered the accomplishments of a noble woman.

the Duchess, in which an almost religious adoration was mingled with audacity, persistence, and aptitude for any crime. The character of his mistress gave him but little hope. Though profoundly wounded by her husband's infidelities, insulted in her pride by the presence of his wanton favourites under her own roof, and assailed by the importunities of the most brilliant profligates in Rome, she held a haughty course, above suspicion, free from taint or stain. Marcello could do nothing but sigh at a distance and watch his opportunity.

At this point, the narrator seems to sacrifice historical accuracy for the sake of combining his chief characters in one intrigue.[31] Though he assumes the tone of a novelist rather than a chronicler, there has hitherto been nothing but what corresponds to fact in his description of the Caraffa cabal. He now explains their downfall; and opens the subject after this fashion: At the beginning of the year 1559, the Pope's confessor ventured to bring before his notice the scandalous behaviour of the Papal nephews. Paul at first refused to credit this report. But an incident happened which convinced him of its truth. On the feast of the Circumcision—a circumstance which aggravated matters in the eyes of a strictly pious Pontiff—Andrea Lanfranchi, secretary to the Duke of Palliano, invited the Cardinal Caraffa to a banquet. One of the loveliest and most notorious courtesans of Rome, Martuccia, was also present; and it so happened that Marcello Capecce at this epoch believed he had more right to her favours than any other man in the capital. That night he sought her in her lodgings, pursued her up and down, and learned at last that she was supping with Lanfranchi and the Cardinal. Attended by armed men, he made his way to Lanfranchi's house, entered the banquet room, and ordered Martuccia to come away with him at once. The Cardinal, who was dressed in secular habit, rose, and, drawing his sword, protested against this high-handed proceeding. Martuccia, by favour of their host, was his partner that evening. Upon this, Marcello called his men; but when they recognised the Cardinal nephew, they refused to employ violence. In the course of the quarrel, Martuccia made her escape, followed by Marcello, Caraffa, and the company. There ensued a street-brawl between the young man and the Cardinal; but no blood was spilt, and the incident need have had but slight importance, if the Duke of Palliano had not thought it necessary to place Lanfranchi and Marcello under arrest. They were soon released, because it became evident that the chief scandal would fall upon the Cardinal, who had clearly been scuffling and crossing swords in a dispute about a common prostitute. The three Caraffa brothers resolved on hushing the affair up. But it was too late. The Pope heard something, which sufficed to confirm his confessor's warnings; and on January 27, he pronounced the famous sentence on his nephews. The Cardinal was banished to Cività Lavinia,

[31] It was a street-brawl, in which the Cardinal Monte played an indecent part, that finally aroused the anger of Paul IV. De Stendhal's MS. shifts the chief blame on to the shoulders of Cardinal Caraffa, who indeed appears to have been in the habit of keeping bad company.

the Duke to Soriano, the Marquis to Montebello. The Duchess took up her abode with her court in the little village of Gallese. It was here that the episode of her love and tragic end ensued.

Violante found herself almost alone in a simple village among mountains, half-way between Rome and Orvieto, surrounded indeed by lovely forest scenery, but deprived of all the luxuries and entertainments to which she was accustomed. Marcello and Diana were at her side, the one eager to pursue his hitherto hopeless suit, and the other to further it for her own profit. One day Marcello committed the apparent imprudence of avowing his passion. The Duchess rejected him with scorn, but disclosed the fact to Diana, who calculated that if she could contrive to compromise her mistress, she might herself be able to secure the end she had in view of marrying Dominiziano. In the solitude of those long days of exile the waiting-woman returned again and again to the subject of Marcello's devotion, his beauty, his noble blood and his manifold good qualities. She arranged meetings in the woods between the Duchess and her lover, and played her cards so well that during the course of the fine summer weeks Violante yielded to Marcello. Diana now judged it wise to press her own suit forward with Dominiziano. But this cold-blooded fellow knew that he was no fit match for a relative of the Marchioness of Montebello. He felt, besides, but little sentiment for his fiery *innamorata*. Dreading the poignard of the Caraffas, if he should presume to marry her, he took the prudent course of slipping away in disguise from the port of Nettuno. Diana, maddened by disappointment, flew to the conclusion that the Duchess had planned her lover's removal, and resolved to take a cruel revenge. The Duke of Palliano was residing at Soriano, only a few miles from Gallese. To bring him secret information of his wife's intrigue was a matter of no difficulty. At first he refused to believe her report. Had not Violante resisted the seductions of all Rome, and repelled the advances even of the Duke of Guise? At last she contrived to introduce him into the bedroom of the Duchess at a moment when Marcello was also there. The circumstances were not precisely indicative of guilt. The sun had only just gone down behind the hills; a maid was in attendance; and the Duchess lay in bed, pencilling some memoranda. Yet they were sufficient to rouse the Duke's anger. He disarmed Marcello and removed him to the prisons of Soriano, leaving Violante under strict guard at Gallese.

The Duke of Palliano had no intention of proclaiming his jealousy or of suggesting his dishonour, until he had extracted complete proof. He therefore pretended to have arrested Marcello on the suspicion of an attempt to poison him. Some large toads, bought by the young man at a high price two or three months earlier, lent colour to this accusation. Meanwhile the investigation was conducted as secretly as possible by the Duke in person, his brother-in-law Count Aliffe, and a certain Antonio Torando, with the sanction of the Podestà of Soriano. After examining several witnesses, they became convinced of Violante's guilt. Marcello was put to the torture, and eventually confessed. The Duke stabbed him to death with his own hands, and afterwards cut Diana's throat for her share in the business. Both bodies were thrown into the prison-sewer. Meanwhile Paul IV. had retained the young Cardinal, Alfonso Caraffa, son of the Marquis of Montebello, near his person. This prelate thought it right to inform his grand-uncle of the occurrences at Soriano. The Pope only answered: 'And the Duchess? What have they done with her?' Paul IV. died in August, and the Conclave, which ended in the election of Pius IV., was opened. During the important intrigues of that moment, Cardinal Alfonso found time to write to the Duke, imploring him not to leave so dark a stain upon his honour, but to exercise justice on a guilty wife. On August 28, 1559, the Duke sent the Count Aliffe, and Don Leonardo del Cardine, with a company of soldiers, to Gallese. They told Violante that they had arrived to kill her, and offered her the offices of two Franciscan monks. Before her death, the Duchess repeatedly insisted on her innocence, and received the sacrament from the hands of Friar Antonio of Pavia. The Count, her brother, then proceeded to her execution. 'He covered her eyes with a handkerchief, which she, with perfect *sang froid*, drew somewhat lower in order to shut his sight out. Then he adjusted the cord to her neck; but finding that it would not exactly fit, he removed it and walked away. The Duchess raised the bandage from her face, and said: "Well! what are we about then?" He answered: "The cord was not quite right, and I am going to get another, in order that you may not suffer." When he returned to the room, he arranged the handkerchief again, fixed the cord, turned the wand in the knot behind her neck, and strangled her. The whole incident, on the part of the Duchess, passed in the tone of ordinary conversation. She died like a good Christian, frequently repeating the words *Credo, Credo.*'

Contrary to the usual custom and opinion of the age, this murder of an erring wife and sister formed part of the accusations brought against the Duke of Palliano and Count Aliffe. It will be remembered that they were executed in Rome, together with the elder Cardinal Caraffa, during the pontificate of Pius IV.

Wife-Murders.

It would be difficult to give any adequate notion of the frequency of wife-murders at this epoch in the higher ranks of society. I will, however, mention a few, noticed by me in the course of study. Donna Pellegrina, daughter of Bianca Capello before her marriage with the Grand Duke of Tuscany, was killed at Bologna in 1598 by four masked assassins, at the order of her husband, Count Ulisse Bentivoglio. She had been suspected or convicted of adultery; and the Court of Florence sent word to the Count, 'che essendo vero quanto scriveva, facesse quello che conveniva a cavaliere di honore.' In the light of open day, together with two of her gentlewomen and her coachman, she was cut to pieces and left on the road.[32] In 1590 at Naples Don Carlo Gesualdo, son of the Prince of Venosta, assassinated his wife and cousin Donna Maria d' Avalos, to-

[32] Mutinelli, *Storia Arcana*, vol. ii. p. 64.

gether with her lover, Fabricio Caraffa, Duke of Andri. This crime was committed in his palace by the husband, attended by a band of cut-throats.[33] In 1577, at Milan, Count Giovanni Borromeo, cousin of the Cardinal Federigo, stabbed his wife, the Countess Giulia Sanseverina, sister of the Countessa di Sala, at table, with three mortal wounds. A mere domestic squabble gave rise to this tragedy.[34] In 1598, in his villa of Zenzalino at Ferrara, the Count Ercole Trotti, with the assistance of a bravo called Jacopo Lazzarini, killed his wife Anna, daughter of the poet Guarini. Her own brother Girolamo connived at the act and helped to facilitate its execution. She was accused—falsely, as it afterwards appeared from Girolamo's confession—of an improper intimacy with the Count Ercole Bevilacqua. I may add that Count Ercole Trotti's father, Alphonso, had murdered his own wife, Michela Granzena, in the same villa.[35]

The Medici

The history of the Medicean family during the sixteenth century epitomises the chief features of social morality upon which I have been dwelling in this chapter. It will be remembered that Alessandro de' Medici, the first Duke of Florence, poisoned his cousin Ippolito, and was himself assassinated by his cousin Lorenzino. To the second of these crimes Cosimo, afterwards Grand Duke of Tuscany, owed the throne of Florence, on which, however, he was not secure until he had removed Lorenzino from this world by the poignard of a bravo. Cosimo maintained his authority by a system of espionage, remorseless persecution, and assassination, which gave colour even to the most improbable of legends.[36] But it is not of him so much as of his children that I have to speak. Francesco, who reigned from 1564 till 1587, brought disgrace upon his line by marrying the infamous Bianca Capello, after authorising the murder of her previous husband. Bianca, though incapable of bearing children, flattered her besotted paramour before this marriage by pretending to have borne a son. In reality, she had secured the co-operation of three women on the point of childbirth; and when one of these was delivered of a boy, she presented this infant to Francesco, who christened him Antonio de' Medici. Of the three mothers who served in this nefarious transaction, Bianca contrived to assassinate two, but not before one of the victims to her dread of exposure made full confession at the point of death. The third escaped. Another woman who had superintended the affair was shot between Florence and Bologna in the valleys of the Apennines. Yet after the manifestation of Bianca's imposture, the Duke continued to recognise Antonio as belonging to the Medicean family; and his successor was

[33] *Ib.* vol. ii. p. 162.
[34] *Ib.* vol. i. p. 343
[35] *I Guarini Famiglia Nobile Ferrarese* (Bologna, Romagnoli, 1870), pp. 83-87
[36] In addition to the victims of his vengeance who perished by the poignard, he publicly executed in Florence forty-two political offenders.

obliged to compel this young man to assume the Cross of Malta, in order to exclude his posterity from the line of princes.[37] The legend of Francesco's and Bianca's mysterious death is well known. The Duchess had engaged in fresh intrigues for palming off a spurious child upon her husband. These roused the suspicions of his brother Cardinal Ferdinando de' Medici, heir presumptive to the crown. An angry correspondence followed, ending in a reconciliation between the three princes. They met in the autumn of 1587 at the villa of Poggio a Cajano. Then the world was startled by the announcement that the Grand Duke had died of fever, after a few days' illness, and that Bianca had almost immediately afterwards followed him to the grave. Ferdinand, on succeeding to the throne, refused her the interment suited to her rank, defaced her arms on public edifices, and for her name and titles in official documents substituted the words, 'la pessima Bianca.' What passed at Poggio a Cajano is not known. It was commonly believed in Italy that Bianca, meaning to poison the Cardinal at supper, had been frustrated in her designs by a blunder which made her husband the victim of this plot, and that she ended her own life in despair or fell a victim to the Cardinal's vengeance. This story is rejected both by Botta and Galluzzi; but Litta has given it a partial credence.[38] Two of Cosimo's sons died previously, in the year 1562, under circumstances which gave rise to similar malignant rumours. Don Garzia and the Cardinal Giovanni were hunting together in the Pisan marshes, when the latter expired after a short illness, and the former in a few days met with a like fate. Report ran that Don Garzia had stabbed his brother, and that Cosimo, in a fit of rage, ran him through the body with his own sword. In this case, although Litta attaches weight to the legend, the balance of evidence is strongly in favour of both brothers having been carried off by a pernicious fever contracted simultaneously during their hunting expedition.[39] Each instance serves, however, to show in what an atmosphere of guilt the Medicean princes were enveloped. No one beleived that they could die except by fraternal or paternal hands. And the authentic crimes of the family certainly justified this popular belief. I have already alluded to the murders of Ippolito, Alessandro, and Lorenzino. I have told how the Court of Florence sanctioned the assassination of Bianca's daughter by her husband at Bologna.[40] I must now proceed to relate the tragic tales of the princesses of the house.

Pietro de' Medici, a fifth of Cosimo's sons, had rendered himself notorious in Spain and Italy by forming a secret society for the most revolting debaucheries.[41] Yet he married the noble lady Eleonora di

[37] See Mutinelli, *Storia Arcana*, vol. ii. pp. 54-56, for Antonio's reception into the Order.

[38] I refer, of course, to Galluzzi's *Storia del Gran Ducato*, vol. iv. pp. 241-244. Botta's *Storia d' Italia*, Book XIV., and Litta's *Famiglie Celebri* under the pedigree of Medici.

[39] See Galluzzi, *op. cit.* vol. iii. p. 25, and Botta, *op. cit.* Book XII.

[40] See above, p. 694.

[41] Litta may be consulted for details; also Galluzzi, *op. cit.* vol. v. p. 174.

Toledo, related by blood to Cosimo's first wife. Neglected and outraged by her husband, she proved unfaithful, and Pietro hewed her in pieces with his own hands at Caffaggiolo. Isabella de' Medici, daughter of Cosimo, was married to the Duke of Bracciano. Educated in the empoisoned atmosphere of Florence, she, like Eleonora di Toledo, yielded herself to fashionable profligacy, and was strangled by her husband at Cerretto.[42] Both of these murders took place in 1576. Isabella's death, as I have elsewhere related, opened the way for the Duke of Bracciano's marriage with Vittoria Accoramboni, which had been prepared by the assassination of her first husband, and which led to her own murder at Padua.[43] Another of Cosimo's daughters, Lucrezia de' Medici, became Duchess of Ferrara, fell under a suspicion of infidelity, and was possibly removed by poison in 1561.[44] The last of his sons whom I have to mention, Don Giovanni, married a dissolute woman of low birth called Livia, and disgraced the name of Medici by the unprincely follies of his life. Eleonora de' Medici, third of his daughters, introduces a comic element into these funereal records. She was affianced to Vincenzo Gonzaga, heir of the Duchy of Mantua. But suspicions, arising out of the circumstances of his divorce from a former wife, obliged him to prove his marital capacity before the completion of the contract. This he did at Venice, before a witness, upon the person of a virgin selected for the experiment.[45] Maria de' Medici, the only child of Duke Francesco, became Queen of France. The history of her amours with Concini forms an episode in French annals.

If now we eliminate the deaths of Don Garzia, Cardinal Giovanni, Duke Francesco, Bianca Capello, and Lucrezia de' Medici, as doubtful, there will still remain the murders of Cardinal Ippolito, Duke Alessandro, Lorenzino de' Medici, Pietro Bonaventuri (Bianca's husband), Pellegrina Bentivoglio (Bianca's daughter), Eleonora di Toledo, Francesco Casi (Eleonora's lover), the Duchess of Bracciano, Troilo Orsini (lover of this Duchess), Felice Peretti (husband of Vittoria Accoramboni), and Vittoria Accoramboni—eleven murders, all occurring between 1535 and 1585, an exact half-century, in a single princely family and its immediate connexions. The majority of these crimes, that is to say seven, had their origin in lawless passion.[46]

[42] It may be worth mentioning that Virginio Orsini, Bracciano's son and heir, married Donna Flavia, grand-niece of Sixtus V., and consequently related to the man his father murdered in order to possess Vittoria Accoramboni. See Mutinelli, *Storia Arcana*, vol. ii. p. 72.

[43] See above, pp. 685-689.

[44] Galluzzi, vol. iii. p. 5, says that she died of a putrid fever. Litta again inclines to the probability of poison. But this must be counted among the doubtful cases.

[45] See Galluzzi, *op. cit.* vol. iv. pp. 195-197, for the account of a transaction which throws curious light upon the customs of the age. It was only stipulated that the trial should not take place upon a Friday. Otherwise, the highest ecclesiastics gave it their full approval.

[46] I have told the stories in this chapter as drily as I could. Yet it would be interesting to analyse the fascination they exercised over our Elizabethan playwrights, some of whose Italian tragedies handle the material with penetrative imagination. For the English mode of interpreting southern passion see my *Italian Byways*, pp. 169 *et seq.*, and a brilliant essay in Vernon Lee's *Euphorion*.

CHAPTER VI

SOCIAL AND DOMESTIC MORALS: PART II

Tales illustrative of Bravi and Banditti—Cecco Bibboni—Ambrogio Tremazzi—Lodovico dall' Armi—Brigandage—Piracy—Plagues—The Plagues of Milan, Venice, Piedmont—Persecution of the Untori—Moral State of the Proletariat—Witchcraft—Its Italian Features—History of Giacomo Centini.

THE stories related in the foregoing chapter abundantly demonstrate the close connexion between the aristocracy and their accomplices—bravi and bandits. But it still remains to consider this connexion from the professional murderer's own point of view. And for this purpose, I will now make use of two documents vividly illustrative of the habits, sentiments, and social status of men who undertook to speculate in bloodshed for reward. They are both autobiographical; and both relate tragedies which occupied the attention of all Italy.

Cecco Bibboni.

The first of these documents is the report made by Cecco Bibboni concerning his method adopted for the murder of Lorenzino de' Medici at Venice in 1546. Lorenzino, by the help of a bravo called Scoroncolo, had assassinated his cousin Alessandro, Duke of Florence, in 1537. After accomplishing this deed, which gained for him the name of Brutus, he escaped from the city; and a distant relative of the murdered and the murderer, Cosimo de' Medici, was chosen Duke in Alessandro's stead. One of the first acts of his reign was to publish a ban of outlawry against Lorenzino. His portrait was painted, according to old Tuscan usage, head-downwards, and suspended by one foot, upon the wall of Alessandro's fortress. His house was cut in twain from roof to pavement, and a narrow passage was driven through it, which received the name of Traitor's Alley—*Chiasso del Traditore.* The price put upon his head was enormous—four thousand golden florins, with a pension of one hundred florins to the murderer and his heirs in perpetuity. The man who should kill Lorenzino was, further, to enjoy amnesty from all offences and to exercise full civic rights; he was promised exemption from taxes, the privilege of carrying arms with two attendants in the whole domain of Florence, and the prerogative of restoring ten outlaws at his choice. If he captured Lorenzino and brought him alive to Florence, the reward would be doubled in each item. There was enough here to raise cupidity and stir the speculative spirit. Cecco Bibboni shall tell us how the business was brought to a successful termination.[1]

'When I returned from Germany,' begins Bibboni, 'where I had been in the pay of the Emperor, I found at Vicenza Bebo da Volterra, who was staying in the house of M. Antonio da Roma, a nobleman of that city. This gentleman employed him because of a great feud he had; and he was mighty pleased, moreover, at my coming, and desired that I too should take up my quarters in his palace.'

Bibboni proceeds to say how another gentleman of Vicenza, M. Francesco Manente, had at this time a feud with certain of the Guazzi and the Laschi, which had lasted several years, and cost the lives of many members of both parties and their following. M. Francesco, being a friend of M. Antonio, besought that gentleman to lend him Bibboni and Bebo for a season; and the two bravi went together with their new master to Celsano, a village in the neighbourhood. 'There both parties had estates, and all of them kept armed men in their houses, so that not a day passed without feats of arms, and always there was some one killed or wounded. One day, soon afterwards, the leaders of our party resolved to attack the foe in their house, where we killed two, and the rest, numbering five men, entrenched themselves in a ground-floor apartment; whereupon we took possession of their harquebusses and other arms, which forced them to abandon the villa and retire to Vicenza; and within a short space of time this great feud was terminated by an ample peace.' After this Bebo took service with the Rector of the University in Padua, and was transferred by his new patron to Milan. Bibboni remained at Vicenza with M. Galeazzo della Seta, who stood in great fear of his life, notwithstanding the peace which had been concluded between the two factions. At the end of ten months he returned to M. Antonio da Roma and his six brothers, 'all of whom being very much attached to me, they proposed that I should live my life with them for good or ill, and be treated as one of the family; upon the understanding that if war broke out and I wanted to take part in it, I should always have twenty-five crowns and arms and horse, with welcome home, so long as I lived; and in case I did not care to join the troops, the same provision for my maintenance.'

From these details we comprehend the sort of calling which a bravo of Bibboni's species followed. Meanwhile Bebo was at Milan. 'There it happened that M. Francesco Vinta, of Volterra, was on embassy from the Duke of Florence. He saw Bebo, and asked him what he was doing in Milan, and Bebo answered that he was a knight errant.' This phrase —derived, no doubt, from the romantic epics then in vogue—was a pretty euphemism for a rogue of Bebo's quality. The ambassador now began cautiously to sound his man, who seems to have been outlawed from the Tuscan duchy, telling him he knew a way by which he might return with favour to his home, and at last disclosing the affair of Lorenzo. Bebo was puzzled at first, but when he understood the matter, he

[1] For the Italian text see *Lorenzino de' Medici*, Daelli, Milano, 1862. The above is borrowed from my *Italian Byways*.

professed his willingness, took letters from the envoy to the Duke of Florence, and, in a private audience with Cosimo, informed him that he was ready to attempt Lorenzino's assassination. He added that 'he had a comrade fit for such a job, whose fellow for the business could not easily be found.'

Bebo now travelled to Vicenza, and opened the whole matter to Bibboni, who weighed it well, and at last, being convinced that the Duke's commission to his comrade was *bona fide*, determined to take his share in the undertaking. The two agreed to have no accomplices. They went to Venice, and 'I,' says Bibboni, 'being most intimately acquainted with all that city, and provided there with many friends, soon quietly contrived to know where Lorenzino lodged, and took a room in the neighbourhood, and spent some days in seeing how we best might rule our conduct.' Bibboni soon discovered that Lorenzino never left his palace; and he therefore remained in much perplexity, until, by good luck, Ruberto Strozzi arrived from France in Venice, bringing in his train a Navarrese servant, who had the nickname of Spagnoletto. This fellow was a great friend of the bravo. They met, and Bibboni told him that he should like to go and kiss the hands of Messer Ruberto, whom he had known in Rome. Strozzi inhabited the same palace as Lorenzino. 'When we arrived there, both Messer Ruberto and Lorenzo were leaving the house, and there were around them so many gentlemen and other persons, that I could not present myself, and both straightway stepped into the gondola. Then I, not having seen Lorenzo for a long while past, and because he was very quietly attired, could not recognise the man exactly, but only as it were between certainty and doubt. Wherefore I said to Spagnoletto, "I think I know that gentleman, but don't remember where I saw him." And Messer Ruberto was giving him his right hand. Then Spagnoletto answered, "You know him well enough; he is Messer Lorenzo. But see you tell this to nobody. He goes by the name of Messer Dario, because he lives in great fear for his safety, and people don't know that he is now in Venice." I answered that I marveled much, and if I could have helped him would have done so willingly. Then I asked where they were going, and he said, to dine with Messer Giovanni della Casa, who was the Pope's Legate. I did not leave the man till I had drawn from him all I required.'

Thus spoke the Italian Judas. The appearance of La Casa on the scene is interesting. He was the celebrated author of the 'Capitolo del Forno,' the author of many sublime and melancholy sonnets, who was now at Venice, prosecuting a charge of heresy against Pier Paolo Vergerio, and paying his addresses to a noble lady of the Quirini family. It seems that on the territory of San Marco he made common cause with the exiles from Florence, for he was himself by birth a Florentine, and he had no objection to take Brutus-Lorenzino by the hand.

After the noblemen had rowed off in their gondola to dine with the Legate, Bibboni and his friend entered their palace, where he found another old acquaintance, the house-steward, or *spenditore* of Lorenzo.

From him he gathered much useful information. Pietro Strozzi it seems, had allowed the tyrannicide one thousand five hundred crowns a year, with the keep of three brave and daring companions (*tre compagni bravi e facinorosi*), and a palace worth fifty crowns on lease. But Lorenzo had just taken another on the Campo di San Polo at three hundred crowns a year, for which swagger (*altura*) Pietro Strozzi had struck a thousand crowns off his allowance. Bibboni also learned that he was keeping house with his uncle, Alessandro Soderini, another Florentine outlaw, and that he was ardently in love with a certain beautiful Barozza. This woman was apparently one of the grand courtesans of Venice. He further ascertained the date when he was going to move into the palace at San Polo, and, 'to put it briefly, knew everything he did, and, as it were, how many times a day he spit.' Such were the intelligences of the servants' hall, and of such value were they to men of Bibboni's calling.

In the Cardinal of 1546 Lorenzo meant to go masqued in the habit of a gipsy woman to the square of San Spirito, where there was to be a joust. Great crowds of people would assemble, and Bibboni hoped to do his business there. The assassination, however, failed on this occasion, and Lorenzo took up his abode in the palace he had hired upon the Campo di San Polo. This Campo is one of the largest open places in Venice, shaped irregularly, with a finely curving line upon the western side, where two of the noblest private houses in the city are still standing. Nearly opposide these, in the south-western angle, stands, detached, the little old church of San Polo. One of its side entrances opens upon the square; the other on a lane which leads eventually to the Frari. There is nothing in Bibboni's narrative to make it clear where Lorenzo hired his dwelling. But it would seem from certain things which he says later on, that in order to enter the church his victim had to cross the square. Meanwhile Bibboni took the precaution of making friends with a shoemaker, whose shop commanded the whole Campo, including Lorenzo's palace. In this shop he began to spend much of his time; 'and oftentimes I feigned to be asleep; but God knows whether I was sleeping, for my mind, at any rate, was wide-awake.'

A second convenient occasion for murdering Lorenzo soon seemed to offer. He was bidden to dine with Monsignor della Casa; and Bibboni, putting a bold face on, entered the Legate's palace, having left Bebo below in the loggia, fully resolved to do the business. 'But we found,' he says, 'that they had gone to dine at Murano, so that we remained with our tabors in their bag.' The island of Murano at that period was a favourite resort of the Venetian nobles, especially of the more literary and artistic, who kept country-houses there, where they enjoyed the fresh air of the lagoons and the quiet of their gardens.

The third occasion, after all these weeks of watching, brought success to Bibboni's schemes. He had observed how Lorenzo occasionally so far broke his rules of caution as to go on foot, past the church of San Polo, to visit the beautiful Barozza; and he resolved, if possible, to catch him on one of these journeys. 'It so chanced on February 28, which was the second Sunday of Lent, that having gone, as was my wont, to pry out whether Lorenzo would give orders for going abroad that day, I entered the shoemaker's shop, and stayed awhile, until Lorenzo came to the window with a napkin round his neck—for he was combing his hair—and at the same moment I saw a certain Giovan Battista Martelli, who kept his sword for the defence of Lorenzo's person, enter and come forth again. Concluding that they would probably go abroad, I went home to get ready and procure the necessary weapons, and there I found Bebo asleep in bed, and made him get up at once, and we came to our accustomed post of observation, by the church of San Polo, where our men would have to pass.' Bibboni now retired to his friend the shoemaker's, and Bebo took up his station at one of the side doors of San Polo; 'and, as good luck would have it, Giovan Battista Martelli came forth, and walked a piece in front, and then Lorenzo came, and then Alessandro Soderini, going the one behind the other, like storks, and Lorenzo, on entering the church, and lifting up the curtain of the door, was seen from the opposite door by Bebo, who at the same time noticed how I had left the shop, and so we met upon the street as we had agreed, and he told me that Lorenzo was inside the church.'

To anyone who knows the Campo di San Polo, it will be apparent that Lorenzo had crossed from the western side of the piazza and entered the church by what is technically called its northern door. Bebo, stationed at the southern door, could see him when he pushed the heavy *stoia* or leather curtain aside, and at the same time could observe Bibboni's movements in the cobbler's shop. Meanwhile Lorenzo walked across the church and came to the same door where Bebo had been standing. 'I saw him issue from the church and take the main street; then came Alessandro Soderini, and I walked last of all; and when we reached the point we had determined on, I jumped in front of Alessandro with the poignard in my hand, crying, "Hold hard, Alessandro, and get along with you, in God's name, for we are not here for you!" He then threw himself around my waist, and grasped my arms, and kept on calling out. Seeing how wrong I had been to try to spare his life, I wrenched myself as well as I could from his grip, and with my lifted poignard struck him, as God willed, above the eyebrow, and a little blood trickled from the wound. He, in high fury, gave me such a thrust that I fell backward, and the ground besides was slippery from having rained a little. Then Alessandro drew his sword, which he carried in its scabbard, and thrust at me in front, and struck me on the corslet, which for my good fortune was of double mail. Before I could get ready I received three passes, which, had I worn a doublet instead of that mailed corslet, would certainly have run me through. At the fourth pass I had regained my strength and spirit, and closed with him, and stabbed him four times in the head, and being so close he could not use his sword, but tried to parry with his hand and hilt, and I, as God willed, struck him at the wrist below the sleeve of mail, and cut his hand off clean, and gave him then one last stroke on his head. Thereupon he begged for God's sake spare his life, and I, in trouble about Bebo, left him in the arms of a Venetian nobleman, who held him back from jumping into the canal.'

Who this Venetian nobleman, found unexpectedly upon the scene, was, does not appear. Nor, what is still more curious, do we hear anything of that Martelli, the bravo, 'who kept his sword for the defence of Lorenzo's person.' The one had arrived accidentally, it seems. The other must have been a coward and escaped from the scuffle.

'When I turned,' proceeds Bibboni, 'I found Lorenzo on his knees. He raised himself, and I, in anger, gave him a great cut across the head, which split it in two pieces, and laid him at my feet, and he never rose again.'

Bebo, meanwhile, had made off from the scene of action. And Bibboni, taking to his heels, came up with him in the little square of San Marcello. They now ran for their lives till they reached the Traghetto di San Spirito, where they threw their poignards into the water, remembering that no man might carry these in Venice under penalty of the galleys. Bibboni's white hose were drenched with blood. He therefore afreed to separate from Bebo, having named a rendezvous. Left alone, his ill luck brought him face to face with twenty constables (*sbirri*). 'In a moment I conceived that they knew everything, and were come to capture me, and of a truth I saw that it was over with me. As swiftly as I could I quickened pace and got into a church, near to which was the house of a Compagnia, and the one opened into the other, and knelt down and prayed, commending myself with fervour to God for my deliverance and safety. Yet while I prayed, I kept my eyes well open and saw the whole band pass the church, except one man who entered, and I strained my sight so that I seemed to see behind as well as in front, and then it was I longed for my poignard, for I should not have heeded being in a church.' But the constable, it soon appeared, was not looking for Bibboni. So he gathered up his courage, and ran for the Church of San Spirito, where the Padre Andrea Volterrano was preaching to a great congregation. He hoped to go in by one door and out by the other, but the crowd prevented him, and he had to turn back and face the *sbirri*. One of them followed him, having probably caught sight of the blood upon his hose. Then Bibboni resolved to have done with the fellow, and rushed at him, and flung him down with his head upon the pavement, and ran like mad, and came at last, all out of breath, to San Marco.

It seems clear that before Bibboni separated from Bebo, they had crossed the water, for the Sestiere di San Polo is separated from the Sestiere di San Marco by the Grand Canal. And this they must have done at the Traghetto di San Spirito. Neither the church nor the traghetto are now in existence, and this part of the story is therefore obscure.[2] Having reached San Marco, he took a gondola at the Ponte

[2] So far as I can discover, the only church of San Spirito in Venice was a building on the island of San Spirito, erected by Sansovino, which belonged to the Sestiere di S. Croce, and which was suppressed in 1656. Its plate and the fine pictures which Titian

della Paglia, where tourists are now want to stand and contemplate the Ducal Palace and the Bridge of Sighs. First, he sought the house of a woman of the town who was his friend; then changed purpose, and rowed to the palace of the Count Salici da Collalto. 'He was a great friend and intimate of ours, because Bebo and I had done him many and great services in times past. There I knocked; and Bebo opened the door, and when he saw me dabbled with blood, he marvelled that I had not come to grief and fallen into the hands of justice, and, indeed, had feared as much because I had remained so long away.' It appears, therefore, that the Palazzo Collalto was their rendezvous. 'The Count was from home; but being known to all his people, I played the master and went into the kitchen to the fire, and with soap and water turned my hose, which had been white, to a grey colour.' This is a very delicate way of saying that he washed out the blood of Alessandro and Lorenzo!

Soon after the Count returned, and 'lavished caresses' upon Bebo and his precious comrade. They did not tell him what they had achieved that morning, but put him off with a story of having settled a *sbirro* in a quarrel about a girl. Then the Count invited them to dinner; and being himself bound to entertain the first physician of Venice, requested them to take it in an upper chamber. He and his secretary served them with their own hands at table. When the physician arrived, the Count went downstairs; and at this moment a messenger came from Lorenzo's mother, begging the doctor to go at once to San Polo, for that her son had been murdered and Soderini wounded to the death. It was now no longer possible to conceal their doings from the Count, who told them to pluck up courage and abide in patience. He had himself to dine and take his siesta, and then to attend a meeting of the Council.

About the hour of vespers, Bibboni determined to seek better refuge. Followed at a discreet distance by Bebo, he first called at their lodgings and ordered supper. Two priests came in and fell into conversation with them. But something in the behaviour of one of these good men roused Bibboni's suspicions. So they left the house, took a gondola, and told the man to row hard to S. Maria Zobenigo. On the way they bade him put them on shore, paid him well, and ordered him to wait for them. They landed near the palace of the Spanish embassy; and here Bibboni meant to seek sanctuary. For it must be remembered that the houses of ambassadors, no less than those of princes of the Church, were inviolable. They offered the most convenient harbouring-places to rascals. Charles V., moreover, was deeply interested in the vengeance taken on Alessandro de' Medici's murderer, for his own natural daughter was Alessandro's widow and Duchess of Florence. In the palace they were received with much courtesy by about forty Spaniards, who showed considerable curiosity, and told them that Lorenzo and Alessandro Soderini had been

painted there were transferred at that date to S. M. della Salute. I cannot help inferring that either Bibboni's memory failed him, or that his words were wrongly understood by printer or amanuensis. If for S. Spirito we substitute S. Stefano, the account would be intelligible.

murdered that morning by two men whose description answered to their appearance. Bibboni put their questions by and asked to see the ambassador. He was not at home. In that case, said Bibboni, take us to the secretary. Attended by some thirty Spaniards, 'with great joy and gladness,' they were shown into the secretary's chamber. He sent the rest of the folk away, 'and locked the door well, and then embraced and kissed us before we had said a word, and afterwards bade us talk freely without any fear.' When Bibboni had told the whole story, he was again embraced and kissed by the secretary, who thereupon left them and went to the private apartment of the ambassador. Shortly after he returned and led them by a winding staircase into the presence of his master. The ambassador greeted them with great honour, told them he would strain all the power of the empire to hand them in safety over to Duke Cosimo, and that he had already sent a courier to the Emperor with the good news.

So they remained in hiding in the Spanish embassy; and in ten days' time commands were received from Charles himself that everything should be done to convey them safely to Florence. The difficulty was how to smuggle them out of Venice, where the police of the Republic were on watch, and Florentine outlaws were mounting guard on sea and shore to catch them. The ambassador began by spreading reports on the Rialto every morning of their having been seen at Padua, at Verona, in Friuli. He then hired a palace at Malghera, near Mestre, and went out daily with fifty Spaniards, and took carriage or amused himself with horse exercise and shooting. The Florentines, who were on watch, could only discover from his people that he did this for amusement. When he thought that he had put them sufficiently off their guard, the ambassador one day took Bibboni and Bebo out by Canaregio to Malghera, concealed in his own gondola, with the whole train of Spaniards in attendance. And though, on landing, the Florentines challenged them, they durst not interfere with an ambassador or come to battle with his men. So Bebo and Bibboni were hustled into a coach, and afterwards provided with two comrades and four horses. They rode for ninety miles without stopping to sleep, and on the day following this long journey reached Trento, having probably threaded the mountain valleys above Bassano, for Bibboni speaks of a certain village where the people talked half German. The Imperial Ambassador at Trento forwarded them next day to Mantua; from Mantua they came to Piacenza; thence passing through the valley of the Taro, crossing the Apennines at Cisa, descending on Pontremoli, and reaching Pisa at night, the fourteenth day after their escape from Venice.

When they arrived at Pisa, Duke Cosimo was supping. So they went to an inn, and next morning presented themselves to his Grace. Cosimo welcomed them kindly, assured them of his gratitude, confirmed them in the enjoyment of their rewards and privileges, and swore that they might rest secure of his protection in all parts of his dominion. We may imagine how the men caroused together after this reception. As Bibboni adds, 'We were now able for the whole time of life left us to live splendidly, without a thought or care.' The last words of his narrative are these: 'Bebo from Pisa, at what date I know not, went home to Volterra, his native town, and there finished his days; while I abode in Florence, where I have had no further wish to hear of wars, but to live my life in holy peace.'

So ends the story of the two bravi. We have reason to believe, from some contemporary documents which Cantù has brought to light, that Bibboni exaggerated his own part in the affair. Luca Martelli, writing to Varchi, says that it was Bebo who clove Lorenzo's skull with a cutlass. He adds this curious detail, that the weapons of both men were poisoned, and that the wound inflicted by Bibboni on Soderini's hand was a slight one. Yet, the poignard being poisoned, Soderini died of it. In other respects Martelli's brief account agrees with that given by Bibboni, who probably did no more, his comrade being dead, than claim for himself, at some expense of truth, the lion's share of their heroic action.

Ambrogio Tremazzi.

In illustration of this narrative, and in evidence that it stands by no means solitary on the records of that century, I shall extract some passages from the report made by Ambrogio Tremazzi of Modigliana concerning the assassination of Troilo Orsini.[3] Troilo, it will be remembered, was the lover of the Medicean Duchess of Bracciano. After the discovery of their amours, and while the lady was being strangled by her husband, with the sanction of her brother, Troilo escaped to France. Ambrogio Tremazzi, knowing that his murder would be acceptable to the Medici, undertook the adventure; moved, as he says, 'solely by the desire of bringing myself into favourable notice with the Grand Duke; for my mind revolted at the thought of money payments, and I had in view the acquisition of honour and praise rather, being willing to risk my life for the credit of my Prince, and not my life only, but also to incur deadly and perpetual feud with a powerful branch of the Orsini family.' On his return from France, having successfully accomplished the mission, Ambrogio Tremazzi found that the friends who had previously encouraged his hopes, especially the Count Ridolfo Isolami, wished to compromise his reward by the settlement of a pension on himself and his associate. Whether he really aimed at a more honourable recognition of his services, or whether he sought to obtain better pecuniary terms, does not appear. But he represents himself as gravely insulted; 'seeing that my tenor of life from boyhood upwards has been always honourable, and thus it ever shall be.' After this exordium in the form of a letter addressed to one Signor Antonio [Serguidi], he proceeds to render account of his proceedings. It seems that Don Piero de' Medici gave him three hundred crowns for his travelling expenses; after which, leaving his son, a boy of twelve years, as hostage in the service of Piero, he set off, and reached

[3] The text is published, from Florentine Archives, in Gnoli's *Vittoria Accoramboni*' pp. 404-414.

Paris on August 12, 1577. There he took lodgings at the sign of the Red Horse, near the Cordeilliers, and began at once to make inquiries for Troilo. He had brought with him from Italy a man called Hieronimo Savorano. Their joint investigations elicited the fact that Troilo had been lately wounded in the service of the King of France, and was expected to arrive in Paris with the Court. It was not until the eve of All Saints' day that the Court returned. Soon afterwards, Ambrogio was talking at the door of a house with some Italian comedians, when a young man, covered with a tawny-coloured mantle, passed by upon a brown horse, bearing a servant behind him on the crupper. This was Troilo Orsini; and Ambrogio marked him well. Troilo, after some minutes' conversation with the players, rode forward to the Louvre. The bravo followed him and discovered from his servant where he lodged. Accordingly, he engaged rooms in the Rue S. Honoré, in order to be nearer to his victim.

Some time, however, elapsed before he was able to ascertain Troilo's daily habits. Chance at last threw them together. He was playing *primiero* one evening in the house of an actress called Vittoria, when Troilo entered, with two gentlemen of Florence. He said he had been absent ten days from Paris. Ambrogio, who had left his harquebuss at home, not expecting to meet him, 'was consequently on that occasion unable to do anything.' Days passed without a better opportunity, till, on November 30, 'the feast of S. Andrew, which is a lucky day for me, I rose and went at once to the palace, and, immediately on my arrival, saw him at the hour when the King goes forth to mass.' Ambrogio had to return as he went; for Troilo was surrounded by too many gentlemen of the French Court; but he made his mind up then and there 'to see the end of him or me.' He called his comrade Hieronimo, posted him on a bridge across the Seine, and proceeded to the Court, where Troilo was now playing racquets with princes of the royal family. Ambrogio hung about the gates until Troilo issued from the lodgings of Monseigneur de Montmorenci, still tracked by his unknown enemy, and thence returned to his own house on horseback, attended by several servants. After waiting till the night fell, Troilo again left home on horseback preceded by his servants with torches. Ambrogio followed at full speed, watched a favourable opportunity, and stopped the horse. 'When I came up with him, I seized the reins with my left hand, and with the right I set my harquebuss against his side, pushing it with such violence that if it had failed to go off it would at any rate have dislodged him from his seat. The gun took effect, and he fell crying out "Eh! Eh!" In the tumult which ensued, I walked away, and do not know what happened afterwards.' Ambrogio then made his way back to his lodgings, recharged his harquebuss, ate some supper and went to bed. He told Hieronimo that nothing had occurred that night. Next day he rose as usual, and returned to the Court, hoping to hear news of Troilo. In the afternoon, at the Italian theatre, he was informed that an Italian had been murdered, at the instance, it was thought, of the Grand Duke of Florence. Hieronimo touched his arm, and whispered that he must have done the deed; but Ambrogio denied the fact. It seems to have been his object to reserve the credit of the murder for himself, and also to avoid the possibility of Hieronimo's treachery in case suspicion fell upon him. Afterwards he learned that Troilo lay dangerously wounded by a harquebuss. Further details made him aware that he was himself suspected of the murder, and that Troilo could not recover. He therefore conferred upon the matter with Hieronimo in Notre Dame, and both of them resolved to leave Paris secretly. This they did at once, relinquishing clothes, arms, and baggage in their lodgings, and reached Italy in safety.

Lodovico dall' Armi.

The relations of trust which bravi occasionally maintained with foreign Courts, supply some curious illustrations of their position in Italian society. One characteristic instance may be selected from documents in the Venetian Archives referring to Lodovico dall' Armi.[4] This man belonged to a noble family of Bologna; and there are reasons for supposing that his mother was sister to Cardinal Campeggi, famous in the annals of the English Reformation. Outlawed from his native city for a homicide, Lodovico adopted the profession of arms and the management of secret diplomacy. He first took refuge at the Court of France, where in 1541 he obtained such credit, especially with the Dauphin, that he was entrusted with a mission for raising revolt in Siena against the Spaniards.[5] His transactions in that city with Giulio Salvi, then aspiring to its lordship, and in Rome with the French ambassador, led to a conspiracy which only awaited the appearance of French troops upon the Tuscan frontier to break out into open rebellion. The plot, however, transpired before it had been matured; and Lodovico took flight through the Florentine territory. He was arrested at Montevarchi and confined in the fortress of Florence, where he made such revelations as rendered the extinction of the Sienese revolt an easy matter. After this we do not hear of him until he reappears at Venice in the year 1545. He was now accredited to the English ambassador with the title of Henry VIII.'s 'Colonel,' and enjoyed the consideration accorded to a powerful monarch's privy agent. His pension amounted to fifty crowns a month, while he kept eight captains at his orders, each of whom received half that sum as pay. These subordinates were people of some social standing. We find among them a Trissino of Vicenza and a Bonifacio of Verona, the one entitled Marquis and the other Count. What the object of Lodovico's residence in Italy might be, did not appear. Though he carried letters of recommendation from the English Court, he laid no claim to the rank of diplomatic envoy. But it was tolerably well known that he employed himself in levying troops. Whether these were meant

[4] See Rawdon Brown's *Calendar of State Papers*, vol. iv.
[5] See Botta, Book IV., for the story of Lodovico's intrigues at Siena.

to be used against France or in favour of Savoy, or whether, as the Court of Rome suggested, Henry had given orders for the murder of his cousin, Cardinal Pole, at Trento, remained an open question. Lodovico might have dwelt in peace under the tolerant rule of the Venetians, had he not exposed himself to a collision with their police. In the month of August he assaulted the captain of the night guard in a street brawl; and it was also proved against him that he had despatched two of his men to inflict a wound of infamy upon a gentleman at Treviso. These offences, coinciding with urgent remonstrances from the Papal Curia, gave the Venetian Government fair pretext for expelling him from their dominions. A ban was therefore published against him and fourteen of his followers. The English ambassador declined to interfere in his behalf, and the man left Italy. At the end of August he appeared at Brussels, where he attempted to excuse himself in an interview with the Venetian ambassador. Now began a diplomatic correspondence between the English Court and the Venetian Council, which clearly demonstrates what kind of importance attached to this private agent. The Chancellor Lord Wriothesley, and the Secretary Sir William Paget, used considerable urgency to obtain a suspension of the ban against Dall' Armi. After four months' negotiation, during which the Papal Court endeavoured to neutralise Henry's influence, the Doge signed a safe-conduct for five years in favour of the bravo. Early in 1546 Lodovico reappeared in Lombardy. At Mantua he delivered a letter signed by Henry himself to the Duke Francesco Gonzaga, introducing 'our noble and beloved familiar Lodovico dall' Armi,' and begging the Duke to assist him in such matters as he should transact at Mantua in the King's service.[6] Lodovico presented this letter in April; but the Duchess, who then acted as regent for her son Francesco, refused to receive him. She alleged that the Duke forbade the levying of troops for foreign service, and declined to complicate his relations with foreign powers. It seems, from a sufficiently extensive correspondence on the affairs of Lodovico, that he was understood by the Italian princess to be charged with some special commission for recruiting soldiers against the French. The peace between England and France, signed at Guines in June, rendered Lodovico's mission nugatory; and the death of Henry VIII. in January 1547 deprived him of his only powerful support. Meanwhile he had contrived to incur the serious displeasure of the Venetian Republic. In the autumn of 1546 they outlawed one of their own nobles, Ser Mafio Bernardo, on the charge of his having revealed State secrets to France. About the middle of November, Bernardo, then living in concealment at Ravenna, was lured into the pine forest by two men furnished with tokens which secured his confidence. He was there murdered, and the assassins turned out to be paid instruments of Lodovico. It now came to light that Lodovico and Ser Mafio Bernardo had for some time past colluded in political intrigue. If, therefore, the murder had a motive, this was found in Lodovico's dread of revelations in the event of Ser Mafio's capture. Submitted to torture in

[6] This letter is dated February 16, 1546.

the prisons of the Ten, Ser Mafio might have incriminated his accomplice both with England and Venice. It was obvious why he had been murdered by Lodovico's men. Dall' Armi was consequently arrested and confined in Venice. After examination, followed by a temporary release, he prudently took flight into the Duchy of Milan. Though they held proof of his guilt in the matter of Ser Mafio's murder, the Venetians were apparently unwilling to proceed to extremities against the King of England's man. Early in February, however, Sir William Paget surrendered him in the name of Lord Protector Somerset to the discretion of S. Mark. Furnished with this assurance that Dall' Armi had lost the favour of England, the Signory wrote to demand his arrest and extradition from the Spanish governor in Milan. He was in fact arrested on February 10. The letter announcing his capture describes him as a man of remarkably handsome figure, accustomed to wear a crimson velvet cloak and a red cap trimmed with gold. It is exactly in this costume that Lodovico has been represented by Bonifazio in a picture of the Massacre of the Innocents. The bravo there stands with his back partly turned, gazing stolidly upon a complex scene of bloodshed. He wears a crimson velvet mantle, scarlet cap and white feather, scarlet stockings, crimson velvet shoes, and rose-coloured silk underjacket. His person is that of a gallant past the age of thirty, high-complexioned, with short brown beard, spare whiskers and moustache. He is good to look at, except that the sharp-set mouth suggests cynical vulgarity and shallow rashness. On being arrested in Milan, Lodovico proclaimed himself a privileged person (*persona pubblica*), bearing credentials from the King of England; and, during the first weeks of his confinement, he wrote to the Emperor for help. This was an idle step. Henry's death had left him without protectors, and Charles V. felt no hesitation in abandoning his suppliant to the Venetians. When the usual formalities regarding extradition had been completed, the Milanese Government delivered Lodovico at the end of April into the hands of the Rector of Brescia, who forwarded him under a guard of two hundred men to Padua. He was handcuffed; and special directions were given regarding his safety, it being even prescribed that if he refused food it should be thrust down his throat. What passed in the prisons of the State, after his arrival at Venice, is not known. But on May 14 he was beheaded between the columns on the Molo.

Venice, at this epoch, incurred the reproaches of her neighbours for harbouring adventurers of Lodovico's stamp. One of the Fregosi of Genoa, a certain Valerio, and Pietro Strozzi, the notorious French agent, all of whom habitually haunted the lagoons, roused sufficient public anxiety to necessitate diplomatic communications between Courts, and to disquiet fretful Italian princelings. Banished from their own provinces, and plying a petty *condottiere* trade, such men, when they came together on a neutral ground, engaged in cross-intrigues which made them politically dangerous. They served no interest but that of their own egotism, and they were notoriously unscrupulous in the means employed to effect immediate objects. At the same time, the protection which they claimed from foreign potentates withdrew them from the customary justice of the State. Bedmar's conspiracy in 1617-18 revealed to Venice the full extent of the peril which this harbourage of ruffians involved; for though grandees of the distinction of the Duke of Ossuna were involved in it, the main agents, on whose ambition and audacity all depended, sprang from those French, English, Spanish, and Italian mercenaries, who crowded the low quarters of the city, alert for any mischief, and inflamed with the wildest projects of self-aggrandisement by policy and bloodshed. Nothing testifies to the social and political decrepitude of Italy in this period more plainly than the importance which folk like Lodovico dall' Armi acquired, and the revolutionary force which a man like Jaffier commanded.

Brigands, Pirates, Plague.

After collecting these stories, which illustrate the manners of the upper classes in society and prove their dependence upon henchmen paid to subserve lawless passions, it would be interesting to lay bare the life of the common people with equal lucidity. This, however, is a more difficult matter. Statistics of dubious value can indeed be gathered regarding the desolation of villages by brigands, the multitudes destroyed by pestilence and famine, and the inroads of Mediterranean pirates. I propose, therefore, to touch lightly upon these points, and specially to use our records of plague in different Italian districts as tests for contrasting the condition of the people at this epoch with that of the same people in the Middle Ages.

Brigandage, though this was certainly a curse of the first magnitude to Central and Southern Italy, cannot be paralleled, either for the miseries it inflicted, or for the ferocity it stimulated, with the municipal warfare of the twelfth, thirteenth, and fourteenth centuries. In those internecine struggles whole cities disappeared, and fertile districts were periodically abandoned to wolves. The bands of an Alfonso Piccolomini or a Sciarra Colonna plundered villages, exacted blackmail, and held prisoners for ransom.[7] But their barbarities were insignificant, when compared with those commonly perpetrated by wandering companies of adventure before the days of Alberigo da Barbiano; nor did brigands cost Italy so much as the mercenary troops, which, after the *condottiere* system had been developed, became a permanent drain upon the resources of the country. The raids of Tunisian and Algerian corsairs were more seriously mischievous; since the whole sea-board from Nice to Reggio lay open to the ravages of such incarnate fiends as Barbarossa and Dragut, while the Adriatic was infested by Uscocchi, and the natives of the Regno not unfrequently turned pirates in emulation of their persecutors.[8]

[7] See Mutinelli, *Storia Arcana*, vol. ii. p. 167, for the pillage of Lucero by Pacchiarotto.

[8] Sarpi's *History of the Uscocchi* may be consulted for this singular episode in the Iliad of human savagery. See Mutinelli, *op. cit.* vol. ii. p. 182, on the case of the son and heir of the Duke of Termoli joining them; and *ibid.* p. 180 on the existence of pirates at Capri.

Yet even these injuries may be reckoned light, when we consider what Italy had suffered between 1494 and 1527 from French, Spanish, German, and Swiss troops in combat on her soil. The pestilences of the Middle Ages, notably the Black Death of 1348, of which Boccaccio has left an immortal description, exceeded in virulence those which depopulated Italian cities during the period of my history. But plagues continued to be frequent; and some of these are so memorable that they require to be particularly noticed. At Venice in 1575-77, a total of about 50,000 persons perished; and in 1630-31, 46,490 were carried off within a space of sixteen months in the city, while the number of those who died at large in the lagoons amounted to 94,235.[9] On these two occasions the Venetians commemorated their deliverance by the erection of the Redentore and S. Maria della Salute churches, which now form principal ornaments of the Giudecca and the Grand Canal. Milan was devastated at the same periods by plagues, of which we have detailed accounts in the despatches of resident Venetian envoys.[10] The mortality in the second of these visitations was terrible. Before September 1629, fourteen thousand had succumbed; between May and August 1630, forty-five thousand victims had been added to the tale.[11] At Naples, in the year 1656, more than fifty thousand perished between May and July; the dead were cast naked into the sea, and the Venetian envoy describes the city as '*non più città ma spelonca di morti*.'[12] In July his diary is suddenly interrupted, whether by departure from the stricken town, or more probably by death, we know not. Savoy was scourged by a fearful pestilence in the years 1598-1600. Of this plague we possess a frightfully graphic picture in the same accurate series of State documents.[13] Simeone Contarini, then resident at Savigliano, relates that more than two-thirds of the population in that province had been swept away before the autumn of 1598, and that the evil was spreading far and wide through Piedmont. In Alpignano, a village of some four hundred inhabitants, only two remained. In Val Moriana, forty thousand expired, out of a total of seventy thousand. The village of San Giovanni counted but twelve survivors from a population of more than four thousand souls. In May 1599, the inhabitants of Turin were reduced by flight and death to four thousand; and of these there died daily numbers gradually rising through the summer from 50 to 180. The streets were encumbered with unburied corpses, the houses infested by robbers and marauders. Some incidents reported of this plague are ghastly in their horror. The infected were treated with inhuman barbarity, and retorted with savage fury, battering their assailants with the pestiferous bodies of unburied victims.

To the miseries of pestilence and its attendant famine were added law-

[9] Mutinelli, *Annali Urbani di Venezia*, pp. 470-483, 549-550.

[10] Mutinelli, *Storia Arcana*, vol. i. pp. 310-340, and vol. xiv. pp. 30-65.

[11] It is worth mentioning that Ripamonte calculates the mortality from plague in Milan in 1524 at 140,000.

[12] Mutinelli, *op. cit.* vol. iii. pp. 229-233. Botta has given an account of this plague in the twenty-sixth book of his *History*.

[13] Mutinelli, *op. cit.* vol. ii. pp. 287-307.

lessness and license, raging fires, and, what was worst of all, the dark suspicion that the sickness had been introduced by malefactors. This belief appears to have taken hold upon the popular mind during the plague of 1598 in Savoy and in Milan.[14] Simeone Contarini reports that two men from Geneva confessed to having come with the express purpose of disseminating infection. He also gives curious particulars of two who were burned, and four who were quartered at Turin in 1600 for this offence.[15] 'These spirits of hell,' as he calls them, indicated a wood in which they declared that they had buried a pestilential liquid intended to be used for smearing houses. The wood was searched, and some jars were discovered. A surgeon at the same epoch confessed to having meant to spread the plague at Mondovi. Other persons, declaring themselves guilty of a similar intention, described a horn filled with poisonous stuff collected from the sores of plague-stricken corpses, which they had concealed outside the walls of Turin. This too was discovered; and these apparent proofs of guilt so infuriated the people that every day some criminals were sacrificed to judicial vengeance.

The name given to the unfortunate creatures accused of this diabolical conspiracy was *Untori*, or the Smearers. The plague of Milan in 1629-30 obtained the name of 'La Peste degli Untori' (as that of 1576 had been called 'La Peste di S. Carlo'), because of the prominent part played in it by the smearers.[16] They were popularly supposed to go about the city daubing walls, doors, furniture, choir-stalls, flowers, and articles of food with plague stuff. They scattered powders in the air, or spread them in circles on the pavement. To set a foot upon one of these circles involved certain destruction. Hundreds of such *untori* were condemned to the most cruel deaths by justice firmly persuaded of their criminality. Exposed to prolonged tortures, the majority confessed palpable absurdities. One woman at Milan said she had killed four thousand people. But, says Pier Antonio Marioni, the Venetian envoy, although tormented to the utmost, none of them was capable of revealing the prime instigators of the plot. So thoroughly convinced was he, together with the whole world, of their guilt, that he never paused to reflect upon the fallacy contained in this remark. The rack-stretched wretches could not reveal their instigators, because there were none; and the acts of which they accused themselves were the delirious figments of their own torture-fretted brains. We possess documents, relating to the trial of the Milanese *Untori*, which make it clear that crimes of this sort must have been imaginary. As in cases of witchcraft, the first accusation was founded upon gossip and delation. The judicial proceedings were ruled by prejudice and cruelty. Fear and physical pain extorted confessions and complicated accusations of their neighbours from multitudes of innocent

[14] See Mutinelli, *op. cit.* p. 241 and p. 289. We hear of the same belief at Milan in 1576, *op. cit.* vol. i. pp. 311-315.

[15] *Ibid.* p. 309. See also vol. iii. p. 254 for a similar narration.

[16] Mutinelli, *op. cit.* vol. ii. pp. 51-65.

people.[17] Indeed the parallel between these unfortunate smearers and no less wretched witches is a close one. I am inclined to think that, as some crazy women fancied they were witches, so some morbid persons of this period in Italy believed in their power of spreading plague, and yielded to the fascination of malignity. Whether such moral mad folk really extended the sphere of the pestilence to any appreciable extent remains a matter for conjecture; and it is quite certain that all but a small percentage of the accused were victims of calumny.

After taking brigandage, piracy, and pestilence into account, the decline of Italy must be attributed to other causes. These I believe to have been the extinction of commercial republics, the decay of free commonwealths, iniquitous systems of taxation, the insane display of wealth by unproductive princes, and the diversion of trade into foreign channels. Florence ceased to be the centre of wool manufacture, Venice lost her hold upon the traffic between East and West.[18] Stagnation fell like night upon the land, and the population suffered from a general atrophy.

The Proletariat.

In what concerns social morality it would be almost impossible to define the position of the proletariat, tillers of the soil, and artisans, at this epoch. These classes vary in their goodness and their badness, in their drawbacks and advantages, from age to age, far less than those who mould the character of marked historical periods by culture. They enjoy indeed a greater or a smaller immunity from pressing miseries. They are innocent or criminal in different degrees. But the groundwork of humanity in them remains comparatively unaltered; and their moral qualities, so far as these may be exceptional, reflect the influences of an upper social stratum. It is clear from the histories related in this chapter that members of the lowest classes were continually mixing with the nobles and the gentry in the wild adventures of that troubled century. They, like their betters, were undergoing a tardy metamorphosis from mediæval to modern conditions, retaining vices of ferocity and grossness, virtues of loyalty and self-reliance, which belonged to earlier periods. They, too, were now infected by the sensuous romance of pietism, the superstitious respect for sacraments and ceremonial observances, which had been wrought by the Catholic Revival into ecstatic frenzy. They shared those correlative yearnings after sacrilegious debauchery, felt those allurements

[17] Cantù's *Ragionamenti sulla Storia Lombarda del Secolo XVII.* (Milano, 1832). The trial may also be read in Mutinelli, *Storia Arcana*, vol. iv. pp. 175-201. Mutinelli inclines to believe in the *Untori*. So do many grave historians, including Nani and Botta. See Cantù, *Storia degli Italiani* (Milano, 1876), vol. ii. p. 215.

[18] Mr. Ruskin has somewhere maintained that the decline of Venice was not due to this cause, but to fornication. He should read the record given by Mutinelli (*Diari Urbani*, p. 157) of Venetian fornication in 1340, at the time when the Ducal Palace was being covered with its sculpture. The public prostitutes were reckoned then at 11,654. Adulteries, rapes, infanticides were matters of daily occurrence. Yet the Renaissance had not begun, and the expansion of Venice, which roused the envious hostility of Europe, had yet to happen.

of magic arts, indulged that perverted sense of personal honour which constituted psychological disease in the century which we are studying. It can, moreover, be maintained that Italian society at no epoch has been so sharply divided into sections as that of the feudalised races. In this period of one hundred years, from 1530 to 1630, when education was a privilege of the few, and when Church and princes combined to retard intellectual progress, the distinction between noble and plebeian, burgher and ploughman, though outwardly defined, was spiritually and morally insignificant. As in the Renaissance, so now, vice trickled downwards from above, infiltrating the masses of the people with its virus. But now, even more decidedly than then, the upper classes displayed obliquities of meanness, baseness, intemperance, cowardice, and brutal violence, which are commonly supposed to characterise villains.

I had thought to throw some light upon the manners of the Italian proletariat by exploring the archives of trials for witchcraft. But I found that these were less common than in Germany, France, Spain, and England at a corresponding period. In Italy, witchcraft, pure and simple, was confined, for the most part, to mountain regions, the Apennines of the Abruzzi, and the Alps of Bergamo and Tyrol.[19] In other provinces it was confounded with crimes of poisoning, the procuring of abortion, and the fomentation of conspiracies in private families. These facts speak much for the superior civilisation of the Italian people considered as a whole. We discover a common fund of intelligence, vice, superstition, prejudice, enthusiasm, craft, devotion, self-assertion, possessed by the race at large. Only in districts remote from civil life did witchcraft assume those anti-social and repulsive features which are familiar to Northern nations. Elsewhere it penetrated, as a subtle poison, through society, lending its supposed assistance to passions already powerful enough to work their own accomplishment. It existed, not as an endemic disease, a permanent delirium of maddened peasants, but as a weapon in the arsenal of malice on a par with poisons and provocatives to lust.

I might illustrate this position by the relation of a fantastic attempt made against the life of Pope Urban VIII.[20] Giacomo Centini, the nephew of Cardinal d'Ascoli, fostered a fixed idea, the motive of his madness being the promotion of his uncle to S. Peter's Chair. In 1633 he applied to a hermit, who professed profound science in the occult arts and close familiarity with demons. The man, in answer to Giacomo's inquiries, said that Urban had still many years to live, that the Cardinal d'Ascoli would certainly succeed him, and that he held it in his power to shorten the Pope's days. He added that a certain Fra Cherubino would be useful, if any matter of grave moment were resolved on; nor did he reject the assistance of other discreet persons. Giacomo, on his side, produced a Fra Domenico; and these four accomplices set to work to

[19] Dandolo's *Streghe Tirolesi*, and Cantù's work on the Diocese of Como, show how much subalpine Italy had in common with Northern Europe in this matter.
[20] See *Rassegna Settimanale*, September 18, 1881.

destroy the reigning Pope by means of sorcery. They caused a knife to be forged, after the model of the Key of Solomon, and had it inscribed with Cabbalistic symbols. A clean virgin was employed to spin hemp into a thread. Then they resorted to a distant room in Giacomo's palace, where a circle was drawn with the mystic thread, a fire was lighted in the centre, and upon it was placed an image of Pope Urban formed of purest wax. The devil was invoked to appear and answer whether Urban had deceased this life after the melting of the image. No infernal visitor responded to the call; and the hermit accounted for this failure by suggesting that some murder had been committed in the palace. As things went at that period, this excuse was by no means feeble, if only the audience, bent on unholy invocation of the power of evil, would accept it as sufficient. Probably more than one murder had taken place there, of which the owner was dimly conscious. The psychological curiosity to note is that avowed malefactors reckoned purity an essential element in their nefarious practice. They tried once more in a vineyard, under the open heavens at night. But no demon issued from the darkness, and the hermit laid this second mischance to the score of bad weather. Giacomo was incapable of holding his tongue. He talked about his undertaking to the neighbours, and promised to make them all cardinals when he should become the Papal nephew. Meanwhile he pressed the hermit forward on the path of folly; and this man, driven to his wits' end for a device, said that they must find seven priests together, one of whom should be assassinated to enforce the spell. It was natural, while the countryside was being raked for seven convenient priests by such a tattler as Giacomo, that suspicions should be generated in the people. Information reached Rome, in consequence of which the persons implicated in this idiotic plot were conveyed thither and given over to the mercies of the Holy Office. The upshot of their trial was that Giacomo lost his head, while the hermit and Fra Cherubino were burned alive, and Fra Domenico went to the galleys for life. Several other men involved in the process received punishments of considerable severity. It must be added in conclusion that the whole story rests upon the testimony of Inquisitorial archives, and that the real method of Giacomo Centini's apparent madness yet remains to be investigated. The few facts that we know about him, from his behaviour on the scaffold and a letter he wrote his wife, prejudice me in his favour.

Enough, and more than enough, perhaps, has been collected in this chapter, to throw light upon the manners of Italians during the Counter-Reformation. It would have been easy to repeat the story of the Countess of Cellant and her murdered lovers, or of the Duchess of Amalfi strangled by her brothers for a marriage below her station. The massacres committed by the Raspanti in Ravenna would furnish a whole series of illustrative crimes. From the deeds of Alfonso Piccolomini, Sciarra and Fabrizio Colonna, details sufficient to fill a volume with records of atrocious savagery could be drawn. The single episode of Elena Campireali, who plighted her troth to a bandit, became Abbess of the Convent at Castro, intrigued with a bishop, and killed herself for shame on the return of her first lover, would epitomise in one drama all the principal features of this social discord. The dreadful tale of the Baron of Montebello might be told again, who assaulted the castle of the Marquis of Pratidattolo, and, by the connivance of a sister whom he subsequently married, murdered the Marquis, with his mother, children, and relatives. The hunted life of Alessandro Antelminelli, pursued through all the States of Europe by assassins, could be used to exemplify the miseries of proscribed exiles. But what is the use of multiplying instances, when every pedigree in Litta, every chronicle of the time, every history of the most insignificant township, swarms with evidence to the same purpose? We need not adopt the opinion that society had greatly altered for the worse.

We must rather decide that mediæval ferocity survived throughout the whole of that period which witnessed the Catholic Revival, and that the piety which distinguished it was not influential in curbing vehement passions.

The conclusions to be drawn from the facts before us seem to be in general these: The link between government and governed in Italy had snapped. The social bond was broken; and the constituents that form a nation were pursuing divers aims. On the one hand stood Popes and princes, founding their claims to absolute authority upon titles that had slight rational or national validity. These potentates were ill combined among themselves, and mutually jealous. On the other side were ranged disruptive forces of the most heterogeneous kinds—remnants from antique party-warfare, fragments of obsolete domestic feuds, new strivings after freer life in mentally down-trodden populations, blending with crime and misery and want and profligacy to compose an opposition which exasperated despotism. These anarchical conditions were due in large measure to the troubles caused by foreign campaigns of invasion. They were also due to the Spanish type of manners imposed upon the ruling classes, which the native genius accepted with fraudulent intelligence, and to which it adapted itself by artifice. We must further reckon the division between cultured and uncultured people, which humanism had effected, and which subsisted after the benefits conferred by humanism had been withdrawn from the race. The retirement of the commercial aristocracy from trade, and their assumption of princely indolence in this period of political stagnation, was another factor of importance. But the truest cause of Italian retrogression towards barbarism must finally be discerned in the sharp check given to intellectual evolution by the repressive forces of the Counter-Reformation.

CHAPTER VII

TORQUATO TASSO

Tasso's Relation to his Age—Balbi on that Period—The Life of Bernardo Tasso—Torquato's Boyhood—Sorrento, Naples, Rome, Urbino—His first Glimpse of the Court—Student Life at Padua and Bologna—The 'Rinaldo'—Dialogues on Epic Poetry—Enters the Service of Cardinal d' Este—The Court of Ferrara—Alfonso II. and the Princesses—Problem of Tasso's Love—Goes to France with Cardinal d' Este—Enters the Service of Duke Alfonso—The 'Aminta'—Tasso at Urbino—Return to Ferrara—Revision of the 'Gerusalemme'—Jealousies at Court—Tasso's Sense of His own Importance—Plans a Change from Ferrara to Florence—First Symptoms of Mental Disorder—Persecutions of the Ferrarese Courtiers—Tasso confined as a Semi-madman—Goes with Duke Alfonso to Belriguardo—Flies in Disguise from Ferrara to Sorrento—Returns to Court Life at Ferrara—Problem of his Madness—Flies again—Mantua, Venice, Urbino, Turin—Returns once more to Ferrara—Alfonso's Third Marriage—Tasso's Discontent—Imprisoned for Seven Years in the Madhouse of S. Anna—Character of Tasso—Character of Duke Alfonso—Nature of the Poet's Malady—His Course of Life in Prison—Released at the Intercession of Vincenzo Gonzaga—Goes to Mantua—The 'Torrismondo'—An Odyssey of Nine Years—Death at Sant Onofrio in Rome—Constantini's Sonnet.

IT was under the conditions which have been set forth in the foregoing chapters that the greatest literary genius of his years in Europe, the poet who ranks among the four first of Italy, was educated, rose to eminence, and suffered. The political changes introduced in 1530, the tendencies of the Catholic Revival, the terrorism of the Inquisition, and the educational energy of the Jesuits had, each and all, their manifest effect in moulding Tasso's character. He represents that period when the culture of the Renaissance was being superseded, when the caries of court-service was eating into the bone and marrow of Italian life, when earlier forms of art were tending to decay, or were passing into the new form of music. Tasso was at once the representative poet of his age and the representative martyr of his age. He was the latter, though this may seem paradoxical, in even a stricter sense than Bruno. Bruno, coming into violent collision with the prejudices of the century, expiated his antagonism by a cruel death. Tasso, yielding to those influences, lingered out a life of irresolute misery. His nature was such, that the very conditions which shaped it sufficed to enfeeble, envenom, and finally reduce it to a pitiable ruin.

Some memorable words of Cesare Balbi may serve as introduction to a sketch of Tasso's life. 'If that can be called felicity which gives to the people peace without activity; to nobles rank without power; to princes undisturbed authority within their States without true independence or full sovereignty; to literary men and artists numerous occasions for writing, painting, making statues, and erecting edifices with the applause of contemporaries but the ridicule of posterity; to the whole nation ease without dignity and facilities for sinking tranquilly into corruption; then no period of her history was so felicitous for Italy as the 140 years which followed the peace of Cateau-Cambrésis. Invasions ceased: her foreign lord saved Italy from intermeddling rivals. Internal struggles ceased: her foreign lord removed their causes and curbed national ambitions. Popular revolutions ceased: her foreign lord bitted and bridled the population of her provinces. Of bravi, highwaymen, vulgar acts of vengeance, tragedies among nobles and princes, we find indeed abundance; but these affected the mass of the people to no serious extent. The Italians enjoyed life, indulged in the sweets of leisure, the sweets of vice, the sweets of making love and dangling after women. From the camp and the council-chamber, where they had formerly been bred, the nobles passed into petty courts and mouldered in a multitude of little capitals. Men bearing historic names, insensible of their own degradation, bowed the neck gladly, grovelled in beatitude. Deprived of power, they consoled themselves with privileges, patented favours, impertinences vented on the common people. The princes amused themselves by debasing the old aristocracy to the mire, depreciating their honours by the creation of new titles, multiplying frivolous concessions, adding class to class of idle and servile dependents on their personal bounty. In one word, the paradise of mediocrities came into being.'

Tasso was born before the beginning of this epoch. But he lived into the last decade of the sixteenth century. In every fibre of his character he felt the influences of Italian decadence, even while he reacted against them. His misfortunes resulted in great measure from his not having wholly discarded the traditions of the Renaissance, though his temperament and acquired habits made him in many points sympathetic to the Counter-Reformation. At the same time, he was not a mediocrity, but the last of an illustrious race of nobly gifted men of genius. Therefore he never patiently submitted to the humiliating conditions which his own conception of the Court, the Prince, the Church, and the Italian gentleman logically involved at that period. He could not be contented with the paradise of mediocrities described by Balbi. Yet he had not strength to live outside its pale. It was the pathos of his situation that he persisted in idealising this paradise, and expected to find in it a paradise of exceptional natures. This it could not be. No one turns Circe's pigsty into a Parnassus. If Tasso had possessed force of character enough to rend the trammels of convention, and to live his own life in a self-constructed sphere, he might still have been unfortunate. Nature condemned him to suffering. But from the study of his history we should then have risen invigorated by the contemplation of heroism, instead of quitting it, as now we do, with pity, but with pity tempered by a slight contempt.

Bernardo, the father of Torquato Tasso, drew noble blood from both his parents. The Tassi claimed to be a branch of that ancient Guelf house of Della Torre, lords of Milan, who were all but extirpated by the Visconti in the fourteenth century. A remnant established themselves in mountain strongholds between Bergamo and Como, and afterwards took rank among the more distinguished families of the former city. Manso affirms that Bernardo's mother was a daughter of those Venetian Cornari who gave a queen to Cyprus.[1] He was born at Venice in the year 1493; and, since he died in 1569, his life covered the whole period of national glory, humiliation, and attempted reconstruction which began with the invasion of Charles VIII. and ended with the closing of the Council of Trent. Born in the pontificate of Alexander VI., he witnessed the reigns of Julius II., Leo X., Clement VII., Paul IV., Pius IV., and died in that of Pius V.

All the illustrious works of Italian art and letters were produced while he was moving in the society of princes and scholars. He saw the Renaissance in its splendour and decline. He watched the growth, progress, and final triumph of the Catholic Revival. Having stated that the curve of his existence led upward from a Borgia and down to a Ghislieri Vicar of Christ, the merest tyro in Italian history knows what vicissitudes it spanned. Though the Tassi were so noble, Bernardo owned no wealth. He was left an orphan at an early age under the care of his uncle, Bishop of Recanati. But in 1520 the poniard of an assassin cut short this guardian's life; and, at the age of seventeen, he was thrown upon the world. After studying at Padua, where he enjoyed the patronage of Bembo, and laid foundations for his future fame as poet, Bernardo entered the service of the Modenese Rangoni in the capacity of secretary. Thus began the long career of servitude to princes, of which he frequently complained, but which only ended with his death.[2] The affairs of his first patrons took him to Paris at the time when a marriage was arranged between Renée of France and Ercole d' Este. He obtained the post of secretary to this princess, and having taken leave of the Rangoni, he next established himself at Ferrara. Only for three years, however; for in 1532 reasons of which we are ignorant, but which may have been connected with the heretical sympathies of Renée, induced him to resign his post. Shortly after this date, we find him attached to the person of Ferrante Sanseverino, Prince ot Salerno, one of the chief feudatories and quasi-independent vassals of the Crown of Naples. In the quality of secretary he attended this patron through the campaign of Tunis in 1535, and accompanied him on all his diplomatic expeditions. The Prince of Salerno treated him more as an honoured friend and confidential adviser than as a paid official. His income was good, and leisure was allowed him for the prosecution of his literary studies. In this flourishing state of his affairs, Bernardo contracted an alliance with Porzia de' Rossi, a lady of a noble house, which came originally from Pistoja, but had been established for some generations in Naples. She was connected by descent or mar-

[1] This is doubtful. Serrassi believed that Bernardo's mother was also a Tasso.

[2] He speaks in his letters of the difficulty 'di sottrarre il collo al difficile noioso arduo giogo della servitù dei Principi.' *Lettere Ined.* (Bologna: Romagnoli), p. 34.

riage with the houses of Gambacorti, Caracciolo, and Caraffa. Their first child, Cornelia, was born about the year 1537. Their second, Torquato, saw the light in March 1544 at Sorrento, where his father had been living some months previously and working at his poem, the 'Amadigi.'

At the time of Torquato's birth Bernardo was away from home, in Lombardy, France, and Flanders, travelling on missions from his prince. However, he returned to Sorrento for a short while in 1545, and then again was forced to leave his family. Married at the mature age of forty-three, Bernardo was affectionately attached to his young wife, and proud of his children. But the exigencies of a courtier's life debarred him from enjoying the domestic happiness for which his sober and gentle nature would have fitted him. In 1547 the events happened which ruined him for life, separated him for ever from Porzia, drove him into indigent exile, and marred the prospects of his children. In that year, the Spanish viceroy, Don Pietro Toledo, attempted to introduce the Inquisition, on its Spanish basis, into Naples. The population resented this exercise of authority with the fury of despair, rightly judging that the last remnants of their liberty would be devoured by the foul monster of the Holy Office. They besought the Prince of Salerno to intercede for them with his master, Charles V., whom he had served loyally up to this time, and who might therefore be inclined to yield to his expostulations. The prince doubted much whether it would be prudent to accept the mission of intercessor. He had two counsellors, Bernardo Tasso and Vincenzo Martelli. The latter, who was an astute Florentine, advised him to undertake nothing so perilous as interposition between the viceroy and the people. Tasso, on the contrary, exhorted him to sacrifice personal interest, honours, and glory, for the duty which he owed his country. The prince chose the course which Tasso recommended. Charles V. disgraced him, and he fled from Naples to France, adopting openly the cause of his imperial sovereign's enemies. He was immediately declared a rebel, with confiscation of his fiefs and property. Bernardo and his infant son were included in the sentence. After twenty-two years of service, Bernardo now found himself obliged to choose between disloyalty to his prince or a disastrous exile. He took the latter course, and followed Ferrante Sanseverino to Paris. But Bernardo Tasso, though proving himself a man of honour in this severe trial, was not of the stuff of Shakspere's Kent; and when the Prince of Salerno suspended payment of his salary he took leave of that master. Some differences arising from the discomforts and irritations of both exiles had early intervened between them. Tasso was miserably poor. 'I have to stay in bed,' he writes, 'to mend my hose; and if it were not for the old arms I brought with me from home, I should not know how to cover my nakedness.'[3] Besides this, he suffered grievously in the separation from his wife, who was detailed at Naples by her relatives—'brothers who, instead of being brothers, are deadly foes, cruel wild beasts rather than men; a mother

[3] *Lett. Ined.* p. 100.

who is no mother, but a fell enemy, a fury from hell rather than a woman.'[4] His wretchedness attained its climax when Porzia died suddenly on February 3, 1556. Bernardo suspected that her family had poisoned her; and this may well have been. His son, Torquato, meanwhile had joined him in Rome; but Porzia's brothers refused to surrender his daughter Cornelia, whom they married to a Sorrentine gentleman, Marzio Sersale, much to Bernardo's disgust, for Sersale was apparently of inferior blood. They also withheld Porzia's dowry and the jointure settled on her by Bernardo—property of considerable value, which neither he nor Torquato was subsequently able to recover. In this desperate condition of affairs, without friends or credit, but conscious of his noble birth and true to honour, the unhappy poet bethought him of the Church. If he could obtain a benefice, he would take orders. But the King of France and Margaret of Valois, on whose patronage he relied, turned him a deaf ear; and when war broke out between Paul IV. and Spain, he felt it prudent to leave Rome. It was at this epoch that Bernardo entered the service of Guidubaldo della Rovere, Duke of Urbino, with whom he remained until 1563, when he accepted the post of secretary from Guglielmo, Duke of Mantua. He died in 1569 at Ostiglia, so poor that his son could scarcely collect money enough to bury him after selling his effects. Manso says that a couple of door-curtains, embroidered with the arms of Tasso and De' Rossi, passed on this occasion into the wardrobe of the Gonzaghi. Thus it seems that the needy nobleman had preserved a scrap of his heraldic trophies till the last, although he had to patch his one pair of breeches in bed at Rome. It may be added, as characteristic of Bernardo's misfortunes, that even the plain marble sarcophagus, inscribed with the words 'Ossa Bernardi Tassi,' which Duke Guglielmo erected to his memory in S. Egidio at Mantua, was removed in compliance with a papal edict ordering that monuments at a certain height above the ground should be destroyed to save the dignity of neighbouring altars!

Such were the events of Bernardo Tasso's life. I have dwelt upon them in detail, since they foreshadow and illustrate the miseries of his more famous son. In character and physical qualities Torquato inherited no little from his father. Bernardo was handsome, well-grown, conscious of his double dignity as a nobleman and poet. From the rules of honour, as he understood them, he deviated in no important point of conduct. Yet the life of Courts made him an incorrigible dangler after princely favours. The 'Amadigi,' upon which he set such store, was first planned and dedicated to Charles V., then altered to suit Henri II. of France, and finally adapted to the flattery of Philip II., according as its author's interests with the Prince of Salerno and the Duke of Urbino varied. No substantial reward accrued to him, however, from its publication. His compliments wasted their sweetness on the dull ears of the despot of Madrid. In misfortune Bernardo sank to neither crime nor baseness, even when he had no clothes to put upon his back. Yet he took the world

[4] *Lettere di Torquato Tasso*, February 15, 1556, vol. ii. p. 157.

to witness of his woes, as though his person ought to have been sacred from calamities of common manhood. A similar dependent spirit was manifested in his action as a man of letters. Before publishing the 'Amadigi' he submitted it to private criticism, with the inevitable result of obtaining feigned praises and malevolent strictures. Irresolution lay at the root of his treatment of Torquato. While groaning under the collar of courtly servitude, he determined that the youth should study law. While reckoning how little his own literary fame had helped him, he resolved that his son should adopt a lucrative profession. Yet no sooner had Torquato composed his 'Rinaldo,' than the fond parent had it printed, and immediately procured a place for him in the train of the Cardinal Luigi d' Este. It is singular that the young man, witnessing the wretchedness of his father's life, should not have shunned a like career of gilded misery and famous indigence. But Torquato was born to reproduce Bernardo's qualities in their feebleness and respectability, to outshine him in genius, and to outstrip him in the celebrity of his misfortunes.

In the absence of his father little Torquato grew up with his mother and sister at Sorrento, under the care of a good man, Giovanni Angeluzzo, who gave him the first rudiments of education. He was a precocious infant, grave in manners, quick at learning, free from the ordinary naughtinesses of childhood. Manso reports that he began to speak at six months, and that from the first he formed syllables with precision. His mother Porzia appears to have been a woman of much grace and sweetness, but timid and incapable of fighting the hard battle of the world. A certain shade of melancholy fell across the boy's path even in these earliest years, for Porzia, as we have seen, met with cruel treatment from her relatives, and her only support, Bernardo, was far away in exile. In 1552 she removed with her children to Naples, where Torquato was sent at once to the school which the Jesuits had opened there in the preceding year. These astute instructors soon perceived that they had no ordinary boy to deal with. They did their best to stimulate his mental faculties and to exalt his religious sentiments; so that he learned Greek and Latin before the age of ten, and was in the habit of communicating at the altar with transports of pious ecstasy in his ninth year.[5] The child recited speeches and poems in public, and received an elementary training in the arts of composition. He was in fact the infant prodigy of those plausible Fathers, the prize specimen of their educational method. As might have been expected, this forcing system overtaxed his nerves. He rose daily before daybreak to attack his books, and when the nights were long he went to morning school attended by a servant carrying torches. Without seeking to press unduly on these circumstances, we may fairly assume that Torquato's character received a permanent impression from the fever of study and the premature pietism excited in him by the Jesuits in Naples. His servile attitude toward speculative thought, that anxious

[5] 'Sentendo in me non so qual nuova insolita contentezza,' 'non so qual segreta divozione.' *Lettere,* vol. ii. p. 90.

dependence upon ecclesiastical authority, that scrupulous mistrust of his own mental faculties, that pretence of solving problems by accumulated citations instead of going to the root of the matter, whereby his philosophical writings are rendered nugatory, may with probability be traced to the mechanical and interested system of the Jesuits. He was their pupil for three years, after which he joined his father in Rome. There he seems to have passed at once into a healthier atmosphere. Bernardo, though a sound Catholic, was no bigot; and he had the good sense to choose an able master for his son—'a man of profound learning, possessed of both the ancient languages, whose method of teaching is the finest and most time-saving that has yet been tried; a gentleman withal, with nothing of the pedant in him.'[6] The boy was lucky also in the companion of his studies, a cousin, Cristoforo Tasso, who had come home from Bergamo to profit by the tutor's care.

The young Tasso's home cannot, however, have been a cheerful one. The elderly hidalgo sitting up in bed to darn his single pair of hose, the absent mother pining for her husband and tormented by her savage brothers' avarice, environed the precocious child of ten with sad presentiments. That melancholy temperament which he inherited from Bernardo was nourished by the half-concealed mysteriously haunting troubles of his parents. And when Porzia died suddenly, in 1556, we can hardly doubt that the father broke out before his son into some such expressions of ungovernable grief as he openly expressed in the letter to Amerigo Sanseverino.[7] Is it possible, then, thought Torquato, that the mother from whose tender kisses and streaming tears I was severed but one year ago,[8] had died of poison—poisoned by my uncles? Sinking into the consciousness of a child so sensitive by nature and so early toned to sadness, this terrible suspicion of a secret death by poison incorporated itself with the very essence of his melancholy humour, and lurked within him to flash forth in madness at a future period of life. That he was well acquainted with the doleful situation of his family is proved by his first extant letter. Addressed to the noble lady Vittoria Colonna on behalf of Bernardo and his sister, this is a remarkable composition for a boy of twelve.[9] His poor father, he says, is on the point of dying of despair, oppressed by the malignity of fortune and the rapacity of impious men. His uncle is bent on marrying Cornelia to some needy gentleman, in order to secure her mother's estate for himself. 'The grief, illustrious lady, of the loss of property is great, but that of blood is crushing. This poor old man has naught but my sister and myself; and now that fortune has deprived him of wealth and of the wife he loved like his own soul, he cannot bear that that man's avarice should rob him of his beloved daughter, with whom he hoped to end in rest these last years of his failing

[6] Bernardo's *Letter to Cav. Giangiacopo Tasso*, December 6, 1554.

[7] Dated February 13, 1556.

[8] See *Opere*, vol. iv. p. 100, for Tasso's description of the farewell to his mother, which he remembered deeply, even in later life.

[9] *Lettere*, vol. i. p. 6.

age. In Naples we have no friends; for my father's disaster makes everyone shy of us: our relatives are our enemies. Cornelia is kept in the house of my uncle's kinsman Giangiacopo Coscia, where no one is allowed to speak to her or give her letters.'

In the midst of these afflictions, which already turned the future poet's utterance to a note of plaintive pathos and ingenuous appeal for aid, Torquato's studies were continued on a sounder plan and in a healthier spirit than at Naples. The perennial consolation of his troubled life, that delight in literature which made him able to anticipate the lines of Goethe—

> That naught belongs to me I know
> Save thoughts that never cease to flow
> From founts that cannot perish,
> And every fleeting shape of bliss
> Which kindly fortune lets me kiss
> Or in my bosom cherish—

now became the source of an inner brightness which not even the 'malignity of fortune,' the 'impiety of men,' the tragedy of his mother's death, the imprisonment of his sister, and the ever-present sorrow of his father, 'the poor gentleman fallen into misery and misfortune through no fault of his own,' could wholly overcloud. The boy had been accustomed in Naples to the applause of his teachers and friends. In Rome he began to cherish a presentiment of his own genius. A 'vision splendid' dawned upon his mind; and every step he made in knowledge and in mastery of language enforced the delightful conviction that 'I too am a poet.' Nothing in Tasso's character was more tenacious than the consciousness of his vocation and the kind of self-support he gained from it. Like the melancholy humour which degenerated into madness, this sense of his own intellectual dignity assumed extravagant proportions, passed over into vanity, and encouraged him to indulge fantastic dreams of greatness. Yet it must be reckoned as a mitigation of his suffering; and what was solid in it at the period of which I now am writing, was the certainty of his rare gifts for art.

The Roman residence was broken by Bernardo's journey to Urbino in quest of the appointment he expected from Duke Guidubaldo. He sent Torquato with his cousin Cristoforo meanwhile to Bergamo, where the boy enjoyed a few months of sympathy and freedom. This appears to have been the only period of his life in which Tasso experienced the wholesome influences of domesticity. In 1557 his father sent for him to Pesaro, and Tasso made his first entrance into a Court at the age of thirteen. This event decided the future of his existence. Urbino was not what it had been in the time of Duke Federigo, or when Castiglione composed his 'Mirror of the Courtier' on its model. Yet it retained the old traditions of gentle living, splendour tempered by polite culture, aristocratic urbanity refined by arts and letters. The evil days of Spanish manners and Spanish bigotry, of exhausted revenues and insane taxation, were but dawning; and the young prince, Francesco Maria, who was destined to survive his heir and transfer a ruined duchy to the mortmain of the Church, was now a boy of eight years old. In fact, though the Court of Urbino laboured already under that manifold disease of waste which drained the marrow of Italian principalities, its atrophy was not apparent to the eye. It could still boast of magnificent pageants, trains of noble youths and ladies moving through its stately palaces and shady villa-gardens, academies of learned men discussing the merits of Homer and Ariosto and discoursing on the principles of poetry and drama. Bernardo Tasso read his 'Amadigi' in the evenings to the Duchess. The days were spent in hunting and athletic exercises; the nights in masquerades or dances. Love and ambition wore an external garb of ceremonious beauty; the former draped itself in sonnets, the latter in rhetorical orations. Torquato, who was assigned as the companion in sport and study to the heir-apparent, shared in all these pleasures of the Court. After the melancholy of Rome, his visionary nature expanded under influences which he idealised with fatal facility. Too young to penetrate below that glittering surface, flattered by the attention paid to his personal charm or premature genius, stimulated by the conversation of politely educated pedants, encouraged in studies for which he felt a natural aptitude, gratified by the comradeship of the young prince whose temperament corresponded to his own in gravity, he conceived that radiant and romantic conception of Courts, as the only fit places of abode for men of noble birth and eminent abilities, which no disillusionment in after life was able to obscure. We cannot blame him for this error, though error it indubitably was. It was one which he shared with all men of his station at that period, which the poverty of his estate, the habits of his father, and his own ignorance of home-life almost forced upon his poet's temperament.

At Urbino Tasso read mathematics under a real master, Federigo Comandino, and carried on his literary studies with enthusiasm. It was probably at this time that he acquired the familiar knowledge of Virgil which so powerfully influenced his style, and that he began to form his theory of epic as distinguished from romantic poetry. After a residence of two years he removed to Venice, where his father was engaged in polishing the 'Amadigi' for publication. Here a new scene of interest opened out for him; and here he first enjoyed the sweets of literary fame. Bernardo had been chosen secretary by an Academy, in which men like Veniero, Molino, Gradenigo, Mocenigo, and Manuzio, the most learned and the noblest Venetians, met together for discussion. The slim lad of fifteen was admitted to their sessions, and surprised these elders by his eloquence and erudition. It is noticeable that at this time he carefully studied and annotated Dante's 'Divine Comedy,' a poem almost neglected by Italians in the Cinque Cento. It seemed good to his father now that he should prosecute his studies in earnest, with a view of choosing a more lucrative profession than that of letters or Court-service. Bernardo, while finishing the 'Amadigi,' which he dedicated to Philip II., sent his son in 1560 to Padua. He was to become a lawyer under the guidance of Guido Panciroli. But Tasso, like Ovid, like Petrarch, like a hundred other poets, felt no inclination for juristic learning. He freely and frankly abandoned himself to the metaphysical conclusions which were being then tried between Piccolomini and Pendasio, the one an Aristotelian dualist, the other a materialist for whom the soul was not immortal. Without force of mind enough to penetrate the deepest problems of philosophy, Tasso was quick to apprehend their bearings. The Paduan school of scepticism, the logomachy in vogue there, unsettled his religious opinions. He began by criticising the doubts of others in his light of Jesuit-instilled belief; next he found a satisfaction for self-esteem in doubting too; finally he called the mysteries of the Creed in question, and debated the articles of creation, incarnation, and immortality. Yet he had not the mental vigour either to cut this Gordian knot, or to untie it by sound thinking. His erudition confused him; and he mistook the lumber of miscellaneous reading for philosophy. Then a reaction set in. He remembered those childish ecstasies before the Eucharist; he recalled the pictures of a burning hell his Jesuit teachers had painted; he heard the trumpets of the Day of Judgment, and the sentence 'Go ye wicked!' On the brink of heresy he trembled and recoiled. The spirit of the coming age, the spirit of Bruno, was not in him. To all appearances he had not heard of the Copernican discovery. He wished to remain a true son of the Church, and was in fact of such stuff as the Catholic Revival wanted. Yet the memory of these early doubts clung to him, principally, we may believe, because he had not force to purge them either by severe science or by vivid faith. Later, when his mind was yielding to disorder, they returned in the form of torturing scruples and vain terrors, which his fervent but superficial pietism, his imaginative but sensuous religion, were unable to efface. Meanwhile, with one part of his mind devoted to these problems, the larger and the livelier was occupied with poetry. To law, the *Brod-Studium* indicated by his position in the world, he only paid perfunctory attention. The consequence was that before he had completed two years of residence in Padua, his first long poem, the 'Rinaldo,' saw the light. In another chapter I mean to discuss the development of Tasso's literary theories and achievements. It is enough here to say that the applause which greeted the 'Rinaldo' conquered his father's opposition. Proud of its success, Bernardo had it printed, and Torquato in the beginning of his nineteenth year counted among the notable romantic poets of his country.

At the end of 1563, Tasso received an invitation to transfer himself from Padua to Bologna. This proposal came from Monsignor Cesi, who had recently been appointed by Pope Pius IV. to superintend public studies in that city. The university was being placed on a new footing, and to secure the presence of a young man already famous seemed desirable. An exhibition was therefore offered as an inducement; and this Tasso readily accepted. He spent about two years at Bologna, studying philosophy and literature, planning his Dialogues on the Art of Poetry, and making projects for an epic on the history of Godfred. Yet in spite of public admiration and official favour, things did not go smoothly with Tasso at Bologna. One main defect of his character, which was a want of tact, began to manifest itself. He showed Monsignor Cesi that he had a poor opinion of his literary judgment, came into collision with the pedants who despised Italian, and finally uttered satiric epigrams in writing on various members of the university. Other students indulged their humour in like pasquinades. But those of Tasso were biting, and he had not contrived to render himself generally popular. His rooms were ransacked, his papers searched; and finding himself threatened with a prosecution for libel, he took flight to Modena. No importance can be attached to this insignificant affair, except in so far as it illustrates the unlucky aptitude for making enemies by want of *savoir vivre* which pursued Tasso through life. His real superiority aroused jealousy; his frankness wounded the self-love of rivals whom he treated with a shadow of contempt. As these were unable to compete with him in eloquence, or to beat him in debate, they soothed their injured feelings by conspiracy and calumny against him.

In an age of artifice and circumspection, while paying theoretical homage to its pedantries, and following the fashion of its compliments, Tasso was nothing if not spontaneous and heedless. This appears in the style of his letters and prose compositions, which have the air of being uttered from the heart. The excellences and defects of his poetry, soaring to the height of song and sinking into frigidity or baldness when the lyric impulse flags, reveal a similar quality. In conduct this spontaneity assumed a form of inconsiderate rashness, which brought him into collision with persons of importance, and rendered universities and Courts, the sphere of his adoption, perilous to the peace of so naturally out-spoken and self-engrossed a man. His irritable sensibilities caused him to suffer intensely from the petty vengeance of the people he annoyed; while a kind of amiable egotism blinded his eyes to his own faults, and made him blame fortune for sufferings of which his indiscretion was the cause.

After leaving Bologna, Tasso became for some months house-guest of his father's earliest patrons, the Modenese Rangoni. With them he seems to have composed his Dialogues on the Art of Poetry. For many years the learned men of Italy had been contesting the true nature of the Epic. One party affirmed that the ancients ought to be followed; and that the rules of Aristotle regarding unity of plot, dignity of style, and subordination of episodes, should be observed. The other party upheld the romantic manner of Ariosto, pleading for liberty of fancy, richness of execution, variety of incident, intricacy of design. Torquato from his earliest boyhood had heard these points discussed, and had watched his father's epic, the 'Amadigi,' which was in effect a romantic poem petrified by classical convention, in process of production. Meanwhile he carefully studied the text of Homer and the Latin epics, examined Horace and Aristotle, and perused the numerous romances of the Italian school. Two conclusions were drawn from this preliminary course of reading: first, that Italy as yet possessed no proper epic; Trissino's 'Italia Liberata' was too tiresome, the 'Orlando Furioso' too capricious; secondly, that the *spolia opima* in this field of art would be achieved by him who should combine the classic and romantic manners in a single work, enriching the unity of the antique epic with the graces of modern romance, choosing a noble and serious subject, sustaining style at a sublime altitude, but gratifying the prevalent desire for beauty in variety by the introduction of attractive episodes and the ornaments of picturesque description. Tasso, in fact, declared himself an eclectic; and the deep affinity he felt for Virgil indicated the lines upon which the Latin language in its romantic or Italian stage of evolution might be made to yield a second Æneid adapted to the requirements of modern taste. He had, indeed, already set before himself the high ambition of supplying this desideratum. The note of prelude had been struck in 'Rinaldo;' the subject of the 'Gerusalemme' had been chosen. But the age in which he lived was nothing if not critical and argumentative. The time had long gone by when Dante's massive cathedral, Boccaccio's pleasure domes, Boiardo's and Ariosto's palaces of enchantment, arose as though unbidden and unreasoned from the maker's brain. It was now impossible to take a step in poetry or art without a theory; and, what was worse, that theory had to be exposed for dissertation and discussion. Therefore Tasso, though by genius the most spontaneous of men, commenced the great work of his life with criticism. Already acclimatised to courts, coteries, academies, formed in the school of disputants and pedants, he propounded his 'Ars Poetica' before establishing it by an example. This was undoubtedly beginning at the wrong end; he committed himself to principles which he was bound to illustrate by practice. In the state of thought at that time prevalent in Italy, burdened as he was with an irresolute and diffident self-consciousness, Tasso could not deviate from the theory he had promulgated. How this hampered him, will appear in the sequel, when we come to notice the discrepancy between his critical and creative faculties. For the moment, however, the Dialogues on Epic Poetry only augmented his fame.

Scipione Gonzaga, one of Tasso's firmest and most illustrious friends, had recently established an Academy at Padua under the name of Gli Eterei. At his invitation the young poet joined this club in the autumn of 1564, assumed the title of Il Pentito in allusion to his desertion of legal studies, and soon became the soul of its society. His dialogues excited deep and wide-spread interest. After so much wrangling between classical and romantic champions, he had transferred the contest to new ground and introduced a fresh principle into the discussion. This principle was, in effect, that of common sense, good taste and instinct. Tasso meant to say: there is no vital discord between classical and romantic art; both have excellences, and it is possible to find defects in both; pedantic adherence to antique precedent must end in frigid failure under the present conditions of intellectual culture; yet it cannot be denied that the cycle of Renaissance poetry was closed by Ariosto; let us therefore attempt creation in a liberal spirit, trained by both these influences. He could not, however, when he put this theory forward in elaborate prose, abstain from propositions, distinctions, deductions, and conclusions, all of which were disputable, and each of which his critics and his honour held him bound to follow. In short, while planning and producing the 'Gerusalemme,' he was involved in controversies on the very essence of his art. These controversies had been started by himself and he could not do otherwise than maintain the position he had chosen. His poet's inspiration, his singer's spontaneity, came thus constantly into collision with his own deliberate utterances. A perplexed self-scrutiny was the inevitable result, which pedagogues who were not inspired and could not sing, but who delighted in minute discussion, took good care to stimulate. The worst, however, was that he had erected in his own mind a critical standard with which his genius was not in harmony. The scholar and the poet disagreed in Tasso; and it must be reckoned one of the drawbacks of his age and education that the former preceded the latter in development. Something of the same discord can be traced in contemporary painting, as will be shown when I come to consider the founders of the Bolognese Academy.

At the end of 1565 Tasso was withdrawn from literary studies and society in Padua. The Cardinal Luigi d' Este offered him a place in his household; and since this opened the way to Ferrara and Court-service, it was readily accepted. It would have been well for Tasso, at this crisis of his fate, if the line of his beloved Æneid—

> Heu, fuge crudeles terras, fuge littus avarum—

that line which warned young Savonarola away from Ferrara, had sounded in his ears, or met his eyes in some Virgilian 'Sortes.' It would have been well if his father, disillusioned by the 'Amadigi's' ill-success, and groaning under the galling yoke of servitude to princes, had forbidden instead of encouraging this fatal step. He might himself have listened to the words of old Speroni, painting the Court as he had learned to know it, a Siren fair to behold and ravishing of song, but hiding in her secret caves the bones of men devoured, and 'mighty poets in their misery dead.' He might even have turned the pages of Aretino's 'Dialogo delle Corti,' and have observed how the ruffian who best could profit by the vices of a Court, refused to bow his neck to servitude in their corruption. But no man avoids his destiny, because few draw wisdom from the past and none foresee the future. To Ferrara Tasso went with a blithe heart. Inclination, the custom of his country, the necessities of that poet's vocation for which he had abandoned a profession, poverty and ambition, vanity and the delights of life, combined to lure him to his ruin.

He found Ferrara far more magnificent than Urbino. Pageants, hunting parties, theatrical entertainments, assumed fantastic forms of splendour in this capital, which no other city of Italy, except Florence and Venice upon rare occasions, rivalled. For a long while past Ferrara had been the centre of a semi-feudal, semi-humanistic culture, out of which the Masque and Drama, music and painting, scholarship and poetry, emerged with brilliant originality, blending mediæval and antique elements in a specific type of modern romance. This culminated in the permanent and monumental work begun by Boiardo in the morning, and completed by Ariosto in the meridian of the Renaissance. Within the circuit of the Court the whole life of the Duchy seemed to concentrate itself. From the frontier of Venice to the Apennines a tract of fertile country, yielding all necessaries of life, corn, wine, cattle, game, fish, in abundance, poured its produce into the palaces and castles of the Duke. He, like other princes of his epoch, sucked each province dry in order to maintain a dazzling show of artificial wealth. The people were ground down by taxes, monopolies of corn and salt, and sanguinary game-laws. Brutalised by being forced to serve the pleasures of their masters, they lived the lives of swine. But why repaint the picture of Italian decadence or dwell again upon the fever of that phthisical consumption? Men like Tasso saw nothing to attract attention in the rotten state of Ferrara. They were only fascinated by the hectic bloom and rouged refinement of its Court. And even the least sympathetic student must confess that the Court at any rate was seductive. A more cunningly combined medley of polite culture, political astuteness, urbane learning, sumptuous display, diplomatic love intrigue, and genial artistic productiveness, never before or since has been exhibited upon a scale so grandiose within limits so precisely circumscribed, or been raised to eminence so high from such inadequate foundations of substantial wealth. Compare Ferrara in the sixteenth with Weimar in the eighteenth century, and reflect how wonderfully the Italians even at their last gasp understood the art of exquisite existence!

Alfonso II., who was always vainly trying to bless Ferrara with an heir, had arranged his second sterile nuptials when Tasso joined the Court in 1565. It was therefore at a moment of more than usual parade of splendour that the poet entered on the scene of his renown and his misfortune. He was twenty-one years of age; and twenty-one years had to elapse before he should quit Ferrara, ruined in physical and mental health—*quantum mutatus ab illo* Torquato! The diffident and handsome stripling, famous as the author of 'Rinaldo,' was welcomed in person with special honours by the Cardinal, his patron. Of such favours as Court-lacqueys prize, Tasso from the first had plenty. He did not sit at the common table of the serving gentlemen, but ate his food apart; and after a short residence, the Princesses, sisters of the Duke, invited him to share their meals. The next five years formed the happiest and most tranquil period of his existence. He continued working at the poem which had then no name, but which we know as the 'Gerusalemme Liberata.' Envies and jealousies had not arisen to mar the serenity in which he basked. Women contended for his smiles and sonnets. He repaid their kindness with somewhat indiscriminate homage and with the verses of occasion which flowed so easily from his pen. It is difficult to trace the history of Tasso's loves through the labyrinth of madrigals, odes, and sonnets which belong to this epoch of his life. These compositions bear, indeed, the mark of a distinguished genius; no one but Tasso could have written them at that period of Italian literature. Yet they lack individuality of emotion, specific passion, insight into the profundities of human feeling. Such shades of difference as we perceive in them, indicate the rhetorician seeking to set forth his motive, rather than the lover pouring out his soul. Contrary to the commonly received legend, I am bound to record my opinion that love played a secondary part in Tasso's destinies. It is true that we can discern the silhouettes of some Court ladies whom he fancied more than others. The first of these was Laura Peperara, for whom he is supposed to have produced some sixty compositions. The second was the Princess Leonora d' Este. Tasso's attachment to her has been so shrouded in mystery, conjecture, and hair-splitting criticism, that none but a very rash man will pronounce confident judgment as to its real nature. Nearly the same may be said about his relations to her sister, Lucrezia. He has posed in literary history as the Rizzio of the one lady and the Chastelard of the other. Yet he was probably in no position at any moment of his Ferrarese existence to be more than the familiar friend and most devoted slave of either. When he joined the Court, Lucrezia was ten and Leonora nine years his senior. Each of the sisters was highly accomplished, graceful, and of royal carriage. Neither could boast of eminent beauty. Of the two Lucrezia possessed the more commanding character. It was she who left her husband, Francesco Maria della Rovere, because his society wearied her, and who helped Clement VIII. to ruin her family, when the Papacy resolved upon the conquest of Ferrara. Leonora's health was sickly. For this reason she refused marriage, living retired in studies, acts of charity, religion, and the company of intellectual men. Something in her won respect and touched the heart at the same moment; so that the verses in her honour, from whatever pen they flowed, ring with more than merely ceremonial compliment. The people revered her like a saint; and in times of difficulty she displayed high courage and the gifts of one born to govern. From the first entrance of Tasso into Ferrara, the sisters took him under their protection. He lived with them on terms of more than courtly intimacy; and for Leonora there is no doubt that he cherished something like a romantic attachment. This is proved by the episode of Sofronia and Olinto in the 'Gerusalemme,' which points in carefully constructed innuendoes to his affection. It can even be conceded that Tasso, who was wont to indulge fantastic visions of unattainable greatness, may have raised his hopes so high as sometimes to entertain the possibility of winning her hand. But if he did dally with such dreams, the realities of his position must in sober moments have convinced him of their folly. Had not a Duchess of Amalfi been murdered for contracting marriage with a gentleman of her household? And Leonora was a granddaughter of France; and the cordon of royalty was being drawn tighter and tighter yearly in the Italy of his day. That a sympathy of no commonplace kind subsisted between this delicate and polished princess and her sensitively gifted poet, is apparent. But it may be doubted whether Tasso had in him the stuff of a grand passion. Mobile and impressible, he wandered from object to object without seeking or attaining permanence. He was neither a Dante nor a Petrarch; and nothing in his 'Rime' reveals solidity of emotion. It may finally be said that had Leonora returned real love, or had Tasso felt for her real love, his earnest wish to quit Ferrara when the Court grew irksome, would be inexplicable. Had their *liaison* been scandalous, as some have fancied, his life would not have been worth two hours' purchase either in the palace or the prison of Alfonso.

Whatever may be thought of Tasso's love-relations to these sisters—and the problem is open to all conjectures in the absence of clear testimony—it is certain that he owed a great deal to their kindness. The marked favour they extended to him was worth much at Court; and their maturer age and wider experience enabled them to give him many useful hints of conduct. Thus, when he blundered into seeming rivalry with Pigna (the Duke's secretary, the Cecil of that little State), by praising Pigna's mistress, Lucrezia Bendidio, in terms of imprudent warmth, it was Leonora who warned him to appease the great man's anger. This he did by writing a commentary upon three of Pigna's leaden Canzoni, which he had the impudence to rank beside the famous three sisters of Petrarch's Canzoniere. The flattery was swallowed, and the peril was averted. Yet in this first affair with Pigna we already hear the grumbling of that tempest which eventually ruined Tasso. So eminent a poet and so handsome a young man was insupportable among a crowd of literary mediocrities and middle-aged gallants. Furthermore, the brilliant being, who aroused the jealousies of rhymesters and of lovers, had one fatal failing—want of tact. In 1568, for example, he set himself up as a target to all malice by sustaining fifty conclusions in the Science of Love before the Academy of Ferrara. As he afterwards confessed, he ran the greatest risks in this adventure; but who, he said, could take up arms against a lover? Doubtless, there were many lovers present; but none of Tasso's eloquence and skill in argument.

In 1569, Tasso was called to his father's sick-bed at Ostiglia on the Po. He found the old man destitute and dying. There was not enough money to bury him decently; and when the funeral rites had been performed by the help of money-lenders, nothing remained to pay for a monument above his grave. What the Romans called *pietas* was a strong feature in Torquato's character. At crises of his life he invariably appealed to the memory of his parents for counsel and support. When the Della Cruscans attacked his own poetry, he answered them with a defence of the 'Amadigi;' and he spent much time and pains in editing the 'Floridante,' which naught but filial feeling could possibly have made him value at the worth of publication.

In the spring of the next year, Lucrezia d' Este made her inauspicious match with the Duke of Urbino, Tasso's former playmate. She was a woman of thirty-four, he a young man of twenty-one. They did not love each other, had no children, and soon parted with a sense of mutual relief. In the autumn Tasso accompanied the Cardinal Luigi d' Este into France, leaving his MSS. in the charge of Ercole Rondinelli. The document drawn up for this friend's instructions in case of his death abroad is interesting. It proves that the 'Gerusalemme,' here called 'Gottifredo,' was nearly finished; for Tasso wished the last six cantos and portions of the first two to be published. He also gave directions for the collection and publication of his love-sonnets and madrigals, but requested Rondinelli to bury 'the others, whether of love or other matters, which were written in the service of some friend,' in his grave. This last commission demands comment. That Tasso should have written verses to oblige a friend, was not only natural but consistent with custom. Light wares like sonnets could be easily produced by a practised man of letters, and the friend might find them valuable in bringing a fair foe to terms. But why should anyone desire to have such verses buried in his grave? The hypothesis which has been strongly urged by those who believe in the gravity of Tasso's *liaison* with Leonora, is that he used this phrase to indicate love-poems which might compromise his mistress. We cannot, however, do more than speculate upon the point. There is nothing to confirm or to refute conjecture in the evidence before us.

Tasso met with his usual fortunes at the Court of Charles IX. That is to say, he was petted and caressed, wrote verses, and paid compliments. It was just two years before the Massacre of S. Bartholomew, and France presented to the eyes of earnest Catholics the spectacle of truly horrifying anarchy. Catherine de' Medici inclined to compromise matters with the Huguenots. The social atmosphere reeked with heresy and cynicism. In that Italianated Court, public affairs and religious questions were treated from a purely diplomatic point of view. Not principle, but practical convenience, ruled conduct and opinion. The large scale on which Machiavellism manifested itself in the discordant realm of France, the apparent breakdown of Catholicism as a national institution, struck Tasso with horror. He openly proclaimed his views, and roundly taxed the Government with dereliction of their duty to the Church. An incurable idealist by temperament, he could not comprehend the stubborn actualities of politics. A pupil of the Jesuits, he would not admit that men like Coligny deserved a hearing. An Italian of the decadence, he found it hard to tolerate the humours of a puissant nation in a state of civil warfare. But his master, Luigi d' Este, well understood the practical difficulties which forced the Valois into compromise, and felt no personal aversion for lucrative transaction with the heretic. Though a prince of the Church he had not taken priest's orders. He kept two objects in view. One was succession to the Duchy of Ferrara, in case Alfonso should die without heirs.[10] The other was election to the Papacy. In the latter event, France, the natural ally of the Estensi, would be of service to him, and the Valois monarchs, his cousins, must therefore be supported in their policy. Tasso had been brought to Paris to look graceful and to write madrigals. It was inconvenient, it was unseemly, that a

[10] Cardinal Ferdinando de' Medici succeeded in a like position to the Grand Duchy of Tuscany. But Luigi d' Este did not survive his brother.

man of letters in the Cardinal's train should utter censures on the Crown, and should profess more Catholic opinions than his patron. Without the scandal of a public dismissal, it was therefore contrived that Tasso should return to Italy; and after this rupture, the suspicious poet regarded Luigi d' Este as his enemy. During his confinement in S. Anna he even threw the chief blame of his detention upon the Cardinal.[11]

After spending a short time at Rome in the company of the Cardinals Ippolito d' Este and Albano, Tasso returned to Ferrara in 1572. Alfonso offered him a place in his own household with an annual stipend worth about 88*l*. of our money. No duties were attached to this post, except the delivery of a weekly lecture in the university. For the rest, Tasso was to prosecute his studies, polish his great poem, and augment the lustre of the Court by his accomplishments.[12] It was of course understood that the 'Gerusalemme,' when completed, should be dedicated to the Duke and shed its splendour on the House of Este. Who was happier than Torquato now? Having recently experienced the discomforts of uncongenial service, he took his place again upon a firmer footing in the city of his dreams. The courtiers welcomed him with smiles. He was once more close to Leonora, basking like Rinaldo in Armida's garden, with golden prospects of the fame his epic would achieve to lift him higher in the coming years. No wonder that the felicity of this moment expanded in a flower of lyric beauty which surpassed all that Tasso had yet published. He produced 'Aminta' in the winter of 1572-3. It was acted with unparalleled applause; for this pastoral drama offered something ravishingly new, something which interpreted and gave a vocal utterance to tastes and sentiments that ruled the age. While professing to exalt the virtues of rusticity, the 'Aminta' was in truth a panegyric of Court life, and Silvia reflected Leonora in the magic mirror of languidly luxurious verse. Poetry melted into music. Emotion exhaled itself in sensuous harmony. The art of the next two centuries, the supreme art of song, of words subservient to musical expression, had been indicated. This explains the sudden and extraordinary success of the 'Aminta.' It was nothing less than the discovery of a new realm, the revelation of a specific faculty which made its author master of the heart of Italy. The very lack of concentrated passion lent it power. Its suffusion of emotion in a shimmering atmosphere toned with voluptuous melancholy, seemed to invite the lutes and viols, the mellow tenors, and the trained suprano voices of the dawning age of melody. We may here remember that Palestrina, seven years earlier in Rome, had already given his 'Mass of Pope Marcello' to the world.

Lucrezia d' Este, now Duchess of Urbino, who was anxious to share the raptures of 'Aminta,' invited Tasso to Pesaro in the summer of 1573, and took him with her to the mountain villa of Casteldurante. She was an unhappy wife, just on the point of breaking her irksome bonds of matrimony. Tasso, if we may credit the deductions which have been

[11] See *Lettere*, vol. ii. p. 80: to Giacomo Buoncompagno.

[12] 'Egli mi disse, allor che suo mi fece: Tu canta, or che se' 'n ozio.'

drawn from passages in his letters, had the privilege of consoling the disappointed woman and of distracting her tedious hours. They roamed together through the villa gardens, and spent days of quiet in the recesses of her apartments. He read aloud passages from his unpublished poem, and composed sonnets in her honour, praising the full-blown beauty of the rose as lovelier than its budding charm. The Duke, her husband, far from resenting this intimacy, heaped favours and substantial gifts upon his former comrade. He had not, indeed, enough affection for his wife to be jealous of her. Yet it is indubitable that if he had suspected her of infidelity, the Italian code of honour would have compelled him to make short work with Tasso.[13]

Meanwhile it seemed as though Leonora had been forgotten by her servant. We possess one letter written to her from Casteldurante on September 3, 1573, in which he encloses a sonnet, disparaging it by comparison with those which he believes she has been receiving from another poet (Guarini probably), and saying that, though the verses were written, not for himself, but 'at the requisition of a poor lover, who, having been for some while angry with his lady, now is forced to yield and crave for pardon,' yet he hopes that they 'will effect the purpose he desires.'[14] Few of Tasso's letters to Leonora have survived. This, therefore, is a document of much importance; and it is difficult to resist the conclusion that he was indirectly begging Leonora to forgive him for some piece of petulance or irritation. At any rate, his position between the two princesses at this moment was one of delicacy, in which a less vain and more cautious man than Tasso might have found it hard to keep his head cool.

Up to the present time his life had been, in spite of poverty and domestic misfortunes, one almost uninterrupted career of triumph. But his fibre had been relaxed in the irresponsible luxurious atmosphere of Courts, and his self-esteem had been inflated by the honours paid to him as the first poet of his age in Europe. Moreover, he had been continuously over-worked and over-wrought from childhood onwards. Now, when he returned to Ferrara with the Duchess of Urbino at the age of twenty-nine, it remained to be seen whether he could support himself with stability upon the slippery foundation of princely favour, whether his health would hold out, and whether he would be able to bring the publication of his long-expected poem to a successful issue.

In 1574 he accompanied Duke Alfonso to Venice, and witnessed the magnificent reception of Henri III. on his return from Poland. A fever,

[13] This is how he wrote in his Diary about Lucrezia. 'Finally the Duke decided upon his marriage with Donna Lucrezia d' Este, which took place, though little to his taste, for she was old enough to have been his mother.' 'The Duchess wished to return to Ferrara, where she subsequently chose to remain, a resolution which gave no annoyance to her husband; for, as she was unlikely to bring him a family, her absence mattered little.' 'February 15, 1598. Heard that Madame Lucrezia d' Este, Duchess of Urbino, my wife, died at Ferrara during the night of the 11th.' (Dennistoun's *Dukes of Urbino*, vol. iii. pp. 127, 146, 156.) Francesco Maria had been attached in Spain to a lady of unsuitable condition, and his marriage with Lucrezia was arranged to keep him out of a *mesalliance*.

[14] *Lettere*, vol. i. p. 47. The sonnet begins, 'Sdegno, debil guerrier.'

contracted during those weeks of pleasure, prevented him from working at the epic for many months. This is the first sign of any serious failure in Tasso's health. At the end of August 1574, however, the 'Gerusalemme' was finished, and in the following February he began sending the MS. to Scipione Gonzaga at Rome. So much depended on its success that doubts immediately rose within its author's mind. Will it fulfil the expectation raised in every Court and literary coterie of Italy? Will it bear investigation in the light of the Dialogues on Epic Poetry? Will the Church be satisfied with its morality; the Holy Office with its doctrine? None of these diffidences assailed Tasso when he flung 'Aminta' negligently forth and found he had produced a masterpiece. It would have been well for him if he had turned a deaf ear to the doubting voice on this occasion also. But he was not of an independent character to start with: and his life had made him sensitively deferent to literary opinion. Therefore, in an evil hour, yielding to Gonzaga's advice, he resolved to submit the 'Gerusalemme' in MS. to four censors—Il Borga, Flaminio de Nobili, vulpine Speroni with his poisoned fang of pedantry, precise Antoniano with his inquisitorial prudery. They were to pass their several criticisms on the plot, characters, diction, and ethics of the 'Gerusalemme;' Tasso was to entertain and weigh their arguments, reserving the right of following or rejecting their advice, but promising to defend his own views. To the number of this committee he shortly after added three more scholars, Francesco Piccolomini, Domenico Veniero, and Celio Magno.[15] Not to have been half maddened by these critics would have proved Tasso more or less than human. They picked holes in the structure of the epic, in its episodes, in its theology, in its incidents, in its language, in its title. One censor required one alteration, and another demanded the contrary. This man seemed animated by an acrid spite; that veiled his malice in the flatteries of candid friendship. Antoniano was for cutting out the love passages: Armida, Sofronia, Erminia, Clorinda, were to vanish or to be adapted to conventual proprieties. It seemed to him more than doubtful whether the enchanted forest did not come within the prohibitions of the Tridentine decrees. As the revision advanced, matters grew more serious. Antoniano threw out some decided hints of ecclesiastical displeasure; Tasso, reading between the lines, scented the style of the Collegium Germanicum. Speroni spoke openly of plagiarism—plagiarism from himself forsooth!—and murmured the terrible words between his teeth, 'Tasso is mad!' He was in fact driven wild, and told his tormentors that he would delay the publication of the epic, perhaps for a year, perhaps for his whole life, so little hope had he of its success.[16] At last he resolved to compose an allegory to explain and moralise the poem. When he wrote the 'Gerusalemme' he had no thought of hidden meanings; but this seemed the only way of preventing

[15] Tasso consulted almost every scholar he could press into his service. But the official tribunal of correction was limited to the above-named four acting in concert with Scipione Gonzaga.

[16] *Lettere*, vol. i. p. 114.

it from being dismembered by hypocrites and pedants.[17] The expedient proved partially successful. When Antoniano and his friends were bidden to perceive a symbol in the enchanted wood and other marvels, a symbol in the loves of heroines and heroes, a symbol even in Armida, they relaxed their wrath. The 'Gerusalemme' might possibly pass muster now before the Congregation of the Index. Tasso's correspondence between March 1575 and July 1576 shows what he suffered at the hands of his revisers, and helps to explain the series of events which rendered the autumn of that latter year calamitous for him.[18] There are, indeed, already indications in the letters of those months that his nerves, enfeebled by the quartan fever under which he laboured, and exasperated by carping or envious criticism, were overstrung. Suspicions began to invade his mind. He complained of headache. His spirits alternated between depression and hysterical gaiety. A dread lest the Inquisition should refuse the imprimatur to his poem haunted him. He grew restless, and yearned for change of scene.

The events of 1575, 1576, and 1577 require to be minutely studied; for upon our interpretation of them must depend the theory which we hold of Tasso's subsequent misfortunes. It appears that early in the year 1575 he was becoming discontented with Ferrara. A party in the Court, led by Pigna, did their best to make his life there disagreeable. They were jealous of the poet's fame, which shone with trebled splendour after the production of 'Aminta.' Tasso's own behaviour provoked, if it did not exactly justify, their animosity. He treated men at least his equals in position with haughtiness, which his irritable temper rendered insupportable. We have it from his own pen that 'he could not bear to live in a city where the nobles did not yield him the first place, or at least admit him to absolute equality;' that 'he expected to be adored by friends, served by serving-men, caressed by domestics, honoured by masters, celebrated by poets, and pointed out by all.'[19] He admitted that it was his habit 'to build castles in the air of honours, favours, gifts, and graces, showered on him by emperors and kings and mighty princes;' that 'the slightest coldness from a patron seemed to him a tacit act of dismissal, or rather an open act of violence.'[20] His blood, he argued, placed him on a level with the aristocracy of Italy; but his poetry lifted him far above the vulgar herd of noble men. At the same time, while claiming so much, he constantly declared himself unfit for any work or office but literary study, and expressed his opinion that princes ought to be his tributaries.[21] Though such pretensions may not have been openly expressed at this period of his life, it cannot be doubted that Tasso's temper made him an unpleasant comrade in Court-service. His sensitiveness, as well as the actual slenderness of his fortunes, exposed him only too obviously to the malevolent tricks and petty bullyings of

[17] *Lettere*, vol. i. p. 192.
[18] *Ib.* vol. i. pp. 55-215.
[19] *Lettere*, vol. iii. p. 41, iv. p. 332.
[20] *Ib.* vol. iii. p. 164, v. p. 6.
[21] *Ib.* vol. iii. pp. 85, 86, 88, 163, iv. pp. 8, 166, v. p. 87.

rivals. One knows what a boy of that stamp has to suffer at public schools, and a Court is after all not very different from an academy.

Such being the temper of his mind, Tasso at this epoch turned his thoughts to bettering himself, as servants say. His friend Scipione Gonzaga pointed out that both the Cardinal de' Medici and the Grand Duke of Tuscany would be glad to welcome him as an ornament of their households. Tasso nibbled at the bait all through the summer; and in November, under the pretext of profiting by the Jubilee, he travelled to Rome. This journey, as he afterwards declared, was the beginning of his ruin.[22] It was certainly one of the principal steps which led to the prison of S. Anna. There were many reasons why Alfonso should resent Tasso's entrance into other service at this moment. The House of Este had treated him with uniform kindness. The Cardinal, the Duke, and the princesses had severally marked him out by special tokens of esteem. In return they expected from him the honours of his now immortal epic. That he should desert them and transfer the dedication of the 'Gerusalemme' to the Medici, would have been nothing short of an insult; for it was notorious that the Estensi and the Medici were bitter foes, not only on account of domestic disagreements and political jealousies, but also because of the dispute about precedence in their titles, which had agitated Italian society for some time past. In his impatience to leave Ferrara, Tasso cast prudence to the winds, and entered into negotiations with the Cardinal de'Medici in Rome. When he travelled northwards at the beginning of 1576, he betook himself to Florence. What passed between him and the Grand Duke is not apparent. Yet he seems to have still further complicated his position by making political disclosures which were injurious to the Duke of Ferrara. Nor did he gain anything by the offer of his services and his poem to Francesco de' Medici. In a letter of February 4, 1576, the Grand Duke wrote that the Florentine visit of that fellow, 'whether to call him a mad or an amusing and astute spirit, I hardly know,' had been throughout a ridiculous affair; and that nothing could be less convenient than his putting the 'Gerusalemme' up to auction among princes.[23] One year later, he said bluntly that 'he did not want to have a madman at his Court.'[24] Thus Tasso, like his father, discovered that a noble poem, the product of his best pains, had but small substantial value. It might, indeed, be worth something to the patron who paid a yearly exhibition to its author; but it was not a gem of such high price as to be wrangled for by dukes who had the cares of State upon their shoulders. He compromised himself with the Estensi, and failed to secure a retreat in Florence.

Meanwhile his enemies at Ferrara were not idle. Pigna had died in the preceding November. But Antonio Montecatino, who succeeded him as ducal secretary, proved even a more malicious foe, and poisoned

[22] Letter to Fabio Gonzaga in 1590 (vol. iv. p. 296).
[23] *Lettere*, vol. iii. p. viii.
[24] *Ib.* vol. iii. p. xxx. note 34.

Alfonso's mind against the unfortunate poet. The two princesses still remained his faithful friends, until Tasso's own want of tact alienated the sympathies of Leonora. When he returned in 1576, he found the beautiful Eleonora Sanvitale, Countess of Scandiano, at Court. Whether he really fell in love with her at first sight, or pretended to do so in order to revive Leonora d' Este's affection by jealousy, is uncertain.[25] At any rate he paid the Countess such marked attentions, and wrote for her and a lady of her suite such splendid poetry, that all Ferrara rang with this amour. A sonnet in Tasso's handwriting, addressed to Leonora d' Este and commented by her own pen, which even Guasti, no credulous believer in the legend of the poet's love, accepts as genuine, may be taken as affording proof that the princess was deeply wounded by her servant's conduct.[26]

It is obvious that, though Tasso's letters at this period show no signs of a diseased mind, his conduct began to strike outsiders as insane. Francesco de' Medici used the plain words *matto* and *pazzo*. The courtiers of Ferrara, some in pity, some in derision, muttered 'Madman,' when he passed. And he spared no pains to prove that he was losing self-control. In the month of January 1577 he was seized with scruples of faith, and conceived the notion that he ought to open his mind to the Holy Office. Accordingly, he appeared before the Inquisitor of Bologna, who, after hearing his confession, bade him be of good cheer, for his self-accusations were the outcome of a melancholy humour. Tasso was, in fact, a Catholic moulded by Jesuit instruction in his earliest childhood; and though, like most young students, he had speculated on the groundwork of theology and metaphysic, there was no taint of heresy or disobedience to the Church in his nature. The terror of the Inquisition was a morbid nightmare, first implanted in his mind by the experience of his father's collision with the Holy Office, enforced by Antoniano's strictures on his poem, and justified to some extent by the sinister activity of the institution which had burned a Carnesecchi and a Paleario. However it grew up, this fancy that he was suspected as a heretic took firm possession of his brain, and subsequently formed a main feature of his mental disease. It combined with the suspiciousness which now became habitual. He thought that secret enemies were in the habit of forwarding delations against him to Rome.

All through these years (1575-1577) his enemies drew tighter cords around him. They were led and directed by Montecatino, the omnipotent persecutor, and hypocritical betrayer. In his heedlessness Tasso left books and papers loose about his rooms. These, he had good reason to suppose, were ransacked in his absence. There follows a melancholy tale of treacherous friends, dishonest servants, false keys, forged correspondence, scraps and fragments of imprudent compositions pieced

[25] Guarini, in a sonnet, hinted at the second supposition. See Rosini's *Saggio sugli Amori*, &c.; vol. xxxiii. of his edition of Tasso, p. 51.

[26] *Lettere*, vol. iii. p. xxxi.

together and brought forth to incriminate him behind his back. These arts were employed all through the year which followed his return to Ferrara in 1576. But they reached their climax in the spring of 1577. He had lost his prestige, and every servant might insult him, every cur snap at his heels. Even the 'Gerusalemme' became an object of derision. It transpired that the revisers, to whom he had confided it, were picking the poem to pieces; and ignoramuses who could not scan a line, went about parroting their pedantries and strictures. At the beginning of 1576 Tasso had begged Alfonso to give him the post of historiographer left vacant by Pigna. It was his secret hope that this would be refused, and that so he would obtain a good excuse for leaving Ferrara.[27] But the Duke granted his request. In the autumn of that year, one of the band of his tormentors, Maddalò de' Frecci, betrayed some details of his love affairs. What these were, we do not know. Tasso resented the insult, and gave the traitor a box on the ears in the courtyard of the castle. Maddalò and his brothers, after this, attacked Tasso on the piazza, but ran away before they reached him with their swords. They were outlawed for the outrage, and the Duke of Ferrara, still benignant to his poet, sent him a kind message by one of his servants. This incident weighed on Tasso's memory. The terror of the Inquisition blended now with two new terrors. He conceived that his exiled foes were plotting to poison him. He wondered whether Maddalò's revelations had reached the Duke's ears, and, if so, whether Alfonso would not inflict sudden vengeance. There is no sufficient reason, however, to surmise that Tasso's conscience was really burdened with a guilty secret touching Leonora d' Este. On the contrary, everything points to a different conclusion. His mind was simply giving way. Just as he conjured up the ghastly spectacle of the Inquisition, so he fancied that the Duke would murder him. Both the Inquisition and the Duke were formidable; but the Holy Office mildly told him to set his morbid doubts at rest, and the Duke on a subsequent occasion coldly wrote: 'I know he thinks I want to kill him. But if indeed I did so, it would be easy enough.' The Duke, in fact, had no sufficient reason and no inclination to tread upon this insect.

In June 1577 the crisis came. On the seventeenth evening of the month Tasso was in the apartments of the Duchess of Urbino. He had just been declaiming on the subject of his imaginary difficulties with the Inquisition, when something in the manner of a servant who passed by aroused his suspicion. He drew a knife upon the man—like Hamlet in his mother's bedchamber. He was immediately put under arrest, and confined in a room of the castle. Next day Maffeo Veniero wrote thus to the Grand Duke of Tuscany about the incident: 'Yesterday Tasso was imprisoned for having drawn a knife upon a servant in the apartment of the Duchess of Urbino. The intention has been to stay disorder and to cure him, rather than to inflict punishment. He suffers under peculiar delusions, believing himself guilty of heresy,

[27] *Lettere*, vol. i. p. 139.

and dreading poison; which state of mind arises, I incline to think, from melancholic blood forced in upon the heart and vapouring to the brain. A wretched case, in truth, considering his great parts and his goodness!'[28]

Tasso was soon released, and taken by the Duke to his villa of Belriguardo. Probably this excursion was designed to soothe the perturbed spirits of the poet. But it may also have had a different object. Alfonso may have judged it prudent to sift the information laid before him by Tasso's enemies. We do not know what passed between them. Whether moral pressure was applied, resulting in the disclosure of secrets compromising Leonora d' Este, cannot now be ascertained; nor is it worth while to discuss the hypothesis that the Duke, in order to secure his family's honour, imposed on Tasso the obligation of feigning madness.[29] There is a something not entirely elucidated, a sediment of mystery in Tasso's fate, after this visit to Belriguardo, which criticism will not neglect to notice, but which no testing, no clarifying process of study, has hitherto explained. All we can rely upon for certain is that Alfonso sent him back to Ferrara to be treated physically and spiritually for derangement; and that Tasso thought his life was in danger. He took up his abode in the Convent of S. Francis, submitted to be purged, and began writing eloquent letters to his friends and patrons. Those which he addressed to the Duke of Ferrara at this crisis, weigh naturally heaviest in the scale of criticism.[30] They turn upon his dread of the Inquisition, his fear of poison, and his diplomatic practice with Florence. While admitting 'faults of grave importance' and 'vacillation in the service of his prince,' he maintains that his secret foes have exaggerated these offences, and have succeeded in prejudicing the magnanimous and clement spirit of Alfonso. He is particularly anxious about the charge of heresy. Nothing indicates that any guilt of greater moment weighed upon his conscience.[31] After scrutinising all accessible sources of information, we are thus driven to accept the prosaic hypothesis that Tasso was deranged, and that his Court-rivals had availed themselves of a favourable opportunity for making the Duke sensible of his insanity.

After the middle of July, the Convent of S. Francis became intolerable to Tasso. His malady had assumed the form of a multiplex fear, which never afterwards relaxed its hold on his imagination. The Inquisition, the Duke, the multitude of secret enemies plotting murder, haunted him day and night like furies. He escaped, and made his way, dis-

[28] *Lettere*, vol. i. p. 228.

[29] This is Rosini's hypothesis in the Essay cited above. The whole of his elaborate and ingenious theory rests upon the supposition that Alfonso at Belriguardo extorted from Tasso an acknowledgment of his *liaison* with Leonora, and spared his life on the condition of his playing a fool's part before the world. But we have no evidence whatever adequate to support the supposition.

[30] *Lettere*, vol. i. pp. 257-262.

[31] Those who adhere to the belief that all Tasso's troubles came upon him through his *liaison* with Leonora, are here of course justified in arguing that on *this* point he could not write openly to the Duke. Or they may question the integrity of the document.

guised in a peasant's costume, avoiding cities, harbouring in mountain hamlets, to Sorrento. Manso, who wrote the history of Tasso's life in the spirit of a novelist, has painted for us a romantic picture of the poet in a shepherd's hut.[32] It recalls Erminia among the pastoral people. Indeed, the interest of that episode in the 'Gerusalemme' is heightened by the fact that its ill-starred author tested the reality of his creation ofttimes in the course of this pathetic pilgrimage. Artists of the Bolognese Academy have placed Erminia on their canvases. But, up to the present time, I know of no great painter who has chosen the more striking incident of Tasso exchanging his Court-dress for sheepskin and a fustian jacket in the smoky cottage at Velletri.

He reached Sorrento safely—'that most enchanting region, which at all times offers a delightful sojourn to men and to the Muses; but at the warm season of the year, when other places are intolerable, affords peculiar solace in the verdure of its foliage, the shadow of its woods, the lightness of the fanning airs, the freshness of the limpid waters flowing from impendent hills, the fertile expanse of tilth, the serene air, the tranquil sea, the fishes and the birds and savoury fruits in marvellous variety; all which delights compose a garden for the intellect and senses, planned by Nature in her rarest mood, and perfected by art with most consummate curiosity.'[33] Into this earthly paradise the wayworn pilgrim entered. It was his birthplace; and here his sister still dwelt with her children. Tasso sought Cornelia's home. After a dramatic scene of suspense, he threw aside his disguise, declared himself to be the poet of Italy and her brother; and for a short while he seemed to forget Courts and schools, pedants and princes, in that genial atmosphere.

Why did he ever leave Sorrento? That is the question which leaps to the lips of a modern free man. The question itself implies imperfect comprehension of Tasso's century and training. Outside the Court, there was no place for him. He had been moulded for Court-life from childhood. It was not merely that he had no money; assiduous labour might have supplied him with means of subsistence. But his friends, his fame, his habits, his engrained sense of service, called him back to Ferrara. He was not simply a man, but that specific sort of man which Italians call *gentiluomo*—a man definitely modified and wound about with intricacies of association. Therefore, he soon began a correspondence with the House of Este. If we may trust Manso, Leonora herself wrote urgently insisting upon his return.[34] Yet in his own letters Tasso says that he addressed apologies to the Duke and both princesses. Alfonso and Lucrezia vouchsafed no answer. Leonora replied coldly that she could not help him.[35]

Anyhow, Ferrara drew him back. It is of some importance here to understand Tasso's own feeling for the Duke, his master. A few months

[32] Rosini's edition of Tasso, vol. xxx. p. 144.
[33] Manso, *ib*. p. 46.
[34] Manso, *ib*. p. 147.
[35] *Lettere*, vol. i. p. 275.

later, after he had once more experienced the miseries of Court-life, he wrote: 'I trusted in him, not as one hopes in men, but as one trusts in God. . . . I was inflamed with the affection for my lord more than ever was man with the love of woman, and became unawares half an idolater. . . . He it was who from the obscurity of my low fortunes raised me to the light and reputation of the Court; who relieved me from discomforts, and placed me in a position of honourable ease; he conferred value on my compositions by listening to them when I read them, and by every mark of favour; he deigned to honour me with a seat at his table and with his familiar conversation; he never refused a favour which I begged for; lastly, at the commencement of my troubles, he showed me the affection, not of a master, but of a father and a brother.'[36] These words, though meant for publication, have the ring of truth in them. Tasso was actually attached to the House of Este, and cherished a vassal's loyalty for the Duke, in spite of the many efforts which he made to break the fetters of Ferrara. At a distance, in the isolation and the ennui of a village, the irksomeness of those chains was forgotten. The poet only remembered how sweet his happier years at Court had been. The sentiment of fidelity revived. His sanguine and visionary temperament made him hope that all might yet be well.

Without receiving direct encouragement from the Duke, Tasso accordingly decided on returning. His sister is said to have dissuaded him; and he is reported to have replied that he was going to place himself in a voluntary prison.[37] He first went to Rome, and opened negotiations with Alfonso's agents. In reply to their communications, the Duke wrote upon March 22, 1578, as follows: 'We are content to take Tasso back; but first he must recognise the fact that he is full of melancholic humours, and that his old notions of enmities and persecutions are solely caused by the said humours. Among other signs of his disorder, he has conceived the idea that we want to compass his death, whereas we have always received him gladly and shown favour to him. It can easily be understood that if we had entertained such a fancy, the execution of it would have presented no difficulty. Therefore let him make his mind up well, before he comes, to submit quietly and unconditionally to medical treatment. Otherwise, if he means to scatter hints and words again as he did formerly, we shall not only give ourselves no further trouble about him, but if he should stay here without being willing to undergo a course of cure, we shall at once expel him from our State with the order not to return.'[38] Words could not be plainer than these. Yet, in spite of them, such was the allurement of the cage for this clipped singing-bird, that Tasso went obediently back to Ferrara. Possibly he had not read the letter written by a greater poet on a similar occasion: 'This is not the way of coming home, my

[36] *Lettere*, vol. i. p. 278, ii. p. 26.

[37] Manso, p. 147. Here again the believers in the Leonora *liaison* may argue that by prison he meant love-bondage, hopeless servitude to the lady from whom he could expect nothing now that her brother was acquainted with the truth.

[38] *Lettere*, vol. i. p. 233.

father! Yet if you or others find one not beneath the fame of Dante and his honour, that will I pursue with no slack step. But if none such give entrance to Florence, I will never enter Florence. How! Shall I not behold the sun and stars from every spot of earth? Shall I not be free to meditate the sweetest truths in every place beneath the sky unless I make myself ignoble, nay, ignominious to the people and the state of Florence? Nor truly will bread fail.' These words, if Tasso had remembered them, might have made his cheek blush for his own servility and for the servile age in which he lived. But the truth is that the fleshpots of Egyptian bondage enticed him; and, moreover, he knew, as half-insane people always know, that he required treatment for his mental infirmities. In his heart of hearts he acknowledged the justice of the Duke's conditions.

An Epistle or Oration addressed by Tasso to the Duke of Urbino, sets forth what happened after his return to Ferrara in 1578.[39] He was aware that Alfonso thought him both malicious and mad. The first of these opinions, which he knew to be false, he resolved to pass in silence. But he openly admitted the latter, 'esteeming it no disgrace to make a third to Solon and Brutus.' Therefore he began to act the madman even in Rome, neglecting his health, exposing himself to hardships, and indulging intemperately in food and wine. By these means, strange as it may seem, he hoped to win back confidence and prove himself a discreet servant of Alfonso. Soon after reaching Ferrara, Tasso thought that he was gaining ground. He hints that the Duke showed signs of raising him to such greatness and showering favours upon him so abundant that the sleeping viper of Court-envy stirred. Montecatino now persuaded his master that prudence and his own dignity indicated a very different line of treatment. If Tasso was to be great and honoured, he must feel that his reputation flowed wholly from the princely favour, not from his studies and illustrious works. Alfonso accordingly affected to despise the poems which Tasso presented, and showed his will that: 'I should aspire to no eminence of intellect, to no glory of literature, but should lead a soft and delicate and idle life immersed in sloth and pleasure, escaping like a runaway from the honour of Parnassus, the Lyceum, and the Academy, into the lodgings of Epicurus, and should harbour in those lodgings in a quarter where neither Virgil nor Catullus nor Horace nor Lucretius himself had ever stayed.' This excited such indignation in the poet's breast that: 'I said oftentimes with open face and free speech that I would rather be a servant of any prince his enemy than submit to this indignity, and in short *odia verbis aspera movi*.' Whereupon, the Duke caused his papers to be seized, in order that the still imperfect epic might be prepared for publication by the hated hypocritical Montecatino. When Tasso complained, he only received indirect answers; and when he tried to gain access to the princesses, he was repulsed by their doorkeepers. At last: 'My infinite patience was exhausted. Leaving my books and

[39] *Ib.* vol. i. pp. 271-290.

writings, after the service of thirteen years, persisted in with luckless constancy, I wandered forth like a new Bias, and betook myself to Mantua, where I met with the same treatment as at Ferrara.'

This account sufficiently betrays the diseased state of Tasso's mind. Being really deranged, yet still possessed of all his literary faculties, he affected that his eccentricity was feigned. The Duke had formed a firm opinion of his madness; and he chose to flatter this whim. Yet when he arrived at Ferrara, he forgot the strict conditions upon which Alfonso sanctioned his return, began to indulge in dreams of greatness, and refused the life of careless ease which formed part of the programme for his restoration to health. In these circumstances he became the laughing-stock of his detractors; and it is not impossible that Alfonso, convinced of his insanity, treated him like a Court-fool. Then he burst out into menaces and mutterings of anger. When he had made himself wholly intolerable, his papers were sequestrated, very likely under the impression that he might destroy them or escape with them into some quarter where they would be used against the interests of his patron. Finally, he so fatigued everybody by his suspicions and recriminations that the Duke forbore to speak with him, and the princesses closed their doors against him.

From this moment Tasso was a ruined man; he had become that worst of social scourges, a courtier with a grievance, a semi-lunatic all the more dangerous and tiresome because his mental powers were not so much impaired as warped. Studying his elaborate apology, we do not know whether to despise the obstinacy of his devotion to the House of Este, or to respect the sentiment of loyalty which survived all real or fancied insults. Against the Duke he utters no word of blame. Alfonso is always magnanimous and clement, excellent in mind and body, good and courteous by nature, deserving the faithful service and warm love of his dependents. Montecatino is the real villain. 'The princes are not tyrants—they are not, no, no: he is the tyrant.'[40]

After quitting Ferrara, Tasso wandered through Mantua, Padua, Venice, coldly received in all these cities; for 'the hearts of men were hardened by their interests against him.' Writing from Venice to the Grand Duke in July, Maffeo Veniero says: 'Tasso is here, disturbed in mind; and though his intellect is certainly not sound, he shows more signs of affliction than of insanity.'[41] The sequestration of his only copy of the 'Gerusalemme' not unnaturally caused him much distress; and Veniero adds that the chief difficulty under which he laboured, was want of money. Veniero hardly understood the case. Even with a competence, it is incredible that Tasso would have been contented to work quietly at literature in a private position.[42] From Venice he

[40] *Lettere*, vol. i. p. 289. [41] *Ib.* vol. i. p. 233.

[42] Tasso declares his inability to live outside the Court. 'Se fra i mali de l' animo, uno de' più gravi è l' ambizione, egli ammalò di questo male già molti anni sono, nè mai è risanato in modo ch' io abbia potuto sprezzare affatto i favori e gli onori del mondc, e chi può dargli' (*Lettere*, vol. iii. p. 56). 'Io non posso acquetarmi in altra fortuna di quella ne la quale già nacqui' (*Ibid.* p. 243).

found his way southward to Urbino, writing one of his sublimest odes upon the road from Pesaro.[43] Francesco Maria della Rovere received him with accustomed kindness; but the spirit of unrest drove him forth again, and after two months we find him once more, an indigent and homeless pedestrian, upon the banks of the Sesia. He wanted to reach Vercelli, but the river was in flood, and he owed a night's lodging to the chance courtesy of a young nobleman. Among the many picturesque episodes in Tasso's wanderings none is more idyllically beautiful than the tale of his meeting with this handsome youth. He has told it himself in the exordium to his Dialogue 'Il Padre di Famiglia.' When asked who he was and whither he was going, he answered: 'I was born in the realm of Naples, and my mother was a Neapolitan; but I draw my paternal blood from Bergamo, a Lombard city. My name and surname I pass in silence: they are so obscure that if I uttered them, you would know neither more nor less of my condition. I am flying from the anger of a prince and fortune. My destination is the state of Savoy.' Upon this pilgrimage Tasso chose the sobriquet of *Omero Fuggiguerra*. Arriving at Turin, he was refused entrance by the guardians of the gate. The rags upon his back made them suspect he was a vagabond infected with the plague. A friend who knew him, Angelo Ingegneri, happened to pass by, and guaranteed his respectability. Manso compares the journey of this penniless and haggard fugitive through the cities of Italy to the meteoric passage of a comet.[44] Wherever he appeared, he blazed with momentary splendour. Nor was Turin slow to hail the lustrous apparition. The Marchese Filippo da Este entertained him in his palace. The Archbishop, Girolamo della Rovere, begged the honour of his company. The Duke of Savoy, Carlo Emanuele, offered him the same appointments as he had enjoyed at Ferrara. Nothing, however, would content his morbid spirit. Flattered and caressed through the months of October and November, he began once more in December to hanker after his old home. Inconceivable as it may seem, he opened fresh negotiations with the Duke; and Alfonso, on his side, already showed a will to take him back. Writing to his sister from Pesaro at the end of September, Tasso says that a gentleman had been sent from Ferrara expressly to recall him.[45] The fact seems to be that Tasso was too illustrious to be neglected by the House of Este. Away from their protection, he was capable of bringing on their name the slur of bad treatment and ingratitude. Nor would it have looked well to publish the 'Gerusalemme' with its praises of Alfonso, while the poet was lamenting his hard fate in every town of Italy. The upshot of these negotiations was that Tasso resolved on retracing his steps. He reached Ferrara again upon February 21, 1579, two days before Margherita Gonzaga, the Duke's new bride, made her pompous entrance into the city. But his reception was far from being

[43] It is addressed to the Metaurus, and begins: 'O del grand' Apennino.'
[44] *Op. cit.* p. 143.
[45] *Lettere*, vol. i. p. 268.

what he had expected. The Duke's heart seemed hardened. Apartments inferior to his quality were assigned him, and to these he was conducted by a courtier with ill-disguised insolence. The princesses refused him access to their lodgings, and his old enemies openly manifested their derision for the kill-joy and the skeleton who had returned to spoil their festival. Tasso, querulous as he was about his own share in the disagreeables of existence, remained wholly unsympathetic to the trials of his fellow-creatures. Self-engrossment closed him in a magic prison-house of discontent. Therefore, when he saw Ferrara full of merry-making guests, and heard the marriage music ringing through the courtyards of the castle, he failed to reflect with what a heavy heart the Duke might now be entering upon his third sterile nuptials. Alfonso was childless, brotherless, with no legitimate heir to defend his duchy from the Church in case of his decease. The irritable poet forgot how distasteful at such a moment of forced gaiety and hollow parade his reappearance, with the old complaining murmurs, the old suspicions, the old restless eyes, might be to the master who had certainly borne much and long with him. He only felt himself neglected, insulted, outraged:

> Questa è la data fede?
> Son questi i miei bramati alti ritorni?[46]

Then he burst out into angry words, which he afterwards acknowledged to have been 'false, mad, and rash.'[47] The Duke's patience had reached its utmost limit. Tasso was arrested, and confined in the hospital for mad folk at S. Anna. This happened in March 1579. He was detained there until July 19, 1586, a period of seven years and four months.

No one who has read the foregoing pages will wonder why Tasso was imprisoned. The marvel is rather that the fact should have roused so many speculations. Alfonso was an autocratic princeling. His favourite minister, Montecatino, fell in one moment from the height of power to irrecoverable ruin. The famous preacher, Panigarola, for whom he negotiated a Cardinal's hat, lost his esteem by seeking promotion at another Court, and had to fly Ferrara. His friend, Ercole Contrario, was strangled in the castle on suspicion of having concealed a murder. Tasso had been warned repeatedly, repeatedly forgiven; and now when he turned up again with the same complaints and the same menaces, Alfonso determined to have done with the nuisance. He would not kill him, but he would put him out of sight and hearing. If he was guilty, S. Anna would be punishment enough. If he was mad, it might be hoped that S. Anna would cure him. To blame the Duke for this exercise of authority, is difficult. Noble as is the poet's calling, and faithful as are the wounds of a devoted friend and servant, there are limits to princely patience. It is easier to blame Tasso for the incurable

[46] From the sonnet, *Sposa regal* (*Opere*, vol. iii. p. 218).
[47] *Lettere*, vol. ii. p. 67.

idealism which, when he was in comfort at Turin, made him pine 'to kiss the hand of his Highness, and recover some part of his favour on the occasion of his marriage.'[48]

Three long letters, written by Tasso during the early months of his imprisonment, discuss the reasons for his arrest.[49] Two of these are directed to his staunch friend Scipione Gonzaga, the third to Giacomo Buoncompagno, nephew of Pope Gregory XIII. Partly owing to omissions made by the editors before publication, and partly perhaps to the writer's reticence, they throw no very certain light even on his own opinion.[50] But this much appears tolerably clear. Tasso was half-mad and altogether irritable. He had used language which could not be overlooked. The Duke continued to resent his former practice with the Medici, and disapproved of his perpetual wanderings. The courtiers had done their utmost to prejudice his mind by calumnies and gossip, raking up all that seemed injurious to Tasso's reputation in the past acts of his life and in the looser verses found among his papers. It may also be conceded that they contrived to cast an unfavourable light upon his affectionate correspondence with the two princesses. Tasso himself laid great stress upon his want of absolute loyalty, upon some lascivious compositions, and lastly upon his supposed heresies. It is not probable that the Duke attached importance to such poetry as Tasso may have written in the heat of youth; and it is certain that he regarded the heresies as part of the poet's hallucinations. It is also far more likely that the Leonora episode passed in his mind for another proof of mental infirmity than that he judged it seriously. It was quite enough that Tasso had put himself in the wrong by petulant abuse of his benefactor and by persistent fretfulness. Moreover, he was plainly brain-sick. That alone justified Alfonso in his own eyes.

And brain-sick Tasso was, without a shadow of doubt.[51] It is hardly needful to recapitulate his terror of the Inquisition, dread of being poisoned, incapacity for self-control in word and act, and other signs of incipient disease. During the residence in S. Anna this malady made progress. He was tormented by spectral voices and apparitions. He believed himself to be under the influence of magic charms. He was haunted by a sprite, who stole his books and flung his MSS. about the

[48] *Ibid.* vol. ii. p. 34.

[49] *Lettere*, pp. 7-62, 80-93.

[50] We are met here as elsewhere in the perplexing problem of Tasso's misfortunes with the difficulty of having to deal with mutilated documents. Still the mere fact that Tasso was allowed to correspond freely with friends and patrons, shows that Alfonso dreaded no disclosures, and confirms the theory that he only kept Tasso locked up out of harm's way.

[51] A letter written by Guarini, the old friend, rival, and constant Court-companion of Tasso at Ferrara, upon the news of his death in 1595, shows how a man of cold intellect judged his case. 'The death by which Tasso has now paid his debt to nature, seems to me like the termination of that death of his in this world which only bore the outer semblance of life.' See Casella's *Pastor Fido*, p. xxxii. Guarini means that when Tasso's mind gave way, he had really died in his own higher self, and that his actual death was a release.

room. A good genius, in the form of a handsome youth, appeared and conversed with him. He lost himself for hours together in abstraction, talking aloud, staring into vacancy and expressing surprise that other people could not see the phantoms which surrounded him. He complained that his melancholy passed at moments into delirium (which he called *frenesia*), after which he suffered from loss of memory and prostration. His own mind became a constant cause of self-torture. Suspicious of others, he grew to be suspicious of himself. And when he left S. Anna, these disorders, instead of abating, continued to afflict him, so that his most enthusiastic admirers were forced to admit that 'he was subject to constitutional melancholy with crises of delirium, but not to actual insanity.'[52] At first, his infirmity did not interfere with intellectual production of a high order, though none of his poetry, after the 'Gerusalemme' was completed in 1574, rose to the level of his earlier work. But in course of time the artist's faculty itself was injured, and the creations of his later life are unworthy of his genius.

The seven years and four months of Tasso's imprisonment may be passed over briefly. With regard to his so-called dungeon, it is certain that, after some months spent in a narrow chamber, he obtained an apartment of several rooms. He was allowed to write and receive as many letters as he chose. Friends paid him visits, and he went abroad under surveillance in the city of Ferrara. To extenuate the suffering which a man of his temper endured in this enforced seclusion would be unjust to Tasso. There is no doubt that he was most unhappy. But to exaggerate his discomforts would be unjust to the Duke. Even Manso describes 'the excellent and most convenient lodgings' assigned him in S. Anna, alludes to the provision for his cure by medicine, and remarks upon the opposition which he offered to medical treatment. According to this biographer, his own endeavours to escape necessitated a strict watch upon his movements.[53] Unless, therefore, we flatly deny the fact of his derangement, which is supported by a mass of testimony, it may be doubted whether Tasso was more miserable in S. Anna than he would have been at large. The subsequent events of his life prove that his release brought no mitigation of his malady.

It was, however, a dreary time. He spent his days in writing letters to all the princes of Italy, to Naples, to Bergamo, to the Roman Curia, declaiming on his wretchedness and begging for emancipation. Occasional poems flowed from his pen. But during this period he devoted his serious hours mainly to prose composition. The bulk of his Dialogues issued from S. Anna. On August 7, 1580, Celio Malaspina published a portion of the 'Gerusalemme' at Venice, under the title of 'Il

[52] Tasso's own letters after the beginning of 1579, and Manso's Life (*op. cit.* pp. 156-176), are the authorities for the symptoms detailed above. Tasso so often alludes to his infirmities that it is not needful to accumulate citations. I will, however, quote two striking examples. 'Sono infermo come soleva, e stanco della infermità, la quale è *non sol malattia del corpo ma de la mente*' (*Lettere*, vol. iii. p. 160). 'Io sono poco sano e tanto maninconico che *sono riputato matto da gli altri e da me stesso*' (*Ib.* p. 262).

[53] *Op. cit.* p. 155.

Gottifredo di M. Torquato Tasso.' In February of the following year, his friend Angelo Ingegneri gave the whole epic to the world. Within six months from that date the poem was seven times reissued. This happened without the sanction or the supervision of the luckless author; and from the sale of the book he obtained no profit. Leonora d' Este died upon February 10, 1581. A volume of elegies appeared on this occasion; but Tasso's Muse uttered no sound.[54] He wrote to Panigarola that 'a certain tacit repugnance of his genius' forced him to be mute.[55] His rival Guarini undertook a revised edition of his lyrics in 1582. Tasso had to bear this dubious compliment in silence. All Europe was devouring his poems; scribes and versifiers were building up their reputation on his fame. Yet he could do nothing. Embittered by the piracies of publishers, infuriated by the impertinence of editors, he lay like one forgotten in that hospital. His celebrity grew daily; but he languished, penniless and wretched, in confinement which he loathed. The strangest light is cast upon his state of mind by the efforts which he now made to place two of his sister's children in Court-service. He even tried to introduce one of them as a page into the household of Alfonso. Eventually, Alessandro Sersale was consigned to Odoardo Farnese, and Antonio to the Duke of Mantua. In 1585 new sources of annoyance rose. Two members of the Della Crusca Academy in Florence, Leonardo Salviati and Bastiano de' Rossi, attacked the 'Gerusalemme.' Their malevolence was aroused by the panegyric written on it by Cammillo Pellegrini, a Neapolitan, and they exposed it to pedantically quibbling criticism. Tasso replied in a dignified apology. But he does not seem to have troubled himself overmuch with this literary warfare, which served meanwhile to extend the fame of his immortal poem. At this time new friends gathered round him. Among these the excellent Benedictine, Angelo Grillo, and the faithful Antonio Constantini demand commemoration from all who appreciate disinterested devotion to genius in distress. At length, in July 1586, Vincenzo Gonzaga, heir-apparent to the Duchy of Mantua, obtained Tasso's release. He rode off with this new patron to Mantua, leaving his effects at S. Anna, and only regretting that he had not waited on the Duke of Ferrara to kiss his hand as in duty bound.[56] Thus to the end he remained an incorrigible courtier; or rather shall we say that, after all his tribulations, he preserved a dog-like feeling of attachment for his master?

The rest of Tasso's life was an Odyssey of nine years. He seemed at first contented with Mantua, wrote dialogues, completed the tragedy of 'Torrismondo' and edited his father's 'Floridante.' But when Vincenzo Gonzaga succeeded to the dukedom, the restless poet felt himself neglected. His young friend had not leisure to pay him due attention. He therefore started on a journey to Loreto, which had long been the

[54] *Lacrime di diversi poeti volgari*, &c. (Vicenza, 1585).

[55] *Lettere*, vol. ii. p. 103. The significance of this message to Panigarola is doubtful. Did Tasso mean that the contrast between past and present was too bitter? 'Most friendship is feigning, most loving mere folly.'

[56] All the letters written from Mantua abound in references to this neglect of duty.

object of his pious aspiration. Loreto led to Rome, where Scipione Gonzaga resided as Patriarch of Jerusalem and Cardinal. Rome suggested Southern Italy, and Tasso hankered after the recovery of his mother's fortune. Accordingly he set off in March 1588 for Naples, where he stayed, partly with the monks of Monte Oliveto, and partly with the Marchese Manso. Rome saw him again in November; and not long afterwards an agent of the Duke of Urbino wrote this pitiful report of his condition: 'Everyone is ready to welcome him to hearth and heart; but his humours render him mistrustful of mankind at large. In the palace of the Cardinal Gonzaga there are rooms and beds always ready for his use, and men reserved for his especial service. Yet he runs away and mistrusts even that friendly lord. In short, it is a sad misfortune that the present age should be deprived of the greatest genius which has appeared for centuries. What wise man ever spoke in prose or verse better than this madman?'[57] In the following August, Scipione Gonzaga's servants, unable to endure Tasso's eccentricities, turned him from their master's house, and he took refuge in a monastery of the Olivetan monks. Soon afterwards he was carried to the hospital of the Bergamasques. His misery now was great, and his health so bad that friends expected a speedy end.[58] Yet the Cardinal Gonzaga again opened his doors to him in the spring of 1590. Then the morbid poet turned suspicious, and began to indulge fresh hopes of fortune in another place. He would again offer himself to the Medici. In April he set off for Tuscany, and alighted at the convent of Monte Oliveto, near Florence. Nobody wanted him; he wandered about the Pitti like a spectre, and the Florentines wrote: '*actum est de eo*.'[59] Some parting compliments and presents from the Grand Duke sweetened his dismissal. He returned to Rome; but each new journey told upon his broken health, and another illness made him desire a change of scene. This time Antonio Costantini offered to attend upon him. They visited Siena, Bologna, and Mantua. At Mantua, Tasso made some halt, and took a new long poem, the 'Gerusalemme Conquistata,' seriously in hand. But the demon of unrest pursued him, and in November 1591 he was off again with the Duke of Mantua to Rome. From Rome he went to Naples at the beginning of the following year, worked at the 'Conquistata,' and began his poem of the 'Sette Giornate.'[60] He was always occupied with the vain hope of recovering a portion of his mother's estate. April saw him once more upon his way to Rome. Clement VIII. had been elected, and Tasso expected patronage from the Papal nephews.[61] He was not disappointed. They received him

[57] *Lettere*, vol. iv. p. 147. [58] *Ibid.* p. 229.

[59] *Ibid.* p. 315.

[60] Yet he now felt that his genius had expired. 'Non posso più fare un verso: la vena è secca, e l' ingegno è stanco' (*Lettere*, vol. v. p. 90).

[61] During the whole period of his Roman residence, Tasso, like his father in similar circumstances, hankered after ecclesiastical honours. His letters refer frequently to this ambition. He felt the parallel between himself and Bernardo Tasso: 'La mia depressa condizione, e la mia infelicità, quasi ereditaria' (vol. iv. p. 288).

into their houses, and for awhile he sojourned in the Vatican. The year 1593 seems, through their means, to have been one of comparative peace and prosperity. Early in the summer of 1594 his health obliged him to seek change of air. He went for the last time to Naples. The Cardinal of S. Giorgio, one of the Pope's nephews, recalled him in November to be crowned poet in Rome. His entrance into the Eternal City was honourable, and Clement granted him a special audience; but the ceremony of coronation had to be deferred because of the Cardinal's ill health.

Meanwhile his prospects seemed likely to improve. Clement conferred on him a pension of one hundred ducats, and the Prince of Avellino, who had detained his mother's estate, compounded with him for a life-income of two hundred ducats. This good fortune came in the spring of 1595. But it came too late; for his death-illness was upon him. On the first of April he had himself transported to the convent of S. Onofrio, which overlooks Rome from the Janiculan hill. Torrents of rain were falling with a furious wind, when the carriage of Cardinal Cinzio was seen climbing the steep ascent. The badness of the weather made the fathers think there must be some grave cause for this arrival. So the prior and others hurried to the gate, where Tasso descended with considerable difficulty, greeting the monks with these words: 'I am come to die among you.'[62] The last of Tasso's letters, written to Antonio Costantini from S. Onofrio, has the quiet dignity of one who struggles for the last time with the frailty of his mortal nature.[63]

'What will my good lord Antonio say when he shall hear of his Tasso's death? The news, as I incline to think, will not be long in coming; for I feel that I have reached the end of life, being unable to discover any remedy for this tedious indisposition which has supervened on the many others I am used to—like a rapid torrent resistlessly sweeping me away. The time is past when I should speak of my stubborn fate, to mention not the world's ingratitude, which, however, has willed to gain the victory of bearing me to the grave a pauper; the while I kept on thinking that the glory which, despite of those that like it not, this age will inherit from my writings, would not have left me wholly without guerdon. I have had myself carried to this monastery of S. Onofrio; not only because the air is commended by physicians above that of any other part of Rome, but also as it were upon this elevated spot and by the conversation of these devout fathers to commence my conversation in heaven. Pray God for me; and rest assured that as I have loved and honoured you always in the present life, so will I perform for you in that other and more real life what appertains not to feigned but to veritable charity. And to the Divine grace I recommend you and myself.'

On April 25, Tasso expired at midnight, with the words *In manus*

[62] Manso, op. cit. p. 215.

[63] This letter proves conclusively that, whatever was the nature of Tasso's malady, and however it had enfeebled his faculties as poet, he was in no vulgar sense a lunatic.

tuas, Domine, upon his lips. Had Costantini, his sincerest friend, been there, he might have said like Kent:

> O, let him pass! he hates him much
> That would upon the rack of this tough world
> Stretch him out longer.

But Costantini was in Mantua; and this sonnet, which he had written for his master, remains Tasso's truest epitaph, the pithiest summary of a life pathetically tragic in its adverse fate—

> Friends, this is Tasso, not the sire but son;
> For he of human offspring had no heed,
> Begetting for himself immortal seed
> Of art, style, genius and instruction.
>
> In exile long he lived and utmost need;
> In palace, temple, school, he dwelt alone;
> He fled, and wandered through wild woods unknown;
> On earth, on sea, suffered in thought and deed.
>
> He knocked at death's door; yet he vanquished him
> With lofty prose and with undying rhyme;
> But fortune not, who laid him where he lies.
>
> Guerdon for singing loves and arms sublime,
> And showing truth whose light makes vices dim,
> Is one green wreath; yet this the world denies.

The wreath of laurel which the world grudged was placed upon his bier; and a simple stone, engraved with the words *Hic jacet Torquatus Tassus*, marked the spot where he was buried.

The foregoing sketch of Tasso's life and character differs in some points from the prevalent conceptions of the poet. There is a legendary Tasso, the victim of malevolent persecution by pedants, the mysterious lover condemned to misery in prison by a tyrannous duke. There is also a Tasso formed by men of learning upon ingeniously constructed systems; Rosini's Tasso, condemned to feign madness in punishment for courting Leonora d' Este with lascivious verses; Capponi's Tasso, punished for seeking to exchange the service of the House of Este for that of the House of Medici; a Tasso who was wholly mad; a Tasso who remained through life the victim of Jesuitical influences. In short, there are as many Tassos as there are Hamlets. Yet these Tassos of the legend and of erudition do not reproduce his self-revealed lineaments. Tasso's letters furnish documents of sufficient extent to make the real man visible, though something yet remains perhaps not wholly explicable in his tragedy.

CHAPTER VIII

THE 'GERUSALEMME LIBERATA'

Problem of Creating Heroic Poetry—The Preface to Tasso's Rinaldo—Subject of 'Rinaldo'—Blending of Romantic Motives with Heroic Style—Imitation of Virgil—Melody and Sentiment—Choice of Theme for the 'Gerusalemme'—It becomes a Romantic Poem after all—Tancredi the real Hero—Nobility of Tone—Virgilian Imitation—Borrowings from Dante—Involved Diction—Employment of Sonorous Polysyllabic Words—Quality of Religious Emotion in this Poem—Rhetoric—Similes—The Grand Style of Pathos—Verbal Music—The Chant d'Amour—Armida—Tasso's Favourite Phrase, Un non so che—His Power over Melody and Tender Feeling—Critique of Tasso's Later Poems—General Survey of his Character.

In a previous portion of this work, I attempted to define the Italian Romantic Epic, and traced the tale of Orlando from Pulci through Boiardo and Ariosto to the burlesque of Folengo. There is an element of humour more or less predominant in the 'Morgante Maggiore,' the 'Orlando Innamorato,' and the 'Orlando Furioso.' This element might almost be regarded as inseparable from the species. Yet two circumstances contributed to alter the character of Italian Romance after the publication of the 'Furioso.' One of these was the unapproachable perfection of that poem. No one could hope to surpass Ariosto in his own style, or to give a fresh turn to his humour without passing into broad burlesque. The romantic poet had therefore to choose between sinking into parody with Folengo and Aretino, or soaring into the sublimities of solemn art. Another circumstance was the keen interest aroused in academic circles by Trissino's unsuccessful epic, and by the discussion of heroic poetry which it stimulated. The Italian nation was becoming critical, and this critical spirit lent itself readily to experiments in hybrid styles of composition which aimed at combining the graces of the Romantic with the dignity of the Heroic poem. The most meritorious of these hybrids was Bernardo Tasso's 'Amadigi,' a long romance in octave stanzas, sustained upon a grave tone throughout, and distinguished from the earlier romantic epics by a more obvious unity of subject. Bernardo Tasso possessed qualities of genius and temper which suited his proposed task. Deficient in humour, he had no difficulty in eliminating that element from the 'Amadigi.' Chivalrous sentiment took the place of irony; scholarly method supplied the want of wayward fancy.

It was just at this point that the young Torquato Tasso made his first essay in poetry. He had inherited his father's temperament, its want of humour, its melancholy, its aristocratic sensitiveness. At the age of seventeen, he was already a ripe scholar, versed in the critical questions which then agitated learned coteries in Italy. The wilding graces and the freshness of the Romantic Epic, as conceived by Boiardo and perfected by Ariosto, had for ever disappeared. To 'recapture that first fine careless rapture' was impossible. Contemporary conditions of society and thought rendered any attempt to do so futile. Italy had passed into a different stage of culture; and the representative poem of Tasso's epoch was imperatively forced to assume a different character. Its type already existed in the 'Amadigi,' though Bernardo Tasso had not the genius to disengage it clearly, or to render it attractive. How Torquato, while still a student in his teens at Padua, attacked the problem of narrative poetry, appears distinctly in his preface to 'Rinaldo.' 'I believe,' he says, 'that you, my gentle readers, will not take it amiss if I have diverged from the path of modern poets, and have sought to approach the best among the ancients. You shall not, however, find that I am bound by the precise rules of Aristotle, which often render those poems irksome which might otherwise have yielded you much pleasure. I have only followed such of his precepts as do not limit your delight: for instance, in the frequent use of episodes, making the characters talk in their own persons, introducing recognitions and peripeties by necessary or plausible motives, and withdrawing the poet as far as possible from the narration. I have also endeavoured to construct my poem with unity of interest and action, not, indeed, in any strict sense, but so that the subordinate portions should be seen to have their due relation to the whole.' He then proceeds to explain why he has abandoned the discourses on moral and general topics with which Ariosto opened his Cantos, and hints that he has taken Virgil, the 'Prince of Poets,' for his model. Thus the Romantic Epic, as conceived by Tasso, was to break with the tradition of the Cantastorie, who told the tale in his own person and introduced reflections on its incidents. It was to aim at unity of subject, and to observe classical rules of art, without, however, sacrificing the charm of variety and those delights which episodes and marvellous adventures yielded to a modern audience. The youthful poet begs that his 'Rinaldo' should not be censured on the one hand by severely Aristotelian critics who exclude pleasure from their ideal, or on the other by amateurs who regard the 'Orlando Furioso' as the perfection of poetic art. In a word, he hopes to produce something midway between the strict Heroic Epic which had failed in Trissino's 'Italia Liberata' through dulness, and the genuine Romantic Epic, which in Ariosto's masterpiece diverged too widely from the rules of classical pure taste. This new species, combining the attractions of romance with the simplicity of epic poetry, was the gift which Tasso at the age of eighteen sought to present in his 'Rinaldo' to Italy.

The 'Rinaldo' fulfilled fairly well the conditions propounded by its author. It had a single hero and a single subject—

> Canto i felici affanni, e i primi ardori,
> Che giovinetto ancor soffrì Rinaldo,
> E come il trasse in perigliosi errori
> Desir di gloria ed amoroso caldo.

The perilous achievements and the passion of Rinaldo in his youth form the theme of a poem which is systematically evolved from the first meeting of the son of Amon with Clarice to their marriage under the auspices of Malagigi. There are interesting episodes like those of young Florindo and Olinda, unhappy Clizia and abandoned Floriana. Rinaldo's combat with Orlando in the Christian camp furnishes an anagnorisis; while the plot is brought to its conclusion by the peripeteia of Clarice's jealousy and the accidents which restore her to her lover's arms. Yet, though observant of his own classical rules, Tasso remained in all essential points beneath the spell of the Romantic Epic. The changes which he introduced were obvious to none but professional critics. In warp and woof the 'Rinaldo' is similar to Boiardo's and Ariosto's tale of chivalry; only the loom is narrower, and the pattern of the web less intricate. The air of artlessness which lent its charm to Romance in Italy has disappeared, yielding place to sustained elaboration of Latinising style. Otherwise the fabric remains substantially unaltered—like a Gothic dwelling furnished with Palladian window-frames. We move in the old familiar sphere of Paladins and Paynims, knights errant and Oriental damsels, magicians and distressed maidens. The action is impelled by the same series of marvellous adventures and felicitous mishaps. There are the same encounters in war and rivalries in love between Christian and Pagan champions; journeys through undiscovered lands and over untracked oceans; fantastic hyperboles of desire, ambition, jealousy, and rage employed as motive passions. Enchanted forests; fairy ships that skim the waves without helm or pilot; lances endowed with supernatural virtues; charmed gardens of perpetual spring; dismal dungeons and glittering palaces, supply the furniture of this romance no less than of its predecessors. Rinaldo, like any other hero of the Renaissance, is agitated by burning thirst for fame and blind devotion to a woman's beauty. We first behold him pining in inglorious leisure:[1]

> Poi, ch' oprar non poss' io che di me s' oda
> Con mia gloria ed onor novella alcuna,
> O cosa, ond' io pregio n' acquisti e loda,
> E mia fama rischiari oscura e bruna.

The vision of Clarice, appearing like Virgil's Camilla, stirs him from this lethargy. He falls in love at first sight, as Tasso's heroes always do, and vows to prove himself her worthy knight by deeds of unexampled daring. Thus the plot is put in motion; and we read in well-

[1] Canto I. 17.

appointed order how the hero acquired his horse Baiardo, Tristram's magic lance, his sword Fusberta from Atlante, his armour from Orlando, the trappings of his charger from the House of Courtesy, the ensign of the lion rampant on his shield from Chiarello, and the hand of his lady after some delays from Malagigi.

No new principle is introduced into the romance. As in earlier poems of this species, the religious motive of Christendom at war with Islam becomes a mere machine; the chivalrous environment affords a vehicle for fanciful adventures. Humour, indeed, is conspicuous by its absence. Charles the Great assumes the sobriety of empire; and his camp, in its well-ordered gravity, prefigures that of Goffredo in the 'Gerusalemme.'[2] Thus Tasso's originality must not be sought in the material of his work, which is precisely that of the Italian romantic school in general, nor yet in its form, which departs from the romantic tradition in details so insignificant as to be inessential. We find it rather in his touch upon the old material, in his handling of the familiar form. The qualities of style, sympathy, sentiment, selection in the use of phrase and image, which determined his individuality as a poet, rendered the 'Rinaldo' a novelty in literature. It will be therefore well to concentrate attention for a while upon those subjective peculiarities by right of which the 'Rinaldo' ranks as a precursor of the 'Gerusalemme.'

The first and the most salient of these is a pronounced effort to heighten style by imitation of Latin poets. The presiding genius of the work is Virgil. Pulci's racy Florentine idiom; Boiardo's frank and natural Lombard manner; Ariosto's transparent and unfettered modern phrase, have been supplanted by a pompous intricacy of construction. The effort to impose Latin rules of syntax on Italian is obvious in such lines as the following:[3]

> Torre ei l' immagin volle, che sospesa
> Era presso l' altar gemmato e sacro,
> Ove in chiaro cristal lampade accesa
> Fea lume di Ciprigna al simulacro:

or in these:

> Umida i gigli e le vermiglie rose
> Del volto, e gli occhi bei conversa al piano,
> Gli occhi, onde in perle accolto il pianto uscia,
> La giovinetta il cavalier seguia.

Virgil is directly imitated, where he is least worthy of imitation, in the details of his battle-pieces. Thus:[4]

> Si riversa Isolier tremando al piano,
> Privo di senso e di vigore ignudo,
> Ed a lui gli occhi oscura notte involve,
> Ed ogni membro ancor se gli dissolve.

---

[2] Canto vi. 64-9.
[3] Canto iii. 40, 45.
[4] Canto ii. 22; iv. 28, 33.

Quel col braccio sospeso in aria stando,
Nè lo movendo a questa o a quella parte,
Chè dalla spada ciò gli era conteso,
Voto sembrava in sacro tempio appeso.

. . . . . .

Mentre ignaro di ciò che 'l ciel destine,
Così diceva ancor, la lancia ultrice
Rinaldo per la bocca entro gli mise,
E la lingua e 'l parlar per mezzo incise.

This Virgilian imitation yields some glowing flowers of poetry in longer passages of description. Among these may be cited the conquest of Baiardo in the second canto, the shipwreck in the tenth, the chariot of Pluto in the fourth, and the supper with Queen Floriana in the ninth. The episode of Floriana, while closely studied upon the 'Æneid,' is also a first sketch for that of Armida. Indeed, it should be said in passing that Tasso anticipates the 'Gerusalemme' throughout the 'Rinaldo.' The murder of Anselmo by Rinaldo (canto xi.) forecasts the murder of Gernando by his namesake, and leads to the same result of the hero's banishment. The shipwreck, the garden of courtesy, the enchanted boat, and the charmed forest, are motives which reappear improved and elaborated in Tasso's masterpiece.[5]

While Tasso thus sought to heighten diction by Latinisms, he revealed another specific quality of his manner in 'Rinaldo.' This is the inability to sustain heroic style at its ambitious level. He frequently drops at the close of the octave stanza into a prosaic couplet, which has all the effect of pathos. Instances are not far to seek:[6]

Già tal insegna acquisitò l' avo, e poi
La portàr molti de' nipoti suoi.

. . . .

E a questi segni ed al crin raro e bianco
Monstrava esser dagli anni oppresso e stanco.

. . . .

Fu qui vicin dal saggio Alchiso il Mago,
Di far qualch' opra memorabil vago.

. . . .

Io son Rinaldo,
Solo di servir voi bramoso e caldo.

The reduplication of epithets, and the occasional use of long sonorous Latin words, which characterise Tasso's later manner, are also noticeable in these couplets. Side by side with such weak endings should be placed some specimens, no less characteristic, of vigorous and noble lines:[7]

Nel cor consiston l' armi,
Onde il forte non è chi mai disarmi.

. . . . .

Si sta placido e cheto,
Ma serba dell' altiero nel mansueto.

---

[5] *Rinaldo*, cantos x. vii. [6] Canto i. 25, 31, 41, 64. [7] Canto ii. 28. 44.

If the 'Rinaldo' prefigures Tasso's maturer qualities of style, it is no less conspicuous for the light it throws upon his eminent poetic faculty. Nothing distinguished him more decidedly from the earlier romantic poets than power over pathetic sentiment conveyed in melodious cadences of oratory. This emerges in Clarice's monologue on love and honour, that combat of the soul which forms a main feature of the lyrics in 'Aminta' and of Erminia's episode in the 'Gerusalemme.'[8] This steeps the whole story of Clizia in a delicious melancholy, foreshadowing the death-scene of Clorinda.[9] This rises in the father's lamentation over his slain Ugone, into the music of a threnody that now recalls Euripides and now reminds us of mediæval litanies.[10] Censure might be passed upon rhetorical conceits and frigid affectations in these characteristic outpourings of pathetic feeling. Yet no one can ignore their liquid melody, their transference of emotion through sound into modulated verse. That lyrical outcry, finding rhythmic utterance for tender sentiment, which may be recognised as Tasso's chief addition to romantic poetry, pierces like a song through many passages of mere narration. Rinaldo, while carrying Clarice away upon Baiardo, with no chaste intention in his heart, bids her thus dry her tears:[11]

> Egli dice: Signora, onde vi viene
> Sì spietato martir, sì grave affanno?
> Perchè le luci angeliche e serene
> Ricopre della doglia oscuro panno?
> Forse fia l' util vostro e 'l vostro bene
> Quel ch' or vi sembra insupportabil danno.
> Deh! per Dio, rasciugate il caldo pianto.
> E l' atroce dolor temprate alquanto.

It is not that we do not find similar lyrical inter-breathings in the narrative of Ariosto. But Tasso developed the lyrism of the octave stanza into something special, lulling the soul upon gentle waves of rising and falling rhythm, foreshadowing the coming age of music in cadences that are untranslatable except by vocal melody. In like manner, the idyll, which had played a prominent part in Boiardo's and in Ariosto's romance, detaches itself with a peculiar sweetness from the course of Tasso's narrative. This appears in the story of Florindo, which contains within itself the germ of the 'Aminta,' the 'Pastor Fido' and the 'Adone.'[12] Together with the bad taste of the artificial pastoral, its preposterous costume (stanza 13), its luxury of tears (stanza 23), we find the tyranny of kisses (stanzas 28, 52), the yearning after the Golden Age (stanza 29), and all the other apparatus of that operatic species. Tasso was the first poet to bathe Arcady in a golden afternoon light of sensuously sentimental pathos. In his idyllic as in his lyrical interbreathings, melody seems absolutely demanded to interpret and

[8] *Rinaldo*, canto ii. 3-11.
[9] Canto vii. 16-51.
[10] Canto vii. 3-11.
[11] Canto iv. 47.
[12] Canto v. 12-57.

complete the plangent rhythm of his dulcet numbers. Emotion so far predominates over intelligence, so yearns to exhale itself in sound and shun the laws of language, that we find already in 'Rinaldo' Tasso's familiar *Non so che* continually used to adumbrate sentiments for which plain words are not indefinite enough.

The 'Rinaldo' was a very remarkable production for a young man of eighteen. It showed the poet in possession of his style and displayed the specific faculties of his imagination. Nothing remained for Tasso now but to perfect and develop the type of art which he had there created. Soon after his first settlement in Ferrara, he began to meditate a more ambitious undertaking. His object was to produce the heroic poem for which Italy had long been waiting, and in this way to rival or surpass the fame of Ariosto. Trissino had chosen a national subject for his epic; but the 'Italia Liberata' was an acknowledged failure, and neither the past nor the present conditions of the Italian people offered good material for a serious poem. The heroic enthusiasms of the age were religious. Revived Catholicism had assumed an attitude of defiance. The Company of Jesus was declaring its crusade against heresy and infidelity throughout the world. Not a quarter of a century had elapsed since Charles V. attacked the Mussulman in Tunis; and before a few more years had passed, the victory of Lepanto was to be won by Italian and Spanish navies. Tasso, therefore, obeyed a wise instinct when he made choice of the First Crusade for his theme, and of Godfrey of Boulogne for his hero. Having to deal with historical facts, he studied the best authorities in chronicles, ransacked such books of geography and travel as were then accessible, paid attention to topography, and sought to acquire what we now call local colouring for the details of his poem. Without the sacrifice of truth in any important point, he contrived to give unity to the conduct of his narrative, while interweaving a number of fictitious characters and marvellous circumstances with the historical personages and actual events of the Crusade. The vital interest of the 'Gerusalemme Liberata' flows from this interpolated material, from the loves of Rinaldo and Tancredi, from the adventures of the Pagan damsels Erminia, Armida, and Clorinda. The 'Gerusalemme' is in truth a Virgilian epic, upon which a romantic poem has been engrafted. Goffredo, idealised into statuesque frigidity, repeats the virtues of Æneas; but the episode of Dido, which enlivens Virgil's hero, is transferred to Rinaldo's part in Tasso's story. The battles of Crusaders and Saracens are tedious copies of the battle in the tenth 'Æneid;' but the duels of Tancredi with Clorinda and Argante breathe the spirit and the fire of chivalry. The celestial and infernal councils, adopted as machinery, recall the rival factions in Olympus; but the force by which the plot moves is love. Pluto and the angel Gabriel are inactive by comparison with Armida, Erminia, and Clorinda. Tasso, in truth, thought that he was writing a religious and heroic poem. What he did write, was a poem of sentiment and passion—a romance. Like Anacreon he might have cried:

> θέλω λέγειν Ἀτρείδας,
> θέλω δὲ Κάδμον ᾄδειν,
> ἁ βάρβιτος δὲ χορδαῖς
> Ἔρωτα μοῦνον ἠχεῖ.

He displayed, indeed, marvellous ingenuity and art in so connecting the two strains of his subject, the stately Virgilian history and the glowing modern romance, that they should contribute to the working of a single plot. Yet he could not succeed in vitalising the former, whereas the latter will live as long as human interest in poetry endures. No one who has studied the 'Gerusalemme' returns with pleasure to Goffredo, or feels that the piety of the Christian heroes is inspired. He skips canto after canto dealing with the Crusade, to dwell upon those lyrical outpourings of love, grief, anguish, vain remorse, and injured affection which the supreme poet of sentiment has invented for his heroines; he recognises the genuine inspiration of Erminia's pastoral idyll, of Armida's sensuous charms, of Clorinda's dying words, of the Siren's song and the music of the magic bird: of all, in fact, which is not pious in the poem.

Tancredi, between Erminia and Clorinda, the one woman adoring him, the other beloved by him—the melancholy graceful modern Tancredi, Tasso's own soul's image—is the veritable hero of the 'Gerusalemme;' and by a curious unintended propriety he disappears from the action before the close, without a word. The force of the poem is spiritualised and concentrated in Clorinda's death, which may be cited as an instance of sublimity in pathos. It is idyllised in the episode of Erminia among the shepherds, and sensualised in the supreme beauty of Armida's garden. Rinaldo ranks second in importance to Tancredi; and Goffredo, on whom Tasso bestows the blare of his Virgilian trumpet from the first line to the last, is poetically of no importance whatsoever. Argante, Solimano, Tisaferno excite our interest, and win the sympathy we cannot spare the saintly hero; and in the death of Solimano Tasso's style, for once, verges upon tragic sublimity.

What Tasso aimed at in the 'Gerusalemme' was nobility. This quality had not been prominent in Ariosto's art. If he could attain it, his ambition to rival the 'Orlando Furioso' would be satisfied. One main condition of success Tasso brought to the achievement. His mind itself was eminently noble, incapable of baseness, fixed on fair and worthy objects of contemplation. Yet the personal nobility which distinguished him as a thinker and a man, was not of the heroic type. He had nothing Homeric in his inspiration, nothing of the warrior or the patriot in his nature. His genius, when it pursued its bias, found instinctive utterance in elegy and idyll, in meditative rhetoric and pastoral melody. In order to assume the heroic strain, Tasso had recourse to scholarship, and gave himself up blindly to the guidance of Latin poets. This was consistent with the tendency of the Classical Revival; but since the subject to be dignified by epic style was Christian and mediæval, a discord between matter and manner amounting almost to insincerity resulted. Some examples will make the meaning of this criticism more apparent. When Goffredo rejects the embassy of Alete and Argante, he declares his firm intention of delivering Jerusalem in spite of overwhelming perils. The Crusaders can but perish:

Noi morirem, ma non morremo inulti. (ii. 86.)

This of course is a reminiscence of Dido's last words, and the difference between the two situations creates a disagreeable incongruity. The nod of Jove upon Olympus is translated to express the fiat of the Almighty (xiii. 74); Gabriel is tricked out in the plumes and colours of Mercury (i. 13-15); the very angels singing round the throne become 'dive sirene' (xiv. 9); the armoury of heaven is described in terms which reduce Michael's spear and the arrows of pestilence to ordinary weapons (vii. 81); hell is filled with harpies, centaurs, hydras, pythons, the common lumber of classical Tartarus (iv. 5); the angel sent to cure Goffredo's wound culls dittany on Ida (xi. 72); the heralds, interposing between Tancredi and Argante, hold pacific sceptres and have naught of chivalry (vi. 51). It may be said that both Dante before Tasso and Milton after him employed similar classical language in dealing with Christian and mediæval motives. But this will hardly serve as an excuse; for Dante and Milton communicate so intense a conviction of religious earnestness that their Latinisms, even though incongruous, are recognised as the mere clothing of profoundly felt ideas. The sublimity, the seriousness, the spiritual dignity is in their thought, not in its expression; whereas Tasso too frequently leaves us with the certainty that he has sought by ceremonious language to realise more than he could grasp with the imagination. In his council of the powers of hell, for instance, he creates monsters of huge dimensions and statuesque distinctness; but these are neither grotesquely horrible like Dante's, nor are they spirits with incalculable capacity for evil like Milton's.

Stampano alcuni il suol di ferine orme,
E in fronte umana han chiome d' angui attorte;
E lor s' aggira dietro immensa coda,
Che quasi sferza si ripiega e snoda.

Against this we have to place the dreadful scene of Satan with his angels transformed to snakes ('Par. Lost,' x. 508-584), and the Dantesque horror of the 'vermo reo che 'l mondo fora' ('Inf.' xxxiv. 108). Again, when Dante cries—

O Sommo Giove,
Che fosti in terra per noi crocifisso!

we feel that the Latin phrase is accidental. The spirit of the poet remains profoundly Christian. Tasso's Jehovah-Jupiter is always 'il Re del Ciel;' and the court of blessed spirits which surrounds his 'gran seggio,' though described with solemn pomp of phrase, cannot be compared with the Mystic Rose of Paradise (ix. 55-60). What Tasso lacks is authenticity of vision; and his heightened style only renders this imaginative poverty, this want of spiritual conviction, more apparent.

His frequent borrowings from Virgil are less unsuccessful when the matter to be illustrated is not of this exalted order. Many similes (vii. 55, vii. 76, viii. 74) have been transplanted with nice propriety. Many descriptions, like that of the approach of night (ii. 96), of the nightingale mourning for her young (xii. 90), of the flying dream (xiv. 6), have been translated with exquisite taste. Dido's impassioned apostrophe to Æneas reappears appropriately upon Armida's lips (xvi. 56). We welcome such culled phrases as the following:

l' orticel dispensa
Cibi non compri alla mia parca mensa (vii. 10).

Premer gli alteri, e sollevar gl' imbelli (x. 76).

E Tisaferno, il folgore di Marte (xvii. 31).

Va, vedi, e vinci (xvii. 38).

Ma mentre dolce parla e dolce ride (iv. 92).

Chè vinta la materia è dal lavoro (xvi. 2).

Non temo io te, nè tuoi gran vanti, o fero:
Ma il Cielo e il mio nemico amor pavento (xix. 73).

It may, however, be observed that in the last of these passages Tasso does not show a just discriminative faculty. Turnus said:

Non me tua fervida terrent
Dicta, ferox: Di me terrent et Jupiter hostis.

From Jupiter to Amor is a descent from sublimity to pathos. In like manner when Hector's ghost reappears in the ghost of Armida's mother,

Quanto diversa, oimè, da quel che pria
Vistro altrove (iv. 49),

the reminiscence suggests ideas that are unfavourable to the modern version.

In his description of battles, the mustering of armies, and military operations, Tasso neither draws from mediæval sources nor from experience, but imitates the battle-pieces of Virgil and Lucan, sometimes with fine rhetorical effect and sometimes with wearisome frigidity. The death of Latino and his five sons is both touching in itself, and a good example of this Virgilian mannerism (ix. 35). The death of Dudone is justly celebrated as a sample of successful imitation (iii. 45):

Cade; e gli occhi, ch' appena aprir si ponno,
Dura quiete preme e ferreo sonno.

The wound of Gerniero, on the contrary, illustrates the peril of seeking after conceits in the inferior manner of the master (ix. 69):

> La destra di Gerniero, onde ferita
> Ella fu pria, manda recisa al piano;
> Tratto anco il ferro, e con tremanti dita
> Semiviva nel suol guizza la mano.

The same may be said about the wound of Algazèl (ix. 78) and the death of Ardonio (xx. 39). In the description of the felling of the forest (iii. 75, 76) and of the mustering of the Egyptian army (xvii. 1-36) Tasso's Virgilian style attains real grandeur and poetic beauty.

Tasso was nothing if not a learned poet. It would be easy to illustrate what he has borrowed from Lucretius, or to point out that the pathos of Clorinda's apparition to Tancredi after death is a debt to Petrarch. It may, however, suffice here to indicate six phrases taken straight from Dante; since the 'Divine Comedy' was little studied in Tasso's age, and his selection of these lines reflects credit on his taste. These are:

> Onorate l' altissimo campione! (iii. 73: 'Inf.' iv.)

> Goffredo intorno gli occhi gravi e tardi (vii. 58: 'Inf.' iv.)

> a riveder le stelle (iv. 18: 'Inf.' xxxiv.)

> Ond' è ch' or tanto ardire in voi s' alletti? (ix. 76: 'Inf.' ix.)

> A guisa di leon quando si posa (x. 56: 'Purg.' vi.)

> e guardi e passi (xx. 43: 'Inf.' iii.)

As in the 'Rinaldo,' so also in the 'Gerusalemme,' Tasso's classical proclivities betrayed him into violation of the clear Italian language. Afraid of what is natural and common, he produced what is artificial and conceited. Hence came involved octaves like the following (vi. 109):

> Siccome cerva, ch' assetata il passo
> Mova a cercar d' acque lucenti e vive,
> Ove un bel fonte distillar da un sasso
> O vide un fiume tra frondose rive,
> Se incontra i cani allor che il corpo lasso
> Ristorar crede all' onde, all' ombre estive,
> Volge indietro fuggendo, e la paura
> La stanchezza obbliar face e l' arsura.

The image is beautiful; but the diction is elaborately intricate, rhetorically indistinct. We find the same stylistic involution in these lines (xii. 6):

> Ma s' egli avverrà pur che mia ventura
> Nel mio ritorno mi rinchiuda il passo,
> D' uom che in amor m' è padre a te la cura
> E delle fide mie donzelle io lasso.

The limpid well of native utterance is troubled at its source by scholastic artifices in these as in so many other passages of Tasso's masterpiece.

Nor was he yet emancipated from the weakness of 'Rinaldo.' Trying to soar upon the borrowed plumes of pseudo-classical sublimity, he often fell back wearied by this uncongenial effort into prose. Lame endings to stanzas, sudden descents from highly wrought to pedestrian diction, are not uncommon in the 'Gerusalemme.' The poet, diffident of his own inspiration, sought inspiration from books. In the magnificence of single lines again, the 'Gerusalemme' reminds us of 'Rinaldo.' Tasso gained dignity of rhythm by choosing Latin adjectives and adverbs with pompous cadences. No versifier before his date had consciously employed the sonorous music of such lines as the following:

> Foro, tentando inaccessibil via (ii. 29).
> Ond' Amor l' arco inevitabil tende (iii. 24).
> Questa muraglia impenetrabil fosse (iii. 51).
> Furon vedute fiammeggiare insieme (v. 28).
> Qual capitan ch' inespugnabil terra (v. 64).
> Sotto l' inevitabile tua spada (xvi. 33).
> Immense solitudini d' arena (xvii. 1).

The last of these lines presents an impressive landscape in three melodious words.

These verbal and stylistic criticisms are not meant to cast reproach on Tasso as a poet. If they have any value, it is the light they throw upon conditions under which the poet was constrained to work. Humanism and the Catholic Revival reduced this greatest genius of his age to the necessity of clothing religious sentiments in scholastic phraseology, with the view of attaining to epic grandeur. But the Catholic Revival was no regeneration of Christianity from living sources; and humanism had run its course in Italy, and was ending in the sands of critical self-consciousness. Thus piety in Tasso appears superficial and conventional rather than profoundly felt or originally vigorous; while the scholarship which supplied his epic style is scrupulous and timid.

The enduring qualities of Tasso as a modern poet have still to be indicated; and to this more grateful portion of my argument I now address myself. Much might be said in the first place about his rhetorical dexterity—the flexibility of language in his hands, and the copiousness of thought, whereby he was able to adorn varied situations and depict diversity of passions with appropriate diction. Whether Alete is subtly pleading a seductive cause, or Goffredo is answering his sophistries with well-weighed arguments; whether Pluto addresses the potentates of hell, or Erminia wavers between love and honour; whether Tancredi pours forth the extremity of his despair, or Armida heaps reproaches on Rinaldo in his flight; the musical and luminously polished stanzas lend themselves without change of style to every gradation of the speaker's mood. In this art of rhetoric, Tasso seems to have taken Livy for his model; and many of the speeches which adorn the graver portions of his poem, are noticeable for compact sententious wisdom.

In fancy Tasso was not so naturally rich and inventive as the author of 'Orlando Furioso.' Yet a gallery of highly finished pictures might be collected from his similes and metaphors. What pride and swiftness mark this vision of a thunderbolt:

> Grande ma breve fulmine il diresti,
> Che inaspettato sopraggiunga e passi;
> Ma del suo corso momentaneo resti
> Vestigio eterno in dirupati sassi (xx. 93).

How delicately touched is this uprising of the morning star from ocean:

> Qual mattutina stella esce dell' onde
> Rugiadosa e stillante; o come fuore
> Spuntò nascendo già dalle feconde
> Spume dell' ocean la Dea d' amore (xv. 60).

Here is an image executed in the style of Ariosto. Clorinda has received a wound on her uncovered head:

> Fu levissima piaga, e i biondi crini
> Rosseggiaron così d' alquante stille,
> Come rosseggia l' or che di rubini
> Per man d' illustre artefice sfaville (iii. 30).

Flowers furnish the poet with exquisite suggestions of colour:

> D'un bel pallor ha il bianco volto asperso,
> Come a gigli sarian miste viole (xii. 69).
> Quale a pioggio d' argento a mattutina
> Si rabbellisce scolorita rosa (xx. 129).

Sometimes the painting is minutely finished like a miniature:

> Così piuma talor, che di gentile
> Amorosa colomba il collo cinge,
> Mai non si scorge a sè stessa simile,
> Ma in diversi colori al sol si tinge:
> Or d' accesi rubin sembra un monile,
> Or di verdi smeraldi il lume finge,
> Or insieme li mesce, e varia e vaga
> In cento modi i riguardanti appaga (xv. 5).

Sometimes the style is broad, the touch vigorous:

> Qual feroce destrier, ch' al faticoso
> Onor dell' arme vincitor sia tolto,
> E lascivo marito in vil riposo
> Fra gli armenti e ne' paschi erri disciolto,
> Se il desta o suon di tromba, o luminoso
> Acciar, colà tosto annitrendo è volto;
> Già già brama l' arringo, e l' uom sul dorso
> Portando, urtato riurtar nel corso (xvi. 28).

I will content myself with referring to the admirably conceived simile of a bulky galleon at sea attacked by a swifter and more agile vessel (xix. 13), which may perhaps have suggested to Fuller his famous comparison of Shakspere and Ben Jonson in their wit encounters.

But Tasso was really himself, incomparable and unapproachable, when he wrote in what musicians would call the *largo e maestoso* mood.

Giace l' alta Cartago; appena i segni
Dell' alte sue ruine il lido serba.
Muoiono le città, muoiono i regni;
Copre i fasti e le pompe arena ed erba;
E l' uomo d' esser mortal par che si sdegni!
Oh nostra mente cupida e superba! (xv. 20).

This is perfect in its measured melancholy, the liquid flow of its majestic simplicity. The same musical breadth, the same noble sweetness, pervade a passage on the eternal beauty of the heavens compared with the brief brightness of a woman's eyes:

oh quante belle
Luci il tempio celeste in sè raguna!
Ha il suo gran carro il dì; le aurate stelle
Spiega la notte e l' argentata luna;
Ma non è chi vagheggi o questa o quelle;
E miriam noi torbida luce e bruna,
Che un girar d' occhi, un balenar di riso
Scopre in breve confin di fragil viso (xviii. 13).

This verbal music culminates in the two songs of earthly joy, the *chants d'amour*, or hymns to pleasure, sung by Armida's ministers (xiv. 60-65, xvi. 12, 13). Boiardo and Ariosto had painted the seductions of enchanted gardens, where valour was enthralled by beauty, and virtue dulled by voluptuous delights. It remained for Tasso to give that magic of the senses vocal utterance. From the myrtle groves of Orontes, from the spell-bound summer amid snows upon the mountains of the Fortunate Isle, these lyrics with their penetrative sweetness, their lingering regret, pass into the silence of the soul. It is eminently characteristic of Tasso's mood and age that the melody of both these honeyed songs should thrill with sadness. Nature is at war with honour; youth passes like a flower away; therefore let us love and yield our hearts to pleasure while we can. 'Sehnsucht,' the soul of modern sentiment, the inner core of modern music, makes its entrance into the sphere of art with these two hymns. The division of the mind, wavering between natural impulse and acquired morality, gives the tone of melancholy to the one chant. In the other, the invitation to self-abandonment is mingled with a forecast of old age and death. Only Catullus, in his song to Lesbia, among the ancients touched this note; only Villon, perhaps, in his Ballade of Dead Ladies, touched it among the moderns before Tasso. But it has gone on sounding ever since through centuries which have enjoyed the luxury of grief in music.

If Tancredi be the real hero of the 'Gerusalemme,' Armida is the heroine. The action of the epic follows her movements. She combines the parts of Angelica and Alcina in one that is original and novel. A sorceress, deputed by the powers of hell to defeat the arms of the Crusaders, Armida falls herself in love with a Christian champion. Love changes her from a beautiful white witch into a woman.[13] When she

[13] I may incidentally point out how often this motive has supplied the plot to modern ballets.

meets Rinaldo in the battle, she discharges all her arrows vainly at the man who has deserted her. One by one, they fly and fall; and as they wing their flight, Love wounds her own heart with his shafts:

> Scocea l' arco più volte, e non fa piaga,
> E, mentre ella saetta, amor lei piaga (xx. 65).

Then she turns to die in solitude. Rinaldo follows, and stays her in the suicidal act. Despised and rejected as she is, she cannot hate him. The man she had entangled in her wiles has conquered and subdued her nature. To the now repentant minister of hell he proposes baptism: and Armida consents:

> Sì parla, e prega; e i preghi bagna e scalda
> Or di lagrime rare, or di sospiri:
> Onde, siccome suol nevosa falda
> Dov' arde il sole, o tepid' aura spiri,
> Così l' ira che in lei parea sì salda,
> Solvesi, e restan sol gli altri desiri.
> *Ecco l' ancilla tua*; d' essa a tuo senno
> Dispon, gli disse, e le fia legge il cenno (xx. 136).

This metamorphosis of the enchantress into the woman in Armida is the climax of the 'Gerusalemme.' It is also the climax and conclusion of Italian romantic poetry, the resolution of its magic and marvels into the truths of human affection. Notice, too, with what audacity Tasso has placed the words of Mary on the lips of his converted sorceress! Deliberately planning a religious and heroic poem, he assigns the spoils of conquered hell to love triumphant in a woman's breast. Beauty, which in itself is diabolical, the servant of the lords of Hades, attains to apotheosis through affection. In Armida we already surmise *das Ewig-Weibliche* of Goethe's Faust, Gretchen saving her lover's soul before Madonna's throne in glory.

What was it, then, that Tasso, this 'child of a later and a colder age,' as Shelley called him, gave of permanent value to European literature? We have seen that the 'Gerusalemme' did not fulfil the promise of heroic poetry for that eminently unheroic period. We know that neither the Virgilian hero nor the laboriously developed theme commands the interest of posterity. We feel that religious emotion is feeble here, and that the classical enthusiasm of the Renaissance is on the point of expiring in those Latinistic artifices. Yet the interwoven romance contains a something difficult to analyse, intangible and evanescent—*un non so che*, to use the poet's favourite phrase—which riveted attention in the sixteenth century, and which harmonises with our own sensibility to beauty. Tasso, in one word, was the poet, not of passion, not of humour, not of piety, not of elevated action, but of that new and undefined emotion which we call sentiment. Unknown to the ancients, implicit in later mediæval art, but not evolved with clearness from romance, alien to the sympathies of the Renaissance as determined by the Classical Revival, sentiment, that *non so che* of modern feeling, waited for its first apocalypse in Tasso's work. The phrase which I have quoted, and which occurs so frequently in this poet's verse, indicates the intrusion of a new element into the sphere of European feeling. Vague, indistinct, avoiding outline, the phrase *un non so che* leaves definition to the instinct of those who feel, but will not risk the limitation of their feeling by submitting it to words. Nothing in antique psychology demanded a term of this kind. Classical literature, in close affinity to sculpture, dealt with concrete images and conscious thoughts. The mediæval art of Dante, precisely, mathematically measured, had not felt the need of it. Boccaccio's clear-cut intaglios from life and nature, Petrarch's compassed melodies, Poliziano's polished arabesques, Ariosto's bright and many-coloured pencillings, were all of them, in all their varied phases of Renaissance expression, distinguished by decision and firmness of drawing. Vagueness, therefore, had hitherto found no place in European poetry or plastic art. But music, the supreme symbol of spiritual infinity in art, was now about to be developed; and the specific touch of Tasso, the musician-poet, upon portraiture and feeling, called forth this quality of vagueness, a vagueness that demanded melody to give what it refused from language to accept. Mendelssohn, when some one asked him what is meant by music, replied that it had meanings for his mind more unmistakable than those which words convey; but what these meanings were, he did not or he could not make clear. This certainty of sentiment, seeming vague only because it floats beyond the scope of language in regions of tone and colour and emotion, is what Tasso's *non so che* suggests to those who comprehend. And Tasso, by his frequent appeal to it, by his migration from the plastic into the melodic realm of the poetic art, proved himself the first genuinely sentimental artist of the modern age. It is just this which gave him a wider and more lasting empire over the heart through the next two centuries than that claimed by Ariosto.

It may not be unprofitable to examine in detail Tasso's use of the phrase to which so much importance has been assigned in the foregoing paragraph. We meet it first in the episode of Olindo and Sofronia. Sofronia, of all the heroines of the 'Gerusalemme,' is the least interesting, notwithstanding her magnanimous mendacity and jesuitical acceptance of martyrdom. Olindo touches the weaker fibres of our sympathy by his feminine devotion to a woman placed above him in the moral scale, whose love he wins by splendid falsehood equal to her own. The episode, entirely idle in the action of the poem, has little to recommend it, if we exclude the traditionally accepted reference to Tasso's love for Leonora d' Este. But when Olindo and Sofronia are standing, back to back, against the stake, Aladino, who has decreed their death by burning, feels his rude bosom touched with sudden pity:

> Un non so che d' inusitato e molle
> Par che nel duro petto al re trapasse:
> Ei presentillo, e si sdengò; nè volle
> Piegarsi, e gli occhi torse, e si ritrasse (ii. 37).

The intrusion of a lyrical emotion, unknown before in the tyrant's breast, against which he contends with anger, and before the force of which he bends, prepares us for the happy *dênouement* brought about by Clorinda. This vague stirring of the soul, this *non so che*, this sentiment, is the real agent in Sofronia's release and Olindo's beatification.

Clorinda is about to march upon her doom. She is inflamed with the ambition to destroy the engines of the Christian host by fire at night; and she calls Argante to her counsels:

> Buona pezza è, signor, che in sè raggira
> On non so che d' insolito e d' audace
> La mia mente inquieta; o Dio l' inspira,
> O l' uom del suo voler suo Dio si face (xii. 5).

Thus at this solemn point of time, when death is certainly in front, when she knows not whether God has inspired her or whether she has made of her own wish a deity, Clorinda utters the mystic word of vague compulsive feeling.

Erminia, taken captive by Tancredi after the siege of Antioch, is brought into her master's tent. He treats her with chivalrous courtesy, and offers her a knight's protection:

> Allora un non so che soave e piano
> Sentii, ch' al cor mi scese, e vi s' affisse,
> Che, serpendomi poi per l' alma vaga,
> Non so come, divenne incendio e piaga (xix. 94).

At that moment, by the distillation of that vague emotion into vein and marrow, Erminia becomes Tancredi's slave, and her future is determined.

These examples are, perhaps, sufficient to show how Tasso, at the turning-points of destiny for his most cherished personages, invoked indefinite emotion to adumbrate the forces with which will contends in vain. But the master phrase rings even yet more tyrannously in the passage of Clorinda's death, which sums up all of sentiment included in romance. Long had Tancredi loved Clorinda. Meeting her in battle, he stood her blows defenceless; for Clorinda was an Amazon, reduced by Tasso's gentle genius to womanhood from the proportions of Marfisa. Finally, with heart surcharged with love for her, he has to cross his sword in deadly duel with this lady. Malign stars rule the hour: he knows not who she is: misadventure makes her, instead of him, the victim of their encounter. With her last breath she demands baptism—the good Tasso, so it seems, could not send so fair a creature of his fancy as Clorinda to the shades without viaticum; and his poetry rises to the sublime of pathos in this stanza:

> Amico, hai vinto: io ti perdon: perdona
> Tu ancora: al corpo no, che nulla pave;
> All' alma sì: deh! per lei prega; e dona
> Battesmo a me ch' ogni mia colpa lave.
> In queste voci languide risuona
> Un non so che di flebile e soave
> Ch' al cor gli serpe, ed ogni sdegno ammorza,
> E gli occhi a lagrimar gl' invoglia e sforza (xii. 66).

Here the vague emotion, the *non so che*, distils itself through Clorinda's voice into Tancredi's being. Afterwards it thrills there like moaning winds in an Æolian lyre, reducing him to despair upon his bed of sickness, and reasserting its lyrical charm in the vision which he has of Clorinda among the trees of the enchanted forest. He stands before the cypress where the soul of his dead lady seems to his misguided fancy prisoned; and the branches murmur in his ears:

> Fremere intanto udia continuo il vento
> Tra le frondi del bosco e tra i virgulti,
> E trarne un suon che flebile concento
> Par d' umani sospiri e di singulti;
> E un non so che confuso instilla al core
> Di pietà, di spavento e di dolore (xiii. 40).

The master word, the magic word of Tasso's sentiment, is uttered at this moment of illusion. The poet has no key to mysteries locked up within the human breast more powerful than this indefinite *un non so che.*

Enough has been said to show how Tasso used the potent spell of vagueness, when he found himself in front of supreme situations. This is in truth the secret of his mastery over sentiment, the spell whereby he brings nature and night, the immense solitudes of deserts, the darkness of forests, the wailings of the winds and the plangent litanies of sea-waves into accord with overstrained humanity. It was a great discovery; by right of it Tasso proved himself the poet of the coming age.

When the 'Gerusalemme' was completed, Tasso had done his best work as a poet. The misfortunes which began to gather round him in his thirty-first year, made him well-nigh indifferent to the fate of the poem which had drained his life-force, and from which he had expected so much glory. It was published without his permission or supervision. He, meanwhile, in the prison of S. Anna, turned his attention to prose composition. The long series of dialogues, with which he occupied the irksome leisure of seven years, interesting as they are in matter and genial in style, indicate that the poet was now in abeyance. It remained to be seen whether inspiration would revive with freedom. No sooner were the bolts withdrawn than his genius essayed a fresh flight. He had long meditated the composition of a tragedy, and had already written some scenes. At Mantua in 1586-7 this work took the form of 'Torrismondo.' It cannot be called a great drama, for it belongs to the rigid declamatory species of Italian tragedy; and Tasso's genius was romantic, idyllic, elegiac, anything but genuinely tragic. Yet the style is eminent for nobility and purity. Just as the 'Aminta' showed how unaffected Tasso could be when writing without preconceived theories of heightened diction, so the 'Torrismondo' displays an unstrained dignity of simple dialogue. It testifies to the plasticity of language in the hands of a master, who deliberately chose and sustained different styles in different species of poetry, and makes us regret that he should have formed his epic manner upon so artificial a type. The last chorus of 'Torrismondo' deserves to be mentioned as a perfect example of Tasso's melancholy elegiac pathos.

Meanwhile he began to be dissatisfied with the 'Gerusalemme,' and in 1588 he resolved upon remodelling his masterpiece. The real vitality of that poem was, as we have seen, in its romance. But Tasso thought otherwise. During the fourteen years which elapsed since its completion, the poet's youthful fervour had been gradually fading out. Inspiration yielded to criticism; piety succeeded to sentiment and enthusiasm for art. Therefore, in this later phase of his maturity, with powers impaired by prolonged sufferings and wretched health, tormented by religious scruples and vague persistent fear, he determined to eliminate the romance from the epic, to render its unity of theme more rigorous, and to concentrate attention upon the serious aspects of the subject. The result of this plan, pursued through five years of wandering, was the 'Gerusalemme Conquistata,' a poem which the world has willingly let die, in which the style of the 'Gerusalemme Liberata' is worsened, and which now serves mainly to establish by comparison the fact that what was immortal in Tasso's art was the romance he ruthlessly rooted out. A further step in this transition from art to piety is marked by the poem upon the Creation of the World, called 'Le Sette Giornate.' Written in blank verse, it religiously but tamely narrates the operation of the Divine Artificer, following the first chapter of Genesis and expanding the motive of each of the seven days with facile rhetoric. Of action and of human interest the poem has none; of artistic beauty little. The sustained descriptive style wearies; and were not this the last work of Tasso, it would not be mentioned by posterity.

Tasso has already occupied us through two chapters. Before passing onward I must, however, invite the reader to pause awhile and reconsider, even at the risk of retrospect and repetition, some of the salient features of his character. And now I remember that of his personal appearance nothing has hitherto been said. 'Tasso was tall, well-proportioned, and of very fair complexion. His thick hair and beard were of a light-brown colour. His head was large, forehead broad and square, eyebrows dark, eyes large, lively and blue, nose large and curved toward the mouth, lips thin and pale.' So writes Manso, the poet's friend and biographer; adding: 'His voice was clear and sonorous; but he read his poems badly, because of a slight impediment in his speech, and because he was short-sighted.' I know not whether I am justified in drawing from this description the conclusion that Tasso was, physically, a man of mixed lymphatic and melancholic temperament, of more than ordinary sensitiveness. Imperfection, at any rate, is indicated by the thin pale lips, the incoherent utterance and the uncertain vision to which his friend in faithfulness bears witness. Of painted portraits representing Tasso in later life there are many; but most of these seem to be based upon the mask taken from his face after death, which still exists at S. Onofrio. Twenty-one years ago I gazed upon this mask, before I knew more than every schoolboy knows of Tasso's life and writings. This is what I wrote about it in my Roman diary: 'The face is mild and weak, especially in the thin short chin and feeble mouth.[14] The forehead round, and ample in proportion to the other features. The eyes are small, but this may be due to the contraction of death. The mouth is almost vulgar, very flat in the upper lip; but this also ought perhaps to be attributed to the relaxation of tissue by death.'

Tasso was constitutionally inclined to pensive moods. His outlook over life was melancholy.[15] The tone of his literary work, whether in prose or poetry, is elegiac—musically, often querulously plaintive. There rests a shadow of dejection over all he wrote and thought and acted. Yet he was finely sensitive to pleasure, thrillingly alive to sentimental beauty.[16] Though the man lived purely, untainted by the license of the age, his genius soared highest when he sang some soft luxurious strain of love. He was wholly deficient in humour. Taking himself and the world of men and things too much in earnest, he weighed heavily alike on art and life. The smallest trifles, if they touched him, seemed to him important.[17] Before imaginary terrors he shook like an aspen. The slightest provocation roused his momentary resentment. The most insignificant sign of neglect or coldness wounded his self-esteem. Plaintive, sensitive to beauty, sentimental, tender, touchy, self-engrossed, devoid of humour—what a sentient instrument was this for uttering Æolian melodies, and straining discords through storm-jangled strings!

From the Jesuits, in childhood, he received religious impressions which might almost be described as mesmeric or hypnotic in their influence upon his nerves. These abode with him through manhood; and in later life morbid scruples and superstitious anxieties about his soul laid hold on his imagination. Yet religion did not penetrate Tasso's nature. As he conceived it, there was nothing solid and supporting in its substance. Piety was neither deeply rooted nor indigenous, neither impassioned nor logically reasoned, in the adult man.[18] What it might have been, but for those gimcrack ecstasies before the Host in boyhood, cannot now be fancied. If he contained the stuff of saint or s mple Christian, this was sterilised and stunted by the clever fathers in their school at Naples.

During the years of his feverishly active adolescence Tasso played for a while with philosophical doubts. But though he read widely and speculated diffusely on the problems of the universe, he failed to pierce

[14] Giov. Imperiale in the *Museum Historicum* describes him thus: 'Perpetuo moerentis et altius cogitantis gessit aspectum, *gracili mento*, facie decolori, conniventibus cavisque oculis.'

[15] 'La mia fiera malinconia' is a phrase which often recurs in his letters.

[16] 'Questo segno mi ho proposto: piacere ed onore' (*Lettere*, vol. v. p. 87).

[17] It should be said that as a man of letters he bore with fools gladly, and showed a noble patience. Of this there is a fine example in his controversy with the Della Cruscans. He was not so patient with the publishers and pirates of his works. No wonder, when they robbed him so!

[18] Tasso's diffuse paraphrase of the *Stabat Mater* might be selected to illustrate the sentimental tenderness rather than strength of his religious feeling.

below the surface of the questions which he handled. His own beliefs had been tested in no red-hot crucible, before he recoiled with terror from their analysis. The man, to put it plainly, was incapable of honest revolt against the pietistic fashions of his age, incapable of exploratory efforts, and yet too intelligent to rest satisfied with gross dogmatism or smug hypocrisy. Neither as a thinker, nor as a Christian, nor yet again as that epicene religious being, a Catholic of the Counter-Reformation, did this noble and ingenuous, but weakly nature attain to thoroughness.

Tasso's mind was lively and sympathetic; not penetrative, not fitted for forming original or comprehensive views. He lived for no great object, whether political, moral, religious, or scientific. He committed himself to no vice. He obeyed no absorbing passion of love or hatred. In his misfortunes he displayed the helplessness which stirs mere pity for a prostrate human being. The poet who complained so querulously, who wept so copiously, who forgot offence so nonchalantly, cannot command admiration.

There is nothing sublimely tragic in Tasso's suffering. The sentiment inspired by it is that at best of pathos. An almost childish self-engrossment restricted his thoughts, his aims and aspirations, to a narrow sphere, within which he wandered incurably idealistic, pursuing prosaic or utilitarian objects—the favour of princes, place at Courts, the recovery of his inheritance—in a romantic and unpractical spirit.[19] Vacillating, irresolute, peevish, he roamed through all the towns of Italy, demanding more than sympathy could give, exhausting friendship, changing from place to place, from lord to lord. Yet how touching was the destiny of this laurelled exile, this brilliant wayfarer on the high-roads of a world he never understood! Shelley's phrase, 'the world's rejected guest,' exactly seems to suit him. And yet he allowed himself to become the spoilt child of his misfortunes. Without them, largely self-created as they were, Tasso could not now appeal to our hearts. Nor does he appeal to us as Dante, eating the salt bread of patrons' tables, does; as Milton, blind and fallen on evil days; as Chatterton, perishing in pride and silence; as Johnson, turning from the stairs of Chesterfield; as Bruno, averting stern eyes from the crucifix; as Leopardi, infusing the virus of his suffering into the veins of humanity; as Heine, motionless upon his mattrass grave. These more potent personalities, bequeathing to the world examples of endurance, have won the wreath of never-blasted bays which shall not be set on Tasso's forehead. We crown him with frailer leaves, bedewed with tears tender as his own sentiment, and aureoled with the light that emanates from pure and delicate creations of his fancy.

Though Tasso does not command admiration by heroism, he wins compassion as a beautiful and finely gifted nature inadequate to cope with the conditions of his century. For a poet to be independent in that age of intellectual servitude was well-nigh impossible. To be

[19] The numerous plaintive requests for a silver cup, a ring, a silk cloak, and such trifles in his later letters indicate something quite childish in his preoccupations.

light-hearted and ironically indifferent lay not in Tasso's temperament. It was no less difficult for a man of his mental education to maintain the balance between orthodoxy and speculation, faith and reason, classical culture and Catholicism, the Renaissance and the Counter-Reformation. He belonged in one sense too much, and in another sense too little, to his epoch. One eminent critic calls him the only Christian of the Italian Renaissance, another with equal justice treats him as the humanistic poet of the Catholic Revival.[20]

Properly speaking, he was the genius of that transition from the Renaissance to the Counter-Reformation, on which I dwelt in the second chapter of this work. By natural inclination he belonged to the line of artists which began with Boccaccio and culminated in Ariosto. But his training and the bias of the times in which he lived, made him break with Boccaccio's tradition. He tried to be the poet of the Council of Trent, without having assimilated hypocrisy or acquired false taste, without comprehending the essentially prosaic and worldly nature of that religious revolution. He therefore lived and worked in a continual discord. This may not suffice to account for the unhingement of his reason. I prefer to explain that by the fatigue of intellectual labour and worry acting on a brain predisposed for melancholia and over-tasked from infancy. But it does account for the moral martyrdom he suffered, and the internal perplexity to which he was habitually subject.

When Tasso first saw the light, the Italians had rejected the Reformation and consented to stifle free thought. The culture of the Renaissance had been condemned; the Spanish hegemony had been accepted. Of this new attitude the concordat between Charles and Clement, the Tridentine Council, the Inquisition and the Company of Jesus were external signs. But these potent agencies had not accomplished their work in Tasso's lifetime. He was rent in twain because he could not react against them as Bruno did, and could not identify himself with them as Loyola was doing. As an artist he belonged to the old order which was passing, as a Christian to the new order which was emerging. His position as a courtier, when the Augustan civility of the earlier Medici was being superseded by dynastic absolutism, complicated his difficulties. While accepting service in the modern spirit of subjection, he dreamed of masters who should be Mæcenases, and fondly imagined that poets might still live, like Petrarch, on terms of equality with princes.

We therefore see in Tasso one who obeyed influences to which his real self never wholly or consciously submitted. He was not so much out of harmony with his age as the incarnation of its still unharmonised contradictions. The pietism instilled into his mind at Naples; the theories of art imbibed at Padua and Venice; the classical lumber absorbed during his precocious course of academical studies; the hypocritical employment of allegory to render sensuous poetry decorous; the deference to critical opinion and the dictates of literary lawgivers;

[20] Carducci, in his essay *Dello Svolgimento della Letteratura Nazionale*; and Quinet, in his *Révolutions d'Italie*.

the reverence for priests and princes interposed between the soul and God: these were principles which Tasso accepted without having properly assimilated and incorporated their substance into his spiritual being. What the poet in him really was, we perceive when he wrote, to use Dante's words, as Love dictates; or as Plato said, when he submitted to the mania of the Muse; or as Horace counselled, when he indulged his genius. It is in the 'Aminta,' in the episodes of the 'Gerusalemme,' in a small percentage of the 'Rime,' that we find the true Tasso. For the rest, he had not the advantages enjoyed by Boiardo and Ariosto in a less self-conscious age, of yielding to natural impulse after a full and sympathetic study of classical and mediæval sources. The analytical labours of the previous century hampered his creativeness. He brought to his task preoccupations of divers and self-contradictory pedantries—pedantries of Catholicism, pedantries of scholasticism, pedantries of humanism in its exhausted phase, pedantries of criticism refined and subtilised within a narrow range of problems. He had, moreover, weighing on his native genius the fears which brooded like feverish exhalations over the evil days in which he lived—fears of Church-censure, fears of despotic princes, fears of the Inquisition, fears of hell, fears of the judgment of academies, fears of social custom and courtly conventionalities. Neither as poet nor as man had he the courage of originality. What he lacked was character. He obeyed the spirit of his age, in so far as he did not, like young David, decline Saul's armour and enter into combat with Philistinism, wielding his sling and stone of native force alone. Yet that native force was so vigorous that, in spite of the panoply of prejudice he wore, in spite of the cumbrous armour lent him by authority, he moved at times with superb freedom. In those rare intervals of personal inspiration he dictated the love-tales of Erminia and Armida, the death-scene of Clorinda, the pastoral of Aminta and Silvia—episodes which created the music and the painting of two centuries, and which still live upon the lips of the people. But inasmuch as his genius laboured beneath the superincumbent weight of precedents and deferences, the poet's nature was strained to the uttermost and his nervous elasticity was overtaxed. No sooner had he poured forth freely what flowed freely from his soul, than he returned on it with scrupulous analysis. The product of his spirit stood before him as a thing to be submitted to opinion, as a substance subject to the test of all those pedantries and fears. We cannot wonder that the subsequent conflict perplexed his reason and sterilised his creative faculty to such an extent that he spent the second half of his life in attempting to undo the great work of his prime. The 'Gerusalemme Conquistata' and the 'Sette Giornate' are thus the splendid triumph achieved by the feebler over the stronger portions of his nature, the golden tribute paid by his genius to the evil genius of the age controlling him. He was a poet who, had he lived in the days of Ariosto, would have created in all senses spontaneously, producing works of Virgilian beauty and divine melancholy to match the Homeric beauty and the divine irony of his great peer. But this was not to be. The spirit of the times which governed his education, with which he was not revolutionary enough to break, which he strove as a critic to assimilate and as a social being to obey, destroyed his independence, perplexed his judgment, and impaired his nervous energy. His best work was consequently of unequal value; pure and base metal mingled in its composition. His worst was a barren and lifeless failure.

CHAPTER IX

GIORDANO BRUNO

Scientific Bias of the Italians checked by Catholic Revival—Boyhood of Bruno—Enters Order of S. Dominic at Naples—Early Accusations of Heresy—Escapes to Rome—Teaches the Sphere at Noli—Visits Venice—At Geneva—At Toulouse—At Paris—His Intercourse with Henri III.—Visits England—The French Ambassador in London—Oxford—Bruno's Literary Work in England—Returns to Paris—Journeys into Germany—Wittenberg, Helmstädt, Frankfort—Invitation to Venice from Giovanni Mocenigo—His Life in Venice—Mocenigo denounces him to the Inquisition—His Trial at Venice—Removal to Rome—Death by Burning in 1600—Bruno's Relation to the Thought of his Age and to the Thought of Modern Europe—Outlines of his Philosophy.

THE humanistic and artistic impulses of the Renaissance were at the point of exhaustion in Italy. Scholarship declined; the passion for antiquity expired. All those forms of literature which Boccaccio initiated—comedy, romance, the idyll, the lyric, and the novel—had been worked out by a succession of great writers. It became clear that the nation was not destined to create tragic or heroic types of poetry. Architecture, sculpture, and painting had performed their task of developing mediæval motives by the light of classic models, and were now entering on the stage of academical inanity. Yet the mental vigour of the Italians was by no means exhausted. Early in the sixteenth century Machiavelli had inaugurated a new method for political philosophy; Pomponazzo at Padua and Telesio at Cosenza disclosed new horizons for psychology and the science of nature. It seemed as though the Renaissance in Italy were about to assume a fresh and more serious character without losing its essential inspiration. That evolution of intellectual energy which had begun with the assimilation of the classics, with the first attempts at criticism, with the elaboration of style and the perfection of artistic form, now promised to invade the fields of metaphysical and scientific speculation. It is true, as we have seen, that the theological problems of the German Reformation took but slight hold on Italians. Their thinkers were already too far advanced upon the paths of modern rationalism to feel the actuality of questions which divided Luther from Zwingli, Calvin from Servetus, Knox from Cranmer. But they promised to accomplish master-works of incalculable magnitude in wider provinces of exploration and investigation. And had this progress not been checked, Italy would have crowned and completed the process commenced by humanism. In addition to the intellectual culture already given to Europe, she might have revealed right methods of mental analysis and physical research. For this further step in the discovery of man and of the world, the nation was prepared to bring an army of new pioneers into the field—the philosophers of the South, and the physicists of the Lombard universities.

Humanism effected the emancipation of intellect by culture. It called attention to the beauty and delightfulness of nature, restored man to a sense of his dignity, and freed him from theological authority. But in Italy, at any rate, it left his conscience, his religion, his sociological ideas, the deeper problems which concern his relation to the universe, the subtler secrets of the world in which he lives, untouched.

These *novi homines* of the later Renaissance, as Bacon called them, these *novatori*, as they were contemptuously styled in Italy, prepared the further emancipation of the intellect by science. They asserted the liberty of thought and speech, proclaimed the paramount authority of that inner light or indwelling deity which man owns in his brain and breast, and rehabilitated nature from the stigma cast on it by Christianity. What the Bible was for Luther, that was the great Book of Nature for Telesio, Bruno, Campanella. The German reformer appealed to the reason of the individual as conscience; the school of Southern Italy made a similar appeal to intelligence. In different ways Luther and these speculative thinkers maintained the direct illumination of the human soul by God, man's immediate dependence on his Maker, repudiating ecclesiastical intervention, and refusing to rely on any principle but earnest love of truth.

Had this new phase of the Italian Renaissance been permitted to evolve itself unhindered, there is no saying how much earlier Europe might have entered into the possession of that kingdom of unprejudiced research which is now secured for us. But it was just at the moment when Italy became aware of the arduous task before her, that the Catholic reaction set in with all its rigour. The still creative spirit of her children succumbed to the Inquisition, the Congregation of the Index, the decrees of Trent, the intellectual submission of the Jesuits, the physical force of Spanish tyranny, and Roman absolutism. Carnesecchi was burned alive; Paleario was burned alive; Bruno was burned alive: these three at Rome. Vanini was burned at Toulouse. Valentino Gentile was executed by Calvinists at Berne. Campanella was cruelly tortured and imprisoned for twenty-seven years at Naples. Galileo was forced to humble himself before ignorant and arrogant monks, and to hide his head in a country villa. Sarpi felt the knife of an assassin, and would certainly have perished at the instigation of his Roman enemies but for the protection guaranteed him by the Signory of Venice. In this way did Italy—or rather, let us say, the Church which dominated Italy—devour her sons of light. It is my purpose in the present chapter to narrate the life of Bruno and to give some account of his philosophy, taking him as the most illustrious example of the school exterminated by reactionary Rome.

Giordano Bruno was born in 1548 at Nola, an ancient Greek city close to Naples. He received the baptismal name of Filippo, which he exchanged for Giordano on assuming the Dominican habit. His parents, though people of some condition, were poor; and this circumstance may perhaps be reckoned the chief reason why Bruno entered the convent of S. Dominic at Naples before he had completed his fifteenth year. It will be remembered that Sarpi joined the Servites at the age of thirteen, and Campanella the Dominicans at that of fourteen. In each of these memorable cases it is probable that poverty had something to do with deciding a vocation so premature. But there were other inducements, which rendered the monastic life not unattractive to a young man seeking knowledge at a period and in a district where instruction was both costly and difficult to obtain. Campanella himself informs us that he was drawn to the order of S. Dominic by its reputation for learning and by the great names of S. Thomas Aquinas and Albertus Magnus. Bruno possibly felt a similar attraction; for there is nothing in the temper of his mind to make us believe that he inclined seriously to the religious life of the cloister.

During his novitiate he came into conflict with the superiors of his convent for the first time. It was proved against him that he had given away certain images of saints, keeping only the crucifix; also that he had told a comrade to lay aside a rhymed version of the Seven Joys of Mary, and to read the lives of the Fathers of the Church instead. On these two evidences of insufficient piety, an accusation was prepared against him which might have led to serious results. But the master of the novices preferred to destroy the document, retaining only a memorandum of the fact for future use in case of need.[1] Bruno, after this event, obeyed the cloistral discipline in quiet, and received priest's orders in 1572.

At this epoch of his life, when he had attained his twenty-fourth year, he visited several Dominican convents of the Neapolitan province, and entered, with the want of prudence which was habitual to him, into disputations on theology. Some remarks he let fall on transubstantiation and the Divinity of Christ exposed him to a suspicion of Arianism, a heresy at that time rife in Southern Italy. Bruno afterwards confessed that from an early age he had entertained speculative doubts upon the metaphysics of the Trinity, though he was always prepared to accept that dogma in faith as a good Catholic. The Inquisition took the matter up in earnest, and began to institute proceedings of so grave a nature that the young priest felt himself in danger. He escaped in his monk's dress, and travelled to Rome, where he obtained admittance for a short while to the convent of the Minerva.

We know very little what had been his occupations up to this date. It is only certain that he had already composed a comedy, 'Il Candelajo:' which furnishes sufficient proof of his familiarity with mundane manners. It is, in fact, one of the freest and most frankly satirical composi-

[1] The final case drawn up against Bruno as heresiarch makes it appear that his record included even these boyish errors. See the letter of Gaspar Schopp in Berti.

tions for the stage produced at that epoch, and reveals a previous study of Aretino. Nola, Bruno's birthplace, was famous for the license of its country folk. Since the day of its foundation by Chalkidian colonists, its inhabitants had preserved their Hellenic traditions intact. The vintage, for example, was celebrated with an extravagance of obscene banter, which scandalised Philip II.'s viceroy in the sixteenth century.[2] During the period of Bruno's novitiate, the ordinances of the Council of Trent for discipline in monasteries were not yet in operation; and it is probable that throughout the thirteen years of his conventual experience, he mixed freely with the people and shared the pleasures of youth in that voluptuous climate. He was never delicate in his choice of phrase, and made no secret of the admiration which the beauty of women excited in his nature. The accusations brought against him at Venice contained one article of indictment implying that he professed distinctly profligate opinions; and though there is nothing to prove that his private life was vicious, the tenor of his philosophy favours more liberty of manners than the Church allowed in theory to her ministers.[3] It is of some importance to dwell upon this topic; for Bruno's character and temper, so markedly different from that of Sarpi, for example, affected in no small measure the form and quality of his philosophy. He was a poet, gifted with keen and lively sensibilities, open at all pores to the delightfulness of nature, recoiling from nothing that is human. At no period of his life was he merely a solitary thinker or a student of books. When he came to philosophise, when the spiritual mistress, Sophia, absorbed all other passions in his breast, his method of exposition retained a tincture of that earlier phase of his experience.

It must not be thought, however, that Bruno prosecuted no serious studies during this period. On the contrary, he seems to have amassed considerable erudition in various departments of learning: a fact which should make us cautious against condemning conventual education as of necessity narrow and pedantic. When he left Naples, he had acquired sufficient knowledge of Aristotle and the Schoolmen, among whom he paid particular attention to S. Thomas and to Raymond Lully. Plato, as expounded by Plotinus, had taken firm hold on his imagination. He was versed in the dialectics of the previous age, had mastered mediæval cosmography and mathematics, and was probably already acquainted with Copernicus. The fragments of the Greek philosophers, especially of Pythagoras and Parmenides, whose metaphysics powerfully influenced his mind, had been assimilated. Perhaps the writings of Cardinal Cusa, the theologian who applied mathematics to philosophy, were also in his hands at the same period. Besides Italian, he possessed the Spanish language, could write and speak Latin with fluency, and

[2] See 'Vita di Don Pietro di Toledo' (*Arch. Stor.* vol. ix. p. 23).

[3] See the passage on polygamy in the *Spaccio della Bestia.* I may here remark that Campanella, though more orthodox than Bruno, published opinions upon the relations of the sexes analogous to those of Plato's *Republic* in his *Città del Sole.* He even recommended the institution of brothels as annexes to schools for boys, in order to avoid the worse evil of unnatural vice in youth.

knew something of Greek. It is clear that he had practised poetry in the vernacular under the immediate influence of Tansillo. Theological studies had not been wholly neglected; for he left behind him at Naples editions of Jerome and Chrysostom with commentaries of Erasmus. These were books which exposed their possessors to the interdiction of the Index.

It seems strange that a Dominican, escaping from his convent to avoid a trial for heresy, should have sought refuge at S. Maria sopra Minerva, then the headquarters of the Roman Inquisition. We must, however, remember that much freedom of movement was allowed to monks, who found a temporary home in any monastery of their order. Without money, Bruno had no roof but that of a religious house to shelter him; and he probably reckoned on evading pursuit till the fatigues of his journey from Naples had been forgotten. At any rate, he made no lengthy stay in Rome. News soon reached him that the prosecution begun at Naples was being transferred to the metropolis. This implied so serious a danger that he determined to quit Rome in secret. Having flung his frock to the nettles, he journeyed—how, we do not know—to Genoa, and thence to Noli on the Riviera. The next time Bruno entered the Dominican convent of S. Maria sopra Minerva, it was as a culprit condemned to death by the Inquisition.

At Noli, Bruno gained a living for about five months by teaching grammar to boys and lecturing in private to some gentlefolk upon the Sphere. The doctrine of the Sphere formed a somewhat miscellaneous branch of mediæval science. It embraced the exposition of Ptolemaic astronomy, together with speculations on the locality of heaven, the motive principle of the world, and the operation of angelical intelligences. Bruno, who professed this subject at various times throughout his wanderings, began now to use it as a vehicle for disseminating Copernican opinions. It is certain that cosmography formed the basis of his philosophy, and this may be ascribed to his early occupation with the Sphere. But his restless spirit would not suffer him to linger in those regions where olive and orange and palm flourish almost more luxuriantly than in his native Nola. The gust of travel was upon him. A new philosophy occupied his brain, vertiginously big with incoherent births of modern thought. What Carlyle called 'the fire in the belly' burned and irritated his young blood. Unsettled, cast adrift from convent moorings, attainted for heresy, out of sympathy with resurgent Catholicism, he became a Vagus Quidam—a wandering student, like the Goliardi of the Middle Ages. From Noli he passed to Savona; from Savona to Turin; from Turin to Venice. There his feet might perhaps have found rest; for Venice was the harbour of all vagrant spirits in that age. But the city was laid waste with plague. Bruno wrote a little book, now lost, on 'The Signs of the Times,' and lived upon the sale of it for some two months. Then he removed to Padua. Here friends persuaded him to reassume the cowl. There were more than 40,000 monks abroad in Italy, beyond the limits of their convent. Why should not he avail himself of house-roof in his travels, a privilege which was always open to friars? From Padua he journeyed rapidly again through Brescia, Bergamo, and Milan to Turin, crossed Mont Cenis, tarried at Chambéry, and finally betook himself to Geneva.

Geneva was no fit resting-place for Bruno. He felt an even fiercer antipathy for dissenting than for orthodox bigotry. The despotism of a belligerent and persecuting sectarian seemed to him more intolerable, because less excusable, than the Catholic despotism from which he was escaping. Galeazzo Caracciolo, Marquis of Vico, who then presided over the Italian refugees in Geneva, came to visit him. At the suggestion of this man Bruno once more laid aside his Dominican attire, and began to earn his bread by working as a reader for the press—a common resort of needy men of learning in those times. But he soon perceived that the Calvinistic stronghold offered no freedom, no security of life even, to one whose mind was bent on new developments of thought. After two months' residence on the shores of Lake Leman he departed for Toulouse, which he entered early in 1577.

We cannot help wondering why Bruno chose that city for his refuge. Toulouse, the only town in France where the Inquisition took firm root and flourished, Toulouse so perilous to Muret, so mortal to Dolet and Vanini, ought, one might have fancied, to have been avoided by an innovator flying from a charge of heresy.[4] Still it must be remembered that Toulouse was French. Italian influence did not reach so far. Nor had Bruno committed himself even in thought to open rupture with Catholicism. He held the opinion, so common at that epoch, so inexplicable to us now, that the same man could countermine dogmatic theology as a philosopher, while he maintained it as a Christian. This was the paradox on which Pomponazzo based his apology, which kept Campanella within the pale of the Church, and to which Bruno appealed for his justification when afterwards arraigned before the Inquisitors at Venice.

It appears from his own autobiographical confessions that Bruno spent some six months at Toulouse, lecturing in private on the peripatetic psychology; after which time he obtained the degree of Doctor in Philosophy, and was admitted to a Readership in the university. This post he occupied two years. It was a matter of some moment to him that professors at Toulouse were not obliged to attend Mass. In his dubious position, as an escaped friar and disguised priest, to partake of the Sacrament would have been dangerous. Yet he now appears to have contemplated the possibility of reconciling himself to the Church, and resuming his vows in the Dominican order. He went so far as to open his mind upon this subject to a Jesuit; and afterwards at Paris he again resorted to Jesuit advice. But these conferences led to nothing. It may be presumed that the trial begun at Naples and removed to Rome, combined with the circumstances of his flight and

[4] On the city, university, and Inquisition of Toulouse in the sixteenth century see Christie's *Etienne Dolet*—a work of sterling merit and sound scholarship.

recusant behaviour, rendered the case too grave for compromise. No one but the Pope in Rome could decide it.

There is no apparent reason why Bruno left Toulouse, except the restlessness which had become a marked feature in his character. We find him at Paris in 1579, where he at once began to lecture at the Sorbonne. It seems to have been his practice now in every town he visited, to combine private instruction with public disputation. His manners were agreeable; his conversation was eloquent and witty. He found no difficulty in gaining access to good society, especially in a city like Paris, which was then thronged with Italian exiles and courtiers. Meanwhile his public lectures met with less success than his private teaching. In conversation with men of birth and liberal culture he was able to expound views fascinating by their novelty and boldness. Before an academical audience it behoved him to be circumspect; nor could he transgress the formal methods of scholastic argumentation.

Two principal subjects seem to have formed the groundwork of his teaching at this period. The first was the doctrine of the Thirty Divine Attributes, based on S. Thomas of Aquino. The second was Lully's Art of Memory and Classification of the Sciences. This twofold material he worked up into a single treatise, called 'De Umbris Idearum,' which he published in 1582 at Paris, and which contains the germ of all his leading speculations. Bruno's metaphysics attracted less attention than his professed Art of Memory. In an age credulous of occult science, when men believed that power over nature was being won by alchemy and magic, there was no difficulty in persuading people that knowledge might be communicated in its essence, and that the faculties of the mind could be indefinitely extended, without a toilsome course of study. Whether Bruno lent himself wittingly to any imposture in his exposition of mnemonics, cannot be asserted. But it is certain that the public were led to expect from his method more than it could give.

The fame of his Art of Memory reached the King's ears; and Henri III. sent for him. 'The King,' says Bruno, 'had me called one day, being desirous to know whether the memory I possessed and professed was natural or the result of magic art. I gave him satisfaction; by my explanations and by demonstrations to his own experience, convincing him that it was not an affair of magic but of science.' Henri, who might have been disappointed by this result, was taken with his teacher, and appointed him Reader Extraordinary—a post that did not oblige Bruno to hear Mass. The Ordinary Readers at Paris had to conform to the usages of the Catholic Church. On his side, Bruno appears to have conceived high admiration for the King's ability. In the 'Cena delle Ceneri' and the 'Spaccio della Bestia Trionfante,' composed and published after he had left France, he paid him compliments in terms of hyperbolical laudation. It would be vain to comment on these facts. No one conversant with French society at that epoch could have been ignorant of Henri's character and vicious life. No one could have pretended that his employment of the kingdom's wealth to enrich unworthy favourites was anything but dishonourable, or have maintained that his flagrant effeminacy was beneficial to society. The fantastic superstition which the King indulged alternately with sensual extravagances, must have been odious to one whose spiritual mistress was divine Sophia, and whose religion was an adoration of the intellect for the One Cause. But Henri had one quality which seemed of supreme excellence to Bruno. He appreciated speculation and encouraged men of learning. A man so enthusiastic as our philosopher may have thought that his own teaching could expel that Beast Triumphant of the vices from a royal heart tainted by bad education in a corrupt Court. Bruno, moreover, it must be remembered, remained curiously inappreciative of the revolution effected in humanity by Christian morals. Much that is repulsive to us in the manners of the Valois, may have been indifferent to him.

Bruno had just passed his thirtieth year. He was a man of middling height, spare figure, and olive complexion, wearing a short chestnut-coloured beard. He spoke with vivacity and copious rhetoric, aiming rather at force than at purity of diction, indulging in trenchant metaphors to adumbrate recondite thoughts, passing from grotesque images to impassioned flights of declamation, blending acute arguments and pungent satires with grave mystical discourses. The impression of originality produced by his familiar conversation rendered him agreeable to princes. There was nothing of the pedant in his nature, nothing about him of the doctor but his title.

After a residence of rather less than four years in Paris, he resolved upon a journey to England. Henri supplied him with letters of introduction to the French ambassador in London, Michel de Castelnau de la Mauvissière. This excellent man, who was then attempting to negotiate the marriage of Elizabeth with the Duke of Anjou, received Bruno into his own family as one of the gentlemen of his suite. Under his roof the wandering scholar enjoyed a quiet home during the two years which he passed in England—years that were undoubtedly the happiest, as they were the most industrious, of his chequered life. It is somewhat strange that Bruno left no trace of his English visit in contemporary literature. Seven of his most important works were printed in London, though they bore the impress of Paris and Venice—for the very characteristic reason that English people only cared for foreign publications. Four of these, on purely metaphysical topics, were dedicated to Michel de Castelnau; two, treating of moral and psychological questions, the famous 'Spaccio della Bestia' and 'Gli Eroici Furori,' were inscribed to Sidney. The 'Cena delle Ceneri' describes a supper party at the house of Fulke Greville; and it is clear from numerous allusions scattered up and down these writings, that their author was admitted on terms of familiarity to the best English society. Yet no one mentions him. Fulke Greville in his 'Life of Sidney' passes him by in silence; nor am I aware that any one of Sidney's panegyrists, the name of whom is legion, alludes to the homage paid him by the Italian philosopher.

On his side, Bruno has bequeathed to us animated pictures of his life in London portraying the English of that period as they impressed a sensitive Italian.[5] His descriptions are valuable, since they dwell on slight particulars unnoticed by ambassadors in their despatches. He was much struck with the filth and unkempt desolation of the streets adjacent to the Thames, the rudeness of the watermen who plied their craft upon the river, and the stalwart beef-eating brutality of prentices and porters. The population of London displayed its antipathy to foreigners by loud remarks, hustled them in narrow lanes, and played at rough and tumble with them after the manners of a bear-garden. But there is no hint that these big fellows shouldering through the crowd were treacherous or ready with their knives. The servants of great houses seemed to Bruno discourteous and savage; yet he says nothing about such subtlety and vice as rendered the retainers of Italian nobles perilous to order. He paints the broad portrait of a muscular and insolently insular people, untainted by the evils of corrupt civilisation. Mounting higher in the social scale, Bruno renders deserved homage to the graceful and unaffected manners of young English noblemen, from whom he singles Sidney out as the star of cultivated chivalry.[6] What he says about the well-born youth of England, shows that the flower of our gentlefolk delighted Southern observers by their mixture of simplicity and sweetness with good breeding and sound sense. For the ladies of England he cannot find words fair enough to extol the beauties of their persons and the purity of their affections. Elizabeth herself he calls a goddess, *diva*, using phrases which were afterwards recited in the terms of his indictment before the Inquisition. What pleased him most in England was the liberty of speech and thought he there enjoyed.[7] Society was so urbane, government was so unsuspicious, that a man could venture to call things by their proper names and speak his heart out without reserve. That Bruno's panegyric was not prompted by any wish to flatter national vanity, is proved by the hard truths he spoke about the grossness of the people, and by his sarcasms on Oxford pedants. He also ventured to condemn in no unmeasured terms some customs which surprised him in domestic intercourse. He drew, for instance, a really gruesome picture of the loving-cup, as it passed round the table, tasted by a mixed assemblage.[8]

A visit paid by Bruno to Oxford forms a curious episode in his English experiences. He found that university possessed by pedants and ignorant professors of the old learning. 'Men of choice,' he calls them, 'trailing their long velvet gowns, this one arrayed with two bright chains of gold around his neck, that one, good heavens! with such a

[5] The 'Cena delle Ceneri,' *Op. It.* vol. i. pp. 137-151.

[6] Signor Berti conjectures that Bruno may have met Sidney first at Milan. But Bruno informs us that he did not become acquainted with him till he came to London: 'Tra' quali è tanto conosciuto, per fama prima quando eravamo in Milano et in Francia, e poi per experienza or che siamo ne la sua patria' (*Op. It.* vol. i. p.145).

[7] Preface to 'Lo Spaccio della Bestia' (*Op. It.* vol. ii. p. 108).

[8] *Op. It.* vol. i. p. 150.

valuable hand—twelve rings upon two fingers, giving him the look of some rich jeweller.'[9] These excellent dons, blest in the possession of fat fellowships, felt no sympathy for an eccentric interloper of Bruno's stamp. They allowed him to lecture on the Soul and the Sphere. They even condescended to dispute with him. Yet they made Oxford so unpleasant a place of residence that after three months he returned to London. The treatment he experienced rankled in his memory. 'Look where you like at the present moment, you will find but doctors in grammar here; for in this happy realm there reigns a constellation of pedantic stubborn ignorance and presumption mixed with a rustic incivility that would disturb Job's patience. If you do not believe it, go to Oxford, and ask to hear what happened to the Nolan, when he disputed publicly with those doctors of theology in the presence of the Polish Prince Alasco.[10] Make them tell you how they answered to his syllogisms; how the pitiful professor, whom they put before them on that grave occasion as the Coryphæus of their university, bungled fifteen times with fifteen syllogisms, like a chicken in the stubble. Make them tell you with what rudeness and discourtesy that pig behaved; what patience and humanity he met from his opponent, who, in truth, proclaimed himself a Neapolitan, born and brought up beneath more genial heavens. Then learn after what fashion they brought his public lectures to an end, those on the Immortality of the Soul and those on the Quintuple Sphere.'[11] The Soul and the Sphere were Bruno's favourite themes. He handled both at this period of life with startling audacity. They had become for him the means of ventilating speculations on terrestrial movement, on the multiplicity of habitable worlds, on the principle of the universe, and on the infinite modes of psychical metamorphosis. Such topics were not calculated to endear him to people of importance on the banks of Isis. That he did not humour their prejudices, appears from a Latin epistle which he sent before him by way of introduction to the Vice-Chancellor.[12] It contains these pompous phrases: 'Philotheus Jordanus Brunus Nolanus magis laboratae theologiae doctor, purioris et innocuae sapientiae professor. In praecipuis Europae academiis notus, probatus et honorifice exceptus philosophus. Nullibi praeterquam apud barbaros et ignobiles peregrinus. Dormitantium animarum excubitor. Praesuntuosae et recalcitrantis ignorantiae domitor. Qui in actibus universis generalem philantropiam protestatur. Qui non magis Italum quam Britannum, marem quam foeminam, mitratum quam coronatum, togatum quam armatum, cucullatum hominem quam sine cucullo virum: sed illum cujus pacatior, civilior, fidelior et utilior est conversatio diligit.' Which may thus be Englished: 'Giordano Bruno of Nola, the God-loving, of the more highly wrought theology doctor, of the purer and harmless wisdom professor. In the

[9] *Ibid.* vol. i. p. 123.
[10] See Wood, *Ath. Oxon.* p. 300.
[11] *Op. It.* vol. i. p. 179.
[12] Printed in the *Explicatio triginta Sigillarum.*

chief universities of Europe known, approved, and honourably received as philosopher. Nowhere save among barbarians and the ignoble a stranger. The awakener of sleeping souls. The trampler upon presuming and recalcitrant ignorance. Who in all his acts proclaims a universal benevolence toward man. Who loveth not Italian more than Briton, male than female, mitred than crowned head, gowned than armed, frocked than frockless; but seeketh after him whose conversation is the more peaceful, more civil, more loyal, and more profitable.' This manifesto, in the style of a mountebank, must have sounded like a trumpet-blast to set the humdrum English doctors with sleepy brains and mouldy science on their guard against a man whom they naturally regarded as an Italian charlatan. What, indeed, was this more highly wrought theology, this purer wisdom? What call had this self-panegyrist to stir souls from comfortable slumbers? What right had he to style the knowledge of his brethren ignorance? Probably he was but some pestilent fellow, preaching unsound doctrine on the Trinity, like Peter Martyr Vermigli, who had been properly hissed out of Oxford a quarter of a century earlier. When Bruno arrived and lectured, their worst prognostications were fulfilled. Did he not maintain a theory of the universe which even that perilous speculator and political schemer, Francis Bacon, sneered at as nugatory?

In spite of academical opposition, Bruno enjoyed fair weather, halcyon months, in England. His description of the Ash Wednesday Supper at Fulke Greville's, shows that a niche had been carved out for him in London, where he occupied a pedestal of some importance. Those gentlemen of Elizabeth's Court did not certainly exaggerate the value of their Italian guest. In Italy, most of them had met with spirits of Bruno's stamp, whom they had not time or opportunity to prove. He was one among a hundred interesting foreigners; and his martyrdom had not as yet set the crown of glory or of shame upon his forehead. They probably accepted him as London society of the present day accepts a theosophist from Simla or Thibet. But his real home at this epoch, the only home, so far as I can see, that Bruno ever had, after he left his mother at the age of thirteen for a convent, was the house of Castelnau. The truest chords in the Italian's voice vibrate when he speaks of that sound Frenchman. To Mme. de Castelnau he alludes with respectful sincerity, paying her the moderate and well-weighed homage which, for a noble woman, is the finest praise. There is no rhetoric in the words he uses to express his sense of obligation to her kindness. They are delicate, inspired with a tact which makes us trust the writer's sense of fitness.[13] But Bruno indulges in softer phrases, drawn from the heart, and eminently characteristic of his predominant enthusiastic mood, when he comes to talk of the little girl, Marie, who brightened the home of the Castelnaus. 'What shall I say of their noble-natured daughter? She has gazed upon the sun barely one lustre and one year; but so far as language goes, I know not how

[13] *Op. It.* vol. i. p. 267.

to judge whether she springs from Italy or France or England! From her hand, touching the instruments of music, no man could reckon if she be of corporate or incorporeal substance. Her perfected goodness makes one marvel whether she be flown from heaven, or be a creature of this common earth. It is at least evident to every man that for the shaping of so fair a body the blood of both her parents has contributed, while for the tissue of her rare spirit the virtues of their heroic souls have been combined.'[14]

It was time to leave these excellent and hospitable friends. 'Forth from the tranquil to the trembling air' Bruno's unquiet impulse drove him. He returned to Paris at the end of 1585, disputed before the Sorbonne with some success of scandal, and then, disquieted by the disorders of the realm, set out for Germany. We find him at Marburg in the following year, ill-received by the university, but welcomed by the Prince. Thence we follow him to Mainz, and afterwards to Wittenberg, where he spent two years. Here he conceived a high opinion of the Germans. He foresaw that when they turned their attention from theology to science and pure speculation, great results might be expected from their solid intellectual capacity. He seems in fact to have taken a pretty accurate measure of the race as it has subsequently shown itself. Wittenberg he called the German Athens. Luther, he recognised as a hero of humanity, who, like himself, defied authority in the defence of truth. Yet he felt no sympathy for the German reformers. When asked by the Inquisitors at Venice what he thought about these men, he replied: 'I regard them as more ignorant than I am. I despise them and their doctrines. They do not deserve the name of theologians, but of pedants.' That this reply was sincere, is abundantly proved by passages in the least orthodox of Bruno's writings. It was the weakness of a philosopher's position at that moment that he derived no support from either of the camps into which Christendom was then divided. Catholics and Protestants of every shade regarded him with mistrust.

A change in the religious policy of Saxony, introduced after the death of the Elector Augustus, caused Bruno to leave Wittenberg for Prague in 1588. From Prague he passed to Helmstädt, where the Duke Heinrich Julius of Brunswick-Wolfenbüttel received him with distinction, and bestowed on him a purse of eighty dollars.[15] Here he conceived two of his most important works, the 'De Monade' and 'De Triplici Minimo,' both written in Latin hexameters.[16] Why he adopted this new form of exposition is not manifest. Possibly he was tired of dialogues, through which he had expressed his thought so freely in England. Possibly a German public would have been indifferent to

[14] *Loc. cit.* p. 267.

[15] It is a curious fact that the single copy of Campanella's poems on which Orelli based his edition of 1834, came from Wolfenbüttel.

[16] They were published at Frankfort, and dedicated to the friendly Prince of Wolfenbüttel.

Italian. Possibly he was emulous of his old masters, Parmenides and Lucretius.

At Helmstädt he came into collision with Boetius, the rector of the Evangelical church, who issued a sentence of excommunication against him. Like a new Odysseus, he set forth once again upon his voyage, and in the spring of 1590 anchored in Frankfort on the Main. A convent (that of the Carmelites) sheltered him in this city, where he lived on terms of intimacy with the printers Wechel and Fischer, and other men of learning. It would appear from evidence laid before the Venetian Inquisitors that the prior of the monastery judged him to be a man of genius and doctrine, devoid of definite religion, addicted to fantastic studies, and bent on the elaboration of a philosophy that should supersede existing creeds.[17] This was a not inaccurate portrait of Bruno as he then appeared to conservatives of commonplace capacity. Yet nothing occurred to irritate him in the shape of persecution or disturbance. Bruno worked in quiet at Frankfort, pouring forth thousands of metaphysical verses, some at least of which were committed to the press in three volumes published by the Wechels.

Between Frankfort and Italy literary communications were kept open through the medium of the great fair, which took place every year at Michaelmas.[18] Books formed one of the principal commodities, and the Italian bibliopoles travelled across the Alps to transact business on these important occasions. It happened by such means that a work of Bruno's, perhaps the 'De Monade,' found its way to Venice.[19] Exposed on the counter of Giambattista Ciotto, then plying the trade of bookseller in that city, this treatise met the eyes of a Venetian gentleman called Giovanni Mocenigo. He belonged to one of the most illustrious of the still surviving noble families in Venice. The long line of their palaces upon the Grand Canal has impressed the mind of every tourist. One of these houses, it may be remarked, was occupied by Lord Byron, who, had he known of Bruno's connexion with the Mocenighi, would undoubtedly have given to the world a poem or a drama on the fate of our philosopher. Giovanni Mocenigo was a man verging on middle life, superstitious, acknowledging the dominion of his priest, but alive in a furtive way to perilous ideas. Morally, he stands before us as a twofold traitor: a traitor to his Church, so long as he hoped to gain illicit power by magic arts; a traitor to his guest, so soon as he discovered that his soul's risk brought himself no profit.[20] He seems to have imagined that Bruno might teach him occult science, or direct him on a royal way to knowledge without strenuous study. Subse-

[17] Brittano's Deposition, Berti's *Vita di G. B.* p. 337.

[18] Sarpi mentions the return of Ciotto from this fair (*Lettere*, vol. i. p. 327).

[19] Ciotto, before the Inquisition, called the book *De Minimo Magno et Mensura.* It might therefore have been the *De Triplici Minimo et Mensura*, and not the *De Monade* (*Vita di G. B.* p. 334).

[20] Mocenigo told Ciotto: 'I wish first to see what I can get from him of those things which he promised me, so as not wholly to lose what I have given him, and afterwards I mean to surrender him to the censure of the Holy Office' (Berti, p. 335).

quent events proved that, though he had no solid culture, he was fascinated by the expectation of discovering some great secret. It was the vice of the age to confound science with sorcery, and Bruno had lent himself to this delusion by his whimsical style. Perhaps the booksellers, who then played a part scarcely less prominent than that of the barbers in diffusing gossip, inflamed Mocenigo's curiosity by painting the author of the puzzling volume in seductive colours. Anyhow, this man sent two letters, one through Ciotto, and one direct to Bruno, praying him to visit Venice, professing his desire for instruction, and offering him an honourable place of residence.

In an evil hour Bruno accepted this invitation. No doubt he longed to see Italy again after so many years of exile. Certainly he had the right to believe that he would find hospitality and a safe refuge in Venice. Had not a Venetian noble pledged his word for the former? Was not the latter a privilege which S. Mark extended to all suppliants? The Republic professed to shield even the outlaws of the Inquisition, if they claimed her jurisdiction. There was therefore no palpable imprudence in the step which Bruno now took. Yet he took it under circumstances which would have made a cautious man mistrustful. Of Mocenigo he knew merely nothing. But he did know that writs from the Holy Office had been out against himself in Italy for many years, during which he had spent his time in conversing with heretics and printing works of more than questionable orthodoxy.[21] Nothing proves the force of the vagrant's impulse which possessed Bruno, more than his light and ready consent to Giovanni Mocenigo's proposal.

He set off at once from Frankfort, leaving the MS. of one of his metaphysical poems in Wechel's hands to print, and found himself at the end of 1591 a guest of his unknown patron. I have already described what Mocenigo hoped to gain from Bruno—the arts of memory and invention, together with glimpses into occult science.[22] We know how little Bruno was able to satisfy an insatiable curiosity in such matters. One of his main weaknesses was a habit of boasting and exaggerating his own powers, which at first imposed upon a vulgar audience and then left them under the impression that he was a charlatan. The bookseller Ciotto learned from students who had conversed with him at Frankfort, that 'he professed an art of memory and other secrets in the sciences, but that all the persons who had dealt with him in such matters, had left him discontented.'[23] Another weakness in his character was extraordinary want of caution. Having lived about the world so long, and changed from town to town, supporting himself as he best could, he had acquired the custom of attracting notice by startling paradoxes. Nor does he seem to have cared to whom he made the

[21] Mere correspondence with heretics exposed an Italian to the Inquisition. Residence in heretical lands, except with episcopal license, was forbidden. The rules of the Index proscribed books in which the name of a heretic was cited with approval.

[22] Bruno speaks himself of 'arte della memoria et inventiva' (*op. cit.* p. 339). Ciotto mentions 'la memoria et altre scientie' (*ib.* p. 334).

[23] *Op. cit.* p. 335.

dangerous confidence of his esoteric beliefs. His public writings, presumably composed with a certain circumspection—since everybody knows the proverb, *litera scripta manet*—contain such perilous stuff that (when we consider what their author may have let fall in unguarded conversation) we are prepared to credit the charges brought against him by Mocenigo. For it must now be said that this man, 'induced by the obligation of his conscience and by order of his confessor,' denounced Bruno to the Inquisition on May 23, 1592.

When the two men, so entirely opposite in their natures, first came together, Bruno began to instruct his patron in the famous art of memory and mathematics. At the same time he discoursed freely and copiously, according to his wont, upon his own philosophy. Mocenigo took no interest in metaphysics, and was terrified by the audacity of Bruno's speculations. It enraged him to find how meagre was Bruno's vaunted method for acquiring and retaining knowledge without pains. In his secret heart he believed that the teacher whom he had maintained at a considerable cost was withholding the occult knowledge he so much coveted. Bruno, meanwhile, attended Andrea Morosini's receptions in the palace at S. Luca, and frequented those of Bernardo Secchini at the sign of the Golden Ship in the Merceria. He made friends with scholars and men of fashion; absented himself for weeks together at Padua; showed that he was tired of Mocenigo; and ended by rousing that man's suspicious jealousy. Mocenigo felt that he had been deceived by an impostor, who, instead of furnishing the wares for which he bargained, put him off with declamations on the nature of the universe. What was even more terrible, he became convinced that this charlatan was an obstinate heretic.

Whether Bruno perceived the gathering of the storm above his head, whether he was only wearied with the importunities of his host, or whether, as he told the Inquisitors, he wished to superintend the publication of some books at Frankfort, does not greatly signify. At any rate, he begged Mocenigo to excuse him from further attendance, since he meant to leave Venice. This happened on Thursday, May 21. Next day, Mocenigo sent his body-servant, together with five or six gondoliers, into Bruno's apartment, seized him, and had him locked up in a ground-floor room of the palace. At the same time he laid hands on all Bruno's effects, including the MS. of one important treatise 'On the Seven Liberal Arts,' which was about to be dedicated to Pope Clement VIII. This, together with other unpublished works, exists probably in the Vatican Archives, having been sent with the papers referring to Bruno's trial from Venice when he was transported to Rome. The following day, which was a Saturday, Mocenigo caused Bruno to be carried to one of those cellars (*magazzeni terreni*) which are used in Venice for storing wood, merchandise or implements belonging to gondolas. In the evening, a Captain of the Council of Ten removed him to the dungeons of the Inquisition. On the same day, May 23, Mocenigo lodged his denunciation with the Holy Office.

The heads of this accusation, extracted from the first report and from two subsequent additions made by the delator, amount to these: Though Bruno was adverse to religions altogether, he preferred the Catholic to any other; but he believed it to stand in need of thorough reform. The doctrines of the Trinity, the miraculous birth of Christ, and transubstantiation, were insults to the Divine Being. Christ had seduced the people by working apparent miracles. So also had the Apostles. To develop a new philosophy which should supersede religions, and to prove his superiority in knowledge over S. Thomas and all the theologians, was Bruno's cherished scheme. He did not believe in the punishment of sins; but held a doctrine of the transmigration of souls, and of the generation of the human soul from refuse. The world he thought to be eternal. He maintained that there were infinite worlds, all made by God, who wills to do what he can do, and therefore produces infinity. The religious orders of Catholicism defile the earth by evil life, hypocrisy, and avarice. All friars are only asses. Indulgence in carnal pleasures ought not to be reckoned sinful. The man confessed to having freely satisfied his passions to the utmost of his opportunities.

One being questioned before the Inquisitors, Mocenigo supported these charges. He added that when he had threatened Bruno with delation, Bruno replied, first, that he did not believe he would betray his confidence by making private conversation the groundwork of criminal charges; secondly, that the utmost the Inquisition could do, would be to inflict some penance and force him to resume the cowl. These, which are important assertions, bearing the mark of truth, throw light on his want of caution in dealing with Mocenigo, and explain the attitude he afterwards assumed before the Holy Office.

Mocenigo's accusations in the main yield evidences of sincerity. They are exactly what we should expect from the distortion of Bruno's doctrines by a mind incapable of comprehending them. In short, they are as veracious as the image of a face reflected on a spoon. Certain gross details (the charges, for example, of having called Christ a *tristo* who was deservedly hung, and of having sneered at the virginity of Mary) may possible have emanated from the delator's own imagination.[24] Bruno emphatically repudiated these; though some passages in his philosophical poems, published at Frankfort, contain the substance of their blasphemies. A man of Mocenigo's stamp probably thought that he was faithfully representing the heretic's views, while in reality he was drawing his own gross conclusions from sceptical utterances about the origins of Christianity which he obscurely understood. It does not seem incredible, however, that Bruno, who was never nice in his choice of language, and who certainly despised historical Christianity, let fall crude witticisms upon such and other points in Mocenigo's presence.

Bruno appeared before the Venetian Inquisition on May 29. His examination was continued at intervals from this date till July 30.

[24] They remind us of the blasphemies imputed to Christopher Marlowe.

His depositions consist for the most part of an autobiographical statement which he volunteered, and of a frank elucidation of his philosophical doctrines in their relation to orthodox belief. While reading the lengthy pages of his trial, we seem to overhear a man conversing confidentially with judges from whom he expected liberal sympathy. Over and over again, he relies for his defence upon the old distinction between philosophy and faith, claiming to have advocated views as a thinker which he does not hold as a Christian. 'In all my books I have used philosophical methods of definition according to the principles and light of nature, not taking chief regard of that which ought to be held in faith; and I believe they do not contain anything which can support the accusation that I have professedly impugned religion rather than that I have sought to exalt philosophy; though I may have expounded many impieties based upon my natural light.'[25] In another place he uses the antithesis, 'speaking like a Christian and according to theology' —'speaking after the manner of philosophy.'[26] The same antithesis is employed to justify his doctrine of metempsychosis: 'Speaking as a Catholic, souls do not pass from one body into another, but go to paradise or purgatory or hell; yet, following philosophical reasonings, I have argued that, the soul being inexistent without the body and inexistent in the body, it can be indifferently in one or in another body, and can pass from one into another, which, if it be not true, seems at any rate probable according to the opinion of Pythagoras.'[27] That he expected no severe punishment appears from the terms of his so-called recantation. 'I said that I wished to present myself before the feet of his Holiness with certain books which I approve, though I have published others which I do not now approve; whereby I meant to say that some works composed and published by me do not meet with my approbation, inasmuch as in these I have spoken and discussed too philosophically, in unseemly wise, not altogether as a good Christian ought; in particular I know that in some of these works I have taught and philosophically held things which ought to be attributed to the power, wisdom, and goodness of God according to the Christian faith, founding my doctrine in such matters on sense and reason, not upon faith.'[28] At the very end of his examination, he placed himself in the hands of his judges, 'confessing his errors with a willing mind,' acknowledging that he had 'erred and strayed from the Church,' begging for such castigation as shall not 'bring public dishonour on the sacred robe which he had worn,' and promising to 'show a noteworthy reform, and to recompense the scandal he had caused by edification at least equal in magnitude.'[29] These professions he made upon his knees, evincing clearly, as it seems to me, that at this epoch he was ready to rejoin the Dominican

[25] *Op. cit.* p. 352.
[26] *Ibid.* p. 355.
[27] *Ibid.* p. 362.
[28] *Ibid.* p. 349.
[29] *Ibid.* p. 384.

order, and that, as he affirmed to Mocenigo, he expected no worse punishment than this.

In attempting to estimate Bruno's recantation, we must remember that he felt no sympathy at all for heretics. When questioned about them, he was able to quote passages from his own works in which he called the Reformation a Deformation of religion.[30] Lutheran and Calvinist theologians were alike pedants in his eyes.[31] There is no doubt that Bruno meant what he said; and had he been compelled to choose one of the existing religions, he would have preferred Catholicism. He was, in fact, at a period of life when he wished to dedicate his time in quiet to metaphysical studies. He had matured his philosophy and brought it to a point at which he thought it could be presented as a peace-offering to the Supreme Pontiff. Conformity to ecclesiastical observances seemed no longer irksome to the world-experienced, wide-reaching mind of the man. Nor does he appear to have anticipated that his formal submission would not be readily accepted. He reckoned strangely, in this matter, without the murderous host into whose clutches he had fallen.

Searching interrogations touching other heads in the evidence against him, as blasphemous remarks on sacred persons, intercourse with heretics, abuse of the religious orders, dealings in magic arts, licentious principles of conduct, were answered by Bruno with a frank assurance, which proves his good conscience in essentials and his firm expectation of a favourable issue to the affair. Mocenigo had described him as *indemoniato*; and considering the manifest peril in which he now stood, there is something scarcely sane in the confidence he showed. For Mocenigo himself he reserved words of bitterest scorn and indignation. When questioned in the usual terms whether he had enemies at Venice, he replied: 'I know of none but Ser Giovanni Mocenigo and his train of servants. By him I have been grievously injured, more so than by living man, seeing he has murdered me in my life, my honour, and my property, having imprisoned me in his own house and stolen all my writings, books, and other effects. And this he did because he not only wished that I should teach him everything I know, but also wished to prevent my teaching it to anyone but him. He has continued to threaten me upon the points of life and honour, unless I should teach him everything I knew.'[32]

The scene closes over Bruno in the Venetian Inquisition on July 30, 1592. We do not behold him again till he enters the Minerva at Rome to receive his death-sentence on February 9 1600. What happened in the interval, is almost a blank. An exchange of letters took place between Rome and Venice concerning his extradition, and the Republic made some show of reluctance to part with a refugee within its jurisdiction. But this diplomatic affair was settled to the satisfaction of

[30] *Op. cit.* p. 364.
[31] *Ibid.* p. 363.
[32] *Ibid.* p. 378.

both parties, and Bruno disappeared into the dungeons of the Roman Inquisition in the month of January 1593.

Seven years of imprisonment was a long period.[33] We find it hard to understand why Bruno's prosecution occupied the Holy Office through this space of time. But conjectures on the subject are now useless. Equally futile is it to speculate whether Bruno offered to conform in life and doctrine to the Church at Rome as he had done at Venice. The temptation to do so must have been great. Most probably he begged for grace, but grace was not accorded on his own terms; and he chose death rather than dishonour and a lie in the last resort, or rather than life long incarceration. It is also singular that but few contemporaries mention the fact of his condemnation and execution. Rome was crowded in the jubilee year of 1600. Bruno was burned in open daylight on the Campo di Fiora. Yet the only eye-witness who records the event is Gaspar Schoppe, or Scioppius, who wrote a letter on the subject to his friend Rittershausen. Kepler, eight years afterwards, informed his correspondent Breugger that Bruno had been really burned: 'He bore his agonising death with fortitude, abiding by the asseveration that all religions are vain, and that God identifies himself with the world, circumference and centre.' Kepler, it may be observed, conceived a high opinion of Bruno's speculations, and pointed him out to Galileo as the man who had divined the infinity of solar systems in their correlation to one infinite order of the universe.[34]

Scioppius was a German humanist of the elder Italianated type, an elegant Latin stylist, who commented indifferently on the 'Priapeia' and the Stoic philosophy. He abjured Protestantism, and, like Muretus, sold his pen to Rome. The Jesuits, in his pompous panegyric, were first saluted as 'the prætorian cohort of the camp of God.' Afterwards, when he quarrelled with their Order, he showered invectives on them in the manner of a Poggio or Filelfo. The literary infamies of the fifteenth century reappeared in his polemical attacks on Protestants, and in his satires upon Scaliger. Yet he was a man of versatile talents and considerable erudition. It must be mentioned in his honour that he visited Campanella in his prison, and exerted himself for his liberation. Campanella dedicated his 'Atheismus Triumphatus' to Scioppius,

[33] These years were not all spent at Rome. From the Records of the Inquisition, it appears that he arrived in Rome on February 27, 1598, and that his trial in form began in February 1599. The Pope ratified his sentence of death on January 20, 1600; this was publicly promulgated on February 8, and carried into effect on the subsequent 17th. Where Bruno was imprisoned between January 1593, and February 1598, is not known.

[34] Doubts have recently been raised as to whether Bruno was really burned. But these are finally disposed of by a succinct and convincing exposition of the evidence by Mr. R. C. Christie, in *Macmillan's Magazine*, October 1885. In addition to Schoppe and Kepler, we have the reference to Bruno's burning published by Mersenne in 1624; but what is far more important, the *Aviso di Roma* for February 19, 1600, records this event as having occurred upon the preceding Thursday. To Signor Berti's two works, *Documenti intorno a G. Bruno* (Roma, 1880), and *Copernico e le vicende*, &c. (Roma, 1876), we owe most of the material which has been lucidly sifted by Mr. R. C. Christie.

calling him 'the dawn-star of our age.' Schoppe was also the first credible authority to warn Sarpi of the imminent peril he ran from Roman hired assassins, as I shall relate in my chapter upon Sarpi's life. This man's letter to his friend is the single trustworthy document which we possess regarding the last hours of Bruno. Its inaccuracies on minor points may be held to corroborate his testimony.

Sciopphius refers to Bruno's early heresies on transubstantiation and the virginity of Mary. He alludes to the 'Spaccio della Bestia Trionfante,' as though it had been a libel on the Pope.[35] He then enumerates Bruno's heterodox opinions, which had been recited in the public condemnation pronounced on the heresiarch. 'Horrible and most utterly absurd are the views he entertained, as, for example, that there are innumerable worlds; that the soul migrates from body to body, yea into another world, and that one soul can inform two bodies; that magic is good and lawful; that the Holy Spirit is nothing but the Soul of the World, which Moses meant when he wrote that it brooded on the waters; that the world has existed from eternity; that Moses wrought his miracles by magic, being more versed therein than the Egyptians, and that he composed his own laws; that the Holy Scriptures are a dream, and that the devils will be saved; that only the Jews descend from Adam and Eve, the rest of men from that pair whom God created earlier; that Christ is not God, but that he was an eminent magician who deluded mankind, and was therefore rightly hanged, not crucified; that the prophets and Apostles were men of naught, magicians, and, for the most part, hanged: in short, without detailing all the monstrosities in which his books abound, and which he maintained in conversation, it may be summed up in one word that he defended every error that has been advanced by pagan philosophers or by heretics of earlier and present times.' Accepting this list as tolerably faithful to the terms of Bruno's sentence, heard by Sciopphius in the hall of the Minerva, we can see how Mocenigo's accusation had been verified by reference to his published works. The 'De Monade' and 'De Triplici' contain enough heterodoxy to substantiate each point.

On February 9, Bruno was brought before the Holy Office at S. Maria sopra Minerva. In the presence of assembled Cardinals, theologians, and civil magistrates, his heresies were first recited. Then he was excommunicated, and degraded from his priestly and monastic offices. Lastly, he was handed over to the secular arm, 'to be punished with all clemency and without effusion of blood.' This meant in plain language to be burned alive. Thereupon Bruno uttered the memorable and monumental words: 'Peradventure ye pronounce this sentence on me with a greater fear than I receive it.' They were the last words he spoke in public. He was removed to the prisons of the State, where he remained eight days, in order that he might have time to repent. But he continued obdurate. Being an apostate priest and a relapsed

[35] 'Londinum profectus, libellum istic edit de Bestia triumphante, b. e. de Papa, quem vestri honoris causa bestiam appellare solent.'

heretic, he could hope for no remission of his sentence. Therefore, on February 17, he marched to a certain and horrible death. The stake was built up on the Campo di Fiora. Just before the wood was set on fire, they offered him the crucifix.[36] He turned his face away from it in stern disdain. It was not Christ but his own soul, wherein he believed the Deity resided, that sustained Bruno at the supreme moment. No cry, no groan, escaped his lips. Thus, as Scioppius affectedly remarked, 'he perished miserably in flames, and went to report in those other worlds of his imagination, how blasphemous and impious men are handled by the Romans.'

Whatever we may think of the good taste of Bruno's sarcasms upon the faith in which he had been bred—and it is certain that he never rightly apprehended Christianity in its essence—there is no doubt he died a valiant martyr to the truth as he conceived it. 'His death like that of Paleario, Carnesecchi, and so many more, no less than countless exiles suffered for religious causes, are a proof that in Italy men had begun to recognise their obligation to a faith, the duty of obedience to a thought: an immense progress, not sufficiently appreciated even by modern historians.'[37] Bruno was a hero in the battle for the freedom of the conscience, for the right of man to think and speak in liberty.[38]

Just five years before this memorable 17th of February, Tasso had passed quietly away in S. Onofrio. 'How dissimilar in genius and fortune,' exclaims Berti, 'were these men, though born under the same skies, though in childhood they breathed the same air! Tasso a Christian and poet of the cross; Bruno hostile to all religious symbols. The one, tired and disillusioned of the world, ends his days in the repose of the convent; the other sets out from the convent to expire upon the scaffold, turning his eyes away from the crucifix.'[39] And yet how much alike in some important circumstances of their lives were these two men! Both wanderers, possessed by that spirit of vagrancy which is the outward expression of an inner restlessness. The unfrocked friar, the courtier out of service, had no home in Italy. Both were pursued by an oestrum corresponding to the intellectual perturbations which closed the sixteenth century, so different from the idyllic calm that rested upon Ariosto and the artists of its opening years. Sufficient justice has not yet been done in history to the Italian wanderers and exiles of this period, men who carried the spirit of the Renaissance

[36] We may remember that while a novice at Naples, he first got into trouble by keeping the crucifix as the only religious symbol which he respected, when he parted with images of saints.

[37] These pregnant words are in Berti's *Vita di G. B.* p. 299.

[38] He well deserves this name, in spite of his recantation at Venice; for it seems incredible that he could not by concessions have purchased life. As Breugger wrote with brutal crudity to Kepler: 'What profit did he gain by enduring such torments? If there were no God to punish crimes, as he believed, could he not have pretended anything to save his life?' We may add that the alternative to death for a relapsed apostate was perpetual incarceration; and seven years of prison may well have made Bruno prefer death with honour.

[39] *Op. cit.* p. 70.

abroad, after the Renaissance had ended in Italy, to the extremest verges of the civilised world. An enumeration of their names, an examination of their services to modern thought, would show how puissant was the intellectual influence of Italy in that period of her political decadence.[40]

Bruno has to be treated from two distinct but interdependent points of view—in his relation to contemporary thought and the Renaissance; and in his relation to the evolution of modern philosophy—as the critic of mediæval speculation and the champion of sixteenth-century enthusiasm; and also as the precursor of Descartes, Spinoza, Leibnitz, Schelling, Hegel, Darwin.

From the former of these two points of view Bruno appears before us as the man who most vitally and comprehensively grasped the leading tendencies of his age in their intellectual essence. He left behind him the mediæval conception of an extra-mundane God, creating a finite world, of which this globe is the centre, and the principal episode in the history of which is a series of events from the Fall, through the Incarnation and Crucifixion, to the Last Judgment.[41] He substituted the conception of an ever-living, ever-acting, ever-self-effectuating God, immanent in an infinite universe, to the contemplation of whose attributes the mind of man ascends by study of Nature and interrogation of his conscience. The rehabilitation of the physical world and of humanity as part of its order, which the Renaissance had already indirectly effected through the medium of arts and literature and modes of life, found in Bruno an impassioned metaphysical supporter. He divinised Nature, not by degrading the Deity to matter, but by lifting matter to participation in the divine existence. The Renaissance had proclaimed the dignity of man considered as a mundane creature, and not in his relation to a hypothetical other-world. It abundantly manifested the beauty and the joy afforded by existence on this planet, and laughingly discarded past theological determinations to the contrary of its new Gospel. Bruno undertook the systematisation of Renaissance intuitions; declared the divine reality of Nature and of man; demonstrated that we cannot speculate God, cannot think ourselves, cannot envisage the universe, except under the form of one living, infinite, eternal, divinely sustained and soul-penetrated complex. He repudiated authority of every sort, refusing to acknowledge the decrees of the Church, freely criticising past philosophers, availing himself of all that seemed to him substantial in their speculations, but appealing in the last resort to that inner witness, that light of reason, which corresponds in the mental order to conscience in the moral. As he deified Nature, so he emancipated man as forming with Nature an integral part of the Supreme Being. He was led upon this path to combat Aristotle and to

[40] Both Berti and Quinet have made similar remarks, which, indeed, force themselves upon a student of the sixteenth century.

[41] This theological conception of history inspired the sacred drama of the Middle Ages, known to us as Cyclical Miracle Plays.

satirise Christian beliefs, with a subtlety of scholastic argumentation and an acerbity of rhetoric that now pass for antiquated. Much that is obsolete in his writings must be referred to the polemical necessities of an age enthralled by peripatetic conceptions, and saturated with the ecclesiastical divinity of the schoolmen. These forces of the philosophy he sought to supersede, had to be attacked with their own weapons, and by methods adapted to the spirit of his age. Simi ar judgment may be passed upon his championship of the Copernican system. That system was the pivot of his metaphysic, the revelation to which he owed his own conception of the universe. His strenuous and ingenious endeavours to prove its veracity, his elaborate and often-repeated refutations of the Ptolemaic theory, appear to modern minds superfluous. But we must remember what a deeply penetrating, widely working revolution Copernicus effected in cosmology, how he dislocated the whole fabric upon which Catholic theology rested, how new and unintelligible his doctrine then seemed, and what vast horizons he opened for speculation on the destinies of man. Bruno was the first fully to grasp the importance of the Copernican hypothesis, to perceive its issues, and to adapt it to the formation of a new ontology. Copernicus, though he proclaimed the central position of the sun in our system, had not ventured to maintain the infinity of the universe. For him, as for the elder physicists, there remained a sphere of fixed stars enclosing the world perceived by our senses within walls of crystal. Bruno broke those walls, and boldly asserted the now recognised existence of numberless worlds in space illimitable. His originality lies in the clear and comprehensive notion he formed of the Copernican discovery, and in his application of its corollaries to the Renaissance apocalypse of deified nature and emancipated man. The deductions he drew were so manifold and so acute that they enabled him to forecast the course which human thought has followed in all provinces of speculation.

This leads us to consider how Bruno is related to modern science and philosophy. The main point seems to be that he obtained a vivid mental picture (*Vorstellung*) of the physical universe, differing but little in essentials from that which has now come to be generally accepted. In reasoning from this concept as a starting-point, he formed opinions upon problems of theology, ontology, biology, and psychology, which placed him out of harmony with mediæval thought, and in agreement with the thought of our own time. Why this was so can easily be explained. Bruno, first of all philosophers, adapted science, in the modern sense of that term, to metaphysic. He was the first to perceive that a revolution in our conception of the material universe, so momentous as that effected by Copernicus, necessitated a new theology and a new philosophical method. Man had ceased to be the centre of all things; this globe was no longer 'the hub of the universe,' but a small speck floating on infinity. The Christian scheme of the Fall and the Redemption, if not absolutely incompatible with the new cosmology, was rendered by it less conceivable in any literal sense. Some of the main points on which the early Christians based their faith, and which had hardened into dogmas through the course of centuries—such, for instance, as the Ascension and the Second Advent—ceased to have their old significance. In a world where there was neither up nor down, the translation of a corporeal Deity to some place above the clouds, whence he would descend to judge men at the last day, had only a grotesque or a symbolic meaning; whereas to the first disciples, imbued with theories of a fixed celestial sphere, it presented a solemn and apparently well-founded expectation. The fundamental doctrine of the Incarnation, in like manner, lost intelligibility and value, when God had to be thought no longer as the Creator of a finite cosmos, but as a Being commensurate with infinity. It was clear to a mind so acute as Bruno's that the dogmas of the Church were correlated to a view of the world which had been superseded; and he drew the logical inference that they were at bottom but poetical and popular adumbrations of the Deity in terms concordant with erroneous physical notions. Aristotle and Ptolemy, the masters of philosophy and cosmography based upon a theory of the universe as finite and circumscribed within fixed limits, lent admirable aid to the theological constructions of the Middle Ages. The Church, adopting their science, gave metaphysical and logical consistency to those earlier poetical and popular conceptions of the religious sense. The *naïf* hopes and romantic mythologies of the first Christians stiffened into syllogisms and ossified in the huge fabric of the 'Summa.' But Aristotle and Ptolemy were now dethroned. Bruno, in a far truer sense than Democritus before him,

extra
Processit longe flammantia moenia mundi.

Bolder even than Copernicus, and nearer in his intuition to the truth, he denied that the universe had 'flaming walls' or any walls at all. That 'immaginata circonferenza,' 'quella margine immaginata del cielo,' on which antique science and Christian theology alike reposed, was the object of his ceaseless satire, his oft-repeated polemic. What, then, rendered Bruno the precursor of modern thought in its various manifestations, was that he grasped the fundamental truth upon which modern science rests, and foresaw the conclusions which must be drawn from it. He speculated boldly, incoherently, vehemently; but he speculated with a clear conception of the universe, as we still apprehend it. Through the course of three centuries we have been engaged in verifying the guesses, deepening, broadening and solidifying the hypotheses, which Bruno's extension of the Copernican theory, and his application of it to pure thought, suggested to his penetrating and audacious intellect.

Bruno was convinced that religion in its higher essence would not suffer from the new philosophy. Larger horizons extended before the human intellect. The soul expanded in more exhilarating regions than the old theologies had offered. The sense of the Divine in Nature, instead of dwindling down to atheism, received fresh stimulus from the immeasurable prospect of an infinite and living universe. Bruno, even more than Spinoza, was a God-intoxicated man. The inebriation of the Renaissance, inspired by golden visions of truth and knowledge close within man's grasp, inflamed with joy at escaping from outworn wearying formulæ into what appeared to be the simple intuition of an everlasting verity, pulses through all his utterances. He has the same cherubic confidence in the renascent age, that charms us in the work of Rabelais. The slow, painful, often thwarted, ever more dubious elaboration of modern metaphysic in *rapport* with modern science—that process which, after completing the cycle of all knowledge and sounding the fathomless depth of all ignorance, has left us in grave disillusionment and sturdy patience—swam before Bruno in a rapturous vision. The Inquisition and the stake put an end abruptly to his dream. But the dream was so golden, so divine, that it was worth the pangs of martyrdom. Can we say the same for Hegel's system, or for Schopenhauer's, or for the encyclopædic ingenuity of Herbert Spencer?

Bruno imagined the universe as infinite space, filled with ether, in which an infinite number of worlds, or solar systems resembling our own, composed of similar materials and inhabited by countless living creatures, move with freedom. The whole of this infinite and complex cosmos he conceived to be animated by a single principle of thought and life. This indwelling force, or God, he described in Platonic phraseology sometimes as the Anima Mundi, sometimes as the Artificer, who by working from within moulds infinite substance into an infinity of finite modes. Though we are compelled to think of the world under the two categories of spirit and matter, these apparently contradictory constituents are for ever reconciled and harmonised in the divine existence, whereof illimitable activity, illimitable volition, and illimitable potentiality are correlated and reciprocally necessary terms. In Aristotelian language, Bruno assumed infinite form and infinite matter as moments of an eternal process, by which the infinite unity manifests itself in concrete reality. This being the case, it follows that nothing exists which has not life, and is not part of God. The universe itself is one immeasurable animal, or animated Being. The solar systems are huge animals; the globes are lesser animals; and so forth down to the monad of molecular cohesion. As the universe is infinite and eternal, motion, place, and time do not qualify it; these are terms applicable only to the finite parts of which it is composed. For the same reason nothing in the universe can perish. What we call birth and death, generation and dissolution, is only the passage of the infinite and homogeneous entity through successive phases of finite and differentiated existence; this continuous process of exchange and transformation being stimulated and sustained by attraction and repulsion, properties of the indwelling divine soul aiming at self-realisation.

Having formed this conception, Bruno supported it by metaphysical demonstration, and deduced conclusions bearing on psychology, religion, ethics. Much of his polemic was directed against the deeply rooted notion of a finite world derived from Aristotle. Much was devoted to the proof of the Copernican discovery. Orthodox theology was indirectly combated or plausibly caressed. There are consequently many pages in his dialogues which do not interest a modern reader, seeing that we have outlived the conditions of thought that rendered them important. In the process of his argument, he established the theory of a philosophical belief, a religion of religions, or 'religione della mente,' as he phrased it, prior to and comprehensive of all historical creeds. He speculated, as probabilities, the transmigration of souls, and the interchangeability of types in living creatures. He further postulated a concordance between the order of thought and the order of existence in the universe, and inclined to the doctrine of necessity in morals. Bruno thus obtained *per saltum* a prospect over the whole domain of knowledge subsequently traversed by rationalism in metaphysics, theology, and ethics. In the course of these demonstrations and deductions he anticipated Descartes' position of the identity of mind and being. He supplied Spinoza with the substance of his reasoned pantheism; Leibnitz with his theory of monadism and pre-established harmony. He laid down Hegel's doctrine of contraries, and perceived that thought was a dialectic process. The modern theory of evolution was enunciated by him in pretty plain terms. He had grasped the physical law of the conservation of energy. He solved the problem of evil by defining it to be a relative condition of imperfect development. He denied that Paradise or a Golden Age is possible for man, or that, if possible, it can be considered higher in the moral scale than organic struggle toward completion by reconciliation of opposites through pain and labour. He sketched in outline the comparative study of religions, which is now beginning to be recognised as the proper basis for theology. Finally, he had a firm and vital hold upon that supreme speculation of the universe, considered no longer as the battleground of dual principles, or as the finite fabric of an almighty designer, but as the self-effectuation of an infinite unity, appearing to our intelligence as spirit and matter—that speculation which in one shape or another controls the course of modern thought.[42]

It must not be supposed that Bruno apprehended these points with distinctness, or that he expressed them precisely in the forms with which we are familiar. The hackneyed metaphor of a Pisgah view across the promised land applies to him with singular propriety. Moreover, as an acute critic has remarked, things old and new are so curi-

[42] It was my intention to support the statements in this paragraph by translating the passages which seem to me to justify them; and I had gone so far as to make English versions of some twenty pages in length, when I found that this material would overweight my book. A study of Bruno as the great precursor of modern thought in its more poetical and widely synthetic speculation must be left for a separate essay. Here I may remark that the most faithful and pithily condensed abstract of Bruno's philosophy is contained in Goethe's poem *Proömium zu Gott und Welt*. Yet this poem expresses Goethe's thought, and it is doubtful whether Goethe had studied Bruno except in the work of his disciple Spinoza.

ously blended in his writings that what at first sight appears modern, is often found upon reflection to be antique, and what is couched in obsolete scholastic terminology, turns out upon analysis to contain the germs of advanced theories.[43] The peculiar forms adopted for the exposition of his thoughts contribute to the difficulty of obtaining a methodical view of Bruno's philosophy. It has, therefore, been disputed whether he was a pantheist or an atheist, a materialist or a spiritualist, a mystic or an agnostic. No one would have contended more earnestly than Bruno himself, that the sage can hold each and all of these apparent contradictions together, with the exception of atheism; which last is a simple impossibility.

The fragmentary and impassioned exposition which Bruno gave to his opinions in a series of Italian dialogues and Latin poems will not discourage those of his admirers who estimate the conspicuous failure made by all elaborate system-builders from Aristotle to Hegel. To fathom the mystery of the world, and to express that mystery in terms of logic, is clearly beyond the faculty of man. Philosophies that aim at universe-embracing, God-explaining, nature-elucidating, man-illuminating comprehensiveness, have justly, therefore, become objects of suspicion. The utmost that man can do, placed as he is at obvious disadvantages for obtaining a complete survey of the whole, is to whet his intelligence upon confessedly insoluble problems, to extend the sphere of his practical experience, to improve his dominion over matter, to study the elevation of his moral nature, and to encourage himself for positive achievements by the indulgence in those glorious dreams from which regenerative creeds and inspiring philosophies have sprung—

> Still climbing after knowledge infinite,
> And ever moving as the restless spheres.

Faith and poetry are the highest regions in which his spirit can profitably move. The study of government, law, and social ethics, the analysis of physical conditions to which he is subject, and over which he has an undefined, though limited, control, form the practical sphere of his intelligence. Bruno traversed these regions; and, forasmuch as the outcome of his exploration was no system, but a congeries of poetic visions, shrewd guesses, profound intuitions, and passionate enthusiasms, bound together and sustained by a burning sense of the Divine unity in nature and in man, we may be permitted to regard him as more fortunate than those cloud-castle-builders whose classifications of absolute existences are successively proved by the advance of relative knowledge to be but catalogues of some few objects apprehended by the vision of each partially instructed age. We have, indeed, reason to marvel how many of Bruno's intuitions have formed the stuff of later more elaborated systems, and still remain the best which these contain. We have reason to wonder how many of his divinations have worked

[43] Spaventa in his *Saggi di Critica.*

themselves into the common fund of modern beliefs, and have become philosophical truisms.

It is probable that if Bruno's career had not been cut short by the dungeon and the stake at the comparatively early age of fifty-two, he might have produced some final work in which his theories would have assumed a formal shape. It is possible that the Vatican even now contains the first sketch for such a studied exposition in the treatise on the Seven Arts, which Giovanni Mocenigo handed over to the Inquisition, and which the philosopher intended to dedicate to Clement VIII. But the loss of this elaborated system is hardly to be regretted, except for the clearer light it must have thrown upon the workings of the most illuminated intellect in the sixteenth century. We know that it could not have revealed to us the secret of things.

Bruno cast his thoughts in two moulds: the dialogue, and Latin hexameters. He was attracted to the latter by his early study of Parmenides and Lucretius. The former seems to have been natural to the man. We must not forget that he was a Neapolitan, accustomed from childhood to the farces of his native land, vividly alive to the comic aspects of existence, and joyously appreciative of reality. His first known composition was a comedy, 'Il Candelajo;' and something of the drama can be traced in all those Italian compositions which distinguish the period of his activity as an author in London. Lucian rather than Plato or Cicero determined the form of his dialogue. An element of the burlesque distinguishes his method of approaching religious and moral problems in the 'Spaccio della Bestia,' and the 'Cavallo Pegaseo.' And though he exchanged the manner of his model for more serious exposition in the trio of metaphysical dialogues, named 'La Cena delle Ceneri,' 'Della Causa,' and 'Dell' Infinito Universo,' yet the irresistible tendency to dramatic satire emerges even there in the description of England and in the characters of the indispensable pedant-buffoon. His dialogue on the 'Eroici Furori' is sustained at a high pitch of aspiring fervour. Mystical in its attempt to adumbrate the soul's thirst for truth and beauty, it adopts the method of a running commentary upon poems, in the manner of a discursive and fantastic 'Vita Nuova.' In his Italian style, Bruno owed much to the fashion set by Aretino. The study of Aretino's comedies is apparent in 'Il Candelajo.' The stringing together of words and ideas in triplets, balanced by a second set of words and ideas in antithetical triplets—this trick of rhetoric, which wearies a modern reader of his prose, seems to have been copied straight from Aretino. The coinage of fantastic titles, of which 'Lo Spaccio della Bestia Trionfante' contributed in some appreciable degree to Bruno's martyrdom, should be ascribed to the same influence. The source of these literary affectations was a bad one. Aretino, Doni, and such folk were no fit masters for Giordano Bruno even in so slight a matter as artistic form. Yet, in this respect, he shared a corrupt taste which was common to his generation, and proved how fully he represented the age in which he lived. It is not improbable that the few contemporary readers of his works, especially in euphuistic England, admired the gewgaws he so plentifully scattered and rendered so brilliant by the coruscations of his wit. When, however, the real divine oestrum descends upon him, he discards those follies. Then his language, like his thought, is all his own: sublime, impassioned, burning, turbid; instinct with a deep volcanic fire of genuine enthusiasm. The thought is simple; the diction direct; the attitude of mind and the turn of expression are singularly living, surprisingly modern. We hear the man speak, as he spoke at Fulke Greville's supper-party, as he spoke at Oxford, as he spoke before the Sorbonne, as he might be speaking now. There is no air of literary effort, no tincture of antiquated style, in these masculine utterances.

CHAPTER X

FRA PAOLO SARPI

Sarpi's Position in the History of Venice—Parents and Boyhood—Entrance into the Order of the Servites—His Personal Qualities—Achievements as a Scholar and Man of Science—His Life among the Servites—In Bad Odour at Rome—Paul V. places Venice under Interdict—Sarpi elected Theologian and Counsellor of the Republic—His Polemical Writings—Views on Church and State—The Interdict Removed—Roman Vengeance—Sarpi attacked by Bravi—His Wounds, Illness, Recovery—Subsequent History of the Assassins—Further Attempts on Sarpi's Life—Sarpi's Political and Historical Works—History of the Council of Trent—Sarpi's Attitude towards Protestantism—His judgment of the Jesuits—Sarpi's Death—The Christian Stoic.

FRA PAOLO was the son of Francesco Sarpi and Isabella Morelli, Venetians of the humbler middle class. He was born in 1552, christened Pietro, and nicknamed Pierino because of his diminutive stature. On entering the Order of the Servites he adopted the religious name of Paolo, which he subsequently rendered famous throughout Europe. Since he died in 1623, Sarpi's life coincided with a period of supreme interest and manifold vicissitudes in the decline of Venice. After the battle of Lepanto in 1571, he saw the nobles of S. Mark welcome their victorious admiral Sebastiano Veniero, and confer on him the honours of the Dogeship. In 1606, he aided the Republic to withstand the thunders of the Vatican and defy the excommunication of a Pope. Eight years later he attended at those councils of state which unmasked the conspiracy, known as Bedmar's, to destroy Venice. In his early manhood Cyprus had been wrested from the hands of S. Mark; and inasmuch as the Venetians alone sustained the cause of Christian civilisation against Turk and pirate in the Eastern seas, he was able before his death to anticipate the ruin which the war of Candia subsequently brought upon his country. During the last eighteen years of his existence Sarpi was the intellect of the Republic; the man of will and mind who gave voice and vigour to her policy of independence; the statesman who most clearly penetrated the conditions of her strength and weakness. This friar incarnated the Venetian spirit at a moment when, upon the verge of decadence, it had attained self-consciousness; and so instinctively devoted are Venetians to their State that in his lifetime he was recognised by them as hero, and after his death venerated as saint.

No sooner had the dispute with Paul V. been compromised, than Sarpi noticed how the aristocracy of Venice yielded themselves to sloth and political indifference. The religious obsequiousness to Rome and the 'peace or rather cowardice of slaves,' which were gradually immersing Italy in mental torpor and luxurious idleness, invaded this last stronghold of freedom. Though Sarpi's Christian Stoicism and practical sagacity saved him from playing the then futile part of public agitator, his private correspondence shows how low his hope had sunk for Italy. Nothing but a general war could free her from the yoke of arrogant Rome and foreign despotism. Meanwhile the Papal Court, Spain, and the House of Austria, having everything to lose by contest, preserved the peace of Italy at any cost. Princes whose petty thrones depended on Spanish and Papal goodwill, dreaded to disturb the equilibrium of servitude; the population, dulled by superstition, emasculated by Jesuitical corruption and intimidated by Church tyranny, slumbered in the gross mud-honey of slavish pleasures. From his cell in the convent of the Servites Sarpi swept the whole political horizon, eagerly anticipating some dawn-star of deliverance. At one time his eyes rested on the Duke of Savoy; but that unquiet spirit failed to steer his course clear between Spanish and French interests, Roman jealousies, and the ill-concealed hostilities of Italian potentates. At another time, like all lovers of freedom throughout Europe, he looked with confidence to Henri IV. But a fanatic's dagger, sharpened by the Jesuits, cut short the monarch's life and gave up France to the government of astute Florentine adventurers. Germany was too distracted by internal dissensions, Holland too distant and preoccupied with her own struggle for existence, to offer immediate aid. It was in vain that Sarpi told his foreign correspondents that the war of liberty in Europe must be carried into the stronghold of absolutism. To secure a victory over the triple forces of Spain, the Papal Court, and Jesuitry, Rome had to be attacked in Italy. His reasoning was correct. But peoples fighting for freedom on their native soil could not risk an adventure which only some central power of the first magnitude like France might have conducted with fair prospect of success. In the meantime what Sarpi called the Diacatholicon, that absolutist alliance of Rome, Spain, and Austria, supported by the Inquisition and the Jesuits, accepted by the States of Italy, and firmly rooted in some parts of Germany, invaded even those provinces where the traditions of independence still survived. After 1610 the Jesuits obtained possession of France; and though they did not effect their re-entrance into Venice, the ruling classes of the Republic allowed themselves to be drugged by the prevalent narcotic. Venice, too, was fighting for her life in the Adriatic and the Levant, while her nobles became daily more supine in aristocratic leisure, more papalising in their private sympathies. Thus the last years of Sarpi's life were overclouded by a deep discouragement, which did not, indeed, extinguish his trust in the Divine Providence or his certain belief that the right would ultimately prevail, but which adds a tragic interest to the old age of this champion of political and moral liberty fallen on evil days.

I have thought it well to preface what I have to say about Sarpi with this forecast of his final attitude. As the Italian who most clearly comprehended the full consequences of the Catholic Revival, and who practically resisted what was evil for his nation in that reactionary movement, he demands a prominent place in this book. On his claims to scientific discoveries and his special service rendered to the Venetian Republic it will suffice to touch but lightly.

Sarpi's father was short of stature, brown-complexioned, choleric and restless. His mother was tall, pale, lymphatic, devoted to religious exercises and austerities. The son of their ill-assorted wedlock inherited something of both temperaments. In his face and eyes he resembled his mother; and he derived from her the piety which marked his course through life. His short, spare person, his vivid, ever-active intellect testified to the paternal impress. This blending of two diverse strains produced in him a singular tenacity of fibre. Man's tenement of clay has rarely lodged a spirit so passionless, so fine, so nearly disembodied. Of extreme physical tenuity, but gifted with inexhaustible mental energy, indefatigable in study, limitless in capacity for acquiring and retaining knowledge, he accentuated the type which nature gave him by the sustained habits of a lifetime. In diet he abstained from flesh and abhorred wine. His habitual weaknesses were those of one who subdues the body to mental government. As costive as Scaliger,[1] Sarpi suffered from hepatic hemorrhage, retention of urine, prolapsus recti, and hemorrhoids. Intermittent fevers reduced his strength, but rarely interfered with his activity. He refused to treat himself as an invalid, never altered his course of life for any illness, and went about his daily avocations when men of laxer tissue would have taken to their bed. His indifference to danger was that of the Stoic or the Mussulman. During a period of fifteen years he knew that restless foes were continually lying in wait to compass his death by poison or the dagger. Yet he could hardly be persuaded to use the most ordinary precautions. 'I am resolved,' he wrote, in 1609, 'to give no thought whatever to these wretchednesses. He who thinks too much of living knows not how to live well. One is bound to die once; to be curious about the day or place or manner of dying is unprofitable. Whatsoever is God's will is good.'[2] As fear had no hold upon his nature, so was he wholly free from the dominion of the senses. A woman's name, if we except that of the Queen of France, is, I think, not once mentioned in his correspondence. Even natural affections seem to have been obliterated; for he records nothing of his mother or his father or a sister who survived their deaths. One suit of clothes sufficed him; and his cell was furnished with three hour-glasses, a picture of Christ in the Garden, and a crucifix raised above a human skull. His physical sensitiveness, developed by austerity of life, was of the highest acuteness. Sight, touch, and taste

[1] We may remind our readers of Henri IV's parting words to Joseph Scaliger: 'Est-il vrai que vous avez été de Paris à Dijon sans aller à la selle?'

[2] *Lettere*, vol. i. p. 239.

in him acquired the most exquisite delicacy. He was wont to say that he feared no poison in his food, since he could discriminate the least adulteration of natural flavours. His mental perspicacity was equally subtle. As a boy he could recite thirty lines of Virgil after hearing them read over once. Books were not so much perused by him as penetrated at a glance; and what he had but casually noticed, never afterwards escaped his memory. In the vast Venetian archives he could lay his hand on any document without referring to registers or catalogues. The minutest details of houses visited or places passed through, remained indelibly engraved upon his memory. The characters of men lay open to his insight through their physiognomy and gestures. When new scientific instruments were submitted to his curiosity, he divined their uses and comprehended their mechanism without effort. Thus endowed with a rare combination of physical and intellectual faculties, it is no wonder that Sarpi became one of the most learned men of his age or of any age. He was an excellent Greek, Latin, and Hebrew scholar; an adequate master of the French and Spanish languages; profoundly versed in canon and civil law; accomplished in the erudition of classical and scholastic philosophy; thoroughly acquainted with secular and ecclesiastical history. Every branch of mathematics and natural science had been explored by him with the enthusiasm of a pioneer. He made experiments in chemistry, mechanics, mineralogy, metallurgy, vegetable and animal physiology. His practical studies in anatomy were carried on by the aid of vivisection. Following independent paths, he worked out some of Gilbert's discoveries in magnetism, and of Da Porta's in optics, demonstrated the valves of the veins, and the function of the uvea in vision, divined the uses of the telescope and thermometer. When he turned his attention to astronomy, he at once declared the futility of judicial astrology; and while recognising the validity of Galileo's system, predicted that this truth would involve its promulgator in serious difficulties with the Roman Inquisition. In his treatises on psychology and metaphysics, he originated a theory of sensationalism akin to that of Locke. There was, in fact, no field of knowledge which he had not traversed with the energy of a discoverer. Only to poetry and *belles lettres* he paid but little heed, disdaining the puerilities of rhetoric then in vogue, and using language as the simplest vehicle of thought. In conversation he was reticent, speaking little, but always to the purpose, and rather choosing to stimulate his collocutors than to make display of eloquence or erudition. Yet his company was eagerly sought, and he delighted in the society, not only of learned men and students, but of travellers, politicians, merchants, and citizens of the world. His favourite places of resort were the saloons of Andrea Morosini, and the shop of the Secchini at the sign of the Nave d' Oro. Here, after days spent in religious exercises, sacerdotal duties, and prolonged studies, he relaxed his mind in converse with the miscellaneous crowd of eminent persons who visited Venice for business or pleasure. A certain subacid humour, combining irony without bitterness, and proverbial pungency without sententiousness, added piquancy to his discourse. We have, unfortunately, no record of the wit-encounters which may have taken place under Morosini's or Secchini's roof between this friar, so punctual in his religious observances, so scrupulously pure in conduct, so cold in temperament, so acute in intellect, so modest in self-esteem, so cautious, so impermeable, and his contemporary, Bruno, the unfrocked friar of genius more daring but less sure, who was mentally in all points, saving their common love of truth and freedom, the opposite to Sarpi.

Sarpi entered the Order of the Servi, or Servants of the Blessed Virgin, at the age of fourteen, renewed his vows at twenty, and was ordained priest at twenty-two.[3] His great worth brought him early into notice, and he filled posts of considerable importance in his Order. Several years of his manhood were spent in Rome, transacting the business and conducting the legal causes of the fathers. At Mantua he gained the esteem of Guglielmo Gonzaga. At Milan he was admitted to familiar intimacy with the sainted Carlo Borromeo, who consulted him upon matters of reform in the diocese, and insisted on his hearing confessions. This duty was not agreeable to Sarpi; and though he habitually in after life said Mass and preached, he abstained from those functions of the priesthood which would have brought him into close relation with individuals. The bent of his mind rendered him averse to all forms of superstition and sacerdotal encroachments upon the freedom of the conscience. As he fought the battle of political independence against ecclesiastical aggression, so he maintained the prerogatives of personal liberty. The arts whereby Jesuits gained hold on families and individuals, inspired in him no less disgust than the illegal despotism of the Papacy. This blending of sincere piety and moral rectitude with a passion for secular freedom and a hatred of priestly craft, has something in it closely akin to the English temperament. Sarpi was a sound Catholic Christian in religion, and in politics what we should call a staunch Whig. So far as it is now possible to penetrate his somewhat baffling personality, we might compare him to a Macaulay of finger edge, to a Dean Stanley of more vigorous build. He was less commonplace than the one, more substantial than the other. But we must be cautious in offering any interpretation of his real opinions. It was not for nothing that he dedicated himself to the monastic life in boyhood, and persevered in it to the end of his long career. The discipline of the convent renders every friar inscrutable; and Sarpi himself assured his friends that he, like all Italians of his day, was bound to wear a mask.[4]

[3] It was under the supervision of the Servites that Sarpi gained the first rudiments of education. Thirst for knowledge may explain his early entrance into their brotherhood. Like Virgil and like Milton, he received among the companions of his youthful studies the honourable nickname of 'The Maiden.' Gross conversation, such as lads use, even in convents, ceased at his approach. And yet he does not seem to have lost influence among his comrades by the purity which marked him out as exceptional.

[4] *Lettere*, vol. i. p. 237.

Be this as it may, Sarpi was not the man to work his way by monkish intrigue or courtly service into high place either in his Order or the Church. Long before he unsheathed the sword in defence of Venetian liberties, he had become an object of suspicion to Rome and his superiors. Some frank words which escaped him in correspondence, regarding the corruption of the Papal Curia, closed every avenue to office. Men of less mark obtained the purple. The meanest and poorest bishoprics were refused to Sarpi. He was thrice denounced, on frivolous charges, to the Inquisition; but on each occasion the indictment was dismissed without a hearing. The General of the Servites accused him of wearing cap and slippers uncanonical in cut, and of not reciting the 'Salve Regina.' After a solemn trial, Sarpi was acquitted; and it came to be proverbially whispered that 'even the slippers of the incorruptible Fra Paolo had been canonised.' Being a sincere Catholic at heart, as well as a man of profound learning and prudent speech, his papalistic enemies could get no grip upon him. Yet they instinctively hated and dreaded one whom they felt to be opposed, in his strength, fearlessness, and freedom of soul, to their exorbitant pretensions and underhand aggressions upon public liberties. His commerce with heretics both in correspondence with learned Frenchmen and in conversation with distinguished foreigners at Venice, was made a ground of accusation, and Clement VIII. declared that this alone sufficed to exclude him from any dignity in the Church.

It does not appear that Sarpi troubled his head about these things. Had he cared for power, there was no distinction to which he might not have aspired by stooping to common arts and by compromising his liberty of conscience. But he was indifferent to rank and wealth. Public business he discharged upon occasion from a sense of duty to his Order. For the rest, so long as he was left to pursue his studies in tranquillity, Sarpi had happiness enough; and his modesty was so great that he did not even seek to publish the results of his discoveries in science. For this reason they have now been lost to the world; only the memory of them surviving in the notes of Foscarini and Grisellini, who inspected his MSS. before they were accidentally destroyed by fire in 1769.

Though renowned through Europe as the *orbis terrae ocellus*, the man sought out by every visitor to Venice as the rarest citizen of the Republic, Sarpi might have quitted this earthly scene with only the faint fame of a thinker whose eminent gifts blossomed in obscurity, had it not been for a public opportunity which forced him to forsake his studies and his cell for a place at the Council-board and for the functions of a polemical writer. That robust manliness of mind, which makes an Englishman hail English virtues in Sarpi, led him to affirm that 'every man of excellence is bound to pay attention to politics.'[5] Yet politics were not his special sphere. Up to the age of fifty-four he ripened in the assiduous studies of which I have made mention, in

[5] *Lettere*, vol. ii. p. 80.

the discharge of his official duties as a friar, and his religious duties as a priest. He had distinguished himself amid the practical affairs of life by judicial acuteness, unswerving justice, infallible perspicacity, and inexhaustible stores of erudition brought to bear with facility on every detail of any matter in dispute. But nature and inclination seemed to mark him out through early manhood for experimental and speculative science rather than for action. Now a demand was made on his deep fount of energy which evolved the latent forces of a character unique in many-sided strength. He had dedicated himself to religion and to the pursuit of knowledge. But he was a Venetian of the Venetians, the very soul of Venice. After God, his Prince and the Republic claimed obedience; and when S. Mark called, Sarpi abandoned science for the service of his country. 'Singularly composed of active and contemplative energies was the life of our Father; yielding to God that which he was able, to his Prince that which duty dictated, and to the domain of Venice more than any law but that of love demanded.'[6]

Paul V. assumed the tiara with the fixed resolve of making good the Papal claims to supremacy. Between Venice and the Holy See numerous disputed points of jurisdiction, relating to the semi-ecclesiastical fief of Ceneda, the investiture of the Patriarch, the navigation of the Po, and the right of the Republic to exercise judgment in criminal cases affecting priests, offered this Pope opportunities of interference. The Venetians maintained their customary prerogatives; and in April 1606 Paul laid them under interdict and excommunication. The Republic denied the legitimacy of this proceeding. The Doge, Leonardo Donato, issued a proclamation to the clergy of all degrees within the domain, appealing to their loyalty and enjoining on them the discharge of their sacerdotal duties in spite of the Papal interdict. Only Jesuits at first disobeyed the ducal mandate. When they refused to say Mass in the excommunicated city, they were formally expelled as contumacious subjects; and the fathers took ship amid the maledictions of the populace: '*Andate in malora.*' Their example was subsequently followed by the reformed Capuchins and the Theatines. Otherwise the Venetian clergy, like the people, remained firm in their allegiance to the State. 'We are Venetians first, Christians afterwards,' was a proverb dating from this incident. Venice, conscious of the justice of her cause, prepared to resist the Pope's arrogant demands if need were with arms, and to exercise religious rites within her towns in spite of Camillo Borghese's excommunication. The Senate, some time before these events happened, had perceived the advantage which would accrue to the Republic from the service of a practised canonist and jurisprudent in ecclesiastical affairs. Sarpi attracted their attention at an early stage of the dispute by a memorial which he drew up and presented to the Doge upon the best means of repelling Papal aggression. After perusing his report, in the month of January 1606, they appointed him Theologian and Canonist to the Republic, with a yearly salary of 200

[6] Sarpi's *Life* by Fra Fulgenzio, p. 64.

ducats. This post he occupied until his death, having at a later period been raised to the still more important office of Counsellor of State, which eventually he filled alone without a single coadjutor.

From the month of January 1606, for the remaining seventeen years of his life, Sarpi was intellectually the most prominent personage of Venice, the man who for the world at large represented her policy of moderate but firm resistance to ecclesiastical tyranny. Greatness had been thrust upon the modest and retiring student; and Father Paul's name became the watchword of political independence throughout Europe.

The Jesuits acting in concert with Spain, as well-informed historians held certain, first inspired Camillo Borghese with his ill-considered attempt upon the liberties of Venice.[7] It was now the Jesuits, after their expulsion from the Republic, who opened the batteries of literary warfare against the Venetian government. They wrote and published manifestoes through the Bergamasque territory, which province acknowledged the episcopal jurisdiction of Milan, though it belonged to the Venetian domain. In these writings it was argued that, so long as the Papal interdict remained in force, all sacraments would be invalid, marriages null, and offspring illegitimate. The population, trained already in doctrines of Papal supremacy, were warned that should they remain loyal to a contumacious State, their own souls would perish through the lack of sacerdotal ministrations, and their posterity would roam the world as bastards and accursed. To traverse this argument of sacerdotal tyranny, exorbitant in any age of the Latin Church, but preposterous after the illumination of the sixteenth century in Europe, was a citizen's plain duty. Sarpi therefore supplied an elegant Italian stylist, Giambattista Leoni, with material for setting forth a statement of the controversy between Venice and Rome. It would have been well if he had taken up the pen with his own hand. But at this early period of his career as publicist, he seems to have been diffident about his literary powers. The result was that Leoni's main defence of the Republic fell flat; and the war was waged for a while upon side issues. Sarpi drew a treatise by Gerson, the learned French champion of Catholic independence, forth from the dust of libraries, translated it into Italian, and gave it to the press accompanied by an introductory letter which he signed.[8] Cardinal Bellarmino responded from Rome with an attack on Sarpi's orthodoxy and Gerson's authority. Sarpi replied in an Apology for Gerson. Then, finding that Leoni's narrative had missed its mark, he poured forth pamphlet upon pamphlet, penning his own 'Considerations on the Censures,' inspiring Fra Fulgenzio Micanzi with a work styled 'Confirmations,' and finally reducing the whole

[7] Fra Fulgenzio's *Vita di F. Poalo*, p. 42. Venetian Despatches in Mutinelli's *Storia Arcana*, vol. iii. p. 67.

[8] The treatise which Sarpi translated was Gerson's *Considerations upon Papal Excommunications*. Gerson's part in the Council of Constance will be remembered. See Creighton's *History of the Papacy* vol. i. p. 211.

matter of the controversy into a book entitled a 'Treatise on the Interdict,' which he signed together with six brother theologians of the Venetian party. It is not needful in this place to institute a minute investigation into the merits of this pamphlet warfare. In its details, whether we regard the haughty claims of delegated omnipotence advanced by Rome, or the carefully studied historical and canonistic arguments built up by Sarpi, the quarrel has lost actuality. Common sense and freedom have so far conquered in Europe that Sarpi's opinions, then denounced as heresies, sound now like truisms; and his candid boast that he was the first to break the neck of Papal encroachments upon secular prerogative, may pass for insignificant in an age which has little to fear from ecclesiastical violence.

Yet we must not forget that, during the first years of the seventeenth century, the Venetian conflict with Papal absolutism, considered merely as a test-case in international jurisprudence, was one of vitally important interest. When we reflect how the Catholic Alliance was then engaged in rolling back the tide of Reformation, how the forces of Rome had been rallied by the Tridentine Council, and how the organism of the Jesuits had been created to promulgate new dogmas of Papal almightiness in Church and State, this, resistance of Venice, stoutly Catholic in creed, valiant in her defence of Christendom against the Moslem, supported by her faithful churchman and accomplished canonist, was no inconsiderable factor in the European strife for light and liberty. The occasion was one of crucial gravity. Reconstituted Rome had not as yet been brought into abrupt collision with any commonwealth which abode in her communion. Had Venice yielded in that issue, the Papacy might have augured for itself a general victory. That Venice finally submitted to Roman influence, while preserving the semblance of independence, detracts, indeed, from the importance of this Interdict affair considered as an episode in the struggle for spiritual freedom. Moreover, we know now that the presumptuous pretensions of the Papacy at large were destined, before many years had passed, to be pared down, diminished, and obliterated by the mere advance of intellectual enlightenment. Yet none of these considerations diminish Sarpi's claim to rank as hero in the forefront of a battle which in his time was being waged with still uncertain prospects.[9] In their comparatively narrow spheres, Venice and Sarpi, not less than Holland, England, Sweden, and the Protestants of Germany, on their wider platform at a later date, were fighting for a principle upon which the liberty of States depended. And they were the first to fight for it upon the ground most perilous to the common adversary. In all his writings Sarpi sought to prove that men might remain sound Catholics and yet

[9] Sarpi's correspondence abundantly proves how very grave was the peril of Papal Absolutism in his days. The tide had not begun to turn with force against the Jesuit doctrines of Papal Supremacy. See Ranke, vol. ii. pp. 4-12, on these doctrines and the counter-theories to which they gave rise. We must remember that the Papal power was now at the height of its ascension; and Sarpi can be excused for not having reckoned on the inevitable decline it suffered during the next century.

resist Roman aggression; that the Roman Court and its modern champions had introduced new doctrine, deviating from the pristine polity of Christendom; that the post-Tridentine theory of Papal Absolutism was a deformation of that order which Christ founded, which the Apostles edified, and which the Councils of a purer age had built into the living temple of God's Church on earth.

A passage from Sarpi's correspondence may be cited, as sounding the keynote to all his writings in this famous controversy. 'I imagine,' he writes to Jacques Gillot in 1609, 'that the State and the Church are two realms, composed, however, of the same human beings. The one is wholly heavenly, the other earthly. Each has its own sovereignty, defended by its own arms and fortifications. Nothing is held by them in common, and there should be no occasion for the one to declare war upon the other. Christ said that he and his disciples were not of this world. S. Paul affirms that our city is in the heavens. I take the word Church to signify an assembly of the faithful, not of priests only; for when we regard it as confined to those, it ceases to be Christ's kingdom, and becomes a portion of the commonwealth in this world, subject to the highest authority of State, as also are the laity.'[10] This emphatic distinction between Church and State, both fulfilling the needs of humanity, but in diverse relations, lay at the root of Sarpi's doctrine. He regarded the claim of the Church to interfere in State management, not only as an infringement of the prince's prerogative, but also as patent rebellion against the law of God which had committed the temporal government of nations in sacred trust to secular rulers. As the State has no call to meddle in the creation and promulgation of dogmas, or to impose its ordinances on the religious conscience of its subjects, so the Church has no right to tamper with affairs of government, to accumulate wealth and arrogate secular power, or to withdraw its ministers from the jurisdiction of the prince in matters which concern the operation of criminal and civil legislature. The ultramontanism of the Jesuits appeared to him destructive of social order; but, more than this, he considered it as impious, as a deflection from the form of Christian economy, as a mischievous seduction of the Church into a slough of self-annihilating cupidity and concupiscence.

Sarpi's views seemed audacious in his own age. But they have become the commonplaces of posterity. We can therefore hardly do justice to the originality and audacity which they displayed at an epoch when only Protestants at war with Rome advanced the like in deadly hatred—when the Catholic pulpits of Europe were ringing with newly promulgated doctrines of Papal supremacy over princes and peoples, of national rights to depose or assassinate excommunicated sovereigns, and of blind unreasoning obedience to Rome as the sole sure method of salvation. Upon the path of that Papal triumph toward the Capitol of world-dominion, Sarpi, the puny friar from his cell at Venice, rose like a spectre announcing certain doom with the irrefragable arguments

[10] *Lettere*, vol. i. p. 312.

of reason. The minatory words he uttered were all the more significant because neither he nor the State he represented sought to break with Catholic traditions. His voice was terrible and mighty, inasmuch as he denounced Rome by an indictment which proclaimed her to be the perturbing power in Christendom, the troubler of Israel, the whore who poured her cup of fornications forth to sup with princes.

After sixteen months, the quarrel of the interdict was compromised. Venice, in duel with Islam, could ill afford to break with Rome, even if her national traditions of eight centuries, intertwined with rites of Latin piety, had not forbidden open rupture. The Papal Court, cowed into resentful silence by antagonism which threatened intellectual revolt through Europe, waived a portion of its claims. Three French converts from Huguenot opinions to Catholicism, Henri IV., the Cardinal du Perron, and M. de Canaye, adjusted matters. The interdict was dismissed from Venice rather than removed—in haughty silence, without the clashing of bells from S. Pietro di Castello and S. Marco, without manifestation of joy in the city which regarded Papal interdicts as illegitimate, without the parade of public absolution by the Pope. Thus the Republic maintained its dignity of self-respect. But Camillo Borghese, while proclaiming a general amnesty, reserved *in petto* implacable animosity against the theologians of the Venetian party. Two of these, Marsilio and Rubetti, died suddenly under suspicion of poison.[11] A third, Fulgenzio Manfredi, was lured to Rome, treated with fair show of favour, and finally hung in the Campo di Fiora by order of the Holy Office.[12] A fourth, Capello, abjured his so-called heresies, and was assigned a pittance for the last days of his failing life in Rome.[13] It remained, if possible, to lay hands on Fra Paolo and his devoted secretary, Fra Fulgenzio Micanzi, of the Servites.

Neither threats nor promises availed to make these friends quit Venice. During the interdict and afterwards, Fulgenzio Micanzi preached the gospel there. He told the people that in the New Testament he had found truth; but he bade them take notice that for the laity this book was even a dead letter through the will of Rome.[14] Paul V. complained in words like these: Fra Fulgenzio's doctrine contains, indeed, no patent heresy, but it rests so clearly on the Bible as to prejudice the Catholic faith.[15] Sarpi informed his French correspondents that Christ and the truth had been openly preached in Venice by this man.[16] Fulgenzio survived the troubles of those times, steadily devoted to his master, of whom he has bequeathed to posterity a faithful portrait in that biography which combines the dove-like simplicity of the fourteenth century with something of Roger North's sagacity and humour.[17] Of Fulgenzio we take no further notice here, having

11 Sarpi's *Letters*, vol. ii. pp. 179, 284. 12 *Ibid.* pp. 100-102.
13 Bianchi Giovini, *Vita di Fra P. Sarpi*, vol. ii. p. 49.
14 A. G. Campbell's *Life of Sarpi*, p. 174.
15 Sarpi's *Letters*, vol. i. pp. 231, 239.
16 *Ibid.* pp. 220, 222, 225.
17 *Vita del Padre F. Paolo Sarpi*, Helmstedt, per Jacopo Mullerl, MDCCXXXXX.

paid him our debt of gratitude for genial service rendered in the sympathetic delineation of so eminent a character as Sarpi's. A side-regret may be expressed that some such simple and affectionate record of Bruno as a man still fails us, and alas! must ever fail. Fulgenzio, by his love, makes us love Sarpi, who otherwise might coldly win our admiration. But for Bruno, that scapegoat of the spirit in the world's wilderness, there is none to speak words of worship and affection.

The first definite warning that his life was in danger came to Sarpi from Caspar Schoppe, the publicist. Scioppius (so his contemporaries called him) was a man of doubtful character and unsteady principles, who, according as his interests varied, used a fluent pen and limpid Latin style for or against the Jesuit faction. History would hardly condescend to notice him but for the singular luck he had of coming at critical moments into contact with the three chief Italian thinkers of his time. We know already that a letter of this man is the one contemporary testimony of an eye-witness to Bruno's condemnation which we possess. He also deserves mention for having visited Campanella in prison and helped to procure his liberation. Now in the year 1607, while passing through Venice, Schoppe sought a private interview with Sarpi, pointed out the odium which Fra Paolo had gained in Rome by his writings, and concluded by asserting that the Pope meant to have him alive or to compass his assassination. If Sarpi wished to make his peace with Paul V., Schoppe was ready to conduct the reconciliation upon honourable terms, having already several affairs of like import in his charge. To this proposal Sarpi replied that the cause he had defended was a just one, that he had done nothing to offend his Holiness, and that all plots against his liberty or life he left within the hands of God. To these words he significantly added that, even in the Pope's grasp, a man was always 'master over his own life'—a sentence which seems to indicate suicide as the last resort of self-defence. In September of the same year the Venetian ambassador at Rome received private information regarding some mysterious design against a person or persons unknown, at Venice, in which the Papal Court were implicated, and which was speedily to take effect.[18] On October 5 Sarpi was returning about five o'clock in the afternoon to his convent at S. Fosca, when he was attacked upon a bridge by five ruffians. It so happened that on this occasion he had no attendant but his servant Fra Marino; Fra Fulgenzio and a man of courage, who usually accompanied him, having taken another route home. The assassins were armed with harquebusses, pistols, and poniards. One of them went straight at Sarpi, while the others stood on guard and held down Fra Marino. Fifteen blows in all were aimed at Sarpi, three of which struck him in the neck and face. The stiletto remained firmly embedded in his cheekbone between the right ear and nose. He fell to the ground senseless; and a cry being raised by some women who had witnessed the outrage

[18] Despatch to Fr. Contarini under date September 25, 1607, quoted in Campbell's *Life of Sarpi*, p. 145.

from a window, the assassins made off, leaving their victim for dead. It was noticed that they took refuge in the palace of the Papal Nuncio, whence they escaped that same evening to the Lido *en route* for the States of the Church. An old Venetian nobleman of the highest birth, Alessandro Malipiero, who bore a singular affection for the champion of his country's liberty, was walking a short way in front of Sarpi beyond the bridge upon which the assault was perpetrated. He rushed to his friend's aid, dragged out the dagger from his face, and bore him to the convent. There Sarpi lay for many weeks in danger, suffering as much, it seems, from his physicians as from the wounds. Not satisfied with the attendance of his own surgeon, Alvise Ragoza, the Venetians insisted on sending all the eminent doctors of the city and of Padua to his bedside. The illustrious Acquapendente formed one of this miscellaneous *cortège*; and when the cure was completed, he received a rich gold chain and knighthood for his service. Every medical man suggested some fresh application. Some of them, suspecting poison, treated the wounds with theriac and antidotes. Others cut into the flesh and probed. Meanwhile the loss of blood had so exhausted Sarpi's meagre frame that for more than twenty days he had no strength to move or lift his hands. Not a word of impatience escaped his lips; and when Acquapendente began to medicate the worst wound in his face, he moved the dozen doctors to laughter by wittily observing, 'And yet the world maintains that it was given *Stilo Romanae Curiae*.'[19] His old friend Malipiero would fain have kept the dagger as a relic. But Sarpi suspended it at the foot of a crucifix in the church of the Servi, with this appropriate inscription, *Dei Filio Liberatori*. When he had recovered from his long suffering, the Republic assigned their Counsellor an increase of pension in order that he might maintain a body of armed guards, and voted him a house in S. Marco for the greater security of his person. But Sarpi begged to be allowed to remain among the friars, with whom he had spent his life, and where his vocation bound him. In the future he took a few obvious precautions, passing in a gondola to the Rialto and thence on foot through the crowded Merceria to the Ducal Palace, and furthermore securing the good offices of his attendants in the convent by liberal gifts of money. Otherwise, he refused to alter the customary tenor of his way.

The State of Venice resented this attack upon their servant as though it had been directed against the majesty of the Republic. A proclamation was immediately issued, offering enormous rewards for the capture or murder of the criminals, especially so worded as to insinuate the belief that men of high position in Rome were implicated. The names of the chief conspirators were as follows: Ridolfo Poma, a broken Vene-

[19] Fulgenzio's *Life*, p. 61. A. G. Campbell asserts that this celebrated *mot* of Sarpi's is not to be found in Fulgenzio's MS. It occurs, however, quite naturally in the published work. The first edition of the Life appeared in 1646, eight years before Fulgenzio's death. The discrepancies between it and the MS. may therefore have been intended by the author.

tian merchant; Alessandro Parrasio of Ancona, outlawed for the murder of his uncle; a priest, Michele Viti of Bergamo; and two soldiers of adventure, Giovanni di Fiorenza and Pasquale di Bitonto. Having escaped to the Lido, they took ship for Ravenna and arrived in due course at Ancona, where they drew 1000 crowns from the Papal Camera, and proceeded to make triumphal progress through Romagna. Their joy was dashed by hearing that Fra Paolo had not been killed. The Venetian *bando* filled them with fears and mutual suspicions, each man's hand being now set against his comrade, and every ruffian on the road having an interest in their capture. Yet after some time they continued their journey to Rome, and sought sanctuary in the palace of Cardinal Colonna. Here their reception was not what they had anticipated. Having failed in the main object and brought scandal on the Church, they were maintained for some months in obscurity, and then coldly bidden to depart with scanty recompense. All this while their lives remained exposed to the Venetian ban. Under these circumstances it is not strange that the men were half-maddened. Poma raged like a wild beast, worshipping the devil in his private chamber, planning schemes of piracy and fresh attacks on Sarpi, even contemplating a last conspiracy against the person of the Pope. He was seized in Rome by the *sbirri* of the government, and one of his sons perished in the scuffle. Another returned to Venice, and ended his days there as a vagrant lunatic. Poma himself died mad in the prison of Cività Vecchia. Viti also died mad in the same prison. Parrasio died in prison at Rome. One of the soldiers was beheaded at Perugia, and the other fell a victim to cut-throats on the high road. Such was the end of the five conspirators against Fra Paolo Sarpi's life.[20] A priest, Franceschi, who had aided and abetted their plot, disappeared soon after the explosion; and we may rest tolerably assured that his was no natural removal to another world.

It is just to add that the instigation of this murderous plot was never brought home by direct testimony to any members of the Papal Court. But the recourse which the assassins first had to the asylum of the Nuncio in Venice, their triumphal progress through cities of the Church, the moneys they drew on several occasions, the interest taken in them by Cardinal Borghese when they finally reached Rome, and their deaths in Papal dungeons, are circumstances of overwhelming cumulative evidence against the Curia. Sarpi's life was frequently attempted in the following years. On one occasion, Cardinal Bellarmino, more mindful of private friendship than of public feud, sent him warning that he must live prepared for fresh attacks from Rome. Indeed, it may be said that he now passed his days in continual expectation of poison or the dagger. This appears plainly in Fulgenzio's biography and in the pages of his private correspondence. The most considerable of these later conspiracies, of which Fra Fulgenzio gives a full account, impli-

[20] A full account of them is given by Bianchi Giovini in his *Biografia*, chap. xvii.

cated Cardinal Borghese and the General of the Servite Order.[21] The history seems in brief to be as follows: One Fra Bernardo of Perugia, who had served the Cardinal during their student days, took up his residence in Rome so soon as Scipione Borghese became a profitable patron. In the course of the year 1609, this Fra Bernardo despatched a fellow-citizen of his, named Fra Giovanni Francesco, to Padua, whence he frequently came across to Venice and tampered with Sarpi's secretary, Fra Antonio of Viterbo. These three friars were all of them Servites; and it appears that the General looked with approval on their undertaking. The upshot of the traffic was that Fra Antonio, having ready access to Sarpi's apartments and person, agreed either to murder him with a razor or to put poison in his food, or, what was finally determined on, to introduce a couple of assassins into his bedchamber at night. An accident revealed the plot, and placed a voluminous cyphered correspondence in the hands of the Venetian Inquisitor of State. Fra Fulgenzio significantly adds that of all the persons incriminated by these letters, none, with the exception of the General of the Servites, was under the rank of Cardinal. The wording of his sentence is intentionally obscure, but one expression seems even to point at the Pope.[22]

At the close of this affair, so disgraceful to the Church and to his Order, Fra Paolo besought the Signory of Venice on his bended knees, as a return for services rendered by him to the State, that no public punishment should be inflicted on the culprits. He could not bear, he said, to be the cause of bringing a blot of infamy upon his religion, or of ruining the career of any man. Fra Giovanni Francesco afterwards redeemed his life by offering weighty evidence against his powerful accomplices. But what he revealed is buried in the oblivion with which the Council of Ten in Venice chose to cover judicial acts of State importance.

It is worth considering that in all the attempts upon Sarpi's life, priests, friars and prelates of high place were the prime agents.[23] Poor devils like Poma and Parrasio lay ready to their hands as sanguinary instruments, which, after work performed, could be broken if occasion served. What, then, was the religious reformation of which the Roman Court made ostentatious display when it secured its unexpected triumph in the Council of Trent? We must reply that in essential points of moral conduct this reformation amounted to almost nothing, and in some points to considerably less than nothing. The Church of God, as Sarpi held, suffered deformation rather than reformation. That is to say, this Church, instead of being brought back to primitive simplicity and purged of temporal abuses, now lay at the mercy of ambitious hypocrites who, with the Supreme Pontiff's sanction, pursued their ends by

[21] *Vita di F. Paolo*, pp. 67-70.

[22] *Vita di F. Paolo*, p. 68: 'Le cose che vennero a pubblica notizia e certe sono: che molte persone nominate in quella cifra, di *Padre* fratelli, e cugini, per le contracifre constò, dal Generale de' Servi in fuori, niuna esser di dignità inferiore alla Cardinalizia.'

[23] Sarpi says that no crime happened in Venice without a friar or priest being mixed in it (*Lettere*, vol. i. p. 351).

treachery and violence. Its hostility to heretics and its new-fangled doctrine of Papal almightiness encouraged the spread of a pernicious casuistry which favoured assassination. Kings at strife with the Catholic Alliance, honest Christians defending the prerogatives of their commonwealth, erudite historians and jurists who disapproved of substituting Popes in Rome for God in heaven, might be massacred or kidnapped by ruffians red with the blood of their nearest relatives and carrying the condemnation of their native States upon their forehead. According to the post-Tridentine morality of Rome, that morality which the Jesuits openly preached and published, which was disseminated in every prelate's antechamber, and whispered in every parish-priest's confessional, enormous sins could be atoned and eternal grace be gained by the merciless and traitorous murder of any notable man who savoured of heresy. If the Holy Office had instituted a prosecution against the victim and had condemned him in his absence, the path was plain. Sentence of excommunication and death publicly pronounced on such a man reduced him to the condition of a wild beast whose head was worth solid coin and plenary absolution to the cut-throat. A private minute recorded on the books of the Inquisitors had almost equal value; and Sarpi was under the impression that some such underhand proceeding against himself had loosed a score of knives. But short of these official or semi-judicial preliminaries, it was maintained upon the best casuistical authority that to take the life of any suspected heretic, of anyone reputed heterodox in Roman circles, should be esteemed a work of merit creditable to the miscreant who perpetrated the deed, and certain, even should he die for it, to yield him in the other world the joys of Paradise. These joys the Jesuits described in language worthy of the Koran. Dabbled in Sarpi's or Duplessis Mornay's blood, quartered and tortured like Ravaillac, the desperado of so pious a crime would swim for ever in oceans of ecstatic pleasure. The priest, ambitious for his hierarchy, fanatical in his devotion to the Church, relying upon privilege if he should chance to be detected, had a plain interest in promoting and directing such conspiracies. Men of blood and bandits, up to the hilts in crimes of violence, rendered reckless by the indiscriminate cruelty of justice in those days, allured by the double hope of pay and spiritual benefit, rushed without a back-thought into like adventures. Ready to risk their lives in an unholy cause, such ruffians were doubly glad to do so when the bait of heaven's felicity was offered to their grosser understanding. These considerations explain, but are far indeed from exculpating, the complicity of clergy and cut-throats in every crime of violence attempted against foes of Papal Rome.

Sarpi's worst enemies could scarcely fix on him the crime of heresy. He was a staunch Catholic; so profoundly versed both in dogmatic theology and in ecclesiastical procedure, that to remain within the straitest limits of orthodoxy, while opposing the presumption of the Papal Court, gave him no trouble. Yet at the time in which he lived, the bare act of resistance to any will or whim of Rome, passed with those doctors who were forging new systems of Pontifical supremacy for heretical. In this arbitrary and uncanonical sense of the phrase Sarpi was undoubtedly a heretic. He had deserved the hatred of the Curia, the Inquisition, the Jesuits, and their myrmidons. Steadily, with caution and a sober spirit, he had employed his energies and vast accumulated stores of knowledge in piling up breakwaters against their pernicious innovations. In all his controversial writings during the interdict Sarpi used none but solid arguments, drawn from Scripture, canon-law, and the Councils of the early Church, in order to deduce one single principle: namely, that both secular and ecclesiastical organisms, the State and the Church, are divinely appointed, but with several jurisdictions and for diverse ends. He pressed this principle home with hammer-strokes of most convincing proof on common-sense and reason. He did so even superfluously to our modern intellect, which is fatigued by following so elaborate a chain of precedents up to a foregone conclusion. But he let no word fall, except by way of passing irony, which could bring contempt upon existing ecclesiastical potentates; and he maintained a dispassionate temper, while dealing with topics which at that epoch inflamed the fiercest party strife. His antagonists, not having sound learning, reason, and the Scripture on their side, were driven to employ the rhetoric of personal abuse and the stiletto. In the end the badness of their cause was proved by the recourse they had to conspiracies of pimps, friars, murderers, and fanatics, in order to stifle that voice of truth which told them of their aberration from the laws of God.

It was not merely by his polemical writings during the interdict that Sarpi won the fame of heretic in ultra-papal circles. In his office as Theologian to the Republic he had to report upon all matters touching the relations of State to Church; and the treatises which he prepared on such occasions assumed the proportions, in many instances, of important literary works. Among these the most considerable is entitled 'Delle Materie Beneficiarie.' Professing to be a discourse upon ecclesiastical benefices, it combines a brief but sufficient history of the temporal power of the Papacy, an inquiry into the arts whereby the Church's property had been accumulated, and a critique of the various devices employed by the Roman Curia to divert that wealth from its original objects. In 'this golden volume,' to use Gibbon's words, 'the Papal system is deeply studied and freely described.' Speaking of its purport, Hallam observes: 'That object was neither more nor less than to represent the wealth and power of the Church as ill-gotten and excessive.' Next in importance is a 'Treatise on the Inquisition,' which gives a condensed sketch of the origin and development of the Holy Office, enlarging upon the special modifications of that institution as it existed in Venice. Here likewise Sarpi set himself to resist ecclesiastical encroachments upon the domain of secular jurisdiction. He pointed out how the right of inquiring into cases of heretical opinion had been gradually wrested from the hands of the bishop and the State, and committed to a specially elected body which held itself only responsible to Rome. He showed how this powerful tribunal was being used to the detriment of States, by extending its operation into the sphere of politics, extruding the secular magistracy from participation in its judgments, and arrogating to itself the cognisance of civil crimes. A third 'Discourse upon the Press' brought the same system of attack to bear upon the Index of prohibited books. Sarpi was here able to demonstrate that a power originally delegated to the bishops of proscribing works pernicious to morality and religion, was now employed for the suppression of sound learning and enlightenment by a Congregation sworn to support the Papacy. Passing from their proper sphere of theology and ethics, these ecclesiastics condemned as heretical all writings which denied the supremacy of Rome over nations and commonwealths, prevented the publication and sale of books which defended the rights of princes and republics, and flooded Europe with doctrines of regicide, Pontifical omnipotence, and hierarchical predominance in secular affairs. These are the most important of Sarpi's minor works. But the same spirit of liberal resistance against Church aggression, supported by the same erudition and critical sagacity, is noticeable in a short tract explaining how the Right of Asylum had been abused to the prejudice of public justice; in a 'Discourse upon the Contributions of the Clergy,' distinguishing their real from their assumed immunities; and in a brief memorandum upon the Greek College in Rome, exposing the mischief wrought in commonwealths and families by the Jesuit system of education.

In all these writings Sarpi held firmly by his main principle, that the State, no less than the Church, exists *jure divino*. The Papal usurpation of secular prerogatives was in his eyes not merely a violation of the divinely appointed order of government, but also a deformation of the ecclesiastical ideal. Those, he argued, are the real heretics who deprave the antique organism of the Church by making the Pope absolute, who preach the deity of the Roman Pontiff as though he were a second God equal in almightiness to God in heaven. 'Nay,' he exclaims in a passage marked by more than usual heat, 'should one drag God from heaven they would not stir a finger, provided the Pope preserved his vice-divinity or rather super-divinity. Bellarmino clearly states that to restrict the Papal authority to spiritual affairs is the same as to annihilate it; showing that they value the spiritual at just zero.'[24] Sarpi saw that the ultra-papalists of his day, by subordinating the State, the family, and the individual to the worldly interests of Rome, by repressing knowledge and liberty of conscience, preaching immoral and anti-social doctrines, encouraging superstition and emasculating education, for the maintenance of those same worldly interests, were advancing steadily upon the path of self-destruction. The essence of Christianity was neglected in this brutal struggle for supremacy; while truth, virtue and religion, those sacred safeguards of humanity, which the Church

[24] *Lettere*, vol. ii. p. 160.

was instituted to preserve, ran no uncertain risk of perishing through the unnatural perversion of its aims.

The work which won for Sarpi a permanent place in the history of literature, and which in his lifetime did more than any other of his writings to expose the Papal system, is the history of the Tridentine Council. It was not published with his name or with his sanction. A manuscript copy lent by him to Marcantonio de Dominis, Archbishop of Spalatro, was taken by that waverer between Catholicism and Protestantism to England, and published in London under the pseudonym of Pietro Soave Polano—an anagram of Paolo Sarpi Veneto—in the year 1619. That Sarpi was the real author admits of no doubt. The book bears every stamp of genuineness. It is written in the lucid, nervous, straightforward style of the man, who always sought for mathematical precision rather than rhetorical elegance in his use of language. Sarpi had taken special pains to collect materials for a History of the Council; and in doing so he had enjoyed exceptional advantages. Early in his manhood he formed at Mantua a close friendship with Camillo Olivo, who had been secretary to the Papal Legate, Cardinal Gonzaga of Mantua, at Trent. During his residence in Rome between 1585 and 1587 he became intimately acquainted with Cardinal Castagna, president of the committee appointed for drawing up the decrees of the Council. In addition to the information afforded by these persons, officially connected with the transactions of the Council, Sarpi had at his command the Archives of Venice, including the despatches of ambassadors, and a vast store of published documents, not to mention numerous details which in the course of his long commerce with society he had obtained from the lips of credible witnesses. All these sources, grasped in their diversity by his powerful memory and animated with his vivid intellect, are worked into an even plain dispassionate narration, which, in spite of the dryness of the subject, forms a truly fascinating whole. That Sarpi was strictly fair in his conception of the Council, can scarcely be maintained; for he wrote in a spirit of distinct antagonism to the ends which it achieved. Yet the more we examine the series of events described by him, the more are we convinced that in its main features the work is just. When Sir Roger Twysden pronounced it 'to be written with so great moderation, learning, and wisdom, as might deserve a place amongst the exactest pieces of ecclesiastic story any age had produced,' he did not overshoot the mark. Nor has the avowedly hostile investigation to which Cardinal Pallavicini submitted it, done more than to confirm its credit by showing that a deadly enemy, with all the arsenal of Roman documents at this command, could only detect inaccuracies in minor details and express rage at the controlling animus of the work.

It was Sarpi's object to demonstrate that the Council of Trent, instead of being a free and open Synod of Christians assembled to discuss points at issue between the Catholic and Protestant Churches, was in reality a closely packed conciliabulum, from which Protestants were excluded, and where Catholics were dominated by the Italian agents of the Roman Court. He made it clear, and in this he is confirmed by masses of collateral proofs, that the presiding spirit of the Council was human diplomacy rather than divine inspiration, and that Roman intrigue conducted its transactions to an issue favourable for Papal supremacy by carefully manipulating the interests of princes and the passions of individuals. 'I shall narrate the causes,' he remarks, in his exordium, 'and the negotiations of an ecclesiastical convocation, during the course of twenty-two years, for divers ends and with varied means; by whom promoted and solicited, by whom impeded and delayed; for another eighteen years, now brought together, now dissolved; always held with various ends; and which received a form and accomplishment quite contrary to the design of those who set it going, as also to the fear of those who took all pains to interrupt it. A clear monition that man ought to yield his thoughts resignedly to God and not to trust in human prudence. Forasmuch as this Council, desired and put in motion by pious men for the reunion of the Church which had begun to break asunder, had so established schism and embittered factions that it has rendered those discords irreconcileable; handled by princes for the reform of the ecclesiastical system, has caused the greatest deformation that hath ever been since the name of Christian came into existence; by bishops with hope expected as that which would restore the episcopal authority, now in large part absorbed by the sole Roman Pontiff, hath been the reason of their losing the last vestige of it and of their reduction to still greater servitude. On the other hand, dreaded and evaded by the Court of Rome, as an efficient instrument for curbing that exorbitant power, which from small beginnings hath arrived by various advances to limitless excess, it has so established and confirmed it over the portion still left subject to it, as that it never was so vast nor so well-rooted.' In treating of what he pithily calls 'the Iliad of our age,' Sarpi promises to observe the truth, and protests that he is governed by no passion. This promise the historian kept faithfully. His animus is never allowed to transpire in any direct tirades; his irony emerges rather in reporting epigrams of others than in personal sarcasms or innuendoes; his own prepossessions and opinions are carefully veiled. After reading the whole voluminous history we feel that it would be as inaccurate to claim Sarpi for Protestantism as to maintain that he was a friend of ultra-papal Catholicism. What he really had at heart was the restoration of the Church of God to unity, to purer discipline and to sincere spirituality. This reconstruction of Christendom upon a sound basis was, as he perceived, rendered impossible by the Tridentine decrees. Yet, though the dearest hope of his heart had been thus frustrated, he set nothing down in malice, nor vented his own disappointment in laments which might have seemed rebellious against the Divine will. Sarpi's personality shows itself most clearly in the luminous discourses with which from time to time he elucidates obscure matters of ecclesiastical history. Those on episcopal residence, pluralism, episcopal jurisdiction, the censure of books, and the mal-appropriation of endowments, are specially valuable.[25] If no other proof existed, these digressions would render Sarpi's authorship of the History unmistakable. They are identical in style and in intention with his acknowledged treatises, firmly but calmly expressing a sound scholar's disapproval of abuses which had grown up like morbid excrescences upon the Church. Taken in connexion with the interpolated summaries of public opinion regarding the Council's method of procedure and its successive decrees, these discourses betray a spirit of hostility to Rome which is nowhere openly expressed. Sarpi illustrated Aretino's cynical sentence: 'How can you speak evil of your neighbour? By speaking the truth, by speaking the truth!'—without rancour and without passion. Nothing, in fact, could have been more damaging to Rome than his precise analysis of her arts in the Council.

I have said that the History of the Tridentine Council, though it confirmed Sarpi's heretical reputation, would not justify us in believing him at heart a Protestant.[26] Very much depends on how we define the word Protestant. If Sarpi's known opinions regarding the worldliness of Rome, ecclesiastical abuses, and Papal supremacy, constitute a Protestant, then he certainly was one. But if antagonism to Catholic dogma, repudiation of the Catholic sacraments and abhorrence of monastic institutions are also necessary to the definition then Sarpi was as certainly no Protestant. He seems to have anticipated the position of those Christians who now are known as Old Catholics. This appears from his vivid sympathy with the Gallican Church, and from his zealous defence of those prerogatives and privileges in which the Venetian Church resembled that of France. We must go to his collected letters in order to penetrate his real way of thinking on the subject of reform. The most important of these are addressed to Frenchmen—Ph. Duplessis Mornay, De l'Isle Groslot, Leschassier, a certain Roux, Gillot, and Casaubon. If we could be quite sure that the text of these familiar letters had not been tampered with before publication, their testimony would be doubly valuable. As it is, no one at all acquainted with Sarpi's style will doubt that in the main they are trustworthy. Here and there it may be that a phrase has been inserted or modified to give

[25] *Opere di Paolo Sarpi*, Helmstadt, 1761, vol. i. pp. 200, 233, 311; vol. ii. pp. 89, 187.

[26] This contradicts the opinion of Hallam and Macaulay, both of whom were convinced that Sarpi was a Protestant at heart. Macaulay wishes that he had thrown off the friar's frock. In a certain sense Sarpi can be classified with the larger minds among the Reformed Churches of his age. But to call him a Protestant who concealed his real faith, argues coarseness of perception, incapacity for comprehending any attitude above and beyond belligerent Catholicism and Protestantism, or of sympathising with the deeply religious feelings of one who, after calculating all chances and surveying all dogmatic differences, thought that he could serve God as well and his country better in that communion which was his by birthright. To an illuminated intellect there was not in the seventeenth century much reason to prefer one of the Reformed Churches to Catholicism, except for the sake of political freedom. It being impossible to change the State-religion in Venice, Sarpi had no inducement to leave his country and to pass his life in exile among prejudiced sectarians.

a stronger Protestant colouring. The frequent allusion to the Court of Rome under the title of *La Meretrice*, especially in letters to Duplessis Mornay, looks suspicious.[27] Yet Dante, Petrarch and Savonarola used similar metaphors, when describing the secular ambition of the Papacy. Having pointed out a weakness in this important series of documents, I will translate some obviously genuine passages which illustrate Sarpi's attitude toward reform.

Writing to Leschassier upon the literary warfare of James I., he says it is a pity that the king did not abstain from theology and confine himself to the defence of his princely prerogatives against the claims of Rome. He has exposed himself to the imputation of wishing to upset the foundations of the faith. 'With regard to our own affairs [*i.e.* in Venice], we do not seek to mix up heaven and earth, things human and things divine. Our desire is to leave the sacraments and all that pertains to religion as they are, believing that we can uphold the secular government in those rights which Scripture and the teaching of the Fathers confirm.'[28] In another place he says: 'I have well considered the reasons which drew Germany and England into changing the observances of religion; but upon us neither these nor others of greater weight will exercise any influence. It is better to suffer certain rules and customs that are not in all points commendable, than to acquire a taste for revolution and to yield to the temptation of confounding all things in chaos.'[29] His own grievance against the Popes, he adds, is that they are innovating and destroying the primitive constitution of the Church. With regard to the possibility of uniting Christendom, he writes that many of the differences between Catholics and Protestants seem to him verbal; many, such as could be tolerated in one communion; and many capable of adjustment. But a good occasion must be waited for.[30] Nothing can be done in Italy without a general war, that shall shake the powers of Spain and Rome.[31] Both Spain and Rome are so well aware of their peril that they use every means to keep Italy in peace.[32] If the Protestants of Europe are bent on victory, they must imitate the policy of Scipio and attack the Jesuits and Rome in their headquarters.[33] 'There is no enterprise of greater moment than to destroy the credit of the Jesuits. When they are conquered, Rome is taken; and without Rome, religion reforms itself spontaneously.'[34] 'Changes in State are inextricably involved in changes of religion;'[35] and Italy will never be free so long as the Diacatholicon lasts. Meanwhile, 'were it not for State policy there would be found hundreds ready

[27] *Lettere*, vol. ii. pp. 3, 18, 96, 109, and elsewhere.
[28] *Ib.* vol. ii. p. 6.
[29] *Ib.* vol. i. p. 237.
[30] *Ib.* p. 268.
[31] *Ib.* vol. ii. pp. 29, 48, 59, 60, 125.
[32] *Ib.* pp. 120, 124.
[33] *Ib.* p. 226.
[34] *Ib.* p. 217.
[35] *Ib.* p. 427.

to leap from this ditch of Rome to the summit of Reform.'[36] The hope of some improvement at Venice depends mainly upon the presence there of embassies from Protestant powers—England, Holland and the Grisons.[37] These give an opportunity to free religious discussion, and to the dissemination of Gospel truth. Sarpi is strong in his praise of Fra Fulgenzio for fearlessly preaching Christ and the truth, and repeats the Pope's complaint that the Bible is injurious to the Catholic faith.[38] He led William Bedell, chaplain to Sir H. Wotton and afterwards Bishop of Kilmore, to believe that Fra Fulgenzio and himself were ripe for Reform. 'These two I know,' writes Bedell to Prince Henry, 'as having practised with them, to desire nothing so much as the Reformation of the Church, and, in a word, for the substance of religion they are wholly ours.'[39] During the interdict Diodati came from Geneva to Venice, and Sarpi informed him that some 12,000 persons in the city wished for rupture with Rome; but the government and the aristocracy being against it, nothing could be done.[40]

Enough has now been quoted to throw some light upon Sarpi's attitude toward Protestantism. That he most earnestly desired the overthrow of ultra-papal Catholicism, is apparent. So also are his sympathies with those reformed nations which enjoyed liberty of conscience and independence of ecclesiastical control. Yet his first duty was to Venice; and since the State remained Catholic, he personally had no intention of quitting the communion into which he had been born and in which he was an ordained priest. All Churches, he wrote in one memorable letter to Casaubon, have their imperfections. The Church of Corinth, in the days of the Apostles, was corrupt.[41] 'The fabric of the Church of God,' being on earth, cannot expect immunity from earthly frailties.[42] Such imperfections and such frailties as the Catholic Church shared with all things of this world, Sarpi was willing to tolerate. The deformation of that Church by Rome and Jesuitry he manfully withstood; but he saw no valid reason why he should abandon her for Protestantism. In his own conscience he remained free to serve God in spirit and in truth. The mind of the man in fact was too far-seeing and too philosophical to exchange old lamps for new without a better prospect of attaining to absolute truth than the dissenters from Catholicism afforded. His interest in Protestant, as separate from Catholic Reform, was rather civil and political than religious or theological. Could those soaring wings of Rome be broken, then and not till then, might the Italians enjoy freedom of conscience, liberty of discussion and research, purer piety, and a healthier activity as citizens.

Side light may be thrown upon Sarpi's judgment of the European

[36] *Ib.* vol. ii. p. 283.
[37] *Ib.* pp. 110, 311.
[38] *Ib.* vol. i. pp. 220, 222, 225, 231, 239.
[39] Campbell's *Life*, p. 132.
[40] Campbell's *Life*, pp. 133, 135.
[41] *Lettere*, vol. ii. p. 86.
[42] *Ib.* vol. i. p. 283.

situation by considering in detail what he said about the Jesuits. This Company, as we have seen, lent its support to Papal absolutism; and during the later years of Sarpi's life it seemed destined to carry the world before it, by control of education, by devotion to Rome, by adroit manipulation of the religious consciousness for anti-social ends and ecclesiastical aggrandisement.

The sure sign of being in the right, said Sarpi, is when one finds himself in contradiction to the Jesuits. They are most subtle masters in ill-doing, men who, if their needs demand, are ready to commit crimes worse than those of which they now are guilty. All falsehood and all blasphemy proceed from them. They have set the last hand at establishing universal corruption. They are a public plague, the plague of the world, chameleons who take their colour from the soil they squat on, flatterers of princes, perverters of youth. They not only excuse but laud lying; their dissimulation is bare and unqualified mendacity; their malice is inestimable. They have the art so to blend their interests and that of Rome, seeking for themselves and the Papacy the empire of the world, that the Curia must needs support them, while it cowers before their inscrutable authority. They are the ruin of good literature and wholesome doctrine by their pitiful pretence of learning and their machinery of false teaching. On ignorance rests their power, and truth is mortal to them. Every vice of which humanity is capable, every frailty to which it is subject, finds from them support and consolation. If S. Peter had been directed by a Jesuit confessor he might have arrived at denying Christ without sin. They use the confessional as an instrument of political and domestic influence, reciprocating its confidences one with the other in their own debates, but menacing their penitents with penalties if a word of their counsel be bruited to the world. Expelled from Venice, they work more mischief there by their intrigues than they did when they were tolerated.[43] They scheme to get a hold on Constantinople and Palestine, in order to establish seminaries of fanatics and assassins. They are responsible for the murder of Henry IV., for if they did not instigate Ravaillac, their doctrine of regicide inspired him. They can creep into any kingdom, any institution, any household, because they readily accept any terms and subscribe to any conditions in the certainty that by the adroit use of flattery, humbug, falsehood, and corruption, they will soon become masters of the situation. In France they are the real Morbus Gallicus. In Italy they are the soul of the Diacatholicon.

The torrent of Sarpi's indignation against the Jesuits, as perverters of sound doctrine in the Church, disturbers of kingdoms, sappers of morality and disseminators of vile customs through society, runs so violently forward that we are fain to check it, while acknowledging its

[43] It is worthy of notice, as a stern Venetian joke, that when the Jesuits eventually returned to the Rialto, they were bade walk in processions upon ceremonial occasions between the Fraternities of S. Marco and S. Teodoro—saints amid whose columns on the Molo criminals were executed.

justice. One passage only, from the many passages bearing on this topic in his correspondence, demands special citation, since it deals directly with the whole material of the present work. Writing to his friend Leschassier, he speaks as follows: 'Nothing can be of more mischief to you in France than the dishonesty of bad confessors and their determination to aggrandise Rome by any means, together with the mistaken zeal of the good sort. We have arrived at a point where cure of the disease must even be despaired of. Fifty years ago things went well in Italy. There was no public system of education for training young men to the profit of the clergy. They were brought up by their parents in private, more for the advantage of their families than for that of the hierarchy. In religious houses, where studies flourished, attention was paid to scholastic logic. The jurisdiction and the authority of the Pope were hardly touched on; and while theology was pursued at leisure, the majority passed their years in contemplation of the Deity and angels. Recently, through the decrees of the Tridentine Council, schools have been opened in every State, which are called Seminaries, where education is concentrated on the sole end of augmenting ecclesiastical supremacy. Furthermore, the prelates of each district, partly with a view of saving their own pockets, and partly that they may display a fashionable show of zeal, have committed the charge of those institutions to Jesuits. This has caused a most important alteration in the aspect of affairs.'[44] It would be difficult to state the changes effected by the Tridentine Council and the commission of education to the Jesuits more precisely and more fairly than in this paragraph. How deeply Sarpi had penetrated the Jesuitical arts in education, can be further demonstrated from another passage in his minor works.[45] In a memoir prepared for the Venetian Signory, he says that the Jesuits are vulgarly supposed to be unrivalled as trainers of youth. But a patent equivocation lurks under this phrase 'unrivalled.' Education must be considered with regard to the utility of the State. 'Now the education of the Jesuits consists in stripping the pupil of every obligation to his father, to his country, and to his natural prince; in diverting all his love and fear toward a spiritual superior, on whose nod, beck and word he is dependent. This system of training is useful for the supremacy of ecclesiastics and for such secular governments as they are ready to submit to; and none can deny that the Jesuits are without equals in their employment of it. Yet in so far as it is advantageous in such cases, so also is it prejudicial to States, the end whereof is liberty and real virtue, and with whom the ecclesiastical faction remains in bad accord. From the Jesuit colleges there never issued a son obedient to his father, devoted to his country, loyal to his prince. The cause of this is that the Jesuits employ their best energies in destroying natural affection, respect for parents, reverence for princes. Therefore they

[44] *Lettere*, vol. i. p. 126; *Opere*, vol. vi. p. 40.
[45] *Opere*, vol. vi. p. 145.

only deserve to be admired by those whose interest it is to subject family, country and government to ecclesiastical interests.'

The Provincial Letters of Pascal, which Sarpi anticipated in so many points, suffice to prove that he was justified in this hostility to ultramontanism backed up by Jesuit artifices. He was writing, be it remembered, at the very high-tide of Papal domination, when Henri IV. had been assassinated, and when the overwhelming forces of secular interests combined with intellectual progress had not as yet set limits on ecclesiastical encroachment. The dread lest Europe should succumb to Rome, now proved by subsequent events an unsubstantial nightmare, was real enough for this Venetian friar, who ran daily risk of assassination in down-trodden servile Italy, with Spanish plots threatening the arsenal, with France delivered into the hands of Florentines and casuists, with England in the grip of Stuarts, and with Germany distracted by intrigues. He could not foresee that in the course of a century the Jesuits would be discredited by their own arts, and that the Papacy would subside into a pacific sovereignty bent on securing its own temporal existence by accommodation.

The end of Sarpi's life consecrated the principles of duty to God and allegiance to his country which had animated its whole course. He fell into a bad state of health; yet nothing would divert him from the due discharge of public business. 'All the signs of the soul's speedy departure from that age-enfeebled body, were visible; but his indefatigable spirit sustained him in such wise that he bore exactly all his usual burdens. When his friends and masters bade him relax his energies, he used to answer: My duty is to serve and not to live; there is some one daily dying in his office.[46] When at length the very sources of existence failed, and the firm brain wandered for a moment, he was once heard to say: 'Let us go to S. Mark, for it is late.'[47] The very last words he uttered, frequently repeated, but scarcely intelligible, were: 'Esto perpetua.'[48] *May Venice last for ever!* This was the dying prayer of the man who had consecrated his best faculties to the service of his country. But before he passed away into that half slumber which precedes death, he made confession to his accustomed spiritual father, received the Eucharist and Extreme Unction, and bade farewell to the Superior of the Servites, in the following sentence: 'Go ye to rest, and I will return to God, from whom I came.' With these words he closed his lips in silence, crossing his hands upon his breast and fixing his eyes upon a crucifix that stood before him.[49]

These words—not the last, for the last were *Esto perpetua*; but the

I will return to God, from whom I came.

[46] Fulgenzio's *Life*, p. 98. [47] *Ibid.* p. 105. [48] *Ibid.*

[49] Letter of the Superior to the Venetian Senate, printed in the *Lettere*, vol. ii. pp. 450-453. It is worth meditating on the contrast between Sarpi's and Bruno's deaths. Sarpi died with the consolations of religion on his bed in the convent which had been his life-long home. Bruno was burned alive, with eyes averted from the crucifix in

last spoken in the presence of his fraternity—have a deep significance for those who would fain understand the soul of Sarpi. When in his lifetime he spoke of the Church, it was always as 'the Church of God.' When he relegated his own anxieties for the welfare of society to a superior power, it was not to Mary, as Jesuits advised, nor even to Christ, but invariably to the Providence of God. Sarpi, we have the right to assume, lived and died a sincere believer in the God who orders and disposes of the universe; and this God, identical in fact though not in form with Bruno's, he worshipped through such symbols of ceremony and religion as had been adopted by him in his youth. An intellect so clear of insight as this, knew that 'God is a spirit, and they that worship him must worship him in spirit and in truth.' He knew that 'neither on this mountain nor yet in Jerusalem,' neither in Protestant communities nor yet in Rome was the authentic God made tangible; but that a loyal human being, created in God's image, could serve him and adore him with life-worship under any of the spiritual shapes which mortal frailty has fashioned for its needs.

To penetrate the abyss of any human personality is impossible. No man truly sees into his living neighbour's, brother's, wife's, nay even his own soul. How futile, therefore, is the effort which we make to seize and sketch the vital lineaments of men long dead, divided from us not merely by the grave which has absorbed their fleshly form and deprived us of their tone of voice, but also by those differences in thought and feeling which separate the centuries of culture! Yet this impossible task lies ever before the historian. Few characters are more patently difficult to comprehend than that of Sarpi. Ultimately, so far as it is possible to formulate a view, I think he may be defined as a Christian Stoic, possessed with two main governing ideas, duty to God and duty to Venice. His last words were for Venice; the penultimate consigned his soul to God. For a mind like his, so philosophically tempered, so versed in all the history of the world to us-wards, the materials of dispute between Catholic and Protestant must have seemed but trifles. He stayed where he had early taken root, in his Servite convent at S. Fosca, because he there could dedicate his life to God and Venice better than in any Protestant conventicle. Had Venice inclined toward rupture with Rome, had the Republic possessed the power to make that rupture with success, Sarpi would have hailed the event gladly, as introducing for Italy the prospect of spiritual freedom, purer piety, and the overthrow of Papal-Spanish despotism. But Venice chose to abide in the old ways, and her Counsellor of State knew better than anyone

bitter scorn, after seven and a half years spent in the prisons of the Inquisition. Sarpi exhaled his last breath amid sympathising friends in the service of a grateful country. Bruno panted his death-pangs of suffocation and combustion out, surrounded by menacing Dominicans, in the midst of hostile Rome celebrating her triumphant jubilee. Sarpi's last thoughts were given to the God of Christendom and the Republic. Bruno had no country; the God in whom he trusted at that grim hour, was the God within his soul, unlocalised, detached by his own reason from every Church and every creed.

that she had not the strength to cope with Spain, Rome, Jesuitry and Islam single-handed. Therefore he possessed his soul in patience, worshipping God under forms and symbols to which he had from youth been used, trusting the while that sooner or later God would break those mighty wings of Papal domination.

CHAPTER XI

GUARINI, MARINO, CHIABRERA, TASSONI

Dearth of Great Men—Guarini a Link between Tasso and the Seventeenth Century—His Biography—The 'Pastor Fido'—Qualities of Guarini as Poet—Marino the Dictator of Letters—His Riotous Youth at Naples—Life at Rome, Turin, Paris—Publishes the 'Adone'—The Epic of Voluptuousness—Character and Action of Adonis—Marino's Hypocrisy—Sentimental Sweetness—Brutal Violence—Violation of Artistic Taste—Great Powers of the Poet—Structure of the 'Adone'—Musical Fluency—Marinism—Marino's Patriotic Verses—Contrast between Chiabrera and Marino—An Aspirant after Pindar—Chiabrera's Biography—His Court Life—Efforts of Poets in the Seventeenth Century to attain to Novelty—Chiabrera's Failure—Tassoni's Life—His Thirst to Innovate—Origin of the 'Secchia Rapita'—Mock-Heroic Poetry—The Plot of this Poem—Its Peculiar Humour—Irony and Satire—Novelty of the Species—Lyrical Interbreathings—Sustained Contrast of Parody and Pathos—The Poet Testi.

Soon after 1600 it became manifest that lapse of years and ecclesiastical intolerance had rendered Italy nearly destitute of great men. Her famous sons were all either dead, murdered or exiled; reduced to silence by the scythe of time or by the Roman 'arguments of sword and halter.' Bruno burned, Vanini burned, Carnesecchi burned, Paleario burned, Bonfadio burned; Campanella banished, after a quarter of a century's imprisonment with torture; the leaders of free religious thought in exile, scattered over northern Europe. Tasso, worn out with misery and madness, rested at length in his tomb on the Janiculan; Sarpi survived the stylus of the Roman Curia with calm inscrutability at S. Fosca; Galileo meditated with closed lips in his watch-tower behind Bello Sguardo. With Michelangelo in 1564, Palladio in 1580, Tintoretto in 1594, the godlike lineage of the Renaissance artists ended; and what children of the sixteenth century still survived to sustain the nation's prestige, to carry on its glorious traditions? The list is but a poor one. Marino, Tassoni, the younger Buonarroti, Boccalini and Chiabrera in literature. The Bolognese Academy in painting. After these men expand arid wildernesses of the Sei Cento—barocco architecture, false taste, frivolity, grimace, affectation—Jesuitry translated into culture. On one bright point, indeed, the eye rests with hope and comfort. Palestrina, when he died in 1594, did not close but opened an age for music. His posterity, those composers, lutists, violists and singers, from whom the modern art of arts has drawn her being, down to the sweet fellowship of Pergolese, Marcello and Jomelli, of Guarneri, Amati and Stradivari, of Farinelli, Caffarielli and La Romanina, were as yet but rising dimly heralded with light of dawn upon their foreheads.

In making the transition from the 'Gerusalemme' to the 'Adone,' from the last great poem of the Cinque Cento to the epic of the Sei Cento, it is indispensable that notice should be taken of the 'Pastor Fido' and its author. Giambattista Guarini forms a link between Tasso and the poets of the seventeenth century. He belonged less to the Renaissance, more to the culture of the age created by the Council of Trent, than did Tasso. His life, in many of its details similar, in others most dissimilar, to that of Tasso, illustrates and helps us in some measure to explain the latter. It must therefore form the subject of a somewhat detailed study.

Guarini drew his blood on the paternal side from the illustrious humanist Guarino of Verona, who settled at Ferrara in the fifteenth century as tutor to Lionello d' Este.[1] By his mother he claimed descent from the Florentine house of Machiavelli. Born in 1537, he was seven years older than Torquato Tasso, whom he survived eighteen years, not closing his long life until 1612. He received a solid education both at Pisa and Padua, and was called at the early age of eighteen to profess moral philosophy in the University of Ferrara. Being of noble birth and inheriting a considerable patrimony, Guarini might have enjoyed a life of uninterrupted literary leisure, if he had chosen to forego empty honours and shun the idle distractions of Courts. But it was the fate of distinguished men in that age to plunge into those quicksands. Guarini had a character and intellect suited to the conduct of state affairs; and he shared the delusion prevalent among his contemporaries, that the petty Italian principalities could offer a field for the exercise of these talents. 'If our country is reduced to the sole government of a prince,' he writes, 'the man who serves his prince will serve his country, a duty both natural and binding upon all.'[2] Accordingly, soon after his marriage to Taddea of the noble Bendedei family, he entered the service of Alfonso II. This was in 1567. Tasso, in his quality of gentleman to Cardinal d' Este, had already shed lustre on Ferrara through the past two years. Guarini first made Tasso's friendship at Padua, where both were Eterei and house-guests of Scipione Gonzaga. The two poets now came together in a rivalry which was not altogether amicable. The genius of Tasso, in the prime of youth and heyday of Court-favour, roused Guarini's jealousy. And yet their positions were so different that Guarini might have been well satisfied to pursue his own course without envy. A married and elder man, he had no right to compete in gallantry with the brilliant young bachelor. Destined for diplomacy and affairs of state, he had no cause to grudge the Court poet his laurels. Writing in 1595, Guarini avers that 'poetry has been my pastime, never my profession;' and yet he made it his business at Ferrara to rival Tasso both as a lyrist and as a servant of dames. Like Tasso, he suffered from the spite of Alfonso's secretaries, Pigna and Montecatino, who seem to have incarnated the malevolence of courtiers

[1] See Vol. I. *The Revival of Learning*, pp. 466-467.

[2] *Lettere del Guarini*, Venezia, 1596, p. 2.

in its basest form. So far, there was a close parallel between the careers of the two men at Ferrara. But Guarini's wealth and avowed objects in life caused the Duke from the first to employ him in a different kind of service. Alfonso sent him as ambassador to Venice, Rome, and Turin, giving him the rank of Cavaliere in order that he might perform his missions with more dignity. At Turin, where he resided for some time, Guarini conceived a just opinion of the growing importance of the House of Savoy. Like all the finest spirits of his age, Tassoni, Sarpi, Chiabrera, Marino, Testi, he became convinced that if Italy were to recover her independence, it could only be by the opposition of the Dukes of Savoy to Spain. How nearly the hopes of these men were being realised by Carlo Emmanuele, and how those hopes were frustrated by Roman intrigues and the jealousy of Italian despots, is matter of history. Yet the student may observe with interest that the most penetrating minds of the sixteenth century already discerned the power by means of which, after the lapse of nearly three hundred years, the emancipation of Italy has been achieved.

In 1574 Guarini was sent to Poland, to congratulate Henri III. upon his election to that monarchy. He went a second time in the following year to conduct more delicate negotiations. The crown of Poland was now thrown open to candidature; and more than one of the Italian Princes thought seriously of competing for this honour. The Grand Duke of Tuscany entertained the notion and abandoned it. But Alfonso II. of Ferrara, who had fought with honour in his youth in Hungary, made it a serious object of ambition. Manolesso, the Venetian envoy in 1575 at Ferrara, relates how the Duke spent laborious hours in acquiring the German language, 'which no one learns for pleasure, since it is most barbarous, nor quickly, but with industry and large expenditure of time.' He also writes: 'The Duke aspires to greatness, nor is satisfied with his present State; and therefore he has entered into the Polish affair, encouraged thereto by his brother the Cardinal and by his ambassador in Poland.'[3]

These embassies were a serious drain upon Guarini's resources; for it appears certain that if he received any appointments, they were inadequate to the expenses of long journeys and the maintenance of a becoming state. He therefore returned to Ferrara, considerably burdened with debts; and this was just the time at which Tasso's mental derangement began to manifest itself. Between 1575 and 1579, the date of Tasso's imprisonment at Sant' Anna, the two men lived together at the Court. Guarini's rivalry induced him at this period to cultivate poetry with such success that, when the author of the 'Gerusalemme' failed, Alfonso commanded him to take the vacant place of Court poet. There is an interesting letter extant from Guarini to his friend Cornelio Bentivoglio, describing the efforts he made to comply with the Duke's pleasure. 'I strove to transform myself into another man, and, like a playactor, to reassume the character, manners and emotions of a past

[3] Alberi, *Relazioni*, serie 2, vol. ii. pp. 423-425.

period. Mature in age, I forced myself to appear young; exchanged my melancholy for gaiety; affected loves I did not feel; turned my wisdom into folly, and, in a word, passed from philosopher to poet.'[4] How ill adapted he was to this masquerade existence may be gathered from another sentence in the same letter. 'I am already in my forty-fourth year, burdened with debts, the father of eight children, two of my sons old enough to be my judges, and with my daughters to marry.'

At last, abandoning this uncongenial strain upon his faculties, Guarini retired in 1582 to the villa which he had built upon his ancestral estate in the Polesine, that delightful rustic region between Adige and Po. Here he gave himself up to the cares of his family, the nursing of his dilapidated fortune, and the composition of the 'Pastor Fido.' It is not yet the time to speak of that work, upon which Guarini's fame as poet rests; for the drama, though suggested by Tasso's 'Aminta,' was not finally perfected until 1602.[5] Yet we may pause to remark upon the circumstances under which he wrote it. A disappointed courtier, past the prime of manhood, feeling his true vocation to be for severe studies and practical affairs, he yet devoted years of leisure to the slow elaboration of a dramatic masterpiece which is worthy to rank with the classics of Italian literature. During this period his domestic lot was not a happy one. He lost his wife, quarrelled with his elder sons, and involved himself in a series of lawsuits.[6] Litigation seems to have been an inveterate vice of his maturity, and he bequeathed to his descendants a coil of legal troubles. Having married one of his daughters, Anna, to Count Ercole Trotti, he had the misery of hearing in 1596 that she had fallen an innocent victim to her husband's jealousy, and that his third son, Girolamo, connived at her assassination. In the midst of these annoyances and sorrows, he maintained a grave and robust attitude, uttering none of those querulous lamentations which flowed so readily from Tasso's pen.

Tasso had used the Pastoral Drama to idealise Courts. Guarini vented all the bitterness of his soul against them in his 'Pastor Fido.' He also wrote from his retirement: 'I am at ease in the enjoyment of liberty, studies, the management of my household.'[7] Yet in 1585, while on a visit to Turin, he again accepted proposals from Alfonso. He had gone there in order to superintend the first representation of his Pastoral, which was dedicated to the Duke of Savoy. Extremely averse to his old servants taking office under other princes, the Duke of Ferrara seems to have feared lest Guarini should pass into the Court of Carlo Emmanuele. He therefore appointed him Secretary of State; and Guarini entered upon the post in the same year that Tasso issued

[4] *Lettere*, p. 195.

[5] In this year it was published with the author's revision by Ciotto at Venice. It had been represented at Turin in 1585, and first printed at Venice in 1590.

[6] Guarini may be compared with Trissino in these points of his private life. See Vol. II. *Italian Literature*, pp. 338, 339.

[7] *Lettere*, p. 196.

from his prison. This reconciliation did not last long. Alfonso took the side of Alessandro Guarini in a lawsuit with his father; and the irritable poet retired in indignation to Florence. The Duke of Ferrara, however, was determined that he should not serve another master. At Florence, Turin, Mantua and Rome, his attempts to obtain firm foothold in offices of trust were invariably frustrated; and Coccapani, the Duke's envoy, hinted that if Guarini were not circumspect, 'he might suffer the same fate as Tasso.' To shut Guarini up in a madhouse would have been difficult. Still he might easily have been despatched by the poniard; and these words throw not insignificant light upon Tasso's terror of assassination.

The Duke Alfonso died in 1597, and Ferrara reverted to the Holy See. Upon this occasion, Guarini was free to follow his own inclinations. He therefore established himself at the Court of the Grand Duke, into whose confidence he entered upon terms of flattering familiarity. Ferdinando de' Medici 'fell in love with him as a man may with a fine woman,' says his son Alessandro in one of his apologetic writings. This, however, meant but little; for compliments passed freely between princes and their courtiers; which, when affairs of purse or honour were at stake, soon turned to discontent and hatred. So it fared with Guarini at Florence. His son, Guarino, made a marriage of which he disapproved, but which the Grand Duke countenanced. So slight a disagreement snapped the ties of friendship, and the restless poet removed to the Court of Urbino. There the last Duke of the House of Rovere, Francesco Maria II., Tasso's schoolfellow and patron, was spending his widowed years in gloomy Spanish pride. The mortmain of the Church was soon to fall upon Urbino, as it had already fallen on Ferrara. Guarini wrote: 'The former Court in Italy is a dead thing. One may see the shadow, but not the substance of it nowadays. Ours is an age of appearances, and one goes a-masquerading all the year.' A sad but sincere epitaph, inscribed by one who had gone the round of all the Courts of Italy, and had survived the grand free life of the Renaissance.

These words close Guarini's career as courtier. He returned to Ferrara in 1604, and in 1605 carried the compliments of that now Pontifical city to Paul V. in Rome on his election to the Papacy. Upon this occasion Cardinal Bellarmino told him that he had inflicted as much harm on Christendom by his 'Pastor Fido' as Luther and Calvin by their heresies. He retorted with a sarcasm which has not been transmitted to us, but which may probably have reflected on the pollution of Christian morals by the Jesuits. In 1612 Guarini died at Venice, whither he was summoned by one of his innumerable and interminable lawsuits.

Bellarmino's censure of the 'Pastor Fido' strikes a modern reader as inexplicably severe. Yet it is certain that the dissolute seventeenth century recognised this drama as one of the most potent agents of corruption. Not infrequent references in the literature of that age to the ruin of families and reputations by its means, warn us to remember how difficult it is to estimate the ethical sensibilities of society in periods remote from our own.[8] In the course of the analysis which I now propose to make of this play, I shall attempt to show how, coming midway between Tasso's 'Aminta' and Marino's 'Adone,' and appealing to the dominant musical enthusiasms of the epoch, Guarini's 'Pastor Fido' may have merited the condemnation of far-sighted moralists. Not censurable in itself, it was so related to the sentimental sensuality of its period as to form a link in the chain of enervation which weighed on Italy.

The 'Pastor Fido' is a tragi-comedy, as its author points out with some elaboration in the critical essay he composed upon that species of the drama. The scene is laid in Arcadia, where according to Guarini it was customary to sacrifice a maiden each year to Diana, in expiation of an ancient curse brought upon the country by a woman's infidelity. An oracle has declared that when two scions of divine lineage are united in marriage, and a faithful shepherd atones for woman's faithlessness, this inhuman rite shall cease. The only youth and girl who fulfil these conditions of divine descent are the daughter of Titiro named Amarilli, and Silvio, the son of the high priest Montano. They have accordingly been betrothed. But Silvio is indifferent to womankind in general, and Amarilli loves a handsome stranger, Mirtillo, supposed to be the son of Carino. The plot turns upon the unexpected fulfilment of the prophecy, in spite of the human means which have been blindly taken to secure its accomplishment. Amarilli is condemned to death for suspected misconduct with a lover; and Mirtillo, who has substituted himself as victim in her place, is found to be the lost son of Montano. This solution of the intrigue, effected by an anagnorisis like that of the 'Œdipus Tyrannus,' supplies a series of dramatic scenes and thrilling situations in the last act. Meanwhile the passion of Dorinda for Silvio, and the accident whereby he is brought to return her affection at the moment when his dart has wounded her, form a picturesque underplot of considerable interest. Both plot and underplot are so connected in the main action and so interwoven by links of mutual dependency that they form one richly varied fabric. Regarded as a piece of cunning mechanism, the complicated structure of the 'Pastor Fido' leaves nothing to be desired. In its kind, this pastoral drama is a monumental work of art, glittering and faultless like a polished bas-relief of hard Corinthian bronze. Each motive has been carefully prepared, each situation amply and logically developed. The characters are firmly traced, and sustained with consistency. The cold and eager hunter Silvio contrasts with tender and romantic Mirtillo. Corisca's meretricious arts and systematised profligacy enhance the pure affection of Amarilli. Dorinda presents another type of love, so impulsive that it conquers maidenly modesty. The Satyr is a creature of rude lust, foiled in its brutal appetite by the courtesan Corisca's wiliness. Carino

[8] *Il Pastor Fido*, per cura di G. Casella (Firenze, Barbèra, 1866), p. liv.

brings the corruption of towns into comparison with the innocence of the country.

In Carino the poet painted his own experience; and here his satire upon the Court of Ferrara is none the less biting because it takes the form of well-weighed and gravely measured censure, instead of vehement invective. The following lines may serve as a specimen of Guarini's style in this species:—

> I' mi pensai che ne' reali alberghi
> Fossero tanto più le genti umane,
> Quant' esse han più di tutto quel dovizia,
> Ond' è l' umanità sì nobil fregio.
> Ma mi trovai tutto 'l contrario, Uranio.
> Gente di nome e di parlar cortese,
> Ma d' opre scarsa e di pietà nemica
> Gente placida in vista e mansueta,
> Ma piu del cupo mar tumida e fera:
> Gente sol d' apparenza, in cui se miri
> Viso di carità, mente d' invidia
> Poi trovi, e 'n dritto sguardo animo bieco,
> E minor fede allor che più lusinga.
> Quel ch' altrove è virtù, quivi è difetto:
> Dir vero, oprar non torto, amar non finto,
> Pietà sincera, invïolabil fede,
> E di core e di man vita innocente,
> Stiman d' animo vil, di basso ingegno,
> Sciocchezza e vanità degna di riso.
> L' ingannare, il mentir, la frode, il furto,
> E la rapina di pietà vestita,
> Crescer col danno e precipizio altrui,
> E far a sè dell' altrui biasimo onore,
> Son le virtù di quella gente infida.
> Non merto, non valor, non riverenza,
> Nè d' età nè di grado nè di legge;
> Non freno di vergogna, non rispetto
> Nè d' amor nè di sangue, non memoria
> Di ricevuto ben; nè, finalmente,
> Cosa sì venerabile o sì santa
> O sì giusta esser può, ch' a quella vasta
> Cupidigia d' onori, a quella ingorda
> Fama d' avere, invïolabil sia.

The 'Pastor Fido' was written in open emulation of Tasso's 'Aminta,' and many of its most brilliant passages are borrowed from that play. Such, for example, is the Chorus on the Golden Age which closes the fourth act. Such, too, is the long description by Mirtillo of the kiss he stole from Amarilli (act ii. sc. 1). The motive here is taken from 'Rinaldo' (canto v.), and the spirit from 'Aminta' (act i. sc. 2). Guarini's Satyr is a studied picture from the sketch in Tasso's pastoral. The dialogue between Silvio and Linco (act i. sc. 1) with its lyrical refrain:

> Lascia, lascia le selve,
> Folle garzon, lascia le fere, ed ama:

reproduces the dialogue between Silvia and Dafne (act i. sc. 1) with its similar refrain:

Cangia, cangia consiglio,
Pazzarella che sei.

In all these instances Guarini works up Tasso's motives into more elaborate forms. He expands the simple suggestions of his model; and employs the artifices of rhetoric where Tasso yielded to inspiration. One example will suffice to contrast the methods of the spontaneous and the reflective poet. Tasso with divine impulse had exclaimed:

Odi quell' usignuolo,
Che va di ramo in ramo
Cantando: Io amo, io amo!

This, in Guarini's hands, becomes:

Quell' augellin, che canta
Sì dolcemente, e lascivetto vola
Or dall' abete al faggio,
Ed or dal faggio al mirto,
S'avesse umano spirto,
Direbbe: Ardo d' amore, ardo d' amore.

Here a laborious effort of the constructive fancy has been substituted for a single flash of sympathetic imagination. Tasso does not doubt that the nightingale is pouring out her love in song. Guarini says that if the bird had human soul, it would exclaim, 'Ardo d' amore.' Tasso sees it flying from branch to branch. Guarini teases our sense of mental vision by particularising pine and beech and myrtle. The same is true of Linco's speech in general when compared with Dafne's on the ruling power of love in earth and heaven.

Of imagination in the true sense of the term Guarini had none. Of fancy, dwelling gracefully, ingeniously, suggestively, upon externals he had plenty. The minute care with which he worked out each vein of thought and spun each thread of sentiment, was that of the rhetorician rather than the poet. Tasso had made Aminta say:

La semplicetta Silvia
Pietosa del mio male,
S'offrì di dar aita
Alla finta ita, ahi lasso! e fece
Più cupa, e più mortale
La mia piaga verace,
Quando le labbra sue
Giunse alle labbra mie.
Nè l' api d' alcun fiore
Colgan si dolce il sugo,
Come fu dolce il mel, ch' allora io colsi
Da quelle fresche rose.

Now listen to Guarini's Mirtillo:

Amor si stava, Ergasto,
Com' ape suol, nelle due fresche rose
Di quelle labbra ascoso;
E mentre ella si stette
Con la baciata bocca

Al baciar della mia
Immobile e ristretta,
La dolcezza del mèl sola gustai;
Ma poichè mi s' offerse anch' ella, e porse
L' una e l' altra dolcissima sua rosa. . . .

This is enough to illustrate Guarini's laborious method of adding touch to touch without augmenting the force of the picture.[9] We find already here the transition from Tasso's measured art to the fantastic prolixity of Marino. And though Guarini was upon the whole chaste in use of language, his rhetorical love of amplification and fanciful refinement not unfrequently betrayed him into Marinistic conceits. Dorinda, for instance, thus addresses Silvio (act iv. sc. 9):

O bellissimo scoglio
Già dall' onda e dal vento
Delle lagrime mie, de' miei sospiri
Si spesso invan percosso!

Sighs are said to be (act i. sc. 2):

impetuosi venti
Che spiran nell' incendio, e 'l fan maggiore
Con turbini d'Amore,
Ch' apportan sempre ai miserelli amanti
Foschi nembi di duol, piogge di pianti.

From this to the style of the 'Adone' there was only one step to be taken.

Though the scene of the 'Pastor Fido' was laid in Arcadia, the play really represented polite Italian society. In the softness of its sentiment, its voluptuous verbal melody, and its reiterated descant upon effeminate love-pleasure, it corresponded exactly to the spirit of its age.[10] This was the secret of its success; and this explains its seduction.

[9] I might have further illustrated this point by quoting the thirty-five lines in which Titiro compares a maiden to the rose which fades upon the spray after the fervours of the noon have robbed its freshness (act. i. sc. 4). To contest the beauty of the comparison would be impossible. Yet when we turn to the two passages in Ariosto (*Orl. Fur.* i. 42, 43, and xxiv. 80) on which it has been modelled, we shall perceive how much Guarini lost in force by not writing with his eye upon the object or with the authenticity of inward vision, but with a self-conscious effort to improve by artifices and refinements upon something he has read. See my essay on 'The Pathos of the Rose' in *Time*, April, 1886.

[10] Even Silvio, the most masculine of the young men, whose heart is closed to love, appears before us thus:

Oh Silvio, Silvio! a che ti diè Natura
Ne' più begli anni tuoi
Fior di beltà si delicato e vago,
Se tu se' tanto a calpestarlo intento?
Che s' avess' io cotesta tua sì bella
E sì fiorita guancia,
Addio selve, direi:
E seguendo altre fere,
E la vita passando in festa e 'n gioco,
Farei la state all' ombra, e 'l verno al foco.

Not Corisca's wanton blandishments and professed cynicism, but Mirtillo's rapturous dithyrambs on kissing, Dorinda's melting moods of tenderness, and Amarilli's delicate regrets that love must be postponed to honour, justified Bellarmino's censure. Without anywhere transgressing the limits of decorum, the 'Pastor Fido' is steeped in sensuousness. The sentiment of love idealised in Mirtillo and Amarilli is pure and self-sacrificing. *Ama l' onestà mia, s' amante sei*, says this maiden to her lover; and he obeys her. Yet, though the drama is dedicated to virtue, no one can read it without perceiving the blandishments of its luxurious rhetoric. The sensual refinement proper to an age of social decadence found in it exact expression, and it became the code of gallantry for the next two centuries.

Meanwhile the literary dictator of the seventeenth century was undoubtedly Marino. On him devolved the sceptre which Petrarch bequeathed to Politian, Politian to Bembo, and Bembo to Torquato Tasso. In natural gifts he was no unworthy successor of these poets, though the gifts he shared with them were conspicuously employed by him for purposes below the scope of any of his predecessors. In artistic achievement he concentrated the less admirable qualities of all, and brought the Italian poetry of the Renaissance to a close by exaggerating its previous defects. Yet, as a man, Marino is interesting, more interesting in many respects than the melancholy discontented Tasso. He accepted the conditions of his age with genial and careless sympathy, making himself at once its idol, its interpreter, and its buffoon. Finally, he illustrates the law of change which transferred to Neapolitans in this age the sceptre which had formerly been swayed by Tuscans and Lombards.[11]

Giovanni Battista Marino was born at Naples in 1569. His father, a jurist of eminence, bred him for the law. But the attractions of poetry and pleasure were irresistible by this mobile son of the warm South—

La lusinga del Genio in me prevalse,
E la toga deposta, altrui lasciai
Parolette smaltir mendaci e false.
Nè dubbi testi interpretar curai,
Nè discordi accordar chiose mi calse,
Quella stimando sol perfetta legge
Che de' sensi sfrenati il fren coregge.

Legge omai più non v' ha la qual per dritto
Punisca il fallo o ricompensi il merto.
Sembra quando è fin quì deciso e scritto
D' opinion confuse abisso incerto.
Dalle calumnie il litigante afflitto
Somiglia in vasto mar legno inesperto.
Reggono il tutto con affetto ingordo,
Passion cieca ed interesse sordo.

[11] Telesio, Bruno, Campanella, Salvator Rosa, Vico, were, like Marino, natives of the Regno.

Such, in the poet's maturity, was his judgment upon law; and probably he expressed the same opinion with frankness in his youth. Seeing these dispositions in his son, the severe parent cast him out of doors, and young Marino was free to indulge vagabond instincts with lazzaroni and loose companions on the quays and strands of Naples. In that luxurious climate a healthy native, full of youth and vigour, needs but little to support existence. Marino set his wits to work, and reaped too facile laurels in the fields of Venus and the Muses. His verses speedily attracted the notice of noble patrons, among whom the Duke of Bovino, the Prince of Conca, and Tasso's friend the Marquis Manso have to be commemorated. They took care that so genuine and genial a poet should not starve. It was in one of Manso's palaces that Marino had an opportunity of worshipping the singer of Armida and Erminia at a distance. He had already acquired dubious celebrity as a juvenile Don Juan and a writer of audaciously licentious lyrics, when disaster overtook him. He assisted one of his profligate friends in the abduction of a girl. For this breach of the law both were thrown together into prison, and Marino only escaped justice by the sudden death of his accomplice. His patrons now thought it desirable that he should leave Naples for a time. Accordingly they sent him with letters of recommendation to Rome, where he was well received by members of the Crescenzio and Aldobrandino families. The Cardinal Pietro Aldobrandino made him private secretary, and took him on a journey to Ravenna and Turin. From the commencement to the end of his literary career Marino's march through life was one triumphal progress. At Turin, as formerly in Naples and Rome, he achieved a notable success. The Duke of Savoy, Carlo Emmanuele, offered him a place at Court, appointed him secretary, and dubbed him Knight of S. Maurice.

> Vidi la corte, e nella corte io vidi
> Promesse lunghe e guiderdoni avari,
> Favori ingiusti e patrocini infidi,
> Speranze dolci e pentimenti amari,
> Sorrisi traditor, vezzi omicidi,
> Ed acquisti dubbiosi e danni chiari,
> E voti vani ed idoli bugiardi,
> Onde il male è sicuro e il ben vien tardi.

It was the custom of all poets in that age to live in Courts and to abuse them, to adulate princes and to vilify these patrons. Marino, however, had real cause to complain of the treachery of courtiers. He appears to have been a man of easy-going temper, popular among acquaintances, and serviceable to the society he frequented. This comradely disposition did not save him, however, from jealousies and hatreds; for he had, besides, a Neapolitan's inclination for satire. There was a Genoese poetaster named Gasparo Murtola established in Court-service at Turin, who had recently composed a lumbering poem, 'Il Mondo Creato.' Marino made fun of it in a sonnet; Murtola retorted; and a warfare of invectives began which equalled for scurrility and filth the duels of Poggio and Valla. Murtola, seeing that he was likely to be worsted by his livelier antagonist, waited for him one day round a corner, gun in hand. The gun was discharged, and wounded, not Marino, but a favourite servant of the Duke. For this offence the assassin was condemned to death; and would apparently have been executed, but for Marino's generosity. He procured his enemy's pardon, and was repaid with the blackest ingratitude. On his release from prison Murtola laid hands upon a satire, 'La Cuccagna,' written some time previously by his rival. This he laid before the Duke, as a seditious attack upon the government of Savoy. Marino now in his turn was imprisoned; but he proved, through the intervention of Manso, that the 'Cuccagna' had been published long before his arrival at Turin. Disgusted by these incidents, he next accepted an invitation from the French Court, and journeyed to Paris in 1615, where the Italianated society of that city received him like a living Phœbus. Maria de' Medici, as Regent, with Concini for her counsellor and lover, was then in all her vulgar glory. Richelieu's star had not arisen to eclipse Italian intrigue and to form French taste by the Academy. D'Urfè and Du Bartas, more marinistic than Marino, more euphuistic than Euphues, gave laws to literature; and the pageant pictures by Rubens, which still adorn the Gallery of the Louvre, marked the full-blown and sensuous splendour of Maria's equipage. Marino's genius corresponded nicely to the environment in which he now found himself; the Italians of the French Court discerned in him the poet who could best express their ideal of existence. He was idolised, glutted with gold, indulged and flattered to the top of his bent. Yearly appointments estimated at 10,000 crowns were augmented by presents in return for complimentary verses or for copies of the poem he was then composing. This poem was the 'Adone,' the theme of which had been suggested by Carlo Emmanuele, and which he now adroitly used as a means of flattering the French throne. First printed at Paris in 1623, its reception both there and in Italy secured apotheosis in his lifetime for the poet.[12] One minor point in this magnificent first folio edition of 'Adone' deserves notice, as not uncharacteristic of the age. Only two Cantos out of the twenty are distinguished by anything peculiar in their engraved decorations. Of these two, the eleventh, displays the shield of France; the thirteenth, which describes Falserina's incantations and enchantments, is ornamented with the symbol of the Jesuits, I.H.S. For this the publishers alone were probably responsible. Yet it may stand as a parable of all-pervasive Jesuitry. Even among the roses and raptures of the most voluptuous poem of the century their presence makes itself felt, as though to hint that the 'Adone' is capable of being used according to Jesuitical rules of casuistry A.M.D.G. One warning voice was raised before the publication of this epic. Cardinal Bentivoglio wrote from Italy beseeching Marino to 'purge it of lasciviousness in such wise that

[12] It is worth noting that Shakspere's *Venus and Adonis* was first printed in 1593, thirty years previously.

it may not have to dread the lash of our Italian censure.' Whether he followed this advice, in other words whether the original MS. of the 'Adone' was more openly licentious than the published poem, I do not know. Anyhow, it was put upon the Index in 1627. This does not, however, appear to have impaired its popularity, or to have injured its author's reputation. Soon after the appearance of 'Adone,' Marino, then past fifty, returned to Naples. He was desirous of reposing on his laurels, wealthy, honoured, and adored, among the scenes from which he fled in danger and disgrace thirty years before. His entrance into Naples was an ovation. The lazzaroni came to meet his coach, dancing and scattering roses; noblemen attended him on horseback; ladies gazed on him from balconies. A banner waving to the wind announced the advent of 'that ocean of incomparable learning, soul of lyres, subject for pens, material for ink, most eloquent, most fertile, phoenix of felicity, ornament of the laurel, of swans in their divine leisure chief and uncontested leader.' At Naples he died in 1625—felicitous in not having survived the fame which attended him through life and reached its climax just before his death.

The 'Adone' strikes us at first sight as the supreme poem of epicene voluptuousness. Its smooth-chinned hero, beautiful as a girl, soft as a girl, sentimental as a girl, with nothing of the man about him—except that 'Nature, as she wrought him, fell adoting'—threads a labyrinth of suggestive adventures, in each of which he is more the patient than the agent of desire. Mercury introduces him to our attention in a series of those fables (tales of Narcissus, Ganymede, Cyparissus, Hylas, Atys) by which antiquity figured the seductiveness of adolescence. Venus woos him, and Falserina tries to force him. Captured in feminine attire by brigands, he is detained in a cave as the mistress of their chief, and doted on by the effeminate companion of his prison. Finally, he contends for the throne of Cyprus with a band of luxurious youths—

Bardassonacci, paggi da taverna.

The crown is destined for the physically fairest. The rival charms of the competitors are minutely noted, their personal blemishes sagaciously detected, by a council of pleasure-sated worldlings. In his death Adonis succumbs to the assault of a boar, fatally inflamed with lust, who wounds the young man in his groin, dealing destruction where the beast meant only amorous caresses. Gods and goddesses console Venus in her sorrow for his loss, each of whom relates the tale of similar disasters. Among these legends Apollo's love for Hyacinth and Phœbus' love for Pampinus figure conspicuously. Thus Marino's Adonis excites unhealthy interest by the spectacle of boyhood exposed to the caprices and allurements of both sexes doting on unfledged virility.

What contributes to this effect, in the central motive of the poem, is that Venus herself is no artless virgin, no innocent Chloe, corresponding to a rustic Daphnis. She is already wife, mother, adulteress, *femme entretenue*, before she meets the lad. Her method of treating him is that of a licentious queen, who, after seducing page or groom, keeps the instrument of her pleasures in seclusion for occasional indulgence during intervals of public business. Vulcan and Mars, her husband and her *cicisbeo*, contest the woman's right to this caprice; and when the god of war compels, she yields him the crapulous fruition of her charms before the eyes of her disconsolate boy-paramour. Her preoccupation with Court affairs in Cythera—balls, pageants, sacrifices, and a people's homage—brings about the catastrophe. Through her temporary neglect, Adonis falls victim to a conspiracy of the gods. Thus the part which the female plays in this amorous epic is that of an accomplished courtesan, highly placed in society. All the pathos, all the attraction of beauty and of sentiment, is reserved for the adolescent male.

This fact, though disagreeable, has to be noted. It is too characteristic of the wave of feeling at that time passing over Europe, to be ignored. The morbid strain which touched the Courts alike of Valois, Medici, and Stuarts; which infected the poetry of Marlowe and of Shakspere; which cast a sickly pallor even over sainthood and over painting in the school of Bologna, cannot be neglected. In Marino's 'Adone' it reaches its artistic climax.[13]

This, however, is not the main point about the poem. The 'Adone' should rather be classed as the epic of voluptuousness in all its forms and species. If the love-poetry of the Italian Renaissance began with the sensuality of Boccaccio's 'Amorosa Visione,' it ended, after traversing the idyll, the novel, the pastoral, the elegy and the romance, in the more complex sensuality of Marino's 'Adone;' for this, like the 'Amorosa Visione,' but far more emphatically, proclaims the beatification of man by sexual pleasure:—

> Tramortiscon di gioia ebbre e languenti
> L' anime stanche, al ciel d' Amor rapite.
> Gl' iterati sospiri, i rotti accenti,
> Le dolcissime guerre e le ferite,
> Narrar non so—fresche aure, onde correnti,
> Voi che il miraste, e ben l' udiste, il dite!
> Voi secretari de' felici amori,
> Verdi mirti, alti pini, ombrosi allori! (Canto viii.)

Thus voluptuousness has its transcendentalism; and Marino finds even his prolific vocabulary inadequate to express the mysteries of this heaven of sensuous delights.[14]

It must not be thought that the 'Adone' is an obscene poem. Marino was too skilful a master in the craft of pleasure to revolt or to regale

[13] Ferrari, in his *Rivoluzioni d' Italia*, vol. iii. p. 563, observes: 'Una Venere sospetta versa lagrime forse maschili sul bellissimo Adonide,' &c. Shakspere's *Venus and Adonis*, in like manner, is so written as to force the reader to feel with Venus the seduction of Adonis.

[14] With the stanza quoted above Marino closes the cycle which Boccaccio in the *Amoroso Visione* (canto xlix.) had opened.

his readers with grossness. He had too much of the Neapolitan's frank self-abandonment to nature for broad indecency in art to afford him special satisfaction; and the taste of his age demanded innuendo. The laureate of Courts and cities saturated with licentiousness knew well that Coan vestments are more provocative than nudity. It was his object to flatter the senses and seduce the understanding rather than to stimulate coarse appetite. Refinement was the aphrodisiac of a sated society, and millinery formed a main ingredient in its love-philtres.[15] Marino, therefore, took the carnal instincts for granted, and played upon them as a lutist plays upon the strings of some lax thrilling instrument. Of moral judgment, of antipathy to this or that form of lust, of prejudice or preference in the material of pleasure, there is no trace. He shows himself equally indulgent to the passion of Mirra for her father, of Jove for Ganymede, of Bacchus for Pampinus, of Venus for Adonis, of Apollo for Hyacinth. He tells the disgusting story of Cinisca with the same fluent ease as the lovely tale of Psyche; passes with the same light touch over Falserina at the bedside of Adonis and Feronia in his dungeon; uses the same palette for the picture of Venus caressing Mars and the struggles of the nymph and satyr. All he demanded was a basis of soft sensuality, from which, as from putrescent soil, might spring the pale and scented flower of artful luxury.

In harmony with the spirit of an age reformed or deformed by the Catholic Revival, Marino parades cynical hypocrisy. The eighth canto of 'Adone' is an elaborately wrought initiation into the mysteries of carnal pleasure. It is a hymn to the sense of touch:[16]

> Ogni altro senso può ben di leggiero
> Deluso esser talor da falsi oggetti:
> Questo sol no, lo qual sempre è del vero
> Fido ministro e padre dei diletti.
> Gli altri non possedendo il corpo intero,
> Ma qualche parte sol, non son perfetti.
> Questo con atto universal distende
> Le sue forze per tutto, e tutto il prende.

We are led by subtle gradations, by labyrinthine delays, to the final beatification of Adonis. Picture is interwoven with picture, each in turn contributing to the panorama of sensual Paradise. Yet while straining all the resources of his art, with intense sympathy, to seduce his reader, the poet drops off set purpose phrases like the following:

> Flora non so, non so se Frine o Taide
> Trovar mai seppe oscenità si laide.

---

[15] On this point I may call attention to the elaborate portraits drawn by Marino (canto xvi.) of the seven young men who contend with Adonis for the prize of beauty and the crown of Cyprus. Quite as many words are bestowed upon their costumes, jewelry and hairdressing as upon their personal charms.

[16] I have pleasure in inviting my readers to study the true doctrine regarding the place of touch among the senses as laid down by Ruskin in *Modern Painters*, part iii. sec. I, chap. ii.

Here the ape masked in the man turns round and grins, gibbering vulgar words to point his meaning, and casting dirt on his pretended decency. While racking the resources of allusive diction to veil and to suggest an immodest movement of his hero (Adonis being goaded beyond the bounds of boyish delicacy by lascivious sights), he suddenly subsides with a knavish titter into prose:

Così il fanciullo all' inonesto gioco.

But the end of all this practice is that innocent Adonis has been conducted by slow and artfully contrived approaches to a wanton's embrace, and that the spectators of his seduction have become, as it were, parties to his fall. To make Marino's cynicism of hypocrisy more glaring, he prefaces each canto with an allegory, declaring that Adonis and Venus symbolise the human soul abandoned to vice, and the allurements of sensuality which work its ruin. In the poem itself, meanwhile, the hero and heroine are consistently treated as a pair of enviable, devoted, and at last unfortunate lovers.[17]

It is characteristic of the mood expressed in the 'Adone' that voluptuousness should not be passionate, but sentimental. Instead of fire, the poet gives us honeyed tears to drink, and rocks the soul upon an ever-rippling tide of Lydian melody. The acme of pleasure, as conceived by him, is kissing. Twenty-three of the most inspired stanzas of the eighth canto are allotted to a panegyric of the kiss, in which delight all other amorous delights are drowned.[18] Tasso's melancholy yearning after forbidden fruit is now replaced by satiety contemplating the image of past joys with purring satisfaction. This quality of self-contented sentiment partly explains why the type of beauty adored is neither womanly nor manly, but adolescent. It has to be tender, fragile, solicitous, unripe; appealing to sensibility, not to passion, by feminine charms in nerveless and soulless boyhood. The most distinctive mark of Adonis is that he has no character, no will, no intellect. He is all sentiment, sighs, tears, pliability, and sweetness. This emasculate nature displays itself with consummate effect in the sobbing farewell, followed by the pretty pettishnesses, of the seventeenth canto.

As a contrast to his over-sweet and cloying ideal of lascivious grace, Marino counterposes extravagant forms of ugliness. He loves to describe the loathsome incantations of witches. He shows Falserina prowling among corpses on a battlefield, and injecting the congealed veins of her resuscitated victim with abominable juices. He crowds

[17] The hypocrisy of the allegory is highly significant for this phase of Italian culture. We have seen how even Tasso condescended to apply it to his noble epic, which needed no such miserable pretence. Exquisitely grotesque was the attempt made by Centorio degli Ortensi to sanctify Bandello's *Novelle* by supplying each one of them with a moral interpretation (ed. Milano: Gio. Antonio degli Antoni, 1560. See Passano's *Novellieri in Prosa*, p. 28).

[18] What I have elsewhere called 'the tyranny of the kiss' in Italian poetry, begins in Tasso's *Rinaldo*, acquires vast proportions in Guarino's *Pastor Fido*, and becomes intolerable in Marino's *Adone*.

the Cave of Jealousy with monsters horrible to sight and sense; depicts the brutality of brigands; paints hideous portraits of eunuchs, deformed hags, unnameable abortions. He gloats over cruelty, and revels in violence.[19] When Mars appears upon the scene, the orchestra of lutes and cymbals with which we had been lulled to sleep, is exchanged for a Corybantic din of dissonances. Orgonte, the emblem of pride, outdoes the hyperboles of Rodomonte and the lunes of Tamburlaine. Nowhere, either in his voluptuousness or in its counterpart of disgust, is there moderation. The Hellenic precept, 'Nothing overmuch,' the gracious Greek virtue of temperate restraint, which is for art what training is for athletes, discipline for soldiers, and pruning for orchard trees, has been violated in every canto, each phrase, the slightest motive of this poem. Sensuality can bear such violation better than sublimity; therefore the perfume of voluptuousness in the 'Adone,' though excessive, is both penetrating and profound; while those passages which aim at inspiring terror or dilating the imagination, fail totally of their effect. The ghastly, grotesque, repulsive images are so overcharged that they cease even to offend. We find ourselves in a region where tact, sense of proportion, moral judgment, and right adjustment of means to ends, have been wantonly abandoned. Marino avowed that he only aimed at surprising his readers:

È del poeta il fin la meraviglia.

But 45,000 verses of sustained astonishment, of industrious and indefatigable appeals to wonder by devices of language, devices of incident, devices of rhodomontade, devices of innuendo, devices of *capricci* and *concetti*, induce the stolidity of callousness. We leave off marvelling, and yield what is left of our sensibility to the fascination of inexhaustible picturesqueness. For, with all his faults, Marino was a master of the picturesque, and did possess an art of fascination. The picturesque, so difficult to define, so different from the pictorial and the poetical, was a quality of the seventeenth century corresponding to its defects of bad taste. And this gift no poet shared in larger measure than Marino.

Granted his own conditions, granted the emptiness of moral and intellectual substance in the man and in his age, we are compelled to acknowledge that his literary powers were rich and various. Few writers, at the same time, illustrate the vices of decadence more luminously than this Protean poet of vacuity. Few display more clearly the 'expense of spirit in a waste of shame.' None teach the dependence of art upon moralised and humane motives more significantly than this drunken Helot of genius. His indifference to truth, his defiance of sobriety, his conviction that the sole end of art is astonishment, have doomed him to oblivion not wholly merited. The critic, whose duty forces him to read through the 'Adone,' will be left bewildered by the

[19] See the climax to the episode of Filauro and Filora.

spectacle of such profuse wealth so wantonly squandered.[20] In spite of fatigue, in spite of disgust, he will probably be constrained to record his opinion that, while Tasso represented the last effort of noble poetry struggling after modern expression under outworn forms of the Classical Revival, it was left for Marino in his levity and license to evoke a real and novel though *rococo* form, which nicely corresponded to the temper of his times, and determined the immediate future of art. For this reason he requires the attention which has here been paid him.

But how, it may be asked, was it possible to expand the story of Venus and Adonis into an epic of 45,000 lines? The answer to this question could best be given by an analysis of the twenty cantos; and since few living students have perused them, such a display of erudition would be pardonable. Marino does not, however, deserve so many pages in a work devoted to the close of the Italian Renaissance. It will suffice to say that the slender narrative of the amour of Venus and her boyish idol, his coronation as king of Cyprus, and his death by the boar's tusk, is ingeniously interwoven with a great variety of episodes. The poet finds occasion to relate the principal myths of Hellenic passion, treating these in a style which frequently reminds us of Ovid's Metamorphoses; he borrows tales from Apuleius, Lucian, and the pastoral novelists; he develops the theme of jealousy in Mars and Vulcan, introduces his own autobiography, digresses into romantic adventures by sea and land, creates a rival to Venus in the sorceress Falserina, sketches the progress of poetry in one canto, and devotes another to a panegyric of Italian princes, extols the House of France and adulates Marie de Medicis, surveys the science of the century, describes fantastic palaces and magic gardens, enters with curious minuteness into the several delights of the five senses, discourses upon Courts, ambition, avarice and honour, journeys over the Mediterranean, conducts a game of chess through fifty brilliant stanzas; in brief, while keeping his main theme in view, is careful to excite and sustain the attention of his readers by a succession of varied and ingeniously suggested novelties. Prolixity, indefatigable straining after sensational effect, interminable description, are the defects of the 'Adone;' but they are defects related to great qualities possessed by the author, to inexhaustible resources, curious knowledge, the improvisatore's facility, the trained rhetorician's dexterity in the use of language, the artist's fervid delight in the exercise of his craft.

[20] In support of this opinion upon Marino's merit as a poet, I will cite the episode of Clizio (canto i. p. 17); the tale of Psyche (iv. 65); the tale of the nightingale and the boy—which occurs both in Ford and Crashaw, by the way (vii. 112); the hymn to pleasure (vii. 116); the passage of Venus and Adonis to the bath (viii. 133); the picture of the nymph and satyr (viii. 135); the personification of the Court (x. 167); the Cave of Jealousy (xii. 204-206); the jewel-garden of Falserina (xii. 218); Falserina watching Adonis asleep (xii. 225); Falserina's incantations (xiii. 233); Mars in the lap of Venus surrounded by the loves (xiii. 245); Venus disguised as a gypsy (xv. 290); the game of chess (xv. 297); the leave-taking of Venus and Adonis (xvii. 332); the phantom of dead Adonis (xviii. 357); the grief of Venus (xviii. 358-362); the tales of Hyacinth and Pampinus (xix. 372-378). The references are to ed. Napoli, Boutteaux, 1861.

Allowing for Marino's peculiar method, his 'Adone' has the excellence of unity which was so highly prized by the poets of his age and nation. Critics have maintained that the whole epic is but a development of the episode of Rinaldo in Armida's garden. But it is more than this. It contains all the main ingredients of the Italian Romance, with the exception of chivalry and war. There is a pastoral episode corresponding to that of Erminia among the shepherds, a magnificent enchantress in the manner of Alcina, an imprisonment of the hero which reminds us of Ruggiero in Atlante's magic castle, a journey like Astolfo's to the moon, a conflict between good and evil supernatural powers, a thread of allegory more or less apparent, a side glance at contemporary history; and these elements are so combined as to render the 'Adone' one of the many poems in the long romantic tradition. It differs mainly from its predecessors in the strict unity of subject, which subordinates each episode and each digression to the personal adventures of the heroine and hero; while the death and obsequies of Adonis afford a tragic close that is lacking to previous poems detached from the Carolingian cycle. Contemporary writers praised it as a poem of peace. But it is the poem of ignoble peace, of such peace as Italy enjoyed in servitude, when a nation of *cicisbei* had naught to occupy their energies but sensual pleasure. Ingenious as Marino truly was in conducting his romance upon so vast a scheme through all its windings to one issue, we feel that the slender tale of a boy's passion for the queen of courtesans and his metamorphosis into the scarlet windflower of the forest supplied no worthy motive for this intricate machinery. The metaphor of an alum basket crystallised upon a petty frame of wire occurs to us when we contemplate its glittering ornaments, and reflect upon the poverty of the sustaining theme. It might in fact stand for a symbol of the intellectual vacancy of the age which welcomed it with rapture, and of the society which formed a century of taste upon its pattern.

In another and higher literary quality the 'Adone' represents that moment of Italian development. A foreigner may hardly pass magisterial judgment on its diction. Yet I venture to remark that Marino only at rare intervals attains to purity of poetic style; even his best passages are deformed, not merely by conceits to which the name of *Marinism* has been given, but also by gross vulgarities and lapses into trivial prose. Notwithstanding this want of distinction, however, he has a melody that never fails. The undulating, evenly on-flowing *cantilena* of his verbal music sustains the reader on a tide of song. That element of poetry, which, as I have observed, was developed with remarkable success by Tasso in some parts of the 'Gerusalemme,' is the main strength of the 'Adone.' With Marino the 'Chant d'Amour' never rises so high, thrills so subtly, touches the soul so sweetly and so sadly, as it does in Tasso's verse. But in all those five thousand octave stanzas it is rarely altogether absent. The singing faculty of the Neapolitan was given to this poet of voluptuousness; and if the song is neither deep nor stirring, neither stately nor sublime, it is because his soul held nothing in its vast vacuity but sensuous joy.[21] A musical Casanova, an unmalignant Aretino, he sang as vulgar nature prompted; but he always kept on singing. His partiality for detonating dissonances, squibs and crackers of pyrotechnical rhetoric, braying trumpets and exploding popguns, which deafen and distract our ears attuned to the suave cadence of the *cantilena*, is no less characteristic of the Neapolitan. Marino had the improvisatory exuberance, the impudence, the superficial passion, the luxurious delight in life, and the noisiness of his birthplace. He also shared its love of the grotesque as complement and contrast to pervading beauty.

A serious fault to be found with Marino's style is its involved exaggeration in description. Who, for instance, can tolerate this picture of a young man's foot shod with a blue buskin?

> L' animato del piè molle alabastro
> Che oscura il latte del sentier celeste
> Stretto alla gamba con purpureo nastro
> Di cuoio azzurro un borsacchin gli veste.

Again he carries to the point of lunacy that casuistical rhetoric, introduced by Ariosto and refined upon by Tasso, with which luckless heroines or heroes announce their doubts and difficulties to the world in long soliloquies. The ten stanzas which set forth Falserina's feelings after she has felt the pangs of love for Adonis, might pass for a parody:

> Ardo, lassa, o non ardo! ahì qual io sento
> Stranio nel cor non conosciuto affetto!
> E forse ardore? ardor non è, chè spento
> L' avrei col pianto; è ben d' ardor sospetto!
> Sospetto no, piuttosto egli è tormento.
> Come tormento fia, se dà diletto?

And so forth through eighty lines in which every conceivable change is rung upon *Amo o non amò? . . . Io vivo e moro pur . . . Io non ho core e lo mio cor n' ha dui.* With all this effort no one is convinced of Falserina's emotion, and her long-winded oration reads like a schoolboy's exercise upon some line of the fourth Æneid. Yet if we allow

[21] There are passages of pure *cantilena* in this poem, where sense is absolutely swallowed up in sound, and words become the mere vehicle for rhythmic melody. Of this verbal music the dirge of the nymphs for Adonis and the threnos of Venus afford excellent examples (xix. pp. 358-361). Note especially the stanza beginning:

> Adone, Adone, o bell' Adon, tu giaci,
> Nè senti i miei sospir, nè miri il pianto!
> O bell' Adone, o caro Adon, tu taci,
> Nè rispondi a colei che amasti tanto!

There is nothing more similar to this in literature than Fra Jacopone's delirium of mystic love:

> Amor amor Jesu, son giunto a porto;
> Amor amor Jesu, tu m' hai menato;
> Amor amor Jesu, dammi conforto;
> Amor amor Jesu, sì m' hai enfiammato.

Only the one is written in a Mixo-Lydian, the other in a Hyper-Phrygian mood.

the sense of rhythmical melody to intervene between our intellectual perception and Marino's language, we shall still be able to translate these outpourings into something which upon the operatic stage would keep its value. False rhetoric and the inability to stop when enough and more than enough has been said upon any theme to be developed, are the incurable defects of Marino. His profuse *fioriture* compared with the simpler descant of Ariosto or Tasso remind us of Rossini's florid roulades beside the grace of Pergolese's or the majesty of Marcello's song.

The peculiar quality of bad taste which is known in Italy as *Marinismo,* consisted in a perpetual straining after effect by antitheses, conceits, plays on words degenerating into equivocation, and such-like rhetorical grimaces. Marino's *ars poetica* was summed up in this sentence: 'Chi non sa far stupir, vada alla striglia.' Therefore, he finds periphrases for the simplest expressions. He calls the nightingale *sirena de' boschi*, gunpowder *l' irreparabil fulmine terreno*, Columbus *il ligure Argonauta*, Galileo *il novello Endimione*. In these instances, what might have been expanded into a simile, is substituted for the proper word in order to surprise the reader. When he alludes to Dante, he poses a conundrum on that poet's surname: *Ben sull' ali liggier tre mondi canta*. The younger Palma is complimented on wresting the *palm* from Titian and Veronese. Guido Reni is apostrophised as: *Reni onde il maggior Reno all' altro cede.*[22] We are never safe in reading his pages from the whirr and whistle of such verbal fireworks. And yet it must be allowed that Marino's style is on the whole freer from literary affectations than that of our own Euphuists. It is only at intervals that the temptation to make a point by clever trickery seems irresistible. When he is seriously engaged upon a topic that stirs his nature to the depth, as in the eighth canto, description flows on for stanza after stanza with limpid swiftness. Another kind of artifice to which he has resort, is the repetition of a dominant word:

> Con tai lusinghe il lusinghiero amante
> La lusinghiera Dea lusinga e prega.
>
> . . . .
>
> Godiamci, amiamci. Amor d' amor mercede,
> Degno cambio d' amore è solo amore.

This play on a word sometimes passes over into a palpable pun, as in the following pretty phrase:

> O mia dorata et adorata Dea.

Still we feel that Shakspere was guilty of precisely the same verbal impertinences. It is only intensity of feeling which prevents such lines as:

> Take all my loves, my love, yea take them all;
> What hast thou then more than thou hadst before?
> No love, my love, that thou may'st true love call:
> All mine was thine, before thou hadst this more:

[22] There is a streamlet called Reno near Bologna.

from being Marinistic. But it must be added that this intensity of feeling renders the artifice employed sublimely natural. Here we lay our finger on the crucial point at issue in any estimate of literary mannerism. What is the force of thought, the fervour of emotion, the acute perception of truth in nature and in man, which lies behind that manneristic screen? If, as in the case of Shakspere, sufficiency or superabundance of these essential elements is palpable, we pardon, we ignore, the euphuism. But should the quality of substance fail, then we repudiate it and despise it. Therefore Marino, who is certainly not more euphuistic than Shakspere, but who has immeasurably less of potent stuff in him, wears the motley of his barocco style in limbo bordering upon oblivion, while the Swan of Avon parades the same literary livery upon both summits of Parnassus. So true it is that poetry cannot be estimated apart from intellectual and moral contents. Had Marino written:

> Prick love for pricking, and you beat love down:

or:

> 'twould anger him
> To raise a spirit in his mistress' circle
> Of some strange nature, letting it there stand
> Till she had laid it and conjured it down:

or:

> The bawdy hand of the dial is now upon
> The prick of noon:

he would have furnished his accusers with far stronger diatribes against words of double meaning and licentious conceits than his own pages offer. But since it was out of the fulness of world-wisdom that Shakspere penned those phrases for Mercutio, and set them as pendents to the impassioned descants upon love and death which he poured from the lips of Romeo, they pass condoned and unperceived.

Only poverty of matter and insincerity of fancy damn in Marino those literary affectations which he held in common with a host of writers—with Gorgias, Æschylus, Chæremon, Philostratus, among Greeks; with Petrarch, Boccaccio, Bembo, Aretino, Tasso, Guarini, among Italians; with Calderon and Cervantes, not to mention Gongora, among Spaniards; with the foremost French and English writers of the Renaissance; with all verbal artists in any age, who have sought unduly to refine upon their material of language. In a word, Marino is not condemned by his so-called Marinism. His true stigma is the inadequacy to conceive of human nature except under a twofold mask of sensuous voluptuousness and sensuous ferocity. It is this narrow and ignoble range of imagination which constitutes his real inferiority, far more than any poetical extravagance in diction. The same mean conception of humanity brands with ignominy the four generations over which he dominated—that brood of eunuchs and courtiers, churchmen and *Cavalieri serventi*, barocco architects and brigands, casuists and bravi, grimacers, hypocrites, confessors, impostors, bastards of the spirit, who controlled Italian culture for a hundred years.

At a first glance we shall be astonished to find that this poet, who may justly be regarded as the coryphæus of Circean orgies in the seventeenth century, left in MS. a grave lament upon the woes of Italy. Marino's 'Pianto d' Italia' has no trace of Marinism. It is composed with sobriety in a pedestrian style of plainness, and it tells the truth without reserve. Italy traces her wretchedness to one sole cause, subjection under Spanish rule.

> Lascio ch' un re che di real non tiene
> Altro che il nome effemminato e vile
> A sua voglia mi reggi, e di catene
> Barbare mi circondi il piè servile.

This tyrant foments jealousy and sows seeds of discord between the Italian states. His viceroys are elected from the cruellest, the most unjust, the most rapacious, and the most luxurious of the courtiers crawling round his throne. The College of Cardinals is bought and sold. No prince dares move a finger in his family or state without consulting the Iberian senate; still less can he levy troops for self-defence. Yet throughout Europe Spanish victories have been obtained by Italian generals; the bravest soldiers in foreign armies are Italian exiles. Perhaps it may be argued that the empty titles which abound in every petty city, the fulsome promises on which those miserable vassals found their hopes, are make-weights for such miseries. Call them rather chains to bind the nation, lures and birdlime such as snarers use. There is but one quarter to which the widowed and discrowned Queen of Nations can appeal for succour. She turns to Carlo Emmanuele, Duke of Savoy, to the hills whence cometh help. It was not, however, until two centuries after Marino penned these patriotic stanzas, that her prayer was answered. And the reflection forced upon us when we read the 'Pianto d' Italia,' is that Marino composed it to flatter a patron who at that moment entertained visionary schemes of attacking the Spanish hegemony.

To make any but an abrupt transition from Marino to Chiabrera would be impossible. It is like passing from some luxurious grove of oranges and roses to a barren hill-top without prospect over sea or champaign. We are fortunate in possessing a few pages of autobiography, from which all that is needful to remember of Gabriello Chiabrera's personal history may be extracted. He was born in 1552 at Savona, fifteen days after his father's death. His mother made a second marriage, and left him to the care of an uncle, with whom at the age of nine he went to reside in Rome. In the house of this bachelor uncle the poor little orphan pined away. Fever succeeded fever, until his guardian felt that companionship with boys in play and study was the only chance of saving so frail a life as Gabriello's. Accordingly he placed the invalid under the care of the Jesuits in their Collegio Romano.

Here the child's health revived, and his education till the age of twenty throve apace. The Jesuits seem to have been liberal in their course of training; for young Chiabrera benefited by private conversation with Paolo Manuzio and Sperone Speroni, while he attended the lectures of Muretus in the university.

How different was this adolescence from that of Marino! Both youths grew to manhood without domestic influences; and both were conspicuous in after life for the want of that affection which abounds in Tasso. But here the parallel between them ends. Marino, running wild upon the streets of Naples, taking his fill of pleasure and adventure, picking up ill-digested information at hap-hazard, and forming his poetic style as nature prompted; Chiabrera, disciplined in piety and morals by Jesuit directors, imbued with erudition by an arid scholar, a formal pedant and an accomplished rhetorician, the three chief representatives of decadent Italian humanism: no contrast can be imagined greater than that which marked these two lads out for diverse paths in literature. The one was formed to be the poet of caprice and license, openly ranking with those

Che la ragion sommettono al talento,

and making *s' ei piace ei lice* his rule of conduct and of art. The other received a rigid bent toward decorum, in religious observances, in ethical severity, and in literature of a strictly scholastic type.

Yet Chiabrera was not without the hot blood of Italian youth. His uncle died, and he found himself alone in the world. After spending a few years in the service of Cardinal Cornaro, he quarrelled with a Roman gentleman, vindicated his honour by some act of violence, and was outlawed from the city. Upon this he retired to Savona; and here again he met with similar adventures. Wounded in a brawl, he took the law into his own hands, and revenged himself upon his assailant. This punctilio proved him to be a true child of his age; and if we may credit his own account of both incidents, he behaved himself as became a gentleman of the period. It involved him, however, in serious annoyances both at Rome and Savona, from which he only extricated himself with difficulty and which impaired his fortune. Up to the age of fifty he remained unmarried, and then took a wife by whom he had no children. He lived to the ripe age of eighty-four, always at Savona, excepting occasional visits to friends in Italian cities, and he died unmolested by serious illness after his first entrance into the Collegio Romano. How he occupied the leisure of that lengthy solitude may be gathered from his published works—two or three thick volumes of lyrics; four bulky poems of heroic narrative; twelve dramas, including two tragedies; thirty satires or epistles; and about forty miscellaneous poems in divers metres. In a word, he devoted his whole life to the art of poetry, for which he was not naturally gifted, and which he pursued in a gravely methodical spirit. It may be said at once that the body of his work, with the exception of some simple pieces of occasion, and a few chastely written epistles, is such as nobody can read without weariness.

Before investigating Chiabrera's claim to rank among Italian poets, it may be well to examine his autobiography in those points which touch upon the temper of society. Short as it is, this document is precious for the light it casts upon contemporary custom. As a writer, Chiabrera was distinguished by sobriety of judgment, rectitude, piety, purity of feeling, justice toward his fellow-workers in literature, and an earnest desire to revive the antique virtues among his countrymen. There is no reason to suppose that these estimable qualities did not distinguish him in private life. Yet eight out of the eighteen pages of his life are devoted to comically solemn details regarding the honours paid him by Italian princes. The Grand Duke of Florence, Ferdinand I., noticed him standing with uncovered head at a theatrical representation in the Pitti Palace. He bade the poet put his cap on and sit down. Cosimo, the heir-apparent, showed the same condescending courtesy. When he was at Turin, Carlo Emmanuele, Duke of Savoy, placed a coach and pair at his disposal, and allowed him 300 lire for travelling expenses to and from Savona. But this prince omitted to appoint him lodgings in the palace, nor did he invite him to cover in the presence. This perhaps is one reason why Chiabrera refused the Duke's offer of a secretaryship at Court. Vincenzo Gonzaga, Duke of Mantua, on the contrary, allotted him rooms and always suffered him to keep his hat on. The Pope, who was an old college friend of Chiabrera, made him handsome presents, and on one delightful occasion allowed him to hear a sermon in the Papal pew. The Doge of Genoa, officially particular in points of etiquette, always took care to bid him cover, although he was a subject born of the Republic.

Basely insignificant as are these details, they serve to show what value was then ascribed even by men of real respectability to trifling princely favours. The unction with which Chiabrera relates them, warming his cold style into a glow of satisfaction, is a practical satire upon his endeavour to resuscitate the virtues of antique republics in that Italy. To do this was his principal aim as a moralist; to revive the grand style of Pindar was his object as an artist. Each attempt involved impossibility, and argued a visionary ambition dimly conscious of its scope. Without freedom, without the living mythology of Hellas, without a triumphant national cause, in the very death of independence, at the end of a long age of glorious but artificial culture, how could Chiabrera dare to pose as Pindar? Instead of the youth of Greece ascending with free flight and all the future of the world before it, decrepit Italy, the Italy so rightly drawn by Marino in his 'Pianto,' lay grovelling in the dust of decaying thrones. Her lyrist had to sing of pallone-matches instead of Panhellenic games; to celebrate the heroic conquest of two Turkish galleys by a Tuscan fleet, instead of Marathon and Salamis; to praise S. Lucy and S. Paul with tepid fervour, instead of telling how Rhodes swam at her god's bidding upward from the waves.

One example will serve as well as many to illustrate the false attitude assumed by Chiabrera when he posed as a new Pindar in the midst of seventeenth-century Italians. I will select the Ode to Don Cesare d' Este. There is something pathetically ridiculous in this would-be swan of the Dircean fount, this apostle of pagan virtues, admonishing the heir of Alfonso II. to prove himself an obedient son of the Church by relinquishing his Duchy of Ferrara to the Holy See. The poet asks him, in fine classic phrases, whether he could bear to look on desecrated altars, confessionals without absolving priests, chapels without choristers, a people barred with bolt and lock from Paradise. How trivial are earthly compared with heavenly crowns! How vulgar is the love of power and gold! The exhortation, exquisite enough in chastened style, closes with this hypocritical appeal to Cesare's aristocratic prejudices:

> Parli la plebe a suo volere, e pensi—
> Non con la plebe hanno da gir gli Estensi.

That is to say, nobility demands that the House of Este should desert its subjects, sacrifice its throne, crawl at a Pontiff's feet, and starve among a crowd of disthroned princes, wrapping the ragged purple of its misery around it till it, too, mixes with the people it contemns.

Hopeless as the venture was, Chiabrera made it the one preoccupation of his life, in these untoward circumstances, to remodel Italian poetry upon the Greek pattern. It was a merit of the Sei Cento, a sign of grace, that the Italians now at last threw orthodox æsthetic precepts to the winds, and avowed their inability to carry the Petrarchistic tradition further. The best of them, Campanella and Bruno, moulded vulgar language like metal in the furnace of a vehement imagination, making it the vehicle of fantastic passion and enthusiastic philosophy. From their crucible the Sonnet and the Ode emerged with no resemblance to academical standards. Grotesque, angular, gnarled, contorted, Gothic even, these antiquated forms beneath their wayward touch were scarcely recognisable. They had become the receptacles of burning, scalding, trenchant realities. Salvator Rosa, next below the best, forced indignation to lend him wings, and scaled Parnassus with brass-bound feet and fury. Marino, bent on riveting attention by surprises, fervid with his own reality of lust, employed the octave stanza as a Turkish Bey might use an odalisque. 'The only rule worth thinking of,' he said, 'is to know how and when and where to break all rules, adapting ourselves to current taste and the fashions of the age.' His epic represents a successful, because a vivid, reaction against conventionality. The life that throbs in it, is incontestable, even though that life may be nothing better than ephemeral. With like brutality of instinct, healthy because natural, the barocco architects embraced ugliness, discord, deformity, spasm, as an escape from harmony and regularity with which the times were satiated. Prose-writers burst the bonds of Bembo, trampled on Boccaccio, revelled in the stylistic debaucheries of Bartolo. Painters, rendered academic in vain by those Fabii of Bologna who had striven to restore the commonwealth of art by temporising, launched themselves upon a sea of massacre and murder, blood and entrails, horrors of dark woods and Bacchanalia of chubby Cupids. The popular Muse of Italy meanwhile emerged with furtive grace and inexhaustible vicacity in dialectic poems, dances, Pulcinello, Bergamasque Pantaloon, and what of parody and satire, Harlequinades, and carnival diversions, any local soil might cherish.[23] All this revolt against precedent, this resurrection of primeval instinct, crude and grinning, took place, let us remember, under the eyes of the Jesuits, within the shadow of the Inquisition, in an age reformed and ordered by the Council of Trent. Art was following Aretino, the reprobate and rebel. He first amid the languors of the golden age—and this is Aretino's merit—discerned that the only escape from its inevitable exhaustion was by passing over into crudest naturalism.

But for Chiabrera, the excellent gentleman, the patronised of princes, scrupulous upon the point of honour, pupil of Jesuits, pious, twisted back on humanism by his Roman tutors, what escape was left for him? Obey the genius of his times he must. Innovate he must. He chose the least indecorous sphere at hand for innovation; and felt therewith most innocently happy. Without being precisely conscious of it, he had discovered a way of adhering to time-honoured precedent while following the general impulse to discard precedent. He threw Petrarch overboard, but he took on Pindar for his pilot. 'When I see anything eminently beautiful, or hear something, or taste something that is excellent, I say: It is Greek Poetry.' In this self-revealing sentence lies the ruling instinct of the man as scholar. The highest praise he can confer upon Italian matters, is to call them Greek Poetry. 'When I have to express my aims in verse, I compare myself to Columbus, who said that he would discover a new world or drown.' Again, in this self-revealing sentence, Chiabrera betrays the instinct which in common with his period he obeyed. He was bound to startle society by a discovery or to drown. For this, be it remembered, was the time in which Pallavicino, like Marino, declared that poetry must make men raise their eyebrows in astonishment. For Chiabrera, educated as he had been, that new world toward which he navigated was a new Hellenic style of Italian poetry; and the Theban was to guide him toward its shores. But on the voyage Chiabrera drowned; drowned for eternity in hyper-atlantic whirlpools of oblivion. Some critics, pitying so lofty, so respectable an ambition, have whispered that he found a little Island of the Blest and there planted modest myrtles of mediocre immortality. Yet this is not the truth. On such a quest there was only failure or success. He did not succeed. His cold mincemeat from Dircean tables, tepid historic parallels, artificially concocted legends, could not create Greek poetry again beneath the ribs of death. The age was destined to be saved by music. License was its only liberty, as the 'Adone'

[23] See Scherillo's two books on the *Commedia dell' Arte* and the *Opera Buffa*.

taught. Unmusical Chiabrera, buckram'd up by old mythologies and sterling precepts, left its life untouched. His antique virtues stood, like stucco gods and goddesses, on pedestals in garden groves, and mouldered. His Pindaric flights were such as a sparrow, gazing upward at a hawk, might venture on. Those abrupt transitions, whereby he sought to simulate the lordly *sprezzatura* of the Theban eagle, 'sailing with supreme dominion through the azure deep of air,' remind us mainly of the hoppings of a frog. Chiabrera failed: failed all the more lamentably because he was so scholarly, so estimable. He is chiefly interesting now as the example of a man devoted to the Church, a pupil of Jesuits, a moralist, and a humanist, in some sense also a patriot, who felt the temper of his time, and strove to innovate in literature. Devoid of sincere sympathy with his academically chosen models, thinking he had discovered a safe path for innovation, he fell flat in the slime and perished.

Marino had human life and vulgar nature, the sensualities and frivolities of the century, to help him. Chiabrera claimed none of these advantages. What had Tassoni for his outfit? Sound common sense, critical acumen, the irony of humour, hatred of tyrants, and humbug, an acrid temper mollified by genial love of letters, a manly spirit of independence. Last, but not least, he inherited something of the old Elysian smile which played upon the lips of Ariosto, from which Tasso's melancholy shrank discomfited, which Marino smothered in the kisses of his courtesans, and Chiabrera banned as too ignoble for Dircean bards. This smile it was that cheered Tassoni's leisure, when, fallen on evil days, he penned the 'Secchia Rapita.'

Alessandro Tassoni was born in 1565 of a noble Modenese family. Before completing his nineteenth year he won the degree of Doctor of Laws, and afterwards spent twelve years in studying at the chief universities of Lombardy. Between 1599 and 1603 he served the Cardinal Ascanio Colonna both in Spain and Rome, as secretary. The insight he then gained into the working of Spanish despotism made him a relentless enemy of that already decadent monarchy. When Carlo Emmanuele, Duke of Savoy, sent back his Collar of the Golden Fleece in 1613 and drew the sword of resistance against Philip III., Tassoni penned two philippics against Spaniards, which are the firmest, most embittered expression of patriotism as it then existed. He had the acuteness to perceive that the Spanish state was no longer in its prime of vigour, and the noble ingenuousness to dream that Italian princes might be roused to sink their rancours in a common effort after independence. As a matter of fact, Estensi, Medici, Farnesi, Gonzaghi, all the reigning houses as yet unabsorbed by Church or Spain, preferred the predominance of a power which sanctioned their local tyrannies, irksome and degrading as that over-lordship was, to the hegemony of Piedmontese Macedon. And like all Italian patriots, strong in mind, feeble in muscle, he failed to reckon with the actual soldierly superiority of Spaniards. Italy could give generals at this epoch to her masters;

but she could not count on levying privates for her own defence. Carlo Emmanuele rewarded the generous ardour of Tassoni by grants of pensions which were never paid, and by offices at Court which involved the poet-student in perilous intrigue. 'My service with the princes of the House of Savoy,' so he wrote at a later period, 'did not take its origin in benefits or favours received or expected. It sprang from a pure spontaneous motion of the soul, which inspired me with love for the noble character of Duke Charles.' When he finally withdrew from that service, he had his portrait painted. In his hands he held a fig, and beneath the picture ran a couplet ending with the words, 'this the Court gave me.' Throughout his life Tassoni showed an independence rare in that century. His principal works were published without dedications to patrons. In the preface to his 'Remarks on Petrarch' he expressed his opinion thus: 'I leave to those who like them the fruitless dedications, not to say flatteries, which are customary nowadays. I seek no protection; for a lie does not deserve it, and truth is indifferent to it. Let such as opine that the shadow of great personages can conceal the ineptitude of authors, make the most of this advantage.' Believing firmly in astrology, he judged that his own horoscope condemned him to ill-success. It appears that he was born under the influence of Saturn, when the sun and moon were in conjunction; and he held that this combination of the heavenly bodies boded 'things noteworthy, yet not felicitous.' It was, however, difficult for a man of Tassoni's condition in that state of society to draw breath outside the circle of a Court. Accordingly, in 1626 he entered the service of the Pope's nephew, Cardinal Lodovisio. He did not find this much to his liking: 'I may compare myself to P. Emilius Metellus, when he was shod with those elegant boots which pinched his feet. Everybody said, Oh what fine boots, how well they fit! But the wretch was unable to walk in them.' On the Cardinal's death in 1632 Tassoni removed to the Court of Francesco I. of Modena, and died there in 1635.

As a writer, Tassoni, in common with the best spirits of his time, aimed at innovation. It had become palpable to the Italians that the Renaissance was over, and that they must break with the traditions of the past. This, as I have already pointed out, was the saving virtue of the early seventeenth century; but what good fruits it might have fostered, had not the political and ecclesiastical conditions of the age been adverse, remains a matter for conjecture. 'It is my will and object to utter new opinions,' he wrote to a friend; and acting upon this principle, he attacked the chief prejudices of his age in philosophy and literature. One of his earliest publications was a miscellaneous collection of 'Divers Thoughts,' in which he derided Aristotle's 'Physics' and propounded speculations similar to those developed by Gassendi. He dared to cast scorn on Homer, as rude and barbarous, poor in the faculty of invention, taxable with at least five hundred flagrant defects. How little Tassoni really comprehended Homer may be judged from his complacent assertion that the episode of Luna and Endymion

('Secchia Rapita,' canto viii.) was composed in the Homeric manner. In truth he could estimate the 'Iliad' and 'Odyssey' no better than Chiabrera could the Pythians and Olympians of Pindar. A just sense of criticism failed the scholars of that age, which was too remote in its customs, too imperfect in its science of history, to understand the essence of Greek art. With equally amusing candour Tassoni passed judgments upon Dante, and thought that he had rivalled the 'Purgatory' in his description of the Dawn ('Secchia Rapita,' viii. 15, the author's note). We must, however, be circumspect and take these criticisms with a grain of salt; for one never knows how far Tassoni may be laughing in his sleeve. There is no doubt, however, regarding the sincerity of his strictures upon the Della Cruscan 'Vocabulary' of 1612, or the more famous inquiry into Petrarch's style. The 'Considerazioni sopra le Rime del Petrarca' were composed in 1602-3 during a sea voyage from Genoa to Spain. They told what now must be considered the plain truth of common sense about the affectations into which a servile study of the *Canzoniere* had betrayed generations of Italian rhymesters. Tassoni had in view Petrarch's pedantic imitators rather than their master; and when the storm of literary fury, stirred up by his work, was raging around him, he thus established his position: 'Surely it is allowable to censure Petrarch's poems, if a man does this, not from malignant envy, but from a wish to remove the supersitions and abuses which beget such evil effects, and to confound the sects of the Rabbins hardened in their perfidy of obsolete opinion, and in particular of such as think they cannot write straight without the *falsariga* of their model.' I may observe in passing that the points in this paragraph are borrowed from a sympathising letter which Marino addressed to the author on his essay. In another place Tassoni stated, 'It was never my intention to speak evil of this poet [Petrarch], whom I have always admired above any lyrist of ancient or modern times.'

So independent in his conduct and so bold in his opinions was the author of the 'Secchia Rapita.' The composition of this poem grew out of the disputes which followed Tassoni's 'Remarks on Petrarch.' He found himself assailed by two scurrilous libels, which were traced to the Count Alessandro Brusantini, feudal lord of Culagna and Bismozza. Justice could not be obtained upon the person of so eminent a noble. Tassoni, with true Italian refinement, resolved to give himself the unique pleasure of ingenious vengeance. The name of the Count's fief supplied him with a standing dish of sarcasm. He would write a satiric poem, of which the Conte Culagna should be the burlesque hero. After ten months' labour, probably in the year 1615, the 'Secchia Rapita' already went abroad in MS.[24] Tassoni sought to pass it off as a product of his youth; but both the style and the personalities which it contained rendered this impossible. Privately issued, the poem had a great success. 'In less than a year,' writes the author, 'more MS. copies were

[24] For the date 1615 see Carducci's learned essay prefixed to his edition of the *Secchia Rapita* (Barbèra, 1861).

in circulation than are usually sent forth from the press in ten years of the most famous works.' One professional scribe made 200 ducats in the course of a few months by reproducing it; and the price paid for each copy was eight crowns. It became necessary to publish the 'Secchia Rapita.' But now arose innumerable difficulties. The printers of Modena and Padua refused; Giuliano Cassiani had been sent to prison in 1617 for publishing some verses of Testi against Spain. The Inquisition withheld its *imprimatur*. Attempts were made to have it printed on the sly at Padua; but the craftsman who engaged to execute this job was imprisoned. At last, in 1622, Tassoni contrived to have the poem published in Paris. The edition soon reached Italy. In Rome it was prohibited, but freely sold; and at last Gregory XV. allowed it to be reprinted with some cancelled passages. There is, in truth, nothing prejudicial either to the Catholic creed or to general morality in the 'Secchia Rapita.' We note, meanwhile, with interest, that it first saw the light at Paris, sharing thus the fortunes of the 'Adone,' which it preceded by one year. If the greatest living Italians at this time were exiles, it appears that the two most eminent poems of their literature first saw the light on foreign shores.

The 'Secchia Rapita' is the first example of heroico-comic poetry. Tassoni claims in print the honour of inventing this new species, and tells his friends that 'though he will not pique himself on being a poet, still he sets some store on having discovered a new kind of poem and occupied a vacant seat.' The seat—and it was no Siege Perilous—stood indeed empty and ready to be won by any free-lance of letters. Folengo had burlesqued romance. But no one as yet had made a parody of that which still existed mainly as the unaccomplished hope of literature. Trissino with his 'Italia Liberata,' Tasso with his 'Gerusalemme Liberata,' tried to persuade themselves and the world that they had succeeded in delivering Italy in labour of an epic. But their maieutic ingenuity was vain. The nation carried no epic in her womb. Trissino's 'Italia' was a weazened changeling of erudition, and Tasso's 'Gerusalemme' a florid bastard of romance. Tassoni, noticing the imposition of these two eminent and worthy writers, determined to give his century an epic or heroic poem in the only form which then was possible. Briefly, he produced a caricature, modelled upon no existing work of modern art, but corresponding to the lineaments of that Desired of the Nation which pedants had prophesied. Unity of action, celestial machinery, races in conflict, contrasted heroes, the wavering chance of war, episodes, bards, heroines, and love subordinated to the martial motive—all these features of the epic he viewed through the distorting medium of his comic art.

In the days of the second Lombard League, when Frederick II. was fighting a losing battle with the Church, Guelf Bologna came into grim conflict with her Ghibelline neighbour Modena. The territory of these two cities formed the *champ clos* of a duel in which the forces of Germany and nearly all Italy took part; and in one engagement, at Fossalta, the Emperor's heir, King Enzo of Sardinia, was taken captive. How he passed the rest of his days, a prisoner of the Bolognese, and how he begat the semi-royal brood of Bentivogli, is matter of history and legend. During this conflict, memorable among the many municipal wars of Italy in the Middle Ages, it happened that some Modenese soldiers, who had pushed their way into the suburbs of Bologna, carried off a bucket and suspended it as a trophy in the bell-tower of their cathedral, where it may still be seen. One of the peculiarities of those mediæval struggles—which roused the rivalry of towns separated from each other by a few miles of fertile country, and which raged through generations till the real interests at issue were confounded in blind animosity of neighbour against neighbour—was the sense of humour and of sarcasm they encouraged. To hurl a dead donkey against your enemy's town-wall passed for a good joke, and discredited his honour more than the loss of a hundred fighting men in a pitched battle. Frontier fortresses received insulting names, like the Perugian *Becca di questo*, or like the Bolognese *Grevalcore*. There was much, in fact, in these Italian wars which reminds one of the hostilities between rival houses in a public school.

Such being the element of humour ready to hand in the annals of his country, Tassoni chose the episode of the Bolognese bucket for the theme of a mock-heroic epic. He made what had been an insignificant incident the real occasion of the war, and grouped the facts of history around it by ingenious distortions of the truth. The bucket is the Helen of his 'Iliad':[25]

> Vedrai, s' al cantar mio porgi l' orecchia,
> Elena trasformarsi in una secchia.

A mere trifle thus becomes a point of dispute capable of bringing gods, popes, emperors, kings, princes, cities, and whole nations into conflict. At the same time the satirist betrays his malice by departing as little as possible from the main current of actual events. History lends verisimilitude to the preposterous assumption that heaven and earth were drawn into a squabble about a bucket; and if there is any moral to be derived from the 'Secchia Rapita' we have it here. At the end of the contention, when both parties are exhausted, it is found that the person of a king weighs in the scale of nations no more than an empty bucket:[26]

> Riserbando ne' patti a i Modanesi
> La secchia, e 'l re de' Sardi ai Bolognesi.

Such is the main subject of the 'Secchia Rapita;' and such is Tassoni's irony, an irony worthy of Aristophanes in its far-reaching indulgent contempt for human circumstance. But the poem has another object. It was written to punish Count Alessandro Brusantini. The leading episode, which occupies about three cantos of the twelve, is an elaborate

[25] Canto i. 2. [26] Canto xii. 77.

vilification of this personal enemy travestied as the contemptible Conte di Culagna.

Tassoni's method of art corresponds to the irony of his inspiration. We find his originality in a peculiar blending of serious and burlesque styles, in abrupt but always well-contrived transitions from heroical magniloquence to plebeian farce and from scurrility to poetic elevation, finally in a frequent employment of the figure which the Greeks called παρὰ προσδοκίαν. His poem is a parody of the Aristophanic type. 'Like a fantastically ironical magic tree, the world-subversive idea which lies at the root of it springs up with blooming ornament of thoughts, with singing nightingales and climbing chattering apes.'[27] To seek a central motive or a sober meaning in this caprice of the satirical imagination would be idle. Tassoni had no intention, as some critics have pretended, to exhibit the folly of those party wars which tore the heart of Italy three centuries before his epoch, to teach the people of his day the miseries of foreign interference, or to strike a death-blow at classical mythology. The lesson which can be drawn from his cantos, that man in warfare disquiets himself in vain for naught, that a bucket is as good a *casus belli* as Helen, the moral which Southey pointed in his ballad of the Battle of Blenheim, emerges, not from the poet's design, but from the inevitable logic of his humour. Pique inspired the 'Secchia Rapita,' and in the despicable character of Count Culagna he fully revenged the slight which had been put upon him. The revenge is savage certainly; for the Count remains 'immortally immerded' in the long-drawn episode which brought to view the shame of his domestic life. Yet while Tassoni drew blood, he never ceased to smile; and Count Culagna remains for us a personage of comedy rather than of satire.

In the next place, Tassoni meant to ridicule the poets of his time. He calls the 'Secchia Rapita' 'an absurd caprice, written to burlesque the modern poets.' His genius was nothing if not critical, and literature afforded him plenty of material for fun. Romance-writers with their jousts and duels and armed heroines, would-be epic poets with their extra-mundane machinery and pomp of phrase, Marino and his hyperbolical conceits, Tuscan purists bent on using only words of the Tre Cento, Petrarchisti spinning cobwebs of old metaphors and obsolete periphrases, all felt in turn the touch of his light lash. The homage paid to Petrarch's stuffed cat at Arquà supplied him with a truly Aristophanic gibe.[28] Society comes next beneath his ferrule. There is not a city of Italy which Tassoni did not wring in the withers of its self-conceit. The dialects of Ferrara, Bologna, Bergamo, Florence, Rome, lend the satirist vulgar phrases when he quits the grand style and, taking Virgil's golden trumpet from his lips, slides off into a *canaille* drawl or sluice of Billingsgate. Modena is burlesqued in her presiding Potta, gibbeted for her filthy streets. The Sienese discover that the world

[27] So Heine wrote of Aristophanes. See my essay in *Studies of the Greek Poets*.

[28] Canto viii. 33, 34.

accounts them lunatics. The Florentines and Perugians are branded for notorious vice. Roman foppery, fantastical in feminine pretentiousness, serves as a foil to drag Culagna down into the ditch of ignominy. Here and there, Tassoni's satire is both venomous and pungent, as when he paints the dotage of the Empire, stabs Spanish pride of sovereignty, and menaces the Papacy with insurrection. But for the most part, like Horace in the phrase of Persius, he plays about the vitals of the victims who admit him to their confidence—*admissus circum præcordia ludit.*

We can but regret that so clear-sighted, so urbane and so truly Aristophanic a satirist had not a wider field to work in. Seventeenth-century Italy was all too narrow for his genius; and if the 'Secchia Rapita' has lost its savour, this is less the poet's fault than the defect of his material. He was strong enough to have brought the Athens of Cleon, the France of Henri III., or the England of James I. within the range of his distorting truth-revealing mirror. Yet, even as it was, Tassoni opened several paths for modern humourists. Rabelais might have owned that caricature of Mars and Bacchus rioting in a tavern bed with Venus travestied as a boy, and in the morning, after breakfasting divinely on two hundred restorative eggs, escaping with the fear of a scandalised host and the police-court before their eyes. Yet Rabelais would hardly have brought this cynical picture of crude debauchery into so fine a contrast with the celestial environment of gods and goddesses. True to his principle of effect by alternation, Tassoni sometimes sketches the deities whom he derides, in the style of Volpato engravings after Guido. They move across his canvas with ethereal grace. What can be more charming than Diana visiting Endymion, and confessing to the Loves that all her past career as huntress and as chaste had been an error? Venus, too, when she takes that sensuously dreamy all-poetic journey across the blue Mediterranean to visit golden-haired King Enzo in his sleep, makes us forget her entrance into Modena disguised as a lad trained to play female parts upon the stage. This blending of true elegance with broad farce is a novelty in modern literature. We are reminded of the songs of the Mystæ on the meadows of Elysium in the 'Frogs.' Scarron and Voltaire, through the French imitators of Tassoni, took lessons from his caricature of Saturn, the old diseased senator, travelling in a sedan chair to the celestial parliament, with a clyster-pipe in front of him and his seat upon a close stool. Molière and Swift, votaries of Cloacina, were anticipated in the climax of Count Culagna's attempt to poison his wife, and in the invention of the enchanted ass so formidable by Parthian discharges on its adversary. Over these births of Tassoni's genius the Maccaronic Muse of Folengo and his Bolognese predecessors presided. There is something Lombard, a smack of sausage, in the humour. But it remained for the Modenese poet to bring this Mafelina into the comity of nations. We are not, indeed, bound to pay her homage. Yet when we find her inspiring such writers as Swift, Voltaire, Sterne and Heine, it is well to remember that Tassoni first evoked her from Mantuan gutters and the tripe-shops of Bologna.

'The fantastically ironical magic tree' of the 'Secchia Rapita' spread its green boughs not merely for chattering baboons. Nightingales sang there. The monkey-like Culagna, with his tricks and antics, disappears. Virtuous Renoppia, that wholesome country lass, the *bourgeois* counterpart of Bradamante, withholds her slipper from the poet's head when he is singing sad or lovely things of human fortune. Our eyes, rendered sensitive by vulgar sights, dwell with unwonted pleasure on the chivalrous beauty of King Enzo. Ernesto's death touches our sympathy with pathos, in spite of the innuendo cast upon his comrade Jaconìa. Paolo Malatesta rides with the shades of doom, the Dantesque cloud of love and destiny, around his forehead, through that motley mock-heroic band of burghers. Manfredi, consumed by an unholy passion for his sister, burns for one moment, like a face revealed by lightning, on our vision and is gone. Finally, when the mood seizes him (for Tassoni persuades us into thinking he is but the creature of caprice), he tunes the soft idyllic harp and sings Endymion's love-tale in strains soft as Marino's, sweet as Tasso's, outdoing Marino in delicacy, Tasso in reserve. This episode moved rigid Alfieri to admiration. It remains embedded in a burlesque poem, one of the most perfectly outlined triumphs of refined Italian romantic art. Yet such was the strength of the master's hand, so loyal was he to his principle of contrast, that he cuts the melodious idyll short with a twang of the guitar-strings, and strikes up a tavern ballad on Lucrezia. The irony which ruled his art demanded this inversion of proprieties. Cynthia wooing Endymion shows us woman in her frailty; Lucrece violated by Tarquin is woman in her dignity. The ironical poet had to adorn the first story with his choicest flowers of style and feeling, to burlesque the second with his grossest realism.

This antithesis between sustained poetry and melodiously worded slang, between radiant forms of beauty and grotesque ugliness, penetrates the 'Secchia Rapita' in every canto and in every detail. We pass from battle-scenes worthy of Ariosto and Tasso at their best into ditches of liquid dung. Ambassadors are introduced with touches that degrade them to the rank of *commis voyageurs*. Before the senate the same men utter orations in the style of Livy. The pomp of war is paraded, its machinery of catapults is put in motion, to discharge a dead ass into a besieged town; and when the beleaguered garrison behold it flying through the air, they do not take the donkey for a taunt, but for a heavenly portent. A tournament is held, and very brave in their attire are all the combatants. But according to its rules the greatest sluggard wins the crown of honour. Even in the similes, which formed so important an element of epic decoration, the same principle of contrast is maintained. Fine vignettes from nature in the style consecrated by Ariosto and Tasso introduce ludicrous incidents. Vulgar details picked up from the streets prepare us for touches of pathos or poetry.

Tassoni takes high rank as a literary artist for the firmness with which he adhered to his principle of irony, and for the facility of vigour which conceals all traces of effort in so difficult a task. I may be thought to have pitched his praise too high. But those will forgive me who enjoy the play of pure sharp-witted fancy, or who reflect upon the sadness of the theme which occupies my pen in these final volumes.

Of the four poets to whom this chapter is devoted, Guarini, Marino, and Tassoni were successful, Chiabrera was a respectable failure. The reason of this difference is apparent. In the then conditions of Italian society, at the close of a great and glorious period of varied culture, beneath the shadow of a score of Spaniardising princelings, with the spies of the Inquisition at every corner, and the drill of the Tridentine Council to be gone through under Jesuitical direction, there was no place for a second Pindar. But there was scope for decorative art, for sensuous indulgence, and for genial irony. Happy the man who paced his vineyards, dreaming musically of Arcadia! Happy the man who rolled in Circe's pigstye! Happy the man who sat in his study and laughed! Therefore the most meritorious productions of the time, Boccalini's 'Ragguagli di Parnaso,' Bracciolini's 'Scherno degli Dei,' have a touch of Tassoni's humour in them; while Achillini and Preti limp somewhat feebly after Marino's Alcibidean swagger, and endless pastorals pullulate from Guarini's tragi-comedy. We need not occupy our minds with these secondary writers, nor do more than indicate the scholarly niceness with which Filicaja in the second half of the seventeenth century continued Chiabrera's tradition. But one word must be said in honour of Fulvio Testi, the Modenese poet and statesman, who paid for the fame of a Canzone with his head. He has a double interest for us: first, because Leopardi esteemed him the noblest of Italian lyrists after Petrarch; secondly, because his fate proved that Tasso's dread of assassination was not wholly an illusion. Reading the ode addressed to Count Raimondo Montecuccoli 'Ruscelletto orgoglioso,' the ode which brought Testi to the block in a dungeon of the Estensi, we comprehend what Leopardi meant by his high panegyric. It is a piece of poetry, lofty in style, grave in movement, pregnant with weighty thought, stern and rugged, steeped in a sublimity of gloom and Stoicism which remind us of the author of 'La Ginestra.' The century produced little that bore a stamp so evident of dignity and greatness.

CHAPTER XII

PALESTRINA AND THE ORIGINS OF MODERN MUSIC

Italy in Renaissance produces no National School of Music—Flemish Composers in Rome—Singers and Orchestra—The Chaotic Indecency of this Contrapuntal Style—Palestrina's Birth and Early History—Decrees of the Tridentine Council upon Church Music—The Mass of Pope Marcello—Palestrina satisfies the Cardinals with his New Style of Sacred Music—Pius IV. and his Partiality for Music—Palestrina and Filippo Neri—His Motetts—The 'Song of Solomon' set to Melody—Palestrina, the Saviour of Music—The Founder of the Modern Style—Florentine Essays in the Oratorio.

It is a singular fact that while Italy led all the European races in scholarship and literature, in the arts of sculpture and painting, in commerce and the sciences of life, she had developed no national school of music in the middle of the sixteenth century. Native melody might indeed be heard in abundance along her shores and hillsides, in city streets and on the squares where men and girls danced together at evening. But such melody was popular; it could not be called artistic or scientific. The music which resounded through the Sistine Chapel, beneath the Prophets of Michelangelo, on high days and festivals, was not Italian. The composers of it came for the most part from Flemish or French provinces, bearing the names of Josquin Desprès, of Andrew Willaert, of Eleazar Genet, of James Arkadelt, of Claude Goudimel; and the performers were in like manner chiefly ultramontanes. Julius II. in 1513 founded a chapel in the Vatican Basilica called the Cappella Giulia for the maintenance of twelve male singers, twelve boys, and two masters of the choristers. In doing so it was his object to encourage a Roman school of music and to free the Chapter of S. Peter's from the inconvenience of being forced to engage foreign choir-men. His scheme, however, had been only partially successful. As late as 1540, we find that the principal composers and musicians in Rome were still foreigners. To three Italians of repute, there were five Flemings, three Frenchmen, three Spaniards, one German, and one Portuguese.[1]

The Flemish style of contrapuntal or figured harmony, which had enchanted Europe by its novelty and grace when Josquin Desprès, in the last quarter of the fifteenth century, brought it into universal vogue, was still dominant in Italy. But this style already showed unmistakable signs of decadence and dissolution. It had become unfit for ecclesiastical uses, and by the exaggeration of its qualities it was

[1] See Baini, *Life of Palestrina*, vol. ii. p. 20.

tending to anarchy. The grand defect of Flemish music, considered as an art of expression, was that it ignored propriety and neglected the libretto. Instead of exercising original invention, instead of suiting melodies to words by appropriate combinations of sound and sense, the composers chose any musical themes that came to hand, and wrought them up into elaborate contrapuntal structures without regard for their book. The first words of a passage from the Creed, for instance, were briefly indicated at the outset of the number: what followed was but a reiteration of the same syllables, and divided in the most arbitrary manner to suit the complicated descant which they had to serve. The singers could not adapt their melodic phrases to the liturgical text, since sometimes passages of considerable length fell upon a couple of syllables, while on the contrary a long sentence might have no more than a bar or even less assigned to it. They were consequently in the habit of drawling out or gabbling over the words, regardless of both sense and sentiment. Nor was this all. The composers of the Flemish school prided themselves on overloading their work with every kind of intricate and difficult ornament, exhibiting their dexterity by canons of many types, inversions, imitations, contrapuntal devices of divers ingenious and distracting species. The verbal theme became a mere basis for the utterance of scientific artifices and the display of vocal gymnastics. The singers, for their part, were allowed innumerable licenses. While the bass sustained the melody, the other voices indulged in extempore descant (*composizione alla mente*) and in extravagances of technical execution (*rifiorimenti*), regardless of the style of the main composition, violating time, and setting even the fundamental tone at defiance.

The composers, to advance another step in the analysis of this strange medley, took particular delight in combining different sets of words, melodies of widely diverse character, antagonistic rhythms, and divergent systems of accentuation in a single piece. They assigned these several ingredients to several parts; and for the further exhibition of their perverse skill, went even to the length of coupling themes in the major and the minor.

The most obvious result of such practice was that it became impossible to understand what words were being sung, and that instead of concord and order in the choir, a confused discord and anarchy of dinning sounds prevailed. What made the matter from an ecclesiastical point of view still worse, was that these scholastically artificial compositions were frequently based on trivial and vulgar tunes, suggesting the tavern, the dancing-room, or even worse places, to worshippers assembled for the celebration of a Sacrament. Masses bore titles adopted from the popular melodies on which they were founded; such, for example, as 'Adieu, mes amours,' 'A l'ombre d'un buissonnet,' 'Baisemoi,' 'L'ami baudichon madame,' 'Le vilain jaloux.' Even the words of love-ditties and obscene ballads in French, Flemish, and Italian, were being squalled out by the tenor while the bass gave utterance to an 'Agnus' or a 'Benedictus,' and the soprano was engaged upon the verses of a Latin hymn. Baini, who examined hundreds of these Masses and motetts in MS., says that the words imported into them from vulgar sources 'make one's flesh creep and one's hair stand on end.' He does not venture to do more than indicate a few of the more decent of these interloping verses; but mentions one 'Kyrie,' in which the tenor sang 'Je ne vis oncques la pareille;' a 'Sanctus,' in which he had to utter 'gracieuse gente mounyere;' and a 'Benedictus,' where the same offender was employed on 'Madame, faites moy sçavoir.' As an augmentation of this indecency, numbers from a Mass or motett which started with the grave rhythm of a Gregorian tone, were brought to their conclusion on the dance measure of a popular *ballata*, so that 'Incarnatus est' or 'Kyrie eleison' went jigging off into suggestions of Masetto and Zerlina at a village ball.

To describe all the impertinences to which the customs of vocal execution then in vogue gave rise, by means of flourishes, improvisations, accelerations of time, and multitudinous artifices derived from the *ad libitum* abuses of the fugal machinery, would serve no purpose. But it may be profitably mentioned that the mischief was not confined to the vocal parts. Organ and orchestra of divers instruments were allowed the same liberty of improvising on the given theme, embroidering these with fanciful *capricci*, and indulging their own taste in symphonies connected with the main structure by slight and artificial links. Instrumental music had not yet taken an independent place in art. The lute, the trumpet, or the stops of the organ, followed and imitated the voice; and thus in this confusion a choir of stringed and wind instruments was placed in competition with the singing choir.[2] It would appear that the composer frequently gave but a ground-sketch of his plan, without troubling himself to distribute written parts to the executants. The efflorescences, excursuses and episodes to which I have alluded, were supplied by artists whom long training in this kind of music enabled to perform their separate sallies and to execute their several antics within certain limits of recognised license. But since each vied with the other to produce striking effects, the choir rivalling the orchestra, the tenor competing with the bass, the organ with the viol, it followed that the din of their accumulated efforts was not unjustly compared to that made by a 'stye of grunting pigs,' the builders of the Tower of Babel, or the 'squalling of cats in January.'[3] 'All their happiness,' writes a contemporary critic, 'consisted in keeping the bass singer to the fugue, while at the same time one voice was shouting out "Sanctus," another "Sabaoth," a third "gloria tua," with howlings, bellowings and squealings that cannot be described.'

[2] While the choir was singing, the orchestra was playing concerted pieces called *ricercari*, in which the vocal parts were reproduced.

[3] See the original passages from contemporary writers quoted by Baini, vol. ii. pp. 102-104. Savonarola went so far as to affirm: 'Che questo canto figuratoll' ha trovato Satanasso,' a phrase quite in the style of a Puritan abusing choirs and organs.

It must not be thought that this almost unimaginable state of things indicated a defect either of intellectual capacity or of artistic skill. It was due rather to the abuse of science and of virtuosity, both of which had attained to a high degree of development. It manifested the decadence of music in its immaturity, through over-confident employment of exuberant resources on an end inadequate for the fulfilment of the art. Music, it must be remembered, unlike literature and plastic art, had no antique tradition to assimilate, no masterpieces of accomplished form to study. In the modern world it was an art without connecting links to bind it to the past. And this circumstance rendered it liable to negligent treatment by a society that prided itself upon the recovery of the classics. The cultivated classes abandoned it in practice to popular creators of melody upon the one hand, and to grotesque scholastic pedants on the other. And from the blending of those ill-accorded elements arose the chaos which I have attempted to describe.

Learned composers in the style developed by the Flemish masters had grown tired of writing simple music for four voices and a single choir. They revelled in the opportunity of combining eight vocal parts and bringing three choirs with accompanying orchestras into play at the same time. They were proud of proving how by counterpoint the most dissimilar and mutually-jarring factors could be wrought into a whole, intelligible to the scientific musician, though unedifying to the public. In the neglect of their art, considered as an art of interpretation and expression, they abandoned themselves to intricate problems and to the presentation of incongruous complexities.

The singers were expert in rendering difficult passages, in developing unpromising motives, and in embroidering the arras-work of the composer with fanciful extravagances of vocal execution. The instrumentalists were trained in the art of copying effects of fugue or madrigal by lutes and viols in concerted pieces. The people were used to dance and sing and touch the mandoline together; in every house were found amateurs who could with voice and string produce the studied compositions of the masters.

What was really lacking, amid this exuberance of musical resources, in this thick jungle of technical facilities, was a controlling element of correct taste, a right sense of the proper function of music as an interpretative art. On the very threshold of its modern development, music had fallen into early decay owing to the misapplication of the means so copiously provided by nature and by exercise. A man of genius and of substantial intuition into the real ends of vocal music was demanded at this moment, who should guide the art into its destined channel. And in order to elicit such a creator of new impulses, such a Nomothetes of the disordered state, it was requisite that external pressure should be brought to bear upon the art. An initiator of the right calibre was found in Palestrina. The pressure from without was supplied by the Council of Trent.

It may here be parenthetically remarked that music, all through modern history, has needed such legislators and initiators of new methods. Considered as an art of expression, she has always tended to elude control, to create for herself a domain extraneous to her proper function, and to erect her resources of mere sound into self-sufficingness. What Palestrina effected in the sixteenth century, was afterwards accomplished on a wider platform by Gluck in the eighteenth, and in our own days the same deliverance has been attempted by Wagner. The efforts of all these epoch-making musicians have been directed toward restraining the tendencies of music to assert an independence, which for herself becomes the source of weakness by reducing her to co-operation with insignificant words, and which renders her subservient to merely technical dexterities.

Giovanni Pier Luigi, called Palestrina from his birthplace in one of the Colonna fiefs near Rome, the ancient Præneste, was born of poor parents, in the year 1524. He went to Rome about 1540, and began his musical career probably as a choir-boy in one of the Basilicas. Claude Goudimel, the Besançon composer, who subsequently met a tragic death at Lyons in a massacre of Huguenots, had opened a school of harmony in Rome, where Palestrina learned the first rudiments of that science. What Palestrina owed to Goudimel is not clear. But we have the right to assume that the Protestant part-songs of the French people which Goudimel transferred to the hymn-books of the Huguenots, had a potent influence upon the formation of his style. They may have been for him what the Chorales of Germany were for the school of Bach.[4] Externally, Palestrina's life was a very uneventful one, and the records collected with indefatigable diligence by his biographer have only brought to light changes from one post to another in several Basilicas, and unceasing industry in composition. The vast number of works published by Palestrina in his lifetime, or left in MS. at his death, or known to have been written and now lost, would be truly astonishing were it not a fact that very eminent creative genius is always copious, and in no province of the arts more fertile than in that of music. Palestrina lived and died a poor man. In his dedications he occasionally remarks with sober pathos on the difficulty of pursuing scientific studies in the midst of domestic anxiety. His pay was very small, and the expense of publishing his works, which does not seem to have been defrayed by patrons, was at that time very great. Yet he enjoyed an uncontested reputation as the first of living composers, the saviour of Church music, the creator of a new style; and on his tomb, in 1594, was inscribed this title: *Princeps Musicæ*.

The state of confusion into which ecclesiastical music had fallen, rendered it inevitable that some notice of so grave a scandal should be taken by the Fathers of the Tridentine Council in their deliberations on reform of ritual. It appears, therefore, that in their twenty-second session (September 17, 1562) they enjoined upon the Ordinaries to

[4] See Michelet, *Histoire de France*, vol. xi. pp. 76, 101; vol. xii. p. 383 (Paris: Lacroix, 1877).

'exclude from churches all such music as, whether through the organ or the singing, introduces anything of impure or lascivious, in order that the house of God may truly be seen to be and may be called the house of prayer.'[5] In order to give effect to this decree of the Tridentine Council, Pius IV. appointed a congregation of eight Cardinals upon August 2, 1564, among whom three deserve especial mention—Michele Ghislieri, the Inquisitor, who was afterwards Pope Pius V.; Carlo Borromeo, the sainted Archbishop of Milan; and Vitellozzo Vitellozzi. It was their business, among other matters of reform, to see that the Church music of Rome was instantly reduced to proper order in accordance with the decree of the Council. Carlo Borromeo was nephew and chief minister of the reigning Pope. Vitellozzo Vitellozzi was a young man of thirty-three years, who possessed a singular passion for music. To these two members of the congregation, as a sub-committee, was deputed the special task of settling the question of ecclesiastical music, it being stipulated that they should by all means see that sufficient clearness were introduced into the enunciation of the liturgical words by the singers.

I will here interrupt the thread of the narration, in order to touch upon the legendary story which connects Palestrina incorrectly with what subsequently happened. It was well known that on the decisions of the sub-committee of the congregation hung the fate of Church music. For some while it seemed as though music might be altogether expelled from the rites of the Catholic Ecclesia. And it soon became matter of history that Palestrina had won the cause of his art, had maintained it in its eminent position in the ritual of Rome, and at the same time had opened a new period in the development of modern music by the production of his Mass called the 'Mass of Pope Marcellus' at this critical moment. These things were true; and when the peril had been overpassed, and the actual circumstances of the salvation and revolution of Church music had been forgotten, the memory of the crisis and the title of the victorious Mass remained to form a mythus. The story ran that the good Pope Marcellus, who occupied the Holy See for only twenty-two days, in the year 1555, determined on the abolition of all music but Plain Song in the Church; hearing of which resolve, Palestrina besought him to suspend his decree until he had himself produced and presented a Mass conformable to ecclesiastical propriety. Marcello granted the chapel-master this request; and on Easter Day, the Mass, which saved Church music from destruction, was performed with the Papal approval and the applause of Rome. It is not necessary to point out the many impossibilities and contradictions involved in this legend, since the real history of the Mass which wrought salvation for Church music, lies before us plainly written in the prolix pages of Baini. Yet it would have vexed me to pass by in silence so interesting and instructive an example of the mode by which the truth of history is veiled in legend.

[5] Baini, i. p. 196.

Truth is always more interesting than fiction, and the facts of this important episode in musical history are not without their element of romance. There is no doubt that there was a powerful party in the Catholic Church imbued with a stern ascetic or puritanical spirit, who would gladly have excluded all but Plain Song from her services. Had Michele Ghislieri instead of the somewhat worldly Angelo de' Medici been on the Papal throne, or had the decision of the musical difficulty been delegated to him by the congregation of eight Cardinals in 1564, Palestrina might not have obtained that opportunity of which he so triumphantly availed himself. But it happened that the reigning Pope was a lover of the art, and had a special reason for being almost superstitiously indulgent to its professors. While he was yet a Cardinal, in the easy-going days of Julius III., Angelo de' Medici had been invited with other princes of the Church to hear the marvellous performances upon the lute and the incomparable improvisations of a boy called Silvio Antoniano. The meeting took place at a banquet in the palace of the Venetian Cardinal Pisani. When the guests were assembled, the Cardinal Rannuccio Farnese put together a bouquet of flowers, and presenting these to the musician, bade him give them to that one of the Cardinals who should one day be chosen Pope. Silvio without hesitation handed the flowers to Angelo de' Medici, and taking up his lute began to sing his praises in impassioned extempore verse. After his election to the Papacy, with the title of Pius IV., Angelo de' Medici took Silvio into his service, and employed him in such honourable offices that the fortunate youth was finally advanced to the dignity of Cardinal under the reign of Clement VIII. in 1598.[6]

It was therefore necessary for the congregation of musical reform to take the Pope's partiality for this art into consideration; and they showed their good will by choosing his own nephew, together with a notorious amateur of music, for their sub-committee. The two Cardinals applied to the College of Pontifical Singers for advice; and these deputed eight of their number—three Spaniards, one Fleming, and four Italians—to act as assistants in the coming deliberations. It was soon agreed that Masses and motetts in which different verbal themes were jumbled, should be prohibited; that musical motives taken from profane songs should be abandoned; and that no countenance should be given to compositions or words invented by contemporary poets. These three conditions were probably laid down as indispensable by the Cardinals in office before proceeding to the more difficult question of securing a plain and intelligible enunciation of the sacred text. When the Cardinals demanded this as the essential point in the proposed reform, the singers replied that it would be impossible in practice. They were so used to the complicated structure of figured music, with its canons, fugal intricacies, imitations and inversions, that they could not even imagine a music that should be simple and straightforward, retaining the essen-

[6] It will be remembered that this Silvio Antoniano was one of the revisers of Tasso's poem, and the one who gave him most trouble.

tial features of vocal harmony, and yet allowing the words on which it was composed to be distinctly heard. The Cardinals rebutted these objections by pointing to the 'Te Deum' of Costanzo Festa (a piece which has been always sung on the election of a new Pope from that day to our own times) and to the 'Improperia' of Palestrina, which also holds its own in the service of the Sistine. But the singers answered that these were exceptional pieces, which, though they might fulfil the requirements of the Congregation of Reform, could not be taken as the sole models for compositions involving such variety and length of execution as the Mass. Their answer proved conclusively to what extent the contrapuntal style had dissociated itself from the right object of all vocal music, that of interpreting, enforcing, and transfiguring the words with which it deals, and how it had become a mere art for the scientific development of irrelevant and often impertinent melodic themes.

In order to avoid an absolute deadlock, which might have resulted in the sacrifice of ecclesiastical harmony, and have inflicted a deathblow on modern music, the committee agreed to refer their difficulties to Palestrina. On the principle of *solvitur ambulando*, he was invited to study the problem, and to produce a trial piece which should satisfy the conditions exacted by the Congregation as well as the requirements of the artists. Literally, he received commission to write a Mass in sober ecclesiastical style, free from all impure and light suggestions in the themes, the melodies and the rhythms, which should allow the sacred words in their full sense to be distinctly heard, without sacrificing vocal harmony and the customary interlacing of fugued passages. If he succeeded, the Cardinals promised to make no further innovation; but if he failed, Carlo Borromeo warned him that the Congregation of Reform would disband the choral establishments of the Pontifical Chapel and the Roman churches, and prohibit the figured style in vogue, in pursuance of the clear decision of the Tridentine Council.

This was a task of Hercules imposed on Palestrina. The art to which he had devoted his lifetime, the fame which he had acquired as a composer, the profession by which he and all his colleagues gained their daily bread, depended on his working out the problem. He was practically commanded to discover a new species of Church music, or to behold the ruin of himself and his companions, the extinction of the art and science he so passionately loved. Truly may his biographer remark: 'I am deliberately of opinion that no artist either before or since has ever found himself in a parallel strait.'

We have no exact record of the spirit in which he approached this labour.[7] But he was a man of sincere piety, a great and enthusiastic

[7] In the Dedication of the *Mass of Pope Marcello* to Philip II. in 1567 Palestrina only says that he had been constrained by the order of men of the highest gravity and most approved piety to apply himself *ad sanctissimum Missæ sacrificium novo modorum genere decorandum*, and that he had performed his task with indefatigable pains and industry (Baini, *op. cit.* vol. i. p. 280). But it is noteworthy that of the three Masses furnished for the approval of the congregation, the first was entitled *Illumina oculos*

servant of art. The command he had received came from a quarter which at that period and in Rome had almost divine authority. He knew that music hung trembling in the balance upon his failure or success. And these two motives, the motive of religious zeal and the motive of devotion to art, inspired him for the creation of a new musical world. Analysis of his work and comparison of it with the style which he was called on to supersede, show pretty clearly what were the principles that governed him. With a view to securing the main object of rendering the text intelligible to the faithful, he had to dispense with the complicated Flemish system of combined melodies in counterpoint, and to employ his scientific resources of fugue and canon with parsimony, so that in future they should subserve and not tyrannise over expression. He determined to write for six voices, two of which should be bass, in order that the fundamental themes should be sustained with dignity and continuity. But what he had principally in view, what in fact he had been called on to initiate, was that novel adaptation of melody and science to verbal phrase and sense, whereby music should be made an art interpretative of religious sentiment, powerful to clothe each shade of meaning in the text with appropriate and beautiful sound, instead of remaining a merely artificial and mechanical structure of sounds disconnected from the words employed in giving them vocal utterance.

Palestrina set to work, and composed three Masses, which were performed upon April 28, 1565, before the eight Cardinals of the congregation in the palace of Cardinal Vitellozzi. All three were approved of; but the first two still left something to be desired. Baini reports that they preserved somewhat too much of the cumbrous Flemish manner; and that though the words were more intelligible, the fugal artifices overlaid their clear enunciation. In the third, however, it was unanimously agreed that Palestrina had solved the problem satisfactorily. 'Its style is always equal, always noble, always alive, always full of thought and sincere feeling, rising and ascending to the climax; not to understand the words would be impossible; the melodies combine to stimulate devotion; the harmonies touch the heart; it delights without distracting; satisfies desire without tickling the senses; it is beautiful in all the beauties of the sanctuary.' So writes Palestrina's enthusiastic biographer; so apparently thought the Cardinals of the congregation; and when this Mass (called the 'Mass of Pope Marcello,' out of grateful tribute to the Pontiff, whose untimely death had extinguished many sanguine expectations) was given to the world, the whole of Italy welcomed it with a burst of passionate applause. Church music had been saved. Modern music had been created. A new and lovely form of art had arisen like a star.

It was not enough that the 'Mass of Pope Marcello' should have satisfied the congregation. It had next to receive the approval of the

meos, and that an anecdote referring to this title relates Palestrina's earnest prayers for grace and inspiration during the execution of the work (*ibid.* p. 223, note).

Pope, who heard it on June 19. On this occasion, if the Court Chronicle be correct, Pius made a pretty speech, declaring that 'of such nature must have been the harmonies of the new song heard by John the Apostle in the heavenly Jerusalem, and that another John had given us a taste of them in the Jerusalem of the Church Militant.' He seems, indeed, to have been convinced that the main problem of preserving clearness of enunciation in the uttered words had been solved, and that there was now no reason to deprive the faithful of the artistic and devotional value of melodious music. He consequently appointed Palestrina to the post of composer for the Papal Chapel, and created a monopoly for the performance of his works. This measure, which roused considerable jealousy among musicians at the moment, had the salutary effect of rendering the new style permanent in usage.

Of Palestrina's voluminous compositions this is not the place to speak. It is enough to have indicated the decisive part which he took in the reformation of Church music at a moment when its very existence was imperilled, and to have described the principles upon which he laid down new laws for the art. I must not, however, omit to dwell upon his subsequent connexion with S. Filippo Neri, since the music he composed for the Oratory of that saint contributed much toward the creation of a semi-lyrical and semi-dramatic style to which we may refer the origins of the modern Oratorio. Filippo Neri was the spiritual director of Palestrina, and appointed him composer to his devout confraternity. For the use of that society the master wrote a series of *Arie Divote* on Italian words. They were meant to be sung by the members, and to supersede the old usages of Laud-music, which had chiefly consisted in adapting popular street-tunes to sacred words.[8]

To the same connexion with the Oratory we owe one of the most remarkable series of Palestrina's compositions. These were written upon the words of an Italian Canzone in thirty octave stanzas, addressed as a prayer to the Virgin. Palestrina set each stanza, after the fashion of a Madrigal, to different melodies; and the whole work proved a manual of devotional music, in the purest artistic taste, and the most delicately sentimental key of feeling. Together with this collection of spiritual songs should be mentioned Palestrina's setting of passages from the 'Song of Solomon' in a series of motetts, which were dedicated to Gregory XIII. in 1584. They had an enormous success. Ten editions between that date and 1650 were poured out from the presses of Rome and Venice, to satisfy the impatience of thousands who desired to feed upon 'the nectar of their sweetness.' Palestrina chose for the motives of his compositions such voluptuous phrases of the Vulgate as the following: *Fasciculus myrrhæ dilectus meus mihi. Fulcite me floribus, stipate me malis, quia amore langueo. Vulnerasti cor meum, soror, sponsa mea.* This was the period when Italy was ringing with the secular sweetnesses of Tasso's 'Aminta' and of Guarini's 'Pastor Fido;' when the devotion of the cloister was becoming languorous and soft; when

[8] See Vol. II. *Italian Literature* pp. 18-19, 44-45.

the cult of the Virgin was assuming the extravagant proportions satirised by Pascal; finally, when manners were affecting a tone of swooning piety blent with sensuous luxuriousness. Palestrina's setting of the 'Canticle' and of the 'Hymn to Mary' provided the public with music which, according to the taste of that epoch, transferred terrestrial emotions into the regions of paradisal bliss, and justified the definition of music as the *Lamento dell' amore o la preghiera agli dei.* The great creator of a new ecclesiastical style, the 'imitator of nature,' as Vincenzo Galileo styled him, the 'prince of music,' as his epitaph proclaimed him, lent his genius to an art, vacillating between mundane sensuality and celestial rapture, which, however innocently developed by him in the sphere of music, was symptomatic of the most unhealthy tendencies of his race and age. While singing these madrigals and these motetts the youth of either sex were no longer reminded, it is true, of tavern ditties or dance measures. But the emotions of luxurious delight or passionate ecstasy deep in their own natures were drawn forth and sanctified by application to the language of effeminate devotion.

I have dwelt upon these two sets of compositions, rather than upon the masses of strictly and severely ecclesiastical music which Palestrina produced with inexhaustible industry, partly because they appear to have been extraordinarily popular, and partly because they illustrate those tendencies in art and manners which the sentimental school of Bolognese painters attempted to embody. They belong to that religious sphere which the Jesuit Order occupied, governed, and administered upon the lines of their prescribed discipline. These considerations are not merely irrelevant. The specific qualities of Italian music for the next two centuries were undoubtedly determined by the atmosphere of sensuous pietism in which it flourished, at the very time when German music was striking far other roots in the Chorales of the Reformation epoch. What Palestrina effected was to substitute in Church music the clear and melodious manner of the secular madrigal for the heavy and scholastic science of the Flemish school, and to produce masterpieces of religious art in his motetts on the Canticles which confounded the lines of demarcation between pious and profane expression. He taught music to utter the emotions of the heart; but those emotions in his land and race were already tending in religion toward the sentimental and voluptuous.

There is no doubt that the peril to which music was exposed at the time of the Tridentine Council was a serious and real one. When we remember how intimate was the connexion between the higher kinds of music and the ritual of the Church, this will be apparent. Nor is it too much to affirm that the art at that crisis, but for the favour shown to it by Pius IV. and for Palestrina's intervention, might have been well-nigh extinguished in Italy. How fatal the results would then have been for the development of modern music, can be estimated by considering the decisive part played by the Italians in the formation of musical style from the end of the sixteenth century onwards to the age of Gluck, Handel, Haydn and Mozart. Had the music of the Church in Italy been confined at that epoch to Plain Song, as the Congregation of Reform threatened, the great Italian school of vocalisation would not have been founded, the Conservatories of Naples and the Scuole of Venice would have been silent, and the style upon which, dating from Palestrina's inventions, the evolution of all species of the art proceeded, would have passed into oblivion.

That this proposition is not extravagant, the history of music in England will suffice to prove. Before the victory of Puritan principles in Church and State, the English were well abreast of other races in this art. During the sixteenth century, Tallis, Byrd, Morley, Wilbye, Dowland and Orlando Gibbons could hold their own against Italian masters. The musical establishments of cathedrals, royal and collegiate chapels, and noble houses were nurseries for artists. Every English home, in that age, like every German home in the eighteenth century, abounded in amateurs who were capable of performing part-songs and concerted pieces on the lute and viol with correctness. Under the *régime* of the Commonwealth this national growth of music received a check from which it never afterwards recovered. Though the seventeenth century witnessed the rising of one eminent composer, Purcell; though the eighteenth was adorned with meritorious writers of the stamp of Blow and Boyce; yet it is obvious that the art remained among us unprogressive, at a time when it was making gigantic strides in Italy and Germany. It is always dangerous to attribute the decline of art in a nation to any one cause. Yet I think it can scarcely be contested that the change of manners and of temperament wrought in England by the prevalence of Puritan opinion, had much to answer for in this premature decay of music. We may therefore fairly argue that if the gloomy passion of intolerant fanaticism which burned in men like Caraffa and Ghislieri had prevailed in Italy—a passion analogous in its exclusiveness to Puritanism—or if no composer, in the place of Palestrina, had satisfied the requirements of the Council and the congregation, the history of music in Italy and Europe to us-wards would have been far different.

These considerations are adduced to justify the importance attached by me to the episode of which Palestrina was the hero. Yet it should not be forgotten that other influences were at work at the same time in Italy, which greatly stimulated the advance of music. If space permitted, it would be interesting to enlarge upon the work of Luca Marenzio, the prince of madrigal-writers, and on the services rendered by Vincenzo Galileo, father of the greatest man of science in his age, in placing the practice of stringed instruments on a sound basis. It should also be remembered that in the society of Filippo Neri at Rome, the Oratorio was taking shape, and emerging from the simple elements of the Spiritual Laud and *Aria Divota*. This form, however, would certainly have perished if the austere party in the Church had prevailed against the lenient for the exclusion of figured music from religious exercises.

There was, moreover, an interesting contemporary movement at Florence, which deserves some detailed mention. A private academy of amateurs and artists formed itself for the avowed purpose of reviving the musical declamation of the Greeks. As the new ecclesiastical style created by Palestrina grew out of the Counter-Reformation embodied in the decrees of the Tridentine Council, so this movement, which eventually resulted in the Opera, attached itself to the earlier enthusiasms of the Classical Revival. The humanists had restored Latin poetry; the architects had perfected a neo-Latin manner; sculptors and painters had profited by the study of antique fragments, and had reproduced the bas-reliefs and arabesques of Roman palaces. It was now, much later in the day, the turn of the musicians to make a similar attempt. Their quest was vague and visionary. Nothing remained of Greek or Roman music. To guide these explorers, there was only a dim instinct that the ancients had declaimed dramatic verse with musical intonation. But, as the alchemists sought the philosopher's stone, and founded modern chemistry; as, according to an ancient proverb, they who search for silver find gold; so it happened that, from the pedantic and ill-directed attempts of this academy proceeded the system on which the modern Oratorio and Opera were based. What is noticeable in these experiments is, that a new form of musical expression, declamatory and continuous, therefore dramatic, as opposed to the lyrical and fugal methods of the contrapuntists, was in process of elaboration. Claudio Monteverde, who may be termed the pioneer of *recitativo*, in his opera of 'Orfeo;' Giacomo Carissimi, in whose 'Jephtha' the form of the Oratorio is already outlined, were the most eminent masters of the school which took its origin in the Florentine Academy of the Palazzo Vernio.

To pursue the subject further, would be to transgress the chronological limits of my theme. It is enough to have attempted in this chapter to show how the destinies of Italian music were secured and its species determined in the last quarter of the sixteenth century. How that art at its climax in the eighteenth century affected the manners, penetrated the whole life, and influenced the literature of the Italians, may be read in an English work of singular ability and originality.[9]

[9] *Studies of the Eighteenth Century in Italy*, by Vernon Lee.

CHAPTER XIII

THE BOLOGNESE SCHOOL OF PAINTERS

Decline of Plastic Art—Dates of the Eclectic Masters—The Mannerists—Baroccio—Reaction started by Lodovico Caracci—His Cousins Annibale and Agostino—Their Studies—Their Academy at Bologna—Their Artistic Aims—Dionysius Calvaert—Guido Reni—The Man and his Art—Domenichino—Ruskin's Criticism—Relation of Domenichino to the Piety of his Age—Caravaggio and the Realists—Ribera—Lo Spagna—Guercino—His Qualities as Colourist—His Terribleness—Private Life—Digression upon Criticism—Reasons why the Bolognese Painters are justly now Neglected.

AFTER tracing the origin of modern music at its fountain head in Palestrina, it requires some courage to approach the plastic arts at this same epoch.

Music was the last real manifestation of the creative genius in Italy. Rarefied to evanescent currents of emotional and sensuous out-breathings, the spirit of the race exhaled itself in song from human throats, in melody on lute and viol, until the whole of Europe thrilled with the marvel and the mystery of this new language of the soul. Music was the fittest utterance for the Italians of the Counter-Reformation period. Debarred from political activity, denied the liberty of thought and speech, that gifted people found an inarticulate vehicle of expression in tone: tone which conveys all meanings to the nerves that feel, advances nothing to the mind that reasons, says everything without formulating a proposition.

Only a sense of duty to my subject, which demands completion, makes me treat of painting in the last years of the sixteenth century. The great Italian cycle, rounded by Lionardo, Raffaello, Michelangelo, Correggio and Tiziano, was being closed at Venice by Tintoretto. After him invention ceased. But there arose at Bologna a school, bent on resuscitating the traditions of an art which had already done its utmost to interpret mind to mind through mediums of lovely form and colour. The founders of the Bolognese Academy, like Medéa operating on decrepit Æson, chopped up the limbs of painting which had ceased to throb with organic life, recombined them by an act of intellect and will, and having pieced them together, set the composite machine in motion on the path of studied method. Their aim was analogous to that of the Church in its reconstitution of Catholicism; and they succeeded in so far as they achieved a partial success, through the inspiration which the Catholic Revival gave them. These painters are known as the Eclectics, and this title sufficiently indicates their effort to revive art by recomposing what lay before them in disintegrated fragments. They did not explore new territory or invent fresh vehicles of expression. They sought to select the best points of Græco-Roman and Italian style, unconscious that the physical type of the Niobids, the voluptuous charm of Correggio, the luminous colour of Titian, the terribleness of Michelangelo, and the serenity of Raphael, being the ultimate expressions of distinct artistic qualities, were incompatible. A still deeper truth escaped their notice—namely, that art is valueless unless the artist has something intensely felt to say, and that where this intensity of feeling exists, it finds for itself its own specific and inevitable form.

> Poems distilled from other poems pass away,
> The swarms of reflectors and the polite pass, and leave ashes;
> Admirers, importers, obedient persons, make but the soil of literature.

These profound sentences are the epitaph, not only of imitative poetry, but also of such eclectic art as the Caracci instituted. Very little of it bears examination now. We regard it with listlessness or loathing. We turn from it without regret. We cannot, or do not, wish to keep it in our memory.

Yet no student of Italian painting will refuse the Caracci that tribute of respect which is due to virile effort. They were in vital sympathy with the critical and analytical spirit of their age—an age mournfully conscious that its sceptre had departed—that

> Nothing can bring back the hour
> Of splendour in the grass, of glory in the flower;

an age incapable as yet of acquiescing in this gloom, strenuously eager by study and by labour to regain the kingdom which belongs alone to inspiration. Science and industry enabled them to galvanise the corpse of art; into this they breathed the breath of the religion *à la mode*, of fashionable sensuousness and prevalent sentimentality.

Michelangelo died in 1564, Paolo Veronese in 1588, Tintoretto in 1594. These were the three latest survivors of the great generation, and each of them had enjoyed a life of activity prolonged into extreme old age. Their intellectual peers had long ago departed; Lionardo in 1520, Raphael in 1522, Correggio in 1534.

> Theirs was the giant race, before the flood.

These dates have to be kept in mind; for the painters of the Bolognese School were all born after 1550, born for the most part at that decisive epoch of the Tridentine Council which might be compared to a watershed of time between the Renaissance and the Counter-Reformation—Lodovico Caracci in 1555, Agostino in 1558, Annibale in 1560, Guido Reni in 1574, Lionello Spada in 1576, Francesco Albani in 1578, Domenichino in 1581, Guercino in 1590.[1] With the last of these men the eclectic impulse was exhausted; and a second generation, derived in part from them, linked the painters of the Renaissance to those of modern times. It is sufficient to mention Nicholas and Gaspar Poussin, Claude Lorraine, Salvator Rosa, Luca Giordano, and Canaletto as chief representatives of this secondary group.[2]

On examining the dates which I have given, it will be noticed that the Bolognese Eclectics, intervening between the age of Michelangelo and the age of Nicholas Poussin, worked during the first fervour of the Catholic Revival. Their art may therefore be taken as fairly representative of the religious temper and the profane culture of the Italians in the period influenced by the Council of Trent. It represents that temper and that culture before the decline of the same influence, when the Counter-Reformation was in active progress, and the Papal pretensions to absolute dominion had received no check.

We should be wrong, however, to treat the Eclectics as though they succeeded without interruption to that 'giant race, before the flood.' Their movement was emphatically one of revival; and revival implies decadence. After 1541, when Michelangelo finished the Last Judgment, and before 1584, when the Caracci were working on their frescoes in the Palazzo Fava at Bologna—that is to say, between the last of the genuine Renaissance paintings and the first of the Revival—nearly half a century elapsed, during which art sank into a slough of slovenly and soulless putrescence.[3] Every city of Italy swarmed with artists, adequately educated in technical methods, and apt at aping the grand style of their masters. But in all their work there is nothing felt, nothing thought out, nothing expressed, nothing imagined. It is a vast vacuity of meaningless and worthless brush-play, a wilderness of hollow trickery and futile fumbling with conventional forms. The Mannerists, as they were called, covered acres of palace and church walls with allegories, histories, and legends, carelessly designed, rapidly executed, but pleasing the eye with crowds of figures and with gaudy colours. Their colours are now faded. Their figures are now seen to be reminiscences of Raphael's, Correggio's, Buonarroti's draughtsmanship. Yet they satisfied the patrons of that time, who required hasty work, and had not much money wherewith to reward the mature labours of a conscientious student. In relation, moreover, to the spiritless and insincere architecture then coming into vogue, this art of the Mannerists can scarcely be judged out of place. When I divulge the names of Giorgio Vasari, Giuseppe Cesari (Cav. d' Arpino), Tempesta, Fontana,

[1] The three founders of the school were thus born precisely during the most critical years of the Council. They felt the Catholic reaction least. That expressed itself most markedly in Domenichino, born seventeen years after its close.

[2] Nich. Poussin, b. 1594; Claude, 1600; Gaspar Poussin, 1613; Salvator Rosa, 1615; Luca Giordano, 1632; Canaletto, 1697.

[3] I of course except Venice, for reasons which I have sufficiently set forth in Vol. I., *The Fine Arts*, 746. Long after other schools of Italy the Venetian was still only adolescent.

Tibaldi, the Zuccari, the Procaccini, the Campi of Cremona, the scholars of Perino del Vaga, I shall probably call up before the reluctant eyes of many of my readers visions of dreary wanderings through weariful saloons and of disconsolate starings up at stuccoed cupolas in Rome and Genoa, in Florence and Naples, and in all the towns of Lombardy.[4]

In an earlier volume I briefly sketched the development of this pernicious mannerism, which now deluged the arts of Italy. Only one painter, outside Venice, seems to have carried on a fairly good tradition. This was Federigo Baroccio (1528-1612), who feebly continued the style of Correggio, with a certain hectic originality, infusing sentimental pietism into that great master's pagan sensuousness. The mixture is disagreeable; and when one is obliged to mention Baroccio as the best in a bad period, this accentuates the badness of his contemporaries. He has, however, historical value from another point of view, inasmuch as nothing more strongly characterises the eclecticism of the Caracci than their partiality for Correggio.[5] Though I have no reason to suppose that Baroccio, living chiefly as he did at Urbino, directly influenced their style, the similarity between his ideal and theirs is certainly striking. It seems to point at something inevitable in the direction taken by the Eclectics.

Such was the state of art in Italy when Lodovico Caracci, the son of a Bolognese butcher, conceived his plan of replacing it upon a sounder system.[6] Instinct led him to Venice, where painting was still alive. The veteran Tintoretto warned him that he had no vocation. But Lodovico obstinately resolved to win by industry what nature seemed to have denied him. He studied diligently at Florence, Parma, Mantua, and Venice, founding his style upon those of Andrea del Sarto, Correggio, Titian, Parmigiano, Giulio Romano, and Primaticcio. When he again settled at Bologna, he induced his two cousins, Agostino and Annibale, the sons of a tailor, to join him in the serious pursuit of art. Agostino was a goldsmith by trade, already expert in the use of the burin, which he afterwards employed more frequently than the brush.[7] Of the three

[4] I have not thought it worth while to write down more than a very few names of the Mannerists. Notice how often they worked in whole families and indistinguishable coteries.

[5] Everyone familiar with European picture-galleries will remember cabinet pieces by the Caracci, especially Ecce Homos, Pietàs, Agonies in the Garden, which look like copies from Correggio with a dash of added sentimentalism.

[6] I have mainly used the encyclopædic work entitled *Felsina Pittrice* (Bologna, 1841, 2 vols.) for my study of the Eclectics. This is based upon the voluminous writings of the Count C. C. Malvasia, who, having been born in 1616, and having enjoyed personal intercourse with the later survivors of the Bolognese Academy, was able to bequeath a vast mass of anecdotical and other material to posterity. The collection contains critical annotations and additions by the hand of Zanotti and later art students, together with many illustrative documents of the highest value. Reading this miscellaneous repertory, we are forced to regret that the same amount of characteristic and authentic information has not been preserved about one of the greater schools of Italy—the Venetian, for example.

[7] He acquired a somewhat infamous celebrity by his obscene engravings in the style of Giulio Romano.

Caracci he was the most versatile, and perhaps the most gifted. There is a note of distinction and attainment in his work. Annibale, the youngest, was a rough, wild, hasty, and hot-tempered lad, of robust build and vigorous intellect, but boorish in his manners, fond of low society, and eaten up with jealousy. They called him the *ragazzaccio*, or 'lout of a boy,' when he began to make his mark at Bologna. Agostino presented a strong contrast to his brother, being an accomplished musician, an excellent dancer, a fair poet, fit to converse with noblemen, and possessed of very considerable culture. Lodovico, the eldest of the cousins, acted as mentor and instructor to the others. He pacified their quarrels, when Annibale's jealousy burst out; set them upon the right methods of study, and passed judgment on their paintings.

Like Lodovico, the brothers served their first apprenticeship in art at Parma and Venice. Annibale's letters from the former place show how Correggio subdued him, and the large copies he there made still preserve for us some shadows of Correggio's time-ruined frescoes. At Venice he executed a copy of Titian's Peter Martyr. This picture, the most dramatic of Titian's works, and the most elaborate in its landscape, was destined to exercise a decisive influence over the Eclectic school. From the Caracci to Domenichino we are able to trace the dominant tone and composition of that masterpiece. No less decisive, as I have already observed, was the influence of Correggio's peculiar style in the choice of type, the light and shade, and the foreshortenings of the Bolognese painters. In some degree, the manner of Paolo Veronese may also be discerned. The Caracci avoided Tintoretto, and at the beginning of their career they derived but little from Raphael or Michelangelo. Theirs was at first a mainly Veneto-Lombardic eclecticism, dashed with something absorbed from Giulio Romano and something from the later Florentines. It must not, however, be supposed that they confined their attention to Italian painters. They contrived to collect casts from antique marbles, coins, engravings of the best German and Italian workmanship, books on architecture and perspective, original drawings, and similar academical appliances. Nor were they neglectful of drawing from the nude, or of anatomy. Indeed, their days and nights were spent in one continuous round of study, which had for its main object the comparison of dead and living nature with the best specimens of art in all ages. It may seem strange that this assiduity and thoroughness of method did not produce work of higher quality. Yet we must remember that even enthusiastic devotion to art will not give inspiration, and that the most thorough science cannot communicate charm. Though the Caracci invented fresh attitudes and showed complete mastery of the human form, their types remained commonplace. Though their chiaroscuro was accurately based on that of Correggio, it lacked his aërial play of semitones. Though they went straight to Titian for colour, they never approached Venetian lucidity and glow. There was something vulgar in their imagination, prosaic in their feeling, leaden in their frigid touch on legend. Who wants those countless gods and goddesses of the Farnese Gallery, those beblubbered saints and colossal Sibyls of the Bolognese Pinacoteca, those chubby cherubs and buxom nymphs, those Satyrs and S. Sebastians, to come down from the walls and live with us? The grace of Raphael's Galatea, the inspiration of Michelangelo's Genii of the Sistine, the mystery of Lionardo's Faun S. John, the wilding grace of Correggio's Diana, the voluptuous fascination of Titian's Venus, the mundane seductiveness of Veronese's Europa, the golden glory of Tintoretto's Bacchus,—all have evanesced, and in their place are hard mechanic figures, excellently drawn, correctly posed, but with no touch of poetry. Where, indeed, shall we find 'the light that never was on sea or land' throughout Bologna?[8]

Part of this failure must be ascribed to a radically false conception of the way to combine studies of nature with studies of art. The Eclectics in general started with the theory that a painter ought to form mental ideals of beauty, strength, dignity, ferocity, and so forth, from the observation of characteristic individuals and acknowledged masterpieces. These ideal types he has to preserve in his memory, and to use living persons only as external means for bringing them into play. Thus, it was indifferent who sat to him as model. He believed that he could invest the ugliest lump of living flesh with the loveliest fancy. Lodovico supplied Annibale Caracci with the fleshy back of a naked Venus. Guido Reni painted his Madonna's heads from any beardless pupil who came handy, and turned his deformed colour-grinder—a man 'with a muzzle like a renegado'—into the penitent Magdalen.[9] It was inevitable that forms and faces thus evolved should bear the stamp of mediocrity, monotony, and dulness on them. Few, very few, painters—perhaps only Michelangelo—have been able to give to purely imagined forms the value and the individuality of persons; and he succeeded best in this perilous attempt when he designed the passionate Genii of the Sistine frescoes. Such flights were far beyond the grasp of the Eclectics. Seeking after the 'grand style,' they fell, as I shall show in the sequel of this chapter, into commonplace vacuity, which makes them now insipid.[10]

[8] Malvasia has preserved, in his *Life of Primaticcio*, a sonnet written by Agostino Caracci, in which the aims of the Eclectics are clearly indicated. The good painter must have at his command Roman or classic design, Venetian movement and shadow, Lombard colouring, the sublimity of Michelangelo, the truth to nature of Titian, the pure and sovereign style of Correggio, Raphael's symmetry, Tibaldi's fitness and solidity, Primaticcio's erudite invention, with something of Parmigianino's grace (*Fels. Pittr.* vol. i. p. 129). Zanotti adds: 'This sonnet is assuredly one which every painter ought to learn by heart and observe in practice.'

[9] See Malvasia, *op. cit.* vol. i. p. 277; vol. ii. p. 57. The odd thing is that Malvasia tells these stories of the Lodovico-Aphrodite and the colour-grinder-Magdalen with applause, as though they proved the mastery of Annibale Caracci and Guido.

[10] The later Eclectics—Spada, Domenichino, Guercino—were to some extent saved by the influences they derived from Caravaggio and the Naturalisti. But they had not the tact to see where the finer point of naturalistic art lies for a delicately minded painter. They added its brutality, as employed by Caravaggio, to the insipidities of the Caracci, and produced such horrors as Domenichino's Martyrdom of S. Agnes.

There was at this time a native of Antwerp named Dionysius Calvaert, a coarse fellow of violent manners, who kept open school in Bologna. The best of the Caracci's pupils—Guido Reni, Domenichino and Albani—emigrated to their academy from this man's workshop. Something, as it seems to me, peculiar in the method of handling oil paint, which all three have in common, may perhaps be ascribed to early training under their Flemish master. His brutality drove them out of doors; and, having sought the protection of Lodovico Caracci, they successively made such progress in the methods of painting as rendered them the most distinguished representatives of the Bolognese Revival. All three were men of immaculate manners. Guido Reni, beautiful as a Sibyl in youth, with blonde hair, blue eyes, and fair complexion, was, to the end of his illustrious career, reputed a virgin. Albani, who translated into delicate oil-painting the sensuousness of the 'Adone,' studied the forms of Nymphs and Venuses from his lovely wife, and the limbs of Amorini from the children whom she bore him regularly every year. Domenichino, a man of shy, retiring habits, preoccupied with the psychological problems which he strove to translate into dramatic pictures, doted on one woman, whom he married, and who lived to deplore his death (as she believed) by poison. Guido was specially characterised by devotion to Madonna. He was a singular child. On every Christmas eve, for seven successive years, ghostly knockings were heard upon his chamber-door; and, every night, when he awoke from sleep the darkness above his bed was illuminated by a mysterious egg-shaped globe of light.[11] His eccentricity in later life amounted to insanity, and at last he gave himself up wholly to the demon of the gaming-table. Domenichino obeyed only one passion, if we except his passion for the wife he loved so dearly, and this was music. He displayed some strangeness of temperament in a morbid dislike of noise and interruptions. Otherwise, nothing disturbed the even current of an existence dedicated to solving questions of art. Albani mixed more freely in the world than Domenichino, enjoyed the pleasures of the table and of sumptuous living, but with Italian sobriety, and expatiated in those spheres of literature which supplied him with motives for his coldly sensual pictures. Yet he maintained the credit of a thoroughly domestic, soundly natured, and vigorously wholesome man.

I have thought it well thus to preface what I have to say about these masters, partly because critics of the modern stamp, trusting more to their subjective impressions than to authoritative records, have painted the moral characters of Guido and Domenichino in lurid colours, and also because there is certainly something in their work which leaves a painful memory of unhealthy sentiment, impassiveness to pain, and polished carnalism on the mind. It may incidentally be recorded that

[11] This tradition of Guido's childhood I give for what it is worth, from Malvasia, *op. cit.* vol. ii. p. 53. In after life, besides being piously addicted to Madonna-worship, he had a great dread of women in general and witches in particular. What some will call spiritual, others effeminate, in his mature work may be due to the temperament thus indicated.

Lodovico Caracci, Guido Reni, and Francesco Albani are all of them, on very good authority, reported to have been even prudishly modest in their use of female models. They never permitted a woman to strip entirely, and Guido carried his reserve to such a pitch that he preferred to leave his studio door open while drawing from a woman.[12] Malevolence might suggest that this was only part and parcel of post-Tridentine hypocrisy; and probably there is truth in the suggestion. I certainly do not reckon such solicitous respect for garments entirely to their credit. But it helps us to understand the eccentric compound of sentiment, sensuality, piety, and uneasy morality which distinguished the age, and which is continually perplexing the student of its art.

Of these three men, Guido was the most genially endowed. He alone derived a true spark from the previous age of inspiration. He wearies us indeed with his effeminacy, and with the reiteration of a physical type sentimentalised from the head and bust of Niobe. But thoughts of real originality and grace not seldom visited his meditations; and he alone deserved the name of colourist among the painters I have as yet ascribed to the Bolognese School.[13] Guido affected a cool harmony of blue, white, and deadened gold, which in the best pictures of his second manner—the Fortune, the Bacchus and Ariadne of S. Luke's in Rome, the Crucifixion at Modena—has a charm akin to that of Metastasio's silvery lyrics. The Samson at Bologna rises above these works both in force of conception and glow of colour. The Aurora of the Rospigliosi Casino attempts a wider scheme of hues, and is certainly, except for some lack of refinement in the attendant Hours, a very noble composition. The S. Michael of the Cappuccini is seductive by its rich bravura style; and the large Pietà in the Bolognese Gallery impresses our mind by a monumental sadness and sobriety of tone. The Massacre of the Innocents, though one of Guido's most ambitious efforts, and though it displays an ingenious adaptation of the Niobe to Raphael's mannerism, fails by falling between two aims—the aim to secure dramatic effect, and the aim to treat a terrible subject with harmonious repose.

Of Albani nothing need be said in detail. Most people know his pictures of the Four Elements, so neatly executed in a style adapting Flemish smoothness of surface to Italian suavity of line. This sort of art delighted the cardinals and Monsignori of the seventeenth century. But it has nothing whatsoever to say to any human soul.

On Domenichino's two most famous pictures at Bologna Mr. Ruskin has written one of his overpoweringly virulent invectives.[14] It is worth inserting here at length. More passionate words could hardly be chosen to express the disgust inspired in minds attuned to earlier Italian art by these once worshipped paintings. Mr. Ruskin's obvious injustice,

[12] Malvasia, *op. cit.* p. 53, p. 178. The latter passage is preceded by a discussion of the nude in art which shows how Malvasia had imbibed Tridentine morality in the middle of Italy glowing with Renaissance masterpieces.

[13] Lo Spada and Guercino, afterwards to be mentioned, were certainly colourists.

[14] *Modern Painters*, vol. i. p. 87.

intemperance, and ostentatious emphasis will serve to point the change of opinion which has passed over England since Sir Joshua Reynolds wrote. His denunciation of the badness of Domenichino's art, though expressed with such a clangour of exaggeration, fairly represents the feeling of modern students. 'The man,' he says, 'who painted the Madonna del Rosario and Martyrdom of S. Agnes in the gallery of Bologna, is palpably incapable of doing anything good, great, or right in any field, way, or kind whatsoever. . . . This is no rash method of judgment, sweeping and hasty as it may appear. From the weaknesses of an artist, or failures, however numerous, we have no right to conjecture his total inability; a time may come when he shall rise into sudden strength, or an instance occur when his efforts shall be successful. But there are some pictures which rank not under the head of failures, but of perpetrations or commissions; some things which a man cannot do or say without sealing for ever his character and capacity. The angel holding the cross with his finger in his eye, the roaring, red-faced children about the crown of thorns, the blasphemous (I speak deliberately and determinedly) head of Christ upon the handkerchief, and the mode in which the martyrdom of the saint is exhibited (I do not choose to use the expressions which alone could characterise it), are perfect, sufficient, incontrovertible proofs that whatever appears good in any of the doings of such a painter must be deceptive, and that we may be assured that our taste is corrupted and false whenever we feel disposed to admire him. I am prepared to support this position, however uncharitable it may seem; a man may be tempted into a gross sin by passion, and forgiven; and yet there are some kinds of sins into which only men of a certain kind can be tempted, and which cannot be forgiven. It should be added, however, that the artistical qualities of these pictures are in every way worthy of the conceptions they realise; I do not recollect any instance of colour or execution so coarse and feelingless.'

We have only to think of the S. Agnes by Tintoretto, or of Luini's S. Catherine, in order to be well aware how far Domenichino, as a painter, deviated from the right path of art.[15] Yet we are bound to acquit him, as a man, of that moral obliquity which Mr. Ruskin seems to impute. Indeed, we know Domenichino to have been an unaffectedly good fellow. He was misled by his dramatic bias, and also by the prevalent religious temper of his age. Jesuitry had saturated the Italian mind; and in a former chapter I have dwelt upon the concrete materialism which formed the basis of the Jesuitical imagination. In portraying the martyrdom of S. Agnes as he has done, Domenichino was only obeying the rules of Loyola's 'Exercitia.' That he belonged to a school which was essentially vulgar in its choice of type, to a city

[15] I allude to the Tintoretto in S. Maria dell' Orto at Venice, and to the Luini in the Monastero Maggiore at Milan. Yet the model of Luini's S. Catherine was the infamous Contessa di Cellant, who murdered her husband and some lovers, and was beheaded for her crimes in Milan. This fact demonstrates the value of the model in the hands of an artist capable of using it.

never distinguished for delicacy of taste, and to a generation which was rapidly losing the sense of artistic reserve, suffices to explain the crude brutality of the conceptions which he formed of tragic episodes.[16] The same may be said about all those horrible pictures of tortures, martyrdoms, and acts of violence which were produced by the dozen in Italy at this epoch. We turn from them with loathing. They inspire neither terror nor pity, only the sickness of the shambles. And yet it would be unjust to ascribe their unimaginative ghastliness to any special love of cruelty. This evil element may be rationally deduced from false dramatic instinct and perverted habits of brooding sensuously on our Lord's Passion, in minds deprived of the right feeling for artistic beauty. Probably Domenichino thought that he was surpassing Titian's Peter Martyr when he painted his hard and hideous parody of that great picture. Yet Titian had already touched the extreme verge of allowable realisation, and his work belonged to the sphere of high pictorial art mainly by right of noble treatment. Of this noble treatment, and of the harmonious colouring which shed a sanctifying splendour over the painful scene, Domenichino stripped his master's design. What he added was grimace, spasm, and the expression of degrading physical terror.

That Domenichino could be, in his own way, stately, is proved by the Communion of S. Jerome, in which he rehandled Agostino Caracci's fine conception. Though devoid of charm, this justly celebrated painting remains a monument of the success which may be achieved by the vigorous application of robust intellectual powers to the working out of a well-conceived and fully developed composition. Domenichino's gigantic saints and Sibyls, with their fleshy limbs, red cheeks, and upturned eyes, though famous enough in the last century, do not demand a word of comment now.[17] So strangely has taste altered, that to our eyes they seem scarcely decorative.

While the Caracci were reviving art at Bologna in the way that I have described, Caravaggio in Rome opposed the Mannerists after his own and a very different fashion.[18] The insipidities of men like Cesari drove him into a crude realism. He resolved to describe sacred and historical events just as though they were being enacted in the Ghetto by butchers and fishwives. This reaction against flimsy emptiness was wholesome; and many interesting studies from the taverns of Italy, portraits of gamesters, sharpers, bravi and the like, remain to prove Caravaggio's mastery over scenes of common life.[19] But when he applied his principles to higher subjects, their vulgarity became appar-

[16] When I assert that the age was losing the sense of artistic reserve, I wish to refer back to what I have written about Marino, the dictator of the age in matters of taste. See above, pp. 852-853.

[17] Go to S. Andrea nella Valle in Rome, to study the best of them.

[18] Michelangelo Amerighi da Caravaggio (1569-1609).

[19] For the historian of manners in seventeenth-century Italy those pictures have a truly precious value, as they are executed with such passion as to raise them above the more careful but more lymphatic transcripts from beer-cellars, in Dutch painting.

ent. Only in one picture, the Entombment, in the Vatican, did he succeed in affecting imagination forcibly by the evident realisation of a tragic scene. His martyrdoms are inexpressibly revolting, without appeal to any sense but savage blood-lust. It seems difficult for realism, either in literature or art, not to fasten upon ugliness, vice, pain, and disease, as though these imperfections of our nature were more real than beauty, goodness, pleasure, and health. Therefore Caravaggio, the leader of a school which the Italians christened Naturalists, may be compared to Zola.

A Spaniard, settled at Naples—Giuseppe Ribera, nicknamed Lo Spagnoletto—carried on Caravaggio's tradition. Spagnoletto surpassed his master in the brutally realistic expression of physical anguish. His Prometheus writhing under the beak of the vulture, his disembowelled martyrs and skinless S. Bartholomews, are among the most nauseous products of a masculine nature blessed with robust health. Were they delirious or hysterical, they would be less disgusting. But no; they are merely vigorous and faithful representations of what anybody might have witnessed, when a traitor like Ravaillac or a Lombard *untore* was being put to death in agony. His firm mental grip on cruelty, and the sombre gloom with which he invested these ghastly transcripts from the torture-chamber, prove Ribera true to his Spanish origin. Caravaggio delighted in colour, and was indeed a colourist of high rank, considering the times in which he lived. Spagnoletto rejoiced in sombre shadows, as though to illustrate the striking sonnet I have quoted in another place from Campanella.[20]

This digression upon the Naturalists was needed partly to illustrate the nature of the attempted revival of the art of painting at this epoch, and partly to introduce two notable masters of the Bolognese School. Lionello Spada, a street-arab of Bologna, found his way into the studio of the Caracci, where he made himself a favourite by roguish ways and ready wit. He afterwards joined Caravaggio, and, when he reappeared in Lombardy, he had formed a manner of his own, more resplendent in colour and more naturalistic than that of the Caracci, but with less of realism than his Roman teacher's. If I could afford space for anecdotical details, the romance of Spada's life would furnish much entertaining material. But I must press on toward Guercino, who represents in a more famous personality this blending of the Bolognese and Naturalistic styles. Giovanni Francesco Barbieri got his nickname of Il Guercino, or the 'Squintling,' from an accident which distorted his right eye in babyhood. Born of poor parents, he was apprenticed to indifferent painters in Bologna at an early age, his father agreeing to pay for the boy's education by a load of grain and a vat of grapes delivered yearly. Thus Guercino owed far less to academical studies than to his own genius. Being Lodovico Caracci's junior by thirty-five years, and Annibale's by thirty, he had ample opportunities for studying the products of their school in Bologna, without joining the Academy.

[20] See above, p. 536.

A generation lay between him and the first Eclectics. Nearly the same space of time separated Guercino from the founder of the Naturalists, and it was universally admitted in his lifetime that he owed to Caravaggio in colouring no less than he derived from the Caracci in sobriety and dignity of conception. These qualities of divergent schools Guercino combined in a manner marked by salient individuality. As a colourist, he approached the Tenebrosi—those lovers of surcharged shadows and darkened hues, whose gloom culminated in Ribera. But we note a fat and buttery *impasto* in Guercino, which distinguishes his work from the drier and more meagre manner of the Roman-Neapolitan painters. It is something characteristic of Bologna, a richness which we might flippantly compare to sausage, or a Flemish smoothness, indicating Calvaert's influence. More than this, Guercino possessed a harmony of tones peculiar to himself, and strongly contrasted with Guido's silver-grey gradations. Guido's colouring, at its best, often reminds one of olive branches set against a blue sea and pale horizon in faintly amber morning light. The empurpled indigos, relieved by smouldering Venetian red, which Guercino loved, suggest thunder-clouds, dispersed, rolling away through dun subdued glare of sunset reflected upward from the west. And this scheme of colour, vivid but heavy, luminous but sullen, corresponded to what contemporaries called the *terribilità* of Guercino's conception. Terribleness was a word which came into vogue to describe Michelangelo's grand manner. It implied audacity of imagination, dashing draughtsmanship, colossal scale, something demonic and decisive in execution.[21] The terrible takes in Guercino's work far lower flights than in the Sistine Chapel. With Michelangelo it soared like an eagle; with Guercino it flitted like a bat. His brawny saints are ponderous, not awe-inspiring. Yet we feel that the man loved largeness, massiveness, and volume; that he was preoccupied with intellectual problems; planning deeply, and constructing strongly, under conditions unfavourable to spiritual freedom.

Guercino lived the life of an anchorite, absorbed in studies, unwived, sober, pious, truthful, sincere in his commerce with the world, unaffectedly virtuous, devoted to his art and God. Some of his pictures bring forcibly before our minds the religious *milieu* created by the Catholic Revival. I will take the single instance of a large oil-painting in the Bolognese Gallery. It represents the reception of a Duke of Aquitaine into monastic orders by S. Bernard. The knightly quality of the hero is adequately portrayed; his piety is masculine. But an accessory to the main subject of the composition arrests attention. A monk, earnestly pleading, emphatically gesticulating, addresses himself to the task of converting a young squire. Perugino, or even Raphael, would have brought the scene quite otherwise before us. The Duke's consecration would of course have occupied a commanding place in the

[21] But the men who used the word failed to perceive that what justified these qualities in Michelangelo's work was piercing, poignant, spiritual passion, of which their age had nothing.

picture. But the episodes would have been composed of comely groups or animated portraits. Guercino, obedient to the religious spirit of the Counter-Reformation, compels sympathy with ecclesiastical propaganda.

Guido exercised a powerful influence over his immediate successors. Guercino felt it when he painted that soulless picture of Abraham and Hagar, in the Brera—the picture which excited Byron's admiration, which has been praised for its accurate delineation of a teardrop, and which, when all is reckoned, has just nothing of emotion in it but a frigid inhumanity. He competed with Guido in the fresco of the Lodovisi Aurora, a substantial work certainly, yet one that lacks the saving qualities of the Rospigliosi ceiling—grace and geniality of fancy.

In the history of criticism there are few things more perplexing than the vicissitudes of taste and celebrity, whereby the idols of past generations crumble suddenly to dust, while the despised and rejected are lifted to pinnacles of glory. Successive waves of æsthetical preference, following one upon the other with curious rapidity, sweep ancient fortresses of fame from their venerable basements, and raise upon the crests of wordy foam some delicate sea-shell that erewhile lay embedded in oblivious sand. During the last half-century, taste has been more capricious, revolutionary, and apparently anarchical than at any previous epoch. The unity of orthodox opinion has broken up. Critics have sought to display originality by depreciating names famous in former ages, and by exalting minor stars to the rank of luminaries of the first magnitude. A man, yet in middle life, can remember with what reverence engravings after Raphael, the Caracci, and Poussin were treated in his boyhood; how Fra Angelico and Perugino ruled at a somewhat later period; how one set of eloquent writers discovered Blake, another Botticelli, and a third Carpaccio; how Signorelli and Bellini and Mantegna received tardy recognition; and now, of late years, how Tiepolo has bidden fair to obtain the European *grido*. He will also bear in mind that the conditions of his own development—studies in the Elgin marbles, the application of photography to works of art, the publications of the Arundel Society, and that genius of new culture in the air which is more potent than all teaching, rendered for himself each oracular utterance interesting but comparatively unimportant—as it were but talk about truths evident to sight.

Meanwhile, amid this gabble of 'sects and schisms,' this disputation which makes a simple mind take refuge in the epigram attributed to Swift on Handel and Bononcini,[22] criticism and popular intelligence have been unanimous upon two points: first, in manifesting a general dislike for Italian art after the date of Raphael's third manner, and a particular dislike for the Bolognese painters; secondly, in an earnest effort to discriminate and exhibit what is sincere and beautiful in works to which our forefathers were unintelligibly irresponsive. A wholesome reaction, in one word, has taken place against academical dogmatism;

[22] 'Strange tha t such difference should be
'Twixt tweedle-dum and tweedle-dee.'

and the study of art has been based upon appreciably better historical and æsthetical principles.

The seeming confusion of the last half-century ought not, therefore, to shake our confidence in the possibility of arriving at stable laws of taste. Radical revolutions, however salutary, cannot be effected without some injustice to ideals of the past, and without some ill-grounded enthusiasm for the ideals of the moment. Nor can so wide a region as that of modern European art be explored except by divers pioneers, each biassed by personal predilections and peculiar sensibilities, each liable to changes of opinion under the excitement of discovery, each followed by a coterie sworn to support their master's *ipse dixit.*

The chief thing is to obtain a clear conception of the mental atmosphere in which sound criticism has to live and move and have its being. 'The form of this world passes; and I would fain occupy myself only with that which constitutes abiding relations.' So said Goethe; and these words have much the same effect as that admonition of his 'to live with steady purpose in the Whole, the Good, the Beautiful.' The true critic must divert his mind from what is transient and ephemeral, must fasten upon abiding relations, *bleibende Verhältnisse.* He notes that one age is classical, another romantic; that *this* swears by Giotto, *that* by the Caracci. Meanwhile, he resolves to maintain that classics and romantics, the Caracci and Giotto, are alike only worthy of regard in so far as they exemplify the qualities which bring art into the sphere of abiding relations. One writer is eloquent for Fra Angelico, another for Rubens; the one has personal sympathy for the Fiesolan monk, the other for the Flemish courtier. Our true critic renounces idiosyncratic whims and partialities, striving to enter with firm purpose into the understanding of universal goodness and beauty. In so far as he finds truth in Angelico and Rubens, will he be appreciative of both.

Aristotle laid it down as an axiom that the ultimate verdict in matters of taste is 'what the man of enlightened intelligence would decide.' The critic becomes a man of enlightened intelligence, a φρόνιμος, by following the line of Goethe's precepts. In working out self-culture, he will derive assistance by the way from the commanding philosophical conception of our century. All things with which we are acquainted are in evolutionary process. Everything belonging to human nature is in a state of organic transition—passing through necessary phases of birth, growth, decline, and death. Art, in any one of its specific manifestations—Italian painting for example—avoids this law of organic evolution, arrests development at the fairest season of growth, averts the decadence which ends in death, no more than does an oak. The oak, starting from an acorn, nourished by earth, air, light, and water, offers indeed a simpler problem than so complex an organism as Italian painting, developed under conditions of manifold diversity. Yet the dominant law controls both equally.

It is not, however, in evolution that we must seek the abiding relations spoken of by Goethe. The evolutionary conception does not supply those to students of art, though it unfolds a law which is permanent and of universal application in the world at large. It forces us to dwell on necessary conditions of mutability and transformation. It leads the critic to comprehend the whole, and encourages the habit of scientific tolerance. We are saved by it from uselessly fretting ourselves because of the ungodly and the inevitable; from mourning over the decline of Gothic architecture into Perpendicular aridity and flamboyant feebleness, over the passage of the sceptre from Sophocles to Euripides or from Tasso to Marino, over the chaos of Mannerism, Eclecticism, and Naturalism into which Italian painting plunged from the height of its maturity. This toleration and acceptance of unavoidable change need not imply want of discriminative perception. We can apply the evolutionary canon in all strictness without ignoring that adult manhood is preferable to senile decrepitude, that Pheidias surpasses the sculptors of Antinous, that one Madonna of Gian Bellini is worth all the pictures of the younger Palma, and that Dossi's portrait of the Ferrarese jester is better worth having than the whole of Annibale Caracci's Galleria Farnesina.[23] It will even lead us to select for models those works which bear the mark of adolescence or vigorous maturity, as supplying more fruitful sources for our own artistic education.

Nevertheless, not in evolution, but in man's soul, his intellectual and moral nature, must be sought those abiding relations which constitute sound art, and are the test of right æsthetic judgment. These are such as truth, simplicity, sobriety, love, grace, patience, modesty, thoughtfulness, repose, health, vigour, brain-stuff, dignity of imagination, lucidity of vision, purity, and depth of feeling. Wherever the critic finds these—whether it be in Giotto at the dawn or in Guido at the evensong of Italian painting, in Homer or Theocritus at the two extremes of Greek poetry—he will recognise the work as ranking with those things from which the soul draws nourishment. At the same time, he may not neglect the claims of craftsmanship. Each art has its own vehicle of expression, and exacts some innate capacity for the use of that vehicle from the artist. Therefore the critic must be also sufficiently versed in technicalities to give them their due value. It can, however, be laid down, as a general truth, that while immature or awkward workmanship is compatible with æsthetic excellence, technical dexterity, however skilfully applied, has never done anything for a soulless painter.

Criticism, furthermore, implies judgment; and that judgment must be adjusted to the special nature of the thing criticised. Art is different from ethics, from the physical world, from sensuality, however refined. It will not, therefore, in the long run, do for the critic of an art to apply the same rules as the moralist, the naturalist, or the hedonist. It will not do for him to be contented with edification, or differentiation of

[23] The great picture by Dosso Dossi, to which I have alluded, is in the Modenese gallery.

species, or demonstrable delightfulness, as the test-stone of artistic excellence. All art is a presentation of the inner human being, his thought and feeling, through the medium of beautiful symbols in form, colour, and sound. Our verdict must therefore be determined by the amount of thought, the amount of feeling, proper to noble humanity, which we find adequately expressed in beautiful æsthetic symbols. And the man who shall pronounce this verdict is, now as in the days of Aristotle, the man of enlightened intelligence, sound in his own nature and open to ideas. Even his verdict will not be final; for no one is wholly free from partialities due to the age in which he lives, and to his special temperament. Still, a consensus of such verdicts eventually forms that voice of the people which, according to an old proverb, is the voice of God. Slowly, and after many successive siftings, the cumulative votes of the φρόνιμοι decide. Insurgents against their judgment, in the case of acknowledged masters like Pheidias, Michelangelo, Shakspere, are doomed to final defeat, because this judgment is really based upon abiding relations between art and human nature.

Our hope with regard to the unity of taste in the future then is, that, all sentimental or academical seekings after the ideal having been abandoned, momentary theories founded upon idiosyncratic or temporary partialities exploded, and nothing accepted but what is solid and positive, the scientific spirit shall make men progressively more and more conscious of those *bleibende Verhältnisse*, more and more capable of living in the whole; also that, in proportion as we gain a firmer hold upon our own place in the world, we shall come to comprehend with more instinctive certitude what is simple, natural, and honest, welcoming with gladness all artistic products that exhibit these qualities. The perception of the enlightened man will then be the taste of a healthy person who has made himself acquainted with the laws of evolution in art and in society, and is able to test the excellence of work in any stage, from immaturity to decadence, by discerning what there is of truth, sincerity, and natural vigour in it.

This digression was forced upon me by the difficulty of properly appreciating the Bolognese Eclectics now. What would be the amused astonishment of Sir Joshua Reynolds, if he returned to London at the present moment, and beheld the Dagon of his esteemed Caracci dashed to pieces by the ark of Botticelli—Carpaccio enthroned—Raffaello stigmatised as the stone of stumbling and the origin of evil? Yet Reynolds had as good a right to his opinion as any living master of the brush, or any living master of language. There is no doubt that the Bolognese painters sufficed for the eighteenth century, whose taste indeed they had created.[24] There is equally no doubt that for the nineteenth they are insufficient.[25] The main business of a critic is to try to answer

[24] The passage from Lodovico Caracci through Poussin to Reynolds is direct and unbroken. 'Poussin,' says Lanzi, 'ranked Domenichino directly next to Raffaello.' *History of Painting in Italy*, Eng. Tr. vol. iii. p. 84.

[25] Perhaps a generation will yet arise which shall take the Caracci and their scholars into favour, even as people of refinement in our own days find a charm in patches,

two questions: first, why did the epoch produce such art, and why did it rejoice in it?—secondly, has this art any real worth beyond a documentary value for the students of one defined historical period; has it enduring qualities of originality, strength, beauty, and inspiration? To the first of these questions I have already given some answer by showing under what conditions the Caracci reacted against mannerism. In the due consideration of the second we are hampered by the culture of our period, which has strongly prejudiced all minds against the results of that reaction.

The painting of the Eclectics was not spontaneous art. It was art mechanically revived during a period of critical hesitancy and declining enthusiasms. It was produced at Bologna, 'la dotta' or 'la grassa,' by Bolognese craftsmen. This is worth remembering; for, except Guido Guinicelli and Francesco Raibolini, no natives of Bologna were eminently gifted for the arts. And Bologna was the city famous for her ponderous learning, famous also for the good cheer of her table, neither erudition nor savoury meats being essential to the artist's temperament. The painting which emerged there at the close of the sixteenth century embodied religion and culture, both of a base alloy. The Christianity of the age was not naïve, simple, sincere, and popular, like that of the thirteenth century; but hysterical, dogmatic, hypocritical, and sacerdotal. It was not Christianity indeed, but Catholicism galvanised by terror into reactionary movement. The culture of the age was on the wane. Men had long lost their first clean perception of classical literature, and the motives of the mediæval past were exhausted. Therefore, though the Eclectics went on painting the old subjects, they painted all alike with frigid superficiality. If we examine the lists of pictures turned out by the Caracci and Guercino, we shall find a pretty equal quantity of saints and Susannas, Judiths and Cleopatras, Davids and Bacchuses, Jehovahs and Jupiters, anchorites and Bassarids, Faiths and Fortunes, cherubs and Cupids. Artistically, all are on the same dead level of inspiration. Nothing new or vital, fanciful or imaginative, has been breathed into antique mythology. What has been added to religious expression is repellent. Extravagantly ideal in ecstatic Magdalens and Maries, extravagantly realistic in martyrdoms and torments, extravagantly harsh in dogmatic mysteries and the ecclesiastical parade of power, extravagantly soft in sentimental tenderness and tearful piety, this new religious element, the element of the Inquisition, the Tridentine Council, and the Jesuits, contradicts the true gospel of Christ. The painting which embodies it belongs to a spirit at strife with what was vital and progressive in the modern world. It is there-

powder, perukes, sedan-chairs, patchouli, and other lumber from the age despised by Keats. I remember visiting a noble English lady at her country seat. We drank tea in her room, decorated by a fashionable 'Queen Anne' artist. She told us that the quaintly pretty furniture of the last century which adorned it had recently been brought down from the attic, whither her forbears had consigned it as tasteless—Gillow in their minds superseding Chippendale.

fore naturally abhorrent to us now; nor can it be appreciated except by those who yearn for the triumph of ultramontane principles.

If we turn from the intellectual content of this art to its external manifestation, we shall find similar reasons for its failure to delight or satisfy. The ambition of the Caracci was to combine in one the salient qualities of earlier masters. This ambition doomed their style to the sterility of hybrids. Moreover, in selecting, they omitted just those features which had given grace and character to their models. The substitution of generic types for portraiture, the avoidance of individuality, the contempt for what is simple and natural in details, deprived their work of attractiveness and suggestion. It is noticeable that they never painted flowers. While studying Titian's landscapes, they omitted the iris and the caper-blossom and the columbine which star the grass beneath Ariadne's feet. The lessons of the rocks and chestnut-trees of his S. Jerome's Solitude were lost on them. They began the false system of depicting ideal foliage and ideal precipices—that is to say, trees which are not trees, and cliffs which cannot be distinguished from cork or stucco. In like manner, the clothes wherewith they clad their personages were not of brocade or satin or broadcloth, but of that empty lie called drapery. The purfled silks of Titian's Lilac Lady, in the Pitti, the embroidered hems of Boccaccini da Cremona, the crimson velvet of Raphael's Joanna of Aragon, Veronese's cloth of silver and shot taffety, are replaced by one monotonous nondescript stuff, differently dyed in dull or glaring colours, but always shoddy. Characteristic costumes have disappeared. We shall not find in any of their Massacres of the Innocents a soldier like Bonifazio's Dall' Armi. In lieu of gems with flashing facets, or of quaint jewels from the Oreficeria, they adorn their kings and princesses with nothing less elevated than polished gold and ropes of pearls. After the same fashion, furniture, utensils, houses, animals, birds, weapons, are idealised—stripped, that is to say, of what in these things is specific and vital.

It would be incorrect to say that there are no exceptions in Eclectic painting to this evil system. Yet the sweeping truth remains that the Caracci returned, not to what was best in their predecessors, but to what was dangerous and misleading.

The 'grand style,' in Sir Joshua's sense of that phrase, denoting style which eliminates specific and characteristic qualities from objects, replacing them by so-called 'ideal' generalities, had already made its appearance in Raphael, Correggio, and Buonarroti. We even find it in Da Vinci's Last Supper. Yet in Raphael it comes attended with divine grace; in Correggio with faun-like radiancy of gladness; in Buonarroti with Sinaitic sublimity; in Da Vinci with penetrative force of psychological characterisation. The Caracci and their followers, with a few exceptions—Guido at his best being the notablest—brought nothing of these saving virtues to the pseudo-grand style.

It was this delusion regarding nobility and elevation in style which betrayed so genial a painter as Reynolds into his appreciation of the

Bolognese masters. He admired them; but he admired Titian, Raphael, Correggio, and Buonarroti more. And he admired the Eclectics because they developed the perilous part of the great Italian tradition. Just as Coleridge recommended young students of dramatic verse to found their style at first on Massinger rather than on Shakspere, so Reynolds thought that the Caracci were sound models for beginners in the science of idealisation. Shakspere and Michelangelo are inimitable; Massinger and the Caracci exhibit the one thing needful to be learned, upon a scale not wholly unattainable by industry and talent. That was the line of argument; and, granted that the pseudo-grand style is a *sine quâ non* of painting, Reynold's position was logical.[26]

The criticism and the art-practice of this century have combined to shake our faith in the grand style. The spirit of the Romantic movement, penetrating poetry first, then manifesting itself in the reflective writings of Rio and Lord Lindsay, Ruskin and Gautier, producing the English landscape-painters and pre-Raphaelites, the French Realists and Impressionists, has shifted the centre of gravity in taste. Science, too, contributes its quota. Histories of painting, like Kugler's, and Crowe and Cavalcaselle's, composed in an impartial and searching spirit of investigation, place students at a point of view removed from prejudice and academical canons of perfection. Only here and there, under special reactionary influences, as in the Düsseldorf and Munich schools of religious purists, has anything approaching to the eighteenth-century 'grand style' delusion reappeared.

Why, therefore, the Eclectics are at present pining in the shade of neglect is now sufficiently apparent. We dislike their religious sentiments. We repudiate their false and unimaginative ideality. We recognise their touch on antique mythology to be cold and lifeless. Superficial imitations of Niobe and the Belvedere Apollo have no attraction for a generation educated by the marbles of the Parthenon. Dull reproductions of Raphael's manner at his worst cannot delight men satiated with Raphael's manner at his best. Whether the whirligig of time will bring about a revenge for the Eclectics yet remains to be seen. Taste is so capricious, or rather the conditions which create taste are so complex and inscrutable, that even this, which now seems impossible, may happen in the future. But a modest prediction can be hazarded that nothing short of the substitution of Catholicism for science and of Jesuitry for truth in the European mind will work a general revolution in their favour.

26 It is only because I am an Englishman, writing a popular book for English folk, that I thus spend time in noticing the opinions of Sir Joshua Reynolds. Addressing a European audience in this year of grace, I should not have thought of eddying about his obsolete doctrine.

CHAPTER XIV

CONCLUSION

The Main Events of European History—Italy in the Renaissance—Germany and Reformation—Catholic Reaction—Its Antagonism to Renaissance and Reformation—Profound Identity of Renaissance and Reformation—Place of Italy in European Civilisation—Want of Sympathy between Latin and Teutonic Races—Relation of Rome to Italy—Macaulay on the Roman Church—On Protestantism—Early Decline of Renaissance Enthusiasms—Italy's Present and Future.

I

THE four main events of European history since the death of Christ are the decline of Græco-Roman civilisation, the triumph of Christianity as a new humanising agency, the intrusion of Teutonic and Slavonic tribes into the comity of nations, and the construction of the modern world of thought by Renaissance and Reformation.

As seems to be inevitable in the progress of our species, each of these changes involved losses, compensated by final gains; for humanity moves like a glacier, plastically, but with alternating phases of advance and retreat, obeying laws of fracture and regelation.

It would thus be easy to deplore the collapse of that mighty and beneficent organism which we call the Roman Empire. Yet without this collapse how could the Catholic Church have supplied inspiration to peoples gifted with fresh faculties, endowed with insight differing from that of Greeks and Romans?

It is tempting to lament the extinction of arts, letters, and elaborated habits of civility, which followed the barbarian invasions. Yet without such extinction, how can we imagine to ourselves the growth of those new arts, original literatures, and varied modes of social culture, to which we give the names of mediæval, chivalrous, or feudal?

It is obvious that we can quarrel with the Renaissance for having put an end to purely Christian arts and letters by imposing a kind of pagan mannerism on the spontaneous products of the later mediæval genius. But without this reversion to the remaining models of antique culture, how could the European races have become conscious of historical continuity; how could the corrupt system of Papal domination have been broken by Reform; how, finally, could Science, the vital principle of our present civilisation, have been evolved?

In all these instances it appears that the old order must yield place to the new, not only because the new is destined to incorporate and supersede it, but also because the old has become unfruitful. Thus, the Roman Empire, having discharged its organising function, was decrepit, and classical civilisation, after exhibiting its strength in season, was decaying when the Latin priesthood and the barbarians entered that closed garden of antiquity, and trampled it beneath their feet. Mediæval religion and modes of thought, in like manner, were at the point of ossifying, when Humanism intervened to twine the threads of past and present into strands that should be strong as cables for the furtherance of future energy.

It is incontestable that the Reformation and the Counter-Reformation, each of them on different grounds antagonistic to the Renaissance, appear to have retarded that emancipation of the reason, begun by Humanism, which is still in progress. Nevertheless, the strife of Protestantism and Catholicism was needed for preserving moral and religious elements which might have been too lightly dropped, and for working these into the staple of the modern consciousness. The process of the last three centuries, attended as it has been by serious drawbacks to the Spanish and Italian peoples, and by a lamentable waste of vigour to the Teutonic nations, has yet resulted in a permeation of the modern compost with the leaven of Christianity. Unchecked, it is probable that the Renaissance would have swept away much that was valuable and deserved to be permanent. Nor, without the flux and reflux of contending principles by which Europe was agitated in the Counter-Reformation period, could the equipoise of reciprocally attracting and repelling States, which constitutes the modern as different from the ancient or the mediæval groundwork of political existence, have been so efficiently established.

II

Permanence and homogeneity are not to be predicated of 'anything that's merely ours and mortal.' We have missed the whole teaching of history if we wail aloud because Greek and Roman culture succumbed to barbarism, out of which mediæval Christianity emerged; because the revival of learning diverted arts and letters in each Occidental nation from their home-ploughed channels; because Protestant theologians and Spanish Jesuits impeded that self-evolution of the reason which Italian humanists inaugurated. No less futile were it to waste declamatory tears upon the strife of absolutism with new-fledged democracy, or to vaticinate a reign of socialistic terror for the immediate future. We have to recognise that man cannot be other than what he makes himself; and he makes himself in obedience to immutable although unwritten laws, whereof he only of late years became dimly conscious. It is well, then, while reflecting on the lessons of some deeply studied epoch in world-history, to regard the developments with which we have been specially occupied, no less than the ephemeral activity of each particular individual, as factors in a universal process, whereof none sees the issue, but which, willing or unwilling, each man helps to further. We shall then acknowledge that a contest between Conservatism and Liberalism, between established order and the order that is destined to replace it, between custom and innovation, constitutes the essence of vitality in human affairs. The nations by turns are protagonists in the drama of progress; by turns are doomed to play the part of obstructive agents. Intermingled in conflict which is active life, they contribute by their phases of declension and resistance, no less than by their forward movements, to the growth of an organism which shall probably in the far future be coextensive with the whole human race.

III

These considerations are suggested to us by the subject I have handled in this work. The first sections were devoted to showing how Italy, in the Renaissance, elaborated a new way of regarding man and the world, a new system of education, new social manners, and a new type of culture for herself and Europe. This was her pioneer's work in the period of transition from the Middle Ages; and while she was engaged in it, all classes, from popes and princes down to poetlings and pedants, seemed for a while to have lost sight of Catholic Christianity. They were equally indifferent to that corresponding and contemporary movement across the Alps, which is known as Reformation. They could not discern the close link of connexion which binds Renaissance to Reformation. Though at root identical in tendency towards freedom, these stirrings of the modern spirit assumed externally such diverse forms as made them reciprocally repellent. Only one European nation received both impulses simultaneously. That was England, which adopted Protestantism and produced the literature of Spenser, Bacon, and Shakspere at the same epoch. France, earlier than England, felt Renaissance influences, and for some while seemed upon the point of joining the Reformation. But while the French were hesitating, Spain proclaimed herself the uncompromising enemy of Protestantism, and Rome, supported by this powerful ally, dragged Italy into the Catholic reaction. That effort aimed at galvanising a decrepit Church into the semblance of vital energy, and, while professing the reformation of its corrupt system, stereotyped all that was antagonistic in its creed and customs to the spirit of the modern world. The Catholic Revival necessitated vigorous reaction, not only against Protestantism, but also against the Liberalism of the Renaissance and the political liberties of peoples. It triumphed throughout Southern Europe chiefly because France chose at length the Catholic side. But the triumph was only partial, condemning Spain and Italy indeed to intellectual barrenness for a season, but not sufficing to dominate and suppress the development of rationalism. The pioneer's work of Italy was over. She joined the ranks of obscurantists and obstructives. Germany, having failed to accomplish the Reformation in time, was distracted by the Catholic reaction, which plunged her into a series of disastrous wars. It remained for England and Holland, not, however, without similar perturbations in both countries, to lead the van of progress through two centuries; after which this foremost post was assigned to France and the United States.

IV

The views which I have maintained throughout my work upon the Renaissance will be found, I think, to be coherent. They have received such varied illustrations that it is difficult to recapitulate the principles on which they rest, without repetition. The main outline of the argument, however, is as follows: During the Middle Ages, Western Christendom recognised, in theory at least, the ideal of European unity under the dual headship of the Papacy and Empire. There was one civil order and one Church. Emperor and Pope, though frequently at strife, were supposed to support each other for the common welfare of Christendom. That mediæval conception has now, in the centuries which we call modern, passed into oblivion; and the period in which it ceased to have effective value we denote as the period of the Renaissance and the Reformation. So long as the ideal held good, it was possible for the Papacy to stamp out heresies and to stifle the earlier stirrings of antagonistic culture. Thus the precursory movements to which I alluded in the first chapter of my 'Age of the Despots,' seemed to be abortive; and no less apparently abortive were the reformatory efforts of Wiclif and Huss. Yet Europe was slowly undergoing mental and moral changes, which announced the advent of a new era. These changes were more apparent in Italy than elsewhere, through the revival of arts and letters early in the fourteenth century. Cimabue, Giotto, and the Pisani, Dante, Petrarch, and Boccaccio, set culture forward on fresh paths divergent from previous mediæval tradition. The gradual enfeeblement of the Empire and the distraction of the Church during the Great Schism prepared the means whereby both Renaissance and Reformation were eventually realised. The Council of Constance brought the Western nations into active diplomatical relations, and sowed seeds of thought which afterwards sprang up in Luther.

Meanwhile a special nidus had been created in the South. The Italian communes freed themselves from all but titular subjection to the Empire, and were practically independent of the Papacy during its exile in Avignon. They succumbed to despots, and from Italian despotism emerged the Machiavellian conception of the State. This conception, modified in various ways, by Sarpi's theory of Church and State, by the Jesuit theory of Papal Supremacy, by the counter-theory of the Divine Right of Kings, by theories of Social Contract and the Divine Right of Nations, superseded the elder ideal of Universal Monarchy. It grew originally out of the specific conditions of Italy in the fifteenth century, and acquired force from that habit of mind, fostered by the Classical Revival, which we call humanism. Humanism had flourished in Italy since the days of Petrarch, and had been communicated by Italian teachers to the rest of Europe. As in the South it generated the new learning and the new culture which I have described in the first five volumes of this work, and acted as a solvent on the mediæval idea of the Empire, so in the North it generated a new religious enthusiasm and acted as a solvent on the mediæval idea of the Church. All through the Middle Ages, nothing seemed more formidable to the European mind than heresy. Any sacrifices were willingly made in order to secure the unity of the Catholic Communion. But now, by the Protestant rebellion, that spell was broken, and the right of peoples to choose their faith, in dissent from a Church declared corrupt, was loudly proclaimed.

So long as we keep this line of reasoning in view, we shall recognise why it is not only uncritical, but also impossible, to separate the two movements severally called Renaissance and Reformation. Both had a common root in humanism, and humanism owed its existence on the one hand to the recovery of antique literature, on the other to the fact that the Papacy, instead of striving to stamp it out as it had stamped out Provençal civilisation, viewed it at first with approval. The new learning, as our ancestors were wont to call it, involved, in Michelet's pregnant formula, the discovery of the world and man, and developed a spirit of revolt against mediævalism in all its manifestations. Its fruits were speedily discerned in bold exploratory studies, sound methods of criticism, audacious speculation, and the free play of the intellect over every field of knowledge. This new learning had time and opportunity for full development in Italy, and for adequate extension to the Northern races, before its real tendencies were suspected. When that happened, the transition from the mediæval to the modern age had been secured. The Empire was obsolete. The Church was forced into reaction. Europe became the battlefield of progressive and retrogressive forces, the scene of a struggle between two parties which can best be termed Liberalism and Conservatism.

Stripping the subject of those artistic and literary associations which we are accustomed to connect with the word Renaissance, these seem to me the most essential points to bear in mind about this movement. Then, when we have studied the diverse antecedent circumstances of the German and Italian races, when we take into account their national qualities, and estimate the different aims and divergent enthusiasms evoked in each by humanistic ardour, we shall perceive how it came to pass that Renaissance and Reformation clashed together in discordant opposition to the Catholic Revival.

V

Italy, through the Roman Republic, the Roman Empire, and the Roman Church, gave discipline, culture, and religion to the Western world. But, during the course of this civilising process, a force arose in Northern Europe which was destined to transfer the centre of gravity from the Mediterranean basin northwards. The Teutonic tribes effaced the Western Empire, adopted Christianity, and profoundly modified what still survived of Latin civility among the Occidental races. A new factor was thus introduced into the European community, which had to be assimilated to the old; and the genius of the Italian people never displayed itself more luminously than in the ability with which the Bishops of Rome availed themselves of this occasion. They separated the Latin from the Greek Church, and, by the figment of the Holy Roman Empire, cemented Southern and Northern Europe into an apparently cohesive whole. After the year A.D. 800 Europe, from the Baltic to the Mediterranean, acknowledged a dual headship; Papacy and Empire ranking as ideals under which the unity of Christendom subsisted in a multiplicity of separate and self-evolving nations.

The concordat between Latin Church and German Empire, the one representing traditions of antique intelligence and Southern habits of State organisation, the other introducing the young energies of half-cultivated peoples and the chivalry of the North, was never perfect. Yet, incomplete as the fusion between Roman and Teuton actually was, it had a common basis in religion, and it enabled the federated peoples to maintain recognised international relations. What we now call Renaissance and Reformation revealed still unreconciled antagonisms between Southern and Northern, Latin and German, factors in this mediæval Europe. Italy, freed for a while from both Papacy and Empire, expressed her intellectual energy in the Revival of Learning, developing that bold investigating spirit to which the names of Humanism or of Rationalism may be given. The new learning, the new enthusiasm for inquiry, the new study of the world and man, as subjects of vital interest irrespective of our dreamed-of life beyond the grave, stimulated in Italy what we know as Renaissance; while in Germany it led to what we know as Reformation. The Reformation must be regarded as the Teutonic counterpart to the Italian Renaissance. It was what emerged from the core of that huge barbarian factor, which had sapped the Roman Empire, and accepted Catholicism, which lent its vigour to the mediæval Empire, and which now participated in the culture of the classical Revival. As Italy restored freedom to human intelligence and the senses by arts and letters and amenities of refined existence, so Germany restored freedom to the soul and conscience by strenuous efforts after religious sincerity and political independence. The one people aiming at a restoration of pagan civility beneath the shadow of Catholicism, the other seeking after a purer Christianity in antagonism to the Papal hierarchy, initiated from opposite points of view that complete emancipation of the modern mind which has not yet been fully realised.

If we inquire why the final end to which both Renaissance and Reformation tended—namely, the liberation of the spirit from mediæval prepossessions and impediments—has not been more perfectly attained, we find the cause of this partial failure in the contradictory conceptions formed by South and North of a problem which was at root one. Both Renaissance and Reformation had their origin in the revival of learning, or rather in that humanistic enthusiasm which was its vital essence. But the race-differences involved in these two movements were so irreconcilable, the objects pursued were so divergent, that Renaissance and Reformation came into the conflict of chemical combination, producing a ferment out of which the intellectual unity of Europe has not as yet clearly emerged. The Latin race, having created a new learning and a new culture, found itself at strife with the Teutonic race, which at the same period developed new religious conceptions and new political energies.

The Church supplied a battlefield for these hostilities. The Renaissance was by no means favourable to the principles of Catholic orthodoxy; and the Italians showed themselves to be Christians by convention and tradition rather than by conviction in the fifteenth century. Yet Italy was well content to let the corrupt hierarchy of Papal Rome subsist, provided Rome maintained the attitude which Leo X. had adopted toward the liberal spirit of the Classical Revival. The Reformation, on the other hand, was openly antagonistic to the Catholic Church. Protestantism repudiated the toleration professed by sceptical philosophers and indulgent free-thinkers in the South, while it repelled those refined persons by theological fervour and moral indignation which they could not comprehend. Thus the Italian and the German children of humanism failed to make common cause against Catholicism, with which the former felt no sympathy and which the latter vehemently attacked. Meanwhile the Church awoke to a sense of her peril. The Papacy was still a force of the first magnitude; and it only required a vigorous effort to place it once more in an attitude of domination and resistance. This effort it made by reforming the ecclesiastical hierarchy, defining Catholic dogma, and carrying on a war of extermination against the two-fold Liberalism of Renaissance and Reformation.

That reactionary movement against the progress of free thought which extinguished the Italian Renaissance and repelled the Reformation, has formed the subject of the concluding section of this work. It could not have been conducted by the Court of Rome without the help of Spain. The Spanish nation, at this epoch paramount in Europe, declared itself fanatically and unanimously for the Catholic Revival. In Italy it lent the weight of arms and overlordship to the Church for the suppression of popular liberties. It provided the Papacy with a spiritual militia specially disciplined to meet the exigencies of the moment. Yet the centre of the reaction was still Rome; and the Spanish hegemony enabled the Roman hierarchy to consolidate an organism which has long survived its own influence in European affairs.

VI

After the close of the Great Schism Rome began to obey the national impulses of the Italians, entered into their confederation as one of the five leading powers, and assumed externally the humanistic culture then in vogue. But the Church was a cosmopolitan institution. Its interests extended beyond the Alps, beyond the Pyrenees, beyond the oceans traversed by Portuguese and Spanish navigators. The Renaissance so far modified its structure that the Papacy continued politically to rank as an Italian power. Its headquarters could not be removed from the Tiber, and by the tacit consent of Latin Catholicism the Supreme Pontiff was selected from Italian prelates. Yet now, in 1530, it began to play a new part more consonant with its mediæval functions and pretensions. Rome indeed had ceased to be the imperial capital of Europe, where the secular head of Christendom assumed the crown of Empire from his peer the spiritual chieftain. The Eternal City in this new phase of modern history, which lasted until Vittorio Emmanuele's entrance into the Quirinal in 1870, gave the Pope a place among Catholic sovereigns. From his throne upon the seven hills he conducted with their approval and assistance the campaign of the Counter-Reformation. Instead of encouraging and developing what yet remained of Renaissance in Italy, instead of directing that movement of the self-emancipating mind beyond the stage of art and humanism into the stage of rationalism and science, the Church used its authority to bring back the Middle Ages and to repress national impulses. It made common cause with Spain for a common object—the maintenance of Italy in a state of political and intellectual bondage, and the subjugation of such provinces in Europe as had not been irretrievably lost to the Catholic cause. The Italians, as a nation, remained passive, but not altogether unwilling or unapproving spectators of the drama which was being enacted under Papal leadership beyond their boundaries. Once again their activity was merged in that of Rome—in the action of that State which had first secured for them the Empire of the habitable globe, and next the spiritual hegemony of the Western races, and from the predominance of which they had partially disengaged themselves during the fourteenth and fifteenth centuries. It was the Papacy's sense of its own danger as a cosmopolitan institution, combined with the crushing superiority of Spain in the peninsula, which determined this phase of Italian history.

The Catholic Revival, like the Renaissance, may in a certain sense be viewed as a product of Italian genius. This is sufficiently proved by the diplomatic history of the Tridentine Council, and by the dedication of the Jesuits to Papal service. It must, however, be remembered that while the Renaissance emanated from the race at large, from its confederation of independent republics and tyrannies, the Catholic Revival emanated from that portion of the race which is called Rome, from the ecclesiastical hierarchy imbued with world-wide ambitions in which national interests were drowned. There is nothing more interesting to the biographer of the Italians than the complicated correlation in which they have always stood to the cosmopolitan organism of Rome, itself Italian. In their antique days of greatness Rome subdued them, and by their native legions won the overlordship of the world. After the downfall of the Empire the Church continued Roman traditions in an altered form, but it found itself unable to dispense with the foreign assistance of Franks and Germans. The price now paid by Italy for spiritual headship in Europe was subjection to Teutonic suzerains and perpetual intriguing interference in her affairs. During the Avignonian captivity and the Great Schism, Italy developed intellectual and confederative unity, imposing her laws of culture and of statecraft even on the Papacy when it returned to Rome. But again at the close of the Renaissance, when Italian independence had collapsed, the Church aspired to spiritual supremacy; and at this epoch she recompensed her Spanish ally by aiding and abetting in the enslavement of the peninsula. Still the Roman Pontiff, who acted as generalissimo of the Catholic armies throughout Europe, was now more than ever recognised as an Italian power.

VII

In his review of Ranke's 'History of the Popes' Lord Macaulay insists with brilliant eloquence upon the marvellous vitality and longevity of the Roman Catholic Church. He describes the insurrection of the intellect against her rule in Provence, and her triumph in the Crusade which sacrificed a nation to the conception of mediæval religious unity. He dwells on her humiliation in exile at Avignon, her enfeeblement during the Great Schism, and her restoration to splendour and power at the close of the Councils. Then he devotes his vast accumulated stores of learning and his force of rhetoric to explain the Reformation, the Catholic Revival, and the Counter-Reformation. He proves abundantly what there was in the organism of the Catholic Church and in the temper of Papal Rome, which made these now reactionary powers more than a match for Protestantism. 'In fifty years from the day on which Luther publicly renounced communion with the Papacy, and burned the bull of Leo before the gates of Wittenberg, Protestantism attained its highest ascendency, an ascendency which it soon lost, and which it never regained.' This sentence forms the theme for Lord Macaulay's survey of the Catholic Revival. Dazzling and fascinating as that survey is, it fails through misconception of one all-important point. Lord Macaulay takes for granted that conflict in Europe, since the publication of Luther's manifesto against Rome, has been between Catholicism and Protestantism. Even after describing the cataclysm of the French Revolution, he winds up his argument with these words: 'We think it a most remarkable fact that no Christian nation, which did not adopt the principles of the Reformation before the end of the sixteenth century, should ever have adopted them. Catholic communities have, since that time, become infidel and Catholic again; but none has become Protestant.' This is tantamount to regarding Protestantism as something fixed and final in itself, as a permanent and necessary form of Christianity. Here lies the fallacy which makes his reasoning, in spite of all its eloquence, but superficial. Protestantism, in truth, has never been more than a half-way house or halting-place between Catholicism and what may variously be described as free thought or science or rationalism. Being in its origin critical—being, as its name implies, a protest and an opposition—Protestantism was doomed to sterility, whenever it hardened into one or other of its dogmatic forms. As critics and insurgents, Luther and Calvin rank among the liberators of the modern intellect. As founders of intolerant and mutually hostile Christian sects, Luther and Calvin rank among the retarders of modern civilisation. Among subsequent thinkers of whom both sects have disapproved, we may recognise the veritable continuators of their work in its best aspect. The Lutheran and Calvinist Churches are but backwaters and stagnant pools, left behind by the subsidence of rivers in flood, separated from the tidal stress of cosmic forces. Macaulay's misconception of the true character of Protestantism, which is to Catholicism what the several dissenting bodies are to the English Establishment, has diverted his attention from the deeper issues involved in the Counter-Reformation. He hardly touches upon Rome's persecution of free thought, upon her obstinate opposition to science. Consequently, he is not sufficiently aware that Copernicus and Bruno were, even in the sixteenth century, far more dangerous foes to Catholicism than were the leaders of the Reformed Churches. Copernicus and Bruno, the lineal ancestors of Helmholtz and Darwin, headed that opposition to Catholicism which has been continuous and potent to the present day, which has never retreated into backwaters or stagnated in slumbrous pools. From this opposition the essence of Christianity, the spirit which Christ bequeathed to his disciples, has nothing to fear. But Catholicism and Protestantism alike, in so far as both are dogmatic and reactionary, clinging to creeds which will not bear the test of scientific investigation, to myths which have lost their significance in the light of advancing knowledge, and to methods of interpreting the Scriptures at variance with the canons of historical criticism, have very much to fear from this opposition. Lord Macaulay thinks it a most remarkable fact that no Christian nation has adopted the principles of the Reformation since the end of the sixteenth century. He does not perceive that, in every race of Europe, all enlightened thinkers, whether we name Bacon or Descartes, Spinoza or Leibnitz, Goethe or Mazzini, have adopted and carried forward those principles in their essence. That they have not proclaimed themselves Protestants unless they happened to be born Protestants, ought not to arouse his wonder, any more than that Washington and Heine did not proclaim themselves Whigs. For Protestantism, when it became dogmatic and stereotyped itself in sects, ceased to hold any vital relation to the forward movement of modern thought. The Reformation, in its origin, was, as I have tried to show, the Northern and Teutonic manifestation of that struggle after intellectual freedom, which in Italy and France had taken shape as Renaissance. But Calvanism, Lutheranism, Zwinglianism, and Anglicanism renounced that struggle only less decidedly than Catholicism; and in some of their specific phases, in Puritanism for example, they showed themselves even more antagonistic to liberal culture and progressive thought than did the Roman Church.

Whatever may be thought about the future of Catholicism (and no prudent man will utter prophecies upon such matters), there can be no doubt that the universal mind of the Christian races, whether Catholic or Protestant, has been profoundly penetrated and permeated with rationalism, which, springing simultaneously in Reformation and Renaissance out of humanism, has supplied the spiritual life of the last four centuries. This has created science in all its branches. This has stimulated critical and historical curiosity. This has substituted sound for false methods of inquiry, the love of truth for attachment to venerable delusion. This has sustained the unconquerable soul of man in its persistent effort after liberty and its revolt against the tyranny of priests and princes. At present, civilisation seems threatened by more potent foes than the Roman Church, nor is it likely that these foes will seek a coalition with Catholicism.

As a final remark upon this topic, it should be pointed out that Protestantism, in spite of the shortcomings I have indicated, has, on the whole, been more favourable to intellectual progress than Catholicism. For Protestantism was never altogether oblivious of its origin in revolt against unjust spiritual domination, while Catholicism has steadily maintained its conservative attitude of self-defence by repression. This suffices to explain another point insisted on by Lord Macaulay—namely, that those nations in which Protestantism took root have steadily advanced, while the decay of Southern Europe can be mainly ascribed to the Catholic Revival. The one group of nations have made progress, not indeed because they were Protestants, but because they were more obedient to the Divine Mind, more in smypathy with the vital principle of movement, more open to rationalism. The other group of nations have declined, because Catholicism, after the year 1530, wilfully separated itself from truth and liberty and living force, and obstinately persisted in serving the false deities of an antiquated religion.

VIII

Few periods in history illustrate the law of reaction and retrogression, to which all processes of civil progress are subject, more plainly and more sadly than the one with which I have been dealing in these volumes. The Renaissance in Italy started with the fascination of a golden dream; and like the music of a dream, it floated over Europe.

But the force which had stimulated humanity to this delightful reawakening of senses and intelligence, stirred also the slumbering religious conscience, and a yearning after personal emancipation. Protestantism arose like a stern reality, plunging the nations into confused and deadly conflict, arousing antagonisms in established orders, unleashing cupidities and passions which had lurked within the breasts of manifold adventurers. The fifteenth century closed to a solemn symphony. After the middle of the sixteenth, discord sounded from every quarter of the Occidental world. Italy lay trampled on and dying. Spain reared her dragon's crest of menacing ambition and remorseless fanaticism. France was torn by factions and devoured by vicious favourites of corrupt kings. Germany heaved like a huge ocean in the grip of a tumultuous gyrating cyclone. England passed through a complex revolution, the issue of which, under the sway of three Tudor monarchs, appeared undecided, until the fourth by happy fate secured the future of her people. It is not to be wondered that, in these circumstances, a mournful discouragement should have descended on the age; that men should have become more dubitative; that arts and letters should have seemed to pine upon unfertile ground. The nutriment they needed was absorbed by plants of fiercer and ranker growth, religious hatreds, political greeds, relentless passions burning in the hearts of princes and of populations.

IX

Italy had already given so much of mental and social civilisation to Europe, that her quiescence at this epoch can scarcely supply a substantial theme for rhetorical lamentations. Marino and Guido Reni prove that the richer veins of Renaissance art and poetry had been worked out. The lives of Aldus the younger and Muretus show that humanism was well-nigh exhausted on its native soil. This will not, however, prevent us from deploring the untimely frost cast by persecution on Italy's budding boughs of knowledge. While we rejoice in Galileo, we must needs shed tears of fiery wrath over the passion of Campanella and the stake of Bruno. Meanwhile the tree of genius was ever green and vital in that Saturnian land of culture. Poetry, painting, sculpture, and architecture, having borne their flowers and fruits, retired to rest. Scholarship faded; science was nipped in its unfolding season by unkindly influences. But music put forth lusty shoots and flourished, yielding a new paradise of harmless joy, which even priests could grudge not to the world, and which lulled tyranny to sleep with silvery numbers.

Thanks be to God that I who pen these pages, and that you who read them, have before us in this year of grace the spectacle of a resuscitated Italy! In this last quarter of the nineteenth century, the work of her heroes, Vittorio Emmanuele, Mazzini, Garibaldi, and Cavour stands firmly founded. The creation of united Italy, that latest birth of the

Italian genius, that most impossible of dreamed-of triumphs through long ages of her glory and greatness, compensates for all that she has borne in these three hundred years. Now that Rome is no longer the seat of a cosmopolitan theocracy, but the capital of a regenerated people; now that Venice joins hands with Genoa, forgetful of Curzola and Chioggia; now that Florence and Pisa and Siena stand like sisters on the sacred Tuscan soil, while Milan has no strife with Naples, and the Alps and sea-waves gird one harmony of cities who have drowned their ancient spites in amity,—the student of the splendid and the bitter past may pause and bow his head in gratitude to Heaven and swear that, after all, all things are well.

X

There is no finality in human history. It is folly to believe that any religions, any social orders, any scientific hypotheses, are more than provisional, and partially possessed of truth. Let us assume that the whole curve of human existence on this planet describes a parabola of some twenty millions of years in duration.[1] Of this we have already exhausted unreckoned centuries in the evolution of prehistoric man, and perhaps five thousand years in the ages of historic records. How much of time remains in front? Through that past period of five thousand years preserved for purblind retrospect in records, what changes of opinion, what peripeties of empire, may we not observe and ponder! How many theologies, cosmological conceptions, polities, moralities, dominions, ways of living and of looking upon life, have followed one upon another! The space itself is brief; compared with the incalculable longevity of the globe, it is but a bare 'scape in oblivion.' And, however ephemeral the persistence of humanity may be in this its earthly dwelling-place, the conscious past sinks into insignificance before those æons of the conscious future, those on-coming and out-rolling waves of further evolution which bear posterity forward. Has any solid gain of man been lost on the stream of time to us-ward? We doubt that. Has anything final and conclusive been arrived at? We doubt that also. The river broadens, as it bears us on. But the rills from which it gathered, and the ocean whereto it tends, are now, as ever in the past, inscrutable. It is therefore futile to suppose, at this short stage upon our journey, while the infant founts of knowledge are still murmuring to our ears, that any form of faith or science has been attained as permanent; that any Pillars of Hercules have been set up against the Atlantic Ocean of experience and exploration. Think of that curve of possibly twenty million years, and of the five thousand years remembered by humanity! How much, how incalculably much longer is the space to be traversed than that which we have left behind! It seems, therefore, our truest, as it is our humblest, wisdom to live by faith and love. 'And now abideth faith, hope, charity, these three;

[1] Twenty millions of years is of course a mere symbol, x or y.

but the greatest of these is charity.' Love is the greatest; and against love man has sinned most in the short but blood-bedabbled annals of his past. Hope is the virtue from which a faithful human being can best afford to abstain, unless hope wait as patient handmaid upon faith. Faith is the steadying and sustaining force, holding fast by which each one of us dares defy change, and gaze with eyes of curious contemplation on the tide which brought us, and is carrying, and will bear us where we see not. 'I know not how I came of you and I know not where I go with you; but I know I came well and I shall go well.' Man can do no better than live in Eternity's Sunrise, as Blake put it. To live in the eternal sunrise of God's presence, ever rising, not yet risen, which will never reach its meridian on this globe, seems to be the destiny, as it should also be the blessing, of mankind.

INDEX

INDEX

MEDICI

TASSO

TASSO

TRANSLATIONS IN VERSE BY AUTHOR